Lecture Notes in Computer Science 14439

The series Lecture Notes in Computer Science (LNCS), including its subseries Lecture Notes in Artificial Intelligence (LNAI) and Lecture Notes in Bioinformatics (LNBI), has established itself as a medium for the publication of new developments in computer science and information technology research, teaching, and education.

LNCS enjoys close cooperation with the computer science R & D community, the series counts many renowned academics among its volume editors and paper authors, and collaborates with prestigious societies. Its mission is to serve this international community by providing an invaluable service, mainly focused on the publication of conference and workshop proceedings and postproceedings. LNCS commenced publication in 1973.

Jian Guo · Ron Steinfeld
Editors

Advances in Cryptology – ASIACRYPT 2023

29th International Conference on the Theory and Application of Cryptology and Information Security Guangzhou, China, December 4–8, 2023 Proceedings, Part II

Springer

Editors
Jian Guo
Nanyang Technological University
Singapore, Singapore

Ron Steinfeld
Monash University
Melbourne, VIC, Australia

ISSN 0302-9743 ISSN 1611-3349 (electronic)
Lecture Notes in Computer Science
ISBN 978-981-99-8723-8 ISBN 978-981-99-8724-5 (eBook)
https://doi.org/10.1007/978-981-99-8724-5

This Springer imprint is published by the registered company Springer Nature Singapore Pte Ltd.
The registered company address is: 152 Beach Road, #21-01/04 Gateway East, Singapore 189721, Singapore

Paper in this product is recyclable.

Preface

The 29th Annual International Conference on the Theory and Application of Cryptology and Information Security (Asiacrypt 2023) was held in Guangzhou, China, on December 4–8, 2023. The conference covered all technical aspects of cryptology, and was sponsored by the International Association for Cryptologic Research (IACR).

We received an Asiacrypt record of 376 paper submissions from all over the world, and the Program Committee (PC) selected 106 papers for publication in the proceedings of the conference. Due to this large number of papers, the Asiacrypt 2023 program had 3 tracks.

The two program chairs were supported by the great help and excellent advice of six area chairs, selected to cover the main topic areas of the conference. The area chairs were Kai-Min Chung for Information-Theoretic and Complexity-Theoretic Cryptography, Tanja Lange for Efficient and Secure Implementations, Shengli Liu for Public-Key Cryptography Algorithms and Protocols, Khoa Nguyen for Multi-Party Computation and Zero-Knowledge, Duong Hieu Phan for Public-Key Primitives with Advanced Functionalities, and Yu Sasaki for Symmetric-Key Cryptology. Each of the area chairs helped to lead discussions together with the PC members assigned as paper discussion lead. Area chairs also helped to decide on the submissions that should be accepted from their respective areas. We are very grateful for the invaluable contribution provided by the area chairs.

To review and evaluate the submissions, while keeping the load per PC member manageable, we selected a record size PC consisting of 105 leading experts from all over the world, in all six topic areas of cryptology. The two program chairs were not allowed to submit a paper, and PC members were limited to submit one single-author paper, or at most two co-authored papers, or at most three co-authored papers all with students. Each non-PC submission was reviewed by at least three reviewers consisting of either PC members or their external sub-reviewers, while each PC member submission received at least four reviews. The strong conflict of interest rules imposed by IACR ensure that papers are not handled by PC members with a close working relationship with the authors. There were approximately 420 external reviewers, whose input was critical to the selection of papers. Submissions were anonymous and their length was limited to 30 pages excluding the bibliography and supplementary materials.

The review process was conducted using double-blind peer review. The conference operated a two-round review system with a rebuttal phase. After the reviews and first round discussions the PC selected 244 submissions to proceed to the second round and the authors were then invited to participate in an interactive rebuttal phase with the reviewers to clarify questions and concerns. The remaining 131 papers were rejected, including one desk reject. The second round involved extensive discussions by the PC members. After several weeks of additional discussions, the committee selected the final 106 papers to appear in these proceedings.

The eight volumes of the conference proceedings contain the revised versions of the 106 papers that were selected. The final revised versions of papers were not reviewed again and the authors are responsible for their contents.

The PC nominated and voted for two papers to receive the Best Paper Awards, and one paper to receive the Best Early Career Paper Award. The Best Paper Awards went to Thomas Espitau, Alexandre Wallet and Yang Yu for their paper "On Gaussian Sampling, Smoothing Parameter and Application to Signatures", and to Kaijie Jiang, Anyu Wang, Hengyi Luo, Guoxiao Liu, Yang Yu, and Xiaoyun Wang for their paper "Exploiting the Symmetry of Z^n: Randomization and the Automorphism Problem". The Best Early Career Paper Award went to Maxime Plancon for the paper "Exploiting Algebraic Structure in Probing Security". The authors of those three papers were invited to submit extended versions of their papers to the Journal of Cryptology. In addition, the program of Asiacrypt 2023 also included two invited plenary talks, also nominated and voted by the PC: one talk was given by Mehdi Tibouchi and the other by Xiaoyun Wang. The conference also featured a rump session chaired by Kang Yang and Yu Yu which contained short presentations on the latest research results of the field.

Numerous people contributed to the success of Asiacrypt 2023. We would like to thank all the authors, including those whose submissions were not accepted, for submitting their research results to the conference. We are very grateful to the area chairs, PC members and external reviewers for contributing their knowledge and expertise, and for the tremendous amount of work that was done with reading papers and contributing to the discussions. We are greatly indebted to Jian Weng and Fangguo Zhang, the General Chairs, for their efforts in organizing the event and to Kevin McCurley and Kay McKelly for their help with the website and review system. We thank the Asiacrypt 2023 advisory committee members Bart Preneel, Huaxiong Wang, Kai-Min Chung, Yu Sasaki, Dongdai Lin, Shweta Agrawal and Michel Abdalla for their valuable suggestions. We are also grateful for the helpful advice and organization material provided to us by the Eurocrypt 2023 PC co-chairs Carmit Hazay and Martijn Stam and Crypto 2023 PC co-chairs Helena Handschuh and Anna Lysyanskaya. We also thank the team at Springer for handling the publication of these conference proceedings.

December 2023

Jian Guo
Ron Steinfeld

Organization

General Chairs

Jian Weng	Jinan University, China
Fangguo Zhang	Sun Yat-sen University, China

Program Committee Chairs

Jian Guo	Nanyang Technological University, Singapore
Ron Steinfeld	Monash University, Australia

Program Committee

Behzad Abdolmaleki	University of Sheffield, UK
Masayuki Abe	NTT Social Informatics Laboratories, Japan
Miguel Ambrona	Input Output Global (IOHK), Spain
Daniel Apon	MITRE Labs, USA
Shi Bai	Florida Atlantic University, USA
Gustavo Banegas	Qualcomm, France
Zhenzhen Bao	Tsinghua University, China
Andrea Basso	University of Bristol, UK
Ward Beullens	IBM Research Europe, Switzerland
Katharina Boudgoust	Aarhus University, Denmark
Matteo Campanelli	Protocol Labs, Denmark
Ignacio Cascudo	IMDEA Software Institute, Spain
Wouter Castryck	imec-COSIC, KU Leuven, Belgium
Jie Chen	East China Normal University, China
Yilei Chen	Tsinghua University, China
Jung Hee Cheon	Seoul National University and Cryptolab Inc, South Korea
Sherman S. M. Chow	Chinese University of Hong Kong, China
Kai-Min Chung	Academia Sinica, Taiwan
Michele Ciampi	University of Edinburgh, UK
Bernardo David	IT University of Copenhagen, Denmark
Yi Deng	Institute of Information Engineering, Chinese Academy of Sciences, China

Patrick Derbez	University of Rennes, France
Xiaoyang Dong	Tsinghua University, China
Rafael Dowsley	Monash University, Australia
Nico Döttling	Helmholtz Center for Information Security, Germany
Maria Eichlseder	Graz University of Technology, Austria
Muhammed F. Esgin	Monash University, Australia
Thomas Espitau	PQShield, France
Jun Furukawa	NEC Corporation, Japan
Aron Gohr	Independent Researcher, New Zealand
Junqing Gong	ECNU, China
Lorenzo Grassi	Ruhr University Bochum, Germany
Tim Güneysu	Ruhr University Bochum, Germany
Chun Guo	Shandong University, China
Siyao Guo	NYU Shanghai, China
Fuchun Guo	University of Wollongong, Australia
Mohammad Hajiabadi	University of Waterloo, Canada
Lucjan Hanzlik	CISPA Helmholtz Center for Information Security, Germany
Xiaolu Hou	Slovak University of Technology, Slovakia
Yuncong Hu	Shanghai Jiao Tong University, China
Xinyi Huang	Hong Kong University of Science and Technology (Guangzhou), China
Tibor Jager	University of Wuppertal, Germany
Elena Kirshanova	Technology Innovation Institute, UAE and I. Kant Baltic Federal University, Russia
Eyal Kushilevitz	Technion, Israel
Russell W. F. Lai	Aalto University, Finland
Tanja Lange	Eindhoven University of Technology, Netherlands
Hyung Tae Lee	Chung-Ang University, South Korea
Eik List	Nanyang Technological University, Singapore
Meicheng Liu	Institute of Information Engineering, Chinese Academy of Sciences, China
Guozhen Liu	Nanyang Technological University, Singapore
Fukang Liu	Tokyo Institute of Technology, Japan
Shengli Liu	Shanghai Jiao Tong University, China
Feng-Hao Liu	Florida Atlantic University, USA
Hemanta K. Maji	Purdue University, USA
Takahiro Matsuda	AIST, Japan
Christian Matt	Concordium, Switzerland
Tomoyuki Morimae	Kyoto University, Japan
Pierrick Méaux	University of Luxembourg, Luxembourg

Mridul Nandi	Indian Statistical Institute, Kolkata, India
María Naya-Plasencia	Inria, France
Khoa Nguyen	University of Wollongong, Australia
Ryo Nishimaki	NTT Social Informatics Laboratories, Japan
Anca Nitulescu	Protocol Labs, France
Ariel Nof	Bar Ilan University, Israel
Emmanuela Orsini	Bocconi University, Italy
Adam O'Neill	UMass Amherst, USA
Morten Øygarden	Simula UiB, Norway
Sikhar Patranabis	IBM Research, India
Alice Pellet-Mary	CNRS and University of Bordeaux, France
Edoardo Persichetti	Florida Atlantic University, USA and Sapienza University, Italy
Duong Hieu Phan	Telecom Paris, Institut Polytechnique de Paris, France
Josef Pieprzyk	Data61, CSIRO, Australia and ICS, PAS, Poland
Axel Y. Poschmann	PQShield, UAE
Thomas Prest	PQShield, France
Adeline Roux-Langlois	CNRS, GREYC, France
Amin Sakzad	Monash University, Australia
Yu Sasaki	NTT Social Informatics Laboratories, Japan
Jae Hong Seo	Hanyang University, South Korea
Yaobin Shen	UCLouvain, Belgium
Danping Shi	Institute of Information Engineering, Chinese Academy of Sciences, China
Damien Stehlé	CryptoLab, France
Bing Sun	National University of Defense Technology, China
Shi-Feng Sun	Shanghai Jiao Tong University, China
Keisuke Tanaka	Tokyo Institute of Technology, Japan
Qiang Tang	University of Sydney, Australia
Vanessa Teague	Thinking Cybersecurity Pty Ltd and the Australian National University, Australia
Jean-Pierre Tillich	Inria, Paris, France
Yosuke Todo	NTT Social Informatics Laboratories, Japan
Alexandre Wallet	University of Rennes, Inria, CNRS, IRISA, France
Meiqin Wang	Shandong University, China
Yongge Wang	UNC Charlotte, USA
Yuyu Wang	University of Electronic Science and Technology of China, China
Qingju Wang	Telecom Paris, Institut Polytechnique de Paris, France

Benjamin Wesolowski	CNRS and ENS Lyon, France
Shuang Wu	Huawei International, Singapore, Singapore
Keita Xagawa	Technology Innovation Institute, UAE
Chaoping Xing	Shanghai Jiao Tong University, China
Jun Xu	Institute of Information Engineering, Chinese Academy of Sciences, China
Takashi Yamakawa	NTT Social Informatics Laboratories, Japan
Kang Yang	State Key Laboratory of Cryptology, China
Yu Yu	Shanghai Jiao Tong University, China
Yang Yu	Tsinghua University, Beijing, China
Yupeng Zhang	University of Illinois Urbana-Champaign and Texas A&M University, USA
Liangfeng Zhang	ShanghaiTech University, China
Raymond K. Zhao	CSIRO's Data61, Australia
Hong-Sheng Zhou	Virginia Commonwealth University, USA

Additional Reviewers

Amit Agarwal
Jooyoung Lee
Léo Ackermann
Akshima
Bar Alon
Ravi Anand
Sarah Arpin
Thomas Attema
Nuttapong Attrapadung
Manuel Barbosa
Razvan Barbulescu
James Bartusek
Carsten Baum
Olivier Bernard
Tyler Besselman
Ritam Bhaumik
Jingguo Bi
Loic Bidoux
Maxime Bombar
Xavier Bonnetain
Joppe Bos
Mariana Botelho da Gama
Christina Boura
Clémence Bouvier
Ross Bowden
Pedro Branco
Lauren Brandt
Alessandro Budroni
Kevin Carrier
André Chailloux
Suvradip Chakraborty
Debasmita Chakraborty
Haokai Chang
Bhuvnesh Chaturvedi
Caicai Chen
Rongmao Chen
Mingjie Chen
Yi Chen
Megan Chen
Yu Long Chen
Xin Chen
Shiyao Chen
Long Chen
Wonhee Cho
Qiaohan Chu
Valerio Cini
James Clements
Ran Cohen
Alexandru Cojocaru
Sandro Coretti-Drayton

Anamaria Costache
Alain Couvreur
Daniele Cozzo
Hongrui Cui
Giuseppe D'Alconzo
Zhaopeng Dai
Quang Dao
Nilanjan Datta
Koen de Boer
Luca De Feo
Paola de Perthuis
Thomas Decru
Rafael del Pino
Julien Devevey
Henri Devillez
Siemen Dhooghe
Yaoling Ding
Jack Doerner
Jelle Don
Mark Douglas Schultz
Benjamin Dowling
Minxin Du
Xiaoqi Duan
Jesko Dujmovic
Moumita Dutta
Avijit Dutta
Ehsan Ebrahimi
Felix Engelmann
Reo Eriguchi
Jonathan Komada Eriksen
Andre Esser
Pouria Fallahpour
Zhiyong Fang
Antonio Faonio
Pooya Farshim
Joël Felderhoff
Jakob Feldtkeller
Weiqi Feng
Xiutao Feng
Shuai Feng
Qi Feng
Hanwen Feng
Antonio Flórez-Gutiérrez
Apostolos Fournaris
Paul Frixons
Ximing Fu
Georg Fuchsbauer
Philippe Gaborit
Rachit Garg
Robin Geelen
Riddhi Ghosal
Koustabh Ghosh
Barbara Gigerl
Niv Gilboa
Valerie Gilchrist
Emanuele Giunta
Xinxin Gong
Huijing Gong
Zheng Gong
Robert Granger
Zichen Gui
Anna Guinet
Qian Guo
Xiaojie Guo
Hosein Hadipour
Mathias Hall-Andersen
Mike Hamburg
Shuai Han
Yonglin Hao
Keisuke Hara
Keitaro Hashimoto
Le He
Brett Hemenway Falk
Minki Hhan
Taiga Hiroka
Akinori Hosoyamada
Chengan Hou
Martha Norberg Hovd
Kai Hu
Tao Huang
Zhenyu Huang
Michael Hutter
Jihun Hwang
Akiko Inoue
Tetsu Iwata
Robin Jadoul
Hansraj Jangir
Dirmanto Jap
Stanislaw Jarecki
Santos Jha

Ashwin Jha
Dingding Jia
Yanxue Jia
Lin Jiao
Daniel Jost
Antoine Joux
Jiayi Kang
Gabriel Kaptchuk
Alexander Karenin
Shuichi Katsumata
Pengzhen Ke
Mustafa Khairallah
Shahram Khazaei
Hamidreza Amini Khorasgani
Hamidreza Khoshakhlagh
Ryo Kikuchi
Jiseung Kim
Minkyu Kim
Suhri Kim
Ravi Kishore
Fuyuki Kitagawa
Susumu Kiyoshima
Michael Klooß
Alexander Koch
Sreehari Kollath
Dimitris Kolonelos
Yashvanth Kondi
Anders Konring
Woong Kook
Dimitri Koshelev
Markus Krausz
Toomas Krips
Daniel Kuijsters
Anunay Kulshrestha
Qiqi Lai
Yi-Fu Lai
Georg Land
Nathalie Lang
Mario Larangeira
Joon-Woo Lee
Keewoo Lee
Hyeonbum Lee
Changmin Lee
Charlotte Lefevre
Julia Len
Antonin Leroux
Andrea Lesavourey
Jannis Leuther
Jie Li
Shuaishuai Li
Huina Li
Yu Li
Yanan Li
Jiangtao Li
Song Song Li
Wenjie Li
Shun Li
Zengpeng Li
Xiao Liang
Wei-Kai Lin
Chengjun Lin
Chao Lin
Cong Ling
Yunhao Ling
Hongqing Liu
Jing Liu
Jiahui Liu
Qipeng Liu
Yamin Liu
Weiran Liu
Tianyi Liu
Siqi Liu
Chen-Da Liu-Zhang
Jinyu Lu
Zhenghao Lu
Stefan Lucks
Yiyuan Luo
Lixia Luo
Jack P. K. Ma
Fermi Ma
Gilles Macario-Rat
Luciano Maino
Christian Majenz
Laurane Marco
Lorenzo Martinico
Loïc Masure
John McVey
Willi Meier
Kelsey Melissaris
Bart Mennink

Charles Meyer-Hilfiger
Victor Miller
Chohong Min
Marine Minier
Arash Mirzaei
Pratyush Mishra
Tarik Moataz
Johannes Mono
Fabrice Mouhartem
Alice Murphy
Erik Mårtensson
Anne Müller
Marcel Nageler
Yusuke Naito
Barak Nehoran
Patrick Neumann
Tran Ngo
Phuong Hoa Nguyen
Ngoc Khanh Nguyen
Thi Thu Quyen Nguyen
Hai H. Nguyen
Semyon Novoselov
Julian Nowakowski
Arne Tobias Malkenes Ødegaard
Kazuma Ohara
Miyako Ohkubo
Charles Olivier-Anclin
Eran Omri
Yi Ouyang
Tapas Pal
Ying-yu Pan
Jiaxin Pan
Eugenio Paracucchi
Roberto Parisella
Jeongeun Park
Guillermo Pascual-Perez
Alain Passelègue
Octavio Perez-Kempner
Thomas Peters
Phuong Pham
Cécile Pierrot
Erik Pohle
David Pointcheval
Giacomo Pope
Christopher Portmann
Romain Poussier
Lucas Prabel
Sihang Pu
Chen Qian
Luowen Qian
Tian Qiu
Anaïs Querol
Håvard Raddum
Shahram Rasoolzadeh
Divya Ravi
Prasanna Ravi
Marc Renard
Jan Richter-Brockmann
Lawrence Roy
Paul Rösler
Sayandeep Saha
Yusuke Sakai
Niels Samwel
Paolo Santini
Maria Corte-Real Santos
Sara Sarfaraz
Santanu Sarkar
Or Sattath
Markus Schofnegger
Peter Scholl
Dominique Schröder
André Schrottenloher
Jacob Schuldt
Binanda Sengupta
Srinath Setty
Yantian Shen
Yixin Shen
Ferdinand Sibleyras
Janno Siim
Mark Simkin
Scott Simon
Animesh Singh
Nitin Singh
Sayani Sinha
Daniel Slamanig
Fang Song
Ling Song
Yongsoo Song
Jana Sotakova
Gabriele Spini

Marianna Spyrakou
Lukas Stennes
Marc Stoettinger
Chuanjie Su
Xiangyu Su
Ling Sun
Akira Takahashi
Isobe Takanori
Atsushi Takayasu
Suprita Talnikar
Benjamin Hong Meng Tan
Ertem Nusret Tas
Tadanori Teruya
Masayuki Tezuka
Sri AravindaKrishnan Thyagarajan
Song Tian
Wenlong Tian
Raphael Toledo
Junichi Tomida
Daniel Tschudi
Hikaru Tsuchida
Aleksei Udovenko
Rei Ueno
Barry Van Leeuwen
Wessel van Woerden
Frederik Vercauteren
Sulani Vidhanalage
Benedikt Wagner
Roman Walch
Hendrik Waldner
Han Wang
Luping Wang
Peng Wang
Yuntao Wang
Geng Wang
Shichang Wang
Liping Wang
Jiafan Wang
Zhedong Wang
Kunpeng Wang
Jianfeng Wang
Guilin Wang
Weiqiang Wen
Chenkai Weng
Thom Wiggers
Stella Wohnig
Harry W. H. Wong
Ivy K. Y. Woo
Yu Xia
Zejun Xiang
Yuting Xiao
Zhiye Xie
Yanhong Xu
Jiayu Xu
Lei Xu
Shota Yamada
Kazuki Yamamura
Di Yan
Qianqian Yang
Shaojun Yang
Yanjiang Yang
Li Yao
Yizhou Yao
Kenji Yasunaga
Yuping Ye
Xiuyu Ye
Zeyuan Yin
Kazuki Yoneyama
Yusuke Yoshida
Albert Yu
Quan Yuan
Chen Yuan
Tsz Hon Yuen
Aaram Yun
Riccardo Zanotto
Arantxa Zapico
Shang Zehua
Mark Zhandry
Tianyu Zhang
Zhongyi Zhang
Fan Zhang
Liu Zhang
Yijian Zhang
Shaoxuan Zhang
Zhongliang Zhang
Kai Zhang
Cong Zhang
Jiaheng Zhang
Lulu Zhang
Zhiyu Zhang

Chang-An Zhao
Yongjun Zhao
Chunhuan Zhao
Xiaotong Zhou
Zhelei Zhou
Zijian Zhou
Timo Zijlstra
Jian Zou
Ferdinando Zullo
Cong Zuo

Sponsoring Institutions

- Gold Level Sponsor: Ant Research
- Silver Level Sponsors: Sansec Technology Co., Ltd., Topsec Technologies Group
- Bronze Level Sponsors: IBM, Meta, Sangfor Technologies Inc.

Contents – Part II

Proof Systems - Succinctness and Foundations

Fiat-Shamir Security of FRI and Related SNARKs

Alexander R. Block[1,2(✉)], Albert Garreta[3], Jonathan Katz[2], Justin Thaler[1,5], Pratyush Ranjan Tiwari[4], and Michał Zając[3]

[1] Georgetown University, Washington, D.C., USA
justin.thaler@georgetown.edu
[2] University of Maryland, College Park, USA
alexander.r.block@gmail.com, jkatz2@gmail.com
[3] Nethermind, London, UK
{albert,michal}@nethermind.io
[4] Johns Hopkins University, Baltimore, USA
pratyush@cs.jhu.edu
[5] A16z Crypto Research, Menlo Park, USA

Abstract. We establish new results on the Fiat-Shamir (FS) security of several protocols that are widely used in practice, and we provide general tools for establishing similar results for others. More precisely, we: (1) prove the FS security of the FRI and batched FRI protocols; (2) analyze a general class of protocols, which we call δ*-correlated*, that use low-degree proximity testing as a subroutine (this includes many "Plonk-like" protocols (e.g., Plonky2 and Redshift), ethSTARK, RISC Zero, etc.); and (3) prove FS security of the aforementioned "Plonk-like" protocols, and sketch how to prove the same for the others.

We obtain our first result by analyzing the round-by-round (RBR) soundness and RBR knowledge soundness of FRI. For the second result, we prove that if a δ-correlated protocol is RBR (knowledge) sound under the assumption that adversaries always send low-degree polynomials, then it is RBR (knowledge) sound in general. Equipped with this tool, we prove our third result by formally showing that "Plonk-like" protocols are RBR (knowledge) sound under the assumption that adversaries always send low-degree polynomials. We then outline analogous arguments for the remainder of the aforementioned protocols.

To the best of our knowledge, ours is the first formal analysis of the Fiat-Shamir security of FRI and widely deployed protocols that invoke it.

1 Introduction

Succinct Non-interactive ARguments of Knowledge (SNARKs) and their zero-knowledge variants (zkSNARKs) are a thriving field of study both in theory and practice. Allowing for fast verification of complex statements made by untrusted parties, zkSNARKs have now been deployed in a myriad of applications. A popular paradigm for constructing (zk)SNARKs is via the following two-step process:

J. Guo and R. Steinfeld (Eds.): ASIACRYPT 2023, LNCS 14439, pp. 3–40, 2023.
https://doi.org/10.1007/978-981-99-8724-5_1

(1) construct a public-coin[1] interactive protocol; and (2) remove all interaction using the Fiat-Shamir (FS) transformation [31], adding zero-knowledge as necessary.

Non-interactivity is essential in many applications of zkSNARKs. In general, interactive protocols are not publicly verifiable and hence cannot be used in settings where anyone in the world should be able to verify the proof. There are various proposals (e.g., [5]) to render interactive protocols publicly verifiable using so-called randomness beacons [61] (i.e., publicly verifiable sources of random bits, such as contents blockchain block headers) and the transaction-ordering functionality offered by public blockchains (which enable the public to verify that the prover sent a message before it knew what the verifier's response to that message would be). However, to the best of our knowledge, such proposals have not been deployed at scale. They are also fraught with performance and security considerations; for example, blockchain headers are at least somewhat biasable [17,57], and splitting an interactive proof across many blockchain blocks can substantially increase latency and fees.

Regardless, the Fiat-Shamir transformation is pervasive and has been used extensively in a variety of schemes beyond zkSNARKs, e.g., signature schemes and non-interactive zero-knowledge [31,54,58], inspiring a rich line of research into understanding both its applicability and pitfalls. The FS transformation is typically modeled and analyzed in the random oracle model (ROM) for security proofs. When using FS in practice, one then assumes that a suitable concrete hash function (e.g., SHA256) is an adequate replacement for said random oracle.

However, there are surprisingly many open problems regarding specific applications of the FS transformation. In particular, the FS transformation is *not* secure in general [3,13,36], even in the random oracle model, when applied to many-round protocols. Specifically, its use can lead to a loss in the number of "bits of security" that is linear in the number of rounds r of the protocol to which it is applied. Here, the number of bits of security roughly refers to the logarithm of the amount of work an attacker has to do to succeed with probability close to 1.

Accordingly, the FS transformation is often applied to many-round protocols without formal security proofs for the resulting SNARKs' security. That is, the security analysis of these protocols is often provided only for their interactive versions. Without further analysis, the security (measured in bits) lost via the FS transformation may be a factor equal to the number of rounds of the protocol. Even a 30% loss in security would be devastating in practical deployments (e.g., reducing the number of bits of security from 100 down to 70), and (more than) such a loss can occur even when Fiat-Shamir is applied to protocols with just two rounds. There are also some works that claim FS-security of their protocols, but in fact show this only under the assumption that certain many-round subprotocols used in the overall protocol are FS-secure [25,26,44].

[1] A protocol is *public-coin* if all messages sent by the verifier are sampled uniformly at random from a challenge space and are independent of all prior prover and verifier messages.

In this work, we fill this gap in these security analyses and provide general tools for doing so for certain varieties of protocols. Specifically, we show that for the protocols we are interested in, the security of the FS-transformed protocol resembles the security of the interactive one (pre-FS) (or more precisely, *what is currently known* about the interactive security). This adds to a recent fruitful line of work has introduced many tools to understand FS security of many-round protocols. These include the notions of state-restoration soundness [9], round-by-round soundness [22], and (generalized) special soundness [2,28,72]. Nonetheless, in the literature on SNARKs, relatively few protocols are known to be FS-secure, despite the above tools existing. These include the GKR protocol [22,37] (or more generally, anything based on the sum-check protocol [49]), the GMW protocol and other natural classes of "commit-and-open" protocols [41], and any protocol satisfying the notion of (generalized) special soundness [2], which includes IPA/Bulletproofs [18,20]. Bulletproofs [18,20] and Sonic [50] have separately been shown to be FS-secure in the algebraic group model [35].

In this introduction, we informally refer to protocols that experience little-to-no loss in the number of bits of security when the FS transformation is applied in the random oracle model as *FS-secure.*

1.1 Our Results

We formally analyze and prove FS-security of the FRI protocol [4] and of some protocols that have wide use in practice which use low-degree proximity testing as a subroutine. For the latter, we build a general tool that allows us to prove FS-security of a certain type of protocol, which we call a δ-correlated IOP, by analyzing its round-by-round soundness assuming an adversary sends low-degree polynomials. We formally apply this tool to "Plonk-like" protocols such as Plonky2 [60], and we outline how the tool can be used on other constructions such as ethSTARK [65]. In particular, we either formally prove or we outline a proof that the security of all these protocols, after applying the Fiat-Shamir transformation, (nearly) matches what is known about its security when run interactively.

As mentioned, we focus on these protocols due to their current popularity. For example, FRI is currently used in various Layer-2 Ethereum projects [59,66] to help secure hundreds of millions of dollars of assets [46]. Some projects are deploying FRI with (at most) 80-bits (dYdX) or 96-bits (those using the SHARP prover) of *interactive security* before the FS transformation is applied [6,65,66]. More precisely, the *best known attacks* on these interactive protocols have success probability 2^{-80} or 2^{-96}. These attacks are conjectured to be optimal [65], though only partial results in this direction are known [6]. Similarly, Plonk-like protocols are utilized in a variety of blockchain networks and Layer 2 Ethereum projects (e.g., [30,51,55,56,67]),

When it comes to the FRI protocol, we *do not* address the gaps between the conjectured and known soundness of the interactive protocol. We merely analyze the security of the FS-compiled protocol as a function of the security of the interactive protocol.

1.2 Technical Details

In a nutshell, we formally establish the *round-by-round (knowledge) soundness* [22] of both FRI and several protocols that rely on a form of low-degree proximity testing. For analyzing round-by-round (RBR) soundness, there is a protocol *state* that can either be "doomed" or not. The state of the protocol starts off as doomed whenever a prover falsely claims that an input is valid. If at the end of interaction the state is doomed, the verifier rejects. The protocol is said to be RBR sound if, whenever the state is doomed, the protocol is still doomed in the next round of interaction, except with negligible probability, no matter what a prover does. RBR knowledge soundness is a similar notion, except that in this case, the protocol always starts off in a doomed state, and after each round, except with negligible probability, it remains doomed unless the prover knows a valid witness; see Sect. 2.1 for more discussion.

By establishing the round-by-round (knowledge) soundness of these protocols, we can then leverage the so-called BCS transformation [9], which (informally) compiles any interactive protocol[2] into a (zk)SNARK via (a variant of) the Fiat-Shamir transformation in the random oracle model. Applying the BCS transformation on a round-by-round (knowledge) sound protocol preserves (knowledge) soundness (yielding a SNARK) [25,26].[3] In fact, round-by-round soundness of the interactive protocol was even shown to imply that the BCS-transformed SNARK is secure against quantum adversaries [25]. Thus, we establish the Fiat-Shamir security of both FRI and the rest of protocols via proving their round-by-round (knowledge) soundness.

Round-by-Round Soundness of FRI. The FRI protocol [4], which stands for **F**ast **R**eed-Solomon **I**nteractive Oracle Proof of Proximity is a logarithmic round *interactive oracle proof.* Briefly, an interactive oracle proof (IOP) [9] is an interactive protocol where the verifier is given oracle (i.e., query) access to the (long) prover messages, and an IOP of Proximity (IOPP) is an IOP for proving proximity of a function to some pre-specified linear error-correcting code [4]. The FRI protocol proves that a function is close to the space of Reed-Solomon codewords [62] of a certain degree over some pre-specified domain over a finite field. This protocol is both of theoretical and practical interest. On the theory side, FRI gives a polylogarithmic-size proof for proving the proximity of messages to some pre-specified Reed-Solomon code, which is an important primitive in many proof systems [4]. On the practical side, FRI is used as a sub-protocol in the design and construction of many SNARKs and has the benefit of being plausibly post-quantum secure due to its avoidance of elliptic curve cryptography (and in fact, it follows from our results that FRI, when run non-interactively via Fiat-Shamir, is unconditionally secure in the quantum random oracle model).

2 More formally, the BCS transformation is applied to *interactive oracle proofs* [9].

3 Actually, [9,25] prove this for *state-restoration soundness*; however, subsequent works observed that round-by-round soundness is an upper bound on state-restoration soundness [22,25,26,44].

Despite intense interest from both theorists and practitioners, we are unaware of any formal security proof for FRI under Fiat-Shamir.

Theorem 1 (Informally Stated; see Theorem 6). *For finite field $\mathbb{F}$, evaluation domain $L \subset \mathbb{F}$ of size 2^n, constants $\rho \in (0,1)$, $\delta \in (0, 1-\sqrt{\rho})$, and positive integer ℓ, the FRI protocol has round-by-round (knowledge) soundness error*

$$\varepsilon_{\mathsf{rbr}}^{\mathsf{FRI}}(\mathbb{F}, \rho, \delta, n, \ell) = \max\{O(2^{2n}/(\rho^{3/2}|\mathbb{F}|)), (1-\delta)^{\ell}\}.$$

Establishing the round-by-round (knowledge) soundness of FRI is a crucial first step to establishing the Fiat-Shamir security of FRI. In particular, given the round-by-round soundness of FRI, we can now apply the BCS transformation [9] to obtain a secure non-interactive argument in the random oracle model using FRI.

Corollary 1 (Informally Stated; see Corollary 4). *For finite field $\mathbb{F}$, evaluation domain $L \subset \mathbb{F}$ of size 2^n, constants $\rho \in (0,1)$, $\delta \in (0, 1-\sqrt{\rho})$, and positive integer ℓ, given a random oracle with κ-bits of output and query bound $Q \geq 1$, compiling FRI with the BCS transformation yields a non-interactive argument in the random oracle model with adaptive soundness error and knowledge error*

$$\varepsilon_{\mathsf{fs}}^{\mathsf{FRI}}(\mathbb{F}, \rho, \delta, n, \ell, Q, \kappa) = Q\varepsilon_{\mathsf{rbr}}^{\mathsf{FRI}}(\mathbb{F}, \rho, \delta, n, \ell) + O(Q^2/2^{\kappa}).$$

Moreover, the transformed non-interactive argument has adaptive soundness error and knowledge error $\Theta(Q \cdot \varepsilon_{\mathsf{fs}}^{\mathsf{FRI}}(\mathbb{F}, \rho, \delta, n, \ell, Q))$ against $O(Q)$-query quantum adversaries.

Extension to Batched FRI. In practice, it is common to run a *Batched FRI* protocol, which allows a prover to simultaneously prove the δ-correlated agreement[4] of t functions $f_1, \ldots, f_t$ by running the FRI protocol on the batched function $G = \sum_i \alpha_i f_i$ for randomly sampled α_i provided by the verifier. We extend our analysis of FRI to this version of Batched FRI and establish its round-by-round (knowledge) soundness.

Theorem 2 (Informally Stated, see Theorem 7). *For finite field $\mathbb{F}$, evaluation domain $L \subset \mathbb{F}$ of size 2^n, constants $\rho \in (0,1)$, $\delta \in (0, 1-\sqrt{\rho})$, and positive integers ℓ, t, the Batched FRI protocol has round-by-round (knowledge) soundness error*

$$\varepsilon_{\mathsf{rbr}}^{\mathsf{bFRI}}(\mathbb{F}, \rho, \delta, n, \ell, t) = \max\{O((2^{2n})/(\rho^{3/2}|\mathbb{F}|)), (1-\delta)^{\ell}\}.$$

As before, establishing round-by-round soundness allows us to securely apply the BCS transformation, obtaining a non-interactive argument in the random oracle model.

[4] Informally, functions have δ-correlated agreement if they are all δ-close to some prespecified Reed-Solomon code and all have the same agreement set; see [14] for full details.

Corollary 2 (Informally Stated; see Corollary 5). *For finite field $\mathbb{F}$, evaluation domain $L \subset \mathbb{F}$ of size 2^n, constants $\rho \in (0, 1)$, $\delta \in (0, 1 - \sqrt{\rho})$, and positive integers ℓ, t, given a random oracle with κ-bits of output and query bound $Q \geq 1$, compiling Batched FRI with the BCS transformation yields a non-interactive argument in the random oracle model with adaptive soundness error and knowledge error*

$$\varepsilon_{\mathsf{fs}}^{\mathsf{bFRI}}(\mathbb{F}, \rho, \delta, n, \ell, t, Q, \kappa) = Q \cdot \varepsilon_{\mathsf{rbr}}^{\mathsf{bFRI}}(\mathbb{F}, \rho, \delta, n, \ell, t) + O(Q^2/2^\kappa).$$

Moreover, the transformed non-interactive argument has adaptive soundness error and knowledge error $\Theta(Q \cdot \varepsilon_{\mathsf{fs}}^{\mathsf{bFRI}}(\mathbb{F}, \rho, \delta, n, \ell, t, Q, \kappa))$ against $O(Q)$-query quantum adversaries.

To the best of our knowledge, our results are the first to establish the security of non-interactive analogs of FRI and Batched FRI in the random oracle model.

A Variant of Batched FRI. To save on communication costs, a variant of Batched FRI is sometimes used, where the batched function G has the form $G = \sum_i \alpha^{i-1} f_i$ for challenge α randomly sampled and sent by the verifier. In both the context of regular soundness and round-by-round soundness, this version of Batched FRI incurs some soundness loss proportional to t. In particular, in Theorem 2, the round-by-round soundness error for this Batched FRI protocol is $\varepsilon_{\mathsf{rbr}}^{\mathsf{bFRI}}(\mathbb{F}, \rho, \delta, n, \ell, t) = \max\{O((2^{2n} \cdot t)/(\rho^{3/2}|\mathbb{F}|)), (1 - \delta)^\ell\}$; see [14] for complete details.

Round-by-Round Soundness Error versus Standard Soundness Error of FRI. Ben-Sasson et al. [6] give the best known provable soundness bounds for (Batched) FRI; in fact, we leverage many tools from their results to show our round-by-round soundness bounds. Roughly speaking, [6] show that the soundness error of (Batched) FRI is $\varepsilon_1 + \varepsilon_2 + \varepsilon_3$, where $\varepsilon_1 = O(2^{2n}/(\rho^{3/2}|\mathbb{F}|))$, $\varepsilon_2 = O((2^n \cdot n\sqrt{\rho})/|\mathbb{F}|)$, and $\varepsilon_3 = (1 - \delta)^\ell$. Then our RBR soundness bound for (Batched) FRI is given by $\max\{\varepsilon_1, \varepsilon_3\}$.

Round-by-Round Knowledge Error. Both FRI and Batched FRI additionally have *round-by-round knowledge error* [25,26,44] identical to the round-by-round soundness errors given in Theorems 1 and 2. The BCS transformation preserves this type of knowledge soundness, yielding a SNARK. See Sect. 2.1 for more discussion.

A General Tool for Proving RBR (Knowledge) Soundness. We go on to analyze proof systems that rely on the FRI protocol as a subroutine. To this end, we introduce a family of IOPs which we call *δ-correlated IOPs*, where $\delta \geq 0$ is a parameter. This family encompasses all of the aforementioned protocols. In a nutshell, we say an IOP is δ-correlated if the prover is supposed to send oracles to maps that are δ-close to low-degree polynomials in a *correlated* manner. Correlation here means that the domain where these maps agree with low-degree polynomials is the same among all the maps. In a δ-correlated IOP, during the verification phase, the verifier: (1) checks some algebraic equalities involving some evaluations of these maps; and (2) verifies that all the received oracles correspond indeed to δ-correlated maps (we assume the verifier has another oracle to perform this check). When $\delta = 0$, a δ-correlated IOPs can be seen as a subclass of RS-encoded IOPs [8,26]. See [14] for a more in-depth comparison.

This points to a "recipe" for building a particular family of SNARKs: first, construct a δ-correlated IOP; then, instantiate the check for δ-correlation using an interactive protocol, e.g., Batched FRI [6]. This produces an IOP as a result. Finally, use the aforementioned BCS transformation on this IOP to produce a succinct non-interactive argument. If this argument is knowledge sound, one has obtained a SNARK. Figure 1 summarizes this construction. It is immediate to see that the previously mentioned protocols (Plonky2, RISC Zero, ethSTARKs, etc.) are actual instantiations of this construction.

$$\delta\text{-correlated IOP} \xrightarrow[\delta\text{-correlation}]{\text{IOPP for}} \text{IOP} \xrightarrow[\text{Transformation}]{\text{BCS}} \text{SNARG/SNARK}$$

Fig. 1. A recipe for building a succinct non-interactive argument.

We then provide general results for proving that the resulting succinct non-interactive argument is knowledge sound. Precisely, we prove the following:

1. **RBR soundness of Batched FRI.** As a general result, we prove that the (Batched) FRI protocol is RBR sound and RBR knowledge sound. We remark that Batched FRI can be used for checking δ-correlated agreement of a collection of maps [6].
2. **From RBR knowledge when the adversary sends low degree polynomials, to general RBR knowledge.** Consider a δ-correlated IOP Π, and suppose attackers always send oracles to low degree polynomials. We prove that if Π is RBR (knowledge) sound under this assumption, then it is also RBR (knowledge) sound in general, and that the soundness error only increases by a (relatively) small factor.
3. **From a RBR knowledge sound δ-correlated IOP to a RBR knowledge sound IOP.** Again let Π be a δ-correlated IOP. By using an interactive protocol Π_{CA} to check for δ-correlation, Π can be turned into a regular IOP Π_{compiled}. We prove that this compilation preserves RBR (knowledge) soundness, assuming Π_{CA} is RBR sound (not necessarily RBR knowledge sound).
4. **From a RBR knowledge sound IOP to a SNARK.** We then apply the BCS compilation results from [9] to obtain a SNARK.

In conclusion, we show that given any succinct non-interactive argument constructed as in Fig. 1 (using Batched FRI to check for δ-correlation), one can show its knowledge soundness simply by proving RBR knowledge soundness of the underlying δ-correlated IOP *under the assumption that the adversary is constrained to sending oracles to low-degree polynomials.* The latter can greatly simplify the analysis since it allows one to work with the simplicity of IOPs (as opposed to arguments) and the convenient properties of polynomials.

Thus, our methods not only allow us to prove FS-security, they also remove the complexity of dealing with maps that are close to low-degree polynomials when using FRI within a protocol. This allows us to analyze the interactive version of these protocols in a similar way as when one studies *Polynomial* IOPs [21], where, by definition, soundness is only considered for adversaries that send low-degree polynomials.

According to our formalism, a δ-correlated IOP where we constrain adversaries to always send low-degree polynomials is in fact a 0-correlated IOP. Then, Item (2) above can be seen as a result that relates the RBR knowledge soundness of a δ-correlated IOP for $\delta = 0$ and for $\delta > 0$. Overall, our security results can be organized and depicted as in Fig. 2; also see Theorem 3.

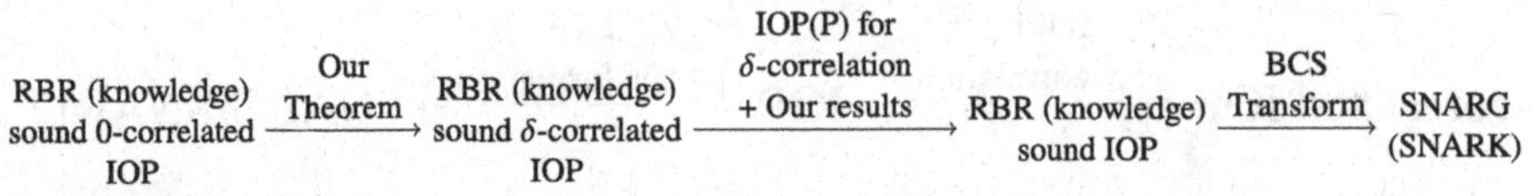

Fig. 2. Another recipe for building a SNARG/SNARK.

Theorem 3 (Informally Stated, see Theorem 8). *Let $\Pi_\delta^{\mathcal{O}}$ be a δ-correlated IOP, where $\mathcal{O}$ is an oracle for δ-correlated agreement. Let $0 < \rho, \eta \leq 1$ and $\delta = 1 - \sqrt{\rho} - \eta$. Assume Π_0 has RBR knowledge soundness with error ε. Then Π_δ has RBR knowledge soundness with error $\varepsilon/(2\sqrt{\rho}\eta)$.*

Moreover, if Π' is an IOP for testing δ-correlated agreement in a Reed-Solomon code with RBR soundness error ε', then the protocol Π_{compiled} obtained by replacing $\mathcal{O}$ in Π_δ with Π' has RBR knowledge soundness with error $\varepsilon_{\mathsf{compiled}} = \max\{\varepsilon/(2\sqrt{\rho}\eta), \varepsilon'\}$. Finally, given a random oracle with κ-bits of output and query bound $Q \geq 1$, compiling Π_{compiled} with the BCS transformation yields a succinct non-interactive argument in the random oracle model with knowledge error $Q \cdot \max\{\varepsilon/(2\sqrt{\rho}\eta), \varepsilon'\} + O(Q^2/2^\kappa)$.

Remark 1. As we mentioned, the notion of δ-correlated IOP is closely related to that of *RS-encoded IOP* from [8,26]. The works of [8,26] also provide a method for compiling a RBR (knowledge) sound RS-encoded IOP into RBR (knowledge sound IOPs); e.g., see [26, Theorem 8.2]. However, our result allows to use a proximity parameter up to the Johnson bound, i.e., we can select $\delta = 1 - \sqrt{\rho} - \eta$ for any arbitrarily small $\eta > 0$, while the compilation results from [8,26] constrain δ to be within the unique decoding radius $\delta < \frac{1-\rho}{2}$. On the other hand, in some sense, RS-encoded IOPs encompass a wider class of protocols than δ-correlated ones. See [14] for further discussion.

Remark 2. Many security analyses of SNARKs obtained by combining Plonk-like protocols with so-called KZG polynomial commitments [43] can assume that an adversary always sends oracles to polynomials of appropriate degree. Intuitively, this is due to the fact that the KZG polynomial commitment scheme ensures that a committed function is indeed a polynomial of appropriate degree.

However, in our scenario, due to the usage of the FRI protocol instead of KZG, adversaries are only constrained to sending (oracles to) maps that are *close to* polynomials of appropriate degree. This makes the soundness analysis of our protocols more subtle. Indeed, as we mentioned, besides showing that FRI itself is RBR sound, most of our work is concerned with reducing the analysis to the case when the adversary actually sends oracles to polynomials of the appropriate degree.

Round-by-Round Soundness of Specific δ-Correlated Proof Systems. We can apply all the tools developed so far to specific protocols whose construction follows the outline from Figs. 1 and 2. In short, these are protocols obtained by compiling a δ-correlated IOP into a succinct non-interactive argument via a protocol for δ-correlated agreement and the BCS transformation. Thanks to Theorems 2 and 3, we can prove the knowledge soundness of these protocols just by proving that the corresponding 0-correlated IOP has RBR knowledge soundness. Recall that in a 0-correlated IOP, the adversary is assumed to always send oracles to low-degree polynomials.

Some of the protocols that fit into this framework are many "Plonk-like" proof systems that use FRI instead of the KZG polynomial commitment scheme; e.g., Plonky2 [60], Redshift [44], and RISC Zero [68]. Here we use the term "Plonk-like" to loosely refer to protocols that use an interactive permutation argument [15,19,47,48,73] as a subroutine (we use the term "Plonk-like" because the Plonk SNARK [34] helped popularize the use of this permutation-checking procedure). Other protocols that fit in our framework but are not "Plonk-like" are ethSTARK or DEEP-ALI [10].

We focus our attention mostly on Plonky2 since we believe that, among all these protocols in 0-correlated IOP form, Plonky2 is the most involved to analyze. Indeed, Plonky2 was designed to be used over a small field (the 64-bit so-called Goldilocks field). Because of this, some checks are repeated in parallel in order to increase its security. The task of correctly designing these parallel repetitions is subtle, and indeed in the full version of our work [14], we describe an (arguably more natural) variation of Plonky2 with dramatically *less* security than Plonky2 itself. To the best of our knowledge, this variation is *not used* in practice—we are highlighting it here to illustrate a potential pitfall to be avoided.

Accordingly, we rigorously define a general "Plonk-like" δ-correlated IOP, which captures many "Plonk-like" protocols that rely on the FRI protocol. We denote this δ-correlated IOP by $\mathsf{OPlonky}(\delta)$. We then formally prove that when $\delta = 0$ (i.e., when adversaries are constrained to sending low-degree polynomials), $\mathsf{OPlonky}(0)$ has RBR soundness and knowledge soundness. Together with our general results and our results on batched FRI, this proves in particular that the SNARK version of Plonky2 is indeed knowledge sound (as well as all other "Plonk-like" protocols of the form $\mathsf{OPlonky}(\delta)$). Adapting Theorem 3 to our abstraction OPlonky, we obtain the following result.

Theorem 4 (Informally Stated, see Lemmas 1 and 3). *Let $\mathbb{F}$ be a finite field and $\mathbb{K}$ be a finite extension of $\mathbb{F}$ and let $D \subseteq \mathbb{F}$ be an evaluation domain for maps. Let $\mathcal{P} = \{P_1, \ldots, P_k\}$ be a list of $2r+\ell$-variate circuit constraint polynomials over $\mathbb{F}$ for $k, r, \ell \geq 1$. For parameters $n, t, u \geq 1$, $s = \lceil r/u \rceil$, and $m \geq 3, \rho = (n+1)/|D| \in (0,1), \eta \in (0, \sqrt{\rho}/2m)$ and $\delta = 1 - \sqrt{\rho} - \eta$, the protocol $\mathsf{OPlonky}^{O}$, when the verifier is given an oracle O for δ-correlated agreement in the Reed-Solomon code $\mathsf{RS}[\mathbb{F}, D, n+1]$, has round-by-round soundness error*

$$\varepsilon_{\mathsf{rbr}}^{\mathsf{OPlonky},O}(\mathbb{F}, \mathbb{K}, D, n, k, r, s, t, u, d, \rho, \eta) = \frac{1}{2\eta\sqrt{\rho}} \cdot \max\left\{O\left(\left(\frac{n(r+u)}{|\mathbb{F}|}\right)^t\right), O\left(\left(\frac{k+st}{|\mathbb{F}|}\right)^t\right), \frac{n \cdot \max\{u+1, d\}}{|\mathbb{K} \setminus D|}\right\},$$

where $d = \max_i\{\deg(P_i)\}$ and D is an evaluation domain for RS codes. Moreover, when $\delta = 0$ then we have

$$\varepsilon_{\mathsf{rbr}}^{\mathsf{OPlonky},O}(\mathbb{F}, \mathbb{K}, D, n, k, r, s, t, u, d, \rho, \eta) = \max\left\{O\left(\left(\frac{n(r+u)}{|\mathbb{F}|}\right)^t\right), O\left(\left(\frac{k+st}{|\mathbb{F}|}\right)^t\right), \frac{n \cdot \max\{u+1, d\}}{|\mathbb{K} \setminus D|}\right\}.$$

Remark 3. The parameter t in Theorem 4 controls the number of times certain checks in OPlonky are performed "in parallel". In most Plonk-like protocols, one uses $t = 1$ and a large field $\mathbb{F}$ to ensure an adequate security level. However, some projects (e.g., Plonky2) currently feature a 64-bit field $\mathbb{F}$, and use $t = 2$ to increase security.

We show in this paper that, if done properly, the resulting FS-transformed protocol does achieve the targeted security level. However, in the full version of our work [14], we explain that this result is surprisingly subtle: certain natural ways of implementing the t-fold repetition actually result in RBR security (and, correspondingly, the post-FS security [2]) that is much lower than the one attained in Theorem 4. While (to our knowledge) all existing projects do implement the t-fold repetition properly so as to ensure FS-security, we highlight this subtlety so that protocol designers continue to avoid this potential pitfall.

We can instantiate the oracle O in Theorem 4 with Batched FRI and obtain the following result.

Theorem 5 (Informally Stated, see Theorem 9). *Let $\mathbb{F}$ be a finite field, $\mathbb{K}$ be a finite extension of $\mathbb{F}$, and $D \subset \mathbb{F}^*$. Let $\mathcal{P} = \{P_1, \ldots, P_k\}$ be a list of $2r + \ell$-variate circuit constraint polynomials over $\mathbb{F}$ for $k, r, \ell, n \geq 1$. For integer $u \geq 1$, $s = \lceil r/u \rceil$, and parameters $\rho, \eta > 0$, $\delta = 1 - \sqrt{\rho} - \eta$, and $N, q \geq 1$, the protocol OPlonky composed with Batched FRI (replacing O) has round-by-round soundness error:*

$$\varepsilon_{\mathsf{rbr}}^{\mathsf{OPlonky}}(\mathbb{F}, \mathbb{K}, D, n, k, r, s, t, u, d, \rho, \eta, N, q) = \max\{\varepsilon_{\mathsf{rbr}}^{\mathsf{OPlonky},O}(\mathbb{F}, \mathbb{K}, D, n, k, r, s, t, u, d, \rho, \eta), \varepsilon_{\mathsf{rbr}}^{\mathsf{bFRI}}(\mathbb{F}, D, \rho, \delta, N, q)\},$$

where $d = \max_i\{\deg(P_i)\}$.

Given the above protocol is a round-by-round sound IOP, as in Theorem 3, we can now apply the BCS transformation to obtain a secure non-interactive argument in the random oracle model.

Corollary 3 (Informally Stated; see [14]). *Let* $\mathbb{F}$ *be a finite field,* $\mathbb{K}$ *be a finite extension of* $\mathbb{F}$*, and* $D \subset \mathbb{F}^*$*. Let* $\mathcal{P} = \{P_1, \ldots, P_k\}$ *be a list of* $2r + \ell$*-variate circuit constraint polynomials over* $\mathbb{F}$ *for* $k, r, \ell, n \geq 1$*. For integers* $u, t \geq 1$*,* $s = \lceil r/u \rceil$*, and parameters* $\rho, \eta > 0$*,* $\delta = 1 - \sqrt{\rho} - \eta$*, and* $N, q \geq 1$*, given a random oracle with* κ*-bits of output and a query bound* $Q \geq 1$*, using the BCS transformation to compile* OPlonky *composed with Batched FRI yields a non-interactive argument in the random oracle model with adaptive soundness error and knowledge error*

$$\varepsilon_{\mathsf{fs}}^{\mathsf{OPlonky}}(\mathbb{F}, \mathbb{K}, D, n, k, r, s, t, u, d, \rho, \eta, N, q, \kappa, Q) = Q\varepsilon_{\mathsf{rbr}}^{\mathsf{OPlonky}}(\mathbb{F}, \mathbb{K}, D, n, k, r, s, t, u, d, \rho, \eta, N, q) + O(Q^2/2^\kappa),$$

where $d = \max_i\{\deg(P_i)\}$*. Moreover, the the transformed non-interactive argument has adaptive soundness error and knowledge error*

$$\Theta(Q \cdot \varepsilon_{\mathsf{fs}}^{\mathsf{OPlonky}}(\mathbb{F}, \mathbb{K}, D, n, k, r, s, t, u, d, \rho, \eta, N, q, \kappa, Q))$$

versus $O(Q)$*-query quantum adversaries.*

Remark 4. We stress that the above theorems do not imply anything for the original work of Plonk [34], or any other Plonk variants that utilize the so-called KZG polynomial commitment scheme [43] as their low-degree test. The tools we leverage to show Fiat-Shamir security of our protocols rely on the low-degree test also being an IOP or an IOP of Proximity, which the KZG scheme is not. While it is likely one can extend our analysis to handle using the KZG scheme, we do not explore that direction in this work.

RISC Zero and ethSTARK. When it comes to RISC Zero and ethSTARK, we sketch why their 0-correlated formulations have RBR knowledge soundness, as opposed to fully formally proving these facts. We do that due to brevity (since formally describing these protocols is a lengthy task), and because proving that these 0-correlated IOPs are RBR knowledge sound is a relatively straightforward task, as our analysis of OPlonky indicates. Moreover, RISC Zero's whitepaper is in draft form at the moment of writing [68]. We hope practitioners can follow the techniques and ideas exposed in this paper to prove in a relatively simple way that their SNARKs are indeed FS-secure.

1.3 Additional Related Work

The Fiat-Shamir (FS) transform [31] has been studied and used extensively to remove interaction from interactive protocols. While it is known that the FS transformation is secure when applied to sound protocols with a constant number of rounds in the random oracle model (ROM) [1,31,58], it is well-known that there exist protocols that are secure under FS in the ROM but insecure for *any* concrete instantiation of the random oracle [3,13,36]. Furthermore, several natural classes of secure interactive protocols are rendered insecure when applying FS (e.g., sequential repetition of a protocol and parallel repetition of certain protocols) [2,22,72], and real-world implementations of FS are often done incorrectly, leading to vulnerabilities [12,29]. Despite this, FS is widely deployed and is a critical component in the majority of SNARG and SNARK constructions.

Recent work has extensively studied which protocols can be securely instantiated under Fiat-Shamir (either in the ROM or using suitable hash-function families). As mentioned before, the general tools of state-restoration soundness [9], round-by-round soundness [22], and special soundness [2,28,72] have been introduced as soundness notions that "behave nicely" under Fiat-Shamir. Prior to these tools, a variety of works [23,40,42] circumvented the impossibility results of [13] by utilizing stronger hardness assumptions to construct Fiat-Shamir compatible hash function families. Another line of work [7,16,27,37,63,64,69,71] follows the frameworks of Kilian [45] and Micali [53] to compile interactive oracle proofs [9] into efficient arguments and SNARKs via collision-resistant hash functions [9,45] or in the random oracle model [9,53].

1.4 Organization

In Sect. 2, we give an overview of our main technical results. Section 3 presents our main results in full detail. Section 4 discusses some future directions. Due to space constraints, most technical details are deferred to the full version of our paper [14].

2 Technical Overview

Our main technical contributions are three-fold. First, we formally prove the round-by-round (knowledge) soundness of the FRI protocol. Second, we build a general tool for proving round-by-round (knowledge) soundness of δ-correlated IOPs. Third, we give a δ-correlated IOP called OPlonky, prove its round-by-round (knowledge) soundness, and showcase how it captures many "Plonk-like" protocols used in practice. Additionally, we sketch how to extend the OPlonky analysis to the ethSTARK protocol. In Sect. 2.1, we briefly discuss round-by-round soundness and its relation to Fiat-Shamir; in Sect. 2.2, we give an overview of the round-by-round soundness of FRI and Batched FRI; in Sect. 2.3, we introduce the concept of δ-correlated IOP and prove our general results about them; in Sect. 2.4, we give an overview of the round-by-round (knowledge) soundness of OPlonky; in Sect. 2.5, we discuss how a similar analysis can be done for the ethSTARK protocol.

2.1 Round-by-Round Soundness and Fiat-Shamir

Our tool of choice for establishing Fiat-Shamir security is *round-by-round soundness* [22]. Informally, a public-coin interactive protocol for a language L is *round-by-round sound* (RBR sound) if at any point during the execution of the protocol, the protocol is in a well-defined state (depending on the protocol execution so far) and some of these states are "doomed", where being "doomed" means that no matter what message the prover sends, with overwhelming probability over the verifier messages, the protocol remains "doomed". A bit more formally, RBR soundness error ε states that: (1) if $x \notin L$ the initial state of the protocol is "doomed"; (2) if the protocol is in a "doomed" state during any non-final round of the protocol, then for any message sent by the prover, the protocol remains doomed with probability at least $1 - \varepsilon$ over the verifier messages; and (3) if the protocol terminates in a "doomed" state, then the verifier rejects. Chiesa et al. [25] extend RBR soundness to *RBR knowledge soundness*, which roughly says that if (1) the protocol is in a "doomed" state during any round of interaction, and (2) *every* prover message can force the protocol to leave this "doomed" state with probability at least ε_k (over the verifier randomness), then an extractor can efficiently extract a witness (with probability 1) simply by examining the current protocol state and the prover's next message.

Canetti et al. [22] introduced RBR soundness as a tool for showing Fiat-Shamir security of interactive proofs [38] when used in conjunction with a suitable family of correlation intractable hash functions [24]. In particular, random oracles are correlation intractable when the set of "doomed" states of a protocol is sufficiently sparse; i.e., for small enough RBR soundness error. RBR soundness readily extends to the language of interactive oracle proofs (IOPs) [9], and hence the Fiat-Shamir compiler result of [22] readily extends to IOPs, and can be readily adapted to the random oracle model as well. However, applying this compiler to IOPs directly introduces some undesirable effects: the constructed non-interactive argument would have proof lengths proportional to the length of the oracle sent by the prover since the compiler of [22] does not compress prover messages in any way. This leads to long proofs and verification times, negating any succinct verification the IOP may have had. Moreover, the transformation of [22] says nothing about the knowledge soundness of the resulting non-interactive argument, even in the random oracle model.

While it is likely that, in the random oracle model, one could argue that the transformation of [22] retains knowledge soundness if the underlying IOP is RBR knowledge sound, we do not prove this fact; moreover, the loss of verifier succinctness is still an issue even if knowledge soundness is retained. Thus to circumvent the above issues, we utilize the BCS transformation [9] for IOPs. Informally, the BCS transformation first compresses oracles sent by the prover using a Merkle tree [52] and then replaces any queries made by the verifier to prover oracles with additional rounds of interaction where the verifier asks the prover its queries, and the prover responds with said queries and Merkle authentication paths to verify consistency. It was shown that if an IOP is round-by-round sound then applying BCS to this IOP gives a SNARK in the random oracle model [25,26]. Thus showing the RBR soundness of FRI and OPlonkyallows us to readily show Fiat-Shamir security of these protocols under the BCS transformation in the random oracle model, yielding our results. Thus in what follows, we give a high-level overview of the round-by-round soundness proofs for both FRI and OPlonky.

2.2 Round-by-Round Soundness of FRI

We give a high-level sketch of the round-by-round soundness of FRI in this section; for full details, see [14]. As previously stated, FRI is an interactive oracle proof of proximity for testing whether or not a polynomial specified by a prover is "close to" a particular space of Reed-Solomon codewords. More formally, for finite field $\mathbb{F}$, multiplicative subgroup $L_0 \subset \mathbb{F}^*$ of size $N = 2^n$, and degree bound $d_0 = 2^k$ for $k \in \mathbb{N}$, $\mathsf{RS} := \mathsf{RS}[\mathbb{F}, L_0, d_0] \subset \mathbb{F}^N$ is the set of all polynomials $f : L_0 \to \mathbb{F}$ of degree at most $d_0 - 1$, and the FRI protocol allows for a prover to succinctly prove to a verifier that a function $G_0 : L_0 \to \mathbb{F}$ is within some proximity bound δ of the RS code. That is, if a verifier accepts the interaction, then the verifier is convinced that there exists $f \in \mathsf{RS}$ such that $\Delta(G_0, f) < \delta N$, where Δ is the Hamming distance between G_0 and f (when viewing them as vectors in $\mathbb{F}^N$). We say that such a G_0 is *δ-close* to RS; otherwise, we say that G_0 is *δ-far* from RS (i.e., $\Delta(G_0, f) \geq \delta N$ for all $f \in \mathsf{RS}$).

To achieve succinct verification, the FRI protocol first interactively compresses G_0 during a *folding phase*,[5] which proceeds as follows. First, the prover sends oracle G_0 to the verifier. Next, the verifier samples $x_0 \in \mathbb{F}$ uniformly at random and sends it to the prover. Now the prover defines new oracle $G_1 : L_1 \to \mathbb{F}$ over the new domain $L_1 = (L_0)^2 := \{z^2 : z \in L_0\}$ of size $N/2$, where for any $s \in L_1$, if $s', s'' \in L_0$ are the square roots of s, then we have

$$G_1(s) = (x_0 - s')(s'' - s')^{-1} G_0(s'') + (x_0 - s'')(s' - s'')^{-1} G_0(s'). \quad (1)$$

Given G_1, the prover and verifier now recursively engage in the above folding procedure with the function G_1, where the claim is that G_1 is δ-close to a new Reed-Solomon code $\mathsf{RS}[\mathbb{F}, L_1, d_1]$ for $d_1 = d_0/2$; this recursion continues $\log(d_0) = k$ times which results in prover oracles $G_0, G_1, \ldots, G_{k-1}$ and verifier challenges $x_0, x_1, \ldots, x_{k-1}$.

After the folding phase, the prover and verifier now engage in the *query phase*. During this phase, the prover sends a constant value $G_k \in \mathbb{F}$ to the verifier, and the verifier samples a uniformly random challenge $s_0 \in L_0$ tto check the consistency of all pairs of functions G_{i-1}, G_i for $i \in \{1, \ldots, k\}$ as follows. The verifier first checks consistency of G_0 and G_1 using Eq. (1); in particular, if we set $s_1 = (s_0)^2$ and let t_0 be the other square root of s_1 (i.e., $(t_0)^2 = s_1$ and $t_0 \neq s_0$), the verifier checks that $G_1(s_1)$ is consistent with $G_0(s_0)$ and $G_0(t_0)$ via Eq. (1). This check is then performed for every pair of functions G_{i-1} and G_i via Eq. (1) using challenge x_{i-1} and $G_i(s_i)$, $G_{i-1}(s_{i-1})$, and $G_{i-1}(t_{i-1})$, where $s_i = (s_{i-1})^2$ and $t_{i-1} \neq s_{i-1}$ is the other square root of s_i. The verifier accepts if and only if all of

[5] [4] refers to this as the *commit phase*. We view the term "folding phase" as more appropriate given the nature of the compression.

these checks pass. More generally, the verifier performs the above query phase (in parallel) $\ell \geq 1$ times and outputs accept if and only if all checks pass.

To show RBR soundness of FRI, we first turn to the prior soundness analyses of FRI. Suppose that G_0 is δ-far from $\mathsf{RS}[\mathbb{F}, L_0, d_0]$, then it turns out a malicious prover has two strategies for fooling the verifier: (1) "luck out" in the sense that for $x_0 \xleftarrow{\$} \mathbb{F}$ sent by the verifier, the new function G_1 is δ-close to $\mathsf{RS}[\mathbb{F}, L_1, d_1]$; or (2) send some $G_1' \neq G_1$ that is δ-close to $\mathsf{RS}[\mathbb{F}, L_1, d_1]$. Intuitively, strategy (2) never increases the probability the prover can fool the verifier since even though G_1' is closer to the Reed-Solomon codespace, this improvement is offset by the fact that G_1 and G_1' will differ at many different points. Thus the optimal prover strategy is to simply behave honestly by sending the correct function during every round using Eq. (1), and hoping to "luck out" from the verifier challenge during that round.

FRI Round-by-Round Soundness Overview. We adapt the above intuition for the RBR soundness of FRI. Let P^* be our (possibly malicious) prover. Let ε_1 be the probability that P^* "lucks out" as described above. First, since G_0 is assumed to be δ-far, and moreover G_0 is honestly sent to the verifier, the protocol, begins in a doomed state. Then if the verifier sends x_0 such that P^* "lucks out" and the function G_1 is δ-close, then we say the protocol is no longer in a doomed state. This happens with probability at most ε_1.

Building on this, suppose the partial transcript so far consists of (G_0, x_0) and suppose that this state is doomed; that is, both G_0 and G_1 are δ-far functions. Now the prover P^* may send some function G_1' that may or may not be equal to G_1 (as given in Eq. (1)), and then the verifier responds with challenge x_1. However, as described before, sending $G_1' \neq G_1$ doesn't increase the probability that the prover fools the verifier, and we want the RBR soundness analysis to reflect this as well. Thus we say that the current state of the protocol, given by (G_0, x_0, G_1', x_1) is not doomed if and only if $G_1' = G_1$ and P^* "lucks out" with the function G_2 (again defined via Eq. (1) using x_1 and G_1). In other words, the protocol remains in a doomed state if: (1) $G_1' \neq G_1$; or G_2 is δ-far (i.e., the prover didn't "luck out"). Thus the protocol leaves its doomed state with probability at most ε_1. This analysis generalizes to all rounds of the folding phase: given any partial transcript $(G_0, x_0, G_1', x_1, \ldots, G_{i-1}', x_{i-1})$ that is in a doomed state, if P^* sends function G_i' and the verifier sends challenge x_i, then the protocol is no longer doomed if and only if (1) the prover "lucked out" and G_{i+1} is δ-close; and (2) *all* $G_j' = G_j$ for $j \in \{1, \ldots, i-1\}$. And again, the protocol is no longer doomed with probability at most ε_1.

To complete the analysis, we now consider the final round of the protocol, which consists of the query phase. Suppose that the partial transcript for this round is given by $(G_0, x_0, G_1', x_1, \ldots, G_{k-1}', x_{k-1})$ and suppose the protocol is in a doomed state. At this point, P^*'s hands are tied: it must send a constant $G_k \in \mathbb{F}$ to the verifier, and the verifier then uniformly samples $s_0^{(1)}, \ldots, s_0^{(\ell)} \in L_0$ and performs its checks. Thus, the only way the protocol can leave the doomed state is if *all* of these checks pass; in particular, if a single check fails then the protocol remains doomed (and, in fact, the verifier rejects). Let ε_2 denote the probability that a single verifier check passes; that is, a single chain of checks depending on $s_0^{(1)}$ passes (i.e., computing the squares and square roots at every level, and checking consistency across all levels with this check). Then the probability P^* can leave the doomed state is exactly ε_2; extending this to ℓ checks (which are performed uniformly and independently at random) gives us that the protocol leaves the doomed state with probability at most ε_2^ℓ. Considering the folding and query phases, the discussion above shows that the FRI protocol has RBR soundness error $\varepsilon_{\mathsf{rbr}}^{\mathsf{FRI}} = \max\{\varepsilon_1, \varepsilon_2^\ell\}$.

Batched FRI Round-by-Round Soundness Overview. Extending the above analysis to Batched FRI is straightforward. Briefly, Batched FRI invokes FRI on a random linear combination of t functions $f_1, \ldots, f_t \colon L_0 \to \mathbb{F}$. In more detail, first the prover sends oracles $f_1, \ldots, f_t$ to the verifier, then the verifier responds with random challenges $\alpha_1, \ldots, \alpha_t$. The prover and verifier then engage in the FRI protocol using function $G_0 = \sum_i \alpha_i f_i$.[6] Finally, Batched FRI modifies the query phase of FRI to also check consistency between f_i and G_0 exactly via the equation $G_0 = \sum_i \alpha_i f_i$. Key to Batched FRI is that if all f_i are δ-close to $\mathsf{RS}[\mathbb{F}, L_0, d_0]$, then G_0 is also δ-close, and if even one f_j is δ-far, then with high probability G_0 is also δ-far.

The RBR soundness analysis of Batched FRI proceeds as follows. Let P^* again denote our (possibly malicious) prover. The protocol begins in a doomed state; namely, there exists at least one f_j that is δ-far from $\mathsf{RS}[\mathbb{F}, L_0, d_0]$. Then P^* honestly sends $f_1, \ldots, f_t$ to the verifier,[7] and the verifier responds with $\alpha_1, \ldots, \alpha_t \in \mathbb{F}$ sampled uniformly and independently at random. Let ε_t be the probability that G_0 is δ-close given that there exists at least one f_j that is δ-far, where the probability is taken over $\alpha_1, \ldots, \alpha_t$. Then we say the protocol is no longer in a doomed state if and only if G_0 is δ-close; thus during this round, P^* can leave the doomed state with probability at most ε_t. Now suppose that $(f_0, \ldots, f_t, \alpha_1, \ldots, \alpha_t)$ is the current protocol state and that this state is doomed. The prover and verifier now engage in FRI using some function G_0' constructed by P^* as input. The observation here is that we can now invoke the RBR soundness analysis of FRI directly, with the following slight change for the first round of FRI. Suppose P^* sends G_0' to the verifier and the verifier responds with x_0. Then the protocol is no longer in a doomed state if and only if $G_0' = G_0$ and G_1 is δ-close, where G_1 is defined via Eq. (1) with respect to the correct function G_0. In particular, the intuition behind the prover's strategy remains the same: if P^* sends some other $G_0' \neq G_0$, then the verifier is more likely to detect this change when checking consistency of G_0' and $f_1, \ldots, f_t$, so P^* can only leaved the doomed state of the protocol if it behaves honestly and "lucks out" with verifier challenge x_0. Finally, we remark

[6] In practice to save on communication, only a single α is sent and the linear combination is computed with $\alpha_i = \alpha^{i-1}$, at the cost of an increased soundness error; see [14] for details.

[7] This is necessary, if a malicious prover is allowed to send dishonest $f_1^*, \ldots, f_t^*$ such that all are δ-close, then the protocol reduces to the honest prover analysis.

that the final round (i.e., the query phase) of Batched FRI with the additional checks between $f_1, \ldots, f_t$ and G_0' has the same RBR soundness error ε_2 as with FRI. Thus the RBR soundness error of Batched FRI is $\varepsilon_{\mathsf{rbr}}^{\mathsf{bFRI}} = \max\{\varepsilon_t, \varepsilon_1, \varepsilon_2^\ell\}$, where ℓ is the number of times the query phase is repeated.

Instantiating ε_1, ε_2, and ε_3. For the query phase, the best one can hope for is $\varepsilon_2 = (1 - \delta)$ [4,6,11,70]; for the folding phase, there is a long line of work done towards improving the bounds on ε_1 [4,6,11]. In our work, we utilize the best known provable bounds on ε_1 given by Ben-Sasson et al. [6], and note that any improvements for ε_1 directly improve the round-by-round soundness error of FRI. In particular, we have $\varepsilon_1 = O(2^{2n}/(\rho \cdot |\mathbb{F}|))$, where $\rho = d_0/|L_0|$ and $|L_0| = 2^n$. This yields our stated round-by-round soundness error in Theorem 1. Finally, [6] also show that $\varepsilon_t = \varepsilon_1$ for Batched FRI, which gives us Batched FRI round-by-round soundness error $\varepsilon_{\mathsf{rbr}}^{\mathsf{bFRI}} = \max\{\varepsilon_1, \varepsilon_2^\ell\}$, yielding our stated round-by-round soundness error in Theorem 2. See [14] for a complete discussion and proof of the round-by-round soundness of FRI and Batched FRI.

FRI Round-by-Round Knowledge Overview. Recall that a protocol has RBR knowledge error ε_{k} if for any "doomed" state of the protocol, if every message the prover can send will put the protocol in a non-"doomed" state with probability at least ε_{k} over the verifier randomness, then an extractor can efficiently recover a witness (with probability 1) when given the current protocol state and the prover's next message. In the context of FRI, RBR knowledge soundness means we can extract a δ-close function G, and for Batched FRI we can extract t functions $f_1, \ldots, f_t$ that are all δ-close. For both FRI and Batched FRI, it turns out we obtain RBR knowledge soundness more or less for free. Recall that both protocols have RBR soundness error $\max\{\varepsilon_1, \varepsilon_2^\ell\}$ from our discussion above. Then we claim that these protocols both have RBR knowledge error exactly $\varepsilon_{\mathsf{k}} = \max\{\varepsilon_1, \varepsilon_2^\ell\}$.

We give an efficient extractor for the RBR knowledge soundness of FRI. First consider any intermediate round i of the folding phase of FRI (the analysis for Batched FRI is identical). Then the current protocol state is doomed and is given by the transcript $(G_0, x_0, G_1', x_1, \ldots, G_{i-1}', x_{i-1})$. Suppose that for any function G_i' sent by the prover, for $x_i \xleftarrow{\$} \mathbb{F}$ sampled by the verifier, the protocol state $(G_0, x_0, G_1', x_1, \ldots, G_i', x_i)$ is not doomed with probability at least ε_{k}. In particular, this happens with probability at least $\varepsilon_1 = O(2^{2n}/(\rho|\mathbb{F}|))$. Then our extractor, given $(G_0, x_0, G_1', x_1, \ldots, G_i')$ simply reads and outputs the oracle G_0. For the query phase, the analysis is identical: let the current protocol state be doomed for transcript $(G_0, x_0, G_1', x_1, \ldots, G_{k-1}', x_{k-1})$. Suppose for every $G_k \in \mathbb{F}$ sent by the prover and verifier challenges $s_{0,1}, \ldots, s_{0,\ell} \xleftarrow{\$} L_0$, the protocol state $(G_0, x_0, G_1', x_1, \ldots, G_k, (s_{0,j})_{j \leq \ell})$ is not doomed with probability at least ε_{k}. In particular, this happens with probability at least $\varepsilon_2^\ell = (1-\delta)^\ell$. Then our extractor again simply reads and outputs oracle G_0.

Now why should we expect G_0 to be a δ-close function? It turns out that by the choices of ε_1 and ε_2, if *all* prover messages can leave the doomed state with the above probabilities, it *unconditionally* implies that G_0 must be δ-close in both cases, a result shown by [6]. First, for any round of the folding, the function G_i' can leave the doomed set if and only if $G_i' = G_i$ (i.e., it is computed as an honest prover would compute it) and G_{i+1} is δ-close. If G_{i+1} is δ-close with probability greater than ε_1 over the verifier randomness, then it unconditionally implies that G_i must have been δ-close as well [6]. This then recursively applies to G_{i-1}, and so on, finally yielding that G_0 must have been δ-close as well. [6] show that a similar result must hold for the query phase: if all verifier checks pass with probability at least ε_2^ℓ during the query phase for any $G_k \in \mathbb{F}$ sent by the prover, then G_0 must be δ-close as well. Thus the RBR knowledge error of FRI is identical to the RBR soundness error. Finally, the above analysis proceeds identically for Batched FRI as well; i.e., if during any round of folding or batching phase the prover can leave with probability at least ε_1, then it unconditionally implies that $f_1, \ldots, f_t$ must be δ-close functions. The Batched FRI query phase is analogous.

2.3 Correlated IOPs and Round-by-Round Knowledge Soundness

To conduct our security analysis beyond FRI, we formulate an abstract type of IOP which we call a *δ-correlated IOP*. This is a notion related and inspired by that of *Reed-Solomon Encoded IOPs* [8,26] (see [14] for further comparison). In a nutshell, when $\delta = 0$, a 0-correlated IOP is an IOP where:

- The verifier has access to an oracle $\mathcal{O}$ that, given any number of maps $f_1, \ldots, f_k : D \to \mathbb{F}$, determines whether each of the f_i is the evaluation map of a polynomial of degree at most d, for any $d < |D|$. Here D is a subset of $\mathbb{F}$, called *evaluation domain.*
  In other words, $\mathcal{O}$ determines whether the maps (or words) f_i belong to the Reed-Solomon code $\mathsf{RS}[\mathbb{F}, D, d+1]$.
- During the interactive phase, the prover sends oracle access to some maps $g_1, \ldots, g_m : D \to \mathbb{F}$ (across several rounds of interaction).
- In the last round of interaction, the verifier sends a field element $\mathfrak{z} \in \mathbb{K} \setminus D$ to the prover, and the prover replies with values

$$\{g_i(k_{i,j}\mathfrak{z}) \mid i \in [m], j \in [n_i]\} \tag{2}$$

  where $k_{i,j}$ are some pre-defined field elements and $n_i \geq 1$ are predefined positive integers. Here $\mathbb{K}$ is either $\mathbb{F}$ or a field extension of $\mathbb{F}$. Importantly, each map g_i appears at least once in the list Eq. (2).
- To decide whether to reject or accept the prover's proof, the verifier:
  - **Check 1.** Asserts that the values $\{g_i(k_{i,j}\mathfrak{z}) \mid i \in [m], j \in [n_i]\}$ satisfy certain polynomial equations.
  - **Check 2.** Uses its oracle $\mathcal{O}$ to check that the following maps belong to $\mathsf{RS}[\mathbb{F}, D, d]$:

$$\mathsf{quotients} := \{(g_i(X) - g_i(k_{i,j}\mathfrak{z}))/(X - \mathfrak{z}) \mid i \in [m], j \in [n_i]\}. \tag{3}$$

When $\delta > 0$, a δ-correlated IOP has the exact same form as above, except that now O is an oracle for checking δ-*correlated agreement* in $\mathsf{RS}[\mathbb{F}, D, d+1]$ for any $d < |D|$. A sequence of maps $g_1, \ldots, g_m : D \to \mathbb{F}$ has δ-correlated agreement if there exists a subset $S \subseteq D$ and polynomials $q_1, \ldots, q_m$ of degree $\leq d$ such that g_i coincides with q_i on S, for all $i \in [m]$, and $|S| \geq (1 - \delta)|D|$.

These type of IOP's are interesting to us because several modern IOP's can be understood as being built on top of a 0-correlated or δ-correlated IOP for $\delta > 0$, e.g., all Plonk-like protocols that use FRI instead of KZG [34,44,60], ethSTARK (or DEEP-ALI) [10,65], RISC Zero [68], etc.

We prove the following results about δ-correlated IOPs:

- **Result 1.** If a 0-correlated IOP Π_0 has round-by-round (RBR) soundness or knowledge ε, then replacing $\delta = 0$ by a larger $\delta > 0$ results in a δ-correlated IOP with RBR soundness or knowledge $\ell\varepsilon$, where ℓ is certain constant related to list decodability of Reed-Solomon (RS) codes. Namely, ℓ is the maximum number of distinct RS codewords that can be δ-close to any given word. Here, by "replacing $\delta = 0$ by a larger $\delta > 0$" we refer to the δ-correlated IOP that results from taking Π_0 and replacing the verifier's oracle for checking membership to $\mathsf{RS}[\mathbb{F}, D, d+1]$ (so, checking 0-correlated agreement) by an oracle that checks for δ-correlated agreement in $\mathsf{RS}[\mathbb{F}, D, d+1]$.
- **Result 2.** Given a δ-correlated IOP Π with RBR soundness or knowledge ε, and given a IOP or IOP of Proximity Π_{CA} for checking δ-correlated agreement, we can construct a new IOP (in the standard sense, i.e., an "uncorrelated IOP"), denoted by Π_{compiled}, by replacing the oracle O with the protocol Π_{CA}. We show that if Π_{CA} has RBR soundness $\varepsilon_{\mathsf{CA}}$, then Π_{compiled} has RBR (knowledge) soundness $\max\{\varepsilon, \varepsilon_{\mathsf{CA}}\}$. Notice that, for RBR knowledge soundness, we don't need Π_{CA} to have RBR knowledge soundness. It suffices for Π to have RBR knowledge soundness, and for Π_{CA} to be RBR sound.

First, we explain how these results can be applied to existing protocols, then give a high-level overview of their proofs.

Using the Above Results. Given these results, one strategy for proving that an IOP Π has RBR (knowledge) soundness is to first try to formulate the IOP as a δ-correlated IOP that has been compiled with the method described above, then prove that the corresponding 0-correlated IOP has RBR (knowledge) soundness. Once this is done, our results provide RBR (knowledge) soundness error bounds for the initial IOP Π. Figure 2 gives an overview of this methodology.

The latter task can be a significant simplification in comparison to analyzing the initial IOP Π directly. This is because when $\delta = 0$, the verifier in Π has an oracle for checking that the maps from the verifier's Check 2 are low-degree polynomials. This effectively forces the prover to send (oracles to) low-degree polynomials throughout the interaction and to provide correct openings in its last message. As a consequence, and roughly speaking, our methods allows to study the IOP as if it was a *Polynomial* IOP (PIOP), with the Batched FRI protocol acting as a Polynomial Commitment Scheme (PCS) used to compile the PIOP into an interactive argument. However, note that FRI cannot be used as a PCS (unless δ lies in the unique decoding radius) since it only guarantees δ-closeness to low-degree polynomials.

Later, we show how these methods can be used on "Plonk-like" protocols, and briefly discuss how to use them on other protocols such as ethSTARK and RISC Zero.

Proof Sketch of Result 1. Let $\delta > 0$, let Π_δ be a δ-correlated IOP, and let Π_0 be the same IOP except that the verifier has access to an oracle for 0-correlated agreement instead of δ-correlated agreement (equivalently, it has an oracle for checking membership to $\mathsf{RS}[\mathbb{F}, D, d' + 1]$ for any $d' < |D|$). Suppose Π_0 is RBR (knowledge) sound with error ε. We first focus on RBR soundness and discuss RBR knowledge soundness later. Let τ be a partial transcript produced during some rounds of interaction between the prover and the verifier from Π_δ. For ease of presentation, assume the prover sends maps to the verifier, as opposed to sending oracle access to these maps. Let $g_1, \ldots, g_k$ be all prover's maps in τ and write $\tau = \tau(g_1, \ldots, g_k)$ to denote that τ contains such maps. Let $\tau' = \tau'(g'_1, \ldots, g'_k)$ be another partial transcript. We informally say τ' is a *low-degree partial transcript* if all of the maps $g'_1, \ldots, g'_k$ are codewords from $\mathsf{RS}[\mathbb{F}, D, d + 1]$. We also say τ' has *δ-correlated agreement* with τ if there is $S \subseteq D$ such that g_i coincides with g'_i on S for all $i \in [k]$ and $|S| \geq (1 - \delta)|D|$. Then we say that τ is "doomed" in Π_δ if and only if one of the following holds:

- All low-degree partial transcripts τ' that are δ-correlated with τ are doomed in Π_0.
- τ is a complete transcript and Check 2 of the verifier fails, i.e., the maps quotients from Eq. (3) do not have δ-correlated agreement in $\mathsf{RS}[\mathbb{F}, D, d + 1]$.

This defines the doomed states for Π_δ, i.e., the doomed states are those where the partial transcript so far is doomed.

Now it remains to be shown that Π_δ has RBR (knowledge) soundness error $\varepsilon/(2\sqrt{\rho}\eta)$ with respect to these doomed states. In what follows, we say that a partial transcript is *doomed in* Π_δ or *doomed in* Π_0 depending on whether it is doomed with respect to the doomed states of Π_δ or Π_0. By a i-round partial transcript we mean a partial transcript where both prover and verifier have sent i messages each.

Let τ be a i-partial transcript after that is doomed in Π_δ. By definition, all low-degree partial transcripts that are δ-correlated with τ are doomed in Π_0. Let m be a prover's message for round $i + 1$. We want to show that the probability that (τ, m, c) is not doomed in Π_δ is at most $\varepsilon/(2\sqrt{\rho}\eta)$, where the probability is taken over the verifier's $(i + 1)$-th message c. Assume (τ, m, c) is not doomed in Π_δ for some c. Then, by definition of the doomed states of Π_δ, there is a low-degre partial transcript ν that is δ-correlated with (τ, m, c) and that is not doomed in Π_0. This transcript must have the form $\nu = (\tau', m', c)$, where τ' is a i-round low-degree partial transcript that is δ-correlated with τ. In particular, τ' is doomed in Π_0.

Since Π_0 is RBR sound with error ε, the fraction of challenges c such that τ' is doomed in Π_0 but (τ', m', c) is not is at most ε. Thus the fraction of challenges

c such that τ is doomed in Π_δ but (τ, m, c) is not doomed in Π_δ is at most $\ell\varepsilon$, where ℓ is the number of i-round low-degree partial transcripts τ' that are δ-correlated with τ. Using a lemma from [65], we can bound ℓ by $1/(2\sqrt{\rho}\eta)$.

It remains to argue that doomed complete transcripts are rejected by the verifier. Let $\tau = \tau(g_1, \ldots, g_m)$ be a doomed complete partial transcript and let $\mathsf{quotients}$ be as in Eq. (3). If the maps $\mathsf{quotients}$ do not have δ-correlated agreement in $\mathsf{RS}[\mathbb{F}, D, d]$, then the verifier rejects and we are done. Hence assume they do have δ-correlated agreement. Thus, for each $i \in [m]$ and $j \in [n_i]$ we have that $(g_i(X) - g_i(k_{i,j}\mathfrak{z}))/(X - k_{i,j}\mathfrak{z})$ agrees with a polynomial $q_{i,j}(X)$ on a set S (this set is the same for all i, j). In other words, $g_i(X)$ agrees with the polynomial $u_{i,j}(X) := q_{i,j}(X)(X - k_{i,j}\mathfrak{z}) + g_i(k_{i,j}\mathfrak{z})$ on S. Moreover, both g_i and $u_{i,j}$ take the same value on $X = k_{i,j}\mathfrak{z}$, i.e., $g_i(k_{i,j}\mathfrak{z}) = u_{i,j}(k_{i,j}\mathfrak{z})$. Additionally, we have $|S| > (1-\delta)|D|$, and by how δ is chosen, $(1-\delta)|D| \geq d+1$. This makes $u_{i,j}(X)$ the same for all $j \in [n_i]$; thus, we denote any $u_{i,j}(X)$ simply as $u_i(X)$.

We have seen so far that $g_i(X)$ agrees with the polynomial $u_i(X)$ on S, for all $i \in [m]$, and that $g_i(k_{i,j}\mathfrak{z}) = u_i(k_{i,j}\mathfrak{z})$, for all i, j. Thus $\tau' = \tau(u_1, \ldots, u_m)$ is a low-degree partial transcript that is δ-correlated with τ. Since τ is a doomed transcript and $\mathsf{quotients}$ have δ-correlated agreement in $\mathsf{RS}[\mathbb{F}, D, d]$, we must have that τ' is doomed in Π_0. Note that τ' is a complete transcript, and so Π_0's verifier rejects it. Clearly, τ' passes the 0-correlated agreement check of Π_0's verifier. Hence the first check of the verifier fails, i.e., the values $\{u_i(k_{i,j}\mathfrak{z}) \mid i \in [m], j \in [n_i]\}$ do not satisfy some required polynomial identities. However, these values coincide with $\{g_i(k_{i,j}\mathfrak{z}) \mid i \in [m], j \in [n_i]\}$, and so the verifier of Π_δ rejects τ for the same reason: the values do not satisfy the appropriate polynomial equations. This proves that Π_δ has the claimed RBR soundness error.

The proof that Π_δ has RBR knowledge soundness uses similar ideas. Precisely, suppose τ is a i-round partial transcript that is doomed in Π_δ. Let m be a prover's $(i+1)$-th round message and assume the probability (over the verifier's $(i+1)$-th challenge c) that (τ, m, c) is not doomed is larger than $\varepsilon/(2\sqrt{\rho}\eta)$. Since, as we argued, there are at most $1/(2\sqrt{\rho}\eta)$ i-round low-degree partial transcripts τ' that are δ-correlated with τ, there must exist at least one such transcript τ' that is doomed in Π_0 such that (τ', m', c) is not doomed in Π_0 with probability larger than ε. Then we can use the RBR knowledge soundness of Π_0 to extract a valid witness from τ'. We can build an extractor that, given τ, computes all low-degree partial transcripts τ' that are δ-correlated with τ. This can be done in polynomial time using a method from [65]. Then for each such τ', the new extractor uses the extractor of Π_0 on τ', until a valid witness is found.

Proof Sketch of Result 2. The second general result stated above can be proved as follows: define a partial transcript τ for Π_{compiled} to be doomed if one of the following hold:

1. τ is a partial transcript for Π and τ is a doomed state in Π.
2. τ is a partial transcript of the form $\tau = (\tau_1, \tau_2)$, where τ_1 is a complete transcript of Π, and τ_2 is a (possibly empty) partial transcript corresponding to some rounds of Π_{CA}, and either

(a) τ_2 is a doomed state in Π_{CA}, or
(b) the verifier V_Π from Π would reject τ_1 due to Check 1 not passing.

We then prove that Π_{compiled} is RBR (knowledge) sound with respect to these doomed states and with error $\max\{\varepsilon, \varepsilon_{\mathsf{CA}}\}$. As before, we discuss first RBR soundness then RBR knowledge.

The key observation is that if τ is a doomed partial transcript of Type 1 above, then it remains doomed in the next round except with probability ε due to the RBR soundness of Π. A similar argument can be used for a partial transcript of Type 2 of the form $\tau = (\tau_1, \tau_2)$, with $\tau_2 \neq \emptyset$. The most noteworthy case is when τ is of Type 2 and of the form $\tau = (\tau_1, \emptyset)$, i.e., the case when τ is exactly a complete transcript for Π. In this case, since τ is doomed, the verifier V_Π in Π would reject τ. Hence τ fails either Check 1 or Check 2 of V_Π. In the first case, the probability of leaving the doomed state in Π_{compiled} is 0 since any partial transcript $\tau' = (\tau_1', \tau_2')$ of Type 2 such that τ_1' fails Check 1 of V_Π is doomed by definition. In the latter case, Π_{CA} is executed with input a set of words that do not have δ-correlated agreement. As such, Π_{CA} starts off in a doomed state and so the probability that the state is not doomed in the next round of interaction is at most $\varepsilon_{\mathsf{CA}}$. This shows that Π_{compiled} is RBR sound with error $\max\{\varepsilon, \varepsilon_{\mathsf{CA}}\}$.

For RBR knowledge soundness, we make the following observations. First, we define doomed states for Π_{compiled} as before, using the doomed states given by the RBR knowledge (as opposed to RBR soundness) for Π, and the doomed states given by the RBR soundness for Π_{CA}. Now, let τ be a doomed partial transcript for Π_{compiled}. Assume the probability θ that τ stops being doomed at the next round is larger than $\max\{\varepsilon_k, \varepsilon_{\mathsf{CA}}\}$, where ε_k is the RBR knowledge error of Π. Then, if τ is of Type 1, we can use the extractor given by the RBR knowledge of Π to obtain a valid witness from τ. On the other hand, if $\theta > \max\{\varepsilon_k, \varepsilon_{\mathsf{CA}}\}$ then $\tau = (\tau_1, \tau_2)$ cannot be of Type 2 because:

- If τ_2 is a doomed state in Π_{CA}, then by definition of RBR soundness, the probability that τ_2 is not doomed in the next round of Π_{CA} is at most $\varepsilon_{\mathsf{CA}}$.
- If τ_1 would be rejected by Π's verifier due to Check 1 failing, then the partial transcript will be doomed at the next round because of the same reason, and so in this case τ has probability 0 of not being doomed in the next round.

In other words, doomed partial transcripts of Type 2 are always doomed at the next round, except with probability at most $\max\{\varepsilon_k, \varepsilon_{\mathsf{CA}}\}$. Thus, we do not need to describe an extractor for this type of partial transcripts.

Remark 5. This approach yields better RBR soundness bounds than some prior known methods. For example, in [44] the authors introduce RedShift, a Plonk-like IOP. The authors obtain a RBR knowledge error (modulo FRI) for RedShift which has a factor of the form, roughly, ℓ^m, where ℓ is the aforementioned "maximum list decoding set size", and m is the number of oracles sent by the prover during the interactive phase. For RedShift, m is set to 6, but similar (though not fully identical) protocols such as Plonky2 [60] use $m \geq 130$. On the contrary, as we mention later in this paper, with our method the factor ℓ^m would be reduced to ℓ. We remark again that [44] also does not obtain FS security of their protocol, as that work does not analyze the FS security of FRI.

In Sect. 2.5 we also point out that, when applied to the ethSTARK protocol, our approach leads to better knowledge soundness error than the one in [65] (this improvement was already demonstrated in [39]).

2.4 Round-by-Round Knowledge of Plonk-Like Protocols

We generalize and abstract Plonk-like protocols as a correlated IOP, which we call OPlonky, where again by "Plonk-like" we specifically mean the interactive oracle proof abstractions underlying the protocols related to and built upon the (IOP underlying the) Plonk SNARK. The abstraction is inspired mostly by Plonky2 [60], which we believe to be one of the most general Plonk-like IOP's currently published.

The protocol OPlonky is an IOP for a Plonk-like relation $\mathbf{R_{ROPlonky}}$ (related to [32]), which generalizes arithmetic circuit satisfiability and seamlessly supports custom gates. Simplifying greatly, an instance of $\mathbf{R_{ROPlonky}}$ is characterized by some multivariate polynomial equations $P_1 = 0, \ldots, P_k = 0$, two integers n, r representing the dimensions of a matrix (usually called *execution trace*), and a permutation $\sigma : [n] \times [r] \to [n] \times [r]$. An input and witness pair $(\mathbb{x}, \mathbb{w})$ satisfies such an instance if $\mathbb{w}$ is a $n \times r$ matrix of field elements, $\mathbb{x}$ is a vector of field elements, and

- The values in each row $\mathbb{w}_i$ of $\mathbb{w}$ satisfy $P_1(\mathbb{w}_i) = \ldots = P_k(\mathbb{w}_i) = 0$.
- Certain pre-specified cells in $\mathbb{w}$ have the values $\mathbb{x}$.
- The entries in $\mathbb{w}$ satisfy the *copy constraints* induced by σ. More precisely, $\mathbb{w}_{(i,j)} = \mathbb{w}_{\sigma(i,j)}$ for all $i, j \in [n] \times [r]$.

The IOP OPlonky proceeds in the following 4-round process. For the sake of presentation, we provide a greatly simplified exposition.

1. **Round 1.** The prover sends r polynomials $a_1(X), \ldots, a_r(X)$ of degree $< n$ to the verifier as oracles. Each of these polynomials is the result of interpolating the columns of $\mathbb{w}$ over a multiplicative subgroup H of $\mathbb{F}$ or order n. The verifier then replies with some random challenges.
2. **Round 2.** The prover uses the verifier randomness from the prior round, to construct and send oracle access to so-called *permutation polynomials* $\pi_1(X), \ldots, \pi_s(X)$ of degree less than n. These polynomials will later be used to (again roughly) check that the copy constraints are satisfied. The verifier responds with a random challenge α.
3. **Round 3.** At this point, the goal of the prover is to convince the verifier that the polynomials $Q_j := P_j(a_1(X), \ldots, a_r(X))$ and certain polynomials of the form $\delta_i(X) := R_i(\pi_1(X), \ldots, \pi_s(X))$ vanish on H, where the R_i is some multivariate polynomial. To this end, the prover *batches* these constraints together by computing

$$d(X) = Q_1(X) + \alpha Q_2(X) + \ldots + \alpha^{k-1} Q_k(X) + \alpha^k \delta_1(X) + \ldots + \alpha^{k+s-1} \delta_s(X) \quad (4)$$

and proving that $d(X)$ vanishes in H. To do so, the prover sends the verifier oracle access to the polynomial $q(X) := d(X)/\mathsf{Z}_H(X)$, where $\mathsf{Z}_H(X)$ is the vanishing polynomial of H. The verifier replies with a random field element $\mathfrak{z}$.

4. **Round 4.** The prover replies with the values $(a_i(\mathfrak{z}))_i, (\pi_j(\mathfrak{z}))_j$ and $q(\mathfrak{z})$.
5. **Verification phase.** The verifier performs two assertions. It accepts the proof if and only if both of them return true.
   - Assert whether $q(\mathfrak{z})\mathsf{Z}_H(\mathfrak{z}) = d(\mathfrak{z})$, where the value $d(\mathfrak{z})$ is obtained by replacing X by $\mathfrak{z}$ in Eq. (4), and querying the oracles to $a_i(X), \pi_j(X)$ for all $i \in [r]$ and $j \in [s]$.
   - Use an oracle to assert whether the following set of words has δ-correlated agreement in some Reed-Solomon code:

$$\left\{\frac{q(X) - q(\mathfrak{z})}{X - \mathfrak{z}}, \left(\frac{a_i(X) - q(\mathfrak{z})}{X - \mathfrak{z}}\right)_i, \left(\frac{\pi_j(X) - q(\mathfrak{z})}{X - \mathfrak{z}}\right)_j\right\}.$$

It is apparent from the description above that $\mathsf{OPlonky}$ is indeed a δ-correlated IOP.

When compiled with the Batched FRI protocol, $\mathsf{OPlonky}_{\mathsf{compiled}}$ becomes almost identical to Plonky2's IOP [60] with some similarities to Redshift [44]. Alternatively, $\mathsf{OPlonky}$ could also be compiled somehow with the KZG commitment scheme (which, in a sense, can act as a protocol for 0-correlated agreement). This would yield generalized versions of the original Plonk protocol and its variations (e.g., TurboPlonk). We leave this as future work.

Round-by-Round Soundness of $\mathsf{OPlonky}$. With the above observations in mind, we then go on to show that $\mathsf{OPlonky}$ with $\delta = 0$ has RBR soundness and knowledge. We now provide an intuitive idea of the proof, focusing on RBR soundness. To do so, we use the simplified description of $\mathsf{OPlonky}$ provided above. As such, our analysis and resulting error bounds are also simplified.

We let $\mathsf{OPlonky}^{\mathcal{O}}$ denote the $\mathsf{OPlonky}$ protocol where the verifier has oracle access to 0-correlated agreement oracle $\mathcal{O}$. To prove that $\mathsf{OPlonky}^{\mathcal{O}}$ has RBR (knowledge) soundness, we need to define a set of "doomed states" the protocol can be in. As a general rule, we will always set the state to "doomed" if the prover has sent the verifier an oracle to a map that is not a polynomial of appropriate degree. As argued in Sect. 2.3, in this scenario it is impossible for a malicious prover to "recover" and eventually convince the verifier, since the verifier will detect the dishonesty when using $\mathcal{O}$ in its Check 2. Moreover, by similar reasons, we can also assume that the prover provides correct openings as its last message.

Next we describe the rest of scenarios in which we set the state to "doomed" and analyze the probabilities of "recovering", i.e., of not being in a doomed set in the next round. We proceed in a round-by-round fashion.

- Given an input $\mathbb{x}$ for the relation $\mathbf{R}_{\mathbf{ROPlonky}}$, if $\mathbb{x}$ is not in the language $\mathcal{L}_{\mathbf{R}_{\mathbf{ROPlonky}}}$ induced by $\mathbf{R}_{\mathbf{ROPlonky}}$, we set the state to "doomed".
- Now assume that at the end of round 1, it is not possible for the prover to compute polynomials $\pi_1(X), \ldots, \pi_s(X)$ of degree $< n$ such that all the polynomials $\delta_i(X)$ vanish on H. Then we set the state to "doomed". We see that if

the state was doomed before round 1, then the chances of receiving verifier randomness such that the state is not doomed at the end of round 1 are, roughly, $\mathsf{r}n/|\mathbb{F}|$. This probability comes from the soundness of permutation checking procedure used in Plonk and many other protocols.
- Now suppose that at the end of round 2, the polynomial $d(X)$ does not vanish on $\mathsf{Z}_H(X)$. Then we set the state to "doomed". In this case, the probability of starting round 2 in a doomed state and finishing it in a non-doomed state is at most, roughly, $(k+s)/|\mathbb{F}|$. This is deduced by taking an arbitrary $x \in H$ and looking at the equality $d(x) = 0$ as a polynomial equation on α. This equation either has degree $\approx k+s$ (on α), or it is identically zero. However, we see that if round 2 started in a doomed state, then $R(x) = 0$ is not identically zero for at least one $x \in H$. Hence, there are at most $\approx k+s$ distinct values of α such that $d(x) = 0$ for all $x \in H$.
- Finally, suppose that at the end of round 3, one has $q(\mathfrak{z})\mathsf{Z}_H(\mathfrak{z}) \neq d(\mathfrak{z})$. Then we set the state to "doomed". In this case, the probability of ending round 3 in a non-doomed state if the state was previously doomed is at most, roughly, $\max_j\{\deg P_j\} \cdot n/|\mathbb{F}|$.[8] This is because either $q(X)Z_H(X) - d(X)$ is the zero polynomial (as it should be), or it is a polynomial of degree $\max_j\{\deg P_j\}n$ and $\mathfrak{z}$ is a root of it. We then see that if the protocol is in a doomed state when round 3 starts, then $q(X)Z_H(X) - d(X)$ is a nonzero polynomial. Notice as well that if the protocol ends in a doomed state as per our definition, then the verifier rejects.

The above argument, at a high-level, establishes the round-by-round security of the 0-correlated hIOP $\mathsf{OPlonky}^{\mathcal{O}}$; complete details are given in the full version of our work [14].

Round-by-Round Knowledge of RISC Zero. RISC Zero [68] is similar to the Plonky2 protocol. More precisely, and modulo technicalities, it can be thought of as being built on top of OPlonky with the addition that RISC Zero implements a lookup argument [33] in the same round as the permutation check is performed. We believe that similar methods as the ones presented in the previous section can be used to establish the RBR knowledge soundness of RISC Zero, and thus, the knowledge soundness of the Fiat-Shamir transformed version of RISC Zero. Since RISC Zero's whitepaper is in draft form at the moment of writing, we leave formally proving this claim as an open task.

2.5 Round-by-Round Knowledge of EthSTARK

We begin by discussing the ethSTARK protocol Π_{ethSTARK} [65], which is a close variation of the DEEP-ALI protocol [10]. We briefly provide a rough overview of the protocol; see [65] for complete details.

---

[8] This is not entirely accurate; for precise bounds, see Theorem 8.

Description of the Protocol. In Π_{ethSTARK}, the honest prover first sends oracle access to a list of degree $\leq d$ polynomials $f_1, \ldots, f_m$ that interpolate the columns of a so-called Algebraic Intermediate Representation (AIR) instance over a multiplicative subgroup H of a field $\mathbb{F}$ (simply put, these polynomials encode the witness). Supposedly, these polynomials are such that certain maps of the form

$$[Q_i(X, f_1(g_{i,1}X), \ldots, f_m(g_{i,m}X))]/Z_{H_i}(X), \quad i \in I, \tag{5}$$

are low-degree polynomials. Here, each $Q_i(X, Y_1, \ldots, Y_m)$ is a pre-specified $(m+1)$-variate polynomial; the $g_{i,j}$'s are field elements; $Z_{H_i}(X)$ is the vanishing polynomial of a subgroup H_i of H; and I is a list of indices.

The verifier replies with $2|I|$ random elements $r_1, r'_1, \ldots, r_{|I|}, r'_{|I|}$ from a field extension $\mathbb{K}$ of $\mathbb{F}$. As its second message, the honest prover sends oracle access to low-degree polynomials $q_1(X), \ldots, q_k(X)$ such that

$$\sum_{i \in I}(r_i + r'_i X^{c_i})[Q_i(X, f_1(g_{i,1}X), \ldots, f_m(g_{i,m}X))]/Z_{H_i}(X) = \sum_{j=1}^{k} X^{j-1} q_j(X^k), \tag{6}$$

where the c_i's are pre-agreed positive integers such that that each summand on the left-hand side of Eq. (6) has the same degree, and k is a conveniently pre-agreed positive integer. The reason why the prover sends k polynomials $q_1(X), \ldots, q_k(X)$ instead of just one polynomial $q(X)$ that equals the left-hand side of Eq. (6) is because the degree of $q(X)$ would be "too large", and hence it is "split" into low-degree polynomials.

The verifier replies with a field element $\mathfrak{z}$ uniformly sampled in a large subset S of $\mathbb{K}$. The honest prover replies with evaluations

$$\{f_1(g_{i,j}\mathfrak{z}), \ldots, f_m(g_{i,j}\mathfrak{z}), q_1(\mathfrak{z}), \ldots, q_k(\mathfrak{z}) \mid i \in I, j \in [m]\}. \tag{7}$$

Then, the verifier checks that Eq. (6) holds after replacing X by $\mathfrak{z}$ (using the purported evaluations in Eq. (7)), and it engages with the prover in the Batched FRI protocol to verify that the following maps have δ-correlated agreement in some Reed-Solomon code:

$$\left\{\frac{f_j(X) - f_j(g_{i,j}\mathfrak{z})}{X - g_{i,j}\mathfrak{z}} \mid i \in I, j \in [m]\right\} \bigcup \left\{\frac{q_t(X) - q_t(\mathfrak{z})}{X - \mathfrak{z}} \mid t \in [k]\right\}. \tag{8}$$

RBR Knowledge Soundness of the ethSTARK Protocol. It is clear that Π_{ethSTARK} is the compilation of a δ-correlated IOP using the Batched FRI protocol for δ-correlated agreement. Thus, one can prove that Π_{ethSTARK} has RBR (knowledge) soundness by showing that the underlying δ-correlated IOP has RBR (knowledge) soundness when $\delta = 0$. Once this is done, we obtain as a consequence that compiling Π_{ethSTARK} with Merkle tree commitments and the Fiat-Shamir transformation (i.e., the BCS transform) yields a knowledge sound succinct non-interactive argument, i.e., a SNARK. Here, the "underlying δ-correlated IOP" is precisely the protocol Π_{ethSTARK} without applying Batched FRI. Instead, we assume the verifier has an oracle that allows for checking δ-correlated agreement of the maps that are batched together in Batched FRI. These are the quotient polynomials in Eq. (8).

As we mentioned, due to our results (Theorem 3), it suffices to analyze RBR knowledge soundness when $\delta = 0$. This corresponds to the case when the verifier has an oracle for checking that the maps of Eq. (8) are low-degree polynomials. Note that if the maps in Eq. (8) have 0-correlated agreement, then so do all the (oracles to) maps sent by the adversary during the protocol execution. This is because if a map of the form $(h(X) - y)/(X - z)$ for constants y, z agree with a polynomial $q(X)$ on a set S, then $h(X)$ agrees with the polynomial $q(X)(X - z) + y$ on the same set S. Moreover, for any map $h(X)$ sent by the prover there is a map of the form $(h(X) - y)/(X - z)$ in the list of Eq. (8). Hence we only need consider adversaries that send (oracles to) low-degree polynomials. Moreover, the check for 0-correlated agreement also forces the prover to provide correct openings for Eq. (7).

We say that a 1-round partial transcript is doomed if the left-hand side of Eq. (6) is not a polynomial of appropriate degree. We say that a 2-round partial transcript is doomed if Eq. (6) does not hold for the received challenge $\mathfrak{z}$. Clearly, if a 1-round partial transcript is doomed, then a 2-round partial transcript is doomed except with probability $d'/|S|$, where d' is the degree of the polynomial equation obtained from Eq. (6) after multiplying it by $Z_H(X)$ on each side. Moreover, any doomed 2-round partial transcript is eventually rejected by the verifier, no matter how it is completed, since Eq. (6) does not hold for $X = \mathfrak{z}$. Finally, if $f_1(X), \ldots, f_m(X)$ do not "encode a valid witness", then by how the AIRs are constructed, not all maps in Eq. (5) are polynomials of appropriate degree. Then we claim there are at most $|\mathbb{K}|^{2|I|-1}$ tuples $(r_1, r'_1, \ldots, r_{|I|}, r'_{|I|})$ such that the right-hand side of Eq. (6) is a polynomial of appropriate degree. If the claim is true, then an incorrect initial message $f_1(X), \ldots, f_m(X)$ leads to a doomed state after Round 1 except with probability $1/|\mathbb{K}|$. To prove the claim, consider the expression

$$\sum_{i \in I} (r_i + r'_i X^{c_i}) Q_i(X, f_1(g_{i,1}X), \ldots, f_m(g_{i,m}X))(Z_H(X)/Z_{H_i}(X)) \tag{9}$$

where we view $Z_H(X)/Z_{H_i}(X)$ as a polynomial since $Z_{H_i}(X)$ divides $Z_H(X)$. Then the right-hand side of Eq. (6) is a polynomial of appropriate degree if and only if Eq. (9) vanishes on H. The latter means that for each $x \in H$, the elements $(r_1, r'_1, \ldots, r_{|I|}, r'_{|I|})$ form a solution to the equation

$$\sum_{i \in I} (r_i + r'_i x^{c_i}) Q_i(x, f_1(g_{i,1}x), \ldots, f_m(g_{i,m}x))(Z_H(x)/Z_{H_i}(x)) = 0$$

on the variables $\{r_i, r'_i \mid i \in I\}$. Unless the right-hand side of the equation is identically zero, there are at most $|\mathbb{K}|^{2|I|-1}$ such solutions. On the other hand, if for all $x \in H$ the right-hand side of the equation was identically zero, then each of the maps Eq. (5) would be polynomials of appropriate degree (recall that the adversary is constrained to sending low-degree polynomials), contradicting the assumption that $f_1(X), \ldots, f_m(X)$ encode an incorrect witness. This proves the claim.

It follows that, in its 0-correlated form, Π_{ethSTARK} has RBR (knowledge) soundness error $\varepsilon_0 := \max\{1/|\mathbb{K}|, d'/|S|\}$. Then, due to the results from Sects. 2.2 and 2.3, Π_{ethSTARK} (as an IOP) has RBR (knowledge) soundness $\varepsilon := \max\{\ell/|\mathbb{K}|, \ell d'/|S|, \varepsilon_{\mathsf{rbr}}^{\mathsf{bFRI}}\}$, where $\ell = 1/(2\sqrt{\rho}\eta)$ (here ρ and η are parameters related to the RS codes used within the protocol), and $\varepsilon_{\mathsf{rbr}}^{\mathsf{bFRI}}$ is the RBR soundness error of batched FRI.

Remark 6. This analysis can slightly improve the knowledge soundness error for Π_{ethSTARK} when compared with [65]. This improvement is already demonstrated in [39]. Using the notation of [65, Theorem 4], the improved knowledge soundness error is

$$(\ell/|\mathbb{K}|) + \ell \cdot (\mathsf{d}_{\mathsf{max}} + 2^{\mathsf{h}} + \mathsf{a})/(|\mathbb{K}| - \mathsf{a} \cdot |D| - |\mathsf{H}_0|) + \varepsilon_{\mathsf{FRI}}.$$

The improvement here is in having the factor ℓ in the second summand, instead of ℓ^2.

2.6 From Round-by-Round Soundness to Fiat-Shamir Security

As stated in Sect. 2.1, we utilize the BCS transformation for IOPs due to Ben-Sasson et al. [9] to compile our round-by-round sound IOPs into secure non-interactive protocols in the random oracle model. At a high level, the transformation works by first compressing oracles sent by the prover with a Merkle tree [52]; i.e., instead of sending oracle f to the verifier, the prover sends M_f, where M_f is the root of the Merkle tree with leaves corresponding to evaluations of f (in some canonical way). Then whenever the verifier would query oracle f at position i, instead the prover provides the verifier with pair $(f(i), \pi_i)$, where π_i is the Merkle authentication path for proving that $f(i)$ is consistent with M_f. Finally, once the IOP is transformed in this way, it is then compressed using Fiat-Shamir to obtain a non-interactive protocol.

Ben-Sasson et al. showed that applying the BCS transformation to an IOP yields a secure non-interactive protocol in the random oracle model if the IOP satisfied a notion of soundness called *state-restoration soundness*, which roughly says that the IOP remains secure even if the prover is allows to rewind the verifier to any prior state at most b times for some upper bound $b \geq 1$; see [9] for full details. However, it is known that round-by-round soundness is an upper bound on state-restoration soundness: in particular, if a protocol has state-restoration soundness error $\varepsilon_{\mathsf{sr}}(b)$ and round-by-round soundness error $\varepsilon_{\mathsf{rbr}}$, then $\varepsilon_{\mathsf{sr}}(b) \leq b\varepsilon_{\mathsf{rbr}}$ [25, 26, 44]. Moreover, Chiesa et al. [25, 26] showed that if an IOP is both round-by-round sound and round-by-round knowledge sound, then the BCS transformed IOP is both (adaptively) sound and (adaptively) knowledge sound versus both classical and quantum adversaries in the random oracle model.

Applying BCS to FRI and Batched FRI directly gives us a SNARK in the random oracle model, establishing the Fiat-Shamir security for FRI and Batched FRI (i.e., Corollary 2). Similarly, for $\mathsf{OPlonky}^{\mathcal{O}}$, we replace the δ-correlated oracle

$\mathcal{O}$ with the Batched FRI protocol, leveraging our δ-correlated IOP techniques to obtain a round-by-round sound IOP. Then again applying BCS to OPlonky composed with Batched FRI gives us a SNARK in the random oracle model, establishing the Fiat-Shamir security of OPlonky composed with Batched FRI (i.e., Corollary 3). Finally, our results allow us to obtain FS security for a variety of Plonk-like protocols; see [14] for details.

3 Our Results

In this section, we formally state all of our results. Due to space constraints, the discussion and proofs for these results can be found in the full version of our work [14].

3.1 Round-by-Round Soundness of FRI and Batched FRI

We formally present the FRI IOPP algorithm in Algorithm 1. The following theorem captures the round-by-round soundness of FRI.

Theorem 6. *Let $\mathbb{F}$ be a finite field, $L_0 \subset \mathbb{F}^*$ be a smooth multiplicative subgroup of size 2^n, $d_0 = 2^k$, $\rho = d_0/|L_0| = 2^{-(n-k)}$, and $\ell \in \mathbb{Z}^+$. For any integer $m \geq 3$, $\eta \in (0, \sqrt{\rho}/(2m))$, $\delta \in (0, 1 - \sqrt{\rho} - \eta)$, and function $G_0\colon L_0 \to \mathbb{F}$ that is δ-far from $\mathsf{RS}[\mathbb{F}, L_0, d_0]$, Algorithm 1 has round-by-round soundness error*

$$\varepsilon_{\mathsf{rbr}}^{\mathsf{FRI}} := \varepsilon_{\mathsf{rbr}}^{\mathsf{FRI}}(\mathbb{F}, L_0, \rho, \delta, m, \ell) = \max\{[(m+1/2)^7|L_0|^2]/[3\rho^{3/2} \cdot |\mathbb{F}|], (1-\delta)^\ell\}.$$

We extend the above theorem to the Batched FRI protocol, a variant of Algorithm 1 where the prover first sends t oracles $f_1, \ldots, f_t$ to the verifier, and the verifier replies with $\alpha_1, \ldots, \alpha_t \xleftarrow{\$} \mathbb{F}$. The prover and verifier then engage in the FRI protocol for polynomial $G_0 = \sum_i \alpha_i f_i$. The following theorem captures the RBR soundness of Batched FRI.

Theorem 7. *Let $\mathbb{F}$ be a finite field, $L_0 \subset \mathbb{F}^*$ be a smooth multiplicative subgroup of size 2^n, $d_0 = 2^k$, $\rho = d_0/|L_0| = 2^{-(n-k)}$, and $\ell \in \mathbb{Z}^+$. For any integer $m \geq 3$, $\eta \in (0, \sqrt{\rho}/(2m))$, $\delta \in (0, 1-\sqrt{\rho}-\eta)$, and functions $f_1^{(0)}, \ldots, f_t^{(0)}\colon L_0 \to \mathbb{F}$ for $t \geq 2$ such that at least one $f_i^{(0)}$ that is δ-far from $\mathsf{RS}^{(0)}$, the Batched FRI protocol has round-by-round soundness error*

$$\varepsilon_{\mathsf{rbr}}^{\mathsf{bFRI}} := \varepsilon_{\mathsf{rbr}}^{\mathsf{bFRI}}(\mathbb{F}, L_0, \rho, \delta, m, \ell, t) = \max\{[(m+1/2)^7|L_0|^2]/[3\rho^{3/2} \cdot |\mathbb{F}|], (1-\delta)^\ell\}.$$

Fiat-Shamir Security of FRI and Batched FRI. Given the BCS transformation [9] (also see [14]), we can apply the BCS transformation to transform both FRI and Batched FRI into SNARKs in the random oracle model. The following corollaries capture this result.

Corollary 4 (FS Security of FRI). *Let $\mathbb{F}$ be a finite field, $L_0 \subset \mathbb{F}^*$ be a smooth multiplicative subgroup of size 2^n, $d_0 = 2^k$, $\rho = d_0/|L_0| = 2^{-(n-k)}$, and $\ell \in \mathbb{Z}^+$. For any integer $m \geq 3$, $\eta \in (0, \sqrt{\rho}/(2m))$, $\delta \in (0, 1 - \sqrt{\rho} - \eta)$, random* *oracle* $\mathcal{H}\colon \{0,1\}^* \to \{0,1\}^\kappa$*, query bound* $Q \in \mathbb{N}$*, and function* $G_0\colon L_0 \to \mathbb{F}$ *that is* δ*-far from* $\mathsf{RS}[\mathbb{F}, L_0, d_0]$*, compiling Algorithm 1 with the BCS transformation [9] gives a non-interactive random oracle proof with adaptive soundness error and knowledge error*

$$\varepsilon_{\mathsf{fs}}^{\mathsf{FRI}} := \varepsilon_{\mathsf{fs}}^{\mathsf{FRI}}(\mathbb{F}, L_0, \rho, \delta, m, \ell, Q, \kappa) = Q \cdot \varepsilon_{\mathsf{rbr}}^{\mathsf{FRI}}(\mathbb{F}, L_0, \rho, \delta, m, \ell) + (3(Q^2+1)/2^\kappa).$$

Moreover, if $\gamma := \gamma(\mathbb{F}, L_0, \rho, \delta, \ell)$ *denotes the length of a FRI proof for parameters* $\mathbb{F}, L_0, \rho, \delta, \ell$*, then the above non-interactive random oracle proof has adaptive soundness error and knowledge error*

$$\varepsilon_{\mathsf{fs\text{-}q}}^{\mathsf{FRI}} := \varepsilon_{\mathsf{fs\text{-}q}}^{\mathsf{FRI}}(\mathbb{F}, L_0, \rho, \delta, m, \ell, Q, \kappa) = \Theta(Q \cdot \varepsilon_{\mathsf{fs}}^{\mathsf{FRI}}(\mathbb{F}, L_0, \rho, \delta, m, \ell, Q, \kappa))$$

against quantum adversaries that can make at most $Q - O(\ell \cdot \log(\gamma))$ *queries.*

Corollary 5 (FS Security of Batched FRI). *Let* $\mathbb{F}$ *be a finite field,* $L_0 \subset \mathbb{F}^*$ *be a smooth multiplicative subgroup of size* 2^n*,* $d_0 = 2^k$*,* $\rho = d_0/|L_0| = 2^{-(n-k)}$*, and* $\ell \in \mathbb{Z}^+$*. For any integer* $m \geq 3$*,* $\eta \in (0, \sqrt{\rho}/(2m))$*,* $\delta \in (0, 1-\sqrt{\rho}-\eta)$*, random oracle* $\mathcal{H}\colon \{0,1\}* \to \{0,1\}\kappa$*, query bound* $Q \in \mathbb{N}$*, and functions* $f_1^{(0)}, \ldots, f_t^{(0)}\colon L_0 \to \mathbb{F}$ *for* $t \geq 2$ *such that at least one* $f_i^{(0)}$ *is* δ*-far from* $\mathsf{RS}[\mathbb{F}, L_0, d_0]$*, compiling Batched FRI with the BCS transformation [9] gives a non-interactive random oracle proof with adaptive soundness error and knowledge error*

$$\varepsilon_{\mathsf{fs}}^{\mathsf{bFRI}} := \varepsilon_{\mathsf{fs}}^{\mathsf{bFRI}}(\mathbb{F}, L_0, \rho, \delta, m, \ell, t, Q, \kappa) = Q\varepsilon_{\mathsf{rbr}}^{\mathsf{bFRI}}(\mathbb{F}, L_0, \rho, \delta, m, \ell, t) + (3(Q^2+1)/2^\kappa).$$

Moreover, if $\gamma := \gamma(\mathbb{F}, L_0, \rho, \delta, \ell, t)$ *denotes the length of a Batched FRI proof for parameters* $\mathbb{F}, L_0, \rho, \delta, \ell, t$*, then the above non-interactive random oracle proof has adaptive soundness error and knowledge error*

$$\varepsilon_{\mathsf{fs\text{-}q}}^{\mathsf{bFRI}} := \varepsilon_{\mathsf{fs\text{-}q}}^{\mathsf{bFRI}}(\mathbb{F}, L_0, \rho, \delta, \ell, t, Q, \kappa) = \Theta(Q \cdot \varepsilon_{\mathsf{fs}}^{\mathsf{bFRI}}(\mathbb{F}, L_0, \rho, \delta, \ell, t, Q, \kappa))$$

against quantum adversaries that can make at most $Q - O(\ell \cdot \log(\gamma))$ *queries.*

Remark 7. A variety of works (e.g., [6,65]) make conjectures about the security of the FRI and Batched FRI protocols. We similarly adapt our above results when assuming these conjectured security bounds; see [14] for full details.

3.2 Correlated IOPs

A key technical tool we introduce is the notion of a δ*-correlated (holographic) interactive oracle proof*, or δ-correlated hIOP in short. A δ-correlated hIOP is an hIOP for indexed $(\mathbb{F}, H, d)$-polynomial oracle relations, where we fix some $0 \leq \delta < 1$ and assume the verifier has an oracle $\mathsf{OCoAgg}(\delta)$ for the correlated agreement relation $\mathbf{CoAgg}(\delta)$ (see [14] for complete details). Furthermore, we assume that the final offline verification process consists of: (1) checking that the oracles sent by the prover satisfy a certain polynomial equation on a random point $\mathfrak{z}$ (not necessarily from H); and (2) using $\mathsf{OCoAgg}(\delta)$ to check that the maps corresponding to certain oracles have correlated agreement in $\mathsf{RS}[\mathbb{F}, H, d]$ (see [14] for details). We denote such a protocol as $\Pi^{\mathsf{OCoAgg}(\delta)}$.

Given a δ-correlated hIOP, our first main result is showing that given a round-by-round sound 0-correlated hIOP, when replacing the oracle $\mathsf{OCoAgg}(0)$ with another suitable IOP, results in a new hIOP that is also round-by-round sound.

Theorem 8. *Let $\Pi^{\mathsf{OCoAgg}(0)} = (\mathsf{Ind}, \mathsf{P}, \mathsf{V}^{\mathsf{OCoAgg}(0)})$ be a μ-round 0-correlated hIOP for an indexed $(\mathbb{F}, D, d)$-polynomial oracle relation $\mathbf{R}$. Let $0 < \delta < 1 - \sqrt{\rho}$, where $\rho = d/|D|$, and let Π_{CA} be a IOPP for δ-correlated agreement in $\mathsf{RS}[\mathbb{F}, D, d]$. Let $\eta > 0$ be such that $\delta = 1 - \sqrt{\rho} - \eta$. Assume Π_{CA} is RBR sound with error $\varepsilon_{\mathsf{CA}}$. Then:*

- *Suppose that $\Pi^{\mathsf{OCoAgg}(0)}$ is RBR sound with error $\varepsilon_{\mathsf{rbr-s}}$. Then there exists a hIOP Π for $\mathbf{R}$ with RBR soundness error $\varepsilon'(\mathbb{i}) := \max\left\{\varepsilon_{\mathsf{rbr-s}}(\mathbb{i})(2\eta\sqrt{\rho}), \varepsilon_{\mathsf{CA}}(\mathbb{i}_{\mathsf{CA}})\right\}$, where $\mathbb{i}_{\mathsf{CA}} = (\mathbb{F}, D, d, \delta, N)$, and N is the number of words whose δ-correlated agreement is checked in the last verification check of $\Pi^{\mathsf{OCoAgg}(\delta)}$.*
- *Suppose $\mu(\mathbb{i}, \mathbb{x}) \geq 1$ for all $\mathbb{i}, \mathbb{x}$ and $\Pi^{\mathsf{OCoAgg}(0)}$ has RBR knowledge error $\varepsilon_{\mathsf{rbr-k}}$, then Π has RBR knowledge error $\max\left\{\varepsilon_{\mathsf{rbr-k}}(\mathbb{i})/(2\eta\sqrt{\rho}), \varepsilon_{\mathsf{CA}}(\mathbb{i}_{\mathsf{CA}})\right\}$, where $\mathbb{i}_{\mathsf{CA}}$ has the same meaning as in above.*

The proof of the above theorem relies on two technical lemmas. The first lemma states that if you have a round-by-round sound 0-correlated hIOP when given access to $\mathsf{OCoAgg}(0)$, then when given access to $\mathsf{OCoAgg}(\delta)$ for $\delta > 0$, the same hIOP is now δ-correlated and is round-by-round sound (with some loss in the soundness error).

Lemma 1. *Let $\Pi^{\mathsf{OCoAgg}(0)} = (\mathsf{Ind}, \mathsf{P}, \mathsf{V}^{\mathsf{OCoAgg}(0)})$ be a μ-round 0-correlated hIOP for an indexed $(\mathbb{F}, D, d)$-polynomial oracle relation $\mathbf{R}$. Let $\delta = 1 - \sqrt{\rho} - \eta$. Then:*

- *Suppose that $\Pi^{\mathsf{OCoAgg}(0)}$ is RBR sound with error $\varepsilon_{\mathsf{rbr-s}}$. Then $\Pi^{\mathsf{OCoAgg}(\delta)}$ has RBR soundness error $\varepsilon_{\mathsf{rbr-s}}(\mathbb{i})/(2\eta\sqrt{\rho})$.*
- *Suppose that $\Pi^{\mathsf{OCoAgg}(0)}$ has RBR knowledge with error $\varepsilon_{\mathsf{rbr-k}}$. Then $\Pi^{\mathsf{OCoAgg}(\delta)}$ has RBR knowledge error $\varepsilon_{\mathsf{rbr-k}}(\mathbb{i})/(2\eta\sqrt{\rho})$,*

The second lemma then states that when one replaces the oracle $\mathsf{OCoAgg}(\delta)$ in the above hIOP with another round-by-round sound IOP for δ-correlated agreement, then the resulting composed protocol remains round-by-round sound.

Lemma 2. *Assume the notation and hypotheses of Theorem 8. Then there exists a hIOP Π_{compiled} for $\mathbf{R}$ with the following properties:*

- *Suppose $\Pi^{\mathsf{OCoAgg}(\delta)}$ has RBR soundness error $\varepsilon_{\mathsf{rbr-s},\delta}$. Then Π_{compiled} has RBR soundness error $\max\left\{\varepsilon_{\mathsf{rbr-s},\delta}(\mathbb{i}), \varepsilon_{\mathsf{CA}}(\mathbb{i}_{\mathsf{CA}})\right\}$.*
- *Suppose $\Pi^{\mathsf{OCoAgg}(\delta)}$ has RBR knowledge soundness error $\varepsilon_{\mathsf{rbr-k},\delta}$. Then Π_{compiled} has RBR knowledge soundness error $\max\left\{\varepsilon_{\mathsf{rbr-k},\delta}(\mathbb{i}), \varepsilon_{\mathsf{CA}}(\mathbb{i}_{\mathsf{CA}})\right\}$.*

3.3 A Plonk-Like Protocol Abstraction OPlonky

Building upon the δ-correlated hIOP framework, we introduce a δ-correlated hIOP we call OPlonky, which abstracts the polynomial IOPs underlying many of the variants of Plonk. This generalization is inspired in part by Plonky2 [60]. Our main technical result is establishing the round-by-round soundness of $\mathsf{OPlonky}(0) := \mathsf{OPlonky}^{\mathsf{OCoAgg}(0)}$, where we assume the verifier has oracle access to the 0-correlated agreement oracle $\mathsf{OCoAgg}(0)$.

Lemma 3. *The 0-correlated agreement encoded hIOP* $\mathsf{OPlonky}(0)$ *has RBR soundness and RBR knowledge error* $\varepsilon(\mathbb{i}) := \max_{i\in[3]}\{\varepsilon_i(\mathbb{i})\}$, *where*

$$\varepsilon_1(\mathbb{i}) := ([3\mathsf{n}(\mathsf{r}' + \mathsf{u})]/|\mathbb{F}|)^{\mathsf{t}}, \quad \varepsilon_2(\mathbb{i}) := ([|\mathcal{P}| + (\mathsf{s}+2)\mathsf{t} - 1]/|\mathbb{F}|)^{\mathsf{t}},$$
$$\varepsilon_3(\mathbb{i}) := \max\{\deg(P_j)_{j\in[|\mathcal{P}|]}, \mathsf{u}+1\} \cdot (\mathsf{n}/|\mathbb{K} \setminus D|)$$

for all index $\mathbb{i} = (\mathcal{P}, \mathcal{Q}, H, \sigma, \mathsf{PI}, \mathsf{r}, \mathsf{r}', \ell, \mathsf{t})$, *any potential input* $\mathbb{x}$, *and* $\mathsf{n} = |H|$.

Given the above lemma and our δ-correlated hIOP results, we obtain our main theorem for OPlonky: compiling $\mathsf{OPlonky}^{\mathsf{OCoAgg}(\delta)}$ with the Batched FRI protocol.

Theorem 9. *Let* $\mathbb{F}$ *be a finite field,* $D \subseteq \mathbb{F}^*$ *a smooth multiplicative subgroup of* $\mathbb{F}$ *of order* 2^n, *and* H *a subgroup of* D *of order* n. *Let* $m \geq 3$, $\delta = 1 - \sqrt{\rho} - \eta$ *for some* $\eta \in (0, \sqrt{\rho}/2m)$, *and let* Plonky2hIOP *be the hIOP obtained from* $\mathsf{OPlonky}(\delta)$ *after compiling it with the Batched FRI protocol (see [14]). Then* Plonky2hIOP *is RBR sound and has RBR knowledge. For each* $\mathbb{i} = (\mathcal{P}, \mathcal{Q}, H, \sigma, \mathsf{PI}, \mathsf{r}, \mathsf{r}', \ell, \mathsf{t})$ *and all* $q \geq 1$, *the error in both cases is given by*

$$\varepsilon_{\mathsf{rbr}}^{\mathsf{OPlonky}}(\mathbb{i}, q) = \max\{\left(\varepsilon_i(\mathbb{i})/(2\eta\sqrt{\rho})\right)_{i\in[3]}, \varepsilon_{\mathsf{rbr}}^{\mathsf{bFRI}}(\mathbb{F}, D, \rho, \delta, N, q)\},$$

where N *is the total number of codewords that are batched together in the batched FRI protocol,* $\varepsilon_{\mathsf{rbr}}^{\mathsf{bFRI}}$ *is the RBR soundness error of* $\varepsilon_{\mathsf{rbr}}^{\mathsf{bFRI}}$ *(which equals its RBR knowledge error, see [14]) and*

$$\varepsilon_1(\mathbb{i}) := ([3\mathsf{n}(\mathsf{r}' + \mathsf{u})]/|\mathbb{F}|)^{\mathsf{t}}, \qquad \varepsilon_2(\mathbb{i}) := ([|\mathcal{P}| + (\mathsf{s}+2)\mathsf{t} - 1]/|\mathbb{F}|)^{\mathsf{t}},$$

$$\varepsilon_3(\mathbb{i}) := \max\{\deg(P_j)_{j\in[|\mathcal{P}|]}, \mathsf{u}+1\}(\mathsf{n}/|\mathbb{K} \setminus D|).$$

Algorithm 1: FRI-IOPP

Input: Finite field $\mathbb{F}$, smooth multiplicative subgroup $L_0 \subset \mathbb{F}^*$ of size 2^n, degree bound $d_0 = 2^k$, and $\ell \in \mathbb{N}$.
P has function $G_0 \colon L_0 \to \mathbb{F}$ and V has oracle $(G_0(z))_{z \in L_0}$.
Output: The verifier V outputs accept or reject.

foreach $i \in [k]$ **do** // *Fold Phase*
  V sends $x_{i-1} \xleftarrow{\$} \mathbb{F}$ to P.
  P and V set $d_i := d_{i-1}/2$ and $L_i := \{z^2 \colon z \in L_{i-1}\}$.
  P computes unique bi-variate polynomial $Q_{i-1}(X, Y)$ such that
    1. $\deg_X(Q_{i-1}) = 1$;
    2. $\deg_Y(Q_{i-1}) < d_i$; and
    3. $G_{i-1}(r) = Q_{i-1}(r, r^2)$ for all $r \in L_{i-1}$.
  P defines $G_i(Y) := Q_{i-1}(x_{i-1}, Y)$.
  if $i = k$ **then** P sends $G_k = C \in \mathbb{F}$ to V.
  else P sends oracle $(G_i(z))_{z \in L_i}$ to V.
forall $j \in [\ell]$ **do** // *Query Phase;* ***processed in parallel***
  V samples $s_{0,j} \xleftarrow{\$} L_0$.
  foreach $i \in [k]$ **do**
    V computes $s_{i,j} = (s_{i-1,j})^2$ and $s'_{i-1,j} \neq s_{i-1,j}$ such that $(s'_{i-1,j})^2 = s_{i,j}$.
    V queries and obtains $q_{i-1,j} = G_{i-1}(s_{i-1,j})$ and $q'_{i-1,j} = G_{i-1}(s'_{i-1,j})$.
    V computes linear polynomial $\widetilde{Q}_{i-1,j}(X)$ via Lagrange interpolation on the set $\{(s_{i-1,j}, q_{i-1,j}), (s'_{i-1,j}, q'_{i-1,j})\}$.
    V checks that $G_i(s_{i,j}) = \widetilde{Q}_{i-1,j}(x_{i-1})$ by querying G_i.
    if $G_i(s_{i,j}) \neq \widetilde{Q}_{i-1,j}(x_{i-1})$ **then** V outputs reject.
V outputs accept.

4 Conclusions and Open Problems

In this work, we formalized the FS-security of FRI and related SNARKs, particularly Plonk-like protocols captured by δ-correlated IOPs. Our results on Plonk-like protocols cover multiple variants, some of which are already in production. There are other protocols that are amenable to our general framework for correlated IOP's, e.g., ethSTARK [65] and RISC Zero [68]. We leave it as future work to perform a RBR soundness/knowledge and FS analysis of these protocols.

Our generalization OPlonky of IOPs using Plonk-like arithmetization along with a protocol for low-degree testing (specifically, FRI) does not address KZG-based Plonk-like schemes. Compiling a 0-correlated IOP with RBR soundness and knowledge using other commitment schemes and the FS-security of such schemes remain open problems.

Acknowledgements. Alexander R. Block was supported by DARPA under Contract Nos. HR00112020022 and HR00112020025. Albert Garreta and Michał Zając were supported by Ethereum Foundation grant FY23-0885. Work of Jonathan Katz was supported by NSF award CNS-2154705 and by DARPA under Contract No. HR00112020025. Work of Justin Thaler was supported by NSF CAREER award CCF-1845125 and by DARPA under Contract No. HR00112020022. Pratyush Ranjan Tiwari was supported by NSF award CNS-1814919 and a Google Security and Privacy research award to Matthew Green. The views, opinions, findings, conclusions, and/or recommendations expressed in this material are those of the authors and should not be interpreted as reflecting the position or policy of DARPA or the United States Government, and no official endorsement should be inferred.

References

1. Abdalla, M., An, J.H., Bellare, M., Namprempre, C.: From identification to signatures via the Fiat-Shamir transform: minimizing assumptions for security and forward-security. In: Knudsen, L.R. (ed.) EUROCRYPT 2002. LNCS, vol. 2332, pp. 418–433. Springer, Heidelberg (2002). https://doi.org/10.1007/3-540-46035-7_28
2. Attema, T., Fehr, S., Klooß, M.: Fiat-Shamir transformation of multi-round interactive proofs. In: Kiltz, E., Vaikuntanathan, V. (eds.) TCC 2022, Part I. LNCS, vol. 13747, pp. 113–142. Springer, Heidelberg (2022). https://doi.org/10.1007/978-3-031-22318-1_5
3. Barak, B.: How to go beyond the black-box simulation barrier. In: 42nd FOCS, pp. 106–115. IEEE Computer Society Press (2001). https://doi.org/10.1109/SFCS.2001.959885
4. Ben-Sasson, E., Bentov, I., Horesh, Y., Riabzev, M.: Fast reed-solomon interactive oracle proofs of proximity. In: Chatzigiannakis, I., Kaklamanis, C., Marx, D., Sannella, D. (eds.) ICALP 2018. LIPIcs, vol. 107, pp. 14:1–14:17. Schloss Dagstuhl (2018). https://doi.org/10.4230/LIPIcs.ICALP.2018.14
5. Ben-Sasson, E., Bentov, I., Horesh, Y., Riabzev, M.: Scalable, transparent, and post-quantum secure computational integrity. Cryptology ePrint Archive, Report 2018/046 (2018). https://eprint.iacr.org/2018/046
6. Ben-Sasson, E., Carmon, D., Ishai, Y., Kopparty, S., Saraf, S.: Proximity gaps for reed-solomon codes. Cryptology ePrint Archive, Paper 2020/654 (2020). https://eprint.iacr.org/2020/654, full version of the same work published at FOCS 2020. https://doi.org/10.1109/FOCS46700.2020.00088
7. Ben-Sasson, E., Chiesa, A., Genkin, D., Tromer, E.: Fast reductions from RAMs to delegatable succinct constraint satisfaction problems: extended abstract. In: Kleinberg, R.D. (ed.) ITCS 2013, pp. 401–414. ACM (2013). https://doi.org/10.1145/2422436.2422481
8. Ben-Sasson, E., Chiesa, A., Riabzev, M., Spooner, N., Virza, M., Ward, N.P.: Aurora: transparent succinct arguments for R1CS. In: Ishai, Y., Rijmen, V. (eds.) EUROCRYPT 2019, Part I. LNCS, vol. 11476, pp. 103–128. Springer, Cham (2019). https://doi.org/10.1007/978-3-030-17653-2_4
9. Ben-Sasson, E., Chiesa, A., Spooner, N.: Interactive oracle proofs. In: Hirt, M., Smith, A. (eds.) TCC 2016, Part II. LNCS, vol. 9986, pp. 31–60. Springer, Heidelberg (2016). https://doi.org/10.1007/978-3-662-53644-5_2
10. Ben-Sasson, E., Goldberg, L., Kopparty, S., Saraf, S.: DEEP-FRI: sampling outside the box improves soundness. In: Vidick, T. (ed.) ITCS 2020, vol. 151, pp. 5:1–5:32. LIPIcs (2020). https://doi.org/10.4230/LIPIcs.ITCS.2020.5

11. Ben-Sasson, E., Kopparty, S., Saraf, S.: Worst-case to average case reductions for the distance to a code. In: Servedio, R.A. (ed.) 33rd Computational Complexity Conference, CCC 2018, 22–24 June 2018, San Diego, CA, USA. LIPIcs, vol. 102, pp. 24:1–24:23. Schloss Dagstuhl - Leibniz-Zentrum für Informatik (2018). https://doi.org/10.4230/LIPIcs.CCC.2018.24
12. Bernhard, D., Pereira, O., Warinschi, B.: How not to prove yourself: pitfalls of the Fiat-Shamir heuristic and applications to Helios. In: Wang, X., Sako, K. (eds.) ASIACRYPT 2012. LNCS, vol. 7658, pp. 626–643. Springer, Heidelberg (2012). https://doi.org/10.1007/978-3-642-34961-4_38
13. Bitansky, N., et al.: Why "Fiat-Shamir for proofs" lacks a proof. In: Sahai, A. (ed.) TCC 2013. LNCS, vol. 7785, pp. 182–201. Springer, Heidelberg (2013). https://doi.org/10.1007/978-3-642-36594-2_11
14. Block, A.R., Garreta, A., Katz, J., Thaler, J., Tiwari, P.R., Zając, M.: Fiat-Shamir security of FRI and related snarks. Cryptology ePrint Archive, Paper 2023/1071 (2023). https://eprint.iacr.org/2023/1071
15. Blum, M., Evans, W., Gemmell, P., Kannan, S., Naor, M.: Checking the correctness of memories. Algorithmica **12**, 225–244 (1994)
16. Blumberg, A.J., Thaler, J., Vu, V., Walfish, M.: Verifiable computation using multiple provers. Cryptology ePrint Archive, Report 2014/846 (2014). https://eprint.iacr.org/2014/846
17. Bonneau, J., Clark, J., Goldfeder, S.: On bitcoin as a public randomness source. IACR Cryptology ePrint Archive, p. 1015 (2015)
18. Bootle, J., Cerulli, A., Chaidos, P., Groth, J., Petit, C.: Efficient zero-knowledge arguments for arithmetic circuits in the discrete log setting. In: Fischlin, M., Coron, J.-S. (eds.) EUROCRYPT 2016, Part II. LNCS, vol. 9666, pp. 327–357. Springer, Heidelberg (2016). https://doi.org/10.1007/978-3-662-49896-5_12
19. Bootle, J., Cerulli, A., Groth, J., Jakobsen, S., Maller, M.: Arya: nearly linear-time zero-knowledge proofs for correct program execution. In: Peyrin, T., Galbraith, S. (eds.) ASIACRYPT 2018. LNCS, vol. 11272, pp. 595–626. Springer, Cham (2018). https://doi.org/10.1007/978-3-030-03326-2_20
20. Bünz, B., Bootle, J., Boneh, D., Poelstra, A., Wuille, P., Maxwell, G.: Bulletproofs: short proofs for confidential transactions and more. In: 2018 IEEE Symposium on Security and Privacy, pp. 315–334. IEEE Computer Society Press (2018). https://doi.org/10.1109/SP.2018.00020
21. Bünz, B., Fisch, B., Szepieniec, A.: Transparent SNARKs from DARK compilers. In: Canteaut, A., Ishai, Y. (eds.) EUROCRYPT 2020, Part I. LNCS, vol. 12105, pp. 677–706. Springer, Cham (2020). https://doi.org/10.1007/978-3-030-45721-1_24
22. Canetti, R., et al.: Fiat-Shamir: from practice to theory. In: Charikar, M., Cohen, E. (eds.) 51st ACM STOC, pp. 1082–1090. ACM Press (2019). https://doi.org/10.1145/3313276.3316380
23. Canetti, R., Chen, Y., Reyzin, L., Rothblum, R.D.: Fiat-Shamir and correlation intractability from strong KDM-secure Encryption. In: Nielsen, J.B., Rijmen, V. (eds.) EUROCRYPT 2018, Part I. LNCS, vol. 10820, pp. 91–122. Springer, Cham (2018). https://doi.org/10.1007/978-3-319-78381-9_4
24. Canetti, R., Goldreich, O., Halevi, S.: The random oracle methodology, revisited. J. ACM **51**(4), 557–594 (2004). https://doi.org/10.1145/1008731.1008734
25. Chiesa, A., Manohar, P., Spooner, N.: Succinct arguments in the quantum random oracle model. In: Hofheinz, D., Rosen, A. (eds.) TCC 2019, Part II. LNCS, vol. 11892, pp. 1–29. Springer, Cham (2019). https://doi.org/10.1007/978-3-030-36033-7_1

26. Chiesa, A., Ojha, D., Spooner, N.: Fractal: post-quantum and transparent recursive proofs from holography. In: Canteaut, A., Ishai, Y. (eds.) EUROCRYPT 2020, Part I. LNCS, vol. 12105, pp. 769–793. Springer, Cham (2020). https://doi.org/10.1007/978-3-030-45721-1_27
27. Cormode, G., Mitzenmacher, M., Thaler, J.: Practical verified computation with streaming interactive proofs. In: Goldwasser, S. (ed.) ITCS 2012, pp. 90–112. ACM (2012). https://doi.org/10.1145/2090236.2090245
28. Cramer, R., Damgård, I., Schoenmakers, B.: Proofs of partial knowledge and simplified design of witness hiding protocols. In: Desmedt, Y.G. (ed.) CRYPTO 1994. LNCS, vol. 839, pp. 174–187. Springer, Heidelberg (1994). https://doi.org/10.1007/3-540-48658-5_19
29. Dao, Q., Miller, J., Wright, O., Grubbs, P.: Weak fiat-shamir attacks on modern proof systems. Cryptology ePrint Archive, Paper 2023/691 (2023). https://eprint.iacr.org/2023/691
30. Dusk Network: Plonkup. https://github.com/dusk-network/plonkup. Accessed 24 May 2023
31. Fiat, A., Shamir, A.: How to prove yourself: practical solutions to identification and signature problems. In: Odlyzko, A.M. (ed.) CRYPTO 1986. LNCS, vol. 263, pp. 186–194. Springer, Heidelberg (1987). https://doi.org/10.1007/3-540-47721-7_12
32. Gabizon, A., Williamson, Z.J.: The turbo-plonk program syntax for specifying snark programs. https://docs.zkproof.org/pages/standards/accepted-workshop3/proposal-turbo_plonk.pdf. Accessed 23 May 2023
33. Gabizon, A., Williamson, Z.J.: plookup: a simplified polynomial protocol for lookup tables. Cryptology ePrint Archive, Paper 2020/315 (2020). https://eprint.iacr.org/2020/315
34. Gabizon, A., Williamson, Z.J., Ciobotaru, O.: PLONK: permutations over lagrange-bases for oecumenical noninteractive arguments of knowledge. Cryptology ePrint Archive, Report 2019/953 (2019). https://eprint.iacr.org/2019/953
35. Ghoshal, A., Tessaro, S.: Tight state-restoration soundness in the algebraic group model. In: Malkin, T., Peikert, C. (eds.) CRYPTO 2021, Part III. LNCS, vol. 12827, pp. 64–93. Springer, Cham (2021). https://doi.org/10.1007/978-3-030-84252-9_3
36. Goldwasser, S., Kalai, Y.T.: On the (in)security of the Fiat-Shamir paradigm. In: 44th FOCS, pp. 102–115. IEEE Computer Society Press (2003). https://doi.org/10.1109/SFCS.2003.1238185
37. Goldwasser, S., Kalai, Y.T., Rothblum, G.N.: Delegating computation: interactive proofs for muggles. In: Ladner, R.E., Dwork, C. (eds.) 40th ACM STOC, pp. 113–122. ACM Press (2008). https://doi.org/10.1145/1374376.1374396
38. Goldwasser, S., Micali, S., Rackoff, C.: The knowledge complexity of interactive proof systems. SIAM J. Comput. **18**(1), 186–208 (1989). https://doi.org/10.1137/0218012
39. Haböck, U.: A summary on the FRI low degree test. Cryptology ePrint Archive, Report 2022/1216 (2022). https://eprint.iacr.org/2022/1216
40. Holmgren, J., Lombardi, A.: Cryptographic hashing from strong one-way functions (or: one-way product functions and their applications). In: Thorup, M. (ed.) 59th FOCS, pp. 850–858. IEEE Computer Society Press (2018). https://doi.org/10.1109/FOCS.2018.00085
41. Holmgren, J., Lombardi, A., Rothblum, R.D.: Fiat-Shamir via list-recoverable codes (or: parallel repetition of GMW is not zero-knowledge). In: Khuller, S., Williams, V.V. (eds.) 53rd ACM STOC, pp. 750–760. ACM Press (2021). https://doi.org/10.1145/3406325.3451116

42. Kalai, Y.T., Rothblum, G.N., Rothblum, R.D.: From obfuscation to the security of Fiat-Shamir for proofs. In: Katz, J., Shacham, H. (eds.) CRYPTO 2017, Part II. LNCS, vol. 10402, pp. 224–251. Springer, Cham (2017). https://doi.org/10.1007/978-3-319-63715-0_8
43. Kate, A., Zaverucha, G.M., Goldberg, I.: Constant-size commitments to polynomials and their applications. In: Abe, M. (ed.) ASIACRYPT 2010. LNCS, vol. 6477, pp. 177–194. Springer, Heidelberg (2010). https://doi.org/10.1007/978-3-642-17373-8_11
44. Kattis, A.A., Panarin, K., Vlasov, A.: RedShift: transparent SNARKs from list polynomial commitments. In: Yin, H., Stavrou, A., Cremers, C., Shi, E. (eds.) ACM CCS 2022, pp. 1725–1737. ACM Press (2022). https://doi.org/10.1145/3548606.3560657
45. Kilian, J.: A note on efficient zero-knowledge proofs and arguments (extended abstract). In: 24th ACM STOC, pp. 723–732. ACM Press (1992). https://doi.org/10.1145/129712.129782
46. L2BEAT: L2BEAT total value locked. https://l2beat.com/scaling/tvl. Accessed 22 May 2023
47. Lipton, R.J.: Fingerprinting sets. Princeton University, Department of Computer Science (1989)
48. Lipton, R.J.: Efficient checking of computations. In: Choffrut, C., Lengauer, T. (eds.) STACS 1990. LNCS, vol. 415, pp. 207–215. Springer, Heidelberg (1990). https://doi.org/10.1007/3-540-52282-4_44
49. Lund, C., Fortnow, L., Karloff, H.J., Nisan, N.: Algebraic methods for interactive proof systems. J. ACM **39**(4), 859–868 (1992). https://doi.org/10.1145/146585.146605
50. Maller, M., Bowe, S., Kohlweiss, M., Meiklejohn, S.: Sonic: Zero-knowledge SNARKs from linear-size universal and updatable structured reference strings. In: Cavallaro, L., Kinder, J., Wang, X., Katz, J. (eds.) ACM CCS 2019, pp. 2111–2128. ACM Press (2019). https://doi.org/10.1145/3319535.3339817
51. Matter Labs: zksync 2.0: Hello ethereum! https://blog.matter-labs.io/zksync-2-0-hello-ethereum-ca48588de179. Accessed 24 May 2023
52. Merkle, R.: Secrecy, authentication, and public key systems (1979)
53. Micali, S.: CS proofs (extended abstracts). In: 35th FOCS, pp. 436–453. IEEE Computer Society Press (1994). https://doi.org/10.1109/SFCS.1994.365746
54. Micali, S.: Computationally sound proofs. SIAM J. Comput. **30**(4), 1253–1298 (2000). https://doi.org/10.1137/S0097539795284959
55. Mina: Mina book: Background on plonk. https://o1-labs.github.io/proof-systems/plonk/overview.html. Accessed 24 May 2023
56. =nil; Foundation: Circuit definition library for =nil; foundation's cryptography suite. https://github.com/NilFoundation/zkllvm-blueprint. Accessed 24 May 2023
57. Pierrot, C., Wesolowski, B.: Malleability of the blockchain's entropy. Cryptogr. Commun. **10**(1), 211–233 (2018)
58. Pointcheval, D., Stern, J.: Security proofs for signature schemes. In: Maurer, U. (ed.) EUROCRYPT 1996. LNCS, vol. 1070, pp. 387–398. Springer, Heidelberg (1996). https://doi.org/10.1007/3-540-68339-9_33
59. Polygon Labs: FRI verification procedures. https://wiki.polygon.technology/docs/miden/user_docs/stdlib/crypto/fri/. Accessed 23 May 2023
60. Polygon Zero Team: Plonky2: Fast recursive arguments with plonk and FRI. https://github.com/mir-protocol/plonky2/tree/main/plonky2
61. Rabin, M.O.: Transaction protection by beacons. J. Comput. Syst. Sci. **27**(2), 256–267 (1983). https://doi.org/10.1016/0022-0000(83)90042-9

62. Reed, I.S., Solomon, G.: Polynomial codes over certain finite fields. J. Soc. Ind. Appl. Math. 8(2), 300–304 (1960). https://doi.org/10.1137/0108018
63. Ron-Zewi, N., Rothblum, R.D.: Local proofs approaching the witness length [extended abstract]. In: 61st FOCS, pp. 846–857. IEEE Computer Society Press (2020). https://doi.org/10.1109/FOCS46700.2020.00083
64. Setty, S.: Spartan: efficient and general-purpose zkSNARKs without trusted setup. In: Micciancio, D., Ristenpart, T. (eds.) CRYPTO 2020, Part III. LNCS, vol. 12172, pp. 704–737. Springer, Cham (2020). https://doi.org/10.1007/978-3-030-56877-1_25
65. StarkWare: ethstark documentation. Cryptology ePrint Archive, Paper 2021/582 (2021). https://eprint.iacr.org/2021/582
66. StarkWare Industries: Starkex documentation: Customers and their deployment contract addresses. https://docs.starkware.co/starkex/deployments-addresses.html. Accessed 22 May 2023
67. Succinct Labs: gnark-plonky2-verifier. https://github.com/succinctlabs/gnark-plonky2-verifier. Accessed 24 May 2023
68. Team, R.Z.: RISC zero's proof system for a zkVM (2023). https://github.com/risc0/risc0. github repository
69. Thaler, J.: Time-optimal interactive proofs for circuit evaluation. In: Canetti, R., Garay, J.A. (eds.) CRYPTO 2013, Part II. LNCS, vol. 8043, pp. 71–89. Springer, Heidelberg (2013). https://doi.org/10.1007/978-3-642-40084-1_5
70. Thaler, J.: Proofs, arguments, and zero-knowledge (2022). https://people.cs.georgetown.edu/jthaler/ProofsArgsAndZK.html
71. Wahby, R.S., Tzialla, I., shelat, a., Thaler, J., Walfish, M.: Doubly-efficient zkSNARKs without trusted setup. In: 2018 IEEE Symposium on Security and Privacy, pp. 926–943. IEEE Computer Society Press (2018). https://doi.org/10.1109/SP.2018.00060
72. Wikström, D.: Special soundness in the random oracle model. Cryptology ePrint Archive, Report 2021/1265 (2021). https://eprint.iacr.org/2021/1265
73. Zhang, Y., Genkin, D., Katz, J., Papadopoulos, D., Papamanthou, C.: vRAM: faster verifiable ram with program-independent preprocessing. In: 2018 IEEE Symposium on Security and Privacy (SP), pp. 908–925. IEEE (2018)

On Black-Box Knowledge-Sound Commit-And-Prove SNARKs

Helger Lipmaa(✉)

University of Tartu, Tartu, Estonia
helger.lipmaa@gmail.com

Abstract. Gentry and Wichs proved that adaptively sound SNARGs for hard languages need non-falsifiable assumptions. Lipmaa and Pavlyk claimed Gentry-Wichs is tight by constructing a non-adaptively sound zk-SNARG FANA for NP from falsifiable assumptions. We show that FANA is flawed. We define and construct a fully algebraic F-position-binding vector commitment scheme VCF. We construct a concretely efficient commit-and-prove zk-SNARK Punic, a version of FANA with an additional VCF commitment to the witness. Punic satisfies *semi-adaptive black-box G-knowledge-soundness*, a new natural knowledge-soundness notion for commit-and-prove SNARKs. We use a new proof technique to achieve global consistency using a functional somewhere-extractable commitment scheme to extract vector commitment's local proofs.

Keywords: Commit-and-prove · falsifiable assumptions · Gentry-Wichs · non-adaptive soundness · QA-NIZK · vector commitment · zk-SNARK

1 Introduction

Gentry and Wichs [24] proved non-falsifiable assumptions are needed to construct (even non-zero-knowledge) adaptively sound SNARGs (*succinct non-interactive arguments*, [23,28,29,43,44,50]) for hard languages under black-box reductions. Their impossibility result balances the following four properties of NIZKs: (1) *Succinctness*: Non-succinct NIZKs are not suitable for many applications. (2) *Falsifiability:* an assumption or a primitive is *falsifiable* if one can efficiently decide whether the adversary broke it. Non-falsifiable assumptions are highly controversial. (3) *Adaptive soundness*: the SNARG is sound even if the malicious prover can choose the statement $\mathbb{x}$ after seeing the CRS. Non-adaptive soundness guarantees security only if $\mathbb{x}$ is independent of the CRS. (4) Many applications need SNARGs for *hard languages* (i.e., languages with hard subset membership problem) like circuit satisfiability.

Assuming black-box reductions, Gentry-Wichs is known to be tight in three aspects: (1) non-succinct falsifiable assumption-based adaptively sound NIZKs are known for NP [18], (2) falsifiable assumption-based adaptively sound

J. Guo and R. Steinfeld (Eds.): ASIACRYPT 2023, LNCS 14439, pp. 41–76, 2023.
https://doi.org/10.1007/978-981-99-8724-5_2

SNARGs are known for P [37], and (3) non-falsifiable assumption-based adaptively sound zk-SNARKs are known for NP [28].

It has been a major open problem *whether Gentry-Wichs is tight in the fourth aspect; that is, whether falsifiable assumption-based non-adaptively sound (even non-zero knowledge) SNARGs for hard languages exist.* Intuitively, it is easier to achieve non-adaptive than adaptive black-box knowledge soundness since, in the former case, the extractor has additional power. Namely, it can rewind the prover to the point after the prover chose the statement, sample a new CRS, and thus obtain many arguments of the same statement under different CRSs.

Sahai and Waters built a non-adaptively sound zk-SNARG for NP [52] using iO, one-way functions, and succinct punctured PRFs. One can use subexponential but falsifiable assumptions to instantiate iO [34]. However, their SNARG has exponential security loss in witness length [35]. Since the reduction can decide the language, their SNARG bypasses the Gentry-Wichs impossibility result (and can achieve adaptive security by complexity leveraging, [35]). Hence, constructing non-adaptively sound SNARGs for NP remains open after [52]. Jain and Jin [35] proposed a SNARG that overcomes this limitation, but only for a subclass of languages in NP ∩ co-NP with a "PV proof of disjointness".

Lipmaa and Pavlyk [46] proposed FANA, an *efficient* (and *polynomial-time challenger*) falsifiable assumption-based non-adaptively sound zk-SNARG for NP. FANA is based on two earlier constructions, DGPRS of [16] and FLPS [17]. DGPRS and FLPS are adaptively sound commit-and-prove (C&P) SNARGs for NP. Since they have non-succinct commitments, Gentry-Wichs does not apply.

By leveraging continuous leakage-resilient one-way functions (that exist under the discrete logarithm assumption [4]), Campanelli et al. [10] proved that non-adaptive black-box extractable SNAR<u>K</u>s (*succinct non-interactive arguments of knowledge*, i.e., *knowledge*-sound arguments) for NP do not exist. Recall that extraction is *black-box* if it extracts a witness from a prover only using its input/output interface, without knowledge about its internal state or code. Note that [10] does not contradict [46] who construct a SNAR<u>G</u>.

Our First Contribution. We show that FANA's security proof is flawed, and FANA is *not* a non-adaptively SNAR<u>G</u>.[1] The main reason why FANA's proof breaks down is that, differently from DGPRS and FLPS, FANA is *not* a C&P SNARG. On the other hand, DGPRS and FLPS rely on a perfectly binding (non-succinct) commitment scheme, i.e., they are not <u>S</u>NARGs.

Main Question. In Table 1, we summarize the state of the art: on top of [10,24] proved that falsifiable assumption-based non-adaptively knowledge-sound SNAR<u>K</u>s for NP do not exist, while [46] (that is insecure) and [52] (with an exponential security loss) constructed falsifiable assumption-based non-adaptively sound SNAR<u>G</u>s for NP. This leaves two open questions: Can one construct falsifiable assumption-based (1) non-adaptively sound SNAR<u>G</u>s, and (2) SNAR<u>K</u>s for NP under a different adaptivity notion?

[1] [53] noted that FANA is insecure (and referred to a private conversation with the authors of [46]), but they did not explain why. We will provide full details.

Table 1. The known possibility and impossibility results for falsifiable assumption-based SNAR(G|K)s for hard languages.

Adaptivity/Knowledge	SNARG	SNARK
Adaptive	✗ [24]	✗ [24]
Non-adaptive	~~✓/✗[46]~~ (✓ with exp. security loss [52])	✗ [10]
Semi-adaptive	✓ This work	✓ This work

We do not know how to answer (1), i.e., formally settle the tightness of Gentry-Wichs. Instead, the current paper aims to find a solution in the latter direction. There, one has the following natural question: For what notion of adaptivity can one construct falsifiable assumption-based black-box knowledge-sound SNAR<u>K</u>s for NP? Moreover, can this be done *efficiently*?

Our (Four More) Contributions. Second, definition. We define *semi-adaptive black-box knowledge-soundness*, a natural security notion for falsifiable assumption-based <u>C&P</u> SNARKs. In a black-box knowledge-sound C&P SNARK, one can black-box extract partial witnesses by rerunning the adversary on a fixed commitment key and commitment C (to the witness) but many CRSs. One can recover the full witness from many succinct arguments and thus overcome an information-theoretical barrier plaguing SNARKs. This is similar to using rewinding in interactive zero-knowledge proofs; indeed, the definition is related to that of witness-extended emulation [42]. Crucially, having a C&P SNARK (i.e., a fixed commitment key and a commitment) lets us avoid the impossibility result of [10]. We emphasize that finding a correct definition is one of the most critical tasks in cryptographic research.

Third, modular proof. We prove black-box knowledge-soundness in two steps, as standard in the *interactive* arguments but unlike [16,17,46]. First, we define *semi-adaptive computational special soundness*, a variant of special soundness [14]. We prove that every semi-adaptively computationally special sound and CRS-indistinguishable C&P zk-SNARK is also semi-adaptively black-box knowledge sound. Thus, we only need to prove the former two properties.

Fourth, the proof technique. We use a perfectly hiding *vector* commitment scheme VC [11,33,41] to create C. Since VC is perfectly hiding, one cannot black-box extract from C. Instead, we use a functional somewhere-extractable (FSE) commitment scheme [17] to black-box extract a *partial witness* (VC's local opening and proof) from a FSE commitment. We then combine many partial witnesses into a full witness. We define and construct *fully algebraic F-position-binding vector commitment schemes* that allow such extractions.

Fifth, construction. We construct a <u>C&P</u> zk-SNAR<u>K</u> Punic that fixes FANA by (re)adding a language parameter $\mathsf{lp} = \mathsf{ck}$ and a succinct (in our case, *vector*) commitment C to $(\mathbb{x}, \mathbb{w})$. We prove Punic is semi-adaptively computationally special-sound and CRS-indistinguishable and thus semi-adaptively black-box knowledge-sound. Since one of our primary goals is efficiency, the special soundness of Punic is based on non-standard yet non-interactive and known falsifiable assumptions.

On Tightness of Gentry-Wichs. The current work opens a novel approach to studying the tightness of Gentry-Wichs in the context of C&P SNARKs. Table 1 summarizes the known results. We emphasize that it is unknown whether one can construct falsifiable assumption-based non-adaptively sound SNARGs for NP with polynomial security loss. We leave it as the open question to state a precise version of Gentry-Wichs for both C&P and non-C&P SNARGs and SNARKs. In particular, is there a separation between SNARGs and black-box knowledge-sound SNARKs?

2 Technical Overview

We will start this section with an overview of DGPRS, FLPS, and FANA. After that, we describe our contributions in more detail.

2.1 Background

In C&P SNARGs and SNARKs, the CRS includes a commitment key ($\Gamma.\mathsf{ck}$, also called a *language parameter* lp, [36]), and the statement includes a Γ-commitment C. Here, Γ is an extractable commitment scheme. Most of the efficient SNARKs (e.g., [9,12,23,29,47,50]) are C&P SNARKs although usually not stated as such; in their knowledge-soundness proof, one uses knowledge assumptions to *non-black-box* extract the full witness from C. Different definitions of C&P SNARGs allow or do not allow dependencies between the commitment key, the language, and the CRS. The definition of C&P QA-SNARG (quasi-adaptive SNARG[2], [16,36]) explicitly requires that one first fixes $\mathsf{lp} = \Gamma.\mathsf{ck}$, defining (for some relation $\mathcal{R}$) the language

$$\mathcal{L}_{\mathsf{lp}} = \{(C, \mathbb{x}) : (\exists \mathbb{w}, r)\, (C = \Gamma.\mathsf{Com}(\Gamma.\mathsf{ck}, (\mathbb{x}, \mathbb{w}); r) \wedge (\mathbb{x}, \mathbb{w}) \in \mathcal{R})\} ,$$

then a CRS crs that may depend on lp (and thus $\mathcal{L}_{\mathsf{lp}}$). Only after that does the prover choose a statement $(C, \mathbb{x})$. Quasi-adaptive soundness is defined for this temporal order: for any honestly generated lp (that fixes $\mathcal{L}_{\mathsf{lp}}$) and crs (that can depend on lp and thus $\mathcal{L}_{\mathsf{lp}}$), it must be hard to generate $(C, \mathbb{x}, \pi)$, such that the verifier accepts $(C, \mathbb{x}, \pi)$ but $(C, \mathbb{x}) \notin \mathcal{L}_{\mathsf{lp}}$.

DGPRS [16] and FLPS [17] are pairing-based C&P QA-SNARGs for certain constraint systems. DGPRS and FLPS use a perfectly binding commitment scheme Γ and two more building blocks:

[2] The initial QA-NIZK constructions were for linear subspaces [36,40]. They (and the bilateral linear subspace QA-SNARG, used in [16,17] and the current paper) have a language parameter that is not a commitment key. We use the acronym QA-SNARG since it fits our framework better.

(1) a succinct functional somewhere-extractable (FSE, [17]) commitment scheme to commit to $(\mathbb{x}, \mathbb{w})$. FSE satisfies the following property: for a small locality parameter q, one can invisibly reprogram FSE's commitment key FSE.ck so that one can later black-box "somewhere-extract" the desired q linear combinations of the coefficients of $[\mathbb{x}, \mathbb{w}]_1$.[3]
(2) a succinct bilateral subspace QA-SNARG argument BLS [25] to prove that a tuple of commitments belongs to a specific subspace (e.g., Γ-commitments and FSE-commitments are to the same $(\mathbb{x}, \mathbb{w})$).

DGPRS and FLPS are falsifiable assumption-based, quasi-adaptively sound, for hard languages, and have a succinct argument. This does not contradict Gentry-Wichs since their statement contains a *non-succinct* commitment C from which the reduction can black-box extract the witness. (See the full version [45].)

Consider their soundness proof to understand why DGPRS and FLPS are quasi-adaptively sound. Assume that an adversary $\mathcal{A}$ broke the quasi-adaptive soundness by outputting an accepting $(C, \mathbb{x}, \pi)$. Thus, either (1) C is not a commitment to $(\mathbb{x}, \mathbb{w})$ for any $\mathbb{w}$, or (2) at least one constraint is unsatisfied (C commits to $(\mathbb{x}, \mathbb{w})$ for some $\mathbb{w}$, but $\mathbb{w}$ is not a correct witness for $\mathbb{x} \in \mathcal{L}_{\mathsf{lp}}$). DGPRS and FLPS define two reductions $\mathcal{B}_1$ and $\mathcal{B}_2$. $\mathcal{B}_1$ is a reduction to the BLS security, guaranteeing in particular that (1) cannot happen.

Let us focus on $\mathcal{B}_2$. $\mathcal{B}_2$ samples a constraint number $\varrho \leftarrow\$ [1, n]$, where n is the number of constraints in the underlying constraint system. $\mathcal{B}_2$ reprograms the CRS to depend on ϱ while $\mathsf{lp} = \Gamma.\mathsf{ck}$ stays unchanged. It follows from the properties of FSE that the CRS hides ϱ. After obtaining $(C, \mathbb{x})$ from $\mathcal{A}$, $\mathcal{B}_2$ black-box extracts from the perfectly binding commitment C all variables, involved in the ϱth constraint. $\mathcal{B}_2$ guesses that the ϱth constraint is unsatisfied and then uses the extracted values to check whether its guess is correct. If the guess is incorrect (i.e., the ϱth constraint is satisfied), then $\mathcal{B}_2$ aborts. Since C is perfectly binding, the adversary's witness $\mathbb{w}$ is fixed by C. Thus, the index of the unsatisfied constraint does not depend on ϱ. (If the adversary can open C to a different message after the CRS reprogramming, one can distinguish the CRSs. The latter is intractable because of the properties of FSE, [16,17].)

Since the index of the unsatisfied constraint does not depend on $\mathcal{B}_2$'s guess ϱ, $\mathcal{B}_2$ aborts with probability $\leq 1 - 1/n$. In the case of non-abortion, $\mathcal{B}_2$ uses FSE's somewhere-extractor to black-box extract a succinct partial witness $[\mathbb{p}^{\varrho}]_1$ from a succinct FSE commitment (also output by $\mathcal{A}$). Here, $[\mathbb{p}^{\varrho}]_1$ is sufficient to verify whether the ϱth constraint of the constraint system is satisfied. The BLS argument (via reduction $\mathcal{B}_1$) guarantees that the values extracted from C are consistent with $[\mathbb{p}^{\varrho}]_1$. $\mathcal{B}_2$ then uses $[\mathbb{p}^{\varrho}]_1$ to break a falsifiable assumption.

FANA. Lipmaa and Pavlyk [46] improve on DGPRS and FLPS in several ways. Their non-C&P zk-SNARG FANA handles the standard R1CS constraint system [23] instead of SSP and SAP used in DGPRS and FLPS, has soundness based on a more plausible falsifiable assumption QALINRES, and is subversion

---

[3] We use the standard additive bracket notation for pairings. For example, for $s \in \mathbb{Z}_p$, $[s]_1 = s[1]_1 \in \mathbb{G}_1$. See Sect. 3.

zero-knowledge [1–3,6,19] (zero-knowledge even when lp and crs are maliciously constructed). [46] claims that FANA is non-adaptively sound and thus Gentry-Wichs is tight. We only focus on the last claim.

FANA omits ck and the commitment C. FANA's security reduction black-box extracts partial witnesses $[\mathbb{p}^{\varrho}]_1$ from the FSE commitment. As in DGPRS and FLPS, extraction is done after reprogramming the CRS. To ensure that $[\mathbb{p}^{\varrho}]_1$ does not covertly depend on ϱ, [46] reverts to non-adaptivity, assuming that the statement $\mathbb{x}$ (recall that there is no commitment C) is fixed before the CRS is created. [46] argues that since $\mathbb{x}$ does not depend on crs, neither does the index ϱ of an unsatisfied constraint; hence, a slight modification of the quasi-adaptive soundness proof of [16,17] goes through.

2.2 FANA Is Not Sound

FANA's soundness proof states that since the statement $\mathbb{x}$ is fixed, the unsatisfied constraint number ϱ does not depend on the CRS. Next, we will explain why one cannot assume that the number ϱ of the (possibly only) unsatisfied constraint did not change after the CRS reprogramming.

If C is a perfectly binding commitment as in DGPRS and FLPS, then one can use the properties of FSE to guarantee that one cannot open C to a different value after the CRS reprogramming. Using a succinct FSE commitment as in FANA, the committed message can change with each CRS reprogramming. So, one cannot ensure that the partial witnesses are consistent. More precisely, one cannot break a falsifiable assumption with a black-box reduction if the partial witnesses are inconsistent (a non-black-box reduction might still be possible). FANA's security proof does not guarantee that the adversary uses the same full witness $\mathbb{w}$ after each reprogramming; in particular, there is no guarantee that ϱ did not change. If ϱ changed, one could not argue that the non-abortion probability in the soundness reduction is at least $1/n$. Indeed, this probability might be zero when the adversary leaves some constraint unsatisfied, but the number of this constraint depends on the CRS in a non-trivial manner.

2.3 Semi-adaptive Black-Box Knowledge-Soundness

An argument system is *black-box knowledge-sound* if, for every PPT prover, there exists a black-box PPT extractor $\mathsf{Ext}_{\mathsf{ks}}$ such that if the prover convinces the verifier to accept a statement $\mathbb{x}$ with a non-negligible probability, then $\mathsf{Ext}_{\mathsf{ks}}$ extracts a witness $\mathbb{w}$ for the validity of $\mathbb{x}$. In an adaptively sound SNARG, since the prover's message is much shorter than the witness, one cannot black-box extract a witness from a single argument. An alternative approach is to extract a witness directly from the code of the prover. In all existing solutions, such *non-black-box extraction* is enabled by non-falsifiable knowledge assumptions.

One can achieve black-box extractable *interactive* succinct arguments by allowing rewinding the prover to earlier rounds. Rewinding gives the extractor power to run the prover with different verifier's randomnesses ϱ and thus obtain many succinct arguments π^{ϱ}. From π^{ϱ}, the extractor can "somewhere extract" a partial witness $\mathbb{p}^{\varrho}$. If the total length of different arguments is larger than the witness length, one does not have the information-theoretic barrier anymore and can thus potentially compute $\mathbb{w}$ from $\{\mathbb{p}^{\varrho}\}$ and thus black-box extract $\mathbb{w}$.

In the interactive case, one usually splits this procedure into two parts: the rewinding step to obtain many transcripts tr^{ϱ} (that, in particular, contain π^{ϱ}) and the gluing step that inputs the transcripts and outputs the full witness $\mathbb{w}$. One formalizes the second step by defining special soundness [14] and saying that the argument is special-sound if the second step succeeds. The first step essentially reduces knowledge-soundness to special soundness. We use the same two-step methodology, albeit for non-interactive semi-adaptive arguments.

In adaptively sound SNARGs, the prover can be rewound to the point before it creates the argument π. The extractor will not have more power since π is not rerandomized by the verifier. In non-adaptively sound SNARGs, one can rewind to the point before the CRS was created. One can then use a new randomness ϱ to create a new CRS crs^{ϱ} and obtain a new succinct argument π^{ϱ}. From π^{ϱ}, the extractor can "somewhere extract" a partial witness $\mathbb{p}^{\varrho}$. Similarly to the interactive case, one can thus breach the information-theoretic barrier. However, a malicious prover can compute each argument using a different witness; this is one intuition behind the impossibility result of [10] that falsifiable assumption-based non-adaptively knowledge-sound SNARKs for NP are impossible.

Local and Global Consistency. If the underlying language is a constraint system, one can think of $\varrho := \mathcal{S}$ as a set of constraints and $\mathbb{p}^{\varrho} = \mathbb{p}_{\mathcal{S}}$ a partial witness that satisfies all constraints in the set $\mathcal{S}$. If this holds for every (small) $\mathcal{S}$, the SNARG satisfies *local consistency* [37]. For *global consistency*, one would like the partial witness $\mathbb{p}_{\mathcal{S}}$ to be consistent with some full witness $\mathbb{w}$, $\mathbb{p}_{\mathcal{S}}(\mathcal{S}) = \mathbb{w}|_{\mathcal{S}}$. In particular, all partial witnesses should be mutually consistent. ([37] does not satisfy global consistency.) We will give more details in Sect. 5.1.

Semi-adaptive Black-Box Knowledge-Soundness. Non-adaptively sound SNARKs can be seen as two-message protocols, where the first message is the CRS, and the second message is the argument. A logical approach to overcome their impossibility result while still staying in the realm of black-box extraction is to increase the number of rewinding points (or messages). C&P SNARKs are a natural way of doing that: they can be seen as four-message protocols, where the first message is a commitment key (also known as the language parameter), the second message is a commitment C and a statement $\mathbb{x}$, the third message is a CRS, and the fourth message is an argument. However, the CRS does not depend on the second message; moreover, the same CRS can be used in different SNARKs by different provers. Thus, semi-adaptivity can be seen as a trust assumption that $(C, \mathbb{x})$ does not depend on the CRS. We use the name *semi-adaptive* since the adversary is allowed to output the statement after seeing ck (the first half of the trusted parameters) and before seeing crs (another half). See Fig. 1.

Again, the extractor can repeatedly use a new ϱ to create a new CRS crs^{ϱ} and obtain a succinct argument π^{ϱ}. From π^{ϱ}, the extractor can "somewhere extract"

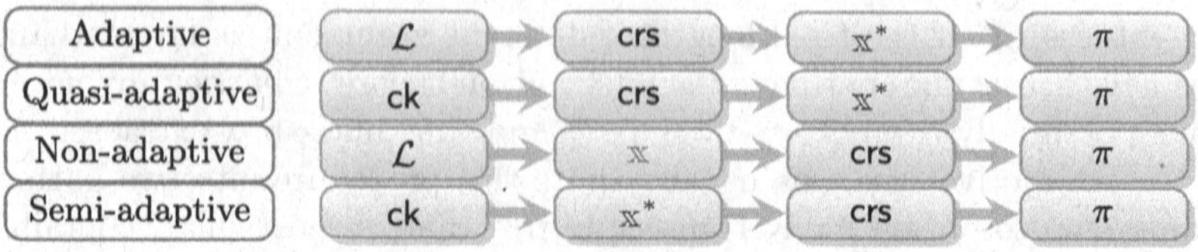

Fig. 1. C&P SNARKs: temporal dependencies. In the case of quasi-adaptive and semi-adaptive soundness, $\mathsf{lp} = \mathsf{ck}$ also fixes the language $\mathcal{L}_{\mathsf{lp}}$. Here, $\mathbb{x}^* = (C, \mathbb{x})$, where C is a commitment. Non-adaptive soundness differs since $\mathbb{x}$ is created before any trusted parameters (ck or crs), which means that $\mathbb{x}$ cannot contain a commitment.

a partial witness $\mathbb{p}^{\varrho}$. In our soundness proof, we do not rewind the creation of ck. The difference with the non-adaptive case is that we have the commitment C that must be the same in different rewindings. So, all partial witnesses must be consistent with C. If they are also consistent with each other, we can compute a full witness $\mathbb{w}$ that is consistent with all partial witnesses and thus satisfies all constraints. Semi-adaptive knowledge-soundness states that this must always be possible. In the soundness proof of the new SNARK, we construct a reduction that works if this is false (i.e., two partial witnesses are not mutually consistent).

Definition. We define a new security notion for C&P SNARKs, *semi-adaptive black-box G-knowledge-soundness* that insists that one can efficiently construct $G(\mathbb{w})$ given oracle access to the prover that outputs arguments corresponding to the fixed ck, C, $\mathbb{x}$ but different CRSs. Its definition is inspired by non-adaptive black-box knowledge-soundness in [10] and witness-extended emulation (WEE, [42]). In particular, if an adversary outputs a single accepting transcript, the black-box extractor outputs both the accepting transcript (from the correct distribution) and $G(\mathbb{w})$ with a similar probability. Here, G is a permutation that plays a similar role to G in Groth-Sahai proofs [31] (that are usually G-extractable) and G-unforgeable signature schemes [5]. In our new SNARK for R1CS, $G(s) := [sy]_1$ for a trapdoor y. When handling SSP [15] (Boolean circuits) instead of R1CS, one can set $G(s) = s$.

Applications of Semi-adaptivity. As argued above, black-box G-knowledge-soundness is a natural security notion that seems to be the best one can do in the context of SNARKs, given the impossibility results of [10,24]. It is a semi-adaptive version of the non-adaptive black-box knowledge-soundness of [10].

Semi-adaptive knowledge-sound SNARKs have natural applications. Consider, for example, e-voting for national institutions like the parliament, where the (universal and updatable) commitment key is made public before elections. The commitment key might be used in other applications and thus has to be created highly securely. In a concrete election, the voters can first commit to their ballot, the trusted third parties can create a non-universal CRS (that may depend on the ballot structure and say the number of voters), and then each voter can construct an argument, proving that the ballot is correct. When using our results, the SNARK relies on falsifiable assumptions. Using weak assumptions is vital for national security. Proving all NP statements is essential in the case of complex ballot structures. Practical efficiency, as provided by Punic, is essential for the SNARK to be used at all. Creating the CRS after the commitment phase seems a natural compromise to achieve all the other properties.

CRS-Indistinguishability. To prove black-box knowledge-soundness, we need that any adversary that makes the verifier accept with a non-negligible probability must succeed with non-negligible probability for *every* argument ϱ to $\mathsf{K}_{\mathsf{crs}}$. Only then will $\mathsf{Ext}_{\mathsf{ks}}$ be able to retrieve all partial witnesses needed to output $G(\mathbb{w})$. To tackle this, it suffices to assume that the CRSs, corresponding to any two values of ϱ, are indistinguishable.

Special Soundness. We define semi-adaptive computational (k, G)-special soundness, stating that there exists a black-box PPT extractor $\mathsf{Ext}_{\mathsf{ss}}$, such that if an adversary outputs k consistent transcripts $\mathsf{tr}^{\varrho} = (C, \mathbb{x}, \mathsf{crs}^{\varrho}, \mathsf{td}^{\varrho}, \pi^{\varrho})$ with pairwise distinct ϱ, then $\mathsf{Ext}_{\mathsf{ss}}$ outputs $G(\mathbb{w})$. We prove that *any* semi-adaptively computationally (k, G)-special-sound and CRS-indistinguishable C&P zk-SNARK is semi-adaptively black-box G-knowledge-sound. Thus, it suffices to prove that a zk-SNARK satisfies the first two properties.

2.4 New SNARK

Construction. Since FANA only uses FSE commitments (with commitment keys reprogrammed by the reduction), it is not semi-adaptively sound. We construct Punic, a falsifiable assumption-based semi-adaptively sound C&P SNARK with a succinct commitment. Punic is CRS-indistinguishable and semi-adaptively black-box G-knowledge-sound for $G(s) := [sy]_1$, where y is a trapdoor. G involves scalar multiplication since the extractor retrieves a group element and the DL is hard; we need y due to using FSE and VCF. Moreover, G is needed since we deal with R1CS (i.e., arithmetic circuits). As we note in Sect. 2.6, in the case of SSP [15] (Boolean circuits), G can be the identity map.

Punic is a variant of FANA, to which we add a language parameter lp (vector commitment scheme's commitment key) and a vector commitment $[C]_1$ to the witness. Alternatively, Punic is an (optimized) variant of FLPS that replaces the perfectly-binding commitment scheme with a well-chosen *vector* commitment scheme VCF. Our completeness, zero-knowledge, and CRS-indistinguishability proofs are relatively straightforward. We will next explain the soundness proof.

Soundness Proof. Recall that it suffices to prove special soundness. In the special soundness proof, we fix $\mathsf{lp} = \mathrm{VCF}.\mathsf{ck}$, where VCF is a new vector commitment scheme, described later. In [16,17], one fixes the adversary's statement (a vector commitment $[C]_1$ to $(\mathbb{x}, \mathbb{w})$, and an R1CS statement $\mathbb{x}$). Then, the reduction $\mathcal{B}$ samples $\varrho \leftarrow\$ [1, n]$, reprograms the CRS accordingly, runs the soundness adversary $\mathcal{A}$ once, and guesses the ϱth constraint is violated. If the guess is wrong, $\mathcal{B}$ aborts. This guarantees local consistency (for every ϱ, a partial witness exists that satisfies the ϱth constraint). [16,17] guarantee soundness (the existence of a full witness $\mathbb{w}$, consistent with each partial witness) by using a perfectly binding commitment to $(\mathbb{x}, \mathbb{w})$ and checking its consistency with partial witnesses.

We use a different proof strategy since we do not have a perfectly binding commitment. Our special soundness reduction $\mathcal{B}$ inputs n transcripts tr^{ϱ}. For each ϱ, $\mathcal{B}$ uses FSE to black-box extract a partial witness $G(\mathbb{p}^{\varrho})$ allowing to check whether the ϱth constraint is satisfied. For this, $\mathcal{B}$ reprograms FSE's commitment key, which is part of Punic's CRS. The verification equation ascertains that $G(\mathbb{p}^{\varrho})$ is consistent with the value committed to by $[C]_1$.

More precisely, we construct a special soundness extractor $\mathsf{Ext}_{\mathsf{ss}}$ that computes $G(\mathbb{w})$ given partial witnesses $G(\mathbb{p}^{\varrho})$ output by the FSE black-box somewhere extractor. When $\mathsf{Ext}_{\mathsf{ss}}$ fails, we construct three reductions, two of which are inspired by the reductions in [16,17,46] (we briefly described them above). The third reduction works when for each ϱ, $\mathbb{p}^{\varrho}$ satisfies the ϱth constraint, but $\mathsf{Ext}_{\mathsf{ss}}$ fails to output $G(\mathbb{w})$ where $\mathbb{w}$ satisfies all constraints. Then, at least two partial witnesses (say, $\mathbb{p}^i$ and $\mathbb{p}^j$) must be inconsistent.

The crux of our solution is using FSE to black-box extract well-defined information, allowing us to build a reduction out of this inconsistency. Let $N(\varrho)$ be the set of witness coefficients used in the ϱth constraint. For all $k \in N(\varrho)$, we use FSE to black-box extract VCF's local opening and local proof for the kth coefficient of the full witness. We need a vector commitment scheme precisely for the existence of local proofs. Since we black-box extract both local openings and local proofs by using FSE, VCF needs to satisfy two novel requirements:

(a) *full algebraicity:* one can compute the vector commitment, the local opening (the claimed vector coefficient), and the local proof from $(\mathbb{x}, \mathbb{w})$ and the commitment randomizer by using linear maps,
(b) *F-position-binding:* position-binding even for an adversary who, instead of coordinates $\eta \neq \eta'$, outputs $F(\eta) \neq F(\eta')$, for a permutation F. We need it since FSE is F-extractable, allowing one to extract only $F(\eta) := [\eta]_1$.

In the ϱth loop of the reduction, we reprogram the CRS so that we can black-box extract $(G(\eta_k^{\varrho}), [\varphi_k^{\varrho}]_1)$ for $k \in N(\varrho)$. Here, $G(\eta_k^{\varrho}) = [\eta_k^{\varrho} y]_1$ and $[\varphi_k^{\varrho}]_1$ are the local opening and the local proof of the full witness $\mathbb{w}^{\varrho}$ the adversary used in the ϱth iteration. If $\mathbb{p}^i \neq \mathbb{p}^j$ for some i, j, then we extract two openings $(G(\eta_k^i), [\varphi_k^i]_1)$ and $(G(\eta_k^j), [\varphi_k^j]_1)$, such that $\eta_k^i \neq \eta_k^j$, breaking G/F-position-binding. Assuming F-position-binding, all extracted partial witnesses are consistent. Using a greedy algorithm, we efficiently compute $G(\mathbb{w})$ from $\{G(\mathbb{p}^{\varrho})\}$. QED.

This is a novel proof technique for handling the case when partial witnesses exist. We hope it will find other applications like in SNARGs for P or batch arguments for NP [13,27,37]. A drawback is that we must extract all coefficients at a constraint, so each R1CS constraint must have a small locality. Any R1CS instance can be modified to be such by introducing new constraints using standard techniques. Such a restriction is well-known and used in several efficient zk-SNARKs, [21,51]. [37] used 3CNF (with locality three) for a similar reason.

Punic's black-box G-knowledge-soundness relies on several falsifiable bilinear group assumptions, of which QALINRES [46] is the most complicated. As proven in [46], QALINRES is secure in the algebraic group model (AGM [20]); for completeness, we reprove this result.

On No-Signaling. Obtaining global consistency *efficiently* from local consistency is a major open problem in constructing falsifiable assumption-based SNARGs. One approach [13,27,37,38] is to use no-signaling PCPs and commitments. However, this approach usually works only for memory-bound computations; one has to use additional techniques in the general case. Our approach to achieving global consistency has direct advantages compared to no-signaling commitments. See the full version [45] for a discussion.

2.5 Fully Algebraic F-Position-Binding Vector Commitment

Punic uses a vector commitment scheme VCF. To use FSE to black-box extract VCF's local openings and local proofs, VCF must be fully algebraic and F-position-binding. Both properties seem novel for vector commitment schemes, though they are similar to known requirements on other primitives (e.g., algebraic commitments and F-unforgeable signature schemes [5]).

VCF is based on the CDHK vector commitment scheme [8]. We show CDHK is fully-algebraic but not F-position-binding. We introduce a new trapdoor y (explaining the choice of G) and a knowledge component without making VCF less efficient. VCF remains fully algebraic. We prove VCF is F-position-binding under a new but standard-looking assumption VCSDH (*Vector Commitment Strong Diffie-Hellman*). We reduce VCSDH to QALINRES.

We hope the new notion of fully-algebraic and/or F-position-binding vector commitments will have independent applications.

2.6 Efficiency

We explicitly strived to make Punic concretely efficient. Its prover computation is dominated by $\Theta(n)$ group operations, and the argument size and verifier computation are $\Theta_\lambda(1)$ with small constants. Notably, using vector commitments allows us (differently from [10,52]) to avoid heavy machinery like FHE, hash trees, iO, PCP, and SNARK recursion. In our application, efficiency is difficult to achieve: having larger argument sizes, one can black-box extract more information at a time, making achieving global consistency less difficult. (See comparison with no-signaling commitments in the full version [45].)

With some loss in efficiency, one can construct a semi-adaptively sound SNARK based on weaker assumptions. One can use (1) better-known somewhere-extractable commitments [32] known to exist under various assumptions instead of FSE commitments and (2) hash trees instead of the new vector commitment scheme. On the other hand, we do not know how to instantiate linear subspace arguments efficiently on general assumptions.

Kilian. In the full version [45], we discuss a solution based on Kilian's seminal interactive zero-knowledge argument. We will leave generalizations for future work.

3 Preliminaries

Let p be a large prime. Denote $\mathbb{F} := \mathbb{Z}_p$. For $\boldsymbol{a} \in \mathbb{F}^m$ and $\mathcal{S} \subseteq [1, m]$, let $\boldsymbol{a}|_{\mathcal{S}} := (a_i)_{i \in \mathcal{S}}$. For two vectors $\boldsymbol{a}$ and $\boldsymbol{b}$, let $\boldsymbol{a} \circ \boldsymbol{b}$ be their Hadamard product, with $(\boldsymbol{a} \circ \boldsymbol{b})_i = a_i b_i$. For a matrix $\boldsymbol{A} = (A_{ij})$, $\boldsymbol{A}_i$ denotes its ith row and $\boldsymbol{A}^{(j)}$ denotes its jth column. Let colspace($\boldsymbol{A}$) be the column space of $\boldsymbol{A}$.

PPT denotes probabilistic polynomial-time; $\lambda \in \mathbb{N}$ is the security parameter. We assume all adversaries are stateful, i.e., keep up a state between different executions. For an algorithm $\mathcal{A}$, range($\mathcal{A}$) is the range of $\mathcal{A}$, i.e., the set of valid outputs of $\mathcal{A}$, $\mathsf{RND}_\lambda(\mathcal{A})$ denotes the random tape of $\mathcal{A}$ (for given λ), and $r \leftarrow\!\!\$ \; \mathsf{RND}_\lambda(\mathcal{A})$ denotes the uniformly random choice of r from $\mathsf{RND}_\lambda(\mathcal{A})$. By $s \leftarrow \mathcal{A}(\mathbb{x}; r)$ we denote the fact that $\mathcal{A}$, given an input $\mathbb{x}$ and a randomizer r, outputs s. Let $\mathsf{negl}(\lambda)$ be an arbitrary negligible function, and $\mathsf{poly}(\lambda)$ be an arbitrary polynomial function. We write $a \approx_\lambda b$ if $|a - b| \leq \mathsf{negl}(\lambda)$.

Assume $n \mid (p-1)$ is a power of two. Let ω be the nth primitive root of unity modulo p and let $\mathbb{H} := \langle \omega \rangle = \{\omega^{i-1}\}_{i=1}^n$ be a subgroup of $\mathbb{F}^*$. Let $Z_{\mathbb{H}}(X) := \prod_{i=1}^n (X - \omega^{i-1}) = X^n - 1$ be the unique degree n monic polynomial, such that $Z_{\mathbb{H}}(\omega^{i-1}) = 0$ for all $i \in [1, n]$. For $i \in [1, n]$, let $\ell_i(X)$ be the *ith Lagrange polynomial*, that is, the unique degree-$(n-1)$ polynomial, such that $\ell_i(\omega^{i-1}) = 1$ and $\ell_i(\omega^{j-1}) = 0$ for $i \neq j$. Then, $\ell_i(X) = (X^n - 1)\omega^{i-1} / \left(n(X - \omega^{i-1})\right)$.

Cryptography. A *bilinear group generator* $\mathsf{Pgen}(1^\lambda)$ returns $(p, \mathbb{G}_1, \mathbb{G}_2, \mathbb{G}_T, \hat{e}, [1]_1, [1]_2)$, where $\mathbb{G}_1$, $\mathbb{G}_2$, and $\mathbb{G}_T$ are additive cyclic (thus, abelian) groups of prime order p, $\hat{e} : \mathbb{G}_1 \times \mathbb{G}_2 \to \mathbb{G}_T$ is an efficient non-degenerate bilinear pairing, and $[1]_\gamma$ is a fixed generator of $\mathbb{G}_\gamma$. While $[1]_\gamma$ is a part of p, for the sake of clarity, we often give it as an explicit input to different algorithms. We assume $n \mid (p-1)$, where n is a large deterministically fixed upper bound on the size of the statements that one handles in this bilinear group. The bilinear pairing is of Type-3; that is, there is no efficient isomorphism between $\mathbb{G}_1$ and $\mathbb{G}_2$. We use the standard bracket notation: for $\gamma \in \{1, 2, T\}$, we write $[a]_\gamma$ to denote $a[1]_\gamma$. We denote $\hat{e}([a]_1, [b]_2)$ by $[a]_1 \bullet [b]_2$. We mix freely bracket and matrix notation, e.g., $\boldsymbol{AB} = \boldsymbol{C}$ iff $[\boldsymbol{A}]_1 \bullet [\boldsymbol{B}]_2 = [\boldsymbol{C}]_T$. We denote $[\boldsymbol{A}]_2 \bullet [\boldsymbol{B}]_1 := [\boldsymbol{AB}]_T = ([\boldsymbol{B}]_1^\intercal \bullet [\boldsymbol{A}]_2^\intercal)^\intercal$.

Let $\gamma \in \{1, 2\}$. *$DDH_{\mathbb{G}_\gamma}$ (Decisional Diffie-Hellman)* holds relative to Pgen, if for all PPT $\mathcal{A}$, $\mathsf{Adv}^{\mathrm{ddh}}_{\mathsf{Pgen}, \mathbb{G}_\gamma, \mathcal{A}}(\lambda) :=$

$$\Pr\left[\mathcal{A}(\mathsf{p}, [x, y, xy + \beta z]_\gamma) = \beta \mid \mathsf{p} \leftarrow \mathsf{Pgen}(1^\lambda); x, y, z \leftarrow\!\!\$ \; \mathbb{F}; \beta \leftarrow\!\!\$ \; \{0, 1\}\right] \approx_\lambda \tfrac{1}{2} \ .$$

Let $\kappa^*, \kappa \in \mathbb{N}_+$, with $\kappa^* \geq \kappa$, be small constants. A PPT-sampleable distribution $\mathcal{D}_{\kappa^*, \kappa}$ is a *matrix distribution* if it samples matrices $\boldsymbol{A} \in \mathbb{F}^{\kappa^* \times \kappa}$ of full rank κ. $\mathcal{D}_{\kappa^*, \kappa}$ is *robust* [36] if it samples matrices $\boldsymbol{A}$ whose upper $\kappa \times \kappa$ submatrix $\bar{\boldsymbol{A}}$ is invertible. Denote the lower $(\kappa^* - \kappa) \times \kappa$ submatrix of $\boldsymbol{A}$ by $\underline{\boldsymbol{A}}$. Let $\mathcal{D}_\kappa := \mathcal{D}_{\kappa+1, \kappa}$. $\mathcal{D}_{\kappa^*, \kappa}$-SKerMDH (Split Kernel Diffie-Hellman, [25]) holds relative to Pgen, if for all PPT $\mathcal{A}$, $\mathsf{Adv}^{\mathrm{skermdh}}_{\mathsf{Pgen}, \mathbb{G}_\gamma, \mathcal{D}_{\kappa^*, \kappa}, \mathcal{A}}(\lambda) :=$

$$\Pr\left[\begin{array}{l|l} \boldsymbol{A}^\intercal(\boldsymbol{x}_1 - \boldsymbol{x}_2) = \boldsymbol{0}_\kappa \wedge & \mathsf{p} \leftarrow \mathsf{Pgen}(1^\lambda); \boldsymbol{A} \leftarrow\!\!\$ \; \mathcal{D}_{\kappa^*, \kappa}; \\ \boldsymbol{x}_1 - \boldsymbol{x}_2 \neq \boldsymbol{0}_{\kappa^*} & ([\boldsymbol{x}_1]_1, [\boldsymbol{x}_2]_2) \leftarrow \mathcal{A}(\mathsf{p}, [\boldsymbol{A}]_1, [\boldsymbol{A}]_2) \end{array}\right] \approx_\lambda 0 \ .$$

The QALINRES Assumption. The new zk-SNARK relies on the n-*Quadratic Arithmetic Linear Residuosity (*n-QALINRES*)* assumption from [46].

Definition 1. n-Quadratic Arithmetic Linear Residuosity (n-QALINRES, *[46]) holds relative to* Pgen*, if for all PPT* $\mathcal{A}$*,* $\mathsf{Adv}^{\mathrm{QALINRES}}_{\mathsf{Pgen},n,\mathcal{A}}(\lambda) :=$

$$\Pr\left[\begin{array}{l|l} \pi = \left(j, [\mathsf{a}, \hat{\eta}_\mathsf{a}, \varphi_\mathsf{a}, \mathsf{c}, \hat{\eta}_\mathsf{c}, \varphi_\mathsf{c}, \mathsf{h}]_1, [\mathsf{b}, \hat{\eta}_\mathsf{b}, \varphi_\mathsf{b}]_2\right) \wedge & \mathsf{p} \leftarrow \mathsf{Pgen}(1^\lambda); \\ \mathsf{a} = \varphi_\mathsf{a}(x - \omega^{j-1}) + \hat{\eta}_\mathsf{a}/y \wedge & x \leftarrow_\$ \mathbb{F} \setminus \mathbb{H}; y \leftarrow_\$ \mathbb{F}^*; \\ \mathsf{b} = \varphi_\mathsf{b}(x - \omega^{j-1}) + \hat{\eta}_\mathsf{b}/y \wedge & \mathsf{ck} \leftarrow ([(x^i)_{i=0}^n, y]_\gamma)_{\gamma=1}^2; \\ \mathsf{c} = \varphi_\mathsf{c}(x - \omega^{j-1}) + \hat{\eta}_\mathsf{c}/y \wedge & \pi \leftarrow \mathcal{A}(\mathsf{ck}) \\ \mathsf{ab} - \mathsf{c} = \mathsf{h}Z_\mathbb{H}(x) \wedge \hat{\eta}_\mathsf{a}\hat{\eta}_\mathsf{b} \neq \hat{\eta}_\mathsf{c} y & \end{array}\right] \approx_\lambda 0 .$$

QALINRES was introduced in [46] as a more realistic version of TSDH-like assumptions used in [16,17]. In particular, it does not rely on $\mathcal{A}$ outputting elements of $\mathbb{G}_T$. See [46] and the full version [45] for a discussion. QALINRES is not publicly verifiable, but it has an efficient challenger.

Lipmaa and Pavlyk [46] proved that QALINRES is secure in the AGM under the PDL assumption. Since [46] does not include this proof, we reprove it in the full version [45]. We stress that while the AGM is an idealized model that can be used to prove non-falsifiable assumptions, QALINRES itself is a falsifiable assumption. QALINRES is non-interactive. Moreover, QALINRES is a "Maurer-game" [54], and thus the specific AGM criticisms of [54,55] do not apply to it.

3.1 Underlying Commitment Schemes

We use several commitment schemes. Each commitment scheme has PPT algorithms $\mathsf{Pgen} : 1^\lambda \mapsto \mathsf{p}$ (for parameter generation), $\mathsf{K_{ck}} : (\mathsf{p}, n) \mapsto (\mathsf{ck}, \mathsf{td})$ (for key generation; here, n is the vector length) and $\mathsf{Com} : (\mathsf{ck}, \boldsymbol{\mu}; r) \mapsto (C, D)$ (for commitment; D is the decommitment information). Let $\mathcal{M}$ be the message space, $\mathcal{C}$ the commitment space, and $\mathcal{R}$ the randomizer space. To simplify notation, we always assume ck implicitly contains p.

Vector Commitment. Let $\mathcal{D}$ be a domain. A vector commitment scheme $\Gamma = (\mathsf{Pgen}, \mathsf{K_{ck}}, \mathsf{Com}, \mathsf{LOpen}, \mathsf{LVer})$ is a commitment scheme, with $\mathcal{M} = \mathcal{D}^n$ for $n \leq \mathsf{poly}(\lambda)$, that has two additional algorithms [11,33,41]:

Local opening: for $\mathsf{p} \in \mathsf{Pgen}(1^\lambda)$, $\mathsf{ck} \in \mathsf{K_{ck}}(\mathsf{p}, n)$, commitment $C \in \mathcal{C}$, index $j \in [1, n]$, and decommitment information D, $\mathsf{LOpen}(\mathsf{ck}, C, j, D)$ returns (η, φ), where η (local opening) is a candidate for μ_j and φ is a local proof.

Local verification: for $\mathsf{p} \in \mathsf{Pgen}(1^\lambda)$, $\mathsf{ck} \in \mathsf{K_{ck}}(\mathsf{p}, n)$, commitment $C \in \mathcal{C}$, index $j \in [1, n]$, candidate value η for μ_j, and local proof φ, $\mathsf{LVer}(\mathsf{ck}, C, j, \eta, \varphi)$ returns either 0 or 1.

Γ must be complete according to the natural definition ($\mathsf{LVer}(\mathsf{p}, \mathsf{ck}, C, j, \eta, \varphi) = 1$ for $(\eta, \varphi) \leftarrow \mathsf{LOpen}(\mathsf{ck}, C, j, D)$ and $(C, D) \leftarrow \mathsf{Com}(\mathsf{ck}, \boldsymbol{\mu}; r)$). Γ must satisfy the following security properties.

$\mathsf{K_{ck}}(\mathsf{p}, n)$: $x \leftarrow\!\!\$\, \mathbb{F} \setminus \mathbb{H}$; $\mathsf{td} \leftarrow x$; $\mathsf{ck} \leftarrow ([(x^i)_{i=0}^n]_\gamma, [1, x]_{3-\gamma})$;
  store $[\mathsf{ck}_\ell]_\gamma \leftarrow [\ell_1(x), \dots, \ell_n(x), Z_{\mathbb{H}}(x)]_\gamma$; return $(\mathsf{ck}, \mathsf{td})$;
$\mathsf{Com}(\mathsf{ck}, \boldsymbol{\mu}; r)$: $r \leftarrow\!\!\$\, \mathbb{F}$; $[C(x)]_\gamma \leftarrow [\mathsf{ck}_\ell]_\gamma \cdot \binom{\boldsymbol{\mu}}{r} = \sum_{i=1}^n \mu_i [\ell_i(x)]_\gamma + r[Z_{\mathbb{H}}(x)]_\gamma$;
  return $([C(x)]_\gamma, (\boldsymbol{\mu}, r))$; // (C, D)
$\mathsf{LOpen}(\mathsf{ck}, [C(x)]_\gamma, j, (\boldsymbol{\mu}, r))$: $\eta \leftarrow \mu_j$; $[\varphi(x)]_\gamma \leftarrow [(C(x) - \eta)/(x - \omega^{j-1})]_\gamma$;
  return $(\eta, [\varphi(x)]_\gamma)$;
$\mathsf{LVer}(\mathsf{ck}, [C(x)]_\gamma, j, \eta, [\varphi(x)]_\gamma)$:
  check that $[C(x) - \eta]_\gamma \bullet [1]_{3-\gamma} = [\varphi(x)]_\gamma \bullet [x - \omega^{j-1}]_{3-\gamma}$;
$\mathsf{Sim}(\mathsf{ck}, \mathsf{td} = x, \{j_i\}_{i \in I}, \{\mu_{j_i}\}_{i \in I})$: $r \leftarrow\!\!\$\, \mathbb{F}$; $r' \leftarrow (\sum_{i \in I} \mu_{j_i} \ell_{j_i}(x))/Z_{\mathbb{H}}(x) + r$;
  $[C(x)]_\gamma \leftarrow \mathsf{Com}(\mathsf{ck}, \mathbf{0}; r') = r'[Z_{\mathbb{H}}(x)]_\gamma$; return $[C(x)]_\gamma$;

Fig. 2. The position-binding vector commitment scheme CDHK.

Position-binding: for all λ, PPT $\mathcal{A}$, and $n \in \mathsf{poly}(\lambda)$, $\mathsf{Adv}^{\mathsf{posb}}_{\mathsf{Pgen},n,\Gamma,\mathcal{A}}(\lambda) :=$

$$\Pr\left[\begin{array}{l|l} \eta_0 \neq \eta_1 \wedge & \mathsf{p} \leftarrow \mathsf{Pgen}(1^\lambda); \\ \mathsf{LVer}(\mathsf{ck}, C, j, \eta_0, \varphi_0) = 1 \wedge & (\mathsf{ck}, \mathsf{td}) \leftarrow \mathsf{K_{ck}}(\mathsf{p}, n); \\ \mathsf{LVer}(\mathsf{ck}, C, j, \eta_1, \varphi_1) = 1 & (C, j, \eta_0, \eta_1, \varphi_0, \varphi_1) \leftarrow \mathcal{A}(\mathsf{ck}) \end{array}\right] \approx_\lambda 0 \ .$$

Perfect zero-knowledge: there exists a PPT simulator Sim, such that for all λ, all $\mathsf{p} \leftarrow \mathsf{Pgen}(1^\lambda)$, all $(\mathsf{ck}, \mathsf{td}) \leftarrow \mathsf{K_{ck}}(\mathsf{p}, n)$, all $\boldsymbol{\mu} \in \mathcal{D}^n$, and any poly-size set $\{j_i \in [1, n]\}_i$, the distributions δ_0 and δ_1 are identical, where

$$\delta_0 := \{(\mathsf{ck}, C, \{\mathsf{LOpen}(\mathsf{ck}, C, j_i, D)\}) : r \leftarrow\!\!\$\, \mathsf{RND}_\lambda(\mathsf{Com}); (C, D) \leftarrow \mathsf{Com}(\mathsf{ck}, \boldsymbol{\mu}; r)\} \ ,$$
$$\delta_1 := \{(\mathsf{ck}, \mathsf{Sim}(\mathsf{ck}, \mathsf{td}, \{j_i\}, \{\mu_{j_i}\}))\} \ .$$

Modeled after the seminal KZG polynomial commitment scheme [39], Camenisch et al. [8] proposed a vector commitment scheme. Let $\mathcal{D} = \mathbb{F}$, $\mathcal{M} = \mathcal{D}^n$, $\mathcal{C} = \mathbb{G}_\gamma$ for $\gamma \in \{1, 2\}$, and $\mathcal{R} = \mathbb{F}$. In Fig. 2, we depict a simplified version CDHK of their scheme. CDHK is position-binding under the standard n-SDH assumption [7]. Straightforwardly, CDHK satisfies perfect zero-knowledge.

FSE *Commitment.* Let $F : \mathcal{M} \to \mathcal{C}$ be a (one-way, p-dependent) permutation. Let $\mathcal{F}$ be a function family, where $f \in \mathcal{F}$ inputs a vector $\boldsymbol{\mu}$ and outputs an element of $\mathcal{C}$. A *functional*[4] *somewhere F-extractable (F-FSE) commitment scheme* [17] $\Gamma = (\mathsf{Pgen}, \mathsf{K_{ck}}, \mathsf{Com}, \mathsf{swExt})$ for $\mathcal{F}$ allows one to commit to a vector $\boldsymbol{\mu}$, s.t. for any $q \leq n$, (1) the commitment key ck depends on q and a function tuple $f_1, \dots, f_q \in \mathcal{F}$, (2) commitment keys corresponding to different function tuples are computationally indistinguishable, and (3) given the extraction key, one can extract from the commitment the vector $(F(f_1(\boldsymbol{\mu})), \dots, F(f_q(\boldsymbol{\mu})))$.

[4] Defined as functional somewhere statistically binding (SSB) commitment in [17]; generalizes SSB hashes [32,48]. In SSB hashes, $\mathcal{F}$ is the family of point functions, and q is always equal to one. On the other hand, we do not need the local opening property, thus obtaining better efficiency. Since extractability is essential, we call them functional SE. DGPRS and FLPS predate [13]. SE commitments have been used to build SNARGs for P and batch-arguments for NP [13,27].

More precisely, an F-FSE *commitment scheme* $\Gamma = (\mathsf{Pgen}, \mathsf{K_{ck}}, \mathsf{Com}, \mathsf{swExt})$ for a function family $\mathcal{F}$ consists of the following (P)PT algorithms.

Parameter generation: $\mathsf{Pgen}(1^\lambda)$ returns p (e.g., the group description).

Commitment key generation: for parameters p, a positive integer $n \leq \mathsf{poly}(\lambda)$, a locality parameter $q \in [1, n]$, and a tuple $\mathcal{S} = (f_1, \ldots, f_{|\mathcal{S}|}) \subseteq \mathcal{F}$ with $|\mathcal{S}| \leq q$, $\mathsf{K_{ck}}(\mathsf{p}, n, q, \mathcal{S})$ outputs a commitment key ck and an extraction key $\mathsf{td} = \mathsf{ek}$. We assume ck and ek implicitly specify p.

Commitment: for a commitment key ck, a message $\boldsymbol{\mu} \in \mathcal{M}^n$, and a randomizer $r \in \mathcal{R}$, $\mathsf{Com}(\mathsf{ck}, \boldsymbol{\mu}; r)$ outputs a commitment $C \in \mathcal{C}$.

Somewhere (black-box) extraction: for $\mathsf{p} \in \mathsf{Pgen}(1^\lambda)$, a positive integer $n \leq \mathsf{poly}(\lambda)$, a locality parameter $q \in [1, n]$, a tuple $\mathcal{S} = (f_1, \ldots, f_{|\mathcal{S}|}) \subseteq \mathcal{F}$ with $1 \leq |\mathcal{S}| \leq q$, $(\mathsf{ck}, \mathsf{ek}) \in \mathsf{K_{ck}}(\mathsf{p}, n, q, \mathcal{S})$, and $C \in \mathcal{C}$, $\mathsf{swExt}(\mathsf{ek}, C)$ returns a tuple $(F(f_1(\boldsymbol{\mu})), \ldots, F(f_{|\mathcal{S}|}(\boldsymbol{\mu}))) \in \mathcal{M}^{|\mathcal{S}|}$.

For $\mathcal{S} = (f_1, \ldots, f_{|\mathcal{S}|}) \subseteq \mathcal{F}$ and a vector $\boldsymbol{\mu}$, denote $f_\mathcal{S}(\boldsymbol{\mu}) = (f_1(\boldsymbol{\mu}), \ldots, f_{|\mathcal{S}|}(\boldsymbol{\mu}))$.

An F-FSE *commitment scheme* Γ for the function family $\mathcal{F}$ can satisfy the following security requirements.

Function-Set Hiding: for all λ, PPT $\mathcal{A}$, $n \in \mathsf{poly}(\lambda)$, and $q \in [1, n]$, $\mathsf{Adv}^{\mathsf{fsh}}_{\mathsf{Pgen},\Gamma,n,q,\mathcal{A}}(\lambda) := 2 \cdot |\varepsilon^{\mathsf{fsh}} - 1/2| \approx_\lambda 0$, where $\varepsilon^{\mathsf{fsh}} :=$

$$\Pr\left[\begin{array}{l} \beta' = \beta \wedge \mathcal{S}_0, \mathcal{S}_1 \subseteq \mathcal{F} \\ \wedge |\mathcal{S}_0|, |\mathcal{S}_1| \leq q \end{array} \middle| \begin{array}{l} \mathsf{p} \leftarrow \mathsf{Pgen}(1^\lambda); (\mathcal{S}_0, \mathcal{S}_1) \leftarrow \mathcal{A}(\mathsf{p}, n, q); \beta \leftarrow_\$ \{0,1\}; \\ (\mathsf{ck}, \mathsf{td}) \leftarrow \mathsf{K_{ck}}(\mathsf{p}, n, q, \mathcal{S}_\beta); \beta' \leftarrow \mathcal{A}(\mathsf{ck}) \end{array}\right] .$$

Intuitively, ck reveals computationally no information about $\mathcal{S}$.

Almost Everywhere Perfectly Hiding (AEPH): for all λ, unbounded $\mathcal{A}$, $n \in \mathsf{poly}(\lambda)$, and $q \in [1, n]$, $\mathsf{Adv}^{\mathsf{aeph}}_{\Gamma,n,q,\mathcal{A}}(\lambda) := 2 \cdot |\varepsilon^{\mathsf{aeph}} - 1/2| = 0$, where $\varepsilon^{\mathsf{aeph}} :=$

$$\Pr\left[\begin{array}{l} \beta' = \beta \wedge \mathcal{S} \subseteq \mathcal{F} \\ \wedge |\mathcal{S}| \leq q \wedge \\ f_\mathcal{S}(\boldsymbol{\mu}_0) = f_\mathcal{S}(\boldsymbol{\mu}_1) \end{array} \middle| \begin{array}{l} \mathsf{p} \leftarrow \mathsf{Pgen}(1^\lambda); \mathcal{S} \leftarrow \mathcal{A}(\mathsf{p}, n, q); \\ (\mathsf{ck}, \mathsf{td}) \leftarrow \mathsf{K_{ck}}(\mathsf{p}, n, q, \mathcal{S}); (\boldsymbol{\mu}_0, \boldsymbol{\mu}_1) \leftarrow \mathcal{A}(\mathsf{ck}); \\ \beta \leftarrow_\$ \{0,1\}; r \leftarrow_\$ \mathcal{R}; (C, D) \leftarrow \mathsf{Com}(\mathsf{ck}, \boldsymbol{\mu}_\beta; r); \\ \beta' \leftarrow \mathcal{A}(C) \end{array}\right] .$$

Intuitively, given ck, that depends on $\mathcal{S}$, the commitment hides perfectly the values of μ_j for $j \notin \mathcal{S}$.

Somewhere F-Extractability: for all λ, $\mathsf{p} \in \mathsf{Pgen}(1^\lambda)$, $n \in \mathsf{poly}(\lambda)$, $q \in [1, n]$, $\mathcal{S} = (f_1, \ldots, f_{|\mathcal{S}|}) \subseteq \mathcal{F}$ with $|\mathcal{S}| \leq q$, $(\mathsf{ck}, \mathsf{ek}) \leftarrow \mathsf{K_{ck}}(\mathsf{p}, n, q, \mathcal{S})$, and PPT $\mathcal{A}$,

$$\Pr\left[\mathsf{swExt}(\mathsf{ek}, C) \neq (F(f_1(\boldsymbol{\mu})), \ldots, F(f_{|\mathcal{S}|}(\boldsymbol{\mu}))) \middle| \begin{array}{l} (\boldsymbol{\mu}, r) \leftarrow \mathcal{A}(\mathsf{ck}); \\ (C, D) \leftarrow \mathsf{Com}(\mathsf{ck}, \boldsymbol{\mu}; r) \end{array}\right] = 0 .$$

I.e., given ck, that depends on $\mathcal{S}$, and an extraction key, one can black-box extract $F(f_\mathcal{S}(\boldsymbol{\mu}))$. ([17] called this property *somewhere perfect F-extractability.*)

$\mathsf{K_{ck}}(\mathsf{p}, n, q, [\boldsymbol{M}]_\gamma \in \mathbb{G}_\gamma^{q \times n})$: // $\mathcal{M} = \mathcal{R} = \mathbb{F}^n$ and $\mathcal{C} = \mathbb{G}_\gamma^{q+1}$
sample a full-rank $\boldsymbol{R} \leftarrow_\$ \mathbb{F}^{(q+1)\times(q+1)}$; $\boldsymbol{\varrho} \leftarrow_\$ \mathbb{F}^n$;
$[\boldsymbol{M}']_\gamma \leftarrow \left[\begin{smallmatrix} \boldsymbol{M} & \boldsymbol{0} \\ \boldsymbol{\varrho}^\top & 1 \end{smallmatrix}\right]_\gamma \in \mathbb{F}^{(q+1)\times(n+1)}$; $\mathsf{ck} \leftarrow \boldsymbol{R}[\boldsymbol{M}']_\gamma \in \mathbb{G}_\gamma^{(q+1)\times(n+1)}$;
$\mathsf{td} = \mathsf{ek} \leftarrow \boldsymbol{R}^{-1}$; **return** $(\mathsf{ck}, \mathsf{td})$;
$\mathsf{Com}(\mathsf{ck}, \boldsymbol{\mu} \in \mathbb{F}^n; r \in \mathbb{F})$: **return** $\mathsf{ck} \cdot \left(\begin{smallmatrix} \boldsymbol{\mu} \\ r \end{smallmatrix}\right)$;
$\mathsf{swExt}(\mathsf{ek}, [\mathbf{c}]_\gamma)$: compute $\left[\begin{smallmatrix} \boldsymbol{M}\boldsymbol{\mu} \\ \boldsymbol{\varrho}^\top\boldsymbol{\mu}+r \end{smallmatrix}\right]_\gamma \leftarrow \mathsf{ek} \cdot [\mathbf{c}]_\gamma$; **return** $[\boldsymbol{M}\boldsymbol{\mu}]_\gamma$.

Fig. 3. The $[\cdot]_\gamma$-FSE commitment scheme FSE_γ for linear maps in $\mathbb{G}_\gamma$.

Construction. Fix $\gamma \in \{1, 2\}$. Let $F : a \mapsto [a]_\gamma$. In Fig. 3, we depict the FSE scheme of [17] for the family of all linear maps. It represents q linear maps by $[\boldsymbol{M}]_\gamma \in \mathbb{G}_\gamma^{q \times n}$, where each row contains coefficients of one map. Clearly, $[\mathbf{c}]_\gamma \leftarrow \mathsf{Com}(\mathsf{ck}, \boldsymbol{\mu}; r)$ is equal to $\mathsf{ck}\left(\begin{smallmatrix} \boldsymbol{\mu} \\ r \end{smallmatrix}\right) = \boldsymbol{R}[\boldsymbol{M}']_\gamma \left(\begin{smallmatrix} \boldsymbol{\mu} \\ r \end{smallmatrix}\right) = \left[\begin{smallmatrix} \boldsymbol{R}\boldsymbol{M}\boldsymbol{\mu} \\ \boldsymbol{R}(\boldsymbol{\varrho}^\top\boldsymbol{\mu}+r) \end{smallmatrix}\right]_\gamma$.

Fact 1 ([17]). *Fix $q < n = \mathsf{poly}(\lambda)$. The scheme in Fig. 3 is (i) function-set hiding relative to* Pgen *under $DDH_{\mathbb{G}_\gamma}$: for each PPT $\mathcal{A}$, there exists a PPT $\mathcal{B}$, such that $\mathsf{Adv}^{\mathrm{fsh}}_{\mathsf{Pgen},\Gamma,n,q,\mathcal{A}}(\lambda) \le \lceil \log_2(q+1) \rceil \cdot \mathsf{Adv}^{\mathrm{ddh}}_{\mathbb{G}_\gamma,\mathsf{Pgen},\mathcal{B}}(\lambda)$. (ii) almost everywhere perfectly-hiding, (iii) somewhere F-extractable for $F = [\cdot]_\gamma$.*

3.2 QA-NIZK

A QA-NIZK argument system [36] Π has public parameters lp (a language parameter, like a commitment key) and crs (a language-dependent common reference string). Π proves membership in the language $\mathcal{L}_{\mathsf{lp}}$ defined by a relation $\mathcal{R}_{\mathsf{lp}} = \{(\mathbb{x}, \mathbb{w})\}$. Both are determined by $\mathsf{lp} \leftarrow_\$ \mathcal{D}_{\mathrm{par}}$ (sampled by PPT K_{lp}), where $\mathcal{D}_{\mathrm{par}}$ is a public distribution. $\mathcal{D}_{\mathrm{par}}$ is *witness-sampleable* [36] if there exists a PPT algorithm K_{lt} that samples $(\mathsf{lp}, \mathsf{lt})$ such that lp is distributed according to $\mathcal{D}_{\mathrm{par}}$, and $\mathsf{lp} \overset{?}{\in} \mathrm{range}(\mathcal{D}_{\mathrm{par}})$ can be efficiently verified given lt.

A *QA-NIZK* for $\mathcal{R}_{\mathrm{par}}$ is a tuple of PPT algorithms $\Pi = (\mathsf{Pgen}, \mathsf{K}_{\mathsf{lp}}, \mathsf{K}_{\mathsf{crs}}, \mathsf{P}, \mathsf{V}, \mathsf{Sim})$. In the case of witness-sampleable languages, K_{lp} is replaced by K_{lt}. Pgen is the parameter generation algorithm, K_{lp} is the language parameter generation algorithm, K_{lt} is the corresponding generation algorithm in the witness-sampleable case that creates lp and lt, $\mathsf{K}_{\mathsf{crs}}$ is the CRS generation algorithm, P is the prover, V is the verifier, and Sim is the simulator. We assume that lp contains p. Sim is a single algorithm that works for each relation in $\mathcal{R}_{\mathrm{par}} := \{\mathcal{R}_{\mathsf{lp}}\}_{\mathsf{lp} \in \mathrm{range}(\mathcal{D}_{\mathrm{par}})}$.

Π can satisfy the following security notions.

<u>*Perfect Completeness:*</u> for all λ and PPT $\mathcal{A}$,

$$\Pr\left[\begin{array}{l} \mathsf{V}(\mathsf{lp}, \mathsf{crs}, \mathbb{x}, \pi) = 0 \wedge \\ (\mathbb{x}, \mathbb{w}) \in \mathcal{R}_{\mathsf{lp}} \end{array} \middle| \begin{array}{l} \mathsf{p} \leftarrow \mathsf{Pgen}(1^\lambda); \mathsf{lp} \leftarrow \mathsf{K}_{\mathsf{lp}}(\mathsf{p}); \\ (\mathsf{crs}, \mathsf{td}) \leftarrow_\$ \mathsf{K}_{\mathsf{crs}}(\mathsf{lp}); (\mathbb{x}, \mathbb{w}) \leftarrow \mathcal{A}(\mathsf{lp}, \mathsf{crs}); \\ \pi \leftarrow \mathsf{P}(\mathsf{lp}, \mathsf{crs}, \mathbb{x}, \mathbb{w}) \end{array}\right] = 0 \ .$$

Computational Quasi-Adaptive Strong Soundness: defined only if lp is witness-sampleable. For any PPT $\mathcal{A}$, $\mathsf{Adv}^{\mathsf{strsound}}_{\mathsf{Pgen},\mathcal{D}_{\mathrm{par}},\mathrm{BLS},\mathcal{A}}(\lambda) :=$

$$\Pr\left[\begin{array}{l|l} \mathsf{V}(\mathsf{lp},\mathsf{crs},\mathbb{x},\pi)=1\wedge & \mathsf{p}\leftarrow\mathsf{Pgen}(1^\lambda);(\mathsf{lp},\mathsf{lt})\leftarrow\mathsf{K}_{\mathsf{lt}}(\mathsf{p}); \\ (\neg\exists\mathbb{w})(\mathbb{x},\mathbb{w})\in\mathcal{R}_{\mathsf{lp}} & (\mathsf{crs},\mathsf{td})\leftarrow\!\!\$\,\mathsf{K}_{\mathsf{crs}}(\mathsf{lp});(\mathbb{x},\pi)\leftarrow\mathcal{A}(\mathsf{lp},\mathsf{lt},\mathsf{crs}) \end{array}\right]\approx_\lambda 0\ .$$

Perfect Zero Knowledge: for all unbounded $\mathcal{A}$, $|\varepsilon_1^{zk}-\varepsilon_2^{zk}|=0$, where $\varepsilon_\beta^{zk} :=$

$$\Pr\left[\mathcal{A}^{\mathcal{O}_\beta(\cdot,\cdot)}(\mathsf{lp},\mathsf{crs})=1\,\middle|\,\mathsf{p}\leftarrow\mathsf{Pgen}(1^\lambda);\mathsf{lp}\leftarrow\mathsf{K}_{\mathsf{lp}}(\mathsf{p});(\mathsf{crs},\mathsf{td})\leftarrow\!\!\$\,\mathsf{K}_{\mathsf{crs}}(\mathsf{lp})\right]\ .$$

Here, $\mathcal{A}$ is given an oracle access to $\mathcal{O}_\beta(\cdot,\cdot)$, where $\mathcal{O}_0(\mathbb{x},\mathbb{w})$ returns 0 (reject) if $(\mathbb{x},\mathbb{w})\notin\mathcal{R}_{\mathsf{lp}}$, and otherwise it returns $\mathsf{P}(\mathsf{lp},\mathsf{crs},\mathbb{x},\mathbb{w})$. Similarly, $\mathcal{O}_1(\mathbb{x},\mathbb{w})$ returns 0 if $(\mathbb{x},\mathbb{w})\notin\mathcal{R}_{\mathsf{lp}}$, and otherwise it returns $\mathsf{Sim}(\mathsf{lp},\mathsf{crs},\mathsf{td},\mathbb{x})$.

C&P *QA-SNARGs.* A QA-NIZK is *succinct* (succinct non-interactive argument, QA-SNARG) if the argument length is sublinear in $\mathsf{poly}(\lambda)\cdot(|\mathbb{x}|+|\mathbb{w}|)$. It is commit-and-prove (C&P) if lp is a commitment key and the statement contains an extractable commitment (to a witness) under this commitment key.

Gentry-Wichs Impossibility Result. Gentry and Wichs [24] proved that if an NP language $\mathcal{L}$ has a sub-exponentially (resp., exponentially) hard subset-membership problem and Π is a complete SNARG in the CRS model with $|\pi|\le\mathsf{poly}(\lambda)\cdot(|\mathbb{x}|+|\mathbb{w}|)^{o(1)}$ (resp., $|\pi|\le\mathsf{poly}(\lambda)\cdot(|\mathbb{x}|+|\mathbb{w}|)^c+o(|\mathbb{x}|+|\mathbb{w}|)$ for some constant $c<1$) for $\mathcal{L}$, then there is a black-box reduction from the adaptive soundness of Π to a falsifiable assumption X only when X is false. [10] clarifies why linear subspace QA-SNARGs do not contradict Gentry-Wichs. In the full version [45], we explain how this relates to the current work.

Bilateral Subspace QA-SNARG. Denote $[\boldsymbol{M}]_* := ([\boldsymbol{M}_1]_1,[\boldsymbol{M}_2]_2)$. A bilateral subspace argument system, with $\mathsf{lp}=[\boldsymbol{M}]_*\in\mathbb{G}_1^{n_1\times m}\times\mathbb{G}_2^{n_2\times m}$, allows to prove that $([\mathbf{c}_1]_1,[\mathbf{c}_2]_2)\in\mathcal{L}_{\mathsf{lp}}$, where

$$\mathcal{L}_{\mathsf{lp}} := \{([\mathbf{c}_1]_1,[\mathbf{c}_2]_2)\in\mathbb{G}_1^{n_1}\times\mathbb{G}_2^{n_2} : (\exists\mathbb{w}\in\mathbb{F}^m)\left(\begin{smallmatrix}\mathbf{c}_1\\ \mathbf{c}_2\end{smallmatrix}\right)=\left(\begin{smallmatrix}\boldsymbol{M}_1\\ \boldsymbol{M}_2\end{smallmatrix}\right)\mathbb{w}\}\ ,$$

that is, $\left(\begin{smallmatrix}\mathbf{c}_1\\ \mathbf{c}_2\end{smallmatrix}\right)\in\mathrm{colspace}\left(\begin{smallmatrix}\boldsymbol{M}_1\\ \boldsymbol{M}_2\end{smallmatrix}\right)$. Note that it does not have the C&P property, unless $[\boldsymbol{M}]_*$ is a commitment key.

For the sake of completeness, in the full version [45], we depict the González-Hevia-Ràfols bilateral subspace QA-SNARG argument system BLS for $\mathcal{L}_{\mathsf{lp}}$. Lipmaa and Pavlyk [46] generalized a theorem by González and Ràfols [25] to any $n_\gamma\times m$ matrices $\boldsymbol{M}_\gamma$ (even if $m>n_\gamma$), given that $\mathrm{rank}\left(\begin{smallmatrix}\boldsymbol{M}_1\\ \boldsymbol{M}_2\end{smallmatrix}\right)<n_1+n_2$. This generalization is important for us since in Punic (see Eq. (4)), $m>n_1,n_2$.

Fact 2 ([25,46]). *Fix λ, n_1, n_2, m. Let $\kappa=2$. Let $\mathcal{D}_{\mathrm{par}}$ be a matrix distribution on $[\boldsymbol{M}]_*\in\mathbb{G}_1^{n_1\times m}\times\mathbb{G}_2^{n_2\times m}$, such that* $\mathrm{rank}\left(\begin{smallmatrix}\boldsymbol{M}_1\\ \boldsymbol{M}_2\end{smallmatrix}\right)<n_1+n_2$. *Then (1)* BLS *is perfectly complete and perfectly zero-knowledge. (2) Assume $\mathcal{D}_{\mathrm{par}}$ is witness-sampleable and $\mathcal{D}_\kappa$ is robust. If $\mathcal{D}_\kappa$-*SKerMDH *holds relative to* Pgen *then* BLS *is computationally quasi-adaptively strongly sound.*

We need $\kappa = 2$ since SKerMDH does not hold for $\kappa = 1$ [25]. The prover's work is dominated by $2m\kappa$ scalar multiplications, the verifier's work is dominated by $(n_1 + n_2 + 2\kappa)\kappa$ pairings, and π consists of 2κ group elements.

4 New Vector Commitment Scheme

We need a pairing-based vector commitment scheme VCF that is fully-algebraic and F-position-binding. Since we use the [17]'s FSE to black-box extract VCF's local openings and local proofs, both novel requirements are needed. W.l.o.g., we consider commitment schemes with an output from $\mathbb{G}_1$.

4.1 Definitions

Fully-Algebraic. Recall that a commitment scheme is *algebraic* if $\mathsf{Com}(\mathsf{ck}, \boldsymbol{\mu}; r) = [\boldsymbol{M}^*]_1 \binom{\boldsymbol{\mu}}{r}$ for a matrix $[\boldsymbol{M}^*]_1$ efficiently computable from ck.

Definition 2. *A vector commitment scheme is* fully-algebraic, *if* $C := \mathsf{Com}(\mathsf{ck}, \boldsymbol{\mu}; r) = [\boldsymbol{M}^*]_1 \binom{\boldsymbol{\mu}}{r}$, $[\eta]_1 = [\boldsymbol{M}_j^\eta]_1 \binom{\boldsymbol{\mu}}{r}$, *and* $[\varphi]_1 = [\boldsymbol{M}_j^\varphi]_1 \binom{\boldsymbol{\mu}}{r}$, *where* $[\eta, \varphi]_1 = \mathsf{LOpen}(\mathsf{ck}, C, j, (\boldsymbol{\mu}, r))$, *for some public matrices* $[\boldsymbol{M}^*]_1$, $[\boldsymbol{M}_j^\eta]_1$, *and* $[\boldsymbol{M}_j^\varphi]_1$ *that can be efficiently computed from* ck *and (in the last two cases)* j.

Let $\boldsymbol{e}_j$ be the jth unit vector. Clearly, $[\eta]_1 = [\mu_j]_1 = [\boldsymbol{e}_j^\top \| 0]_1 \cdot \binom{\boldsymbol{\mu}}{r}$ holds for any vector commitment scheme. Thus, the existence of $\boldsymbol{M}_j^\eta$ is trivial and one needs to only show $\mathsf{Com}(\mathsf{ck}, \boldsymbol{\mu}; r) = [\boldsymbol{M}^*]_1 \binom{\boldsymbol{\mu}}{r}$ and $[\varphi]_1 = [\boldsymbol{M}_j^\varphi]_1 \binom{\boldsymbol{\mu}}{r}$.

The vector commitment scheme of Catalano and Fiore [11] is fully algebraic, but it has a commitment key of $\Theta(n^2)$ group elements and is thus inefficient. The more efficient vector commitment scheme of Libert et al. [33,41] is not fully algebraic. The CDHK [8] vector commitment scheme is efficient and algebraic but not known to be fully algebraic. In Sect. 4.2, we show that CDHK is fully algebraic. However, it does not satisfy the following requirement.

***F*-Position-Binding.** In Punic, we use FSE to black-box extract $F(\eta) = F(\mu_j)$ for a one-way permutation F. Thus, we need the vector commitment scheme to be position-binding even if the position-binding adversary outputs $F(\eta)$ instead of η. This is similar to how F-unforgeable signature schemes [5] is defined when the adversary outputs $F(\boldsymbol{\mu})$ instead of the message $\boldsymbol{\mu}$. F-position-binding suffices in our case since in the soundness proof of Punic, we are not interested in the value of η but only in testing whether two local openings are equal. Since F is a permutation, such testing can be performed on $F(\eta)$ and $F(\eta')$.

Definition 3. *An* F-position-binding vector commitment scheme *is a commitment scheme that has the following additional algorithms:*

Local F-opening: *for* $\mathsf{p} \in \mathsf{Pgen}(1^\lambda)$, $\mathsf{ck} \in \mathsf{K_{ck}}(\mathsf{p}, n)$, *a commitment* $C \in \mathcal{C}$, *a coordinate* $j \in [1, n]$, *and a decommitment information* D, $\mathsf{LOpen}_F(\mathsf{ck}, C, j, D)$ *returns* $(F(\eta), \varphi)$, *where* η *is a local opening (a candidate value of* μ_j*) and* φ *is a local proof.*

Local F-verification: *for* $\mathsf{p} \in \mathsf{Pgen}(1^\lambda)$, $\mathsf{ck} \in \mathsf{K_{ck}}(\mathsf{p}, n)$, *a commitment* $C \in \mathcal{C}$, *a coordinate* $j \in [1, n]$, *a local opening* $F(\eta)$, *and a local proof* φ, $\mathsf{LVer}_F(\mathsf{ck}, C, j, F(\eta), \varphi)$ *returns either* 0 *or* 1.

It must be complete and satisfy the following security notion:

F-position-binding: *for all* λ, *PPT* $\mathcal{A}$, *and* $n \in \mathsf{poly}(\lambda)$, $\mathsf{Adv}^{\mathrm{fposb}}_{\mathsf{Pgen},F,n,\Gamma,\mathcal{A}}(\lambda) :=$

$$\Pr\left[\begin{array}{l} \eta_0 \neq \eta_1 \wedge \\ \mathsf{LVer}_F(\mathsf{ck}, C, j, F(\eta_0), \varphi_0) = 1 \wedge \\ \mathsf{LVer}_F(\mathsf{ck}, C, j, F(\eta_1), \varphi_1) = 1 \end{array} \middle| \begin{array}{l} \mathsf{p} \leftarrow \mathsf{Pgen}(1^\lambda); (\mathsf{ck}, \mathsf{td}) \leftarrow \mathsf{K_{ck}}(\mathsf{p}, n); \\ (C, j, F(\eta_0), F(\eta_1), \varphi_0, \varphi_1) \leftarrow \mathcal{A}(\mathsf{ck}) \end{array}\right]$$

is negligible.

We will omit the subscript F when it is clear from the context. In Punic, F is such that the FSE commitment scheme is somewhere F-extractable. In the case of the FSE commitment scheme of [17], $F = [\cdot]_1$ or $F = [\cdot]_2$.

$\mathsf{K_{ck}}(\mathsf{p}, n)$: $x \leftarrow\!\!\$\ \mathbb{F} \setminus \mathbb{H}$; $y \leftarrow\!\!\$\ \mathbb{F}^*$; $\mathsf{td} \leftarrow (x, y)$;
  $\mathsf{ck} \leftarrow ([(x^i)_{i=0}^n, y]_\gamma, [(x^i)_{i=0}^n, y, xy]_{3-\gamma})$; // Private verif.: $[xy]_\gamma \notin \mathsf{ck}$
  compute and store $[\mathsf{ck}_\ell]_\gamma \leftarrow [\ell_1(x), \ldots, \ell_n(x), Z_\mathbb{H}(x)]_\gamma$;
  return $(\mathsf{ck}, \mathsf{td})$;
$\mathsf{Com}(\mathsf{ck}, \boldsymbol{\mu}; r)$: $r \leftarrow\!\!\$\ \mathbb{F}$; $[C(x)]_\gamma \leftarrow [\mathsf{ck}_\ell]_\gamma \cdot \binom{\boldsymbol{\mu}}{r} = \sum_{i=1}^n \mu_i [\ell_i(x)]_\gamma + r[Z_\mathbb{H}(x)]_\gamma$;
  return $([C(x)]_\gamma, (\boldsymbol{\mu}, r))$; // (C, D)
$\mathsf{LOpen}(\mathsf{ck}, [C(x)]_\gamma, j, (\boldsymbol{\mu}, r))$: $[\hat{\eta}]_\gamma \leftarrow \mu_j [y]_\gamma$; // $\mu_j = C(\omega^{j-1})$
  $[\mathsf{ck}_{\ell,j}]_\gamma \leftarrow [Q_{\ell_1,j}(x), \ldots, Q_{\ell_n,j}(x), Q_{Z_\mathbb{H},j}(x)]_\gamma$;
  $[\varphi(x)]_\gamma \leftarrow [\mathsf{ck}_{\ell,j}]_\gamma \cdot \binom{\boldsymbol{\mu}}{r} = \sum_{i=1}^n \mu_i [Q_{\ell_i,j}(x)]_\gamma + r[Q_{Z_\mathbb{H},j}(x)]_\gamma$;
  return $[\hat{\eta}, \varphi(x)]_\gamma$.
$\mathsf{LVer}(\mathsf{ck}, [C(x)]_\gamma, j, [\hat{\eta}, \varphi(x)]_\gamma)$: check $[C(x)]_\gamma \bullet [y]_{3-\gamma} - [\hat{\eta}]_\gamma \bullet [1]_{3-\gamma} = [\varphi(x)]_\gamma \bullet ([xy]_{3-\gamma} - \omega^{j-1}[y]_{3-\gamma})$; // Public verification only
$\mathsf{Sim}(\mathsf{ck}, \mathsf{td} = x, \{j_i\}_{i \in I}, \{\mu_{j_i}\}_{i \in I})$: $r \leftarrow\!\!\$\ \mathbb{F}$; $r' \leftarrow (\sum_{i \in I} \mu_{j_i} \ell_{j_i}(x))/Z_\mathbb{H}(x) + r$; return $[C(x)]_\gamma \leftarrow \mathsf{Com}(\mathsf{ck}, \mathbf{0}; r') = r'[Z_\mathbb{H}(x)]_\gamma$;

Fig. 4. The new $[\cdot]_\gamma$-position-binding vector commitment scheme VCF_γ.

4.2 Construction

CDHK is clearly algebraic. We will show that it is fully algebraic by showing that $[\varphi(x)]_1$ can be computed by using a linear map.

For a polynomial $f(X) \in \mathbb{F}[X]$ and an integer $j \in [1, n]$, let $Q_{f,j}(X)$ be the quotient of $(f(X) - f(\omega^{j-1}))/(X - \omega^{j-1})$. Clearly, $\deg Q_{f,j} = \deg f - 1$.

Lemma 1. *Fix* $j \in [1, n]$. *For* $C(X) = \sum_{i=1}^n \mu_i \ell_i(X) + r Z_\mathbb{H}(X) \in \mathbb{F}[X]$, $Q_{C,j}(X) = \frac{C(X) - C(\omega^{j-1})}{X - \omega^{j-1}}$. *Then,* $[Q_{C,j}(x)]_1 = [\mathsf{ck}_{\ell,j}(x)]_1 \cdot \binom{\boldsymbol{\mu}}{r}$, *where* $\mathsf{ck}_{\ell,j}(X) := (Q_{\ell_1,j}(X), \ldots, Q_{\ell_n,j}(X), Q_{Z_\mathbb{H},j}(X))$. *Thus,* CDHK *is fully-algebraic.*

Proof. Clearly, $Q_{C,j}(X) = (C(X) - C(\omega^{j-1}))/(X - \omega^{j-1})$ is equal to $(\sum_{i=1}^{n} \mu_i \ell_i(X) + r Z_{\mathbb{H}}(X) - \mu_j)/(X - \omega^{j-1})$. Since $\sum_{i=1}^{n} \mu_i \ell_i(\omega^{j-1}) = \mu_j$ and $Z_{\mathbb{H}}(\omega^{j-1}) = 0$, $Q_{C,j}(X) = \sum_{i=1}^{n} \mu_i Q_{\ell_i,j}(X) + r Q_{Z_{\mathbb{H}},j}(X) = \mathsf{ck}_{\ell,j}(X) \cdot \binom{\mu}{r}$. □

Making CDHK $[\cdot]_\gamma$-Position-Binding. One can easily break $[\cdot]_\gamma$-position-binding of CDHK (see Fig. 2) by outputting $([C]_\gamma, j, [\eta, \eta']_\gamma, [\varphi, \varphi']_\gamma)$, where $[C]_\gamma = [x - \omega^{j-1}]_\gamma$, $[\eta]_\gamma = [0]_\gamma$, $[\eta']_\gamma = [x - \omega^{j-1}]_\gamma$, $[\varphi]_\gamma = [1]_\gamma$, and $[\varphi']_\gamma = [0]_\gamma$. Clearly, $C - \eta = \varphi(x - \omega^{j-1})$ and $C - \eta' = \varphi'(x - \omega^{j-1})$.

We avoid such attacks by guaranteeing that $[\eta, \eta']_\gamma$ do not depend on x. We achieve this by making the local opening depend on a new trapdoor y and not adding $[x^i y]_\gamma$ to ck for $i > 0$. (However, $[y]_1, [y]_2, [y, xy]_{3-\gamma}$ must be in ck for VCF to be publicly verifiable.) Importantly, the communication does not increase. In Fig. 4, we depict the new vector commitment scheme VCF_γ. Clearly, $C(x) = (x - \omega^{j-1})\varphi(x) + \hat{\eta}/y$ since the remainder of $\ell_i(X)/(X - \omega^{j-1})$ is 1 if $i = j$ and 0, otherwise. The local opening is $G_\gamma(\mu_j) = G_\gamma(\eta)$ for $G_\gamma(s) := [sy]_\gamma$.

The soundness proofs (but not the constructions) of QA-SNARGs of [16,17] use *implicitly* a version of VCF but without defining the used primitive as a vector commitment scheme or writing down the needed security properties. Their implicit vector commitment scheme is less efficient, requiring the local opening to output both $\mu_j[1]_\gamma$ and $\mu_j[y]_\gamma$. Their constructions also use a perfectly-hiding commitment scheme, while we use only VCF.

Private-Verifiability. Punic uses both VCF_1 and VCF_2. We need to use the same trapdoor in both cases, and thus want to have the same ck when defining VCF_γ. Thus, although this is not necessary for VCF_γ itself, we add $[(x^i)_{i=0}^n]_{3-\gamma}$ to the commitment key. However, we cannot add $[xy]_\gamma$ to ck since that would break VCF's security. To overcome this, one possibility is to reuse the trapdoor x but have separate trapdoors y_1 and y_2 in VCF_1 and VCF_2. We opted for a simpler possibility: since in Punic, VCF_γ does not have to be publicly verifiable, one can omit $[xy]_\gamma$ (only used in verification) from ck. This allows us to reuse the same trapdoor y in both VCF_1 and VCF_2. From now on, we will always use the privately verifiable version of VCF_γ with $\mathsf{ck} \leftarrow ([(x^i)_{i=0}^n, y]_\gamma, [(x^i)_{i=0}^n, y]_{3-\gamma})$.

4.3 Security Analysis

VCF_γ is clearly perfectly zero-knowledge. From a position-binding collision $([C(x)]_\gamma, j, [\hat{\eta}, \hat{\eta}']_\gamma, [\varphi, \varphi']_\gamma)$ with $\hat{\eta} \neq \hat{\eta}'$, we get $[\hat{\eta}' - \hat{\eta}]_\gamma \bullet [1]_{3-\gamma} = [\varphi - \varphi']_\gamma \bullet [(x - \omega^{j-1})y]_{3-\gamma}$ and thus $[\varphi - \varphi']_\gamma = \frac{1}{(x-\omega^{j-1})y}[\hat{\eta}' - \hat{\eta}]_\gamma$. We define a new assumption n-VCSDH that states that it is difficult to output $[\varphi - \varphi']_\gamma$ and $[\hat{\eta}' - \hat{\eta}]_\gamma \neq [0]_\gamma$ that satisfy the above equation.

Definition 4. *n-Vector-Commitment Strong Diffie-Hellman (n-VCSDH) holds relative to* Pgen *in* $\mathbb{G}_\gamma$, *if for all PPT* $\mathcal{A}$, $\mathsf{Adv}^{\mathrm{VCSDH}}_{\mathsf{Pgen},\gamma,n,\mathcal{A}}(\lambda) :=$

$$\Pr\left[\begin{array}{l} \hat{\eta} \neq 0 \wedge \\ [\varphi]_\gamma = \frac{1}{(x-\omega^{j-1})y}[\hat{\eta}]_\gamma \end{array} \middle| \begin{array}{l} \mathsf{p} \leftarrow \mathsf{Pgen}(1^\lambda); x \leftarrow_\$ \mathbb{F} \setminus \mathbb{H}; y \leftarrow_\$ \mathbb{F}^*; \\ \mathsf{ck} \leftarrow ([(x^i)_{i=0}^n, y]_1, [(x^i)_{i=0}^n, y]_2); \\ (j, [\hat{\eta}, \varphi]_\gamma) \leftarrow \mathcal{A}(\mathsf{ck}) \end{array}\right] \approx_\lambda 0 .$$

The following lemma is straightforward.

Lemma 2. *Privately-verifiable* VCF_1 *is* $[\cdot]_\gamma$*-position-binding iff* n-VCSDH *holds relative to* Pgen.

VCSDH is similar to known SDH-like [7] assumptions like RSDH [26]. VCSDH is privately-verifiable but clearly falsifiable. It is intuitively secure since $[\hat{\eta}]_\gamma$ cannot depend on xy, and thus $\varphi(x, y)$ is not a polynomial. Next, prove that VCSDH follows from QALINRES, which was proven in [46] to be secure in the AGM, [20]. Thus, VCSDH is secure in the AGM and falsifiable. Punic relies on QALINRES and not on VCSDH directly.

Lemma 3. *Fix* $n = \mathsf{poly}(\lambda)$. *If* n-QALINRES *holds, then* n-VCSDH *holds.*

See the full version [45] for the proof.

QALINRES can restated as an algebraic security property of privately-verifiable VCF_γ, observing that say $\mathsf{a} = \varphi_\mathsf{a}(x - \omega^{j-1}) + \hat{\eta}_\mathsf{a}/y$ iff $\mathrm{VCF}_1.\mathsf{LVer}(\mathsf{ck}, [\mathsf{a}]_1, j, [\hat{\eta}_\mathsf{a}]_1, [\varphi_\mathsf{a}]_1)$. Privately-verifiable VCF_1 and VCF_2 share the commitment key; this is possible since we do not require QALINRES to be publicly-verifiable.

4.4 Committing to Linear Maps

We need the following result. See the full version [45] for the proof.

Lemma 4. *Let* VCF_1 *be as in Fig. 4 Let* $\boldsymbol{\mu} \in \mathbb{F}^m$ *and* $\boldsymbol{U} \in \mathbb{F}^{n\times m}$. *Let* $u_j(X) := \sum_{i=1}^n U_{ij}\ell_i(X)$ *be the interpolating vector of* $\boldsymbol{U}^{(j)}$, $\mathsf{ck}_u := (u_1(x)\|\dots\|u_m(x)\|Z_\mathbb{H}(x)) = \mathsf{ck}_\ell \cdot \left(\begin{smallmatrix} U & 0 \\ 0 & 0 \end{smallmatrix}\right)$, $[\mathsf{ck}_{e,j}]_1 := G(\boldsymbol{e}_j^\top\|0)$, *and* $\mathsf{ck}_{u,j} := (Q_{u_1,j}(x)\|\dots\|Q_{u_m,j}(x)\|Q_{Z_\mathbb{H},j}(x))$. *Then,* $[C(x)]_1 \leftarrow \mathsf{Com}(\mathsf{ck}, \boldsymbol{U}\boldsymbol{\mu}; r)$ *and* $(G(\eta), [\varphi]_1) \leftarrow \mathsf{LOpen}(\mathsf{ck}, [C(x)]_1, j, D = (\boldsymbol{U}\boldsymbol{\mu}, r))$ *are linear maps of* $\left(\begin{smallmatrix} \boldsymbol{\mu} \\ r \end{smallmatrix}\right)$:

$$[C(x)]_1 = [\mathsf{ck}_u]_1 \cdot \left(\begin{smallmatrix} \boldsymbol{\mu} \\ r \end{smallmatrix}\right)\ , \quad G(\eta) = G(\mathsf{ck}_{e,j}) \cdot \left(\begin{smallmatrix} \boldsymbol{\mu} \\ r \end{smallmatrix}\right)\ , \quad [\varphi]_1 = [\mathsf{ck}_{u,j}]_1 \cdot \left(\begin{smallmatrix} \boldsymbol{\mu} \\ r \end{smallmatrix}\right)\ .$$

Thus, one can compute the commitment to $\boldsymbol{U}\boldsymbol{\mu}$ and its local proof as $[\mathsf{ck}_u]_1\left(\begin{smallmatrix} \boldsymbol{\mu} \\ r \end{smallmatrix}\right)$ and $[\mathsf{ck}_{u,j}]_1\left(\begin{smallmatrix} \boldsymbol{\mu} \\ r \end{smallmatrix}\right)$ given public matrices that depend on x, $\boldsymbol{U}$, and j.

5 New C&P Zk-SNARK Security Notions

The new C&P zk-SNARK satisfies a novel soundness notion, semi-adaptive black-box G-knowledge-soundness. As motivated in Sect. 2.3, semi-adaptivity is a natural version of non-adaptivity for C&P SNARKs. Black-box G-knowledge-soundness is stronger than local consistency (Kalai et al., [37]). Semi-adaptive black-box G-knowledge-soundness is a semi-adaptive variant of the non-adaptive black-box knowledge-soundness of [10]. Moreover, we need Punic to be CRS-indistinguishable. Next, we define the new security notions.

5.1 R1CS and R1CS$_\mathfrak{f}$

Let n be the number of constraints, m be the number of variables, and $m_\mathbb{x} < m$ be the number of public inputs and outputs. Let $\boldsymbol{U}, \boldsymbol{V}, \boldsymbol{W} \in \mathbb{F}^{n \times m}$ be instance-dependent matrices and let $\binom{\mathbb{x}}{\mathbb{w}} \in \mathbb{F}^m$. An R1CS [23] instance $\mathfrak{I} = (\mathbb{F}, m_\mathbb{x}, \boldsymbol{U}, \boldsymbol{V}, \boldsymbol{W})$ defines the following relation[5]:

$$\mathcal{R}_\mathfrak{I} = \{(\mathbb{x}, \mathbb{w}) : \mathbb{x} \in \mathbb{F}^{m_\mathbb{x}} \wedge \mathbb{w} \in \mathbb{F}^{m - m_\mathbb{x}} \wedge \boldsymbol{U}\binom{\mathbb{x}}{\mathbb{w}} \circ \boldsymbol{V}\binom{\mathbb{x}}{\mathbb{w}} = \boldsymbol{W}\binom{\mathbb{x}}{\mathbb{w}}\} \ . \qquad (1)$$

We say $(\mathbb{x}, \mathbb{w})$ *satisfies* $\mathfrak{I}$ if $(\mathbb{x}, \mathbb{w}) \in \mathcal{R}_\mathfrak{I}$. Crucially, one can check that $(\mathbb{x}, \mathbb{w}) \in \mathcal{R}_\mathfrak{I}$ by checking a conjugation of local constraints. For a constraint $\varrho \in [1, n]$,

$$N_\mathfrak{I}(\varrho) := \{j : U_{\varrho j} \neq 0 \vee V_{\varrho j} \neq 0 \vee W_{\varrho j} \neq 0\}$$

(the *ϱth neighborhood*) is the set of variables in the neighborhood of the constraint ϱ. We usually omit the subscript $\mathfrak{I}$. W.l.o.g., assume that the set of neighborhoods covers the whole range $[1, m]$. Otherwise, some variables are not used in the instance and can thus be omitted. For $\mathfrak{f} \geq 1$, let R1CS$_\mathfrak{f}$ be the language of instances $\mathfrak{I}$, such that $|N(\varrho)| \leq \mathfrak{f}$ for all ϱ.

Fix $\varrho \in [1, n]$. Let $\mathbb{p}^\varrho : N(\varrho) \to \mathbb{F}$ be an assignment of variables from $N(\varrho)$. We say that $(\mathbb{x}, \mathbb{p}^\varrho)$ *locally satisfies* the instance $\mathfrak{I}$ iff

(1) $\mathbb{p}^\varrho$ agrees with the statement $\mathbb{x}$: $(\forall j \in ([1, m_\mathbb{x}] \cap N(\varrho)))\, \mathbb{p}^\varrho(j) = \mathbb{x}_j$, and
(2) $\mathbb{p}^\varrho$ satisfies the ϱth constraint:

$$(\textstyle\sum_{j \in N(\varrho)} U_{\varrho j} \mathbb{p}^\varrho(j)) \cdot (\sum_{j \in N(\varrho)} V_{\varrho j} \mathbb{p}^\varrho(j)) = \sum_{j \in N(\varrho)} W_{\varrho j} \mathbb{p}^\varrho(j) \ .$$

If only 1 holds, we say that $\mathbb{p}^\varrho$ satisfies the ϱth constraint. If both 1 and 2 hold, we write $(\mathbb{x}, \mathbb{p}^\varrho) \in \mathcal{R}^\varrho_{\mathsf{loc}, \mathfrak{I}}$, where $\mathcal{R}^\varrho_{\mathsf{loc}, \mathfrak{I}} :=$

$$\left\{ (\mathbb{x}, \mathbb{p}^\varrho) \,\middle|\, \begin{array}{l} ((\forall j \in ([1, m_\mathbb{x}] \cap N(\varrho)))\, \mathbb{p}^\varrho(j) = \mathbb{x}_j) \wedge \\ ((\sum_{j \in N(\varrho)} U_{\varrho j} \mathbb{p}^\varrho(j)) \cdot (\sum_{j \in N(\varrho)} V_{\varrho j} \mathbb{p}^\varrho(j)) = (\sum_{j \in N(\varrho)} W_{\varrho j} \mathbb{p}^\varrho(j))) \end{array} \right\} . \qquad (2)$$

Note that the second element of $(\mathbb{x}, \mathbb{w}) \in \mathcal{R}_\mathfrak{I}$ is a full witness while the second element of $(\mathbb{x}, \mathbb{p}^\varrho) \in \mathcal{R}^\varrho_{\mathsf{loc}, \mathfrak{I}}$ is a partial witness. Moreover, one can use pairings to check $(\mathbb{x}, \mathbb{p}^\varrho) \in^? \mathcal{R}^\varrho_{\mathsf{loc}, \mathfrak{I}}$ even if only given $(\mathbb{x}, [\mathbb{p}^\varrho]_1)$.

For $i, j \in [1, n]$, we define the *consistency predicate*

$$\mathsf{Cons}(\mathbb{p}^i, \mathbb{p}^j) := (\forall k \in (N(i) \cap N(j)))\, \mathbb{p}^i(k) = \mathbb{p}^j(k) \ ,$$

Remark 1. Fix $\mathbb{x}$. Clearly, there exists a full witness $\mathbb{w} \in \mathcal{R}_\mathfrak{I}$ that satisfies all constraints and agrees with all partial assignments $\mathbb{p}^\varrho$ if

(1) for each constraint ϱ, $(\mathbb{x}, \mathbb{p}^\varrho)$ is locally satisfied,
(2) for all constraints i, j, $\mathsf{Cons}(\mathbb{p}^i, \mathbb{p}^j) = \mathsf{true}$.

[5] $(\boldsymbol{U}, \boldsymbol{V}, \boldsymbol{W})$ is a part of the instance and thus our SNARKs are non-universal. The most efficient known universal SNARKs [30] in the standard model (without random oracles) have quadratic size CRS and are thus too inefficient for practice.

Fix a commitment scheme and instance $\mathfrak{J}$. We assume the statement is $\mathbb{x}^\dagger := (C, \mathbb{x})$ and the witness is $\mathbb{w}^\dagger := (r_C, \mathbb{w})$, where C is a commitment and r_C is a commitment randomness. For a fixed $\mathsf{lp} = \mathsf{ck}$, we define

$$\mathcal{R}_{\mathsf{lp}} := \{((C, \mathbb{x}), (r_C, \mathbb{w})) : C = \mathsf{Com}\left(\left(\begin{smallmatrix}\mathbb{x}\\ \mathbb{w}\end{smallmatrix}\right); r_C\right) \wedge (\mathbb{x}, \mathbb{w}) \in \mathcal{R}_{\mathfrak{J}}\}$$

to be the relation $\mathcal{R}_{\mathsf{lp}}$ from Sect. 3.2.

5.2 Security Definitions

We redefine C&P zk-SNARKs for R1CS$_{\mathfrak{f}}$ allowing $\mathsf{K_{crs}}$ to depend on a constraint number ϱ, where an honest execution sets $\varrho \leftarrow 0$ while the reductions use non-zero ϱ's. (An alternative approach is to define two different $\mathsf{K_{crs}}$'s.) Fix a (vector) commitment scheme Γ. Then, $\mathsf{lp} = \mathsf{ck}$ is a commitment key. We also assume that there exists a black-box somewhere-extractor $\mathsf{Ext_{ks}}$.

The modified (QA-)SNARK security definitions follow. We highlight the changes to the definition in Sect. 3.2. We require that completeness holds for all choices of ϱ while zero-knowledge holds for the value of ϱ, $\varrho = 0$, used in the honest case. Computational zero-knowledge for *any* ϱ follows from this and the CRS-indistinguishability. The latter (see Definition 5) guarantees that the CRSs corresponding to different constraints are computationally indistinguishable.

<u>*Perfect Completeness:*</u> for all λ, PPT $\mathcal{A}$, and $\varrho \in [1, n]$,

$$\Pr\left[\begin{array}{l|l} \mathsf{V}(\mathsf{lp}, \mathsf{crs}, \mathbb{x}^\dagger, \pi) = 0 & \mathsf{p} \leftarrow \mathsf{Pgen}(1^\lambda); \mathsf{lp} \leftarrow \mathsf{K_{lp}}(\mathsf{p}); \\ \wedge (\mathbb{x}, \mathbb{w}) \in \mathcal{R}_{\mathfrak{J}} & (\mathsf{crs}, \mathsf{td}) \leftarrow\!\!\$\; \mathsf{K_{crs}}(\mathsf{lp}, \mathcal{R}_{\mathfrak{J}}, \varrho); \\ & (\mathbb{x}, \mathbb{w}, r_C) \leftarrow \mathcal{A}(\mathsf{lp}, \mathsf{crs}); C \leftarrow \mathsf{Com}(\left(\begin{smallmatrix}\mathbb{x}\\ \mathbb{w}\end{smallmatrix}\right); r_C); \\ & \mathbb{x}^\dagger \leftarrow (C, \mathbb{x}); \mathbb{w}^\dagger \leftarrow (r_C, \mathbb{w}); \pi \leftarrow \mathsf{P}(\mathsf{lp}, \mathsf{crs}, \mathbb{x}^\dagger, \mathbb{w}^\dagger) \end{array}\right] = 0 .$$

<u>*Perfect Zero Knowledge:*</u> for all unbounded $\mathcal{A}$, $|\varepsilon_1^{zk} - \varepsilon_2^{zk}| = 0$, where $\varepsilon_\beta^{zk} :=$

$$\Pr\left[\mathcal{A}^{\mathcal{O}_\beta(\cdot,\cdot)}(\mathsf{lp}, \mathsf{crs}) = 1 \middle| \mathsf{p} \leftarrow \mathsf{Pgen}(1^\lambda); \mathsf{lp} \leftarrow \mathsf{K_{lp}}(\mathsf{p}); (\mathsf{crs}, \mathsf{td}) \leftarrow\!\!\$\; \mathsf{K_{crs}}(\mathsf{lp}, \mathcal{R}_{\mathfrak{J}}, 0)\right] .$$

$\mathcal{A}$ is given an oracle access to $\mathcal{O}_\beta(\cdot, \cdot)$, where $\mathcal{O}_0(\mathbb{x}^\dagger, \mathbb{w}^\dagger)$ returns 0 if $(\mathbb{x}^\dagger, \mathbb{w}^\dagger) \notin \mathcal{R}_{\mathsf{lp}}$; otherwise, it returns $\mathsf{P}(\mathsf{lp}, \mathsf{crs}, \mathbb{x}^\dagger, \mathbb{w}^\dagger)$. Similarly, $\mathcal{O}_1(\mathbb{x}^\dagger, \mathbb{w}^\dagger)$ returns 0 if $(\mathbb{x}^\dagger, \mathbb{w}^\dagger) \notin \mathcal{R}_{\mathsf{lp}}$; otherwise, it returns $\mathsf{Sim}(\mathsf{lp}, \mathsf{crs}, \mathsf{td}, \mathbb{x}^\dagger)$.

We define a new knowledge soundness notion that has two aspects. First, *semi-adaptivity*. In the quasi-adaptive case, the statement can depend on lp and crs, while in the semi-adaptive case, it can only depend on lp. Second, in local consistency [27,37,49] it is required that, given $\mathsf{crs}^\varrho \leftarrow\!\!\$\; \mathsf{K_{crs}}(\mathsf{lp}, \mathcal{R}_{\mathfrak{J}}, \varrho)$, one can black-box somewhere-extract a partial witness that satisfies the ϱth constraint. We strengthen this by requiring one to black-box extract a full witness that satisfies all constraints.

Definition 5 is inspired by non-adaptive black-box knowledge-soundness in [10] and witness-extended emulation (WEE, [42]). Let G be a permutation. Definition 5 formalizes our expected ability to black-box extract $G(\mathbb{w})$, where $\mathbb{w}$ satisfies all constraints, by running the adversary with many different CRSs

crs^{ϱ}, where crs^{ϱ} is output by $\mathsf{K_{crs}}(\mathsf{lp}, \mathcal{R}_{\mathfrak{I}}, \varrho)$, and then gluing the adversary's outputs to $G(\mathbb{w})$. We relate the probability that an adversary outputs an accepting transcript to the probability that the black-box extractor outputs an accepting transcript together with $G(\mathbb{w})$. For falsifiability, we require that one can test whether $(\mathbb{x}, \mathbb{w}) \notin \mathcal{R}_{\mathfrak{I}}$ when only given $(\mathbb{x}, G(\mathbb{w}))$. This holds in our applications.

Definition 5 (Semi-Adaptive Black-Box G-Knowledge-Soundness). *Let $\mathfrak{I}$ be an R1CS instance with $n = n(\lambda)$ constraints. There exists a black-box expected (deterministic) PT extractor* $\mathsf{Ext_{ks}}$*, such that for all non-uniform PPT $\mathcal{A}_1$, $\mathcal{D}$ and DPT $\mathcal{A}_2$,* $\mathsf{Adv}^{\mathsf{bbks}}_{\mathsf{Pgen},G,\Pi,\mathsf{Ext_{ks}},\mathcal{A}}(\lambda) := |\varepsilon_2(\lambda) - \varepsilon_1(\lambda)| \approx_\lambda 0$, *where*

$$\varepsilon_1(\lambda) := \Pr\left[\mathcal{D}(\mathsf{lp}, \mathsf{tr}) = 1 \,\middle|\, \begin{array}{l} \mathsf{p} \leftarrow \mathsf{Pgen}(1^\lambda); \mathsf{lp} \leftarrow \mathsf{K_{lp}}(\mathsf{p}); \\ ((C, \mathbb{x}), \mathsf{st}) \leftarrow \mathcal{A}_1(\mathsf{lp}, \mathcal{R}_{\mathfrak{I}}); (\mathsf{crs}, \mathsf{td}) \leftarrow_\$ \mathsf{K_{crs}}(\mathsf{lp}, \mathcal{R}_{\mathfrak{I}}, 0); \\ \pi \leftarrow \mathcal{A}_2(\mathsf{st}, \mathsf{crs}); \mathsf{tr} \leftarrow (C, \mathbb{x}, \mathsf{crs}, \pi) \end{array}\right],$$

$$\varepsilon_2(\lambda) := \Pr\left[\begin{array}{c} \mathcal{D}(\mathsf{lp}, \mathsf{tr}) = 1 \wedge \\ \begin{pmatrix} \mathsf{V}(\mathsf{ck}, \mathsf{tr}) = 1 \Rightarrow \\ (\mathbb{x}, \mathbb{w}) \notin \mathcal{R}_{\mathfrak{I}} \end{pmatrix} \end{array} \,\middle|\, \begin{array}{l} \mathsf{p} \leftarrow \mathsf{Pgen}(1^\lambda); \mathsf{lp} \leftarrow \mathsf{K_{lp}}(\mathsf{p}); \\ ((C, \mathbb{x}), \mathsf{st}) \leftarrow \mathcal{A}_1(\mathsf{lp}, \mathcal{R}_{\mathfrak{I}}); \\ (\mathsf{crs}, \pi, G(\mathbb{w})) \leftarrow \mathsf{Ext_{ks}}^{\mathcal{A}_2(\mathsf{st}, \cdot)}(\mathsf{lp}, \mathcal{R}_{\mathfrak{I}}, C, \mathbb{x}, \mathsf{st}); \\ \mathsf{tr} \leftarrow (C, \mathbb{x}, \mathsf{crs}, \pi) \end{array}\right].$$

$\mathsf{Ext_{ks}}$ *is an oracle machine that makes an expected polynomial number of (adaptive or non-adaptive) queries. Before each query,* $\mathsf{Ext_{ks}}$ *chooses $\varrho \in [1, n]$ and samples* $(\mathsf{crs}^{\varrho}, \mathsf{td}^{\varrho}) \leftarrow_\$ \mathsf{K_{crs}}(\mathsf{lp}, \mathcal{R}_{\mathfrak{I}}, \varrho)$. $\mathsf{Ext_{ks}}$ *then calls* $\mathcal{A}_2(\mathsf{st}, \mathsf{crs}^{\varrho})$, *obtaining some (possibly invalid) argument π^{ϱ} (*st *is not updated between $\mathcal{A}_2$ queries).*

We allow $\mathsf{Ext_{ks}}$ to use the same ϱ several times, but each time, $\mathsf{Ext_{ks}}$ can use a different crs. In this case, π^{ϱ} depends on crs^{ϱ} and not only ϱ, but we will mostly ignore this detail. Let $\mathcal{Q}$ be the set of ϱ-s, actually used by $\mathsf{Ext_{ks}}$. A C&P zk-SNARK is a C&P *SA-SNARK (semi-adaptive SNARK)* if it meets Definition 5.

Comparison to WEE. Compared to standard WEE [42], there are several differences. We can think of a semi-adaptive SNARG as a three-round protocol with a trusted setup, where the CRS is the verifier's second message. However, (1) the CRS is not public-coin, and (2) the CRS does not depend on the first message — it instead depends on the constraint number ϱ. Thus, our soundness notion and proof differ from the classical WEE ones. We use the name of black-box knowledge-soundness, although WEE might be more apt.

Comparison to [13]. In the context of (non-C&P) SNARGs for NP, Choudhuri et al. [13] define semi-adaptivity differently. Choudhuri et al. do not consider C&P arguments, but they allow for CRS reprogramming. In their semi-adaptivity game, the adversary first maliciously chooses the constraint ϱ, the CRS is programmed to use ϱ, and finally, the adversary outputs a statement and an argument. In our case, ϱ must stay hidden from the adversary; hence, we introduce the requirement of CRS-indistinguishability.

On G in G-Knowledge-Soundness. Since the lack of a trapdoor prevents one from efficiently computing $\mathbb{w}$ from $G(\mathbb{w})$, G-knowledge-soundness is a standard notion in many pairing-based schemes like Groth-Sahai. See [5,22] for further discussions. Since we work in the pairing-based setting, we set $G(s) := [sy]_1$ (we need y for compatibility with VCF). Involving $[\cdot]_1$ is a usual restriction in the pairing-based setting due to the hardness of the discrete logarithm.

A C&P SA-SNARK must satisfy one more requirement. $\mathsf{Ext_{ks}}$ in Definition 5 can query $\mathcal{A}_2$ with CRSs corresponding to different constraints ϱ. The adversary's success is the difference between the probabilities of acceptance and extraction. In our case, it is crucial that if the adversary succeeds with a non-negligible probability, it does so for *any* $\varrho \in \mathcal{Q}$. Otherwise, the extractor might "miss" two inconsistent partial witnesses. We solve this by requiring CRS indistinguishability: CRSs for different ϱ are computationally indistinguishable. If that holds, the acceptance probability is roughly the same for different ϱ; hence, if the verifier accepts with a non-negligible probability, it does so for every ϱ. Crucially, the values extracted by the FSE somewhere-extractor when using different ϱ's do not have to be consistent; the reduction $\mathcal{B}_{\mathsf{fposb}}$ (see Sect. 6) handles this case.

Definition 6 (CRS-Indistinguishability). *For all* λ, *PPT* $\mathcal{A}$, *and* $\varrho \in [1, n]$, $\mathsf{Adv}^{\mathsf{crsind}}_{\mathsf{Pgen},\varrho,\Pi,\mathcal{A}}(\lambda) :=$

$$\Pr\left[\beta' = \beta \,\middle|\, \begin{array}{l} \mathsf{p} \leftarrow \mathsf{Pgen}(1^\lambda); \mathsf{lp} \leftarrow \mathsf{K_{lp}}(\mathsf{p}); \beta \leftarrow\!\!\$\; \{0,1\}; \\ (\mathsf{crs}, \mathsf{td}) \leftarrow\!\!\$\; \mathsf{K_{crs}}(\mathsf{lp}, \mathcal{R}_{\mathfrak{I}}, \beta \cdot \varrho); \beta' \leftarrow \mathcal{A}(\mathsf{lp}, \mathsf{crs}) \end{array}\right] \approx_\lambda \frac{1}{2} \ .$$

Special Soundness. We define a tailored special soundness [14] notion, semi-adaptive computational (k, G)-special soundness. Defining special soundness is a common step for interactive arguments but novel for non-interactive ones. We prove that any semi-adaptively computationally (n, G)-specially-sound and CRS-indistinguishable QA-SNARG Π is semi-adaptively black-box G-knowledge-sound. As typical in similar reductions, the knowledge-soundness extractor is only *expected* PPT. Later, we prove that the new zk-SNARK Punic is semi-adaptively computationally (n, G)-specially-sound under three (strict) PPT computational assumptions.

Definition 7 (Semi-adaptive Computational (k, G)-Special Soundness). *Fix* $k \in \mathsf{poly}(\lambda)$. *There exists a black-box PPT extractor* $\mathsf{Ext_{ss}}$, *such that for any PPT adversary* $\mathcal{A}_{\mathsf{ss}}$, $\mathsf{Adv}^{\mathsf{specsound}}_{\mathsf{Pgen},G,\Pi,k,\mathsf{Ext_{ss}},\mathcal{A}_{\mathsf{ss}}}(\lambda) :=$

$$\Pr\left[\begin{array}{l} \mathbf{tr} = (\mathsf{tr}^j)_{j=1}^k \wedge \\ \forall j \in [1,k]. \left(\begin{array}{c} \mathsf{tr}^j = (C, \mathbb{x}, \mathsf{crs}^j, \mathsf{td}^j, \pi^j) \\ \wedge (\mathsf{crs}^j, \mathsf{td}^j) \leftarrow\!\!\$\; \mathsf{K_{crs}}(\mathsf{lp}, \mathcal{R}_{\mathfrak{I}}, \varrho^j) \\ \wedge \mathsf{V}(\mathsf{lp}, \mathsf{crs}^j, (C, \mathbb{x}), \pi^j) = 1 \end{array}\right) \\ \wedge \left(\forall i \neq j. \varrho^i \neq \varrho^j\right) \wedge (\mathbb{x}, \mathbb{w}) \notin \mathcal{R}_{\mathfrak{I}} \end{array} \,\middle|\, \begin{array}{l} \mathsf{p} \leftarrow \mathsf{Pgen}(1^\lambda); \\ \mathsf{lp} \leftarrow \mathsf{K_{lp}}(\mathsf{p}); \\ \mathbf{tr} \leftarrow \mathcal{A}_{\mathsf{ss}}(\mathsf{lp}, \mathcal{R}_{\mathfrak{I}}); \\ G(\mathbb{w}) \leftarrow \mathsf{Ext_{ss}}(\mathsf{lp}, \mathbf{tr}) \end{array}\right] \approx_\lambda 0 \ .$$

Intuitively, Definition 7 states that if $\mathcal{A}_{\mathsf{ss}}$ produces an accepting admissible k-tuple $\mathbf{tr}$ (meaning that $\mathbf{tr}$ satisfies all conditions on the left-hand side), then one can—except with a negligible probability—black-box extract $G(\mathbb{w})$, such that $(\mathbb{x}, \mathbb{w}) \in \mathcal{R}_{\mathfrak{I}}$. The transcripts include trapdoors, needed in the special soundness proof of Punic. We assume that td^j contains ϱ^j.

The following result is related to yet different from classical reductions of WEE to special soundness. Note that $\mathcal{A}_{\mathsf{ss}}$ in the full version [45] works in expected PPT. One can use Markov's inequality to make $\mathcal{A}_{\mathsf{ss}}$ to be strict PPT but with some loss in the probability. The latter technique is standard, and we will not elaborate on it. See the full version [45] for the proof of Theorem 1.

Theorem 1. *Let G be a permutation. If Π is semi-adaptively computationally (n, G)-special-sound and CRS-indistinguishable, then it is semi-adaptively black-box G-knowledge-sound for any family of instances $\mathfrak{J} = \mathfrak{J}(\lambda)$ with $n = n(\lambda)$ constraints. More precisely, there exists a black-box expected PPT extractor $\mathsf{Ext}_{\mathsf{ks}}$ and an expected PPT adversary $\mathcal{A}_{\mathsf{ss}}$, such that for any PPT $\mathsf{Ext}_{\mathsf{ss}}$ and $\mathcal{A}_{\mathsf{ks}} = (\mathcal{A}_1, \mathcal{A}_2)$, $\mathsf{Adv}^{\mathrm{bbks}}_{\mathsf{Pgen},G,\Pi,\mathsf{Ext}_{\mathsf{ks}},\mathcal{A}_{\mathsf{ks}}}(\lambda) \le \mathsf{Adv}^{\mathrm{specsound}}_{\mathsf{Pgen},G,\Pi,n,\mathsf{Ext}_{\mathsf{ss}},\mathcal{A}_{\mathsf{ss}}}(\lambda)$.*

6 New C&P SA-SNARK Punic

Next, we propose a C&P SA-SNARK Punic for $\mathrm{R1CS}_{\mathfrak{f}}$ by following ideas from [16,17,46]. We will use a new proof technique based on fully algebraic F-position-binding vector commitments and new security notions.

6.1 Intuition

We construct a C&P SA-SNARK Punic for $\mathrm{R1CS}_{\mathfrak{f}}$ for a small constant $\mathfrak{f}$. Let $\mathsf{lp} = \mathsf{VCF.ck}$ and (x, y) be the VCF trapdoor key. The prover's statement is $([C(x)]_1, \mathbb{x})$, where $[C(x)]_1$ is a succinct VCF commitment to $\mathbb{z} = \binom{\mathbb{x}}{\mathbb{w}}$. Notably, (honest) crs is independent of the statement. Thus, crs can be created before the statement; we only prove soundness if the statement does not depend on crs.

The argument π includes three VCF commitments ($[\mathsf{a}(x), \mathsf{c}(x)]_1$ and $[\mathsf{b}(x)]_2$ to $\boldsymbol{U}\mathbb{z}$, $\boldsymbol{W}\mathbb{z}$, and $\boldsymbol{V}\mathbb{z}$) and a group element $[\mathsf{h}(x)]_1$. Here, $\mathsf{h}(X) = (\mathsf{a}(X)\mathsf{b}(X) - \mathsf{c}(X))/Z_{\mathbb{H}}(X)$. Intuitively, $[\mathsf{h}(x)]_1$ is the randomizer of the VCF commitment $[\mathsf{a}(x)\mathsf{b}(x) - \mathsf{c}(x)]_1$, Many non-universal zk-SNARKs, e.g. [23,29,50], have commitments $[\mathsf{a}(x), \mathsf{c}(x)]_1$ and $[\mathsf{b}(x)]_2$ and possibly the proof element $[\mathsf{h}(x)]_1$. Our novelty is using VCF, a *vector* commitment. Following [16,17], we prove that the commitments are correct (in particular, they commit to the correct public input) by using a BLS argument BLS.π that we add to Punic's argument.

The black-box extractor in our soundness proof extracts the local proofs corresponding to these three vector commitments. We follow [16,17] and add to the argument two FSE commitments $[\mathsf{d}(x)]_1$ and $[\mathsf{e}(x)]_2$ that allow us to black-box somewhere-extract one partial witness. For black-box extraction to succeed, the length of FSE commitments needs to be at least $\mathfrak{f}$ group elements.

Soundness Proof. Following the discussion of Sect. 5.2, we aim for Punic to be semi-adaptively $[\cdot]_1$-knowledge-sound—a different soundness notion than in [16,17]. Since we proved in Theorem 1 that this notion follows from special soundness, we will explain next how we prove special soundness. This helps to motivate the choice of primitives (VCF, FSE, and BLS).

In the honest case, $[C]_1$ is a VCF commitment to a statement-witness pair. We construct a special soundness extractor $\mathsf{Ext}_{\mathsf{ss}}$ (see the full version [45]). We also construct three reductions that work when the extractor $\mathsf{Ext}_{\mathsf{ss}}$ fails. These three reductions each call $\mathsf{Ext}_{\mathsf{ss}}$ to obtain a tuple of admissible transcripts $\mathbf{tr}$. Let $G(s) := [sy]_1$ to be G_1 from Sect. 4.2. Denote $G(\mathbb{p}^{\varrho}) := G(\mathbb{p}^{\varrho}(N(\varrho)))$. Each reduction loops over $\varrho \in [1, n]$. For each $\varrho \in [1, n]$, some of the reductions use FSE to black-box somewhere-extract $G(\mathbb{p}^{\varrho}) = G(\eta|_{N(\varrho)})$ together with $[\varphi|_{N(\varrho)}]_1$. Here, $\eta|_{N(\varrho)}$ is an assignment of variables from $N(\varrho)$, $[\varphi|_{N(\varrho)}]_1$ is a tuple of VCF local proofs for every coefficient in $N(\varrho)$, and $\mathsf{LVer}(\mathrm{VCF}_1.\mathsf{ck}, [C(x)]_1, k, G(\eta_k), [\varphi_k]_1) = 1$ for all $k \in N(\varrho)$. (We extract more values, but they are immaterial for this subsection.)

The first reduction $\mathcal{B}_{\mathsf{bls}}$ (see the full version [45]) is to the security of BLS. $\mathcal{B}_{\mathsf{bls}}$ guarantees three things: (1) the adversary uses the correct statement $\mathbb{x}$, (2) commitments like $[\mathsf{a}(x)]_1$ in the argument (see Fig. 5) are correctly formed, and (3) the extracted variables contain correctly computed local openings and local proofs of the vector commitment. Assuming that (1–3) holds, the second reduction $\mathcal{B}_{\mathsf{qal}}$ (see the full version [45]) handles the case when there exists a ϱ such that $\mathbb{p}^{\varrho}$ does not satisfy the ϱth coefficient. By the first two reductions, we obtain a guarantee for local consistency: for all ϱ, $(\mathbb{x}, \mathbb{p}^{\varrho})$ locally satisfies the instance. The first two reductions are related to the reductions in [16,17], see the full version [45] for more.

The third reduction $\mathcal{B}_{\mathsf{fposb}}$ (see the full version [45]) handles the case when partial witnesses exist, but $\mathsf{Ext}_{\mathsf{ks}}$ fails to black-box extract a full witness satisfying all constraints. By Remark 1, then there must exist two indices $i \neq j$, such that:

(1) $\mathbb{p}^i$ satisfies the ith constraint and $\mathbb{p}^j$ satisfies the jth constraint.
(2) $\mathsf{Cons}(\mathbb{p}^i, \mathbb{p}^j) = \mathsf{false}$; that is, $(\exists k \in (N(i) \cap N(j)))\, \mathbb{p}^i(k) \neq \mathbb{p}^j(k)$.

Given all extracted $G(\mathbb{p}^{\varrho})$-s, $\mathcal{B}_{\mathsf{fposb}}$ can efficiently recover i, j, k. $\mathcal{B}_{\mathsf{fposb}}$ returns the position k and two different local openings $\eta^i_k \neq \eta^j_k$ of $[C(x)]_1$ with local proofs φ^i_k and φ^j_k. Thus, $\mathcal{B}_{\mathsf{fposb}}$ breaks the $[\cdot]_1$-position-binding property.

Recall that FSE can black-box somewhere-extract group elements. Moreover, the extracted group elements must be linear maps of $\mathbb{z}$, that is, of the form $[\boldsymbol{M}]_{\gamma}\mathbb{z}$ for some public matrix $[\boldsymbol{M}]_{\gamma}$. Thus, the vector commitment scheme must be F-position-binding and fully-algebraic, which motivates the use of VCF.

In the ϱth iteration, we need to black-box extract η^{ϱ}_k and φ^{ϱ}_k for all $k \in N(\varrho)$. Since the length of an FSE commitment depends on the number of extracted values, we must limit the maximum number of such coefficients for the sake of efficiency. Thus, we can only handle $\mathrm{R1CS}_{\mathfrak{f}}$ for a small $\mathfrak{f}$.

We need protection against adversaries who make the verifier accept only for specific values of ϱ, which makes it impossible to construct $\mathbb{p}^{\varrho}$ for all ϱ. As explained in Sect. 5.2, it suffices to prove that Punic is CRS-indistinguishable.

See comparison with no-signaling commitments in the full version [45].

6.2 Description of Punic

Prerequisites. Punic uses VCF in $\mathbb{G}_1$ and $\mathbb{G}_2$ to commit. We use its local opening only in the soundness proof and not in the construction. Punic also uses FSE and BLS. Punic handles $\mathrm{R1CS}_\mathfrak{f}$, where $\mathfrak{f} \in \mathbb{N}$ is a small integer. Zk-SNARG(K)s for similarly restricted constraint systems are well-known; see, e.g., [21,37,51]. Using small $\mathfrak{f}$ only affects the efficiency: the restriction on $\mathfrak{f}$ is like to bounding the fan-in and fan-out in arithmetic circuits; it is easy to transform arithmetic circuits to circuits with bounded fan-in and fan-out efficiently.

Since we need to black-box extract the neighborhood of any given constraint, FSE has larger locality parameters than [16,17,46]. We set

$$q_1 = 2 + 2\mathfrak{f} \text{ and } q_2 := 2 \ . \tag{3}$$

We explain this choice in the soundness proof, see Sect. 7. We use q_γ as the locality parameter for FSE_γ.

Description. In Fig. 5, we depict Punic for an $\mathrm{R1CS}_\mathfrak{f}$ instance $\mathfrak{J}$. The language parameter lp is the commitment key of VCF. For $\varrho \in [0, n]$ (in the honest case, $\varrho = 0$), Punic's CRS $\mathsf{crs} \leftarrow\$ \mathsf{K}_{\mathsf{crs}}(\mathsf{lp}, \mathcal{R}_\mathfrak{J}, \varrho)$ contains instance-dependent values BLS.lp and BLS.crs (BLS's language parameter and CRS). Furthermore, BLS.$\mathsf{lp} = [\boldsymbol{M}]_*$ contains as submatrices FSE commitment keys, together with commitment keys like ck_u required to locally open linear maps (see Lemma 4).

The FSE commitment keys are created as in Fig. 3 from ϱ-dependent extraction matrices $[\boldsymbol{E}_1^\varrho]_1$ and $[\boldsymbol{E}_2^\varrho]_2$. Here, $[\boldsymbol{E}_1^0]_1 = [\boldsymbol{0}_{q_1 \times (m+3)}]_1$ and $[\boldsymbol{E}_2^0]_2 = [\boldsymbol{0}_{q_2 \times (m+1)}]_2$. In the knowledge-soundness proof, we invoke $\mathsf{K}_{\mathsf{crs}}$ with a non-zero $\varrho \in [1, n]$. If $\varrho \neq 0$, then each row of $[\boldsymbol{E}_1^\varrho]_1/[\boldsymbol{E}_2^\varrho]_2$ contains an extraction key used in the soundness proof to black-box extract local openings and local proofs. We describe the algorithm for creating $[\boldsymbol{E}_1^\varrho]_1/[\boldsymbol{E}_2^\varrho]_2$ in Fig. 7. (We postpone it to Sect. 7 since the case $\varrho \neq 0$ is only used in the soundness proof.) Similarly, $[\boldsymbol{M}]_*$ is created by using the algorithm in Fig. 6. In Figs. 6 and 7, the first row (small, blue font) denotes the elements of the vector that the matrices will be multiplied with. "Empty" entries mean zeros. We explain the construction of these matrices in Sect. 7.1.

Efficiency. Clearly, $\mathrm{FSE}_1.\mathsf{ck} \in \mathbb{G}_1^{(q_1+1)\times(m+3)}$ and $\mathrm{FSE}_2.\mathsf{ck} \in \mathbb{G}_2^{(q_2+1)\times(m+2)}$. Using $\hat{\ell}_i(X)$ instead of $\ell_i(X)$ helps us to prove efficiently that the prover used the correct $\mathrm{R1CS}_\mathfrak{f}$ statement $(\mathbb{z}_1, \dots, \mathbb{z}_{m_\mathbb{x}})^\top = \mathbb{x}$. Assuming we have an instance of $\mathrm{R1CS}_\mathfrak{f}$ for $\mathfrak{f} = o(|\mathbb{w}|)$, the Punic argument π is succinct, consisting of $7 + 2\mathfrak{f}$ elements of $\mathbb{G}_1$ and 5 elements of $\mathbb{G}_2$. Choosing a larger $\mathfrak{f}$ potentially decreases the number of constraints, while a smaller $\mathfrak{f}$ decreases the argument size.

SSP. In the full version [45], we note that Punic can be simplified significantly by targeting SSP [15] instead of R1CS [23].

$\mathsf{K_{lp}}(\mathsf{p})$: // $\mathrm{VCF}_2.\mathsf{ck} = \mathrm{VCF}_1.\mathsf{ck}$, $\mathrm{VCF}_2.\mathsf{td} = \mathrm{VCF}_1.\mathsf{td}$ by design
  $(\mathrm{VCF}_1.\mathsf{ck}, \mathrm{VCF}_1.\mathsf{td}) \leftarrow \mathrm{VCF}_1.\mathsf{K_{ck}}(\mathsf{p}, n)$; // $\mathrm{VCF}_1.\mathsf{td}$ contains x, y
  return $\mathsf{lp} \leftarrow \mathrm{VCF}_1.\mathsf{ck} = \mathrm{VCF}_2.\mathsf{ck}$;

$\mathsf{K_{crs}}(\mathsf{lp}, \mathcal{R}_{\mathfrak{I}}, \varrho)$: // n is implicit in $\mathsf{p}, \mathcal{R}_{\mathfrak{I}}$; honest case: $\varrho = 0$
  $([\boldsymbol{E}_1^{\varrho}]_1, [\boldsymbol{E}_2^{\varrho}]_2) \leftarrow \mathsf{CreateE}(\mathsf{lp}, \mathcal{R}_{\mathfrak{I}}, \varrho)$; // FSE extraction matrices
  $(\mathrm{FSE}_1.\mathsf{ck}, \mathrm{FSE}_1.\mathsf{td}) \leftarrow \mathrm{FSE}_1.\mathsf{K_{ck}}(\mathsf{p}, m+3, q_1, [\boldsymbol{E}_1^{\varrho}]_1)$; // As in Fig. 3
  $(\mathrm{FSE}_2.\mathsf{ck}, \mathrm{FSE}_2.\mathsf{td}) \leftarrow \mathrm{FSE}_2.\mathsf{K_{ck}}(\mathsf{p}, m+1, q_2, [\boldsymbol{E}_2^{\varrho}]_2)$;
  $\mathrm{BLS}.\mathsf{lp} = [\boldsymbol{M}]_* \leftarrow \mathsf{CreateM}(\mathsf{lp}, \mathcal{R}_{\mathfrak{I}}, \mathrm{FSE}_1.\mathsf{ck}, \mathrm{FSE}_2.\mathsf{ck})$;
  $(\mathrm{BLS}.\mathsf{crs}, \mathrm{BLS}.\mathsf{td}) \leftarrow \mathrm{BLS}.\mathsf{K_{crs}}(\mathsf{p}, \mathrm{BLS}.\mathsf{lp})$;
  $\mathsf{crs} \leftarrow (\mathrm{BLS}.\mathsf{lp}, \mathrm{BLS}.\mathsf{crs})$;
  $\mathsf{ek} \leftarrow (\mathrm{FSE}_1.\mathsf{ek}, \mathrm{FSE}_2.\mathsf{ek})$; $\mathsf{td} \leftarrow (\mathrm{BLS}.\mathsf{td}, \mathsf{ek})$;
  return $(\mathsf{crs}, \mathsf{td})$;

$\mathsf{P}(\mathsf{lp}, \mathsf{crs}, ([C(x)]_1, \mathbb{x} \in \mathbb{F}^{m_{\mathbb{x}}}), (r_C, \mathbb{w} \in \mathbb{F}^{m-m_{\mathbb{x}}}))$:
  // $\mathbb{z} = \binom{\mathbb{x}}{\mathbb{w}}$; $[C(x)]_1 \leftarrow \mathrm{VCF}_1.\mathsf{Com}(\mathrm{VCF}_1.\mathsf{ck}, \mathbb{z}, r_C)$
  1. $r_\mathsf{a}, r_\mathsf{b}, r_\mathsf{c}, r_\mathsf{d}, r_\mathsf{e} \leftarrow\$ \mathbb{F}$;
  2. $[\mathsf{a}(x)]_1 \leftarrow \mathrm{VCF}_1.\mathsf{Com}(\mathrm{VCF}_1.\mathsf{ck}, \boldsymbol{U}\mathbb{z}; r_\mathsf{a})$;
  3. $[\mathsf{b}(x)]_2 \leftarrow \mathrm{VCF}_2.\mathsf{Com}(\mathrm{VCF}_2.\mathsf{ck}, \boldsymbol{V}\mathbb{z}; r_\mathsf{b})$;
  4. $[\mathsf{c}(x)]_1 \leftarrow \mathrm{VCF}_1.\mathsf{Com}(\mathrm{VCF}_1.\mathsf{ck}, \boldsymbol{W}\mathbb{z}; r_\mathsf{c})$;
  5. $\mathsf{h}(X) \leftarrow (\mathsf{a}(X)\mathsf{b}(X) - \mathsf{c}(X))/Z_{\mathbb{H}}(X)$; // $[\mathsf{h}(x)]_1 \leftarrow \sum_{i=0}^{n-2} h_i [x^i]_1$
  6. $[\mathsf{d}(x)]_1 \leftarrow \mathrm{FSE}_1.\mathsf{Com}(\mathrm{FSE}_1.\mathsf{ck}, (\mathbb{z}^\intercal, r_C, r_\mathsf{a}, r_\mathsf{c})^\intercal; r_\mathsf{d})$;
  7. $[\mathsf{e}(x)]_2 \leftarrow \mathrm{FSE}_2.\mathsf{Com}(\mathrm{FSE}_2.\mathsf{ck}, \binom{\mathbb{z}}{r_\mathsf{b}}; r_\mathsf{e})$;
  8. $[C^*(x)]_1 \leftarrow [C(x)]_1 - \sum_{i=1}^{m_{\mathbb{x}}} \mathbb{x}_i [\ell_i(x)]_1$;
  9. $\mathrm{BLS}.\mathbb{x} \leftarrow ([C^*(x), \mathsf{a}(x), \mathsf{c}(x), \mathsf{d}(x)]_1, [\mathsf{b}(x), \mathsf{e}(x)]_2)^\intercal$;
  10. $\mathrm{BLS}.\pi \leftarrow \mathrm{BLS}.\mathsf{P}(\mathrm{BLS}.\mathsf{lp}, \mathrm{BLS}.\mathsf{crs}, \mathrm{BLS}.\mathbb{x}, (\mathbb{z}, r_C, r_\mathsf{a}, r_\mathsf{b}, r_\mathsf{c}, r_\mathsf{d}, r_\mathsf{e}))$;
  11. $\pi \leftarrow ([\mathsf{a}(x), \mathsf{c}(x), \mathsf{d}(x), \mathsf{h}(x)]_1, [\mathsf{b}(x), \mathsf{e}(x)]_2, \mathrm{BLS}.\pi)$;

$\mathsf{V}(\mathsf{lp}, \mathsf{crs}, ([C(x)]_1, \mathbb{x} \in \mathbb{F}^{m_{\mathbb{x}}}), \pi)$: Parse π as in 11;
  1. $[C^*(x)]_1 \leftarrow [C(x)]_1 - \sum_{i=1}^{m_{\mathbb{x}}} \mathbb{x}_i [\ell_i(x)]_1$;
  2. $\mathrm{BLS}.\mathbb{x} \leftarrow ([C^*(x), \mathsf{a}(x), \mathsf{c}(x), \mathsf{d}(x)]_1, [\mathsf{b}(x), \mathsf{e}(x)]_2)^\intercal$;
  3. check $\mathrm{BLS}.\mathsf{V}(\mathrm{BLS}.\mathsf{lp}, \mathrm{BLS}.\mathsf{crs}, \mathrm{BLS}.\mathbb{x}, \mathrm{BLS}.\pi) = 1$;
  4. check $[\mathsf{a}(x)]_1 \bullet [\mathsf{b}(x)]_2 - [\mathsf{c}(x)]_1 \bullet [1]_2 = [\mathsf{h}(x)]_1 \bullet [Z_{\mathbb{H}}(x)]_2$;

$\mathsf{Sim}(\mathsf{lp}, \mathsf{crs}, \mathsf{td} = (\mathrm{BLS}.\mathsf{td}, \mathsf{ek}), ([C(x)]_1, \mathbb{x} \in \mathbb{F}^{m_{\mathbb{x}}}))$:
  1. $r_\mathsf{a}, r_\mathsf{b}, r_\mathsf{c}, r_\mathsf{d}, r_\mathsf{e} \leftarrow\$ \mathbb{F}$;
  2. $[\mathsf{a}(x)]_1 \leftarrow \mathrm{VCF}_1.\mathsf{Com}(\mathrm{VCF}_1.\mathsf{ck}, \boldsymbol{0}; r_\mathsf{a})$; // $= r_\mathsf{a}[Z_{\mathbb{H}}(x)]_1$
  3. $[\mathsf{b}(x)]_2 \leftarrow \mathrm{VCF}_2.\mathsf{Com}(\mathrm{VCF}_2.\mathsf{ck}, \boldsymbol{0}; r_\mathsf{b})$; // $= r_\mathsf{b}[Z_{\mathbb{H}}(x)]_2$
  4. $[\mathsf{c}(x)]_1 \leftarrow \mathrm{VCF}_1.\mathsf{Com}(\mathrm{VCF}_1.\mathsf{ck}, \boldsymbol{0}; r_\mathsf{c})$; // $= r_\mathsf{c}[Z_{\mathbb{H}}(x)]_1$
  5. $[\mathsf{h}(x)]_1 \leftarrow r_\mathsf{a} r_\mathsf{b} [Z_{\mathbb{H}}(x)]_1 - r_\mathsf{c}[1]_1$;
  6. $[\mathsf{d}(x)]_1 \leftarrow \mathrm{FSE}_1.\mathsf{Com}(\mathrm{FSE}_1.\mathsf{ck}, \boldsymbol{0}_{m+3}; r_\mathsf{d})$;
  7. $[\mathsf{e}(x)]_2 \leftarrow \mathrm{FSE}_2.\mathsf{Com}(\mathrm{FSE}_2.\mathsf{ck}, \boldsymbol{0}_{m+1}; r_\mathsf{e})$;
  8. $[C^*(x)]_1 \leftarrow [C(x)]_1 - \sum_{i=1}^{m_{\mathbb{x}}} \mathbb{x}_i [\ell_i(x)]_1$;
  9. $\mathrm{BLS}.\mathbb{x} \leftarrow ([C^*(x), \mathsf{a}(x), \mathsf{c}(x), \mathsf{d}(x)]_1, [\mathsf{b}(x), \mathsf{e}(x)]_2)^\intercal$;
  10. $\mathrm{BLS}.\pi \leftarrow \mathrm{BLS}.\mathsf{Sim}(\mathrm{BLS}.\mathsf{lp}, \mathrm{BLS}.\mathsf{crs}, \mathrm{BLS}.\mathsf{td}, \mathrm{BLS}.\mathbb{x})$;
  11. $\pi \leftarrow ([\mathsf{a}(x), \mathsf{c}(x), \mathsf{d}(x), \mathsf{h}(x)]_1, [\mathsf{b}(x), \mathsf{e}(x)]_2, \mathrm{BLS}.\pi)$;

Fig. 5. New semi-adaptively black-box $[\cdot]_1$-knowledge-sound C&P SA-SNARK Punic.

1. let $\hat{\ell}_j(X) = \ell_j(X)$ for $m_{\mathbb{x}} < j \leq n$ and $\hat{\ell}_j(X) = 0$ for $j \leq m_{\mathbb{x}}$ or $j > n$;
   // W.l.o.g., we assume $m \geq n$
2. let $u_j(X), v_j(X), w_j(X)$ interpolate column vectors $\boldsymbol{U}^{(j)}, \boldsymbol{V}^{(j)}, \boldsymbol{W}^{(j)}$;
3. $[\mathsf{ck}_{\hat{\ell}}]_1 \leftarrow [\hat{\ell}_1(x), \dots, \hat{\ell}_m(x), Z_{\mathbb{H}}(x)]_1$; $[\mathsf{ck}_u]_1 \leftarrow [u_1(x), \dots, u_m(x), Z_{\mathbb{H}}(x)]_1$;
4. $[\mathsf{ck}_v]_2 \leftarrow [v_1(x), \dots, v_m(x), Z_{\mathbb{H}}(x)]_2$; $[\mathsf{ck}_w]_1 \leftarrow [w_1(x), \dots, v_m(x), Z_{\mathbb{H}}(x)]_1$;
5. let $n_1 := q_1 + 4$, $n_2 := q_2 + 2$;
6. return $[\boldsymbol{M}]_* \in \mathbb{G}_1^{n_1 \times (m+6)} \times \mathbb{G}_2^{n_2 \times (m+6)}$, where

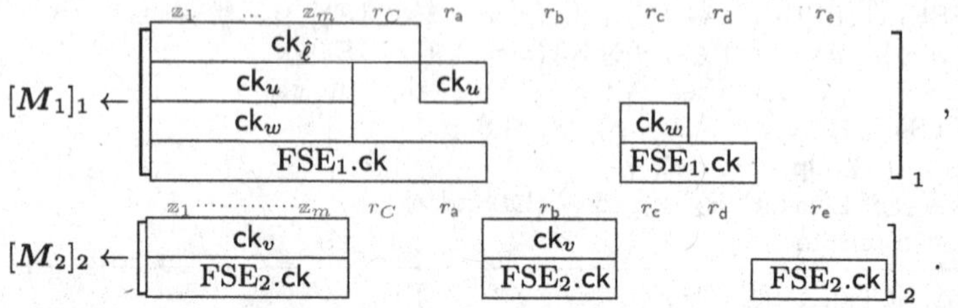

(4)

Fig. 6. Algorithm $\mathsf{CreateM}(\mathsf{lp}, \mathcal{R}_{\mathfrak{I}}, \mathrm{FSE}_1.\mathsf{ck}, \mathrm{FSE}_2.\mathsf{ck})$.

1. if $\varrho = 0$ then $\boldsymbol{E}_1^\varrho \leftarrow \boldsymbol{0}_{q_1 \times (m+3)}$; $\boldsymbol{E}_2^\varrho \leftarrow \boldsymbol{0}_{q_2 \times (m+1)}$; return $([\boldsymbol{E}_1^\varrho]_1, [\boldsymbol{E}_2^\varrho]_2)$;
2. $(\beta_1, \dots, \beta_{\mathfrak{f}}) \leftarrow N(\varrho)$; // Duplicate some entries when $|N(\varrho)| < \mathfrak{f}$
3. let $u_j(X)$, $v_j(X)$, $w_j(X)$ interpolate column vectors $\boldsymbol{U}^{(j)}$, $\boldsymbol{V}^{(j)}$, $\boldsymbol{W}^{(j)}$;
4. as in Lemma 1, let $[\mathsf{ck}_{\ell,\beta_i}]_1 \leftarrow [Q_{\ell_1,\beta_i}(x) \| \dots \| Q_{\ell_m,\beta_i}(x) \| Q_{Z_{\mathbb{H}},\beta_i}(x)]_1^\top$.
5. as in Lemma 4, let $[\mathsf{ck}_u^\varrho]_1 \leftarrow [Q_{u_1,\varrho}(x) \| \dots \| Q_{u_m,\varrho}(x) \| Q_{Z_{\mathbb{H}},\varrho}(x)]_1^\top$; similarly, define $[\mathsf{ck}_v^\varrho]_2$, $[\mathsf{ck}_w^\varrho]_1$;
6. return $([\boldsymbol{E}_1^\varrho]_1, [\boldsymbol{E}_2^\varrho]_2)$, $\boldsymbol{E}_1^\varrho \in \mathbb{F}^{q_1 \times (m+3)}$, $\boldsymbol{E}_2^\varrho \in \mathbb{F}^{q_2 \times (m+1)}$, where

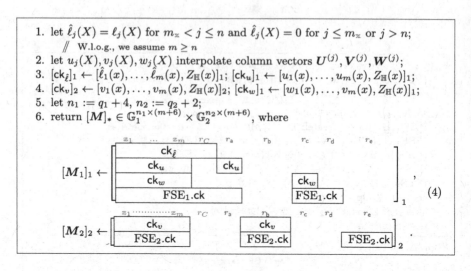

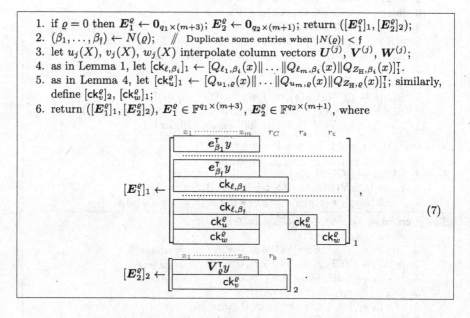

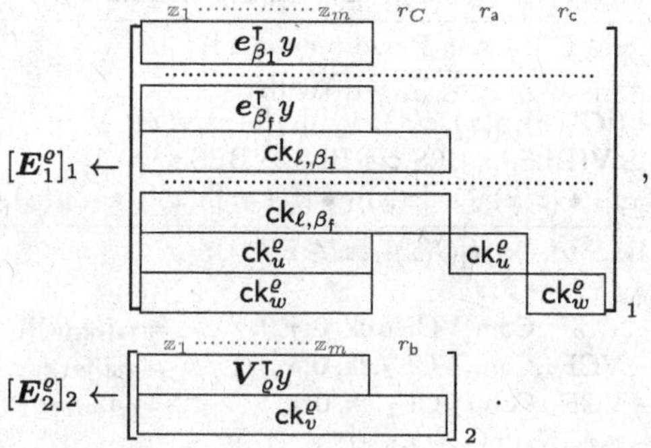

(7)

Fig. 7. Algorithm $\mathsf{CreateE}(\mathsf{lp}, \mathcal{R}_{\mathfrak{I}}, \varrho)$, where $\varrho \in [0, n]$.

7 Security of Punic

We postpone the following two proofs to the full version [45].

Theorem 2. *(1) Punic is perfectly complete. (2) If* VCF_1 *and* VCF_2 *are perfectly zero-knowledge,* BLS *is perfectly zero-knowledge, and* FSE_1 *and* FSE_2 *are almost everywhere perfectly-hiding then Punic is perfectly zero-knowledge.*

Theorem 3. *Let m, q_1, and q_2 be as above. If FSE_γ is function-set hiding for $\gamma \in \{1,2\}$, then Punic is CRS-indistinguishable. More precisely, there exist PPT $\mathcal{B}_1$ and $\mathcal{B}_2$, such that for every PPT $\mathcal{A}$ and ϱ,* $\mathsf{Adv}^{\mathsf{crsind}}_{\mathsf{Pgen},\varrho,\mathrm{Punic},\mathcal{A}}(\lambda) \leq \mathsf{Adv}^{\mathsf{fsh}}_{\mathsf{Pgen},\mathrm{FSE}_1,m+3,q_1,\mathcal{B}_1}(\lambda) + \mathsf{Adv}^{\mathsf{fsh}}_{\mathsf{Pgen},\mathrm{FSE}_2,m+1,q_2,\mathcal{B}_2}(\lambda)$.

7.1 Semi-adaptive Computational (n, G)-Special-Soundness

On M_γ. For $\mathrm{BLS}.\mathsf{lp} = [\boldsymbol{M}]_*$ defined as in Eq. (4), we use BLS to show that

$$\mathrm{BLS}.\mathbb{x} := ([C^*(x), \mathsf{a}(x), \mathsf{c}(x), \mathsf{d}(x)]_1, [\mathsf{b}(x), \mathsf{e}(x)]_2)^\top \in \mathrm{colspace}\begin{pmatrix} [\boldsymbol{M}_1]_1 \\ [\boldsymbol{M}_2]_2 \end{pmatrix} . \quad (5)$$

Equation (5) holds iff there exists $\mathrm{BLS}.\mathbb{w} = (\mathbb{z} = \binom{\mathbb{x}}{\mathbb{w}}, r_C, r_\mathsf{a}, r_\mathsf{b}, r_\mathsf{c}, r_\mathsf{d}, r_\mathsf{e})$, such that (here, $[C(x)]_1$ follows from $[C^*(x)]_1$)

$$\begin{aligned}
[C^*(x)]_1 &= \mathrm{VCF}_1.\mathsf{ck} \cdot \begin{pmatrix} \mathbf{0} \\ \mathbb{w} \\ r_C \end{pmatrix} , \\
[C(x)]_1 &= \mathrm{VCF}_1.\mathsf{ck} \cdot \binom{\mathbb{z}}{r_C} = \mathrm{VCF}_1.\mathsf{Com}(\mathrm{VCF}_1.\mathsf{ck}, \mathbb{z}, r_C) , \\
[\mathsf{a}(x)]_1 &= \mathrm{VCF}_1.\mathsf{ck} \cdot \binom{\boldsymbol{U}\mathbb{z}}{r_\mathsf{a}} = \mathrm{VCF}_1.\mathsf{Com}(\mathrm{VCF}_1.\mathsf{ck}, \boldsymbol{U}\mathbb{z}; r_\mathsf{a}) , \\
[\mathsf{c}(x)]_1 &= \mathrm{VCF}_1.\mathsf{ck} \cdot \binom{\boldsymbol{W}\mathbb{z}}{r_\mathsf{c}} = \mathrm{VCF}_1.\mathsf{Com}(\mathrm{VCF}_1.\mathsf{ck}, \boldsymbol{W}\mathbb{z}; r_\mathsf{c}) , \\
[\mathsf{d}(x)]_1 &= \mathrm{FSE}_1.\mathsf{ck} \cdot (\mathbb{z}^\top, r_C, r_\mathsf{a}, r_\mathsf{c}, r_\mathsf{d})^\top \\
&= \mathrm{FSE}_1.\mathsf{Com}(\mathrm{FSE}_1.\mathsf{ck}, (\mathbb{z}^\top, r_C, r_\mathsf{a}, r_\mathsf{c})^\top; r_\mathsf{d}) , \\
[\mathsf{b}(x)]_2 &= \mathrm{VCF}_2.\mathsf{ck} \cdot \binom{\boldsymbol{V}\mathbb{z}}{r_\mathsf{b}} = \mathrm{VCF}_2.\mathsf{Com}(\mathrm{VCF}_2.\mathsf{ck}, \boldsymbol{V}\mathbb{z}; r_\mathsf{b}) , \\
[\mathsf{e}(x)]_2 &= \mathrm{FSE}_2.\mathsf{ck} \cdot (\mathbb{z}^\top, r_\mathsf{b}, r_\mathsf{e})^\top = \mathrm{FSE}_2.\mathsf{Com}(\mathrm{FSE}_2.\mathsf{ck}, \binom{\mathbb{z}}{r_\mathsf{b}}; r_\mathsf{e}) .
\end{aligned} \quad (6)$$

By Fact 2, for BLS to be strongly sound, we need the distribution of $[\boldsymbol{M}]_*$ to be witness-sampleable; this is clearly the case. We also need that $\mathrm{rank}\binom{\boldsymbol{M}_1}{\boldsymbol{M}_2} < n_1 + n_2$. This is fine since $\mathrm{BLS}.\mathbb{w}$ *always* exists when $n_1 + n_2 = \mathrm{rank}\binom{\boldsymbol{M}_1}{\boldsymbol{M}_2}$.

On E_γ. Assume $\varrho \neq 0$, $(\mathsf{crs}^\varrho, \mathsf{td}^\varrho) \leftarrow\$ \mathsf{K}_{\mathsf{crs}}(\mathsf{lp}, \mathcal{R}_\mathfrak{J}, \varrho)$, and that P computes the argument π^ϱ honestly by using an ϱ-dependent full witness $\mathbb{w}^\varrho$ and randomizers like r^ϱ_a. (BLS will guarantee the latter.) Then, $\mathrm{FSE}_1.\mathsf{swExt}(\mathrm{FSE}_1.\mathsf{ek}, [\mathsf{d}(x)]_1)$ and $\mathrm{FSE}_2.\mathsf{swExt}(\mathrm{FSE}_2.\mathsf{ek}, [\mathsf{e}(x)]_2)$ output

$$\begin{pmatrix} G(\boldsymbol{\eta}^\varrho) \\ \begin{bmatrix} \boldsymbol{\varphi}^\varrho \\ \varphi^\varrho_\mathsf{a} \\ \varphi^\varrho_\mathsf{c} \end{bmatrix}_1 \end{pmatrix} \leftarrow [\boldsymbol{E}^\varrho_1]_1 \cdot \begin{pmatrix} \mathbb{z}^\varrho \\ r^\varrho_C \\ r^\varrho_\mathsf{a} \\ r^\varrho_\mathsf{c} \end{pmatrix} \quad \text{and} \quad \begin{pmatrix} G_2(\eta^\varrho_\mathsf{b}) \\ [\varphi^\varrho_\mathsf{b}]_2 \end{pmatrix} \leftarrow [\boldsymbol{E}^\varrho_2]_2 \cdot \begin{pmatrix} \mathbb{z}^\varrho \\ r^\varrho_\mathsf{b} \end{pmatrix} , \quad (8)$$

where $G_2(X) := [Xy]_2$. From Lemma 1, the security of BLS, and Eq. (7) it follows $G(\boldsymbol{\eta}^\varrho|_{N(\varrho)}) = G(\mathbb{p}^\varrho|_{N(\varrho)})$ is a tuple of local openings and $\boldsymbol{\varphi}^\varrho = (\varphi^\varrho_j)|_{N(\varrho)}$ is the corresponding tuple of local proofs, with

$$(G(\eta^\varrho_j), [\varphi^\varrho_j]_1) = \mathrm{VCF}_1.\mathsf{LOpen}(\mathsf{ck}, [C(x)]_1, j, D = (\mathbb{z}^\varrho, r^\varrho))$$

for some $\mathbb{z}^\varrho$ and r^ϱ. (Recall that dependency from y is required to construct a reduction to $[\cdot]_1$-position-binding.) Define $G(\eta^\varrho_\mathsf{a}) \leftarrow \sum_{j \in N(\varrho)} U_{\varrho j} G(\eta^\varrho_j)$ and $G(\eta^\varrho_\mathsf{c}) \leftarrow \sum_{j \in N(\varrho)} W_{\varrho j} G(\eta^\varrho_j)$. Equations (7) and (8) and Lemma 4 imply that

$$(G(\eta^\varrho_\mathsf{a}), [\varphi^\varrho_\mathsf{a}]_1) = \mathrm{VCF}_1.\mathsf{LOpen}(\mathsf{ck}, [\mathsf{a}(x)]_1, j, D = (\boldsymbol{U}\mathbb{z}^\varrho, r^\varrho_\mathsf{a}))$$

and $(G(\eta_{\mathsf{c}}^{\varrho}), [\varphi_{\mathsf{c}}^{\varrho}]_1) = \mathrm{VCF}_1.\mathsf{LOpen}(\mathsf{ck}, [\mathsf{c}(x)]_1, j, D = (\boldsymbol{W}\mathbb{z}^{\varrho}, r_{\mathsf{c}}^{\varrho}))$. Note that we black-box extract $[\varphi_{\mathsf{b}}^{\varrho}]_2$ by using FSE.

For $\varrho \in [0, n]$, let $\mathcal{D}_{\mathrm{par}}^{\varrho}$ be the distribution of $[\boldsymbol{M}]_*$ in Eq. (4). We postpone the special soundness proof to the full version [45].

Theorem 4. *Let n be the number of $R1CS_{\mathfrak{f}}$ constraints. Assume* FSE_γ *is somewhere $[\cdot]_\gamma$-extractable for $\gamma \in \{1, 2\}$,* BLS *is quasi-adaptively strongly sound for $\mathcal{D}_{\mathrm{par}}^{\varrho}$ where $\varrho \in [1, n]$,* VCF_1 *is $[\cdot]_1$-position-binding, and n-*QALINRES *holds. Then, Punic is semi-adaptively computationally (n, G)-special-sound. More precisely, there exist an expected PPT* $\mathsf{Ext}_{\mathsf{ss}}$ *and PPT $\mathcal{B}_{\mathsf{fposb}}$, $\mathcal{B}_{\mathsf{qal}}$, and $\mathcal{B}_{\mathsf{bls}}^{\varrho}$ for $\varrho \in [1, n]$, such that for any PPT $\mathcal{A}_{\mathsf{ss}}$,*

$$\mathsf{Adv}^{\mathrm{specsound}}_{\mathsf{Pgen},G,\mathrm{Punic},n,\mathsf{Ext}_{\mathsf{ss}},\mathcal{A}_{\mathsf{ss}}}(\lambda) \le \textstyle\sum_{\varrho=1}^{n} \mathsf{Adv}^{\mathrm{strsound}}_{\mathsf{Pgen},\mathcal{D}_{\mathrm{par}}^{\varrho},\mathrm{BLS},\mathcal{B}_{\mathsf{bls}}^{\varrho}}(\lambda) + \mathsf{Adv}^{\mathrm{fposb}}_{\mathsf{Pgen},[\cdot]_1,n,\mathrm{VCF}_1,\mathcal{B}_{\mathsf{fposb}}}(\lambda) + \mathsf{Adv}^{\mathrm{QALINRES}}_{\mathsf{Pgen},n,\mathcal{B}_{\mathsf{qal}}}(\lambda) \enspace .$$

Acknowledgment and History. The author became aware of the error in FANA in December 2021; the error was (partially) caused by the fact that he was severely sick when submitting [46] and its camera-ready version. We thank Daniel Wichs and anonymous reviewers for helpful comments.

References

1. Abdolmaleki, B., Baghery, K., Lipmaa, H., Zając, M.: A subversion-resistant SNARK. In: Takagi, T., Peyrin, T. (eds.) ASIACRYPT 2017, Part III. LNCS, vol. 10626, pp. 3–33. Springer, Cham (2017). https://doi.org/10.1007/978-3-319-70700-6_1
2. Abdolmaleki, B., Lipmaa, H., Siim, J., Zając, M.: On QA-NIZK in the BPK model. In: Kiayias, A., Kohlweiss, M., Wallden, P., Zikas, V. (eds.) PKC 2020, Part I. LNCS, vol. 12110, pp. 590–620. Springer, Cham (2020). https://doi.org/10.1007/978-3-030-45374-9_20
3. Abdolmaleki, B., Lipmaa, H., Siim, J., Zajac, M.: On Subversion-Resistant SNARKs. J. Cryptology **34**(3), 1–42 (2021). https://doi.org/10.1007/s00145-021-09379-y
4. Agrawal, S., Dodis, Y., Vaikuntanathan, V., Wichs, D.: On continual leakage of discrete log representations. In: Sako, K., Sarkar, P. (eds.) ASIACRYPT 2013, Part II. LNCS, vol. 8270, pp. 401–420. Springer, Heidelberg (2013). https://doi.org/10.1007/978-3-642-42045-0_21
5. Belenkiy, M., Chase, M., Kohlweiss, M., Lysyanskaya, A.: P-signatures and noninteractive anonymous credentials. In: Canetti, R. (ed.) TCC 2008. LNCS, vol. 4948, pp. 356–374. Springer, Heidelberg (2008). https://doi.org/10.1007/978-3-540-78524-8_20
6. Bellare, M., Fuchsbauer, G., Scafuro, A.: NIZKs with an Untrusted CRS: Security in the Face of Parameter Subversion. In: Cheon, J.H., Takagi, T. (eds.) ASIACRYPT 2016, Part II. LNCS, vol. 10032, pp. 777–804. Springer, Heidelberg (2016). https://doi.org/10.1007/978-3-662-53890-6_26
7. Boneh, D., Boyen, X.: Short signatures without random oracles and the SDH assumption in bilinear groups. J. Cryptol. **21**(2), 149–177 (2008). https://doi.org/10.1007/s00145-007-9005-7

8. Camenisch, J., Dubovitskaya, M., Haralambiev, K., Kohlweiss, M.: Composable and modular anonymous credentials: definitions and practical constructions. In: Iwata, T., Cheon, J.H. (eds.) ASIACRYPT 2015, Part II. LNCS, vol. 9453, pp. 262–288. Springer, Heidelberg (2015). https://doi.org/10.1007/978-3-662-48800-3_11
9. Campanelli, M., Faonio, A., Fiore, D., Querol, A., Rodríguez, H.: Lunar: a toolbox for more efficient universal and updatable zkSNARKs and commit-and-prove extensions. In: Tibouchi, M., Wang, H. (eds.) ASIACRYPT 2021, Part III. LNCS, vol. 13092, pp. 3–33. Springer, Cham (2021). https://doi.org/10.1007/978-3-030-92078-4_1
10. Campanelli, M., Ganesh, C., Khoshakhlagh, H., Siim, J.: Impossibilities in succinct arguments: black-box extraction and more. In: Duquesne, S., Feo, L.D., Mrabet, N.E. (eds.) AFRICACRYPT 2023. LNCS, vol. 14064, pp. 465–489. Springer, Cham (2023). https://doi.org/10.1007/978-3-031-37679-5_20
11. Catalano, D., Fiore, D.: Vector commitments and their applications. In: Kurosawa, K., Hanaoka, G. (eds.) PKC 2013. LNCS, vol. 7778, pp. 55–72. Springer, Heidelberg (2013). https://doi.org/10.1007/978-3-642-36362-7_5
12. Chiesa, A., Hu, Y., Maller, M., Mishra, P., Vesely, N., Ward, N.: Marlin: preprocessing zkSNARKs with universal and updatable SRS. In: Canteaut, A., Ishai, Y. (eds.) EUROCRYPT 2020, Part I. LNCS, vol. 12105, pp. 738–768. Springer, Cham (2020). https://doi.org/10.1007/978-3-030-45721-1_26
13. Choudhuri, A.R., Jain, A., Jin, Z.: SNARGs for $\mathcal{P}$ from LWE. In: FOCS 2021, Denver, Colorado, USA, pp. 68–79. IEEE, IEEE Computer Society Press (2021)
14. Cramer, R., Damgård, I., Schoenmakers, B.: Proofs of partial knowledge and simplified design of witness hiding protocols. In: Desmedt, Y.G. (ed.) CRYPTO 1994. LNCS, vol. 839, pp. 174–187. Springer, Heidelberg (1994). https://doi.org/10.1007/3-540-48658-5_19
15. Danezis, G., Fournet, C., Groth, J., Kohlweiss, M.: Square span programs with applications to succinct NIZK arguments. In: Sarkar, P., Iwata, T. (eds.) ASIACRYPT 2014, Part I. LNCS, vol. 8873, pp. 532–550. Springer, Heidelberg (2014). https://doi.org/10.1007/978-3-662-45611-8_28
16. Daza, V., González, A., Pindado, Z., Ràfols, C., Silva, J.: Shorter quadratic QA-NIZK proofs. In: Lin, D., Sako, K. (eds.) PKC 2019, Part I. LNCS, vol. 11442, pp. 314–343. Springer, Cham (2019). https://doi.org/10.1007/978-3-030-17253-4_11
17. Fauzi, P., Lipmaa, H., Pindado, Z., Siim, J.: Somewhere statistically binding commitment schemes with applications. In: Borisov, N., Diaz, C. (eds.) FC 2021, Part I. LNCS, vol. 12674, pp. 436–456. Springer, Heidelberg (2021). https://doi.org/10.1007/978-3-662-64322-8_21
18. Feige, U., Lapidot, D., Shamir, A.: Multiple non-interactive zero knowledge proofs based on a single random string (extended abstract). In: 31st FOCS, pp. 308–317. IEEE Computer Society Press (1990). https://doi.org/10.1109/FSCS.1990.89549
19. Fuchsbauer, G.: Subversion-zero-knowledge SNARKs. In: Abdalla, M., Dahab, R. (eds.) PKC 2018, Part I. LNCS, vol. 10769, pp. 315–347. Springer, Cham (2018). https://doi.org/10.1007/978-3-319-76578-5_11
20. Fuchsbauer, G., Kiltz, E., Loss, J.: The algebraic group model and its applications. In: Shacham, H., Boldyreva, A. (eds.) CRYPTO 2018, Part II. LNCS, vol. 10992, pp. 33–62. Springer, Cham (2018). https://doi.org/10.1007/978-3-319-96881-0_2
21. Gabizon, A., Williamson, Z.J., Ciobotaru, O.: PLONK: Permutations over lagrange-bases for oecumenical noninteractive arguments of knowledge. Cryptology ePrint Archive, Report 2019/953 (2019). https://eprint.iacr.org/2019/953

22. Ganesh, C., Khoshakhlagh, H., Parisella, R.: NIWI and new notions of extraction for algebraic languages. In: Galdi, C., Jarecki, S. (eds.) SCN 2022. LNCS, vol. 13409, pp. 687–710. Springer, Cham (2022). https://doi.org/10.1007/978-3-031-14791-3_30
23. Gennaro, R., Gentry, C., Parno, B., Raykova, M.: Quadratic span programs and succinct NIZKs without PCPs. In: Johansson, T., Nguyen, P.Q. (eds.) EUROCRYPT 2013. LNCS, vol. 7881, pp. 626–645. Springer, Heidelberg (2013). https://doi.org/10.1007/978-3-642-38348-9_37
24. Gentry, C., Wichs, D.: Separating succinct non-interactive arguments from all falsifiable assumptions. In: Fortnow, L., Vadhan, S.P. (eds.) 43rd ACM STOC, pp. 99–108. ACM Press (2011). https://doi.org/10.1145/1993636.1993651
25. González, A., Hevia, A., Ràfols, C.: QA-NIZK arguments in asymmetric groups: new tools and new constructions. In: Iwata, T., Cheon, J.H. (eds.) ASIACRYPT 2015, Part I. LNCS, vol. 9452, pp. 605–629. Springer, Heidelberg (2015). https://doi.org/10.1007/978-3-662-48797-6_25
26. González, A., Ràfols, C.: Shorter pairing-based arguments under standard assumptions. In: Galbraith, S.D., Moriai, S. (eds.) ASIACRYPT 2019, Part III. LNCS, vol. 11923, pp. 728–757. Springer, Cham (2019). https://doi.org/10.1007/978-3-030-34618-8_25
27. González, A., Zacharakis, A.: Fully-succinct publicly verifiable delegation from constant-size assumptions. In: Nissim, K., Waters, B. (eds.) TCC 2021, Part I. LNCS, vol. 13042, pp. 529–557. Springer, Cham (2021). https://doi.org/10.1007/978-3-030-90459-3_18
28. Groth, J.: Short pairing-based non-interactive zero-knowledge arguments. In: Abe, M. (ed.) ASIACRYPT 2010. LNCS, vol. 6477, pp. 321–340. Springer, Heidelberg (2010). https://doi.org/10.1007/978-3-642-17373-8_19
29. Groth, J.: On the size of pairing-based non-interactive arguments. In: Fischlin, M., Coron, J.-S. (eds.) EUROCRYPT 2016. LNCS, vol. 9666, pp. 305–326. Springer, Heidelberg (2016). https://doi.org/10.1007/978-3-662-49896-5_11
30. Groth, J., Kohlweiss, M., Maller, M., Meiklejohn, S., Miers, I.: Updatable and universal common reference strings with applications to zk-SNARKs. In: Shacham, H., Boldyreva, A. (eds.) CRYPTO 2018. LNCS, vol. 10993, pp. 698–728. Springer, Cham (2018). https://doi.org/10.1007/978-3-319-96878-0_24
31. Groth, J., Sahai, A.: Efficient non-interactive proof systems for bilinear groups. In: Smart, N. (ed.) EUROCRYPT 2008. LNCS, vol. 4965, pp. 415–432. Springer, Heidelberg (2008). https://doi.org/10.1007/978-3-540-78967-3_24
32. Hubacek, P., Wichs, D.: On the communication complexity of secure function evaluation with long output. In: Roughgarden, T. (ed.) ITCS 2015, pp. 163–172. ACM (2015). https://doi.org/10.1145/2688073.2688105
33. Izabachène, M., Libert, B., Vergnaud, D.: Block-wise P-signatures and non-interactive anonymous credentials with efficient attributes. In: Chen, L. (ed.) 13th IMA International Conference on Cryptography and Coding. LNCS, vol. 7089, pp. 431–450. Springer, Heidelberg (Dec (2011). https://doi.org/10.1007/978-3-642-25516-8_26
34. Jain, A., Lin, H., Sahai, A.: Indistinguishability obfuscation from well-founded assumptions. In: Khuller, S., Williams, V.V. (eds.) 53rd ACM STOC, pp. 60–73. ACM Press (2021). https://doi.org/10.1145/3406325.3451093
35. Jain, A., Jin, Z.: Indistinguishability obfuscation via mathematical proofs of equivalence. In: 63rd FOCS, pp. 1023–1034. IEEE Computer Society Press (2022). https://doi.org/10.1109/FOCS54457.2022.00100

36. Jutla, C.S., Roy, A.: Shorter quasi-adaptive NIZK proofs for linear subspaces. In: Sako, K., Sarkar, P. (eds.) ASIACRYPT 2013, Part I. LNCS, vol. 8269, pp. 1–20. Springer, Heidelberg (2013). https://doi.org/10.1007/978-3-642-42033-7_1
37. Kalai, Y.T., Paneth, O., Yang, L.: How to delegate computations publicly. In: Charikar, M., Cohen, E. (eds.) 51st ACM STOC, pp. 1115–1124. ACM Press (2019). https://doi.org/10.1145/3313276.3316411
38. Kalai, Y.T., Raz, R., Rothblum, R.D.: How to delegate computations: the power of no-signaling proofs. In: Shmoys, D.B. (ed.) 46th ACM STOC, pp. 485–494. ACM Press (2014). https://doi.org/10.1145/2591796.2591809
39. Kate, A., Zaverucha, G.M., Goldberg, I.: Constant-size commitments to polynomials and their applications. In: Abe, M. (ed.) ASIACRYPT 2010. LNCS, vol. 6477, pp. 177–194. Springer, Heidelberg (2010). https://doi.org/10.1007/978-3-642-17373-8_11
40. Kiltz, E., Wee, H.: Quasi-adaptive NIZK for linear subspaces revisited. In: Oswald, E., Fischlin, M. (eds.) EUROCRYPT 2015, Part II. LNCS, vol. 9057, pp. 101–128. Springer, Heidelberg (2015). https://doi.org/10.1007/978-3-662-46803-6_4
41. Libert, B., Yung, M.: Concise mercurial vector commitments and independent zero-knowledge sets with short proofs. In: Micciancio, D. (ed.) TCC 2010. LNCS, vol. 5978, pp. 499–517. Springer, Heidelberg (2010). https://doi.org/10.1007/978-3-642-11799-2_30
42. Lindell, Y.: Parallel coin-tossing and constant-round secure two-party computation. In: Kilian, J. (ed.) CRYPTO 2001. LNCS, vol. 2139, pp. 171–189. Springer, Heidelberg (2001). https://doi.org/10.1007/3-540-44647-8_10
43. Lipmaa, H.: Progression-free sets and sublinear pairing-based non-interactive zero-knowledge arguments. In: Cramer, R. (ed.) TCC 2012. LNCS, vol. 7194, pp. 169–189. Springer, Heidelberg (2012). https://doi.org/10.1007/978-3-642-28914-9_10
44. Lipmaa, H.: Succinct non-interactive zero knowledge arguments from span programs and linear error-correcting codes. In: Sako, K., Sarkar, P. (eds.) ASIACRYPT 2013, Part I. LNCS, vol. 8269, pp. 41–60. Springer, Heidelberg (2013). https://doi.org/10.1007/978-3-642-42033-7_3
45. Lipmaa, H.: On Black-Box Knowledge-Sound Commit-And-Prove SNARKs. Technical report 2023/?, IACR (2023). https://eprint.iacr.org/2023/?
46. Lipmaa, H., Pavlyk, K.: Gentry-Wichs is tight: a falsifiable non-adaptively sound SNARG. In: Tibouchi, M., Wang, H. (eds.) ASIACRYPT 2021. LNCS, vol. 13092, pp. 34–64. Springer, Cham (2021). https://doi.org/10.1007/978-3-030-92078-4_2
47. Lipmaa, H., Siim, J., Zajac, M.: Counting vampires: from univariate sumcheck to updatable ZK-SNARK. In: Agrawal, S., Lin, D. (eds.) ASIACRYPT 2022, Part II. LNCS, vol. 13792, pp. 249–278. Springer, Heidelberg (2022). https://doi.org/10.1007/978-3-031-22966-4_9
48. Okamoto, T., Pietrzak, K., Waters, B., Wichs, D.: New realizations of somewhere statistically binding hashing and positional accumulators. In: Iwata, T., Cheon, J.H. (eds.) ASIACRYPT 2015, Part I. LNCS, vol. 9452, pp. 121–145. Springer, Heidelberg (2015). https://doi.org/10.1007/978-3-662-48797-6_6
49. Paneth, O., Rothblum, G.N.: On zero-testable homomorphic encryption and publicly verifiable non-interactive arguments. In: Kalai, Y., Reyzin, L. (eds.) TCC 2017, Part II. LNCS, vol. 10678, pp. 283–315. Springer, Cham (2017). https://doi.org/10.1007/978-3-319-70503-3_9
50. Parno, B., Howell, J., Gentry, C., Raykova, M.: Pinocchio: nearly practical verifiable computation. In: 2013 IEEE Symposium on Security and Privacy, pp. 238–252. IEEE Computer Society Press (2013). https://doi.org/10.1109/SP.2013.47

51. Ràfols, C., Zapico, A.: An algebraic framework for universal and updatable SNARKs. In: Malkin, T., Peikert, C. (eds.) CRYPTO 2021. LNCS, vol. 12825, pp. 774–804. Springer, Cham (2021). https://doi.org/10.1007/978-3-030-84242-0_27
52. Sahai, A., Waters, B.: How to use indistinguishability obfuscation: deniable encryption, and more. In: Shmoys, D.B. (ed.) 46th ACM STOC, pp. 475–484. ACM Press (2014). https://doi.org/10.1145/2591796.2591825
53. Waters, B., Wu, D.J.: Batch arguments for sfNP and more from standard bilinear group assumptions. In: Dodis, Y., Shrimpton, T. (eds.) CRYPTO 2022, Part II. LNCS, vol. 13508, pp. 433–463. Springer, Heidelberg (2022). https://doi.org/10.1007/978-3-031-15979-4_15
54. Zhandry, M.: To label, or not to label (in generic groups). In: Dodis, Y., Shrimpton, T. (eds.) CRYPTO 2022, Part III. LNCS, vol. 13509, pp. 66–96. Springer, Heidelberg (2022). https://doi.org/10.1007/978-3-031-15982-4_3
55. Zhang, C., Zhou, H.S., Katz, J.: An analysis of the algebraic group model. In: Agrawal, S., Lin, D. (eds.) ASIACRYPT 2022, Part IV. LNCS, vol. 13794, pp. 310–322. Springer, Heidelberg (2022). https://doi.org/10.1007/978-3-031-22972-5_11

Protostar: Generic Efficient Accumulation/Folding for Special-Sound Protocols

Benedikt Bünz[1,2] and Binyi Chen[1](✉)

[1] Espresso Systems, Middletown, USA
binyi@espressosys.com
[2] New York University, New York, USA

Abstract. Accumulation is a simple yet powerful primitive that enables incrementally verifiable computation (IVC) without the need for recursive SNARKs. We provide a generic, efficient accumulation (or folding) scheme for any $(2k-1)$-move special-sound protocol with a verifier that checks ℓ degree-d equations. The accumulation verifier only performs $k+2$ elliptic curve multiplications and $k + d + O(1)$ field/hash operations. Using the compiler from BCLMS21 (Crypto 21), this enables building efficient IVC schemes where the recursive circuit only depends on the number of rounds and the verifier degree of the underlying special-sound protocol but not the proof size or the verifier time. We use our generic accumulation compiler to build PROTOSTAR. PROTOSTAR is a non-uniform IVC scheme for Plonk that supports high-degree gates and (vector) lookups. The recursive circuit is dominated by 3 group scalar multiplications and a hash of d^* field elements, where d^* is the degree of the highest gate. The scheme does not require a trusted setup or pairings, and the prover does not need to compute any FFTs. The prover in each accumulation/IVC step is also only logarithmic in the number of supported circuits and independent of the table size in the lookup.

1 Introduction

Incrementally Verifiable Computation [30] is a powerful primitive that enables a possibly infinite computation to be run, such that the correctness of the state of the computation can be verified at any point. IVC, and it's generalization to DAGs, PCD [12], have many applications, including distributed computation [3,13], blockchains [5,18], verifiable delay functions [4], verifiable photo editing [25], and SNARKs for machine-computations [2]. An IVC-based VDF construction is the current candidate VDF for Ethereum [19]. One of the most exciting applications of IVC and PCD is the ZK-EVM. This is an effort to build a proof system that can prove that Ethereum blocks, as they exist today, are valid [10].

Accumulation and Folding. Historically, IVC was built from recursive SNARKs, proving that the previous computation step had a valid SNARK that proves correctness up to that point. Recently, an exciting new approach was initiated

J. Guo and R. Steinfeld (Eds.): ASIACRYPT 2023, LNCS 14439, pp. 77–110, 2023.
https://doi.org/10.1007/978-981-99-8724-5_3

by Halo [6] and has led to a series of significant advances [8,9,22]. The idea is related to batch verification. Instead of verifying a SNARK at every step of the computation, we can instead *accumulate* the SNARK verification check with previous checks. We define an *accumulator*[1] such that we can combine a new SNARK and an old accumulator into a new accumulator. Checking or *deciding* the new accumulator implies that all previously accumulated SNARKs were valid. Now the recursive statement just needs to ensure the accumulation was performed correctly. Amazingly, this accumulation step can be significantly cheaper than SNARK verification [6,9]. Even more surprising, this process does not even require a SNARK but instead can be instantiated with a non-succinct NARK [8], as long as there exists an efficient accumulation scheme for that NARK. The most efficient accumulation (aka folding) scheme constructions yield IVC constructions, where the recursive circuit is dominated by as few as 2 elliptic curve scalar multiplications [8,22]. These constructions only require the discrete logarithm assumption in the random oracle model and, unlike many efficient SNARK-based IVCs, do not require a trusted setup, pairings, or FFTs. These constructions build an accumulation scheme for one fixed (but universal) R1CS language by taking a random linear combination between the accumulator and a new proof. R1CS is a minimal expression of NP, defined by three matrices A, B, C, that close resembles arithmetic circuits with addition and multiplication gates. However, it has limited flexibility, especially as the current constructions require fixing R1CS matrices that are used for all computation steps. These limitations are especially problematic for ZK-EVMs. In a ZK-EVM, each VM instruction (OP-CODE) is encoded in a different circuit. Each circuit uses high-degree gates, instead of just multiplication, and so-called lookup gates [16]. These lookup gates enable looking up that a circuit value is in some table, simplifying range proofs and bit-operations. These R1CS-based accumulation schemes contrast non-IVC SNARK developments, with an increased focus on high-degree gate [11,16] and lookup support [15]. For lookups, a recent line of work has shown that if the table can be pre-computed, we can perform n lookups in a table of size T in time $O(n \log n)$, independent of T [14,27,33,34].

More Expressive Accumulation. There have been efforts to build accumulation schemes that overcome the limitations of fixed R1CS. SuperNova [21] enables selecting the appropriate R1CS instance at runtime without a recursive circuit that is linear in all R1CS instances. The approach, however, still has limitations. The recursive circuit still requires many (though a constant number of) hashes and a hash-to-group gadget, and additionally, the accumulator, and thus the final proof, is still linear in the total size of all instances.

Sangria [24] describes an accumulation scheme for a Plonk-like [16] constraint system with degree-2 gates. It also proposes a solution for higher-degree gates in the future work section but without security proof. Moreover, as the gate degree d increases, the number of group operations in Sangria grows by a factor of d, which cancels out the advantages of using the more expressive high-degree

[1] Unrelated to set accumulators.

gates. Origami [35] recently introduced a folding scheme for lookups using a product check and degree 7 polynomials. These accumulation schemes are built from simple underlying protocols performing a linear combination between an accumulator and a proof. However, the constructions seem ad hoc and need individual security proof. This leads us to our main research questions:

Recipe for accumulation. Is there a general recipe for building accumulation schemes? Can we formalize this recipe, simplifying the task of constructing secure and efficient accumulation schemes?

Efficient accumulation for ZK-EVM. Can we build an accumulation/folding scheme for a language that combines the benefits of the most advanced proof systems today? Can we support multiple circuits, high-degree, and lookup gates?

We answer both questions positively. Firstly we show a general compiler that takes any $(2k-1)$-move special-sound interactive argument for an NP-complete relation $\mathcal{R}_{\mathsf{NP}}$ with an algebraic degree d verifier and construct an efficient IVC-scheme from it. This is done in 4 simple steps.

1. We compress the prover message by committing to them in a homomorphic commitment scheme.
2. Then we apply the Fiat-Shamir transform to yield a secure NARK. [1,31]
3. We build a simple and efficient accumulation scheme that samples a random challenge α and takes a linear combination between the current accumulator and the new NARK.
4. We apply the compiler by [8] to yield a secure IVC scheme.

The recursive circuit of this transformation is dominated by only $d + k - 1$ scalar multiplications in the additive group of the commitment scheme[2] for a protocol with k prover messages and a degree d verifier. For R1CS, where $k = 1$ and $d = 2$, this yields the same protocol and efficiency as Nova [22]. We can further reduce the size of the recursive circuit to only $k + 2$ group scalar multiplication, by compressing all verification equations using a random linear combination.

Efficient Simple Protocols for $\mathcal{R}_{mplkup}$. Equipped with this compiler, we design PROTOSTAR, a simple and efficient IVC scheme for a highly expressive language $\mathcal{R}_{\mathsf{mplkup}}$ that supports multiple non-uniform circuits and enables high degree and lookup gates. The schemes can be instantiated from any linearly homomorphic vector commitment, e.g., the discrete logarithm-based Pedersen commitment [26], and do not require a trusted setup or the computation of large FFTs. The protocol has several advantages over prior schemes:

Non-uniform IVC without overhead. Each iteration has a program counter **pc** that selects one out of I circuits. Part of the circuit constrains **pc**; e.g.,

[2] When instantiated with elliptic curve Pedersen commitments, this translates to $d + k - 1$ elliptic curve multiplications. This is usually the largest component of the recursive statement.

pc could depend on the iteration or indicate which instruction within a VM is executed. The IVC-prover, including the recursive statement, only requires one exponentiation per non-zero bit in the witness. The prover's computation is independent of I.

Flexible high degree gates. Our protocol supports Plonk-like constraint systems with degree d gates instead of just addition and multiplication. The recursive statement consists of 3 group scalar multiplications and $d + O(1)$ hash and field operations. Unlike in traditional Plonk, there is no additional cost for additional gate types (of degree less than d) and additional selectors. This enables a high level of non-uniformity, even within a circuit.

Lookups, linear and independent of table size. PROTOSTAR supports lookup gates that ensure a value is in some precomputed table T. In each computation step, the prover commits to 2 vectors of length ℓ_{lk}, where ℓ_{lk} is the number of lookups. The prover, in each step, is independent of the table size (assuming free indexing in T). We also support tables that store tuples of size v using 1 additional challenge computations within the recursive circuit.

Table 1. The comparison between IVCs.

	PROTOSTAR	HyperNova	SuperNova
Language	Degree d Plonk/CCS	Degree d CCS	R1CS (degree 2)
Non-uniform	yes	no	yes
P native	$\lvert\mathbf{w}\rvert\,\mathbb{G}$ $O(\lvert\mathbf{w}\rvert d\log^2 d)\,\mathbb{F}$	$\lvert\mathbf{w}\rvert\,\mathbb{G}$ $O(\lvert\mathbf{w}\rvert d\log^2 d)\,\mathbb{F}$	$\lvert\mathbf{w}\rvert\,\mathbb{G}$
extra P native w/ lookup	$O(\lvert\ell_{\mathsf{lk}}\rvert)\,\mathbb{G}$	$O(T)\,\mathbb{F}$	N/A
P recursive	$3\mathbb{G}$ $(d+O(1))\mathsf{H}+\mathsf{H}_{\mathsf{in}}$ $(d+O(1))\,\mathbb{F}$	$1\mathbb{G}$ $d\log n\mathsf{H}+\mathsf{H}_{\mathsf{in}}$ $O(d\log n)\mathbb{F}$	$2\mathbb{G}$ $\mathsf{H}_{\mathsf{in}}+O(1)\mathsf{H}+1\mathsf{H}_{\mathbb{G}}$
extra P recursive w/ lookup	$1\mathsf{H}$	$O(\log T)\,\mathsf{H}$ $O(\ell_{\mathsf{lk}}\log T)\,\mathbb{F}$	N/A

Our protocols are built of multiple small building blocks. In the protocol for high-degree gates, the prover simply sends the witness, and the degree d verifier checks the circuit with degree d gates. For lookup, we leverage an insight by Haböck [17] on logarithmic derivates. This yields a protocol where a prover performing ℓ_{lk} in a table of size T only needs to commit to two vectors of length ℓ_{lk}, independent of T. This is the most efficient lookup protocol today. While the verification is linear time, it is low degree (2) and thus compatible with our generic compiler. Combining all these yields PROTOSTAR, a new IVC-scheme for $\mathcal{R}_{\mathsf{mplkup}}$. We compare PROTOSTAR, with SuperNova [21] and HyperNova [20], in Table 1 (for more detail see Corollary 1): P native is the running time of the accumulation prover and P recursive refers to the cost of implementing the accumulation verifier as a circuit. In the table, $|\mathbf{w}|$ is the number of non-zero entries of the witness for circuit i, and ℓ_{lk} is the number of lookups in a table of size T. $\mathbb{G}$ is the cost of a group scalar multiplication. $\mathbb{F}$ is the cost of a field multiplication. $d\,\mathsf{H}$ denotes the cost of hashing d λ-bit numbers. We assume that the cost scales linearly with the size of the input and output. In PROTOSTAR d field elements are hashed once and in HyperNova d field elements are hashed $\log(n)$ times. $\mathsf{H}_{\mathbb{G}}$ is the cost of a hash-to-group function. H_{in} is the cost of hashing the public input and the accumulator instance. Note that the $O(1)\,\mathsf{H}$ in SuperNova's recursive circuit involves constant number of hashes to the input of two accumulator instances and one circuit verification key, by using multiset-based offline memory checking in a circuit [28].

Concurrent Work. In a paper concurrent with this work, Kothapalli and Setty [20] introduce an IVC for high degree relations. They use a generalization of R1CS called customizable constraint systems (CCS) [29] that covers the Plonkish relations. It also enables gates with a high additive fan-in. PROTOSTAR also has no restriction to the fan-in an individual gate has, but we subsequently showed that our compiler can also be directly applied to CCS (See full version [7]). HyperNova is based on so-called multi-folding schemes. They also provide a lookup argument suitable for recursive arguments. However, they do not explicitly explain how to integrate lookup to Plonk/CCS in their IVC scheme or provide any explicit constructions for non-uniform computations. Their scheme is built using sumchecks [23] and the resulting IVC recursive circuit is dominated by 1 group scalar multiplication, $d\log n + \ell_{\mathsf{in}}$ hash operations and $O(d\log n + \ell_{\mathsf{in}})$ field multiplications where d is the custom gate degree, n is the number of gates and ℓ_{in} is the public input length. In comparison, our IVC recursive circuit, even with lookup and non-uniformity support, is only dominated by 3 group scalar multiplications and $O(\ell_{\mathsf{in}} + d)$ field/hash operations, entirely independent of n. The 2 additional group operations compared to HyperNova are likely offset by the additional lookup support [32] and the significantly fewer hashes and non-native field operations (d vs. $d\log(n)$). A detailed comparison is given in Table 1.

For a lookup relation with table size T and ℓ_{lk} lookup gates, their accumulation/folding scheme leads to an accumulation prover whose work is dominated by $O(T)$ field operations and an accumulation verifier whose work is dominated by $O(\ell_{\mathsf{lk}}\log T)$ field operations and $O(\log T)$ hashes. This is undesirable when the table size $T \gg \ell_{\mathsf{lk}}$. In comparison, our scheme has prover complexity $O(\ell_{\mathsf{lk}})$ and the verifier is only dominated by 3 group scalar multiplications, 2 hashes and 2 field multiplications. Moreover, the lookup support adds almost no overhead to the IVC scheme for high-degree Plonk relations. In particular, it adds no group scalar multiplications. Lastly, their lookup scheme does not support vector-valued lookups, which is essential for applications like ZK-EVM and encoding bit-wise operations in circuits.

1.1 Technical Overview

Given an NP-complete relation $\mathcal{R}$, we introduce a generic framework for constructing efficient incremental verifiable computation (IVC) schemes with predicates expressed in $\mathcal{R}$. For $\mathcal{R}$ being the non-uniform Plonkup circuit satisfiability relation, we obtain an efficient (non-uniform) IVC scheme for proving correct program executions on stateful machines (e.g., EVM). The framework starts by designing a simple special-sound protocol Π_{sps} for relation $\mathcal{R}$, which is easy to analyze. Next, we use a generic compiler to transform Π_{sps} into a Non-interactive Argument of Knowledge Scheme (NARK) whose verification predicate is easy to accumulate/fold. Finally, we build an efficient accumulation/folding scheme for the NARK verifier, and apply the generic compiler from [8] to obtain the IVC/PCD scheme for relation $\mathcal{R}$. We describe the workflow in Fig. 1.

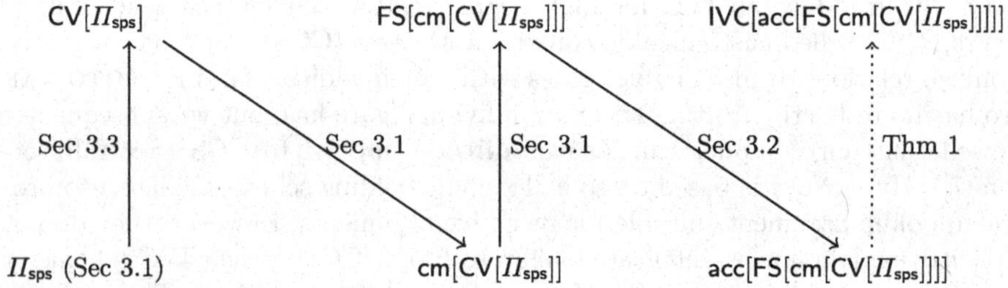

Fig. 1. The workflow for building an IVC from a special sound protocol. We start from a special-sound protocol Π_{sps} for an NP-complete relation $\mathcal{R}_{\mathsf{NP}}$, and transform it to $\mathsf{CV}[\Pi_{\mathsf{sps}}]$ with a compressed verifier check. $\mathsf{CV}[\Pi_{\mathsf{sps}}]$ is converted to a NARK $\mathsf{FS}[\mathsf{cm}[\mathsf{CV}[\Pi_{\mathsf{sps}}]]]$ via commit-and-open and the Fiat-Shamir transform. We then build a generic accumulation scheme for the NARK and apply Theorem 1 from [8] to obtain the IVC scheme. This last connection is dotted as it requires heuristically replacing random oracles with cryptographic hash functions.

The paper begins by describing the compiler from special-sound protocols to NARKs in Sect. 3, and presents an efficient accumulation scheme for the compiled NARK verifier in Sect. 3.2. Next, we describe simple and efficient special-sound protocols for Plonkup circuit-satisfiability relations and extend it to support non-uniform computation in Sect. 5. Similarly, we extend the CCS relation [29] to support non-uniform computation and lookup (see full version [7]). We give an overview of our approach below.

Efficient IVCs from Special-Sound Protocols. Let Π_{sps} be any *multi-round* special-sound protocol for some relation $\mathcal{R}$, in which the verifier is *algebraic*, that is, the verifier algorithm only checks algebraic equations over the input and the prover messages. E.g., the following naive protocol for the Hadamard product relation over vectors $\mathbf{a}, \mathbf{b}, \mathbf{c} \in \mathbb{F}^n$ is special-sound and has a degree-2 algebraic verifier: The prover simply sends the vectors $\mathbf{a}$, $\mathbf{b}$, $\mathbf{c}$ to the verifier, and the verifier checks that $a_i \cdot b_i = c_i$ for all $i \in [n]$. However, as shown in the example, the prover message can be large in Π_{sps} and the folding scheme can be expensive if we directly accumulate the verifier predicate. Inspired by the splitting accumulation scheme [8], to enable efficient accumulation/folding, we split each prover message into a short instance and a large opening, where the short instance is built from the homomorphic commitment to the prover message. Next, we use the Fiat-Shamir transform to compile the protocol into a NARK where the verifier challenges are generated from a random oracle.

Now we can view the NARK transcript as an accumulator (or a relaxed NP instance-witness pair in the language of folding schemes), where the accumulator instance consists of the prover message commitments and the verifier challenges; while the accumulator witness consists of the prover messages (i.e., the opening to the commitments). Note we also need to introduce an error vector/commitment into the accumulator witness/instance to absorb the "noise" that arises after each accumulation/folding step.

In the accumulation scheme, given two accumulators (or NARK proofs), the prover folds the witnesses and the instances of both accumulators via a random linear combination and generates a list of d "error-correcting terms" as accumulation proof (d is the degree of the NARK verifier); the verifier only needs to check that the folded accumulator instance is consistent with the accumulation proof and the original instances being folded, both of which are small. After finishing all the accumulation steps, a decider applies a final check to the accumulator, scrutinizing that (i) the accumulator witness is consistent with the commitments in the accumulator instance, and (ii) the "relaxed" NARK verifier check still passes. Here by "relaxed" we mean that the algebraic equation also involves the error vector in the accumulator. If the decider accepts, this implies that all accumulated NARKs were valid and thus that all accumulated statements are in $\mathcal{R}$ (and the prover knows witnesses for these statements).

Finally, given the accumulation scheme, if the relation $\mathcal{R}$ is NP-complete, we can apply the compiler in [8] to obtain an efficient IVC scheme with predicates expressed in $\mathcal{R}$.

In Theorem 3, we show that for any $(2k-1)$-move[3] special-sound protocols with degree-d verifiers, the resulting IVC recursive circuit only involves $k + d + O(1)$ hashes, $k+1$ non-native field operations and $k+d-1$ commitment group scalar multiplications. We also introduce a generic approach for further reducing the number of group operations to $k+2$ in Sect. 3.3. This is favorable for $d \geq 3$. The idea is to compress all ℓ degree d verification checks into a single verification check using a random linear combination with powers of a challenge β. This means that error-correcting terms are field elements and, thus, can be sent directly without committing to them. The prover also sends a single commitment to powers of β and powers of $\beta^{\sqrt{\ell}}$. The verification equation uses one power of β and one power of $\beta^{\sqrt{\ell}}$, which increases the degree of the verification check to $d+2$. The verifier also checks the correctness of the powers of β using $2\sqrt{\ell}$ degree 2 checks.

[3] k prover messages, $k-1$ challenges.

Special-Sound Protocols for (Non-uniform) Plonkup Relations. Given the generic compiler above, our ultimate goal of constructing a (non-uniform) IVC scheme for zkEVM becomes much easier. It is now sufficient to design a multi-round special-sound protocol for the (non-uniform) Plonkup relation. We describe the components of the special-sound protocol in Fig. 2. Note we also extend CCS relation [29] to support lookup and non-uniform computation and build a special-sound protocol for it (See Fig. 2). Recall that a Plonkup circuit-satisfiability relation consists of three modular relations, namely, (i) a high-degree gate relation checking that each custom gate is satisfied; (ii) a permutation (wiring-identity) relation checking that different gate values are consistent if the same wire connects them, and (iii) a lookup relation checking that a subset of gate values belongs to a preprocessed table. The special-sound protocols for the permutation and high-degree gate relations are trivial, where the prover directly sends the witness to the verifier, and the verifier checks that the permutation/high-degree gate relation holds. The degree of the permutation check is only 1, and the degree of the gate-check is the highest degree in the custom gate formula.

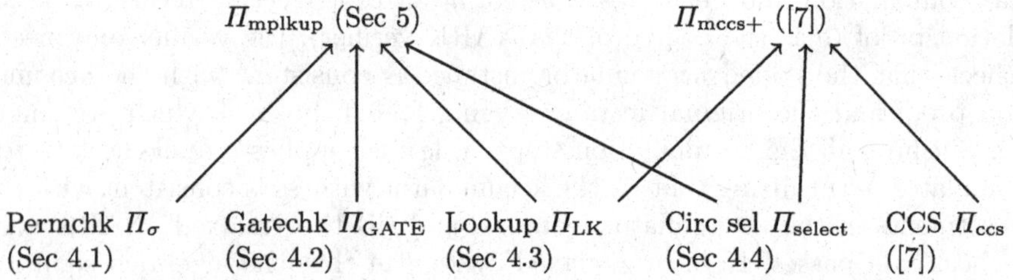

Fig. 2. The special-sound protocols for PROTOSTAR and PROTOSTAR$_{\mathsf{ccs}}$. The special-sound protocol Π_{mplkup} for the multi-circuit Plonkup relation $\mathcal{R}_{\mathsf{mplkup}}$ consists of the sub-protocols for permutation, high-degree custom gate, lookup, and circuit selection relations. The special-sound protocol $\Pi_{\mathsf{mccs+}}$ for the extended CCS relation $\mathcal{R}_{\mathsf{mccs+}}$ consists of the sub-protocols for lookup, circuit selection, as well as the CCS relation [29]. From Π_{mplkup} or $\Pi_{\mathsf{mccs+}}$, we can apply the workflow described in Fig. 1 to obtain the IVC schemes PROTOSTAR or PROTOSTAR$_{\mathsf{ccs}}$.

The special-sound protocol for the lookup relation $\mathcal{R}_{\mathsf{LK}}$ is more interesting as the statement of the lookup relation is not algebraic. Inspired by the log-derivative lookup scheme [17], in Sect. 4.3, we design a simple 3-move special-sound protocol Π_{LK} for $\mathcal{R}_{\mathsf{LK}}$, in which the verifier degree is only 2. A great feature of Π_{LK} is that the number of non-zero elements in the prover messages is only proportional to the number of lookups, but independent of the table size. Thus the IVC prover complexity for computing the prover message commitments is independent of the table size, which is advantageous when the table size is much larger than the witness size. However, the prover work for computing the error terms is not independent of the table size because the accumulator is not sparse. Fortunately, we observe that the prover can efficiently update the error term commitments without recomputing the error term vectors from scratch, thus preserving the efficiency of the accumulation prover. Moreover, we extend Π_{LK} in Sect. 4.3 to further support vector-valued lookup, where each table entry is a vector of elements. This feature is useful in applications like zkEVM and for simulating bit operations in circuits.

Given the special-sound protocols for permutation/high-degree gate/lookup relations, the special-sound protocol Π_{plonkup} for Plonkup is just a parallel composition of the three protocols. Furthermore, in Sect. 5, we apply a simple trick to support *non-uniform* IVC. More precisely, let $\{\mathcal{C}_i\}_{i=1}^{I}$ be I different branch circuits (e.g., the set of supported instructions in EVM), let $\mathsf{pi} := (pc, \mathsf{pi}')$ be the public input where $pc \in [I]$ is a program counter indicating which instruction/branch circuit is going to be executed in the next IVC step. Our goal is to prove that $(\mathsf{pi}, \mathbf{w})$ is in the relation $\mathcal{R}_{\mathsf{mplkup}}$ in the sense that $\mathcal{C}_{pc}(\mathsf{pi}, \mathbf{w}) = 0$ for witness $\mathbf{w}$. The relation statement can also add additional constraints on pc depending on the applications. The special-sound protocol for $\mathcal{R}_{\mathsf{mplkup}}$ is almost identical to Π_{plonkup} for the Plonkup relation, except that the prover further sends a bool vector $\mathbf{b} \in \mathbb{F}^I$, and the verifier uses $2I$ degree 2 equations to check that $b_{pc} = 1$ and $b_i = 0 \forall i \neq pc$. Additionally, each algebraic equation $\mathcal{G}$ checked in Π_{plonkup} is replaced with $\sum_{i=1}^{I} \mathcal{G}_i \cdot b_i$ where $\mathcal{G}_i$ $(1 \le i \le I)$ is the corresponding gate in the i-th branch circuit. The resulting special-sound protocol has 3 moves, and the verifier degree is $d+1$, where d is the highest degree of the custom gates. This means that the IVC scheme for the non-uniform Plonkup relation adds negligible overhead to that for the Plonkup relation.

2 Preliminaries

The definitions of special-sound protocols and non-interactive arguments follow from [1]. We defer the definition of Fiat-Shamir transform and commitment schemes to the full version [7].

Lemma 1 (Fiat-Shamir transform of Special-sound Protocols [1]**).** *The Fiat-Shamir transform of a $(\alpha_1, \ldots, \alpha_\mu)$-out-of-$N$ special-sound interactive proof Π is knowledge sound with knowledge error*

$$\kappa_{\mathsf{fs}}(Q) = (Q+1)\kappa$$

where $\kappa = 1 - \prod(1 - \frac{\alpha_i}{N})$ is the knowledge error of the interactive proof Π.

2.1 Incremental Verifiable Computation (IVC)

We adapt and simplify the definition from [8,22].

Definition 1 (IVC). *An incremental verifiable computation (IVC) scheme for function predicates expressed in a circuit-satisfiability relation $\mathcal{R}_{\mathsf{NP}}$ is a tuple of algorithms $\mathsf{IVC} = (\mathsf{P}_{\mathsf{IVC}}, \mathsf{V}_{\mathsf{IVC}})$ with the following syntax and properties:*

- $\mathsf{P}_{\mathsf{IVC}}(m, z_0, z_m, z_{m-1}, \mathbf{w}_{\mathsf{loc}}, \pi_{m-1}]) \to \pi_m$. *The IVC prover $\mathsf{P}_{\mathsf{IVC}}$ takes as input a program output z_m at step m, local data $\mathbf{w}_{\mathsf{loc}}$, initial input z_0, previous program output z_{m-1} and proof π_{m-1} and outputs a new IVC proof π_m.*

– $\mathsf{V}_{\mathsf{IVC}}(m, z_0, z_m, \pi_m) \rightarrow b$. *The IVC verifier* $\mathsf{V}_{\mathsf{IVC}}$ *takes the initial input* z_0*, the output* z_m *at step* m*, and an IVC proof* π_m*, 'accepts' by outputting* $b = 0$ *and 'rejects' otherwise.*

The scheme IVC *has perfect adversarial completeness if for any function predicate* ϕ *expressible in* $\mathcal{R}_{\mathsf{NP}}$*, and any, possibly adversarially created,* $(m, z_0, z_m, , z_{m-1}, \mathbf{w}_{\mathsf{loc}}, \pi_{m-1})$ *such that*

$$\phi(z_0, z_m, z_{m-1}, \mathbf{w}_{\mathsf{loc}}) \wedge (\mathsf{V}_{\mathsf{IVC}}(m-1, z_0, z_{m-1}, \pi_{m-1}) = 0)$$

it holds that $\mathsf{V}_{\mathsf{IVC}}(m, z_0, z_m, \pi_m)$ *accepts for proof* $\pi_m \leftarrow \mathsf{P}_{\mathsf{IVC}}(m, z_0, z_{m-1}, z_m, \mathbf{w}_{\mathsf{loc}}, \pi_{m-1})$.

The scheme IVC *has knowledge soundness if for every expected polynomial-time adversary* P^**, there exists an expected polynomial-time extractor* $\mathsf{Ext}_{\mathsf{P}^*}$ *such that*

$$\Pr\left[\begin{array}{c} \mathsf{V}_{\mathsf{IVC}}(m, z_0, z, \pi_m) = 0 \wedge \\ ([\exists i \in [m], \neg\phi(z_0, z_i, z_{i-1}, \mathbf{w}_i)] \\ \vee z \neq z_m) \end{array} \middle| \begin{array}{c} [\phi, (m, z_0, z, \pi_m)] \leftarrow \mathsf{P}^* \\ [z_i, \mathbf{w}_i]_{i=1}^m \leftarrow \mathsf{Ext}_{\mathsf{P}^*} \end{array}\right] \leq \mathsf{negl}(\lambda) .$$

Here m *is a constant.*

Efficiency. The runtime of $\mathsf{P}_{\mathsf{IVC}}$ *and* $\mathsf{V}_{\mathsf{IVC}}$ *as well as the size of* π_{IVC} *only depend on* $|\phi|$ *and are independent on the number of iterations.*

Recently, [21] introduced the notion of non-uniform IVC, where the predicate ϕ is selected from a fixed set of predicates at every step of the computation. The selection depends on the current state of the computation. Non-uniform IVC fits into our model by simply setting the predicate to be the union of all predicates, including the selection circuit. The one key difference is an additional efficiency requirement that the IVC prover in step i only depends on the size of the predicate that is being executed in step i. Our PROTOSTAR construction achieves this requirement.

2.2 Simple Accumulation

We take definitions and proofs from [8].

Definition 2 (Accumulation Scheme). *An accumulation scheme for a NARK* $(\mathsf{P}_{NARK}, \mathsf{V}_{NARK})$ *is a triple of algorithms* $\mathsf{acc} = (\mathsf{P}_{\mathsf{acc}}, \mathsf{V}_{\mathsf{acc}}, D)$*, all of which have access to the same random oracle* ρ_{acc} *as well as* ρ_{NARK}*, the oracle for the NARK. The algorithms have the following syntax and properties:*

– $\mathsf{P}_{\mathsf{acc}}(\mathsf{pi}, \pi = (\pi.x, \pi.\mathbf{w}), \mathsf{acc} = (\mathsf{acc}.x, \mathsf{acc}.\mathbf{w})) \rightarrow \{\mathsf{acc}' = (\mathsf{acc}'.x, \mathsf{acc}'.\mathbf{w}), \mathsf{pf}\}$. *The accumulation prover* $\mathsf{P}_{\mathsf{acc}}$ *takes as input a statement* pi*, NARK proof* π*, and an accumulator* acc *and outputs a new accumulator* acc′ *and correction terms* pf.

- $\mathsf{V}_{\mathsf{acc}}(\mathsf{pi}, \pi.x, \mathsf{acc}.x, \mathsf{acc}'.x, \mathsf{pf}) \to v$. *The accumulation verifier takes as input the statement* pi*, the instances of the NARK proof, the old and new accumulator, the correction terms, and 'accepts' by outputting* 0 *and 'rejects' otherwise.*
- $D(\mathsf{acc}) \to v$. *The decider on input* acc *'accepts' by outputting* 0 *and 'rejects' otherwise.*

An accumulation scheme has knowledge-soundness with knowledge error κ *if the RO-NARK* $(\mathsf{P}', \mathsf{V}')$ *has knowledge error* κ *for the relation*

$$\mathcal{R}_{\mathsf{acc}}((\mathsf{pi}, \pi.x, \mathsf{acc}.x); (\pi.\mathbf{w}, \mathsf{acc}.\mathbf{w})) : (\mathsf{V}_{NARK}(\mathsf{pi}, \pi) = 0 \wedge D(\mathsf{acc}) = 0) ,$$

where P' *outputs* $\mathsf{acc}', \mathsf{pf}$ *and* V' *on input* $((\mathsf{pi}, \pi.x, \mathsf{acc}.x), (\mathsf{acc}', \mathsf{pf}))$ *accepts if* $D(\mathsf{acc}')$ *and* $\mathsf{V}_{\mathsf{acc}}(\mathsf{pi}, \pi.x, \mathsf{acc}.x, \mathsf{acc}'.x, \mathsf{pf}) = 0$.

The scheme has perfect completeness if the RO-NARK $(\mathsf{P}', \mathsf{V}')$ *has perfect completeness for* $\mathcal{R}_{\mathsf{acc}}$.

Theorem 1 (IVC from accumulation [8]**).** *Given a standard-model NARK for circuit-satisfiability and a standard-model accumulation scheme (Definition 2) for that NARK, both with negligible knowledge error, there exists an efficient transformation that outputs an IVC scheme (see Sect. 3.2 of* [8]*) for constant-depth compliance predicates, assuming that the circuit complexity of the accumulation verifier* $\mathsf{V}_{\mathsf{acc}}$ *is sub-linear in its input.*

Random Oracle. Note that both the NARK and accumulation scheme we construct are in the random oracle model. However, Theorem 1 requires a NARK and an accumulation scheme in the standard model. It remains an open problem to construct such schemes. However, we can heuristically instantiate the random oracle with a cryptographic hash function and assume that the resulting schemes still have knowledge soundness.

Definition 3 (Fiat-Shamir Heuristic). *The Fiat-Shamir Heuristic, relative to a secure cryptographic hash function* H*, states that a random oracle NARK with negligible knowledge error yields a NARK that has negligible knowledge error in the standard (CRS) model if the random oracle is replaced with* H.

Complexity. The IVC transformation from [8] recursively proves that the accumulation was performed correctly. To do that, it implements $\mathsf{V}_{\mathsf{acc}}$ as a circuit and proves that the previous accumulation step was done correctly. Note that this recursive circuit is independent of the size of $\pi.\mathbf{w}, \mathsf{acc}.\mathbf{w}$ and the runtime of D. The IVC prover is linear in the size of the recursive circuit plus the size of the IVC computation step expressed as a circuit. The final IVC verifier and the IVC proof size are linear in these components. This can be reduced using an additional SNARK as in [22].

PCD. IVC can be generalized to arbitrary DAGs instead of just path graphs in a primitive called proof-carrying data [3]. Accumulation schemes can be compiled into full PCD if they support accumulating an arbitrary number of accumulators and proofs [8,9]. For simplicity, we only build accumulation for one proof and one accumulator, as well as for two accumulators. This enables PCD for DAGs of degree two. By transforming higher degree graphs into degree two graphs (by converting each degree d node into a $\log_2(d)$ depth tree), we can achieve PCD for these graphs.

Outsourcing the Decider. In the accumulation to IVC transformation, the IVC proof is linear in the accumulator, and the IVC verifier runs the decider. The accumulation schemes we construct are linear in the witness of a single computation step. However, we can outsource the decider by providing a SNARK that, given $\mathsf{acc}.x$, proves knowledge of $\mathsf{acc}.\mathbf{w}$, such that $D(\mathsf{acc}) = 0$. Nova [22] constructs a custom, concretely efficient SNARK for their accumulation/folding scheme.

3 Protocols

3.1 Special-Sound Protocols and Their Basic Transformations

In this section, we describe a class of special-sound protocols whose verifier is algebraic. The protocol Π_{sps} has 3 essential parameters $k, d, \ell \in \mathbb{N}$, meaning that Π_{sps} is a $(2k-1)$-move protocol with verifier degree d and output length ℓ (i.e. the verifier checks ℓ degree d algebraic equations). In each round i $(1 \le i \le k)$, the prover $\mathsf{P}_{\mathsf{sps}}(\mathsf{pi}, \mathbf{w}, [\mathbf{m}_j, r_j]_{j=1}^{i-1})$ generates the next message $\mathbf{m}_i$ on input the public input pi, the witness $\mathbf{w}$, and the current transcript $[\mathbf{m}_j, r_j]_{j=1}^{i-1}$, and sends $\mathbf{m}_i$ to the verifier; the verifier replies with a random challenge $r_i \in \mathbb{F}$. After the final message $\mathbf{m}_k$, the verifier computes the algebraic map $\mathsf{V}_{\mathsf{sps}}$ and checks that the output is a zero vector of length ℓ. More precisely, $\deg(\mathsf{V}_{\mathsf{sps}}) = d$, s.t.

$$\mathsf{V}_{\mathsf{sps}}(\mathsf{pi}, [\mathbf{m}_i]_{i=1}^{k}, [r_i]_{i=1}^{k-1}) := \sum_{j=0}^{d} f_j^{\mathsf{V}_{\mathsf{sps}}}(\mathsf{pi}, [\mathbf{m}_i]_{i=1}^{k}, [r_i]_{i=1}^{k-1}),$$

where $f_j^{\mathsf{V}_{\mathsf{sps}}}$ is a homogeneous degree-j algebraic map that outputs a vector of ℓ field elements.

Commit and Open. For a commitment scheme $\mathsf{cm} = (\mathsf{Setup}, \mathsf{Commit})$, consider the following relation $\mathcal{R}_{\mathsf{cm}}^{\mathcal{R}} = (x; \mathbf{w}, \mathbf{m} \in \mathcal{M}, \mathbf{m}' \in \mathcal{M}) : \{(x, \mathbf{w}) \in \mathcal{R} \vee (\mathsf{Commit}(\mathbf{m}) = \mathsf{Commit}(\mathbf{m}') \wedge \mathbf{m} \neq \mathbf{m}')\}$. The relation's witness is either a valid witness for $\mathcal{R}$ or a break of the commitment scheme cm. We now design a special-sound protocol $\Pi_{\mathsf{cm}} = (\mathsf{P}_{\mathsf{cm}}, \mathsf{V}_{\mathsf{cm}})$ for $\mathcal{R}_{\mathsf{cm}}^{\mathcal{R}}$ given $\Pi_{\mathsf{sps}} = (\mathsf{P}_{\mathsf{sps}}, \mathsf{V}_{\mathsf{sps}})$, a special-sound protocol for $\mathcal{R}$. P_{cm} runs $\mathsf{P}_{\mathsf{sps}}$ to generate the ith message and then commits to the message. Along with the final message, P_{cm} sends the opening to the commitment. The verifier V_{cm} checks the correctness of the commitments and runs $\mathsf{V}_{\mathsf{sps}}$ on the commitment openings.

Lemma 2 (Π_{cm} is $(a_1, \ldots, a_\mu)$-special-sound). *Let Π_{sps} be an $(a_1, \ldots, a_\mu)$-out-of-N special-sound protocol for relation $\mathcal{R}$, where the prover messages are all in a set $\mathcal{M}$. Let $(\mathsf{Setup}, \mathsf{Commit})$ be a binding commitment scheme for messages in $\mathcal{M}$. For $\mathsf{ck} \leftarrow \mathsf{Setup}_{\mathsf{cm}}(1^\lambda)$ let $\mathcal{R}_{\mathsf{cm}} = (\mathsf{pi}; \mathbf{w}, m \in \mathcal{M}, m' \in \mathcal{M}) : (\mathsf{pi}; \mathbf{w}) \in \mathcal{R} \vee (\mathsf{Commit}(\mathsf{ck}, m) = \mathsf{Commit}(\mathsf{ck}, m') \wedge m \neq m')$. Then $\Pi_{\mathsf{cm}} = \mathsf{cm}[\Pi_{\mathsf{sps}}]$ is an $(a_1, \ldots, a_\mu)$-out-of-N special-sound protocol for $\mathcal{R}_{\mathsf{cm}}^{\mathcal{R}}$.*

We defer the proof to the full version [7].

Fiat-Shamir Transform. Let ρ_{NARK} be a random oracle. Let Π_{cm} be the commit-and-open protocol for the special-sound protocol $\Pi_{\mathsf{sps}} = (\mathsf{P}_{\mathsf{sps}}, \mathsf{V}_{\mathsf{sps}})$. The Fiat-Shamir Transform $\mathsf{FS}[\Pi_{\mathsf{cm}}]$ of the protocol Π_{cm} is the following. The prover generates the round challenges by computing ρ_{NARK} on input the challenge and the prover message commitment in the previous round. The prover then sends the proof as the list of prover messages and the corresponding commitments. The verifier checks the proof by recomputing the challenges and runs the verifier for Π_{cm}. By Lemma 1, $\mathsf{FS}[\Pi_{\mathsf{cm}}]$ is knowledge sound if Π_{sps} is special-sound.

3.2 Accumulation Scheme for $\mathsf{V}_{\mathsf{NARK}}$

Let ρ_{acc} and ρ_{NARK} be two random oracles, and let $\mathsf{V}_{\mathsf{NARK}}$ be the verifier of $\mathsf{FS}[\Pi_{\mathsf{cm}}]$ in Sect. 3.1, whose underlying special-sound protocol is $\Pi_{\mathsf{sps}} = (\mathsf{P}_{\mathsf{sps}}, \mathsf{V}_{\mathsf{sps}})$ for a relation $\mathcal{R}$. We describe the accumulation scheme for $\mathsf{V}_{\mathsf{NARK}}$.

The accumulated predicate. The predicate to be accumulated is the "relaxed" verifier check of the NARK scheme $\mathsf{FS}[\Pi_{\mathsf{cm}}]$ for relation $\mathcal{R}$. Namely, given public input $\mathsf{pi} \in \mathcal{M}^{\ell_{\mathsf{in}}}$, random challenges $[r_i]_{i=1}^{k-1} \in \mathbb{F}^{k-1}$, a NARK proof

$$\pi.x = [C_i]_{i=1}^k, \; \pi.\mathbf{w} = [\mathbf{m}_i]_{i=1}^k$$

where $[C_i]_{i=1}^k \in \mathcal{C}^k$ are commitments and $[\mathbf{m}_i]_{i=1}^k$ are prover messages in the special-sound protocol Π_{sps}, and a slack variable μ, the predicate checks that (i) $r_i = \rho_{\mathsf{NARK}}(r_{i-1}, C_i)$ for all $i \in [k-1]$ (where $r_0 := \rho_{\mathsf{NARK}}(\mathsf{pi})$), (ii) $\mathsf{Commit}(\mathsf{ck}, \mathbf{m}_i) = C_i$ for all $i \in [k]$, and (iii)

$$\mathsf{V}_{\mathsf{sps}}(\mathsf{pi}, \pi.x, \pi.\mathbf{w}, [r_i]_{i=1}^{k-1}, \mu) := \sum_{j=0}^{d} \mu^{d-j} \cdot f_j^{\mathsf{V}_{\mathsf{sps}}}(\mathsf{pi}, \pi.\mathbf{w}, [r_i]_{i=1}^{k-1}) = \mathbf{e}$$

where $\mathbf{e} = \mathbf{0}^\ell$ and $\mu = 1$ for the NARK verifier $\mathsf{V}_{\mathsf{NARK}}$. Here $f_j^{\mathsf{V}_{\mathsf{sps}}}$ is a degree-j homogeneous algebraic map that outputs ℓ field elements. Degree-j homogeneity says that each monomial term of $f_j^{\mathsf{V}_{\mathsf{sps}}}$ has degree exactly j.

Remark 1. Without loss of generality, we assume that the public input pi is of constant size, as otherwise, we can set it as the hash of the original public input.

Accumulator. The accumulator has the following format:

- *Accumulator instance* $\mathsf{acc}.x := \{\mathsf{pi}, [C_i]_{i=1}^k, [r_i]_{i=1}^{k-1}, E, \mu\}$, where $\mathsf{pi} \in \mathcal{M}^{\ell_{\mathsf{in}}}$ is the accumulated public input, $[C_i]_{i=1}^k \in \mathcal{C}^k$ are the accumulated commitments, $[r_i]_{i=1}^{k-1} \in \mathbb{F}^{k-1}$ are the accumulated challenges, $E \in \mathcal{C}$ is the accumulated commitment to the error terms, and $\mu \in \mathbb{F}$ is a slack variable.
- *Accumulator witness* $\mathsf{acc}.\mathbf{w} := \{[\mathbf{m}_i]_{i=1}^k\}$, where $[\mathbf{m}_i]_{i=1}^k$ are the accumulated prover messages.

Accumulation Prover. On input commitment key ck (which can be hardwired in the prover's algorithm), accumulator acc, an instance-proof pair (pi, π) where

$$\mathsf{acc} := (\mathsf{acc}.x = \{\mathsf{pi}', [C_i']_{i=1}^k, [r_i']_{i=1}^{k-1}, E, \mu\}, \mathsf{acc}.\mathbf{w} = \{[\mathbf{m}_i']_{i=1}^k\}),$$
$$\pi := (\pi.x = [C_i]_{i=1}^k, \pi.\mathbf{w} = [\mathbf{m}_i]_{i=1}^k),$$

the accumulation prover $\mathsf{P}_{\mathsf{acc}}$ works as in Fig. 3.

Accumulation Verifier. On input public input pi, NARK proof instance $\pi.x$, accumulator instance $\mathsf{acc}.x$, accumulation proof pf, and the updated accumulator instance $\mathsf{acc}'.x := \{\mathsf{pi}'', [C_i'']_{i=1}^k, [r_i'']_{i=1}^k, E', \mu'\}$, the accumulation verifier $\mathsf{V}_{\mathsf{acc}}$ works as in Fig. 3.

Decider. On input the commitment key ck (which can be hardwired) and an accumulator

$$\mathsf{acc} = (\mathsf{acc}.x = \{\mathsf{pi}, [C_i]_{i=1}^k, [r_i]_{i=1}^{k-1}, E, \mu\}, \mathsf{acc}.\mathbf{w} = \{[\mathbf{m}_i]_{i=1}^k\}),$$

the decider does the checks described in Fig. 4.

Theorem 2. *Let* $(\mathsf{P}_{\mathsf{NARK}}, \mathsf{V}_{\mathsf{NARK}})$ *be the RO-NARK defined in Sect. 3.1. Let* $\mathsf{cm} = (\mathsf{Setup}, \mathsf{Commit})$ *be a binding, homomorphic commitment scheme. Let* ρ_{acc} *be another random oracle. The accumulation scheme* $(\mathsf{P}_{\mathsf{acc}}, \mathsf{V}_{\mathsf{acc}}, D_{\mathsf{acc}})$ *for* $\mathsf{V}_{\mathsf{NARK}}$ *satisfies perfect completeness and has knowledge error* $(Q+1)\frac{d+1}{|\mathbb{F}|} + \mathsf{negl}(\lambda)$ *as defined in Definition 2, against any randomized polynomial-time Q-query adversary.*

Proof. **Completeness:** Consider any tuple $((\mathsf{pi}, \pi), \mathsf{acc}) \in \mathcal{R}_{\mathsf{acc}}$, that is, $\mathsf{V}_{\mathsf{NARK}}(\mathsf{pi}, \pi)$ and $D(\mathsf{acc})$ both accept. Let $(\mathsf{acc}', \mathsf{pf})$ denote the output of the accumulation prover $\mathsf{P}_{\mathsf{acc}}(\mathsf{ck}, \mathsf{acc}, (\mathsf{pi}, \pi))$. We argue that both the decider $D(\mathsf{acc}')$ and the accumulation verifier $\mathsf{V}_{\mathsf{acc}}(\mathsf{pi}, \pi.x, \mathsf{acc}.x, \mathsf{pf}, \mathsf{acc}'.x)$ will accept, which finishes the proof of perfect completeness by Definition 2.

$\mathsf{V}_{\mathsf{acc}}$ accepts as $\mathsf{P}_{\mathsf{acc}}$ and $\mathsf{V}_{\mathsf{acc}}$ go through the same process of computing challenges $[r_i]_{i=1}^{k-1}$ and α, thus the linear combinations of $\mathsf{acc}.x$ and $(\mathsf{pi}, \pi.x; \mathsf{pf}, [r_i]_{i=1}^{k-1})$ via α will be consistent.

We prove that $D(\mathsf{acc}')$ accepts by scrutinizing the following decider checks.

The check $\mathsf{acc}'.C_i \stackrel{?}{=} \mathsf{Commit}(\mathsf{ck}, \mathsf{acc}'.\mathbf{m}_i)$ succeeds for all $i \in [k]$. This is because

$$\mathsf{acc}'.\{C_i, \mathbf{m}_i\} = \mathsf{acc}.\{C_i, \mathbf{m}_i\} + \alpha \cdot \pi.\{C_i, \mathbf{m}_i\}$$

$\mathsf{P}_{\mathsf{acc}}^{\rho_{\mathsf{acc}},\rho_{\mathsf{NARK}}}(\mathsf{ck}, \mathsf{acc}, (\mathsf{pi}, \pi))$

1. $r_i \leftarrow \rho_{\mathsf{NARK}}(r_{i-1}, C_i) \forall i \in [k-1]$ where $r_0 := \rho_{\mathsf{NARK}}(\mathsf{pi})$.
2. Compute $[\mathbf{e}_j]_{j=1}^{d-1} \in (\mathbb{F}^\ell)^{d-1}$, such that

$$\sum_{j=0}^{d}(X+\mu)^{d-j} \cdot f_j^{\mathsf{V_{sps}}}(X \cdot \mathsf{pi} + \mathsf{pi}', [X \cdot \mathbf{m}_i + \mathbf{m}'_i]_{i=1}^k, [X \cdot r_i + r'_i]_{i=1}^{k-1})$$
$$= \sum_{j=0}^{d} \mu^{d-j} f_j^{\mathsf{V_{sps}}}(\mathsf{pi}', [\mathbf{m}'_i]_{i=1}^k, [r'_i]_{i=1}^{k-1}) + X^d \cdot \mathsf{V_{NARK}}(\mathsf{pi}, [\mathbf{m}_i]_{i=1}^k, [r_i]_{i=1}^{k-1}) + \sum_{j=1}^{d-1} \mathbf{e}_j X^j$$
$$= \mathbf{e} + \sum_{j=1}^{d-1} \mathbf{e}_j X^j$$

3. $E_j \leftarrow \mathsf{Commit}(\mathsf{ck}, \mathbf{e}_j) \forall j \in [d-1]$
4. $\alpha \leftarrow \rho_{\mathsf{acc}}(\mathsf{acc}.x, \mathsf{pi}, \pi.x, [E_j]_{j=1}^{d-1}) \in \mathbb{F}$
5. Set vectors

$$\mathbf{v} := \left(1, \mathsf{pi}, [r_i]_{i=1}^{k-1}, [C_i]_{i=1}^k, [\mathbf{m}_i]_{i=1}^k\right), \; \mathbf{v}' := \left(\mu, \mathsf{pi}', [r'_i]_{i=1}^{k-1}, [C'_i]_{i=1}^k, [\mathbf{m}'_i]_{i=1}^k\right).$$

6. $\mathbf{v}'' := (\mu', \mathsf{pi}'', [r''_i]_{i=1}^{k-1}, [C''_i]_{i=1}^k, [\mathbf{m}''_i]_{i=1}^k) \leftarrow \alpha \cdot \mathbf{v} + \mathbf{v}'$.
7. $E' \leftarrow E + \sum_{j=1}^{d-1} \alpha^j \cdot E_j$.
8. Set $\mathsf{acc}'.x := \{\mathsf{pi}'', [C''_i]_{i=1}^k, [r''_i]_{i=1}^k, E', \mu'\}$, $\mathsf{acc}'.\mathbf{w} := \{[\mathbf{m}''_i]_{i=1}^k\}$.
9. Set accumulation proof $\mathsf{pf} := [E_j]_{j=1}^{d-1}$

$\mathsf{V}_{\mathsf{acc}}^{\rho_{\mathsf{acc}},\rho_{\mathsf{NARK}}}(\mathsf{pi}, \pi.x = [C_i]_{i=1}^k, \mathsf{acc}.x = (\mathsf{pi}', [C'_i]_{i=1}^k, [r'_i]_{i=1}^{k-1}, E, \mu), \mathsf{pf} = [E_j]_{j=1}^{d-1}, \mathsf{acc}'.x)$

1. $r_i \leftarrow \rho_{\mathsf{NARK}}(r_{i-1}, C_i) \forall i \in [k-1]$ where $r_0 := \rho_{\mathsf{NARK}}(\mathsf{pi})$.
2. $\alpha \leftarrow \rho_{\mathsf{acc}}(\mathsf{acc}.x, \mathsf{pi}, \pi.x, \mathsf{pf})$
3. Set vectors

$$\mathbf{v} := \left(1, \mathsf{pi}, [r_i]_{i=1}^{k-1}, [C_i]_{i=1}^k\right), \; \mathbf{v}' := \mathsf{acc}.x.\left(\mu, \mathsf{pi}', [r'_i]_{i=1}^{k-1}, [C'_i]_{i=1}^k\right).$$

4. Check $\mathsf{acc}'.x.\,(\mu', \mathsf{pi}'', [r''_i]_{i=1}^{k-1}, [C''_i]_{i=1}^k) \stackrel{?}{=} \alpha \cdot \mathbf{v} + \mathbf{v}'$.
5. Check $\mathsf{acc}'.x.E' \stackrel{?}{=} \mathsf{acc}.x.E + \sum_{j=1}^{d-1} \alpha^j \cdot E_j$.

Fig. 3. Accumulation Prover/Verifier for low-degree Fiat-Shamired NARKs

$D_{\mathsf{acc}}(\mathsf{acc} = (\mathsf{acc}.x = \{\mathsf{pi}, [C_i]_{i=1}^k, [r_i]_{i=1}^{k-1}, E, \mu\}, \mathsf{acc}.\mathbf{w} = \{[\mathbf{m}_i]_{i=1}^k\}))$

1. $C_i \stackrel{?}{=} \mathsf{Commit}(\mathsf{ck}, \mathbf{m}_i)$ for all $i \in [k]$.
2. $\mathbf{e} \leftarrow \sum_{j=0}^{d} \mu^{d-j} f_j^{\mathsf{V_{sps}}}(\mathsf{pi}, [\mathbf{m}_i]_{i=1}^k, [r_i]_{i=1}^{k-1})$ where $f_j^{\mathsf{V_{sps}}}$ is the degree-j homogeneous algebraic map described in the accumulated predicate.
3. $E \stackrel{?}{=} \mathsf{Commit}(\mathsf{ck}, \mathbf{e})$.

Fig. 4. Accumulation Decider for low-degree Fiat-Shamired NARKs

for all $i \in [k]$, where $\pi.C_i = \mathsf{Commit}(\mathsf{ck}, \pi.\mathbf{m}_i)$ because $\mathsf{V}_{\mathsf{NARK}}(\mathsf{pi}, \pi)$ accepts, and $\mathsf{acc}.C_i = \mathsf{Commit}(\mathsf{ck}, \mathsf{acc}.\mathbf{m}_i)$ because $D(\mathsf{acc})$ accepts. Thus the check succeeds by the homomorphism of the commitment scheme.

The decider computes $\mathbf{e}' \leftarrow \sum_{j=0}^{d} (\mathsf{acc}'.\mu)^{d-j} f_j^{\mathsf{V}_{\mathsf{sps}}}(\mathsf{acc}'.\{\mathsf{pi}, [\mathbf{m}_i]_{i=1}^{k}, [r_i]_{i=1}^{k-1}\})$ such that for $\mathbf{e} = \sum_{j=0}^{d} \mathsf{acc}.\mu^{(d-j)} \cdot f_j^{\mathsf{V}_{\mathsf{sps}}}(\mathsf{acc}.\{\mathsf{pi}, [\mathbf{m}_i]_{i=1}^{k}, [r_i]_{i=1}^{k-1}\})$, it holds that

$$\mathbf{e}' = \mathbf{e} + \sum_{j=1}^{d-1} \alpha^j \cdot \mathsf{pf}.\mathbf{e}_j$$

$$= \sum_{j=0}^{d} (\alpha + \mathsf{acc}.\mu)^{d-j} \cdot f_j^{\mathsf{V}_{\mathsf{sps}}}(\alpha \cdot \{\mathsf{pi}, \pi.[\mathbf{m}_i]_{i=1}^{k}, [r_i]_{i=1}^{k-1}\} + \mathsf{acc}.\{\mathsf{pi}, [\mathbf{m}_i]_{i=1}^{k}, [r_i]_{i=1}^{k-1}\}).$$

By the definition of $\mathsf{pf}.\mathbf{e}_j$ and the homomorphism of the commitment scheme, and because $D(\mathsf{acc})$ accepts and checks $E = \mathsf{Commit}(\mathsf{ck}, \mathbf{e})$, we have that $E' = \mathsf{Commit}(\mathsf{ck}, \mathbf{e}')$.

Knowledge-Soundness: We show that the scheme has knowledge-soundness by showing that there exists an underlying $(d + 1)$-special-sound protocol and then applying the Fiat-Shamir transform to show that the accumulation scheme is knowledge sound. Consider the public-coin interactive protocol $\Pi_I = (\mathsf{P}_I(\mathsf{pi}, \pi, \mathsf{acc}), \mathsf{V}_I(\mathsf{pi}, \pi.x, \mathsf{acc}.x))$ where P_I sends $\mathsf{pf} = [E_j]_{j=1}^{d-1} \in \mathbb{G}^{d-1}$ as computed by $\mathsf{P}_{\mathsf{acc}}$ to V_I. The verifier sends a random challenge $\alpha \in \mathbb{F}$, and the prover P_I responds with acc' as computed by $\mathsf{P}_{\mathsf{acc}}$. V_I accepts if $D_{\mathsf{acc}}(\mathsf{acc}') = 0$ and $\mathsf{V}_{\mathsf{acc}}(\mathsf{pi}, \pi.x, \mathsf{acc}.x, \mathsf{pf}, \mathsf{acc}'.x) = 0$ using the random challenge α, instead of a Fiat-shamir challenge.

Claim 1: Π_I is $(d+1)$-special-sound Consider the relation $\mathcal{R}_{\mathsf{acc}}$ where $\mathcal{R}_{\mathsf{acc}}$ is defined in Definition 2. Consider $d+1$ accepting transcripts for Π_I :

$$\{\mathcal{T}_i := (\mathsf{pi}, \pi.x, \mathsf{acc}.x; \mathsf{acc}'_i, \mathsf{pf}_i)\}_{i=1}^{d+1}.$$

We construct an extractor $\mathsf{Ext}_{\mathsf{acc}}$ that extracts a witness for $\mathcal{R}_{\mathsf{acc}}(\mathsf{pi}.\pi.x, \mathsf{acc}.x)$ given $\mathcal{T}$.

For all $i \in [d+1]$,

$$(\mathsf{acc}'_i) = (\mu'_i, \mathsf{pi}'_i, [C'_{i,j}]_{j=1}^{k}, [r_{i,j}]_{j=1}^{k-1}, E'_i, [\mathbf{m}'_{i,j}]_{j=1}^{k})$$

and $\mathsf{pf}_i = \mathsf{pf} = [E_j]_{j=1}^{d-1}$.

Given that the transcripts are accepting, i.e. both $\mathsf{V}_{\mathsf{acc}}$ and D_{acc} accept, we have that $\mathsf{Commit}(\mathsf{ck}, \mathbf{e}'_i) = E'_i = \mathsf{acc}.E + \sum_{j=1}^{d-1} \alpha_i^j E_j$ for all $i \in [d+1]$, whereas

$$\mathbf{e}'_i := \sum_{j=0}^{d} \mu_i'^{d-j} f_j^{\mathcal{R}}(\pi'_i, [\mathbf{m}'_{i,j}]_{j=1}^{k}, [r_{i,j}]_{j=1}^{k-1}).$$

Using a Vandermonde matrix of the challenges $\alpha_1, \ldots, \alpha_d$ we can compute $\mathbf{e}, [\mathbf{e}_j]_{j=1}^{d-1}$ such that $E_j = \mathsf{Commit}(\mathsf{ck}, \mathbf{e}_j)$ and $\mathsf{acc}.E = \mathsf{Commit}(\mathsf{ck}, \mathbf{e})$ from the equations above. Therefore we have that $\mathbf{e}'_i = \mathbf{e} + \sum_{j=1}^{d-1} \alpha_i^j \mathbf{e}_j$ for all $i \in [d+1]$.

Additionally using two challenges (α_1, α_2), $\mathsf{Ext}_{\mathsf{acc}}$ can compute $\pi.\mathbf{w} = [\mathbf{m}_j]_{j=1}^k = [\frac{\mathsf{acc}'.\mathbf{m}_{1,j} - \mathsf{acc}'.\mathbf{m}_{2,j}}{\alpha_1 - \alpha_2}]_{j=1}^k$. It holds that $\mathsf{acc}.\mathbf{m}_j = \mathsf{acc}'.\mathbf{m}_{1,j} - \alpha_1 \cdot \pi.\mathbf{m}_j \forall j \in [k]$, such that $\pi.C_j = \mathsf{Commit}(\mathsf{ck}, \pi.\mathbf{m}_j)$ and $\mathsf{acc}.C_j = \mathsf{Commit}(\mathsf{ck}, \mathsf{acc}.\mathbf{m}_j)$. If for any other challenge and any j, $\mathsf{acc}'.\mathbf{m}_j \neq \alpha\pi.\mathbf{m}_j + \mathsf{acc}.\mathbf{m}_j$, then this can be used to compute a break of the commitment scheme cm. This happens with negligible probability by assumption.

Otherwise, we have that $\sum_{j=0} \mu_i^{d-j} f_j^{\mathcal{R}}(\pi_j, [\mathbf{m}_{i,j}]_{i=1}^k, [r_{i,j}]_{i=1}^{k-1}) - \mathbf{e}_i = 0$ for all $i \in [d+1]$. Together this implies that the degree d polynomial

$$p(X) = \sum_{j=0}^{d} (X + \mathsf{acc}.\mu)^{d-j} \cdot f_j^{\mathsf{V}_{\mathsf{sps}}}(X \cdot \mathsf{pi} + \mathsf{acc}.\mathsf{pi}, [X \cdot \mathbf{m}_i + \mathsf{acc}.\mathbf{m}_i]_{i=1}^k, [X \cdot r_i + \mathsf{acc}.r_i]_{i=1}^{k-1})$$
$$- \mathbf{e} - \sum_{j=1}^{d-1} \mathbf{e}_j X^j, \tag{1}$$

is zero on $d+1$ points $(\alpha_1, \ldots, \alpha_{d+1})$, i.e. is zero everywhere. The constant term of this polynomial is

$$\sum_{j=0}^{d} \mathsf{acc}.\mu^{d-j} \cdot f_j^{\mathsf{V}_{\mathsf{sps}}}(\mathsf{acc}.\mathsf{pi}, [\mathsf{acc}.\mathbf{m}_i]_{i=1}^k, [\mathsf{acc}.r_i]_{i=1}^{k-1}) - \mathbf{e}.$$

It being 0 implies that $D(\mathsf{acc}) = 0$. Additionally, the degree d term of the polynomial is

$$\sum_{j=0}^{d} f_j^{\mathsf{V}_{\mathsf{sps}}}(\mathsf{pi}, [\pi.\mathbf{m}_i]_{i=1}^k, [\pi.r_i]_{i=1}^{k-1}).$$

Together with $\mathsf{V}_{\mathsf{acc}}$ checking that the challenges r_i are computed correctly this implies that $\mathsf{V}_{\mathsf{NARK}}(\mathsf{pi}, \pi) = 0$. Ext thus outputs a valid witness $(\pi.\mathbf{w}, \mathsf{acc}.\mathbf{w}) \in \mathcal{R}_{\mathsf{acc}}(\mathsf{pi}, \pi.x, \mathsf{acc}.x)$ and thus Π_I is $(d+1)$-special-sound. Using Lemma 1, we have that $\Pi_{AS} = \mathsf{FS}[\Pi_I]$ is a NARK for $\mathcal{R}_{\mathsf{acc}}$ with knowledge soundness $(Q+1) \cdot \frac{d+1}{|\mathbb{F}|} + \mathsf{negl}(\lambda)$. This implies that acc is an accumulation scheme with $((Q+1) \cdot \frac{d+1}{|\mathbb{F}|} + \mathsf{negl}(\lambda))$-knowledge soundness. □

3.3 Compressing Verification Checks for High-Degree Verifiers

Observe that the accumulation prover needs to perform $\Omega(d\ell)$ group operations to commit to the $d-1$ error vectors $\mathbf{e}_j \in \mathbb{F}^\ell$ $(1 \leq j < d)$; and the accumulation verifier needs to check the combination of d error vector commitments. This can be a bottleneck when the verifier degree d is high. In this circumstance, we can optimize the accumulation complexity by transforming the underlying special-sound protocol Π_{sps} into a new special-sound protocol $\mathsf{CV}[\Pi_{\mathsf{sps}}]$ for the same relation $\mathcal{R}$. This optimization compresses the ℓ degree-d equations checked by the verifier into a single degree-$(d+2)$ equation using a random linear combination, with the tradeoff of additionally checking $2\sqrt{\ell}$ degree-2 equations. We describe the generic transformation below.

Compressing Verification Checks. W.l.o.g. assume ℓ is a perfect square, then we can transform Π_{sps} into a special-sound protocol $\mathsf{CV}[\Pi_{\mathsf{sps}}]$ where the $\mathsf{V}_{\mathsf{sps}}$ reduces from ℓ degree-d checks to 1 degree-$(d+2)$ check and additionally $2\sqrt{\ell}$ degree-2 checks. Instead of checking the output of $\mathsf{V}_{\mathsf{sps}}$ to be ℓ zeroes, we take a random linear combination of the ℓ verification equations using powers of a challenge β. For example, if the map is $\mathsf{V}_{\mathsf{sps}}(x_1, x_2) := (\mathsf{V}_{\mathsf{sps},1}(x_1, x_2), \mathsf{V}_{\mathsf{sps},2}(x_1, x_2)) = (x_1 + x_2, x_1 x_2)$ we can set the new algebraic map as $\mathsf{V}'_{\mathsf{sps}}(x_1, x_2, \beta) := \mathsf{V}_{\mathsf{sps},1}(x_1, x_2) + \beta \cdot \mathsf{V}_{\mathsf{sps},2}(x_1, x_2) = (x_1 + x_2) + \beta x_1 x_2$ for a random β. Doing this naively reduces the output length to 1 but also requires the verifier to compute the appropriate powers of β. This would increase the degree by ℓ, an undesirable tradeoff. To mitigate this, we can have the prover precompute powers of β, i.e. $\beta, \beta^2, \ldots, \beta^\ell$ and send them to the verifier. The verifier then only needs to check consistency between the powers of β, which can be done using a degree 2 check, e.g. $\beta^{i+1} = \beta^i \cdot \beta$ and the degree d verification equation increases in degree by 1. This mitigates the degree increase but requires the prover to send another message of length ℓ. To achieve a more optimal tradeoff, we write each $i = j + k \cdot \sqrt{\ell}$ for $j, k \in [1, \sqrt{\ell}]$. The prover then sends $\sqrt{\ell}$ powers of β and $\sqrt{\ell} - 1$ powers of $\beta^{\sqrt{\ell}}$. From these, each power of β from 1 to ℓ can be recomputed using just one multiplication. This results in the prover sending an additional message of length $2\sqrt{\ell}$, the original ℓ verification checks being transformed into a single degree $d+2$ check and additionally $2\sqrt{\ell}$ degree 2 checks for the consistency of the powers of β.

Transformed Protocol $\mathsf{CV}[\Pi_{\mathsf{sps}}] = (\mathsf{P}_{\mathsf{sps}}, \mathsf{V}'_{\mathsf{sps}})$ for relation $\mathcal{R}$

Prover $\mathsf{P}_{\mathsf{sps}}(\mathsf{pi}, \mathbf{w})$		**Verifier** $\mathsf{V}'_{\mathsf{sps}}(\mathsf{pi})$
$\mathbf{m}_i \leftarrow \mathsf{P}_{\mathsf{sps}}(\mathsf{pi}, \mathbf{w}, [\mathbf{m}_j, r_j]_{j=1}^{i-1})$	$\xrightarrow{\mathbf{m}_i}$	
	$\xleftarrow{r_i}$	$r_i \leftarrow\$ \mathbb{F}$
Repeat $k-1$ time		Repeat $k-1$ time
	$\xrightarrow{\text{Message } \mathbf{m}_k}$	
	$\xleftarrow{\beta}$	$\beta \leftarrow\$ \mathbb{F}$
$[\beta_i \leftarrow \beta^i]_{i=1}^{\sqrt{\ell}-1}$	$\xrightarrow{\mathbf{m}_{k+1} = [\beta_i, \beta'_i]_{i=1}^{\sqrt{\ell}-1}}$	
$[\beta'_j \leftarrow \beta^{j\sqrt{\ell}}]_{j=1}^{\sqrt{\ell}-1}$		$\mathsf{V}'_{\mathsf{sps}}(\mathsf{pi}, [\mathbf{m}_i]_{i=1}^{k+1}, ([r_i]_{i=1}^{k-1}, \beta)) \stackrel{?}{=} 0$
		$\beta_{i+1} = \beta_i \cdot \beta \forall i \in [1, \sqrt{\ell} - 2]$
		$\beta'_{i+1} = \beta'_i \cdot \beta'_1 \forall i \in [1, \sqrt{\ell} - 2]$
		$\beta_1 = \beta, \beta'_1 = \beta_{\sqrt{\ell}-1} \cdot \beta$

Fig. 5. Compressed verification of Π_{sps}.

We describe the transformed protocol in Fig. 5, where

$$\mathsf{V}'_{\mathsf{sps}}(\mathsf{pi}, [\mathbf{m}_i]_{i=1}^{k+1}, ([r_i]_{i=1}^{k-1}, \beta)) := \sum_{i=0}^{\sqrt{\ell}-1} \sum_{j=0}^{\sqrt{\ell}-1} \beta_i \cdot \beta'_j \cdot \mathsf{V}_{\mathsf{sps},i+j\sqrt{\ell}}(\mathsf{pi}, [\mathbf{m}_i]_{i=1}^{k}, [r_i]_{i=1}^{k-1})$$
$$= \sum_{j=0}^{\ell-1} \beta^j \cdot \mathsf{V}_{\mathsf{sps},j}(\mathsf{pi}, [\mathbf{m}_i]_{i=1}^{k}, [r_i]_{i=1}^{k-1})$$

and $\mathsf{V}_{\mathsf{sps},j}(\mathsf{pi}, [\mathbf{m}_i]_{i=1}^{k}, [r_i]_{i=1}^{k-1})$ is the $(j+1)$-th $(0 \leq j < \ell)$ equation checked by $\mathsf{V}_{\mathsf{sps}}$. The transformed protocol is a $(2k+1)$-move special-sound protocol for the same relation $\mathcal{R}$. The transformed verifier now checks 1 degree-$(d+2)$ equation and additionally $2\sqrt{\ell}$ degree-2 equations.

Lemma 3. *Let Π_{sps} be a $(2k-1)$-move protocol for relation $\mathcal{R}$ with $(a_1, \ldots, a_{k-1})$-special-soundness, in which the verifier outputs ℓ elements. The transformed protocol $\mathsf{CV}[\Pi_{\mathsf{sps}}]$ of Π_{sps} is $(a_1, \ldots, , a_{k-1}, \ell)$-special-sound.*

We defer the proof to the full version [7].

High-Low Degree Accumulation. After the transformation, the error vectors $\mathbf{e}_j$ $(1 \leq j \leq d+1)$ become single field elements, and we can use the trivial commitment $E_j := \mathsf{Commit}(\mathsf{ck}, e_j) := e_j$ without group operations. Additionally, we can use a separate error vector $\mathbf{e}' \in \mathbb{F}^{2\sqrt{\ell}}$ to keep track of the error terms for the $2\sqrt{\ell}$ degree-2 checks, and set $E' := \mathsf{Commit}(\mathsf{ck}, \mathbf{e}') \in \mathbb{G}$ to be the corresponding error commitment. The accumulation prover only needs to perform $O(\sqrt{\ell})$ additional group operations to commit $\mathbf{m}_{k+1}$ and $\mathbf{e}'$, and compute the coefficients of a degree-$(d+2)$ univariate polynomial, which is described as the sum of $O(\ell)$ polynomials. The accumulator instance needs to include one more challenge β and two commitments (for $\mathbf{m}_{k+1}$ and $\mathbf{e}'$). The accumulator verifier needs to do only $k+2$ (rather than $k+d-1$) group scalar multiplications, with the tradeoff of 1 more hash and $O(d)$ more field operations. This high-low degree accumulation is described in detail in the full version [7].

Theorem 3 (IVC for high-degree special-sound protocols). *Let $\mathbb{F}$ be a finite field, such that $|\mathbb{F}| \geq 2^\lambda$ and $\mathsf{cm} = (\mathsf{Setup}, \mathsf{Commit})$ be a binding homomorphic commitment scheme for vectors in $\mathbb{F}$. Let $\Pi_{\mathsf{sps}} = (\mathsf{P}_{\mathsf{sps}}, \mathsf{V}_{\mathsf{sps}})$ be a special-sound protocol for an NP-complete relation $\mathcal{R}_{\mathsf{NP}}$ with the following properties:*

- *It's $(2k-1)$ move.*
- *It's $(a_1, \ldots, a_{k-1})$-out-of-$|\mathbb{F}|$ special-sound. Such that the knowledge error $\kappa = 1 - \prod_{i=1}^{k-1}(1 - \frac{a_i}{|\mathbb{F}|}) = \mathsf{negl}(\lambda)$*
- *The inputs are in $\mathbb{F}^{\ell_{\mathsf{in}}}$*
- *The verifier is degree $d = \mathsf{poly}(\lambda)$ with output in $\mathbb{F}^\ell$*

Then, under the Fiat-Shamir heuristic for a cryptographic hash function H (Definition 3), there exist two IVC schemes $\mathsf{IVC} = (\mathsf{P}_{\mathsf{IVC}}, \mathsf{V}_{\mathsf{IVC}})$ and $\mathsf{IVC}_{\mathsf{CV}} = (\mathsf{P}_{\mathsf{CV,IVC}}, \mathsf{V}_{\mathsf{CV,IVC}})$ with predicates expressed in $\mathcal{R}_{\mathsf{NP}}$ with the following efficiencies:

	No CV	CV
$\mathsf{P_{IVC}}$ *native*	$\sum_{i=1}^{k} \lvert\mathbf{m}_i^*\rvert + (d-1)\ell\mathbb{G}$ $\mathsf{P_{sps}} + L(\mathsf{V_{sps}}, d)$	$\sum_{i=1}^{k} \lvert\mathbf{m}_i^*\rvert + O(\sqrt{\ell})\mathbb{G}$ $\mathsf{P_{sps}} + L'(\mathsf{V_{sps}}, d+2)$
$\mathsf{P_{IVC}}$ *recursive*	$k+d-1\mathbb{G}$ $k+\ell_{\mathsf{in}}\mathbb{F}$ $(k+d+O(1))\mathsf{H} + 1\mathsf{H_{in}}$	$k+2\mathbb{G}$ $k+\ell_{\mathsf{in}}+d+1\mathbb{F}$ $(k+d+O(1))\mathsf{H} + 1\mathsf{H_{in}}$
$\mathsf{V_{IVC}}$:	$\ell + \sum_{i=1}^{k} \lvert\mathbf{m}_i\rvert\mathbb{G}$ $\mathsf{V_{sps}}$	$O(\sqrt{\ell}) + \sum_{i=1}^{k} \lvert\mathbf{m}_i\rvert\mathbb{G}$ $O(\ell) + \mathsf{V_{sps}}$
$\lvert\pi_{\mathsf{IVC}}\rvert$:	$k+\ell_{\mathsf{in}}\mathbb{F}$ $k+1\mathbb{G}$ $\sum_{i=1}^{k} \lvert\mathbf{m}_i\rvert$	$k+\ell_{\mathsf{in}}+1\mathbb{F}$ $k+2\mathbb{G}$ $\sum_{i=1}^{k} \lvert\mathbf{m}_i\rvert + O(\sqrt{\ell})$

The first row displays the native operations of the IVC *prover (i.e., the complexity of running the accumulation prover). The second row describes the size of the recursive statement representing the accumulation verifier for which* $\mathsf{P_{IVC}}$ *creates a proof. The third row is the computation of* $\mathsf{V_{IVC}}$*, and the last row is the size of the proof. In the table,* $|\mathbf{m}_i|$ *denotes the prover message length;* $|\mathbf{m}_i^*|$ *is the number of non-zero elements in* $\mathbf{m}_i$*;* $\mathbb{G}$ *for rows 1–3 is the total length of the messages committed using* Commit*.* $\mathbb{F}$ *are field operations.* H *denotes the total input length to a cryptographic hash, and* $\mathsf{H_{in}}$ *is the hash to the public input and accumulator instance.* $\mathsf{P_{sps}}$ *(and* $\mathsf{V_{sps}}$*) is the cost of running the prover (and the algebraic verifier) of the special-sound protocol, respectively.* $L(\mathsf{V_{sps}}, d)$ *is the cost of computing the coefficients of the degree d polynomial*

$$\mathbf{e}(X) := \sum_{j=0}^{d} (\mu + X)^{d-j} \cdot f_j^{\mathsf{V_{sps}}}(\mathsf{acc} + X \cdot \pi), \tag{2}$$

and $L'(\mathsf{V_{sps}}, d+2)$ *is the cost of computing the coefficients of the degree* $d+2$ *polynomial*

$$e(X) := \sum_{a=0}^{\sqrt{\ell}-1} \sum_{b=0}^{\sqrt{\ell}-1} (X \cdot \pi.\beta_a + \mathsf{acc}.\beta_a)(X \cdot \pi.\beta'_b + \mathsf{acc}.\beta'_b) \sum_{j=0}^{d} (\mu + X)^{d-j} \cdot f_{j,a+b\sqrt{\ell}}^{\mathsf{V_{sps}}}(\mathsf{acc} + X \cdot \pi), \tag{3}$$

where all inputs are linear functions in a formal variable X[4]*, and* $f_{j,i}^{\mathsf{V_{sps}}}$ *is the ith* $(0 \le i \le \ell - 1)$ *component of* $f_j^{\mathsf{V_{sps}}}$*'s output. For the proof size,* $\mathbb{G}$ *and* $\mathbb{F}$ *are the number of commitments and field elements, respectively.*

[4] For example if $f_d = \prod_{i=1}^{d}(a_i + b_i \cdot X)$ then a naive algorithm takes $O(d^2)$ time but using FFTs it can be computed in time $O(d \log^2 d)$ [11].

Proof. The construction first defines the two NARKs

$$\Pi_{\mathsf{NARK}} = (\mathsf{P}_{\mathsf{NARK}}, \mathsf{V}_{\mathsf{NARK}}) = \mathsf{FS}[\mathsf{cm}[\Pi_{\mathsf{sps}}]],$$

and

$$\Pi_{\mathsf{NARK,CV}} = (\mathsf{P}_{\mathsf{NARK}}, \mathsf{V}_{\mathsf{NARK}}) = \mathsf{FS}[\mathsf{cm}[\mathsf{CV}[\Pi_{\mathsf{sps}}]]].$$

Then we construct the accumulation scheme $(\mathsf{P}_{\mathsf{acc}}, \mathsf{V}_{\mathsf{acc}}) = \mathsf{acc}[\Pi_{\mathsf{NARK}}]$ using the accumulation scheme from Sect. 3.2 and $(\mathsf{P}_{\mathsf{acc,HL}} \mathsf{V}_{\mathsf{acc,HL}}) = \mathsf{acc}_{\mathsf{HL}}[\Pi_{\mathsf{NARK,CV}}]$ using the accumulation scheme described in Sect. 3.3. Then we apply the transformation from Theorem 1 to construct the IVC schemes IVC and $\mathsf{IVC}_{\mathsf{CV}}$.

Security: By Lemmas 1, 2, we have that Π_{NARK} has $(Q+1)\cdot\left[1-\prod_{i=1}^{k-1}(1-\frac{a_i}{|\mathbb{F}|})\right]$ knowledge error for relation $\mathcal{R}_{\mathsf{cm}}^{\mathcal{R}_{\mathsf{NP}}}$ for a polynomial-time Q-query RO-adversary. Witnesses for $\mathcal{R}_{\mathsf{cm}}^{\mathcal{R}_{\mathsf{NP}}}$ are either a witness for $\mathcal{R}_{\mathsf{NP}}$ or a break of the binding property of cm. Assuming that cm is a binding commitment scheme, the probability that a polynomial time adversary and a polynomial time extractor can compute such a break is $\mathsf{negl}(\lambda)$. Thus Π_{NARK} has knowledge error $\kappa = (Q+1)\cdot\left[1-\prod_{i=1}^{k-1}(1-\frac{a_i}{|\mathbb{F}|})\right] + \mathsf{negl}(\lambda)$ for $\mathcal{R}_{\mathsf{NP}}$. Analogously and using Lemma 3, $\Pi_{\mathsf{NARK,CV}}$ has knowledge soundness with knowledge error $\kappa' = (Q+1)\cdot\left[1-(1-\frac{\ell}{|\mathbb{F}|})\prod_{i=1}^{k-1}(1-\frac{a_i}{|\mathbb{F}|})\right] + \mathsf{negl}(\lambda)$ for $\mathcal{R}_{\mathsf{NP}}$. By assumption, κ and κ' are negligible in λ. Using Theorem 2 and the high-low degree accumulation scheme described previously, we can construct accumulation schemes acc and $\mathsf{acc}_{\mathsf{CV}}$ for Π_{NARK} and $\Pi_{\mathsf{NARK,CV}}$, respectively. The accumulation schemes have negligible knowledge error as $d = \mathsf{poly}(\lambda)$. Under the Fiat-Shamir heuristic for H we can turn the NARKs and the accumulation schemes into secure schemes in the standard model.

By Theorem 1, this yields IVC and $\mathsf{IVC}_{\mathsf{CV}}$, secure IVC schemes with predicates expressed in $\mathcal{R}_{\mathsf{NP}}$.

Efficiency: We first analyze the efficiency for IVC. The IVC-prover runs $\mathsf{P}_{\mathsf{sps}}$ to compute all prover messages. It also commits to all the $\mathsf{P}_{\mathsf{sps}}$ messages using cm. Finally, it needs to compute all error terms $\mathbf{e}_1, \ldots, \mathbf{e}_{d-1}$ and commit to them. The error terms are computed by symbolically evaluating the polynomial $e(X)$ in Eq. 3 with linear functions as inputs. The recursive circuit combines a new proof $\pi.x$ with an accumulator $\mathsf{acc}.x$. The size of the accumulator instance is ℓ_{in} field elements for the input, $k-1$ field elements for the interactive-proof challenges, 1 field element for the accumulator challenge, and k commitments for the $\mathsf{P}_{\mathsf{sps}}$ messages and $d-1$ commitments for the error terms. The IVC verifier checks the correctness of the commitments and runs $\mathsf{V}_{\mathsf{sps}}$.

For $\mathsf{IVC}_{\mathsf{CV}}$, the prover needs to additionally commit to a message $\mathbf{m}_{k+1}$ with length $O(\sqrt{\ell})$; the number of error terms also increases from $d-1$ to $d+1$. Fortunately, the error terms are only one element in $\mathbb{F}$, so we can use the identity function as the trivial commitment scheme. Thus, there is no cost for committing to the $d+1$ error terms when using CV. However, there is another separate error term $\mathbf{e}' \in \mathbb{F}^{2\sqrt{\ell}}$ for the additional $O(\sqrt{\ell})$ degree-2 checks, thus the prover needs to commit to $E' = \mathsf{Commit}(\mathbf{e}')$. The size of the accumulator instance is ℓ_{in} field elements for the input, k field elements for the interactive-proof challenges, 1 field element for the accumulator challenge, $k+1$ commitments for the prover messages, $d+1$ field elements for the error terms of the high-degree checks, and 1 commitment for the additional error term $\mathbf{e}'$. □

3.4 Computation of Error Terms

We now give an explicit algorithm for efficiently computing the error terms, that is, computing the polynomial $e(X)$ as defined in (3) (the degree of $e(X)$ is $d' = d+2$). The algorithm has similarities with computing the round polynomials in a single round of the sumcheck protocol [23].

1. For each $i = 0$ to d define

$$e^{(i)}(X) := \sum_{a=0}^{\sqrt{\ell}-1} \sum_{b=0}^{\sqrt{\ell}-1} (X \cdot \pi.\beta_a + \mathsf{acc}.\beta_a)(X \cdot \pi.\beta'_b + \mathsf{acc}.\beta'_b) \cdot f^{\mathsf{V}_{\mathsf{sps}}}_{i,a+b\sqrt{\ell}}(\mathsf{acc} + X \cdot \pi) \tag{4}$$

2. Compute $e^{(i)}(j)$ for all $j \in [0, i+2]$. Use these evaluations to interpolate $e^{(i)}(X)$ using fast interpolation methods, e.g. an iFFT
3. Compute the coefficient form of $e(X) = \sum_{i=0}^{d} e^{(i)}(X) \cdot (\mu + X)^{d-i}$. This is done by computing the coefficients of $e^{(i)}(X) \cdot (\mu + X)^{d-i}$ for every $i \in [0, d]$ using FFTs, and recover $e(X)$ using coefficient-wise addition. The complexity is $O(d^2 \log d)$.

In the worst case, this algorithm is equivalent to evaluating the circuit at $d+2$ different inputs. However, it can perform much better in practice. The reason is that many of the n gates may only be low degree. E.g. 90% of the gates are degree 1 or 2 addition and multiplication gates, and 10% are more high degree gates. Then the prover only has to evaluate the 10% of the circuit at $d+2$ points and 90% of the circuit only at 4 points. Note that the selector polynomials are static in the classification of NP plonkup. This means that each gate has precisely the degree of the active component. This stands in contrast to relations such as high-degree Plonk, where the selectors are pre-processed, and the selectors are preprocessed witnesses. In Plonk and related systems, each gate essentially has the same degree.

Dealing with Branched Gates. In some scenarios, the NARK proof π has the property that each gate $f^{\mathsf{V}_{\mathsf{sps}}}_{i,a+b\sqrt{\ell}}(\mathsf{acc} + X \cdot \pi)$ in Formula 4 can be represented as the sum of I parts where at most one part is related to π, that is, for some gates $g_1, \dots, g_I$ and some index $pc \in [I]$,

$$f^{\mathsf{V}_{\mathsf{sps}}}_{i,a+b\sqrt{\ell}}(\mathsf{acc} + X \cdot \pi) = g_{pc}(\mathsf{acc} + X \cdot \pi) + \sum_{j \in [I] \setminus \{pc\}} g_j(\mathsf{acc}).$$

In this case, for any gate $f^{\mathsf{V}_{\mathsf{sps}}}_{i,a+b\sqrt{\ell}}$, we present a caching algorithm for evaluating $f^{\mathsf{V}_{\mathsf{sps}}}_{i,a+b\sqrt{\ell}}(\mathsf{acc} + k \cdot \pi)$ at all evaluation points $k \in [0, i+2]$. The complexity is only proportional to the evaluation complexity of g_{pc} rather than $f^{\mathsf{V}_{\mathsf{sps}}}_{i,a+b\sqrt{\ell}}$.

1. For every $j \in [I]$, initialize $U_j := g_j(\mathsf{acc})$, and store $V := \sum_{j=1}^{I} U_j$.
2. Upon receiving a new NARK proof π during accumulation, for every $k \in [0, i+2]$, compute $f^{\mathsf{V}_{\mathsf{sps}}}_{i,a+b\sqrt{\ell}}(\mathsf{acc} + k \cdot \pi) = V + g_{pc}(\mathsf{acc} + k \cdot \pi) - U_{pc}$.
3. After the accumulation, let $\alpha \in \mathbb{F}$ be the folding challenge and let $U'_{pc} = g_{pc}(\mathsf{acc} + \alpha \cdot \pi)$, update $V \leftarrow V + U'_{pc} - U_{pc}$ and update $U_{pc} \leftarrow U'_{pc}$.

The algorithm is correct because V is always $\sum_{j\in[I]} g_j(\mathsf{acc})$ where acc is the current accumulator.

4 Special-Sound Subprotocols for ProtoStar

In this section, we present special-sound protocols for permutation, high-degree gate, circuit selection and lookup relations, which are the building blocks for the (non-uniform) Plonkish circuit-satisfiability relations. We can build accumulation schemes for (and thus IVCs from) these special-sound protocols via the framework presented in Sect. 3.

4.1 Permutation Relation

Definition 4. *Let $\sigma : [n] \to [n]$ be a permutation, the relation $\mathcal{R}_\sigma$ is the set of tuples $\mathbf{w} \in \mathbb{F}^n$ such that $\mathbf{w}_i = \mathbf{w}_{\sigma(i)}$ for all $i \in [n]$.*

Special-sound protocol Π_σ for permutation relation $\mathcal{R}_\sigma$

Prover $\mathsf{P}(\sigma, \mathbf{w} \in \mathbb{F}^n)$		**Verifier** $\mathsf{V}(\sigma)$
	$\xrightarrow{\mathbf{w}}$	
		Check $\mathbf{w}_i - \mathbf{w}_{\sigma(i)} = 0 \forall i \in [n]$

Complexity. Π_σ is a 1-move protocol (i.e. $k = 1$); the degree of the verifier is 1.

4.2 High-Degree Custom Gate Relation

Definition 5. *Given configuration $\mathcal{C}_{GATE} := (n, c, d, [\mathbf{s}_i \in \mathbb{F}^n, G_i]_{i=1}^m)$ where n is the number of gates, c is the arity per gate, d is the gate degree, $[\mathbf{s}_i]_{i=1}^m$ are the selector vectors, and $[G_i]_{i=1}^m$ are the gate formulas, the relation $\mathcal{R}_{GATE}$ is the set of tuples $\mathbf{w} \in \mathbb{F}^{cn}$ such that $\sum_{j=1}^m \mathbf{s}_{j,i} \cdot G_j(\mathbf{w}_i, \mathbf{w}_{i+n}, \ldots, \mathbf{w}_{i+(c-1)\cdot n}) = 0$ for all $i \in [n]$.*

Special-sound protocol Π_{GATE} for relation $\mathcal{R}_{\mathrm{GATE}}$

Prover $\mathsf{P}(\mathcal{C}_{\mathbf{GATE}}, \mathbf{w} \in \mathbb{F}^{cn})$		**Verifier** $\mathsf{V}(\mathcal{C}_{\mathbf{GATE}})$
	$\xrightarrow{\mathbf{w}}$	
		$\sum_{j=1}^{m} \mathbf{s}_{j,i} \cdot G_j(\mathbf{w}_i, \mathbf{w}_{i+n}, \ldots, \mathbf{w}_{i+(c-1)\cdot n}) \stackrel{?}{=} 0 \forall i \in [n]$

Complexity. Π_{GATE} is a 1-move protocol (i.e. $k = 1$) with verifier degree d.

4.3 Lookup Relation

Definition 6. *Given configuration $\mathcal{C}_{LK} := (T, \ell, \mathbf{t})$ where ℓ is the number of lookups and $\mathbf{t} \in \mathbb{F}^T$ is the lookup table, the relation $\mathcal{R}_{LK}$ is the set of tuples $\mathbf{w} \in \mathbb{F}^\ell$ such that $\mathbf{w}_i \in \mathbf{t}$ for all $i \in [\ell]$.*

We recall a useful lemma for lookup relation from [17], and present a special-sound protocol for the lookup relation.

Lemma 4 (Lemma 5 of [17]). *Let $\mathbb{F}$ be a field of characteristic $p > \max(\ell, T)$. Given two sequences of field elements $[\mathbf{w}_i]_{i=1}^\ell$ and $[\mathbf{t}_i]_{i=1}^T$, we have $\{\mathbf{w}_i\} \subseteq \{\mathbf{t}_i\}$ as sets (with multiples of values removed) if and only if there exists a sequence $[\mathbf{m}_i]_{i=1}^T$ of field elements such that*

$$\sum_{i=1}^{\ell} \frac{1}{X + \mathbf{w}_i} = \sum_{i=1}^{T} \frac{\mathbf{m}_i}{X + \mathbf{t}_i}. \tag{5}$$

Special-sound protocol Π_{LK} for $\mathcal{R}_{\mathrm{LK}}$

Prover $\mathsf{P}(\mathcal{C}_{\mathbf{LK}}, \mathbf{w} \in \mathbb{F}^{\ell})$ **Verifier** $\mathsf{V}(\mathcal{C}_{\mathbf{LK}})$

Compute $\mathbf{m} \in \mathbb{F}^T$ such that

$$\mathbf{m}_i := \sum_{j=1}^{\ell} \mathbb{1}(\mathbf{w}_j = \mathbf{t}_i) \forall i \in [T] \xrightarrow{\mathbf{w}, \mathbf{m}}$$

$$\xleftarrow{r} \quad r \leftarrow\$ \mathbb{F}$$

Compute $\mathbf{h} \in \mathbb{F}^{\ell}$, $\mathbf{g} \in \mathbb{F}^T$

$$\mathbf{h}_i := \frac{1}{\mathbf{w}_i + r} \forall i \in [\ell]$$

$$\mathbf{g}_i := \frac{\mathbf{m}_i}{\mathbf{t}_i + r} \forall i \in [T] \xrightarrow{\mathbf{h}, \mathbf{g}}$$

$$\sum_{i=1}^{\ell} \mathbf{h}_i \stackrel{?}{=} \sum_{i=1}^{T} \mathbf{g}_i$$

$$\mathbf{h}_i \cdot (\mathbf{w}_i + r) \stackrel{?}{=} 1 \forall i \in [\ell]$$

$$\mathbf{g}_i \cdot (\mathbf{t}_i + r) \stackrel{?}{=} \mathbf{m}_i \forall i \in [T]$$

Achieving Perfect Completeness. Note that the protocol does not have perfect completeness. If there exists an $\mathbf{w}_i$ or $\mathbf{t}_i$ such that $\mathbf{w}_i + r = 0$ $\mathbf{t}_i + r = 0$ then the prover message is undefined. We can achieve perfect completeness by having the verifier set $\mathbf{h}_i = 0$ or $\mathbf{g}_i = 0$ in this case and changing the verification equations to

$$(\mathbf{w}_i + r) \cdot (\mathbf{h}_i \cdot (\mathbf{w}_i + r) - 1) = 0$$

and

$$(\mathbf{t}_i + r) \cdot (\mathbf{g}_i \cdot (\mathbf{t}_i + r) - \mathbf{m}_i) = 0\,.$$

These checks ensure that either $\mathbf{h}_i = \frac{1}{\mathbf{w}_i + r}$ or $\mathbf{w}_i + r = 0$. The checks increase the verifier degree to 3. Without these checks, the protocol has a negligible completeness error of $\frac{\ell + T}{|\mathbb{F}|}$. This completeness error can likely be ignored in practice, and these checks do not need to be implemented. However, to achieve the full definition of PCD (which has perfect completeness) and use Theorem 1 by [8], we require that all protocols have perfect completeness.

Complexity. Π_{LK} is a 3-move protocol (i.e. $k = 2$); the degree of the verifier is 2; the number of non-zero elements in the prover message is at most 4ℓ.

Accumulation with $O(\ell)$ Prover Complexity. The prover complexity of Π_{LK} is due to the sparseness of $\mathbf{g} \in \mathbb{F}^T$ and $\mathbf{m} \in \mathbb{F}^T$. However, there is no guarantee that when building an accumulation scheme for Π_{LK}, the accumulated $\mathsf{acc}.\mathbf{g}$ and $\mathsf{acc}.\mathbf{m}$ are sparse. This is an issue, as the prover needs to compute the error term $\mathbf{e}_1$. If we expand the accumulation procedures, we see that the three verification checks lead to three components of the error term $\mathbf{e}_1$:

$$\mathbf{e}_1^{(1)} = \left(\sum_{i=1}^{\ell} \mathsf{acc}.\mathbf{h}_i - \sum_{i=1}^{T} \mathsf{acc}.\mathbf{g}_i\right) + \mu \left(\sum_{i=1}^{\ell} \pi.\mathbf{h}_i - \sum_{i=1}^{T} \pi.\mathbf{g}_i\right) \in \mathbb{F}$$

$$\mathbf{e}_1^{(2)} = \mathsf{acc}.\mathbf{h} \circ (\pi.\mathbf{w} + \pi.r \cdot \mathbf{1}^\ell) + \pi.\mathbf{h} \circ (\mathsf{acc}.\mathbf{w} + \mathsf{acc}.r \cdot \mathbf{1}^\ell) - 2\mu \cdot \mathbf{1}^\ell \in \mathbb{F}^\ell$$

$$\mathbf{e}_1^{(3)} = \mathsf{acc}.\mathbf{g} \circ (\mathbf{t} + \pi.r \cdot \mathbf{1}^T) + \pi.\mathbf{g} \circ (\mu \cdot \mathbf{t} + \mathsf{acc}.r \cdot \mathbf{1}^T) - \mu \cdot \pi.\mathbf{m} - \mathsf{acc}.\mathbf{m} \in \mathbb{F}^T.$$

We examine all three components below.

For $\mathbf{e}_1^{(1)}$, we see that $(\sum_{i=1}^{\ell} \pi.\mathbf{h}_i - \sum_{i=1}^{T} \pi.\mathbf{g}_i) = 0$ by the assumption that π is valid, and $(\sum_{i=1}^{\ell} \mathsf{acc}.\mathbf{h}_i - \sum_{i=1}^{T} \mathsf{acc}.\mathbf{g}_i) = \mathsf{acc}.\mathbf{e}^{(1)}/\mathsf{acc}.\mu$ (where $\mathsf{acc}.\mathbf{e}^{(1)}$ is the first component of the error vector for acc). Thus $\mathbf{e}_1^{(1)} = \mathsf{acc}.\mathbf{e}^{(1)}/\mathsf{acc}.\mu$. We observe that since in IVC the accumulator $\mathsf{acc}.\mathbf{e}^{(1)}$ is initiated with 0, this implies that for all iterations $\mathbf{e}_1^{(1)} = 0$.

For $\mathbf{e}_1^{(2)}$, it is computed from terms of size ℓ, so can be computed in time $O(\ell)$.

For $\mathbf{e}_1^{(3)}$, note that $\mathsf{acc}.\mu$, $\mathsf{acc}.r$ and $\pi.r$ are all scalars. Also note that the accumulation prover only needs to compute the commitment $E_1 = \mathsf{Commit}(\mathsf{ck}, \mathbf{e}_1) = \mathsf{Commit}(\mathsf{ck}, \mathbf{e}_1^{(1)}) + \mathsf{Commit}(\mathsf{ck}, 0||\mathbf{e}_1^{(2)}) + \mathsf{Commit}(\mathsf{ck}, \mathbf{0}^{\ell+1}||\mathbf{e}_1^{(3)})$, not the actual vector $\mathbf{e}_1$. We will compute $E_1^{(3)} = \mathsf{Commit}(\mathsf{ck}, \mathbf{e}_1^{(3)})$ homomorphically from the commitments below (dropping the zero padding for readability):

1. $G = \mathsf{Commit}(\mathsf{ck}, \pi.\mathbf{g})$, $G' = \mathsf{Commit}(\mathsf{ck}, \mathsf{acc}.\mathbf{g})$,
2. $M = \mathsf{Commit}(\mathsf{ck}, \pi.\mathbf{m})$, $M' = \mathsf{Commit}(\mathsf{ck}, \mathsf{acc}.\mathbf{m})$,
3. $GT = \mathsf{Commit}(\mathsf{ck}, \pi.\mathbf{g} \circ \mathbf{t})$, $GT' = \mathsf{Commit}(\mathsf{ck}, \mathsf{acc}.\mathbf{g} \circ \mathbf{t})$.

Given these commitments, we can compute

$$E_1^{(3)} = GT' + \pi.r \cdot G' + \mathsf{acc}.\mu \cdot GT + \mathsf{acc}.r \cdot G - \mathsf{acc}.\mu \cdot M - M'.$$

This reduces the problem to the problem of efficiently computing and updating the commitments. G, M and GT are all commitments to ℓ-sparse vectors, thus can be efficiently computed. The prover can cache the commitments G', M', and GT' and efficiently update them during accumulation. That is $G'' \leftarrow G' + \alpha G$, $M'' \leftarrow M' + \alpha M$ and $GT'' \leftarrow GT' + \alpha GT$. Additionally, we need to update the accumulation witnesses: $\mathsf{acc}'.\mathbf{m} \leftarrow \mathsf{acc}.\mathbf{m} + \alpha\pi.\mathbf{m}$ and $\mathsf{acc}'.\mathbf{g} \leftarrow \mathsf{acc}.\mathbf{g} + \alpha\pi.\mathbf{g}$. Again because $\pi.\mathbf{g}, \pi.\mathbf{m}$ are sparse this can be done in time $O(\ell)$ independent of $T = |\mathbf{t}|$.

When Π_{LK} is used in composition with another special-sound protocol with a higher degree d, the accumulation is made homogeneous using a $(X + \mu)^{d-2}$ factor when computing the error terms. The contribution to the error terms $\mathbf{e}_i$ $(1 \leq i \leq d - 1)$ is still a linear function in $\mathsf{acc}.\mathbf{g}$, $\mathsf{acc}.\mathbf{m}$ and $\mathsf{acc}.\mathbf{g} \circ \mathbf{t}$, and thus can be computed homomorphically from commitments to these values.

Finally, we note that the algorithm above can be generalized to support polynomial $\mathbf{e}(X)$ with more general formats and with higher degrees. We refer to the full version [7] for more details.

Special-Soundness. We prove special-soundness for the perfect complete version of Π_{LK}, the proof for Π_{LK} is almost identical (but even simpler).

Lemma 5. *The perfect complete version of Π_{LK} is $2(\ell+T)$-special-sound.*

We defer the proof to the full version [7].

The Special-Sound Protocol for Plonkup. The special-sound protocol for the Plonkup relation is the parallel composition of Π_σ, Π_{GATE} and Π_{LK}. We refer to the full version [7] for more detailed descriptions.

Vector-Valued Lookup. In some applications (e.g., simulating bit operations in circuits), we need to support lookup for a vector, i.e., each table value is a vector of field elements. In this section, we adapt the scheme in Sect. 4.3 to support vector lookups.

Definition 7. *Consider configuration $\mathcal{C}_{VLK} := (T, \ell, v \in \mathbb{N}, \mathbf{t})$ where ℓ is the number of lookups, and $\mathbf{t} \in (\mathbb{F}^v)^T$ is a lookup table in which the ith $(1 \le i \le T)$ entry is*

$$\mathbf{t}_i := (\mathbf{t}_{i,1}, \ldots, \mathbf{t}_{i,v}) \in \mathbb{F}^v .$$

A sequence of vectors $\mathbf{w} \in (\mathbb{F}^v)^\ell$ is in relation $\mathcal{R}_{VLK}$ if and only if for all $i \in [\ell]$,

$$\mathbf{w}_i := (\mathbf{w}_{i,1}, \ldots, \mathbf{w}_{i,v}) \in \mathbf{t} .$$

As noted in Sect. 3.4 of [17], we can extend Lemma 4 and replace Eq. 5 with

$$\sum_{i=1}^{\ell} \frac{1}{X + w_i(Y)} = \sum_{i=1}^{T} \frac{\mathbf{m}_i}{X + t_i(Y)} \tag{6}$$

where the polynomials are defined as

$$w_i(Y) := \sum_{j=1}^{v} \mathbf{w}_{i,j} \cdot Y^{j-1}, \quad t_i(Y) := \sum_{j=1}^{v} \mathbf{t}_{i,j} \cdot Y^{j-1},$$

which represent the witness vector $\mathbf{w}_i \in \mathbb{F}^v$ and the table vector $\mathbf{t}_i \in \mathbb{F}^v$. We, therefore, can describe a special-sound protocol for the vector lookup relation as follows.

Special-sound protocol Π^v_{VLK} for $\mathcal{R}_{\mathrm{VLK}}$

Prover $\mathsf{P}(\mathcal{C}_{\mathbf{VLK}}, \mathbf{w} \in (\mathbb{F}^v)^\ell)$ — **Verifier** $\mathsf{V}(\mathcal{C}_{\mathbf{VLK}})$

Compute $\mathbf{m} \in \mathbb{F}^T$ such that

$$\mathbf{m}_i := \sum_{j=1}^{\ell} \mathbb{1}(\mathbf{w}_j = \mathbf{t}_i) \forall i \in [T]$$

Prover → Verifier: $\mathbf{w}, \mathbf{m}$

Verifier: $\beta \leftarrow \$ \mathbb{F}$; Verifier → Prover: β

Prover → Verifier: $\perp$

Verifier: $r \leftarrow \$ \mathbb{F}$; Verifier → Prover: r

Compute $[\beta_i = \beta^{i-1}]_{i=1}^v$

and $\mathbf{h} \in \mathbb{F}^\ell$, $\mathbf{g} \in \mathbb{F}^T$

$$\mathbf{h}_i := \frac{1}{w_i(\beta) + r} \forall i \in [\ell]$$

$$\mathbf{g}_i := \frac{\mathbf{m}_i}{t_i(\beta) + r} \forall i \in [T]$$

Prover → Verifier: $[\beta_i]_{i=1}^v, \mathbf{h}, \mathbf{g}$

Verifier checks:

$$\sum_{i=1}^{\ell} \mathbf{h}_i \stackrel{?}{=} \sum_{i=1}^{T} \mathbf{g}_i$$

$$\mathbf{h}_i \cdot [(\sum_{j=1}^{v} \mathbf{w}_{i,j} \cdot \beta_j) + r] \stackrel{?}{=} 1 \forall i \in [\ell]$$

$$\mathbf{g}_i \cdot [(\sum_{j=1}^{v} \mathbf{t}_{i,j} \cdot \beta_j) + r] \stackrel{?}{=} \mathbf{m}_i \forall i \in [T]$$

$$\beta_{i+1} \stackrel{?}{=} \beta_i \cdot \beta \forall i \in [v-1], \beta_1 \stackrel{?}{=} 1$$

Achieving Perfect Completeness. We can use the same trick in Sect. 4.3 to achieve perfect completeness for Π^v_{VLK}. Namely, the verifier sets $\mathbf{h}_i = 0$ or $\mathbf{g}_i = 0$ when $w_i(\beta) + r = 0$ or $t_i(\beta) + r = 0$ respectively. The verification equations become

$$(w_i(\beta_1, \ldots, \beta_v) + r) \cdot (\mathbf{h}_i \cdot (w_i(\beta_1, \ldots, \beta_v) + r) - 1) = 0$$

and

$$(t_i(\beta_1, \ldots, \beta_v) + r) \cdot (\mathbf{g}_i \cdot (t_i(\beta_1, \ldots, \beta_v) + r) - \mathbf{m}_i) = 0,$$

where $w_i(\beta_1, \ldots, \beta_v) := \left(\sum_{j=1}^v \mathbf{w}_{i,j} \cdot \beta_j\right)$ and $t_i(\beta_1, \ldots, \beta_v) := \left(\sum_{j=1}^v \mathbf{t}_{i,j} \cdot \beta_j\right)$. The degree of the verifier is 5. In practice, the negligible completeness error can likely be ignored without implementing these checks.

Accumulation Complexity. Π_{VLK} is a 5-move protocol (i.e. $k = 3$) with the 2nd prover message being empty; the degree of the verifier is 3; the number of non-zero elements in the prover message is at most $(v + 3)\ell + v$. To ensure that the accumulation procedure only requires $O(v\ell)$ operations independent of T, we can apply the same trick as in Sect. 4.3.

Special-Soundness. The perfect complete version of Π^v_{VLK} is special-sound.

Lemma 6. *For any $v \in \mathbb{N}$, the perfect complete version of Π^v_{VLK} is $[1 + (v - 1) \cdot (\ell + T - 1), 2(\ell + T)]$-special-sound.*

We defer the proof to the full version [7].

4.4 Circuit Selection

We provide a sub-protocol for showing that a vector has a single one-bit (and zeros otherwise) at the location of a program counter pc. This is later used to select the appropriate circuit.

Definition 8. *For an integer n the relation $\mathcal{R}_{select}$ is the set of tuples $(\mathbf{b}, pc) \in \mathbb{F}^n \times \mathbb{F}$ such that $b_i = 0 \forall i \in [n] \setminus \{pc\}$ and if $pc \in [n]$ then $b_{pc} = 1$.*

Special-sound protocol Π_{select} for circuit selecting relation $\mathcal{R}_{\text{select}}$

Prover $\mathsf{P}(\mathbf{b} \in \mathbb{F}^n, pc \in \mathbb{F})$ **Verifier** V

$$\xrightarrow{\mathbf{b}, pc}$$

$$b_i \cdot (pc - i) \stackrel{?}{=} 0 \forall i \in [n]$$

$$b_i \cdot (b_i - 1) \stackrel{?}{=} 0 \forall i \in [n]$$

$$\sum_{i \in [n]} b_i \stackrel{?}{=} 1$$

Complexity and security. Π_{select} is a 1-move protocol (i.e. $k = 1$); the degree of the verifier is 2.

The protocol trivially satisfies completeness. Note that the protocol is also sound: the checks $b_i \cdot (b_i - 1) = 0$ ensure that the vector $\mathbf{b}$ is Boolean; the checks $b_i \cdot (pc - i) = 0$ ensures that $b_i = 0$ if $i \neq pc$; finally, the last check guarantees that $b_{pc} = 1 - \sum_{i \in [n] \setminus \{pc\}} b_i = 1$ as $b_i = 0$ for all $i \in [n] \setminus \{pc\}$.

5 Protostar

In this section, we describe PROTOSTAR, which is built using a special-sound protocol for capturing non-uniform Plonkup circuit computations. In particular, the relation is checking that *one* of the I circuits is satisfied, where the index of the target circuit is determined by a part of the public input called program counter pc. The non-uniform Plonkup circuit can add arbitrary constraints on input pc.

For ease of exposition, we assume that the I circuits have the same number of (i) gates n, (i) gate arity c, (ii) gate degree d, (iii) gate types m, (iv) public inputs ℓ_{in} and (v) lookup gates ℓ_{lk}.

The scheme naturally extends when different branch circuits have different parameters.

Definition 9. *Consider configuration* $\mathcal{C}_{mplkup} := (\mathsf{pp} = [n, T, c, d, m, \ell_{\mathsf{in}}, \ell_{\mathsf{lk}}]; [\mathcal{C}_i]_{i=1}^{I}; \mathbf{t})$ *where the ith* $(1 \le i \le I)$ *branch circuit has configuration* $\mathcal{C}_i := (\mathsf{pp}, \sigma_i, [\mathbf{s}_{i,j}, G_{i,j}]_{j=1}^{m}, L_i)$, *and* $\mathbf{t} \in \mathbb{F}^T$ *is the global lookup table. For a public input* $\mathsf{pi} := (pc, \mathsf{pi}') \in \mathbb{F}^{\ell_{\mathsf{in}}}$ *where* $pc \in [I]$ *is a program counter, we say that* $(\mathsf{pi}, \mathbf{w} \in \mathbb{F}^{cn})$ *is in the relation* $\mathcal{R}_{mplkup}$ *if and only if* $(\mathsf{pi}, \mathbf{w}) \in \mathcal{R}_{plonkup}$ *w.r.t. circuit configuration* $(\mathcal{C}_{pc}, \mathbf{t})$.

Protocol $\Pi_{\mathbf{mplkup}} = \langle \mathsf{P}(\mathcal{C}_{\mathbf{mplkup}}, \mathsf{pi}, \mathbf{w}), \mathsf{V}(\mathcal{C}_{\mathbf{mplkup}}, \mathsf{pi} = (pc \in [I], \mathsf{pi}')) \rangle$:

1. P sends V vector $\mathbf{b} = (0, \ldots, 0, b_{pc} = 1, 0, \ldots, 0) \in \mathbb{F}^I$.
2. V checks that $b_i \cdot (1 - b_i) \stackrel{?}{=} 0$ and $b_i \cdot (i - pc) \stackrel{?}{=} 0$ for all $i \in [I]$, and $\sum_{i \in [I]} b_i \stackrel{?}{=} 1$.
3. P sends vector $\mathbf{m} \in \mathbb{F}^T$ such that $\mathbf{m}_i := \sum_{j \in L_{pc}} \mathbb{1}(\mathbf{w}_j = \mathbf{t}_i) \forall i \in [T]$.
4. P sends V a sparse vector $\mathbf{w}^* := (\mathbf{w}^{(1)}, \ldots, \mathbf{w}^{(I)}) \in \mathbb{F}^{Icn}$ where $\mathbf{w}^{(i)} = 0^{cn}$ for all $i \in [I] \setminus \{pc\}$ and $\mathbf{w}^{(pc)} = \mathbf{w}$.
5. V checks that
   Permutation check: $\sum_{j=1}^{I} b_j (\mathbf{w}_i^{(j)} - \mathbf{w}_{\sigma_j(i)}^{(j)}) \stackrel{?}{=} 0$ for all $i \in [cn]$.
   Public input check: $\sum_{j=1}^{I} b_j \cdot \mathbf{w}^{(j)}[1..\ell_{\mathsf{in}}] \stackrel{?}{=} \mathsf{pi}$.
   Gate check: for all $i \in [n]$, it holds that
   $$\sum_{j=1}^{I} b_j \cdot \mathsf{GT}_{j,i}\left(\mathbf{w}_i^{(j)}, \ldots, \mathbf{w}_{i+cn-n}^{(j)}\right) = 0$$
   where $\mathsf{GT}_{j,i}(x_1, \ldots, x_c) := \sum_{k=1}^{m} \mathbf{s}_{j,k}[i] \cdot G_{j,k}(x_1, \ldots, x_c)$.
6. V samples and sends P random challenge $r \leftarrow\$ \mathbb{F}$.
7. P computes vectors $\mathbf{h} \in \mathbb{F}^{\ell_{\mathsf{lk}}}$, $\mathbf{g} \in \mathbb{F}^T$ such that
   $$\mathbf{h}_i := \frac{1}{\mathbf{w}_{L_{pc}[i]} + r} \forall i \in [\ell_{\mathsf{lk}}], \qquad \mathbf{g}_i := \frac{\mathbf{m}_i}{\mathbf{t}_i + r} \forall i \in [T].$$
8. V checks that $\sum_{i=1}^{\ell_{\mathsf{lk}}} \mathbf{h}_i \stackrel{?}{=} \sum_{i=1}^{T} \mathbf{g}_i$ and
   $$\sum_{j=1}^{I} b_j \cdot \left[\mathbf{h}_i \cdot (\mathbf{w}_{L_j[i]}^{(j)} + r)\right] \stackrel{?}{=} 1 \quad \forall i \in [\ell_{\mathsf{lk}}],$$
   $$\mathbf{g}_i \cdot (\mathbf{t}_i + r) \stackrel{?}{=} \mathbf{m}_i \quad \forall i \in [T]$$

We present the special-sound protocol $\Pi_{\mathbf{mplkup}}$ for the multi-circuit Plonkup relation.

Remark 2. The public input check $\sum_{j=1}^{I} b_j \cdot \mathbf{w}^{(j)}[1..\ell_{\mathsf{in}}] \stackrel{?}{=} \mathsf{pi}$ is equivalent to $\mathbf{w}[1..\ell_{\mathsf{in}}] = \mathbf{w}_{pc}[1..\ell_{\mathsf{in}}] \stackrel{?}{=} \mathsf{pi}$ if the vector $\mathbf{b}$ passes the check at Step 2. Thus we guarantee that $\mathbf{w}[1] = pc$, and the circuit relation can add constraints on pc depending on the applications.

Special-Soundness. We prove the special-soundness property of $\Pi_{\mathbf{mplkup}}$ below.

Lemma 7. *Π_{mplkup} is $2(T+\ell_{\mathsf{lk}})$-special-sound.*

We defer the proof to the full version [7].

We will now use Π_{mplkup} and our compiler described in Theorem 3 to design PROTOSTAR. Before that, we address two efficiency issues regarding supporting multiple branch circuits and combining high-degree gates with sparse lookups.

Efficient Accumulation for Supporting Many Branch Circuits. Let I be the number of branch circuits. At first glance, the message $\mathbf{w}^*$ has length $O(In)$ and seems the accumulation prover needs to take $O(In)$ time to fold the witness. Fortunately, the prover message $\mathbf{w}^* := (\mathbf{w}^{(1)}, \ldots, \mathbf{w}^{(I)}) \in \mathbb{F}^{Icn}$ is sparse: only the witness $\mathbf{w}^{(pc)}$ for the single activated branch circuit $\mathcal{C}_{pc}$ is non-zero (where $\mathbf{w}^{(pc)}$ can be determined at runtime). Thus, using the commitment to $\mathsf{acc}.\mathbf{w}^*$ and the commitments homomorphism, the complexity for the prover to fold $\mathbf{w}^*$ onto $\mathsf{acc}.\mathbf{w}^*$ is only $O(n)$.

On the other hand, the accumulation prover also needs to compute the error terms $[\mathbf{e}_j]_{j=1}^{d-1}$ described at Step 2 of Fig. 3. Note that each gate check can be split into I parts where at most one part is active, that is, $\sum_{j=1}^{I} b_j \cdot \mathsf{GT}_{j,i}(\mathbf{w}_i^{(j)}, \ldots, \mathbf{w}_{i+cn-n}^{(j)})$ can be split into I branch gates where the j-th $(1 \leq j \leq I)$ branch gate is $b_j \cdot \mathsf{GT}_{j,i}(\mathbf{w}_i^{(j)}, \ldots, \mathbf{w}_{i+cn-n}^{(j)})$. Thus we can use the caching algorithm described in Sect. 3.4 to achieve $O(d|\mathcal{C}_{pc}|)$ computational complexity rather than $O(d(|\mathcal{C}_1| + \cdots + |\mathcal{C}_I|))$ where $\mathcal{C}_i$ $(1 \leq i \leq I)$ is the evaluation cost of the i-th branch circuit.

Next, we address the issue of combining the high-degree gate and sparse lookup protocols with the generic transform CV in Sect. 3.3.

Efficient Accumulation of $\mathsf{CV}[\Pi_{mplkup}]$. $\mathsf{CV}[\Pi_{\mathrm{GATE}}]$ reduces the number of degree-d verification checks in Π_{GATE} from n to 1, with the tradeoff of $O(\sqrt{n})$ additional degree-2 checks. In the resulting accumulation scheme, the error terms for high-degree gates are, thus, only of length 1. This enables using the trivial identity commitment for these error terms and thus reduces the number of group operations by the accumulation verifier. Unfortunately, applying CV to mplkup seems to have a major tradeoff. The number of verification checks is $n + \ell_{\mathsf{lk}} + T + c \cdot n$. This requires using a) CV[mplkup] and b) is not composable with the sparseness optimizations for lookup described in Sect. 4.3. These optimizations make the prover computation independent of T.

Fortunately, a closer look at the verification of mplkup reveals that only n of these verification checks are of high degree d, namely the checks in Π_{GATE}. The other checks are of degree 2 or lower. With a slight abuse of notation, we can define $\mathsf{CV}[\Pi_{\mathsf{mplkup}}]$ as applying the generic transform CV only to the Π_{GATE} part of Π_{mplkup}. This means that there are $d+1$ cross error vectors (each of length 1) for the degree $d+2$ check in $\mathsf{CV}[\Pi_{\mathrm{GATE}}]$; and 1 cross error vector of length $T + \ell_{\mathsf{lk}} + cn + O(\sqrt{n})$ for the rest checks—namely the low-degree checks in Π_{mplkup} and the $O(\sqrt{n})$ degree-2 checks in $\mathsf{CV}[\Pi_{\mathrm{GATE}}]$. By leveraging the error separation technique described in Sect. 3.3, we can use the identity function to commit to the field elements and a vector commitment to commit to the long error term. Again we leverage homomorphism as described in Sect. 4.3 to make the prover independent of T.

Corollary 1 (Protostar protocol). *Consider the configuration*

$$\mathcal{C}_{mplkup} := (n, T, c, d, m, \ell_{\mathsf{in}}, \ell_{\mathsf{lk}}; [\mathcal{C}_i]_{i=1}^{I}; \mathbf{t}).$$

Given a binding homomorphic commitment scheme $\mathsf{cm} = (\mathsf{Setup}, \mathsf{Commit})$, *and under the Fiat-Shamir Heuristic (Definition 3) for a hash function* H, *there exists an IVC scheme* PROTOSTAR *for* $\mathcal{R}_{mplkup}$ *relations with the following efficiencies for* $m = 1$ *(i.e. each circuit has a single degree-d gate type), public input length* $\ell_{\mathsf{in}} = 1$*: (we omit cost terms that are negligible compared to the dominant parts)*

$\mathsf{P}_{\text{PROTOSTAR}}$ *native*	$\mathsf{P}_{\text{PROTOSTAR}}$ *recursive*	$\mathsf{V}_{\text{PROTOSTAR}}$	$\lvert\pi_{\text{PROTOSTAR}}\rvert$
$O(\lvert\mathbf{w}\rvert + \ell_{\mathsf{lk}})\mathbb{G}$ $L'(\mathcal{C}_{pc}, d+2) + 2\ell_{\mathsf{lk}}\mathbb{F}$	$3\mathbb{G}$ $d + 4\mathbb{F}$ $d + O(1)H + 1\mathsf{H}_{\mathsf{in}}$	$O(c \cdot n + T + \ell_{\mathsf{lk}})\mathbb{G}$ $n + \sum_{i=1}^{I} \mathcal{C}_i + T + \ell_{\mathsf{lk}}\mathbb{F}$	$O(c \cdot n + T + \ell_{\mathsf{lk}})$

Here $\lvert\mathbf{w}\rvert \le cn$ *is the number of non-zero entries in the witness,* $\sum_{i=1}^{I} \mathcal{C}_i$ *is the cost of evaluating all circuits on some random input, and* $L'(\mathcal{C}_{pc}, d)$ *is the cost of computing the coefficients of the polynomial* $\mathsf{e}(X)$ *defined in Eq. 3 using techniques from Sect. 5.*[5] H_{in} *is the cost of hashing the public input and the (constant-sized) accumulator instance.*

We defer the proof to the full version [7].

References

1. Attema, T., Fehr, S., Klooß, M.: Fiat-Shamir transformation of multi-round interactive proofs. In: Kiltz, E., Vaikuntanathan, V. (eds.) TCC 2022, Part I. LNCS, vol. 13747, pp. 113–142. Springer, Cham (2022). https://doi.org/10.1007/978-3-031-22318-1_5
2. Ben-Sasson, E., Chiesa, A., Tromer, E., Virza, M.: Scalable zero knowledge via cycles of elliptic curves. In: Garay, J.A., Gennaro, R. (eds.) CRYPTO 2014, Part II. LNCS, vol. 8617, pp. 276–294. Springer, Heidelberg (2014). https://doi.org/10.1007/978-3-662-44381-1_16
3. Bitansky, N., Canetti, R., Chiesa, A., Tromer, E.: Recursive composition and bootstrapping for SNARKS and proof-carrying data. In: Boneh, D., Roughgarden, T., Feigenbaum, J. (eds.) 45th ACM STOC, pp. 111–120. ACM Press (2013). https://doi.org/10.1145/2488608.2488623
4. Boneh, D., Bonneau, J., Bünz, B., Fisch, B.: Verifiable delay functions. In: Shacham, H., Boldyreva, A. (eds.) CRYPTO 2018, Part I. LNCS, vol. 10991, pp. 757–788. Springer, Cham (2018). https://doi.org/10.1007/978-3-319-96884-1_25

[5] As noted in Theorem 3, $L'(\mathcal{C}_{pc}, d+2)$ is bounded by $O(nd\log^2(d))$.

5. Bonneau, J., Meckler, I., Rao, V., Shapiro, E.: Coda: decentralized cryptocurrency at scale. Cryptology ePrint Archive, Report 2020/352 (2020). https://eprint.iacr.org/2020/352
6. Bowe, S., Grigg, J., Hopwood, D.: Halo: recursive proof composition without a trusted setup. Cryptology ePrint Archive, Report 2019/1021 (2019). https://eprint.iacr.org/2019/1021
7. Bünz, B., Chen, B.: Protostar: generic efficient accumulation/folding for special sound protocols. In: Cryptology ePrint Archive (2023)
8. Bünz, B., Chiesa, A., Lin, W., Mishra, P., Spooner, N.: Proof-carrying data without succinct arguments. In: Malkin, T., Peikert, C. (eds.) CRYPTO 2021, Part I. LNCS, vol. 12825, pp. 681–710. Springer, Cham (2021). https://doi.org/10.1007/978-3-030-84242-0_24
9. Bünz, B., Chiesa, A., Mishra, P., Spooner, N.: Recursive proof composition from accumulation schemes. In: Pass, R., Pietrzak, K. (eds.) TCC 2020, Part II. LNCS, vol. 12551, pp. 1–18. Springer, Cham (2020). https://doi.org/10.1007/978-3-030-64378-2_1
10. Buterin, V.: The different types of ZK EVM (2022). https://vitalik.ca/general/2022/08/04/zkevm.html. Accessed 27 Apr 2023
11. Chen, B., Bünz, B., Boneh, D., Zhang, Z.: HyperPlonk: plonk with linear-time prover and high-degree custom gates. Cryptology ePrint Archive, Report 2022/1355 (2022). https://eprint.iacr.org/2022/1355
12. Chiesa, A., Tromer, E.: Proof-carrying data and hearsay arguments from signature cards. In: Chi-Chih, A. (ed.) ICS 2010, pp. 310–331. Yao, Tsinghua University Press (2010)
13. Chiesa, A., Tromer, E., Virza, M.: Cluster computing in zero knowledge. In: Oswald, E., Fischlin, M. (eds.) EUROCRYPT 2015, Part II. LNCS, vol. 9057, pp. 371–403. Springer, Heidelberg (2015). https://doi.org/10.1007/978-3-662-46803-6_13
14. Eagen, L., Fiore, D., Gabizon, A.: cq: cached quotients for fast lookups. Cryptology ePrint Archive, Report 2022/1763 (2022). https://eprint.iacr.org/2022/1763
15. Gabizon, A., Williamson, Z.J.: plookup: a simplified polynomial protocol for lookup tables. Cryptology ePrint Archive, Report 2020/315 (2020). https://eprint.iacr.org/2020/315
16. Gabizon, A., Williamson, Z.J., Ciobotaru, O.: PLONK: permutations over lagrange-bases for oecumenical noninteractive arguments of knowledge. Cryptology ePrint Archive, Report 2019/953 (2019). https://eprint.iacr.org/2019/953
17. Haböck, U.: Multivariate lookups based on logarithmic derivatives. Cryptology ePrint Archive, Report 2022/1530 (2022). https://eprint.iacr.org/2022/1530
18. Kattis, A., Bonneau, J.: Proof of necessary work: succinct state verification with fairness guarantees. Cryptology ePrint Archive, Report 2020/190 (2020). https://eprint.iacr.org/2020/190
19. Khovratovich, D., Maller, M., Tiwari, P.R.: MinRoot: candidate sequential function for ethereum VDF. Cryptology ePrint Archive, Report 2022/1626 (2022). https://eprint.iacr.org/2022/1626
20. Kothapalli, A., Setty, S.: HyperNova: recursive arguments for customizable constraint systems. In: Cryptology ePrint Archive (2023)
21. Kothapalli, A., Setty, S.: SuperNova: proving universal machine executions without universal circuits. Cryptology ePrint Archive, Report 2022/1758 (2022). https://eprint.iacr.org/2022/1758

22. Kothapalli, A., Setty, S., Tzialla, I.: Nova: recursive zero-knowledge arguments from folding schemes. In: Dodis, Y., Shrimpton, T. (eds.) CRYPTO 2022, Part IV. LNCS, vol. 13510, pp. 359–388. Springer, Cham (2022). https://doi.org/10.1007/978-3-031-15985-5_13
23. Lund, C., Fortnow, L., Karloff, H.J., Nisan, N.: Algebraic methods for interactive proof systems. In: 31st FOCS, pp. 2–10. IEEE Computer Society Press (1990). https://doi.org/10.1109/FSCS.1990.89518
24. Mohnblatt, N.: Sangria: a folding scheme for PLONK (2023). https://github.com/geometryresearch/technical_notes/blob/main/sangria_folding_plonk.pdf. Accessed 27 Apr 2023
25. Naveh, A., Tromer, E.: PhotoProof: cryptographic image authentication for any set of permissible transformations. In: 2016 IEEE Symposium on Security and Privacy, pp. 255–271. IEEE Computer Society Press (2016). https://doi.org/10.1109/SP.2016.23
26. Pedersen, T.P.: Non-interactive and information-theoretic secure verifiable secret sharing. In: Feigenbaum, J. (ed.) CRYPTO 1991. LNCS, vol. 576, pp. 129–140. Springer, Heidelberg (1992). https://doi.org/10.1007/3-540-46766-1_9
27. Posen, J., Kattis, A.A.: Caulk+: table-independent lookup arguments. Cryptology ePrint Archive, Report 2022/957 (2022). https://eprint.iacr.org/2022/957
28. Setty, S., Angel, S., Gupta, T., Lee, J.: Proving the correct execution of concurrent services in zero-knowledge. In: 13th USENIX Symposium on Operating Systems Design and Implementation (OSDI 2018), pp. 339–356 (2018)
29. Setty, S., Thaler, J., Wahby, R.: Customizable constraint systems for succinct arguments. Cryptology ePrint Archive (2023)
30. Valiant, P.: Incrementally verifiable computation or proofs of knowledge imply time/space efficiency. In: Canetti, R. (ed.) TCC 2008. LNCS, vol. 4948, pp. 1–18. Springer, Heidelberg (2008). https://doi.org/10.1007/978-3-540-78524-8_1
31. Wikström, D.: Special soundness in the random oracle model. Cryptology ePrint Archive, Report 2021/1265 (2021). https://eprint.iacr.org/2021/1265
32. Xiong, A.L., et al.: VERI-ZEXE: decentralized private computation with universal setup. Cryptology ePrint Archive, Report 2022/802 (2022). https://eprint.iacr.org/2022/802
33. Zapico, A., Buterin, V., Khovratovich, D., Maller, M., Nitulescu, A., Simkin, M.: Caulk: lookup arguments in sublinear time. In: Yin, H., Stavrou, A., Cremers, C., Shi, E. (eds.) ACM CCS 2022, pp. 3121–3134. ACM Press (2022). https://doi.org/10.1145/3548606.3560646
34. Zapico, A., Gabizon, A., Khovratovich, D., Maller, M., Ràfols, C.: Baloo: nearly optimal lookup arguments. Cryptology ePrint Archive, Report 2022/1565 (2022). https://eprint.iacr.org/2022/1565
35. Zhang, Y.X., Vark, A.: Origami - a folding scheme for Halo2 lookups (2023). https://hackmd.io/@aardvark/rkHqa3NZ2. Accessed 12 July 2023

Polynomial IOPs for Memory Consistency Checks in Zero-Knowledge Virtual Machines

Yuncong Zhang[1], Shi-Feng Sun[1(✉)], Ren Zhang[2], and Dawu Gu[1(✉)]

[1] Shanghai Jiao Tong University, Shanghai, China
{shjdzhangyuncong,shifeng.sun,dwgu}@sjtu.edu.cn
[2] Cryptape Co. Ltd. and Nervos, Hangzhou, China
ren@nervos.org

Abstract. Zero-Knowledge Virtual Machines (ZKVMs) have gained traction in recent years due to their potential applications in a variety of areas, particularly blockchain ecosystems. Despite tremendous progress on ZKVMs in the industry, no formal definitions or security proofs have been established in the literature. Due to this lack of formalization, existing protocols exhibit significant discrepancies in terms of problem definitions and performance metrics, making it difficult to analyze and compare these advancements, or to trust the security of the increasingly complex ZKVM implementations.

In this work, we focus on random-access memory, an influential and expensive component of ZKVMs. Specifically, we investigate the state-of-the-art protocols for validating the correct functioning of memory, which we refer to as the *memory consistency checks*. Isolating these checks from the rest of the system allows us to formalize their definition and security notion. Furthermore, we summarize the state-of-the-art constructions using the Polynomial IOP model and formally prove their security. Observing that the bottleneck of existing designs lies in sorting the entire memory trace, we break away from this paradigm and propose a novel memory consistency check, dubbed Permem. Permem bypasses this bottleneck by introducing a technique called the address cycle method, which requires fewer building blocks and—after instantiating the building blocks with state-of-the-art constructions—fewer online polynomial oracles and evaluation queries. In addition, we propose gcq, a new construction for the lookup argument—a key building block of the memory consistency check, which costs fewer online polynomial oracles than the state-of-the-art construction cq.

Keywords: Proof System · SNARK · ZKVM · Random Access Memory

1 Introduction

Zero-Knowledge Virtual Machine (ZKVM) [zkS22, TV22, Pol22, Scr22, Mid22, Ris22, GPR21] is a type of program execution system that can produce a proof

J. Guo and R. Steinfeld (Eds.): ASIACRYPT 2023, LNCS 14439, pp. 111–141, 2023.
https://doi.org/10.1007/978-981-99-8724-5_4

of the validity of the execution without revealing any secret inputs. These proofs can be verified quickly without re-executing the program. ZKVMs are considered more user-friendly than traditional circuit-based SNARKs [Gro16, CHM+20, GWC19] for programmers, because ZKVMs support instruction-based programs that can be easily constructed from high-level languages. Some ZKVMs [zkS22, Pol22, Scr22], often referred to as zkEVMs, are designed to be compatible with the Ethereum Virtual Machine (EVM), and have the potential to improve the scalability and privacy of Ethereum, a decentralized platform with the second-largest market value as of 2023, the time of this writing. Other ZKVMs support various types of machine architectures, such as RISC-V [Ris22] for wider applications, or SNARK-friendly machines [TV22, Scr22, GPR21] for increased efficiency.

Constructing a ZKVM involves designing protocols for checking the consistent functioning of all its components, including the instruction fetcher, register file, arithmetic logic unit, and memory. The most technically challenging protocol among them is the *memory consistency check (MCC)*, whose complexity roots in the *history-dependent* nature of memory: the output of memory access depends on the entire history of its inputs. This characteristic causes the MCC to be more resource-intensive than other protocols. Consequently, many ZKVM projects such as Scroll [Scr22] and Triton VM [TV22] devoted continuing efforts to optimizing the MCC.

However, there is an absence of literature discussing recent advances in MCC, as the constructions have mostly been developed in a haphazard manner and tightly connected to their engineering projects. This leads to a lack of agreement on the formal definition of the security goals, the context of protocol design, and the performance metrics, rendering it challenging to analyze and compare different constructions. Furthermore, it is uncertain whether they contain vulnerabilities due to their lack of formal security analysis. Although there is a family of related works investigating RAM-based SNARKs [BCGT13, BCG+13, BCTV13, BBC+17, BBHR18, BCG+18], recent implementations adopt a richer and more advanced family of new techniques not covered in this literature. To address the above issues, *it is crucial to formalize the problem of MCC and to conduct a systematic examination of existing solutions*, which can help deepen our understanding of the problem, eliminate potential security risks, and identify and address the performance bottleneck.

1.1 Our Contributions

This work offers a formal analysis of the MCCs employed in popular ZKVMs in the industry and improves their performance via a new design method and a new building block. Specifically, we provide a formal definition of MCC and its security, formulated within the Polynomial IOP (PIOP) model [BFS20], which is a widely used SNARK construction model in the literature [GWC19, CHM+20, CBBZ22, SZ22, ZSZ+22]. We also extract and formalize the underlying techniques of existing MCCs in PIOPs and prove their security. Inspired by our formalization, we propose (1) a more efficient construction method called the

Table 1. Comparing the MCCs, our Permem achieves the largest memory size with fewer building blocks and online polynomials outside of the building blocks. The protocols are sorted by the address space, from the most limited contiguous memory to the largest full space read-write memory. "Sort." stands for the sorting paradigm, and "AC." stands for the address cycle method, which is extracted from Arya [BCG+18] and formalized in this paper. The constant $c \geq 1$ is a user-selected integer, but $c = 1$ usually suffices as $\mathbb{F}$'s size is usually 256-bit or larger. N is the number of execution steps, which is usually orders of magnitude less than 2^{32}. **Perm.** is the number of permutation arguments. **Lookup** is the number of lookup arguments (one "Double" lookup argument achieves the same result as two "Single" lookup arguments with smaller amortized cost). **Poly.** is the number of polynomial oracles sent to the verifier online *excluding those in the building blocks.* **Queries** is the number of evaluation queries issued by the verifier *excluding those in the building blocks.*

Protocol	Method	Address Space	Writable	Build blocks		Poly.	Queries
				Perm.	Lookup		
Cairo [GPR21]	Sort.	Contiguous	×	1	0	4	0
AryaMem (optimized based on [BCG+18])	AC.	[1..N]	✓	2	1 Single	4	0
Miden [Mid22] etc.	Sort.	32k-bit	✓	1	2k Double	$7 + 2k$	0
Triton [TV22]	Sort.	$\mathbb{F}^c$	✓	1	1 Single	$10 + c$	2
Permem	AC.	$\mathbb{F}^c$	✓	1	1 Single	$6 + c$	2

address cycle method, which instantiates into a novel MCC named Permem, and (2) a new lookup argument called gcq. Our main contributions are as follows.

- We formally define the notion *memory consistency check* and its security (Sect. 3), and formalize the state-of-the-art constructions in PIOPs with security proofs under our definition (Sect. 4). Specifically, observing that all these constructions follow a common pattern, which we refer to as the *sorting paradigm*, we identify the key subprotocol (*sorting check*) that differentiates these constructions. We summarize all the sorting checks into three PIOPs, each for a different memory model, respectively: (a) contiguous read-only memory (Sect. 4.1), used by Cairo [GPR21]; (b) memory with 32- or 256-bit addresses (Sect. 4.2), used by Miden [Mid22], RiscZero [Ris22], and all zkEVMs; and (c) memory with the *full address space*, i.e., $\mathbb{F}^c$ for $c \geq 1$ (Sect. 4.3), used by Triton VM [TV22], which supports memory spaces larger than 32- or even 256-bit address with less cost.
- Next, observing the bottleneck of the sorting paradigm, we introduce a more efficient method for constructing MCCs, named *address cycle method* (Sect. 5.1). We extract the address-shifting permutation of Arya [BCG+18], a zero-knowledge proof for TinyRAM [BCG+13], and develop it into a method for constructing MCCs. This general method reduces the MCC construction into designing a *distinctness check*, which is to prove that all entries in a vector are distinct. This reduction not only simplifies the design workflow

Table 2. Comparing the MCCs with different instantiations of the lookup argument, our new lookup argument gcq reduces the number of polynomials and queries by ≈ 3 compared to the state-of-the-art construction cq (the rows without the gcq mark). Here double-gcq is the batched version of gcq with smaller amortized costs. The protocols are sorted by the address space (column **A. Space**), from the most limited contiguous memory to the largest full space read-write memory. The star "*" means the double-gcq is alternatively constructed where the grand-sum vector $\tilde{\mathbf{u}}$ is split (see Sect. 6 for details). N is the number of executed steps of the machine. **Deg.** is the maximal degree of the polynomial oracles sent from the prover. **Poly.** is the number of polynomial oracles sent to the verifier online. **Queries** is the number of evaluation queries. **Dist.** is the number of distinct evaluation points.

Protocol	A. Space	Deg.	Poly.	Queries	Dist.
Cairo [GPR21]	Contiguous	N	5	8	2
AryaMem (optimized based on [BCG+18])	$[1..N]$	2N	13	20	2
AryaMem (gcq)	$[1..N]$	2N	10	18	2
Miden etc. [Mid22, Scr22, Pol22, Ris22, zkS22]	$32k$-bit	2N	$14 + 4k$	$20 + 5k$	2
Miden etc. (double-gcq)	$32k$-bit	5N	$12 + 3k$	$19 + 4k$	2
Miden etc. (double-gcq*)	$32k$-bit	3N	$12 + 4k$	$19 + 5k$	2
Triton [TV22]	$\mathbb{F}$	2N	18	26	3
Triton (gcq)	$\mathbb{F}$	2N	15	24	3
Permem	$\mathbb{F}$	2N	15	23	3
Permem (gcq)	$\mathbb{F}$	2N	12	21	3

but also improves the performance of MCC. Using our method, we propose a new MCC, called Permem (Sect. 5.1); it supports the *full address space* as Triton VM does, by extracting the core of the *contiguity check* of Triton VM and formalizing it into a distinctness check, which may also be useful in constructing PIOPs other than MCC. As shown in Table 1 and 2, Permem costs fewer building blocks, thus fewer online polynomial oracles and evaluation queries compared to Triton VM and $32k$-bit ZKVMs. Note that, as it is hard to compare Permem directly with Arya, which is constructed in the ILC model [BCG+17], we adapt the memory component of Arya in the PIOP model, named AryaMem, and include it in our tables along with the recent ZKVMs.

- Finally, we propose a novel lookup argument, which is an essential building block for most MCCs and is widely used in SNARKs [PFM+22, ABST22, CBBZ22]. We name it gcq for *grand-sum version of* cq [EFG22]. The key idea behind gcq is to replace the univariate sumcheck of cq with the grand-sum check; this technique is simple but effective, because the grand-sum check fits perfectly in the context of cq, especially when cq is used in MCC. Table 2 and 3 show that when the lookup argument is instantiated with gcq, the MCCs use fewer online polynomial oracles and evaluation queries (by 2 to 10), and has

Table 3. Comparing the MCCs with the PIOP instantiated with KZG [KZG10], our new lookup argument gcq reduces the proof sizes by $2 \sim 10$ group and field elements, and the prover costs by $2 \sim 10$ FFTs/MSMs, compared to the state-of-the-art construction cq (the rows without the gcq mark). Here double-gcq is the batched version of gcq with smaller amortized costs. The protocols are sorted by the address space, from the most limited contiguous memory to the largest full space read-write memory. The star "*" means the double-gcq is alternatively constructed where the grand-sum vector $\tilde{\mathbf{u}}$ is split (see Sect. 6 for details). N is the number of executed steps of the machine. The prover is dominated by FFT ($O(N \log N)$), MSM ($O(N \cdot \lambda / \log N)$), and MPE (multi-point evaluation, $O(S \log^2 S)$), where the unit is field operations, and S is the number of addresses touched by the program in the execution. In practice, S is usually at least an order of magnitude smaller than N. For all protocols, the cost of the verifier is dominated by one pairing, which is omitted from the table.

Protocol	Address Space	SRS		Proof		Prover		
		$\mathbb{G}_1$	$\mathbb{G}_2$	$\mathbb{G}_1$	$\mathbb{F}$	FFT	MSM	MPE
Cairo [GPR21]	Contiguous	N	2	7	8	5	7	0
AryaMem (optimized based on [BCG+18])	$[1..N]$	2N	2	15	20	13	15	0
AryaMem (gcq)	$[1..N]$	2N	2	12	18	10	12	0
Miden [Mid22] etc	$32k$-bit	2N	2	$16+4k$	$20+5k$	$14+4k$	$16+4k$	0
Miden etc. (double-gcq)	$32k$-bit	5N	2	$14+3k$	$19+4k$	$12+3k$	$14+3k$	0
Miden etc. (double-gcq*)	$32k$-bit	3N	2	$14+4k$	$19+5k$	$12+4k$	$14+4k$	0
Triton [TV22]	$\mathbb{F}$	2N	2	21	26	18	21	1
Triton (gcq)	$\mathbb{F}$	2N	2	18	24	15	18	1
Permem	$\mathbb{F}$	2N	2	18	23	15	18	1
Permem (gcq)	$\mathbb{F}$	2N	2	15	21	12	15	1

smaller proof sizes (by 2 to 10 group and field elements), compared to using the state-of-the-art construction cq[1].

1.2 Technical Overview

To better understand the protocols presented in this work, we provide an overview of the underlying intuitions. We start by introducing the necessary background concepts.

[1] Strictly speaking, the corresponding PIOP protocol behind cq is without the KZG-specific optimizations.

PIOP. Almost all SNARKs, including ZKVMs, follow the PIOP pipeline, which designs a PIOP and then compiles it into a non-interactive scheme via cryptographic tools [BFS20]. A PIOP is an interactive protocol between two parties, the prover and the verifier. The prover is able to send polynomials, e.g., $f(X) \in \mathbb{F}[X]$, which may be much larger than the verifier's storage. The verifier, however, only has oracle access to $f(X)$, meaning it is able to query for $y = f(z)$ for any given $z \in \mathbb{F}$. This oracle access allows the verifier to check if the polynomials satisfy certain relations, using the Swartz-Zippel Lemma. For example, by checking $f(z) + g(z) = h(z)$ for uniformly random z, the verifier ensures $f(X) + g(X) = h(X)$.

PIOPs can also be used to verify relations between vectors besides polynomials, by exploiting the natural transformations between polynomials and vectors. One popular transformation is the polynomial interpolation over a specific domain $\mathbb{D}$ of size $N = 2^\mu$. With this correspondence, the verifier can verify a vector equation, e.g., $\mathbf{a} + \mathbf{b} \circ \mathbf{c} = \mathbf{0}$, where "$\circ$" is the entrywise product between vectors. This vector equation is equivalent to the polynomial equation $f_{\mathbf{a}}(X) + f_{\mathbf{b}}(X) \cdot f_{\mathbf{c}}(X) = q(X) \cdot Z(X)$ for some quotient polynomial $q(X)$, where $Z(X) := \prod_{x \in \mathbb{D}} (X - x)$ is the vanishing polynomial over $\mathbb{D}$. Apart from the above vector equations, the verifiers can also check more complex relations such as:

- *The permutation relation* [GWC19], which states that two vectors are permutations of each other. For example, $\mathbf{a} = (1, 2, 2, 3)^\mathsf{T}$ and $\mathbf{b} = (2, 3, 1, 2)^\mathsf{T}$, denoted by $\mathbf{a} \sim \mathbf{b}$ for convenience.
- *The lookup relation* [GW20], which states that all the elements in one vector are contained in the other vector. For example, $\mathbf{a} = (1, 2, 2, 3)^\mathsf{T}$ and $\mathbf{b} = (1, 2, 3, 4)^\mathsf{T}$, denoted by $\mathbf{a} \subset \mathbf{b}$ for convenience.

The protocols for checking these relations are referred to as *permutation arguments* [GWC19] and *lookup arguments* [GW20], respectively. These arguments can be extended to apply to tuples of vectors, also referred to as *tables*. For example, $(\mathbf{a}, \mathbf{b}, \mathbf{c}) \sim (\mathbf{a}', \mathbf{b}', \mathbf{c}') \in \mathbb{F}^{N \times 3}$ means these two tables have the same multiset of rows in potentially different orders, i.e., the multisets of tuples $\{(\mathbf{a}_{[i]}, \mathbf{b}_{[i]}, \mathbf{c}_{[i]})\}_{i=1}^N$ and $\{(\mathbf{a}'_{[i]}, \mathbf{b}'_{[i]}, \mathbf{c}'_{[i]})\}_{i=1}^N$ are equal to each other.

A PIOP can be compiled into a SNARK by standard techniques [BFS20], i.e., instantiating the polynomial oracles with cryptographic constructions such as polynomial commitment scheme (PCS) [KZG10]. The performance of the resulting SNARK is determined by that of the PIOP in various aspects.

Next, we present a high-level overview of ZKVMs and our systemization over the current state of MCCs.

Workflow of ZKVM. On input $\mathbf{x}$, a machine $\mathbf{M}$ executes for T steps and produces an output $\mathbf{y} := \mathbf{M}(\mathbf{x})$. For simplicity, throughout this work, we assume $T = N$, the size of interpolation domain $\mathbb{D}$[2]. Assume the machine has m field elements as

[2] For example, the machine can be designed such that executing the last instruction (e.g., a STOP instruction) does not change the state of the machine, so that this instruction can be repeated as many times as needed until T reaches N.

the internal state. The *execution trace* of the machine is a table $(\mathbf{v}^{(1)}, \cdots, \mathbf{v}^{(m)}) \in \mathbb{F}^{T \times m}$ where the t-th row represents the state values at step t. Given the pair $\mathbf{x}$ and $\mathbf{y}$, proving that $\mathbf{y} = \mathbf{M}(\mathbf{x})$ is equivalent to proving the existence of an execution trace that is consistent with $\mathbf{x}$, $\mathbf{y}$ and the architecture of the machine. Since we are in the PIOP model, the prover, after executing the program, may directly send the execution trace to the verifier, without exhausting the verifier's storage and computational resources.

After sending the execution trace, the prover tries to convince the verifier that these vectors are consistent with the machine. In practice, the machine is broken down into smaller components, such as instruction fetching, decoding, arithmetic logic unit, and memory access. Each component's consistency is formalized using building blocks including vector equations, permutation relation, and lookup relation. We focus on the memory component, whose checking protocol is the most challenging to design for reasons that will be explained later.

Memory Consistency Check. Although the memory is typically modeled as a dictionary that maps from the address space to the value space, we describe its functionality via an alternative approach that matches our definition of memory consistency. This model involves three variables $\mathbf{op}_{[t]}, \mathbf{addr}_{[t]}, \mathbf{val}_{[t]}$ representing the *operator*, the *address*, and the *value*, respectively. For step t from 1 to N, the machine computes two state variables $\mathbf{op}_{[t]}$ and $\mathbf{addr}_{[t]}$ from the current instruction or other internal states of the machine. The variable $\mathbf{op}_{[t]}$ is either Read or Write, which are constant field elements specified by the machine. The machine then computes another variable $\mathbf{val}_{[t]}$ as follows:

- If $\mathbf{op}_{[t]} = \mathsf{Read}$, find the maximal $t' < t$ such that $\mathbf{addr}_{[t']} = \mathbf{addr}_{[t]}$, then set $\mathbf{val}_{[t]} = \mathbf{val}_{[t']}$. If no satisfying t' is found, set $\mathbf{val}_{[t]}$ arbitrarily.
- If $\mathbf{op}_{[t]} = \mathsf{Write}$, compute $\mathbf{val}_{[t]}$ from the other internal states of the machine by a specified procedure. However, to decouple the memory from this potentially complex procedure, we consider $\mathbf{val}_{[t]}$ to be an arbitrary value set by the machine executor.

Given the traces of these variables, namely the vectors $\mathbf{op}, \mathbf{addr}, \mathbf{val}$ of size N, the memory consistency check should ensure that they represent a consistent execution trace of the memory, where the consistency can be informally defined as follows: for every t, $\mathbf{val}_{[t]}$ is honestly computed from $\mathbf{op}_{[t]}$, $\mathbf{addr}_{[1]}, \cdots, \mathbf{addr}_{[t]}$, $\mathbf{val}_{[1]}, \cdots, \mathbf{val}_{[t-1]}$ by the above procedure.

Among all the components of the machine, memory is the only one that is *history-dependent*[3]: the next state depends on the entire history of the machine states, instead of only on the previous state. This characteristic complicates the consistency checking protocol for the following reason. Without history dependency, the consistency of the entire trace can be decomposed into a sequence

[3] Except for some special-purpose components designed particularly for ZKVMs, e.g., the hash table in Triton VM and some builtins in Cairo, that are not in a traditional CPU architecture. The stack in stack-based architectures like EVM can be considered as a simpler version of random-access memory, whose consistency checks are similar to those for memories.

of *local relations* between adjacent rows in the trace. These local relations can be captured by one or more low-degree multivariate polynomials that verify the transition between adjacent states. The number of variables in these polynomials has only the size of two states. This allows efficient verification using the vector equation checks. However, if the current state of the machine depends on the entire history, capturing the relations between dependent states would require multivariate polynomials with $O(N)$ variables, which renders the vector equation check infeasible.

The Sorting Paradigm. The reason for memory consistency being history-dependent is that different memory addresses are accessed in an interleaved manner. This observation inspires the idea of sorting the memory execution trace by address. After sorting the table $(\mathsf{op}, \mathsf{addr}, \mathsf{val})$ into $(\widetilde{\mathsf{op}}, \widetilde{\mathsf{addr}}, \widetilde{\mathsf{val}})$ using the column $\widetilde{\mathsf{addr}}$ as the key, accesses to identical addresses are grouped together, and as a result, $\widetilde{\mathsf{val}}_{[t]}$ depends only on $\widetilde{\mathsf{op}}_{[t]}, \widetilde{\mathsf{addr}}_{[t]}, \widetilde{\mathsf{addr}}_{[t-1]}$ and $\widetilde{\mathsf{val}}_{[t-1]}$.

The above idea is formalized as the *sorting paradigm*, which captures the MCCs in all ZKVMs as of 2023, the time of this writing. This paradigm is described by the following procedure:

1. The prover sorts $\mathsf{op}, \mathsf{addr}, \mathsf{val}$ by the entries in addr and obtains $\widetilde{\mathsf{op}}, \widetilde{\mathsf{addr}}, \widetilde{\mathsf{val}}$. These sorted vectors are sent to the verifier.
2. The verifier confirms that $\mathsf{op}, \mathsf{addr}, \mathsf{val}$ and $\widetilde{\mathsf{op}}, \widetilde{\mathsf{addr}}, \widetilde{\mathsf{val}}$ are permutations of each other.
3. The verifier ensures the expected local property of the sorted memory trace using one or more vector equations.
4. The final step varies in different ZKVMs, but all involve proving that $\widetilde{\mathsf{op}}$, $\widetilde{\mathsf{addr}}$, $\widetilde{\mathsf{val}}$ is the sorting of $\mathsf{op}, \mathsf{addr}, \mathsf{val}$ by addr.

In current ZKVMs, step 4—the sorting check—is accomplished using one of the following three protocols, each for a different memory model:

1. *Contiguous read-only memory.* This model requires that the values in the vector addr span a contiguous region in $\mathbb{F}$ and that $\mathsf{op}_{[t]}$ is always Read. With these requirements, $\widetilde{\mathsf{addr}}_{[t-1]} \leq \widetilde{\mathsf{addr}}_{[t]}$ is equivalent to $\widetilde{\mathsf{addr}}_{[t]} - \widetilde{\mathsf{addr}}_{[t-1]} \in \{0, 1\}$, which is captured by the vector equation $(\widetilde{\mathsf{addr}}_{[t]} - \widetilde{\mathsf{addr}}_{[t-1]}) \cdot (\widetilde{\mathsf{addr}}_{[t]} - \widetilde{\mathsf{addr}}_{[t-1]} - 1) = 0$.
2. *Read-write memory with 32k-bit addresses.* For this memory model, the constraint $\widetilde{\mathsf{addr}}_{[t-1]} \leq \widetilde{\mathsf{addr}}_{[t]}$ is checked by a $32k$-bit range check over the vector $\widetilde{\mathsf{addr}}^{\leftarrow 1} - \widetilde{\mathsf{addr}}$, where $\widetilde{\mathsf{addr}}^{\leftarrow 1}$ is the cyclic left-shifting of $\widetilde{\mathsf{addr}}$ by one position.
3. *Read-write memory with full address space:* $\mathbb{F}^c$ for $c \geq 1$. Since the case $c > 1$ can be reduced to $c = 1$ by random linear combination, we proceed assuming that $c = 1$. The statement that $\widetilde{\mathsf{addr}}$ is sorted is proved by the *contiguity check*, designed by Triton VM [TV22], explained as follows. Given the vector $\widetilde{\mathsf{addr}}$, initialize the polynomial $f(X) = X - \widetilde{\mathsf{addr}}_{[1]}$, then for each t from 2 to

N, if $\widetilde{\textsf{addr}}_{[t]} \neq \widetilde{\textsf{addr}}_{[t-1]}$, multiply $f(X)$ by $X - \widetilde{\textsf{addr}}_{[t]}$, otherwise do nothing. Obviously, the vector **addr** is *contiguous* (which means repeated elements fall in contiguous regions; this is equivalent to $\widetilde{\textsf{addr}}$ being sorted by some custom order over $\mathbb{F}$) if and only if no monomial $X - \widetilde{\textsf{addr}}_{[t]}$ is multiplied to $f(X)$ more than once, if and only if $f(X)$ has no multiple roots. The prover sends the polynomial $f(X)$ to the verifier, who checks that $f(X)$ is correctly computed and that $\gcd(f(X), Df(X)) = 1$, where $Df(X)$ is the formal derivative of $f(X)$.

For read-write memories, there is an additional issue: as **addr** may contain duplicate elements, multiple permutations exist for sorting the memory execution trace. However, the sorting technique works only if the permutation is the unique one that preserves the order of rows with identical addresses as in the original table. This unique permutation is referred to as the *canonical sorting*. To ensure that the sorting is canonical, the following modifications should be applied to the second and third protocols: the memory execution trace is sorted together with the incrementing vector $\textsf{incs} = (1, 2, \cdots, N)$. The verifier then ensures that if $\widetilde{\textsf{addr}}_{[t]} = \widetilde{\textsf{addr}}_{[t-1]}$, the difference $\widetilde{\textsf{incs}}_{[t]} - \widetilde{\textsf{incs}}_{[t-1]}$ must be in the range $1, 2, \cdots, N$, by a lookup relation.

Our Improvement: Address Cycle Method. Note that in the sorting paradigm, the prover sends at least four vectors to the verifier, each for a column in the sorted memory trace. This is somewhat wasteful because, compared to the unsorted memory trace, the additional information conveyed in these four vectors is no more than a single permutation. We propose an alternative way that saves these costs. Instead of reordering the memory execution trace, we *redefine* the meaning of *adjacency* such that identical addresses become adjacent under this new definition. This insight is extracted from Arya [BCG+18], a zero-knowledge protocol for TinyRAM [BCG+13]. We name this technique the *address cycle method.*

This method involves defining a permutation σ over the index set $\{1, \cdots, N\}$. The permutation σ maps each index t to the previous time when $\textsf{addr}_{[t]}$ was accessed, i.e. $\sigma(t) = \max\{j < t | \textsf{addr}_{[j]} = \textsf{addr}_{[t]}\}$, if such maximal value is well-defined. If otherwise, this maximal value does not exist, i.e., $\textsf{addr}_{[t]}$ is accessed for the first time, $\sigma(t)$ maps it to the last time the same address was accessed, i.e., in this case, $\sigma(t) = \max\{j \leq N | \textsf{addr}_{[j]} = \textsf{addr}_{[t]}\}$. This way, for each distinct address, all the positions where it appears are linked into a cycle by σ. Obviously, **addr** is invariant under the permutation σ.

Now we observe the behavior of **val** as it is permuted by σ. By definition, if the memory trace is consistent, then **val** is *almost* invariant under the permutation. Specifically, $\textsf{val}_{[\sigma(t)]} = \textsf{val}_{[t]}$ for every t except for those with $\textsf{op}_{[t]} = \textsf{Write}$ or $\textsf{addr}_{[t]}$ is accessed the first time.

It turns out that the aforementioned behaviors of **addr** and **val** when permuted by σ suffice to guarantee memory consistency, as shown in Theorem 7. To summarize, the MCC can be accomplished by proving the existence of a permutation σ with the following properties:

1. There exists a vector $\textsf{first} \in \{0,1\}^N$ such that $t > \sigma(t)$ for every t except for those t where $\textsf{first}_{[t]} = 1$.
2. $\textsf{addr}$ is invariant under σ and $\textsf{val}$ is almost invariant: $\textsf{val}_{[\sigma(t)]} = \textsf{val}_{[t]}$ for every t except for those with $\textsf{op}_{[t]} = \textsf{Write}$ or $\textsf{first}_{[t]} = 1$.
3. For every address a, all the positions where a appears in $\textsf{addr}$ fall in the same cycle of σ.

The first two properties are simple to check, as they are captured by vector equations, permutation relations, and lookup relations. See Sect. 5.1 for details. Checking the last property is the most challenging part of this method. We proved in Lemma 3 (Sect. 5.1) that this property can be ensured by showing that the elements $\{\textsf{addr}_{[t]} | 1 \leq t \leq N, \textsf{first}_{[t]} = 1\}$ are distinct. Therefore, our address cycle method reduces the MCC problem to the *distinctness check* problem, which is the key component of different constructions. Here we present two constructions for this component.

1. *Permem.* We note that the contiguity check of Triton VM can be generalized into a distinctness check that does not pose any restriction on the address space. This distinctness check protocol produces a new MCC with full address space, i.e., $\mathcal{A} = \mathbb{F}^c$ for any $c \geq 1$. We name this new MCC Permem.
2. *AryaMem.* For a clear comparison between Permem and Arya, which is originally described in the ILC model [BCG+17], we adapt the memory component of Arya into a PIOP, called AryaMem, which is optimized with the standard PIOP techniques. We remark that the memory component of the original Arya does not strictly follow the pattern of our address cycle method, whereas AryaMem is adapted to follow this method strictly. In particular, in Arya, the last property of σ is not verified via distinctness check, but instead by a protocol called blookup, which is constructed with two lookup arguments. We replace this blookup protocol with a distinctness check, which is much simpler thanks to Arya's limited memory address space (the set $\{1, 2, \cdots, M\}$ for $M \approx N$). Specifically, to prove that $\textsf{addr}$ satisfies the distinctness condition, it suffices to show that there exists a vector that is both a permutation of $(1, 2, \cdots, M)$ and is identical to $\textsf{addr}$ in places where $\textsf{first}_{[t]} = 1$. This can be implemented using a single permutation argument.

Lookup Argument. The lookup argument is an influential building block in most MCCs. We construct a new lookup argument, named gcq for *grand-sum version of* cq [EFG22], based on the *logarithmic derivative* technique. The insight of logarithmic derivative is that every element in $A = \{a_1, \cdots, a_n\}$ appears in $B = \{b_1, \cdots, b_n\}$ if and only if $\sum \left(\frac{1}{X - a_i} - \frac{m_i}{X - b_i}\right) = 0$, where $m_i \geq 0$ is the number of times b_i appears in A. Proving that this sum is zero is the core of the logarithmic derivative technique. In cq, this is accomplished by the popular univariate sumcheck protocol [BCR+19], which is also extensively used in building general-purpose SNARKs [BCR+19, CHM+20, COS20, RZ21].

However, we notice that a simpler technique, called *grand-sum check*, has multiple benefits which are, somewhat surprisingly, undervalued in the literature[4]. Compared to the univariate sumcheck, the grand-sum check has the following three advantages: (1) it works in both monomial basis and Lagrange basis; (2) it does not require an individual degree bound of the PIOP; and (3) most importantly, the grand-sum check contributes (almost) no additional cost at all, in terms of the number of online polynomials and evaluation queries, which is explained as follows. Note that: (1) for any vector $\mathbf{u}$, the vector $\mathbf{u}^{\leftarrow 1} - \mathbf{u} + s \cdot \mathbf{e}_1$ is guaranteed to have sum s, where $\mathbf{u}^{\leftarrow 1}$ is $\mathbf{u}$ circularly left-shifted by one position; and (2) for any vector $\mathbf{v}$, we can always find $\tilde{v}$ such that $\mathbf{v} = \widetilde{\mathbf{v}}^{\leftarrow 1} - \widetilde{\mathbf{v}} + s \cdot \mathbf{e}_1$, e.g., $\widetilde{\mathbf{v}} := (v_1, v_1 + v_2, \cdots, \sum v_i)$, the grand-sum vector of $\mathbf{v}$. Therefore, the prover could have directly sent $\widetilde{\mathbf{v}}$, without sending $\mathbf{v}$ in the first place, and the verifier simulates the polynomial oracle for $\mathbf{v}$ using that of $\widetilde{\mathbf{v}}$ wherever $\mathbf{v}$ appears.

Although the grand-sum check has some disadvantages compared to the univariate check, which may partially explain the rare usage of grand-sum check, these disadvantages are avoided in the context of MCCs:

- Grand-sum check involves shifting the vector $\tilde{\mathbf{v}}$ by one position, which requires simulating the polynomial oracle $f_{\tilde{\mathbf{v}}}(\omega X)$, causing one additional distinct evaluation point ωz in the PIOP. However, this is not a problem in MCC, as ωz is already required by the permutation check.
- It is unclear how to exploit the KZG-specific optimizations in grand-sum check, which is interesting for future research. In particular, cq exploits these techniques to allow the prover cost to depend only on the size N of the execution trace and independent of the lookup table size. However, in Permem, the lookup table also has size N, rendering the table-size-independence unnecessary.
- The grand-sum check does not look intuitive when the polynomial oracle $f_{\mathbf{v}}(X)$ has a degree greater than N, in which case the simulation additionally involves the quotient polynomial $q(X)$. However, the grand-sum check still saves one polynomial oracle compared to the univariate sumcheck in this scenario. Moreover, in cq or gcq, the target polynomials of the sumcheck have degrees bounded by the domain size, so the quotient polynomials are unnecessary.

For the above reasons, grand-sum check fits perfectly in MCC, especially in our Permem. Table 2 shows that the MCCs use three fewer online polynomials and two fewer evaluation queries by replacing cq (that uses univariate sum-check) with gcq (that uses grand-sum check).

Zero knowledge. We will not address the zero-knowledge aspect in this work for the following two reasons. First, despite the "ZK" in the name, ZKVMs are more valued for their succinctness than their zero-knowledge property. This preference is evident from the fact that currently ZKVMs are mainly used in zkRollups [zkS22, Azt22, Pol22, Loo22], which prioritize scalability over privacy.

[4] It is indeed used in some works, but very rarely, e.g., in Flookup [GK22]. It is used only in a small component of Flookup, where univariate sumcheck is unusable.

Second, zero-knowledge can be achieved as an added property in SNARKs using standard techniques such as adding a masking polynomial $\delta(X) \cdot Z(X)$ to the interpolated polynomials, where $\delta(X)$ is a uniformly random small polynomial. It is unnecessary to repeat these standard techniques, so we omit them for clarity and simplicity.

1.3 Related Works

Although there is a lack of literature discussing the recent developments in ZKVMs [zkS22, TV22, Pol22, Scr22, Mid22, Ris22, GPR21], these ZKVMs are the result of more than ten years of progress in the field of verifiable computations (VC) [GGP10]. VC constructions can be categorized based on their model of computation, primarily the circuit model and the RAM model. Circuit-based VCs, particularly SNARKs, have gained greater attention and undergone active research since 2018 [PHGR13, Gro16, CHM+20, GWC19, Set20, XZZ+19, BDFG20, BBB+18, Eag22, SL20, BFS20, ZSZ+22, SZ22, ZXZS20, BFH+20, COS20, BCR+19, WTS+18]. Nonetheless, they have a significant drawback as circuits are inconvenient to program for, especially when branching and loops are involved.

Although RAM-based VCs potentially support more intuitive programming interfaces like high-level programming languages, they are more inefficient than the circuit-based ones, with MCC being a major bottleneck. The Merkle-tree-based memory check [BFR+13] is barely practical, and outperformed by the sorting technique, which is initially based on routing networks [BCGT13, BCG+13, BCTV13, BBC+17, BBHR18] and later adopts the more efficient permutation argument developed in circuit-based SNARKs [GWC19], as in [ZGK+18, BCG+18]. Many works only support memory space as small as $\{1, \cdots, M\}$ for $M = O(T)$, and those supporting 32-bit memory addresses tend to be quite slow.

The recent rapid development of ZKVMs has been largely aided by the introduction of lookup arguments [GW20, ZBK+22, PK22, GK22, ZGK+22, EFG22, Hab22, CBBZ22, SLST23], which have significantly boosted the efficiency of 32- and 64-bit MCCs. However, 256-bit memory checks remain very expensive. Triton VM [TV22] mitigates this issue by its MCC with full address space, which is sufficiently large to cover the functionality of 256-bit memory. Our new protocol, Permem, further reduces the number of online polynomials of Triton VM.

Recent lookup arguments based on logarithmic derivatives [Hab22, EFG22, SLST23] are a promising new approach, offering both high performance and appealing properties such as homomorphic additions. Our new lookup argument gcq improves the state-of-the-art construction cq, costing fewer online polynomials and evaluation queries.

2 Preliminaries

Let λ be the security parameter. For $n \in \mathbb{N}$, $[n]$ denotes the set $\{1, 2, \cdots, n\}$. For $i \leq j$, $[i..j]$ denotes $\{i, \cdots, j\}$. Throughout the paper, we use a unique finite field $\mathbb{F} = \mathbb{F}_p$ where p is a prime of $O(\lambda)$ bits. When the context is clear, we use integers and field elements interchangeably, so the sets $[n], [i..j]$ may also represent the corresponding $\mathbb{F}$ elements after reducing modulo p. For algorithm A, $\mathsf{A} \to c$ means the algorithm outputs c.

An *indexed relation* $\mathcal{R}$ is a set of triples $(\mathbb{i}, \mathbb{x}, \mathbb{w})$, where $\mathbb{i}$ is called the index, $\mathbb{x}$ is the instance, and $\mathbb{w}$ is the witness. The language induced from $\mathcal{R}$ is $\mathcal{L}(\mathcal{R}) := \{(\mathbb{i}, \mathbb{x}) : \exists\ \mathbb{w}, s.t.\ (\mathbb{i}, \mathbb{x}, \mathbb{w}) \in \mathcal{R}\}$.

2.1 Vectors and Polynomials

A vector of length N over $\mathbb{F}$ is denoted by $\mathbf{v} \in \mathbb{F}^N$. The length of $\mathbf{v}$ is $|\mathbf{v}|$. The i-th entry of the vector $\mathbf{v}$ is denoted by $\mathbf{v}_{[i]}$. The subvector of $\mathbf{v}$ from index i to j is denoted by $\mathbf{v}_{[i..j]}$. Let $\mathsf{Elems}(\mathbf{v})$ be the set of *distinct* elements in $\mathbf{v}$, and $\mathsf{MultiElems}(\mathbf{v})$ be the *multiset* of the elements in $\mathbf{v}$. We write $a \in \mathbf{v}$ if $a \in \mathsf{Elems}(\mathbf{v})$ and $\mathbf{u} \subset \mathbf{v}$ if $\mathsf{Elems}(\mathbf{u}) \subseteq \mathsf{Elems}(\mathbf{v})$. We say $\mathbf{u}$ and $\mathbf{v}$ are permutations of each other if $\mathsf{MultiElems}(\mathbf{u}) = \mathsf{MultiElems}(\mathbf{v})$. For permutation σ over $[N]$ and $\mathbf{v} \in \mathbb{F}^N$, define $\sigma(\mathbf{v}) := (\mathbf{v}_{[\sigma(t)]})_{t=1}^N$. For vectors $\mathbf{u}, \mathbf{v}$ with $|\mathbf{u}| = |\mathbf{v}|$, $\mathbf{u} \circ \mathbf{v}$ is their *Hadamard product* (entry-wise product). $\mathbf{u}\|\mathbf{v}$ is the concatenation of two vectors. $\mathbf{v}^{\leftarrow k} := \mathbf{v}_{[k+1..N]}\|\mathbf{v}_{[1..k]}$ is the circular shift of $\mathbf{v}$ by k positions to the left or $-k$ positions to the right if $k < 0$. Let $\mathbf{v}_1, \cdots, \mathbf{v}_c \in \mathbb{F}^N$, then the tuple $(\mathbf{v}_1, \cdots, \mathbf{v}_c)$ is a *table* with N rows and c columns. The notations for tables, including $\sigma(\mathbf{v}_1, \cdots, \mathbf{v}_c)$, $(a_1, \cdots, a_c) \in (\mathbf{v}_1, \cdots, \mathbf{v}_c)$ and $(\mathbf{u}_1, \cdots, \mathbf{u}_c) \subset (\mathbf{v}_1, \cdots, \mathbf{v}_c)$, are defined similarly as for vectors. Particularly, let $\mathsf{Rows}(\mathbf{v}_1, \cdots, \mathbf{v}_c)$ denote the set of *distinct* tuples $\{(a_1, \cdots, a_c) \in (\mathbf{v}_1, \cdots, \mathbf{v}_c)\}$, and $\mathsf{MultiRows}(\mathbf{v}_1, \cdots, \mathbf{v}_c)$ be the *multiset* of the tuples $\{(a_1, \cdots, a_c) \in (\mathbf{v}_1, \cdots, \mathbf{v}_c)\}$.

For any constant $C \in \mathbb{F}$, let $\mathbf{C}^N$ be a shorthand of the size-N vector consisting of only C. In particular, $\mathbf{0}^N, \mathbf{1}^N$ are the vectors consisting of N zeros or ones. Let $\mathbf{e}_i^N := \mathbf{0}^{i-1}\|1\|\mathbf{0}^{N-i}$ be the i-th unit vector. The superscript may be omitted if the length is clear from the context.

Let $f(X) \in \mathbb{F}[X]$ denote a polynomial over $\mathbb{F}$. We call a subset $\mathbb{D} \subset \mathbb{F}$ a *domain*. Given a domain $\mathbb{D}$ of size N where the elements are ordered by $a_1, \cdots, a_N$, let $f(\mathbb{D})$ be the vector $(f(a_1), \cdots, f(a_N))$. Given a vector $\mathbf{v}$ of size $|\mathbb{D}|$, we can find at least one polynomial $f_{\mathbf{v}}(X)$ such that $f_{\mathbf{v}}(\mathbb{D}) = \mathbf{v}$, and call it an interpolation of $\mathbf{v}$ over $\mathbb{D}$. We usually take $\mathbb{D} = \{1, \omega, \cdots, \omega^{N-1}\}$ where ω is the N-th root of unity. In this setting, the polynomial interpolation of $\mathbf{e}_i$ is $f_{\mathbf{e}_i}(X) = \frac{\omega^{i-1}.(X^N-1)}{N\cdot(X-\omega^{i-1})}$ and can be evaluated by $O(\log(N))$ field operations. The identity polynomial $f_{\mathbf{id}}(X) := X$ corresponds to the vector $\mathbf{id} := (1, \omega, \cdots, \omega^{N-1})$.

2.2 Interactive Proof System

An interactive proof system [GMR85] is a protocol between two parties, the prover P and the verifier V. The prover tries to convince the verifier of a statement $(\mathbb{i}, \mathbb{x}) \in \mathcal{L}$. In this work, we consider arguments of knowledge with preprocessing. That is, before the protocol starts, the index $\mathbb{i}$ is preprocessed offline by the indexer I, which produces helpful information for both the prover and the verifier, such that the verifier does not need to learn the entire index, but only the preprocessed information.

Definition 1 (Preprocessing Proof System). *A preprocessing proof system for indexed relation $\mathcal{R}$ is a triple of PPT algorithms* $(\mathsf{I}, \mathsf{P}, \mathsf{V})$. *For any triple* $(\mathbb{i}, \mathbb{x}, \mathbb{w})$, *the indexer* I *takes as input* $\mathbb{i}$, *and outputs* $\mathbb{i}_P$ *and* $\mathbb{i}_V$. *The prover* P *takes as input* $\mathbb{i}_P, \mathbb{x}, \mathbb{w}$, *and the verifier* V *takes as input* $\mathbb{i}_V, \mathbb{x}$, *and they interact with each other. At the end of the interaction, the verifier outputs* $b \in \{0, 1\}$, *indicating if it accepts* $(b = 1)$ *or rejects* $(b = 0)$. *Denote this procedure by* $\langle \mathsf{I}(\mathbb{i}), \mathsf{P}(\mathbb{x}, \mathbb{w}), \mathsf{V}(\mathbb{x})\rangle \to b$.

The protocols should satisfy the following properties:

- *Completeness. For any* $(\mathbb{i}, \mathbb{x}, \mathbb{w}) \in \mathcal{R}$,

$$\Pr[b = 0 | \langle \mathsf{I}(\mathbb{i}), \mathsf{P}(\mathbb{x}, \mathbb{w}), \mathsf{V}(\mathbb{x})\rangle \to b] \le e_c$$

  where e_c *is a negligible value called the completeness error. If* e_c *is zero, then we say this protocol has perfect completeness.*
- *Soundness. For any* $(\mathbb{i}, \mathbb{x}) \notin \mathcal{L}(\mathcal{R})$ *and unbounded algorithm* P^*,

$$\Pr[b = 1 | \langle \mathsf{I}(\mathbb{i}), \mathsf{P}^*, \mathsf{V}(\mathbb{x})\rangle \to b] \le e_s$$

  where e_s *is a negligible value called the soundness error. If* e_s *is zero, then we say this protocol has perfect soundness.*

Moreover, a proof system may also enjoy other properties:

- *public coin*, if all the verifier messages are fresh random coins;
- *statistical honest-verifier zero-knowledge*, if there exists a simulator S such that for any $(\mathbb{i}, \mathbb{x}, \mathbb{w}) \in \mathcal{R}$ and any unbounded distinguisher D

$$|\Pr[\mathsf{D}(\mathsf{View}(\mathbb{i}, \mathbb{x}, \mathbb{w}))] - \Pr[\mathsf{D}(\mathsf{S}(\mathbb{i}, \mathbb{x}))]| = \mathsf{negl}$$

  where $\mathsf{View}(\mathbb{i}, \mathbb{x}, \mathbb{w})$ is the view of the verifier during the execution.
- *succinctness*, if the verification time and/or the online communication cost is sublinear with respect to the size of the witness;
- *proof (resp. argument[5]) of knowledge*, if for any $\mathbb{i}$ and (resp. PPT) prover P^*, there exists a PPT extractor E, which has access to the same input and random tape of P^*, such that for any efficient adversary A

$$\Pr[b = 1 \wedge (\mathbb{i}, \mathbb{x}, \mathbb{w}) \notin \mathcal{R} | \mathsf{A} \to \mathbb{x}, \langle \mathsf{I}(\mathbb{i}), \mathsf{P}^*, \mathsf{V}(\mathbb{x})\rangle \to b, \mathsf{E}^{\mathsf{P}^*}(\mathbb{i}) \to \mathbb{w}] \le e_s.$$

A public coin argument of knowledge can be transformed into a non-interactive argument of knowledge via the Fiat-Shamir heuristic [FS86]. If the protocol is also succinct (and zero-knowledge), then the resulting non-interactive scheme is called a SNARK (or zkSNARK).

[5] If soundness holds only against a polynomial-bounded prover, then we say this protocol is an *argument*.

2.3 Polynomial IOP

A Polynomial Interactive Oracle Proof (PIOP) [BFS20] is a type of interactive proof system where the prover's messages sent to the verifier are restricted to be polynomial oracles or field elements. PIOPs can be converted into conventional interactive proofs through cryptographic compilers [BFS20] based on polynomial comitments [KZG10, BFS20].

Definition 2 (Polynomial IOP). *Given a finite field $\mathbb{F}$, a preprocessing PIOP of degree bound D for indexed relation $\mathcal{R}$ is a triple of PPT algorithms* $(\mathsf{I}, \mathsf{P}, \mathsf{V})$ *such that:*

- $(\mathsf{I}, \mathsf{P}, \mathsf{V})$ *is a public coin preprocessing interactive proof system for $\mathcal{R}$ with completeness error e_c and soundness error e_s;*
- I, P *sends polynomials $f_i(X) \in \mathbb{F}[X]$ of degree at most D to* V*;*
- V *sends challenges $\alpha_k \in \mathbb{F}$ to* P*;*
- V *is an oracle machine with access to a list of oracles, which contains one oracle for each polynomial received from* I *and* P*;*
- *on receiving a query $z \in \mathbb{F}$, the oracle for $f_i(X)$ responds with $f_i(z)$.*

Having oracle access to $f(X)$ gives the verifier the ability to evaluate $f(X)$ at arbitrary point z without learning the content of $f(X)$ itself. Moreover, given oracle access to $f(X)$ and $g(X)$, the verifier also gains the ability to evaluate other polynomials, e.g., $a \cdot f(X) + b \cdot g(X)$ and $f(c \cdot X)$. We say the verifier *simulates the oracle access* to these polynomials. The verifier may also simulate the oracle access to polynomials that admit fast evaluation. For example, the constant polynomial $f(X) = C$, the identity polynomial $f_{\mathsf{id}}(X) = X$, and the polynomial $\frac{\omega^{i-1} \cdot (X^N - 1)}{N \cdot (X - \omega^{i-1})}$, i.e., the polynomial obtained from interpolating $\mathbf{e}_i$ over $\mathbb{D}$.

We adopt the following notations for describing a PIOP:

- "I sends $f(X)$" means the indexer sends $f(X)$ to the prover and the oracle access of $f(X)$ to the verifier, and "P sends $f(X)$" means the prover sends the oracle access of $f(X)$ to the verifier.
- "V samples $\alpha \xleftarrow{\$} \mathbb{F}$" implies that V sends a uniformly random α to P.
- "V checks $f(z) \cdot g(z) = h(z)$" (or similar equations) means the verifier queries the oracles for $f(X), g(X), h(X)$ at point z, receives y_f, y_g, y_h respectively, and checks if $y_f \cdot y_g = y_h$.

2.4 PIOP for Vector Languages

Exploiting the polynomial interpolation, we may describe a PIOP as if the parties are communicating with vectors instead of polynomials. We adopt the following change of notations for ease of description:

- We say "I sends $\mathbf{v}$" or "P sends $\mathbf{v}$" in place of "I sends $f_{\mathbf{v}}(X)$" or "P sends $f_{\mathbf{v}}(X)$", where $f_{\mathbf{v}}(X)$ is an interpolation of $\mathbf{v}$ over $\mathbb{D}$.

- Vector expressions stand for polynomials: $\mathbf{u} \circ \mathbf{v}$ for $f_{\mathbf{u}}(X) \cdot f_{\mathbf{v}}(X)$, $a \cdot \mathbf{u} + b \cdot \mathbf{v}$ for $a \cdot f_{\mathbf{u}}(X) + b \cdot f_{\mathbf{v}}(X)$, and $\mathbf{v}^{\leftarrow k}$ for $f_{\mathbf{v}}(\omega^k X)$.
- We say "V checks $\mathbf{u}+\mathbf{v}\circ\mathbf{w}^{\leftarrow k} = \mathbf{0}$" (or other vector equations) when the verifier samples $z \in \mathbb{F}$ uniformly, the prover sends $q(X) = \frac{f_{\mathbf{u}}(X)+f_{\mathbf{v}}(X)\cdot f_{\mathbf{w}}(\omega^k X)}{Z(X)}$, and the verifier checks $f_{\mathbf{u}}(z)+f_{\mathbf{v}}(z)\cdot f_{\mathbf{w}}(\omega^k z) = q(z)\cdot Z(z)$, where $Z(X) = X^N - 1$ is the vanishing polynomial over $\mathbb{D}$. When a protocol contains more than one such checks, say $F_i = \mathbf{0}$ for i from 1 to m, where F_i is a vector expression, the verifier samples $\beta \in \mathbb{F}$ and checks $\sum_{i=1}^{m} \beta^{i-1} F_i = \mathbf{0}$ instead. By Schwartz-Zippel Lemma, this check incurs a soundness error of $(d + m - 1)/|\mathbb{F}|$, where d is the degree of the polynomial divided by $Z(X)$.

Although a PIOP may involve polynomial oracles in its execution, the parties of a PIOP cannot take polynomial oracles as inputs, because the relation $\mathcal{R}$ is not well-defined when oracles are involved. However, in constructing a PIOP, we frequently encounter situations where it would be convenient to design a building-block *subprotocol* for proving statements that involve polynomial oracles, e.g., "given the oracle access to $f(X)$ that was previously sent from the prover, $f(X)$ satisfies certain property". In fact, all the PIOPs presented in this work are such subprotocols, including the MCC, which works as a building block of the entire ZKVM protocol. To formally define such subprotocols in the PIOP model, we introduce the notion *vector languages*.

Definition 3 (Vector Language). *Let m, N be positive integers. A vector language $\mathcal{R}$ of width m and length N is a set of vector tuples, where each tuple contains m vectors and each vector has length N.*

Definition 4 (PIOP for Vector Language). *Let $\mathcal{R}$ be a vector language of width m and length N. We say a PIOP $\Pi = (\mathsf{I}, \mathsf{P}, \mathsf{V})$ is a PIOP for $\mathcal{R}$ if I takes inputs the description of $\mathcal{R}$, and for any vectors $\mathbf{v}_1, \cdots, \mathbf{v}_m$, P takes inputs $\mathbf{v}_1, \cdots, \mathbf{v}_m$, and V has oracle access to $f_{\mathbf{v}_1}(X), \cdots, f_{\mathbf{v}_m}(X)$ at the start. The PIOP is complete if for any tuple $(\mathbf{v}_1, \cdots, \mathbf{v}_m) \in \mathcal{R}$, V accepts except with probability at most e_c. The PIOP is sound if for any $(\mathbf{v}_1, \cdots, \mathbf{v}_m) \notin \mathcal{R}$, V accepts with probability no more than e_s.*

2.5 Building Blocks

MCCs have two key building blocks: the permutation argument and the lookup argument. Given $\mathbf{u}_1, \cdots, \mathbf{u}_m$ and $\mathbf{v}_1, \cdots, \mathbf{v}_m$, the *permutation argument* [GWC19] (also referred to as the *multi-set check* [CBBZ22]) allows the verifier to check that the tables $(\mathbf{u}_1, \cdots, \mathbf{u}_m)$ and $(\mathbf{v}_1, \cdots, \mathbf{v}_m)$ have the same *multi-set* of rows, potentially in different orders. Formally, a permutation argument is a PIOP, referred to as Perm, for the vector language

$$\mathcal{R}_{\mathsf{Perm}} := \left\{ (\{\mathbf{u}_i \in \mathbb{F}^N\}_{i=1}^m, \{\mathbf{v}_i \in \mathbb{F}^N\}_{i=1}^m) \,\middle|\, \begin{array}{l} \mathsf{MultiRows}(\mathbf{u}_1, \cdots, \mathbf{u}_m) = \\ \mathsf{MultiRows}(\mathbf{v}_1, \cdots, \mathbf{v}_m) \end{array} \right\}$$

with completeness error $e_{c,\mathsf{Perm}}$ and soundness error $e_{s,\mathsf{Perm}}$. PLONK [GWC19] provides an example construction of the permutation argument. The idea of the

PLONK construction is to prove that for given random values $\alpha_0, \cdots, \alpha_m$, the two grand products $\prod_i(\alpha_0+\alpha_1 \cdot \mathbf{u}_{1,[i]}+\cdots+\alpha_m \cdot \mathbf{u}_{m,[i]})$ and $\prod_i(\alpha_0+\alpha_1 \cdot \mathbf{v}_{1,[i]}+\cdots+\alpha_m \cdot \mathbf{v}_{m,[i]})$ are equal. We denote the vectors satisfying the permutation relation by $(\mathbf{u}_1, \cdots, \mathbf{u}_m) \sim (\mathbf{v}_1, \cdots, \mathbf{v}_m)$, and we say "V checks $(\mathbf{u}_1, \cdots, \mathbf{u}_m) \sim (\mathbf{v}_1, \cdots, \mathbf{v}_m)$" when the parties run the Perm protocol with inputs $\mathbf{u}_1, \cdots, \mathbf{u}_m, \mathbf{v}_1, \cdots, \mathbf{v}_m$.

The *lookup argument* [GW20] allows the verifier to confirm that the set of rows of the table $(\mathbf{u}_1, \cdots, \mathbf{u}_m)$ is contained in the set of rows of the table $(\mathbf{v}_1, \cdots, \mathbf{v}_m)$. In ZKVM design, it is often necessary to prove this relationship for only a selected subset of the rows in $(\mathbf{u}_1, \cdots, \mathbf{u}_m)$. To deal with this, we modify the traditional lookup relation by introducing a selector vector $\mathbf{b}$ with values of either 0 or 1. This selector vector is used to specify the positions of the rows to be selected. Formally, for any table $(\mathbf{u}_1, \cdots, \mathbf{u}_m)$ and vector $\mathbf{b} \in \{0,1\}^N$, let $\mathsf{Rows}_{\mathbf{b}}(\mathbf{u}_1, \cdots, \mathbf{u}_m)$ denote the set of tuples $\{(\mathbf{u}_{1,[j]}, \cdots, \mathbf{u}_{m,[j]}) | j \in [N], \mathbf{b}_{[j]} = 1\}$. Then a lookup argument is a PIOP for the vector language

$$\mathcal{R}_{\mathsf{Lookup}} := \left\{ \left(\begin{matrix} \{\mathbf{u}_i \in \mathbb{F}^N\}_{i=1}^m, \{\mathbf{v}_i \in \mathbb{F}^N\}_{i=1}^m, \\ \mathbf{b} \in \{0,1\}^N \end{matrix} \right) \middle| \begin{matrix} \mathsf{Rows}_{\mathbf{b}}(\mathbf{u}_1, \cdots, \mathbf{u}_m) \subseteq \\ \mathsf{Rows}(\mathbf{v}_1, \cdots, \mathbf{v}_m) \end{matrix} \right\}$$

with completeness error $e_{c,\mathsf{Lookup}}$ and soundness error $e_{s,\mathsf{Lookup}}$. We denote the vectors satisfying the lookup relation by $(\mathbf{u}_1, \cdots, \mathbf{u}_m) \subset_{\mathbf{b}} (\mathbf{v}_1, \cdots, \mathbf{v}_m)$, and we say "V checks $(\mathbf{u}_1, \cdots, \mathbf{u}_m) \subset_{\mathbf{b}} (\mathbf{v}_1, \cdots, \mathbf{v}_m)$" when the parties run the Lookup protocol with inputs $\mathbf{u}_1, \cdots, \mathbf{u}_m, \mathbf{v}_1, \cdots, \mathbf{v}_m, \mathbf{b}$. We omit $\mathbf{b}$ when $\mathbf{b} = \mathbf{1}$.

Although existing lookup argument constructions [GW20, ZBK+22, PK22, GK22, ZGK+22, EFG22, Hab22, CBBZ22, SLST23] do not involve the selector vector $\mathbf{b}$, they can be adapted to take $\mathbf{b}$ into consideration. We will present our construction in Sect. 5.2.

A widely used application of the lookup argument is the range check, particularly 32-bit range checks in ZKVMs. Formally, a 32-bit range check is a PIOP, referred to as Range32, for the vector language

$$\mathcal{R}_{\mathsf{R32}} = \{(\mathbf{v} \in \mathbb{F}^N, \mathbf{b} \in \{0,1\}^N) | \forall t \in [N], \mathbf{b}_{[t]} = 0 \vee \mathbf{v}_{[t]} \in [0..2^{32}-1]\}$$

with completeness error $e_{c,\mathsf{Range32}}$ and soundness error $e_{s,\mathsf{Range32}}$.

3 The Memory Consistency Check Problem

We start from defining the problem of memory consistency check (MCC). We call a table $(\mathbf{op}, \mathbf{addr}, \mathbf{val}) \in \mathbb{F}^{N \times 3}$ a consistent memory trace if the value $\mathbf{val}_{[t]}$ for each row with $\mathbf{op}_{[t]} = \mathsf{Read}$ is equal to the value associated with the address $\mathbf{addr}_{[t]}$ the last time it was accessed. This concept is formalized in Definition 5, where we set $\mathsf{Read} = 0$ and $\mathsf{Write} = 1$ for simplicity and without loss of generality.

Definition 5 (Memory Consistency Check). *Let N be an integer and $\mathcal{A} \subset \mathbb{F}$. A memory consistency check for memory address space $\mathcal{A}$ is a PIOP $\Pi = (\mathsf{I}, \mathsf{P}, \mathsf{V})$ for the following vector language:*

$$\mathcal{R}_{\mathsf{Mem}}^{\mathcal{A}} := \left\{ \begin{matrix} \mathbf{op} \in \{0,1\}^N, \\ \mathbf{addr} \in \mathcal{A}^N, \\ \mathbf{val} \in \mathbb{F}^N \end{matrix} \middle| \begin{matrix} \forall t \in [N], \textit{either } \mathbf{op}_{[t]} = 1 \textit{ or} \\ \mathsf{prev}(t; \mathbf{addr}) = \perp \textit{ or} \\ \mathbf{val}_{[t]} = \mathbf{val}_{[\mathsf{prev}(t;\mathbf{addr})]} \end{matrix} \right\} \textit{ where}$$

$$\mathsf{prev}(t;\mathbf{addr}) := \begin{cases} \max J := \{t' \mid t' < t \wedge \mathbf{addr}_{[t']} = \mathbf{addr}_{[t]}\}, & \textit{if } J \neq \emptyset \\ \perp, & \textit{otherwise} \end{cases}.$$

We may write $\mathsf{prev}(t)$ instead of $\mathsf{prev}(t;\mathbf{addr})$ for simplicity when the choice of **addr** is unambiguous. Intuitively, $\mathsf{prev}(t)$ maps t to the previous time t' when the same address appeared. The memory consistency requires that $\mathbf{val}_{[t]}$ is equal to $\mathbf{val}_{[t']}$, unless the current instruction is writing ($\mathbf{op}_{[t]} = 1$) or this address was never accessed before ($t' = \perp$).

Next, we will explain the mainstream approach for constructing MCCs, which is referred to as the *sorting paradigm* and is used in all of the ZKVM projects discussed in this work.

4 The Sorting Paradigm

The main challenge in MCCs is handling the *history-dependency* of the memory: the value retrieved from a memory operation is dependent on previous operations that may be far ahead. A natural solution to this challenge is to sort the table $(\mathbf{op}, \mathbf{addr}, \mathbf{val})$ to group related operations together. To avoid affecting the consistency of this trace, the sorting should satisfy the following criterion: it should *never* swap the order between two rows with the same address. The sortings that follow this criterion are formalized by the following definitions. See the full version of this paper for the more formal definitions.

Definition 6 (Sorting, Informal). *A sorting of table* $(\mathbf{v}^{(1)}, \cdots, \mathbf{v}^{(m)}) \in \mathbb{F}^{N\times m}$ *by keys* $\mathbf{v}^{(k_1)}, \cdots, \mathbf{v}^{(k_\ell)}$ *is another table* $(\widetilde{\mathbf{v}}^{(1)}, \cdots, \widetilde{\mathbf{v}}^{(m)}) \in \mathbb{F}^{N\times m}$ *that is a permutation of the original table such that the rows in the table* $(\widetilde{\mathbf{v}}^{(k_1)}, \cdots, \widetilde{\mathbf{v}}^{(k_\ell)})$ *are sorted lexigraphically.*

Definition 7 (Canonical Sorting, Informal). *The canonical sorting of table* $(\mathbf{v}^{(1)}, \cdots, \mathbf{v}^{(m)}) \in \mathbb{F}^{N\times m}$ *by keys* $\mathbf{v}^{(k_1)}, \cdots, \mathbf{v}^{(k_\ell)}$ *is one of its sorting* $(\widetilde{\mathbf{v}}^{(1)}, \cdots, \widetilde{\mathbf{v}}^{(m)}) \in \mathbb{F}^{N\times m}$ *such that for any two rows with identical keys, these two rows are ordered respecting their orders in the original table.*

With the above definition of sorted tables, we now describe how to sort the memory trace. Let $\preceq_{\mathbf{addr}}$ be any total order over the address space $\mathcal{A}$ and $\mathcal{R}^{\mathcal{A}}_{\mathsf{CN}}(\preceq_{\mathbf{addr}})$ denote the vector language that consists of all the vector tuples ($\mathbf{op}$, $\mathbf{addr}$, $\mathbf{val}$, $\widetilde{\mathbf{op}}$, $\widetilde{\mathbf{addr}}$, $\widetilde{\mathbf{val}}$) such that $(\widetilde{\mathbf{op}}, \widetilde{\mathbf{addr}}, \widetilde{\mathbf{val}})$ is the canonical sorting of $(\mathbf{op}, \mathbf{addr}, \mathbf{val})$ by the key **addr** with total order $\preceq_{\mathbf{addr}}$. Let $\mathcal{R}^{\mathcal{A}}_{\mathsf{CN}}(\mathbf{addr})$ be the union of all these vector languages, i.e., $\mathcal{R}^{\mathcal{A}}_{\mathsf{CN}}(\mathbf{addr}) := \bigcup_{\preceq_{\mathbf{addr}}} \mathcal{R}^{\mathcal{A}}_{\mathsf{CN}}(\preceq_{\mathbf{addr}})$. The following theorem is the central idea behind the sorting technique for MCCs.

Theorem 1. *Given any* $\mathcal{A} \subset \mathbb{F}$ *and tuple* $((\mathbf{op}, \mathbf{addr}, \mathbf{val}), (\widetilde{\mathbf{op}}, \widetilde{\mathbf{addr}}, \widetilde{\mathbf{val}})) \in \mathcal{R}^{\mathcal{A}}_{\mathsf{CN}}(\mathbf{addr})$, $(\mathbf{op}, \mathbf{addr}, \mathbf{val}) \in \mathcal{R}^{\mathcal{A}}_{\mathsf{Mem}}$ *if and only if* $(\widetilde{\mathbf{op}}, \widetilde{\mathbf{addr}}, \widetilde{\mathbf{val}}) \in \mathcal{R}^{\mathcal{A}}_{\mathsf{Mem}}$.

Proof (Sketch). The conclusion follows from the fact that any canonical sorting can be obtained by repeatedly swapping rows with different keys, i.e., $\mathbf{addr}_{[t]}$, and that such swaps do not affect the membership of $\mathcal{R}^{\mathcal{A}}_{\mathsf{Mem}}$. The full proof is left to the full version.

Based on Theorem 1, Algorithm 1 shows the common workflow of all the MCCs using the sorting technique, where the $\mathsf{CSort}_{\mathcal{A}}$ protocol is decided by the concrete constructions. We call this workflow the *sorting paradigm*. In Algorithm 1, we use the following trick for proving a statement of the form "if $r = 0 \wedge s = t$ then $u = v$". We note that this statement is equivalent to "$\exists a, b$ such that $a \cdot r + b \cdot (s - t) = u - v$". We use this trick to prove the statement that whenever $\mathbf{op}$ is 0 for reading and the sorted address matches with the previous one, then the value should also match.

Theorem 2. *If* $\mathsf{CSort}_{\mathcal{A}}$ *is a PIOP for the vector language* $\mathcal{R}^{\mathcal{A}}_{\mathsf{CN}}(\preceq_{\mathbf{addr}})$ *with completeness error* e_c *and soundness error* e_s*, where* $\preceq_{\mathbf{addr}}$ *is any total order over* $\mathcal{A}$*, then the* $\mathsf{CSortMCC}_{\mathcal{A}}$ *protocol in Algorithm 1 is an MCC for* $\mathcal{A}$ *with completeness error* e_c *and soundness error* $e_s + (2N+1)/|\mathbb{F}|$.

For the proof please refer to the full version of this paper.

In the following subsections, we will introduce three different constructions of the CSort protocol, each for a different memory model.

Algorithm 1. Sorting Paradigm

---

procedure $\mathsf{CSortMCC}_{\mathcal{A}}(\mathbf{op}, \mathbf{addr}, \mathbf{val})$

P sends $\widetilde{\mathbf{op}}, \widetilde{\mathbf{addr}}, \widetilde{\mathbf{val}}$, the canonical sorting of $(\mathbf{op}, \mathbf{addr}, \mathbf{val})$;

P sends $\mathbf{a}, \mathbf{b}$ such that $\forall t \in [N-1]$, $\mathbf{a}_{[t]} \cdot \widetilde{\mathbf{op}}_{[t+1]} + \mathbf{b}_{[t]} \cdot (\widetilde{\mathbf{addr}}_{[t+1]} - \widetilde{\mathbf{addr}}_{[t]}) = \widetilde{\mathbf{val}}_{[t+1]} - \widetilde{\mathbf{val}}_{[t]}$;

V checks $\mathbf{op} \circ \mathbf{op} = \mathbf{op}$;

V checks $(\mathbf{id} - \mathbf{1}) \circ (\mathbf{a} \circ \widetilde{\mathbf{op}}^{\leftarrow 1} + \mathbf{b} \circ (\widetilde{\mathbf{addr}}^{\leftarrow 1} - \widetilde{\mathbf{addr}}) - (\widetilde{\mathbf{val}}^{\leftarrow 1} - \widetilde{\mathbf{val}})) = \mathbf{0}$ where $\mathbf{id} = \{1, \omega, \cdots, \omega^{N-1}\}$ is the evaluation of $f(X) := X$ over $\mathbb{D}$;

P and V run the $\mathsf{CSort}_{\mathcal{A}}$ protocol with inputs $\mathbf{op}$, $\mathbf{addr}$, $\mathbf{val}$, $\widetilde{\mathbf{op}}$, $\widetilde{\mathbf{addr}}$, $\widetilde{\mathbf{val}}$.

4.1 Contiguous Read-Only Memory

We start from the simplest case—the *contiguous read-only* memory setting, which is adopted by Cairo [GPR21]. In this setting, there is no writing operation, which means $\mathbf{op}$ is restricted to be the zero vector, hence "read-only". Moreover, all accessed memory addresses form a contiguous region, which means $\mathsf{Elems}(\mathbf{addr}) = \{s, s+1, \cdots, s+S-1\}$ for some $s \in \mathbb{F}$ and $S \in \mathbb{N}$. Formally, all valid execution traces for contiguous read-only memory constitute the vector language

$$\mathcal{R}_{\mathsf{CROM}} := \left\{(\mathbf{addr}, \mathbf{val}) \,\middle|\, (\mathbf{0}, \mathbf{addr}, \mathbf{val}) \in \mathcal{R}^{\mathbb{F}}_{\mathsf{Mem}}, \mathbf{addr} \in \mathcal{R}_{\mathsf{CONT}}\right\}$$

where $\mathcal{R}_{\mathsf{CONT}} = \left\{\mathbf{addr} \,\middle|\, \exists s \in \mathbb{F}, S \in [N], \mathsf{Elems}(\mathbf{addr}) = \{s+i\}_{i=0}^{S-1}\right\}$.

Contiguous read-only memories are more restricted and have fewer capabilities compared to read-write memories, thus the programming process is more challenging for programmers. On the positive side, the contiguous read-only memory model enables a much simpler protocol for checking memory consistency. Being read-only, the vectors $\mathbf{op}$, $\widetilde{\mathbf{op}}$ and $\mathbf{a}$ are eliminated from Algorithm 1, and every sorting of $(\mathbf{0}, \mathbf{addr}, \mathbf{val})$ is the canonical sorting. By contiguity, $\widetilde{\mathbf{addr}}$ satisfies that adjacent addresses differ by at most one. These observations lead to Algorithm 2. In this protocol, the vector equation checked by the verifier ensures that $\widetilde{\mathbf{addr}}_{[t]} - \widetilde{\mathbf{addr}}_{[t+1]}$ is either 0 or 1, except for the edge case $t = N$, which is eliminated by multiplying the vector $\mathbf{id} - \omega^{N-1} \cdot \mathbf{1} = (1 - \omega^{N-1}, \omega - \omega^{N-1}, \cdots, \omega^{N-1} - \omega^{N-1})$, which is zero only at $t = N$.

Algorithm 2. Canonical Sort for Contiguous Read-Only Memory

---

procedure CROMSort($\mathbf{addr}, \mathbf{val}, \widetilde{\mathbf{addr}}, \widetilde{\mathbf{val}}$)
  V checks $(\mathbf{addr}, \mathbf{val}) \sim (\widetilde{\mathbf{addr}}, \widetilde{\mathbf{val}})$;
  V checks $(\mathbf{id} - \omega^{N-1} \cdot \mathbf{1}) \circ (\overleftarrow{\widetilde{\mathbf{addr}}}^{1} - \widetilde{\mathbf{addr}}) \circ (\overleftarrow{\widetilde{\mathbf{addr}}}^{1} - \widetilde{\mathbf{addr}} - \mathbf{1}) = \mathbf{0}$.

Theorem 3. *Assuming the input vectors satisfy* $\forall t \in [N-1]$, $\widetilde{\mathbf{addr}}_{[t]} \neq \widetilde{\mathbf{addr}}_{[t+1]} \vee \widetilde{\mathbf{val}}_{[t]} = \widetilde{\mathbf{val}}_{[t+1]}$, *then the* CROMSort *protocol in Algorithm 2 is a PIOP for the vector language*

$$\mathcal{R}_{\mathsf{CN}}^{\mathsf{CROM}} := \left\{ (\mathbf{addr}, \mathbf{val}, \widetilde{\mathbf{addr}}, \widetilde{\mathbf{val}}) \;\middle|\; \begin{array}{l} \mathbf{addr} \in \mathcal{R}_{\mathsf{CONT}} \\ (\mathbf{0}, \mathbf{addr}, \mathbf{val}, \mathbf{0}, \widetilde{\mathbf{addr}}, \widetilde{\mathbf{val}}) \in \mathcal{R}_{\mathsf{CN}}^{\mathcal{A}}(\preceq_{\mathbf{addr}}) \end{array} \right\}$$

with completeness error $e_{c,\mathsf{Perm}}$ *and soundness error* $e_{s,\mathsf{Perm}} + 2N/|\mathbb{F}|$, *where* $\preceq_{\mathbf{addr}}$ *is the total order over* $\mathsf{Elems}(\mathbf{addr}) = \{s+i\}_{i=1}^{S}$ *such that* $s+i \preceq_{\mathbf{addr}} s+j \Leftrightarrow i \leq j$ *for every pair of* $(i, j) \in [0..S-1]^2$.

The proof is left to the full version.

Next, we handle the most popular case where the memory is writable and the memory address space is the set of 32-bit integers.

4.2 Read-Write Memory with 32-Bit Addresses

We explain how to construct CSort when $\mathcal{A} = [0..2^{32} - 1]$. This 32-bit address space is adopted by Miden [Mid22] and 32-bit RiscZero [Ris22]. The techniques can also be extended to 64- and 256-bit address spaces; the later is used in zkEVMs, e.g., Scroll [Scr22], Polygon Hermez [Pol22], zkSync [zkS22].

In the 32-bit randomly accessible memory, the differences between adjacent entries in the sorted addresses $\widetilde{\mathbf{addr}}$ are no longer restricted to $\{0, 1\}$, but fall in a larger range, namely $[0..2^{32} - 1]$. Therefore, the boolean check in Algorithm 2 is replaced with the 32-bit range check. Moreover, without the read-only setting, the canonicity of the sorting is no longer automatically guaranteed. Instead, the prover sorts the memory trace together with the vector $\mathbf{incs} = (1, 2, \cdots, N)$ and the verifier ensures the sorted vector $\widetilde{\mathbf{incs}}$ satisfies certain properties, as detailed in Algorithm 3. In this protocol, the vectors $\widetilde{\mathbf{inv}}$ and $\widetilde{\mathbf{diff}}$ are used to indicate the positions where $\widetilde{\mathbf{addr}}_{[t+1]}$ differs from $\widetilde{\mathbf{addr}}_{[t]}$, i.e. $\widetilde{\mathbf{addr}}_{[t+1]} - \widetilde{\mathbf{addr}}_{[t]}$ is invertible. The second Range32 in Algorithm 3 uses the tricks from Hermez and Miden, which applies the 32-bit range check simultaneously to two vectors, exploiting the fact that we only need to ensure $\widetilde{\mathbf{incs}}_{[t+1]} - \widetilde{\mathbf{incs}}_{[t]} \in [0, 2^{32})$ for $\mathbf{diff}_{[t]} = 0$ and $\widetilde{\mathbf{addr}}_{[t+1]} - \widetilde{\mathbf{addr}}_{[t]} \in [0, 2^{32})$ for $\mathbf{diff}_{[t]} = 1$. The masking vector $\mathbf{1} - \mathbf{e}_N$ excludes the case $t = N$ from the range check.

Theorem 4. *The* RW32Sort *protocol in Algorithm 3 is a PIOP for the vector language* $\mathcal{R}_{\mathsf{CN}}^{[0..2^{32}-1]}(\preceq_{\mathbf{addr}})$ *with completeness error* $e_{c,\mathsf{Perm}} + 2 \cdot e_{c,\mathsf{Range32}}$ *and soundness error* $(2N+1)/|\mathbb{F}| + e_{s,\mathsf{Perm}} + 2 \cdot e_{s,\mathsf{Range32}}$*, where* $\preceq_{\mathbf{addr}}$ *is the natural order over integers.*

The proof is left to the full version.

The above protocol can be extended to $32k$-bit address space for arbitrary k, as long as $|\mathbb{F}| > 2^{32k+1}$. In practice, we are interested in cases where $k = 1, 2, 4$ and 8. However, the cost also grows linearly with k, particularly the number of online polynomial oracles and queries. In comparison, an MCC protocol with the full address space, i.e., $\mathcal{A} = \mathbb{F}$, provides a sufficiently large space with a smaller cost. We introduce the related techniques next.

Algorithm 3. Canonical Sort for 32-bit Read-Write Memory

---

procedure RW32Sort($\mathbf{op}, \mathbf{addr}, \mathbf{val}, \widetilde{\mathbf{op}}, \widetilde{\mathbf{addr}}, \widetilde{\mathbf{val}}$)
  I sends $\mathbf{incs} = (1, 2, \cdots, N)$;
  P sends $\widetilde{\mathbf{incs}}$ satisfying $(\mathbf{incs}, \mathbf{op}, \mathbf{addr}, \mathbf{val}) \sim (\widetilde{\mathbf{incs}}, \widetilde{\mathbf{op}}, \widetilde{\mathbf{addr}}, \widetilde{\mathbf{val}})$;
  P sends $\mathbf{inv}$ such that for every $t \in [N]$, $\mathbf{inv}_{[t]} = 0$ if $\widetilde{\mathbf{addr}}_{[t+1]} = \widetilde{\mathbf{addr}}_{[t]}$, and $\mathbf{inv}_{[t]} = (\widetilde{\mathbf{addr}}_{[t+1]} - \widetilde{\mathbf{addr}}_{[t]})^{-1}$ elsewhere, where $\widetilde{\mathbf{addr}}_{[N+1]}$ is treated as $\widetilde{\mathbf{addr}}_{[1]}$;
  P sends $\mathbf{diff}$ such that for every $t \in [N]$, $\mathbf{diff}_{[t]} = 0$ if $\widetilde{\mathbf{addr}}_{[t+1]} = \widetilde{\mathbf{addr}}_{[t]}$, and $\mathbf{diff}_{[t]} = 1$ elsewhere, where $\widetilde{\mathbf{addr}}_{[N+1]}$ is treated as $\widetilde{\mathbf{addr}}_{[1]}$;
  V checks $(\mathbf{incs}, \mathbf{op}, \mathbf{addr}, \mathbf{val}) \sim (\widetilde{\mathbf{incs}}, \widetilde{\mathbf{op}}, \widetilde{\mathbf{addr}}, \widetilde{\mathbf{val}})$;
  V checks $(\overleftarrow{\widetilde{\mathbf{addr}}}^{1} - \widetilde{\mathbf{addr}}) \circ \mathbf{inv} = \mathbf{diff}$ and $\mathbf{diff} \circ (\overleftarrow{\widetilde{\mathbf{addr}}}^{1} - \widetilde{\mathbf{addr}}) = \overleftarrow{\widetilde{\mathbf{addr}}}^{1} - \widetilde{\mathbf{addr}}$;
  P and V run the Range32 protocol with inputs $\mathbf{addr}, \mathbf{1}$;
  P and V run the Range32 protocol with inputs $(\mathbf{1} - \mathbf{diff}) \circ (\overleftarrow{\widetilde{\mathbf{incs}}}^{1} - \widetilde{\mathbf{incs}}) + \mathbf{diff} \circ (\overleftarrow{\widetilde{\mathbf{addr}}}^{1} - \widetilde{\mathbf{addr}})$ and $\mathbf{1} - \mathbf{e}_N$.

4.3 Read-Write Memory with the Full Address Space

We present the canonical sorting extracted from Triton VM [TV22], which, at the time of writing, is the *only* ZKVM that adopts the setting with both full address space (i.e., $\mathcal{A} = \mathbb{F}$) and a read-write memory. This address space covers the functionalities of both 64-bit and 256-bit memories[6]. In cases where $|\mathbb{F}| < 2^{256}$,

[6] Unless for extremely special cases where the program relies on the memory check to decide whether to abort or not.

one can use two or more field elements as a memory address, making $\mathcal{A} = \mathbb{F}^c$ for $c > 1$, and linearly combine the c address traces with random challenges supplied by the verifier. Each extra address trace enlarges the memory space by a factor of $|\mathbb{F}|$ with the cost of only one online polynomial oracle. For simplicity, we assume $c = 1$ in the rest of this section.

When $\mathcal{A} = \mathbb{F}$, the greatest challenge is to define a total order over $\mathsf{Elems}(\mathbf{addr})$ that is efficiently verifiable, since $\mathsf{Elems}(\mathbf{addr})$ is neither contiguous nor restricted to a small subset. Triton VM overcomes this issue by designing a new technique for showing that $\widetilde{\mathbf{addr}}$ is sorted by any total order, which we summarize in Algorithm 4. Algorithm 4 is slightly different from that of Triton VM, dropping the engineering-related details. Moreover, we extract the core of the Triton VM memory protocol, the *contiguity check*, and generalize and reformulate it as the *distinctness check*, which will also be used in our construction in the next section.

The contiguity check of Triton VM relies on the following lemma, which presents an equivalent condition for a vector being sorted.

Lemma 1. *Given any vector* $\mathbf{v} \in \mathbb{F}^N$, *the following two statements are equivalent:*

1. *There exists a total order "$\preceq$" over $\mathbb{F}$ such that $\mathbf{v}$ is sorted by "$\preceq$".*
2. *There exists a vector $\mathbf{b} \in \{0,1\}^N$ such that*
   - $\mathbf{b}_{[1]} = 1$, *and for every* $t \in [N-1]$, *either* $\mathbf{v}_{[t]} = \mathbf{v}_{[t+1]}$ *or* $\mathbf{b}_{[t+1]} = 1$;
   - *the elements* $\{\mathbf{v}_{[t]} | t \in [N], \mathbf{b}_{[t]} = 1\}$ *are distinct.*

The proof is left to the full version.

Lemma 1 reduces the problem of proving that $\mathbf{v}$ is sorted to proving that the elements in certain positions of $\mathbf{v}$ are distinct, where the positions are specified by $\mathbf{b}$. This problem is then handled by the following lemma.

Lemma 2 (Proposition 6.6 of [Mig92]**).** *Let $\mathbb{F}$ be a finite field and $f(X) = \sum_{i=0}^{d} f_i X^i \in \mathbb{F}[X]$. Then $f(X)$ is squarefree if and only if* $\gcd(f(X), Df(X)) = 1$, *where $Df(X)$ is the shorthand for formal derivative of $f(X)$, i.e., $Df(X) := \frac{d(f(X))}{dX} = \sum_{i=0}^{d-1}(i+1)f_{i+1}X^i$.*

Lemma 2 inspires the protocol $\mathsf{DstFull}$ in Algorithm 4, which proves that given $\mathbf{b} \in \{0,1\}^N$, the elements $\{\mathbf{v}_{[i]} | i \in [N], \mathbf{b}_{[i]} = 1\}$ are distinct. This protocol exploits the formulae of logarithmic derivative $Df(X) = f(X) \cdot D(\log(f(X)))$ and $D(\log \prod_i (X - v_i)) = \sum_i \frac{1}{X - v_i}$ from calculus. The vectors $\mathbf{f}$ and $\mathbf{u}$ in this protocol are constructed so that their last entries are exactly $f(\beta)$ and $g(\beta)/f(\beta)$, respectively. Based on the $\mathsf{DstFull}$ protocol, we construct the $\mathsf{FullSort}$ protocol, as presented in Algorithm 4.

Theorem 5. *The* $\mathsf{DstFull}$ *protocol in Algorithm 4 is a PIOP for the vector language*

$$\mathcal{R}_{\mathsf{Distinct}} := \left\{ (\mathbf{v} \in \mathbb{F}^N, \mathbf{b} \in \{0,1\}^N) \,|\, \forall (i,j) \in [N]^2, (\mathbf{b}_{[i]}, \mathbf{b}_{[j]}) \neq (1,1) \vee \mathbf{v}_{[i]} \neq \mathbf{v}_{[j]} \right\}$$

with completeness error $e_{c,\mathsf{DstFull}} = N/|\mathbb{F}|$ and soundness error $e_{s,\mathsf{DstFull}} = (4N + D + 4)/|\mathbb{F}|$ where D is the degree bound of PIOP.

The proof is left to the full version.

Theorem 6. *The* FullSort *protocol in Algorithm 4 is a PIOP for the relation* $\mathcal{R}_{\mathsf{CN}}^{\mathbb{F}}(\mathbf{addr})$ *with completeness error* $e_{c,\mathsf{Perm}} + e_{c,\mathsf{Lookup}} + e_{c,\mathsf{DstFull}}$ *and soundness error* $(2N+1)/|\mathbb{F}| + e_{s,\mathsf{Perm}} + e_{s,\mathsf{Lookup}} + e_{s,\mathsf{DstFull}}$.

The proof is left to the full version.

5 Permem: New Construction with the Full Address Space

Inspired by our systemization of existing protocols, we propose several ways to optimizing the performance of previous works. First, observing the bottleneck of the sorting paradigm, in which the sorted vectors inevitably cost four online polynomials, we propose an alternative method for addressing the history-dependency of memory, called *address cycle method*, that avoids these costs. Then, using this method, we propose Permem, a more efficient MCC that supports the full memory address space. Finally, observing the significant impact of lookup arguments on the efficiency of MCCs, which is also an independently important target of research [GW20, ZBK+22, PK22], we propose a more efficient lookup argument gcq.

5.1 Address Cycle Method and Permem

As an alternative to the sorting paradigm, we propose a new method for addressing the history-dependency issue of MCC, which we call the address cycle method. This method is extracted from Arya [BCG+18]. Using this method, we construct a new MCC protocol, named Permem.

The insight behind the address cycle method is the following observation on the definition of $\mathcal{R}_{\mathsf{Mem}}$. The consistency of the memory trace $\mathbf{op}, \mathbf{addr}, \mathbf{val}$ is equivalent to a series of equality checks over elements in $\mathbf{val}$, where these equality checks are determined by $\mathbf{op}$ and $\mathbf{addr}$. The equality checks can be accomplished using the technique of PLONK [GWC19] that checks if $\mathbf{val}$ remains invariant under some permutation σ. However, unlike in PLONK, the permutation σ here is kept secret from the verifier. As a result, the prover must demonstrate, in the online phase, that the committed permutation is consistent with $\mathbf{op}$ and $\mathbf{addr}$.

Multiple permutations exist that capture the equality checks induced by $\mathcal{R}_{\mathsf{Mem}}$. We choose the following one that is conceptually simpler.

Definition 8 (Previous Access Permutation). *The* previous access permutation *of* $\mathbf{addr} \in \mathbb{F}^N$ *is the permutation over* $[N]$ *defined by*

$$\sigma_{\mathbf{addr}}(t) = \begin{cases} \mathsf{prev}(t; \mathbf{addr}), & \textit{if } \mathsf{prev}(t; \mathbf{addr}) \neq \perp \\ \max\{j \in [N] | \mathbf{addr}_{[j]} = \mathbf{addr}_{[t]}\}, & \textit{otherwise} \end{cases},$$

where $\mathsf{prev}(t; \mathbf{addr})$ *is defined as in Definition 5.*

Algorithm 4. Canonical Sort for Full Address Space

procedure DstFull($\mathbf{v}, \mathbf{b}$)

P locally computes $f(X) = \prod_{i \in [N], \mathbf{b}_{[i]}=1}(X - \mathbf{v}_{[i]})$, $g(X) = Df(X)$;

P sends $s(X), t(X)$ such that $s(X)f(X) + t(X)g(X) = 1$ computed as follows:

V Let $\{r_1, \cdots, r_k\} = \{\mathbf{v}_{[i]} | i \in [N], \mathbf{b}_{[i]} = 1\}$;

V Compute $t_i = 1/g(r_i)$ for $i \in [k]$ by multi-point evaluation and batched inversion;

V Interpolate $t(X)$ such that $t(r_i) = t_i$, and compute $s(X) = \frac{1-t(X)g(X)}{f(X)}$;

V samples $\beta \xleftarrow{\$} \mathbb{F}$ and queries for $s(\beta), t(\beta)$;

P sends $\mathbf{f}, \mathbf{u}$ where $\mathbf{f}_{[i]} = \begin{cases} (\beta - \mathbf{v}_{[1]}) \cdot \mathbf{b}_{[1]} + 1 - \mathbf{b}_{[1]}, & i = 1 \\ \mathbf{f}_{[i-1]} \cdot \left((\beta - \mathbf{v}_{[i]}) \cdot \mathbf{b}_{[i]} + 1 - \mathbf{b}_{[i]}\right), & i > 1 \end{cases}$ and $\mathbf{u}_{[i]} = \left\{ \frac{\mathbf{b}_{[1]}}{\beta - \mathbf{v}_{[1]}}, \text{ for } i = 1 \text{ or } \mathbf{u}_{[i-1]} + \frac{\mathbf{b}_{[i]}}{\beta - \mathbf{v}_{[i]}}, \text{ for } i > 1 \right.$;

V checks $\mathbf{b} \circ \mathbf{b} = \mathbf{b}$ and $(\mathbf{f} \circ (s(\beta) \cdot \mathbf{1} + t(\beta) \cdot \mathbf{u}) - \mathbf{1}) \circ \mathbf{e}_N = \mathbf{0}$;

V checks $\mathbf{e}_1 \circ ((\beta - \mathbf{v}) \circ \mathbf{b} + \mathbf{1} - \mathbf{b} - \mathbf{f}) = \mathbf{0}$;

V checks $(\mathbf{id} - \mathbf{1}) \circ \left(\mathbf{f}^{\leftarrow -1} \circ ((\beta - \mathbf{v}) \circ \mathbf{b} + \mathbf{1} - \mathbf{b}) - \mathbf{f}\right) = \mathbf{0}$;

V checks $(\mathbf{id} - \mathbf{1}) \circ ((\mathbf{u} - \mathbf{u}^{\leftarrow -1}) \circ (\beta - \mathbf{v}) - \mathbf{b}) = \mathbf{0}$.

procedure FullSort($\mathbf{op}, \mathbf{addr}, \mathbf{val}, \widetilde{\mathbf{op}}, \widetilde{\mathbf{addr}}, \widetilde{\mathbf{val}}$)

I sends $\mathbf{incs} = (1, 2, \cdots, N)$;

P sends $\widetilde{\mathbf{incs}}$ as in Algorithm 3 and $\mathbf{b}$ computed from $\widetilde{\mathbf{addr}}$ as in Lemma 1;

V checks $\mathbf{b} \circ \mathbf{e}_1 = \mathbf{e}_1$ and $(\widetilde{\mathbf{addr}} - \widetilde{\mathbf{addr}}^{\leftarrow -1}) \circ (\mathbf{1} - \mathbf{b}) = \mathbf{0}$;

V checks $(\mathbf{incs}, \mathbf{op}, \mathbf{addr}, \mathbf{val}) \sim (\widetilde{\mathbf{incs}}, \widetilde{\mathbf{op}}, \widetilde{\mathbf{addr}}, \widetilde{\mathbf{val}})$ and $\widetilde{\mathbf{incs}} - \widetilde{\mathbf{incs}}^{\leftarrow -1} \subset_{\mathbf{1-b}} \mathbf{incs}$;

P and V run the DstFull protocol with inputs $\widetilde{\mathbf{addr}}, \mathbf{b}$.

Given this permutation, $(\mathbf{op}, \mathbf{addr}, \mathbf{val}) \in \mathcal{R}_{\mathsf{Mem}}$ is equivalent to the following statement: the vector $\sigma_{\mathbf{addr}}(\mathbf{val}) - \mathbf{val}$ should be zero except at positions where $\mathsf{prev}(t; \mathbf{addr}) \neq \perp$ or $\mathbf{op}_{[t]} = 1$, as demonstrated in the following theorem.

Theorem 7. *Given* $\mathbf{op} \in \{0,1\}^N$, $\mathbf{addr} \in \mathcal{A}^N$, $\mathbf{val} \in \mathbb{F}^N$. *Let* $\mathbf{first} \in \{0,1\}^N$ *be defined as* $\mathbf{first}_{[t]} = 1$ *if and only if* $\mathbf{addr}_{[t]} \notin \mathbf{addr}_{[1..t-1]}$. *Then* $(\mathbf{op}, \mathbf{addr}, \mathbf{val}) \in \mathcal{R}^{\mathcal{A}}_{\mathsf{Mem}}$ *if and only if* $(\sigma_{\mathbf{addr}}(\mathbf{val}) - \mathbf{val}) \circ (\mathbf{1} - \mathbf{first}) \circ (\mathbf{1} - \mathbf{op}) = \mathbf{0}$, *where* $\sigma_{\mathbf{addr}}$ *is the previous access permutation of* $\mathbf{addr}$.

Proof. Note that $\mathbf{first}_{[t]} = 1$ is equivalent to $\mathsf{prev}(t; \mathbf{addr}) = \perp$. Then according to definitions of $\mathcal{R}^{\mathcal{A}}_{\mathsf{Mem}}$ and $\sigma_{\mathbf{addr}}$, $(\mathbf{op}, \mathbf{addr}, \mathbf{val}) \in \mathcal{R}^{\mathcal{A}}_{\mathsf{Mem}}$ if and only if for every $t \in [N]$, $\mathbf{first}_{[t]} = 1$ or $\mathbf{op}_{[t]} = 1$ or $\mathbf{val}_{[t]} = \mathbf{val}_{[\sigma_{\mathbf{addr}}(t)]}$, which is equivalent to the claimed vector equation.

The following lemma shows the properties of $\sigma_{\mathbf{addr}}$ with which the prover can prove to the verifier that a committed permutation is indeed $\sigma_{\mathbf{addr}}$. Theorem 7 and Lemma 3 together leads to our new MCC, which we call the address cycle method, in Algorithm 5, where the Distinct protocol is yet to instantiate. Note that the notation "$\subset_{\mathbf{1-first}}$" flips "$\subset_{\mathbf{first}}$" in the sense that the lookup check is only applied to the subset of positions where $\mathbf{first}_{[i]} = 0$ instead of $\mathbf{first}_{[i]} = 1$.

Lemma 3. *Given* $\mathbf{addr} \in \mathbb{F}^N$*, the previous access permutation* $\sigma_{\mathbf{addr}}$ *of* $\mathbf{addr}$ *is the unique permutation over* $[N]$ *that satisfies the following properties: (a)* $\sigma_{\mathbf{addr}}(\mathbf{addr}) = \mathbf{addr}$*; and (b) for any pair* $t \neq t'$ *such that* $\sigma_{\mathbf{addr}}(t) \geq t$ *and* $\sigma_{\mathbf{addr}}(t') \geq t'$, $\mathbf{addr}_{[t]} \neq \mathbf{addr}_{[t']}$.

The proof is left to the full version.

Theorem 8. *Let* $\mathcal{A} \subseteq \mathbb{F}$ *be the set of addresses. Assume that* $\mathsf{Distinct}_{\mathcal{A}}$ *is a PIOP for the vector language*

$$\mathcal{R}_{\mathsf{Distinct},\mathcal{A}} := \left\{ (\mathbf{v} \in \mathbb{F}^N, \mathbf{b} \in \{0,1\}^N) \;\middle|\; \begin{array}{l} \forall (i,j) \in [N]^2,\ \textit{if}\ \mathbf{b}_{[i]} = \mathbf{b}_{[j]} = 1 \\ \textit{then}\ (\mathbf{v}_{[i]}, \mathbf{v}_{[j]}) \in \mathcal{A}^2 \wedge \mathbf{v}_{[i]} \neq \mathbf{v}_{[j]} \end{array} \right\}$$

with completeness error $e_{c,\mathsf{Distinct}}$ *and soundness error* $e_{s,\mathsf{Distinct}}$*, then the* $\mathsf{ACMCC}_{\mathcal{A}}$ *protocol in Algorithm 5 is a PIOP for* $\mathcal{R}^{\mathcal{A}}_{\mathsf{Mem}}$ *with completeness error* $e_{c,\mathsf{Perm}} + e_{c,\mathsf{Lookup}} + e_{c,\mathsf{Distinct}}$ *and soundness error* $(3N+1)/|\mathbb{F}| + e_{s,\mathsf{Perm}} + e_{s,\mathsf{Lookup}} + e_{s,\mathsf{Distinct}}$.

The proof is left to the full version.

We then provide two instantiations of the address cycle method.

Full Memory Address Space. Note that $\mathcal{R}_{\mathsf{Distinct},\mathcal{A}}$ in Theorem 8 becomes the same as $\mathcal{R}_{\mathsf{Distinct}}$ in Theorem 5 when $\mathcal{A} = \mathbb{F}$. Therefore, the DstFull protocol in Algorithm 4 satisfies the requirement of $\mathsf{Distinct}_{\mathbb{F}}$. Placing this protocol directly into the address cycle method produces a new MCC which we name Permem.

Linear-Size Memory Address Space. When the memory address space $\mathcal{A}$ is the set $[M]$ for memory size $M \approx N$, as in Arya, there exists a simpler and more efficient construction of $\mathsf{Distinct}_{\mathcal{A}}$, denoted by DistLinear. Combining this distinctness check with the address cycle method gives us AryaMem, which roughly follows the same pattern as the memory component of Arya but adopts many PIOP-specific techniques. See the DistLinear protocol in the full version.

Algorithm 5. Address Cycle Method

---

procedure $\mathsf{ACMCC}_{\mathcal{A}}(\mathbf{op}, \mathbf{addr}, \mathbf{val})$
- I sends $\mathbf{incs} = (1, 2, \cdots, N)$;
- P computes σ_{addr} as in Definition 8;
- P sends $\boldsymbol{\sigma}_{\mathsf{addr}} := (\sigma_{\mathsf{addr}}(1), \cdots, \sigma_{\mathsf{addr}}(N))$;
- P sends $\mathbf{sval} := \sigma_{\mathbf{addr}}(\mathbf{val})$ (which is $(\mathbf{val}_{[\sigma_{\mathbf{addr}}(1)]}, \cdots, \mathbf{val}_{[\sigma_{\mathbf{addr}}(N)]})$)
- P sends $\mathbf{first}$ where $\mathbf{first}_{[t]} = 1$ if $\mathbf{addr}_{[t]} \notin \mathbf{addr}_{[1..t-1]}$, otherwise $\mathbf{first}_{[t]} = 0$;
- V checks $(\boldsymbol{\sigma}_{\mathsf{addr}}, \mathbf{addr}, \mathbf{sval}) \sim (\mathbf{incs}, \mathbf{addr}, \mathbf{val})$ and $\mathbf{incs} - \boldsymbol{\sigma}_{\mathsf{addr}} \subset_{\mathbf{1}-\mathbf{first}} \mathbf{incs}$;
- V checks $\mathbf{op} \circ \mathbf{op} = \mathbf{op}$ and $(\mathbf{1} - \mathbf{first}) \circ (\mathbf{1} - \mathbf{op}) \circ (\mathbf{sval} - \mathbf{val}) = \mathbf{0}$;
- P and V run the $\mathsf{Distinct}_{\mathcal{A}}$ protocol (Theorem 8), with inputs $\mathbf{addr}$ and $\mathbf{first}$.

5.2 Grand-Sum-Based Lookup Argument

Observing that the lookup argument presents an influential factor in the efficiency of most MCCs, we provide gcq, in Algorithm 6, a novel lookup argument with improved performance. Our protocol takes inspiration from cq [EFG22] and differs from cq by replacing the univariate sumcheck with the grand-sum check, resulting in a smaller number of online polynomials. Our protocol assumes that the invoker will ensure that the input vector $\mathbf{b}$ is a boolean vector, as is the case in the MCCs. Our protocol exploits the following technique from the grand-sum check: a vector $\mathbf{a}$ satisfies $\sum_{i=1}^{N} \mathbf{a}_{[i]} = 0$ if and only if there exists vector $\mathbf{c}$ such that $\mathbf{a} = \mathbf{c}^{\rightarrow 1} - \mathbf{c}$. Therefore, we can simply eliminate $\mathbf{a}$ from the protocol, and simulate it using $\mathbf{c}^{\rightarrow 1} - \mathbf{c}$ wherever $\mathbf{a}$ is needed.

Theorem 9. *Assume that* $\mathbf{b} \in \{0,1\}^N$ *is guaranteed. The* single-gcq *protocol in Algorithm 6 is a PIOP for* $\mathcal{R}_{\mathsf{Lookup}}^{(m=1)}$ *(defined in Sect. 2.5) with completeness error* $2N/|\mathbb{F}|$ *and soundness error* $7N/|\mathbb{F}|$*. The* gcq *protocol is a PIOP for* $\mathcal{R}_{\mathsf{Lookup}}$ *with completeness error* $2N/|\mathbb{F}|$ *and soundness error* $(m+8N)/|\mathbb{F}|$.

The proof is left to the full version.

Algorithm 6. Lookup Argument

---

procedure $\mathsf{gcq}(\mathbf{u}_1, \cdots, \mathbf{u}_m, \mathbf{v}_1, \cdots, \mathbf{v}_m, \mathbf{b})$
  V samples $\alpha \xleftarrow{\$} \mathbb{F}$;
  P and V run the single-gcq protocol with inputs $\sum_{i=1}^{m} \alpha^{i-1}\mathbf{u}_i$, $\sum_{i=1}^{m} \alpha^{i-1}\mathbf{v}_i$, $\mathbf{b}$.
procedure $\mathsf{single\text{-}gcq}(\mathbf{u}, \mathbf{v}, \mathbf{b})$
  P sends $\mathbf{m} = (m_i)_{i=1}^{N}$ where $m_i = |\{j \in [N] | \mathbf{u}_{[j]} = \mathbf{v}_{[i]}, \mathbf{b}_{[j]} = 1\}|$;
  V samples $\beta \xleftarrow{\$} \mathbb{F}$;
  P sends $\mathbf{c} := \left(\sum_{j=1}^{i}\left(\frac{\mathbf{b}_{[j]}}{\mathbf{u}_{[j]}+\beta} - \frac{\mathbf{m}_{[j]}}{\mathbf{v}_{[j]}+\beta}\right)\right)_{i=1}^{N}$;
  V checks $(\mathbf{u}+\beta) \circ (\mathbf{v}+\beta) \circ (\mathbf{c} - \mathbf{c}^{\leftarrow -1}) = \mathbf{b} \circ (\mathbf{v}+\beta) - \mathbf{m} \circ (\mathbf{u}+\beta)$.

Our protocol can be extended to achieve smaller amortized costs for k lookup arguments with the same superset $\mathbf{v}$. Specifically, the extended version requires $\lceil \frac{k+1}{2} \rceil$ online polynomial oracles, compared to $2k$ for naïvely invoking single-gcq by k times. The example for $k = 2$, called double-gcq, is presented in the full version. We write "V checks $(\mathbf{u}\|\mathbf{u}') \subset_{\mathbf{b}\|\mathbf{b}'} \mathbf{v}$" when the parties run the double lookup argument. An immediate application is the Range32 protocol for the 32-bit range check, which can be directly extended to 64- or 256-bit ranges.

6 Efficiency Analysis

We evaluate and compare the performance of the different MCCs. We measure their performance based on two factors: the number of times building blocks Perm and Lookup are used, and the number of online polynomial oracles and evaluation queries outside of these building blocks. A summary of these costs is presented in Table 1.

For more concrete comparisons, we instantiate the permutation argument with the construction from PLONK [GWC19], and the lookup argument with two constructions respectively: the state-of-the-art construction cq [EFG22] and our gcq. See the full version of this paper for the PIOP version of cq after applying the standard optimization techniques and adding the masking vector **b**. We also analyze the performance of the $32k$-bit memory with a different tradeoff between the maximal degree and the number of online polynomials. This alternative approach is characterized by not merging the grand-sum vectors in double-gcq. The concrete performance results are summarized in Table 2.

We present in Table 3 the estimated proof sizes and the costs of the prover and the verifier after instantiating the PIOP with the KZG polynomial commitment scheme. These numbers are the costs of the memory consistency checks when they are compiled into a SNARK as a standalone PIOP. They can only partially reflect the additional costs these protocols contribute to the entire ZKVM, as batching is extensively used in the compilation. Specifically, MCC can share the verifier-sampled evaluation point z with the other parts, and the proof for opening polynomial commitments can be batched with those for the rest of the PIOP, just like other building blocks like permutation/lookup arguments. Therefore, the additional cost brought by MCC in practice would be smaller than the numbers shown in Table 3.

Comparison Among Prior MCCs. As Table 2 shows, the simplest memory model, contiguous read-only memory, has the most efficient MCC protocols with either instantiation of the building blocks. For non-contiguous read-write memories, the Triton VM MCC requires roughly the same number of online polynomial oracles and evaluation queries as the check for 32-bit memory. However, for 256-bit memory, the Triton VM check costs approximately 20 to 30 fewer online polynomial oracles and evaluation queries. Although AryaMem has the fewest polynomials and queries, its memory space is also the most limited among the read-write memories.

Performance of Permem. Our new protocol costs three fewer online oracles and three fewer evaluation queries compared to Triton VM. Both Permem and Triton VM cost one more distinct evaluation point—the β in the DstFull protocol (Algorithm 4), compared to all other works. This additional evaluation point and the $O(S \cdot \log^2 S)$ complexity of multi-point evaluation seems inevitable for achieving the full address space.

Compared to all existing works with read-write memories, Permem is outperformed only by AryaMem, which is also based on the address cycle method. In detail, Permem costs three more polynomials and two more evaluation queries, in exchange for the larger memory address space.

Comparison between Lookup Arguments. When used in MCCs, our new lookup argument gcq reduces the number of online polynomial oracles by 2 to 10 and the number of online queries by 1 to 9, compared to the state-of-the-art construction cq. In particular, the performance of the MCCs with the full address space has overall improvements when instantiated with gcq.

7 Conclusion

In this work, we have analyzed the current methods for performing MCCs, a crucial and expensive component in ZKVMs, and formalized all of them as variants of the sorting paradigm. Our study provides a comprehensive overview of the various techniques used to build MCCs. Inspired by the techniques covered in this systemization, we suggest improvements to existing protocols in two aspects: a novel MCC protocol Permem that costs fewer building blocks, and a new lookup argument also with improved efficiency.

We hope that our work will inspire further research that explores new combinations of these techniques or improves existing components. In particular, for full address space, the DstFull protocol presents a bottleneck in terms of performance. It requires four online polynomials, one distinct evaluation point, and has a prover cost of $O(S \log^2 S)$. Improving its performance or eliminating the dependence on this protocol would be a valuable avenue for future work.

Acknowledgement. This work is partially supported by the National Key Research and Development Project (Grant No. 2020YFA0712300) and the National Natural Science Foundation of China (Grant No. 62272294). We thank Alan Szepieniec and the anonymous reviewers for their valuable comments.

References

[ABST22] Ambrona, M., Beunardeau, M., Schmitt, A.-L., Toledo, R.R.: aPlonK: aggregated PlonK from multi-polynomial commitment schemes. https://eprint.iacr.org/2022/1352 (2022)

[Azt22] Team of Aztec. Aztec (2022). https://zk.money/

[BBB+18] Bünz, B., Bootle, J., Boneh, D., Poelstra, A., Wuille, P., Maxwell, G.: Bulletproofs: short proofs for confidential transactions and more. In: SP 2018, Proceedings, pp. 315–334. IEEE Computer Society (2018)

[BBC+17] Ben-Sasson, E., et al.: Computational integrity with a public random string from quasi-linear PCPs. In: Coron, J.S., Nielsen, J. (eds.) EUROCRYPT 2017. LNCS, vol. 10212, pp. 551–579. Springer, Cham (2017). https://doi.org/10.1007/978-3-319-56617-7_19

[BBHR18] Ben-Sasson, E., Bentov, I., Horesh, Y., Riabzev, M.: Scalable, transparent, and post-quantum secure computational integrity. IACR Cryptol. ePrint Arch., 2018:46 (2018). http://eprint.iacr.org/2018/046

[BCG+13] Ben-Sasson, E., Chiesa, A., Genkin, D., Tromer, E., Virza, M.: SNARKs for C: verifying program executions succinctly and in zero knowledge. In: Canetti, R., Garay, J.A. (eds.) CRYPTO 2013. LNCS, vol. 8043, pp. 90–108. Springer, Heidelberg (2013). https://doi.org/10.1007/978-3-642-40084-1_6

[BCG+17] Bootle, J., Cerulli, A., Ghadafi, E., Groth, J., Hajiabadi, M., Jakobsen, S.K.: Linear-time zero-knowledge proofs for arithmetic circuit satisfiability. In: Takagi, T., Peyrin, T. (eds.) ASIACRYPT 2017. LNCS, vol. 10626, pp. 336–365. Springer, Cham (2017). https://doi.org/10.1007/978-3-319-70700-6_12

[BCG+18] Bootle, J., Cerulli, A., Groth, J., Jakobsen, S., Maller, M.: Arya: nearly linear-time zero-knowledge proofs for correct program execution. In: Peyrin, T., Galbraith, S. (eds.) ASIACRYPT 2018. LNCS, vol. 11272, pp. 595–626. Springer, Cham (2018). https://doi.org/10.1007/978-3-030-03326-2_20

[BCGT13] Ben-Sasson, E., Chiesa, A., Genkin, D., Tromer, E.: Fast reductions from RAMs to delegatable succinct constraint satisfaction problems: extended abstract. In: ITCS 2013, pp. 401, Berkeley, California, USA. ACM Press (2013). http://dl.acm.org/citation.cfm?doid=2422436.2422481

[BCR+19] Ben-Sasson, E., Chiesa, A., Riabzev, M., Spooner, N., Virza, M., Ward, N.P.: Aurora: transparent succinct arguments for R1CS. In: Ishai, Y., Rijmen, V. (eds.) EUROCRYPT 2019. LNCS, vol. 11476, pp. 103–128. Springer, Cham (2019). https://doi.org/10.1007/978-3-030-17653-2_4

[BCTV13] Ben-Sasson, E., Chiesa, A., Tromer, E., Virza, M.: Succinct Non-Interactive Zero Knowledge for a von Neumann Architecture. Technical report 879 (2013). https://eprint.iacr.org/2013/879

[BDFG20] Boneh, D., Drake, J., Fisch, B., Gabizon, A.: Halo infinite: recursive zk-SNARKs from any additive polynomial commitment scheme. Technical report 1536 (2020). http://eprint.iacr.org/2020/1536

[BFH+20] Bhadauria, R., Fang, Z., Hazay, C., Venkitasubramaniam, M., Xie, T., Zhang, Y.: Ligero++: a new optimized sublinear IOP. In: CCS 2020, pp. 2025–2038 (2020)

[BFR+13] Braun, B., Feldman, A.J., Ren, Z., Setty, S., Blumberg, A.J., Walfish, M.: Verifying computations with state. In: Proceedings of the Twenty-Fourth ACM Symposium on Operating Systems Principles, Farminton Pennsylvania, November 2013, pp. 341–357. ACM (2013). https://dl.acm.org/doi/10.1145/2517349.2522733

[BFS20] Bünz, B., Fisch, B., Szepieniec, A.: Transparent SNARKs from DARK compilers. In: Canteaut, A., Ishai, Y. (eds.) EUROCRYPT 2020. LNCS, vol. 12105, pp. 677–706. Springer, Cham (2020). https://doi.org/10.1007/978-3-030-45721-1_24

[CBBZ22] Chen, B., Bünz, B., Boneh, D., Zhang, Z.: HyperPlonk: plonk with linear-time prover and high-degree custom gates (2022). https://eprint.iacr.org/2022/1355

[CHM+20] Chiesa, A., Hu, Y., Maller, M., Mishra, P., Vesely, N., Ward, N.: Marlin: preprocessing zkSNARKs with universal and updatable SRS. In: Canteaut, A., Ishai, Y. (eds.) EUROCRYPT 2020. LNCS, vol. 12105, pp. 738–768. Springer, Cham (2020). https://doi.org/10.1007/978-3-030-45721-1_26

[COS20] Chiesa, A., Ojha, D., Spooner, N.: Fractal: post-quantum and transparent recursive proofs from holography. In: Canteaut, A., Ishai, Y. (eds.) EUROCRYPT 2020. LNCS, vol. 12105, pp. 769–793. Springer, Cham (2020). https://doi.org/10.1007/978-3-030-45721-1_27

[Eag22] Eagen, L.: Bulletproofs++. Technical report 510 (2022). https://eprint.iacr.org/2022/510

[EFG22] Eagen, L., Fiore, D., Gabizon A.:. CQ: Cached quotients for fast lookups (2022). https://eprint.iacr.org/2022/1763

[FS86] Fiat, A., Shamir, A.: How to prove yourself: practical solutions to identification and signature problems. In: Odlyzko, A.M. (ed.) CRYPTO 1986. LNCS, vol. 263, pp. 186–194. Springer, Heidelberg (1987). https://doi.org/10.1007/3-540-47721-7_12

[GGP10] Gennaro, R., Gentry, C., Parno, B.: Non-interactive verifiable computing: outsourcing computation to untrusted workers. In: Rabin, T. (ed.) CRYPTO 2010. LNCS, vol. 6223, pp. 465–482. Springer, Heidelberg (2010). https://doi.org/10.1007/978-3-642-14623-7_25

[GK22] Gabizon, A., Khovratovich, D.: Flookup: fractional decomposition-based lookups in quasi-linear time independent of table size (2022). https://eprint.iacr.org/2022/1447

[GMR85] Goldwasser, S., Micali, S., Rackoff, C.: The knowledge complexity of interactive proof-systems. In: Proceedings of the Seventeenth Annual ACM Symposium on Theory of Computing - STOC 1985, pp. 291–304, Providence, Rhode Island, United States. ACM Press (1985). http://portal.acm.org/citation.cfm?doid=22145.22178

[GPR21] Goldberg, L., Papini, S., Riabzev, M.: Cairo – a turing-complete STARK-friendly CPU architecture. Technical report 1063 (2021). http://eprint.iacr.org/2021/1063

[Gro16] Groth, J.: On the size of pairing-based non-interactive arguments. In: Fischlin, M., Coron, J.-S. (eds.) EUROCRYPT 2016. LNCS, vol. 9666, pp. 305–326. Springer, Heidelberg (2016). https://doi.org/10.1007/978-3-662-49896-5_11

[GW20] Gabizon, A., Williamson, Z.J.: Plookup: a simplified polynomial protocol for lookup tables. Technical report 315 (2020). http://eprint.iacr.org/2020/315

[GWC19] Gabizon, A., Williamson, Z.J., Ciobotaru, O.: PLONK: permutations over Lagrange-bases for Oecumenical noninteractive arguments of knowledge. Technical report 953 (2019). https://eprint.iacr.org/2019/953

[Hab22] Haböck, U.: Multivariate lookups based on logarithmic derivatives (2022). https://eprint.iacr.org/2022/1530

[KZG10] Kate, A., Zaverucha, G.M., Goldberg, I.: Constant-size commitments to polynomials and their applications. In: Abe, M. (ed.) ASIACRYPT 2010. LNCS, vol. 6477, pp. 177–194. Springer, Heidelberg (2010). https://doi.org/10.1007/978-3-642-17373-8_11

[Loo22] Team of Loopring. Loopring - zkRollup Layer2 for Trading and Payment (2022). https://loopring.org/#/

[Mid22] Team of Miden. Miden VM Documentation (2022). https://maticnetwork.github.io/miden/

[Mig92] Mignotte, M.: Mathematics for Computer Algebra. Springer, New York (1992). https://doi.org/10.1007/978-1-4613-9171-5

[PFM+22] Pearson, L., Fitzgerald, J., Masip, H., Bellés-Mutextasciitilde noz, M., noz-Tapia, J.L.M.: PlonKup: reconciling PlonK with plookup. Technical report 086 (2022). https://eprint.iacr.org/2022/086

[PHGR13] Parno, B., Howell, J., Gentry, C., Raykova, M.: Pinocchio: nearly practical verifiable computation. In: SP 2013, pp. 238–252, Berkeley, CA, May 2013. IEEE (2013). http://ieeexplore.ieee.org/document/6547113/

[PK22] Posen, J., Kattis, A.A.: Caulk+: table-independent lookup arguments. Cryptology ePrint Archive (2022). https://eprint.iacr.org/2022/957

[Pol22] Team of Polygon. Polygon Hermez (2022). https://polygon.technology/solutions/polygon-hermez/

[Ris22] Team of RiscZero. RISC Zero: General-Purpose Verifiable Computing (2022). https://risczero.com/

[RZ21] Ràfols, C., Zapico, A.: An algebraic framework for universal and updatable SNARKs. In: Malkin, T., Peikert, C. (eds.) CRYPTO 2021. LNCS, vol. 12825, pp. 774–804. Springer, Cham (2021). https://doi.org/10.1007/978-3-030-84242-0_27

[Scr22] Team of Scroll. Scroll (2022). https://scroll.io/

[Set20] Setty, S.: Spartan: efficient and general-purpose zkSNARKs without trusted setup. In: Micciancio, D., Ristenpart, T. (eds.) CRYPTO 2020. LNCS, vol. 12172, pp. 704–737. Springer, Cham (2020). https://doi.org/10.1007/978-3-030-56877-1_25

[SL20] Setty, S., Lee, J.: Quarks: Quadruple-efficient transparent zkSNARKs. Technical report 1275 (2020). http://eprint.iacr.org/2020/1275

[SLST23] Szepieniec, A., Lemmens, A., Sauer, J.F., Threadbare, B.: The Tip5 Hash Function for Recursive STARKs (2023). https://eprint.iacr.org/2023/107

[SZ22] Szepieniec, A., Zhang, Y.: Polynomial IOPs for linear algebra relations. In: Hanaoka, G., Shikata, J., Watanabe, Y. (eds.) PKC 2022. LNCS, vol. 13177, pp. 523–552. Springer, Cham (2022). https://doi.org/10.1007/978-3-030-97121-2_19

[TV22] Team of Triton VM. Triton VM. Triton VM, September 2022. https://github.com/TritonVM/triton-vm

[WTS+18] Wahby, R.S., Tzialla, I., Shelat, A., Thaler, J., Walfish, M.: Doubly-Efficient zkSNARKs without trusted setup. In: SP 2018, pp. 926–943 (2018)

[XZZ+19] Xie, T., Zhang, J., Zhang, Y., Papamanthou, C., Song, D.: Libra: succinct zero-knowledge proofs with optimal prover computation. In: Boldyreva, A., Micciancio, D. (eds.) CRYPTO 2019. LNCS, vol. 11694, pp. 733–764. Springer, Cham (2019). https://doi.org/10.1007/978-3-030-26954-8_24

[ZBK+22] Zapico, A., Buterin, V., Khovratovich, D., Maller, M., Nitulescu, A., Simkin, M.: Caulk: lookup arguments in sublinear time. Technical report 621 (2022). https://eprint.iacr.org/2022/621

[ZGK+18] Zhang, Y., Genkin, D., Katz, J., Papadopoulos, D., Papamanthou, C.: vRAM: faster verifiable RAM with program-independent preprocessing. In: SP 2018, pp. 908–925. IEEE (2018)

[ZGK+22] Zapico, A., Gabizon, A., Khovratovich, D., Maller, M., Ràfols, C.: Baloo: nearly optimal lookup arguments (2022). https://eprint.iacr.org/2022/1565

[zkS22] Team of zkSync. zkSync (2022). https://zksync.io/

[ZSZ+22] Zhang, Y., Szepeniec, A., Zhang, R., Sun, S.F., Wang, G., Gu, D.: VOProof: efficient zkSNARKs from vector oracle compilers. In: CCS 2022, CCS 2022, New York, NY, USA, November 2022, pp. 3195–3208 (2022). https://doi.org/10.1145/3548606.3559387

[ZXZS20] Zhang, J., Xie, T., Zhang, Y., Song, D.: Transparent polynomial delegation and its applications to zero knowledge proof. In: SP 2020, pp. 859–876. IEEE (2020)

Weak Zero-Knowledge via the Goldreich-Levin Theorem

Dakshita Khurana[1(✉)], Giulio Malavolta[2,3], and Kabir Tomer[1]

[1] UIUC, Urbana-Champaign, USA
{dakshita,ktomer2}@illinois.edu
[2] Bocconi University, Milan, Italy
[3] Max Planck Institute for Security and Privacy, Bochum, Germany
giulio.malavolta@hotmail.it

Abstract. Obtaining three round zero-knowledge from standard cryptographic assumptions has remained a challenging open problem. Meanwhile, there has been exciting progress in realizing useful relaxations such as weak zero-knowledge, strong witness indistinguishability and witness hiding in two or three rounds. In particular, known realizations from generic assumptions obtain: (1) security against *adaptive* verifiers assuming fully homomorphic encryption among other standard assumptions (Bitansky et. al., STOC 2019), and (2) security against *non-adaptive* verifiers in the distributional setting from oblivious transfer (Jain et. al., Crypto 2017).

This work builds three round weak zero-knowledge for NP in the non-adaptive setting from doubly-enhanced injective trapdoor functions. We obtain this result by developing a new distinguisher-dependent simulation technique that makes crucial use of the Goldreich-Levin list decoding algorithm, and may be of independent interest.

Keywords: Distinguisher · Simulation · Zero-knowledge · Goldreich-Levin

1 Introduction

Zero-knowledge (ZK) proofs are among the most widely used cryptographic primitives, with a rich history of study. In particular there has been significant recent interest in understanding the round complexity of zero-knowledge and its variants.

Zero-knowledge protocols are typically defined via the simulation paradigm. A simulator Sim is a polynomial-time algorithm that mimics the interaction of an adversarial verifier $\mathcal{V}^*$ with an honest prover $\mathcal{P}$. Sim has access to the verifier $\mathcal{V}^*$ and knows the statement, i.e., $x \in \mathcal{L}$, for an instance x of an NP language $\mathcal{L}$. Importantly, the simulator does not have access to any other "secret" information, including the (typically hard to find) NP witness for x.

The goal of the simulator is to generate a simulated view for the verifier $\mathcal{V}^*$, given only the information that $x \in \mathcal{L}$, such that this is indistinguishable

J. Guo and R. Steinfeld (Eds.): ASIACRYPT 2023, LNCS 14439, pp. 142–173, 2023.
https://doi.org/10.1007/978-981-99-8724-5_5

from the view that the verifier would have obtained in its real interaction with the honest prover $\mathcal{P}$. Informally, a protocol is zero-knowledge (ZK) iff there exists a simulator Sim that with access to $\mathcal{V}^*$ generates a view, which fools all distinguishers $\mathcal{D}^*$ that may be trying to distinguish a simulated view from a real one.

Weak Zero-knowledge [10]**.** The definition of *weak zero-knowledge* (WZK) relaxes ZK by reversing the order of quantifiers: it requires that for every verifier-distinguisher pair $(\mathcal{V}^*, \mathcal{D}^*)$, there exists a simulator Sim that fools this pair. This removes the need for a universal simulator that fools all distinguishers. In applications, this reversal of quantifiers does not necessarily incur a large privacy cost: e.g., this still guarantees that no $(\mathcal{V}^*, \mathcal{D}^*)$ can recover the NP witness, or any predicate of the NP witness. In fact, it also implies the following relaxations.

- **Witness Hiding** [12] loosely guarantees that a malicious verifier cannot recover a witness from a proof unless the witness can be efficiently computed from the statement alone.
- **Strong Witness Indistinguishability (Strong WI)** [13] requires that for two indistinguishable statement distributions $\mathcal{D}_0, \mathcal{D}_1$, a proof (or argument) for statement $d_0 \leftarrow \mathcal{D}_0$ must be indistinguishable from a proof (or argument) for statement $d_1 \leftarrow \mathcal{D}_1$.
- **Witness indistinguishability (WI)** [12] ensures that proofs of the *same statement* generated using different witnesses are indistinguishable. WI does not hold for statements sampled from different distributions, and is meaningless for statements that have a unique witness associated with them.

Prior Techniques to Realize Weak ZK. Unlike zero-knowledge, weak ZK (and therefore all the other relaxations it implies) *has been shown to be achievable* in three rounds assuming the existence of *unleveled fully-homomorphic encryption* [4]. In a more relaxed "non-adaptive" setting, where the instance is sampled from an entropic distribution only *after the verifier's challenge is fixed*, three round weak ZK (and similarly, all other relaxations) can be obtained from weaker assumptions: namely any *statistically sender-private* (SSP) oblivious transfer. This type of OT can be instantiated from algebraic assumptions such as DDH [1,22], QR, N^{th} residuosity [18], LWE [5], and most recently even LPN [3]. Similarly, while the primary contribution of [4] is to remove the non-adaptivity requirement via fully homomorphic encryption, a pared-down version of their protocol yields weak ZK in the *non-adaptive* setting from *random self-reducible* public-key encryption (which can also be viewed as a type of homomorphism) as opposed to OT. Finally, a recent work [6] obtains a realization of distinguisher-dependent simulation under the *specific* assumption that factoring is hard.

At a high level, all the above works build strategies that *enable a simulator to learn a trapdoor* by making repeated queries to a distinguisher, called *distinguisher-dependent simulation.* This technique has subsequently had had applications to non-malleable cryptography [21] and MPC [2], to low-communication laconic protocols [7] and new types of oblivious transfer [8,20].

Despite its applicability, we lack an understanding of the *generic assumptions* under which this technique is instantiable.

This work: Non-adaptive Distinguisher-Dependent Simulation from Doubly-Enhanced Injective TDFs. This work focuses on improving our understanding of the generic assumptions that can be used to realize distinguisher-dependent simulation. In particular, while existing realizations from generic assumptions require schemes with homomorphic capabilities, we ask whether there are other classes of generic assumptions that imply three-round weak zero-knowledge protocols.

We obtain a positive answer to this question, obtaining non-adaptive weak ZK/strong witness indistinguishable/witness hiding arguments assuming the existence of enhanced, injective trapdoor functions and two-message witness indistinguishable arguments. The latter can themselves be based on doubly-enhanced injective trapdoor functions (with efficiently verifiable keys) [9] or an array of assumptions such as (subexponentially hard versions of) DDH, QR, N^{th} residuosity, LWE. Under the same assumptions, we also obtain three round *arguments of knowledge* that satisfy weak zero-knowledge, strong witness indistinguishability and witness hiding properties in the non-adaptive setting. Even in the non-adaptive setting, these systems are already known to have several applications, including to multiparty computation [19] and non-malleable commitments [21].

2 Our Techniques

The starting point of our work is the following template for distinguisher-dependent simulation, that abstracts out and generalizes ideas underlying existing frameworks.

A Template for Distinguisher-Dependent Simulation: Encrypted Proofs. Suppose a prover $\mathcal{P}$ wants to convince a verifier $\mathcal{V}$ that an instance $x \in \mathcal{L}$, for some NP language $\mathcal{L}$.

- The verifier $\mathcal{V}$ will first sample a puzzle together with a corresponding solution – which we will call the secret. $\mathcal{V}$ will send the puzzle to the prover $\mathcal{P}$, while keeping the secret hidden.
- Given a verifier message containing the puzzle, $\mathcal{P}$ will encrypt its proof in such a way that anyone that holds the secret corresponding to this puzzle can decrypt and check the proof.

For security, we will require that:

- Any proof encrypted to a puzzle cannot be decrypted without *knowledge* of the corresponding secret, and
- Given a random puzzle, its corresponding secret is hard to find.

The first requirement on *knowledge* can be made more precise: consider any distinguisher $\mathcal{D}^*$ that distinguishes between encrypted proofs generated by an honest prover, and proofs sampled (efficiently) by a simulator from a public distribution. Then it should be possible to *extract* a secret from this distinguisher by building an efficient *search* algorithm $\mathcal{S}^*$. In more detail, $\mathcal{S}^*$ on input a random puzzle should be able to use $\mathcal{D}^*$ to efficiently find the secret for $\mathcal{V}^*$'s puzzle.

Finally, using known techniques [11], this protocol can be designed to allow a simulator to easily generate simulated views once it knows the secret. In summary, for any $\mathcal{D}^*$, either

- Proofs sampled by Sim from a public distribution already fool $\mathcal{D}^*$, and if not, then
- Sim can use the search algorithm $\mathcal{S}^*$ (which itself runs the verifier, and the distinguisher $\mathcal{D}^*$) to extract a secret that will enable Sim to fool $\mathcal{D}^*$.

What are some generic assumptions under which this template can be instantiated? To begin with, we observe that the template does appear necessitate (a form of) public-key encryption. Injective trapdoor functions are among the weakest generic primitives that are known to imply public-key encryption. In this work, we will aim to understand whether this template can be instantiated from trapdoored variants of injective one-way functions. Before studying this question, a few remarks about prior works are in order.

First, we note that in retrospect, prior works [4,6,19] can be viewed as instantiations of the generic template above under very specific homomorphic-style assumptions. For example, the protocol in [19] uses two-round oblivious transfer (OT) to ensure that a verifier obtains one out of two possible challenge openings for a $\Sigma-$protocol[1]. At a very high level, the simulation technique in [19] builds on the fact that (1) either simulated "garbage" $\Sigma-$protocol openings will already fool a distinguisher, or (2) if the distinguisher is able to meaningfully recover one (and only one, due to OT security) out of two $\Sigma-$protocol openings, then a simulator can find which of the two is being recovered by running such a distinguisher repeatedly, and this information can then be used to complete simulation. The work of [4] instead relies on random-self-reducible encryption towards a similar end: namely, (1) either a distinguisher cannot distinguish encryptions of 0 from encryptions of 1, or (2) if the distinguisher is able to distinguish between these encryptions, then it can be used to decrypt a specific challenge ciphertext, thereby helping the simulator find a trapdoor. As such, while the generic template discussed above itself does not appear to necessitate any homomorphic properties, these prior instantiations [4,19] require certain flavors of homomorphism (e.g., oblivious transfer is roughly equivalent to homomorphic encryption for certain linear functions) to reduce solving specific instances to solving random instances of a similar problem.

In contrast, in this work, we aim to add to the class of assumptions yielding distinguisher-dependent simulation, by relying new types of generic assumptions which do not a-prior satisfy self-reducibility or homomorphic properties. This requires us to rely on other mechanisms for search-to-decision: in particular, we

1 This basic protocol is repeated in parallel in [19] to reduce soundness error.

develop new techniques that build on the Goldreich-Levin algorithm to enable distinguisher-dependent simulation.

Towards Distinguisher-Dependent Simulation from Trapdoor One-way Functions. The Goldreich-Levin list decoding theorem provides a natural search to decision strategy for encryption schemes: it guarantees that any adversary that has better than negligible advantage in predicting the hardcore bit $\langle a, s \rangle$ for fixed secret a and random s, can be used to *find* a with overwhelming probability.

Our first idea is to encrypt proofs in the template discussed above, via Goldreich-Levin hardcore bits. Let us imagine that the prover (in an as-yet unspecified manner) generates an initial proof π attesting to the fact that x is in L. Each bit π_i of π will be encrypted by XOR-ing it with Goldreich-Levin hardcore bits, i.e., the prover will send for each i, the ciphertext

$$\mathsf{ct}_i = f(a_i), \pi_i \oplus \langle a_i, s_i \rangle, s_i$$

for $a_i, s_i \leftarrow \{0,1\}^\kappa$, and where f denotes an (injective) one-way function. Any $\mathcal{D}^*$ that distinguishes honestly generated encrypted proofs from encryptions of junk values implies a search algorithm $\mathcal{S}^*$ that inverts f. However, there is no way for an *honest* verifier to *decrypt* and check the proof π.

To remedy this, we set f to be a family of *trapdoored* functions, where the verifier samples the function family and the corresponding trapdoor. Namely, our protocol is modified so that the verifier samples

$$(\mathsf{pk}, \mathsf{sk}) \leftarrow \mathsf{KeyGen}(1^\kappa)$$

obtained by running the key generation algorithm for a trapdoor (injective) one-way function family, and sends pk to the prover. Next, the prover computes

$$\mathsf{ct}_i = f_{\mathsf{pk}}(a_i), \pi_i \oplus \langle a_i, s_i \rangle, s_i$$

and the verifier decrypts these ciphertexts to obtain π given the corresponding secret key sk.

Now, given any $\mathcal{D}^*$ that distinguishes ciphertexts that encrypt well-formed proofs from ciphertexts that encrypt 0, it becomes possible to extract *inverses* $a_1, \ldots a_n$ of the one-way function outputs $f(a_1), \ldots f(a_n)$ contained in the ciphertexts.

We can label these values $(a_1, \ldots a_n)$ as the secret, and use these to provide an alternative path to simulation. Namely, we will modify the proof itself (also simplifying it along the way to use only one a value) so that the verifier sends the prover a public key pk as before. Next, the prover computes

$$\mathsf{ct} = (y_1, y_2) \text{ for } y_1 = f_{\mathsf{pk}}(a), y_2 = 0 \oplus \langle a, s \rangle, s$$

as an encryption of 0, and additionally computes a witness indistinguishable (WI) proof attesting to the fact that

"either $x \in L$, or ct *encrypts* 1*, or the prover knows an inverse 'a' of y_1"*

The verifier accepts this proof if the WI proof accepts, and also ct decrypts to 0 (the verifier can decrypt ct since it knows the trapdoor for the one-way function).

Fixing Soundness via Coin-Tossing and Enhanced TDFs. To ensure that the prover cannot get away with generating accepting proofs for $x \notin L$, we must ensure that the prover actually *does not* know the inverse a of y_1. This is not true for the protocol described so far – in particular, the prover can always first sample a, then sample y_1 as $f_{\mathsf{pk}}(a)$. To prevent this, we modify the protocol to perform a *coin-toss* between the prover and verifier, namely, $\mathcal{P}$ first commits to randomness r_0, then $\mathcal{V}$ sends randomness r_1, and finally $\mathcal{P}$ outputs a WI proof attesting to the fact that

"*either* $x \in L$, *or* ct *encrypts* 1, *or the prover knows an inverse* 'a' *of* $r_0 \oplus r_1$"

With this modification, it becomes possible to show that $r_0 \oplus r_1$ appears sufficiently random to the prover, and the prover is unable to find an inverse of $r_0 \oplus r_1$. However, to allow simulation to go through, we still need such an inverse to *exist* for most choices of $r_0 \oplus r_1$, which may not be true if we simply treat $r_0 \oplus r_1$ as an element of the co-domain.

As such, instead of requiring the prover to find an inverse a of $r_0 \oplus r_1$, we will have the prover use randomness $r = r_0 \oplus r_1$ to sample an element y_1 from the *image of the trapdoor function*, and the WI proof will ask to find an inverse a of y_1. That is, the prover (as before) computes

$$\mathsf{ct} = (y_1, y_2) \text{ for } y_1 = f_{\mathsf{pk}}(a), y_2 = 0 \oplus \langle a, s \rangle, s$$

as an encryption of 0, and computes a witness indistinguishable (WI) proof attesting to the updated statement

"*either* $x \in L$, *or* ct *encrypts* 1,
or the prover knows an inverse 'a' *of* y_1 *for* y_1 *sampled from the image using randomness* $r_0 \oplus r_1$"

As before, the verifier accepts this proof if the WI accepts, and also ct decrypts to 0 (the verifier can decrypt ct since it has a trapdoor for the one-way function).

With this modification, we are able to prove soundness assuming that it is hard to invert such a y_1, even given the randomness r used to sample y_1 (a trapdoor function satisfying this property is called an *enhanced* trapdoor function [16]).

Building a Distinguisher-Dependent Simulator. A simulator Sim given a statement x (and without knowing a witness w for $x \in L$), has the following options:

- Generate ct as an encryption of 1, and use this as witness for the WI proof. If $\mathcal{D}^*$ cannot distinguish such a ciphertext from an honestly generated ciphertext (encrypting 0), then this option succeeds and the simulator's job is done.

- On the other hand, suppose the first option fails because $\mathcal{D}^*$ distinguishes a ciphertext encrypting 1 from the honestly generated one (encrypting 0). Then the Goldreich-Levin theorem suggests that $\mathcal{D}^*$ can be used by Sim to compute inverses. In particular Sim can generate $\mathsf{ct} = (y_1', y_2')$ for $y_1' = r_0 \oplus r_1$, and then use $\mathcal{D}^*$ to find its inverse a. This also requires Sim to sample other instance-witness pairs from the distribution on its own, which is why our techniques are limited to the non-adaptive setting. Finally, Sim can use a extracted above as a witness for the WI proof, thereby successfully completing simulation.

A Technical Subtlety. We discuss one additional technical subtlety that requires us to further modify the protocol sketched above. First, the definition of enhanced trapdoor function families guarantees that *honestly sampled keys* $(\mathsf{pk}, \mathsf{sk})$ lead to invertible distributions on y. But a malicious verifier may sample pk for which y values sampled as above *do not* have an inverse. This would cause the simulation strategy described above to break down.

We address this issue by relying on two-round witness indistinguishable (WI) arguments. In particular, the protocol above is modified to have the verifier generate two sets of keys $(\mathsf{pk}_1, \mathsf{sk}_1)$ and $(\mathsf{pk}_2, \mathsf{sk}_2)$ and prove (via a WI argument) that one of these pairs is well-formed, and will necessarily lead to invertible samples. We show that the resulting protocol is both simulatable and an argument of knowledge by combining all the techniques discussed above with the two-key technique [23].

This completes an overview of our protocol, where we assumed the existence of (1) enhanced trapdoor functions and (2) two-round witness indistinguishable arguments. For the sake of brevity, we swept some additional technical details under the rug; we point the reader to Sect. 4 for a more detailed description of our protocol. We conclude this section with a couple of natural problems that would be useful to address in future research.

Open Problems and Directions for Future Work. A natural open problem given our work and prior works, is to understand whether distinguisher-dependent simulation can be realized based on any public-key encryption scheme. Second, in light of the generic template discussed earlier in the overview, it is reasonable to wonder whether distinguisher-dependent simulation can be realized in minicrypt, or if public-key encryption is *necessary*. We conjecture that two-round proofs with distinguisher-dependent simulation imply public-key cryptography, but leave a formal exploration of this question for future work. As these questions demonstrate, there remain gaps in our understanding of what assumptions are necessary and sufficient for (non-trivial) distinguisher-dependent protocols in two or three rounds. Nevertheless, we believe that demonstrating the utility of the Goldreich-Levin search-to-decision reduction as is done in this work may be a useful step towards answering some of these questions.

3 Preliminaries

Notation. Given an NP relation R, we denote the NP language associated with it as $L_R := \{x : \exists w \text{ such that } R(x, w) = 1\}$.

3.1 Goldreich-Levin List Decoding

In what follows, we recall the Goldreich-Levin Theorem [15], borrowing some text verbatim from [17].

Definition 1 (Goldreich-Levin Bit Prediction Algorithm [15]). *Fix $\varepsilon > 0$ and a secret $x \in \{0,1\}^\kappa$. A probabilistic Goldreich-Levin prediction algorithm* $\mathsf{GL.Pred}$ *for secret x with advantage ε takes input $r \in \{0,1\}^\kappa$ and outputs a value in $\{0,1\}$ such that:*

$$\Pr_{r \xleftarrow{R} \{0,1\}^\kappa} [\mathsf{GL.Pred}(r) = \langle x, r\rangle] \geq 1/2 + \varepsilon$$

where probability is taken over r and the randomness of $\mathsf{GL.Pred}$.

Theorem 1 (Goldreich-Levin Theorem [15]). *For any given $\varepsilon > 0$ and any polynomial-time computable function $f : \{0,1\}^\kappa \to \{0,1\}^{poly(\kappa)}$, there exists an algorithm* $\mathsf{GL.Inv}$ *that runs in time $poly(1/\varepsilon, \kappa)$ with the following property.*

Let $\mathsf{GL.Pred}$ *be a Goldreich-Levin prediction algorithm for secret x with advantage ε (Definition 1). Then* $\mathsf{GL.Inv}$*, given oracle access to* $\mathsf{GL.Pred}$*, queries the oracle at most $poly(1/\varepsilon, \kappa)$ times and outputs x with probability $1 - 2^{-\Omega(\kappa)}$. That is,*

$$\Pr[\mathsf{GL.Inv}^{\mathsf{GL.Pred}}(f(x)) = x] \geq 1 - \mathsf{negl}(\kappa)$$

where probability is taken over the randomness of $\mathsf{GL.Inv}$.

3.2 Building Blocks

Definition 2 (Enhanced trapdoor injective one-way functions [14]). *A family of enhanced trapdoor injective one-way functions is a collection of injective functions $f_\alpha : \{D_\alpha \to R_\alpha\}$ such that:*

- **Syntax.** *There exist randomized PPT algorithms:*
  - *I such that $I(1^n) \to (\alpha, \tau)$ where α is the index of the injective function f_α, and τ is a corresponding trapdoor for the function.*
    We will denote by $I_1(\cdot)$ the function that runs $I(\cdot)$ and only outputs the first coordinate α, and by $I_2(\cdot)$ the function that runs $I(\cdot)$ and only outputs the second coordinate τ.
  - *S_D that on input α outputs an element from the domain D_α of the function f_α.*
  - *S_R that on input α outputs an element from the range R_α of f_α.*
- **Enhancement.** *For every $\alpha \in \mathsf{Supp}(I_1)$, the distributions $S_R(\alpha)$ and $f_\alpha(S_D(\alpha))$ are computationally indistinguishable.*
- **Efficiency.** *There exists a deterministic polynomial-time algorithm F such that for all $\alpha \leftarrow I_1(1^\kappa)$, and for all $x \in D_\alpha$, $F(\alpha, x) = f_\alpha(x)$.*
- **Trapdoor Inversion.** *There exists a deterministic polynomial-time algorithm B such that for all $(\alpha, \tau) \leftarrow I(1^\kappa)$, and for all $y \in R_\alpha$, $B(\tau, y)$ outputs an x such that $f_\alpha(x) = y$.*

- **Security (Hardness of Inversion).** *This guarantees that samples output by the* range sampler S_R *are hard to invert, even given the randomness used to sample them.*

$$\Pr\left[f_\alpha(x') = y \;\middle|\; \begin{array}{c} \alpha \leftarrow I_1(1^n) \\ r \xleftarrow{R} \{0,1\}^* \\ y \leftarrow S_R(\alpha; r) \\ x' \leftarrow A(\alpha, r) \end{array} \right] \leq \mathsf{negl}(n)$$

We note that these types of definitions have previously naturally arisen in the study of oblivious transfer and non-interactive zero-knowledge, where sometimes a strengthening to *permutations* is considered. It is shown in [16] that natural versions of the RSA and Rabin collections of trapdoor functions satisfy the definition above, and in fact also yield doubly enhanced trapdoor permutations. In this work, we will not require permutations, and can work with the weaker definition above (this weakening has also been considered previously, e.g., in [16]).

Definition 3 (Perfectly Binding Non-Interactive Bit-Commitments). *A perfectly binding non-interactive bit-commitment scheme consists of a PPT algorithm* com *such that:*

- **Perfect Binding:** *For all* $\kappa \in \mathbb{N}$, $\forall r_0, r_1 \in \{0,1\}^\kappa$, *and* $\forall b_0, b_1 \in \{0,1\}$*:*

$$(\mathsf{com}(b_0; r_0) = \mathsf{com}(b_1; r_1)) \implies (b_0 = b_1)$$

- **Computational Hiding:** *For all non-uniform PPT adversaries* A*, there exists a negligible function* μ *such that for all* $\kappa \in \mathbb{N}$*:*

$$\Pr_{r \xleftarrow{R} \{0,1\}^\kappa, b \xleftarrow{R} \{0,1\}} [b' = b \,|\, b' \leftarrow A(1^\kappa, \mathsf{com}(b; r))] \leq \frac{1}{2} + \mu(\kappa)$$

Bit commitments can be used to commit to strings of length $\mathsf{poly}(\kappa)$ by separately committing to each bit of the string. This preserves perfect binding and computational hiding.

Furthermore, perfectly binding non-interactive bit-commitments can be based on any injective one-way trapdoor function family, simply by masking the input with the Goldreich-Levin hardcore bit of the function.

3.3 Proof Systems

In this section, we recall definitions of proof systems, including delayed-input protocols and weak-zero knowledge following [19].

Definition 4 (Delayed-Input Interactive Protocols [19]). *An* n*-round delayed-input interactive protocol* (P, V) *for deciding a language* L *associated with the relation* R_L *is an interactive protocol for the same where:*

- *To prove $x \in L$, the prover and the verifier initially receive the size of the instance and execute the first $n-1$ rounds of the protocol.*
- *At the start of the last round, the prover receives $(x, w) \in R_L$ and the verifier receives x. They then execute the last round of the protocol.*

Definition 5 (Delayed-Input Interactive Arguments [19]**).** *An n-round delayed-input interactive argument (P, V) for deciding a language L associated with the relation R_L is an interactive protocol such that it satisfies the following:*

- **Completeness:** *For all $(x, w) \in R_L$,*

$$\Pr[\langle P, V\rangle(x, w) = 1] \geq 1 - \mathsf{negl}(\kappa)$$

where probability is taken over the randomness of P and V.
- **Adaptive Soundness:** *For every κ, for every PPT P^* that chooses an $x \in \{0,1\}^\kappa \setminus L$ adaptively after the first $n-1$ rounds of the protocol,*

$$\Pr[\langle P^*, V\rangle(x) = 1] \leq \mathsf{negl}(\kappa)$$

where probability is taken over the randomness of P^* and V.

Definition 6 (Witness Indistinguishability [19]**).** *An n-round delayed-input interactive argument (P, V) for deciding a language L associated with the relation R_L is said to be witness-indistinguishable if for every non-uniform PPT verifier V^* and all (x, w_1, w_2) where $w_1, w_2 \in R_L(x)$, the following ensembles are computationally indistinguishable:*

$$\{\langle P, V^*\rangle(x, w_1)\} \text{ and } \{\langle P, V^*\rangle(x, w_2)\}$$

Two-round witness indistinguishable arguments can be based on the existence of doubly-enhanced injective trapdoor functions [9,16].

Definition 7 (Argument of Knowledge). *A delayed-input interactive argument is an argument of knowledge if there exists a polynomial time extractor E such that for any polynomial-size prover P^*, there exists a negligible μ such that for any security parameter $\kappa \in \mathbb{N}$,*

$$\Pr\left[\begin{array}{l|l} V(x;\tau) = 1 \wedge & (x,\tau) \leftarrow \langle P^*, V\rangle \\ w \notin R_L(x) & w \leftarrow E^{P^*}(x,\tau) \end{array}\right] \leq \mu(\kappa).$$

A *witness indistinguishable argument of knowledge* is a proof system that satisfies both the witness indistinguishability and the argument of knowledge properties above. We now define what it means for an argument of knowledge to satisfy reusable witness indistinguishability.

Definition 8 (Reusable Witness Indistinguishable Argument of Knowledge [19]**).** *An n-round delayed input interactive argument of knowledge (P, V) for a language L is Reusable Witness Indistinguishable if for all PPT V^*, all $k = \mathsf{poly}(\kappa)$, $\Pr[b = b'] \leq 1/2 + \mathsf{negl}(\kappa)$ for the following game.*

- (P, V^*) *initially receive the size of the instance and execute the first* $n-1$ *rounds.*
- V^* *then outputs* $(x^1, w^1), (x^2, w^2), ..., (x^{k-1}, w^{k-1})$.
- P *generates the* n^{th} *message of the delayed-input witness indistinguishable argument of knowledge for the instances* $(x^1, x^2, ..., x^{k-1})$ *using the witnesses* $(w^1, w^2, ...w^{k-1})$ *and sends them to* V^*.
- V^* *outputs* (x^k, w_1^k, w_2^k).
- P *samples a single bit* b *and generates the* n^{th} *message of the delayed-input WIAoK for the instance* x^k *using witness* w_b^k.
- V^* *outputs* b'.

Reusable WI arguments of knowledge can be based on the existence of two-round witness indistinguishable arguments (ZAPs), as shown in [19].

Definition 9 (Non-adaptive Distributional ϵ-Weak Zero Knowledge [19]). *A delayed-input interactive argument* (P, V) *for a language* L *is said to be* distributional ϵ-weak zero knowledge against non-adaptive verifiers *if there exists a simulator* $\mathcal{S}$, *which is an oracle-aided machine that runs in time* $\mathsf{poly}(\kappa, \epsilon)$ *such that for every efficiently sampleable distribution* $(\mathcal{X}_\kappa, \mathcal{W}_\kappa)$ *on* R_L, *i.e.,* $\mathsf{Supp}(\mathcal{X}_\kappa, \mathcal{W}_\kappa) = \{(x, w) : x \in L \cap \{0,1\}^\kappa, w \in R_L(x)\}$, *every non-adaptive polynomial-size verifier* V^*, *every polynomial-size distinguisher* $\mathcal{D}$, *and every* $\epsilon = 1/\mathsf{poly}(\kappa)$,

$$\left| \Pr_{(x,w)\leftarrow(\mathcal{X}_\kappa,\mathcal{W}_\kappa)} \left[\mathcal{D}(x, \mathsf{View}_{V^*}[\langle P, V^*\rangle(x,w)]) = 1\right] - \Pr_{(x,w)\leftarrow(\mathcal{X}_\kappa,\mathcal{W}_\kappa)} \left[\mathcal{D}(x, \mathcal{S}^{V^*,D}(x)) = 1\right] \right| \leq \epsilon(\kappa),$$

where the probability is over the random choices of (x, w) *as well as the random coins of the parties.*

4 Construction

In this section, we describe our protocol. We will use the following ingredients.

- Let f be a family of enhanced one-way trapdoor functions according to Definition 2, and denote the index sampler, domain and range samplers, function description and inversion function respectively by $(I = (I_1, I_2), S_D, S_R, F, B)$.
- Let com be a non-interactive, statistically binding, computationally hiding commitment scheme (Definition 3).
- Let $\mathsf{ZAP} = (\mathsf{ZAP}_1, \mathsf{ZAP}_2, \mathsf{ZAP}_{\mathsf{verify}})$ denote the verifier and prover next-message functions, and the verification algorithm respectively for a two-round witness indistinguishable argument (Definition 6) for NP. This will be used to prove membership in the language L_{zap} defined below.

- Let $\mathsf{WI} = (\mathsf{WI}_1, \mathsf{WI}_2, \mathsf{WI}_3, \mathsf{WI}_{\mathsf{verify}})$ denote the prover, verifier, and prover next-message functions, and the verification algorithm respectively for a 3-round delayed-input reusable witness indistinguishable argument of knowledge (Definition 8) for NP. This will be used to prove membership in the language L_{wi} defined below.

We fix the following predicates for notational convenience.

- Intuitively, the first predicate ϕ_{chal} takes in two tuples $(y_d, \mathsf{ik}_d, \mathsf{chal}_d)$ for $d \in \{0,1\}$, and ensures that for each d, chal_d "encrypts" b_d where $b_0 \neq b_1$, i.e. chal_d is of the form $F(\mathsf{ik}_d, y_d), b_d \oplus \langle y_d, r_d \rangle, r_d$. That is,

$$\phi_{\mathsf{chal}}(y_0, y_1, \mathsf{ik}_0, \mathsf{ik}_1, \mathsf{chal}_0, \mathsf{chal}_1) = 1$$
$$\iff \exists \widetilde{r}_0, \widetilde{r}_1, b_0, b_1 \text{ s.t. } \begin{pmatrix} \mathsf{chal}_0 = [F(\mathsf{ik}_0, y_0), b_0, \widetilde{r}_0] \ \wedge \\ \mathsf{chal}_1 = [F(\mathsf{ik}_1, y_1), b_1, \widetilde{r}_1] \ \wedge \\ b_0 \oplus b_1 = \langle y_0, \widetilde{r}_0 \rangle \oplus \langle y_1, \widetilde{r}_1 \rangle \oplus 1 \end{pmatrix}$$

- The second predicate ϕ_{inv} on input a commitment c and strings r_0, r_1, s checks that c is a commitment to r_0 with randomness s; and that its remaining input z is an inverse of $r_0 \oplus r_1$ with respect to atleast one of its two input index keys $\mathsf{ik}_0, \mathsf{ik}_1$. Formally,

$$\phi_{\mathsf{inv}}(r_0, s, z, r_1, \mathsf{ik}_0, \mathsf{ik}_1, c) = 1$$
$$\iff (c = \mathsf{com}(r_0; s)) \wedge \begin{pmatrix} F(\mathsf{ik}_0, z) = S_R(\mathsf{ik}_0; r_0 \oplus r_1) \ \vee \\ F(\mathsf{ik}_1, z) = S_R(\mathsf{ik}_1; r_0 \oplus r_1) \end{pmatrix}$$

We also define the following two languages.

- Let L_{zap} be a language with corresponding relation $R_{L_{\mathsf{zap}}}$ defined as:

$$R_{L_{\mathsf{zap}}}(x_{\mathsf{zap}}, r_{\mathsf{zap}}) = 1 \iff (x_0 = I_1(r_{\mathsf{zap}})) \vee (x_1 = I_1(r_{\mathsf{zap}}))$$

  where x_{zap} is parsed as (x_0, x_1).
- Let L_{wi} be a language with corresponding relation $R_{L_{\mathsf{wi}}}$ defined as:

$$R_{L_{\mathsf{wi}}}(x_{\mathsf{wi}}, w_{\mathsf{wi}}) = 1 \iff \begin{pmatrix} (x, w) \in R_L \ \vee \\ \phi_{\mathsf{chal}}(y_0, y_1, \mathsf{ik}_0, \mathsf{ik}_1, \mathsf{chal}_0, \mathsf{chal}_1) \ \vee \\ \phi_{\mathsf{inv}}(r_0, s, z, r_1, \mathsf{ik}_0, \mathsf{ik}_1, c) \end{pmatrix}$$

  where L is a given language, x_{wi} is parsed as $(x, \mathsf{chal}_0, \mathsf{chal}_1, \mathsf{ik}_0, \mathsf{ik}_1, r_1, c)$ and w_{wi} is parsed as (w, y_0, y_1, r_0, s, z).

5 Proof of Security

In this section, we prove the following theorem.

Theorem 2. *Assuming the existence of enhanced injective trapdoor functions satisfying Definition 2 and two-round witness indistinguishable arguments satisfying Definition 6, the protocol in Fig. 1 satisfies non-adaptive distributional ϵ-weak zero knowledge.*

Weak Zero-Knowledge

Prover Input: An instance $x \in L$ and witness w s.t. $R_L(x, w) = 1$
Verifier Input: Language L

- **Prover Message:**
  1. Sample $r_0 \xleftarrow{R} \{0,1\}^\kappa, s \xleftarrow{R} \{0,1\}^\kappa, r_{\mathsf{wi}} \leftarrow \{0,1\}^\kappa$.
  2. Compute $c := \mathsf{com}(r_0; s), \mathsf{zap}_1 \leftarrow \mathsf{ZAP}_1(1^\kappa), \mathsf{wi}_1 \leftarrow \mathsf{WI}_1(1^\kappa; r_{\mathsf{wi}})$.
  3. Send message $m_1 := (c, \mathsf{zap}_1, \mathsf{wi}_1)$ to the verifier.
- **Verifier Message:**
  1. Sample $r_1 \xleftarrow{R} \{0,1\}^\kappa$
  2. Sample $(\mathsf{ik}_0, \tau_0) \xleftarrow{R} I(1^\kappa; r_{\mathsf{ik}_0})$ and $(\mathsf{ik}_1, \tau_1) \xleftarrow{R} I(1^\kappa; r_{\mathsf{ik}_1})$ where r_{ik_0} and r_{ik_1} are uniformly sampled strings.
  3. Set $x_{\mathsf{zap}} := (\mathsf{ik}_0, \mathsf{ik}_1)$ and $w_{\mathsf{zap}} := r_{\mathsf{ik}_0}$
  4. Compute $\mathsf{wi}_2 \leftarrow \mathsf{WI}_2(\mathsf{wi}_1)$ and $\mathsf{zap}_2 \leftarrow \mathsf{ZAP}_2(\mathsf{zap}_1, x_{\mathsf{zap}}, w_{\mathsf{zap}})$ proving that $R_{L_{\mathsf{zap}}}(x_{\mathsf{zap}}, w_{\mathsf{zap}}) = 1$
  5. Send message $m_2 := (r_1, \mathsf{ik}_0, \mathsf{ik}_1, \mathsf{wi}_2, \mathsf{zap}_2)$ to the prover.
- **Prover Message:**
  1. If $\mathsf{ZAP}_{\mathsf{verify}}(\mathsf{zap}_1, \mathsf{zap}_2)$ rejects, abort execution.
  2. Sample $q_0 \xleftarrow{R} S_D(\mathsf{ik}_0)$, $q_1 \xleftarrow{R} S_D(\mathsf{ik}_1)$, $\widetilde{r}_0, \widetilde{r}_1 \xleftarrow{R} \{0,1\}^\kappa$
  3. Compute $\mathsf{chal}_0 = [F(\mathsf{ik}_0, q_0), \langle q_0, \widetilde{r}_0 \rangle, \widetilde{r}_0]$, $\mathsf{chal}_1 = [F(\mathsf{ik}_1, q_1), \langle q_1, \widetilde{r}_1 \rangle, \widetilde{r}_1]$
  4. Set $x_{\mathsf{wi}} := (x, \mathsf{chal}_0, \mathsf{chal}_1, \mathsf{ik}_0, \mathsf{ik}_1, r_1, c)$ and $w_{\mathsf{wi}} := w$.
  5. Compute $\mathsf{wi}_3 \leftarrow \mathsf{WI}_3(r_{\mathsf{wi}}, \mathsf{wi}_2, x_{\mathsf{wi}}, w_{\mathsf{wi}})$ proving that $R_{L_{\mathsf{wi}}}(x_{\mathsf{wi}}, w_{\mathsf{wi}}) = 1$.
  6. Send $m_3 := (x, \mathsf{chal}_0, \mathsf{chal}_1, \mathsf{wi}_3)$ to the verifier.
- **Verifier Output:** The verifier uses the inversion trapdoors τ_0, τ_1 to perform the following checks, and outputs 1 iff
  - There exist y_0, y_1 s.t. $\mathsf{chal}_0 = [F(\mathsf{ik}_0, y_0), \langle y_0, \widetilde{r}_0 \rangle, \widetilde{r}_0]$, $\mathsf{chal}_1 = [F(\mathsf{ik}_1, y_1), \langle y_1, \widetilde{r}_1 \rangle, \widetilde{r}_1]$, and
  - $\mathsf{WI}_{\mathsf{verify}}(\mathsf{wi}_1, \mathsf{wi}_2, \mathsf{wi}_3)$ accepts.

Fig. 1. A Non-adaptive Distributional ϵ-weak Zero Knowledge Argument

5.1 Simulator

For language L with corresponding NP relation R_L, an efficiently sampleable distribution $(\mathcal{X}_\kappa, \mathcal{W}_\kappa)$ on R_L, an adversarial verifier A, a distinguisher $\mathcal{D}$, and an $\epsilon = 1/\mathsf{poly}(\kappa)$, we describe the following $\mathsf{poly}(\kappa, \epsilon)$ time simulator S, where $\epsilon' := \epsilon/7$. The simulator is described in stages below.

Initialization:
In this section the simulator behaviour is identical to an honest prover.

- Receive x as input.
- Sample $r_0 \xleftarrow{R} \{0,1\}^\kappa$, $s \xleftarrow{R} \{0,1\}^\kappa$, $r_{\mathsf{wi}} \xleftarrow{R} \{0,1\}^\kappa$
- Compute $c = \mathsf{com}(r_0; s)$, $\mathsf{zap}_1 \leftarrow \mathsf{ZAP}_1(1^\kappa)$, $\mathsf{wi}_1 \xleftarrow{R} \mathsf{WI}_1(1^\kappa; r_{\mathsf{wi}})$

Algorithm $\mathsf{Pred}_{\gamma,\mathcal{Q},\mathsf{b}}(r)$

The algorithm $\mathsf{Pred}_{\gamma,\mathcal{Q},\mathsf{b}}$ takes an input r and is parameterised by the inversion target γ, the state $\mathcal{Q}$ and the bit b that chooses an index key.

$\mathcal{Q}$ is parsed as $(r_{\mathsf{wi}}, m_1, m_2, Q)$ where m_1 is parsed as $(c, \mathsf{zap}_1, \mathsf{wi}_1)$ and m_2 as $(r_1, \mathsf{ik}_0, \mathsf{ik}_1, \mathsf{wi}_2, \mathsf{zap}_2)$.

Pred does the following:

- Initialize A to state Q.
- Sample $\widetilde{b} \xleftarrow{R} \{0,1\}$
- Sample $q \xleftarrow{R} S_{\mathcal{D}}(\mathsf{ik}_{1-\mathsf{b}})$.
- Sample $r' \xleftarrow{R} \{0,1\}^{\kappa}$
- Sample $(x', w') \xleftarrow{R} (\mathcal{X}, \mathcal{W})$
- Compute $\mathsf{chal}_{\mathsf{b}} = \left[\gamma, \widetilde{b}, r\right]$, $\mathsf{chal}_{1-\mathsf{b}} = \left[f_{\mathsf{ik}_{1-\mathsf{b}}}(q), \langle q, r' \rangle, r'\right]$
- Set $x'_{\mathsf{wi}} := (x', \mathsf{chal}_0, \mathsf{chal}_1, \mathsf{ik}_0, \mathsf{ik}_1, r_1, c)$ and $w'_{\mathsf{wi}} := (w', \bot, \bot, \bot, \bot, \bot)$.
- Compute $\mathsf{wi}_3 \leftarrow \mathsf{WI}_3(r_{\mathsf{wi}}, \mathsf{wi}_2, x'_{\mathsf{wi}}, w'_{\mathsf{wi}}, L_{\mathsf{wi}})$.
- Send $x', \mathsf{chal}_0, \mathsf{chal}_1, \mathsf{wi}_3$ to the verifier.

If the output of $\mathcal{D}$ on input the view of the verifier is 1, output $\widetilde{b}$, else output $1-\widetilde{b}$

Fig. 2. Predicting the hardcore bit for γ w.r.t. ik_{b}. Intuitively, m_1 and m_2 represent the first two messages of an execution of the protocol from Fig. 1, and Q is the state of the verifier $\mathcal{A}$ from the protocol just before $\mathcal{A}$ receives the third message, after having received m_1 and sent m_2. r_{wi} is interpreted as the randomness used to generate the first WI message wi_1. Pred uses the distinguisher $\mathcal{D}$ to guess the Goldreich-Levin hardcore bit for challenge γ for input r, w.r.t. ik_{b}.

- Send $m_1 = (c, \mathsf{zap}_1, \mathsf{wi}_1)$ to a freshly initialised instance of the adversary A.
- Receive m_2, parsed as $(r_1, \mathsf{ik}_0, \mathsf{ik}_1, \mathsf{wi}_2, \mathsf{zap}_2)$.
- Verify that $\mathsf{ZAP}_{\mathsf{verify}}(\mathsf{zap}_1, \mathsf{zap}_2)$ accepts. Output verifier view if verification fails.

Let Q be the state of the adversary after the above. Define $\mathcal{Q} := (r_{\mathsf{wi}}, m_1, m_2, Q)$.

Key Check Stage:
The simulator will perform a test on both index keys in order to choose one to use for inversion. The test aims to choose a key ik *such that* $\mathcal{D}$ *does not distinguish between a challenge ciphertext generated by calling* f_{ik} *on the output of* $S_{\mathcal{D}}(\mathsf{ik})$ *or one generated by* $S_{\mathcal{R}}(\mathsf{ik})$.

- Compute $b \xleftarrow{R} \mathsf{ik\text{-}check}_{\mathcal{Q}}$ (from Fig. 4) , where $b \in \{0, 1, \bot\}$
- If $b = \bot$, return $\bot$
- Else, continue onto the next stage.

Algorithm $\mathsf{Inv}(\gamma, \mathcal{Q}, \mathsf{b}, \varepsilon)$

The algorithm Inv takes as input r, inversion target γ, state $\mathcal{Q}$, a bit b that chooses an index key, and prediction advantage ε.

$\mathcal{Q}$ is parsed as $(r_{\mathsf{wi}}, m_1, m_2, Q)$ where m_1 is parsed as $(c, \mathsf{zap}_1, \mathsf{wi}_1)$ and m_2 as $(r_1, \mathsf{ik}_0, \mathsf{ik}_1, \mathsf{wi}_2, \mathsf{zap}_2)$.

Inv runs GL.Inv from Theorem 1 with oracle access to $\mathsf{Pred}_{\gamma,\mathcal{Q},\mathsf{b}}$. More formally, Inv performs the following steps:

- For advantage ε and the polytime-computable function $f_{\mathsf{ik_b}} : D_{\mathsf{ik_b}} \to R_{\mathsf{ik_b}}$, let GL.Inv be the Goldreich-Levin inversion algorithm given by Theorem 1.
- Construct an oracle P that answers queries by executing algorithm $\mathsf{Pred}_{\gamma,\mathcal{Q},\mathsf{b}}$.
- Compute $x = \mathsf{GL.Inv}^P(\gamma)$
- If $f_{\mathsf{ik_b}}(x) = \gamma$ return x, else return $\perp$.

Fig. 3. Inverting the trapdoor one-way function using Pred and Goldreich-Levin.

Inversion Stage:
The simulator will try to use the adversarial verifier and distinguisher to compute q' *such that* $f_{\mathsf{ik}_b}(q') = (S_R(\mathsf{ik}_b; r_0 \oplus r_1))$*, where* b *is the output of* ik-check *in the previous stage.*

- Run $\mathsf{Inv}(S_R(\mathsf{ik}_b; r_0 \oplus r_1), \mathcal{Q}, b, \epsilon'/2)$ (from Fig. 3).
- If Inv succeeds and outputs some q' and proceed to the *Success Stage*.
- If Inv fails, proceed to *Failure Stage*.

Failure Stage:
If Inv *fails to invert during the Inversion Stage, then intuitively the distinguisher output does not depend on the Goldreich-Levin hardcore bit in the challenge with sufficient probability. This can be used to produce a transcript using the second branch of* WI*, by modifying the challenge. This requires knowledge of the inverse of the challenge. Since the inverse is not known for the previous challenge, a new challenge that fails inversion must be found.*

For each $i \in [\kappa/\epsilon']$:

- Rewind the adversary to state Q (unless already in state Q).
- Sample $\widetilde{q}_i \xleftarrow{R} S_D(\mathsf{ik}_b)$
- Run $\mathsf{Inv}(f_{\mathsf{ik}_b}(\widetilde{q}_i), \mathcal{Q}, b, \epsilon'/2)$.
- If Inv fails:
  - Rewind the adversary to state Q.
  - Sample $\widetilde{r}_0, \widetilde{r}_1 \xleftarrow{R} \{0,1\}^\kappa$, $q_{1-b} \xleftarrow{R} S_D(\mathsf{ik}_{1-b})$.
  - Compute $\mathsf{chal}_b = [F(\mathsf{ik}_b, \widetilde{q}_i), \langle \widetilde{q}_i, \widetilde{r}_b \rangle \oplus 1, \widetilde{r}_b]$.

Algorithm $\mathsf{ik\text{-}check}_{\mathcal{Q}}$

The algorithm $\mathsf{ik\text{-}check}_{\mathcal{Q}}$ is parameterized by a state $\mathcal{Q}$ parsed as $(r_{\mathsf{wi}}, m_1, m_2, Q)$ where m_1 is parsed as $(c, \mathsf{zap}_1, \mathsf{wi}_1)$ and m_2 as $(r_1, \mathsf{ik}_0, \mathsf{ik}_1, \mathsf{wi}_2, \mathsf{zap}_2)$.

- Initial A in state Q.
- Let $n' := (4/\epsilon')^3$ and $t := n'\epsilon'/4$
- Initialize $c_{0,D} \leftarrow 0, c_{0,R} \leftarrow 0, c_{1,D} \leftarrow 0, c_{1,R} \leftarrow 0$
- For $i \in [n']$:
  - Sample $q_0 \xleftarrow{R} S_D(\mathsf{ik}_0), q_1 \xleftarrow{R} S_D(\mathsf{ik}_1)$
  - Sample $\gamma_0 \xleftarrow{R} S_R(\mathsf{ik}_0), \gamma_1 \xleftarrow{R} S_R(\mathsf{ik}_1)$
  - Run $\mathsf{Inv}(f_{\mathsf{ik}_0}(q_0), \mathcal{Q}, 0, \epsilon'/2)$ and add 1 to $c_{0,D}$ if it succeeds.
  - Run $\mathsf{Inv}(f_{\mathsf{ik}_1}(q_1), \mathcal{Q}, 1, \epsilon'/2)$ and add 1 to $c_{1,D}$ if it succeeds.
  - Run $\mathsf{Inv}(\gamma_0, \mathcal{Q}, 0, \epsilon'/2)$ and add 1 to $c_{0,R}$ if it succeeds.
  - Run $\mathsf{Inv}(\gamma_1, \mathcal{Q}, 1, \epsilon'/2)$ and add 1 to $c_{1,R}$ if it succeeds.
- Compute $\Delta_0 := |c_{0,D} - c_{0,R}|$
- Compute $\Delta_1 := |c_{1,D} - c_{1,R}|$

We say ik_b passes the check if $\Delta_b \leq t$. The algorithm always outputs a b such that ik_b passes the check. It outputs $\perp$ if both fail.

- If $\Delta_0 \leq t$ and $\Delta_1 \leq t$ return a random bit.
- If $\Delta_0 \leq t$, return 0.
- If $\Delta_1 \leq t$, return 1.
- Return $\perp$.

Fig. 4. Checking index keys: ik-check interacts with a copy of the adversarial verifier $\mathcal{A}$ initialised to state Q. Intuitively, the algorithm compares (for some fixed index key) the distribution resulting from generating a domain element via S_D and applying f, with the distribution resulting from generating a range element via S_R. If the index key is honestly generated, both distributions should be close. ik-check performs this comparison for both index keys the verifier $\mathcal{A}$ supplies in m_2. A key passes the check if both distributions appear sufficiently close, and ik-check can only output a key (or a bit indicating a key) that passes the check.

- Compute $\mathsf{chal}_{1-b} = [F(\mathsf{ik}_{1-b}, q_{1-b}), \langle q_{1-b}, \widetilde{r}_{1-b}\rangle, \widetilde{r}_{1-b}]$
- Set $x_{\mathsf{wi}} := (x, \mathsf{chal}_0, \mathsf{chal}_1, \mathsf{ik}_0, \mathsf{ik}_1, r_1, c)$ and $w_{\mathsf{wi}} := (\perp, \widetilde{q}_i, q_{1-b}, \perp, \perp, \perp)$.
- Compute $\mathsf{wi}_3 \leftarrow \mathsf{WI}_3(r_{\mathsf{wi}}, \mathsf{wi}_2, x_{\mathsf{wi}}, w_{\mathsf{wi}})$.
- Send $m_3 := (x, \mathsf{chal}_0, \mathsf{chal}_1, \mathsf{wi}_3)$ to the verifier.
- Output the view of the verifier for the current session, i.e. for m_1, m_2, m_3, and halt execution.

Output $\perp$

Success Stage:
If Inv *successfully inverts, we can use the output* q' *to produce a transcript using the third branch of* wi_3*. To do so, the simulator searches for a new challenge that also successfully inverts.*

For each $i \in [\kappa/\epsilon']$:

- Rewind the adversary to state Q (unless already in state Q).
- Sample $\widetilde{q}_i \xleftarrow{R} S_D(\mathsf{ik}_b)$
- Run $\mathsf{Inv}(f_{\mathsf{ik}_b}(\widetilde{q}_i), \mathcal{Q}, b, \epsilon'/2)$.
- If Inv succeeds:
  - Rewind the adversary to state Q.
  - Sample $\widetilde{r}_0, \widetilde{r}_1 \xleftarrow{R} \{0,1\}^\kappa$, $q_{1-b} \xleftarrow{R} S_D(\mathsf{ik}_{1-b})$.
  - Compute $\mathsf{chal}_b = [F(\mathsf{ik}_b, \widetilde{q}_i), \langle \widetilde{q}_i, \widetilde{r}_b \rangle, \widetilde{r}_b]$
  - Compute $\mathsf{chal}_{1-b} = [F(\mathsf{ik}_{1-b}, q_{1-b}), \langle q_{1-b}, \widetilde{r}_{1-b} \rangle, \widetilde{r}_{1-b}]$
  - Set $x_{\mathsf{wi}} := (x, \mathsf{chal}_0, \mathsf{chal}_1, \mathsf{ik}_0, \mathsf{ik}_1, r_1, c)$ and $w_{\mathsf{wi}} := (\perp, \perp, \perp, r_0, s, q')$
  - Compute $\mathsf{wi}_3 \leftarrow \mathsf{WI}_3(r_{\mathsf{wi}}, \mathsf{wi}_2, x_{\mathsf{wi}}, w_{\mathsf{wi}})$.
  - Send $m_3 = (x, \mathsf{chal}_0, \mathsf{chal}_1, \mathsf{wi}_3)$.
  - Output the view of the verifier for the current session, i.e. for m_1, m_2, m_3, and halt execution.

Output $\perp$

5.2 Proof of Theorem 2

Proof. Given the simulator described above, we will now prove the main theorem by contradiction: suppose there exists a distinguisher $\mathcal{D}$ that along with an adversarial verifier $\mathcal{A}$ distinguishes between experiments where the prover generates a proof using witness w versus an experiment where the proof is simulated, with advantage greater than ϵ, where $\epsilon = 1/poly(\kappa)$. We define $\epsilon' := \epsilon/7$ and consider a sequence of eight hybrid experiments, indexed by error parameter ϵ' where the first hybrid corresponds to the honest execution and the final hybrid corresponds to the simulated execution. $\mathcal{D}$ must necessarily distinguish some two consecutive hybrids in the sequence with advantage greater than $\epsilon' = \epsilon/7$. This leads to a contradiction, because we prove that the advantage of the distinguisher $\mathcal{D}$ for any two consecutive hybrids is always less than ϵ'.

In what follows, we let the random variable $\mathcal{D}(H_i^{\epsilon'})$ denote the output of the distinguisher upon receiving as input the view of the verifier in hybrid $H_i^{\epsilon'}$.

Hybrid $H_0^{\epsilon'}$:

This hybrid outputs the view of the verifier $\mathcal{A}$ when it interacts with an honest prover that generates a proof for x using witness w. The hybrid interacts with $\mathcal{A}$ acting as a prover for the protocol in the following manner:

- Sample $x, w \xleftarrow{R} \mathcal{X}_\kappa, \mathcal{W}_\kappa$.

- Sample $r_0 \xleftarrow{R} \{0,1\}^\kappa$, $s \xleftarrow{R} \{0,1\}^\kappa$, $r_{\mathsf{wi}} \xleftarrow{R} \{0,1\}^\kappa$
- Compute $c = \mathsf{com}(r_0; s)$, $\mathsf{zap}_1 \leftarrow \mathsf{ZAP}_1(1^\kappa)$, $\mathsf{wi}_1 \xleftarrow{R} \mathsf{WI}_1(1^\kappa; r_{\mathsf{wi}})$
- Send $m_1 = (c, \mathsf{zap}_1, \mathsf{wi}_1)$ to a freshly initialised instance of the adversary $\mathcal{A}$.
- Receive m_2, parsed as $(r_1, \mathsf{ik}_0, \mathsf{ik}_1, \mathsf{wi}_2, \mathsf{zap}_2)$.
- Verify that $\mathsf{ZAP}_{\mathsf{verify}}(\mathsf{zap}_1, \mathsf{zap}_2)$ accepts. Output $\perp$ if verification fails.
- Sample $q_0 \xleftarrow{R} S_D(\mathsf{ik}_0)$, $q_1 \xleftarrow{R} S_D(\mathsf{ik}_1)$
- Sample $\widetilde{r}_0, \widetilde{r}_1 \xleftarrow{R} \{0,1\}^\kappa$
- Compute $\mathsf{chal}_0 = [F(\mathsf{ik}_0, q_0), \langle q_0, \widetilde{r}_0\rangle, \widetilde{r}_0]$ and $\mathsf{chal}_1 = [F(\mathsf{ik}_1, q_1), \langle q_1, \widetilde{r}_1\rangle, \widetilde{r}_1]$
- Set $x_{\mathsf{wi}} := (x, \mathsf{chal}_0, \mathsf{chal}_1, \mathsf{ik}_0, \mathsf{ik}_1, r_1, c)$ and $w_{\mathsf{wi}} := (w, \perp, \perp, \perp, \perp, \perp)$
- Compute $\mathsf{wi}_3 \leftarrow \mathsf{WI}_3(r_{\mathsf{wi}}, \mathsf{wi}_2, x_{\mathsf{wi}}, w_{\mathsf{wi}})$
- Send $m_3 = (x, \mathsf{chal}_0, \mathsf{chal}_1, \mathsf{wi}_3)$.
- Output the view of the verifier for the current session, i.e. for m_1, m_2, m_3, and halt execution.

Hybrid $H_1^{\epsilon'}$:

This hybrid differs from $H_0^{\epsilon'}$ in that it runs an additional algorithm ik-check once just after receiving the verifier's message. If ik-check outputs $\perp$, the hybrid aborts, else, it continues as in $H_0^{\epsilon'}$.

Interacting with $\mathcal{A}$ as a prover for the protocol, $H_1^{\epsilon'}$ performs the following:

- Sample $x, w \xleftarrow{R} \mathcal{X}_\kappa, \mathcal{W}_\kappa$.
- Sample $r_0 \xleftarrow{R} \{0,1\}^\kappa$, $s \xleftarrow{R} \{0,1\}^\kappa$, $r_{\mathsf{wi}} \xleftarrow{R} \{0,1\}^\kappa$
- Compute $c = \mathsf{com}(r_0; s)$, $\mathsf{zap}_1 \leftarrow \mathsf{ZAP}_1(1^\kappa)$, $\mathsf{wi}_1 \xleftarrow{R} \mathsf{WI}_1(1^\kappa; r_{\mathsf{wi}})$
- Send $m_1 = (c, \mathsf{zap}_1, \mathsf{wi}_1)$ to a freshly initialised instance of the adversary $\mathcal{A}$.
- Receive m_2, parsed as $(r_1, \mathsf{ik}_0, \mathsf{ik}_1, \mathsf{wi}_2, \mathsf{zap}_2)$.
- Verify that $\mathsf{ZAP}_{\mathsf{verify}}(\mathsf{zap}_1, \mathsf{zap}_2)$ accepts. Output $\perp$ if verification fails. Let the state of $\mathcal{A}$ at this point be Q.
- Define $\mathcal{Q} := (r_{\mathsf{wi}}, m_1, m_2, Q)$ and compute $b \xleftarrow{R} \mathsf{ik\text{-}check}_{\mathcal{Q}}$, where $b \in \{0, 1, \perp\}$
- If $b = \perp$, return $\perp$
- Sample $q_0 \xleftarrow{R} S_D(\mathsf{ik}_0)$, $q_1 \xleftarrow{R} S_D(\mathsf{ik}_1)$
- Sample $\widetilde{r}_0, \widetilde{r}_1 \xleftarrow{R} \{0,1\}^\kappa$
- Compute $\mathsf{chal}_0 = [F(\mathsf{ik}_0, q_0), \langle q_0, \widetilde{r}_0\rangle, \widetilde{r}_0]$ and $\mathsf{chal}_1 = [F(\mathsf{ik}_1, q_1), \langle q_1, \widetilde{r}_1\rangle, \widetilde{r}_1]$
- Set $x_{\mathsf{wi}} := (x, \mathsf{chal}_0, \mathsf{chal}_1, \mathsf{ik}_0, \mathsf{ik}_1, r_1, c)$ and $w_{\mathsf{wi}} := (w, \perp, \perp, \perp, \perp, \perp)$
- Compute $\mathsf{wi}_3 \leftarrow \mathsf{WI}_3(r_{\mathsf{wi}}, \mathsf{wi}_2, x_{\mathsf{wi}}, w_{\mathsf{wi}})$
- Send $m_3 = (x, \mathsf{chal}_0, \mathsf{chal}_1, \mathsf{wi}_3)$.
- Output the view of the verifier for the current session, i.e. for m_1, m_2, m_3, and halt execution.

Lemma 1. $\left|\Pr[\mathcal{D}(H_0^{\epsilon'}) = 1] - \Pr[\mathcal{D}(H_1^{\epsilon'}) = 1]\right| \leq \epsilon'$

Proof. (Overview) Note that the hybrids differ only if ik-check outputs $b = \bot$, and are identical conditioned on $b \in \{0,1\}$. Therefore, the probability of distinguishing the hybrids is bounded by the probability of $b = \bot$. We show that this probability is negligible in the full version of this paper, and omit the proof here due to space. Intuitively, this is because ik-check tests whether samples obtained by $f_{\mathsf{ik}}(S_D(\mathsf{ik}))$ and $S_R(\mathsf{ik})$ are indistinguishable to the adversary. ZAP ensures that with high probability atleast one of the index keys is sampled correctly, and by the enhancement property the samples will be indistinguishable. Therefore with high probability atleast one key will pass the test.

Hybrid $H_2^{\epsilon'}$:

This hybrid differs from $H_1^{\epsilon'}$ in that it runs $\mathsf{Inv}(f_{\mathsf{ik}_b}(q_b), \mathcal{Q}, b, \epsilon'/2)$ just before computing m_3 and ignores the output, here represented as following the same steps independent of the output.

Interacting with $\mathcal{A}$ as a prover for the protocol, $H_2^{\epsilon'}$ performs the following:

- Sample $x, w \xleftarrow{R} \mathcal{X}_\kappa, \mathcal{W}_\kappa$.
- Sample $r_0 \xleftarrow{R} \{0,1\}^\kappa$, $s \xleftarrow{R} \{0,1\}^\kappa$, $r_{\mathsf{wi}} \xleftarrow{R} \{0,1\}^\kappa$
- Compute $c = \mathsf{com}(r_0; s)$, $\mathsf{zap}_1 \leftarrow \mathsf{ZAP}_1(1^\kappa)$, $\mathsf{wi}_1 \xleftarrow{R} \mathsf{WI}_1(1^\kappa; r_{\mathsf{wi}})$
- Send $m_1 = (c, \mathsf{zap}_1, \mathsf{wi}_1)$ to a freshly initialised instance of the adversary $\mathcal{A}$.
- Receive m_2, parsed as $(r_1, \mathsf{ik}_0, \mathsf{ik}_1, \mathsf{wi}_2, \mathsf{zap}_2)$.
- Verify that $\mathsf{ZAP}_{\mathsf{verify}}(\mathsf{zap}_1, \mathsf{zap}_2)$ accepts. Output $\bot$ if verification fails. Let the state of $\mathcal{A}$ at this point be Q.
- Define $\mathcal{Q} := (r_{\mathsf{wi}}, m_1, m_2, Q)$ and compute $b \xleftarrow{R} \mathsf{ik\text{-}check}_{\mathcal{Q}}$, where $b \in \{0, 1, \bot\}$
- If $b = \bot$, return $\bot$
- Sample $q_0 \xleftarrow{R} S_D(\mathsf{ik}_0)$, $q_1 \xleftarrow{R} S_D(\mathsf{ik}_1)$
- Run $\mathsf{Inv}(f_{\mathsf{ik}_b}(q_b), \mathcal{Q}, b, \epsilon'/2)$
- If Inv succeeds and outputs q' :
  - Sample $\widetilde{r}_0, \widetilde{r}_1 \xleftarrow{R} \{0,1\}^\kappa$
  - Compute $\mathsf{chal}_0 = [F(\mathsf{ik}_0, q_0), \langle q_0, \widetilde{r}_0\rangle, \widetilde{r}_0]$ and $\mathsf{chal}_1 = [F(\mathsf{ik}_1, q_1), \langle q_1, \widetilde{r}_1\rangle, \widetilde{r}_1]$
  - Set $x_{\mathsf{wi}} := (x, \mathsf{chal}_0, \mathsf{chal}_1, \mathsf{ik}_0, \mathsf{ik}_1, r_1, c)$ and $w_{\mathsf{wi}} := (w, \bot, \bot, \bot, \bot, \bot)$
  - Compute $\mathsf{wi}_3 \leftarrow \mathsf{WI}_3(r_{\mathsf{wi}}, \mathsf{wi}_2, x_{\mathsf{wi}}, w_{\mathsf{wi}})$
  - Send $m_3 = (x, \mathsf{chal}_0, \mathsf{chal}_1, \mathsf{wi}_3)$.
  - Output the view of the verifier for the current session, i.e. for m_1, m_2, m_3, and halt execution.
- If Inv fails:
  - Sample $\widetilde{r}_0, \widetilde{r}_1 \xleftarrow{R} \{0,1\}^\kappa$
  - Compute $\mathsf{chal}_0 = [F(\mathsf{ik}_0, q_0), \langle q_0, \widetilde{r}_0\rangle, \widetilde{r}_0]$ and $\mathsf{chal}_1 = [F(\mathsf{ik}_1, q_1), \langle q_1, \widetilde{r}_1\rangle, \widetilde{r}_1]$
  - Set $x_{\mathsf{wi}} := (x, \mathsf{chal}_0, \mathsf{chal}_1, \mathsf{ik}_0, \mathsf{ik}_1, r_1, c)$ and $w_{\mathsf{wi}} := (w, \bot, \bot, \bot, \bot, \bot)$
  - Compute $\mathsf{wi}_3 \leftarrow \mathsf{WI}_3(r_{\mathsf{wi}}, \mathsf{wi}_2, x_{\mathsf{wi}}, w_{\mathsf{wi}})$

- Send $m_3 = (x, \mathsf{chal}_0, \mathsf{chal}_1, \mathsf{wi}_3)$.
- Output the view of the verifier for the current session, i.e. for m_1, m_2, m_3, and halt execution.

Lemma 2. $\left|\Pr[\mathcal{D}(H_1^{\epsilon'}) = 1] - \Pr[\mathcal{D}(H_2^{\epsilon'}) = 1]\right| = 0$

Proof. The distributions of m_1, m_2, m_3 in $H_1^{\epsilon'}$ and $H_2^{\epsilon'}$ are identical because the output Inv is effectively ignored, therefore the adversary's view is identically distributed between both hybrids.

Hybrid $H_3^{\epsilon'}$:

This hybrid differs from $H_2^{\epsilon'}$ in that instead of computing the protocol execution using the same q_b for which Inv was called, it attempts to sample some $\widetilde{q}$ identically distributed to q_b given the output of Inv, and completes protocol execution using $\widetilde{q}$ if it succeeds.

Interacting with $\mathcal{A}$ as a prover for the protocol, $H_3^{\epsilon'}$ performs the following:

- Sample $x, w \xleftarrow{R} \mathcal{X}_\kappa, \mathcal{W}_\kappa$.
- Sample $r_0 \xleftarrow{R} \{0,1\}^\kappa$, $s \xleftarrow{R} \{0,1\}^\kappa$, $r_{\mathsf{wi}} \xleftarrow{R} \{0,1\}^\kappa$
- Compute $c = \mathsf{com}(r_0; s)$, $\mathsf{zap}_1 \leftarrow \mathsf{ZAP}_1(1^\kappa)$, $\mathsf{wi}_1 \xleftarrow{R} \mathsf{WI}_1(1^\kappa; r_{\mathsf{wi}})$
- Send $m_1 = (c, \mathsf{zap}_1, \mathsf{wi}_1)$ to a freshly initialised instance of the adversary $\mathcal{A}$.
- Receive m_2, parsed as $(r_1, \mathsf{ik}_0, \mathsf{ik}_1, \mathsf{wi}_2, \mathsf{zap}_2)$.
- Verify that $\mathsf{ZAP}_{\mathsf{verify}}(\mathsf{zap}_1, \mathsf{zap}_2)$ accepts. Output $\perp$ if verification fails. Let the state of $\mathcal{A}$ at this point be Q.
- Define $\mathcal{Q} := (r_{\mathsf{wi}}, m_1, m_2, Q)$ and compute $b \xleftarrow{R} \mathsf{ik\text{-}check}_{\mathcal{Q}}$, where $b \in \{0, 1, \perp\}$
- If $b = \perp$, return $\perp$
- Sample $q_0 \xleftarrow{R} S_D(\mathsf{ik}_0), q_1 \xleftarrow{R} S_D(\mathsf{ik}_1)$
- Run $\mathsf{Inv}(f_{\mathsf{ik}_b}(q_b), \mathcal{Q}, b, \epsilon'/2)$
- If Inv succeeds and outputs q', for each $i \in [\kappa/\epsilon']$:
  - Rewind the adversary to state Q (unless already in state Q).
  - Sample $\widetilde{q}_i \xleftarrow{R} S_D(\mathsf{ik}_b)$
  - Run $\mathsf{Inv}(f_{\mathsf{ik}_b}(\widetilde{q}_i), \mathcal{Q}, b, \epsilon'/2)$.
  - If Inv succeeds:
    * Rewind the adversary to state Q.
    * Sample $\widetilde{r}_0, \widetilde{r}_1 \xleftarrow{R} \{0,1\}^\kappa$, $q_{1-b} \xleftarrow{R} S_D(\mathsf{ik}_{1-b})$.
    * Compute $\mathsf{chal}_b = [F(\mathsf{ik}_b, \widetilde{q}_i), \langle \widetilde{q}_i, \widetilde{r}_b \rangle, \widetilde{r}_b]$
    * Compute $\mathsf{chal}_{1-b} = [F(\mathsf{ik}_{1-b}, q_{1-b}), \langle q_{1-b}, \widetilde{r}_{1-b} \rangle, \widetilde{r}_{1-b}]$
    * Set $x_{\mathsf{wi}} := (x, \mathsf{chal}_0, \mathsf{chal}_1, \mathsf{ik}_0, \mathsf{ik}_1, r_1, c)$ and $w_{\mathsf{wi}} := (w, \perp, \perp, \perp, \perp, \perp)$
    * Compute $\mathsf{wi}_3 \leftarrow \mathsf{WI}_3(r_{\mathsf{wi}}, \mathsf{wi}_2, x_{\mathsf{wi}}, w_{\mathsf{wi}})$
    * Send $m_3 = (x, \mathsf{chal}_0, \mathsf{chal}_1, \mathsf{wi}_3)$.

  * Output the view of the verifier for the current session, i.e. for m_1, m_2, m_3, and halt execution.
- Else if Inv fails, for each $i \in [\kappa/\epsilon']$:
  - Rewind the adversary to state Q (unless already in state Q).
  - Sample $\widetilde{q}_i \xleftarrow{R} S_D(\mathsf{ik}_b)$
  - Run $\mathsf{Inv}(f_{\mathsf{ik}_b}(\widetilde{q}_i), \mathcal{Q}, b, \epsilon'/2)$.
  - If Inv fails:
    * Rewind the adversary to state Q.
    * Sample $\widetilde{r}_0, \widetilde{r}_1 \xleftarrow{R} \{0,1\}^\kappa$, $q_{1-b} \xleftarrow{R} S_D(\mathsf{ik}_{1-b})$.
    * Compute $\mathsf{chal}_b = [F(\mathsf{ik}_b, \widetilde{q}_i), \langle \widetilde{q}_i, \widetilde{r}_b \rangle, \widetilde{r}_b]$
    * Compute $\mathsf{chal}_{1-b} = [F(\mathsf{ik}_{1-b}, q_{1-b}), \langle q_{1-b}, \widetilde{r}_{1-b} \rangle, \widetilde{r}_{1-b}]$
    * Set $x_{\mathsf{wi}} := (x, \mathsf{chal}_0, \mathsf{chal}_1, \mathsf{ik}_0, \mathsf{ik}_1, r_1, c)$ and $w_{\mathsf{wi}} := (w, \bot, \bot, \bot, \bot, \bot)$
    * Compute $\mathsf{wi}_3 \leftarrow \mathsf{WI}_3(r_{\mathsf{wi}}, \mathsf{wi}_2, x_{\mathsf{wi}}, w_{\mathsf{wi}})$
    * Send $m_3 = (x, \mathsf{chal}_0, \mathsf{chal}_1, \mathsf{wi}_3)$.
    * Output the view of the verifier for the current session, i.e. for m_1, m_2, m_3, and halt execution.
- Output $\bot$

Lemma 3. $\left|\Pr[\mathcal{D}(H_2^{\epsilon'}) = 1] - \Pr[\mathcal{D}(H_3^{\epsilon'}) = 1]\right| \leq \epsilon'$

Proof. Note that conditioned on successfully finding an appropriate $\widetilde{q}$, the adversary's view is identically distributed in both hybrids. The hybrid distinguishing probability is therefore bounded by the probability of failing to find $\widetilde{q}$.
For a fixed $(\mathcal{Q}, b)$, let p be defined as follows:

$$p(\mathcal{Q}, b) = \Pr_{\widetilde{q} \xleftarrow{R} S_D(\mathsf{ik}_b)} [\mathsf{Inv}(f_{\mathsf{ik}_b}(\widetilde{q}), \mathcal{Q}, b, \epsilon'/2) \text{ succeeds}]$$

We omit the parameters in the remaining discussion. Summing the probabilities of failing to find $\widetilde{q}$:

$$\left|\Pr[\mathcal{D}(H_2^{\epsilon'}) = 1] - \Pr[\mathcal{D}(H_3^{\epsilon'}) = 1]\right| \leq p(1-p)^{\kappa/\epsilon'} + (1-p)p^{\kappa/\epsilon'}$$

If $p \leq \epsilon'/2$, then:

$$p(1-p)^{\kappa/\epsilon'} + (1-p)p^{\kappa/\epsilon'} \leq \epsilon'/2 + (1-p)p^{\kappa/\epsilon'} \leq \epsilon'/2 + (\epsilon'/2)^{\kappa/\epsilon'} \leq \epsilon'$$

If $p > \epsilon'/2$, then:

$$p(1-p)^{\kappa/\epsilon'} + (1-p)p^{\kappa/\epsilon'} \leq \left(1 - \frac{\epsilon'}{2}\right)^{\kappa/\epsilon'} + (\epsilon'/2)^{\kappa/\epsilon'}$$

By the Taylor series expansion, we have:

$$\log\left(1 - \frac{\epsilon'}{2}\right)/\epsilon' \leq -\frac{1}{2}$$

which imples

$$\left(1-\frac{\epsilon'}{2}\right)^{\kappa/\epsilon'} = e^{\frac{\kappa}{\epsilon'}\log\left(1-\frac{\epsilon'}{2}\right)} \leq \frac{1}{e^{\kappa/2}}$$

Since $\epsilon' = 1/\mathsf{poly}(\kappa)$, for sufficiently large κ :

$$\left(1-\frac{\epsilon'}{2}\right)^{\kappa/\epsilon'} + (\epsilon'/2)^{\kappa/\epsilon'} \leq \frac{1}{e^{\kappa/2}} + \epsilon'/2 \leq \epsilon'$$

This completes the proof.

Hybrid $H_4^{\epsilon'}$:

This hybrid differs from $H_3^{\epsilon'}$ in that the adversary flips the hardcore bit for chal_b in the case where Inv fails.
Interacting with $\mathcal{A}$ as a prover for the protocol, $H_4^{\epsilon'}$ performs the following:

- Sample $x, w \xleftarrow{R} \mathcal{X}_\kappa, \mathcal{W}_\kappa$.
- Sample $r_0 \xleftarrow{R} \{0,1\}^\kappa$, $s \xleftarrow{R} \{0,1\}^\kappa$, $r_{\mathsf{wi}} \xleftarrow{R} \{0,1\}^\kappa$
- Compute $c = \mathsf{com}(r_0; s)$, $\mathsf{zap}_1 \leftarrow \mathsf{ZAP}_1(1^\kappa)$, $\mathsf{wi}_1 \xleftarrow{R} \mathsf{WI}_1(1^\kappa; r_{\mathsf{wi}})$
- Send $m_1 = (c, \mathsf{zap}_1, \mathsf{wi}_1)$ to a freshly initialised instance of the adversary $\mathcal{A}$.
- Receive m_2, parsed as $(r_1, \mathsf{ik}_0, \mathsf{ik}_1, \mathsf{wi}_2, \mathsf{zap}_2)$.
- Verify that $\mathsf{ZAP}_{\mathsf{verify}}(\mathsf{zap}_1, \mathsf{zap}_2)$ accepts. Output $\perp$ if verification fails. Let the state of $\mathcal{A}$ at this point be Q.
- Define $\mathcal{Q} := (r_{\mathsf{wi}}, m_1, m_2, Q)$ and compute $b \xleftarrow{R} \mathsf{ik\text{-}check}_{\mathcal{Q}}$, where $b \in \{0, 1, \perp\}$
- If $b = \perp$, return $\perp$
- Sample $q_0 \xleftarrow{R} S_D(\mathsf{ik}_0), q_1 \xleftarrow{R} S_D(\mathsf{ik}_1)$
- Run $\mathsf{Inv}(f_{\mathsf{ik}_b}(q_b), \mathcal{Q}, b, \epsilon'/2)$
- If Inv succeeds and outputs q', for each $i \in [\kappa/\epsilon']$:
  - Rewind the adversary to state Q (unless already in state Q).
  - Sample $\widetilde{q}_i \xleftarrow{R} S_D(\mathsf{ik}_b)$
  - Run $\mathsf{Inv}(f_{\mathsf{ik}_b}(\widetilde{q}_i), \mathcal{Q}, b, \epsilon'/2)$.
  - If Inv succeeds:
    * Rewind the adversary to state Q.
    * Sample $\widetilde{r}_0, \widetilde{r}_1 \xleftarrow{R} \{0,1\}^\kappa$, $q_{1-b} \xleftarrow{R} S_D(\mathsf{ik}_{1-b})$.
    * Compute $\mathsf{chal}_b = [F(\mathsf{ik}_b, \widetilde{q}_i), \langle \widetilde{q}_i, \widetilde{r}_b \rangle, \widetilde{r}_b]$
    * Compute $\mathsf{chal}_{1-b} = [F(\mathsf{ik}_{1-b}, q_{1-b}), \langle q_{1-b}, \widetilde{r}_{1-b} \rangle, \widetilde{r}_{1-b}]$
    * Set $x_{\mathsf{wi}} := (x, \mathsf{chal}_0, \mathsf{chal}_1, \mathsf{ik}_0, \mathsf{ik}_1, r_1, c)$ and $w_{\mathsf{wi}} := (w, \perp, \perp, \perp, \perp, \perp)$
    * Compute $\mathsf{wi}_3 \leftarrow \mathsf{WI}_3(r_{\mathsf{wi}}, \mathsf{wi}_2, x_{\mathsf{wi}}, w_{\mathsf{wi}})$
    * Send $m_3 = (x, \mathsf{chal}_0, \mathsf{chal}_1, \mathsf{wi}_3)$.
    * Output the view of the verifier for the current session, i.e. for m_1, m_2, m_3, and halt execution.
- Else if Inv fails, for each $i \in [\kappa/\epsilon']$:
  - Rewind the adversary to state Q (unless already in state Q).
  - Sample $\widetilde{q}_i \xleftarrow{R} S_D(\mathsf{ik}_b)$

- Run $\mathsf{Inv}(f_{\mathsf{ik}_b}(\widetilde{q}_i), \mathcal{Q}, b, \epsilon'/2)$.
- If Inv fails:
  - ∗ Rewind the adversary to state Q.
  - ∗ Sample $\widetilde{r}_0, \widetilde{r}_1 \xleftarrow{R} \{0,1\}^\kappa$, $q_{1-b} \xleftarrow{R} S_D(\mathsf{ik}_{1-b})$.
  - ∗ Compute $\mathsf{chal}_b = \left[F(\mathsf{ik}_b, \widetilde{q}_i), \boxed{\langle \widetilde{q}_i, \widetilde{r}_b\rangle \oplus 1}, \widetilde{r}_b\right]$
  - ∗ Compute $\mathsf{chal}_{1-b} = [F(\mathsf{ik}_{1-b}, q_{1-b}), \langle q_{1-b}, \widetilde{r}_{1-b}\rangle, \widetilde{r}_{1-b}]$
  - ∗ Set $x_{\mathsf{wi}} := (x, \mathsf{chal}_0, \mathsf{chal}_1, \mathsf{ik}_0, \mathsf{ik}_1, r_1, c)$ and $w_{\mathsf{wi}} := (w, \bot, \bot, \bot, \bot, \bot)$
  - ∗ Compute $\mathsf{wi}_3 \leftarrow \mathsf{WI}_3(r_{\mathsf{wi}}, \mathsf{wi}_2, x_{\mathsf{wi}}, w_{\mathsf{wi}})$
  - ∗ Send $m_3 = (x, \mathsf{chal}_0, \mathsf{chal}_1, \mathsf{wi}_3)$.
  - ∗ Output the view of the verifier for the current session, i.e. for m_1, m_2, m_3, and halt execution.

- Output $\bot$

Lemma 4. $\left|\Pr[\mathcal{D}(H_3^{\epsilon'}) = 1] - \Pr[\mathcal{D}(H_4^{\epsilon'}) = 1]\right| \leq \epsilon'$

Proof. (Overview) Due to lack of space, we defer the proof to the full version. Intuitively, since the inversion algorithm fails for $\widetilde{q}_i$, the distinguisher does not distinguish between correct and incorrect hardcore bits. Since the only difference between hybrids is the hardcore bit, we show it is safe to send incorrect bits.

Hybrid $H_5^{\epsilon'}$:

This hybrid differs from $H_4^{\epsilon'}$ in that the adversary attempts to invert a randomly sampled $S_R(\mathsf{ik}_b)$ instead of $f_{\mathsf{ik}_b}(q_b)$. Since this change means that q_b is unused, it is no longer sampled. Interacting with $\mathcal{A}$ as a prover for the protocol, $H_5^{\epsilon'}$ performs the following:

- Sample $x, w \xleftarrow{R} \mathcal{X}_\kappa, \mathcal{W}_\kappa$.
- Sample $r_0 \xleftarrow{R} \{0,1\}^\kappa$, $s \xleftarrow{R} \{0,1\}^\kappa$, compute $c = \mathsf{com}(r_0; s)$, compute the first message zap_1 of a ZAP, the first message wi_1 of a WI, and send $m_1 = (c, \mathsf{zap}_1, \mathsf{wi}_1)$ to the adversary.
- Receive m_2, parsed as $(r_1, \mathsf{ik}_0, \mathsf{ik}_1, \mathsf{wi}_2, \mathsf{zap}_2)$.
- Verify that $\mathsf{ZAP}_{\mathsf{verify}}(\mathsf{zap}_1, \mathsf{zap}_2)$ accepts. Output $\bot$ if verification fails. Let the state of $\mathcal{A}$ at this point be Q.
- Define $\mathcal{Q} := (r_{\mathsf{wi}}, m_1, m_2, Q)$ and compute $b \xleftarrow{R} \mathsf{ik\text{-}check}_{\mathcal{Q}}$, where $b \in \{0, 1, \bot\}$
- If $b = \bot$, return $\bot$
- Sample $q_b \xleftarrow{R} S_D(\mathsf{ik}_b)$
- Run $\mathsf{Inv}(\boxed{S_R(\mathsf{ik}_b; \widehat{r})}, \mathcal{Q}, b, \epsilon'/2)$ $\boxed{\text{for } \widehat{r} \xleftarrow{R} \{0,1\}^\kappa}$.
- If Inv succeeds and outputs q', for each $i \in [\kappa/\epsilon']$:
  - Rewind the adversary to state Q (unless already in state Q).
  - Sample $\widetilde{q}_i \xleftarrow{R} S_D(\mathsf{ik}_b)$
  - Run $\mathsf{Inv}(f_{\mathsf{ik}_b}(\widetilde{q}_i), \mathcal{Q}, b, \epsilon'/2)$.
  - If Inv succeeds:
    - ∗ Rewind the adversary to state Q.

  * Sample $\widetilde{r}_0, \widetilde{r}_1 \xleftarrow{R} \{0,1\}^\kappa$, $q_{1-b} \xleftarrow{R} S_D(\mathsf{ik}_{1-b})$.
  * Compute $\mathsf{chal}_b = [F(\mathsf{ik}_b, \widetilde{q}_i), \langle \widetilde{q}_i, \widetilde{r}_b \rangle, \widetilde{r}_b]$
  * Compute $\mathsf{chal}_{1-b} = [F(\mathsf{ik}_{1-b}, q_{1-b}), \langle q_{1-b}, \widetilde{r}_{1-b} \rangle, \widetilde{r}_{1-b}]$
  * Set $x_{\mathsf{wi}} := (x, \mathsf{chal}_0, \mathsf{chal}_1, \mathsf{ik}_0, \mathsf{ik}_1, r_1, c)$ and $w_{\mathsf{wi}} := (w, \perp, \perp, \perp, \perp, \perp)$
  * Compute $\mathsf{wi}_3 \leftarrow \mathsf{WI}_3(r_{\mathsf{wi}}, \mathsf{wi}_2, x_{\mathsf{wi}}, w_{\mathsf{wi}})$
  * Send $m_3 = (x, \mathsf{chal}_0, \mathsf{chal}_1, \mathsf{wi}_3)$.
  * Output the view of the verifier for the current session, i.e. for m_1, m_2, m_3, and halt execution.

– Else if Inv fails, for each $i \in [\kappa/\epsilon']$:
  - Rewind the adversary to state Q (unless already in state Q).
  - Sample $\widetilde{q}_i \xleftarrow{R} S_D(\mathsf{ik}_b)$
  - Run $\mathsf{Inv}(f_{\mathsf{ik}_b}(\widetilde{q}_i), \mathcal{Q}, b, \epsilon'/2)$.
  - If Inv fails:
    * Rewind the adversary to state Q.
    * Sample $\widetilde{r}_0, \widetilde{r}_1 \xleftarrow{R} \{0,1\}^\kappa$, $q_{1-b} \xleftarrow{R} S_D(\mathsf{ik}_{1-b})$.
    * Compute $\mathsf{chal}_b = [F(\mathsf{ik}_b, \widetilde{q}_i), \langle \widetilde{q}_i, \widetilde{r}_b \rangle \oplus 1, \widetilde{r}_b]$
    * Compute $\mathsf{chal}_{1-b} = [F(\mathsf{ik}_{1-b}, q_{1-b}), \langle q_{1-b}, \widetilde{r}_{1-b} \rangle, \widetilde{r}_{1-b}]$
    * Set $x_{\mathsf{wi}} := (x, \mathsf{chal}_0, \mathsf{chal}_1, \mathsf{ik}_0, \mathsf{ik}_1, r_1, c)$ and $w_{\mathsf{wi}} := (w, \perp, \perp, \perp, \perp, \perp)$
    * Compute $\mathsf{wi}_3 \leftarrow \mathsf{WI}_3(r_{\mathsf{wi}}, \mathsf{wi}_2, x_{\mathsf{wi}}, w_{\mathsf{wi}})$
    * Send $m_3 = (x, \mathsf{chal}_0, \mathsf{chal}_1, \mathsf{wi}_3)$.
    * Output the view of the verifier for the current session, i.e. for m_1, m_2, m_3, and halt execution.

– Output $\perp$

Lemma 5. $\left|\Pr[\mathcal{D}(H_4^{\epsilon'}) = 1] - \Pr[\mathcal{D}(H_5^{\epsilon'}) = 1]\right| \leq \epsilon'$

Proof. Note that the behaviour of both hybrids for a given outcome of the first Inv call (success or failure) is identical. If a difference arises, it must be in the probability of Inv succeeding. Fix any $\mathcal{Q} := (r_{\mathsf{wi}}, m_1, m_2, Q)$, where m_1 is parsed as $(c, \mathsf{zap}_1, \mathsf{wi}_1)$ and m_2 is parsed as $(r_1, \mathsf{ik}_1, \mathsf{ik}_2, \mathsf{wi}_2, \mathsf{zap}_2)$. Define predicates p_0, p_1, and p as:

$$p_0(b) = \Pr\left[\mathsf{Inv}(f_{\mathsf{ik}_b}(q_b), \mathcal{Q}, b, \epsilon'/2) \text{ succeeds.}\right]$$

$$p_1(b) = \Pr\left[\mathsf{Inv}(S_R(\mathsf{ik}_b), \mathcal{Q}, b, \epsilon'/2) \text{ succeeds.}\right]$$

$$p(b) = |p_0(b) - p_1(b)|$$

Further, define p as zero whenever $b = \perp$. If we let $\Pr[b]$ be the probability that $\mathsf{ik\text{-}check}_{\mathcal{Q}}$ outputs b in either hybrid:

$$\left|\Pr[\mathcal{D}(H_4^{\epsilon'}) = 1] - \Pr[\mathcal{D}(H_5^{\epsilon'}) = 1]\right| \leq \max_{\mathcal{Q}} \left(\sum_b \Pr[b] * p(b)\right)$$

where we consider $b \in \{0,1\}$ since p is zero if $b = \perp$. Let $\{X_i\}_{i \in [n']}$ be n' iid random variables that take values $\in \{0,1\}$, and $\Pr[X_i = 1] = p_1(m_1, m_2, Q, b)$. Similarly, let $\{Y_i\}_{i \in [n']}$ be n' iid random variables that take values $\in \{0,1\}$, and $\Pr[Y_i = 1] = p_0(m_1, m_2, Q, b)$. Let $Z = \sum_{i\in[n']} X_i - Y_i$. Then $\Pr[Z \leq t] = \Pr[\mathsf{ik}_b \text{ passes key-check}]$. Since (m_1, m_2, Q, b) are fixed for the following discussion, we omit the parameters from p_0, p_1, p. Note that $E[Z] = pn'$ and $Var[Z] = n'(Var[X] + Var[Y]) = n'p_1(1-p_1) + n'p_0(1-p_0) \leq 2n'$.

Now, consider the case when $p \geq \epsilon'/2$. By applying Chebyshev's Inequality to Z we obtain:

$$\Pr\left[Z \leq E[Z] - k\sqrt{Var[Z]}\right] \leq 1/k^2$$

$E[Z] = n'p$ and $Var[Z] \leq 2n'$, therefore:

$$\Pr\left[Z \leq n'p - k\sqrt{2n'}\right] \leq 1/k^2$$

Since $p \geq \epsilon'/2$:

$$\Pr\left[Z \leq n'\epsilon'/2 - k\sqrt{2n'}\right] \leq 1/k^2$$

Setting $k = n'\epsilon'/\sqrt{32n'}$:

$$\Pr[Z \leq n'\epsilon'/4] = \Pr[Z \leq t] \leq \frac{32}{n'(\epsilon')^2}$$

Since $n' = (4/\epsilon')^3$:

$$\Pr[Z \leq t] \leq \epsilon'/2$$

$$\Pr[\mathsf{ik}_b \text{ passes key-check}] \leq \epsilon'/2$$

We use this result to show that the hybrid distinguishing probability is also bounded by ϵ'. If $p(b) \geq \epsilon'/2$, then probability of ik_b passing the check is no more than $\epsilon'/2$, which implies that $\Pr[b] \leq \epsilon'/2$. Therefore, $\Pr[b] * p(b) \leq \epsilon'/2$, which in turn implies $\sum_b \Pr[b] * p(b) \leq \epsilon'$. This completes the proof.

Hybrid $H_6^{\epsilon'}$:

This hybrid differs from $H_5^{\epsilon'}$ in that the adversary uses $r_0 \oplus r_1$ instead of fresh randomness to sample from $S_R(\mathsf{ik}_b)$.

Interacting with $\mathcal{A}$ as a prover for the protocol, $H_6^{\epsilon'}$ performs the following:

- Sample $x, w \xleftarrow{R} \mathcal{X}_\kappa, \mathcal{W}_\kappa$.
- Sample $r_0 \xleftarrow{R} \{0,1\}^\kappa$, $s \xleftarrow{R} \{0,1\}^\kappa$, $r_{\mathsf{wi}} \xleftarrow{R} \{0,1\}^\kappa$
- Compute $c = \mathsf{com}(r_0; s)$, $\mathsf{zap}_1 \leftarrow \mathsf{ZAP}_1(1^\kappa)$, $\mathsf{wi}_1 \xleftarrow{R} \mathsf{WI}_1(1^\kappa; r_{\mathsf{wi}})$
- Send $m_1 = (c, \mathsf{zap}_1, \mathsf{wi}_1)$ to a freshly initialised instance of the adversary $\mathcal{A}$.
- Receive m_2, parsed as $(r_1, \mathsf{ik}_0, \mathsf{ik}_1, \mathsf{wi}_2, \mathsf{zap}_2)$.
- Verify that $\mathsf{ZAP}_{\mathsf{verify}}(\mathsf{zap}_1, \mathsf{zap}_2)$ accepts. Output $\bot$ if verification fails. Let the state of $\mathcal{A}$ at this point be Q.
- Define $\mathcal{Q} := (r_{\mathsf{wi}}, m_1, m_2, Q)$ and compute $b \xleftarrow{R} \mathsf{ik\text{-}check}_{\mathcal{Q}}$, where $b \in \{0, 1, \bot\}$
- If $b = \bot$, return $\bot$

- Sample $q_b \xleftarrow{R} S_D(\mathsf{ik}_b)$
- Run $\mathsf{Inv}(\ S_R(\mathsf{ik}_b; r_0 \oplus r_1)\ , \mathcal{Q}, b, \epsilon'/2)$.
- If Inv succeeds and outputs q', for each $i \in [\kappa/\epsilon']$:
  - Rewind the adversary to state Q (unless already in state Q).
  - Sample $\widetilde{q}_i \xleftarrow{R} S_D(\mathsf{ik}_b)$
  - Run $\mathsf{Inv}(f_{\mathsf{ik}_b}(\widetilde{q}_i), \mathcal{Q}, b, \epsilon'/2)$.
  - If Inv succeeds:
    * Rewind the adversary to state Q.
    * Sample $\widetilde{r}_0, \widetilde{r}_1 \xleftarrow{R} \{0,1\}^\kappa$, $q_{1-b} \xleftarrow{R} S_D(\mathsf{ik}_{1-b})$.
    * Compute $\mathsf{chal}_b = [F(\mathsf{ik}_b, \widetilde{q}_i), \langle \widetilde{q}_i, \widetilde{r}_b \rangle, \widetilde{r}_b]$
    * Compute $\mathsf{chal}_{1-b} = [F(\mathsf{ik}_{1-b}, q_{1-b}), \langle q_{1-b}, \widetilde{r}_{1-b} \rangle, \widetilde{r}_{1-b}]$
    * Set $x_{\mathsf{wi}} := (x, \mathsf{chal}_0, \mathsf{chal}_1, \mathsf{ik}_0, \mathsf{ik}_1, r_1, c)$ and $w_{\mathsf{wi}} := (w, \perp, \perp, \perp, \perp, \perp)$
    * Compute $\mathsf{wi}_3 \leftarrow \mathsf{WI}_3(r_{\mathsf{wi}}, \mathsf{wi}_2, x_{\mathsf{wi}}, w_{\mathsf{wi}})$
    * Send $m_3 = (x, \mathsf{chal}_0, \mathsf{chal}_1, \mathsf{wi}_3)$.
    * Output the view of the verifier for the current session, i.e. for m_1, m_2, m_3, and halt execution.
- Else if Inv fails, for each $i \in [\kappa/\epsilon']$:
  - Rewind the adversary to state Q (unless already in state Q).
  - Sample $\widetilde{q}_i \xleftarrow{R} S_D(\mathsf{ik}_b)$
  - Run $\mathsf{Inv}(f_{\mathsf{ik}_b}(\widetilde{q}_i), \mathcal{Q}, b, \epsilon'/2)$.
  - If Inv fails:
    * Rewind the adversary to state Q.
    * Sample $\widetilde{r}_0, \widetilde{r}_1 \xleftarrow{R} \{0,1\}^\kappa$, $q_{1-b} \xleftarrow{R} S_D(\mathsf{ik}_{1-b})$.
    * Compute $\mathsf{chal}_b = [F(\mathsf{ik}_b, \widetilde{q}_i), \langle \widetilde{q}_i, \widetilde{r}_b \rangle \oplus 1, \widetilde{r}_b]$
    * Compute $\mathsf{chal}_{1-b} = [F(\mathsf{ik}_{1-b}, q_{1-b}), \langle q_{1-b}, \widetilde{r}_{1-b} \rangle, \widetilde{r}_{1-b}]$
    * Set $x_{\mathsf{wi}} := (x, \mathsf{chal}_0, \mathsf{chal}_1, \mathsf{ik}_0, \mathsf{ik}_1, r_1, c)$ and $w_{\mathsf{wi}} := (w, \perp, \perp, \perp, \perp, \perp)$
    * Compute $\mathsf{wi}_3 \leftarrow \mathsf{WI}_3(r_{\mathsf{wi}}, \mathsf{wi}_2, x_{\mathsf{wi}}, w_{\mathsf{wi}})$
    * Send $m_3 = (x, \mathsf{chal}_0, \mathsf{chal}_1, \mathsf{wi}_3)$.
    * Output the view of the verifier for the current session, i.e. for m_1, m_2, m_3, and halt execution.
- Output $\perp$

Lemma 6. $\left|\Pr[\mathcal{D}(H_5^{\epsilon'}) = 1] - \Pr[\mathcal{D}(H_6^{\epsilon'}) = 1]\right| \leq \epsilon'$

Proof. (Overview) Due to lack of space, we defer the proof to the full version. Intuitively, we switch from inverting a uniformly random string to inverting $r_0 \oplus r_1$. Since r_0 is also sampled uniformly, the adversary's view is identical apart from the commitment to r_0 in the first round. We therefore show that an adversary that distinguishes the hybrids must be breaking the hiding of the commitment scheme.

Hybrid $H_7^{\epsilon'}$:

This hybrid differs from $H_6^{\epsilon'}$ in that the hybrid uses the q' obtained by Inv to compute wi_3 by the third branch in the success case.

Interacting with $\mathcal{A}$ as a prover for the protocol, $H_7^{\epsilon'}$ performs the following:

- Sample $x, w \xleftarrow{R} \mathcal{X}_\kappa, \mathcal{W}_\kappa$.
- Sample $r_0 \xleftarrow{R} \{0,1\}^\kappa$, $s \xleftarrow{R} \{0,1\}^\kappa$, $r_{\mathsf{wi}} \xleftarrow{R} \{0,1\}^\kappa$
- Compute $c = \mathsf{com}(r_0; s)$, $\mathsf{zap}_1 \leftarrow \mathsf{ZAP}_1(1^\kappa)$, $\mathsf{wi}_1 \xleftarrow{R} \mathsf{WI}_1(1^\kappa; r_{\mathsf{wi}})$
- Send $m_1 = (c, \mathsf{zap}_1, \mathsf{wi}_1)$ to a freshly initialised instance of the adversary $\mathcal{A}$.
- Receive m_2, parsed as $(r_1, \mathsf{ik}_0, \mathsf{ik}_1, \mathsf{wi}_2, \mathsf{zap}_2)$.
- Verify that $\mathsf{ZAP}_{\mathsf{verify}}(\mathsf{zap}_1, \mathsf{zap}_2)$ accepts. Output $\perp$ if verification fails. Let the state of $\mathcal{A}$ at this point be Q.
- Define $\mathcal{Q} := (r_{\mathsf{wi}}, m_1, m_2, Q)$ and compute $b \xleftarrow{R} \mathsf{ik\text{-}check}_{\mathcal{Q}}$, where $b \in \{0, 1, \perp\}$
- If $b = \perp$, return $\perp$
- Sample $q_b \xleftarrow{R} S_D(\mathsf{ik}_b)$
- Run $\mathsf{Inv}(S_R(\mathsf{ik}_b; r_1 \oplus r_2), \mathcal{Q}, b, \epsilon'/2)$.
- If Inv succeeds and outputs q', for each $i \in [\kappa/\epsilon']$:
  - Rewind the adversary to state Q (unless already in state Q).
  - Sample $\widetilde{q}_i \xleftarrow{R} S_D(\mathsf{ik}_b)$
  - Run $\mathsf{Inv}(f_{\mathsf{ik}_b}(\widetilde{q}_i), \mathcal{Q}, b, \epsilon'/2)$.
  - If Inv succeeds:
    * Rewind the adversary to state Q.
    * Sample $\widetilde{r}_0, \widetilde{r}_1 \xleftarrow{R} \{0,1\}^\kappa$, $q_{1-b} \xleftarrow{R} S_D(\mathsf{ik}_{1-b})$.
    * Compute $\mathsf{chal}_b = [F(\mathsf{ik}_b, \widetilde{q}_i), \langle \widetilde{q}_i, \widetilde{r}_b \rangle, \widetilde{r}_b]$
    * Compute $\mathsf{chal}_{1-b} = [F(\mathsf{ik}_{1-b}, q_{1-b}), \langle q_{1-b}, \widetilde{r}_{1-b} \rangle, \widetilde{r}_{1-b}]$
    * Set $x_{\mathsf{wi}} := (x, \mathsf{chal}_0, \mathsf{chal}_1, \mathsf{ik}_0, \mathsf{ik}_1, r_1, c)$ and $w_{\mathsf{wi}} := (\perp, \perp, \perp, r_0, s, q')$
    * Compute $\mathsf{wi}_3 \leftarrow \mathsf{WI}_3(r_{\mathsf{wi}}, \mathsf{wi}_2, x_{\mathsf{wi}}, w_{\mathsf{wi}})$
    * Send $m_3 = (x, \mathsf{chal}_0, \mathsf{chal}_1, \mathsf{wi}_3)$.
    * Output the view of the verifier for the current session, i.e. for m_1, m_2, m_3, and halt execution.
- Else if Inv fails, for each $i \in [\kappa/\epsilon']$:
  - Rewind the adversary to state Q (unless already in state Q).
  - Sample $\widetilde{q}_i \xleftarrow{R} S_D(\mathsf{ik}_b)$
  - Run $\mathsf{Inv}(f_{\mathsf{ik}_b}(\widetilde{q}_i), \mathcal{Q}, b, \epsilon'/2)$.
  - If Inv fails:
    * Rewind the adversary to state Q.
    * Sample $\widetilde{r}_0, \widetilde{r}_1 \xleftarrow{R} \{0,1\}^\kappa$, $q_{1-b} \xleftarrow{R} S_D(\mathsf{ik}_{1-b})$.
    * Compute $\mathsf{chal}_b = [F(\mathsf{ik}_b, \widetilde{q}_i), \langle \widetilde{q}_i, \widetilde{r}_b \rangle \oplus 1, \widetilde{r}_b]$
    * Compute $\mathsf{chal}_{1-b} = [F(\mathsf{ik}_{1-b}, q_{1-b}), \langle q_{1-b}, \widetilde{r}_{1-b} \rangle, \widetilde{r}_{1-b}]$
    * Set $x_{\mathsf{wi}} := (x, \mathsf{chal}_0, \mathsf{chal}_1, \mathsf{ik}_0, \mathsf{ik}_1, r_1, c)$ and $w_{\mathsf{wi}} := (w, \perp, \perp, \perp, \perp, \perp)$
    * Compute $\mathsf{wi}_3 \leftarrow \mathsf{WI}_3(r_{\mathsf{wi}}, \mathsf{wi}_2, x_{\mathsf{wi}}, w_{\mathsf{wi}})$
    * Send $m_3 = (x, \mathsf{chal}_0, \mathsf{chal}_1, \mathsf{wi}_3)$.
    * Output the view of the verifier for the current session, i.e. for m_1, m_2, m_3, and halt execution.
- Output $\perp$

Lemma 7. $\left|\Pr[\mathcal{D}(H_6^{\epsilon'}) = 1] - \Pr[\mathcal{D}(H_7^{\epsilon'}) = 1]\right| \leq \epsilon'$

Proof.

$$\Pr_{\substack{r_{\mathsf{wi}} \xleftarrow{R} \{0,1\}^\kappa, b_{\mathsf{wi}} \xleftarrow{R} \{0,1\} \\ R_1, R_2, R_3, \mathsf{WI}_3}} \left[b' = b_{\mathsf{wi}} \;\middle|\; \begin{array}{r} \mathsf{wi}_1 \leftarrow \mathsf{WI}_1(1^\kappa; r_{\mathsf{wi}}) \\ \mathsf{wi}_2, \{x_{\mathsf{wi},i}, w_{\mathsf{wi},i}\}_i, \tau \leftarrow R_1(\mathsf{wi}_1) \\ \{\mathsf{wi}_{3,i}\}_i \leftarrow \{\mathsf{WI}_3(r_{\mathsf{wi}}, \mathsf{wi}_2, x_{\mathsf{wi},i}, w_{\mathsf{wi},i})\}_i \\ (x_{\mathsf{wi}}, w_0, w_1) \leftarrow R_2(\{\mathsf{wi}_{3,i}\}_i, \tau) \\ b' \leftarrow R_3(\mathsf{WI}_3(r_{\mathsf{wi}}, \mathsf{wi}_2, x_{\mathsf{wi}}, w_{b_{\mathsf{wi}}})) \end{array} \right] \geq \frac{1}{2} + \frac{\epsilon'}{2}$$

Apart from the final construction of wi_3, WI_3 is always called during a call to Pred, which in turn is called during a call to Inv. This means that WI_3 is called for some $x'_{\mathsf{wi}} := (x', \mathsf{chal}_0, \mathsf{chal}_1, \mathsf{ik}_0, \mathsf{ik}_1, r_1, c)$ and $w'_{\mathsf{wi}} := (w', \perp^5)$. Here, x' and w' are chosen randomly each time, while $\mathsf{ik}_0, \mathsf{ik}_1, r_1$ and c are fixed by m_1 and m_2 before any WI_3 call is made. Only the distributions of chal_0 and chal_1 change between Pred calls. For any fixed b, the distributions of chal will be independent of the output of any Pred call. The only interdependence will be dependence on the bit b. This can be remedied by choosing two sets of inputs, one for $b = 0$ and one for $b = 1$. The outputs of one set may be later discarded depending on the value of b. Therefore, all inputs may be chosen together immediately after receiving m_2. We represent this set of WI_3 inputs as $S_{\mathsf{wi}} := \{x_{\mathsf{wi}_i}, w_{\mathsf{wi},i}\}_{i \in [\mathsf{poly}(\kappa)]}$.

We build a reduction R that interacts with an external challenger for WI by running $H_6^{\epsilon'}$ with the following modifications:

1. Instead of computing the first message of WI, receive wi_1 from the external challenger.
2. Send wi_2 parsed from m_2 to the external verifier.
3. Choose the set S_{wi} as specified above and send to the external verifier immediately after sending wi_2.
4. Receive $P_{\mathsf{wi}} := \{\mathsf{wi}_{3,i}\}_{i \in [\mathsf{poly}(\kappa)]}$ from the challenger immediately after sending S_{wi}, consisting of third WI messages for each $(x_{\mathsf{wi},i}, w_{\mathsf{wi},i})$ pair in S_{wi}.
5. Proceed with hybrid execution until just before wi_3 is computed, replacing every WI_3 call with its corresponding $\mathsf{wi}_{3,i}$.
6. Compute w_{wi} as in $H_6^{\epsilon'}$ and label it w_0.
7. Compute w_{wi} as in $H_7^{\epsilon'}$ and label it w_1.
8. Send $(x_{\mathsf{wi}}, w_0, w_1)$ to the external challenger and receive wi_3 as response.
9. Continue with hybrid execution using wi_3 received from the challenger.
10. If the distinguisher returns 1, output 1. If not, or if any step fails, output 0.

The view of the adversarial verifier $\mathcal{A}$ in R is identical to the view in $H_6^{\epsilon'}$ when $b_{\mathsf{wi}} = 0$ and the view in $H_7^{\epsilon'}$ when $b_{\mathsf{wi}} = 1$. If we denote the event that R outputs $b' = b_{\mathsf{wi}}$ as R succeeding:

$$\Pr[R \text{ succeeds} | b_{\mathsf{wi}} = 1] = \Pr[\mathcal{D}(H_7^{\epsilon'}) = 1]$$

$$\Pr[R \text{ succeeds} | b_{\mathsf{wi}} = 0] = \Pr[\mathcal{D}(H_6^{\epsilon'}) \neq 1] = 1 - \Pr[\mathcal{D}(H_6^{\epsilon'}) = 1]$$

Since b_{wi} is chosen uniformly:

$$\Pr[R \text{ succeeds}] = \frac{1}{2}\left(1 + \left(\Pr[\mathcal{D}(H_7^{\epsilon'}) = 1] - \Pr[\mathcal{D}(H_6^{\epsilon'}) = 1]\right)\right) \geq \frac{1}{2} + \frac{\epsilon'}{2}$$

which contradicts the security of wi since $\epsilon'/2$ is non-negligible.

Hybrid $H_8^{\epsilon'}$:

This hybrid differs from $H_7^{\epsilon'}$ in that the hybrid uses the $\widetilde{q}$ for which Inv fails to compute wi_3 via the third branch in the failure case.

Interacting with $\mathcal{A}$ as a prover for the protocol, $H_8^{\epsilon'}$ performs the following:

- Sample $x, w \xleftarrow{R} \mathcal{X}_\kappa, \mathcal{W}_\kappa$.
- Sample $r_0 \xleftarrow{R} \{0,1\}^\kappa$, $s \xleftarrow{R} \{0,1\}^\kappa$, $r_{\mathsf{wi}} \xleftarrow{R} \{0,1\}^\kappa$
- Compute $c = \mathsf{com}(r_0; s)$, $\mathsf{zap}_1 \leftarrow \mathsf{ZAP}_1(1^\kappa)$, $\mathsf{wi}_1 \xleftarrow{R} \mathsf{WI}_1(1^\kappa; r_{\mathsf{wi}})$
- Send $m_1 = (c, \mathsf{zap}_1, \mathsf{wi}_1)$ to a freshly initialised instance of the adversary $\mathcal{A}$.
- Receive m_2, parsed as $(r_1, \mathsf{ik}_0, \mathsf{ik}_1, \mathsf{wi}_2, \mathsf{zap}_2)$.
- Verify that $\mathsf{ZAP}_{\mathsf{verify}}(\mathsf{zap}_1, \mathsf{zap}_2)$ accepts. Output $\perp$ if verification fails. Let the state of $\mathcal{A}$ at this point be Q.
- Define $\mathcal{Q} := (r_{\mathsf{wi}}, m_1, m_2, Q)$ and compute $b \xleftarrow{R} \mathsf{ik\text{-}check}_{\mathcal{Q}}$, where $b \in \{0, 1, \perp\}$
- If $b = \perp$, return $\perp$
- Sample $q_b \xleftarrow{R} S_D(\mathsf{ik}_b)$
- Run $\mathsf{Inv}(S_R(\mathsf{ik}_b; r_1 \oplus r_2), \mathcal{Q}, b, \epsilon'/2)$.
- If Inv succeeds and outputs q', for each $i \in [\kappa/\epsilon']$:
  - Rewind the adversary to state Q (unless already in state Q).
  - Sample $\widetilde{q}_i \xleftarrow{R} S_D(\mathsf{ik}_b)$
  - Run $\mathsf{Inv}(f_{\mathsf{ik}_b}(\widetilde{q}_i), \mathcal{Q}, b, \epsilon'/2)$.
  - If Inv succeeds:
    * Rewind the adversary to state Q.
    * Sample $\widetilde{r}_0, \widetilde{r}_1 \xleftarrow{R} \{0,1\}^\kappa$, $q_{1-b} \xleftarrow{R} S_D(\mathsf{ik}_{1-b})$.
    * Compute $\mathsf{chal}_b = [F(\mathsf{ik}_b, \widetilde{q}_i), \langle \widetilde{q}_i, \widetilde{r}_b \rangle, \widetilde{r}_b]$
    * Compute $\mathsf{chal}_{1-b} = [F(\mathsf{ik}_{1-b}, q_{1-b}), \langle q_{1-b}, \widetilde{r}_{1-b} \rangle, \widetilde{r}_{1-b}]$
    * Set $x_{\mathsf{wi}} := (x, \mathsf{chal}_0, \mathsf{chal}_1, \mathsf{ik}_0, \mathsf{ik}_1, r_1, c)$ and $w_{\mathsf{wi}} := (\perp, \perp, \perp, r_0, s, q')$
    * Compute $\mathsf{wi}_3 \leftarrow \mathsf{WI}_3(r_{\mathsf{wi}}, \mathsf{wi}_2, x_{\mathsf{wi}}, w_{\mathsf{wi}})$
    * Send $m_3 = (x, \mathsf{chal}_0, \mathsf{chal}_1, \mathsf{wi}_3)$.
    * Output the view of the verifier for the current session, i.e. for m_1, m_2, m_3, and halt execution.
- Else if Inv fails, for each $i \in [\kappa/\epsilon']$:
  - Rewind the adversary to state Q (unless already in state Q).
  - Sample $\widetilde{q}_i \xleftarrow{R} S_D(\mathsf{ik}_b)$
  - Run $\mathsf{Inv}(f_{\mathsf{ik}_b}(\widetilde{q}_i), \mathcal{Q}, b, \epsilon'/2)$.
  - If Inv fails:
    * Rewind the adversary to state Q.
    * Sample $\widetilde{r}_0, \widetilde{r}_1 \xleftarrow{R} \{0,1\}^\kappa$, $q_{1-b} \xleftarrow{R} S_D(\mathsf{ik}_{1-b})$.
    * Compute $\mathsf{chal}_b = [F(\mathsf{ik}_b, \widetilde{q}_i), \langle \widetilde{q}_i, \widetilde{r}_b \rangle \oplus 1, \widetilde{r}_b]$
    * Compute $\mathsf{chal}_{1-b} = [F(\mathsf{ik}_{1-b}, q_{1-b}), \langle q_{1-b}, \widetilde{r}_{1-b} \rangle, \widetilde{r}_{1-b}]$
    * Set $x_{\mathsf{wi}} := (x, \mathsf{chal}_0, \mathsf{chal}_1, \mathsf{ik}_0, \mathsf{ik}_1, r_1, c)$
    * If $b = 0$:
      · Set $w_{\mathsf{wi}} := (\perp, \widetilde{q}_i, q_{1-b}, \perp, \perp, \perp)$

* If $b = 1$:
    * Set $w_{\mathsf{wi}} := (\bot, q_{1-b}, \widetilde{q}_i, \bot, \bot, \bot)$
* Compute $\mathsf{wi}_3 \leftarrow \mathsf{WI}_3(r_{\mathsf{wi}}, \mathsf{wi}_2, x_{\mathsf{wi}}, w_{\mathsf{wi}})$
* Send $m_3 = (x, \mathsf{chal}_0, \mathsf{chal}_1, \mathsf{wi}_3)$.
* Output the view of the verifier for the current session, i.e. for m_1, m_2, m_3, and halt execution.

- Output $\bot$

Lemma 8. $\left|\Pr[\mathcal{D}(H_8^{\epsilon'}) = 1] - \Pr[\mathcal{D}(H_7^{\epsilon'}) = 1]\right| \leq \epsilon'$

Proof. The proof proceeds identically to the proof of Lemma 7, except that in R, w_0 is computed as wi_3 in $H_7^{\epsilon'}$ instead of as in $H_6^{\epsilon'}$ and w_1 is computed as wi_3 in $H_8^{\epsilon'}$ instead of as in $H_7^{\epsilon'}$.

The view of the adversary in the final hybrid $H_8^{\epsilon'}$ is identically distributed to the simulated view of the adversary. Since $\mathcal{D}$ is unable to distinguish any two consecutive hybrids with probability greater than ϵ', it cannot distinguish the view of the adversary in an honest execution from the simulated view with probability greater than ϵ.

5.3 Argument of Knowledge Property

Theorem 3. *Assuming enhanced injective trapdoor functions secure against PPT adversaries, the protocol in Fig. 1 is an argument of knowledge.*

Proof. (Overview) Due to lack of space, we defer the proof to the full version. Intuitively, the extractor uses the argument of knowledge property of WI to extract a witness. Since an honest verifier will check challenge bits, this will either yield a witness for $x \in L$ or an inverse of $r_0 \oplus r_1$, which we show implies breaking one-wayness of f. One subtlety is that the inverse may be with respect to either index key. We show that we may obtain an inverse with respect to the desired index key by swapping the order of keys, which is undetectable by the witness indistinguishability of ZAP.

Acknowledgments. D. Khurana and K. Tomer were supported in part by NSF CAREER CNS-2238718, DARPA SIEVE and a gift from Visa Research. This material is based upon work supported by the Defense Advanced Research Projects Agency through Award HR00112020024. G. Malavolta was funded by the Deutsche Forschungsgemeinschaft (DFG, German Research Foundation) under Germany's Excellence Strategy - EXC 2092 CASA - 390781972.

References

1. Aiello, W., Ishai, Y., Reingold, O.: Priced oblivious transfer: how to sell digital goods. In: Pfitzmann, B. (ed.) EUROCRYPT 2001. LNCS, vol. 2045, pp. 119–135. Springer, Heidelberg (May (2001)
2. Badrinarayanan, S., Goyal, V., Jain, A., Khurana, D., Sahai, A.: Round optimal concurrent MPC via strong simulation. IACR Cryptology ePrint Archive **2017**, 597 (2017)
3. Bitansky, N., Freizeit, S.: Statistically sender-private OT from LPN and derandomization. CRYPTO (2022)
4. Bitansky, N., Khurana, D., Paneth, O.: Weak zero-knowledge beyond the black-box barrier. SIAM J. Comput. Special Sect. STOC 2019, pp. STOC19-156-STOC19-199 (2022)
5. Brakerski, Z., Döttling, N.: Two-message statistically sender-private OT from LWE. In: Beimel, A., Dziembowski, S. (eds.) TCC 2018. LNCS, vol. 11240, pp. 370–390. Springer, Cham (2018). https://doi.org/10.1007/978-3-030-03810-6_14
6. Deng, Y.: Individual simulations. In: Moriai, S., Wang, H. (eds.) Individual simulations. LNCS, vol. 12493, pp. 805–836. Springer, Cham (2020). https://doi.org/10.1007/978-3-030-64840-4_27
7. Döttling, N., Garg, S., Goyal, V., Malavolta, G.: Laconic conditional disclosure of secrets and applications. In: FOCS, pp. 661–685. IEEE Computer Society (2019)
8. Döttling, N., Garg, S., Hajiabadi, M., Masny, D., Wichs, D.: Two-round oblivious transfer from CDH or LPN. In: Canteaut, A., Ishai, Y. (eds.) .: Two-round oblivious transfer from CDH or LPN. LNCS, vol. 12106, pp. 768–797. Springer, Cham (2020). https://doi.org/10.1007/978-3-030-45724-2_26
9. Dwork, C., Naor, M.: Zaps and their applications. SIAM J. Comput. **36**(6), 1513–1543 (2007)
10. Dwork, C., Naor, M., Reingold, O., Stockmeyer, L.J.: Magic functions. J. ACM **50**(6), 852–921 (2003)
11. Feige, U., Lapidot, D., Shamir, A.: Multiple non-interactive zero knowledge proofs based on a single random string (extended abstract). In: STOC, pp. 308–317. IEEE Computer Society (1990)
12. Feige, U., Shamir, A.: Witness indistinguishable and witness hiding protocols. In: Proceedings of the 22nd Annual ACM Symposium on Theory of Computing, May 13–17, 1990, Baltimore, Maryland, USA, pp. 416–426. ACM (1990)
13. Goldreich, O.: The Foundations of Cryptography - Basic Techniques, vol. 1. Cambridge University Press, Cambridge (2001)
14. Goldreich, O.: The Foundations of Cryptography - Volume 2: Basic Applications. Cambridge University Press (2004)
15. Goldreich, O., Levin, L.A.: A hard-core predicate for all one-way functions. In: Johnson, D.S. (ed.) Proceedings of the 21st Annual ACM Symposium on Theory of Computing, May 14–17, 1989, Seattle, Washington, USA, pp. 25–32. ACM (1989)
16. Goldreich, O., Rothblum, R.D.: Enhancements of trapdoor permutations. J. Cryptol. **26**, 484–512 (2013)
17. Goyal, V., Richelson, S.: Non-malleable commitments using goldreich-levin list decoding. In: Zuckerman, D. (ed.) 60th IEEE Annual Symposium on Foundations of Computer Science, FOCS 2019, Baltimore, Maryland, USA, November 9–12, 2019, pp. 686–699. IEEE Computer Society (2019)
18. Halevi, S., Kalai, Y.T.: Smooth projective hashing and two-message oblivious transfer. J. Cryptol. **25**(1), 158–193 (2012)

19. Jain, A., Kalai, Y.T., Khurana, D., Rothblum, R.: Distinguisher-dependent simulation in two rounds and its applications. In: Katz, J., Shacham, H. (eds.) Distinguisher-dependent simulation in two rounds and its applications. LNCS, vol. 10402, pp. 158–189. Springer, Cham (2017). https://doi.org/10.1007/978-3-319-63715-0_6
20. Kalai, Y.T., Khurana, D., Sahai, A.: Statistical witness indistinguishability (and more) in two messages. In: Nielsen, J.B., Rijmen, V. (eds.) Advances in Cryptology - EUROCRYPT 2018–37th Annual International Conference on the Theory and Applications of Cryptographic Techniques, Tel Aviv, Israel, April 29 - May 3, 2018 Proceedings, Part III. Lecture Notes in Computer Science, vol. 10822, pp. 34–65. Springer (2018). https://doi.org/10.1007/978-3-319-78372-7_2
21. Khurana, D.: Round optimal concurrent non-malleability from polynomial hardness. In: Kalai, Y., Reyzin, L. (eds.) TCC 2017. LNCS, vol. 10678, pp. 139–171. Springer, Cham (2017). https://doi.org/10.1007/978-3-319-70503-3_5
22. Naor, M., Pinkas, B.: Efficient oblivious transfer protocols. In: Proceedings of the Twelfth Annual Symposium on Discrete Algorithms, January 7–9, 2001, Washington, DC, USA, pp. 448–457 (2001)
23. Naor, M., Yung, M.: Public-key cryptosystems provably secure against chosen ciphertext attacks. In: 22nd ACM STOC, pp. 427–437. ACM Press (1990)

A Simple and Efficient Framework of Proof Systems for NP

Yuyu Wang[1], Chuanjie Su[1], Jiaxin Pan[2,3], and Yu Chen[4,5,6](✉)

[1] University of Electronic Science and Technology of China, Chengdu, China
wangyuyu@uestc.edu.cn, chuanjie.su@hotmail.com
[2] University of Kassel, Kassel, Germany
[3] Department of Mathematical Sciences, NTNU - Norwegian University of Science and Technology, Trondheim, Norway
jiaxin.pan@ntnu.no
[4] School of Cyber Science and Technology, Shandong University, Qingdao 266237, China
[5] State Key Laboratory of Cryptology, P.O. Box 5159, Beijing 100878, China
[6] Key Laboratory of Cryptologic Technology and Information Security, Ministry of Education, Shandong University, Qingdao 266237, China
yuchen@sdu.edu.cn

Abstract. In this work, we propose a simple framework of constructing efficient non-interactive zero-knowledge proof (NIZK) systems for all NP. Compared to the state-of-the-art construction by Groth, Ostrovsky, and Sahai (J. ACM, 2012), our resulting NIZK system reduces the proof size and proving and verification cost without any trade-off, i.e., neither increasing computation cost, CRS size nor resorting to stronger assumptions.

Furthermore, we extend our framework to construct a batch argument (BARG) system for all NP. Our construction remarkably improves the efficiency of BARG by Waters and Wu (Crypto 2022) without any trade-off.

Keywords: Non-interactive zero-knowledge · batch argument · NP language · pairing-based cryptography

1 Introduction

1.1 Motivation

Zero-knowledge proof systems introduced by Goldwasser, Micali, and Rackoff [25] allow a prover to convince a verifier for the validity of an NP statement, without revealing anything beyond that. As its round-optimal variant, non-interactive zero-knowledge proof (NIZK) allows a prover to convince the verifier by sending out a single message. Due to this nice property, NIZK is a very interesting topic in both practical and theoretical cryptography, and it has been used as an important building block for countless cryptographic primitives and protocols.

J. Guo and R. Steinfeld (Eds.): ASIACRYPT 2023, LNCS 14439, pp. 174–207, 2023.
https://doi.org/10.1007/978-981-99-8724-5_6

NIZKs for all NP were firstly proposed in [7,19] based on the quadratic residuosity assumption and the existence of trapdoor permutation. While these results demonstrate the feasibility of NIZKs for NP under standard assumptions, they are not very efficient.

For better efficiency, Groth, Ostrovsky, and Sahai [29] proposed a framework of efficient pairing-based constructions (GOS-NIZK). It provides constructions with prime-order and composite-order pairings. Their security is based on the Decisional Linear (DLIN) assumption and the subgroup decision assumption, depending on which pairing group they are constructed in. Their constructions have tight security and compact common reference strings (CRS), namely, a CRS contains a constant number of group elements. Moreover, they achieve perfect soundness and computationally zero-knowledge, or computational soundness and perfect zero-knowledge, depending on the CRS. This is referred to as the dual-mode property. Perfect soundness and perfect zero-knowledge can provide "everlasting security" and are interesting for certain applications. For instance, a NIZK with perfect soundness always rejects an invalid proof and can protect messages that are valuable for a limited time and can be published or deleted later. Additionally, the dual mode with perfect zero-knowledge continuously protects secrets and prevents adversaries from breaking soundness at the time where an honest proof is generated, thereby ensuring security by letting the system reject users who have timed out when attempting to generate proofs.

To further improve the efficiency of GOS-NIZK, a sequence of works have been proposed. These works either restrict to algebraic languages (e.g., [15,30, 33,34,39]) or base their security on non-falsifiable assumptions (e.g., [17,23,26, 28,40]). In this paper, we are interested in constructions based on standard assumptions in pairing groups. By "standard assumptions", we refer to static and falsifiable assumptions, such as the (Matrix) Diffie-Hellman assumption [18]. The reason of using standard assumptions is that they are well-studied and provide more reliable security guarantee. Recently, a notable work by Katsumata et al. [37,38] (KNYY) shortened the proof size of pairing-based NIZKs for all NP based on standard assumptions. Their proof size is additive, e.g., $s + \mathsf{poly}(\lambda)$ rather than $s \cdot \mathsf{poly}(\lambda)$ as in GOS-NIZK, where s is the number of gates. However, its security is based on a particular computational Diffie-Hellman assumption, CDH^*, which is the CDH assumption in a subgroup of $\mathbb{Z}_p^*$ (where prime p is the group order).[1] As noted by the authors themselves, it is unclear how to instantiate their construction under the standard CDH assumption in a pairing group. Also, their construction suffers from non-compact CRSs and significant security loss, and lacks both perfect zero-knowledge and perfect soundness.

Summing up the above discussion, we ask the following question:

Is it possible to improve the efficiency of GOS-NIZK without any trade-off?

Non-interactive batch arguments. Another line of research focuses on non-interactive batch arguments (BARG), which are sound proof systems amortizing

[1] This particular assumption was not included in their proceeding version [37], but in their later full version [38].

Table 1. Comparison of pairing-based NIZKs for all NP under standard assumptions. GOS12 is the original GOS-NIZK which is only with symmetric pairings, and GOS12* is its variant with asymmetric pairings (see Appendix A). t and s are the number of wires and gates in the statement circuit respectively. In column "**Sound.**" (respectively, "**ZK**"), comp. and perf. mean computation and perfect soundness (respectively, zero-knowledge) respectively. In columns "**Prov. Cost**", "**Ver. Cost**" we measure the numbers of exponentiations and pairings for the proving and verification cost respectively (since they dominate the overall performance of proving and verification). "**Assump.**" means the underlying assumption.

Scheme	Sound.	ZK	CRS Size	Proof Size	Prov. Cost	Ver. Cost	Assump.
GOS12 [29] (sym. pair.)	comp. perf.	perf. comp.	$5\|\mathbb{G}\|$	$(9t+6s)\|\mathbb{G}\|$	$15t+12s$	$18(s+t)$	DLIN
GOS12* (asym. pair.)	comp. perf.	perf. comp.	$4\|\mathbb{G}_1\|+4\|\mathbb{G}_2\|$	$(6t+4s)\|\mathbb{G}_1\|+(6t+6s)\|\mathbb{G}_2\|$	$18t+16s$	$12(s+t)$	SXDH
Ours	comp. perf.	perf. comp.	$4\|\mathbb{G}_1\|+4\|\mathbb{G}_2\|$	$(2t+8s)\|\mathbb{G}_1\|+10s\|\mathbb{G}_2\|$	$2t+30s$	$24s$	SXDH

the cost of verification across multiple statements. Specifically, a BARG allows a prover to generate a proof of the validity of multiple statements where the proof size scales sublinearly with the number of statements.

Up until now most works are devoted to constructions in idealized models [2,11,12,28,42,46] or non-standard assumptions [3–6,8,16,23,27,36,41,44]. Recently, Choudhuri et al. [13,14] proposed a construction under both quadratic residue and the subexponentially hard Diffie-Hellman assumption and a construction under the learning with errors assumption. Subsequently, a breakthrough work by Waters and Wu [48] proposed the first BARG (WW-BARG) for all NP over prime-order bilinear maps under the matrix Diffie-Hellman (MDDH) assumption [18]. They also gave a composite-order group version under the subgroup decision assumption. The proof sizes of both constructions are independent of the number of statements. As applications of WW-BARG, they proposed the first succinct non-interactive argument (SNARG) for P with sublinear-sized CRS and the first aggregated signature from standard assumptions over bilinear maps. A recent work by Kalai et al. [35] shows a bootstrapping technique that can generally convert BARGs into ones where CRSs grow polylogarithmically with the number of statements. As a trade-off, the proof sizes grow polylogarithmically as well.

Due to the versatility of BARGs over bilinear maps, it is natural to ask the same question on GOS-NIZK mentioned above for the state-of-the-art BARG by Waters and Wu, i.e. whether we can improve its efficiency without any trade-off. Such an improvement will immediately yields a more efficient BARGs with short CRSs via the bootstrapping technique by Kalai et al. [35].

1.2 Our Contributions

Improvement on GOS-NIZK without Trade-Off. In this work, we improve the efficiency of GOS-NIZK with asymmetric Type-3 pairings by proposing a new and simple framework of constructing efficient NIZKs for NP. We consider Type-3 pairings, since it is the most efficient one among all different types of pairings [20]. Moreover, cryptanalysis [31,32] against symmetric pairing groups with small characteristic curves motivate cryptographic schemes in Type-3 pairings (for instance, [1,10]).

We note that the original GOS-NIZK was proposed with symmetric pairings under the decisional linear (DLIN) assumption. For a fair comparison with our scheme, we give its variant in the asymmetric pairing explicitly in Appendix A. In the rest of this section, we refer GOS-NIZK to be the one in the Type-3 setting, unless stated otherwise.

By instantiating our scheme based on the SXDH assumption, our resulting NIZK proofs consist of $2t + 8s$ group elements in $\mathbb{G}_1$ and $10s$ elements in $\mathbb{G}_2$, where t and s respectively denote the numbers of wires and gates of the statement circuit (the statement represented by fan-in-2 and unbounded fan-out NAND gates). We denote this as $(2t + 8s, 10s)$. Notice that for each multiple fan-out gate, we only increment the count of wires t by 1 for its output wires, since all output wires of the gate are assigned the same value and serves as input wires for multiple other gates. For proving and verification, we use $2t + 30s$ exponentiations and $24s$ pairings respectively. We note that any circuit can be converted to one with only NAND gates.[2] For GOS-NIZK, its proof size, proving cost, and verification cost are $(6t + 4s, 6t + 6s)$, $18t + 16s$ exponentiations, and $12(t+s)$ pairings respectively, which are strictly larger than ours. This is because t is larger (or even much larger in many cases) than s, since each gate has at least 1 output wire. Indeed, $t - s$ corresponds to the number of input wires (with no gates outputting them) and it cannot be very small. Otherwise, the witness will be very short and an adversary can guess it with large probability. As an instance, for a statement circuit consisting only of fan-in-2 and fan-out-1 gates, we have $t = 2s$ (without counting the final ouput wire) since each time when adding a gate from the bottom to the top in a circuit, s and t increase by 1 and 2 respectively. In this case, our scheme uses $(12s, 10s)$ group elements in the proof, $34s$ exponentiations for proving, and $24s$ pairings for verification, which is much more efficient than GOS-NIZK using $(16s, 18s)$ elements in a proof, $52s$ exponentiations for proving, and $36s$ pairings for verification.

---

[2] Notice that this conversion does not affect the fairness of the comparison. The reason is that in an original statement circuit consisting of AND, OR, and NOT gates, each AND or OR gate can be represented as the combination of one NAND gate and several NOT gates, while NOT gates are "free" in the sense that they do not increase the proof size in both the GOS-NIZK and ours. Indeed, converting the statement circuits into ones consisting only of NAND gates is unnecessary in practice. This conversion is just used for conceptual simplicity, as we will discuss at the end of Sect. 3. The same arguments can be made for the BARGs mentioned later.

In Table 1, we give comparison of the security quality, CRS size, proof size, proving and verification cost, and the underlying assumptions of our NIZK and the ones by GOS. For being general, we present the schemes and proofs in the technical part with the MDDH assumption [18], which is an algebraic generalization of the DLIN and SXDH assumptions. The security of all the instantiations are tight. For the experimental results on the cost and proof size, which are consistent with our comparison in Table 1, we refer the reader to Sect. 5.

Table 2. Comparison of pairing-based BARGs for all NP. WW22 is WW-BARG in the asymmetric pairing, and WW22* is its symmetric pairing version. m denotes the number of statement instances. t and s denote the number of wires and gates in the relation circuit respectively. We assume that all provers take as input m statements. All the instantiations satisfy somewhere argument of knowledge. In columns "**Prov. Cost**", "**Ver. Cost**", we measure the numbers of multiplications and pairings for the proving and verification cost respectively (since they dominate the overall performance of proving and verification). "**Assump.**" means the underlying assumption.

Scheme	CRS Size	Proof Size	Prov. Cost	Ver. Cost	Assump.
WW22 [48] (asym. pair.)	$(4+2m^2)\|\mathbb{G}_1\|+$ $(4+2m^2)\|\mathbb{G}_2\|$	$(4t+4s)\|\mathbb{G}_1\|+$ $(4t+4s)\|\mathbb{G}_2\|$	$4m^2t+4m(m-1)s$	$24t+32s$	SXDH
WW22* [48] (sym. pair.)	$(1+m^2)\|\mathbb{G}\|$	$(2t+s)\|\mathbb{G}\|$	$m^2t+\frac{m(m-1)}{2}s$	$2t+3s$	Subgroup decision
Ours (asym. pair.)	$(4+2m^2)\|\mathbb{G}_1\|+$ $(4+2m^2)\|\mathbb{G}_2\|$	$(2t+6s)\|\mathbb{G}_1\|+$ $(2t+6s)\|\mathbb{G}_2\|$	$4mt+6m(m-1)s$	$40s$	SXDH
Ours (sym. pair.)	$(1+m^2)\|\mathbb{G}\|$	$(t+2s)\|\mathbb{G}\|$	$mt+m(m-1)s$	$4s$	Subgroup decision

Given that our construction improves the proving and verification costs of state-of-the-art constructions without any trade-off, it is recommended that any applications of GOS-NIZK utilize our construction as a drop-in replacement. Shorter proofs are always better, particularly in distributed settings. In such scenarios, proofs may need to be stored permanently and can significantly impact bandwidth usage. Therefore, even a constant rate of communication cost holds significant importance. This is exemplified by ZKB++ [9], which successfully reduces the proof size of ZKBoo [24] in the random oracle model by a factor of 2. Also, similar to GOS-NIZK, via the generic construction in [29], our NIZK can be converted into a (more efficient) non-interactive zap, which has witness-indistinguishability and uses no CRS. As far as we know, this is the most efficient non-interactive zap based on standard assumptions by now. It provides perfect subversion-resistance and is important for distributed systems where trusted CRS is not desirable. Moreover, it can be converted into a leakage-resilient NIZK via the generic construction by Garg-Jain-Sahai [21], which in turn implies a (more efficient) fully leakage-resilient signature.

Extension to BARG. We further extend our framework to improve the efficiency of WW-BARG without making compromises. Similar to our NIZK, we present our BARG with the MDDH assumptions. Under the SXDH assumption, we obtain a BARG with each proof consisting of $(6s + 2t, 6s + 2t)$ elements. It is shorter than that in WW-BARG with $(4s + 4t, 4s + 4t)$ elements. Transplanting our BARG into composite-order bilinear groups derives a BARG with the proof size $2s + t$, while the proof size of the composite-order construction by Waters and Wu is $2t + s$. Moreover, our proving and verifying costs are less than WW-BARG in both the prime-order and composite-order groups.

In Table 2, we give comparison of our constructions and the ones by Waters and Wu. All the instantiations in the table satisfy the (tight) security of somewhere extractability argument of knowledge (see Definition 7), which in turn implies non-adaptive soundness, namely, soundness for statements independent of the CRS. For the experimental results on the cost and proof size, which are consistent with our comparison in Table 2, we refer the reader to Sect. 5.

Similar to our NIZK construction, we recommend using our BARG construction as a drop-in replacement for WW-BARG in any of its applications. For instance, it provides the most efficient SNARG for P with optimal succinctness on CRS and proof sizes, through conversions by Waters-Wu and Kalai et al. [35].

1.3 Technical Overview

Let $\mathsf{C}(\mathsf{x}, \cdot)$ be a statement circuit represented by NAND gates, where x is the statement hardwired in C. We briefly recall that, in the GOS-NIZK, to prove the existence of a witness w such that $\mathsf{C}(\mathsf{x}, \mathsf{w}) = 1$, a prover first extends the witness to contain the bits for all wires of $\mathsf{C}(\mathsf{x}, \cdot)$. Then it hides all bits in w with an additively homomorphic commitment and makes the commitment for the final output wire a fixed one corresponding to 1. In this way anyone can check it. Since for each gate $G_\ell = (d_1, d_2, d_3)$, $((\mathsf{w}_{d_1}, \mathsf{w}_{d_2}), \mathsf{w}_{d_3})$ is a valid input/output tuple if and only if

$$\mathsf{w}_{d_1} + \mathsf{w}_{d_2} + 2\mathsf{w}_{d_3} - 2 \in \{0, 1\}. \quad (1)$$

Here by $G_\ell = (d_1, d_2, d_3)$ we mean that the left and right input wires of the gate G_ℓ are indexed as d_1 and d_2 respectively, while the output wire of G_ℓ is indexed as d_3. The prover can use an OR-proof system to prove that the plaintexts of all the commitments satisfy such a relation. Additionally, the prover has to prove the validity of each wire, namely, each commitment commits to a bit (rather than some other value).

Our approach of NIZK for all NP. In our construction, we also commit to the value of each wire and prove that the committed values are valid for each gate. Different to the GOS-NIZK, we adopt the following consistency relation to improve the efficiency:

$$(-1 + \mathsf{w}_{d_1} + \mathsf{w}_{d_3} = 0 \wedge -1 + \mathsf{w}_{d_2} = 0) \ \vee \ (-1 + \mathsf{w}_{d_3} = 0 \wedge \mathsf{w}_{d_2} = 0). \quad (2)$$

One can check that when the computations are over $GF(2)$, Relation (2) holds if and only if the input/output pair is binary. Only proving this relation of committed values for each gate can be done by using a simple OR-proof, and this indeed yields shorter proof size in total, compared with the GOS-NIZK. However, when considering a large field, only satisfying this relation may seem meaningless. Specifically, when $\mathsf{w}_{d_2} = 1$, w_{d_1} and w_{d_3} might be large numbers with sum "happening to be" 1, and when $\mathsf{w}_{d_2} = 0$, the situation seems worse: there is no restriction on w_{d_1} at all. Hence, without proving the wires are binary, a valid proof for such a relation does not necessarily mean the validity of a statement. A natural approach is to additionally generate proofs of wire validity for $\mathsf{w}_{d_1}, \mathsf{w}_{d_3} \in \{0, 1\}$. However, this results in longer proofs than the GOS-NIZK. To overcome this, we develop a new method for soundness without additional wire validity checking procedure.

A new witness-extraction strategy. To maintain both security and efficiency, we propose a new *witness-extraction strategy* for proving soundness, which does not require additional wire validity checks when adopting Relation (2). Specifically, this strategy helps us extract a witness from any valid proof only proving that committed values satisfy Relation (2) for each gate. The strategy uses two phases.

In the first phase, given a valid proof, we use a trapdoor to decrypt all commitments. The decryption result for the final output wire must be 1, and those for other wires could be any value (not necessarily in $\{0, 1\}$). The soundness of the underlying OR-proof system only guarantees that all the decryption results satisfy Relation (2) for each gate.

In the next phase, we start to pick up useful values from the decryption results. This procedure starts from the final output wire to the input wires. Let $((\mathsf{w}_{d_1}, \mathsf{w}_{d_2}), \mathsf{w}_{d_3})$ be the decryption results for the final gate G_t. We must have $\mathsf{w}_{d_3} = 1$, and $\mathsf{w}_{d_2} \in \{0, 1\}$ according to Relation (2). If $\mathsf{w}_{d_2} = 1$, $\mathsf{w}_{d_1} = 0$ must hold, and we set $((\mathsf{w}_{d_1}, \mathsf{w}_{d_2}), \mathsf{w}_{d_3})$ as the input/output values for G_t. The problem is that when $\mathsf{w}_{d_2} = 0$, w_{d_1} could be any large value. Our trick is not to assign any number to this wire and leave it blank for now. The point is that no matter which in $\{0, 1\}$ will be assigned to the left-input wire, as long as $\mathsf{w}_{d_2} = 0$ and $\mathsf{w}_{d_3} = 1$, $((\mathsf{w}_{d_1}, \mathsf{w}_{d_2}), \mathsf{w}_{d_3})$ will be a valid pair for G_t. Next, for each gate where we have previously assigned a value in $\{0, 1\}$ to its output wire, we assign values to its input-wire(s) in a similar way. By doing this recursively from the bottom to the top of the circuit, we eventually obtain values for part of the input wires of the whole statement circuit. Now notice that these values will lead the circuit to output 1 anyway, no matter what the rest of the input wires (left as blank) will be. By setting these rest of the input wires as, say 0, we obtain a value witness.

For better understanding, we give an example of the witness-extraction procedure for the statement circuit in Fig. 1. In the decryption result of a valid proof, the final output must be 1, and the right inputs of all gates must be in $\{0, 1\}$ according to Relation (2). Without loss of generality, we assume that the right inputs of (G_1, G_2, G_4, G_5) are $(0, 1, 1, 0)$ respectively. Here we do not care about the right input of G_3 since it does not affect the final output as we will see. Then we extract the witness from the bottom to the top. For G_5, we leave its left input as blank. Then for G_4, its left input must be 1 according to Relation (2). Next, according to the same rule, we leave the left input of G_1 as blank and set the left input of G_2 as 0. One can see that by now, we have found a path (remarked as red wires in Fig. 1) leading the whole circuit to output 1. By setting the rest of the input wires assigned $\perp$ as 0, we immediately obtain a valid witness, which is 000001. One can check that it leads the circuit to output 1. For the full details, we refer the reader to Sect. 3.

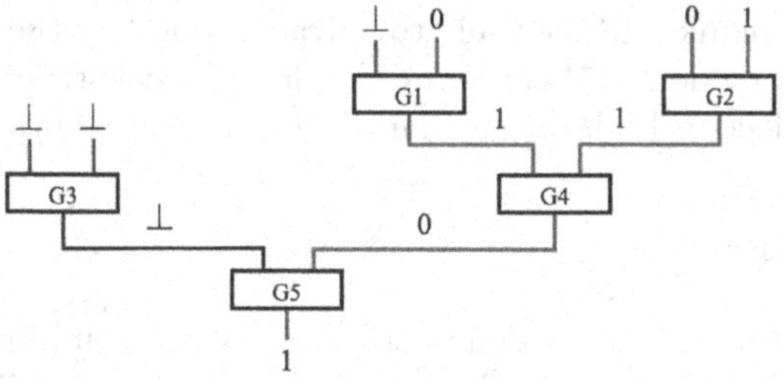

Fig. 1. An instance of the witness-extraction procedure. Without loss of generality, all the gates $\{G_i\}_{i\in[5]}$ in the statement circuit are set as NAND gates. The procedure starts from the bottom to the top. By setting the (blue) input wires assigned $\perp$ as 0, we extract a valid witness 000001 leading the circuit to output 1. (Color figure online)

Extension to batch argument for all NP. We now explain how to combine our witness-extraction strategy with the WW-BARG proposed by Waters and Wu in [48] to achieve a BARG with shorter proofs.

To prove the existence of witnesses $(\mathsf{w}_i)_{i\in[m]}$ such that $\mathsf{C}(\mathsf{x}_i, \mathsf{w}_i) = 1$ for m statements x_i, WW-BARG first extends each $(\mathsf{x}_i, \mathsf{w}_i)$ to $(\mathsf{w}_{i,j})_{j\in[t]}$ containing bits of all wires in the circuit C. Then it commits to $(\mathsf{w}_{i,j})_{i\in[m]}$ with an additively homomorphic (de-randomized) vector commitment for each wire. Next it generates succinct proofs of wire validity and gate consistency, i.e., for all $i \in [m]$, it proves that $\mathsf{w}_{i,j} \in \{0,1\}$ for each $j \in [t]$ and $1 - \mathsf{w}_{i,d_1}\mathsf{w}_{i,d_2} = \mathsf{w}_{i,d_3}$ for each gate $G_\ell = (d_1, d_2, d_3)$. The final proof size is independent of m.

Alternatively, if we can prove gate consistency with respect to Relation (2) as in the case of NIZK, then we can adopt our aforementioned witness-extraction strategy to avoid generating proofs of wire validity and achieve soundness with shorter proofs. However, we do not have an explicit "batch OR-proof" for doing this. To overcome this, we observe that WW-BARG essentially provides us with a way to prove $\mathsf{w}_{i,1}\mathsf{w}_{i,2} = 0$ for all $i \in [m]$ given two commitments to $(\mathsf{w}_{i,1})_{i\in[m]}$ and $(\mathsf{w}_{i,2})_{i\in[m]}$ respectively. Then for each gate $G_\ell = (d_1, d_2, d_3)$, we let the prover homomorphically evaluate commitments to $(1-\mathsf{w}_{i,d_1}-\mathsf{w}_{i,d_3})_{i\in[m]}$, $(1-\mathsf{w}_{i,d_3})_{i\in[m]}$, and $(1-\mathsf{w}_{i,d_2})_{i\in[m]}$ respectively, and extend WW-BARG to adopt the following relation for consistency checks:

$$(1 - \mathsf{w}_{i,d_1} - \mathsf{w}_{i,d_3})\mathsf{w}_{i,d_2} = 0 \ \wedge \ (1 - \mathsf{w}_{i,d_3})(1 - \mathsf{w}_{i,d_2}) = 0. \tag{3}$$

One can check that Relation (3) implies

$$(1 - \mathsf{w}_{i,d_3} = 0 \wedge \mathsf{w}_{i,d_2} = 0) \vee (1 - \mathsf{w}_{i,d_1} - \mathsf{w}_{i,d_3} = 0 \wedge 1 - \mathsf{w}_{i,d_2} = 0),$$

which is equivalent to Relation (2), or

$$\mathsf{w}_{i,d_1} = 0 \wedge 1 - \mathsf{w}_{i,d_3} = 0.$$

Then for any valid proof, we can extract the extended witness from the bottom to the top of the circuit in a similar way to the witness-extraction strategy for our NIZK. Here, a main difference is that there is a new case $\mathsf{w}_{i,d_1} = 0 \wedge 1 - \mathsf{w}_{i,d_3} = 0$ captured by Relation (3) but not captured by Relation (2). When this happens, we just leave w_{i,d_2} blank and continue to extract values for the gate outputting w_{i,d_1}. We refer the readers to Sect. 4 for the detailed construction and security analysis, which reflects a bulk of our main technical contribution.

2 Preliminaries

Notations. We use $x \xleftarrow{\$} \mathcal{S}$ to denote the process of sampling an element x from set $\mathcal{S}$ uniformly at random. All our algorithms are probabilistic polynomial time unless we stated otherwise. If $\mathcal{A}$ is a probabilistic algorithm, then we write $a \xleftarrow{\$} \mathcal{A}(b)$ to denote the random variable that outputted by $\mathcal{A}$ on input b. By $\mathsf{negl}(\cdot)$ we mean an unspecified negligible function.

2.1 Pairing Groups and Matrix Diffie-Hellman Assumptions

Let GGen be a probabilistic polynomial time (PPT) algorithm that on input 1^λ returns a description $\mathcal{G} := (\mathbb{G}_1, \mathbb{G}_2, \mathbb{G}_T, p, P_1, P_2, e)$ of asymmetric pairing groups where $\mathbb{G}_1, \mathbb{G}_2, \mathbb{G}_T$ are cyclic groups of order p for a λ-bit prime p, P_1 and P_2 are generators of $\mathbb{G}_1$ and $\mathbb{G}_2$, respectively, and $e : \mathbb{G}_1 \times \mathbb{G}_2 \to \mathbb{G}_T$ is an efficiently computable (non-degenerate) bilinear map. Define $P_T := e(P_1, P_2)$, which is a generator in $\mathbb{G}_T$. Unless stated otherwise, we consider Type III pairings, where $\mathbb{G}_1 \neq \mathbb{G}_2$ and there is no efficient homomorphism between them.

We use implicit representation of group elements as in [18]. For $s \in \{1, 2, T\}$ and $a \in \mathbb{Z}_p$ define $[a]_s = aP_s \in \mathbb{G}_s$ as the implicit representation of a in $\mathbb{G}_s$. Similarly, for a matrix $\mathbf{A} = (a_{ij}) \in \mathbb{Z}_p^{n \times m}$ we define $[\mathbf{A}]_s$ as the implicit representation of $\mathbf{A}$ in $\mathbb{G}_s$. $\mathsf{Span}(\mathbf{A}) := \{\mathbf{Ar} | \mathbf{r} \in \mathbb{Z}_p^m\} \subset \mathbb{Z}_p^n$ denotes the linear span of $\mathbf{A}$, and similarly $\mathsf{Span}([\mathbf{A}]_s) := \{[\mathbf{Ar}]_s | \mathbf{r} \in \mathbb{Z}_p^m\} \subset \mathbb{G}_s^n$. Note that it is efficient to compute $[\mathbf{AB}]_s$ given $([\mathbf{A}]_s, \mathbf{B})$ or $(\mathbf{A}, [\mathbf{B}]_s)$ with matching dimensions. We define $[\mathbf{A}]_1 \circ [\mathbf{B}]_2 := e([\mathbf{A}]_1, [\mathbf{B}]_2) = [\mathbf{AB}]_T$, which can be efficiently computed given $[\mathbf{A}]_1$ and $[\mathbf{B}]_2$.

Next we recall the definition of the Matrix Decisional Diffie-Hellman (MDDH) [18] and related assumptions [43].

Definition 1 (Matrix distribution). *Let $k, \ell \in \mathbb{N}$ with $\ell > k$. We call $\mathcal{D}_{\ell,k}$ a matrix distribution if it outputs matrices in $\mathbb{Z}_p^{\ell \times k}$ of full rank k in polynomial time. By $\mathcal{D}_k$ we denote $\mathcal{D}_{k+1,k}$.*

For a matrix $\mathbf{A} \xleftarrow{\$} \mathcal{D}_{\ell,k}$, we define the set of kernel matrices of $\mathbf{A}$ as

$$\mathsf{ker}(\mathbf{A}) := \{\mathbf{A}^\perp \in \mathbb{Z}_p^{\ell \times (\ell - k)} \mid (\mathbf{A}^\perp)^\top \cdot \mathbf{A} = \mathbf{0} \in \mathbb{Z}_p^{(\ell-k) \times k} \text{ and } \mathbf{A} \text{ has rank } (\ell - k)\}.$$

Given a matrix $\mathbf{A}$ over $\mathbb{Z}_p^{\ell \times k}$, it is efficient to sample an $\mathbf{A}^\perp$ from $\mathsf{ker}(\mathbf{A})$.

The $\mathcal{D}_{\ell,k}$-Matrix Diffie-Hellman problem is to distinguish the two distributions $([\mathbf{A}], [\mathbf{Aw}])$ and $([\mathbf{A}], [\mathbf{u}])$ where $\mathbf{A} \xleftarrow{\$} \mathcal{D}_{\ell,k}$, $\mathbf{w} \xleftarrow{\$} \mathbb{Z}_p^k$ and $\mathbf{u} \xleftarrow{\$} \mathbb{Z}_p^\ell$.

Definition 2 ($\mathcal{D}_{\ell,k}$-matrix decisional Diffie-Hellman assumption *[18]***).** *Let $\mathcal{D}_{\ell,k}$ be a matrix distribution and $s \in \{1, 2, T\}$. We say that the $\mathcal{D}_{\ell,k}$-Matrix Diffie-Hellman ($\mathcal{D}_{\ell,k}$-*MDDH*) is hard relative to* GGen *in group $\mathbb{G}_s$ if for all PPT adversaries $\mathcal{A}$, it holds that*

$$|\Pr[1 \xleftarrow{\$} \mathcal{A}(\mathcal{G}, [\mathbf{A}]_s, [\mathbf{Aw}]_s)] - \Pr[1 \xleftarrow{\$} \mathcal{A}(\mathcal{G}, [\mathbf{A}]_s, [\mathbf{u}]_s)]| \leq \mathsf{negl}(\lambda),$$

where $\mathcal{G} \xleftarrow{\$} \mathsf{GGen}(\mathsf{par})$, $\mathbf{A} \xleftarrow{\$} \mathcal{D}_{\ell,k}$, $\mathbf{w} \xleftarrow{\$} \mathbb{Z}_p^k$ and $\mathbf{u} \xleftarrow{\$} \mathbb{Z}_p^\ell$.

2.2 Non-Interactive Zero-Knowledge Proof

Let $\lambda \in \mathbb{N}$ be the security parameter determining a public parameter par. We define NIZK as follows.

Definition 3 (Non-interactive zero-knowledge proof [30]**).** *A* non-interactive zero-knowledge proof (NIZK) *for a family of languages $\{\mathcal{L}_{\mathsf{par}}\}$ consists of three PPT algorithms* NIZK = (NGen, NProve, NVer) *such that:*

- $\mathsf{NGen}(1^\lambda, \mathsf{par})$ *returns a common reference string* crs.
- $\mathsf{NProve}(\mathsf{crs}, \mathsf{C}, \mathsf{x}, \mathsf{w})$ *returns a proof π.*
- $\mathsf{NVer}(\mathsf{crs}, \mathsf{C}, \mathsf{x}, \pi)$ *returns* 1 *(accept) or* 0 *(reject). Here,* NVer *is deterministic.*

Completeness *is satisfied if for all $(\mathsf{C}, \mathsf{x}) \in \mathcal{L}_{\mathsf{par}}$ and all* w *such that* $\mathsf{C}(\mathsf{x}, \mathsf{w}) = 1$, *all* $\mathsf{crs} \in \mathsf{NGen}(1^\lambda, \mathsf{par})$, *and all* $\pi \in \mathsf{NProve}(\mathsf{crs}, \mathsf{x}, \mathsf{w})$, *we have* $\mathsf{NVer}(\mathsf{crs}, \mathsf{x}, \pi) = 1$.

Definition 4 (Composable zero-knowledge). *A NIZK* NIZK = (NGen, NProve, NVer) *is said to satsify* composable zero-knowledge *if there exist a simulator consisting of two PPT algorithms* (NTGen, NSim) *such that*

- $\mathsf{NTGen}(1^\lambda, \mathsf{par})$ *returns* crs *and a trapdoor* td,
- $\mathsf{NSim}(\mathsf{crs}, \mathsf{td}, \mathsf{C}, \mathsf{x})$ *returns a proof π,*

and for any PPT adversary $\mathcal{A}$, we have

$$|\Pr[1 \xleftarrow{\$} \mathcal{A}(\mathsf{crs})|\mathsf{crs} \xleftarrow{\$} \mathsf{NGen}(1^\lambda, \mathsf{par})] - \Pr[1 \xleftarrow{\$} \mathcal{A}(\mathsf{crs})|(\mathsf{crs}, \mathsf{td}) \xleftarrow{\$} \mathsf{NTGen}(1^\lambda, \mathsf{par})]| \leq \mathsf{negl}(\lambda),$$

and for all (x, w) *such that* $\mathsf{C}(\mathsf{x}, \mathsf{w}) = 1$, *the following distributions are identical.*

$$\pi \xleftarrow{\$} \mathsf{NProve}(\mathsf{crs}, \mathsf{C}, \mathsf{x}, \mathsf{w}) \text{ and } \pi \xleftarrow{\$} \mathsf{NSim}(\mathsf{crs}, \mathsf{td}, \mathsf{C}, \mathsf{x}),$$

where $(\mathsf{crs}, \mathsf{td}) \xleftarrow{\$} \mathsf{NTGen}(1^\lambda, \mathsf{par})$.

Definition 5 (Perfect soundness). *A NIZK* NIZK = (NGen, NProve, NVer) *is said to satisfy* perfect soundness *if for all* $\mathsf{x} \notin \mathcal{L}_{\mathsf{par}}$, *all* $\mathsf{crs} \in \mathsf{NGen}(1^\lambda, \mathsf{par})$, *and all π, we have* $\mathsf{NVer}(\mathsf{crs}, \mathsf{C}, \mathsf{x}, \pi) = 0$.

Witness-extractor. One can easily see that for any statement, if there exists a (possibly inefficient) witness-extractor that can extract a valid witness from any valid proof passing the verification, then perfect soundness is satisfied.

Dual mode. A NIZK defined as above satisfies computational zero-knowledge and perfect soundness. By generating CRSs with NTGen instead of NGen, we immediately achieve its dual mode with perfect zero-knowledge but computational soundness.

2.3 Batch Argument

Let $\lambda \in \mathbb{N}$ be the security parameter determining a public parameter par. We define batch argument as follows.

Definition 6 (Batch argument). *A* batch argument (BARG) *for a family of languages* $\{\mathcal{L}_{\mathsf{par}}\}$ *consists of three PPT algorithms* $\mathsf{BARG} = (\mathsf{BGen}, \mathsf{BProve}, \mathsf{BVer})$ *such that*

- $\mathsf{BGen}(1^\lambda, \mathsf{par}, 1^m)$ *returns a common reference string* crs.
- $\mathsf{BProve}(\mathsf{crs}, \mathsf{C}, (\mathsf{x}_i)_{i\in[m]}, (\mathsf{w}_i)_{i\in[m]})$ *returns a proof* π.
- $\mathsf{BVer}(\mathsf{crs}, \mathsf{C}, (\mathsf{x}_i)_{i\in[m]}, \pi)$ *returns* 1 *(accept) or* 0 *(reject). Here,* BVer *is deterministic.*

Completeness *is satisfied if for all* $\lambda, m \in \mathbb{N}$, *all* $(\mathsf{C}, (\mathsf{x}_i)_{i\in[m]}) \in \mathcal{L}_{\mathsf{par}}$, *all* $(\mathsf{w}_i)_{i\in[m]})$ *such that* $\mathsf{C}(\mathsf{x}_i, \mathsf{w}_i) = 1$ *for all* $i \in [m]$, *all* $\mathsf{crs} \in \mathsf{BGen}(1^\lambda, \mathsf{par}, 1^m)$, *and all* $\pi \in \mathsf{BProve}(\mathsf{crs}, \mathsf{C}, (\mathsf{x}_i)_{i\in[m]}, (\mathsf{w}_i)_{i\in[m]})$, *we have* $\mathsf{BVer}(\mathsf{crs}, \mathsf{C}, (\mathsf{x}_i)_{i\in[m]}, \pi) = 1$.

Definition 7 (Somewhere argument of knowledge). *A BARG* $\mathsf{BARG} = (\mathsf{BGen}, \mathsf{BProve}, \mathsf{BVer})$ *for* $\{\mathcal{L}_{\mathsf{par}}\}$ *is said to be a* somewhere argument of knowledge *if there exist two PPT algorithms* $(\mathsf{BTGen}, \mathsf{BExt})$ *such that*

- $\mathsf{BTGen}(1^\lambda, \mathsf{par}, 1^m, i^*)$ *returns a common reference string* crs *and a trapdoor* td,
- $\mathsf{BExt}(\mathsf{td}, \mathsf{C}, (\mathsf{x}_i)_{i\in[m]}, \pi)$ *returns a witness* w^*. *Here,* BExt *is deterministic,*

and $(\mathsf{BTGen}, \mathsf{BExt})$ *satisfy the following two properties.*

CRS indistinguishability*: for all* $\lambda, m \in \mathbb{N}$, *all* $i^* \in [m]$, *and all PPT adversary* $\mathcal{A}$, *we have*

$$\begin{aligned}&|\Pr[1 \xleftarrow{\$} \mathcal{A}(\mathsf{crs}) | \mathsf{crs} \xleftarrow{\$} \mathsf{BGen}(1^\lambda, \mathsf{par}, 1^m)] \\ &- \Pr[1 \xleftarrow{\$} \mathcal{A}(\mathsf{crs}) | (\mathsf{crs}, \mathsf{td}) \xleftarrow{\$} \mathsf{BTGen}(1^\lambda, \mathsf{par}, 1^m, i^*)]| \leq \mathsf{negl}(\lambda).\end{aligned}$$

Somewhere extractability in trapdoor mode*: for all polynomial* $m = m(\lambda)$, *all* $i^* \in [m]$, *and all adversary* $\mathcal{A}$, *we have*

$$\begin{aligned}&\Pr[\mathsf{BVer}(\mathsf{crs}^*, \mathsf{C}, (\mathsf{x}_i)_{i\in[m]}, \pi) = 1 \wedge C(\mathsf{x}_{i^*}, \mathsf{w}_{i^*}) \neq 1 | \\ &(\mathsf{crs}^*, \mathsf{td}) \xleftarrow{\$} \mathsf{BTGen}(1^\lambda, \mathsf{par}, 1^m, i^*), (\mathsf{C}, (\mathsf{x}_i)_{i\in[m]}, \pi) \xleftarrow{\$} \mathcal{A}(\mathsf{crs}^*), \\ &\qquad \mathsf{w}_{i^*} \xleftarrow{\$} \mathsf{BExt}(\mathsf{td}, \mathsf{C}, (\mathsf{x}_i)_{i\in[m]}, \pi)] \leq \mathsf{negl}(\lambda).\end{aligned}$$

As noted in [48], somewhere extractability implies non-adaptive soundness, i.e., soundness for statements independent of the CRS (see [48] for the formal definition), by a standard hybrid argument.[3]

[3] A security loss of $O(m)$ occurs in the hybrid argument.

Definition 8 (Succinctness). *A batch argument* $\mathsf{BARG} = (\mathsf{BGen}, \mathsf{BProve}, \mathsf{BVer})$ *for* $\{\mathcal{L}_{\mathsf{par}}\}$ *is said to satisfy* succinctness *if there exists a fixed polynomial* $\mathsf{poly}(\cdot,\cdot,\cdot)$ *such that for all* $\lambda, m \in \mathbb{N}$, *all* $\mathsf{crs} \in \mathsf{BGen}(1^\lambda, \mathsf{par}, 1^m)$, *and all* $(\mathsf{C} : \{0,1\}^n \times \{0,1\}^h \to \{0,1\}, (\mathsf{x}_i)_{i\in[m]}) \in \mathcal{L}_{\mathsf{par}}$, *the following properties hold:*

Succinct proofs: all $\pi \in \mathsf{BProve}(\mathsf{crs}, \mathsf{C}, (\mathsf{x}_i)_{i\in[m]}, (\mathsf{w}_i)_{i\in[m]})$ *where* $\mathsf{C}(\mathsf{x}_i, \mathsf{w}_i) = 1$ *for all* $i \in [m]$ *satisfies* $|\pi| \leq \mathsf{poly}(\lambda, \log m, s)$.

Succinct CRS: all $\mathsf{crs} \in \mathsf{Gen}(1^\lambda, \mathsf{par}, 1^m)$ *satisfies* $|\mathsf{crs}| \leq \mathsf{poly}(\lambda, m, n) + \mathsf{poly}(\lambda, \log m, s)$.

Succinct verification: BVer *runs in time* $\mathsf{poly}(\lambda, m, n) + \mathsf{poly}(\lambda, \log m, s)$.

Above by s *we denote the number of gates in* C.

3 Simple NIZK from OR-Proof

In this section, we recall an efficient instantiation of OR-proof and give a new framework for converting an OR-proof into an efficient NIZK for circuit satisfiability in NP.

3.1 NIZK for OR-Language

We now recall the OR-proof system based on the MDDH assumptions presented in [39,45] and implicitly given in [29]. As far as we know, this is the most efficient OR-proof by now in the standard model.

For the language

$$\mathsf{L}^{\mathsf{or}}_{[\mathbf{A}]_1} = \{(\mathsf{C}_{[\mathbf{A}]_1}, ([\mathbf{x}_0]_1, [\mathbf{x}_1]_1)) | \exists \mathbf{w} \in \mathbb{Z}_p^t : \mathsf{C}_{[\mathbf{A}]_1}([\mathbf{x}_0, \mathbf{x}_1]_1, \mathbf{w}) = 1\},$$

where $[\mathbf{A}]_1 \in \mathbb{G}_1^{n\times t}$ is public and $\mathsf{C}_{[\mathbf{A}]_1}$ is a Boolean circuit on input $([\mathbf{x}_0, \mathbf{x}_1]_1, \mathbf{w})$ outputting 1 iff $[\mathbf{x}_0]_1 = [\mathbf{A}]_1\mathbf{w} \vee [\mathbf{x}_1]_1 = [\mathbf{A}]_1\mathbf{w}$, the OR-proof system ORNIZK with each public parameter containing $\mathsf{par} = (\mathcal{G} \xleftarrow{\$} \mathsf{GGen}(1^\lambda))$ is defined as in Fig. 2.

Lemma 1. *If the* $\mathcal{D}_k$-MDDH *assumption holds in the group* $\mathbb{G}_2$, *then the proof system* $\mathsf{ORNIZK} = (\mathsf{NGen_{or}}, \mathsf{NTGen_{or}}, \mathsf{NProve_{or}}, \mathsf{NVer_{or}}, \mathsf{NSim_{or}})$ *is a NIZK with perfect completeness, perfect soundness, and composable zero-knowledge. For any adversary* $\mathcal{A}$ *against the composable zero-knowledge of* ORNIZK, *there exists a tight reduction algorithm breaking the* MDDH *assumption by using* $\mathcal{A}$ *in a black-box way with security loss* $O(1)$.

We refer the reader to [39,45] for the detailed proof.

3.2 Our NIZK for NP

Before giving our NIZK for NP, we first introduce the notion of circuit satisfiability.

$\underline{\mathsf{NGen}_{\mathsf{or}}(1^\lambda, \mathsf{par})\text{:}}$
$\mathbf{D} \stackrel{\$}{\leftarrow} \mathcal{D}_k$, $\mathbf{z} \stackrel{\$}{\leftarrow} \mathbb{Z}_p^{k+1} \backslash \mathsf{Span}(\mathbf{D})$
Return $\mathsf{crs} = (\mathsf{par}, [\mathbf{D}]_2, [\mathbf{z}]_2)$

$\underline{\mathsf{NProve}_{\mathsf{or}}(\mathsf{crs}, \mathsf{C}_{[\mathbf{A}]_1}, ([\mathbf{x}_0]_1, [\mathbf{x}_1]_1), \mathbf{r})\text{:}}$
let $j \in \{0,1\}$ s.t. $[\mathbf{x}_j]_1 = [\mathbf{A}]_1 \cdot \mathbf{r}$
$\mathbf{v} \stackrel{\$}{\leftarrow} \mathbb{Z}_p^k$, $[\mathbf{z}_{1-j}]_2 = [\mathbf{D}]_2 \cdot \mathbf{v}$, $[\mathbf{z}_j]_2 = [\mathbf{z}]_2 - [\mathbf{z}_{1-j}]_2$, $\mathbf{S}_0, \mathbf{S}_1 \stackrel{\$}{\leftarrow} \mathbb{Z}_p^{t \times k}$
$[\mathbf{C}_j]_2 = \mathbf{S}_j \cdot [\mathbf{D}]_2^\top + \mathbf{r} \cdot [\mathbf{z}_j]_2^\top \in \mathbb{G}_2^{t \times (k+1)}$, $[\pi_j]_1 = [\mathbf{A}]_1 \cdot \mathbf{S}_j \in \mathbb{G}_1^{n \times k}$
$[\mathbf{C}_{1-j}]_2 = \mathbf{S}_{1-j} \cdot [\mathbf{D}]_2^\top$, $[\pi_{1-j}]_1 = [\mathbf{A}]_1 \cdot \mathbf{S}_{1-j} - [\mathbf{x}_{1-j}]_1 \cdot \mathbf{v}^\top$
Return $\pi = ([\mathbf{z}_0]_2, ([\mathbf{C}_i]_2, [\pi_i]_1)_{i \in \{0,1\}})$

$\underline{\mathsf{NVer}_{\mathsf{or}}(\mathsf{crs}, \mathsf{C}_{[\mathbf{A}]_1}, [\mathbf{x}]_1, \pi)\text{:}}$
$[\mathbf{z}_1]_2 = [\mathbf{z}]_2 - [\mathbf{z}_0]_2$
If for all $i \in \{0,1\}$ it holds $[\mathbf{A}]_1 \circ [\mathbf{C}_i]_2 = [\pi_i]_1 \circ [\mathbf{D}^\top]_2 + [\mathbf{x}_i]_1 \circ [\mathbf{z}_i^\top]_2$, return 1
Else return 0

$\underline{\mathsf{NTGen}_{\mathsf{or}}(1^\lambda, \mathsf{par})\text{:}}$
$\mathbf{D} \stackrel{\$}{\leftarrow} \mathcal{D}_k$, $\mathbf{u} \stackrel{\$}{\leftarrow} \mathbb{Z}_p^k$, $\mathbf{z} = \mathbf{D} \cdot \mathbf{u}$
Return $(\mathsf{crs} = (\mathsf{par}, [\mathbf{D}]_2, [\mathbf{z}]_2), \mathsf{td} = \mathbf{u}$

$\underline{\mathsf{NSim}_{\mathsf{or}}(\mathsf{crs}, \mathsf{td}, \mathsf{C}_{[\mathbf{A}]_1}, ([\mathbf{x}_0]_1, [\mathbf{x}_1]_1))\text{:}}$
$\mathbf{v} \stackrel{\$}{\leftarrow} \mathbb{Z}_p^k$, $[\mathbf{z}_0]_2 = [\mathbf{D}]_2 \cdot \mathbf{v}$, $[\mathbf{z}_1]_2 = [\mathbf{z}]_2 - [\mathbf{z}_0]_2$
$\mathbf{S}_0, \mathbf{S}_1 \stackrel{\$}{\leftarrow} \mathbb{Z}_p^{t \times k}$, $[\mathbf{C}_0]_2 = \mathbf{S}_0 \cdot [\mathbf{D}]_2^\top$, $[\pi_0]_1 = [\mathbf{A}_0]_1 \cdot \mathbf{S}_0 - [\mathbf{x}_0]_1 \cdot \mathbf{v}^\top$
$[\mathbf{C}_1]_2 = \mathbf{S}_1 \cdot [\mathbf{D}]_2^\top$, $[\pi_1]_1 = [\mathbf{A}]_1 \cdot \mathbf{S}_1 - [\mathbf{x}_1]_1 \cdot (\mathbf{u} - \mathbf{v})^\top$
Return $\pi = ([\mathbf{z}_0]_2, ([\mathbf{C}_i]_2, [\pi_i]_1)_{i \in \{0,1\}})$

Fig. 2. Construction of $\mathsf{ORNIZK} = (\mathsf{NGen}_{\mathsf{or}}, \mathsf{NProve}_{\mathsf{or}}, \mathsf{NVer}_{\mathsf{or}})$ with the simulator $(\mathsf{NTGen}_{\mathsf{or}}, \mathsf{NSim}_{\mathsf{or}})$.

Definition 9 (Circuit satisfiability). *Let λ be the security parameter. The* circuit satisfiability *language is defined as*

$$\mathcal{L}_\lambda^{\mathsf{CSAT}} = \{(\mathsf{C}, \mathsf{x}) | \exists \mathsf{w} \in \{0,1\}^h : \mathsf{C}(\mathsf{x}, \mathsf{w}) = 1\},$$

where $\mathsf{C} : \{0,1\}^n \times \{0,1\}^h \to \{0,1\}$ is any Boolean circuit with polynomial size in λ and $\mathsf{x} \in \{0,1\}^n$ is the instance. Without loss of generality, we assume that C consists only of fan-in-2 NAND gates.

Let λ be the security parameter and $\mathsf{par} = \mathcal{G}$ be the public parameter, where $\mathcal{G} = (\mathbb{G}_1, \mathbb{G}_2, \mathbb{G}_T, p, [1]_1, [1]_2, e) \stackrel{\$}{\leftarrow} \mathsf{GGen}(1^\lambda)$. Let $\mathsf{ORNIZK} = (\mathsf{NGen}_{\mathsf{or}}, \mathsf{NProve}_{\mathsf{or}}, \mathsf{NVer}_{\mathsf{or}})$ be an OR-proof with the simulator $(\mathsf{NTGen}_{\mathsf{or}}, \mathsf{NSim}_{\mathsf{or}})$, where each public parameter is comprised of $\mathcal{G}$. Let $\mathsf{L}^{\mathsf{or}}_{[\mathbf{M}']_1}$ be the following language it supports.

$$\mathsf{L}^{\mathsf{or}}_{[\mathbf{M}']_1} = \{(\mathsf{C}_{[\mathbf{M}']_1}, ([\mathbf{x}_0]_1, [\mathbf{x}_1]_1)) | \exists \mathbf{w} \in \mathbb{Z}_p^{2k} : \mathsf{C}_{[\mathbf{M}']_1}(([\mathbf{x}_0]_1, [\mathbf{x}_1]_1), \mathbf{w}) = 1\},$$

where $\mathsf{C}_{[\mathbf{M}']_1} : \mathbb{G}_1^{2k+2} \times \mathbb{G}_1^{2k+2} \times \mathbb{Z}_p^{2k} \to \{0,1\}$ is a Boolean circuit on input $((\mathbf{x}_0, \mathbf{x}_1), \mathbf{w})$ outputting 1 iff $[\mathbf{x}_0]_1 = [\mathbf{M}']_1 \mathbf{w} \vee [\mathbf{x}_1]_1 = [\mathbf{M}']_1 \mathbf{w}$ for $\mathbf{M}' = \begin{pmatrix} \mathbf{M} & \mathbf{0} \\ \mathbf{0} & \mathbf{M} \end{pmatrix}$

and $\mathbf{M} \in \mathcal{D}_k$. We give our NIZK for $\mathcal{L}_\lambda^{\mathsf{CSAT}}$ in Fig. 3. Roughly, we first extend the witness to all wires, commit to all the values, and use the OR-proof to prove that committed values satisfy Relation (2) (see Sect. 1.3) for each gate.[4]

$\underline{\mathsf{NGen}(1^\lambda, \mathsf{par})\text{:}}$

$\mathbf{M} \xleftarrow{\$} \mathcal{D}_k$, $\mathbf{z} \xleftarrow{\$} \mathbb{Z}_p^{k+1} \backslash \mathsf{Span}(\mathbf{M})$, $\mathsf{crs}_{\mathsf{or}} \xleftarrow{\$} \mathsf{NGen}_{\mathsf{or}}(1^\lambda, \mathsf{par})$

Return $\mathsf{CRS} = (\mathsf{crs}_{\mathsf{or}}, [\mathbf{M}]_1, [\mathbf{z}]_1)$

$\underline{\mathsf{NProve}(\mathsf{CRS}, \mathsf{C}, \mathsf{x}, \mathsf{w})\text{:}}$

Hardwire x in C to obtain the circuit $\mathsf{C}(\mathsf{x}, \cdot) : \{0,1\}^h \to \{0,1\}$

Define s and t to be the numbers of gates and wires of $\mathsf{C}(\mathsf{x}, \cdot)$ respectively

Extend w to $(\mathsf{w}_i)_{i\in[t]}$ containing the bits of all wires in $\mathsf{C}(\mathsf{x}, \cdot)$

Compute $\mathbf{r}_i \xleftarrow{\$} \mathbb{Z}_p^k$ and $\mathsf{cm}_i = [\mathbf{M}]_1\mathbf{r}_i + [\mathbf{z}]_1\mathsf{w}_i$ for all $i \in [t-1]$

Set $\mathbf{r}_t = \mathbf{0}$ and $\mathsf{cm}_t = [\mathbf{z}]_1$ for the output wire

For each NAND gate $G_\ell = (d_1, d_2, d_3) \in [t]^3$ where $\ell \in [s]$, run

- $\mathsf{x}_{\ell,1} = \begin{pmatrix} -[\mathbf{z}]_1 + \mathsf{cm}_{d_1} + \mathsf{cm}_{d_3} \\ -[\mathbf{z}]_1 + \mathsf{cm}_{d_2} \end{pmatrix}$, $\mathbf{r}'_{\ell,1} = \begin{pmatrix} \mathbf{r}_{d_1} + \mathbf{r}_{d_3} \\ \mathbf{r}_{d_2} \end{pmatrix}$
- $\mathsf{x}_{\ell,2} = \begin{pmatrix} -[\mathbf{z}]_1 + \mathsf{cm}_{d_3} \\ \mathsf{cm}_{d_2} \end{pmatrix}$, $\mathbf{r}'_{\ell,2} = \begin{pmatrix} \mathbf{r}_{d_3} \\ \mathbf{r}_{d_2} \end{pmatrix}$
- $\pi_\ell \xleftarrow{\$} \mathsf{NProve}_{\mathsf{or}}(\mathsf{crs}_{\mathsf{or}}, \mathsf{C}_{[\mathbf{M}']_1}, (\mathsf{x}_{\ell,1}, \mathsf{x}_{\ell,2}), \mathbf{r}'_b)$ if $\mathsf{x}_{\ell,b} = [\mathbf{M}']_1\mathbf{r}'_{\ell,b}$ for $b \in \{1,2\}$ and abort otherwise

Return $\Pi = ((\mathsf{cm}_i)_{i\in[t]}, (\pi_\ell)_{\ell\in[s]})$

$\underline{\mathsf{NVer}(\mathsf{CRS}, \mathsf{C}, \mathsf{x}, \Pi)\text{:}}$

Hardwire x in C to obtain $\mathsf{C}(\mathsf{x}, \cdot)$ in the same way as NProve does

Check that all wires in $\mathsf{C}(\mathsf{x}, \cdot)$ have a corresponding commitment and $\mathsf{cm}_t = [\mathbf{z}]_1$

Check that all NAND gates have a valid OR-proof of compliance

Return 1 iff all checks pass

Fig. 3. Definition of $\mathsf{NIZK} = (\mathsf{NGen}, \mathsf{NProve}, \mathsf{NVer})$. By $G_\ell = (d_1, d_2, d_3)$ we mean that the left and right input wires of the gate G_ℓ are indexed as d_1 and d_2 respectively, while the output wire of G_ℓ is indexed as d_3. Notice that for each multiple fan-out gate, we only increment the count of wires t by 1 for its output wires and generate only one commitment for these wires, since all output wires of the gate are assigned the same value and serves as input wires for multiple other gates. The same argument is also made for all other proof systems given later.

Theorem 1 (Completeness). *If* ORNIZK *is complete, then* NIZK *is complete.*

Proof. Let w_{d_1} and w_{d_2} be the input bits of a NAND gate, and w_{d_3} be the true output. We must have

$$(-1 + \mathsf{w}_{d_1} + \mathsf{w}_{d_3} = 0 \wedge -1 + \mathsf{w}_{d_2} = 0) \text{ or } (-1 + \mathsf{w}_{d_3} = 0 \wedge \mathsf{w}_{d_2} = 0).$$

[4] Notice that we do not define the commitment and its properties in advance since we use a concrete construction based on the MDDH assumption in a non-black-box way.

Let $\mathsf{cm}_{d_1} = [\mathbf{M}\mathbf{r}_{d_1} + \mathbf{z}\mathsf{w}_{d_1}]_1$ and $\mathsf{cm}_{d_2} = [\mathbf{M}\mathbf{r}_{d_2} + \mathbf{z}\mathsf{w}_{d_2}]_1$ be the input commitments and $\mathsf{cm}_{d_3} = [\mathbf{M}\mathbf{r}_{d_3} + \mathbf{z}\mathsf{w}_{d_3}]_1$ be the output commitment. We have

$$\mathsf{x}_{\ell,1} = \begin{pmatrix} -[\mathbf{z}]_1 + \mathsf{cm}_{d_1} + \mathsf{cm}_{d_3} \\ -[\mathbf{z}]_1 + \mathsf{cm}_{d_2} \end{pmatrix} = [\mathbf{M}']_1 \begin{pmatrix} \mathbf{r}_{d_1} + \mathbf{r}_{d_3} \\ \mathbf{r}_{d_2} \end{pmatrix} + \begin{pmatrix} [\mathbf{z}]_1(-1 + \mathsf{w}_{d_1} + \mathsf{w}_{d_3}) \\ [\mathbf{z}]_1(-1 + \mathsf{w}_{d_2}) \end{pmatrix}$$
$$= [\mathbf{M}']_1 \begin{pmatrix} \mathbf{r}_{d_1} + \mathbf{r}_{d_3} \\ \mathbf{r}_{d_2} \end{pmatrix}$$

$$\text{or} \quad \mathbf{x}_{\ell,2} = \begin{pmatrix} -[\mathbf{z}]_1 + \mathsf{cm}_{d_3} \\ \mathsf{cm}_{d_2} \end{pmatrix} = [\mathbf{M}']_1 \begin{pmatrix} \mathbf{r}_{d_3} \\ \mathbf{r}_{d_2} \end{pmatrix} + \begin{pmatrix} [\mathbf{z}]_1(-1 + \mathsf{w}_{d_3}) \\ [\mathbf{z}]_1 \mathsf{w}_{d_2} \end{pmatrix} = [\mathbf{M}']_1 \begin{pmatrix} \mathbf{r}_{d_3} \\ \mathbf{r}_{d_2} \end{pmatrix}.$$

Therefore, we have $\mathsf{x}_{\ell,1} \in \mathsf{Span}([\mathbf{M}']_1)$ if $\mathsf{w}_{d_2} = 1$ and $\mathsf{x}_{\ell,2} \in \mathsf{Span}([\mathbf{M}']_1)$ otherwise. Then the completeness of NIZK follows from the completeness of ORNIZK, completing the proof of Theorem 1. □

Theorem 2 (Composable zero-knowledge). *Under the* $\mathcal{D}_k$-MDDH *assumption, if* ORNIZK *satisfies composable zero-knowledge, then* NIZK *satisfies composable zero-knowledge.*

NTGen$(1^\lambda, \mathsf{par})$:
$\mathbf{M} \xleftarrow{\$} \mathcal{D}_k$, $\mathbf{u} \xleftarrow{\$} \mathbb{Z}_p^k$, $\mathbf{z} = \mathbf{M} \cdot \mathbf{u}$, $(\mathsf{crs}_{\mathsf{or}}, \mathsf{td}_{\mathsf{or}}) \xleftarrow{\$} \mathsf{NTGen}_{\mathsf{or}}(1^\lambda, \mathsf{par})$
Return $\mathsf{CRS} = (\mathsf{crs}_{\mathsf{or}}, [\mathbf{M}]_1, [\mathbf{z}]_1)$ and $\mathsf{TD} = \mathsf{td}_{\mathsf{or}}$

NSim(CRS, TD, C, x):
Hardwire x in C to obtain $\mathsf{C}(\mathsf{x}, \cdot)$ in the same way as NProve does
Define s and t to be the numbers of gates and wires of $\mathsf{C}(\mathsf{x}, \cdot)$ respectively
Compute $\mathbf{r}_i \xleftarrow{\$} \mathbb{Z}_p^k$ and $\mathsf{cm}_i = [\mathbf{M}\mathbf{r}_i]_1$ for all $i \in [t-1]$
Set $\mathsf{cm}_t = [\mathbf{z}]_1$ for the output wire
For each NAND gate $G_\ell = (d_1, d_2, d_3) \in [t]^3$ where $\ell \in [s]$, run
– $\mathsf{x}_{\ell,1} = \begin{pmatrix} -[\mathbf{z}]_1 + \mathsf{cm}_{d_1} + \mathsf{cm}_{d_3} \\ -[\mathbf{z}]_1 + \mathsf{cm}_{d_2} \end{pmatrix}$, $\mathsf{x}_{\ell,2} = \begin{pmatrix} -[\mathbf{z}]_1 + \mathsf{cm}_{d_3} \\ \mathsf{cm}_{d_2} \end{pmatrix}$
– $\pi_\ell \xleftarrow{\$} \mathsf{NSim}_{\mathsf{or}}(\mathsf{crs}_{\mathsf{or}}, \mathsf{td}_{\mathsf{or}}, \mathsf{C}_{[\mathbf{M}']_1}, (\mathsf{x}_{\ell,1}, \mathsf{x}_{\ell,2}))$
Return $\Pi = ((\mathsf{cm}_i)_{i \in [t]}, (\pi_\ell)_{\ell \in [s]})$

Fig. 4. Definition of the simulator (NTGen, NSim).

Proof. We define the simulator (NTGen, NSim) as in Fig. 4.

First we note that the distribution of $\mathbf{z} \xleftarrow{\$} \mathbb{Z}_p^{k+1} \backslash \mathsf{Span}(\mathbf{M})$ is $1/p$-statistically close to the uniform distribution over $\mathbb{Z}_p^{k+1}$. Then the indistinguishability of CRSs generated by $\mathsf{NGen}(1^\lambda, \mathsf{par})$ and $\mathsf{NTGen}(1^\lambda, \mathsf{par})$ follows immediately from the $\mathcal{D}_k$-MDDH assumption and the composable zero-knowledge of ORNIZK (which says that $\mathsf{crs}_{\mathsf{or}}$ generated by $\mathsf{NGen}_{\mathsf{or}}$ and $\mathsf{NTGen}_{\mathsf{or}}$ are computationally close).

Next we define a modified prover NProve', which is exactly the same as NProve except that for each NAND gate, π_ℓ is generated as

$$\pi_\ell \xleftarrow{\$} \mathsf{NSim}_{\mathsf{or}}(\mathsf{crs}_{\mathsf{or}}, \mathsf{td}_{\mathsf{or}}, \mathsf{C}_{[\mathbf{M}']_1}, (\mathsf{x}_{\ell,1}, \mathsf{x}_{\ell,2})).$$

The following distributions are identical due to the composable zero-knowledge of ORNIZK.

$$\Pi \xleftarrow{\$} \mathsf{NProve}(\mathsf{CRS}, \mathsf{C}, \mathsf{x}, \mathsf{w}) \text{ and } \Pi \xleftarrow{\$} \mathsf{NProve}'(\mathsf{CRS}, \mathsf{C}, \mathsf{x}, \mathsf{w})$$

for $(\mathsf{CRS}, \mathsf{TD}) \xleftarrow{\$} \mathsf{NTGen}(1^\lambda, \mathsf{par})$ and any (x, w) such that $\mathsf{C}(\mathsf{x}, \mathsf{w}) = 1$.

Moreover, since the distribution of $\mathsf{cm}_i = [\mathbf{M}\mathbf{r}_i]_1$ is identical to that of $\mathsf{cm}_i = [\mathbf{M}\mathbf{r}_i + \mathbf{z}\mathsf{w}_i]_1$ for $\mathbf{r}_i \xleftarrow{\$} \mathbb{Z}_p^\lambda$ when $\mathbf{z} \in \mathsf{Span}(\mathbf{M})$, the distributions of

$$\Pi \xleftarrow{\$} \mathsf{NProve}'(\mathsf{CRS}, \mathsf{C}, \mathsf{x}, \mathsf{w}) \text{ and } \Pi \xleftarrow{\$} \mathsf{NSim}(\mathsf{CRS}, \mathsf{TD}, \mathsf{C}, \mathsf{x}),$$

where $(\mathsf{CRS}, \mathsf{TD}) \xleftarrow{\$} \mathsf{NTGen}(1^\lambda, \mathsf{par})$ and $\mathsf{C}(\mathsf{x}, \mathsf{w}) = 1$, are identical as well, completing the proof of Theorem 2. □

Theorem 3 (Soundness). *If* ORNIZK *is perfectly sound, then* NIZK *is perfectly sound.*

Proof. To prove perfect soundness, we just have to show that we can extract a valid witness from any proof passing the verification. Let $\mathbf{k}$ be the vector in the kernel of $\mathbf{M}$ such that $\mathbf{k}^\top \mathbf{z} = 1$, which must exist when $\mathbf{z} \notin \mathsf{Span}(\mathbf{M})$. We define an extractor as in Fig. 5. For any valid statement/proof pair (x, Π), we argue that the extractor must be able to extract a valid witness w for x as below.

Due to the perfect soundness of ORNIZK, for each NAND gate with input commitments $(\mathsf{cm}_{d_1}, \mathsf{cm}_{d_2})$ and an output commitment cm_{d_3} in a valid proof, we have

$$\mathsf{x}_{\ell,1} = \begin{pmatrix} -[\mathbf{z}]_1 + \mathsf{cm}_{d_1} + \mathsf{cm}_{d_3} \\ -[\mathbf{z}]_1 + \mathsf{cm}_{d_2} \end{pmatrix} \in \mathsf{Span}([\mathbf{M}']_1)$$

$$\text{or} \quad \mathbf{x}_{\ell,2} = \begin{pmatrix} -[\mathbf{z}]_1 + \mathsf{cm}_{d_3} \\ \mathsf{cm}_{d_2} \end{pmatrix} \in \mathsf{Span}([\mathbf{M}']_1).$$

Then we have

$$\begin{aligned} \mathbf{k}^\top(-[\mathbf{z}]_1 + \mathsf{cm}_{d_1} + \mathsf{cm}_{d_3}) &= -[1]_1 + \mathbf{k}^\top \mathsf{cm}_{d_1} + \mathbf{k}^\top \mathsf{cm}_{d_3} = [0]_1 \\ \wedge \mathbf{k}^\top(-[\mathbf{z}]_1 + \mathsf{cm}_{d_2}) &= -[1]_1 + \mathbf{k}^\top \mathsf{cm}_{d_2} = [0]_1 \end{aligned}$$

$\mathsf{Ext}_{\mathsf{NIZK}}(\mathsf{C}(\mathsf{x}, \cdot), \Pi)$:
Initialize the values for all wires in $\mathsf{C}(\mathsf{x}, \cdot)$ as $\perp$.
Run $\mathsf{F}_{\mathsf{NIZK}}(\mathbf{k}, \mathsf{C}, G_t, \Pi)$, where G_t is the gate for the final output, to assign values for each wire in the circuit $\mathsf{C}(\mathsf{x}, \cdot)$
For each input wire with index i assigned $\perp$, set $\mathsf{w}_i = 0$
Return the witness $\mathsf{w} = (\mathsf{w}_i)_{i \in [h]}$ (containing all the bits for input values)

Fig. 5. Definition of $\mathsf{Ext}_{\mathsf{NIZK}}$. $\mathsf{F}_{\mathsf{NIZK}}$ is the recursion algorithm defined as in Fig. 6.

$\mathsf{F}_{\mathsf{NIZK}}(\mathbf{k}, \mathsf{C}, G_\ell = (d_1, d_2, d_3), \Pi)$:
Compute $\mathsf{temp}_i = \mathbf{k}^\top \mathsf{cm}_i$ for $i = 1, 2, 3$
If $\mathsf{temp}_2 = [0]_1$ and $\mathsf{temp}_3 = [1]_1$:
- set $(\mathsf{w}_{d_1}, \mathsf{w}_{d_2}) = (\bot, 0)$
- stop if $\mathsf{Parent}_r(G_\ell) = \bot$
- run $\mathsf{F}_{\mathsf{NIZK}}(\mathbf{k}, \mathsf{C}, \mathsf{Parent}_r(G_\ell), \Pi)$

If $\mathsf{temp}_2 = [1]_1$ and $[\mathsf{temp}_1 + \mathsf{temp}_3]_1 = [1]_1$:
- if $\mathsf{temp}_3 \notin \{[0]_1, [1]_1\}$, abort $\mathsf{Ext}_{\mathsf{NIZK}}$
- set $(\mathsf{w}_{d_1}, \mathsf{w}_{d_2}) = (b, 1)$ where $[b]_1 = \mathsf{temp}_1$ and $b \in \{0, 1\}$
- stop if $\mathsf{Parent}_l(G_\ell) = \bot$ and $\mathsf{Parent}_r(G_\ell) = \bot$
- run $\mathsf{F}_{\mathsf{NIZK}}(\mathbf{k}, \mathsf{C}, \mathsf{Parent}_l(G_\ell), \Pi)$ and $\mathsf{F}_{\mathsf{NIZK}}(\mathbf{k}, \mathsf{C}, \mathsf{Parent}_r(G_\ell), \Pi)$

Otherwise, abort $\mathsf{Ext}_{\mathsf{NIZK}}$

Fig. 6. Definition of $\mathsf{F}_{\mathsf{NIZK}}$. Parent_l (repsectively, Parent_r) denotes the gate whose output is the left (respectively, right) input to G_ℓ.

$$\text{or } \mathbf{k}^\top(-[\mathbf{z}]_1 + \mathsf{cm}_{d_3}) = -[1]_1 + \mathbf{k}^\top \mathsf{cm}_{d_3} = [0]_1 \wedge \mathbf{k}^\top \mathsf{cm}_{d_2} = [0]_1.$$

Moreover, we must have $\mathbf{k}^\top \mathsf{cm}_t = \mathbf{k}^\top [\mathbf{z}]_1 = [1]_1$ for the output wire. As a result, for a valid proof, $\mathsf{F}_{\mathsf{NIZK}}$ (see Fig. 6) will never abort during the execution of $\mathsf{Ext}_{\mathsf{NIZK}}$, and running $\mathsf{F}_{\mathsf{NIZK}}$ recursively will result in bits for input wires leading the statement circuit to output 1. Notice that after running $\mathsf{F}_{\mathsf{NIZK}}(\mathbf{k}, \mathsf{C}, G_t, \Pi)$, there might be some input wires assigned $\bot$. However, these wires do not affect the final output and we can just assign 0 to them.

As a result, we can extract the bits for all wires consisting of valid input/output pairs for all NAND gates and leading the statement circuit to output 1. Therefore, for all proofs passing the verification, there must exist a valid witness for the statement x, i.e., $\mathsf{x} \in \mathcal{L}_\lambda^{\mathsf{CSAT}}$, completing the proof of Theorem 3.[5] □

Remark on the representation of circuits. We represent the circuits by NAND gates only for conceptual simplicity. In practice, this conversion is unnecessary. For any original circuit represented as AND, OR, NOT gates, the NOT gates are free, and by slightly changing Relation 2 on Page 6, we can directly adopt the OR-proof for AND and OR gates. Concretely, for AND gates, we prove $(\mathsf{w}_{d_1} - \mathsf{w}_{d_3} = 0 \wedge -1 + \mathsf{w}_{d_2} = 0) \vee (\mathsf{w}_{d_3} = 0 \wedge \mathsf{w}_{d_2} = 0)$, and for OR gates, we prove $(\mathsf{w}_{d_1} - \mathsf{w}_{d_3} = 0 \wedge \mathsf{w}_{d_2} = 0) \vee (\mathsf{w}_{d_3} = 1 \wedge \mathsf{w}_{d_2} = 1)$. Then our new technique saves overhead for AND and OR gates with our witness-extraction strategy in the same way as for NAND-gates. The same argument can also be made for our BARG given later.

Instantiation of our NIZK. By instantiating the OR-proof system as in Sect. 3.1 under the SXDH assumption, each proof of our NIZK consists of $(2t+8s)$

[5] One can see that our construction is also a NIZK proof of knowledge, i.e., we can generate the extraction key $\mathbf{k}$ along with a binding CRS and use it to extract a valid witness from any valid proof.

elements in $\mathbb{G}_1$ and $10s$ elements in $\mathbb{G}_2$, where t and s are the number of wires and gates in the statement circuit respectively. Compared to the GOS-NIZK given in Appendix A, which requires $(6t + 4s)$ elements in $\mathbb{G}_1$ and $(6t + 6s)$ elements in $\mathbb{G}_2$ for each proof, our proof size is strictly smaller since t must be larger than s in any circuit. Moreover, the numbers of exponentiations and pairing products required in our proving and verification procedures are only $2t + 30s$ and $24s$ respectively, while those in the GOS-NIZK are $18t+16s$ and $12(s+t)$. Notice that when adopting the OR-proof in our construction, the statement $\mathbf{M}'$ determining the language has half of the entries being $[0]_1$. We do not count exponentiations of these entries and pairing products between these entries and other elements in verification, since the computing results can always be fixed as $[0]_1$ or $[0]_T$.

More instantiations. By instantiating the underlying OR-proof system based on the Extended-Kernel Matrix Diffie-Hellman assumption, which holds unconditionally in the generic group model and implied by the discrete logarithm assumption in the algebraic group model, as in Fig. 6 of [15], we can further reduce the OR-proof size used by our construction by 5 elements in $\mathbb{G}_2$, compared to our SXDH based instantiation (see Table 1). While this also works for the GOS-NIZK in Appendix A, its OR-proof size can only be reduced by 3 elements in $\mathbb{G}_2$.

Extension to non-interactive zaps. In [29], Groth, Sahai, and Ostrovsky gave a generic conversion from any NIZK with verifiable correlated key generation into a non-interactive zap, i.e., non-interactive witness-indistinguishability proof systems in the plain model. To date, this is the only known non-interactive zap for NP based on standard assumptions. Here, verifiable correlated key generation refers to the ability to efficiently generate two correlated common reference strings (CRSs) along with one trapdoor. One CRS is binding, meaning it provides perfect soundness, while the other CRS is hiding, meaning it offers perfect zero-knowledge and corresponds to the trapdoor. It is crucial that a PPT adversary cannot distinguish which CRS is hiding when given both of them. Additionally, it is required that a verification algorithm exist such that honestly sampled CRS pairs always pass verification, and for any CRS pair that passes verification, one of them must be binding. We refer the reader to [29] for a detailed description of the conversion method, while we argue that our NIZK proof system satisfies the requirements for verifiable correlated key generation as outlined above. Consequently, it can be converted into a non-interactive zap, thereby improve the construction in [29] without any trade-offs. As far as we know, this results in the most efficient non-interactive zap based on standard assumptions.

To show that our NIZK has verifiable correlated key generation, we first recall that in both our NIZK and the GOS-NIZK, each CRS essentially consists of a CRS from the underlying NIZK and a key for a homomorphic commitment. Since both parts have the same distribution, we can combine them into a single tuple $(\mathsf{par}, [\mathbf{M}]_1, [\mathbf{z}_{\mathsf{bind}}]_1)$, where $\mathsf{par} = (\mathcal{G} \xleftarrow{\$} \mathsf{GGen}(1^\lambda))$, $\mathbf{M} \xleftarrow{\$} \mathcal{D}_k$, and $\mathbf{z}_{\mathsf{bind}} \xleftarrow{\$} \mathbb{Z}_p^{k+1} \backslash \mathsf{Span}(\mathbf{M})$, without compromising security. In the hiding mode, we replace $\mathbf{z}_{\mathsf{bind}}$ with $\mathbf{z}_{\mathsf{hide}} = \mathbf{M}\mathbf{u}$ where $\mathbf{u} \xleftarrow{\$} \mathbb{Z}_p^k$. We can further change the distribution of $\mathbf{z}_{\mathsf{bind}}$ to that of $\mathbf{z}_{\mathsf{hide}} + \mathbf{f}$, where $\mathbf{f}$ is some fixed vector outside $\mathsf{Span}(\mathbf{M})$. One can easily see that changed $\mathbf{z}_{\mathsf{bind}}$ remains binding due to non-linearility and composable zero-knowledge still holds due to the MDDH assumption. Then we can set the correlated CRSs as $(\mathsf{par}, [\mathbf{M}, \mathbf{z}_{\mathsf{bind}}]_1)$ and $(\mathsf{par}, [\mathbf{M}, \mathbf{z}_{\mathsf{hide}} = \mathbf{z}_{\mathsf{bind}} - \mathbf{f}]_1)$ and set $\mathbf{u}$ as the trapdoor. Due to the MDDH assumption, any PPT adversary cannot tell which one is hiding. The verification algorithm given the two CRSs checks the validity of par and $[\mathbf{M}]_1$ and whether $\mathbf{z}_{\mathsf{bind}} + \mathbf{z}_{\mathsf{hide}} = \mathbf{f}$ holds. For any two CRS $(\mathsf{par}, [\mathbf{M}, \mathbf{z}_0]_1)$ and $(\mathsf{par}, [\mathbf{M}, \mathbf{z}_1]_1)$ passing the verification, we must have either $[\mathbf{z}_0]_1 \notin \mathsf{Span}([\mathbf{M}]_1)$ or $[\mathbf{z}_1]_1 \notin \mathsf{Span}([\mathbf{M}]_1)$, i.e., one of them must be binding. Therefore, our NIZK proof system, as well as the GOS-NIZK in the asymmetric pairing setting, has verifiable correlated key generation.

4 Batch Argument for NP

In this section, we extend our framework for NIZK to give an efficient construction of BARG for batch circuit satisfiability in NP.

Definition 10 (Batch circuit satisfiability). *Let λ be the security parameter. The* batch circuit satisfiability *language for an integer $m \in \mathbb{N}$ is defined as follows.*

$$\mathcal{L}_{\lambda}^{\mathsf{BatchCSAT}} = \{(\mathsf{C}, (\mathsf{x}_i)_{i\in[m]}) | \forall i \in [m] : \exists \mathsf{w}_i \in \{0,1\}^h : C(\mathsf{x}_i, \mathsf{w}_i) = 1\},$$

where $\mathsf{C} : \{0,1\}^n \times \{0,1\}^h \to \{0,1\}$ is any Boolean circuit with polynomial size in λ and $\mathsf{x}_1, \cdots, \mathsf{x}_m \in \{0,1\}^n$ are the statements. Without loss of generality, we assume that C *consists only of fan-in-2* NAND *gates.*

Let $\mathsf{par} = \mathcal{G}$ be the public parameter, where $\mathcal{G} = (\mathbb{G}_1, \mathbb{G}_2, \mathbb{G}_T, p, [1]_1, [1]_2, e) \xleftarrow{\$} \mathsf{GGen}(1^\lambda)$. We give our BARG for $\mathcal{L}_{\lambda}^{\mathsf{BatchCSAT}}$ in Fig. 7.

Theorem 4 (Completeness). BARG *is complete.*

Proof. **Validity of statement.** Since the first n wires corresponds to the statement, for honestly generated $([\mathbf{u}_d]_1 = \sum_{i\in[m]} \mathsf{w}_{i,d}[\mathbf{a}_i]_1)_{d\in[t]}$ and $([\mathbf{u}_d^*]_1 = \sum_{i\in[m]} \mathsf{x}_{i,d}[\mathbf{a}_i]_1)_{d\in[n]}$, we must have $\mathsf{x}_{i,d} = \mathsf{w}_{i,d}$ for all $i \in [m]$ and $d \in [n]$. Hence, we have $[\mathbf{u}_d]_1 = [\mathbf{u}_d^*]_1$ for all $d \in [n]$. Similarly, we have $[\hat{\mathbf{u}}_d]_2 = [\hat{\mathbf{u}}_d^*]_2$ for all $d \in [n]$. Moreover, when the witnesses are valid, we must have $\mathsf{w}_{i,t} = 1$ for all $i \in [m]$ for the output wire. Hence, we have $[\mathbf{u}_t]_1 = [\sum_{i\in[m]} \mathbf{a}_i]_1 = [\mathbf{a}]_1$ and $[\hat{\mathbf{u}}_t]_2 = [\sum_{i\in[m]} \hat{\mathbf{a}}_i]_2 = [\hat{\mathbf{a}}]_2$.

Validity of gate computation. For witnesses $(\mathsf{w}_i)_{i\in[m]}$, for each gate $G_\ell = (d_1, d_2, d_3)$, we have $(-1 + \mathsf{w}_{i,d_1} + \mathsf{w}_{i,d_3} = 0 \wedge -1 + \mathsf{w}_{i,d_2} = 0)$ or $(-1 + \mathsf{w}_{i,d_3} = 0 \wedge \mathsf{w}_{i,d_2} = 0)$ for all $i \in [m]$, which in turn implies

$$(-1 + \mathsf{w}_{i,d_1} + \mathsf{w}_{i,d_3})\mathsf{w}_{i,d_2} = 0 \text{ and } (-1 + \mathsf{w}_{i,d_3})(-1 + \mathsf{w}_{i,d_2}) = 0.$$

$\underline{\mathsf{BGen}(1^\lambda, \mathsf{par}, 1^m)}$:
Sample $\mathbf{M}, \hat{\mathbf{M}} \xleftarrow{\$} \mathcal{D}_k$ and $\alpha_i, \hat{\alpha}_i \xleftarrow{\$} \mathbb{Z}_p^k$ for all $i \in [m]$
Set $\mathbf{a}_i = \mathbf{M}\alpha_i$ and $\hat{\mathbf{a}}_i = \hat{\mathbf{M}}\hat{\alpha}_i$ for all $i \in [m]$, $\mathbf{a} = \sum_{i\in[m]} \mathbf{a}_i$, and $\hat{\mathbf{a}} = \sum_{i\in[m]} \hat{\mathbf{a}}_i$
For each $i, j \in [m]$ such that $i \neq j$, sample $\mathbf{R}_{i,j} \xleftarrow{\$} \mathbb{Z}_p^{k\times k}$, and set $\mathbf{B}_{i,j} = \mathbf{M}(\alpha_i\hat{\alpha}_j^\top + \mathbf{R}_{i,j})$ and $\hat{\mathbf{B}}_{i,j} = -\hat{\mathbf{M}}\mathbf{R}_{i,j}^\top$
Return $\mathsf{crs} = (\mathsf{par}, [\mathbf{M}]_1, [\hat{\mathbf{M}}]_2, [\mathbf{a}]_1, [\hat{\mathbf{a}}]_2, ([\mathbf{a}_i]_1, [\hat{\mathbf{a}}_i]_2)_{i\in[m]}, \{[\mathbf{B}_{i,j}]_1, [\hat{\mathbf{B}}_{i,j}]_2\}_{i\neq j})$

$\underline{\mathsf{BProve}(\mathsf{crs}, \mathsf{C} : \{0,1\}^n \times \{0,1\}^h \to \{0,1\}, (\mathsf{x}_i)_{i\in[m]}, (\mathsf{w}_i)_{i\in[m]})}$:
Define s and t to be the numbers of gates and wires of C respectively
For all $i \in [m]$, extend $(\mathsf{x}_i, \mathsf{w}_i)$ to $(\mathsf{w}_{i,j})_{j\in[t]}$ containing the bits of all wires in C
For each $d \in [t]$, set $[\mathbf{u}_d]_1 = \sum_{i\in[m]} \mathsf{w}_{i,d}[\mathbf{a}_i]_1$ and $[\hat{\mathbf{u}}_d]_2 = \sum_{i\in[m]} \mathsf{w}_{i,d}[\hat{\mathbf{a}}_i]_2$
For each gate $G_\ell = (d_1, d_2, d_3) \in [t]^3$ where $\ell \in [s]$, set

- $[\mathbf{V}_{\ell,1}]_1 = \sum_{i\neq j}(1 - \mathsf{w}_{i,d_1} - \mathsf{w}_{i,d_3})\mathsf{w}_{j,d_2}[\mathbf{B}_{i,j}]_1$
- $[\hat{\mathbf{V}}_{\ell,1}]_2 = \sum_{i\neq j}(1 - \mathsf{w}_{i,d_1} - \mathsf{w}_{i,d_3})\mathsf{w}_{j,d_2}[\hat{\mathbf{B}}_{i,j}]_2$
- $[\mathbf{V}_{\ell,2}]_1 = \sum_{i\neq j}\left(\mathsf{w}_{i,d_2} - (\mathsf{w}_{i,d_1} + \mathsf{w}_{i,d_3})\mathsf{w}_{j,d_2}\right)[\mathbf{B}_{i,j}]_1$
- $[\hat{\mathbf{V}}_{\ell,2}]_2 = \sum_{i\neq j}\left(\mathsf{w}_{i,d_2} - (\mathsf{w}_{i,d_1} + \mathsf{w}_{i,d_3})\mathsf{w}_{j,d_2}\right)[\hat{\mathbf{B}}_{i,j}]_2$
- $[\mathbf{W}_\ell]_1 = \sum_{i\neq j}(1 - \mathsf{w}_{i,d_3})(1 - \mathsf{w}_{j,d_2})[\mathbf{B}_{i,j}]_1$
- $[\hat{\mathbf{W}}_\ell]_2 = \sum_{i\neq j}(1 - \mathsf{w}_{i,d_3})(1 - \mathsf{w}_{j,d_2})[\hat{\mathbf{B}}_{i,j}]_2$

Return $\Pi = (([\mathbf{u}_d]_1, [\hat{\mathbf{u}}_d]_2)_{d\in[t]}, ([\mathbf{V}_{\ell,i}]_1, [\hat{\mathbf{V}}_{\ell,i}]_2)_{\ell\in[s],i\in[2]}, ([\mathbf{W}_\ell]_1, [\hat{\mathbf{W}}_\ell]_2)_{\ell\in[s]})$

$\underline{\mathsf{BVer}(\mathsf{crs}, \mathsf{C}, (\mathsf{x}_i)_{i\in[m]}, \Pi)}$:

- $\underline{\mathsf{GenVK}(\mathsf{crs}, (\mathsf{x}_i)_{i\in[m]})}$:
  Parse $\mathsf{x}_i = (\mathsf{x}_{i,1}, \cdots, \mathsf{x}_{i,n})$ for all $i \in [m]$
  For each $d \in [n]$, set $[\mathbf{u}_d^*]_1 = \sum_{i\in[m]} \mathsf{x}_{i,d}[\mathbf{a}_i]_1$ and $[\hat{\mathbf{u}}_d^*]_2 = \sum_{i\in[m]} \mathsf{x}_{i,d}[\hat{\mathbf{a}}_i]_2$
  Output $\mathsf{vk} = ([\mathbf{u}_d^*]_1, [\hat{\mathbf{u}}_d^*]_2)_{d\in[n]}$
- $\underline{\mathsf{OnlineVer}(\mathsf{vk}, \mathsf{C}, \Pi)}$:
  Check that $[\mathbf{u}_d]_1 = [\mathbf{u}_d^*]_1$ and $[\hat{\mathbf{u}}_d]_2 = [\hat{\mathbf{u}}_d^*]_2$ for all $d \in [n]$
  Check that $[\mathbf{u}_t]_1 = [\mathbf{a}]_1$ and $[\hat{\mathbf{u}}_t]_2 = [\hat{\mathbf{a}}]_2$
  For all $\ell \in [s]$, check that
  - $[\mathbf{a} - \mathbf{u}_{d_1} - \mathbf{u}_{d_3}]_1 \circ [\hat{\mathbf{u}}_{d_2}^\top]_2 = [\mathbf{M}]_1 \circ [\hat{\mathbf{V}}_{\ell,1}^\top]_2 + [\mathbf{V}_{\ell,1}]_1 \circ [\hat{\mathbf{M}}^\top]_2$
  - $[\mathbf{u}_{d_2}]_1 \circ [\hat{\mathbf{a}}^\top]_2 - [\mathbf{u}_{d_1} + \mathbf{u}_{d_3}]_1 \circ [\hat{\mathbf{u}}_{d_2}^\top]_2 = [\mathbf{M}]_1 \circ [\hat{\mathbf{V}}_{\ell,2}^\top]_2 + [\mathbf{V}_{\ell,2}]_1 \circ [\hat{\mathbf{M}}^\top]_2$
  - $[\mathbf{a} - \mathbf{u}_{d_3}]_1 \circ [\hat{\mathbf{a}}^\top - \hat{\mathbf{u}}_{d_2}^\top]_2 = [\mathbf{M}]_1 \circ [\hat{\mathbf{W}}_\ell^\top]_2 + [\mathbf{W}_\ell]_1 \circ [\hat{\mathbf{M}}^\top]_2$

  Return 1 iff all checks pass

Fig. 7. Definition of $\mathsf{BARG} = (\mathsf{BGen}, \mathsf{BProve}, \mathsf{BVer})$.

Moreover, for the CRS, we have

$$\mathbf{B}_{i,j}\hat{\mathbf{M}}^\top + \mathbf{M}\hat{\mathbf{B}}_{i,j}^\top = \mathbf{M}(\alpha_i\hat{\alpha}_j^\top + \mathbf{R}_{i,j})\hat{\mathbf{M}}^\top - \mathbf{M}\mathbf{R}_{i,j}\hat{\mathbf{M}}^\top = \mathbf{M}\alpha_i\hat{\alpha}_j^\top\hat{\mathbf{M}}^\top = \mathbf{a}_i\hat{\mathbf{a}}_j^\top.$$

Then for $((\mathbf{u}_d, \hat{\mathbf{u}}_d)_{d\in[t]}, ([\mathbf{V}_{\ell,i}, \mathbf{W}_\ell]_1, [\hat{\mathbf{V}}_{\ell,i}, \hat{\mathbf{W}}_\ell]_2)_{\ell\in[s],i\in[2]})$ in a valid proof, we have

$$\begin{aligned}(\mathbf{a} - \mathbf{u}_{d_1} - \mathbf{u}_{d_3})\hat{\mathbf{u}}_{d_2}^\top &= \sum_{i\in[m]}(1 - \mathsf{w}_{i,d_1} - \mathsf{w}_{i,d_3})\mathbf{a}_i \sum_{i\in[m]}\mathsf{w}_{i,d_2}\hat{\mathbf{a}}_i^\top \\ &= \Big(\underbrace{\sum_{i\in[m]}(1 - \mathsf{w}_{i,d_1} - \mathsf{w}_{i,d_3})\mathsf{w}_{i,d_2}\mathbf{a}_i\hat{\mathbf{a}}_i^\top}_{=0} + \sum_{i\neq j}(1 - \mathsf{w}_{i,d_1} - \mathsf{w}_{i,d_3})\mathsf{w}_{j,d_2}\mathbf{a}_i\hat{\mathbf{a}}_j^\top\Big) \\ &= \sum_{i\neq j}(1 - \mathsf{w}_{i,d_1} - \mathsf{w}_{i,d_3})\mathsf{w}_{j,d_2}\underbrace{(\mathbf{B}_{i,j}\hat{\mathbf{M}}^\top + \mathbf{M}\hat{\mathbf{B}}_{i,j}^\top)}_{=\mathbf{a}_i\hat{\mathbf{a}}_j^\top} = \mathbf{M}\hat{\mathbf{V}}_{\ell,1}^\top + \mathbf{V}_{\ell,1}\hat{\mathbf{M}}^\top,\end{aligned}$$

$$\begin{aligned}&\mathbf{u}_{d_2}\hat{\mathbf{a}}^\top - (\mathbf{u}_{d_1} + \mathbf{u}_{d_3})\hat{\mathbf{u}}_{d_2}^\top \\ &= \sum_{i\in[m]}\mathsf{w}_{i,d_2}\mathbf{a}_i \sum_{i\in[m]}\hat{\mathbf{a}}_i^\top - \sum_{i\in[m]}(\mathsf{w}_{i,d_1} + \mathsf{w}_{i,d_3})\mathbf{a}_i \sum_{i\in[m]}\mathsf{w}_{i,d_2}\hat{\mathbf{a}}_i^\top \\ &= \Big(\underbrace{\sum_{i\in[m]}(1 - \mathsf{w}_{i,d_1} - \mathsf{w}_{i,d_3})\mathsf{w}_{i,d_2}\mathbf{a}_i\hat{\mathbf{a}}_i^\top}_{=0} + \sum_{i\neq j}\big(\mathsf{w}_{i,d_2} - (\mathsf{w}_{i,d_1} + \mathsf{w}_{i,d_3})\mathsf{w}_{j,d_2}\big)\mathbf{a}_i\hat{\mathbf{a}}_j^\top\Big) \\ &= \sum_{i\neq j}\big(\mathsf{w}_{i,d_2} - (\mathsf{w}_{i,d_1} + \mathsf{w}_{i,d_3})\mathsf{w}_{j,d_2}\big)\underbrace{(\mathbf{B}_{i,j}\hat{\mathbf{M}}^\top + \mathbf{M}\hat{\mathbf{B}}_{i,j}^\top)}_{=\mathbf{a}_i\hat{\mathbf{a}}_j^\top} = \mathbf{M}\hat{\mathbf{V}}_{\ell,2}^\top + \mathbf{V}_{\ell,2}\hat{\mathbf{M}}^\top,\end{aligned}$$

$$\begin{aligned}&(\mathbf{a} - \mathbf{u}_{d_3})(\hat{\mathbf{a}}^\top - \hat{\mathbf{u}}_{d_2}^\top) \\ &= \sum_{i\in[m]}(1 - \mathsf{w}_{i,d_3})\mathbf{a}_i \sum_{i\in[m]}(1 - \mathsf{w}_{i,d_2})\hat{\mathbf{a}}_i^\top \\ &= \Big(\underbrace{\sum_{i\in[m]}(1 - \mathsf{w}_{i,d_3})(1 - \mathsf{w}_{i,d_2})\mathbf{a}_i\hat{\mathbf{a}}_i^\top}_{=0} + \sum_{i\neq j}(1 - \mathsf{w}_{i,d_3})(1 - \mathsf{w}_{j,d_2})\mathbf{a}_i\hat{\mathbf{a}}_j^\top\Big) \\ &= \sum_{i\neq j}(1 - \mathsf{w}_{i,d_3})(1 - \mathsf{w}_{j,d_2})\underbrace{(\mathbf{B}_{i,j}\hat{\mathbf{M}}^\top + \mathbf{M}\hat{\mathbf{B}}_{i,j}^\top)}_{=\mathbf{a}_i\hat{\mathbf{a}}_j^\top} = \mathbf{M}\hat{\mathbf{W}}_\ell^\top + \mathbf{W}_\ell\hat{\mathbf{M}}^\top.\end{aligned}$$

This completes the proof of completeness. □

Theorem 5 (Succinctness). BARG *is succinct.*

Proof. For our BARG in Fig. 7, we check the succinctness as follows.

Proof size. Each proof π consists of $t(k+1)+3s(k+1)k$ group elements in each of $\mathbb{G}_1$ and $\mathbb{G}_2$, where each group element can be represented in $\mathsf{poly}(\lambda)$ bits and k is constant. Since $t = \mathsf{poly}(s)$, we have $|\pi| = \mathsf{poly}(\lambda, s)$.

CRS size. Each CRS crs consists of the group description and $(k+1)k+(m+1)(k+1)+m(m-1)/2\cdot(k+1)k = O(k^2m^2)$ elements in each of $\mathbb{G}_1$ and $\mathbb{G}_2$. Thus we have $|\mathsf{crs}| = m^2 \cdot \mathsf{poly}(\lambda)$.

Verification key. Each verification key vk output by GenVK consists of $n(k+1)$ elements in each of $\mathbb{G}_1$ and $\mathbb{G}_2$. Thus we have $|\mathsf{vk}| = n \cdot \mathsf{poly}(\lambda)$.

Verification key generation time. GenVK performs $2mn(k+1)$ group operations, which requires $\mathsf{poly}(\lambda, m, n)$ time.

Online verification time. The OnlineVer consists of 3 steps in total, where the running time of each step is bounded by $nk\cdot\mathsf{poly}(\lambda)$, $k\cdot\mathsf{poly}(\lambda)$, and $sk^3\cdot\mathsf{poly}(\lambda)$ respectively. Since $n = \mathsf{poly}(s)$, the total running time is bounded by $\mathsf{poly}(s,\lambda)$

Putting all the above together, Theorem 5 immediately follows. □

Theorem 6 (Somewhere argument of knowledge). *Under the* $\mathcal{D}_k$-MDDH *assumption,* BARG *is a somewhere argument of knowledge.*

Proof. We define the trapdoor setup and extraction algorithms as in Fig. 8.

CRS indistinguishability. We prove the CRS indistinguishability by defining a sequence of intermediate games.

Let $\mathcal{A}$ be any PPT adversary against the CRS indistinguishability of BARG for some index $i^* \in [m]$. It receives a CRS crs generated by the challenger $\mathcal{CH}$ in each game as defined in Fig. 10.

Game G_0 and G_1. Game G_0 is the game where $\mathcal{CH}$ on receiving the index i^* from the adversary returns crs generated as $\mathsf{crs} \xleftarrow{\$} \mathsf{BGen}(1^\lambda, \mathsf{par}, 1^m)$ to $\mathcal{A}$. Game G_1 is exactly the same as G_0 except that $\mathbf{B}_{i,j}$ and $\hat{\mathbf{B}}_{i,j}$ are generated in a different way. □

Lemma 2. $\Pr[\mathsf{G}_0^{\mathcal{A}} \Rightarrow 1] = \Pr[\mathsf{G}_1^{\mathcal{A}} \Rightarrow 1]$.

Proof. For $j \neq i^*$, the distributions of $\mathbf{B}_{i,j}$ in Games G_0 and G_1 are identical, since

$$\mathbf{M}(\alpha_i\hat{\alpha}_j^\top + \mathbf{R}_{i,j}) = (\mathbf{M}\alpha_i)\hat{\alpha}_j^\top + \mathbf{M}\mathbf{R}_{i,j} = \mathbf{a}_i\hat{\alpha}_j^\top + \mathbf{M}\mathbf{R}_{i,j}.$$

For $j = i^*$, in G_0, we have $\mathbf{B}_{i,j} = \mathbf{M}(\alpha_i\hat{\alpha}_j^\top + \mathbf{R}_{i,j})$ and

$$\hat{\mathbf{B}}_{i,j} = -\hat{\mathbf{M}}\mathbf{R}_{i,j}^\top = \hat{\mathbf{M}}(\alpha_i\hat{\alpha}_j^\top)^\top - \hat{\mathbf{M}}(\mathbf{R}_{i,j} + \alpha_i\hat{\alpha}_j^\top)^\top = \hat{\mathbf{a}}_j\alpha_i^\top - \hat{\mathbf{M}}(\mathbf{R}_{i,j} + \alpha_i\hat{\alpha}_j^\top).$$

Since the distribution of $\mathbf{R}_{i,j} + \alpha_i\hat{\alpha}_j^\top$ is uniformly distributed, the distribution of $\mathbf{B}_{i,j}$ and $\hat{\mathbf{B}}_{i,j}$ is identical to that in G_1, completing this part of proof. □

$\underline{\mathsf{BTGen}(1^\lambda, \mathsf{par}, 1^m, i^*)}$:
Sample $\mathbf{M}, \hat{\mathbf{M}} \xleftarrow{\$} \mathcal{D}_k$ and $\alpha_i, \hat{\alpha}_i \xleftarrow{\$} \mathbb{Z}_p^k$ for all $i \neq i^*$
Sample $\mathbf{a}_{i^*} \xleftarrow{\$} \mathbb{Z}_p^{k+1} \backslash \mathsf{Span}(\mathbf{M})$ and $\hat{\mathbf{a}}_{i^*} \xleftarrow{\$} \mathbb{Z}_p^{k+1} \backslash \mathsf{Span}(\hat{\mathbf{M}})$
Set $\mathbf{a}_i = \mathbf{M}\alpha_i$ and $\hat{\mathbf{a}}_i = \hat{\mathbf{M}}\hat{\alpha}_i$ for all $i \neq i^*$, $\mathbf{a} = \sum_{i \in [m]} \mathbf{a}_i$, and $\hat{\mathbf{a}} = \sum_{i \in [m]} \hat{\mathbf{a}}_i$
For each $i, j \in [m]$ such that $i \neq j$,
- sample $\mathbf{R}_{i,j} \xleftarrow{\$} \mathbb{Z}_p^{k \times k}$
- set $\mathbf{B}_{i,j} = \mathbf{a}_i \hat{\alpha}_j^\top + \mathbf{M}\mathbf{R}_{i,j}$ and $\hat{\mathbf{B}}_{i,j} = -\hat{\mathbf{M}}\mathbf{R}_{i,j}^\top$ for all $i, j \in [m]$ and $j \neq i^*$
- set $\mathbf{B}_{i,j} = \mathbf{M}\mathbf{R}_{i,j}$ and $\hat{\mathbf{B}}_{i,j} = \hat{\mathbf{a}}_j \alpha_i^\top - \hat{\mathbf{M}}\mathbf{R}_{i,j}^\top$ for all $i \in [m]$ and $j = i^*$

Compute a non-zero vector $\tau \in \mathbb{Z}_p^{k+1}$ such that $\tau^\top \mathbf{M} = 0$ and $\tau^\top \mathbf{a}_{i^*} = 1$, which must exist and can be efficiently computed since $\mathbf{M}$ is of rank k
Return $\mathsf{crs} = (\mathsf{par}, [\mathbf{M}]_1, [\hat{\mathbf{M}}]_2, [\mathbf{a}]_1, [\hat{\mathbf{a}}]_2, ([\mathbf{a}_i]_1, [\hat{\mathbf{a}}_i]_2)_{i \in [m]}, \{[\mathbf{B}_{i,j}]_1, [\hat{\mathbf{B}}_{i,j}]_2\}_{i \neq j})$ and $\mathsf{td} = \tau$

$\underline{\mathsf{Ext}_{\mathsf{BARG}}(\mathsf{td}, \mathsf{C}, (\mathsf{x}_i)_{i \in [m]}, \Pi)}$:
Initialize the values for all wires in $\mathsf{C}(\mathsf{x}_{i^*}, \cdot)$ as $\perp$.
Run $\mathsf{F}_{\mathsf{BARG}}(\mathsf{td}, \mathsf{C}, G_t, \Pi)$, where G_t is the gate for the final output, to assign values for each wire in the circuit $\mathsf{C}(\mathsf{x}_{i^*}, \cdot)$
For each input wire $d \in [t]$ assigned with $\perp$, set $\mathsf{w}_{i^*,d} = 0$
Return the witness $\mathsf{w}_{i^*} = (\mathsf{w}_{i^*,i})_{i \in [h]}$ containing all bits for input values of $\mathsf{C}(\mathsf{x}_{i^*}, \cdot)$

Fig. 8. Definition of $(\mathsf{BTGen}, \mathsf{Ext}_{\mathsf{BARG}})$. $\mathsf{F}_{\mathsf{BARG}}$ is the recursion algorithm defined as in Fig. 9.

$\underline{\mathsf{F}_{\mathsf{BARG}}(\mathsf{td}, \mathsf{C}, G_\ell = (d_1, d_2, d_3), \Pi)}$:
Compute $\mathsf{temp}_i = \tau^\top [\mathbf{u}_{d_i}]_1$ for all $i = 1, 2, 3$
If $\mathsf{temp}_2 = [0]_1$ and $\mathsf{temp}_3 = [1]_1$:
- set $(\mathsf{w}_{i^*,d_1}, \mathsf{w}_{i^*,d_2}) = (\perp, 0)$
- stop if $\mathsf{Parent}_r(G_\ell) = \perp$, and run $\mathsf{F}_{\mathsf{BARG}}(\mathsf{td}, \mathsf{C}, \mathsf{Parent}_r(G_\ell), \Pi)$ otherwise

If $\mathsf{temp}_2 = [1]_1$ and $\mathsf{temp}_1 + \mathsf{temp}_3 = [1]_1$:
- if $\mathsf{temp}_3 \notin \{[0]_1, [1]_1\}$, abort $\mathsf{Ext}_{\mathsf{BARG}}$
- set $(\mathsf{w}_{i^*,d_1}, \mathsf{w}_{i^*,d_2}) = (b, 1)$ where $[b]_1 = \mathsf{temp}_1$ and $b \in \{0, 1\}$
- stop if $\mathsf{Parent}_l(G_\ell) = \perp$ and $\mathsf{Parent}_r(G_\ell) = \perp$
- run $\mathsf{F}_{\mathsf{BARG}}(\mathsf{td}, \mathsf{C}, \mathsf{Parent}_l(G_\ell), \Pi)$ and $\mathsf{F}_{\mathsf{BARG}}(\mathsf{td}, \mathsf{C}, \mathsf{Parent}_r(G_\ell), \Pi)$

If $\mathsf{temp}_1 = [0]_1$ and $\mathsf{temp}_3 = [1]_1$:
- set $(\mathsf{w}_{i^*,d_1}, \mathsf{w}_{i^*,d_2}) = (0, \perp)$
- stop if $\mathsf{Parent}_l(G_\ell) = \perp$
- run $\mathsf{F}_{\mathsf{BARG}}(\mathsf{td}, \mathsf{C}, \mathsf{Parent}_l(G_\ell), \Pi)$ otherwise

Otherwise, abort $\mathsf{Ext}_{\mathsf{BARG}}$

Fig. 9. Definition of $\mathsf{F}_{\mathsf{BARG}}$. Parent_l (repsectively, Parent_r) denotes the gate whose output is the left (respectively, right) input to G_ℓ.

Game G_2. G_2 is the same as G_1 except that $\mathbf{a}_{i^*}$ is randomly sampled outside the span of $\mathbf{M}$.

Lemma 3. *There exists an adversary* $\mathcal{B}_1$ *breaking the* $\mathcal{D}_k$-MDDH *assumption in* $\mathbb{G}_1$ *with probability at least* $|\Pr[\mathsf{G}_2^{\mathcal{A}} \Rightarrow 1] - \Pr[\mathsf{G}_1^{\mathcal{A}} \Rightarrow 1]| - 1/p$.

$\underline{\mathcal{CH}(\mathsf{par}, 1^m, i^*)}$: G_0, $\boxed{\mathsf{G}_1}$, G_2, G_3

Sample $\mathbf{M}, \hat{\mathbf{M}} \xleftarrow{\$} \mathcal{D}_k$ and $\alpha_i, \hat{\alpha}_i \xleftarrow{\$}$ for all $i \in [m]$

Set $\mathbf{a}_i = \mathbf{M}\alpha_i$ for all $i \in [m]$

Set $\mathbf{a}_i = \mathbf{M}\alpha_i$ for all $i \neq i^*$ and sample $\mathbf{a}_{i^*} \xleftarrow{\$} \mathbb{Z}_p^{k+1} \backslash \mathsf{Span}(\mathbf{M})$

Set $\hat{\mathbf{a}}_i = \hat{\mathbf{M}}\hat{\alpha}_i$ for all $i \in [m]$

Set $\hat{\mathbf{a}}_i = \hat{\mathbf{M}}\hat{\alpha}_i$ for all $i \neq i^*$ and sample $\hat{\mathbf{a}}_{i^*} \xleftarrow{\$} \mathbb{Z}_p^{k+1} \backslash \mathsf{Span}(\hat{\mathbf{M}})$

Set $\mathbf{a} = \sum_{i \in [m]} \mathbf{a}_i$ and $\hat{\mathbf{a}} = \sum_{i \in [m]} \hat{\mathbf{a}}_i$

For each $i, j \in [m]$ such that $i \neq j$,

- sample $\mathbf{R}_{i,j} \xleftarrow{\$} \mathbb{Z}_p^{k \times k}$
- set $\mathbf{B}_{i,j} = \mathbf{M}(\alpha_i \hat{\alpha}_j^\top + \mathbf{R}_{i,j})$ and $\hat{\mathbf{B}}_{i,j} = -\hat{\mathbf{M}}\mathbf{R}_{i,j}^\top$
- $\boxed{\text{set } \mathbf{B}_{i,j} = \mathbf{a}_i \hat{\alpha}_j^\top + \mathbf{M}\mathbf{R}_{i,j} \text{ and } \hat{\mathbf{B}}_{i,j} = -\hat{\mathbf{M}}\mathbf{R}_{i,j}^\top \text{ for all } j \neq i^*}$
- $\boxed{\text{set } \mathbf{B}_{i,j} = \mathbf{M}\mathbf{R}_{i,j} \text{ and } \hat{\mathbf{B}}_{i,j} = \hat{\mathbf{a}}_j \alpha_i^\top - \hat{\mathbf{M}}\mathbf{R}_{i,j}^\top \text{ for } j = i^*}$

Return $\mathsf{crs} = (\mathsf{par}, [\mathbf{M}]_1, [\hat{\mathbf{M}}]_2, [\mathbf{a}]_1, [\hat{\mathbf{a}}]_2, ([\mathbf{a}_i]_1, [\hat{\mathbf{a}}_i]_2)_{i \in [m]}, \{[\mathbf{B}_{i,j}]_1, [\hat{\mathbf{B}}_{i,j}]_2\}_{i \neq j})$

Fig. 10. Challenger $\mathcal{CH}$ in the intermediate games.

Proof. We build $\mathcal{B}_1$ as follows.

$\mathcal{B}_1$ runs in exactly the same way as the challenger of G_1 except that instead of generating $[\mathbf{a}_{i^*}]_1$ by itself, it takes as input $[\mathbf{a}_{i^*}]_1$ generated as $\mathbf{a}_{i^*} \xleftarrow{\$} \mathbb{Z}_p^{k+1}$ or $\mathbf{a}_{i^*} = \mathbf{M}\alpha_{i^*}$ where $\alpha_{i^*} \xleftarrow{\$} \mathbb{Z}_p^k$ from its own challenger. When $\mathcal{A}$ outputs $\beta \in \{0, 1\}$, $\mathcal{B}_1$ outputs β as well.

If $\mathbf{a}_{i^*}$ is generated as $\mathbf{a}_{i^*} = \mathbf{M}\alpha_{i^*}$ where $\alpha_{i^*} \xleftarrow{\$} \mathbb{Z}_p^k$, the view of $\mathcal{A}$ is the same as its view in G_1. Otherwise, the view of $\mathcal{A}$ is $1/p$-statistically close to its view in G_2. Hence, the probability that $\mathcal{B}_1$ breaks the $\mathcal{D}_k$-MDDH assumption is at least $|\Pr[\mathsf{G}_2^{\mathcal{A}} \Rightarrow 1] - \Pr[\mathsf{G}_1^{\mathcal{A}} \Rightarrow 1]| - 1/p$, completing this part of proof. □

Game G_3. G_3 is the game $\mathcal{CH}$ returns crs generated by $\mathsf{BTGen}(1^\lambda, \mathsf{par}, 1^m, i^*)$. It is exactly the same as G_2 except that $\hat{\mathbf{a}}_{i^*}$ is randomly sampled outside the span of $\hat{\mathbf{M}}$.

Lemma 4. *There exists an adversary* $\mathcal{B}_2$ *breaking the* $\mathcal{D}_k$-MDDH *assumption in* $\mathbb{G}_2$ *with probability at least* $|\Pr[\mathsf{G}_3^{\mathcal{A}} \Rightarrow 1] - \Pr[\mathsf{G}_2^{\mathcal{A}} \Rightarrow 1]| - 1/p$.

Proof. We build $\mathcal{B}_2$ as follows.

$\mathcal{B}_2$ runs in exactly the same way as the challenger of G_2 except that instead of generating $[\hat{\mathbf{a}}_{i^*}]_2$ by itself, it takes as input $[\hat{\mathbf{a}}_{i^*}]_2$ generated as $\hat{\mathbf{a}}_{i^*} \xleftarrow{\$} \mathbb{Z}_p^{k+1}$ or $\hat{\mathbf{a}}_{i^*} = \hat{\mathbf{M}}\hat{\alpha}_{i^*}$ where $\hat{\alpha}_{i^*} \xleftarrow{\$} \mathbb{Z}_p^k$ from its own challenger. When $\mathcal{A}$ outputs $\beta \in \{0, 1\}$, $\mathcal{B}_2$ outputs β as well.

If $\hat{\mathbf{a}}_{i^*}$ is generated as $\hat{\mathbf{a}}_{i^*} = \hat{\mathbf{M}}\hat{\alpha}_{i^*}$ where $\hat{\alpha}_{i^*} \xleftarrow{\$} \mathbb{Z}_p^k$, the view of $\mathcal{A}$ is the same as its view in G_2. Otherwise, the view of $\mathcal{A}$ is $1/p$-statistically close to G_3. Hence, the probability that $\mathcal{B}_2$ breaks the k-MDDH assumption is $|\Pr[\mathsf{G}_3^{\mathcal{A}} \Rightarrow 1] - \Pr[\mathsf{G}_2^{\mathcal{A}} \Rightarrow 1]| - 1/p$, completing this part of proof. □

Putting all the above together, the CRS indistinguishability of BARG immediately follows.

Somewhere extractability in the trapdoor mode. We now argue that for any valid statement/proof pair $((\mathsf{x}_i)_{i\in[m]}, \Pi)$, the extractor must be able to extract a valid witness w_{i^*} for x_{i^*}.

For each NAND gate G_ℓ with commitments $(\mathbf{u}_{d_i}, \hat{\mathbf{u}}_{d_i})_{i\in[3]}$ and proof $(([\mathbf{V}_{\ell,i}]_1, [\hat{\mathbf{V}}_{\ell,i}]_2)_{i\in[2]}, [\mathbf{W}_\ell, \hat{\mathbf{W}}_\ell]_1)$, we have

$$[\mathbf{a} - \mathbf{u}_{d_1} - \mathbf{u}_{d_3}]_1 \circ [\hat{\mathbf{u}}_{d_2}^\top]_2 = [\mathbf{M}]_1 \circ [\hat{\mathbf{V}}_{\ell,1}^\top]_2 + [\mathbf{V}_{\ell,1}]_1 \circ [\hat{\mathbf{M}}^\top]_2,$$

$$[\mathbf{u}_{d_2}]_1 \circ [\hat{\mathbf{a}}^\top]_2 - [\mathbf{u}_{d_1} + \mathbf{u}_{d_3}]_1 \circ [\hat{\mathbf{u}}_{d_2}^\top]_2 = [\mathbf{M}]_1 \circ [\hat{\mathbf{V}}_{\ell,2}^\top]_2 + [\mathbf{V}_{\ell,2}]_1 \circ [\hat{\mathbf{M}}^\top]_2,$$

$$[\mathbf{a} - \mathbf{u}_{d_3}]_1 \circ [\hat{\mathbf{a}}^\top - \hat{\mathbf{u}}_{d_2}^\top]_2 = [\mathbf{M}]_1 \circ [\hat{\mathbf{W}}_{\ell,1}^\top]_2 + [\mathbf{W}_{\ell,1}]_1 \circ [\hat{\mathbf{M}}^\top]_2.$$

Recall that τ is the trapdoor in Fig. 8, and let $\hat{\tau}$ be the vector in the kernel of $\hat{\mathbf{M}}$ such that $\hat{\tau}^\top \hat{\mathbf{a}}_{i^*} = 1$, which must exist when $\hat{\mathbf{a}}_{i^*} \notin \mathsf{Span}(\hat{\mathbf{M}})$. Since $\tau^\top \mathbf{a} = \hat{\tau}^\top \hat{\mathbf{a}} = 1$ and $\tau^\top \mathbf{M} = \hat{\tau}^\top \hat{\mathbf{M}}$, where τ is the trapdoor in Fig. 8, the above equations imply

$$[1 - \tau^\top \mathbf{u}_{d_1} - \tau^\top \mathbf{u}_{d_3}]_1 \circ [\hat{\mathbf{u}}_{d_2}^\top \hat{\tau}]_2 = [0]_T \tag{4}$$

$$[\tau^\top \mathbf{u}_{d_2}]_1 \circ [1]_2 - [\tau^\top \mathbf{u}_{d_1} + \tau^\top \mathbf{u}_{d_3}]_1 \circ [\hat{\mathbf{u}}_{d_2}^\top \hat{\tau}]_2 = [0]_T, \tag{5}$$

$$[1 - \tau^\top \mathbf{u}_{d_3}]_1 \circ [1 - \hat{\mathbf{u}}_{d_2}^\top \hat{\tau}]_2 = [0]_T. \tag{6}$$

The quotient of the Eqs. (4) and (5) yields $[\tau^\top \mathbf{u}_{d_2}]_T = [\hat{\mathbf{u}}_{d_2}^\top \hat{\tau}]_T$. Then, combining Eqs. (4) and (6) yields $1 - \tau^\top \mathbf{u}_{d_1} - \tau^\top \mathbf{u}_{d_3} = 0 \wedge 1 - \tau^\top \mathbf{u}_{d_2} = 0$ or $1 - \tau^\top \mathbf{u}_{d_3} = 0 \wedge \tau^\top \mathbf{u}_{d_2} = 0$ or $1 - \tau^\top \mathbf{u}_{d_1} - \tau^\top \mathbf{u}_{d_3} = 0 \wedge 1 - \tau^\top \mathbf{u}_{d_3} = 0$, i.e., $1 - \tau^\top \mathbf{u}_{d_3} = 0 \wedge \tau^\top \mathbf{u}_{d_1} = 0$. Moreover, we must have $\tau^\top \mathbf{u}_{d_t} = \tau^\top [\mathbf{a}]_1 = [1]_1$ for the output wire. As a result, for a valid proof, $\mathsf{F}_{\mathsf{BARG}}$ (see Fig. 9) will never abort during the execution of $\mathsf{Ext}_{\mathsf{BARG}}$, and running $\mathsf{F}_{\mathsf{BARG}}$ recursively will result in bits for input wires leading the statement circuit to output 1. Notice that after running $\mathsf{F}_{\mathsf{BARG}}(\mathsf{td}, \mathsf{C}, G_t, \Pi)$, there might be some input wires assigned with $\perp$. However, these wires do not affect the final output and can be assigned with 0.

As a result, we can extract the bits for all wires consisting of valid input/output pairs for all NAND gates and leading the statement circuit to output 1, completing the proof of perfect soundness.

Putting all the above together, Theorem 6 immediately follows. □

Proof size and proving and online verification cost. By instantiating our construction under the SXDH assumption, each proof of our BARG consists of $(2t+6s)$ elements in both $\mathbb{G}_1$ and $\mathbb{G}_2$, where t and s are the numbers of wires and gates in the statement circuit respectively. The proof size is strictly smaller than that of WW-BARG, which require $(4t+4s)$ elements in both $\mathbb{G}_1$ and $\mathbb{G}_2$. Moreover, the proving and online verification procedures in our construction require only $4mt + 6m(m-1)s$ multiplications and $40s$ pairing products respectively. In contrast, those in WW-BARG require $4m^2t + 4m(m-1)s$ multiplications and $24t + 32s$ pairing products (after merging items with multiplication in $\mathbb{G}_1$ and $\mathbb{G}_2$).

Construction in the symmetric pairing. Transplanting our construction to the setting of symmetric composite-order pairing groups yields a BARG under the subgroup decision assumption. Compared to the WW-BARG, we reduce the proof size by $(2t + s) - (t + 2s) = t - s$ group elements in $\mathbb{G}$. Also, the number of multiplications and pairing products required in the proving and online verification procedures are reduced by $m(m-1)t - (m(m-1)/2)s$ and $(2t + 3s) - 4s = 2t - s$ respectively. We refer the reader to the full paper for the construction and security proof.

Bootstrapping to reduce CRS size. Similar to WW-BARG, by using the bootstrapping technique in [48], we can reduce the CRS size of our BARG to $m^c \cdot \mathsf{poly}(\lambda, s)$ for any $c > 0$. As a trade-off, the proof size will be dependent on $\log(m)$. A recent work by Kalai et al. [35] shows a general construction to convert BARGs into ones having both CRSs and proofs of size $\mathsf{poly}(\lambda, \log m, s)$. Instantiating the underlying BARG with ours immediately an efficient construction with both succinct CRSs and succinct proofs.

5 Experimental Performance

In this section, we experimentally evaluate the proving cost, verification cost, and the proof size of our NIZK and BARG for NP and compare them with GOS-NIZK and WW-BARG respectively. We focus on SXDH based implementations in asymmetric Type-3 pairings, since it is the most efficient one amongst all different types of pairings as mentioned in the introduction. The GOS-NIZK and WW-BARG are implemented by ourselves since the open sourced implementations are not available.

We implement NIZK and BARG schemes in C++ atop pairing-friendly curve `bls12-381` in the `mcl` library [47]. Parameters of all schemes are set to achieve 128-bit security level. All experiments are carried on a Macbook Pro with Intel i5-7360U CPU (2.30 GHz) and 16 GB, where a single exponentiation and pairing respectively take about 0.08 ms and 0.8 ms.

In Tables 3 and 4, we present experimental results regarding the proving and verification costs and the proof sizes of our NIZK and GOS-NIZK. The comparisons are carried out for both schemes under different ratios between the number of gates and wires, namely 2.00, 1.50, and 1.06. We also evaluated their performance across statement circuit sizes ranging from 2^8 to 2^{12}. Our prover is 1.52×, 1.32×, and 1.11× faster than GOS-NIZK when the ratios are 2.00, 1.50, and 1.06 respectively. For the same ratios, our verifier is 1.44×, 1.21×, and 1.02× faster. Additionally, our proof sizes are 1.62×, 1.38×, and 1.16× smaller. One can see that our scheme outperforms GOS-NIZK in every aspect, and the significance of our improvement increases as the ratio becomes larger. Additionally, we note

Table 3. Comparison of the proving and verification cost (in seconds) between GOS-NIZK and our NIZK.

Scheme	Ratio	Proving Cost (seconds)					Verification Cost (seconds)				
		2^8	2^9	2^{10}	2^{11}	2^{12}	2^8	2^9	2^{10}	2^{11}	2^{12}
GOS12 [29]	2.00	1.38	2.69	5.39	10.81	21.72	12.55	25.80	50.57	101.11	201.95
Ours		0.87	1.82	3.51	6.99	14.37	8.68	17.38	37.23	70.04	138.70
GOS12 [29]	1.50	1.17	2.23	4.55	9.27	17.87	10.61	21.15	42.28	84.91	168.13
Ours		0.85	1.69	3.49	6.74	13.75	8.61	17.27	34.74	68.60	141.79
GOS12 [29]	1.06	0.91	1.83	3.65	7.32	14.65	8.61	17.25	34.49	69.01	138.28
Ours		0.83	1.65	3.30	6.64	13.25	8.58	17.12	34.81	68.53	137.28

Table 4. Comparison of the proof size (in MB) between GOS-NIZK and our NIZK.

Scheme	Proof Size (MB) (Ratio: 2.00)					Proof Size (MB) (Ratio: 1.50)					Proof Size (MB) (Ratio: 1.06)				
	2^8	2^9	2^{10}	2^{11}	2^{12}	2^8	2^9	2^{10}	2^{11}	2^{12}	2^8	2^9	2^{10}	2^{11}	2^{12}
GOS12 [29]	0.61	1.22	2.44	4.87	9.75	0.50	1.01	2.01	4.03	8.06	0.41	0.82	1.64	3.29	6.58
Ours	0.37	0.75	1.50	3.00	6.00	0.36	0.73	1.45	2.90	5.81	0.35	0.70	1.41	2.82	5.65

that the ratio tends to be 2 (i.e., its upper bound) when most gates do not share common input wires, and the ratio tends to be close to 1 (i.e., its lower bound) when most gates share common input wires, which may happen when most gates have multiple fan-out and the witness size is very small. Similar same argument can also be made for our BARG.

In Tables 5 and 6, we present experimental results regarding the proving and verification costs and the proof sizes of our BARG and WW-BARG when proving 50 and 100 statements. The comparisons are carried out for both schemes under different ratios between the number of gates and wires, namely 2.00, 1.50, and 1.06. We also evaluated their performance across statement circuit sizes ranging from 2^8 to 2^{12}. For proving 100 statement instances, our prover is 2.27×, 1.63×, and 1.35× faster than WW-BARG when the ratios are 2.00, 1.50, and 1.06 respectively. For the same ratios, the verifier is 2.70×, 2.35×, and 1.92× faster. For proving 50 statement instances with respect to these ratios, our prover is 2.13×, 1.51×, and 1.28× faster, and our verifier is 2.63×, 2.27×, and 1.94× faster. Additionally, our proof sizes are 1.20×, 1.11×, and 1.02× smaller, regardless of the number of statement instances. As a result, our scheme outperforms WW-BARG in every aspect.

Table 5. Comparison of the proving and verification costs (in seconds) between WW-BARG and our BARG. "stats." means statement instances.

Scheme	Ratio	Proving Cost (seconds)					Verification Cost (seconds)				
		2^8	2^9	2^{10}	2^{11}	2^{12}	2^8	2^9	2^{10}	2^{11}	2^{12}
WW22 [48] (100 stats.)	2.00	2.50	4.64	9.93	18.36	37.44	15.69	30.23	65.45	123.66	255.95
Ours (100 stats.)		1.07	2.02	4.10	8.00	16.91	5.90	11.61	23.38	46.41	94.46
WW22 [48] (50 stats.)	2.00	0.61	1.22	2.46	4.71	9.74	16.43	31.16	62.21	118.37	253.20
Ours (50 stats.)		0.29	0.55	1.20	2.05	4.67	5.68	11.44	23.40	46.56	95.28
WW22 [48] (100 stats.)	1.50	1.51	3.11	6.06	12.61	25.43	13.38	26.69	52.00	108.68	212.98
Ours (100 stats.)		1.02	1.87	4.09	7.56	16.57	5.95	11.20	22.94	44.92	92.28
WW22 [48] (50 stats.)	1.50	0.39	0.82	1.56	3.39	6.49	12.56	26.17	52.23	108.45	211.41
Ours (50 stats.)		0.26	0.57	1.03	2.23	4.30	6.25	11.90	23.27	46.47	93.22
WW22 [48] (100 stats.)	1.06	1.84	3.80	7.67	14.80	30.73	15.27	30.21	62.68	119.36	248.12
Ours (100 stats.)		1.00	1.99	3.82	8.53	15.95	5.81	12.19	23.11	46.63	96.11
WW22 [48] (50 stats.)	1.06	0.42	0.67	1.30	2.61	5.40	11.51	22.91	43.82	94.81	182.75
Ours (50 stats.)		0.25	0.50	1.13	2.08	4.13	6.16	11.86	23.97	47.32	93.92

Table 6. Comparison of the proof size (in MB) between WW-BARG and our BARG. "stats." means statement instances.

Scheme	Proof Size (MB) (Ratio: 2.00)					Proof Size (MB) (Ratio: 1.50)					Proof Size (MB) (Ratio: 1.06)				
	2^8	2^9	2^{10}	2^{11}	2^{12}	2^8	2^9	2^{10}	2^{11}	2^{12}	2^8	2^9	2^{10}	2^{11}	2^{12}
WW22 [48] (100 stats.)	0.42	0.84	1.69	3.37	6.75	0.35	0.70	1.41	2.81	5.62	0.29	0.58	1.16	2.32	4.64
Ours (100 stats.)	0.35	0.70	1.41	2.81	5.62	0.32	0.63	1.26	2.53	5.06	0.28	0.57	1.14	2.28	4.57
WW22 [48] (50 stats.)	0.42	0.84	1.69	3.37	6.75	0.35	0.70	1.41	2.81	5.62	0.29	0.58	1.16	2.32	4.64
Ours (50 stats.)	0.35	0.70	1.41	2.81	5.62	0.32	0.63	1.26	2.53	5.06	0.28	0.57	1.14	2.28	4.57

Acknowledgement. Parts of Yuyu Wang's work was supported by the National Natural Science Foundation for Young Scientists of China under Grant Number 62002049, the Natural Science Foundation of Sichuan under Grant Number 2023NSFSC0472, the Sichuan Science and Technology Program under Grant Number 2022YFG0037, and the National Key Research and Development Program of China under Grant Number 2022YFB3104600. Parts of Jiaxin Pan's work was supported by the Research Council of Norway under Project No. 324235. Parts of Yu Chen's work was supported by the National Key Research and Development Program of China under Grant Number 2021YFA1000600, the National Natural Science Foundation of China under Grant Numbers 62272269 and 61932019, Taishan Scholar Program of Shandong Province.

Appendix

A GOS-NIZK in the Asymmetric Pairing Setting

The original GOS-NIZK [29] was proposed in the symmetric pairing setting. In this section, we give the GOS-NIZK in the asymmetric pairing setting. It was previously indicated by [22,45] but has never been treated explicitly.

Let λ be the security parameter and $\mathsf{par} = \mathcal{G}$ be the public parameter, where $\mathcal{G} = (\mathbb{G}_1, \mathbb{G}_2, \mathbb{G}_T, p, [1]_1, [1]_2, e) \stackrel{\$}{\leftarrow} \mathsf{GGen}(1^\lambda)$, and $\mathsf{ORNIZK} = (\mathsf{NGen}_{\mathsf{or}}, \mathsf{NProve}_{\mathsf{or}}, \mathsf{NVer}_{\mathsf{or}})$ be a NIZK with the simulator $(\mathsf{NTGen}_{\mathsf{or}}, \mathsf{NSim}_{\mathsf{or}})$. Let $\mathsf{L}^{\mathsf{or}}_{[\mathbf{M}]_1}$ be the following language it supports.

$$\mathsf{L}^{\mathsf{or}}_{[\mathbf{M}]_1} = \{(\mathsf{C}_{[\mathbf{M}]_1}, ([\mathbf{x}_0]_1, [\mathbf{x}_1]_1)) | \exists \mathbf{w} \in \mathbb{Z}_p^{2k} : \mathsf{C}_{[\mathbf{M}]_1}(([\mathbf{x}_0]_1, [\mathbf{x}_1]_1), \mathbf{w}) = 1\},$$

where $\mathsf{C}_{[\mathbf{M}]_1} : \mathbb{G}_1^{k+1} \times \mathbb{G}_1^{k+1} \times \mathbb{Z}_p^k \rightarrow \{0,1\}$ is a Boolean circuit on input $((\mathbf{x}_0, \mathbf{x}_1), \mathbf{w})$ outputting 1 iff $[\mathbf{x}_0]_1 = [\mathbf{M}]_1\mathbf{w} \vee [\mathbf{x}_1]_1 = [\mathbf{M}]_1\mathbf{w}$ for $\mathbf{M} \in \mathcal{D}_k$. We give the NIZK NIZK^* in Fig. 11.

Theorem 7 (Completeness). *If* ORNIZK *is complete, then* NIZK^* *is complete.*

Proof. Let w_{d_1} and w_{d_2} be the input bits of a NAND gate, and w_{d_3} be the true output. We must have $\mathsf{w}_{d_1} + \mathsf{w}_{d_2} + 2\mathsf{w}_{d_3} - 2 \in \{0,1\}$. Let $\mathsf{cm}_{d_1} = [\mathbf{M}\mathbf{r}_{d_1} + \mathbf{z}\mathsf{w}_{d_1}]_1$ and $\mathsf{cm}_{d_2} = [\mathbf{M}\mathbf{r}_{d_2} + \mathbf{z}\mathsf{w}_{d_2}]_1$ be the input commitments and $\mathsf{cm}_{d_3} = [\mathbf{M}\mathbf{r}_{d_3} + \mathbf{z}\mathsf{w}_{d_3}]_1$ be the output commitment. We have

$$\begin{aligned}\mathsf{x}_\ell &= \mathsf{cm}_{d_1} + \mathsf{cm}_{d_2} + 2\mathsf{cm}_{d_3} - [\mathbf{z} \cdot 2]_1 \\ &= [\mathbf{M}]_1(\mathbf{r}_{d_1} + \mathbf{r}_{d_2} + 2\mathbf{r}_{d_3}) + [\mathbf{z}]_1(\mathsf{w}_{d_1} + \mathsf{w}_{d_2} + 2\mathsf{w}_{d_3} - 2).\end{aligned}$$

Therefore, for all $\ell \in [s]$, we must have $\mathsf{x}_\ell \in \mathsf{Span}([\mathbf{M}]_1)$ or $\mathsf{x}_\ell - [\mathbf{z}]_1 \in \mathsf{Span}([\mathbf{M}]_1)$. Moreover, for all $i \in [t]$, we have $\mathsf{cm}_i \in \mathsf{Span}([\mathbf{M}]_1)$ or $\mathsf{cm}_i - [\mathbf{z}]_1 \in \mathsf{Span}([\mathbf{M}]_1)$. Then the completeness of NIZK follows from the completeness of ORNIZK, completing the proof of Theorem 7. □

Theorem 8 (Composable zero-knowledge). *Under the* $\mathcal{D}_k$-MDDH *assumption, if* ORNIZK *is a NIZK with composable zero-knowledge, then* NIZK *is a NIZK with composable zero-knowledge.*

$\underline{\mathsf{NGen}^*(1^\lambda, \mathsf{par})}$:
$\mathbf{M} \xleftarrow{\$} \mathcal{D}_k$, $\mathsf{crs}_{\mathsf{or}} \xleftarrow{\$} \mathsf{NTGen}_{\mathsf{or}}(\mathsf{par}, \mathsf{C}_{[\mathbf{M}]_1})$, $\mathbf{z} \xleftarrow{\$} \mathbb{Z}_p^{k+1} \backslash \mathsf{Span}(\mathbf{M})$
Return $\mathsf{CRS} = (\mathsf{crs}_{\mathsf{or}}, [\mathbf{M}]_1, [\mathbf{z}]_1)$

$\underline{\mathsf{NProve}^*(\mathsf{CRS}, \mathsf{C}, \mathsf{x}, \mathsf{w})}$:
Hardwire x in C to obtain the circuit $\mathsf{C}(\mathsf{x}, \cdot) : \{0,1\}^h \to \{0,1\}$
Define s and t to be the numbers of gates and wires of $\mathsf{C}(\mathsf{x}, \cdot)$ respectively
Extend w to $(\mathsf{w}_i)_{i \in [t]}$ containing the bits of all wires in $\mathsf{C}(\mathsf{x}, \cdot)$
Compute $\mathbf{r}_i \xleftarrow{\$} \mathbb{Z}_p^{k+1}$ and $\mathsf{cm}_i = [\mathbf{M}]_1 \mathbf{r}_i + [\mathbf{z}]_1 \mathsf{w}_i$ for all $i \in [t-1]$
Set $\mathbf{r}_t = \mathbf{0}$ and $\mathsf{cm}_t = [\mathbf{z}]_1$ for the output wire
Compute $\hat{\pi}_i \xleftarrow{\$} \mathsf{NProve}_{\mathsf{or}}(\mathsf{crs}_{\mathsf{or}}, \mathsf{C}_{[\mathbf{M}]_1}, (\mathsf{cm}_i, \mathsf{cm}_i - [\mathbf{z}]_1), \mathbf{r}_i)$ for all $i \in [t]$
For each NAND gate $G_\ell = (d_1, d_2, d_3) \in [t]^3$ where $\ell \in [s]$, run
- $\mathsf{x}_\ell = \mathsf{cm}_{d_1} + \mathsf{cm}_{d_2} + 2\mathsf{cm}_{d_3} - [\mathbf{z} \cdot 2]_1$, $\mathsf{r}_\ell = \mathbf{r}_{d_1} + \mathbf{r}_{d_2} + 2\mathbf{r}_{d_3}$
- $\pi_\ell \xleftarrow{\$} \mathsf{NProve}_{\mathsf{or}}(\mathsf{crs}_{\mathsf{or}}, \mathsf{C}_{[\mathbf{M}]_1}, (\mathsf{x}_\ell, \mathsf{x}_\ell - [\mathbf{z}]_1), \mathsf{r}_\ell)$

Return $\Pi = ((\mathsf{cm}_i, \hat{\pi}_i)_{i \in [t]}, (\pi_\ell)_{\ell \in [s]})$

$\underline{\mathsf{NVer}^*(\mathsf{CRS}, \mathsf{C}, \mathsf{x}, \Pi)}$:
Hardwire x in C to obtain $\mathsf{C}(\mathsf{x}, \cdot)$ in the same way as NProve^* does
Check that all wires in $\mathsf{C}(\mathsf{x}, \cdot)$ have a corresponding commitment and $\mathsf{cm}_t = [\mathbf{z}]_1$
Check that all NAND gates have a valid NIZK proof of compliance
Return 1 iff all checks pass

Fig. 11. Definition of $\mathsf{NIZK}^* = (\mathsf{NGen}^*, \mathsf{NProve}^*, \mathsf{NVer}^*)$.

Proof. We define the simulator $(\mathsf{NTGen}^*, \mathsf{NSim}^*)$ as in Fig. 12.

First we note that the distribution of $\mathbf{z} \xleftarrow{\$} \mathbb{Z}_p^{k+1} \backslash \mathsf{Span}(\mathbf{M})$ is $1/p$-statistically close to the uniform distribution over $\mathbb{Z}_p^{k+1}$. Then the indistinguishability of CRSs generated by NGen^* and NTGen^* follows immediately from the $\mathcal{D}_k$-MDDH assumption and the composable zero-knowledge of ORNIZK (which says that $\mathsf{crs}_{\mathsf{or}}$ generated by $\mathsf{NGen}_{\mathsf{or}}(1^\lambda, \mathsf{par})$ and $\mathsf{NTGen}_{\mathsf{or}}(1^\lambda, \mathsf{par})$ are computationally close).

Next we define a modified prover $\mathsf{NProve}^{*\prime}$, which is exactly the same as NProve^* except that $\hat{\pi}_i$ is generated as

$$\hat{\pi}_i \xleftarrow{\$} \mathsf{NSim}_{\mathsf{or}}(\mathsf{crs}_{\mathsf{or}}, \mathsf{td}_{\mathsf{or}}, \mathsf{C}_{[\mathbf{M}]_1}, (\mathsf{cm}_i, \mathsf{cm}_i - [\mathbf{z}]_1))$$

for $i \in [t]$, and for each NAND gate π_ℓ is generated as

$$\pi_\ell \xleftarrow{\$} \mathsf{NSim}_{\mathsf{or}}(\mathsf{crs}_{\mathsf{or}}, \mathsf{td}_{\mathsf{or}}, \mathsf{C}_{[\mathbf{M}]_1}, (\mathsf{x}_\ell, \mathsf{x}_\ell - [\mathbf{z}]_1)).$$

The following distributions are identical due to the composable zero-knowledge of ORNIZK.

$$\Pi \xleftarrow{\$} \mathsf{NProve}^*(\mathsf{CRS}, \mathsf{C}, \mathsf{x}, \mathsf{w}) \text{ and } \Pi \xleftarrow{\$} \mathsf{NProve}^{*\prime}(\mathsf{CRS}, \mathsf{C}, \mathsf{x}, \mathsf{w})$$

for $(\mathsf{CRS}, \mathsf{TD}) \xleftarrow{\$} \mathsf{NTGen}^*(1^\lambda, \mathsf{par})$ and any (x, w) such that $\mathsf{C}(\mathsf{x}, \mathsf{w}) = 1$.

Moreover, since the distribution of $\mathsf{cm}_i = [\mathbf{M}\mathbf{r}_i]_1$ is identical to that of $\mathsf{cm}_i = [\mathbf{M}\mathbf{r}_i + \mathbf{z}\mathsf{w}_i]_1$ for $\mathbf{r}_i \xleftarrow{\$} \mathbb{Z}_p^\lambda$ when $\mathbf{z} \in \mathsf{Span}(\mathbf{M})$, the distributions of

$$\Pi \xleftarrow{\$} \mathsf{NProve}^{*\prime}(\mathsf{CRS}, \mathsf{C}, \mathsf{x}, \mathsf{w}) \text{ and } \Pi \xleftarrow{\$} \mathsf{NSim}^*(\mathsf{CRS}, \mathsf{TD}, \mathsf{C}, \mathsf{x}),$$

$\underline{\mathsf{NTGen}^*(1^\lambda, \mathsf{par})\text{:}}$
$(\mathsf{crs_{or}}, \mathsf{td_{or}}) \xleftarrow{\$} \mathsf{NTGen_{or}}(\mathsf{par})$, $\mathbf{M} \xleftarrow{\$} \mathcal{D}_k$, $\mathbf{u} \xleftarrow{\$} \mathbb{Z}_p^k$, $\mathbf{z} = \mathbf{M} \cdot \mathbf{u}$
Return $\mathsf{CRS} = (\mathsf{crs_{or}}, \mathbf{M}, [\mathbf{z}]_1)$ and $\mathsf{TD} = \mathsf{td_{or}}$

$\underline{\mathsf{NSim}^*(\mathsf{CRS}, \mathsf{TD}, \mathsf{C}, \mathsf{x})\text{:}}$
Hardwire x in C to obtain $\mathsf{C}(\mathsf{x}, \cdot)$ in the same way as NProve^* does
Define s and t to be the numbers of gates and wires of $\mathsf{C}(\mathsf{x}, \cdot)$ respectively
Compute $\mathbf{r}_i \xleftarrow{\$} \mathbb{Z}_p^\lambda$ and $\mathsf{cm}_i = [\mathbf{M}\mathbf{r}_i]_1$ for all $i \in [t-1]$
Set $\mathsf{cm}_t = [\mathbf{z}]_1$ for the output wire
Compute $\hat{\pi}_i \xleftarrow{\$} \mathsf{NSim_{or}}(\mathsf{crs_{or}}, \mathsf{td_{or}}, [\mathbf{M}]_1, (\mathsf{cm}_i, \mathsf{cm}_i - [\mathbf{z}]_1))$ for $i \in [t]$
For each NAND gate $G_\ell = (d_1, d_2, d_3) \in [t]^3$ where $\ell \in [s]$, run
- $\mathsf{x}_\ell = \mathsf{cm}_{d_1} + \mathsf{cm}_{d_2} + 2\mathsf{cm}_{d_3} - [\mathbf{z} \cdot 2]_1$
- $\pi_\ell \xleftarrow{\$} \mathsf{NSim_{or}}(\mathsf{crs_{or}}, \mathsf{td_{or}}, [\mathbf{M}]_1, (\mathsf{x}_\ell, \mathsf{x}_\ell - [\mathbf{z}]_1))$

Return $\Pi = ((\mathsf{cm}_i, \hat{\pi}_i)_{i \in [t]}, (\pi_\ell)_{\ell \in [s]})$

Fig. 12. Definition of the simulator $(\mathsf{NTGen}^*, \mathsf{NSim}^*)$.

where $(\mathsf{CRS}, \mathsf{TD}) \xleftarrow{\$} \mathsf{NTGen}^*(1^\lambda, \mathsf{par})$ and $\mathsf{C}(\mathsf{x}, \mathsf{w}) = 1$, are identical as well, completing the proof of Theorem 8. □

Theorem 9 (Soundness). *If* ORNIZK *is perfectly sound, then* NIZK^* *is perfectly sound.*

Proof. Due to the perfect soundness of ORNIZK, for each NAND gate with input commitments $(\mathsf{cm}_{d_1}, \mathsf{cm}_{d_2})$ and an output commitment cm_{d_3} in a valid proof, we have $\mathsf{cm}_d \in \mathsf{Span}([\mathbf{M}]_1)$ or $\mathsf{cm}_d - [\mathbf{z}]_1 \in \mathsf{Span}([\mathbf{M}]_1)$ for $d \in \{d_1, d_2, d_3\}$, and

$$\mathsf{x}_\ell = (\mathsf{cm}_{d_1} + \mathsf{cm}_{d_2} + \mathsf{cm}_{d_3} - [\mathbf{z} \cdot 2]_1) \in \mathsf{Span}([\mathbf{M}]_1)$$

$$\text{or} \quad \mathsf{x}_\ell = (\mathsf{cm}_{d_1} + \mathsf{cm}_{d_2} + \mathsf{cm}_{d_3} - [\mathbf{z} \cdot 2]_1) - [\mathbf{z}]_1 \in \mathsf{Span}([\mathbf{M}]_1).$$

Let $\mathbf{k}$ be the vector in the kernel of $\mathbf{M}$ such that $\mathbf{k}^\top \mathbf{z} = 1$, which must exist when $\mathbf{z} \notin \mathsf{Span}(\mathbf{M})$. We have $\mathbf{k}^\top \mathsf{cm}_{d_1}, \mathbf{k}^\top \mathsf{cm}_{d_2}, \mathbf{k}^\top \mathsf{cm}_{d_3} \in \{[0]_1, [1]_1\}$ and

$$\mathbf{k}^\top \mathsf{cm}_{d_1} + \mathbf{k}^\top \mathsf{cm}_{d_2} + \mathbf{k}^\top \mathsf{cm}_{d_3} - [2]_1 \in \{[0]_1, [1]_1\}.$$

As a result, we can extract the bits for all wires consisting of valid input/output pairs for all NAND gates and leading the statement circuit to output 1, completing the proof of Theorem 9. □

Instantiation of the OR-proof system. The underlying OR-proof system can be instantiated as in [22,45] (see Sect. 3.1 for the instantiation). Under the SXDH assumption, each CRS consists of 4 elements in $\mathbb{G}_2$ and each proof consists of 4 and 6 elements in $\mathbb{G}_1$ and $\mathbb{G}_2$ respectively. In this case, the proof size of the resulting NIZK consists of $6t+4s$ elements in $\mathbb{G}_1$ and $6t+6s$ elements in $\mathbb{G}_2$, where t and s are the number of wires and gates in the statement circuit respectively.

References

1. Abe, M., Hoshino, F., Ohkubo, M.: Design in Type-I, Run in Type-III: fast and scalable bilinear-type conversion using integer programming. In: Robshaw, M., Katz, J. (eds.) CRYPTO 2016. LNCS, vol. 9816, pp. 387–415. Springer, Heidelberg (2016). https://doi.org/10.1007/978-3-662-53015-3_14
2. Ben-Sasson, E., Bentov, I., Horesh, Y., Riabzev, M.: Scalable, transparent, and post-quantum secure computational integrity. IACR Cryptol. ePrint Arch, p. 46 (2018)
3. Bitansky, N., et al.: The hunting of the SNARK. J. Cryptol. **30**(4), 989–1066 (2017)
4. Bitansky, N., Canetti, R., Chiesa, A., Tromer, E.: From extractable collision resistance to succinct non-interactive arguments of knowledge, and back again. In: Goldwasser, S. (ed.) ITCS 2012, pp. 326–349. ACM (2012)
5. Bitansky, N., Canetti, R., Paneth, O., Rosen, A.: On the existence of extractable one-way functions. In: Shmoys, D.B. (ed.) 46th ACM STOC, pp. 505–514. ACM Press (2014)
6. Bitansky, N., Chiesa, A., Ishai, Y., Paneth, O., Ostrovsky, R.: Succinct non-interactive arguments via linear interactive proofs. In: Sahai, A. (ed.) TCC 2013. LNCS, vol. 7785, pp. 315–333. Springer, Heidelberg (2013). https://doi.org/10.1007/978-3-642-36594-2_18
7. Blum, M., Feldman, P., Micali, S.: Non-interactive zero-knowledge and its applications (extended abstract). In: STOC, pp. 103–112. ACM (1988)
8. Boneh, D., Ishai, Y., Sahai, A., Wu, D.J.: Lattice-based SNARGs and their application to more efficient obfuscation. In: Coron, J.-S., Nielsen, J.B. (eds.) EUROCRYPT 2017. LNCS, vol. 10212, pp. 247–277. Springer, Cham (2017). https://doi.org/10.1007/978-3-319-56617-7_9
9. Chase, M., et al.: Post-quantum zero-knowledge and signatures from symmetric-key primitives. In: Thuraisingham, B.M., Evans, D., Malkin, T., Xu, D. (eds.) ACM CCS 2017, pp. 1825–1842. ACM Press (2017)
10. Chatterjee, S., Menezes, A.: Type 2 structure-preserving signature schemes revisited. In: Iwata, T., Cheon, J.H. (eds.) ASIACRYPT 2015. LNCS, vol. 9452, pp. 286–310. Springer, Heidelberg (2015). https://doi.org/10.1007/978-3-662-48797-6_13
11. Chiesa, A., Hu, Y., Maller, M., Mishra, P., Vesely, N., Ward, N.: Marlin: preprocessing zkSNARKs with universal and updatable SRS. In: Canteaut, A., Ishai, Y. (eds.) EUROCRYPT 2020. LNCS, vol. 12105, pp. 738–768. Springer, Cham (2020). https://doi.org/10.1007/978-3-030-45721-1_26
12. Chiesa, A., Ojha, D., Spooner, N.: Fractal: post-quantum and transparent recursive proofs from holography. In: Canteaut, A., Ishai, Y. (eds.) EUROCRYPT 2020, Part I. LNCS, vol. 12105, pp. 769–793. Springer, Heidelberg (May (2020). https://doi.org/10.1007/978-3-030-45721-1_27
13. Choudhuri, A.R., Jain, A., Jin, Z.: Non-interactive batch arguments for NP from standard assumptions. In: Malkin, T., Peikert, C. (eds.) CRYPTO 2021. LNCS, vol. 12828, pp. 394–423. Springer, Cham (2021). https://doi.org/10.1007/978-3-030-84259-8_14
14. Choudhuri, A.R., Jain, A., Jin, Z.: Snargs for $\mathcal{P}$ from LWE. In: FOCS, pp. 68–79. IEEE (2021)
15. Couteau, G., Hartmann, D.: Shorter non-interactive zero-knowledge arguments and ZAPs for algebraic languages. In: Micciancio, D., Ristenpart, T. (eds.) CRYPTO 2020. LNCS, vol. 12172, pp. 768–798. Springer, Cham (2020). https://doi.org/10.1007/978-3-030-56877-1_27

16. Damgård, I., Faust, S., Hazay, C.: Secure two-party computation with low communication. In: Cramer, R. (ed.) TCC 2012. LNCS, vol. 7194, pp. 54–74. Springer, Heidelberg (2012). https://doi.org/10.1007/978-3-642-28914-9_4
17. Danezis, G., Fournet, C., Groth, J., Kohlweiss, M.: Square span programs with applications to succinct NIZK arguments. In: Sarkar, P., Iwata, T. (eds.) ASIACRYPT 2014. LNCS, vol. 8873, pp. 532–550. Springer, Heidelberg (2014). https://doi.org/10.1007/978-3-662-45611-8_28
18. Escala, A., Herold, G., Kiltz, E., Ràfols, C., Villar, J.: An algebraic framework for Diffie-Hellman assumptions. In: Canetti, R., Garay, J.A. (eds.) CRYPTO 2013. LNCS, vol. 8043, pp. 129–147. Springer, Heidelberg (2013). https://doi.org/10.1007/978-3-642-40084-1_8
19. Feige, U., Lapidot, D., Shamir, A.: Multiple noninteractive zero knowledge proofs under general assumptions. SIAM J. Comput. **29**(1), 1–28 (1999)
20. Galbraith, S., Paterson, K., Smart, N.: Pairings for cryptographers. Cryptology ePrint Archive, Report 2006/165 (2006). https://eprint.iacr.org/2006/165
21. Garg, S., Jain, A., Sahai, A.: Leakage-resilient zero knowledge. In: Rogaway, P. (ed.) CRYPTO 2011. LNCS, vol. 6841, pp. 297–315. Springer, Heidelberg (2011). https://doi.org/10.1007/978-3-642-22792-9_17
22. Gay, R., Hofheinz, D., Kohl, L., Pan, J.: More efficient (almost) tightly secure structure-preserving signatures. In: Nielsen, J.B., Rijmen, V. (eds.) EUROCRYPT 2018. LNCS, vol. 10821, pp. 230–258. Springer, Cham (2018). https://doi.org/10.1007/978-3-319-78375-8_8
23. Gennaro, R., Gentry, C., Parno, B., Raykova, M.: Quadratic span programs and succinct NIZKs without PCPs. In: Johansson, T., Nguyen, P.Q. (eds.) EUROCRYPT 2013. LNCS, vol. 7881, pp. 626–645. Springer, Heidelberg (2013). https://doi.org/10.1007/978-3-642-38348-9_37
24. Giacomelli, I., Madsen, J., Orlandi, C.: ZKBoo: faster zero-knowledge for Boolean circuits. In: Holz, T., Savage, S. (eds.) USENIX Security 2016, pp. 1069–1083. USENIX Association (2016)
25. Goldwasser, S., Micali, S., Rackoff, C.: The knowledge complexity of interactive proof systems. SIAM J. Comput. **18**(1), 186–208 (1989)
26. Groth, J.: Short non-interactive zero-knowledge proofs. In: Abe, M. (ed.) ASIACRYPT 2010. LNCS, vol. 6477, pp. 341–358. Springer, Heidelberg (2010). https://doi.org/10.1007/978-3-642-17373-8_20
27. Groth, J.: Short pairing-based non-interactive zero-knowledge arguments. In: Abe, M. (ed.) ASIACRYPT 2010. LNCS, vol. 6477, pp. 321–340. Springer, Heidelberg (2010). https://doi.org/10.1007/978-3-642-17373-8_19
28. Groth, J.: On the size of pairing-based non-interactive arguments. In: Fischlin, M., Coron, J.-S. (eds.) EUROCRYPT 2016. LNCS, vol. 9666, pp. 305–326. Springer, Heidelberg (2016). https://doi.org/10.1007/978-3-662-49896-5_11
29. Groth, J., Ostrovsky, R., Sahai, A.: New techniques for noninteractive zero-knowledge. J. ACM **59**(3), 11:1–11:35 (2012)
30. Groth, J., Sahai, A.: Efficient noninteractive proof systems for bilinear groups. SIAM J. Comput. **41**(5), 1193–1232 (2012)
31. Joux, A.: Faster index calculus for the medium prime case application to 1175-bit and 1425-bit finite fields. In: Johansson, T., Nguyen, P.Q. (eds.) EUROCRYPT 2013. LNCS, vol. 7881, pp. 177–193. Springer, Heidelberg (2013). https://doi.org/10.1007/978-3-642-38348-9_11
32. Joux, A.: A new index calculus algorithm with complexity $L(1/4 + o(1))$ in very small characteristic. Cryptology ePrint Archive, Report 2013/095 (2013). https://eprint.iacr.org/2013/095

33. Jutla, C.S., Roy, A.: Switching lemma for bilinear tests and constant-size NIZK proofs for linear subspaces. In: Garay, J.A., Gennaro, R. (eds.) CRYPTO 2014. LNCS, vol. 8617, pp. 295–312. Springer, Heidelberg (2014). https://doi.org/10.1007/978-3-662-44381-1_17
34. Jutla, C.S., Roy, A.: Shorter quasi-adaptive NIZK proofs for linear subspaces. J. Cryptol. **30**(4), 1116–1156 (2017)
35. Kalai, Y., Lombardi, A., Vaikuntanathan, V., Wichs, D.: Boosting batch arguments and RAM delegation. In: STOC, pp. 1545–1552. ACM (2023)
36. Kalai, Y.T., Paneth, O., Yang, L.: How to delegate computations publicly. In: Charikar, M., Cohen, E. (eds.) 51st ACM STOC, pp. 1115–1124. ACM Press (2019)
37. Katsumata, S., Nishimaki, R., Yamada, S., Yamakawa, T.: Compact NIZKs from standard assumptions on bilinear maps. In: Canteaut, A., Ishai, Y. (eds.) EUROCRYPT 2020. LNCS, vol. 12107, pp. 379–409. Springer, Cham (2020). https://doi.org/10.1007/978-3-030-45727-3_13
38. Katsumata, S., Nishimaki, R., Yamada, S., Yamakawa, T.: Compact NIZKs from standard assumptions on bilinear maps. Cryptology ePrint Archive, Report 2020/223 (2020). https://eprint.iacr.org/2020/223
39. Kiltz, E., Wee, H.: Quasi-adaptive NIZK for linear subspaces revisited. In: Oswald, E., Fischlin, M. (eds.) EUROCRYPT 2015. LNCS, vol. 9057, pp. 101–128. Springer, Heidelberg (2015). https://doi.org/10.1007/978-3-662-46803-6_4
40. Lipmaa, H.: Progression-free sets and sublinear pairing-based non-interactive zero-knowledge arguments. In: Cramer, R. (ed.) TCC 2012. LNCS, vol. 7194, pp. 169–189. Springer, Heidelberg (2012). https://doi.org/10.1007/978-3-642-28914-9_10
41. Lipmaa, H.: Succinct non-interactive zero knowledge arguments from span programs and linear error-correcting codes. In: Sako, K., Sarkar, P. (eds.) ASIACRYPT 2013. LNCS, vol. 8269, pp. 41–60. Springer, Heidelberg (2013). https://doi.org/10.1007/978-3-642-42033-7_3
42. Micali, S.: Computationally sound proofs. SIAM J. Comput. **30**(4), 1253–1298 (2000)
43. Morillo, P., Ràfols, C., Villar, J.L.: The kernel matrix Diffie-Hellman assumption. In: Cheon, J.H., Takagi, T. (eds.) ASIACRYPT 2016. LNCS, vol. 10031, pp. 729–758. Springer, Heidelberg (2016). https://doi.org/10.1007/978-3-662-53887-6_27
44. Parno, B., Howell, J., Gentry, C., Raykova, M.: Pinocchio: nearly practical verifiable computation. In: 2013 IEEE Symposium on Security and Privacy, pp. 238–252. IEEE Computer Society Press (2013)
45. Ràfols, C.: Stretching Groth-Sahai: NIZK proofs of partial satisfiability. In: Dodis, Y., Nielsen, J.B. (eds.) TCC 2015. LNCS, vol. 9015, pp. 247–276. Springer, Heidelberg (2015). https://doi.org/10.1007/978-3-662-46497-7_10
46. Setty, S.: Spartan: efficient and general-purpose zkSNARKs without trusted setup. In: Micciancio, D., Ristenpart, T. (eds.) CRYPTO 2020. LNCS, vol. 12172, pp. 704–737. Springer, Cham (2020). https://doi.org/10.1007/978-3-030-56877-1_25
47. Shigeo, M.: A portable and fast pairing-based cryptography library. https://github.com/herumi/mcl
48. Waters, B., Wu, D.J.: Batch arguments for sfNP and more from standard bilinear group assumptions. In: CRYPTO 2022, Part II, pp. 433–463. LNCS, Springer, Heidelberg (2022)

Sigma Protocols from Verifiable Secret Sharing and Their Applications

Min Zhang[1,2,3], Yu Chen[1,2,3](✉), Chuanzhou Yao[1,2,3], and Zhichao Wang[4,5]

[1] School of Cyber Science and Technology, Shandong University, Qingdao 266237, China
[2] State Key Laboratory of Cryptology, P.O. Box 5159, Beijing 100878, China
[3] Key Laboratory of Cryptologic Technology and Information Security of Ministry of Education, Shandong University, Qingdao 266237, China
{zm_min,yaochuanzhou}@mail.sdu.edu.cn, yuchen@sdu.edu.cn
[4] State Key Laboratory of Information Security, Institute of Information Engineering, Chinese Academy of Sciences, Beijing 100085, China
[5] School of Cyber Security, University of Chinese Academy of Sciences, Beijing 100049, China
wangzhichao2022@iie.ac.cn

Abstract. Sigma protocols are one of the most common and efficient zero-knowledge proofs (ZKPs). Over the decades, a large number of Sigma protocols are proposed, yet few works pay attention to the common design principal. In this work, we propose a generic framework of Sigma protocols for algebraic statements from verifiable secret sharing (VSS) schemes. Our framework provides a general and unified approach to understanding Sigma protocols. It not only neatly explains the classic protocols such as Schnorr, Guillou-Quisquater and Okamoto protocols, but also leads to new Sigma protocols that were not previously known. Furthermore, we show an application of our framework in designing ZKPs for composite statements, which contain both algebraic and non-algebraic statements. We give a generic construction of non-interactive ZKPs for composite statements by combining Sigma protocols from VSS and ZKPs following MPC-in-the-head paradigm in a seamless way via a technique of *witness sharing reusing*. Our construction has advantages of requiring no "glue" proofs for combining algebraic and non-algebraic statements. By instantiating our construction using Ligero++ (Bhadauria et al., CCS 2020) and designing an associated Sigma protocol from VSS, we obtain a concrete ZKP for composite statements which achieves a tradeoff between running time and proof size, thus resolving the open problem left by Backes et al. (PKC 2019).

Keywords: Sigma protocols · Verifiable secret sharing · Composite statements · MPC-in-the-head

J. Guo and R. Steinfeld (Eds.): ASIACRYPT 2023, LNCS 14439, pp. 208–242, 2023.
https://doi.org/10.1007/978-981-99-8724-5_7

1 Introduction

Zero-knowledge proofs (ZKPs), introduced by Goldwasser, Micali and Rackoff [GMR85], allow a prover to convince a verifier that a statement is true without revealing any further information. Goldreich, Micali, and Wigderson [GMW86] further showed that ZKP exists for every $\mathcal{NP}$ language, making it an extremely powerful tool in modern cryptography. Since its introduction in the mid 1980s, ZKPs have been used as an instrumental building block in a myriad of cryptographic protocols/schemes like identification protocols [FFS87], digital signatures [BCC+16, Sch91], CCA-secure public-key encryption [NY90, Sah99], anonymous credentials [CL01], voting [CF85], maliciously secure multi-party computation [GMW87], and privacy-preserving cryptocurrency [GK15, BCG+14].

In the realm of ZKPs[1], there are three types of statements. The first is algebraic statements, which are defined by relations over algebraic groups like prime-order groups and RSA-type groups, such as knowledge of discrete logarithm or modular root. The second is non-algebraic statements, which are expressed by arithmetic/boolean circuits, such as knowledge of preimage of SHA256 or knowledge of plaintext of AES encryption. The third is composite statements that mix algebraic and non-algebraic statements, e.g. the value w committed by Com also satisfies $C(w) = 1$, where the predicate C represents an arithmetic/boolean circuit. Below we briefly survey ZKPs for the three types of statements.

ZKPs for Non-algebraic Statements. Since boolean/arithmetic circuits can describe arbitrary computations, ZKPs for non-algebraic statements are usually referred to as general-purpose. The last decade has seen tremendous progress in designing and implementing efficient general-purpose ZKPs (see [Tha22] for a comprehensive survey). These efforts can be roughly divided into four categories according to the underlying machinery.

The first is built upon probabilistic checkable proof (PCP). Following the seminal works of Kilian [Kil92] and Micali [Mic94] based on classical PCPs, recent works [AHIV17, BBHR18, BCR+19, ZXZS20, COS20, Set20] begin to build general-purpose ZKP from interactive variants of PCP, first in the model of interactive PCP [KR08] and then in the more general model of interactive oracle proofs [BCS16, RRR16]. ZKPs of this category have the advantages of not relying on public-key cryptography, not requiring trusted setup, and offering conjectured post-quantum security. The second is based on linear PCP, initiated by Ishai, Kushilevitz, and Ostrovsky [IKO07], and followed by a sequence of works [Gro10, Lip12, GGPR13, Gro16, MBKM19, CHM+20]. ZKPs of this category are featured with constant size proofs and fast verification, but they are quite slow on the prover side and require long and "toxic" common reference string. The third is based on inner product arguments. Initial work [Gro09] of this line has square root size proof and linear verification time. Followup works [BCC+16, BBB+18] managed to achieve logarithmic size proof, and the

[1] For the sake of convenience, we will not distinguish between computational and information-theoretic soundness, and thus refer to both proofs and arguments as "proofs".

verification cost is finally reduced to logarithmic complexity [Lee21]. The fourth is based on garbled circuits. The original protocol due to Jawurek, Kerschbaum and Orlandi [JKO13] is secret-coin in nature. Recently, Cui and Zhang [CZ21] showed how to tweak the JKO protocol to public-coin. ZKPs of this category require linear prover time, proof size and verification time.

ZKPs for Algebraic Statements. Almost exclusively, the most common and efficient ZKPs for algebraic statements fall into a class known as Sigma protocols, introduced by Cramer [Cra96]. Let L be an $\mathcal{NP}$ language associated with relation R, i.e., $L = \{x \mid \exists w \text{ s.t. } \mathsf{R}(x, w) = 1\}$. A Sigma ($\Sigma$) protocol for L is a 3-move public coin interactive proof system that allows a prover to convince a verifier that he knows a witness w of a public instance x without disclosing w. The Greek letter Σ visualizes the 3-move structure (commit, challenge and response). The prover sends an initial message a called a commitment to the verifier, the verifier replies with a uniformly and independently random chosen challenge e from some finite challenge space, and the prover answers with a response z as the final message. Finally, the verifier decides whether to accept or reject the statement based on the transcript (a, e, z).

Sigma protocols are very appealing due to many attractive properties. First, Sigma protocols are extremely efficient for algebraic statements. They yield short proof sizes, only require a constant number of public-key operations and do not need trusted common reference string generation. Although seemingly specific, Sigma protocols for algebraic statements cover a wide variety of tasks arise from practice such as proving the knowledge of discrete logarithm/modular root, a tuple is of the Diffie-Hellman type, an ElGamal/Paillier encryption is to a certain value, and many more. Second, Sigma protocols are closed under parallel composition, and thus it is possible to efficiently combine several simple Sigma protocols to prove compound statements. This further increases the usability of Sigma protocols. Third, the so-called special soundness make Sigma protocols easy to work with by providing a simple way to establish proof of knowledge property. Moreover, Sigma protocols can be made non-interactive using the Fiat-Shamir heuristic [FS86]. The above properties make Sigma protocols an incredibly powerful tool for various cryptographic tasks.

In contrast to the state of affairs of general-purpose ZKP, though Sigma protocols have been intensively studied in the last four decades, few attentions are paid to generic constructions. This is probably because that the design of Sigma protocols is relatively easier than that of general-purpose ZKPs. Sigma protocols in the literature such as the classic Schnorr [Sch91], Batching Schnorr [GLSY04], Guillou-Quisquater [GQ88], and Okamato protocol [Oka92] are ingenious but hand-crafted, and they came with a separate proof. It is curious to know whether there exists a common design principal.

ZKPs for Composite Statements. A composite statement is one that contains both algebraic and non-algebraic statements, e.g., x is a Pederden commitment to w such that SHA256(w) $= y$. As noted in [CGM16, AGM18, BHH+19], ZKPs for composite statements have various applications, such as proof of solvency for Bitcoin exchanges, anonymous credentials based on RSA and (EC-)DSA signatures, and 2PC with authenticated inputs.

To prove composite statements, a naïve approach is transforming composite statements into a single form, namely either algebraic or non-algebraic form, and then using only Sigma protocols or general-purpose ZKPs to prove it. In one direction, one could turn the non-algebraic statements expressed as a circuit into algebraic statements by expressing each gate of the circuit as an algebraic relation between input and output, and then use Sigma protocols to prove these relations. However, it would cost several public-key operations and group elements per gate, which is prohibitively expensive when the circuit is large. As noted by [AGM18], in case of hash functions and block-ciphers, it costs tens of thousands of exponentiations and group elements when proving the associated algebraic relations of the circuits. In the other direction, one could turn the algebraic statements into non-algebraic statements and then use general-purpose ZKPs to prove it. But this results in a substantial increase in the size of the statements. For example, the circuit for computing a single exponentiation could be of thousands or millions of gates depending on the group size. This in turn increases the overheads of both prover's/verifier's work and proof size. As mentioned before, the computation cost and proof size of all transparent general-purpose ZKPs grow with the circuit size. General-purpose ZKPs based on linear PCP offer efficient verification and constant proof size, while the prover's work is still heavy and they require a trusted setup.

A better approach, employed by most of prior works on this direction, is that: using Sigma protocols to prove the algebraic part, using off-the-shelf efficient general-purpose ZKPs to prove the non-algebraic part, then additionally designing customized protocols as a "glue" to link the two parts. "Glue" proofs play a crucial role in this approach. Without "glue" proofs, a cheating prover can easily generate proofs of the two parts using inconsistent witnesses (e.g., a cheating prover may give a proof π_1 for proving knowledge of w_1 such that $\mathsf{Com}(w_1) = x$ and a proof π_2 for proving knowledge of w_2 such that $\text{SHA256}(w_2) = y$ where $w_1 \neq w_2$). The resulting proof systems will inherit the advantages and disadvantages of the underlying general-purpose ZKPs. For instance, [CGM16] presented two tailor-made "glue" proofs to link Sigma protocols with the JKO protocol [JKO13], yielding ZKPs which have a fast prover and verifier while they are private-coin inherently; [AGM18,CFQ19,ABC+22] each gave a generic construction of "glue" proofs to link Sigma protocols with ZKPs based on linear PCP, yielding proofs which are featured with constant size proofs and fast verification, but they are quite slow on the prover side and require a trusted setup; [BHH+19] customized two "glue" proofs to link Sigma protocols with the ZKBoo [GMO16]/ZKB++ [CDG+17] protocols, yielding transparent ZKPs which have a fast prover, but the proof size is linear in the circuit size.

However, this approach servers from two main drawbacks. First, "glue" proofs inevitably introduce additional overheads in both computation cost and proof size to enforce the witness consistency. Second, "glue" proofs must be tailored in a specific way to align with the general-purpose ZKPs, limiting the space of possible general-purpose ZKPs we can use. Particularly, "glue" proofs in [BHH+19] are tailored for the ZKBoo [GMO16]/ZKB++ [CDG+17] and they could not be applied to other similar proof systems like

Ligero [AHIV17]/Ligero++ [BFH+20]. The authors left a more efficient and compact ZKP for composite statements using Ligero/Ligero++ as an open problem[2]. Therefore, an intriguing question is that whether the seemingly indispensable "glue" proofs are necessary when designing ZKPs for composite statements.

The above discussion motivates the main questions that we study in this paper:

Is there a generic framework of Sigma protocols?
Can this framework help to give a generic construction of efficient ZKPs for composite statements without "glue" proofs?

1.1 Our Contributions

In this work, we positively answer the above two questions and summarize our contributions as below.

1.1.1 A Framework of Sigma Protocols for Algebraic Statements

We present a framework of Sigma protocols for algebraic statements from verifiable secret sharing (VSS) schemes. Our framework not only neatly explains existing classic Sigma protocols including the Schnorr, Batching Schnorr, GQ, and Okamoto protocols, but also provides a unified paradigm of designing Sigma protocols for proving knowledge of openings of algebraic commitments.

MPC-in-the-head paradigm revisit. Ishai et al. [IKOS07] showed how to build general-purpose ZKPs by using MPC in a black-box manner. In a nutshell, to prove the knowledge of w such that $C(y, w) = 1$ for a circuit C and a value y, their construction proceeds as below: the prover simulate an execution of an n-party secure-computation protocol Π_f that evaluates the function $f_y(w_1, \ldots, w_n)$ which outputs "1" iff $C(y, w) = 1$ with $w = w_1 \oplus \cdots \oplus w_n$, and commit the views of the parties in the protocol. The verifier then picks and asks a random subset of those parties, and the prover opens the corresponding views. The verifier finally accepts if the opened views all output "1" and are consistent with each other. Their approach, known as MPC-in-the-head, presents a generic connection between ZKP and MPC, and gives rise to a rich line of transparent general-purpose ZKPs with continually improved performance, including ZKBoo [GMO16], ZKB++ [CDG+17], KKW [KKW18], Ligero [AHIV17], Ligero++ [BFH+20] and more, forming a promising subclass of general-purpose ZKPs based on PCP machinery. Interestingly, we find that the ZKPs from the MPC-in-the-head paradigm also follow the commit-challenge-response pattern. In light of this observation, the MPC-in-the-head paradigm actually gives a generic construction of Sigma protocols for non-algebraic statements. This suggests that when seeking for a generic framework of Sigma protocols for algebraic statements, one may start from some lite machinery than MPC.

[2] Actually, it is hard to give a more efficient ZKP for composite statement using Ligero/Ligero++ than those using ZKBoo/ZKB++, since the former two protocols reduce the proof size, at the cost of increasing the computation.

VSS-in-the-Head. An (n, t_p, t_f)-verifiable secret sharing (VSS) scheme allows a dealer to distribute a secret s among n participants, in such a way that no group of up to t_p participants could learn anything about s, any group of at least t_f participants could recover the secret, and the cheating behaviors of both the dealer and the participants can be detected. VSS is an essential building block employed for numerous MPC protocols with malicious players [GMW87, BGW88, CCD88, RB89]. Based on the above reasoning, VSS is arguably the right backbone of Sigma protocols for algebraic statements.

A REFINED DEFINITION OF VSS. In this work, we restrict ourselves to non-interactive VSS schemes. For simplicity, we will omit non-interactive hereafter when the context is clear. Before describing the framework, we first give a refined definition of VSS, which differs from the original definition proposed by Feldman [Fel87] in both syntax and security properties. In terms of syntax, there are two primary differences as below: (1) The secret is committed rather than being encrypted, such relaxation makes our definition more general; (2) The sharing algorithm is asked to additionally output *authentication information*, denoted by *aut*, which essentially commits to the sharing method (e.g., in the case of Feldman's VSS scheme, it is a vector of commitments to the polynomial's coefficients), and will later be used to check the validity of each share. This kind of information does not appear in the original definition. In terms of security properties, there are two differences as follows: (1) For correctness, the secrets recovered by different groups of participants are not stipulated to be consistent as in [Fel87], instead the recovered secrets are required to be an opening of the commitment. This property is crucial in this work and is actually met by many existing VSS schemes, but it has never been formally defined; (2) For privacy, we provide a simulation-based definition instead of a game-based one, making it more convenient to use in the context of ZKP and MPC. See Sect. 3.1 for the details of the refined definition.

SIGMA PROTOCOLS FROM VSS. Having settled on a satisfactory definition of VSS, we are ready to describe the framework of Sigma protocols for algebraic statements-"given a commitment x, prove the knowledge of an opening (s, r) such that $\mathsf{Com}(s; r) = x$". Our framework is built upon (n, t_p, t_f)-VSS schemes with respect to Com. Roughly speaking, in the commit phase, the prover shares the witness (s, r) into n pieces of shares $v_1, \ldots, v_n$ "in his head" and generates the associated authentication information *aut*, then sends *aut* to the verifier. In the challenge phase, the verifier picks a random subset I from the challenge space $[n]$, where $|I| \leq t_p$, and acts as the set of participants in I to query their private shares. In the response phase, the prover answers with corresponding shares $(v_i)_{i \in I}$. Finally, the verifier decides to accept or reject the statement by checking whether each v_i is a valid share for participant P_i. For the security of the resulting Sigma protocols, the *special soundness* property follows from the *correctness* of VSS and the *special honest verifier zero-knowledge property* follows from the *privacy* of VSS.

The above framework from VSS encompasses almost all the classic Sigma protocols for proving knowledge of openings of algebraic commitments. As a concrete example, we show how to derive the celebrated Schnnor protocol from our framework. The start point is the Feldman's (n, t_p, t_f)-VSS scheme [Fel87] where $t_f = t_p + 1$: to distribute a secret $s \in \mathbb{F}_p$ among n participants $P_1, \ldots, P_n$, the dealer first computes a commitment $c = g^s$ to secret s, chooses a t_p-degree polynomial $f(x) = a_0 + a_1 x + \cdots + a_{t_p} x^{t_p}$ where $a_0, \ldots, a_{t_p-1} \xleftarrow{R} \mathbb{F}_p$ and $a_{t_p} = s$ (the coefficients of the polynomial could be viewed as the compact description of the sharing method), and sets the private share v_i for P_i as $f(i)$, then generates the commitment of the randomnesses as the authentication information, i.e., $aut = (c_0, \ldots, c_{t_p-1})$ where $c_j = g^{a_j}$ for $0 \leq j \leq t_p - 1$. The dealer then broadcasts c and aut, and sends v_i to P_i in private. Upon receiving the share, each participant checks the validity of the share with respect to c and aut, and rejects if it is invalid. The secret s can be recovered by pooling more than t_p valid shares. By setting the number of participants n to p (the size of the field $\mathbb{F}_p$), the privacy threshold t_p to 1, we immediately recover the classic Schnorr protocol. More examples can be found in Sect. 4.

1.1.2 A Framework of ZKPs for Composite Statements

To demonstrate the usefulness of our framework, we show its application in designing ZKPs for composite statements. Among various types of composite statements, *commit-and-prove*, i.e., a committed value w satisfies a circuit C, is the most common one. According to [CGM16, BHH+19], it is an building block for some other types. Therefore, we restrict ourselves to the *commit-and-prove* type.

In this work, we show that by reusing the witness sharing process, Sigma protocols from VSS and ZKPs following MPC-in-the-head paradigm can be combined seamlessly, yielding a generic construction of ZKPs for composite statements without "glue" proofs. Our generic construction enjoys two benefits: (i) eliminating the cost introduced by "glue" proofs; (ii) expanding the space of possible general-purpose ZKPs that we can use.

Enforcing Consistency via Witness Sharing Reusing. As mentioned before, ZKPs from MPC bear strong resemblance with Sigma protocols, as both of them follow the same commit-challenge-response pattern. This implies that ZKPs from MPC might be easily coupled with Sigma protocols from VSS to prove composite statements. However, if we combine them as the mainstream approach, "glue" proofs are still necessary. A key observation is that ZKPs from MPC and Sigma protocols from VSS not only follow the same pattern but also share a common *witness sharing procedure*: at the very beginning, the provers share the witnesses into n shares in their heads; in the challenge phase, the verifiers ask to reveal a subset of witness shares; in the response phase, the provers reply with corresponding shares (albeit in ZKPs from MPC, the shares are included as a part of parties' views), and finally the verifiers use the received shares to check the verification equations. This suggests that when combining Sigma protocols from VSS and ZKPs from MPC to prove composite statements, the *witness sharing procedure* of them are able to be reused. More precisely, the prover shares the witness only once, the verifier picks and asks only one challenge I, and then the prover responds with only one subset of shares, whereas the verifier accepts if and only if the shares pass verifications of both algebraic and non-algebraic parts. Such "reusing" enforces the prover to use a consistent witness without any additional "glue" proofs. From the perspective of security proof, one can construct an extractor Ext of ZKPs for composite statements by invoking extractors Ext_{Σ} of Sigma protocols from VSS and $\mathsf{Ext}_{\mathrm{ZKP}}$ of ZKPs from MPC as subroutines, both of which run the same recovering algorithm on the same input, and thus output the same witness satisfying both algebraic and non-algebraic statements. When implementing the above high-level idea, we encounter the following two main technical obstacles.

A Generalization of MPC-in-the-Head Paradigm. One obstacle comes from the MPC-in-the-Head Paradigm. Recall that the secret sharing mechanism in the original ZKPs from MPC [IKOS07] sticks to the XOR-based secret sharing (SS) schemes, which is a special case of $(n, n-1, n)$-SS, making it hard to interact with (n, t_p, t_f)-VSS schemes. To address this issue, we generalize the MPC-in-the-head paradigm by extending the XOR-based SS scheme to the (n, t_p, t_f)-SS schemes. Specifically, in the commit phase the prover P shares the witness w into n shares $w_1, \ldots, w_n$ by running SS.$\mathsf{Share}(w)$, which does not fix to picking n shares satisfying $w = w_1 \oplus \cdots \oplus w_n$. This, in turn, requires an MPC protocol Π that evaluates n-party function f satisfying $f_y(w_1, \ldots, w_n) = 1$ iff $C(y, \cdot) = 1$ on input $w =$ SS.$\mathsf{Recover}(w_1, \ldots, w_n)$. The proof of knowledge property is not explicitly given in [IKOS07]. In this work, we rigorously prove this property, which is crucial for our construction of ZKPs for composite statements and might be of independent interest.

Separable VSS Schemes. The other obstacle is that the relationship between VSS and SS is unclear, making it difficult to reuse the common witness sharing procedure. To overcome this obstruction, we introduce a mild property called *separability* for VSS which has been satisfied by many existing VSS schemes. Roughly speaking, we say a VSS scheme satisfies *separability* if its procedure of generating shares $(v_1, \ldots, v_n)$ and authentication information aut could be separated. Particularly, we say a VSS scheme aligns with an SS scheme if it generates the shares as per this SS scheme. Such delicate dissection allows us to distill the common secret sharing mechanism used in Sigma protocols from VSS and ZKPs from MPC, paving the way to implement the *witness sharing reusing* technique.

An Efficient Instantiation. We instantiate above framework of ZKPs for composite statements by choosing Ligero++ [BFH+20] as the underlying general-purpose ZKPs and designing a Sigma protocol from VSS which aligns with the SS component underlying Ligero++. The resulting protocol requires no trusted setup and no "glue" proofs, and achieves a tradeoff between proof size and running time. Concretely, the proof size is polylogarithmic to the circuit size and the number of expensive public-key operations required by prover and verifier is independent of the circuit size. See Sect. 6.2 for a detailed efficiency analysis.

Table 1 shows a brief comparison between closely related works. Among them, the protocols in [BHH+19] and [BBB+18] are the only two that are both public-coin and transparent. Compared to [BHH+19], our instantiation achieves asymptotically smaller proof size, thus settling the open problem in [BHH+19]: whether a more compact ZKP for composite statements can be constructed by using Ligero/Ligero++. Though the work [BBB+18] also proposed a proof system that achieves succinct proof size, the prover's work is still expensive. As noted in [Tha22, Section 19.3.2], for circuits with small size, $O(|C|\log(|C|))$ field operations are likely to be faster than $O(|C|)$ group operations. Thus, our instantiation is likely to have better prover performance when the circuit size is small.

Table 1. Comparisons among ZKPs for composite statements

Protocols	Prover time	Verifier time	Proof size
[CGM16] Constr.1 *	$O(\|w\|)$ pub $O(\|C\|)$ sym	$O(\|w\|)$ pub $O(\|C\|)$ sym	$O(\|C\| + \|w\|)$
[CGM16] Constr.2 *	$O(\lambda)$ pub $O(\|C\| + \|w\|\lambda)$ sym	$O(\lambda)$ pub $O(\|C\| + \|w\|\lambda)$ sym	$O(\|C\| + \|w\|\lambda)$
[BBB+18]	$O(\|C\|)$ pub	$O(\frac{\|C\|}{\log(\|C\|)})$ pub	$O(\log(\|C\|))$
[AGM18]†	$O(\|C\| + \lambda)$ pub.	$O(\|w\| + \lambda)$ pub	$O(1)$
[BHH+19]	$O((\|w\| + \lambda)$ pub $O(\|C\| \cdot \lambda)$ sym	$O((\|w\| + \lambda)$ pub $O(\|C\| \cdot \lambda)$ sym	$O(\|C\|\lambda + \|w\|)$
[CFQ19] LegoAC1†	$O(\|C\|)$ pub $O(\|C\|\log(\|C\|))$ sym	$O(\|w\|)$ pub	$O(1)$
[ABC+22]†	$O(\|C\| + \|w\|)$ pub	$O(\|w\|)$ pub	$O(\log(\|w\|))$
This work	$O(\lambda)$ pub$O(\|C\|\log(\|C\|))$ sym	$O(\frac{(\|w\|+\lambda)^2}{\log(\|w\|+\lambda)})$ pub $O(\|C\|)$ sym	$O(\mathsf{polylog}(\|C\|) + \lambda)$

* Means being private-coin. † Means requiring a trusted setup. We use pub to indicate a public-key operation, sym to a symmetric-key operation. We denote by $|C|$ the circuit size, by $|w|$ the witness length, by λ the security parameter.

1.2 Related Work

Sigma Protocols. The notion was first proposed by Cramer [Cra96] as an abstraction of Schnorr protocol [Sch91] for proving knowledge of discrete logarithm and Guillou-Quisquater protocol [GQ88] for proving knowledge of modular root. Since its introduction, Sigma protocols have received much attention due to their simplicity and high efficiency, and a great deal of works have focused on improving the efficiency or extending the functionality of Sigma protocols. For example, Beullens [Beu20] introduced a new notion called *sigma protocols with helper*, referring to the Sigma protocols where the prover and the verifier are assisted by a trusted third party, and further improved the efficiency of several Sigma protocols using the new notion. Cramer, Damgård and Schoenmakers (CDS) [CDS94] applied the secret sharing technique to construct proofs of partial knowledge, i.e., given n statements $x_1, \ldots, x_n$, convincing the verifier that the prover knows a witness w for at least one of the statements. Our framework seems like a dual construction of theirs. In their construction, the prover shares the challenge e rather than the witness w, while in ours, the prover shares the witness w instead of the challenge e. In any case, we both showed that (verifiable) secret sharing is an important technique for constructing Sigma protocols. Abe et al. [AAB+20] then improved the CDS technique by letting the prover hash the shares before using them as challenges, resulting in several significant benefits. Abe et al. [AAB+21] also introduced a model of monotone computation called *acyclicity program* (ACP), and proposed an alternative method for proving partial knowledge based on the ACP.

However, few works study the common design principal of Sigma protocols. To our knowledge, [Mau15] is the only work on this direction. In [Mau15], Maurer proposed a template for building Sigma protocols for algebraic statements that can be captured by preimage of a group homomorphism. Despite a large number of classic Sigma protocols can be explained by this template, it still has deficiencies in generality and utility. First, Maurer's template is tied to group homomorphism, and is less flexible cause it imposes fixed formats on three move messages. For instance, it fails to encompass the variant Schnorr and the batching Schnorr protocol introduced in [GLSY04] where the initial message is not computed using the same homomorphism as the statement. Second, Maurer's template does not establish connection between Sigma protocols and other cryptographic primitives. The shed light on the machinery of Sigma protocols is still unclear.

ZKPs for Composite Statements. This line of research started with the work of Chase et al. [CGM16]. They gave two efficient ZKPs for proving composite statement, of which the number of expensive public-key operations is independent of the size of the circuit C. However, both of the two constructions are based on the general-purpose ZKPs from garbled circuits proposed by [JKO13], which makes the protocols interactive inherently. Agrawal et al. [AGM18] further presented non-interactive protocols, which use the QAP-based succinct non-interactive arguments of knowledge (SNARK) to prove the non-algebraic part of the statement. Their protocols take advantage of having a small proof size and fast verification time, while require a trusted setup for generating the structured common reference string (CRS). Backes et al. [BHH+19] presented non-interactive protocols which require no trusted setup, and have efficient prover and verifier running time. However, their protocol makes use of the ZKBoo [GMO16]/ZKB++ [CDG+17] protocols which follow the MPC-in-the-head paradigm to prove the non-algebraic statement, thus resulting in a large proof size that is linear to $|C|$. Campanelli et al. [CFQ19] proposed a framework of ZKPs for composite statements utilizing pairing-based general-purpose ZKPs, achieving succinct proof size while all the instantiations they given require a trusted setup. Among these instantiations, the one reported in Table 1 has the shortest proof size and the most efficient verifier. Recently, Aranha et al. [ABC+22] proposed a general method of compiling Algebraic Holographic Proofs into ZKPs for composite statements, whose proof size is logarithmic to the number of commitments in the statements while also requiring a trusted setup. See Table 1 for a brief comparison between these works.

All the works above used customized "glue" proofs for proving consistency, which severely limit the space of general-purpose ZKPs that can be used and also causes additional overheads in both computation and communication. Aside from the works mentioned above, general-purpose ZKPs based on inner product arguments, such as [BBB+18,HKR19] are able to be combined with Pedersen commitments without any "glue" proofs. However, the algebraic parts of them are fixed to Pedersen commitments with some certain constraints, making the construction semi-generic. For example, the algebraic part of [BBB+18] is fixed to $|\mathbf{w}|$ Pedersen commitments, each of which commits to an entry of the witness $\mathbf{w}$. Once the algebraic part changes to a single vector commitment to $\mathbf{w}$, an additional "glue" proof is required. What's more, the prover's work is still expensive, since the number of public-key operations required by the prover is linear to the circuit size. To our knowledge, there is no generic construction of ZKPs for composite statements that is without "glue" proofs.

2 Preliminaries

Notations. For an integer n, we use $[n]$ to denote the set $\{1, \ldots, n\}$. For a set X and integer t, we use $|X|$ to denote the size of X, use X_t to indicate the set consisting of all t-sized subsets of X, and use $x \xleftarrow{R} X$ to denote sampling x uniformly at random from X. We use the abbreviation PPT to indicate probabilistic polynomial-time. We denote a negligible function in λ by $\mathsf{negl}(\lambda)$.

2.1 Commitment Schemes

We first recall the definition of commitment schemes.

Definition 1 (Commitment Schemes). *A commitment scheme is a triple of polynomial time algorithms as below:*

- $\mathsf{Setup}(1^\lambda)$*: on input a security parameter* λ*, outputs the public commitment key pp, which includes the descriptions of the message space* M*, randomness space* R*, and commitment space* C*.*
- $\mathsf{Com}(m; r)$*: on input a message* $m \in M$ *and a randomness* $r \in R$*, outputs a commitment* c*.*
- $\mathsf{Verify}(c, m, r)$*: on input a commitment* $c \in C$*, a message* $m \in M$ *and a randomness* $r \in R$*, outputs "1" if* $\mathsf{Com}(m; r) = c$ *and "0" otherwise.*

Additionally, we require the following properties of a commitment scheme.

Correctness. *For any pp* $\leftarrow \mathsf{Setup}(1^\lambda)$*, any* $m \in M$ *and any* $r \in R$*, it holds that* $\mathsf{Verify}(\mathsf{Com}(m; r), m, r) = 1$.

Hiding. *A commitment* $\mathsf{Com}(m; r)$ *should reveal no information about* m*. Formally, it is computationally (resp. statistically) hiding if for any PPT (resp.*

unbounded) adversary $\mathcal{A}$, it holds that:

$$\Pr\left[b' = b : \begin{array}{l} pp \leftarrow \mathsf{Setup}(1^\lambda); \\ (m_0, m_1) \leftarrow \mathcal{A}(pp); \\ b \xleftarrow{\text{R}} \{0,1\}, r \xleftarrow{\text{R}} R, c \leftarrow \mathsf{Com}(m_b; r); \\ b' \leftarrow \mathcal{A}(c); \end{array}\right] \leq \frac{1}{2} + \mathsf{negl}(\lambda).$$

For commitment schemes with deterministic Com *algorithm, namely the randomness is null, we consider a weaker security notion called one-way hiding, which can be defined similarly as above. Roughly speaking, we say a commitment scheme is one-way hiding if the adversary only takes a negligible probability to open a randomly chosen commitment.*

Binding. *A commitment can not be opened to two different messages. Formally, it is computationally (resp. statistically) binding if for any PPT (resp. unbounded) adversary $\mathcal{A}$, it holds that:*

$$\Pr\left[\begin{array}{c} m_0 \neq m_1 \wedge \\ \mathsf{Com}(m_0; r_0) = \mathsf{Com}(m_1; r_1) \end{array} : \begin{array}{c} pp \leftarrow \mathsf{Setup}(1^\lambda); \\ (m_0, r_0, m_1, r_1) \leftarrow \mathcal{A}(pp); \end{array}\right] \leq \mathsf{negl}(\lambda).$$

2.2 Sigma Protocols

Let L be an $\mathcal{NP}$ language and R be the associated binary relation. We say an instance x lies in L if and only if there exists a witness w such that $(x, w) \in \mathsf{R}$. Consider following three-move interaction between two PPT algorithms P and V: (1) Commit: P sends an initial message to V; (2) Challenge: V sends a challenge e to P; (3) Response: P replies with a response z. A formal definition of Sigma protocols is presented as below.

Definition 2 (Sigma Protocols). *A Sigma protocol for a relation* R *is a three-move public-coin protocol with above communication pattern and satisfies the following three properties:*

Completeness. *If P and V follow the protocol on input x and private input w to P where $(x, w) \in \mathsf{R}$, then V always accepts the transcript.*

n-Special soundness. *There exists a PPT extraction algorithm* Ext *that on input any instance x and any n accepting transcripts $(a, e_1, z_1), \ldots, (a, e_n, z_n)$ for x where all e_i's are distinct, outputs a witness w for x.*

Special honest-verifier zero-knowledge (SHVZK). *There exists a PPT simulator* Sim *that on input any instance x and any challenge e, generates a transcript (a, e, z) such that the triple is distributed identically to an accepting transcript generated by a real protocol run between the honest $P(x, w)$ and $V(x)$.*

Lemma 1 ([ACK21, GMO16]). *Let n be a positive integer bounded by a polynomial and $\langle P, V\rangle$ be a Sigma protocol with n-special soundness. If the verifier V samples the challenge uniformly at random from the challenge space C, then $\langle P, V\rangle$ is knowledge sound with knowledge error bounded by $(n-1)/|C|$.*

2.3 Secure Multiparty Computation

A multiparty computation (MPC) protocol allows n parties $P_1, \ldots, P_n$ to jointly compute an n-party function f over their inputs while maintaining the privacy of their inputs. For a set of parties $I \subseteq [n]$, we denote by f_I the outputs of parties in I after the joint computation of f. Let $view_i$ be the view of P_i during the execution of an MPC protocol, including its private input, randomness and the received messages. Below, we recall some important definitions and lemmas of MPC protocols from [IKOS07].

Definition 3 (Consistent Views). *We say a pair of views* $(view_i, view_j)$ *are consistent, with respect to the protocol* Π *and some public input* x*, if the outgoing messages implicit in* $view_i$, x *are identical to the incoming messages reported in* $view_j$ *and vice versa.*

Lemma 2 (Local vs. Global Consistency). *Let* Π *be an* n*-party protocol,* x *be a public input and* $view_1, \ldots, view_n$ *be* n *(possible incorrect) views. Then all pairs of views are consistent with respect to* Π *and* x *if and only if there exists an honest execution of* Π *with public input* x *(and some choice of private inputs and random inputs).*

In the semi-honest model, the security of an MPC protocol can be divided into the following two requirements.

Definition 4 (Correctness). *An MPC protocol* Π *realizes an* n*-party functionality* $f(x, w_1, \ldots, w_n)$ *with perfect correctness, if for all inputs* $x, w_1, \ldots, w_n$*, the probability that the outputs of some players are different from the output of* f *is 0.*

Definition 5 (t-privacy). *Let* $1 \leq t < n$*. We say an MPC protocol* Π *realizes an* n*-party functionality* f *with perfect* t*-privacy, if there exists a PPT simulator* Sim *such that for any inputs* $x, w_1, \ldots, w_n$*, and any set of parties* $I \subset [n]$ *where* $|I| \leq t$*, the joint view of parties in* I *is distributed identically to* $\mathsf{Sim}(I, x, (w_i)_{i \in I}, f_I(x, w_1, \ldots, w_n))$.

2.4 (Verifiable) Secret Sharing

A secret sharing (SS) scheme [Sha79] among a dealer and n participants $P_1, \ldots, P_n$ consists of two phases, called *Sharing* and *Reconstruction*. In the *Sharing* phase, the dealer shares a secret s (either a single value or a vector) among n participants, in such a way that no unauthorized subsets of participants can learn anything about the secret, while any authorized subsets of participants can recover the secret in the *Reconstruction* phase. The formal definition is as below.

Definition 6 (Secret Sharing). *A secret sharing scheme consists of three polynomial-time algorithms as follows:*

- $\mathsf{Setup}(1^\lambda)$*: on input a security parameter* λ*, outputs the system parameters* pp*, including descriptions of secret space* M*, share space* S*, the number of participants* n*, the privacy threshold* t_p *and the fault-tolerance threshold* t_f*, where all the three parameters* n*,* t_p *and* t_f *are positive integers and hold that* $n \geq t_f > t_p$*.*
- $\mathsf{Share}(s)$*: on input the secret* $s \in M$*, outputs* n *shares* $(s_i)_{i\in[n]} \in S^n$*.*
- $\mathsf{Recover}(I, (s_i)_{i\in I})$*: on input a set of participants* $I \subseteq [n]$ *and a vector of shares* $(s_i)_{i\in I}$ *where* $s_i \in S$*, outputs a secret* $s \in M$ *or a special reject symbol* $\perp$ *denoting failure.*

An SS scheme should satisfy the following two properties:

t_f***-Correctness.*** *In Reconstruction phase, any group of at least* t_f *participants can recover the secret. Formally, for any* $pp \leftarrow \mathsf{Setup}(1^\lambda)$ *where* pp *include the fault-tolerance threshold* t_f*, any secret* $s \in M$*, any* $(s_i)_{i\in[n]} \leftarrow \mathsf{Share}(s)$ *and any subset* $I \subseteq [n]$ *where* $|I| \geq t_f$*, it holds that* $\mathsf{Recover}(I, (s_i)_{i\in I}) = s$*.*

t_p***-Privacy.*** *In Sharing phase, the joint view of at most* t_p *participants reveals nothing about the secret. Formally, for any* $pp \leftarrow \mathsf{Setup}(1^\lambda)$ *where* pp *include the privacy threshold* t_p*, any* $s \in M$ *and any set* $I \subset [n]$ *where* $|I| \leq t_p$*, there exists a simulator* Sim *such that the distributions of the outputs of* $\mathsf{Sim}(I)$ *and* $(s_i)_{i\in I}$ *that generated by a real execution of* $\mathsf{Share}(s)$ *are identical.*

Verifiable Secret Sharing. Note that a secret sharing scheme only considers semi-honest dealer and participants, while in many applications, a scheme which is able to prevent malicious behaviours from them is needed. Thereby, Chor et al. [CGMA85] put forward a stronger notion called verifiable secret sharing (VSS) schemes, where each participant is able to check the validity of the received share, such that the behavior of delivering invalid shares will be detected. Feldman [Fel87] further introduced the concept of non-interactive VSS schemes, where each participant could check the validity of his own share without interaction between other participants.

3 A Framework of Sigma Protocols from VSS

3.1 A Refined Definition of VSS Schemes

Before describing the framework, we first give a refined definition of VSS, adapted from the definition in [Fel87].

Definition 7 (Verifiable Secret Sharing). *A verifiable secret sharing scheme consists of following four algorithms:*

- $\mathsf{Setup}(1^\lambda)$*: on input the security parameter* λ*, outputs system parameters* pp*, including descriptions of secret space* M*, share space* S*, randomness space* R *(if there is any), commitment space* C*, the number of participants* n*, the privacy threshold* t_p *and the fault-tolerance threshold* t_f*, where all the three parameters* n*,* t_p *and* t_f *are positive integers and hold that* $n \geq t_f > t_p$*.*

- $\mathsf{Share}(s)$*: on input a secret* $s \in M$*, outputs a commitment* $c \in C$*,* n *shares* $(v_i)_{i\in[n]} \in S^n$ *and the authentication information* aut*. For ease of exposition, we describe the process by two algorithms:*

$$c \leftarrow \mathsf{Com}(s; r),$$
$$((v_i)_{i\in[n]}, aut) \leftarrow \mathsf{Share}^*(s, r),$$

where the randomness r *could be null in some settings.*
- $\mathsf{Check}(i, v_i, c, aut)$*: on input* P_i*'s index* i *and share* v_i*, a commitment* c *and the authentication information* aut*, outputs "1" iff* v_i *is valid for* P_i *w.r.t.* c *and* aut*; outputs "0", otherwise.*
- $\mathsf{Recover}(I, (v_i)_{i\in I})$*: on input a set of participants* $I \subseteq [n]$ *and a vector of shares* $(v_i)_{i\in I}$ *where* $v_i \in S$*, outputs a secret* $s \in M$ *and a randomness* $r \in R$ *(if there is any), or a special reject symbol* $\perp$ *denoting failure.*

A VSS scheme should satisfy following three properties:

Acceptance. *If the dealer honestly shares the secret, then all honest participants who receive correct shares will output "accept" in the end of Sharing phase. Formally, for any* $pp \leftarrow \mathsf{Setup}(1^\lambda)$*,* $s \in M$*,* $(c, (v_i)_{i\in[n]}, aut) \leftarrow \mathsf{Share}(s)$*, it holds that* $\mathsf{Check}(i, v_i, c, aut) = 1$ *for all* $1 \leq i \leq n$*.*

t_f***-Correctness.*** *Any group with at least* t_f *honest participants who output "accept" at the end of Sharing phase can recover a secret via algorithm* $\mathsf{Recover}$ *and the reconstructed secret must be an opening of the public commitment. Formally, for any* $pp \leftarrow \mathsf{Setup}(1^\lambda)$ *where* pp *include the fault-tolerance threshold* t_f*, any* $c \in C$*, any* aut *and any vector of shares* $(v_i)_{i\in I} \in S^{|I|}$ *where* $I \subseteq [n]$ *and* $|I| \geq t_f$*, if for all* $1 \leq j \leq m$*, it holds that* $\mathsf{Check}(i, v_i, c, aut) = 1$*, then for* $(s, r) \leftarrow \mathsf{Recover}(I, (v_i)_{i\in I})$*, it satisfies* $\mathsf{Com}(s; r) = c$*.*

t_p***-Privacy.*** *The joint view of* t_p *or less participants reveals nothing about the secret except a commitment to it. Formally, for any* $pp \leftarrow \mathsf{Setup}(1^\lambda)$ *where* pp *include the privacy threshold* t_p*, any* $s \in M$*, any* $c \leftarrow \mathsf{Com}(s; r)$ *and any set* $I \subset [n]$ *where* $|I| \leq t_p$*, there exists a simulator* Sim *such that the distributions of the output of* $\mathsf{Sim}(c, I)$ *and* $((v_i)_{i\in I}, aut)$ *that generated by the real execution of* $\mathsf{Share}^*(s, r)$ *are identical.*

For notation convenience, we denote (n, t_p, t_f)-(V)SS by (verifiable) secret sharing schemes with number of participants n, privacy threshold t_p and fault-tolerance threshold t_f. Particularly, we say a verifiable secret sharing scheme VSS is with respect to a commitment scheme Com, if VSS.Share runs Com.Com as a subroutine to commit to the secret.

A Dissection of Share^* **Algorithm.** In conventional syntax of VSS, Share^* algorithm outputs all shares $(v_1, ..., v_n)$ in one shot, where n denotes the maximum number of possible participants. Such syntax is fine when n is polynomial in λ. But, it is problematic when n is superpolynomial[3] in λ because

[3] The value n could even be exponential in security parameter λ (e.g. the size of a finite field).

Share^* algorithm becomes inefficient. To fix this issue, we further dissect Share^* algorithm as below:

(i) $\mathsf{Share\text{-}in\text{-}Mind}(s, r)$: on input a secret s and a randomness r, outputs a compact description of the sharing method SH_{cpt} and the associated authentication information aut. Both of their sizes are no larger than $\mathsf{poly}(\lambda)$.
(ii) $\mathsf{Distribute}(s, r, SH_{\text{cpt}}, i)$: on input the secret s, the randomness r, the compact description of the sharing method SH_{cpt} and an index i, generates share v_i for participant P_i as per the prefixed sharing method. This step is analogous to the private key extraction algorithm in identity-based cryptography, which generates the private keys for users on-the-fly upon request.

Evidently, our refined syntax can precisely captures all VSS schemes, while the conventional syntax is only suitable for VSS schemes with polynomial size n.

Flexible Design of VSS. The VSS schemes can be designed in a flexible manner. For example, when the secret s is a vector, the commitment c could either be a single vector commitment committing to the multiple entries of the secret at once (e.g., using Pedersen vector commitment [Ped91,BBB+18]), or a vector of commitments committing to each entry of the secret (e.g., the VSS scheme in Sect. 4.2). Meanwhile, the shares v_i's could either be packed shares of the multiple entries of s (e.g., being generated by using packed Shamir's secret sharing scheme [FY92] as the VSS scheme in Sect. 4.2), or be a collection of separate shares of each entry of the secret. Moreover, the authentication information aut could be viewed as a commitment to the sharing procedure, which possibly are in the form of polynomial commitments, non-interactive zero-knowledge proofs or something else.

3.2 The Framework of Sigma Protocols

Having settled a satisfactory definition of VSS, we are ready to describe our framework of Sigma protocols. Let Com = ($\mathsf{Setup}, \mathsf{Com}, \mathsf{Verify}$) be an algebraic commitment scheme, and VSS = ($\mathsf{Setup}, \mathsf{Share}, \mathsf{Check}, \mathsf{Recover}$) be an (n, t_p, t_f)-VSS scheme w.r.t Com. The framework of Sigma protocols for relation $\mathsf{R}_{\text{Com}} = \{(x; s, r) : \mathsf{Com}(s; r) = x\}$ proceeds as below (see Fig. 1 for a pictorial view).

- **Commit:** the prover P runs $((v_i)_{i\in[n]}, aut) \leftarrow \mathsf{VSS.Share}^*(s, r)$ "in his head", and then sends the authentication information aut to the verifier V;
- **Challenge:** V chooses a random set of participants $I \subset [n]$ subject to $|I| = t_p$, and queries P for corresponding shares;
- **Response:** P replies with the shares $(v_i)_{i\in I}$.

Finally, V verifies whether $(v_i)_{i\in I}$ are valid shares for $(P_i)_{i\in I}$ w.r.t. aut and x, and outputs *accept* iff $\mathsf{Check}(i, v_i, x, aut) = 1$ for all $i \in I$.

Theorem 1. *Suppose* VSS *is an* (n, t_p, t_f)*-VSS scheme where* $t_f \log t_f = O(\log \lambda)$, *then the protocol described in Fig. 1 is a Sigma protocol for* $\mathcal{NP}$ *relation* R_{Com} *with* $\left(\binom{t_f-1}{t_p} + 1\right)$*-special soundness.*

$$\mathsf{Com}(s;r) = x$$

$\underline{P(x; s, r)}$		$\underline{V(x)}$
$((v_i)_{i\in[n]}, aut) \leftarrow \mathsf{VSS.Share}^*(s, r)$	$\xrightarrow{aut}$	
		$I \xleftarrow{R} [n]_{t_p}$
	$\xleftarrow{I}$	
	$\xrightarrow{(v_i)_{i\in I}}$	accept iff $\forall i \in I$, $\mathsf{VSS.Check}(i, v_i, x, aut) = 1$

Fig. 1. A framework of Sigma protocols for algebraic commitments

Proof. We separately argue its completeness, special soundness and SHVZK.

Completeness. This follows readily from the acceptance property of the underlying VSS schemes.

Special Soundness. We argue this by constructing a PPT extractor Ext as below. For notation convenience, let $k = \binom{t_f-1}{t_p} + 1$. Since $t_f \log t_f = O(\log \lambda)$, k is bounded by $\mathsf{poly}(\lambda)$. Given any k accepting transcripts $(aut, I_j, (v_i)_{i\in I_j})_{j\in[k]}$, where $|I_j| = t_p$ and $I_j \neq I_{j'}$ for all $j \neq j'$, first note that, there exist at least t_f distinct indices $i_1, \ldots, i_{t_f} \in [n]$ along with corresponding shares $v_{i_1}, \ldots, v_{i_{t_f}}$ (which are possibly not unique) subject to $\mathsf{VSS.Check}(i_j, v_{i_j}, x, aut) = 1$ for all $j \in [t_f]$. This is because if not, then there must be a $(t_f - 1)$-sized set T, such that all I_j's are subsets of T. Since the total number of t_p-sized subsets of T is $\binom{t_f-1}{t_p} < \binom{t_f-1}{t_p} + 1$, there must exist two sets $I_j = I_{j'}$ where $j \neq j'$ by the pigeonhole principle. This contradicts to the hypothesis that $I_j \neq I_{j'}$ for all $j \neq j'$. Thus, Ext can extract a witness simply through running $\mathsf{VSS.Recover}$ on input $(i_j)_{j\in[t_f]}, (v_{i_j})_{j\in[t_f]}$ and taking the output (s, r) as its own output. By the correctness of VSS scheme, the reconstructed witness (s, r) must hold that $\mathsf{Verify}(x, s, r) = 1$. This implies that the soundness error of the Sigma protocol in Fig. 1 is $\binom{t_f-1}{t_p}/\binom{n}{t_p}$, which is no greater than $(t_f/n)^{t_p}$.

SHVZK. We prove the SHVZK property by constructing a simulator Sim as below. Given the statement x and a challenge $I \in [n]_{t_p}$, the simulator Sim invokes the simulator of VSS scheme $\mathsf{Sim}_{\mathsf{VSS}}$ on input (x, I) and outputs the same as $\mathsf{Sim}_{\mathsf{VSS}}$ does, which includes the joint views of parties in I, namely the shares $(v_i)_{i\in I}$ and the authentication information aut. Based on the t_p-privacy of VSS scheme, the simulated transcript is distributed identically to real one.

A More Detailed Framework. In the light of the dissection of Share^* algorithm in Sect. 3.1, the framework of Sigma protocols from VSS could also be dissected. Specifically, in the *Commit* phase, P runs the algorithm $(SH_{\text{cpt}}, aut) \leftarrow \mathsf{VSS.Share\text{-}in\text{-}Mind}(s, r)$ and sends aut to V. In the *Challenge* phase, V chooses and sends random set $I \subset [n]$ as before. In the *Response* phase, P runs $v_i \leftarrow \mathsf{VSS.Distribute}(s, r, SH_{\text{cpt}}, i)$ for all $i \in I$. In fact, this framework could yield more efficient Sigma protocols, since the prover only needs to compute the requested shares, not all the shares. Sigma protocols in Sects. 4.2 to 4.4 all follow this framework.

Parameters Selection. The three parameters n, t_p, t_f of the underlying VSS schemes could be any positive integers subject to $|\mathbb{F}| \geq n \geq t_f > t_p$ where $\mathbb{F}$ is the field to which parameters n, t_p, t_f belong. However, there are two caveats that warrant attention:

1. When n is superpolynomial in the security parameter λ, the Sigma protocols from such VSS schemes follow the detailed version of the framework. This is because, the underlying Share^* algorithm in this case must be dissected for efficiency reasons.
2. If the soundness error $(t_f/n)^{t_p}$ in a single execution of the protocol is not negligible in the security parameter λ, one should repeat the protocol in parallel to amplify soundness. To achieve soundness error of $2^{-\lambda}$, one should set the repetition number $\rho = \frac{\lambda}{t_p(\log n - \log t_f)}$.

Size of I. For the sake of simplicity, we set the size of I to t_p, which is equal to the privacy threshold of the VSS scheme. Actually, it is possible to set the size of I to be an arbitrary positive number k smaller than t_p, thus leading to Sigma protocols with $\left(\binom{t_f-1}{k}+1\right)$-special soundness. This can be proved similarly as in the proof of Theorem 1.

4 Instantiations of Our Framework

In this section, we demonstrate the generality of our framework by recovering the classic Schnorr [Sch91], Batching Schnorr [GLSY04], Okamoto [Oka92] and GQ [GQ88] protocols from corresponding VSS schemes.

4.1 Proof of Knowledge of a Discrete Logarithm

Let $\mathbb{G}$ be a cyclic group with generator g and prime order p, define $\mathsf{Com}(s) = g^s$. Given a commitment $x \in \mathbb{G}$, we show how to prove knowledge of s such that $g^s = x$. In Sect. 1.1.1, we have showed how to recover the classic Schnorr protocol from Feldman's VSS scheme. Below, we present another Sigma protocol from the following additive VSS scheme.

- $\mathsf{Setup}(1^\lambda)$: runs $(\mathbb{G}, p, g) \leftarrow \mathsf{GroupGen}(1^\lambda)$, sets the total number of participants $n \leq p$, the privacy threshold $t_p = n-1$ and the fault-tolerance threshold $t_f = n$, outputs $pp = ((\mathbb{G}, p, g), n, t_p, t_f)$.

- Share(s): computes commitment $c = g^s$, picks $s_1, \ldots, s_n \xleftarrow{\text{R}} \mathbb{Z}_p$ subject to $s = \sum_{i=1}^{n} s_i \mod p$, then sets P_i's share $v_i = s_i$ and $aut = (c_1, \ldots, c_{n-1})$ where $c_i = g^{s_i}$ for $i \in [n-1]$, outputs the vector $(c, (v_i)_{i \in [n]}, aut)$.
- Check(i, v_i, c, aut): parses $aut = (c_1, \ldots, c_{n-1})$, if $i \in [1, n-1]$, then outputs "1" iff $g^{v_i} = c_i$ and outputs "0" otherwise; if $i = n$, then outputs "1" if $g^{v_i} = c / \prod_{j=1}^{n-1} c_j$ and "0" otherwise.
- Recover($I, (v_i)_{i \in I}$): outputs $s = \sum_{i \in I} v_i \mod p$.

Theorem 2. *The above VSS scheme satisfies acceptance, n-correctness and $(n-1)$-privacy properties.*

By plugging the above VSS scheme into our framework, we obtain a variant of Schnorr protocol for proving knowledge of a discrete logarithm (as depicted in Fig. 2).

$$x = g^s$$

$\underline{P(x; s)}$ $\hfill$ $\underline{V(x)}$

$s_1, \ldots, s_n \xleftarrow{\text{R}} \mathbb{Z}_p$
s.t. $s = \sum_{i=1}^{n} s_i \mod p$ $\qquad \xrightarrow{\quad aut = (c_1, \ldots, c_{n-1}) \quad}$
for $i \in [n-1]$, $c_i = g^{s_i}$ $\hfill I \xleftarrow{\text{R}} [n]_{n-1}$

$\xleftarrow{\qquad\qquad I \qquad\qquad}$

$\xrightarrow{\quad (s_i)_{i \in I} \quad}$ $\qquad$ accept iff for $i \in I$,
$\hfill$ if $i \in [1, n-1]$, $g^{s_i} = c_i$,
$\hfill$ if $i = n$, $g^{s_i} = x / \prod_{j=1}^{n-1} c_j$

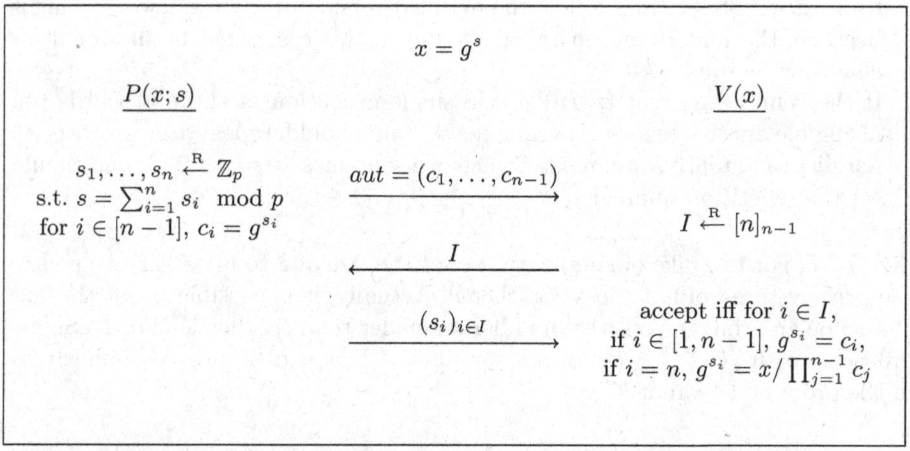

Fig. 2. A Sigma protocol for proving knowledge of a discrete logarithm

4.2 Proof of Knowledge of Several Discrete Logarithms

Define $\mathsf{Com}(\mathbf{s}) = (g^{s_j})_{j \in \{1, \ldots, |\mathbf{s}|\}}$. Given a vector of commitments $\mathbf{x} = (x_j)_{j \in [\ell]}$, we show how to prove knowledge of $\mathbf{s} = (s_j)_{j \in [\ell]}$ such that $g^{s_j} = x_j$ for all $j \in [\ell]$. Consider following VSS scheme:

- Setup(1^λ): runs $(\mathbb{G}, p, g) \leftarrow \mathsf{GroupGen}(1^\lambda)$, picks a positive number $\ell \in \mathbb{Z}_p^*$, sets the total number of participants $n \le p$ and the privacy threshold t_p and the fault-tolerance threshold $t_f = t_p + \ell$, outputs $pp = ((\mathbb{G}, p, g), n, t_p, t_f, \ell)$.
- Share($\mathbf{s}$): on input the secret $\mathbf{s} = (s_j)_{j \in [\ell]}$, runs following three algorithms and outputs $(\mathbf{c}, SH_{\mathrm{cpt}}, aut)$:

- $\mathsf{Com}(\mathbf{s})$: computes $c_j = g^{s_j}$ for $j \in [\ell]$, outputs $\mathbf{c} = (c_j)_{j\in[\ell]} \in \mathbb{G}^\ell$;
- $\mathsf{Share\text{-}in\text{-}Mind}(\mathbf{s})$: selects $a_1, \ldots, a_{t_p} \xleftarrow{R} \mathbb{Z}_p^*$, defines a polynomial $A(x) = \sum_{j=1}^{t_p+\ell} a_j \cdot x^{j-1}$ where $a_{t_p+j} = s_j$ for all $j \in [\ell]$, sets $SH_{\text{cpt}} = (a_j)_{j\in[t_p]}$ and $aut = (\widetilde{c}_j)_{j\in[t_p]}$ where $\widetilde{c}_j = g^{a_j}$ for $j \in [t_p]$, outputs (SH_{cpt}, aut);
- $\mathsf{Distribute}(\mathbf{s}, SH_{\text{cpt}}, i)$: parses $\mathbf{s} = (s_j)_{j\in[\ell]}$ and $SH_{\text{cpt}} = (a_j)_{j\in[t_p]}$, sets $a_{t_p+j} = s_j$ for $j \in [\ell]$, computes $v_i = \sum_{j=1}^{t_p+\ell} a_j \cdot i^{j-1} \mod p$, outputs v_i. (This algorithm is run upon request.)

- $\mathsf{Check}(i, v_i, \mathbf{c}, aut)$: parses $\mathbf{c} = (c_j)_{j\in[\ell]}$ and $aut = (\widetilde{c}_j)_{j\in[t_p]}$, outputs "1" if it holds that $g^{v_i} = \left(\prod_{j=1}^{t_p} \widetilde{c}_j^{\,i^{j-1}}\right) \cdot \left(\prod_{j=1}^{\ell} c_j^{\,i^{t_p+j-1}}\right)$ and "0" otherwise.
- $\mathsf{Rec}(I, (v_i)_{i\in I})$: computes a polynomial $A(x)$ such that $A(i) = v_i$ for all $i \in I$, sets s_j be the $(t_p + j)$-th coefficient of A, outputs $(s_j)_{j\in[\ell]}$.

Theorem 3. *Above VSS scheme satisfies acceptance, $(t_p + \ell)$-correctness and t_p-privacy.*

By plugging the above VSS scheme into our framework, we obtain a Sigma protocol for proving knowledge of several discrete logarithms (as depicted in Fig. 3). By setting parameters $n = p$ and $t_p = 1$, we recover the Batching Schnorr protocol [GLSY04].

$$x_1 = g^{s_1}, \ldots, x_\ell = g^{s_\ell}$$

$P((x_j)_{j\in[\ell]}; (s_j)_{j\in[\ell]})$		$V((x_j)_{j\in[\ell]})$
$a_1, \ldots, a_{t_p} \xleftarrow{R} \mathbb{Z}_p^*$ for $j \in [t_p]$, $\widetilde{c}_i = g^{a_i}$	$\xrightarrow{aut = (\widetilde{c}_j)_{j\in[t_p]}}$	
	$\xleftarrow{I}$	$I \xleftarrow{R} [n]_{t_p}$
for $i \in I$, $v_i = \sum_{j=1}^{t_p} a_j \cdot i^{j-1} + \sum_{j=1}^{\ell} s_j \cdot i^{t_p+j-1}$	$\xrightarrow{(v_i)_{i\in I}}$	accept iff for $i \in I$, $g^{v_i} = \prod_{j=1}^{t_p} \widetilde{c}_j^{\,i^{j-1}} \cdot \prod_{j=1}^{\ell} x_j^{\,i^{t_p+j-1}}$

Fig. 3. A Sigma protocol for proving knowledge of several discrete logarithms

4.3 Proof of Knowledge of a Representation

Define $\mathsf{Com}(s; r) = g^s h^r$ where g, h are two different generators of group $\mathbb{G}$. Given a commitment x, we show how to prove knowledge of (s, r) such that $g^s h^r = x$ from the Pedersen's VSS scheme [Ped91] as below:

- $\mathsf{Setup}(1^\lambda)$: runs $(\mathbb{G}, p, g, h) \leftarrow \mathsf{GroupGen}(1^\lambda)$, sets the total number of participants $n \leq p$, the privacy threshold t_p and the fault-tolerance threshold $t_f = t_p + 1$, outputs $pp = ((\mathbb{G}, p, g, h), n, t_p, t_f)$.
- $\mathsf{Share}(s)$: on input the secret s, runs following three algorithms and outputs $(c, SH_{\text{cpt}}, aut)$:
  - $\mathsf{Com}(s; r)$: picks a random element $r \xleftarrow{R} \mathbb{Z}_p^*$, outputs $c = g^s h^r$;
  - $\mathsf{Share\text{-}in\text{-}Mind}(s, r)$: picks two random t_p-degree polynomials $A(x) = \sum_{i=0}^{t_p} a_i \cdot x^i$ and $B(x) = \sum_{i=0}^{t_p} b_i \cdot x^i$ subject to $a_{t_p} = s$ and $b_{t_p} = r$, computes $c_j = g^{a_j} h^{b_j}$ for $0 \leq j \leq t_p - 1$, sets $SH_{\text{cpt}} = (a_j, b_j)_{0 \leq j \leq t_p - 1}$ and $aut = (c_j)_{0 \leq j \leq t_p - 1}$, outputs (SH_{cpt}, aut);
  - $\mathsf{Distribute}(s, r, SH_{\text{cpt}}, i)$: parses $SH_{\text{cpt}} = (a_j, b_j)_{0 \leq j \leq t_p - 1}$, sets $a_{t_p} = s$ and $b_{t_p} = r$, computes $s_i = \sum_{j=0}^{t_p} a_j \cdot i^j \mod p$ and $r_i = \sum_{j=0}^{t_p} b_j \cdot i^j \mod p$, outputs $v_i = (s_i, r_i)$. (This algorithm is run upon request.)
- $\mathsf{Check}(i, v_i, c, aut)$: parses $v_i = (s_i, r_i)$ and $aut = (c_j)_{0 \leq j \leq t_p - 1}$, outputs "1" if $g^{s_i} h^{r_i} = c^{i^{t_p}} \cdot \prod_{j=0}^{t_p - 1} c_j^{i^j}$ and "0" otherwise.
- $\mathsf{Recover}(I, (v_i)_{i \in I})$: parses $v_i = (s_i, r_i)$, constructs two polynomials $A(x)$, $B(x)$ such that $A(i) = s_i$ and $B(i) = r_i$ for all $i \in I$, sets s be the coefficient of the t_p-degree term of A and r be that of B, outputs (s, r).

Theorem 4. *Pedersen's VSS scheme satisfies acceptance, $(t_p + 1)$-correctness and t_p-privacy.*

By plugging the above VSS scheme into our framework, we obtain a Sigma protocol for proving knowledge of a representation (as depicted in Fig. 4). By setting parameters $n = p$ and $t_p = 1$, we recover the classic Okamoto protocol [Oka92].

$$x = g^s h^r$$

$\underline{P(x; s, r)}$ $\qquad\qquad$ $\underline{V(x)}$

$a_0, \ldots, a_{t_p - 1} \xleftarrow{R} \mathbb{Z}_p^*$;
$b_0, \ldots, b_{t_p - 1} \xleftarrow{R} \mathbb{Z}_p^*$;
for $0 \leq j \leq t_p - 1$, $c_j = g^{a_j} h^{b_j}$ $\quad \xrightarrow{aut = (c_j)_{0 \leq j \leq t_p - 1}}$

$\qquad\qquad I \xleftarrow{R} [n]_{t_p}$

$\xleftarrow{\quad I \quad}$

for $i \in I$, compute
$s_i = s \cdot i^{t_p} + \sum_{j=0}^{t_p - 1} a_j \cdot i^j \mod p$ $\quad \xrightarrow{(s_i, r_i)_{i \in I}}$ $\quad$ accept iff $\forall i \in I$, $g^{s_i} h^{r_i} = x^{i^{t_p}} \cdot \prod_{j=0}^{t_p - 1} c_j^{i^j}$
$r_i = r \cdot i^{t_p} + \sum_{j=0}^{t_p - 1} b_j \cdot i^j \mod p$

Fig. 4. A Sigma protocol for proving knowledge of a representation

4.4 Proof of Knowledge of An *e*th Root

Let GenRSA be a PPT algorithm that on input security parameter λ, outputs an RSA public key (N, e), where e is prime. Given an $x \in \mathbb{Z}_N^*$, we show how to prove knowledge of s such that $x = s^e \mod N$ from following VSS scheme:

- $\mathsf{Setup}(1^\lambda)$: runs $(N; e) \leftarrow \mathsf{GenRSA}(1^\lambda)$, where e is prime, sets the total number of participants $n \leq e$, and sets the privacy threshold $t_p = 1$ and the fault-tolerance threshold $t_f = 2$, outputs $pp = ((N, e), n, t_p, t_f)$.
- $\mathsf{Share}(s)$: on input a secret $s \in \mathbb{Z}_N^*$, runs following three algorithms and outputs $(c, SH_{\text{cpt}}, aut)$:
  - $\mathsf{Com}(s)$: computes the commitment $c = s^e \mod N$, outputs c;
  - $\mathsf{Share\text{-}in\text{-}Mind}(s)$: picks a random element $a \in \mathbb{Z}_N^*$, defines a function $f(x) = a \cdot s^x \mod N$, sets $SH_{\text{cpt}} = a$, computes $aut = a^e \mod N$, outputs (SH_{cpt}, aut);
  - $\mathsf{Distribute}(s, SH_{\text{cpt}}, i)$: parses $SH_{\text{cpt}} = a$, computes $s_i = a \cdot s^i \mod N$, outputs $v_i = s_i$. (This algorithm is run upon request.)
- $\mathsf{Check}(i, v_i, c, aut)$: outputs "1" if $v_i^e = aut \cdot c^i \mod N$ and "0" otherwise.
- $\mathsf{Recover}(I, (v_i)_{i \in I}, c)$: if $|I| < 2$ outputs $\perp$; else, runs the extended Euclidean algorithm yields integers $\alpha, \beta \in \mathbb{Z}_N^*$ such that $\alpha \cdot e + \beta \cdot (i_2 - i_1) = 1$, outputs $s = c^\alpha (v_{i_2}/v_{i_1})^\beta \mod N$.

Theorem 5. *The above VSS scheme satisfies acceptance,* 2*-correctness and* 1*-privacy properties.*

By plugging the above VSS scheme into our framework, we obtain a Sigma protocol for proving knowledge of an e-th root (as depicted in Fig. 5). By setting the parameter $n = e$, we recover the classic GQ protocol [GQ88].

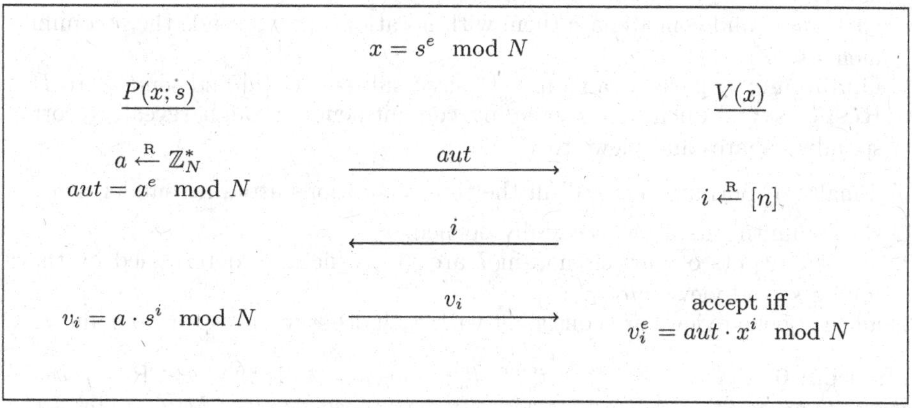

Fig. 5. A Sigma protocol for proving knowledge of an e-th root

5 A Framework of ZKPs for Composite Statements

In this section, we are going to show the application of the Sigma protocols from VSS in giving a generic construction of efficient ZKPs for composite statements. In this work, we focus on a common form of composite statement where given a commitment x and a value y, the prover wants to prove the knowledge of (s, r) such that $\mathsf{Com}(s; r) = x \wedge C(s) = y$, where C is an arithmetic/boolean circuit. In a nutshell, we use Sigma protocols from VSS to prove the algebraic parts, use ZK protocols from MPC to prove the non-algebraic parts, and enforce consistency between the witnesses used in two parts via *witness sharing reusing*.

5.1 A Generalization of MPC-in-the-Head Paradigm

Before designing the framework of ZKPs for composite statements, we first generalize the MPC-in-the-head paradigm introduced by Ishai et al. [IKOS07] via extending the XOR-based secret sharing scheme to an (n, t_p, t_f)-SS scheme. Precisely, to construct a ZK protocol for $\mathcal{NP}$ relation $\mathsf{R}_C = \{(y; s) : C(s) = y\}$ using MPC-in-the-head technique, we need three building blocks: a secret sharing scheme, an MPC protocol and a commitment scheme.

Let SS $=$ (Setup, Share, Recover) be an $(n, t_p^{\mathrm{ss}}, t_f)$-secret sharing scheme, $\widehat{\mathsf{Com}} = (\mathsf{Setup}, \mathsf{Com}, \mathsf{Verify})$ be a commitment scheme and Π_f be a t_p^{mpc}-private n-party protocol that realizes a n-party function f, where $f(y, s_1, \ldots, s_n) = 1$ if and only if $C(\mathsf{Recover}([n], (s_i)_{i\in[n]})) = y$, and integers $t_p^{\mathrm{mpc}} < t_p^{\mathrm{ss}}$. Then, ZK protocols following MPC-in-the-head paradigm proceeds as below (as depicted in Fig. 6):

- **Commit:** the prover P shares the witness s into n shares $s_1, \ldots, s_n$ by running SS.Share(s), then runs MPC protocol Π_f "in his head" with shares $s_1, \ldots, s_n$ as input of n virtual parties, then commits to each party's share s_i and view $view_i$ (without loss of generality, we separate P_i's input s_i from his view $view_i$ and concatenate them with notation $||$), and sends the n commitments to V;
- **Challenge:** V picks a random t_p^{mpc}-sized subset I of $[n]$ and sends it to P;
- **Response:** P opens corresponding commitments through revealing corresponding shares and views to V.

Finally, V outputs "accept" iff the three conditions listed hereunder hold:

1. the commitments are successfully opened;
2. all the outputs of participants in I are "1", which are determined by their inputs s_i and views $view_i$;
3. all the opened views are consistent with each other with respect to y and Π_f.

Theorem 6. *Let $n > 2$, $t_p^{\mathrm{ss}} \geq t_p^{\mathrm{mpc}}$, $t_p^{\mathrm{mpc}} \cdot \log n = O(\log \lambda)$, and R_C, f be as above. Suppose SS is an $(n, t_p^{\mathrm{ss}}, t_f)$-secret sharing scheme, the MPC protocol Π_f realizes the n-party functionality f with correctness and t_p^{mpc}-privacy and $\widehat{\mathsf{Com}}$ is a commitment scheme, then the protocol in Fig. 6, is a Sigma protocol for relation R_C with $\left(\binom{n-2}{t_p^{\mathrm{mpc}}} + 2\binom{n-2}{t_p^{\mathrm{mpc}}-1} + 1\right)$-special soundness.*

$$C(s) = y$$

$P(y; s)$ 　　　　　　　　　　　　　　　　　　　　　　$V(y)$

$(s_i)_{i \in [n]} \leftarrow \mathsf{SS.Share}(s)$
$(s_i \| view_i)_{i \in [n]} \leftarrow \Pi_{f(y, s_1, \dots, s_n)}$ 　$\xrightarrow{\quad c_1 \dots, c_n \quad}$
$\forall i \in [n], c_i \leftarrow \widehat{\mathsf{Com}}.\mathsf{Com}(s_i \| view_i)$ 　　　　　　　　　　　　$I \xleftarrow{\;\mathrm{R}\;} [n]_{t_p^{\mathrm{mpc}}}$
　　　　　　　　　　　　　$\xleftarrow{\qquad I \qquad}$

　　　　　　　　　　　$\xrightarrow{\;(s_i \| view_i)_{i \in I}\;}$ 　accept iff $\forall i \in I$
　　　　　　　　　　　　　　　　　　　$\widehat{\mathsf{Com}}.\mathsf{Verify}(c_i, s_i \| view_i) = 1$
　　　　　　　　　　　　　　　　　　　$\Pi_{f_y}(P_i, s_i \| view_i) = 1$
　　　　　　　　　　　　　　　　　　　$s_i \| view_i$ is consistent with others

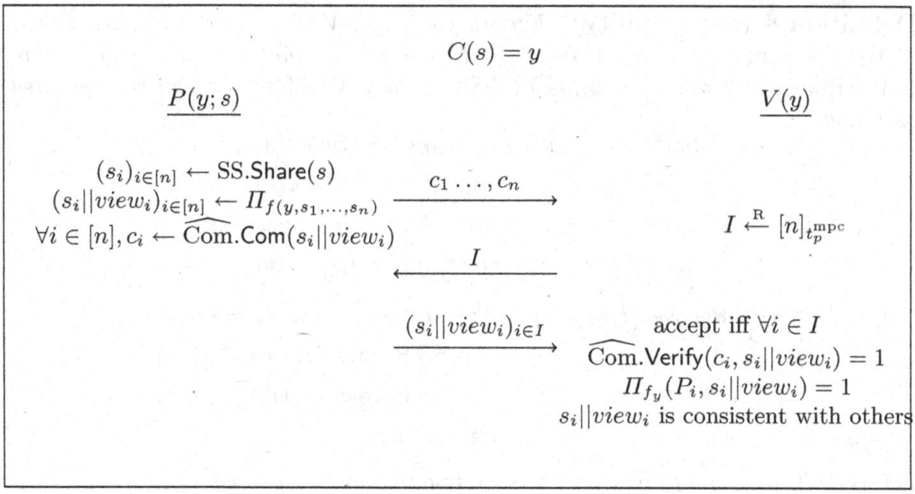

Fig. 6. ZKP from MPC-in-the-head paradigm

5.2 Separable VSS Schemes

As discussed in Sect. 1, in order to combine Sigma protocols from VSS and ZK protocols from MPC seamlessly, we are interested in VSS schemes which satisfy a mild property called *Separability*. Since the parameter n in the MPC-in-the-head paradigm is bounded by $\mathsf{poly}(\lambda)$, we consider the separability of VSS schemes simply using the syntax in Definition 7. Informally, for a VSS scheme, we say it satisfies *Separability* if the following two conditions hold:

1. The algorithm $\mathsf{Share}^*(s, r)$ could be separated into two sub-algorithms, one for generating the shares $(v_i)_{i \in [n]}$ and the other for generating the authentication information aut. Particularly, the shares $(v_i)_{i \in [n]}$ are generated as per some secret sharing schemes and aut is generated by committing to the sharing method (i.e., the shares $(v_i)_{i \in [n]}$ in the syntax in Definition 7 or the compact description of the sharing method SH_{cpt} in the dissected version).
2. If the randomness r is not a dummy value, then each share v_i could be divided into two values s_i and r_i, where the former is a share of the secret s and the later is a share of the randomness r. That is, s and r are secret-shared separately.

Below, we formally define the *Separability* property.

Definition 8 (Separability). *For an* (n, t_p, t_f)*-VSS scheme* VSS*, we say it satisfies separability if there is an* (n, t_p, t_f)*-SS scheme* SS *and an algorithm* AutGen *such that the algorithms* VSS.Share* *and* VSS.Recover *can be separated as below:*

$$\begin{aligned}\mathsf{VSS.Share}^*(s, r) : (s_i)_{i\in[n]} &\leftarrow \mathsf{SS.Share}(s)\\ (r_i)_{i\in[n]} &\leftarrow \mathsf{SS.Share}(r)\\ aut &\leftarrow \mathsf{AutGen}((s_i, r_i)_{i\in[n]})\\ &\mathit{return}\ ((s_i, r_i)_{i\in[n]}, aut)\end{aligned}$$

$$\begin{aligned}\mathsf{VSS.Recover}(I, (v_i)_{i\in I}) : &\forall 1 \le j \le |I|,\ \text{parse } v_i = (s_i, r_i)\\ &s \leftarrow \mathsf{SS.Recover}(I, (s_i)_{i\in[n]})\\ &r \leftarrow \mathsf{SS.Recover}(I, (r_i)_{i\in[n]})\\ &\mathit{return}\ (s, r)\end{aligned}$$

If r *is null, then only the* s *will be secret-shared and recovered.*

Particularly, we say a VSS scheme aligns with an SS scheme if it generates the shares as per this SS scheme.

Remark 1. More generally, in such separable VSS schemes, the SS schemes used to share secret s and randomness r could be different in some settings.

5.3 Generic Construction of ZKPs for Composite Statements

Now, we proceed to describe the generic construction of ZKPs for composite statements. Formally, let Com be an algebraic commitment algorithm and C be an arbitrary circuit, we give a zero-knowledge proof for relation:

$$\mathsf{R_{cs}} = \{(x, y; s, r) : \mathsf{Com}(s; r) = x \wedge C(s) = y\}.$$

Let Π_C^{MPC} be a Sigma protocol for $\{(y; s) : C(s) = y\}$ from MPC as depicted in Fig. 6 and using building blocks: an $(n, t_p^{\mathrm{ss}}, t_f)$-SS scheme SS, a commitment scheme $\widehat{\mathsf{Com}}$, and a t_p^{mpc}-private n-party protocol Π_f. Let $\Pi_{\mathrm{Com}}^{\mathrm{VSS}}$ be a Sigma protocol for $\{(x; s, r) : \mathsf{Com}(s; r) = x\}$ following the framework as in Fig. 1 and using building blocks: an $(n, t_p^{\mathrm{vss}}, t_f)$-VSS scheme VSS w.r.t. Com and SS. Below, we show how to obtain a ZK protocol $\Pi_{\mathrm{Com},C}$ for composite statements through combining Π_C^{MPC} and $\Pi_{\mathrm{Com}}^{\mathrm{VSS}}$, which is also a Sigma protocol. The full protocol is presented in Fig. 7 and the overlap between Π_C^{MPC} and $\Pi_{\mathrm{Com}}^{\mathrm{VSS}}$ are highlighted in rectangles.

- **Commit:** P proceeds as in $\Pi_{\mathrm{Com}}^{\mathrm{VSS}}$, running algorithm $((s_i, r_i)_{i\in[n]}, aut) \leftarrow$ VSS.Share*(s, r), which can be separated into three algorithms $(s_i)_{i\in[n]} \leftarrow$ SS.Share(s), $(r_i)_{i\in[n]} \leftarrow$ SS.Share(r) and $aut \leftarrow$ AutGen$((s_i, r_i)_{i\in[n]})$. Then, P proceeds as in Π_C^{MPC} while reusing the shares $(s_i)_{i\in[n]}$. Next, P sends $c_1, \ldots, c_n$ and aut to V.
- **Challenge:** V picks a random t_{mpc}-sized subset I of $[n]$ as in Π_C^{MPC}.

- **Response:** P responds with participants' inputs and views $(s_i\|view_i)_{i\in I}$ as in Π_C^{MPC} and shares of randomness $(r_i)_{i\in I}$ as in $\Pi_{\mathrm{Com}}^{\mathrm{VSS}}$.

Finally, V outputs "accept" iff $(s_i\|view_i)_{i\in I}$ pass the verification of Π_C^{MPC} and $(s_i, r_i)_{i\in I}$ pass the verification of $\Pi_{\mathrm{Com}}^{\mathrm{VSS}}$.

$$\mathsf{Com}(s;r) = x \wedge C(s) = y$$

$$\underline{P(x,y;s,r)} \qquad\qquad\qquad\qquad\qquad\qquad \underline{V(x,y)}$$

$\boxed{(s_i)_{i\in[n]} \leftarrow \mathsf{SS.Share}(s)}$
$(r_i)_{i\in[n]} \leftarrow \mathsf{SS.Share}(r)$
$aut \leftarrow \mathsf{AutGen}((s_i, r_i)_{i\in[n]})$ $\qquad c_1\ldots,c_n, aut$
$(s_i\|view_i)_{i\in[n]} \leftarrow \widehat{\Pi_{f(y,s_1,\ldots,s_n)}} \xrightarrow{\qquad\qquad\qquad\qquad}$
$\forall i \in [n], c_i \leftarrow \widehat{\mathsf{Com.Com}}(s_i\|view_i)$ $\qquad\qquad\qquad\qquad\qquad I \xleftarrow{\mathrm{R}} [n]_{t_p^{\mathrm{mpc}}}$

$\xleftarrow{\qquad\qquad I \qquad\qquad}$

$(r_i, \boxed{s_i}\|view_i)_{i\in I}$ $\qquad$ accept iff $\forall i \in I,$
$\xrightarrow{\qquad\qquad\qquad\qquad}$ $\widehat{\mathsf{Com}}.\mathsf{Verify}(c_i, s_i\|view_i) = 1$
$\qquad\qquad\qquad\qquad\qquad \Pi_f(P_i, s_i\|view_i) = 1$
$\qquad\qquad\qquad\qquad s_i\|view_i$ is consistent with others
$\qquad\qquad\qquad\qquad \mathsf{VSS.Check}(i, (s_i, r_i), x, aut) = 1$

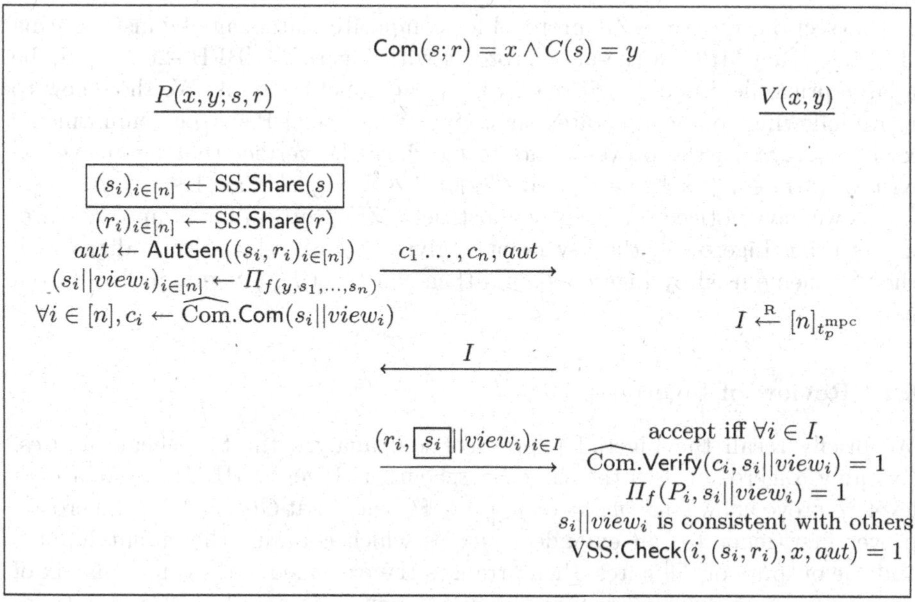

Fig. 7. A ZKP for composite statements

Theorem 7. *Let $n > 2$, $t_p^{\mathrm{ss}} \geq t_p^{\mathrm{mpc}}$, $t_p^{\mathrm{mpc}} \cdot \log n = O(\log \lambda)$. Suppose the protocol Π_C^{MPC} constructed as in Fig. 6 using building blocks SS, $\widehat{\mathsf{Com}}$ and Π_f as above, is a Sigma protocol for relation $\{(y;s) : C(s) = y\}$ with $\left(\binom{n-2}{t_p^{\mathrm{mpc}}} + 2\binom{n-2}{t_p^{\mathrm{mpc}}-1} + 1\right)$- special soundness, protocol $\Pi_{\mathrm{Com}}^{\mathrm{VSS}}$ constructed as in Fig. 1 using building block VSS which is with respect to Com and aligns with SS, is a Sigma protocol for relation $\{(x;s,r) : \mathsf{Com}(s;r) = x\}$, then the protocol $\Pi_{\mathrm{Com},C}$ constructed as in Fig. 7 is a Sigma protocol for R_{cs} with $\left(\binom{n-2}{t_p^{\mathrm{mpc}}} + 2\binom{n-2}{t_p^{\mathrm{mpc}}-1} + 1\right)$-special soundness.*

Remark 2 (Key element required for combining). In order to get better efficiency, some practical protocols in the MPC-in-the-head paradigm slightly deviate from the template in Sect. 5.1, depending on the concrete MPC protocols they used. For example, the KKW protocol [KKW18] utilizes an MPC protocol designed in the preprocessing model and the Ligero [AHIV17]/Ligero++ [BFH+20] protocols make use of a particular type of MPC protocols in the malicious model.

Nevertheless, they all retain the secret sharing procedure (though different secret sharing schemes are employed), which is the key element that is required for combining with our Sigma protocols framework in Sect. 3.2.

6 An Instantiation of ZKP for Composite Statements

In this section, we give a ZK protocol for composite statements by instantiating the underlying MPC-in-the-head protocol with Ligero++ [BFH+20]. Let $\mathbb{F}_p$ be a large prime field and $C : \mathbb{F}_p^m \to \mathbb{F}_p$ be an arithmetic circuit. We show how to prove following composite statements: given a vector of Pedersen commitments $\mathbf{x} = (x_1, \ldots, x_m)$, the prover wants to convince the verifier that he knows the witness $(\mathbf{s}, \mathbf{r}) \in \mathbb{F}_p^m \times \mathbb{F}_p^m$ such that $C(\mathbf{s}) = 1 \wedge x_i = g^{s_i} h^{r_i}$ for $1 \leq i \leq m$.

As we have noticed, in order to construct a ZK protocol for composite statements using Ligero++, the key point is giving a VSS scheme that aligns with the SS scheme used by Ligero++, and then constructing a Sigma protocol from it.

6.1 Review of Ligero++

We briefly recall the Ligero++ protocol and analyze the SS scheme it uses. (Notably, Ligero++ uses the same SS scheme as Ligero [AHIV17].) At a high level, to prove knowledge of $\mathbf{s} = (s_i)_{i \in [m]} \in \mathbb{F}_p^m$ such that $C(\mathbf{s}) = 1$, the Ligero++ prover first generates an extended witness which contains the circuit input $\mathbf{s}$ and the outputs of $|C|$ gates, then arranges the extended witness in a matrix of size $\frac{C}{\mathsf{polylog}|C|} \times \mathsf{polylog}|C|$ (where the first m entries are $(s_i)_{i \in [m]}$) and encodes each row using Reed-Solomon (RS) Code. The verifier challenges the prover to reveal the linear combinations of the rows of the codeword matrix, and checks its consistency through invoking inner-product argument (IPA) protocols on $\tilde{t}$ randomly picked columns. As mentioned in [BFH+20], to remain zero-knowledge during the consistency check, it is desirable to either utilize zero-knowledge IPA protocols or make the encoding randomized. For further consideration, we use a randomized RS encoding to ensure zero knowledge. The formal definition of RS code is presented below.

Definition 9 (Reed-Solomon Code). *For positive integers n, k, a finite field $\mathbb{F}$, and a vector $\eta = (\eta_1, \ldots, \eta_n)$ of distinct elements of $\mathbb{F}$, the code $\mathsf{RS}_{\mathbb{F},n,k,\eta}$ is the $[n, k, n-k+1]$ linear code over $\mathbb{F}$ that consists of all n-tuples $(P(\eta_1), \ldots, P(\eta_n))$ where P is a polynomial of degree $< k$ over $\mathbb{F}$.*

Definition 10 (Encoded message). *Let $L = \mathsf{RS}_{\mathbb{F},n,k,\eta}$ be an RS code and $\zeta = (\zeta_1, \ldots, \zeta_\ell)$ be a vector of distinct elements of $\mathbb{F}$ for $\ell \leq k$. For a codeword $u = (u_1, \ldots, u_n) \in L$, we say it encodes (or rather, can be decodes to) the message $(P_u(\zeta_1), \ldots, P_u(\zeta_\ell))$, where P_u is the polynomial (of degree $< k$) corresponding to u.*

Encoding and Sharing. We can simply make the RS code $\mathsf{RS}_{\mathbb{F},n,k,\eta}$ randomized via increasing the degree of polynomials by $\widetilde{t}$ where $\widetilde{t} < k$, and it is evident that the randomized RS code $\mathsf{RS}_{\mathbb{F},n,k,\eta}$ can be viewed as the (variant) packed Shamir's SS scheme [FY92] with number of participants n, privacy threshold $t_p = \widetilde{t}$ and the fault-tolerance $t_f = k$. That is, encoding a message is equivalent to sharing the message: to encode (resp., share) a message $(s_i)_{i\in[\ell]}$ using randomized $\mathsf{RS}_{\mathbb{F},n,k,\eta}$ (resp., packed Shamir's SS scheme), one first selects $\widetilde{t}$ random elements $\alpha_1, \ldots, \alpha_{\widetilde{t}} \in \mathbb{F}$ where $\ell + \widetilde{t} = k$ and generates a polynomial $P(x)$ with degree $< \ell + \widetilde{t}$ such that $P(\zeta_i) = s_i$ for all $i \in [\ell]$ and $P(\zeta_{\ell+i}) = \alpha_i$ for all $i \in [\widetilde{t}]$, then sets the codeword (resp., shares) to be $(P(\eta_1), \ldots, P(\eta_n))$. Therefore, the codeword matrix aforementioned is also the shares matrix.

Modifications to Ligero++. As mentioned before, the Ligero++ protocol does not strictly conform to the generalized MPC-in-the-head paradigm in Sect. 5.1, due to the different MPC model it used. There are two main differences that could pose challenges in combining Ligero++ with Sigma protocols. First, the witness to be shared is an expanded version that encompasses the input of circuit and the outputs of all circuit gates, rather than only the input itself, making the shares opened later be an expanded version as well. Second, the $\widetilde{t}$ random columns of shares matrix will not be opened directly due to the invocation of IPA protocols, causing obstructions of reusing witness shares. Fortunately, both of them can be overcame with a few modifications to Ligero++: dividing the shares matrix into two vertically concatenated sub-matrices and handling them differently when in the consistency check. Specifically, the two sub-matrices and their respective handling methods are as follows:

- The first sub-matrix is the first m/ℓ rows of the shares matrix (WLOG., we assume $m = c \cdot \ell$ for some integer $c > 0$), which in fact is the shares of circuit input $\mathbf{s}$. When in the consistency check, the prover opens its $\widetilde{t}$ entries directly to the verifier and the verifier computes the inner product of these entries with random vectors directly. Thereby, the shares of circuit input $\mathbf{s}$ could be reused later. Since the encoding is randomized, the openings leak nothing about the witness.
- The second sub-matrix is the remaining rows of the shares matrix, which are the shares of outputs of gates. When in the consistency check, the prover inputs its $\widetilde{t}$ entries on IPA protocols as originally while the inner product checked in IPA protocols should be modified according to the opened entries of the first sub-matrix.

By doing so, the shares of inputs $\mathbf{s}$ and shares of gates' outputs are separated. Moreover, it makes witness shares reusing available while maintaining the advantage of utilizing IPA technique.

6.2 A Sigma Protocol for Pedersen Commitments

Having specified the SS scheme that Ligero++ employs, we are now ready to present a VSS scheme that aligns with this SS scheme and later give a corresponding Sigma protocol from it.

Since the parameter n in the SS scheme used by Ligero++ is bounded by $\mathsf{poly}(\lambda)$, we describe the VSS scheme simply using the syntax in Definition 7. The VSS scheme consists following four algorithms:

- $\mathsf{Setup}(1^\lambda)$: runs $(\mathbb{G}, p, g, h) \leftarrow \mathsf{GroupGen}(1^\lambda)$, sets the total number of participants n, the privacy threshold t_p, the fault-tolerance threshold $t_f = \ell + t_p$, picks two disjoint vectors $\boldsymbol{\zeta} = (\zeta_j)_{j\in[\ell+t_p]} \in \mathbb{F}_p^{\ell+t_p}$ and $\boldsymbol{\eta} = (\eta_i)_{i\in[n]} \in \mathbb{F}_p^n$, and both $\boldsymbol{\zeta}, \boldsymbol{\eta}$ contain distinct elements, outputs $pp = ((\mathbb{G}, p, g, h), n, t_p, t_f, \ell, \boldsymbol{\zeta}, \boldsymbol{\eta})$.
- $\mathsf{Share}(\mathbf{s})$: on input a vector of secret $\mathbf{s} = (s_j)_{j\in[\ell]} \in \mathbb{F}_p^\ell$, runs following two algorithms and outputs $(\mathbf{c}, (v_i)_{i\in[n]}, aut)$:
  - $\mathsf{Com}(\mathbf{s}; \mathbf{r})$: selects a vector of randomness $\mathbf{r} = (r_j)_{j\in[\ell]} \xleftarrow{\text{R}} \mathbb{F}_p^\ell$, outputs a vector of commitments $\mathbf{c} = (c_j)_{j\in[\ell]}$, where $c_j = g^{s_j} h^{r_j}$ for all $j \in [\ell]$.
  - $\mathsf{Share}^*(\mathbf{s}, \mathbf{r})$: chooses two random vectors $(\alpha_j)_{j\in[t_p]}, (\beta_j)_{j\in[t_p]} \xleftarrow{\text{R}} \mathbb{F}_p^{t_p}$, interpolates two polynomials $A(x)$ and $B(x)$ such that

$$\begin{aligned} &\forall 1 \leq j \leq \ell,\ A(\zeta_j) = s_j,\ B(\zeta_j) = r_j; \\ &\forall \ell + 1 \leq j \leq \ell + t_p,\ A(\zeta_j) = \alpha_{j-\ell},\ B(\zeta_j) = \beta_{j-\ell}, \end{aligned} \tag{1}$$

    outputs shares $(v_i)_{i\in[n]}$ where $v_i = (A(\eta_i), B(\eta_i))$ for all $i \in [n]$ and $aut = (\widetilde{c}_j)_{j\in[t_p]}$ where $\widetilde{c}_j = g^{\alpha_j} h^{\beta_j}$ for all $j \in [t_p]$.
- $\mathsf{Check}(i, v_i, \mathbf{c}, aut)$: parses $v_i = (v_{i1}, v_{i2})$ and $aut = (\widetilde{c}_j)_{j\in[t_p]}$, computes $h_k = \left(\prod_{j=1}^{\ell} c_j^{\delta_{k,j}}\right) \cdot \left(\prod_{j=1}^{t_p} \widetilde{c}_j^{\delta_{k,\ell+j}}\right)$ for $k \in [\ell + t_p]$, where the matrix $(\delta_{k,j})_{1\leq k,j\leq \ell+t_p}$ is equal to $\mathbf{V}(\boldsymbol{\zeta})^{-1}$, outputs "1" if $g^{v_{i1}} h^{v_{i2}} = \prod_{k=1}^{\ell+t_p} h_k^{\eta_i^{k-1}}$ and "0" otherwise.
- $\mathsf{Recover}(I, (v_i)_{i\in I})$: parses $v_i = (v_{i1}, v_{i2})$, uses Lagrange Interpolation to compute polynomials $A(x)$ and $B(x)$ such that $A(\eta_i) = v_{i1}$ and $B(\eta_i) = v_{i2}$ for all $i \in I$, outputs $(\mathbf{s}, \mathbf{r})$ where $(s_j, r_j) = (A(\zeta_j), B(\zeta_j))$ for $j \in [\ell]$.

Theorem 8. *The VSS scheme described above satisfies acceptance, $(\ell + t_p)$-correctness and t_p-privacy.*

By plugging the above VSS scheme into the framework in Sect. 1.1.1, we obtain a Sigma protocol (as depicted in Fig. 8) for proving knowledge of openings of several Pedersen commitments.

Parameters Selection. In order to combine with Ligero++, some of the public parameters of above VSS scheme, including p, n, t_p, ℓ, $\boldsymbol{\zeta}$ and $\boldsymbol{\eta}$, should be in line with that of Ligero++. Since Ligero++ performs interpolation and evaluation using fast Fourier transform (FFT), above VSS scheme should be implemented using elliptic curves whose scalar fields $\mathbb{F}_p$ are FFT-friendly. One can refer to [AHG22] for a suitable elliptic curve.

Security Analysis. Based on Lemma 1, Theorem 1 and Theorem 8, it is straightforward that the protocol in Fig. 8 is a Sigma protocol with soundness error $\binom{t_f-1}{t_p}/\binom{n}{t_p}$. When setting $n = c \cdot t_f$ for some constant $c \geq 1$, we must set $t_p = \lambda/\log c$ to achieve a soundness error of $2^{-\lambda}$ without repetition. Since

$$x_1 = g^{s_1}h^{r_1}, \ldots, x_\ell = g^{s_\ell}h^{r_\ell}$$

$P((x_j)_{j\in[\ell]}; (s_j, r_j)_{j\in[\ell]})$		$V((x_j)_{j\in[\ell]})$
$(\alpha_j)_{j\in[t_p]}, (\beta_j)_{j\in[t_p]} \xleftarrow{R} \mathbb{F}_p^{t_p}$ compute $A(x)$, $B(x)$ as in (1) $\forall\, i \in [n]$: $s_i = A(\eta_i)$, $r_i = B(\eta_i)$ $\forall\, j \in [t_p]$, $\widetilde{c}_j = g^{\alpha_j}h^{\beta_j}$	$aut = (\widetilde{c}_j)_{j\in[t_p]}$ $\longrightarrow$	
	$\longleftarrow$ I	$I \xleftarrow{R} [n]_{t_p}$
	$(s_i, r_i)_{i\in I}$ $\longrightarrow$	$(\delta_{k,j})_{1\le k,j\le \ell+t_p} = \mathbf{V}(\zeta)^{-1}$ $\forall k \in [\ell + t_p]$, $h_k = \prod_{j=1}^{\ell} x_j^{\delta_{k,j}} \cdot \prod_{j=\ell+1}^{\ell+t_p} \widetilde{c}_{j-\ell}^{\delta_{k,j}}$ accept iff $\forall i \in I$, $g^{s_i}h^{r_i} = \prod_{k=1}^{\ell+t_p} h_k^{\eta_i^{k-1}}$

Fig. 8. A Sigma protocol for Pedersen commitments

$\binom{t_f-1}{t_p}/\binom{n}{t_p}$ is smaller than the soundness error of Ligero++, the soundness error of ZK protocols for composite statements, obtained by combining Sigma protocols in Fig. 8 and Ligero++, is dominated by the soundness error of Ligero++.

Efficiency Analysis. Let λ be the security parameter, $\ell_{\mathbb{G}}$ be the length of a group element, $\ell_{\mathbb{F}}$ be the length of a field element and $\ell = |\mathbf{x}|$ be the number of commitments in the statement. Fix parameters n, t_p, t_f where $n = c \cdot t_f$ for some constant $c \geq 1$ and $t_f = \ell + t_p$. Then, the proof size is $t_p \cdot \ell_{\mathbb{G}} + 2t_p \cdot \ell_{\mathbb{F}})$, which asymptotically is $O(\lambda)$. The prover's work includes the computations of c_k's, which need $O(t_p)$ group operations; interpolation and evaluation of polynomials, which need $O((\ell + t_p) \cdot \log(\ell + t_p)$ field operations by using FFT. The verifier's work includes the computations of matrix $(\delta_{k,j})$, which need $O((\ell + t_p)^2)$ field operations; the computations of h_k's, which need $O(\ell + t_p)$ multi-exponentiations of size $\ell + t_p$; and the computations in the verification equations, which need $O(t_p)$ multi-exponentiations of size $\ell + t_p$. (Pippenger's [Pip80] algorithm could be used to accelerate the computations of multi-exponentiations.)

Having given the Sigma protocol for Pedersen commitments, it is not difficult to combine it with the Ligero++ protocol and get a ZK protocol for composite statements, following the method in Sect. 5.3, and we omit the details in this paper. The efficiency of the final ZK protocol reported in Table 1 is obtained by directly summing the costs of Ligero++ and above Sigma protocol. Since the underlying SS components are identical in Ligero and Ligero++, the Sigma protocol could also be combined with Ligero seamlessly by choosing appropriate parameters. This will lead to a faster prover while a larger proof size.

7 Conclusion

Sigma protocols are the most efficient ZKPs for proving knowledge of openings of algebraic commitments, which are defined as relations over algebraic groups. They have now become an important building block for a variety of cryptosystems. In this work, we presented a framework of Sigma protocols for algebraic statements from verifiable secret sharing schemes. This framework neatly explains the design principal underlying those classic Sigma protocols, including the Schnorr, Batching Schnorr, GQ and Okamoto protocol. In addition, it gives a generic construction of Sigma protocols for proving knowledge of algebraic commitments, thus being able to lead to new Sigma protocols that were not previously known. Furthermore, we also showed its application in designing ZKPs for composite statements. By using the *witness sharing reusing* technique, we combined the Sigma protocols from VSS and general-purpose ZKPs following MPC-in-the-head paradigm seamlessly, yielding a generic construction of ZKPs for composite statements which enjoys the advantages of requiring no "glue" proofs. Through instantiating the underlying general-purpose ZKPs with Ligero++ and tailoring a corresponding Sigma protocol, we obtain a concrete ZKP for composite statements, which achieves a tradeoff between running time and proof size, thus resolving the open problem left by Backes et al. (PKC 2019).

Acknowledgements. We thank the anonymous reviewers for their valuable comments. This work was supported by the National Key Research and Development Program of China (Grant No. 2021YFA1000600), the National Natural Science Foundation of China (Grant No. 62272269, No. 61932019, and No. 62372447), Taishan Scholar Program of Shandong Province, and Beijing Natural Science Foundation (Grant No. M22003).

References

[AAB+20] Abe, M., Ambrona, M., Bogdanov, A., Ohkubo, M., Rosen, A.: Non-interactive composition of sigma-protocols via share-then-hash. In: Moriai, S., Wang, H. (eds.) ASIACRYPT 2020. LNCS, vol. 12493, pp. 749–773. Springer, Cham (2020). https://doi.org/10.1007/978-3-030-64840-4_25

[AAB+21] Abe, M., Ambrona, M., Bogdanov, A., Ohkubo, M., Rosen, A.: Acyclicity programming for sigma-protocols. In: Nissim, K., Waters, B. (eds.) TCC 2021. LNCS, vol. 13042, pp. 435–465. Springer, Cham (2021). https://doi.org/10.1007/978-3-030-90459-3_15

[ABC+22] Aranha, D.F., Bennedsen, E.M., Campanelli, M., Ganesh, C., Orlandi, C., Takahashi, A.: ECLIPSE: enhanced compiling method for Pedersen-committed zkSNARK engines. In: Hanaoka, G., Shikata, J., Watanabe, Y. (eds.) PKC 2022. LNCS, vol. 13177, pp. 584–614. Springer, Cham (2022)

[ACK21] Attema, T., Cramer, R., Kohl, L.: A compressed Σ-protocol theory for lattices. In: Malkin, T., Peikert, C. (eds.) CRYPTO 2021. LNCS, vol. 12826, pp. 549–579. Springer, Cham (2021). https://doi.org/10.1007/978-3-030-84245-1_19

[AGM18] Agrawal, S., Ganesh, C., Mohassel, P.: Non-interactive zero-knowledge proofs for composite statements. In: Shacham, H., Boldyreva, A. (eds.) CRYPTO 2018. LNCS, vol. 10993, pp. 643–673. Springer, Cham (2018). https://doi.org/10.1007/978-3-319-96878-0_22

[AHG22] Aranha, D.F., El Housni, Y., Guillevic, A.: A survey of elliptic curves for proof systems. IACR Cryptology ePrint Archive (2022)

[AHIV17] Ames, S., Hazay, C., Ishai, Y., Venkitasubramaniam, M.: Lightweight sublinear arguments without a trusted setup. In: ACM CCS, Ligero (2017)

[BBB+18] Bünz, B., Bootle, J., Boneh, D., Poelstra, A., Wuille, P., Maxwell, G.: Short proofs for confidential transactions and more. In: IEEE S&P, Bulletproofs (2018)

[BBHR18] Ben-Sasson, E., Bentov, I., Horesh, Y., Riabzev, M.: Scalable, transparent, and post-quantum secure computational integrity (2018). http://eprint.iacr.org/2018/046

[BCC+16] Bootle, J., Cerulli, A., Chaidos, P., Groth, J., Petit, C.: Efficient zero-knowledge arguments for arithmetic circuits in the discrete log setting. In: Fischlin, M., Coron, J.-S. (eds.) EUROCRYPT 2016. LNCS, vol. 9666, pp. 327–357. Springer, Heidelberg (2016). https://doi.org/10.1007/978-3-662-49896-5_12

[BCG+14] Ben-Sasson, E., Chiesa, A., Garman, C., Green, M., Miers, I., Tromer, E., Virza, M.: Decentralized anonymous payments from bitcoin. In: IEEE S&P, Zerocash (2014)

[BCR+19] Ben-Sasson, E., Chiesa, A., Riabzev, M., Spooner, N., Virza, M., Ward, N.P.: Aurora: transparent succinct arguments for R1CS. In: Ishai, Y., Rijmen, V. (eds.) EUROCRYPT 2019. LNCS, vol. 11476, pp. 103–128. Springer, Cham (2019). https://doi.org/10.1007/978-3-030-17653-2_4

[BCS16] Ben-Sasson, E., Chiesa, A., Spooner, N.: Interactive oracle proofs. In: Hirt, M., Smith, A. (eds.) TCC 2016. LNCS, vol. 9986, pp. 31–60. Springer, Heidelberg (2016). https://doi.org/10.1007/978-3-662-53644-5_2

[Beu20] Beullens, W.: Sigma protocols for MQ, PKP and SIS, and fishy signature schemes. In: Canteaut, A., Ishai, Y. (eds.) EUROCRYPT 2020. LNCS, vol. 12107, pp. 183–211. Springer, Cham (2020). https://doi.org/10.1007/978-3-030-45727-3_7

[BFH+20] Bhadauria R., Fang Z., Hazay C., Venkitasubramaniam M., Xie T., Zhang Y.: Ligero++: a new optimized sublinear IoP. In: ACM CCS (2020)

[BGW88] Ben-Or, M., Goldwasser, S., Wigderson, A.: Completeness theorems for non-cryptographic fault-tolerant distributed computation (extended abstract). In: STOC (1988)

[BHH+19] Backes, M., Hanzlik, L., Herzberg, A., Kate, A., Pryvalov, I.: Efficient non-interactive zero-knowledge proofs in cross-domains without trusted setup. In: Lin, D., Sako, K. (eds.) PKC 2019. LNCS, vol. 11442, pp. 286–313. Springer, Cham (2019). https://doi.org/10.1007/978-3-030-17253-4_10

[CCD88] Chaum, D., Crépeau, C., Damgård, I.: Multiparty unconditionally secure protocols (extended abstract). In: STOC (1988)

[CDG+17] Chase, M., et al.: Post-quantum zero-knowledge and signatures from symmetric-key primitives. In: ACM CCS (2017)

[CDS94] Cramer, R., Damgård, I., Schoenmakers, B.: Proofs of partial knowledge and simplified design of witness hiding protocols. In: Desmedt, Y.G. (ed.) CRYPTO 1994. LNCS, vol. 839, pp. 174–187. Springer, Heidelberg (1994). https://doi.org/10.1007/3-540-48658-5_19

[CF85] Cohen, J.D., Fischer, M.J.: A robust and verifiable cryptographically secure election scheme (extended abstract). In: FOCS (1985)

[CFQ19] Campanelli, M., Fiore, D., Querol, A.: Modular design and composition of succinct zero-knowledge proofs. In: ACM CCS, Legosnark (2019)

[CGM16] Chase, M., Ganesh, C., Mohassel, P.: Efficient zero-knowledge proof of algebraic and non-algebraic statements with applications to privacy preserving credentials. In: Robshaw, M., Katz, J. (eds.) CRYPTO 2016. LNCS, vol. 9816, pp. 499–530. Springer, Heidelberg (2016). https://doi.org/10.1007/978-3-662-53015-3_18

[CGMA85] Chor, B., Goldwasser, S., Micali, S., Awerbuch, B.: Verifiable secret sharing and achieving simultaneity in the presence of faults. In: FOCS (1985)

[CHM+20] Chiesa, A., Hu, Y., Maller, M., Mishra, P., Vesely, N., Ward, N.: Marlin: preprocessing zkSNARKs with universal and updatable srs. In: Canteaut, A., Ishai, Y. (eds.) EUROCRYPT 2020. LNCS, vol. 12105, pp. 738–768. Springer, Cham (2020). https://doi.org/10.1007/978-3-030-45721-1_26

[CL01] Camenisch, J., Lysyanskaya, A.: An efficient system for non-transferable anonymous credentials with optional anonymity revocation. In: Pfitzmann, B. (ed.) EUROCRYPT 2001. LNCS, vol. 2045, pp. 93–118. Springer, Heidelberg (2001). https://doi.org/10.1007/3-540-44987-6_7

[COS20] Chiesa, A., Ojha, D., Spooner, N.: FRACTAL: post-quantum and transparent recursive proofs from holography. In: Canteaut, A., Ishai, Y. (eds.) EUROCRYPT 2020. LNCS, vol. 12105, pp. 769–793. Springer, Cham (2020). https://doi.org/10.1007/978-3-030-45721-1_27

[Cra96] Cramer, R.: Modular design of secure yet practical cryptographic protocols. Ph.D. thesis (1996)

[CZ21] Cui, H., Zhang, K.: A simple post-quantum non-interactive zero-knowledge proof from garbled circuits. In: Yu, Yu., Yung, M. (eds.) Inscrypt 2021. LNCS, vol. 13007, pp. 269–280. Springer, Cham (2021). https://doi.org/10.1007/978-3-030-88323-2_14

[Fel87] Feldman, P.: A practical scheme for non-interactive verifiable secret sharing. In: FOCS (1987)

[FFS87] Feige, U., Fiat, A., Shamir, A.: Zero knowledge proofs of identity. In: STOC (1987)

[FS86] Fiat, A., Shamir, A.: How to prove yourself: practical solutions to identification and signature problems. In: Odlyzko, A.M. (ed.) CRYPTO 1986. LNCS, vol. 263, pp. 186–194. Springer, Heidelberg (1987). https://doi.org/10.1007/3-540-47721-7_12

[FY92] Franklin, M.K., Yung, M.: Communication complexity of secure computation (extended abstract). In: STOC (1992)

[GGPR13] Gennaro, R., Gentry, C., Parno, B., Raykova, M.: Quadratic span programs and succinct NIZKs without PCPs. In: Johansson, T., Nguyen, P.Q. (eds.) EUROCRYPT 2013. LNCS, vol. 7881, pp. 626–645. Springer, Heidelberg (2013). https://doi.org/10.1007/978-3-642-38348-9_37

[GK15] Groth, J., Kohlweiss, M.: One-out-of-many proofs: or how to leak a secret and spend a coin. In: Oswald, E., Fischlin, M. (eds.) EUROCRYPT 2015. LNCS, vol. 9057, pp. 253–280. Springer, Heidelberg (2015). https://doi.org/10.1007/978-3-662-46803-6_9

[GLSY04] Gennaro, R., Leigh, D., Sundaram, R., Yerazunis, W.: Batching Schnorr identification scheme with applications to privacy-preserving authorization and low-bandwidth communication devices. In: Lee, P.J. (ed.) ASIACRYPT 2004. LNCS, vol. 3329, pp. 276–292. Springer, Heidelberg (2004). https://doi.org/10.1007/978-3-540-30539-2_20

[GMO16] Giacomelli, I., Madsen, J., Orlandi, C.: Faster zero-knowledge for Boolean circuits. In: USENIX, Zkboo (2016)

[GMR85] Goldwasser, S., Micali, S., Rackoff, C.: The knowledge complexity of interactive proof-systems (extended abstract). In: STOC (1985)

[GMW86] Goldreich, O., Micali, S., Wigderson, A.: How to prove all NP statements in zero-knowledge and a methodology of cryptographic protocol design (extended abstract). In: Odlyzko, A.M. (ed.) CRYPTO 1986. LNCS, vol. 263, pp. 171–185. Springer, Heidelberg (1987). https://doi.org/10.1007/3-540-47721-7_11

[GMW87] Goldreich, O., Micali, S., Wigderson, A.: How to play any mental game or a completeness theorem for protocols with honest majority. In: STOC (1987)

[GQ88] Guillou, L.C., Quisquater, J.-J.: A "paradoxical" indentity-based signature scheme resulting from zero-knowledge. In: Goldwasser, S. (ed.) CRYPTO 1988. LNCS, vol. 403, pp. 216–231. Springer, New York (1990). https://doi.org/10.1007/0-387-34799-2_16

[Gro09] Groth, J.: Linear algebra with sub-linear zero-knowledge arguments. In: Halevi, S. (ed.) CRYPTO 2009. LNCS, vol. 5677, pp. 192–208. Springer, Heidelberg (2009). https://doi.org/10.1007/978-3-642-03356-8_12

[Gro10] Groth, J.: Short pairing-based non-interactive zero-knowledge arguments. In: Abe, M. (ed.) ASIACRYPT 2010. LNCS, vol. 6477, pp. 321–340. Springer, Heidelberg (2010). https://doi.org/10.1007/978-3-642-17373-8_19

[Gro16] Groth, J.: On the size of pairing-based non-interactive arguments. In: Fischlin, M., Coron, J.-S. (eds.) EUROCRYPT 2016. LNCS, vol. 9666, pp. 305–326. Springer, Heidelberg (2016). https://doi.org/10.1007/978-3-662-49896-5_11

[HKR19] Hoffmann, M., Klooß, M., Rupp, A.: Efficient zero-knowledge arguments in the discrete log setting, revisited. In: ACM CCS (2019)

[IKO07] Ishai, Y., Kushilevitz, E., Ostrovsky, R.: Efficient arguments without short PCPs. In: IEEE CCC (2007)

[IKOS07] Ishai, Y., Kushilevitz, E., Ostrovsky, R., Sahai, A.: Zero-knowledge from secure multiparty computation. In: STOC (2007)

[JKO13] Jawurek, M., Kerschbaum, F., Orlandi, C.: Zero-knowledge using garbled circuits: how to prove non-algebraic statements efficiently. In: ACM CCS (2013)

[Kil92] Kilian, J.: A note on efficient zero-knowledge proofs and arguments (extended abstract). In: STOC (1992)

[KKW18] Katz, J., Kolesnikov, V., Wang, X.: Improved non-interactive zero knowledge with applications to post-quantum signatures. In: ACM CCS (2018)

[KR08] Kalai, Y.T., Raz, R.: Interactive PCP. In: ICALP (2008)

[Lee21] Lee, J.: Dory: efficient, transparent arguments for generalised inner products and polynomial commitments. In: Nissim, K., Waters, B. (eds.) TCC 2021. LNCS, vol. 13043, pp. 1–34. Springer, Cham (2021). https://doi.org/10.1007/978-3-030-90453-1_1

[Lip12] Lipmaa, H.: Progression-free sets and sublinear pairing-based non-interactive zero-knowledge arguments. In: Cramer, R. (ed.) TCC 2012. LNCS, vol. 7194, pp. 169–189. Springer, Heidelberg (2012). https://doi.org/10.1007/978-3-642-28914-9_10

[Mau15] Maurer, U.: Zero-knowledge proofs of knowledge for group homomorphisms. Des. Codes Cryptogr. **77**, 663–676 (2015)

[MBKM19] Maller, M., Bowe, S., Kohlweiss, M., Meiklejohn, S.: Sonic: zero-knowledge snarks from linear-size universal and updatable structured reference strings. : ACM CCS (2019)

[Mic94] Micali, S.: CS proofs (extended abstracts). In: FOCS (1994)

[NY90] Naor, M., Yung, M.: Public-key cryptosystems provably secure against chosen ciphertext attacks. In: STOC (1990)

[Oka92] Okamoto, T.: Provably secure and practical identification schemes and corresponding signature schemes. In: Brickell, E.F. (ed.) CRYPTO 1992. LNCS, vol. 740, pp. 31–53. Springer, Heidelberg (1993). https://doi.org/10.1007/3-540-48071-4_3

[Ped91] Pedersen, T.P.: Non-interactive and information-theoretic secure verifiable secret sharing. In: Feigenbaum, J. (ed.) CRYPTO 1991. LNCS, vol. 576, pp. 129–140. Springer, Heidelberg (1992). https://doi.org/10.1007/3-540-46766-1_9

[Pip80] Pippenger, N.: On the evaluation of powers and monomials. SIAM J. Comput. (1980)

[RB89] Rabin, T., Ben-Or, M.: Verifiable secret sharing and multiparty protocols with honest majority (extended abstract). In: STOC (1989)

[RRR16] Reingold, O., Rothblum, G.N., Rothblum, R.D.: Constant-round interactive proofs for delegating computation. In: STOC (2016)

[Sah99] Sahai, A.: Non-malleable non-interactive zero knowledge and adaptive chosen-ciphertext security. In: FOCS (1999)

[Sch91] Schnorr, C.-P.: Efficient signature generation by smart cards. J. Cryptol. (1991)

[Set20] Setty, S.: Spartan: efficient and general-purpose zkSNARKs without trusted setup. In: Micciancio, D., Ristenpart, T. (eds.) CRYPTO 2020. LNCS, vol. 12172, pp. 704–737. Springer, Cham (2020). https://doi.org/10.1007/978-3-030-56877-1_25

[Sha79] Shamir, A.: How to share a secret. CACM (1979)

[Tha22] Thaler, J.: Proofs, arguments, and zero-knowledge. Found. Trends® Privacy Secur. (2022)

[ZXZS20] Zhang, J., Xie, T., Zhang, Y., Song, D.: Transparent polynomial delegation and its applications to zero knowledge proof. In: IEEE S&P (2020)

Anonymity

Anonymous Counting Tokens

Fabrice Benhamouda[1], Mariana Raykova[2(✉)], and Karn Seth[2]

[1] Amazon Web Services, Seattle, USA
[2] Google, Menlo Park, USA
marianar@google.com

Abstract. We introduce a new primitive called *anonymous counting tokens* (ACTs) which allows clients to obtain blind signatures or MACs (aka tokens) on messages of their choice, while at the same time enabling users to enforce rate limits on the number of tokens that a client can obtain for each message. Our constructions enforce that each client will be able to obtain only one token per message and we show a generic transformation to support other rate limiting as well. We achieve this new property while maintaining the unforgeability and unlinkability properties required for anonymous tokens schemes. We present four ACT constructions with various trade-offs for their efficiency and underlying security assumptions. One construction uses factorization-based primitives and a cyclic group. It is secure in the random oracle model under the q-DDHI assumption (in a cyclic group) and the DCR assumption. Our three other constructions use bilinear maps: one is secure in the standard model under q-DDHI and SXDH, one is secure in the random oracle model under SXDH, and the most efficient of the three is secure in the random oracle model and generic bilinear group model.

1 Introduction

Counting unique users can be a useful signal for different applications to measure service usage and user interest. In many contexts, however, the content for which we want to measure interest may be sensitive, so we would like to guarantee anonymity for the user while still providing accurate counts. The anonymity property becomes challenging when untrustworthy users may try to inflate the counts. As a concrete example, we consider the k-anonymity server developed in the context of Privacy Sandbox [Gra22]. The goal of this server is to count how many users have joined different user interest groups. Users should not be linkable to any specific interest groups. At the same time, it is important to obtain an accurate count of the number of users in each interest group. In particular, each user should not be counted multiple times. In addition, users should be allowed to join as many interest groups as they wish.

There is seemingly a tension between the desirable anonymity that does not allow mapping the count contribution to the user identity and the ability to

F. Benhamouda—Work done while employed at Algorand Foundation, prior to joining Amazon.

J. Guo and R. Steinfeld (Eds.): ASIACRYPT 2023, LNCS 14439, pp. 245–278, 2023.
https://doi.org/10.1007/978-981-99-8724-5_8

bound contributions from each user. Multiparty computation (MPC) [Ode09] and in particular secure aggregation constructions [BIK+17,BBG+20] enable computing aggregates over user inputs while maintaining privacy for concrete contributions. However, these solutions do not allow users to be anonymous while at the same time limiting the rate of their input contributions.

Anonymous credential tools such as blind signatures [Cha82] and anonymous tokens [DGS+18,KLOR20,SS22] provide capabilities to convey trust across different contexts while providing anonymity. In the setting of anonymous tokens, during token issuance, the user identity is known to an issuer who can provide a token that encodes a limited amount of information. The token is associated with a user-provided message or a random message that the issuer should not learn. In our initial example of counting the number of users in each interest group, the message would be the interest group name. The token can later be redeemed in a different context where the user is anonymous. At redemption, the message is revealed. In order to be able to use these tokens to count the number of users in each interest group, it is crucial that each user can only contribute a single token. In other words, anonymous tokens redemption (or issuance) should be restricted (or rate limited) to a single token per user and per message. More generally, anonymous tokens allowing redemption of a small fixed number of tokens per user and per message can be considered.

A recent IETF draft proposed by four large tech companies (Google, Apple, Cloudflare, Fastly) [HIP+22] is highlighting two other applications of such rate-limited or counting tokens: rate-limiting anonymous tokens per website (or "origin") to avoid abuse, and implementing metered paywall for a given website. In both cases, anonymous tokens need to be associated with the website, and rate limits need to be applied per message. The IETF draft proposes a solution that relies on two non-colluding servers: an attester and an issuer. The attester sees the information used for rate limiting in the clear (that is the "origin" or website in the applications above). Instead, if we were able to design an anonymous token scheme restricting each user to only receive a small number of tokens per (hidden, underlying) message, we could provide a solution for the IETF draft applications without the need for two separate servers.

The challenge in designing the rate-limiting capability on the private message authenticated in anonymous tokens lies in the following fact: users should be able to obtain blind tokens for many messages (e.g., be able to contribute to the counts for many different user interest groups in the first example, or visiting many different paywall-metered websites in the last example). And all these messages should remain hidden from the issuer. Only violations of the rate-limiting rules should be detectable before such tokens are redeemed. At the same time, different users should be able to obtain anonymous tokens for the same message, as many users will join the same interest group or visit the same website. Therefore tokens for the same message from different users need to be distinct. In particular, tokens cannot computed deterministically from the message (as it is the case in Privacy Pass [DGS+18]).

We note that anonymous tokens with public or private metadata such as [SS22,CDV23] do not help building the applications above. Indeed, in these schemes the metadata needs to be revealed to the issuer in order for the issuer to be able to apply rate limits. In the interest group example, this means the issuer would know which interest group a user is joining.

Contributions. In this paper we propose a new notion of anonymous tokens which we call *anonymous counting tokens* (ACTs). This primitive offers an additional rate-limiting property that guarantees that no user will be able to redeem with the same verifier more than one token for the same message. Conceptually there are two approaches to enforcing the rate-limiting property in the anonymous token functionality. This can be done either at issuance by enabling the issuer to detect repeated token requests for the same message from the same user, or at redemption by enabling the verifier to identify if two tokens for the same message were issued to the same user. With the first approach, the challenge is to preserve the blind property of the requests as long as there are no repeating message requests, and to reveal only the one bit information whether a message in a request has been queried before. With the second approach, the challenge is to enable the verifier to detect when the two tokens for the same message were issued to the same user while preserving the unlinkability property.

We present two conceptual approaches for building ACTs. One enables rate limiting at issuance and one enables it at redemption. Both of them assume that each user registers a public key with the issuer and this public key enables the rate limiting of one token per message per user. Recall that at issuance, users identify themselves to the issuer and can thus be associated to their registered public keys. Note that such registration is necessary: if there was no registration mechanism, tokens would information theoretically be completely independent of the user identity and it would be impossible to ensure a given user does not create and redeem two tokens for the same message (unless tokens are deterministic functions of messages in which case the issuer could know when two different users ask the same message, which in turn would break unlinkability).

Our first construction uses a PRF evaluation as the token issuance mechanism. This mechanism has been leveraged in previous anonymous token constructions [DGS+18,KLOR20,SS22]. Our first construction is in the random oracle model (ROM) and relies on the q-Decisional Diffie-Hellman Inversion assumption (q-DDHI) assumption in a group of prime order.

Our second set of constructions leverages the notion of equivalence class signatures (EQS) [FG18,FHS19] to construct an ACT scheme. Existing EQS schemes rely on bilinear maps. We present three instantiations of our EQS-based ACT construction. The first one is in the standard model and assumes the SXDH and q-DDHI assumptions over bilinear groups to support short $O(\log \lambda)$ messages (λ is the security parameter). The second instantiation is proven in the ROM under just the SXDH assumption and supports any length of message. The last instantiation uses much stronger security assumptions: it is only proven in the ROM and generic bilinear group model (GBGM) but achieves significantly shorter tokens. Our three instantiations are based on two generic transforms of EQS into ACT, however, our third instantiation is an optimization whose security is proven directly in the ROM and GBGM and does not directly follow from the security of the generic transform.

Tables 1 and 2 summarize the communication costs and assumptions tradeoffs of our constructions. Our four constructions are the four first constructions of anonymous counting tokens: there are no prior such constructions. We provide four different constructions as parties implementing anonymous counting tokens may have different preferences for cryptographic assumptions and tools used in the constructions. For example, in enterprise products (targeted by the IETF draft [HIP+22]), adding pairing-based libraries can be quite challenging due to non-technical reasons (e.g., audit requirements, complex approval process, etc.).

Table 1 and 2 also contain comparisons to selected related works which do *not* achieve the anonymous *counting* tokens property. We include them for an informative comparison of what it takes to add the additional properties we need. Privacy Pass [DGS+18] achieves unforgeability and unlinkability, but has no notion of an underlying message on which rate limiting can be done. [TCR+22] extends Privacy Pass to support public metadata, which can be viewed as a message. However, the public metadata is revealed to both the issuer and the verifier and thus cannot be used in our context. [FHS19] enables multi-show anonymous credentials, a very different primitive that allows a user to get a credential on a set of messages, but without blind issuance. The credential can be redeemed multiple times while remaining unlinkable with the issuance and the other redemptions. Several of our constructions can be seen as extensions of [FHS19] to support blind issuance and a throttling mechanism, so we include it to give a sense of the extra cost incurred for these additional properties. We note that the costs in Table 2 for [FHS19] are for a single message or attribute, but their scheme supports vectors of messages/attributes.

Table 1. Summary of our constructions and selected previous work

Cons.	PubV	Assumptions	|msg|	Extra
4.1	×	ROM + DCR + q-DDHI	any	**counting**
5.1	✓	SXDH + $2^{\|msg\|}$-DDHI$_{\mathbb{G}_1}$	$\mathcal{O}(\log(\lambda))$	**counting**
5.2	✓	ROM + SXDH	any	**counting**
6.1	✓	ROM + GBGM	any	**counting**
[DGS+18]	×	ElGamal-OMD	n/a	n/a
[TCR+22]	×	ROM + OM-Gap-SDHI	any	public metadata
[FHS19]	✓	ROM + GBGM	any	multi-show

Extra properties are properties beyond anonymous token base properties. Our constructions are the only anonymous counting tokens. See text for detail. PubV refers to public verifiability (i.e., whether anyone can verify a token from the public parameters).
Assumptions: DCR = decisional composite residuosity assumption, SXDH = symmetric external decisional Diffie-Hellman assumption, q-DDHI = decisional Diffie-Hellman inversion assumption (q is the number of signature queries made by the adversary), ROM = random oracle model, GBGM = generic bilinear group model, all of our constructions but the first one use pairings. ElGamal-OMD = ElGamal One-More-Decryption assumption. OM-Gap-SDHI = (m,n) One-More-Gap-Strong Diffie-Hellman Inversion assumption.

1.1 Technical Approach

Next, we overview the main technical challenges and ideas for our constructions.

Table 2. Performance of our constructions and selected previous work

Cons	|blindRequest|	|blindToken|	|tok|
4.1	$5 \times \mathsf{Ped} + 4 \times \mathsf{CS} + 12 \times \mathbb{Z}_p + 11 \times \mathbb{Z}_N$	$1 \times \mathsf{Ped} + 1 \times \mathbb{Z}_p + 3 \times \mathbb{Z}_N$	$1 \times \mathbb{G}$
5.1	$7 \times \mathbb{G}_1 + 6 \times \mathbb{G}_2$	$5 \times \mathbb{G}_1 + 1 \times \mathbb{G}_2$	$23 \times \mathbb{G}_1 + 12 \times \mathbb{G}_2$
5.2	$2 \times \mathbb{Z}_p + 3 \times \mathbb{G}_1$	$5 \times \mathbb{G}_1 + 1 \times \mathbb{G}_2$	$23 \times \mathbb{G}_1 + 12 \times \mathbb{G}_2$
6.1	$2 \times \mathbb{Z}_p + 2 \times \mathbb{G}_1$	$2 \times \mathbb{G}_1 + 1 \times \mathbb{G}_2$	$3 \times \mathbb{G}_1 + 1 \times \mathbb{G}_2$
[DGS+18]	$1 \times \mathbb{G}$	$1 \times \mathbb{G} + 2 \times \mathbb{Z}_p$	λ
[TCR+22]	$1 \times \mathbb{G} + 1 \times \mathbb{Z}_p$	$1 \times \mathbb{G} + 2 \times \mathbb{Z}_p$	$1 \times \mathbb{G}$
[FHS19]	$\mathbb{Z}_p + \mathbb{G}_1$	$2 \times \mathbb{G}_1 + \mathbb{G}_2$	$3 \times \mathbb{G}_1 + \mathbb{G}_2 + 2 \times \mathbb{Z}_p$

Only our four constructions are anonymous **counting** tokens. The other constructions are just for reference and do not achieve the counting property. See text for detail.
Constructions 5.1 and 5.2 (long version) are instantiated using the EQS construction from Sect. 6.1., full version [BRS23], and the element M'_1 and M'_3 are not included in tok as they can be recomputed.
$\mathbb{G}$ denotes a cyclic group (and by extension a group element from $\mathbb{G}$) with order p, $\mathbb{G}_1$ and $\mathbb{G}_2$ are asymmetric bilinear maps groups, CS is a Camenish-Shoup ciphertext, Ped is a Pedersen commitment on a strong RSA group.
Using Edwards25519 [BDL+12] for $\mathbb{G}$, $1 \times \mathbb{G} = 32$ bytes. Using BLS12-381 [Bow17] as bilinear group, $1 \times \mathbb{G}_1 = 48$ bytes, $1 \times \mathbb{G}_2 = 96$ bytes. For both Edwards25519 and BLS12-381, $1 \times \mathbb{Z}_p = 32$ bytes. Using the NIST recommendation [Bar16] for 128-bit safe-RSA modulus (that is 3072 bits), $1 \times \mathsf{Ped} = 384$ bytes and $1 \times \mathsf{CS} = 1{,}536$ bytes. N refers to this RSA modulus, and $\log(N) = 3072$ bits.

ACT from PRF. We start with our first construction. It follows the idea of previous anonymous tokens schemes to make the tokens be PRF evaluations under the issuer's secret key. A first construction attempt might be to make the anonymous tokens deterministic. This is what Privacy Pass [DGS+18] does, where tokens are PRF evaluations of the users' messages. This, however, is possible in Privacy Pass only because the tokens there do not correspond to messages that have meaning for the application and instead are sampled at random for every token issuance. For our ACT scheme, we need the user to be able to choose the message. If the tokens are a deterministic function of the message alone (and not of the user identity), then the issuer will know when two users ask for the same message which would violate the unlinkability. Thus, we need to have a randomized issuance algorithm.

To give insight into our construction, we start with an overview of some unsuccessful ideas for building anonymous counting tokens from the randomized version of the Okamoto-Schnorr Privacy Pass tokens introduced by Kreuter et al. [KLOR20]. Contrary to Privacy Pass, tokens generated by these schemes are randomized (and not deterministic). Like in Privacy Pass, the client sends the following blinded request to the issuer: $\mathsf{r} \cdot \mathsf{H}(\mathsf{msg})$, where r is chosen a random in $\mathbb{Z}_p$ by the client and where H is a hash function into a cyclic group $\mathbb{G}$ of order p (where DDH is hard). H is modeled as a random oracle in the proof and we use the additive notation for $\mathbb{G}$.

A first idea to construct an ACT is to have each client always use the same fixed randomness r to blind their requests. This would allow the issuer to detect when the same user makes two requests for the same message. We would argue the unlinkability of the requests by remarking those can also be seen as PRF evaluations using the key r, which is only known by the client. The client could provide the issuer with a commitment to this PRF key r (as part of the registration process). And the client would then prove the correctness of the message included in each blinded request with respect to the committed key, using a zero-knowledge proof.

This idea would actually work. Unfortunately, the resulting protocol would be quite inefficient as the zero-knowledge proof made by the client requires proving the correct evaluation of the hash function H. We note that the Pedersen hash ($\mathsf{H}(m) = m_1G_1 + \cdots + m_nG_n$, where m_i is the i-th bit of the message m and G_i is a generator of $\mathbb{G}$) has good algebraic properties which may allow for an efficient zero-knowledge proof. However, it cannot be used in this setting since its linear properties enable an attack on the rate limiting as follows: $\mathsf{H}(1||0||\ldots||0) + \mathsf{H}(0||1||0||\ldots||0) = \mathsf{H}(1||1||0||\ldots||0)$, which allows to get a fresh token on $1||1||0||\ldots||0$ by querying messages $1||0||\ldots||0$ and $0||1||\ldots||0$.

Another option could be to use SNARK/STARK/Bulletproofs-friendly hash functions such as MiMC [AGR+16] and Poseidon [GKR+21]. However, this would first introduce the new non-standard assumptions that are used for the security of these hash functions. Additionally, depending on the proof system used, there will be a need for more assumptions (for example non-falsifiable assumptions for SNARKs). Furthermore, those proof techniques are generic and use circuits. This significantly increases the prover's complexity (which is used in the token request that is computed by weak user devices, in many cases). Furthermore, the proof needs to prove not only correct hash evaluation, but also mapping to the elliptic curve, and exponentiation/scalar multiplication. The Poseidon costs in Sect. 6 of [GKR+21] report around 40ms for a SNARK just proving correct Poseidon hash evaluation: the subsequent scalar multiplication would at least double this time to > 80ms. These costs appeared to be much higher than our approach. In addition, without a trusted setup, only STARKs and Bulletproofs can be used and they are about 10x more expensive than SNARKs for Poseidon evaluation.

Yet another tempting way to get an efficient scheme would be to only require the client to prove the blinded request is of the form $\mathsf{r} \cdot \mathsf{T}$ for some group element T, and not proving knowledge of msg such that $\mathsf{T} = \mathsf{H}(\mathsf{msg})$. We may think we can argue unforgeability since the client will only be able to extract a valid signature if they know a correct hash preimage of T (due to the form of the tokens in [KLOR20]).

While the above reasoning does guarantee the regular unforgeability property, it fails to protect against the adversary being able to obtain two tokens for the same value, which is required by ACT. The issue stems from the fact that the resulting tokens are of the form $x\mathsf{H}(\mathsf{msg}) + yS$ where (x, y) is the secret key of the issuer and S is a random element that comes with the token. Now, we can observe that the token is additively homomorphic with respect to the hash of the message. With this observation, an attacker can obtain a token for message msg without directly asking for it, by additively sharing $\mathsf{H}(\mathsf{msg})$ as $A + B = \mathsf{H}(\mathsf{msg})$. Then the client can request two tokens, sending blind requests $\mathsf{r}A$ and $\mathsf{r}B$. The client can prove correctness for its requests as long as it does not have to prove knowledge of hash preimages of A and B. Then, using the additive properties of the tokens, it can recover a token for $\mathsf{H}(\mathsf{msg})$ which will be different from any previous token issued directly for that value.

Thus, we adopt a different pseudorandom function which has a structure that facilitates composition with sigma protocols for proof of correctness of evaluation (in particular, it does not involve a hash function). This is the Dodis-Yampolskiy verifiable pseudorandom function [DY05]. We instantiate it in a single group as a PRF without public verifiability, as in the work of Miao et al. [MPR+20]. However, this on its own does not solve the question of the randomized issuance algorithm. One option is to add to the message a random value, which changes for every issuance, and make the token the PRF evaluation under the issuer's key on the message plus randomness. To ensure the rate limiting we will use a different PRF which the user evaluates only on the message under its registered key and provides this to the issuer during issuance to prove non-repeating message requests.

The way we choose to combine message and randomness as input for the PRF evaluation (to generate the token) leverages the function $\mathsf{F}(\mathsf{sk} = (\mathsf{u}, \mathsf{y}), \mathsf{msg}; \mathsf{r}) = (\mathsf{msg} + \mathsf{u} + \mathsf{r} \cdot \mathsf{y})$, which is used by Boneh and Boyen to construct short signatures without random oracle [BB04]. In the proof of their construction, they show how this function no longer has the limitation to short messages of the Dodis-Yampolskiy's variant as long as r is chosen at random and can be controlled by the reduction.

We further observe that the randomness r for the issuance needs to be chosen jointly by the client and the issuer. If the client can choose the randomness on its own, then it can force homomorphism of the tokens, which could create forgery issues similar to the one discussed above. If the issuer controls the randomness, then this becomes an easy fingerprinting mechanism, which violates unlinkability. While we can generate the randomness with an interactive coin-tossing protocol, we observe that the issuer's randomness does not need to be private with respect to the client since we just want to enforce that the randomness is chosen honestly. Thus, we apply the Fiat-Shamir transformation to generate the issuer's randomness in a non-interactive manner [FS87, AFK22].

ACT from EQS. The second general construction approach for ACT that we present views the tokens as signatures with certain homomorphic properties which allow the client to adapt a signature for a message $\vec{\mathsf{M}}$ to a signature of a transformed message $\vec{\mathsf{M}}' = f(\vec{\mathsf{M}})$. The set of allowed transformation f is limited and fixed. In particular, equivalence class (EQS) signatures [FG18, FHS19] enable the client to sign vectors of messages and the adaptation functionality allows the client to transform the signature into a signature of a new vector that is in the linear span of the signed message. This transformation is used as part of the blinding and unblinding operations in previous anonymous tokens and blind signatures constructions.

Taking this approach, of course, creates challenges for the rate-limiting property. Seemingly a client might be able to create multiple tokens from the same initial signature. To prevent this we need to embed the rate-limiting check but this time during redemption. This can be achieved similarly to the above construction using a PRF evaluation on the message with a key that each user commits with the issuer. The challenge when doing this check during redemption is to remove the link to the client identity while maintaining the ability to verify that the PRF value was generated by a key registered by a real client.

Our approach to satisfy the above requirements is to have the client embed a PRF evaluation on the message under their registered key in the blind signature request. We show how we can do this using two different PRF constructions $\mathsf{PRF}(\mathsf{u}, \mathsf{msg}) = \mathsf{u} \cdot \mathsf{H}(\mathsf{msg})$ and $\mathsf{PRF}(\mathsf{u}, \mathsf{msg}) = (\mathsf{msg} + \mathsf{u})^{-1} \cdot \mathsf{G}$ (the latter being the Dodis-Yampolskiy PRF). In the first case, unlike our first PRF-based ACT construction, we are able to use a random-oracle-based PRF without having to proof correct evaluation (in zero-knowledge) of the hash function H. Concretely, the EQS construction allows us to sign vectors of messages. And we sign a vector of the form $\mu \cdot (\mathsf{G}, \mathsf{H}(\mathsf{msg}), \mathsf{u} \cdot \mathsf{H}(\mathsf{msg}))$. Thus, the client just needs to prove the DDH relation between $(\mathsf{H}(\mathsf{msg}), \mathsf{u} \cdot \mathsf{H}(\mathsf{msg}))$ and the registered client key $(\mathsf{G}, \mathsf{u} \cdot \mathsf{G})$. Combining the unforgeability of EQS (for messages that are not a multiple of a signed message) with a check by the verifier that the first message in the redeemed token signature is G, we can guarantee that the client can create only one valid token from each blinded response it gets from the issuer. In the second case (i.e., the Dodis-Yampolskiy PRF case), the client can directly efficiently prove that the message in its blinded request is of the form $\mu \cdot (\mathsf{G}, (\mathsf{msg} + \mathsf{u}) \cdot \mathsf{G}, \mathsf{msg} \cdot \mathsf{G})$.

The above two constructions are generic transformations from any EQS to ACT. Instantiating them yields multiple concrete efficient ACT constructions under various security assumptions. In particular, we obtain an ACT construction with security in the standard model based on the SXDH and q-DDHI assumption, using the Dodis-Yampolskiy PRF construction together with the following EQS construction. The EQS signature is a normal signature. The adaptation of the signature of a message $\vec{\mathsf{M}}$ to a message $\vec{\mathsf{M}}' = \rho\vec{\mathsf{M}}$ is a ZK proof of knowledge of a valid signature on $\vec{\mathsf{M}}$ and of a scalar ρ such that $\vec{\mathsf{M}}' = \rho\vec{\mathsf{M}}$. For the concrete efficient instantiation of this EQS construction we use the efficient Jutla-Roy structure-preserving signatures [JR17] together with Groth-Sahai zero-knowledge proofs [GS08,EG14]. This construction has a restriction that it can support only short messages of length $O(\log \lambda)$ because the Dodis-Yampolskiy function is an adaptively secure PRF only over polynomial-size domains. The message length restriction can be solved by hashing the message using a hash function modeled as a random oracle. Hashing the message this way, makes Dodis-Yampolskiy adaptively secure because, instead of having to guess the message forged by the adversary, the reduction just needs to guess which random oracle query will be used for the forgery. However, if we are willing to use the random oracle model, our second generic transformation (based on the random-oracle-based PRF $\mathsf{PRF}(\mathsf{u}, \mathsf{msg}) = \mathsf{u} \cdot \mathsf{H}(\mathsf{msg})$ instead of the Dodis-Yampolskiy PRF) is more efficient.

Finally, we present an optimized ACT construction with security in the generic bilinear group model (GBGM) and random oracle model (ROM). Conceptually this construction can be viewed as an optimization of the instantiation of our ACT from EQS which relies on $\mathsf{u} \cdot \mathsf{H}(\mathsf{msg})$ as PRF and uses the EQS from Fuchsbauer et al. [FHS19] and Fiat-Shamir transforms of Sigma protocols as ZK proofs. We prove the resulting scheme directly in the ROM and GBGM.

Other Related Work. We remark that the EQS scheme from [FHS19] has been used in [HS21] to construct anonymous credentials that are also "tag-based" and "aggregatable". However, we do not know how to use these extra properties to construct anonymous counting tokens, because, like metadata, the tag has to be known by the issuer, which would break unlinkability.

1.2 Organization of the Paper

After recalling preliminaries in Sect. 2, we define formally the notion of ACT in Sect. 3. We then present our construction of anonymous counting tokens (ACT) from Oblivious PRF in Sect. 4 and our two generic transforms of ACT from equivalence-class signature schemes (EQS) in Sect. 5. Combined with the EQS schemes in the full version of the paper [BRS23], these two generic transforms yield our concrete constructions of ACT from EQS that do not rely on the generic bilinear group model (GBGM). In Sect. 6 we show that an optimization of the second transform from Sect. 5 can be instantiated very efficiently in the GBGM.

2 Preliminaries

We denote by λ the security parameter. PPT means probabilistic polynomial time. $\mathsf{negl}(\lambda)$ indicates a quantity negligible in the security parameter, that is, for any positive integer k and for any large enough λ, $\mathsf{negl}(\lambda) \leq 1/\lambda^k$.

2.1 Cyclic Groups, Bilinear Groups, and Associated Assumptions

Our constructions make use of cyclic groups and bilinear groups. We denote by G the generator of a cyclic group $\mathbb{G}$ of prime order p. We use additive notation. We denote by $\mathbb{G}^*$ the set $\mathbb{G} \setminus \{0\}$.

A bilinear group is a set of three groups $(\mathbb{G}_1, \mathbb{G}_2, \mathbb{G}_T)$, all of order p with generators $(\mathsf{G}_1, \mathsf{G}_2, \mathsf{G}_T)$, so that there exists an efficient bilinear map $e : \mathbb{G}_1 \times \mathbb{G}_2 \to \mathbb{G}_T$ (called a pairing) such that $e(\mathsf{G}_1, \mathsf{G}_2) = \mathsf{G}_T$. The target group $\mathbb{G}_T$ is also denoted additively and we use $\bullet$ to denote the pairing operation: $e(\mathsf{G}_1, \mathsf{G}_2) = \mathsf{G}_1 \bullet \mathsf{G}_2$.

The symmetric external Diffie-Hellman (SXDH) assumption in a bilinear group $(\mathsf{G}_1, \mathsf{G}_2, \mathsf{G}_T)$ states that the decisional Diffie-Hellman (DDH) assumption holds in G_1 and G_2. The DDH assumption in $\mathbb{G}$ states that PPT adversaries $\mathcal{A}$:

$$\Big| \Pr\left[x, y \leftarrow \mathbb{Z}_p,\ \mathcal{A}(\mathsf{G},\ x\mathsf{G},\ y\mathsf{G},\ (xy) \cdot \mathsf{G}) = 1\right] - \Pr\left[x, y, z \leftarrow \mathbb{Z}_p,\ \mathcal{A}(\mathsf{G},\ x\mathsf{G},\ y\mathsf{G},\ z \cdot \mathsf{G}) = 1\right] \Big| \leq \mathsf{negl}(\lambda).$$

The q-decisional Diffie-Hellman inversion (q-DDHI) assumption in the group $\mathbb{G}$ states that for any PPT adversaries $\mathcal{A}$:

$$\Big| \Pr\left[x \leftarrow \mathbb{Z}_p,\ \mathcal{A}(\mathsf{G}, x\mathsf{G}, \ldots, x^q\mathsf{G}, (1/x)\cdot \mathsf{G}) = 1\right] \\ - \Pr\left[x, y \leftarrow \mathbb{Z}_p,\ \mathcal{A}(\mathsf{G}, x\mathsf{G}, \ldots, x^q\mathsf{G}, y\cdot \mathsf{G}) = 1\right] \Big| \leq \mathsf{negl}(\lambda).$$

2.2 Pseudorandom Function

A pseudorandom function $\mathsf{PRF} : \mathcal{K} \times \mathcal{X} \to \mathcal{Y}$ is a function such that

$$\left| \Pr\left[\mathsf{K} \leftarrow\!\!\$\, \mathcal{K},\ \mathcal{A}^{\mathsf{PRF}(\mathsf{K},\cdot)}(1^\lambda) = 1\right] - \Pr\left[\mathcal{A}^{\mathsf{O}(\cdot)}(1^\lambda) = 1\right] \right| \leq \mathsf{negl}(\lambda)$$

where $\mathsf{O} : \mathcal{X} \to \mathcal{Y}$ is a random oracle.

We need to consider a stronger definition where $\mathcal{A}$ is also given some public information $\mathsf{pk_K}$ derived from $\mathsf{K} \leftarrow\!\!\$\, \mathcal{K}$, e.g., $\mathsf{pk_K} = \mathsf{K}\cdot\mathsf{G}$ where G is a generator of a cyclic group:

$$\left| \Pr\left[\mathsf{K} \leftarrow\!\!\$\, \mathcal{K},\ \mathcal{A}^{\mathsf{PRF}(\mathsf{K},\cdot)}(\mathsf{pk_K}) = 1\right] - \Pr\left[\mathsf{K} \leftarrow\!\!\$\, \mathcal{K},\ \mathcal{A}^{\mathsf{O}(\cdot)}(\mathsf{pk_K}) = 1\right] \right| \leq \mathsf{negl}(\lambda) \tag{1}$$

Finally, we also consider a *selective* version where $\mathcal{A}$ must make all its query to its oracle PRF/O before receiving any answer and before seeing $\mathsf{pk_K}$.

Dodis-Yampolskiy Pseudorandom Function. The Dodis-Yampolskiy function [BB04, DY05] is defined by $\mathcal{F}_{\mathsf{DY}}(\mathsf{u}, \mathsf{msg}) = \frac{1}{\mathsf{u}+\mathsf{msg}}\mathsf{G}$, with key $\mathsf{K} = \mathsf{u}$. We recall the following two lemmas that follow from the proof of weakly unforgeable signature scheme in Boneh-Boyen [BB04] and the pseudorandomness of the VRF in Dodis-Yampolskiy [DY05].[1]

Lemma 2.1. *If the q-DDHI assumption holds in group* $\mathbb{G}$ *with generator* G*, the function* $\mathcal{F}_{\mathsf{DY}}(\mathsf{u}, \mathsf{msg}) = (\mathsf{u} + \mathsf{msg})^{-1} \cdot \mathsf{G}$ *is a* selectively *pseudorandom function (when the adversary can make up to q queries), even when the adversaries sees* $\mathsf{pk_u} = \mathsf{u}\cdot\mathsf{G}$ *after its selective queries.*

Using the same idea as in [DY05], we also get the following lemma:

Lemma 2.2. *If the* 2^α*-DDHI assumption holds in group* $\mathbb{G}$ *with generator* G*, the function* $\mathcal{F}_{\mathsf{DY}}(\mathsf{u}, \mathsf{msg}) = (\mathsf{u} + \mathsf{msg})^{-1} \cdot \mathsf{G}$ *is pseudorandom function when* $\mathsf{msg} \in \{0,1\}^\alpha$*, even when the adversaries sees* $\mathsf{pk_u} = \mathsf{u}\cdot\mathsf{G}$ *(see Eq. (1)).*

[1] Contrary to [BB04], we use a decisional assumption instead of the computational q-SDH because we want pseudorandomness and not unpredictability. Contrary to [DY05], we have the PRF value in $\mathbb{G}_1$ instead of $\mathbb{G}_T$ and our assumption is thus q-DDHI instead of q-DBDHI, and we do not need to have a bilinear map. Appendix A of Miao et al. [MPR+20] shows the proof under q-DDHI. The only difference with our case is that we allow the adversary to see $\mathsf{pk} = \mathsf{u}\cdot\mathsf{G}$, which can easily be simulated the same way as in [DY05]. Simulating $\mathsf{pk} = \mathsf{u}\cdot\mathsf{G}$ is why we rely on q-DDHI instead of just $(q-1)$-DDHI as would [MPR+20] require.

In particular, the Dodis-Yampolskiy PRF is pseudorandom under a standard assumption for input message sizes that are logarithmic in the security parameter.

2.3 Camenisch-Shoup Encryption

The homomorphic encryption introduced by Camenisch and Shoup [CS03] is an additively homomorphic encryption. It additionally supports verifiable decryption, which enables a party holding the decryption key to prove the correctness of the decryption of a given ciphertext. Here, we define the encryption and decryption algorithms. We use the verifiable decryption proofs implicitly in our constructions. We use the additive notation for the CS algorithms except for decryption. That is, we write the multiplicative group $\mathbb{Z}_{N^2}^*$ additively, except in the description of the decryption algorithm. Later, in our constructions, we will refer only to the decryption algorithm by name and never use the multiplicative notation.

- $\mathsf{CS.Gen}(1^\lambda)$: Generate two ℓ-bit primes p' and q' such that $p = 2p' + 1$ and $q = 2q' + 1$ are primes and set $N = pq$. Choose random $\mathsf{R} \leftarrow\$ \mathbb{Z}_{N^2}^*$ and set $\mathsf{G} = 2N\mathsf{R}$ be a $2N$-th residue.[2] Choose random $x \leftarrow\$ \mathbb{Z}_{\lfloor N/4 \rfloor}$ and set $\mathsf{Y} = x\mathsf{G}$. Set $\mathsf{H} = 1 + N \mod N^2$, $\mathsf{PK} \leftarrow (N, \mathsf{G}, \mathsf{Y}, \mathsf{H})$ and $\mathsf{SK} \leftarrow x$. Remark that H is a generator of the subgroup of order N of $\mathbb{Z}_{N^2}^*$.
- $\mathsf{CS.Enc}(\mathsf{PK}, m \in \mathbb{Z}_n)$: Output $(r\mathsf{G}, m\mathsf{H} + r\mathsf{Y}) \in \mathbb{Z}_{N^2}^* \times \mathbb{Z}_{N^2}^*$ where $r \leftarrow\$ \mathbb{Z}_{\lfloor N/4 \rfloor}$.
- $\mathsf{CS.Dec}(\mathsf{SK}, \mathsf{ct} = (u, e))$: Output $m = \frac{(\frac{e}{u^x} - 1) \mod N^2}{N}$ (in multiplicative notation).

2.4 Non-interactive Zero-Knowledge Argument of Knowledge

A (non-interactive) zero-knowledge argument has the following algorithms:

- $\mathsf{crs} \leftarrow \mathsf{ZK.Setup}(\mathcal{R})$: generates public parameters (common random string) $\mathsf{ZK.crs}$ for the prove relationship $\mathcal{R}$. (We assume $\mathcal{R}$ implicitly defines the security parameter λ).
- $\pi \leftarrow \mathsf{ZK.Prove}(\mathcal{R}, \mathsf{crs}, \phi, w)$: generates a proof π that the prover knows a witness w such that the input statement ϕ satisfies the relation $\mathcal{R}(\phi, w)$.
- **false**/**true** $\leftarrow \mathsf{ZK.Verify}(\mathcal{R}, \mathsf{crs}, \phi, \pi)$: verifies the correctness of the proof for a statement ϕ.

Relation $\mathcal{R}$ and CRS $\mathsf{ZK.crs}$ are omitted when clear from the context (or not used). To simplify notation, we also often write:

$$\mathsf{ZK}\{\exists w : \phi\} \quad \text{or} \quad \mathsf{ZK}\{\reflectbox{K} w : \phi\}$$

[2] Recall this is using additive notation for $\mathbb{Z}_{N^2}^*$. In usual multiplicative notation, this corresponds to: $\mathsf{G} = \mathsf{R}^{2N} \mod N^2$.

instead of $\mathsf{ZK.Prove}(\mathcal{R}, \mathsf{crs}, \phi, w)$. "$\exists\!\!\!/$" is used instead of "$\exists$" when the ZK argument is an argument of knowledge and satisfies computational knowledge soundness. We abuse notation and do not explicitly include as part of the witness random coins of algorithms in the statement. For example, we may write:

$$\mathsf{ZK}\{\exists x : c = \mathsf{Enc}(\mathsf{pk}, x),\ \mathsf{com} = \mathsf{Commit}(\mathsf{prm}, x)\}$$

without making explicit the randomness used by the encryption and commitment algorithms.

For some of the ZK arguments in this work, completeness holds for a smaller language than soundness. In that case, the notation above corresponds to the soundness language. The language for completeness is implicitly defined by the way the statement is constructed. See the full version [BRS23] for complete ZK properties..

In our construction we use Sigma protocols [Cra97, CDS94] and Groth-Sahai proofs [GS08], which we defined in detail in the full version [BRS23].

2.5 Commitment Schemes

We define commitment schemes as a pair of two algorithms $\mathsf{COM} = (\mathsf{COM.Setup}, \mathsf{Commit})$ where $\mathsf{Setup}(1^\lambda)$ outputs (public) commitment parameters prm, and $\mathsf{Commit}(\mathsf{prm}, \mathsf{msg}; t)$ returns a commitment com of message msg using randomness t. Public parameters are often omitted when clear from the context.

Pedersen Commitments. We will use the Pedersen commitment scheme when we need binding and hiding properties. We use Pedersen commitment over a group $\mathbb{G}$ where the Strong RSA assumption [BP97, FO97] holds. This will be needed since, in some cases, the committed values come from groups of different orders. The parameters for the commitment are group generators $\mathsf{G}, \mathsf{H} \in \mathbb{Z}_N^*$, where N is a Strong RSA modulus. As for Camenisch-Shoup (Sect. 2.3), we use the additive notation for $\mathbb{Z}_N^*$ instead of the multiplication notation. The commitment of a value x is of the form $\mathsf{Commit}(x; r) = x\mathsf{G} + r\mathsf{H}$ where $r \leftarrow\!\!\$\ \mathbb{Z}_{\lfloor N/4 \rfloor}$. The binding property of the commitment scheme requires that the prover does not know the discrete log relation between the generators G and H.

Extractable Commitments. These are commitments that have an extractable mode in which the commitment parameters are generated together with a trapdoor trap. There exists an extractor $\mathcal{E}$ which can extract the committed value $m \leftarrow \mathcal{E}(\mathsf{trap}, \mathsf{Commit}(m))$ using the trapdoor trap. We will use the Camenisch-Shoup encryption as an extractable commitment where in the normal mode, the secret key (i.e. the discrete log of Y) is not known, while in the trapdoor mode, the secret key is the trapdoor.

2.6 Equivalence-Class Signature Schemes (EQS)

Equivalence class signatures (EQS) [FHS19] are signatures for equivalence classes where a signature for a representative of the equivalence class can be transformed into a signature for any other representative in the same class using only public parameters. The EQS schemes that we use allow signing messages that are vectors of group elements $\vec{\mathsf{M}} \in \mathbb{G}_1^{*\ell}$ and provide the following signature adaptation property: a signature for $\vec{\mathsf{M}}$ can be adapted into signatures of any multiple $\mu\vec{\mathsf{M}}$, for $\mu \in \mathbb{Z}_p^*$. We exclude the 0 element for all coordinates of $\vec{\mathsf{M}}$ as well as for μ to match [FHS19].

As in [FG18], we use a slightly weaker definition than the original EQS notion: we allow the adapted signatures to be of a different format than the original signatures. The original signatures are called pre-signatures. We also only require computational signature adaptation instead of perfect signature adaptation: an adversary cannot computationally distinguish an (adapted) signature on the same message computed from two different pre-signatures, even if the adversary generated the secret key. We also allow for a common reference string (that is generated by a trusted party).

EQS. An equivalence class signature scheme consists of the following algorithms:

- $\mathsf{crs} \leftarrow \mathsf{EQS.Setup}(\mathcal{PG})$: on input a bilinear group $\mathcal{PG}$, generate a CRS crs.
- $(\mathsf{pk}, \mathsf{sk}) \leftarrow \mathsf{EQS.KGen}(\mathsf{crs})$: on input a CRS crs generates secret and public keys which define pre-signature space $\mathcal{R}$ and signature space $\mathcal{S}$.
- $\rho \leftarrow \mathsf{EQS.Sign}(\mathsf{crs}, \mathsf{sk}, \vec{\mathsf{M}} \in \mathbb{G}_1^{*\ell})$: generates a pre-signature ρ for the representative $\vec{\mathsf{M}} = \vec{m}G_1 \in \mathbb{G}_1^{*\ell}$ of the class $\mathsf{Span}(\vec{\mathsf{M}}) = \mathsf{Span}(\vec{m}) \cdot G_1$.
- $\sigma \leftarrow \mathsf{EQS.Adapt}(\mathsf{crs}, \mathsf{pk}, \vec{\mathsf{M}} \in \mathbb{G}_1^{*\ell}, \rho \in \mathcal{R}, \mu \in \mathbb{Z}_p^*)$: transforms a pre-signature ρ for a representative $\vec{\mathsf{M}}$ into a signature for $\vec{\mathsf{M}}' = \mu \cdot \vec{\mathsf{M}}$.
- **false**/**true** $\leftarrow \mathsf{EQS.Verify}(\mathsf{crs}, \mathsf{pk}, \vec{\mathsf{M}}' \in \mathbb{G}_1^{*\ell}, \sigma \in \mathcal{S})$: verifies signature σ for representative $\vec{\mathsf{M}}'$ using the public key pk.

When clear from the context, crs is omitted. Compared with [FG18], $\mathsf{EQS.Adapt}$ also takes as input $\vec{\mathsf{M}}$ (wlog since $\vec{\mathsf{M}}$ could also be included in ρ).

Perfect Correctness. An EQS is correct if, for any honestly generated pre-signature, any resulting adapted signature verifies. That is, for any $\vec{\mathsf{M}} \in \mathbb{G}_1^{*\ell}$ and $\mu \in \mathbb{Z}_p^*$:

$$\mathsf{crs} \leftarrow \mathsf{EQS.Setup}(\mathcal{PG}), \qquad (\mathsf{pk}, \mathsf{sk}) \leftarrow \mathsf{EQS.KGen}(\mathsf{crs}),$$
$$\rho \leftarrow \mathsf{EQS.Sign}(\mathsf{crs}, \mathsf{sk}, \vec{\mathsf{M}}), \qquad \sigma \leftarrow \mathsf{EQS.Adapt}(\mathsf{crs}, \mathsf{pk}, \vec{\mathsf{M}}, \rho, \mu)$$

we have:

$$\mathbf{true} = \mathsf{EQS.Verify}(\mathsf{crs}, \mathsf{pk}, \mu \cdot \vec{\mathsf{M}}, \sigma).$$

Existential Unforgeability. We recall the notion of existential unforgeability under chosen-message attacks from [FHS19].

Definition 2.3. *An EQS scheme* $\mathsf{EQS} = (\mathsf{Setup}, \mathsf{KGen}, \mathsf{Sign}, \mathsf{Adapt}, \mathsf{Verify})$ *satisfies existential unforgeability under chosen-message attacks (EUF-CMA) if for all PPT adversaries* $\mathcal{A}$*:*

Game $\text{EUF-CMA}_{\mathcal{A}}(\lambda)$

$\mathcal{PG} \leftarrow \mathsf{GGen}(\lambda)$
$(\mathsf{crs}, \mathsf{trap}) \leftarrow \mathsf{EQS.Setup}(\mathcal{PG})$
$(\mathsf{pk}, \mathsf{sk}) \leftarrow \mathsf{EQS.KGen}(\mathsf{crs})$
$\mathcal{Q}_{\mathsf{Sign}} := \emptyset$
$(\vec{\mathsf{M}}'^{*} \in \mathbb{G}_1^{*\ell}, \sigma^* \in \mathcal{S}) \leftarrow \mathcal{A}^{\mathsf{Sign}(\cdot)}(\mathsf{crs}, \mathsf{pk})$
return true $= \mathsf{Verify}(\mathsf{pk}, \vec{\mathsf{M}}'^{*}, \sigma^*)$ **and**
$\quad \forall \vec{\mathsf{M}} \in \mathcal{Q}_{\mathsf{Sign}}, \vec{\mathsf{M}}'^{*} \notin \mathsf{Span}(\vec{\mathsf{M}})$

Oracle $\mathsf{Sign}(\vec{\mathsf{M}} \in \mathbb{G}_1^{*\ell})$

$\mathcal{Q}_{\mathsf{Sign}} := \mathcal{Q}_{\mathsf{Sign}} \cup \{\vec{\mathsf{M}}\}$
$\rho \leftarrow \mathsf{EQS.Sign}(\mathsf{crs}, \mathsf{sk}, \vec{\mathsf{M}})$
return ρ

Game $\text{SIG-ADP}_{\mathcal{A}}(\lambda)$

$\mathcal{PG} \leftarrow \mathsf{GGen}(\lambda)$
$\mathsf{crs} \leftarrow \mathsf{EQS.Setup}(\mathcal{PG})$
$(\mathsf{pk}, \vec{\mathsf{M}}, \rho, \mu, \rho', \mathsf{state}) \leftarrow \mathcal{A}(\mathsf{crs})$
$\mathsf{b_{chl}} \leftarrow\!\$\ \{0, 1\}$
$\sigma_0 \leftarrow \mathsf{EQS.Adapt}(\mathsf{crs}, \mathsf{pk}, \vec{\mathsf{M}}, \rho, \mu)$
$\sigma_1 \leftarrow \mathsf{EQS.Adapt}(\mathsf{crs}, \mathsf{pk}, \mu\vec{\mathsf{M}}, \rho', 1)$
abort if $\sigma_0 = \perp$ or $\sigma_1 = \perp$
$\mathsf{b_{guess}} \leftarrow \mathcal{A}(\mathsf{state}, \sigma_{\mathsf{b_{chl}}})$
return $(\mathsf{b_{chl}} == \mathsf{b_{guess}})$

Fig. 1. EUF-CMA and signature adaptation security game for EQS

$$\mathsf{Adv}^{\text{euf-cma}}_{\mathsf{EQS},\mathcal{A}}(\lambda) := \Pr[\text{EUF-CMA}_{\mathcal{A}}(\lambda) = 1] = \mathsf{negl}(\lambda),$$

where $\text{EUF-CMA}_{\mathcal{A}}(\lambda)$ *is defined in Fig. 1.*

Fuchsbauer and Gay introduced a weaker EUF-CoMA notion in [FG18]. This notion requires the adversary in the security game to provide the discrete logarithms of all group elements. In our first construction of ACT from EQS (Construction 5.1), we could use this weak EUF-CoMA definition if we add a ZK proof of knowledge of the discrete logarithms of the message elements. However, such proof is very expensive (unless using Fiat-Shamir in the generic group model or the algebraic group model, but such proofs are much harder since extraction in the GGM or the AGM requires careful consideration of how the proof of the full scheme works).

Signature Adaptation. An EQS satisfies signature adaptation if a malicious signer cannot distinguish between two signatures on the same message $\vec{\mathsf{M}}' \in \mathbb{G}_1^{*\ell}$ adapted from two pre-signatures on two potentially different messages. Contrary to [FHS19], we allow signature adaptation to hold only computationally. We also implicitly assume that $\mathsf{EQS.Adapt}$ fails if the pre-signature ρ is invalid, which is why we don't have a verification algorithm for ρ. More formally, we define signature adaptation as follows.

Definition 2.4. *An EQS scheme* $\mathsf{EQS} = (\mathsf{Setup}, \mathsf{KGen}, \mathsf{Sign}, \mathsf{Adapt}, \mathsf{Verify})$ *satisfies signature adaptation if for all PPT adversaries* $\mathcal{A}$*:*

$$\mathsf{Adv}^{\text{sig-adp}}_{\mathsf{EQS},\mathcal{A}}(\lambda) := |\Pr[\text{SIG-ADP}_{\mathcal{A}}(\lambda) = 1] - 1/2| = \mathsf{negl}(\lambda),$$

where the game $\text{SIG-ADP}_{\mathcal{A}}(\lambda)$ *is defined in Fig. 1.*

3 Definitions

In this section, we define *anonymous counting tokens* (ACTs) with public (respectively private) key verifiability. The private key verifiability version includes the grey-background text, while the public verifiability version does not.

Definition 3.1 (ACT). *An anonymous counting token (ACT) scheme with private key verifiability consists of the following algorithms:*

- $(\mathsf{pprm}_\mathsf{S}, \mathsf{privprm}_\mathsf{S}) \leftarrow \mathsf{ACT.GenParam}(1^\lambda)$*: generates parameters for the ACT scheme. These are parameters that will be reused throughout the execution of token issuance. Outputs private parameters* $\mathsf{privprm}_\mathsf{S}$ *for the token issuer and public parameters* pprm_S *for the ACT scheme.*
- $(\mathsf{pprm}_\mathsf{C}, \mathsf{privprm}_\mathsf{C}) \leftarrow \mathsf{ACT.ClientRegister}(\mathsf{pprm}_\mathsf{S})$*: on input the public parameters for the ACT scheme, this algorithm generates private parameters* $\mathsf{privprm}_\mathsf{C}$ *for the client and public parameters* pprm_C.
- $(\mathsf{blindRequest}, \mathsf{rand}_\mathsf{msg}) \leftarrow \mathsf{ACT.Request}(\mathsf{pprm}_\mathsf{S}, \mathsf{privprm}_\mathsf{C}, \mathsf{msg})$*: on input the public parameters* pprm_S *for the ACT scheme, the private parameters for a client* pprm_C *and a message* msg*, generate a blinded token issuance request* $\mathsf{blindRequest}$ *and state information* $\mathsf{rand}_\mathsf{msg}$.
- $(\mathsf{blindToken}, \boxed{\mathit{tag}}) \leftarrow \mathsf{ACT.Sign}(\mathsf{privprm}_\mathsf{S}, \mathsf{pprm}_\mathsf{C}, \mathsf{blindRequest})$*. on input the private parameters for the issuer server* $\mathsf{privprm}_\mathsf{S}$*, the public parameters for the client* pprm_C *and the blinded request* $\mathsf{blindRequest}$*, generate a blinded token. There is an optional output* tag *which the issuer can use for throttling one token per message per client.*
- $(\mathsf{msg}, \mathsf{tok}) \leftarrow \mathsf{ACT.Unblind}(\mathsf{pprm}_\mathsf{S}, \mathsf{privprm}_\mathsf{C}, \mathsf{blindToken}, \mathsf{rand}_\mathsf{msg})$*: on inputs the public parameters* pprm_S *for the ACT scheme and the private parameters for a client* pprm_C *and a blind token* $\mathsf{blindToken}$ *and randomness* $\mathsf{rand}_\mathsf{msg}$ *used to blind the request for the message, generate the unblinded token* tok *for message* msg).
- $(\mathsf{bit}, \boxed{\mathit{tag}}) \leftarrow \mathsf{ACT.Verify}(\mathsf{vrfyprm}, \mathsf{msg}, \mathsf{tok})$*: on input the verification parameters for the ACT scheme* $\mathsf{vrfyprm} := (\mathsf{pprm}_\mathsf{S}, \mathsf{privprm}_\mathsf{S})$*, which consist of the public parameters* pprm_S *for the ACT scheme, the private parameter for the issuer server* $\mathsf{privprm}_\mathsf{S}$*, a message* msg *and a token* tok*, output verification bit* bit*. There is an optional output* tag *which the issuer can use for throttling one token per message per client.*

Figure 2 presents the interactions between a client and an issuer server during token issuance and verification using the algorithms of the ACT scheme. The client has the public parameters of the scheme and the server has the public keys $\mathcal{C}$ registered by clients as well as a set of tags $\mathcal{T}$ which it uses to throttle issuance at a single token per message per client. In order for the server to be able to enforce that each client gets at most one token per message, the server will obtain a tag that allows it to detect when the same client tries to obtain more than one token per message. This tag will be related to the message and the client's registered key but will only reveal whether more than one token per message is obtained/used by the same client. An ACT construction may enforce

$\mathsf{Client}(\mathsf{pprm_S}, \mathsf{privprm_C}, \mathsf{msg})$		$\mathsf{Issuer}(\mathsf{privprm_S}, \mathcal{C}, \mathcal{T})$
$(\mathsf{bR}, \mathsf{r}) \leftarrow \mathsf{ACT.Request}(\mathsf{pprm_S}, \mathsf{privprm_C}, \mathsf{msg})$ $\mathsf{state} \leftarrow \mathsf{state} \cup (\mathsf{msg}, \mathsf{r})$		
	$\xrightarrow{\mathsf{bR}}$	
		$(\mathsf{bT}, \boxed{\mathsf{tag}}\ )$ $\leftarrow \mathsf{ACT.Sign}(\mathsf{privprm_S}, \mathsf{pprm_C}, \mathsf{bR})$ **if** $\exists$ tag, **if** $\mathsf{tag} \in \mathcal{T}$, **abort, else** $\mathcal{T} = \mathcal{T} \cup \mathsf{tag}$
	$\xleftarrow{\mathsf{bT}}$	
$(\mathsf{msg}, \mathsf{t}) \leftarrow \mathsf{ACT.Unblind}(\mathsf{pprm_S}, \mathsf{privprm_C}, \mathsf{bT}, \mathsf{r})$		
	$\xrightarrow{\mathsf{msg}, \mathsf{t}}$	
		$(\mathsf{bit}, \boxed{\mathsf{tag}}\ ) \leftarrow \mathsf{ACT.Verify}(\mathsf{vrfyprm}, \mathsf{msg}, \mathsf{t})$ **if** $\exists$ tag, **if** $\mathsf{tag} \in \mathcal{T}, ;$ **abort, else** $\mathcal{T} = \mathcal{T} \cup \mathsf{tag}$ **if** $\mathsf{bit} =$ **false, abort**

Fig. 2. Token issuance and verification for ACT (Definition 3.1).

the throttling property either at issuance (i.e., the client cannot obtain a second token for the same message) or during verification where a client cannot redeem more than one token for the same message. For each of our constructions, we will specify which of the two functionalities it provides.

ACT Correctness. An ACT scheme is correct if any honestly generated token verifies. That is for any sets of issuer's and client's parameters

$$(\mathsf{pprm_S}, \mathsf{privprm_S}) \leftarrow \mathsf{ACT.GenParam}(\lambda),$$
$$(\mathsf{pprm_C}, \mathsf{privprm_C}) \leftarrow \mathsf{ACT.ClientRegister}(\mathsf{pprm_S}),$$

and any message msg, the following holds

$$(\mathsf{blindRequest}, \mathsf{rand_{msg}}) \leftarrow \mathsf{ACT.Request}(\mathsf{pprm_S}, \mathsf{privprm_C}, \mathsf{msg})$$
$$\mathsf{blindToken} \leftarrow \mathsf{ACT.Sign}(\mathsf{privprm_S}, \mathsf{pprm_C}, \mathsf{blindRequest})$$
$$(\mathsf{msg}, \mathsf{tok}) \leftarrow \mathsf{ACT.Unblind}(\mathsf{pprm_S}, \mathsf{privprm_C}, \mathsf{blindToken}, \mathsf{rand_{msg}})$$
$$\mathbf{true} \leftarrow \mathsf{ACT.Verify}(\mathsf{vrfyprm}, \mathsf{msg}, \mathsf{tok}).$$

3.1 Security Properties

Unforgeability. The first security property is unforgeability, which guarantees that an adversary cannot generate tokens for more messages than the ones it has requested signatures and it also cannot generate more than one signature for a message per registered client key. This holds even when the adversary can register public parameters for many clients.

Definition 3.2 (Unforgeability). *An anonymous counting token scheme* ACT *is* unforgeable *if for any* PPT *adversary* $\mathcal{A}$ *and any* $\max(\mathsf{T}) \geq 0$, $\max(\mathsf{R}) \geq 0$ *(the maximum number of queries):*

$$\mathsf{Adv}^{\mathsf{omuf}}_{\mathsf{ACT},\mathcal{A}}(\lambda) := \Pr\left[\mathrm{OMUF}_{\mathsf{ACT},\mathcal{A}}(\lambda) = 1\right] = \mathsf{negl}(\lambda).$$

where $\mathrm{OMUF}_{\mathsf{ACT},\mathcal{A}}(\lambda)$ *is defined in Fig. 3.*

Game $\mathrm{OMUF}_{\mathsf{ACT},\mathcal{A}}(\lambda)$

$(\mathsf{pprm_S}, \mathsf{privprm_S}) \leftarrow \mathsf{ACT.GenParam}(1^\lambda)$
$\mathsf{R} \leftarrow 0,\ \mathsf{T} \leftarrow 0,\ \mathsf{state} \leftarrow \{\},\ \mathsf{tags} \leftarrow \{\}$
$\mathsf{output} \leftarrow \mathcal{A}^{\mathsf{Register}(\cdot),\mathsf{Sign}(\cdot),\mathsf{Verify}(\cdot)}(\mathsf{pprm_S})$
$(\mathsf{msg}_i, \mathsf{tok}_i)_{i\in[\mathsf{T}+1]} := \mathsf{output}$
return
$\quad \forall\, i \neq j \in [\mathsf{T}+1], (\mathsf{msg}_i, \mathsf{tok}_i) \neq (\mathsf{msg}_j, \mathsf{tok}_j)$
$\quad$ **and**
$\quad ($ // Type 1 forgery:
$\quad\big(\forall i \in [\mathsf{T}+1],$
$\quad\quad \mathsf{ACT.Verify}(\mathsf{vrfyprm}, \mathsf{msg}_i, \mathsf{tok}_i) = (\mathbf{true}, \boxed{\mathsf{tag}_i}),$
$\quad\quad \boxed{\forall\, i \neq j \in [\mathsf{T}+1], (\mathsf{msg}_i, \mathsf{tag}_i) \neq (\mathsf{msg}_j, \mathsf{tag}_j)}\big)$
$\quad\quad$ **or**
$\quad\quad$ // Type 2 forgery:
$\quad\big(\exists\, S \subset [\mathsf{T}], \exists \mathsf{msg} : |S| > \mathsf{R}$ **and**
$\quad\quad \forall i \in S, \mathsf{msg}_i = \mathsf{msg}$ **and**
$\quad\quad \forall i \in S, \mathsf{ACT.Verify}(\mathsf{vrfyprm}, \mathsf{msg}_i, \mathsf{tok}_i) = \mathbf{true}\big)$
$\quad)$

Oracle $\mathsf{Register}(\mathsf{pprm_C})$

$\mathsf{state} \leftarrow \mathsf{state} \cup \mathsf{pprm_C}$
$\mathsf{R} \leftarrow \mathsf{R}+1$

Oracle $\mathsf{Sign}(\mathsf{pprm_C}, \mathsf{bR})$

if $\mathsf{pprm_C} \notin \mathsf{state}$, **return** $\bot$
$\mathsf{T} = \mathsf{T}+1$
$(\mathsf{bT}, \boxed{\mathsf{tag}})$
$\quad \leftarrow \mathsf{ACT.Sign}(\mathsf{privprm_S}, \mathsf{pprm_C}, \mathsf{bR})$
$\boxed{\textbf{if } \mathsf{tag} \in \mathsf{tags}, \textbf{return } \bot}$
$\boxed{\mathsf{tags} \leftarrow \mathsf{tags} \cup \mathsf{tag}}$
return bT

Oracle $\mathsf{Verify}(\mathsf{msg}, \mathsf{tok})$

$\mathsf{bit} \leftarrow \mathsf{ACT.Verify}(\mathsf{vrfyprm}, \mathsf{msg}, \mathsf{tok})$
return bit

Fig. 3. Unforgeability game for an ACT scheme. The appropriate $\boxed{\text{boxed}}$ instructions are included depending on whether rate limiting is done at issuance (boxed instructions in Sign) or at redemption (boxed instruction in main game).

Unlinkability. The next ACT property is *unlinkability* which guarantees that even the issuer cannot link client token requests with redeemed tokens, except if it can trivially do so. Definition relies on $\mathrm{UNLINK}_{\mathsf{ACT},\mathcal{A}}(\lambda)$ is defined in Fig. 4.

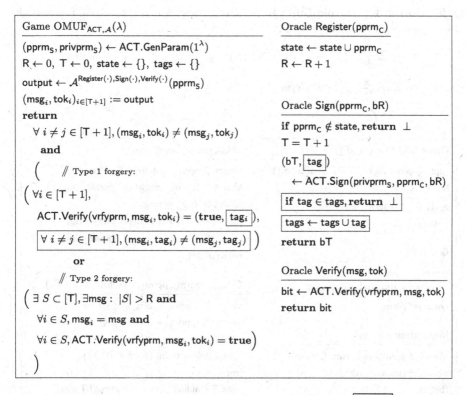

The high-level idea of the game is the following. The adversary plays the role of the issuer, can register as many clients as it wants in via the GetPrm oracle, and can ask those clients to generate blind token requests for messages of its choice via the Request oracle. It needs to be distinguish blind token requests bT for two different client/message pairs (oracle $\mathsf{Chl}_{\mathsf{issue}}$); or it needs to distinguish redeemed/unblind tokens for the same message but two different issuance sessions (oracle $\mathsf{Chl}_{\mathsf{redeem}}$). As the adversary can always provide wrong blindToken (as issuer), in that latter, we request that ACT.Unblind succeeds on both the blind tokens provided by the adversary.

Our unlinkability notion assumes that the issuer parameters pprm_S and $\mathsf{privprm}_\mathsf{S}$ are honestly generated. We informally discuss how to remove this requirement in each of our constructions.

Definition 3.3 (Unlinkability). *An anonymous token scheme* ACT *is* unlinkable *if for any* PPT *adversary* $\mathcal{A}$*:*

$$\mathsf{Adv}^{UNLINK}_{\mathsf{ACT},\mathcal{A}}(\lambda) := \left|2\Pr\left[\mathrm{UNLINK}_{\mathsf{ACT},\mathcal{A}}(\lambda) = 1\right] - 1\right| = \mathsf{negl}(\lambda),$$

where $\mathrm{UNLINK}_{\mathsf{ACT},\mathcal{A}}(\lambda)$ *is defined in Fig. 4.*

Game $\mathrm{UNLINK}_{\mathsf{ACT},\mathcal{A}}(\lambda)$

$(\mathsf{pprm}_\mathsf{S}, \mathsf{privprm}_\mathsf{S}) \leftarrow \mathsf{ACT.GenParam}(1^\lambda)$
$\mathsf{b}_{\mathsf{chl}} \leftarrow\!\!\$\ \{0,1\}$
$\mathsf{b}_{\mathsf{guess}} \leftarrow \mathcal{A}^{O}(\mathsf{pprm}_\mathsf{S}, \mathsf{privprm}_\mathsf{S})$
return $(\mathsf{b}_{\mathsf{chl}} == \mathsf{b}_{\mathsf{guess}})$

$\mathsf{GetPrm}()$

$(\mathsf{pprm}_\mathsf{C}, \mathsf{privprm}_\mathsf{C})$
  $\leftarrow \mathsf{ACT.ClientRegister}(\mathsf{pprm}_\mathsf{S})$
return pprm_C

$\mathsf{Request}(\mathsf{pprm}_\mathsf{C}, \mathsf{msg})$

abort if pprm_C not from GetPrm
abort if $(\mathsf{pprm}_\mathsf{C}, \mathsf{msg}) \in \mathcal{Q}'$
$(\mathsf{bR}, \mathsf{r})$
  $\leftarrow \mathsf{ACT.Request}(\mathsf{pprm}_\mathsf{S}, \mathsf{privprm}_\mathsf{C}, \mathsf{msg})$
$\mathcal{Q} = \mathcal{Q} \cup (\mathsf{pprm}_\mathsf{C}, \mathsf{msg}, \mathsf{bR}, \mathsf{r})$
$\mathcal{Q}' = \mathcal{Q}' \cup (\mathsf{pprm}_\mathsf{C}, \mathsf{msg})$
return bR

$\mathsf{Chl}_{\mathsf{issue}}(\mathsf{pprm}_\mathsf{C}, \mathsf{msg}_0, \mathsf{msg}_1)$

abort if pprm_C not from GetPrm
abort if $(\mathsf{pprm}_\mathsf{C}, \mathsf{msg}_0)$ or $(\mathsf{pprm}_\mathsf{C}, \mathsf{msg}_1) \in \mathcal{Q}'$
abort if $\mathsf{msg}_0 = \mathsf{msg}_1$
$(\mathsf{bR}, \mathsf{r}) \leftarrow \mathsf{ACT.Request}(\mathsf{privprm}_\mathsf{C}, \mathsf{msg}_{\mathsf{b}_{\mathsf{chl}}})$
$\mathcal{Q}' = \mathcal{Q}' \cup (\mathsf{pprm}_\mathsf{C}, \mathsf{msg}_0) \cup (\mathsf{pprm}_\mathsf{C}, \mathsf{msg}_1)$
return bR

$\mathsf{Chl}_{\mathsf{redeem}}(\mathsf{pprm}_0, \mathsf{pprm}_1, \mathsf{bR}_0, \mathsf{bR}_1, \mathsf{bT}_0, \mathsf{bT}_1)$

abort if $(\mathsf{pprm}_0, \star, \mathsf{bR}_0, \star) \notin \mathcal{Q}$
abort if $(\mathsf{pprm}_1, \star, \mathsf{bR}_1, \star) \notin \mathcal{Q}$
Find $(\mathsf{pprm}_b, \mathsf{msg}_b, \mathsf{bR}_b, \mathsf{r}_b) \in \mathcal{Q}$
  and delete them (for $b \in \{0,1\}$)
$(\mathsf{msg}'_0, \mathsf{tok}_0) \leftarrow$
  $\mathsf{ACT.Unblind}(\mathsf{pprm}_\mathsf{S}, \mathsf{privprm}_0, \mathsf{bT}_0, \mathsf{r}_0)$
$(\mathsf{msg}'_1, \mathsf{tok}_1) \leftarrow$
  $\mathsf{ACT.Unblind}(\mathsf{pprm}_\mathsf{S}, \mathsf{privprm}_1, \mathsf{bT}_1, \mathsf{r}_1)$
abort if $\mathsf{msg}_0 \neq \mathsf{msg}_1$
abort if $\mathsf{msg}'_0 \neq \mathsf{msg}_0$ or $\mathsf{msg}'_1 \neq \mathsf{msg}_1$
return $\mathsf{tok}_{\mathsf{b}_{\mathsf{chl}}}$

Fig. 4. Unlinkability game for an ACT scheme, where $\mathcal{A}$ has access to oracles $O =$ $\mathsf{GetPrm}(\cdot), \mathsf{Request}(\cdot), \mathsf{Chl}_{\mathsf{issue}}(\cdot), \mathsf{Chl}_{\mathsf{redeem}}(\cdot)$

4 Anonymous Counting Tokens from Oblivious PRF

In this section, we present our first anonymous counting tokens construction which leverages oblivious pseudorandom functions. We make use of the extended Boneh-Boyen PRF function $\mathcal{F}(\mathsf{sk} = (\mathsf{u}, \mathsf{y}), \mathsf{msg}, \mathsf{r}) = (\mathsf{msg} + \mathsf{u} + \mathsf{r} \cdot \mathsf{y})^{-1} \cdot \mathsf{G}$ where G is a generator of a group $\mathbb{G}$, which was used by Boneh and Boyen [BB04] to construct short signatures without oracles. The Dodis-Yampolskiy function [DY05] $\mathcal{F}_{\mathsf{DY}}(\mathsf{u}, \mathsf{msg}) = (\mathsf{msg} + \mathsf{u})^{-1} \cdot \mathsf{G}$ can be viewed as a special case of this function where the key y is set to zero. For our construction and proofs, we need the property that $\mathcal{F}$ is pseudorandom when evaluated on adversarially chosen messages and on randomness that is sampled uniformly at random. We prove the properties for this function in the full version of the paper [BRS23].

We will need to evaluate obliviously the function $\mathcal{F}(\mathsf{sk} = (\mathsf{u}, \mathsf{y}), \mathsf{msg}, \mathsf{r}) = (\mathsf{msg} + \mathsf{u} + \mathsf{r} \cdot \mathsf{y})^{-1} \cdot \mathsf{G}$: one party has the secret key sk while the other party has a message $(\mathsf{msg}, \mathsf{r})$ as input. We call the resulting protocol a verifiable oblivious pseudorandom function (VOPRF). The VOPRF algorithms $\mathsf{VOPRF} = (\mathsf{VOPRF.GenParam}, \mathsf{VOPRF.EncodeMsg}, \mathsf{VOPRF.Eval}, \mathsf{VOPRF.Decode})$ are informally defined as follow. Given public parameters and assuming inputs are committed, we consider the following protocol: the client runs $\mathsf{EncodeMsg}$ with a message $(\mathsf{msg}, \mathsf{r})$ and gets back a digest, the server runs Eval on digest (and the server's key) to get a blinded PRF value. The client can then run Decode to obtain the output $\mathcal{F}(\mathsf{msg}, \mathsf{r})$ on the message msg. Informally, the VOPRF security property (that we will be proving in the ACT proof) states that this protocol is a maliciously secure computation protocol, where the client receives the output $\mathcal{F}(\mathsf{msg}, \mathsf{r})$ and the server learns nothing.

We are constructing a VOPRF in Sect. 4.2. We also present a stand-alone definition in the full version of the paper [BRS23]. The VOPRF primitive is introduced mostly for readability. It is used as part of the final ACT protocol, where we implicitly assume inputs and keys to be previously committed. We do not prove separate properties for it but we prove directly the ACT security properties.

4.1 ACT Construction

Assuming we have a VOPRF (with the right properties) for the extended Boneh-Boyen PRF function $\mathcal{F}(\mathsf{sk} = (\mathsf{u}, \mathsf{y}), \mathsf{msg}, \mathsf{r}) = (\mathsf{msg} + \mathsf{u} + \mathsf{r} \cdot \mathsf{y})^{-1} \cdot \mathsf{G}$, we construct an ACT from this VOPRF.

Constructions 4.1 (ACT from VOPRF). Let $\mathbb{G}$ be a cyclic group of prime order p with generator G, $\mathsf{VOPRF} = (\mathsf{VOPRF.GenParam}, \mathsf{VOPRF.EncodeMsg}, \mathsf{VOPRF.Eval}, \mathsf{VOPRF.Decode})$ be the verifiable oblivious pseudorandom function defined in Construction 4.2, $\mathsf{COM}_{\mathsf{Ped}} = (\mathsf{COM}_{\mathsf{Ped}}.\mathsf{Setup}, \mathsf{Commit}_{\mathsf{Ped}})$ be the Pedersen commitment scheme over a strong-RSA group (a hiding and binding commitment scheme), $\mathsf{COM}_{\mathsf{Ext}} = (\mathsf{COM}_{\mathsf{Ext}}.\mathsf{Setup}, \mathsf{Commit}_{\mathsf{Ext}})$ be an extractable commitment scheme defined as the CS encryption scheme (see Sect. 2.5), $\mathcal{F}_{\mathsf{DY}}$ be the

Dodis-Yampolskiy (selective) PRF over $\mathbb{G}$,[3] and ZK be a sound zero-knowledge argument scheme. We construct an anonymous counting token scheme ACT as follows:

ACT.GenParam(1^λ): Generate

1. $(\mathsf{PK_{VOPRF}}, \mathsf{SK_{VOPRF}}) \leftarrow \mathsf{VOPRF.GenParam}(1^\lambda)$. Note that $\mathsf{PK_{VOPRF}}$ contains (public) parameters $\mathsf{prm_{Ext}}$ for the extractable commitment scheme and $\mathsf{prm_{Ped}}$ for the Perdersen hiding and binding commitment.

$$\textbf{Output:}\quad \begin{aligned}\mathsf{pprm_S} &\leftarrow \mathsf{PK_{VOPRF}}\\ \mathsf{privprm_S} &\leftarrow \mathsf{SK_{VOPRF}}\end{aligned}$$

ACT.ClientRegister($\mathsf{pprm_S}$): Generate

1. a Dodis-Yampolskiy PRF key $\mathsf{u_C} \leftarrow\$\, \mathbb{Z}_p$,
2. a commitment $\mathsf{com_{u_C}} \leftarrow \mathsf{Commit_{Ped}}(\mathsf{u_C}; t_{\mathsf{u_C}})$

$$\textbf{Output:}\quad \begin{aligned}\mathsf{pprm_C} &\leftarrow \mathsf{com_{u_C}}\\ \mathsf{privprm_C} &\leftarrow \mathsf{u_C}\end{aligned}$$

ACT.TokenRequest($\mathsf{pprm_S}, \mathsf{privprm_C}, \mathsf{msg}$):

1. Compute a commitment to the message $\mathsf{com_{msg}} \leftarrow \mathsf{Commit_{Ext}}(\mathsf{H}(\mathsf{msg}); r_{\mathsf{msg}})$.
2. Compute
   - Dodis-Yampolskiy PRF evaluation $\mathsf{v} \leftarrow \mathcal{F}_{\mathsf{DY}}(\mathsf{u_C}, \mathsf{H}(\mathsf{msg}))$.
   - Proof of correct PRF evaluation

$$\pi_{\mathsf{v}} : \mathsf{ZK}\{\exists h, \mathsf{u_C}, t_{\mathsf{msg}}, t_{\mathsf{u_C}} : \mathsf{v} = \mathcal{F}_{\mathsf{DY}}(\mathsf{u_C}, h),\\ \mathsf{com_{msg}} = \mathsf{Commit_{Ext}}(h; t_{\mathsf{msg}}),\ \mathsf{com_{u_C}} = \mathsf{Commit_{Ped}}(\mathsf{u_C}; t_{\mathsf{u_C}})\}$$

3. Generate a random $\mathsf{r_C}$ and commitment $\mathsf{com_{r_C}} \leftarrow \mathsf{Commit_{Ext}}(\mathsf{r_C}; t_{\mathsf{r_C}})$.
4. Hash the transcript to get random value $\mathsf{r_S} \leftarrow \mathsf{H}(\mathsf{trnc})$ where

$$\mathsf{trnc} = (\mathsf{pprm_S}, \mathsf{com_{u_C}}, \mathsf{com_{msg}}, \mathsf{v}, \mathsf{com_{r_C}}).$$

5. Compute $\mathsf{r} \leftarrow \mathsf{r_C} + \mathsf{r_S}$, commit $\mathsf{com_r} \leftarrow \mathsf{Commit_{Ped}}(\mathsf{r}; t_{\mathsf{r}})$ and generate a proof:

$$\pi_{\mathsf{r}} : \mathsf{ZK}\{\exists\ \mathsf{r_C}, t_{\mathsf{r_C}}, t_{\mathsf{r}} :\ \mathsf{r} = \mathsf{r_C} + \mathsf{r_S},\\ \mathsf{com_{r_C}} = \mathsf{Commit_{Ext}}(\mathsf{r_C}, t_{\mathsf{r_C}}), \mathsf{com_r} = \mathsf{Commit_{Ped}}(\mathsf{r}; t_{\mathsf{r}})\}.$$

(The above 3 steps are used to create a random value r that neither the issuer nor the client control as explained in Section 1.1.)

[3] This PRF is used for the rate limitation of the client. VOPRF does not evaluate this PRF but rather evaluates $\mathcal{F}$ defined in Sect. 4.

6. Compute first OPRF message on input msg with randomness r

$$(\mathsf{VOPRF.,}, \mathsf{VOPRF.digest}) \leftarrow \mathsf{VOPRF.EncodeMsg}(\mathsf{PK}_{\mathsf{VOPRF}}, (\mathsf{H}(\mathsf{msg}), \mathsf{r}), (t_{\mathsf{msg}}, t_{\mathsf{r}})).$$

Output: $\mathsf{blindRequest} \leftarrow (\mathsf{com}_{\mathsf{msg}}, \mathsf{v}, \pi_{\mathsf{v}}, \mathsf{com}_{\mathsf{rc}}, \mathsf{com}_{\mathsf{r}}, \pi_{\mathsf{r}}, \mathsf{VOPRF.digest})$
$\mathsf{rand}_{\mathsf{msg}} \leftarrow (\mathsf{msg}, \mathsf{r}, \mathsf{VOPRF.})$

ACT.Sign($\mathsf{privprm}_{\mathsf{S}}, \mathsf{pprm}_{\mathsf{C}}, \mathsf{blindRequest}$)

1. Parse $\mathsf{blindRequest} = (\mathsf{com}_{\mathsf{msg}}, \mathsf{v}, \pi_{\mathsf{v}}, \mathsf{com}_{\mathsf{rc}}, \mathsf{com}_{\mathsf{r}}, \pi_{\mathsf{r}}, \mathsf{VOPRF.digest})$.
2. Parse $\mathsf{privprm}_{\mathsf{S}} = \mathsf{sk}_{\mathsf{OPRF}}$.
3. Compute $\mathsf{r}_{\mathsf{S}} \leftarrow \mathsf{H}(\mathsf{trnc})$ as in ACT.Request.
4. Verify the proofs π_{v} and π_{r} and abort if any of them doesn't verify.
5. Compute the second message of the VOPRF evaluation

$$\mathsf{blindPRF} \leftarrow \mathsf{VOPRF.Eval}(\mathsf{sk}_{\mathsf{VOPRF}}, \mathsf{VOPRF.digest}).$$

Output: $\mathsf{blindToken} \leftarrow \mathsf{blindPRF}$
$\mathsf{tag} \leftarrow \mathsf{v}$

ACT.Unblind($\mathsf{pprm}_{\mathsf{S}}, \mathsf{privprm}_{\mathsf{C}}, \mathsf{blindToken}, \mathsf{rand}_{\mathsf{msg}}$)

1. Parse $\mathsf{blindToken} = \mathsf{blindPRF}$.
2. Parse $\mathsf{rand}_{\mathsf{msg}} = (\mathsf{msg}, \mathsf{r}, \mathsf{VOPRF.})$.
3. Decode the returned token (implicitly verifying its correctness):

$$\tau \leftarrow \mathsf{VOPRF.Decode}(\mathsf{VOPRF.}, \mathsf{blindPRF}).$$

4. Set the signature $\mathsf{tok} \leftarrow (\mathsf{r}, \tau)$

Output: $(\mathsf{msg}, \mathsf{tok})$

ACT.Verify($\mathsf{pprm}_{\mathsf{S}}, \mathsf{privprm}, \mathsf{msg}, \mathsf{tok}$)

1. Parse $\mathsf{privprm}_{\mathsf{S}} = \mathsf{sk}_{\mathsf{VOPRF}}$ and $\mathsf{tok} = (\mathsf{r}, \tau)$. Set bit $\leftarrow$ **false**.
2. If $\mathcal{F}(\mathsf{sk}_{\mathsf{VOPRF}}, \mathsf{H}(\mathsf{msg}), \mathsf{r}) = \tau$, set bit $\leftarrow$ **true**.

Output: bit

4.2 Verifiable Oblivious Pseudorandom Function Construction

Next, we present our construction of a verifiable oblivious pseudorandom function which closely follows the construction of distributed oblivious PRF of Miao et al. [MPR+20]. The main difference is that [MPR+20] relies on the selective pseudorandom property of the Dodis-Yampolskiy function while we use the extended Boneh-Boyen PRF function $\mathcal{F}(\mathsf{sk} = (\mathsf{u}, \mathsf{y}), \mathsf{msg}, \mathsf{r}) = (\mathsf{msg}+\mathsf{u}+\mathsf{r}\cdot\mathsf{y})^{-1}\cdot\mathsf{G}$.

Constructions 4.2. Let $\mathsf{COM}_{\mathsf{Ped}}$ be the Pedersen commitment scheme, CS be the Camenisch-Shoup encryption scheme, and $\mathsf{COM}_{\mathsf{Ext}}$ be extractable commitment instantiated as CS encryption (but with a different public key, whose secret key is known by the issuer, contrary to the secret key of $\mathsf{COM}_{\mathsf{Ext}}$). We assume for simplicity that we use the same modulus N for CS, $\mathsf{COM}_{\mathsf{Ext}}$, and $\mathsf{COM}_{\mathsf{Ped}}$. We construct an VOPRF ($\mathsf{VOPRF.GenParam}$, $\mathsf{VOPRF.EncodeMsg}$, $\mathsf{VOPRF.Eval}$, $\mathsf{VOPRF.Decode}$) as follows:

VOPRF.GenParam(1^λ):

1. Generate CS parameters $(\mathsf{pk}_{\mathsf{CS}} \leftarrow (N, \mathsf{G}_{\mathsf{CS}}, \mathsf{Y}_{\mathsf{CS}}, \mathsf{H}_{\mathsf{CS}}), \mathsf{sk}_{\mathsf{CS}} \leftarrow x) \leftarrow \mathsf{CS.Gen}(1^\lambda)$.
2. Generate extractable commitment parameters $\mathsf{prm}_{\mathsf{Ext}} \leftarrow \mathsf{COM}_{\mathsf{Ext}}.\mathsf{Setup}(1^\lambda)$.
3. Generate Pedersen commitment parameters $\mathsf{prm}_{\mathsf{Ped}} \leftarrow \mathsf{COM}_{\mathsf{Ped}}.\mathsf{Setup}(1^\lambda)$. We use the same modulus N for the two commitment schemes and the CS scheme above.
4. Sample random keys $\mathsf{u}, \mathsf{y} \leftarrow\$ \mathbb{Z}_{|\mathsf{G}|}$ for the function $\mathcal{F}$.
5. Encrypt $\mathsf{ct}_{\mathsf{u}} \leftarrow \mathsf{CS.Enc}(\mathsf{pk}_{\mathsf{CS}}, \mathsf{u}) = (r_{\mathsf{u}}\cdot\mathsf{G}_{\mathsf{CS}}, \mathsf{u}\cdot\mathsf{H}_{\mathsf{CS}}+r_{\mathsf{u}}\cdot\mathsf{Y}_{\mathsf{CS}})$ where $r_{\mathsf{u}} \leftarrow\$ \mathbb{Z}_{\lfloor N/4 \rfloor}$.
6. Encrypt $\mathsf{ct}_{\mathsf{y}} \leftarrow \mathsf{CS.Enc}(\mathsf{pk}_{\mathsf{CS}}, \mathsf{y}) = (r_{\mathsf{y}}\cdot\mathsf{G}_{\mathsf{CS}}, \mathsf{y}\cdot\mathsf{H}_{\mathsf{CS}}+r_{\mathsf{y}}\cdot\mathsf{Y}_{\mathsf{CS}})$ where $r_{\mathsf{y}} \leftarrow\$ \mathbb{Z}_{\lfloor N/4 \rfloor}$.

Output: $\mathsf{pprm}_{\mathsf{S}} \leftarrow (\mathsf{pk}_{\mathsf{CS}}, \mathsf{prm}_{\mathsf{Ped}}, \mathsf{prm}_{\mathsf{Ext}}, \mathsf{ct}_{\mathsf{u}}, \mathsf{ct}_{\mathsf{y}})$
$\mathsf{privprm}_{\mathsf{S}} \leftarrow (\mathsf{u}, \mathsf{y}, \mathsf{sk}_{\mathsf{CS}})$

VOPRF.EncodeMsg($\mathsf{pprm}_{\mathsf{S}}$, $(\mathsf{msg}, r) \in \mathbb{Z}^2_{|\mathsf{G}|}$, (t_{msg}, t_r)):[4]

1. Commit $\mathsf{com}_{\mathsf{msg}} \leftarrow \mathsf{Commit}_{\mathsf{Ext}}(\mathsf{msg}; t_{\mathsf{msg}})$, $\mathsf{com}_r \leftarrow \mathsf{Commit}_{\mathsf{Ped}}(r; t_r)$.
2. Sample $a \leftarrow\$ \mathbb{Z}_p$ and $b \leftarrow\$ \mathbb{Z}_{p^2 \cdot 2^\lambda}$.
3. Compute commitments with randomness $t_a, t_b, t_r \leftarrow\$ \mathbb{Z}_{\lfloor N/4 \rfloor}$
$\mathsf{com}_a \leftarrow \mathsf{Commit}_{\mathsf{Ext}}(a; t_a), \mathsf{com}_b \leftarrow \mathsf{Commit}_{\mathsf{Ped}}(b; t_b)$,
$\mathsf{com}_r \leftarrow \mathsf{Commit}_{\mathsf{Ped}}(r; t_r)$.
4. Let $\alpha = a \cdot \mathsf{msg}$, $\gamma = a \cdot r$. Compute commitments:
$$\mathsf{com}_\alpha \leftarrow \mathsf{Commit}_{\mathsf{Ped}}(\alpha, t_\alpha), \ \ \mathsf{com}_\alpha \leftarrow \mathsf{Commit}_{\mathsf{Ped}}(\gamma, t_\gamma)$$
5. Compute encryption of $\beta = a \cdot \mathsf{msg} + a \cdot (\mathsf{u} + r \cdot \mathsf{y}) + b \cdot p$ (implicitly defined):
$$\mathsf{ct}_\beta = \mathsf{CS.Enc}(\mathsf{pk}_{\mathsf{CS}}, \beta) = \mathsf{Enc}(\mathsf{pk}_{\mathsf{CS}}, a \cdot \mathsf{msg} + b \cdot p) + a \cdot \mathsf{ct}_{\mathsf{u}} + a \cdot r \cdot \mathsf{ct}_{\mathsf{y}}.$$

6. Generate a ZK proof

$$\begin{aligned}\pi = \mathsf{ZK}\{\exists\, & a, b, \mathsf{msg}, r, \alpha, \gamma, t_a, t_b, t_{\mathsf{msg}}, t_r, t_\alpha, t_\gamma \text{ s.t.}:\\ & \mathsf{ct}_\beta = \mathsf{Enc}(\mathsf{pk}_{\mathsf{CS}}, a\cdot \mathsf{msg} + b\cdot p) + a\cdot \mathsf{ct}_{\mathsf{u}} + a\cdot r\cdot \mathsf{ct}_{\mathsf{y}},\\ & \mathsf{com}_a = \mathsf{Commit}_{\mathsf{Ext}}(a; t_a),\ \mathsf{com}_b = \mathsf{Commit}_{\mathsf{Ped}}(b; t_b),\\ & \mathsf{com}_r = \mathsf{Commit}_{\mathsf{Ped}}(r; t_r),\ \mathsf{com}_{\mathsf{msg}} = \mathsf{Commit}_{\mathsf{Ext}}(\mathsf{msg}; t_{\mathsf{msg}}),\\ & \mathsf{com}_\alpha = \mathsf{Commit}_{\mathsf{Ped}}(a\cdot \mathsf{msg}; t_\alpha),\ \mathsf{com}_\gamma = \mathsf{Commit}_{\mathsf{Ped}}(a\cdot r; t_\gamma),\\ & a < p\cdot 2^{2\lambda+1}, \alpha < p\cdot 2^{2\lambda+1}, r < p\cdot 2^{2\lambda+1}, b < p^2\cdot 2^{3\lambda+1}\}.\end{aligned}$$

Output: $\mathsf{digest} \leftarrow (\mathsf{ct}_\beta, \mathsf{com}_a, \mathsf{com}_b, \mathsf{com}_{\mathsf{msg}}, \mathsf{com}_r, \mathsf{com}_\alpha, \mathsf{com}_\gamma, \pi)$
$\mathsf{state} \leftarrow (a, b)$

VOPRF.Eval($\mathsf{privprm}_{\mathsf{S}}, \mathsf{digest}$):

1. Parse $\mathsf{digest} \leftarrow (\mathsf{ct}, \pi)$. If π does not verify, abort.
2. Compute $\beta \leftarrow \mathsf{CS.Dec}(\mathsf{sk}_{\mathsf{CS}}, \mathsf{ct})$. If $\beta \geq p^3 2^{\lambda+1}$, abort.
3. Compute commitment $\mathsf{com}_\beta = \mathsf{Commit}_{\mathsf{Ped}}(\beta; r_\beta)$ where $r_\beta \leftarrow\!\$\, \mathbb{Z}_{\lfloor N/4 \rfloor}$.
4. Set $\mathsf{F} = \beta^{-1}\cdot \mathsf{G}$.
5. Generate a ZK proof

$$\begin{aligned}\pi = \mathsf{ZK}\{\beta, r_\beta, \mathsf{sk}_{\mathsf{CS}} \text{ s.t.}: \mathsf{ct} = (\mathsf{G}', \beta\cdot \mathsf{H}_{\mathsf{CS}} + \mathsf{sk}_{\mathsf{CS}}\cdot \mathsf{G}'), \mathsf{Y}_{\mathsf{CS}} = \mathsf{sk}_{\mathsf{CS}}\cdot \mathsf{G}_{\mathsf{CS}},\\ \mathsf{com}_\beta = \mathsf{Commit}_{\mathsf{Ped}}(\beta; r_\beta), \mathsf{F} = \beta^{-1}\cdot \mathsf{G}, \beta < p^3\cdot 2^{3\lambda+1}\}.\end{aligned}$$

Output: $\mathsf{blindPRF} \leftarrow (\mathsf{F}, \mathsf{com}_\beta, \pi)$

VOPRF.Decode($, \mathsf{blindPRF}$):

1. Parse $\mathsf{blindPRF} = (\mathsf{F}, \mathsf{com}_\beta, \pi), = (a, b)$.
2. If π does not verify, abort.
3. Set $\mathsf{F}' = a\cdot \mathsf{F}$.

Output: $\tau \leftarrow \mathsf{F}'$

Security Proof. We start with the intuition for our security proof. The first observation is that in the case of a single client, an ACT forgery corresponds to generating a new evaluation of the PRF $\mathcal{F}$ on a message that has not been queried. To formalize this, we leverage the result of Miao et al. [MPR+20, Theorem B.1] which constructs a distributed oblivious PRF evaluation protocol with malicious security on committed inputs for the Dodis-Yampolskiy

[4] Note that when called from the ACT, msg will actually be a hash of some message H(msg).

PRF. Their result essentially shows that the VOPRF Construction 4.2 with $\mathcal{F}_{\mathsf{DY}}(\mathsf{u}, \mathsf{msg}) = (\mathsf{u} + \mathsf{msg})^{-1} \cdot \mathsf{G}$ is a secure two-party computation protocol where the client obtains $\mathsf{PRF}(\mathsf{u}, \mathsf{msg})$ and the server has no output. This means that if we instantiated the ACT construction with this VOPRF construction, then the ACT scheme will be unforgeable for a single client who chooses its messages selectively. Then, we show how we can reduce the unforgeability of the ACT construction with PRF $\mathcal{F}_{\mathsf{DY}}(\mathsf{u}, \mathsf{y}, \mathsf{msg}, \mathsf{r}) = (\mathsf{u} + \mathsf{msg} + \mathsf{r} \cdot \mathsf{y})^{-1} \cdot \mathsf{G}$ to the single client unforgeability of the ACT with the Dodis-Yampolskiy PRF. This reduction will follow the ideas of the reduction from unforgeability to weak unforgeability for the Boneh-Boyen signatures [BB04].

The unlinkability of the scheme follows from the selective pseudorandom property of the Dodis-Yampolskiy PRF. It indeed shows that the unlinkability adversary only obtains pseudorandom tokens that do not reveal any information about the underlying input messages. We provide all proof details and a concrete instantiation with efficiency cost estimates in the full version of the paper [BRS23].

5 ACTs from Equivalence-Class Signature

In this section, we present ACT constructions from equivalence-class signatures (EQS). Note that these constructions will have the functionality where the rate-limiting of a single token per message per client will be enforced during token redemption. In particular, the ACT verification will output the verification bit of the validity of the token and a tag that is a pseudorandom value derived from the client's key and the message. The issuer can compare this tag against its database of redeemed message tags and reject the token if this value occurs there. However, this latter rate-limiting step is not part of the ACT verification algorithm itself.

We present two ACT constructions which differ in the type of PRF used to enforce the rate-limiting property. The first one is based on the Dodis-Yampolskiy PRF and can be instantiated in the standard model but is limited to messages of size logarithmic in the security parameter. The second one has two versions: the long version is provably secure in the random oracle model, while the short version is provably secure in the generic bilinear group and random oracle model when instantiated with a specific scheme.

5.1 ACT from EQS and Dodis-Yampolskiy PRF for Small Messages

We start with an ACT construction from EQS and the Dodis-Yampolskiy PRF.

Constructions 5.1 (ACT from EQS and Dodis-Yampolskiy). Let $\mathsf{EQS} = (\mathsf{EQS.Setup}, \mathsf{EQS.KGen}, \mathsf{EQS.Sign}, \mathsf{EQS.Adapt}, \mathsf{EQS.Verify})$ be an equivalence-class signature scheme over a bilinear group $\mathcal{PG} = (\mathbb{G}_1, \mathbb{G}_2, \mathbb{G}_T)$. We use the Dodis-Yampolskiy pseudorandom function $\mathcal{F}_{\mathsf{DY}}(\mathsf{u}, x) = (\mathsf{u} + x)^{-1} \cdot \mathsf{G}_1$ over the cyclic group $\mathbb{G}_1$. We assume messages msg are in a subset of $\mathbb{Z}_p^*$ of size polynomial in the security parameter λ. An anonymous counting token construction ACT consists of the following algorithms:

ACT.GenParam(1^λ): Generate

1. a bilinear group $\mathcal{PG} \leftarrow \mathsf{GGen}(1^\lambda)$ and an extra random generator $\mathsf{G}_1' \in \mathbb{G}_1$
2. ZK argument CRS $\mathsf{ZK.crs} \leftarrow \mathsf{ZK.Setup}(\mathcal{R})$ where $\mathcal{R}$ is implicitly defined in ACT.Request (ZK.crs is used implicitly when generating and verifying ZK proofs),
3. EQS CRS $\mathsf{crs} \leftarrow \mathsf{EQS.Setup}(\mathcal{PG})$, and EQS keys $(\mathsf{pk}, \mathsf{sk}) \leftarrow \mathsf{EQS.KGen}(\mathsf{crs})$.

Output: $\mathsf{pprm_S} \leftarrow (\mathsf{ZK.crs}, \mathsf{crs}, \mathsf{pk})$
$\mathsf{privprm_S} \leftarrow (\mathsf{pprm_S}, \mathsf{sk})$.

ACT.ClientRegister$(\mathsf{pprm_S})$:

1. Generate a Dodis-Yampolskiy PRF key $\mathsf{u_C} \leftarrow\$ \mathbb{Z}_p$,
2. Set $\mathsf{U_C} = \mathsf{u_C} \cdot \mathsf{G}_1$.

Output: $\mathsf{pprm_C} \leftarrow \mathsf{U_C}$
$\mathsf{privprm_C} \leftarrow \mathsf{u_C}$

ACT.TokenRequest$(\mathsf{pprm_S}, \mathsf{privprm_C}, \mathsf{msg} \in \mathbb{Z}_p^*)$:

1. Generate a random value $\mu \leftarrow\$ \mathbb{Z}_p^*$.
2. Set $\vec{\mathsf{M}} \leftarrow (\mathsf{M}_1 = \mu^{-1} \cdot \mathsf{G}_1,\ \mathsf{M}_2 = \mu^{-1} \cdot \mathcal{F}_{\mathsf{DY}}(\mathsf{u_C}, \mathsf{msg}),\ \mathsf{M}_3 = (\mu^{-1}\mathsf{msg}) \cdot \mathsf{G}_1')$.
3. Generate a proof $\pi_{\vec{\mathsf{M}}}$:

$$\pi_{\vec{\mathsf{M}}} : \mathsf{ZK}\{\exists\ \mu^{-1}, \mathsf{u_C} \in \mathbb{Z}_p : \mathsf{M}_1' = \mu^{-1} \cdot \mathsf{G}_1,\ \mathsf{M}_2' = \mu^{-1}(\mathsf{u_C} + \mathsf{msg})^{-1} \cdot \mathsf{G}_1,\ \mathsf{M}_3 = (\mu^{-1}\mathsf{msg}) \cdot \mathsf{G}_1,\ \mathsf{U_C} = \mathsf{u_C} \cdot \mathsf{G}_1\}$$

Output: $\mathsf{blindRequest} \leftarrow (\vec{\mathsf{M}}, \pi_{\vec{\mathsf{M}}})$
$\mathsf{rand_{msg}} \leftarrow (\mathsf{msg}, \vec{\mathsf{M}}, \mu)$

ACT.Sign$(\mathsf{privprm_S}, \mathsf{pprm_C}, \mathsf{blindRequest})$

1. Parse $\mathsf{blindRequest} = (\vec{\mathsf{M}}, \pi_{\vec{\mathsf{M}}})$.
2. If verification of $\pi_{\vec{\mathsf{M}}}$ fails, abort.
3. Run $\rho \leftarrow \mathsf{EQS.Sign}(\mathsf{crs}, \mathsf{sk}, \vec{\mathsf{M}})$.

Output: $\mathsf{blindToken} \leftarrow \rho$

ACT.Unblind($\mathsf{pprm_S}, \mathsf{privprm_C}, \mathsf{blindToken}, \mathsf{rand_{msg}}$)

1. Parse $\mathsf{rand_{msg}} = (\mathsf{msg}, \vec{\mathsf{M}}, \mu)$, $\mathsf{blindToken} = \rho$.
2. Set $\vec{\mathsf{M}}' \leftarrow (\mathsf{G}_1, \mathcal{F}_{\mathsf{DY}}(\mathsf{u_C}, \mathsf{msg}), \mathsf{msg} \cdot \mathsf{G}'_1)$.
3. Compute $\sigma \leftarrow \mathsf{EQS.Adapt}(\mathsf{crs}, \mathsf{pk}, \vec{\mathsf{M}}, \rho, \mu)$.
4. If $\sigma = \perp$, abort.

Output: $\left(\mathsf{msg},\ \mathsf{tok} \leftarrow (\vec{\mathsf{M}}', \sigma)\right)$

ACT.Verify($\mathsf{pprm_S}, \mathsf{privprm}, \mathsf{msg}, \mathsf{tok}$)

1. Set $\mathsf{bit} \leftarrow$ **true**.
2. Parse $\mathsf{tok} = (\vec{\mathsf{M}}' = (\mathsf{M}'_1, \mathsf{M}'_2, \mathsf{M}'_3), \sigma)$.
3. If $\mathsf{M}'_1 \neq \mathsf{G}_1$ or $\mathsf{M}'_3 \neq \mathsf{msg} \cdot \mathsf{G}'_1$, set $\mathsf{bit} \leftarrow$ **false**.
4. If **false** $= \mathsf{EQS.Verify}(\mathsf{pk}, \vec{\mathsf{M}}', \sigma)$, set $\mathsf{bit} \leftarrow$ **false**.

Output: $(\mathsf{bit},\ \mathsf{M}_2)$

Perfect correctness is straightforward.

We provide the unforgeability and unlinkability proofs in the full version [BRS23]. We note that unforgeability does not rely on the pseudorandomness of the Dodis-Yampolskiy PRF.

Parameter Generation for Unlinkability. Unlinkability assumes that the ACT parameters are generated honestly and the issuer only sees the secret key. To alleviate this requirement, we can instead work in the CRS model, where the ZK and EQS CRS are put in the CRS and generated by a trusted party. The EQS signature adaptation holds even for maliciously generated pk, but our unlinkability proof uses sk. Therefore, we would also need that the issuer includes in $\mathsf{pprm_S}$ a zero-knowledge proof of knowledge of the EQS secret key sk for the unlinkability proof above to go through. This can be done efficiently using either Groth-Sahai proofs or Fiat-Shamir proofs.

The same discussion applies to Construction 5.2.

Instantiation. The construction in Construction 5.1 can be instantiated in the standard model using the EQS from Sect. 6.1. in the full version of the paper [BRS23] and using Groth-Sahai proofs for the ZK argument. Following the notations from [EG14], the Groth-Sahai proof will need to make (with the cost in the number of group elements):

- $3 \times \mathsf{sca}_{\mathbb{G}_2}$ for the commitments to μ^{-1}, $\mathsf{u_C}$, and msg
  $\hookrightarrow$ cost $= 6 \times \mathbb{G}_2$
- $4 \times \mathsf{MConst}_{G_2}$ to prove the following 4 equations:

$$\mathsf{M}_1' \bullet \mathsf{G}_2 = \mathsf{G}_1 \bullet (\mu^{-1} \cdot \mathsf{G}_2) \quad \mathsf{M}_2' \bullet (\mathsf{u_C} \cdot \mathsf{G}_2) + \mathsf{M}_2' \bullet (\mathsf{msg} \cdot \mathsf{G}_2) = \mathsf{G}_1 \bullet (\mu^{-1} \cdot \mathsf{G}_2)$$
$$\mathsf{M}_3' \bullet \mathsf{G}_2 = \mathsf{M}_1' \bullet (\mathsf{msg} \cdot \mathsf{G}_2) \quad \mathsf{U_C} \bullet \mathsf{G}_2 = \mathsf{G}_1 \bullet (\mathsf{u_C} \cdot \mathsf{G}_2)$$

  $\hookrightarrow$ cost $= 4 \times \mathbb{G}_1$

5.2 ACT from EQS and a Random-Oracle-Based PRF

The second ACT construction from EQS leverages the PRF in the RO model $\mathsf{PRF}(\mathsf{K}, x) = \mathsf{K} \cdot \mathsf{H}(x)$ where $\mathsf{H} : \{0,1\}^* \to \mathbb{G}_1$ is a hash function that can be modeled as a random oracle. This PRF was folklore and has been formally defined in [NPR99].

The ACT construction is similar to Construction 5.1 but the message $\vec{\mathsf{M}}$ generated by $\mathsf{ACT.Request}$ is generated as:

$$\vec{\mathsf{M}} \leftarrow \left(\mathsf{M}_1 = \mu^{-1} \cdot \mathsf{G}_1,\ \mathsf{M}_2 = \mu^{-1} \cdot \mathsf{u_C} \cdot \mathsf{H}(\mathsf{msg}),\ \mathsf{M}_3 = \mu^{-1} \cdot \mathsf{H}(\mathsf{msg})\right)$$

instead of

$$\vec{\mathsf{M}} \leftarrow \left(\mathsf{M}_1 = \mu^{-1} \cdot \mathsf{G}_1,\ \mathsf{M}_2 = \mu^{-1} \cdot (\mathsf{u_C} + \mathsf{msg})^{-1} \cdot \mathsf{G}_1,\ \mathsf{M}_3 = (\mu^{-1}\mathsf{msg}) \cdot \mathsf{G}_1\right).$$

Note that in both cases $\mathsf{M}_2 = \mathsf{PRF}(\mathsf{u_C}, \mathsf{msg})$, but with a different PRF. Importantly the statements proven by the ZK proof in this new construction do not need to evaluate the hash function H, so they can be still efficiently instantiated with Fiat-Shamir or Groth-Sahai.

We present two versions: the long version uses dimension-3 vectors $\vec{\mathsf{M}}$ and includes M_1 (like the Dodis-Yampolkiy-based construction), while the short version uses dimension-2 vectors without M_1. The short version is not proven unforgeable but we show that a specific instantiation of it is unforgeable in Sect. 6, in the generic (bilinear) group model.

Constructions 5.2 (ACT from EQS and Random Oracle (long and short versions)). Let ($\mathsf{EQS.Setup}$, $\mathsf{EQS.KGen}$, $\mathsf{EQS.Sign}$, $\mathsf{EQS.Adapt}$, $\mathsf{EQS.Verify}$) be an equivalence-class signature scheme. An anonymous counting token construction ACT consists of the following algorithms:

ACT.GenParam(1^λ): Generate

1. a bilinear group $\mathcal{PG} \leftarrow \mathsf{GGen}(1^\lambda)$,
2. ZK argument CRS $\mathsf{ZK.crs} \leftarrow \mathsf{ZK.Setup}(\mathcal{R})$ where $\mathcal{R}$ is implicitly define in $\mathsf{ACT.Request}$ ($\mathsf{ZK.crs}$ is used implicitly when generating and verifying ZK proofs),

3. EQS CRS $\mathsf{crs} \leftarrow \mathsf{EQS.Setup}(\mathcal{PG})$, and EQS keys $(\mathsf{pk}, \mathsf{sk}) \leftarrow \mathsf{KGen}(\mathsf{crs})$.

Output: $\mathsf{pprm}_\mathsf{S} \leftarrow (\mathsf{ZK.crs}, \mathsf{crs}, \mathsf{pk})$
$\mathsf{privprm}_\mathsf{S} \leftarrow (\mathsf{pprm}_\mathsf{S}, \mathsf{sk})$.

ACT.ClientRegister(pprm_S):

1. Generate a PRF key $\mathsf{u}_\mathsf{C} \leftarrow\$ \mathbb{Z}_p$.
2. Set $\mathsf{U}_\mathsf{C} = \mathsf{u}_\mathsf{C} \cdot \mathsf{G}_1$.

Output: $\mathsf{pprm}_\mathsf{C} \leftarrow \mathsf{U}_\mathsf{C}$
$\mathsf{privprm}_\mathsf{C} \leftarrow \mathsf{u}_\mathsf{C}$

ACT.TokenRequest($\mathsf{pprm}_\mathsf{S}, \mathsf{privprm}_\mathsf{C}, \mathsf{msg}$):

1. Generate a random value $\mu \leftarrow\$ \mathbb{Z}_p^*$.
2. Compute $\mathsf{M}'_3 \leftarrow \mathsf{H}(\mathsf{msg})$ and $\mathsf{M}'_2 \leftarrow \mathsf{u}_\mathsf{C} \cdot \mathsf{H}(\mathsf{msg})$.
3. Set $\vec{\mathsf{M}} \leftarrow (\mathsf{M}_1 = \mu^{-1} \cdot \mathsf{G}_1, \mathsf{M}_2 = \mu^{-1} \cdot \mathsf{M}'_2, \mathsf{M}_3 = \mu^{-1} \cdot \mathsf{M}'_3)$.
4. Generate a proof $\pi_{\vec{\mathsf{M}}}$:

$$\pi_{\vec{\mathsf{M}}} : \mathsf{ZK}\{\exists \mathsf{u}_C \in \mathbb{Z}_p : \mathsf{M}_2 = \mathsf{u}_\mathsf{C} \cdot \mathsf{M}_3 \textbf{ and } \mathsf{U}_\mathsf{C} = \mathsf{u}_\mathsf{C} \cdot \mathsf{G}_1)\}$$

Output: $\mathsf{blindRequest} \leftarrow (\vec{\mathsf{M}}, \pi_{\vec{\mathsf{M}}})$
$\mathsf{rand}_\mathsf{msg} \leftarrow (\mathsf{msg}, \vec{\mathsf{M}}, \mu)$

ACT.Sign($\mathsf{privprm}_\mathsf{S}, \mathsf{pprm}_\mathsf{C}, \mathsf{blindRequest}$)

1. Parse $\mathsf{blindRequest} = (\vec{\mathsf{M}}, \pi_{\vec{\mathsf{M}}})$.
2. If verification of $\pi_{\vec{\mathsf{M}}}$ fails, abort.
3. Run $\rho \leftarrow \mathsf{EQS.Sign}(\mathsf{crs}, \mathsf{sk}, \vec{\mathsf{M}})$.

Output: $\mathsf{blindToken} \leftarrow \rho$

ACT.Unblind($\mathsf{pprm}_\mathsf{S}, \mathsf{privprm}_\mathsf{C}, \mathsf{blindToken}, \mathsf{rand}_\mathsf{msg}$)

1. Parse $\mathsf{rand}_\mathsf{msg} = (\mathsf{msg}, \vec{\mathsf{M}}, \mu)$, $\mathsf{blindToken} = \rho$.
2. Set $\vec{\mathsf{M}}' \leftarrow (\mathsf{G}_1, \mathsf{u}_\mathsf{C} \cdot \mathsf{H}(\mathsf{msg}), \mathsf{H}(\mathsf{msg}))$.
3. Compute $\sigma \leftarrow \mathsf{EQS.Adapt}(\mathsf{crs}, \mathsf{pk}, \vec{\mathsf{M}}, \rho, \mu)$.
4. If $\sigma = \perp$, abort.

Output: $\left(\mathsf{msg}, \mathsf{tok} \leftarrow (\vec{\mathsf{M}}', \sigma)\right)$

ACT.Verify(pprm$_S$, privprm, msg, tok)

1. Set bit $\leftarrow$ **true**.
2. Parse tok $= (\vec{\mathsf{M}}' = (\mathsf{M}_1', \mathsf{M}_2', \mathsf{M}_3'), \sigma)$.
3. If $\mathsf{M}_1' \neq \mathsf{G}_1$ or $\mathsf{M}_3' \neq \mathsf{H}(\mathsf{msg})$, set bit $\leftarrow$ **false**.
4. If **false** $=$ EQS.Verify(crs, pk, $\vec{\mathsf{M}}', \sigma$), set bit $\leftarrow$ **false**.

Output: (bit, M_2)

Perfect correctness is straightforward. We provide the unforgeability and unlinkability proofs in the full version of the paper [BRS23].

Instantiation. The long version of Construction 5.2 can be instantiated in the random oracle model using the EQS from Sect. 6.1. in the full version of the paper [BRS23] and using a Fiat-Shamir proof for the ZK argument.

Concretely, the Fiat-Shamir proof needs to prove that $\log_{\mathsf{G}_1}(\mathsf{U}_\mathsf{C}) = \log_{\mathsf{M}_3}(\mathsf{M}_2)$ and consists of the following:

- Generate random scalar $v \leftarrow\$ \mathbb{Z}_p^*$.
- Compute the Fiat-Shamir commitments: $V \leftarrow v \cdot \mathsf{G}_1$, $W \leftarrow v \cdot \mathsf{M}_3$.
- Derive the Fiat-Shamir challenge: $c \leftarrow \mathsf{H}'(\mathsf{U}_\mathsf{C}, \vec{\mathsf{M}}, V, W)$, where $\mathsf{H}' : \{0,1\}^* \rightarrow \mathbb{Z}_p$ is a hash function that will be modeled as a random oracle.
- Compute the Fiat-Shamir response: $\xi \leftarrow v + c \cdot \mathsf{u}_\mathsf{C}$.
- Set the proof to be: $\pi_{\vec{\mathsf{M}}} \leftarrow (\xi, c) \in \mathbb{Z}_p^2$.[5]

The proof is verified by computing $V' \leftarrow \xi \cdot \mathsf{G}_1 - c \cdot \mathsf{U}_\mathsf{C}$ and $W' \leftarrow \xi \cdot \mathsf{M}_3 - c \cdot \mathsf{M}_2$, and then checking whether $c = \mathsf{H}'(\mathsf{U}_\mathsf{C}, \vec{\mathsf{M}}, V', W')$.

6 ACTs in the Generic Bilinear Group Model

In this section, we show that the short variant of Construction 5.2 is unforgeable in the generic bilinear group model and random oracle model, when implemented with the EQS scheme from [FHS19] and Fiat-Shamir for equality of discrete logarithms for the ZK proof in ACT.Sign (as in the instantiation in Sect. 5.2). It achieves better concrete efficiency than all our other constructions at the cost of security holding in the generic bilinear group model (GBGM).

For the sake of completeness, we describe the full protocol below.

[5] Actually the challenge c can be reduced to λ bits while keeping the security of the Fiat-Shamir transform.

Constructions 6.1 (ACT in GBGM). Let $\mathcal{PG} = (\mathbb{G}_1, \mathbb{G}_2, \mathbb{G}_T)$ be a bilinear group, $\mathsf{H} : \{0,1\}^* \to \mathbb{G}_1$ and $\mathsf{H}' : \{0,1\}^* \to \mathbb{Z}_p$ be two hash functions that will be modeled as two random oracles. In this construction, we denote elements from $\mathbb{G}_2$ with a hat, e.g., $\hat{X}_2$, matching notation from [FHS19] (except the generators G_1 and G_2). Vectors $\vec{\mathsf{M}}$ have two elements indexed 2 and to match Construction 5.2. Recall that $\mathbb{G}_T$ is also written additively and that we use $\bullet$ to denote the pairing operation $e(\mathsf{X}, \hat{\mathsf{Y}}) = \mathsf{X} \bullet \hat{\mathsf{Y}}$. An anonymous counting token construction ACT consists of the following algorithms:

ACT.GenParam(1^λ): Generate

1. a bilinear group $\mathcal{PG} \leftarrow \mathsf{GGen}(1^\lambda)$
2. EQS secret key $\mathsf{sk} = (x_2, x_3) \leftarrow\$ (\mathbb{Z}_p^*)^2$
3. EQS public key $\mathsf{pk} \leftarrow (\hat{\mathsf{X}}_2 \leftarrow x_2 \cdot \mathsf{G}_2,\ \hat{\mathsf{X}}_3 \leftarrow x_3 \cdot \mathsf{G}_2)$

Output: $\mathsf{pprm}_\mathsf{S} \leftarrow \mathsf{pk}$,
$\mathsf{privprm}_\mathsf{S} \leftarrow \mathsf{sk}$.

ACT.ClientRegister$(\mathsf{pprm}_\mathsf{S})$:

1. Generate a PRF key $\mathsf{u}_\mathsf{C} \leftarrow\$ \mathbb{Z}_p$,
2. Set $\mathsf{U}_\mathsf{C} \leftarrow \mathsf{u}_\mathsf{C} \cdot \mathsf{G}_1$

Output: $\mathsf{pprm}_\mathsf{C} \leftarrow \mathsf{U}_\mathsf{C}$
$\mathsf{privprm}_\mathsf{C} \leftarrow \mathsf{u}_\mathsf{C}$

ACT.TokenRequest$(\mathsf{pprm}_\mathsf{S}, \mathsf{privprm}_\mathsf{C}, \mathsf{msg})$:

1. Generate random scalars $v, \mu \leftarrow\$ \mathbb{Z}_p^*$.
2. Compute $\mathsf{M}_3' \leftarrow \mathsf{H}(\mathsf{msg})$ and $\mathsf{M}_2' \leftarrow \mathsf{u}_\mathsf{C} \cdot \mathsf{H}(\mathsf{msg})$.
3. Set $\vec{\mathsf{M}} \leftarrow (\mathsf{M}_2 = \mu^{-1}\mathsf{M}_2',\ \mathsf{M}_3 = \mu^{-1}\mathsf{M}_3')$
4. Compute the Fiat-Shamir commitments: $V = v \cdot \mathsf{G}_1$, $W = v \cdot \mathsf{M}_3$.
5. Derive the Fiat-Shamir challenge: $c \leftarrow \mathsf{H}'(\mathsf{U}_\mathsf{C}, \vec{\mathsf{M}}, V, W)$.
6. Compute the Fiat-Shamir response: $\xi \leftarrow v + c \cdot \mathsf{u}_\mathsf{C}$.
7. Set the proof to be: $\pi_{\vec{\mathsf{M}}} \leftarrow (\xi, c)$.

Output: $\mathsf{blindRequest} \leftarrow (\vec{\mathsf{M}}, \pi_{\vec{\mathsf{M}}})$
$\mathsf{rand}_\mathsf{msg} \leftarrow (\mathsf{msg}, \vec{\mathsf{M}}, \mu)$

ACT.Sign$(\mathsf{privprm}_\mathsf{S}, \mathsf{pprm}_\mathsf{C}, \mathsf{blindRequest})$

1. Parse $\mathsf{blindRequest} = (\vec{\mathsf{M}},\ \pi_{\vec{\mathsf{M}}} = (\xi, c))$.

2. Verify the ZK proof $\pi_{\vec{\mathsf{M}}}$: namely compute $V' \leftarrow \xi \mathsf{G}_1 - c\mathsf{U}_\mathsf{C}$, $W' \leftarrow \xi \mathsf{M}_3 - c\mathsf{M}_2$, and abort if $c \neq \mathsf{H}'(\mathsf{U}_\mathsf{C}, \vec{\mathsf{M}}, \mathsf{V}', \mathsf{W}')$.
3. Generate a random $y \leftarrow_R \mathbb{Z}_p^*$.
4. Compute the EQS signature: $\mathsf{Z} \leftarrow y \cdot (x_2 \cdot \mathsf{M}_2 + x_3 \cdot \mathsf{M}_3)$, $\mathsf{Y} \leftarrow y^{-1} \cdot \mathsf{G}_1$, and $\hat{\mathsf{Y}} \leftarrow y^{-1} \cdot \mathsf{G}_2$.

Output: $\mathsf{blindToken} \leftarrow \rho = (\mathsf{Z}, \mathsf{Y}, \hat{\mathsf{Y}})$

ACT.Unblind$(\mathsf{pprm_S}, \mathsf{privprm_C}, \mathsf{blindToken}, \mathsf{rand_{msg}})$

1. Parse $\mathsf{rand_{msg}} = (\mathsf{msg}, \vec{\mathsf{M}}, \mu)$, $\mathsf{blindToken} = \rho = (\mathsf{Z}, \mathsf{Y}, \hat{\mathsf{Y}})$.
2. Generate a random scalar $\psi \leftarrow\$ \mathbb{Z}_p^*$.
3. Compute $\sigma \leftarrow (\mathsf{Z}' \leftarrow \mu\psi\mathsf{Z},\ \mathsf{Y}' \leftarrow \psi^{-1}\mathsf{Y},\ \hat{\mathsf{Y}}' \leftarrow \psi^{-1}\hat{\mathsf{Y}})$
4. Set $\vec{\mathsf{M}}' \leftarrow (\mathsf{u_C} \cdot \mathsf{H}(\mathsf{msg}),\ \mathsf{H}(\mathsf{msg}))$.
5. Abort if $\mathsf{M}_2' \bullet \hat{\mathsf{X}}_2 + \mathsf{M}_3' \bullet \hat{\mathsf{X}}_3 \neq \mathsf{Z} \bullet \hat{\mathsf{Y}}$ or if $\mathsf{Y} \bullet \mathsf{G}_2 \neq \mathsf{G}_1 \bullet \hat{\mathsf{Y}}$ or $\mathsf{Y} = 0$ or $\hat{\mathsf{Y}} = 0$.

Output: $\left(\mathsf{msg},\ \mathsf{tok} \leftarrow (\mathsf{M}_2',\ \sigma \leftarrow (\mathsf{Z}', \mathsf{Y}', \hat{\mathsf{Y}}'))\right)$

ACT.Verify$(\mathsf{pprm_S}, \mathsf{privprm}, \mathsf{msg}, \mathsf{tok})$

1. Parse $\mathsf{tok} = (\mathsf{M}_2',\ \sigma = (\mathsf{Z}', \mathsf{Y}', \hat{\mathsf{Y}}'))$.
2. Compute $\mathsf{M}_3' \leftarrow \mathsf{H}(\mathsf{msg})$.
3. Set bit $\leftarrow$ **true**.
4. If $\mathsf{M}_2' \bullet \hat{\mathsf{X}}_2 + \mathsf{M}_3' \bullet \hat{\mathsf{X}}_3 \neq \mathsf{Z} \bullet \hat{\mathsf{Y}}$ or $\mathsf{Y} \bullet \mathsf{G}_2 \neq \mathsf{G}_1 \bullet \hat{\mathsf{Y}}$ or $\mathsf{Y} = 0$ or $\hat{\mathsf{Y}} = 0$, set bit $\leftarrow$ **false**.

Output: (bit, tag $\leftarrow \mathsf{M}_2'$).

Correctness and unlinkability follow from correctness and unlinkability of Construction 5.2. See the full version of the paper [BRS23] for the proof of unforgeability.

References

[AFK22] Attema, T., Fehr, S., Klooß, M.: Fiat-Shamir transformation of multi-round interactive proofs. In: Kiltz, E., Vaikuntanathan, V. (eds.) TCC 2022, Part I. LNCS, vol. 13747, pp. 113–142. Springer, Heidelberg (2022). https://doi.org/10.1007/978-3-031-22318-1_5

[AGR+16] Albrecht, M., Grassi, L., Rechberger, C., Roy, A., Tiessen, T.: MiMC: efficient encryption and cryptographic hashing with minimal multiplicative complexity. In: Cheon, J.H., Takagi, T. (eds.) ASIACRYPT 2016. LNCS, vol. 10031, pp. 191–219. Springer, Heidelberg (2016). https://doi.org/10.1007/978-3-662-53887-6_7

[Bar16] Barker, E.: Recommendation for key management, part 1: General, 2016-01-28 (2016)

[BB04] Boneh, D., Boyen, X.: Short signatures without random oracles. In: Cachin, C., Camenisch, J.L. (eds.) EUROCRYPT 2004. LNCS, vol. 3027, pp. 56–73. Springer, Heidelberg (2004). https://doi.org/10.1007/978-3-540-24676-3_4

[BBG+20] Bell, J.H., Bonawitz, K.A., Gascón, A., Lepoint, T., Raykova, M.: Secure single-server aggregation with (poly)logarithmic overhead. In: Ligatti, J., Ou, X., Katz, J., Vigna, G. (eds.) ACM CCS 2020, pp. 1253–1269. ACM Press, November 2020

[BDL+12] Bernstein, D.J., Duif, N., Lange, T., Schwabe, P., Yang, B.-Y.: High-speed high-security signatures. J. Cryptogr. Eng. **2**(2), 77–89 (2012)

[BIK+17] Bonawitz, K., et al.: Practical secure aggregation for privacy-preserving machine learning. In: Thuraisingham, B.M., Evans, D., Malkin, T., Xu, D. (eds.) ACM CCS 2017, pp. 1175–1191. ACM Press, October/November 2017

[Bow17] Bowe, S.: Bls12-381: New zk-snark elliptic curve construction, March 2017. https://electriccoin.co/blog/new-snark-curve/

[BP97] Barić, N., Pfitzmann, B.: Collision-free accumulators and fail-stop signature schemes without trees. In: Fumy, W. (ed.) EUROCRYPT 1997. LNCS, vol. 1233, pp. 480–494. Springer, Heidelberg (1997). https://doi.org/10.1007/3-540-69053-0_33

[BRS23] Benhamouda, F., Raykova, M., Seth, K.: Anonymous counting tokens. Cryptology ePrint Archive, Paper 2023/320 (2023). https://eprint.iacr.org/2023/320

[CDS94] Cramer, R., Damgård, I., Schoenmakers, B.: Proofs of partial knowledge and simplified design of witness hiding protocols. In: Desmedt, Y.G. (ed.) CRYPTO 1994. LNCS, vol. 839, pp. 174–187. Springer, Heidelberg (1994). https://doi.org/10.1007/3-540-48658-5_19

[CDV23] Chase, M., Durak, F.B., Vaudenay, S.: Anonymous tokens with stronger metadata bit hiding from algebraic MACs. In: Handschuh, H., Lysyanskaya, A. (eds.) CRYPTO 2023. LNCS, vol. 14082, pp. 418–449. Springer, Cham (2023). https://doi.org/10.1007/978-3-031-38545-2_14

[Cha82] Chaum, D.: Blind signatures for untraceable payments. In: Chaum, D., Rivest, R.L., Sherman, A.T. (eds.) Advances in Cryptology, pp. 199–203. Springer, Boston, MA (1983). https://doi.org/10.1007/978-1-4757-0602-4_18

[Cra97] Cramer, R.: Modular design of secure yet practical cryptographic protocols. Ph.D. thesis, University of Amsterdam (1997)

[CS03] Camenisch, J., Shoup, V.: Practical verifiable encryption and decryption of discrete logarithms. In: Boneh, D. (ed.) CRYPTO 2003. LNCS, vol. 2729, pp. 126–144. Springer, Heidelberg (2003). https://doi.org/10.1007/978-3-540-45146-4_8

[DGS+18] Davidson, A., Goldberg, I., Sullivan, N., Tankersley, G., Valsorda, F.: Privacy pass: bypassing internet challenges anonymously. PoPETs **2018**(3), 164–180 (2018)

[DY05] Dodis, Y., Yampolskiy, A.: A verifiable random function with short proofs and keys. In: Vaudenay, S. (ed.) PKC 2005. LNCS, vol. 3386, pp. 416–431. Springer, Heidelberg (2005). https://doi.org/10.1007/978-3-540-30580-4_28

[EG14] Escala, A., Groth, J.: Fine-tuning Groth-Sahai proofs. In: Krawczyk, H. (ed.) PKC 2014. LNCS, vol. 8383, pp. 630–649. Springer, Heidelberg (2014). https://doi.org/10.1007/978-3-642-54631-0_36

[FG18] Fuchsbauer, G., Gay, R.: Weakly secure equivalence-class signatures from standard assumptions. In: Abdalla, M., Dahab, R. (eds.) PKC 2018. LNCS, vol. 10770, pp. 153–183. Springer, Cham (2018). https://doi.org/10.1007/978-3-319-76581-5_6

[FHS19] Fuchsbauer, G., Hanser, C., Slamanig, D.: Structure-preserving signatures on equivalence classes and constant-size anonymous credentials. J. Cryptol. **32**(2), 498–546 (2019)

[FO97] Fujisaki, E., Okamoto, T.: Statistical zero knowledge protocols to prove modular polynomial relations. In: Kaliski, B.S. (ed.) CRYPTO 1997. LNCS, vol. 1294, pp. 16–30. Springer, Heidelberg (1997). https://doi.org/10.1007/BFb0052225

[FS87] Fiat, A., Shamir, A.: How To prove yourself: practical solutions to identification and signature problems. In: Odlyzko, A.M. (ed.) CRYPTO 1986. LNCS, vol. 263, pp. 186–194. Springer, Heidelberg (1987). https://doi.org/10.1007/3-540-47721-7_12

[GKR+21] Grassi, L., Khovratovich, D., Rechberger, C., Roy, A., Schofnegger, M.: Poseidon: a new hash function for zero-knowledge proof systems. In: Bailey, M., Greenstadt, R. (eds.) USENIX Security 2021, pp. 519–535. USENIX Association, August 2021

[Gra22] Graney, K.: Privacy Sandbox k-anonymity Server (2022). https://github.com/WICG/turtledove/blob/main/FLEDGE_k_anonymity_server.md#privacy-enhancements-we-are-exploring

[GS08] Groth, J., Sahai, A.: Efficient non-interactive proof systems for bilinear groups. In: Smart, N. (ed.) EUROCRYPT 2008. LNCS, vol. 4965, pp. 415–432. Springer, Heidelberg (2008). https://doi.org/10.1007/978-3-540-78967-3_24

[HIP+22] Hendrickson, S., Iyengar, J., Pauly, T., Valdez, S., Wood, C.A.: Rate-Limited Token Issuance Protocol (2022). https://datatracker.ietf.org/doc/draft-privacypass-rate-limit-tokens/

[HS21] Hanzlik, L., Slamanig, D.: With a little help from my friends: constructing practical anonymous credentials. In: Vigna, G., Shi, E. (eds.) ACM CCS 2021, pp. 2004–2023. ACM Press, November 2021

[JR17] Jutla, C.S., Roy, A.: Improved structure preserving signatures under standard bilinear assumptions. In: Fehr, S. (ed.) PKC 2017, Part II. LNCS, vol. 10175, pp. 183–209. Springer, Heidelberg (2017). https://doi.org/10.1007/978-3-662-54388-7_7

[KLOR20] Kreuter, B., Lepoint, T., Orrù, M., Raykova, M.: Anonymous tokens with private metadata bit. In: Micciancio, D., Ristenpart, T. (eds.) CRYPTO 2020, Part I. LNCS, vol. 12170, pp. 308–336. Springer, Cham (2020). https://doi.org/10.1007/978-3-030-56784-2_11

[MPR+20] Miao, P., Patel, S., Raykova, M., Seth, K., Yung, M.: Two-sided malicious security for private intersection-sum with cardinality. In: Micciancio, D., Ristenpart, T. (eds.) CRYPTO 2020, Part III. LNCS, vol. 12172, pp. 3–33. Springer, Cham (2020). https://doi.org/10.1007/978-3-030-56877-1_1

[NPR99] Naor, M., Pinkas, B., Reingold, O.: Distributed pseudo-random functions and KDCs. In: Stern, J. (ed.) EUROCRYPT 1999. LNCS, vol. 1592, pp. 327–346. Springer, Heidelberg (1999). https://doi.org/10.1007/3-540-48910-X_23

[Ode09] Oded, G.: Foundations of Cryptography: Volume 2, Basic Applications, 1st edn. Cambridge University Press, Cambridge (2009)

[SS22] Silde, T., Strand, M.: Anonymous tokens with public metadata and applications to private contact tracing. In: Eyal, I., Garay, J.A. (eds.) FC 2022. LNCS, vol. 13411, pp. 179–199. Springer, Heidelberg (2022). https://doi.org/10.1007/978-3-031-18283-9_9

[TCR+22] Tyagi, N., Celi, S., Ristenpart, T., Sullivan, N., Tessaro, S., Wood, C.A.: A fast and simple partially oblivious PRF, with applications. In: Dunkelman, O., Dziembowski, S. (eds.) EUROCRYPT 2022. LNCS, vol. 13276, pp. 674–705. Springer, Cham (2022). https://doi.org/10.1007/978-3-031-07085-3_23

Predicate Aggregate Signatures and Applications

Tian Qiu(✉) and Qiang Tang

The University of Sydney, Sydney, Australia
tqiu4893@uni.sydney.edu.au, qiang.tang@sydney.edu.au

Abstract. Motivated by applications in anonymous reputation systems and blockchain governance, we initiate the study of predicate aggregate signatures (PAS), which is a new primitive that enables users to sign multiple messages, and these individual signatures can be aggregated by a combiner, preserving the anonymity of the signers. The resulting PAS discloses only a brief description of signers for each message and provides assurance that both the signers and their description satisfy the specified public predicate.

We formally define PAS and give a construction framework to yield a logarithmic size signature, and further reduce the verification time also to logarithmic. We also give several instantiations for several concrete predicates that may be of independent interest.

To showcase its power, we also demonstrate its applications to multiple settings including multi-signatures, aggregate signatures, threshold signatures, (threshold) ring signatures, attribute-based signatures, etc, and advance the state of the art in all of them.

1 Introduction

Anonymous reputation systems are widely used in many applications. For example, on online platforms, for Internet peers to jointly establish accumulated ratings on the merchants/service providers or certain products, so that users that are not familiar with them, can have some context to make a better choice. Since the main necessary information is the accumulated rating, ensuring anonymity plays a crucial role to allow users to participate in the reputation systems. More specifically, in YouTube, each user registers at YouTube, and then gives his rating on each content as an "I like it" (like +1) or not, then there will be an accumulated content score shown in the platform. The accumulated score not only serves as a succinct representation/description, but also *hides the identities* of the voters. To reduce the reliance on fully trusting the platform, other important requirements are that the accumulated score should be *publicly verifiable*, so that users may have stronger confidence that the score is not manipulated by the platform; furthermore, in the anonymous setting, one potential threat arises when a malicious platform attempts to manipulate the ratings by repeatedly counting one user's vote for many times. Therefore, *additional measures* must

J. Guo and R. Steinfeld (Eds.): ASIACRYPT 2023, LNCS 14439, pp. 279–312, 2023.
https://doi.org/10.1007/978-981-99-8724-5_9

be taken to assure the verifier that each voter's contribution to the accumulated score is limited to a single vote.[1]

Naturally, individual votes can be realized via digital signatures from legitimate users (e.g., registered identities). To obtain a succinct accumulated score k, say up-votes, we would like to aggregate the corresponding identities and signatures to be a short "proof". The proof needs to ensure that indeed there are at least k signatures on "I like it" from k *distinct* identities.

The one-user-one-vote requirement above can be seen as a special policy that was put on the identities of those signatures. In broader applications, there could be more complex voting policies that could be expressed as a predicate on the voter identities. For example, in blockchain governance (e.g., Decentralized autonomous organizations (DAOs) [4]), decisions could be made by the whole community whose accounts hold sufficient amount of tokens. The final decision needs to be attested with a short proof that the voting result is indeed following the governing policy, and the proof would be stored onchain. Voting processes in DAOs offer a remarkable degree of flexibility and customization. These processes can be tailored and programmed to accommodate a wide range of requirements and preferences. For example, quadratic voting [1,2] allows the voter have budgets of credits which are converted to counted votes according to their square root. Delegated voting [5] allows users to delegate their voting power to trusted individuals or entities. Property-based voting [3] differentiates signers based on the properties of their non-fungible tokens used in voting.

Introducing Predicate Aggregate Signatures. Motivated by above applications and many other relevant ones, in this paper, we are studying a general problem for aggregating signatures and keys on multiple messages, while ensuring that the signers satisfy some public predicate without disclosing their identities. We call such a cryptographic primitive *predicate aggregate signatures*, PAS for short.

More specifically, let us consider a set of users denoted as $\mathcal{U} = \{u_i\}_{i\in[n]}$ and a collection of messages $\mathcal{M} = \{m_j\}_{j\in[k]}$ drawn from a predefined message space. Users choose the messages to sign. There is also a combiner, who aggregates the corresponding signatures and signer identities/public keys into one succinct certificate/proof/signature and shows a description Δ of signers (like the number) on each message. The signature also confirms the legitimacy of both the signers and signatures, ensuring that the signers and the description adhere to a particular public predicate P, i.e., $P(S_1, \dots, S_k, \Delta) = 1$, where each $S_i \subseteq \mathcal{U}$ is a subset of users.

For example, in the anonymous reputation system, the rate-once policy requires that each signer can only sign once at most. It means there is no duplicate signer in each subset, and all subsets are disjoint, i.e., $S_i \cap S_j = \emptyset$ for any $i \neq j$. Another example is the onchain voting system with special policy.

[1] There are also other types of rating systems, such as Uber/Airbnb, that are based on accumulation on each transaction, so each user may rate on the same service provider more than once. We only consider the common version as a motivational example for our primitive.

Besides showing the number of voters, the property policy [3] requires that some of the voters have special properties. By representing the property via index, the combiner can assure the policy is satisfied by proving that some voters' indices belong to a specific range, e.g., there is at least one voter in the subset who is a senior member with an index smaller than 50.

Inefficiencies of Existing Primitives. Despite that there are many relevant research on signature aggregation, anonymous authentication, and others, none of them gives a PAS in a satisfying way (as shown in Table 1). We first give a simple categorization of existing relevant primitives, and briefly describe insufficiency of each type, and defer a more detailed comparison to the full version. Besides that most of the primitives do not support a general policy validation on the signers, each of them lack some other critical properties. Jumping ahead, we will show that some of concrete instantiations of our PAS directly advance the state of the art of several of those well-studied primitives, see Table 2.

Table 1. Comparisons of relevant primitives.

Primitives	Trans. setup	Flexi. thld.	Agg across msgs[a]	Anony.	Signer Policy
Thld Sig. [37]	×	×	×	✓	×
Multi-Sig [13]	✓	✓	×	×	×
Agg-Sig. [14]	✓	✓	✓	×	×
Graded Sig. [10,28]	✓	✓	×	✓	×
Compact Cert. [33]	✓	✓	×	×	×
Thld-ring Sig. [18]	✓	×	×	✓	×
Attri-based Sig. [32]	×	×	×	✓	✓[b]
Our PAS	✓	✓	✓	✓	✓

[a] Agg across msgs means signatures can be compressed among different messages.
[b] The predicate in this setting is applied to one single user's attribute set, while we consider predicate across multiple users.

Signature Aggregations. Multi-signatures [13], aggregate signatures [14], threshold signatures [37] and several other relevant ones allow one to compress signatures from different users. Besides they usually have no anonymity guarantee, the former two have to explicitly provide the signer identities/public keys thus the total proof size and verification cost still remains at least linear to the threshold (which is usually linear to the total number of users); threshold signature, on the other hand, can have one single public key for verification, but via a trusted setup, when its threshold is fixed, and it does not support signature aggregation across multiple messages. Multi-key homomorphic signatures [29] evaluates the messages signed by different users but it does not protect the privacy of signers. All signers' identities are public which is not suitable for our anonymous setting.

Anonymous Primitives. Anonymity oriented signatures such as ring signatures [17,35] and the linkable [31] and threshold versions [18], usually do not require the identities of the ring being aggregated, and often with a fixed threshold. Scored anonymous credential [21] is used for privacy-preserving reputation enforcement. The user's reputation is decided by some service provider. While we are considering the reputation voting setting where a set of users rate a product by signing.

Attribute-based signatures (ABS) [32] allow a user to attest that his attributes satisfy certain predicate. Anonymity can be implicitly ensured if two users have the same attribute set. However, ABS requires a trusted key generation center, it does not consider signature aggregations, or policies across multiple users. In our context, each user independently generates their own keys, and our goal is to have the flexibility to aggregate signatures and apply predicates across multiple users.

Generic Constructions. Generic zk-SNARKs could certainly provide a path for feasibility. By collecting numerous signatures from signers, the combiner can create a zk-SNARK proof that guarantees the existence of sufficient valid partial signatures satisfying the public predicate, while concealing the signers' identities and revealing only the counts. However, the generation of zk-SNARK proofs remains prohibitively expensive, and it relies on trusted setups and unfalsifiable assumptions. Some recent efforts have focused on constructing *dynamic threshold* signatures[2] [22,27] directly in the AGM model [26], whose actual security is not well-understood, and may have subtle vulnerabilities [38]. While we focus on building the PAS on classical and more standard assumptions.

1.1 Our Contributions

In this article, we formulate, construct and analyze the new primitive of predicate aggregate signatures to address remaining issues.

Formulating PAS. We give a formal definition and security models for predicate aggregate signatures.

As mentioned above, it allows registered users (public keys, identities known and made public) to sign on multiple messages and these signatures can be aggregated by a combiner who hides these signers' identities. The final signature only reveals a description of signers and guarantees that the signers and this description satisfy the public predicate.[3]

We formally define the security model of predicate aggregate signatures. It enjoys the following features simultaneously which advances existing primitives.

---

[2] They are a kind of special threshold signature that supports the *dynamic choice* of thresholds for each time of signature generation.

[3] In later, we would use the *dynamic threshold* as an example of the description. It reveals the number of users who have signed on the message. We choose it as the example for three reasons: (1) For a simpler presentation that shows how we can get our final construction step by step; (2) the dynamic threshold is a natural feature of our motivated anonymous reputation system; (3) the dynamic threshold aggregate signature itself might be of independent interests, and indeed it already advances the state of the art of several relevant signatures.

- *Transparent setup*: users generate pk, sk on their own, and a setup algorithm only publishes public parameters for the system.
- *Signer anonymity*: the adversary (not the combiner) cannot get any information about each individual signer identity/public key (e.g., whether he signed on a particular message) except the public description from the final signature, even if the adversary corrupts *all* users, including the target himself.
- *Unforgeability*: the adversary cannot convince the verifier, if it does not collect enough signatures, or the predicate is not satisfied. To facilitate such a notion, we generalize the classical proof of knowledge, and define a signer identity extractor.

Efficient Constructions from Standard Assumptions. We proceed in several steps towards the full construction, with concrete efficient instantiations. Our starting point is the BLS aggregate signature [14]. It allows the combiner to aggregate a set of partial signatures on multiple messages.

Transparent Setup. First of all, each user generates his secret-public key pair $(sk_i = x_i, pk_i = g^{x_i})$, and registers pk_i. To avoid the known rogue-key attacks [14], we first let each user run proof of knowledge of x_i during the registration. The system simply includes $pk_1, \ldots, pk_n$ and some common parameter $g_1, \ldots, g_n$ as public parameters and makes them available to everyone.

Succinct Size Solution. We start with the core building block of dynamic threshold aggregate signature. This can be considered as the special case where the predicate only requires the threshold counting is correct.

An intuitive idea is letting the combiner do more work: not only the partial signatures are aggregated, but their respective public keys are also compressed into a compact version. To protect signer anonymity, it also adds some blind factors to the compressed public keys and signatures. However, anonymity introduces a concern regarding the correctness of compressed public keys. Specifically, there is no guarantee that these compressed public keys are part of the legitimate/registered public key set.

Therefore, the combiner needs to produce an additional proof for the membership relation and duplication checks (that there are indeed t signatures from t *distinct* signing keys). A naïve attempt for the latter would be proving pairwise difference on all the compressed signing keys, which will yield a *quadratic* size proof. Some techniques in relevant primitives such as graded signatures [28] and signature of reputation [10] got around the challenge and sorted the public keys first, to do a sequential proof that $pk_i \neq pk_{i+1}$, which can push down the proof size to be *linear*. However, that is still quite cumbersome.

Alternatively, we observe that instead of proving relations among signer keys directly, we may leverage the published public keys in the public parameter. First, we can represent the included keys as a binary vector $\boldsymbol{b} = (b_1, ..., b_n)$, i.e., $b_i = 1$, if pk_i is in (has signed on the message), and 0 otherwise, and commit $\boldsymbol{b}$ in a succinct way (via vector commitment). Then we can prove an alternative statement that the committed vector is indeed *binary*. Now the Hamming weight of this vector will be corresponding to the threshold. Two remaining parts: (i) each bit value is assigned correctly; (ii) Hamming weight is correctly computed.

For (i), observe that when each pk_i is directly taken in as part of the system parameter, the "aggregated public keys" $\widehat{pk} = \Pi_i pk_i^{b_i}$ can be seemed as another "commitment" to the binary vector. We can establish the validity of the bit assignment by demonstrating that the previously committed binary vector is identical to the one contained in $\widehat{pk}$. While for (ii), Hamming weight can again be derived directly from inner product of the bit vector and all 1 vector, and proven using the efficient inner product argument from Bulletproofs [19].

Now we have a construction framework from the inner product argument and "binary" proof (that proves a committed vector is binary), which can be instantiated via Bulletproofs [19], yielding a signature of *logarithmic size* relative to the number of all users.

In the multiple (say k) messages setting, signers are divided into multiple sets depending on the message they have signed. A natural method is running the above proof generation for k times, so the total communication cost would have a multiplicative factor of k. Fortunately, by exploring the above technique further, we can generate a proof for k values on the knowledge of n-length binary vectors. In this way, these k proofs can be aggregated into one single proof for a $(k \cdot n)$-length binary vector. As a result, we achieve a communication cost of $O(k + \log n + \log k)$, comprising k aggregated public keys and additional proofs of size $O(\log n + \log k)$.

Reduce Verification Time. However, the above signature still requires a linear verification time (for example, even reading in all the public keys). To also reduce verification time, we propose a new proof system for the inner product and binary relations with structured parameters, that can reduce the verification time also to logarithmic.

There were previous efforts improving verification cost [23,30], in [23], the authors achieve logarithmic size and logarithmic verification time for inner product argument and range proof using *structured* reference string with highly correlated parameters in the form of $g, g^{x_1}, g^{x_2}, \ldots, g^{x_{\log n}}, g^{x_1 \cdot x_2}, g^{x_1 \cdot x_3}, g^{x_2 \cdot x_3}, g^{x_1 \cdot x_2 \cdot x_3} \ldots$, that separates the parameter into two parts: linear proving parameter and logarithmic verification parameter.

Unfortunately, as we would like a transparent setup, and public keys are generated by users themselves randomly, and then included as the public parameter, which clearly inconsistent with these structured parameters.

To work around this, we need to redesign the parameter generation and the statement for the proof. Besides the binary vector, we also commit the public keys via structure preserving commitment of [6] (also called AFGHO commitment). Introducing structured parameters into it is still compatible with the random generated public keys. Given these two commitments, we can prove another element is the inner pairing product of the two committed vectors. We observe that demonstrating the well-formedness of the aggregated public key is equivalent to proving that its bilinear map is equal to the inner pairing product between a binary vector and all public keys. Now we prove the validity of $\widehat{pk}$ by directly leveraging inner product argument between two committed vectors. One of these vectors is a binary vector, whose correctness is guaranteed by a binary proof, while the other comprises all the public keys. By adjusting the AFGHO commitment with structured parameters, these proofs achieve efficiency with logarithmic communication costs and verification times. We refer detailed description in Sect. 4.1.

Achieve Anonymity. In the anonymous setting with a blind factor r, where $\widehat{pk} = \Pi_i pk_i^{b_i} \cdot \tilde{g}^r$, several challenges arise when applying the previous method. These challenges include proving the last position of the binary vector is 1 and handling commitments of public keys together with the random factor $\tilde{g}^r$. These challenges are exacerbated by the anonymity requirements. See Sect. 4.1 for detailed discussion.

To mitigate these issues, a new approach is proposed. First, $\boldsymbol{b}$ and r are committed separately using distinct commitment keys, and proofs are generated for each. Then, by combining these two commitments, we can prove the presence of both a binary vector and a blind factor in specific positions. Subsequently, an inner pairing product argument is applied to these vectors, ensuring the well-formedness of the blinded aggregated public key.

Generic Predicate. Then to lift the construction to support any arithmetic predicate on the signer identities, we observe that both techniques for the core building block is via Fiat-Shamir transformation on Σ-protocols. We can add the extra proof of predicate satisfaction similarly via Bulletproof with our optimized verification time, then use the classical And proof to bind them. The final proof is with logarithmic size and verification time, while its security can be based on the standard SXDH assumption.

Efficient Instantiations for Concrete Predicates. As discussed above, such a special PAS with dynamic threshold already gives a better construction of multiple relevant signatures, as shown in Table 2.

We also give a concrete construction for the concrete predicate that all signer sets are also disjoint (that denotes the rate-once policy in the motivational application of anonymous reputation system).

It is a challenging task for the combiner to demonstrate the disjoint nature of all of these subsets of signers. In general, it would require comparing every pair of them and proving that they are indeed disjoint. However, this approach would necessitate a quadratic number of comparisons, leading to additional significant communication and computation cost.

It is worth noting that the binary feature can also be utilized in this case. Specifically, each public key subset can be represented as a binary vector. The addition of two binary vectors corresponds to the union of the corresponding subsets, including duplicate elements if any. In case the resulting sum vector remains binary, it implies that there are no duplicate elements in the union set, thereby indicating that the two sets are disjoint. By extending this approach to the k-subsets scenario, where we add all these binary vectors, we can demonstrate that all of the public key subsets are indeed disjoint.

Applications and Extensions. Our PAS (including the building block alone) implies many interesting primitives such as threshold signature, aggregate signature, multi-signature, ring signature, threshold ring signature, etc; more importantly, our efficient construction with different instantiations of concrete predicates, can improve the state of the art of all those primitives. More specifically, when using our dynamic threshold aggregate signature, we can directly yield the first multi-signature, aggregate signature, graded signature and threshold signature with both $O(\log n)$ communication and verification cost, while the state-of-the-art construction of them (from standard assumptions except zk-SNARKs or AGM directly) are all having linear costs. See Table 2.

Table 2. Advancing relevant primitives. (In the comparison, we restrict only to the single message case in our PAS. If there are k messages to be signed, all others have a *multiplicative* factor k, while we only have an *additive* factor.)

Primitives	Commun. Cost	Verify Cost.	Generation Cost.
Multi-Sig. [13]	$O(n)$[a]	$O(n)$	$O(n)$
Agg-Sig. [14]	$O(n)$[a]	$O(n)$	$O(n)$
Graded Sig. [10,28]	$O(n)$	$O(n)$	$O(n)$
Thld-ring Sig. [7]	$O(\log n)$	$O(n)$	$O(n)$
Using our PAS*	$O(\log n)$	$O(\log n)$	$O(n)$

[a] Although their signatures can be aggregated, the signers' identities should also be transmitted which leads to linear communication cost, except recent ones [22,27] that rely on zk-SNARKs or AGMs directly.
⋆ The last row means using our PAS with dynamic threshold as Δ, it implies the above primitives and advances their performance.

For multiple users and multiple messages, the combiner generates a PAS with threshold t_j for each m_j. It implies the aggregate signature and hides the signers' identities. For multiple users and one message, a PAS with threshold t implies that t different signers have signed on the message. It implies the threshold signature with transparent setup and dynamic threshold t and threshold ring signature with threshold t. It also naturally implies the multi-signature with t signers and the graded signature which indicates there are t different signers. When there is only one signer and one message, it implies the ring signature and attribute-based signature. The signer himself works as the combiner and shows the threshold is 1 with the proof of satisfying the predicate. It is equivalent to validating the signer's attribute. More details can be found in Sect. 6.

Anonymous Reputation Systems. Recent works on the anonymous reputation systems [11,12,24] achieve full anonymity at the cost of linear communication cost and quadratic verification complexity. We allow the combiner to know the signer identities and let the number of signers be the description. It generates a PAS which reveals the reputation states and its size is just logarithmic and can be verified in logarithmic time.

Onchain Voting System. Certain voting policies necessitate that voters possess a particular property [3], and it can be denoted by their identity index. For instance, within an organization, senior members are associated with indices smaller than a threshold. The combiner's task is to demonstrate that among the signers, there is at least one whose index is lower than a specified threshold. In our design, relying on the binary vector, the combiner only needs to prove the existence of a single position in the vector where the value is 1 and the position is smaller than a specified threshold.

Extensions. We can also easily support further advanced properties such as *dynamic join, weighted, accountability* and more.

- New users can seamlessly join the system without causing any disruptions to existing users. The process of joining is transparent and does not have any adverse effects on other users. It just involves changing a single global public key in a publicly verifiable way.
- In the PAS scheme, each user can associate their public key with a weight and the Δ is defined as the total weight of the signers. As a result, when generating the PAS signature, it discloses the total weight of the signers involved. So our PAS also supports the weight aggregation feature like [20,22,33].
- Our PAS can be extended to support the accountability by adding an extra identities encryption layer. It is similar with the method of TAPS [15].

2 Preliminary

We use bold letter for vector, for example $\boldsymbol{a} = (a_1, ..., a_n) \in \mathbb{Z}_q^n$. We use $\circ$ to denote the Hadamard product: $\boldsymbol{a} \circ \boldsymbol{b} = (a_1 \cdot b_1, ..., a_n \cdot b_n)$ for $\boldsymbol{a}, \boldsymbol{b} \in \mathbb{Z}_q^n$. We use $[k]$ to denote the integers in $\{1, 2, ..., k\}$. On input the security parameter 1^λ, a group generator $\mathsf{G.Gen}(1^\lambda)$ produces public parameters $\mathsf{G.pp} = (q, \mathbb{G}, g)$, where q is a prime of length λ, and $\mathbb{G}$ is a cyclic group of order q with generator g. Similarly, a bilinear group generator $\mathsf{BG.Gen}(1^\lambda)$ produces public parameters $\mathsf{BG.pp} = (q, \mathbb{G}_1, \mathbb{G}_2, \mathbb{G}_T, g, \tilde{g}, e)$ where $\mathbb{G}_1 = \langle g \rangle, \mathbb{G}_2 = \langle \tilde{g} \rangle, \mathbb{G}_T$ are groups of order q. The map $e : \mathbb{G}_1 \times \mathbb{G}_2 \rightarrow \mathbb{G}_T$ defines $g_T = e(g, \tilde{g})$, the map is bilinear, (for all $a, b \in \mathbb{Z}_q$, $e(g^a, \tilde{g}^b) = e(g, \tilde{g})^{ab}$) and non-degenerate (for all generators g of $\mathbb{G}_1$, $\tilde{g}$ of $\mathbb{G}_2$, $\mathbb{G}_T = \langle e(g, \tilde{g}) \rangle$). We assume $\mathbb{G}_1 \neq \mathbb{G}_2$ and we are working on Type III groups [6] who do not have efficiently computable homomorphisms between $\mathbb{G}_1$ and $\mathbb{G}_2$. We use $[a]_1, [b]_2, [c]_T$ denotes the element $g^a, \tilde{g}^b, g_T^c$ in $\mathbb{G}_1, \mathbb{G}_2, \mathbb{G}_T$ respectively. We use $[\boldsymbol{x}]_1$ denotes the vector $(g^{x_1}, ..., g^{x_n}) \in \mathbb{G}_1^n$ for $\boldsymbol{x} = (x_1, ..., x_n) \in \mathbb{Z}_q^n$. We write all groups additively, e.g., $[a]_1 + [b]_1 = [a + b]_1$ denotes $g^a \cdot g^b = g^{a+b}$, $b \cdot [a]_1 = [ab]_1$ denotes $(g^a)^b = g^{ab}$, $[\boldsymbol{x}]_1 + [\boldsymbol{y}]_1 = [\boldsymbol{x} + \boldsymbol{y}]_1$ denotes $(g^{x_1}, ..., g^{x_n}) \circ (g^{y_1}, ..., g^{y_n}) = (g^{x_1+y_1}, ..., g^{x_n+y_n})$, $[\boldsymbol{x}]_1 \circ \boldsymbol{y} = (g^{x_1 y_1}, ..., g^{x_n y_n})$, $[\boldsymbol{x}]_1^{\boldsymbol{y}} = \sum_{i=1}^n y_i \cdot [x_i]_1 = \Pi_{i=1}^n g^{x_i y_i}$. For $\boldsymbol{a}, \boldsymbol{b} \in \mathbb{Z}_q^n$, let $\langle \boldsymbol{a}, \boldsymbol{b} \rangle := \sum_{i=1}^n a_i \cdot b_i$ denote the inner product between $\boldsymbol{a}, \boldsymbol{b}$. For $[\boldsymbol{a}]_1 \in \mathbb{G}_1^n$ and $[\boldsymbol{b}]_2 \in \mathbb{G}_2^n$, let $\langle [\boldsymbol{a}]_1, [\boldsymbol{b}]_2 \rangle := e([\boldsymbol{a}]_1, [\boldsymbol{b}]_2) = \sum_{i=1}^n e([a_i]_1, [b_i]_2)$ denote the inner pairing product between $[\boldsymbol{a}]_1, [\boldsymbol{b}]_2$. Given a vector $\boldsymbol{v} = (v_1, ..., v_n)$ with even n, we denote $\boldsymbol{v}_\ell = (v_1, ..., v_{n/2})$ and $\boldsymbol{v}_r = (v_{n/2+1}, ..., v_n)$. For $k \in \mathbb{Z}_q^*$ we use $\boldsymbol{k}^n$ to denote the vector containing the first n powers of k, i.e., $\boldsymbol{k}^n = (1, k, k^2, ..., k^{n-1})$.

2.1 Assumptions

Definition 1 (DDH assumption). *Let* $(q, \mathbb{G}, g) \leftarrow \mathsf{G.Gen}(1^\lambda)$ *be a group generator. The DDH assumption holds for* $\mathsf{G.Gen}$ *if the following distributions are indistinguishable:* $(g, g^a, g^b, g^{ab} : a, b \leftarrow_\$ \mathbb{Z}_q)$ *and* $(g, g^a, g^b, g^c : a, b, c \leftarrow_\$ \mathbb{Z}_q)$

Definition 2 (DLOG assumption). *Let* $(q, \mathbb{G}, g) \leftarrow \mathsf{G.Gen}(1^\lambda)$ *be a group generator. The DLOG assumption holds for* $\mathsf{G.Gen}$ *if for all PPT adversary* $\mathcal{A}$ *we have:* $\Pr[\mathcal{A}(q, \mathbb{G}, g, X) = x | (q, \mathbb{G}, g) \leftarrow \mathsf{G.Gen}(1^\lambda), x \leftarrow_\$ \mathbb{Z}_q, X = g^x] \leq negl(\lambda)$

Definition 3 (SXDH assumption [6]**).** *Let* $(q, \mathbb{G}_1, \mathbb{G}_2, \mathbb{G}_T, e, g, \tilde{g}) \leftarrow \mathsf{BG.Gen}(1^\lambda)$ *be a bilinear group generator. The SXDH assumption holds for* $\mathsf{BG.Gen}$ *if DDH assumption holds for* $\mathbb{G}_1$ *and* $\mathbb{G}_2$*.*

Definition 4 (co-CDH assumption [14]**).** *Let* $(q, \mathbb{G}_1, \mathbb{G}_2, \mathbb{G}_T, e, g, \tilde{g}) \leftarrow \mathsf{BG.Gen}(1^\lambda)$ *be a bilinear group generator. The co-CDH assumption holds for* $\mathsf{BG.Gen}$ *if for all PPT* $\mathcal{A}$*, given* $[a]_1, [b]_2$ *where* $a, b \leftarrow_\$ \mathbb{Z}_q$*, the probability that* $\mathcal{A}$ *can produce* $[ab]_1$ *is negligible.*

Definition 5 (DPair assumption [6]**).** *Let* $(q, \mathbb{G}_1, \mathbb{G}_2, \mathbb{G}_T, e, g, \tilde{g}) \leftarrow \mathsf{BG.Gen}(1^\lambda)$ *be a bilinear group generator,* $n = poly(\lambda)$*. The double-pairing (DPair) assumption holds for* $\mathsf{BG.Gen}$ *if for all PPT adversary* $\mathcal{A}$*, given* $[r]_1 \leftarrow_\$ \mathbb{G}_1$*, the probability that* $\mathcal{A}$ *can produce* $[a]_2, [b]_2 \in \mathbb{G}_2$ *s.t.* $e([r]_1, [a]_2) + e(g, [b]_2) = [0]_T$ *and* $a, b \neq 0$ *is negligible.*

Definition 6 (ML-Find-Rep assumption [23]**).** *Let* $(q, \mathbb{G}, g) \leftarrow \mathsf{G.Gen}(1^\lambda)$ *be a group generator,* $n = poly(\lambda)$ *which a power of 2,* $\nu = \log n$*. The ML-Find-Rep assumption holds for* $\mathsf{G.Gen}$ *if for all PPT adversary* $\mathcal{A}$ *we have:* $\Pr[\mathcal{A}(q, \mathbb{G}, [\boldsymbol{r}], X) \rightarrow \boldsymbol{a} \in \mathbb{Z}_q^n \text{ s.t. } [\boldsymbol{r}]^{\boldsymbol{a}} = [0] \wedge \boldsymbol{a} \neq \boldsymbol{0} | (q, \mathbb{G}, g) \leftarrow \mathsf{G.Gen}(1^\lambda), (x_1, ..., x_\nu) \leftarrow_\$ \mathbb{Z}_q^\nu, \boldsymbol{r} = (1, x_1, x_2, x_1x_2, ..., x_1 \cdots x_\nu)] \leq negl(\lambda)$.

Definition 7 (DPair-ML assumption). *Let* $(q, \mathbb{G}_1, \mathbb{G}_2, \mathbb{G}_T, e, g, \tilde{g}) \leftarrow \mathsf{BG.Gen}(1^\lambda)$ *be a bilinear group generator,* $n = poly(\lambda)$ *which a power of 2. The DPair-ML assumption holds for* $\mathsf{BG.Gen}$ *if for all PPT adversary* $\mathcal{A}$*, given* $[\boldsymbol{r}]_1 \in \mathbb{G}_1^n$*, where* $\boldsymbol{r} = (1, x_1, x_2, x_1x_2, ..., x_1 \cdots x_\nu)$ *for* $(x_1, ..., x_\nu) \leftarrow_\$ \mathbb{Z}_q^\nu$*, the probability that* $\mathcal{A}$ *can produce* $[\boldsymbol{s}]_2 \in \mathbb{G}_2^n$ *s.t.* $e([\boldsymbol{r}]_1, [\boldsymbol{s}]_2) = [0]_T$ *is negligible.*

The DPair-ML assumption is implied by the SXDH assumption and ML-Find-Rep assumption.

2.2 Cryptographic Primitives

Due to space constraints, we introduce some cryptographic primitives here briefly and defer the detailed preliminaries to the full version.

Commitment. A commitment scheme allows one to commit to a chosen value secretly, with the ability to only open to the same committed value later. A commitment scheme Π_{cmt} consists of the following PPT algorithms:

$\mathsf{Setup}(1^\lambda) \to pp$: generates the public parameter pp.
$\mathsf{Com}(m; r) \to com$: generates the commitment for the message m using the randomness r.
Hiding. A commitment scheme is said to be hiding if the commitment does not reveal any information about the committed value.
Binding. A commitment scheme is said to be binding if a commitment can only be opened to one value.
Additively Homomorphic. A commitment is additively homomorphic if for any values m_1, m_2 and randomness r_1, r_2: $\mathsf{Com}(m_1; r_1) + \mathsf{Com}(m_2; r_2) = \mathsf{Com}(m_1 + m_2; r_1 + r_2)$.

Pedersen Commitment. For messages $\boldsymbol{m} \in \mathbb{Z}_q^n$ and any $i \in \{1, 2, T\}$, the Pedersen commitment is defined by:
$\mathsf{Setup}(1^\lambda) \to pp$: $\boldsymbol{g} \leftarrow_\$ \mathbb{G}_i^n, h \leftarrow_\$ \mathbb{G}_i$.
$\mathsf{Com}(\boldsymbol{m}; r) \to com$: $\mathsf{Com}(\boldsymbol{m}; r) = \boldsymbol{g}^{\boldsymbol{m}} \cdot h^r \in \mathbb{G}_i$ where $r \leftarrow_\$ \mathbb{Z}_p$.

The Pedersen commitment is additively homomorphic, perfectly hiding and computationally binding under the DLOG assumption.

AFGHO Commitment. Abe et al. [6] defined a structure preserving commitment to group elements. In this case we have the message space $\mathbb{G}_2^n$:
$\mathsf{Setup}(1^\lambda) \to pp$: Run $(q, \mathbb{G}_1, \mathbb{G}_2, \mathbb{G}_T, e, g, \tilde{g}) \leftarrow \mathcal{G}(1^\lambda)$, the commitment key $\mathsf{ck}_1 := \boldsymbol{g} \leftarrow_\$ \mathbb{G}_1^n$.
$\mathsf{Com}(\boldsymbol{m}; r) \to com$: for $[\boldsymbol{m}]_2 \in \mathbb{G}_2^n$, $\mathsf{Com}([\boldsymbol{m}]_2; [r]_2) = \langle \mathsf{ck}_1, [\boldsymbol{m}]_2 \rangle + e(g, [r]_2)$ where $[r]_2 \leftarrow_\$ \mathbb{G}_2$.

To commit to messages in $\mathbb{G}_1$, we can just interchange the role of $\mathbb{G}_1$ and $\mathbb{G}_2$ in the above construction with $\mathsf{ck}_2 \in \mathbb{G}_2^n$.

The AFGHO commitment is additively homomorphic, perfectly hiding and computationally binding under the SXDH assumption.

Structured AFGHO. Based on the updatable common reference string technique of Daza et al. [23], we give the modified AFGHO commitment with structured commitment keys $\mathsf{ck}_1, \mathsf{ck}_2$ which are generated as below.

$$(pp, [r]_1 \in \mathbb{G}_1, \mathsf{ck}_1 = [\boldsymbol{r}]_1 \in \mathbb{G}_1^n, \mathsf{vk}_1 = [\boldsymbol{x}]_2 \in \mathbb{G}_2^\nu) \in \mathcal{L}_{\mathsf{Com}}^1 \Leftrightarrow$$
$$[r_1]_1 = [r]_1 \wedge \forall i \in [\nu], \forall j \in [2^{i-1}], [r_{2^{i-1}+j}]_1 = x_i [r_j]_1$$

$$(pp, [s]_2 \in \mathbb{G}_2, \mathsf{ck}_2 = [\boldsymbol{s}]_2 \in \mathbb{G}_2^n, \mathsf{vk}_2 = [\boldsymbol{y}]_1 \in \mathbb{G}_1^\nu) \in \mathcal{L}_{\mathsf{Com}}^2 \Leftrightarrow$$
$$[s_1]_2 = [s]_2 \wedge \forall i \in [\nu], \forall j \in [2^{i-1}], [s_{2^{i-1}+j}]_2 = y_i [s_j]_2$$

where $r, x_i \leftarrow_\$ \mathbb{Z}_q$ and $s, y_i \leftarrow_\$ \mathbb{Z}_q$ for all $i \in [\nu]$.

The structured AFGHO commitment is additively homomorphic, perfectly hiding and computationally binding under the SXDH and DPair-ML assumptions.

Zero-Knowledge Arguments of Knowledge (ZKAoK). A zero-knowledge argument of knowledge is a cryptographic protocol involving two parties: a prover and a verifier. In this protocol, the prover's objective is to provide convincing proof to the verifier that a certain statement is true, without revealing any information about the underlying witness.

It consists of three PPT algorithms Setup, $\mathcal{P}$, and $\mathcal{V}$. The setup algorithm outputs a common reference string σ on inputting a security parameter λ. The prover $\mathcal{P}$ and the verifier $\mathcal{V}$ are interactive algorithms. As the output of this protocol, we use the notation $\langle \mathcal{P}, \mathcal{V} \rangle = b$, where $b = 1$ if $\mathcal{V}$ accepts and $b = 0$ if $\mathcal{V}$ rejects. The proof is *public coin* if an honest verifier generates his responses to $\mathcal{P}$ uniformly.

Argument of Knowledge. ($\mathbf{Setup}, \mathcal{P}, \mathcal{V}$) is called an argument of knowledge for the relation $\mathcal{R}$ if it satisfies the following two definitions.

Perfect Completeness. The prover can persuade the verifier if it possesses a witness that attests to the truth of the statement.

Computational Witness-Extended Emulation. Whenever an adversary that produces an acceptable argument with some probability, there exist an emulator who can produce a similar argument with the same probability and provide a witness w simultaneously. It implies *soundness* which asserts that no PPT adversary can persuade the verifier when the statement is false. It also assures *knowledge soundness* which guarantees the existence of an extractor capable of producing a valid witness for the statement.

Honest-Verifier Special Zero-Knowledge (HVSZK). Given the verifier's challenge values, it is possible to simulate the entire argument without witness efficiently.

BLS Aggregate Signature. We briefly review the BLS signature scheme and its signature aggregation mechanism [14]. Given an efficiently computable non-degenerate pairing $e : \mathbb{G}_1 \times \mathbb{G}_2 \to \mathbb{G}_T$ in groups $\mathbb{G}_1, \mathbb{G}_2, \mathbb{G}_T$ of prime order q. Let g and $\tilde{g}$ be generators of $\mathbb{G}_1$ and $\mathbb{G}_2$ respectively, a hash function $H : \mathcal{M} \to \mathbb{G}_1$:

- **KeyGen**(): the user chooses $sk \leftarrow_{\$} \mathbb{Z}_q$, outputs (pk, sk) for $pk \leftarrow \tilde{g}^{sk} \in \mathbb{G}_2$.
- **Sign**(sk, m): output $\sigma \leftarrow H(m)^{sk} \in \mathbb{G}_1$.
- **Vrfy**(pk, m, σ): output 1 if $e(\sigma, \tilde{g}) = e(H(m), pk)$, otherwise, output 0.
- **Signature Aggregation**: Given triples (pk_i, m_i, σ_i) for $i \in [n]$, anyone can aggregate the signatures $\sigma_1, ..., \sigma_n$ into a single group element $\hat{\sigma} \leftarrow \Pi_{i\in[n]}\sigma_i \in \mathbb{G}_1$. Verification can be done by checking that if

$$e(\hat{\sigma}, \tilde{g}) = e(H(m_1), pk_1) \cdots e(H(m_n), pk_n).$$

  For all same messages it just needs to check if $e(\hat{\sigma}, \tilde{g}) = e(H(m_1), \Pi_{i=1}^{n} pk_i)$. It is *unforgeable* under the co-CDH assumption.

The Rogue Public-Key Attack and Defense. Note that the aggregate public key $\Pi_{i=1}^{n} pk_i$ suffers the rogue public-key attack [9]. To prevent it, we use the Proof-of-Possession (PoP) mechanism [34] in the *registered key model.* In this approach, each party is required to provide a proof that they possess the private key corresponding to their public key. This proof can be included during the setup phase and ensures that only legitimate key owners can participate. In this paper, we implicitly assume the presence of PoP proofs for the public keys.

3 Predicate Aggregate Signatures

In this section, we formalize the predicate aggregate signatures and establish the security model for this concept. Predicate aggregate signatures enable users to sign multiple messages according to some predefined public policy, and these individual signatures can be aggregated by a combiner, preserving the anonymity of the signers. The resulting aggregate signature discloses only a brief description of the involved signers (e.g., count of signers for each message, total weight of signers, etc.) and provides assurance that these signers and the description satisfy the specified policy denoted by a public predicate function.

This notion addresses the need for efficient and privacy-preserving signature schemes that allow for the signing of multiple messages while ensuring adherence to a given predicate. The security model encompasses the privacy of signers and the unforgeability of the predicate aggregate signature.

3.1 Syntax

In general, there are three parties in the system: signers who sign on the message; the combiner, who generates a predicate aggregate signature with a public description of the involved signers and proves that these signers and the description satisfy a public predicate; the verifier who verifies the correctness of the predicate aggregate signature.

- $\mathsf{Setup}(1^\lambda)$: On the security parameter λ, the system public parameters pp are generated. The message space is set as $M = \{m_j\}_{j\in[k]}$. There is a public policy Ω which decides the computation rule of the signers description Δ and the predicate function P_Ω.
  It also includes the key generation of users. Each user u_i generates his secret key sk_i and public key pk_i pair and broadcasts the public key. The combiner (or any other parties) collects the public keys and publishes the aggregation key ak and verification key vk which contains P_Ω.
- $\mathsf{ParSign}(sk_i, m_j)$: For a message m_j chosen from M, the user i signs on it using his secret key sk_i and sends (pk_i, m_j, σ_{ij}) to the combiner.
- $\mathsf{ParVrfy}(pk, m_j, \sigma)$: On receiving (pk_i, m_j, σ), anyone can verify it.
- $\mathsf{Combine}(ak, \{S_j\}_{j\in[k]}, \{\{\sigma_{ij}\}_{i\in S_j}\}_{j\in[k]}, \{m_j\}_{j\in[k]})$: When receiving sets of signatures $\{\{\sigma_{ij}\}_{i\in S_j}\}_{j\in[k]}$ on the message m_j from different signers w.r.t. index sets $\{S_j\}_{j\in[k]}$ (called signer sets) where each $S_j \subseteq [n]$, the combiner generates a signature Σ for the message set $M = \{m_j\}_{j\in[k]}$ with corresponding description Δ of these signer sets. It also proves that the signer sets and Δ satisfy the public predicate P_Ω decided by some policy Ω, i.e., $P_\Omega(S_1, ..., S_k, \Delta) = 1$.
- $\mathsf{Verify}(vk, M, \Delta, \Sigma)$: Given the verification key vk, messages $M = \{m_j\}_{j\in[k]}$, description Δ, the PAS signature Σ, anyone can check the validness by running $\mathsf{Verify}(vk, M, \Delta, \Sigma)$ and outputs one bit $b \in \{0, 1\}$ indicating if it is valid.

Remark 1 Δ is the description of signers in $S_1, ..., S_k$ whose partial signatures are used to generate the final PAS signature. It is computed via a *deterministic* function F specified in the policy Ω from the signer sets: $\Delta = F(S_1, ..., S_k)$. Note that it cannot display the signer identities plainly, since it ruins the anonymity directly. Although it is computed deterministically, in many cases, it leaks very little information about the signers. For example, it could be the size of each signer set, the combined weight of signers within each signer set, or simply demonstrating that the number exceeds a certain minimum threshold.

Remark 2 P_Ω is the predicate decided by the public policy Ω which takes the signer sets and a description as input. $P_\Omega(S_1, ..., S_k, \Delta) = 1$ indicates that $S_1, ..., S_k, \Delta$ satisfy the rule according to Ω.

3.2 Model

Correctness. If enough valid signatures under different public keys are used to produce the signature Σ on the messages m_j for $j \in [k]$, the description Δ and the signer sets satisfy the public predicate $P_\Omega(S_1, ..., S_k, \Omega) = 1$, then the verification for (M, Δ, Σ) always outputs 1.

Anonymity. The signer identities are hidden from the public. The PAS signature only discloses a description of the signer sets and whether they satisfy the predicate according to the public policy. Given any two valid signatures Σ_0, Σ_1 with the *same* descriptions and predicates from different signer sets on the same messages set M, they are indistinguishable even to some of these signers.

Unforgeability. The adversary cannot generate a valid signature on multiple messages if it does not have enough signatures from different signers on each message, or the signer sets and the description do not satisfy the predicate.

Oracles. We define the following oracles to model the adversary's ability. There is an honest user table HU, a corrupted user table CU and a queried message table QM which are initialized as empty.

- **add**(i): Add a new user u_i to the system. If i has not been queried before, run the key generation algorithm $(pk^*, sk^*) \leftarrow \mathsf{KeyGen}$, set $(pk_i, sk_i) = (pk^*, sk^*)$ and output pk_i. Add (u_i, pk_i, sk_i) to the honest user table HU.
- **corrupt**(pk_i): Corrupt an honest user in the system. If $pk_i \in \mathsf{HU}$, output sk_i, delete (u_i, pk_i, sk_i) from HU and add (u_i, pk_i, sk_i) to CU.
- **sign**(pk_i, m): If $pk_i \notin \mathsf{HU}$, ignore it. Otherwise, run $\sigma \leftarrow \mathsf{ParSign}(sk_i, m)$ and add (pk_i, m) to QM, output σ.

Anonymity. This property ensures that signer identities are hidden from the public. Only the combiner knows the signer identities. Others just know the description of the signers and the signer sets with the description satisfy the public predicate. Formally speaking, given any two valid signatures Σ_0, Σ_1 from different signer sets on the same messages M with the same description Δ and both satisfy the predicate, nobody can distinguish them except the combiner.

In the anonymity definition, even the signers will not be able to distinguish two PAS signatures for the maliciously chosen messages with same thresholds. The anonymity experiment $\text{Exp}^{\mathsf{anony}}$ between an adversary $\mathcal{A}$ and a challenger $\mathcal{C}$ is formalized as follows.

- $\mathcal{A}$ receives the public parameters including the description function F and public predicate P_Ω specified by the policy Ω.
- $\mathcal{A}$ adds users to the system, it can query signatures of any signers on any messages and even corrupt all users. The global aggregation key ak and verification key vk are setup and given to $\mathcal{A}$.
- $\mathcal{A}$ chooses a set of messages $M = \{m_j\}_{j\in[k]}$, and two sets of index sets $S^0 = \{S_j^0\}_{j\in[k]}$ and $S^1 = \{S_j^1\}_{j\in[k]}$ where each $S_j^0, S_j^1 \subseteq [n]$. Then it generates partial signatures $\sigma_{u,j} \leftarrow \mathsf{ParSign}(sk_u, m_j)$, $\sigma_{v,j} \leftarrow \mathsf{ParSign}(sk_v, m_j)$ for all $j \in [k], u \in S^0$ and $v \in S^1$ and let $D_0 = \{\{\sigma_{u,j}\}_{u\in S^0}\}_{j\in[k]}, D_1 = \{\{\sigma_{v,j}\}_{v\in S^1}\}_{j\in[k]}$. It sends (M, S^0, S^1, D_0, D_1) to $\mathcal{C}$.
- $\mathcal{C}$ computes $\Delta_0 = F(S^0)$, $\Delta_1 = F(S^1)$ and checks these partial signatures. It aborts, if there exists any invalid partial signature or $S^0 = S^1$ or $\Delta_0 \neq \Delta_1$ or $P_\Omega(S^0, \Delta_0) \neq 1$ or $P_\Omega(S^1, \Delta_1) \neq 1$. Otherwise, continue.
- $\mathcal{C}$ randomly chooses one bit $b \leftarrow \{0,1\}$ and sends $\mathcal{A}$ a predicate aggregate signature Σ with M generated from signatures of D_b by running $\Sigma \leftarrow \mathsf{Combine}(ak, S^b, D_b, M)$.
- $\mathcal{A}$ outputs a guess b'.
- Outputs 1 if $b' == b$, otherwise, outputs 0.

Definition 8 *A predicate aggregate signature is anonymous if any PPT adversary in the* $\text{Exp}^{\mathsf{anony}}$ *can only guess the bit correctly with probability negligibly close to* $\frac{1}{2}$, *i.e.,* $|\Pr[\text{Exp}^{\mathsf{anony}}(\mathcal{A}, \lambda) = 1] - \frac{1}{2}| \leq negl(\lambda)$.

Unforgeability. This property ensures that given the public policy, any adversary cannot generate a valid signature on multiple messages if it does not have enough signatures on the messages or the signer sets and their description do not satisfy the predicate.

It contains two properties: (1). $\mathcal{A}$ can not produce a valid PAS signature which contains an honest signer who has never signed on that message. (2). All signer sets w.r.t. the messages must adhere to the specified predicate. It is infeasible for $\mathcal{A}$ to generate a valid PAS signature with a signer sets description but the signer sets and the description are unsatisfied for the predicate.

Note that due to the anonymity requirement, the signer identities are hidden and only their description is shown. So it is hard to decide whether $\mathcal{A}$ has broken the predicate satisfaction property. To address this dilemma, we introduce an extractor $\mathcal{E}$ that has the ability to reveal the signers' identities for each message from the predicate aggregate signature. It is inspired by the knowledge extractor for the knowledge soundness in zero-knowledge proof of knowledge.

Formally speaking, the unforgeability experiment $\text{Exp}^{\mathsf{unforge}}$ works as follows:

- $\mathcal{A}$ receives the public parameters and the public predicate.

- $\mathcal{A}$ can add users to the system then gets the aggregation key ak and verification key vk.
- $\mathcal{A}$ is an adaptive adversary, it can interact with $\mathcal{E}$ via querying oracles. It can then query signatures of any signers on any messages and corrupt users.
- $\mathcal{A}$ outputs a tuple (M, Δ, Σ).
- On a valid (M, Δ, Σ), $\mathcal{E}$ outputs the signers' identities $S_1, ..., S_k$.

$\mathcal{A}$ wins and the experiment outputs 1 only if (M, Δ, Σ) is valid w.r.t. vk and at least one of the following conditions is satisfied:

- $\exists\, i_j \in S_j$, such that $i_j \in \mathsf{HU}$ and $(pk_{i_j}, m_j) \notin \mathsf{QM}$;
- $P_\Omega(S_1, ..., S_k, \Delta) \neq 1$.

The first condition means $\mathcal{A}$ has never queried the **corrupt** oracle on pk_{i_j} or **sign** oracle on (pk_{i_j}, m_j). It models that $\mathcal{A}$ generates a valid PAS signature without enough valid partial signatures.

Definition 9 *A predicate aggregate signature is unforgeable if any PPT adversary in the above experiment can only win with negligible probability, i.e.,* $\Pr[\mathsf{Exp}^{\mathsf{unforge}}(\mathcal{A}, \lambda) = 1] \leq negl(\lambda)$.

4 Constructions

In this section, we give the construction of the predicate aggregate signature. Formally speaking, the combiner aims to prove the knowledge of signatures and signers satisfying the following relation:

$$\begin{aligned} R_{\mathsf{PAS}} = \{ & pk_1, \ldots, pk_n, m_1, \ldots, m_k, \Omega, \Delta; \{\sigma_{i1}\}_{i \in S_1}, \ldots, \{\sigma_{ik}\}_{i \in S_k} : \\ & \mathsf{ParVrfy}(pk_i, m_j, \sigma_{ij}) = 1 \ \forall i \in S_j, j \in [k]; \\ & S_j \subseteq [n], \forall j \in [k]; P_\Omega(S_1, ..., S_k, \Delta) = 1\} \end{aligned}$$

where $pk_1, \ldots, pk_n$ are all the public keys, $m_1, \ldots, m_k$ are the candidate messages, S_j contains the indices of users who have signed on the message m_j, σ_{ij} is the signature from user i on message m_j. P_Ω is the predicate function decided by the public policy Ω.

The predicate function can be very simple that outputs 1 as long as the description Δ is correct and there is no other requirements on the policy. For any general policy that can be described by an arithmetic circuit, the predicate can be converted into a circuit and proved using the efficient zero-knowledge argument for arbitrary arithmetic circuits which have been studied in [16,19,23].

In this section, we mainly consider the anonymous reputation system with the rate-once policy as a non-trivial example. Here the description is the number of signers in each subset ($\Delta = \{t_j\}_{j \in [k]}$ where $t_j = |S_j|$) and all users can only sign once even for different messages. It means the signer sets for all messages are disjoint. We define the public predicate as follows:

$$P_\Omega(S_1, ..., S_k, \Delta) = \begin{cases} 1, \text{if } \Delta = \{t_j\}_{j \in [k]}, S_j \subseteq [n], |S_j| = t_j, \forall j \in [k]; \\ \quad \wedge S_{j_0} \cap S_{j_1} = \emptyset, \ \forall j_0, j_1 \in [k], j_0 \neq j_1 \\ 0, \text{otherwise.} \end{cases} \quad (1)$$

4.1 Construction Overview

Our starting point is the pairing-based BLS aggregate signature (see Sect. 2.2). Let n be the number of users in the system. On receiving a set of partial signatures σ_{ij} on each message $m_j \in M$ from signer $i \in [n]$, the combiner generates the aggregate signature $\hat{\sigma}$ and publishes it with the index set $S_j \in [n]$ of signers on message m_j for verification. The verifier computes the verification key for m_j w.r.t. S_j: $\widehat{pk}_j = \Pi_{i \in S_j} pk_i$ for $j \in [k]$. Subsequently, it verifies the validity of $\hat{\sigma}$.

An intuitive idea is letting the combiner also compress the public keys into a compact version which can be used for verifying the aggregated signature. To protect the privacy of signers, it also adds *blind factors* to the compressed public keys and respective aggregated signatures. The crux of our construction now revolves around proving the correctness of the compressed public keys without using linear descriptions while still enabling duplication checks.

We start from the single message case. Given all the public keys $\boldsymbol{pk} = (pk_1, ..., pk_n) \in \mathbb{G}_2^n$ and a set $S \subseteq [n]$, let $\boldsymbol{pk}_S = \{pk_i\}_{i \in S} \subseteq \{pk_i\}_{i \in [n]}$ to denote a subset of all public keys w.r.t. S. The blinded aggregation of public keys of $\boldsymbol{pk}_S$ is: $\widehat{pk}_S = \Pi_{i \in S} pk_i \cdot \tilde{g}^{r_S}$ where r_S is the blind factor. Note that S determines a binary vector $\boldsymbol{b}_S = (b_1, ..., b_n)$, $b_i = 1$ if $i \in S$, otherwise, $b_i = 0$.

The combiner (or prover $\mathcal{P}$) computes a commitment B on $\boldsymbol{b}_S$ and proves that the committed $\boldsymbol{b}_S$ is a binary vector whose Hamming weight is t. Then $\mathcal{P}$ proves that $\widehat{pk}_S$ can be expressed in the form of $\boldsymbol{pk}^{\boldsymbol{v}} \cdot \tilde{g}^r$ where $\boldsymbol{v}$ is same as the $\boldsymbol{b}_S$ in B and it knows the blind factor r. It means that $\widehat{pk}_S$ contains t different signers. Combined with an aggregate signature $\hat{\sigma}$ and a message m, the valid tuple $(\widehat{pk}_S, m, \hat{\sigma})$, the verifier can be convinced that the message has been signed by t different users.

For multiple messages $m_1, ..., m_k$ case, the index set of signers who have signed on m_j is S_j and their aggregated public keys are $\widehat{pk}_j$ for $j \in [k]$. Here $\mathcal{P}$ proves the knowledge of corresponding binary vectors $\boldsymbol{b}_j$ whose Hamming weight is t_j and the knowledge of blind factor r_j and the signer sets $S = \{S_1, ..., S_k\}$ and thresholds $T = \{t_1, ..., t_k\}$ satisfy the public predicate P_Ω.

Considering the rate-once policy in the anonymous reputation system as a concrete example, the predicate is denoted by $P_\Omega(S, T) := |S_j| = t_j, \forall j \in [k] \wedge S_{j_0} \cap S_{j_1} = \emptyset$, $\forall j_0, j_1 \in [k], j_0 \neq j_1$. Due to the binary feature, we observe that proving subsets disjoint can be achieved by demonstrating that the summation of all binary vectors is still binary with a Hamming weight $t = \sum_{j \in [k]} t_j$.

In summary, we formulate this process in the following relation:

$$\begin{aligned} R_1 = \{ & \{\widehat{pk}_j, m_j, t_j\}_{j=1}^k, \hat{\sigma}; \boldsymbol{b}_1, \ldots, \boldsymbol{b}_k, r_1, ..., r_k : \\ & e(\hat{\sigma}, \tilde{g}) = e(H(m_1), \widehat{pk}_1) \cdots e(H(m_k), \widehat{pk}_k) \\ & \wedge\ \widehat{pk}_j = \boldsymbol{pk}^{\boldsymbol{b}_j} \cdot \tilde{g}^{r_j} \ \wedge\ \boldsymbol{b}_j \in \{0,1\}^n \ \wedge\ t_j = \langle \boldsymbol{1}^n, \boldsymbol{b}_j \rangle, \forall j \in [k] \\ & \wedge\ \boldsymbol{b} = \Sigma_{j \in [k]} \boldsymbol{b}_j \in \{0,1\}^n \} \end{aligned} \quad (2)$$

Strawman Scheme from Bulletproofs. In general, the public keys are group elements. It can be integrated with the public parameters of Bulletproofs which are also group elements. Then we use Pederson commitment to commit the binary vector and prove the correctness of the aggregated public keys. The combiner has $\widehat{pk} = \Pi_{i=1}^{n} pk_i^{b_i} \cdot g^r$ and generates $B = \Pi_{i=1}^{n} g_i^{b_i} \cdot h^r$. It generates binary proof on B with parameter $(g_1, ..., g_n, h)$ and another binary proof on $B \cdot \widehat{pk}$ with parameter $(g_1 \cdot pk_1, ..., g_n \cdot pk_n, h \cdot g)$. It implies that $\widehat{pk}$ shares the same binary vector and randomness in B, so it is well-formed. Here the binary proof can be constructed from Bulletproofs [19] with logarithmic size. The final construction comes with almost the same cost.

For multiple k messages case, instead of generating k individual proofs, we generate a proof for k values on the knowledge of n-length binary vectors. It aggregates k proofs into one proof of a kn-length binary vector ($k \cdot n$ bits) via a random challenge value z and Schwartz-Zippel lemma. It is similar with the aggregated range proofs of Sec. 4.3 in [19]. As a result, we achieve a communication cost of $O(k + \log n + \log k)$ which is just logarithmic to the parameter n. However, the verification time scales linearly with the total bit length, denoted as $O(k \cdot n)$. This places a significant burden on the verifier, prompting us to explore more efficient construction methods that offer sublinear verification times.

Construction with Logarithmic Verifier. Daza et al. [23] improves Bulletproofs to achieve both logarithmic size and verification time. But it cannot be applied to our setting in the same way as above. Since it relies on structured parameters which are incompatible with the randomly chosen public keys. Integrating the public keys with these parameters would violate their structure and render the technique useless.

Plain Case Without Anonymity. We start from the single message case without anonymity. We assume that the proof of possession has been done to prove the knowledge of secret key for each public key. We aim to prove that a given $\widehat{pk} \in \mathbb{G}_2$ can be expressed in the form of $\boldsymbol{pk}^{\boldsymbol{b}}$ where $\boldsymbol{b}$ is a binary vector. Note that the pairing $e(g, \boldsymbol{pk}^{\boldsymbol{b}}) = \sum_{i=1}^{n} e(g, pk_i^{b_i}) = \sum_{i=1}^{n} e([b_i]_1, pk_i) = \langle [\boldsymbol{b}]_1, \boldsymbol{pk} \rangle$. Instead of directly proving the form of $\widehat{pk}$, we compute the map $e(g, \widehat{pk})$ at first. By the bilinear property, it is sufficient to prove that the map result is also an inner pairing product between $[\boldsymbol{b}]_1$ and $\boldsymbol{pk}$. To this end, we leverage an inner pairing product (IPP) argument. It asserts that a given element in $\mathbb{G}_T$ is the inner pairing product between two vectors in $\mathbb{G}_1^n$ and $\mathbb{G}_2^n$ which are committed with AFGHO commitments. By imposing a specific structure on the commitment key (similar to [23], as we introduced in Sect. 2.2), the verification time is reduced to logarithmic in relation to n.

The remaining issue is proving the form of these two committed vectors. $\boldsymbol{pk}$ are public, so the commitment can be verified publicly. For $[\boldsymbol{b}]_1$, we develop a binary proof in which the verification time is also logarithmic to n. It proves the committed vector consists of elements which is either $[0]_1$ or $[1]_1$. Thus, $\boldsymbol{b} \in \{0, 1\}^n$.

Anonymous Case. Now we consider the anonymous setting with a blind factor r: $\widehat{pk} = \boldsymbol{pk}^{\boldsymbol{b}} \cdot \tilde{g}^r$ and $e(g, \widehat{pk}) = \langle ([\boldsymbol{b}]_1, g), (\boldsymbol{pk}, \tilde{g}^r) \rangle$. When we attempt to follow the above method, some issues happen. The combiner needs to take additional work on proving: (i) the last position of the binary vector is 1; (ii) the public keys are committed together with a random element $\tilde{g}^r$ and he knows r. The first task requires another invocation of binary proof and it is unclear how to prove the discrete logarithm of a committed group element without leaking r or $\tilde{g}^r$.

By the bilinear property, we also have $e(g, \widehat{pk}) = \langle([\boldsymbol{b}]_1, g^r), (\boldsymbol{pk}, \tilde{g})\rangle$. Even though the latter vector $(\boldsymbol{pk}, \tilde{g})$ is publicly known, the situation remains challenging because the binary proof mechanism does not inherently support proving the presence of a random value within the vector. Another observation is that $e(g, \widehat{pk}) = \langle[\boldsymbol{b}]_1, \boldsymbol{pk}\rangle + r \cdot e_T$. One may consider to extract $r \cdot e_T$ and prove the knowledge of r. But it would leak $\boldsymbol{b}$ and violate the anonymity.

To mitigate these issues, we commit $\boldsymbol{b}$ and r with different commitment keys and generate the proofs for them separately. Afterward, by combining these two commitments, we can ascertain the presence of both a binary vector and a blind factor in designated positions. Then we can apply the inner pairing product argument on these vectors and proves the well-formedness of the blinded aggregated public key.

For k messages setting with k aggregated public keys, the aggregation technology on kn-length binary vector can also be applied as we outlined in the strawman scheme.

In the next section, we introduce our inner pairing product argument and binary proof with logarithmic communication cost and logarithmic verification time. They can be rendered non-interactive by applying the Fiat-Shamir heuristic [25]. In Sect. 4.3, we present our PAS signature scheme with the rate-once policy in the anonymous reputation system.

4.2 Succinct Proofs with Logarithmic Verifier

Inner Pairing Product Argument. We consider an argument for inner pairing product between two vectors $\boldsymbol{v}_i \in \mathbb{G}_i^n$ committed with structured AFGHO commitments with generators $(\mathsf{ck}_{3-i}, e_H) \in \mathbb{G}_i^n \times \mathbb{G}_T$ for $i \in \{1,2\}$ where $e_H = e(g_H, \tilde{g}), g_H \leftarrow_\$ \mathbb{G}_1$. In this section, we assume that the dimension n is a power of 2. If necessary, it is straightforward to add padding to the inputs to ensure this condition is met. Formally, we define a language:

$$\begin{aligned}(pp, P, C_1, C_2, [r]_1, \mathsf{ck}_1, \mathsf{vk}_1, [s]_2, \mathsf{ck}_2, \mathsf{vk}_2, e_H) \in \mathcal{L}_{\mathsf{IPP}} \Leftrightarrow \\ ([r]_1, \mathsf{ck}_1, \mathsf{vk}_1) \in \mathcal{L}^1_{\mathsf{Com}} \wedge ([s]_2, \mathsf{ck}_2, \mathsf{vk}_2) \in \mathcal{L}^2_{\mathsf{Com}} \wedge \\ \exists \boldsymbol{v}_1 \in \mathbb{G}_1^n, \boldsymbol{v}_2 \in \mathbb{G}_2^n, r_{C_1}, r_{C_2}, r_P \in \mathbb{Z}_q : \\ C_1 = \langle \boldsymbol{v}_1, \mathsf{ck}_2\rangle + r_{C_1} \cdot e_H \wedge C_2 = \langle \mathsf{ck}_1, \boldsymbol{v}_2\rangle + r_{C_2} \cdot e_H \wedge \\ P = \langle \boldsymbol{v}_1, \boldsymbol{v}_2\rangle + r_P \cdot e_H\end{aligned}$$

Common input: $(pp, [r]_1, [s]_2, \mathsf{vk}_1, \mathsf{vk}_2, e_H), P, C_1, C_2 \in \mathbb{G}_T$
$\mathcal{P}$ input: $(\mathsf{ck}_1, \mathsf{ck}_2)$, $\boldsymbol{v}_1 \in \mathbb{G}_1^n, \boldsymbol{v}_2 \in \mathbb{G}_2^n, r_{C_1}, r_{C_2}, r_P \in \mathbb{Z}_q$
Statement: $(pp, P, C_1, C_2, [r]_1, \mathsf{ck}_1, \mathsf{vk}_1, [s]_2, \mathsf{ck}_2, \mathsf{vk}_2, e_H) \in \mathcal{L}_{\mathsf{IPP}}$
$\mathcal{P}$ and $\mathcal{V}$ proceed the protocol Π_{IPP} as follows:
If $n = 1$:

$$C_1 = e(v_1, \mathsf{ck}_2) + r_{C_1} \cdot e_H, C_2 = e(\mathsf{ck}_1, v_2) + r_{C_2} \cdot e_H, P = e(v_1, v_2) + r_P \cdot e_H \ .$$

- $\mathcal{P}$ samples $s_1 \leftarrow_\$ \mathbb{G}_1, s_2 \leftarrow_\$ \mathbb{G}_2, r_{D_1}, r_{D_2}, r_{T_1}, r_{T_2} \leftarrow_\$ \mathbb{Z}_q$ and computes:
$D_1 = e(s_1, \mathsf{ck}_2) + r_{D_1} \cdot e_H, D_2 = e(\mathsf{ck}_1, s_2) + r_{D_2} \cdot e_H$
$T_1 = e(s_1, v_2) + e(v_1, s_2) + r_{T_1} \cdot e_H, T_2 = e(s_1, s_2) + r_{T_2} \cdot e_H$
- $\mathcal{P}$ sends D_1, D_2, T_1, T_2 to $\mathcal{V}$
- $\mathcal{V}$ replies with $c \leftarrow_\$ \mathbb{Z}_q^*$
- $\mathcal{P}$ computes and sends:
$u_1 = v_1 + c \cdot s_1,\ u_2 = v_2 + c \cdot s_2,$
$r_1 = r_{C_1} + c \cdot r_{D_1},\ r_2 = r_{C_2} + c \cdot r_{D_2},\ r_3 = r_P + c \cdot r_{T_1} + c^2 \cdot r_{T_2}$
- $\mathcal{V}$ accepts if:
$C_1 + c \cdot D_1 = e(u_1, \mathsf{ck}_2) + r_1 \cdot e_H \wedge$
$C_2 + c \cdot D_2 = e(\mathsf{ck}_1, u_2) + r_2 \cdot e_H \wedge$
$P + c \cdot T_1 + c^2 \cdot T_2 = e(u_1, u_2) + r_3 \cdot e_H$

Else $n > 1$, the reduce procedure:
- $\mathcal{P}$ samples $r_{1\ell}, r_{2\ell}, r_{P\ell}, r_{1r}, r_{2r}, r_{Pr} \leftarrow_\$ \mathbb{Z}_q$ and computes:
$C_{1\ell} \leftarrow \langle \boldsymbol{v}_{1\ell}, \mathsf{ck}_{2r} \rangle + r_{1\ell} \cdot e_H,\ C_{2\ell} \leftarrow \langle \mathsf{ck}_{1r}, \boldsymbol{v}_{2\ell} \rangle + r_{2\ell} \cdot e_H,$
$P_\ell \leftarrow \langle \boldsymbol{v}_{1r}, \boldsymbol{v}_{2\ell} \rangle + r_{P\ell} \cdot e_H,$
$C_{1r} \leftarrow \langle \boldsymbol{v}_{1r}, \mathsf{ck}_{2\ell} \rangle + r_{1r} \cdot e_H,\ C_{2r} \leftarrow \langle \mathsf{ck}_{1\ell}, \boldsymbol{v}_{2r} \rangle + r_{2r} \cdot e_H,$
$P_r \leftarrow \langle \boldsymbol{v}_{1\ell}, \boldsymbol{v}_{2r} \rangle + r_{Pr} \cdot e_H$
- $\mathcal{P}$ sends $C_{1\ell}, C_{2\ell}, P_\ell, C_{1r}, C_{2r}, P_r$
- $\mathcal{V}$ replies with $c \leftarrow_\$ \mathbb{Z}_q^*$
- $\mathcal{P}$ computes:
$\boldsymbol{v}_1' \leftarrow \boldsymbol{v}_{1\ell} c + \boldsymbol{v}_{1r} c^{-1} \in \mathbb{G}_1^{n'},\ \boldsymbol{v}_2' \leftarrow \boldsymbol{v}_{2\ell} c^{-1} + \boldsymbol{v}_{2r} c \in \mathbb{G}_2^{n'},$
$r_{C_1}' = r_{C_1} + r_{1\ell} \cdot c^2 + r_{1r} \cdot c^{-2},\ r_{C_2}' = r_{C_2} + r_{2\ell} \cdot c^{-2} + r_{2r} \cdot c^2,$
$r_P' = r_P + r_{P\ell} \cdot c^{-2} + r_{Pr} \cdot c^2$
$\mathsf{ck}_1' = c\mathsf{ck}_{1\ell} + c^{-1}\mathsf{ck}_{1r},\ \mathsf{ck}_2' = c^{-1}\mathsf{ck}_{2\ell} + c\mathsf{ck}_{2r},$
$[r']_1 \leftarrow \{\mathsf{ck}_1'\}_1,\ [s']_2 \leftarrow \{\mathsf{ck}_2'\}_1$ (picks the first elements of $\mathsf{ck}_1', \mathsf{ck}_2'$)
- $\mathcal{P}$ sends $[r']_1, [s']_2$ to $\mathcal{V}$.
- $\mathcal{V}$ checks the following equations and aborts if any fails:

$$e([r']_1 - c[r]_1, [1]_2) = e(c^{-1}[r]_1, [x_\nu]_2),\ e([1]_1, [s']_2 - c^{-1}[s]_2) = e([y_\nu]_1, c[s]_2)$$

Update $\mathsf{vk}_1' = [\boldsymbol{x}']_2 \leftarrow ([x_i]_2)_{i \in [\nu-1]}$ and $\mathsf{vk}_2' = [\boldsymbol{y}']_1 \leftarrow ([y_i]_1)_{i \in [\nu-1]}$
- Both compute
$C_1' \leftarrow c^2 C_{1\ell} + C_1 + c^{-2} C_{1r},\ C_2' \leftarrow c^{-2} C_{2\ell} + C_2 + c^2 C_{2r},$
$P' = c^{-2} P_\ell + P + c^2 P_r,$
- The reduced statement is $(pp, P', C_1', C_2', [r']_1, \mathsf{ck}_1', \mathsf{vk}_1', [s']_2, \mathsf{ck}_2', \mathsf{vk}_2', g_H, e_H) \in \mathcal{L}_{\mathsf{IPP}}$ with the new witnesses $(\boldsymbol{v}_1', \boldsymbol{v}_2', r_1', r_2', r_P')$.

Theorem 1 *The protocol presented is a Public Coin, HVSZK, interactive argument of knowledge for the relation $\mathcal{L}_{\mathsf{IPP}}$ with $O(\log n)$ round complexity, $O(n)$ prover complexity, and $O(\log n)$ communication and verification complexity under the SXDH and DPair-ML assumptions.*

The proof for Theorem 1 follows a similar structure to those found in [19, 23, 30]. Due to page constraints, we refer readers to the full version for detailed elaboration.

Binary Proofs with Logarithmic Verifier. We consider an argument for a binary vector $\boldsymbol{b} = (b_1, \ldots, b_n) \in \{0,1\}^n$ with Hamming weight t. This binary vector is equivalent to a vector $\boldsymbol{v} \in \mathbb{G}_1^n$ where each element is either $[0]_1$ or $[1]_1$, and the number of $[1]_1$ is precisely t. Formally, we define a language:

$$(C, [r]_2, \mathsf{ck}_2, \mathsf{vk}_2, e_H, t) \in \mathcal{L}_{\mathsf{Bin}} \Leftrightarrow$$
$$([r]_2, \mathsf{ck}_2, \mathsf{vk}_2) \in \mathcal{L}^1_{\mathsf{Com}} \wedge$$
$$\exists \boldsymbol{b} \in \{0,1\}^n, r_C \in \mathbb{Z}_q, s.t. :$$
$$C = \langle [\boldsymbol{b}]_1, \mathsf{ck}_2 \rangle + r_C \cdot e_H \wedge \langle \mathbf{1}^n, \boldsymbol{b} \rangle = t_j,$$

$\mathcal{P}$ proves that $\langle \mathbf{1}^n, \boldsymbol{b} \rangle = t \wedge \boldsymbol{b} \circ \boldsymbol{b}' = \mathbf{0}^n \wedge \boldsymbol{b}' = \boldsymbol{b} - \mathbf{1}^n$. Using random $y, \tau \in \mathbb{Z}_q^*$ from $\mathcal{V}$, these constraints can be re-written as:

$$\langle \boldsymbol{b} - \tau \cdot \mathbf{1}^n, \boldsymbol{y}^n \circ (\boldsymbol{b}' + \tau \cdot \mathbf{1}^n + \tau^2 \cdot \mathbf{1}^n) \rangle = \tau^2 \cdot t + \delta(y, \tau)$$

where $\delta(y,\tau) = (\tau - \tau^2) \cdot \langle \mathbf{1}^n, \boldsymbol{y}^n \rangle - \tau^3 \langle \mathbf{1}^n, \mathbf{1}^n \rangle \in \mathbb{Z}_q$. Thus the binary proof can be reduced to one inner pairing product argument. Concretely, $\mathcal{P}$ and $\mathcal{V}$ engage in the following protocol Π_{Bin}:

- On input $\boldsymbol{b} \in \{0,1\}^n$, $\mathcal{P}$ computes:
$\boldsymbol{b}' = \boldsymbol{b} - \mathbf{1}^n$, $[\boldsymbol{b}]_1 \in \mathbb{G}_1^n$ and $[\boldsymbol{b}']_2 \in \mathbb{G}_2^n$, $r_{B_1}, r_{B_2} \leftarrow_{\$} \mathbb{Z}_q$,
commits to $[\boldsymbol{b}]_1$ and $[\boldsymbol{b}']_2$:
$C = B_1 = \langle [\boldsymbol{b}]_1, \mathsf{ck}_2 \rangle + r_{B_1} \cdot e_H$, $B_2 = \langle \mathsf{ck}_1, [\boldsymbol{b}']_2 \rangle + r_{B_2} \cdot e_H$,
chooses blinding vectors and commits them:
$\boldsymbol{u}_1, \boldsymbol{u}_2 \leftarrow_{\$} \mathbb{Z}_q^n$, $r_{U_1}, r_{U_2} \leftarrow_{\$} \mathbb{Z}_q$,
$U_1 = \langle [\boldsymbol{u}_1]_1, \mathsf{ck}_2 \rangle + r_{U_1} \cdot e_H, U_2 = \langle \mathsf{ck}_1, [\boldsymbol{u}_2]_2 \rangle + r_{U_2} \cdot e_H$,
sends B_1, B_2, U_1, U_2 to $\mathcal{V}$
- $\mathcal{V}$ sends challenges $y, \tau \leftarrow_{\$} \mathbb{Z}_q^*$ to $\mathcal{P}$
- $\mathcal{P}$ computes $\mathsf{ck}_1' \leftarrow \mathsf{ck}_1 \circ \boldsymbol{y}^{-n}$,
define the following polynomials:

$$l(X) = \boldsymbol{b} - \tau \cdot \mathbf{1}^n + \boldsymbol{u}_1 \cdot X \in \mathbb{Z}_q^n[X]$$

$$r(X) = \boldsymbol{y}^n \circ (\boldsymbol{b}' + \tau \cdot \mathbf{1}^n + \boldsymbol{u}_2 \cdot X) + \tau^2 \cdot \mathbf{1}^n \in \mathbb{Z}_q^n[X]$$

$$p(X) = \langle l(X), r(X) \rangle = p_0 + p_1 \cdot X + p_2 \cdot X^2 \in \mathbb{Z}_q^n[X]$$

Next, $\mathcal{P}$ needs to convince $\mathcal{V}$ that $p_0 = t \cdot \tau^2 + \delta(y, \tau)$.
- $\mathcal{P}$ chooses $\phi_1, \phi_2 \leftarrow_{\$} \mathbb{Z}_q^*$ and computes:
$P_1 = p_1 \cdot e(g, \tilde{g}) + \phi_1 \cdot e_H$, $P_2 = p_2 \cdot e(g, \tilde{g}) + \phi_2 \cdot e_H$
- $\mathcal{P}$ sends $P_1, P_2 \in \mathbb{G}_T$ to $\mathcal{V}$
- $\mathcal{V}$ sends $x \leftarrow_{\$} \mathbb{Z}_q^*$ to $\mathcal{P}$
- $\mathcal{P}$ computes:
$[\boldsymbol{l}]_1 = [l(x)]_1 = [\boldsymbol{b} - \tau \cdot \mathbf{1}^n + \boldsymbol{u}_1 \cdot x]_1 \in \mathbb{G}_1^n$,
$[\boldsymbol{r}]_2 = [r(x)]_2 = [\boldsymbol{y}^n \circ (\boldsymbol{b}' + \tau \cdot \mathbf{1}^n + \boldsymbol{u}_2 \cdot x) + \tau^2 \cdot \mathbf{1}^n]_2 \in \mathbb{G}_2^n$
$P = \langle [\boldsymbol{l}]_1, [\boldsymbol{r}]_2 \rangle \in \mathbb{G}_T$, $\phi_x = \phi_2 \cdot x^2 + \phi_1 \cdot x \in \mathbb{Z}_q$
$\mu_1 = r_{B_1} + r_{U_1} \cdot x, \mu_2 = r_{B_2} + r_{U_2} \cdot x \in \mathbb{Z}_q$
$\mathcal{P}$ sends $[\boldsymbol{l}]_1, [\boldsymbol{r}]_2, P, \phi_x, \mu_1, \mu_2$ to $\mathcal{V}$

$\mathcal{V}$ computes $\mathsf{ck'}_1$ in the same way and computes:
$Q_1 = B_1 + x \cdot U_1 - \tau \cdot \langle [\mathbf{1}]_1, \mathsf{ck}_2 \rangle$, $Q_2 = B_2 + x \cdot U_2 + \tau \cdot \langle \mathsf{ck}'_1, [\boldsymbol{y}^n]_2 \rangle + \tau^2 \cdot \langle \mathsf{ck}'_1, [\mathbf{1}^n]_2 \rangle$
checks whether

$$P + \phi_x \cdot e_H \stackrel{?}{=} (t \cdot \tau^2 + \delta(y, \tau)) \cdot e(g, \tilde{g}) + x \cdot P_1 + x^2 \cdot P_2$$

$$Q_1 \stackrel{?}{=} \langle [\boldsymbol{l}]_1, \mathsf{ck}_2 \rangle + \mu_1 \cdot e_H, \; Q_2 \stackrel{?}{=} \langle \mathsf{ck'}_1, [\boldsymbol{r}]_2 \rangle + \mu_2 \cdot e_H$$

Note that the communication and verification cost are linear to n. To reduce them, $\mathcal{P}$ does not send $[\boldsymbol{l}]_1, [\boldsymbol{r}]_2$ directly, and $\mathcal{V}$ just computes $\mathsf{vk}'_1 \leftarrow \mathsf{vk}_1 \circ \bar{\boldsymbol{y}}$, where $\bar{\boldsymbol{y}} = (1, y^{-1}, \cdots, y^{-2^{\nu-1}})$, rather than ck'_1. To make sure $\mathcal{V}$ still can compute Q_2, $\mathcal{P}$ computes $Y = \langle \mathsf{ck}'_1, [\boldsymbol{y}^n]_2 \rangle = \langle \mathsf{ck}_1, [\mathbf{1}^n]_2 \rangle$ and $\Gamma = \langle \mathsf{ck}'_1, [\mathbf{1}^n]_2 \rangle$.

$\mathcal{P}$ sends Γ to $\mathcal{V}$ and proves its correctness as follows:
Let $\Gamma_\nu = \Gamma$, $\mathsf{ck}'_{1\nu} = \mathsf{ck}'_1$, for $i = \nu - 1$ to 1:
$\mathcal{P}$ sends $M_i = \mathsf{ck'}_{1i}^{\mathbf{1}^{2^i}} \in \mathbb{G}_1$, where $\mathsf{ck}'_{1i} \in \mathbb{G}_1^{2^i}$ is the left half of $\mathsf{ck}'_{1(i+1)}$;
$\mathcal{V}$ aborts if $e(M_i, ([1]_2 + \mathsf{vk}'_{1(i+1)})) \neq \Gamma_{i+1}$,
where $\mathsf{vk}'_{1(i+1)}$ is the $i+1$-th element of vk'_1,
otherwise let $\Gamma_i = e(M_i, [1]_2)$ and continue;
After $\nu - 1$ steps without abort, $\mathcal{V}$ can be convinced that Γ is correct:
$\Gamma = \langle \mathsf{ck}'_1, [\mathbf{1}^n]_2 \rangle$ and its computation time is $O(\nu) = O(\log n)$.
Thus, $\mathcal{V}$ can compute $Q_2 = B_2 + x \cdot U_2 + \tau \cdot Y + \tau^2 \cdot \Gamma$ in $O(\log n)$ time.
Thereafter, $\mathcal{P}$ runs the inner pairing product argument protocol Π_{IPP} with $\mathcal{V}$: $\mathcal{L}_{\mathsf{IPP}}(pp, P, Q_1, Q_2, [r]_1, \mathsf{ck}'_1, \mathsf{vk}'_1, [s]_2, \mathsf{ck}_2, \mathsf{vk}_2)$

Theorem 2 *The binary proof has perfect completeness, HVSZK and computational witness extended emulation under the SXDH and DPair-ML assumptions.*

Proof The binary proof is a special case of the aggregated binary proof in Theorem 3 with $k = 1$. It can be regarded as a corollary of Theorem 3.

Aggregated Binary Proofs. The prover is similar to the prover for a binary proof with $k \cdot n$ bits except the following modifications. Without loss of generality, we assume that $k \cdot n$ is still a power of 2. It proves that the committed values are $k \cdot n$ bits and they are the concatenation of k blocks. The number of 1's in the j-th block is t_j: $\boldsymbol{b} = (\boldsymbol{b}_1 || \cdots || \boldsymbol{b}_k)$ for all $j \in [k]$ where $\boldsymbol{b}_j \in \{0,1\}^n$ and $\langle \mathbf{1}^n, \boldsymbol{b}_j \rangle = t_j$. Formally, we define a language:

$$\begin{aligned}(C, [r]_2, \mathsf{ck}_2, \mathsf{vk}_2, e_H, \{t_j\}_{j \in [k]}) \in \mathcal{L}_{\mathsf{aBin}} \Leftrightarrow \\ ([r]_2, \mathsf{ck}_2, \mathsf{vk}_2) \in \mathcal{L}^1_{\mathsf{Com}} \wedge \\ \exists \boldsymbol{b} \in \{0,1\}^n, r_C \in \mathbb{Z}_q, s.t.: \\ C = \langle [\boldsymbol{b}]_1, \mathsf{ck}_2 \rangle + r_C \cdot e_H \wedge \langle \mathbf{1}^n, \boldsymbol{b}_j \rangle = t_j, \forall j \in [k].\end{aligned}$$

We convert $\boldsymbol{b}$ to $[\boldsymbol{b}]_1 \in \mathbb{G}_1^{kn}$, and commit it into $B = \langle [\boldsymbol{b}]_1, \mathsf{ck}_2 \rangle + r_B \cdot e_H$ where $r_B \leftarrow_\$ \mathbb{Z}_q$ and all t_j are public. The protocol in the former section is modified as follows:

$$l(X) = \boldsymbol{b} - \tau \cdot \mathbf{1}^{k \cdot n} + \boldsymbol{u}_1 \cdot X \in \mathbb{Z}_q^{k \cdot n}[X]$$

$$r(X) = \boldsymbol{y}^{k\cdot n} \circ (\boldsymbol{b}' + \tau \cdot \boldsymbol{1}^{k\cdot n} + \boldsymbol{u}_2 \cdot X) + \sum_{j=1}^{k} \tau^{j+1} \cdot (\boldsymbol{0}^{(j-1)\cdot n} || \boldsymbol{1}^n || \boldsymbol{0}^{(k-j)\cdot n}) \in \mathbb{Z}_q^{k\cdot n}[X]$$

$\delta(y, \tau) = (\tau - \tau^2) \cdot \langle \boldsymbol{1}^{k\cdot n}, \boldsymbol{y}^{k\cdot n} \rangle - \sum_{j=1}^{k} \tau^{j+2} \cdot \langle \boldsymbol{1}^n, \boldsymbol{1}^n \rangle$
The verification check needs to include each t_j:

$$P + \phi_x \cdot e_H = ((\sum_{j=1}^{k} (t_j \cdot \tau^{j+1}) + \delta(y, \tau)) \cdot e(g, \tilde{g}) + x \cdot P_1 + x^2 \cdot P_2$$

Q_2 needs to be updated to

$$Q_2 = B_2 + x \cdot U_2 + \tau \cdot Y + \sum_{j=1}^{k} \tau^{(j+1)} \cdot \langle \mathsf{ck}'_{1j}, [\boldsymbol{1}^n]_2 \rangle$$

where ck'_{1j} consists of the $((j-1) \cdot n + 1)$-th element to the $(j \cdot n)$-th element of ck'_1.

Theorem 3 *The aggregated binary proof has perfect completeness, HVSZK and computational witness extended emulation under the SXDH and DPair-ML assumptions.*

The proof is analogous to that of the Range proof in [19], Appendix C. Due to page limitations, we defer the formal proof to the full version.

4.3 Efficient Construction from BLS Signatures

- **Setup**(1^λ) In this phase, the system parameters are generated, especially, the common reference string. On input the security parameter 1^λ, it produces the public parameters for the BLS scheme $pp_{bls} = \{\mathbb{G}_1, \mathbb{G}_2, \mathbb{G}_T, e(\cdot,\cdot), H_1(\cdot)\}$. Here $\mathbb{G}_1, \mathbb{G}_2$ are asymmetric groups, $e : \mathbb{G}_1 \times \mathbb{G}_2 \rightarrow \mathbb{G}_T$ is the Type III bilinear pairing operation, and $H_1 : \{0,1\}^* \rightarrow \mathbb{G}_1$ is the hash function. $H_2 : \{0,1\}^* \rightarrow \mathbb{Z}_q$ is another hash function. Let k be the number of potential messages, n be the maximum number of users. W.l.o.g., we assume they are power of 2. The setup algorithm additionally outputs the structured common reference string $\mathsf{crs} = (pp_{\mathsf{com}}, [r]_1, \mathsf{ck}_1, \mathsf{vk}_1, [s]_2, \mathsf{ck}_2, \mathsf{vk}_2)$ as we described in Sect. 2.2. Note that $\mathsf{ck}_1 = (\mathsf{ck}_1^1 || \cdots || \mathsf{ck}_1^j || \cdots || \mathsf{ck}_1^k || \cdots || \mathsf{ck}_1^{2k}) \in \mathbb{G}_1^{2kn}$, ck_1^j denotes the $((j-1)n+1)$-th element to the jn-th element of ck_1. $\mathsf{ck}_2 = (\mathsf{ck}_2^1 || \cdots || \mathsf{ck}_2^k || \cdots || \mathsf{ck}_2^{2k}) \in \mathbb{G}_2^{2kn}$. Especially, let $\mathsf{ck}'_1 = (\mathsf{ck}_1^1 || \cdots || \mathsf{ck}_1^k) \in \mathbb{G}_1^{kn}$, $\mathsf{ck}'_2 = (\mathsf{ck}_2^1 || \cdots || \mathsf{ck}_2^k) \in \mathbb{G}_2^{kn}$ and we use $\mathsf{ck}_1^*, \mathsf{ck}_2^*$ to denote the first element of $\mathsf{ck}_1^{k+1}, \mathsf{ck}_2^{k+1}$ respectively. Output $pp = (pp_{bls}, \mathsf{crs}, H_2)$.
  Each user generates his secret key $sk_i \leftarrow_\$ \mathbb{Z}_q$ and public key $pk_i = [sk_i]_2 \in \mathbb{G}_2$ and broadcasts the public key with proof of knowledge of secret key.
  The combiner or any other parties collects the public keys $\boldsymbol{pk} = (pk_1, ..., pk_n)$ and publishes the commitments of them as $K_1 = \langle \mathsf{ck}_1^1, \boldsymbol{pk} \rangle, ..., K_k = \langle \mathsf{ck}_1^k, \boldsymbol{pk} \rangle$. It also publish the aggregation key $ak = (pp, \boldsymbol{pk})$ and the verification key $vk = (pp_{\mathsf{com}}, pp_{bls}, [r]_1, \mathsf{vk}_1, [s]_2, \mathsf{vk}_2, K_1, ..., K_k)$

- **ParSign**(m_j, sk_i) For a message m_j chosen from the message space $\mathcal{M}$, the user u_i signs on it using his secret key sk_i and sends (pk_i, m_j, σ_{ij}) to the combiner where $\sigma_{ij} = H(m_j)^{sk_i}$.
- **ParVrfy**(pk_i, m_j, σ_{ij}) On receiving (pk_i, m_j, σ_{ij}), the combiner verifies it. Output 1 if $e(H(m_j), pk_i) = e(\sigma_{ij}, \tilde{g})$, otherwise output 0.
- **Combine**$(ak, \{pk_i, m_j, \sigma_{ij}\}_{j\in[k]})$ When collecting a set of $\{pk_i, m_j, \sigma_i\}$, the combiner verifies them one by one. If all of them are valid, the combiner does as follows:
  - Let $S_j \subseteq [n]$ be the indices of signers who have signed on m_j, set $\boldsymbol{b}_j = (b_{1j}, ..., b_{nj}) \in \{0,1\}^n$, such that $b_{ij} = 1$ if $i \in S_j$, otherwise, $b_{ij} = 0$ and $t_j = \sum_{i=1}^{n} b_{ij}$;
  - Let $\boldsymbol{b} = (\boldsymbol{b}_1 || \cdots || \boldsymbol{b}_k)$, compute the commitment to $[\boldsymbol{b}]_1 \in \mathbb{G}_1^{kn}$: $B = \langle [\boldsymbol{b}]_1, \mathsf{ck}_2' \rangle + r_B \cdot e_H$ where $r_B \leftarrow_{\$} \mathbb{Z}_q$ and generate the binary proof π_{aBin} from Π_{aBin} w.r.t. the language $\mathcal{L}_{\mathsf{aBin}}(C, [r]_2, \mathsf{ck}_2', \mathsf{vk}_2', e_H, \{t_j\}_{j\in[k]})$;
  - For $j = 1$ to k, $m_j \in M$, choose $r_j \leftarrow_{\$} \mathbb{Z}_q$, compute sub-aggregated public keys $\widehat{pk}_j = \Pi_{i\in S_j} pk_i \cdot \tilde{g}^{r_j} = \Pi_{i=1}^{n} pk_i^{b_{ij}} \cdot \tilde{g}^{r_j} = \boldsymbol{pk}^{\boldsymbol{b}_j} \cdot \tilde{g}^{r_j}$ and sub-aggregated signatures $\hat{\sigma}_j = \Pi_{i\in S_j} \sigma_i \cdot H(m_j)^{r_j}$;
  - For the k sub-aggregated public keys $\widehat{pk}_j$, compute $\widehat{PK} = \Pi_{j=1}^{k} \widehat{pk}_j^{\,z^{(j-1)}} = \boldsymbol{pk}^{b_1} \cdot \boldsymbol{pk}^{z b_2} \cdots \boldsymbol{pk}^{z^{k-1} b_k} \cdot \tilde{g}^{r^*} = (\boldsymbol{pk} || \boldsymbol{pk}^{z} || \cdots || \boldsymbol{pk}^{z^{k-1}})^{(b_1||\cdots||b_k)} \cdot \tilde{g}^{r^*}$, where $z = H_2(\{\widehat{pk}_j, \widehat{\sigma}_j\}_{j\in[k]}, B, \pi_{\mathsf{aBin}})$ and $r^* = \sum_{j=1}^{k} r_j \cdot z^{j-1}$.
  - Compute $X = r^* \cdot e(g, \mathsf{ck}_2^*) + r_X \cdot e_H$ and generate π_{pok} (via the Schnorr's protocol [36]) to prove the knowledge of r^* and r_X;
  - Compute $Q = B + X = \langle [\boldsymbol{b}]_1, \mathsf{ck}_2' \rangle + e(g^{r^*}, \mathsf{ck}_2^*) + (r_B + r_X) \cdot e_H$, it means $Q = \langle ([\boldsymbol{b}]_1, g^{r^*}), (\mathsf{ck}_2', \mathsf{ck}_2^*) \rangle + (r_B + r_X) \cdot e_H \in \mathbb{G}_T$, so we know Q is the commitment of a binary vector and a randomness;
  - Compute $K = \langle (\mathsf{ck}_1', \mathsf{ck}_1^*), (\boldsymbol{pk}^{\mathbf{z}^k}, \tilde{g}) \rangle$, $E = \langle [\boldsymbol{b}]_1, \boldsymbol{pk}^{\mathbf{z}^k} \rangle + r^* \cdot e(g, \tilde{g}) \in \mathbb{G}_T$, where $\boldsymbol{pk}^{\mathbf{z}^k} = (\boldsymbol{pk} || \boldsymbol{pk}^{z} || ... || \boldsymbol{pk}^{z^{k-1}}) \in \mathbb{G}_2^{kn}$;
  - Based on E, Q, K, generates π_{IPP} from Π_{IPP} w.r.t. the language $\mathcal{L}_{\mathsf{IPP}}(E, Q, K, \mathsf{ck}_1, \mathsf{vk}_1, \mathsf{ck}_2, \mathsf{vk}_2, e_H)$ to prove that E is the *inner pairing product* of vectors $\boldsymbol{v}_1, \boldsymbol{v}_2$ which are committed in Q and K: $E = \langle \boldsymbol{v}_1, \boldsymbol{v}_2 \rangle + r_E \cdot e_H$, where $\boldsymbol{v}_1 = (g^{b_1}, ..., g^{b_{kn}}, g^{r^*}, [0]_1, ..., [0]_1) \in \mathbb{G}_1^{2kn}$ and $b_i \in \{0,1\}$, $r^* \in \mathbb{Z}_q$ which has been proved via π_{aBin} and π_{pok}, $\boldsymbol{v}_2 = (\boldsymbol{pk}^{\mathbf{z}^k}, \tilde{g}, [0]_2, ..., [0]_2) \in \mathbb{G}_2^{2kn}$ which is public.[4]
  - Generate the proof π_{disj} to prove all signer sets are disjoint: $S_{j_0} \cap S_{j_1} = \emptyset, \forall j_0, j_1 \in [k], j_0 \neq j_1$. It requires the combiner additionally prove that $\widehat{PK}' = \prod_{j=1}^{k} \widehat{pk}_j$ can be expressed in the form of $\boldsymbol{pk}^{\boldsymbol{b}'} \cdot \tilde{g}^{r'}$ using the same method as above, where $r' = \sum_{j=1}^{k} r_j$, $\boldsymbol{b}' = \sum_{j=1}^{k} \boldsymbol{b}_j$ is also a binary vector with $\sum_{j\in[k]} t_j$ ones.
  - Output the signature $\Sigma \leftarrow (\{\widehat{pk}_j, \widehat{\sigma}_j\}_{j\in[k]}, B, z, X, \pi_{\mathsf{aBin}}, \pi_{\mathsf{pok}}, \pi_{\mathsf{IPP}}, \pi_{\mathsf{disj}})$ with the thresholds $T = \{t_j\}_{j\in[k]}$ as Δ.

[4] We pad 'zeros' in $\boldsymbol{v}_1, \boldsymbol{v}_2$ since the dimension of commitment keys for $\mathcal{L}_{\mathsf{IPP}}$ is $2kn$, which is a power of 2.

- **Verify**(vk, M, T, Σ) Parse $\Sigma = (\{\widehat{pk}_j, \widehat{\sigma}_j\}_{j\in[k]}, B, z, X, \pi_{\mathsf{aBin}}, \pi_{\mathsf{pok}}, \pi_{\mathsf{IPP}}, \pi_{\mathsf{disj}})$, $T = \{t_j\}_{j\in[k]}$, compute:
  $z' = H_2(\{\widehat{pk}_j, \widehat{\sigma}_j\}_{j\in[k]}, B, \pi_{\mathsf{aBin}})$, $\widehat{\sigma} = \prod_{j\in[k]} \widehat{\sigma}_j$, $Q = B + X$,
  $K = K_1 + \cdots + K_j^{z'^{j-1}} + \cdots + K_k^{z'^{k-1}} + e(\mathsf{ck}_1^*, \tilde{g})$,
  $\widehat{PK} = \prod_{j=1}^k \widehat{pk}_j^{z'(j-1)}$, $E = e(g, \widehat{PK})$, $\widehat{PK}' = \prod_{j=1}^k \widehat{pk}_j$, $\hat{t} = \sum_{j\in[k]} t_j$.
  Accept if all the following conditions are satisfied:
  - $z' = z$;
  - **Vrfy**$(\{\widehat{pk}_j, m_j\}_{j\in[k]}, \hat{\sigma}) = 1$;
  - π_{aBin} is valid w.r.t. B, T;
  - π_{pok} is valid w.r.t. X;
  - π_{IPP} is valid w.r.t. Q, K, E;
  - π_{disj} are valid w.r.t. $\widehat{PK}', \hat{t}$.

General Predicate Satisfiability Proofs. In our specific setting, where we aim to prove the predicate regarding the relations among signer sets, we focus on the committed binary vector. It serves as the representation of signers for different messages and plays a crucial role in our proof construction.

Recall that Daza et al. [23] proves that the committed vectors satisfy some circuits. By following the protocol of zero-knowledge SNARK for circuit satisfiability in [23] but with AFGHO commitment (which is also homomorphic same as the Pedersen commitment), we can obtain a circuit satisfiability proof that is compatible with our previous inner pairing product and binary proofs. Both communication cost and verification complexity are logarithmic to the size of the circuit.

5 Analysis

5.1 Performance Analysis

We first analyze the performance related to the inner pairing product and binary proofs. The inner pairing product and binary proof protocols require $\nu = \log(k{\cdot}n)$ rounds, where each round involves communication and computations. In each round, the size of the witness is halved. It leads to a communication complexity of $O(\nu)$ since the communication cost is constant in each round. The prover's computation complexity in round i is $O(2^{\nu-i+1})$. As a result, the overall prover complexity is $O(2^\nu)$ since ν rounds are performed. On the other hand, the verifier's computation cost remains constant at $O(1)$ since it only needs to perform a fixed number of operations in each round. Consequently, the verifier's overall complexity is $O(\nu)$. For the predicate satisfaction proof with generic arithmetic circuit, the communication cost and verification complexity are logarithmic to the size of the circuit, which is $O(\log|\mathcal{C}|)$. The prover's computation complexity is $O(|\mathcal{C}|)$.

In the $\mathsf{Combine}$ phase, the combiner needs to verify the partial signatures, generate the sub-aggregated public keys and sub-aggregated signatures and the computation cost is $O(n)$. The final signature contains additional aggregated public keys and signatures and thresholds w.r.t. each message. It leads to $O(k)$ communication cost. On the final signature, the verifier checks the sub-aggregated signatures with the respective message and sub-aggregated public key. It involves the $O(k)$ computation complexity. Then it verifies the correctness of these sub-aggregated public keys by checking these proofs.

In summary, the communication cost is $O(k + \nu + \log|\mathcal{C}|) = O(k + \log k + \log n + \log|\mathcal{C}|)$, the prover complexity is $O(2^\nu + |\mathcal{C}|) = O(k \cdot n + |\mathcal{C}|)$, and the verifier complexity is $O(\nu + \log|\mathcal{C}|) = O(\log k + \log n + \log|\mathcal{C}|)$. For the special case of rate-once policy, the communication cost is $O(k+\log k+\log n)$, the prover complexity is $O(k \cdot n)$, and the verifier complexity is $O(k + \log k + \log n)$.

5.2 Security Analysis

Theorem 4 (Anonymity) *The predicate aggregate signature is anonymous in the random oracle model under the SXDH assumption.*

Proof. Based on the rate-once policy in the anonymous reputation system, the predicate has been explained in Eq. (1) and the description Δ is defined as $\Delta = T = \{t_j\}_{j\in[k]}$. In the anonymous experiment, $\Delta_0 = T_0, \Delta_1 = T_1$ and it is required that $T_0 = T_1$ for the challenge sets S^0, S^1. Given the signature $\Sigma = (\{\widehat{pk}_j, \widehat{\sigma}_j\}_{j\in[k]}, B, z, X, \pi_{\mathsf{aBin}}, \pi_{\mathsf{pok}}, \pi_{\mathsf{IPP}}, \pi_{\mathsf{disj}})$, and thresholds $T = \{t_j\}_{j\in[k]}$. Note that T, K leak nothing since they are the same in both challenges with identity sets S^0, S^1. We design the hybrid games as follows:

- $\mathsf{G}_{\mathsf{real}}$: This game is the same as the experiment, challenger chooses $b \leftarrow_{\$} \{0,1\}$ and generates the signature Σ_b honestly under the identities in S^b.
- G_1 : This game is similar with G_0 except that the proofs $\pi_{\mathsf{aBin}}, \pi_{\mathsf{pok}}, \pi_{\mathsf{IPP}}, \pi_{\mathsf{disj}}$ are simulated without witness.
- G_2 : This game is similar with G_1 except that the sub-aggregated public keys and signatures are generated randomly without using b as follows: for $j \in [k]$, choose $u_j \leftarrow_{\$} \mathbb{Z}_q$ and set $\widehat{pk}'_j = \tilde{g}^{u_j} \in \mathbb{G}_2$ and $\hat{\sigma}'_j = H(m_j)^{u_j} \in \mathbb{G}_1$ such that $e(H(m_j), \widehat{pk}'_j) = e(\hat{\sigma}'_j, \tilde{g})$.
- G_3: This game is similar with G_2 except that B, X are also chosen randomly independently: $B', X' \leftarrow_{\$} \mathbb{G}_T$. Note that the proofs $\pi_{\mathsf{aBin}}, \pi_{\mathsf{pok}}, \pi_{\mathsf{IPP}}, \pi_{\mathsf{disj}}$ are simulated without using witnesses. They can still be verified.

Compare G_1 with $\mathsf{G}_{\mathsf{real}}$, the only difference is that these proofs are simulated. Since these proofs are zero-knowledge under the SXDH assumptions in the random oracle model, the probability of distinguishing G_1 from $\mathsf{G}_{\mathsf{real}}$ is negligible. We have that $|\Pr[\mathsf{G}_{\mathsf{real}}(\mathcal{A}, \lambda) = 1] - \Pr[\mathsf{G}_1(\mathcal{A}, \lambda) = 1]| \leq negl(\lambda)$.

Compare G_2 with G_1, in G_1, $\widehat{pk}_j = \Pi_{i\in S^b_j} pk_i \cdot \tilde{g}^{r_j}$, $\widehat{\sigma}_j = \Pi_{i\in S^b}\sigma_i \cdot H(m_j)^{r_j}$ where $r_j \leftarrow_{\$} \mathbb{Z}_q$, so they are uniformly random and each pair satisfies $e(H(m_j), \widehat{pk}_j) = e(\hat{\sigma}_j, \tilde{g})$. In G_1, $\widehat{pk}'_j$ and $\hat{\sigma}'_j$ are also random elements in $\mathbb{G}_1, \mathbb{G}_2$ respectively, and satisfy the same kinds of relation. $\widehat{PK}'$ is generated from these random $\widehat{pk}'_j$ and z, so is E'. Thus $(\{\widehat{pk}_j, \widehat{\sigma}_j\}_{j\in[k]}, z, \widehat{pk}, E)$ and

$(\{\widehat{pk}'_j, \widehat{\sigma}'_j\}_{j\in[k]}, z', \widehat{PK}', E')$ have the same distribution. The probability that they can be distinguished is 0. We have that $|\Pr[\mathsf{G}_1(\mathcal{A},\lambda) = 1] - \Pr[\mathsf{G}_2(\mathcal{A},\lambda) = 1]| = 0$.

Compare G_3 with G_2, in G_2, B is the structured AFGHO commitment of $[\boldsymbol{b}]_1$, X is the Pedersen commitment of r^*. Since these commitments are perfect hiding, they are indistinguishable from the random B', X' in G_3. We have that $|\Pr[\mathsf{G}_2(\mathcal{A},\lambda) = 1] - \Pr[\mathsf{G}_3(\mathcal{A},\lambda) = 1]| = 0$.

In G_3, $\mathcal{A}$'s view is independent of b. Thus, $\mathcal{A}$ just outputs a random guess $\hat{b}$ in G_3, so its advantage is 0: $\Pr[\mathsf{G}_3(\mathcal{A},\lambda) = 1] - 1/2 = 0$. In summary, we have

$$\begin{aligned}&|\Pr[\mathrm{Exp}^{\mathsf{anony}}(\mathcal{A},\lambda) = 1] - 1/2| = |\Pr[\mathsf{G}_{\mathsf{real}}(\mathcal{A},\lambda) = 1] - 1/2|\\ \le&|\Pr[\mathsf{G}_{\mathsf{real}}(\mathcal{A},\lambda) = 1] - \Pr[\mathsf{G}_1(\mathcal{A},\lambda) = 1]| + |\Pr[\mathsf{G}_1(\mathcal{A},\lambda) = 1] - \Pr[\mathsf{G}_2(\mathcal{A},\lambda) = 1]|\\ &+ |\Pr[\mathsf{G}_2(\mathcal{A},\lambda) = 1] - \Pr[\mathsf{G}_3(\mathcal{A},\lambda) = 1]| + |\Pr[\mathsf{G}_3(\mathcal{A},\lambda) = 1] - 1/2| \le negl(\lambda)\end{aligned}$$

Theorem 5 (Unforgeability) *The predicate aggregate signature is unforgeable in the random oracle model under the co-CDH, SXDH and DPair-ML assumptions.*

Proof. First of all, we assume that the proof of possession has been done to prove the knowledge of secret key for each public key. Based on the rate-once policy in the anonymous reputation system, the predicate has been explained as in Eq. (1). So in the unforgeability experiment, the adversary $\mathcal{A}$ wins if for the extracted identities sets $S_1, ..., S_k$, at least one of the following happens:

1. $\exists\ i_j \in S_j$, such that $\mathcal{A}$ has never queried the **corrupt** oracle on pk_{i_j} or **sign** oracle on (pk_{i_j}, m_j);
2. $\exists\ j \in [k]$, s.t. $t_j \neq |S_j|$;
3. $\exists\ i_j \in S_j$ and it appears more than once in S_j;
4. $\exists\ S_i$ and S_j which overlap: $S_i \cap S_j \neq \emptyset$.

We reduce the security of our scheme to the security of the underlying BLS signature which is unforgeable under co-CDH assumption, and non-interactive ZKAoK which is sound and knowledge sound under SXDH and DPair-ML assumptions. We elaborate it case by case.

Extract the Identities and Randomness: $\mathcal{A}$ outputs a non-trivial PAS forgery $\Sigma = (\{\widehat{pk}_j, \widehat{\sigma}_j\}_{j\in[k]}, B, z, X, \pi_{\mathsf{aBin}}, \pi_{\mathsf{pok}}, \pi_{\mathsf{IPP}}, \pi_{\mathsf{disj}})$ on message set $M = \{m_j\}_{j=1}^k$ with threshold $T = \{t_j\}_{j=1}^k$. Due to the witness extended emulation of $\Pi_{\mathsf{aBin}}, \Pi_{\mathsf{IPP}}$ and the knowledge soundness of Π_{pok}, there exists an extractor $\mathcal{E}$ who can extract the signer identities $\boldsymbol{b}_j$, r_j such that $\widehat{pk}_j = \boldsymbol{pk}^{\boldsymbol{b}_j} \cdot \tilde{g}^{r_j}$ as follows.

$\mathcal{E}$ can run the extractor χ_{aBin} for π_{aBin} to extract the committed elements $[\boldsymbol{b}]_1 \in \mathbb{G}_1^{kn}$ and randomness $r_B \in \mathbb{Z}_q$ s.t. $B = \langle [\boldsymbol{b}]_1, \mathsf{ck}_2\rangle + r_B \cdot e_H$ and $\boldsymbol{b} \in \{0,1\}^{kn}$. $\mathcal{E}$ can rewind $\mathcal{A}$ on different z. For each z, $\mathcal{E}$ runs the extractor χ_{pok} for π_{pok} to extract the committed element $r^* \in \mathbb{Z}_q$ and randomness $r_X \in \mathbb{Z}_q$ s.t. $X = r^* \cdot e(g, \mathsf{ck}_2^*) + r_X \cdot e_H$ and runs the extractor χ_{IPP} for π_{IPP} to extract the committed elements $\boldsymbol{v}_1 \in \mathbb{G}_1^{2kn}, \boldsymbol{v}_2 \in \mathbb{G}_2^{2kn}$ and randomness $r_Q, r_K, r_E \in \mathbb{Z}_q$

s.t. $E = \langle \boldsymbol{v}_1, \boldsymbol{v}_2\rangle + r_E \cdot e_H$, $Q = \langle \boldsymbol{v}_1, (\mathsf{ck}_2, \mathsf{ck}_2^*)\rangle + r_Q \cdot e_H$, $K = \langle (\mathsf{ck}_1, \mathsf{ck}_1^*), \boldsymbol{v}_2\rangle + r_K \cdot e_H$. We know that $\boldsymbol{v}_1 = ([\boldsymbol{b}]_1, [r^*]_1, [0]_1, ..., [0]_1)$, $\boldsymbol{v}_2 = (\boldsymbol{pk}^{\boldsymbol{z}^k}, \tilde{g}, [0]_2, ..., [0]_2)$. Otherwise, it breaks the DPair-ML assumption. So $E = \langle \boldsymbol{v}_1, \boldsymbol{v}_2\rangle + r_E \cdot e_H = e(g, \widehat{G}) + e(g_H, \tilde{g}^{r_E})$, where $\widehat{G} = \boldsymbol{pk}^{\boldsymbol{z}^k \boldsymbol{b}} \cdot \tilde{g}^{r^*}$. We also have $\widehat{PK} = \prod_{j=1}^k \widehat{pk}_j^{z^{(j-1)}} \in \mathbb{G}_2$ s.t. $E = e(g, \widehat{PK})$. It means that $\widehat{PK} = \widehat{G}$ and $r_E = 0$, otherwise, it breaks the DPair assumption by finding a non-trivial pair $(N_1, N_2) = (\widehat{G}/\widehat{PK}, \tilde{g}^{r_e}) \in \mathbb{G}_2^2$ s.t. $e(g, N_1) + e(g_H, N_2) = [0]_T$. Thus $\widehat{PK}$ can be expressed in the form of $\boldsymbol{pk}^{\boldsymbol{z}^k \boldsymbol{b}} \cdot \tilde{g}^{r^*}$.

Repeating this for k different challenges z with the randomness r^*, we can compute r_j for $j \in [k]$ s.t. $r^* = \sum_{j=1}^k r_j \cdot z^{j-1}$ for each challenge and each sub-aggregated public key $\widehat{pk}_j$ is in the form of $\boldsymbol{pk}^{\boldsymbol{b}_j} \cdot \tilde{g}^{r_j}$ by Schwartz-Zippel lemma, where $\boldsymbol{b}_j$ is the j-th block in the extracted $\boldsymbol{b}$.

(1) Suppose that P_1=Pr[$\mathcal{A}$ wins and violates condition 1] is non-negligible. We prove that if $\mathcal{A}$ wins, we can use it in a black-box manner to construct an attacker $\mathcal{B}$ to break the unforgeability of the underlying BLS signature. $\mathcal{B}$ receives the BLS parameter pp_{bls} and the target BLS public key pk^*. It can also query the BLS signing oracle $\mathbf{Sign}_{\mathsf{bls}}(\cdot)$ on pk^* and any message. $\mathcal{B}$ can emulate the experiment for $\mathcal{A}$ as follows.

Setup: $\mathcal{B}$ generates crs and sets $pp = (pp_{bls}, \mathsf{crs})$. $\mathcal{B}$ chooses an index $\hat{i} \leftarrow_\$ [n]$ and sets $pk_{\hat{i}} = pk^*$. For other $i \in [n], i \neq \hat{i}$, it generates the secret keys $sk_i \leftarrow_\$ \mathbb{Z}_q$ and sets public keys $pk_i = [sk_i]_2 \in \mathbb{G}_2$. $\mathcal{B}$ sends pp and all public keys to $\mathcal{A}$.

Emulate Corrupt and Sign oracles: For corruption oracle $\mathbf{corrupt}(\cdot)$: if $\mathcal{A}$ corrupts $pk_{\hat{i}}$, $\mathcal{B}$ aborts. Otherwise, for other identity corruption, $\mathcal{B}$ responds with the secret key sk_i. Note that $\mathcal{A}$ is not allowed to corrupt all public keys.

For signing oracle $\mathbf{sign}(\cdot,\cdot)$: if $\mathcal{A}$ queries on $(pk_{\hat{i}}, m)$, $\mathcal{B}$ forwards m to its $\mathbf{Sign}_{bls}$ oracle and replies $\mathcal{A}$ with the signature it received. Otherwise, for other signer identities, $\mathcal{B}$ generates the signature on the message using secret key sk_i.

Breaking BLS Unforgeability: $\mathcal{A}$ outputs a non-trivial PAS forgery Σ on message set $M = \{m_j\}_{j=1}^k$ with threshold $T = \{t_j\}_{j=1}^k$. By the knowledge soundness, $\mathcal{B}$ can works like $\mathcal{E}$ as above to extract the signer identities $\boldsymbol{b}_j$, r_j such that $\widehat{pk}_j = \boldsymbol{pk}^{\boldsymbol{b}_j} \cdot \tilde{g}^{r_j}$. Based on each $\boldsymbol{b}_j$, we obtain the identity subset $S_j = \{i | b_{ji} = 1, b_{ji} \in \boldsymbol{b}_j\}$ for $j = 1$ to k and $S = \cup_{j=1}^k S_j$. Note that the non-triviality of the forgery implies that S includes at least one honest signer, who $\mathcal{A}$ did not corrupt. Otherwise, it proceeds as follows. $\mathcal{B}$ aborts if the target identity $\hat{i}$ is not included in S or $\hat{i} \in S_j$ w.r.t. a message m_j but $\mathcal{A}$ has queried $\mathbf{sign}$ oracle on $(pk_{\hat{i}}, m_j)$. Otherwise, $\mathcal{B}$ can locate the identity subset $S_{\hat{j}}$ w.r.t. the message $m_{\hat{j}}$ in which the target identity $\hat{i} \in S_{\hat{j}}$ and $\widehat{pk}_{\hat{j}} = \boldsymbol{pk}^{\boldsymbol{b}_{\hat{j}}} \cdot \tilde{g}^{r_{\hat{j}}}$. Given $\hat{\sigma}_j$, the randomness r_j and all other identities $i_j \in S_{\hat{j}}, i_j \neq \hat{i}$, $\mathcal{B}$ can computes their signatures σ_{i_j} on the message $m_{\hat{j}}$ and gets $\sigma_{i_j^*} = \hat{\sigma}/(\prod_{i \in S_j^* \setminus \{i_j^*\}} \sigma_i \cdot H(m_{\hat{j}})^{r_j})$ which is a valid signature of the target identity on $m_{\hat{j}}$ that $\mathcal{A}$ has never queried. So it is a successful BLS forgery and $\mathcal{B}$ wins.

Success Probability: Let $\epsilon_{\mathcal{A}}$ be the probability with which $\mathcal{A}$ outputs a valid forgery. It is easy to see that $\mathcal{B}$ breaks the unforgeability of BLS signature if it does not abort. We compute the lower bound of the probability with which $\mathcal{B}$ does not abort. Firstly, since $\hat{i}$ is chosen uniformly at random, $\mathcal{A}$ does not corrupt $pk_{\hat{i}}$ with probability at least $1/n$. Let δ be the probability with which $\mathcal{B}$ extracts the witness successfully. Then the probability that $\hat{i} \in I$ is at least $1/n$. Let q_H be the number of queries on the random oracle, q_S be the number of queries on the signing oracle, the probability that $\mathcal{A}$ has never queried on $(pk_{\hat{i}}, m_{\hat{j}})$ is at least $(1 - \frac{1}{n \cdot q_H}) \cdot (1 - \frac{1}{n \cdot q_H - 1}) \cdots (1 - \frac{1}{n \cdot q_H - q_S}) = \frac{n \cdot q_H - q_S - 1}{n \cdot q_H}$. Finally, we obtain the success probability of $\mathcal{B}$ is $\epsilon_{\mathcal{B}} \geq \epsilon_{\mathcal{A}} \cdot \frac{n \cdot q_H - q_S - 1}{n^3 \cdot q_H}$. Due to the unforgeability of the BLS signature, $\epsilon_{\mathcal{B}}$ is negligible, so $\epsilon_{\mathcal{A}}$ is also negligible.

(2) Suppose that P_2=Pr[$\mathcal{A}$ wins and violates condition 2] is non-negligible. It implies that $\mathcal{A}$ generates a valid binary proof for t_j with an incorrect witness whose Hamming weight is not t_j. It contradicts with the statement of π_{aBin} which breaks the soundness of the underlying ZKAoK.
(3) Suppose that P_3=Pr[$\mathcal{A}$ wins and violates condition 3] is non-negligible. It implies that $\mathcal{A}$ generates a valid binary proof with an incorrect witness which contains a number larger than 1. It also contradicts to the statement of π_{aBin}, so the soundness is broken.
(4) Suppose that P_4=Pr[$\mathcal{A}$ wins and violates condition 4] is non-negligible. It implies that $\mathcal{A}$ generates a valid binary proof for the sum of commitments with an incorrect witness which contains a number larger than 1. It contradicts to the statement of π_{disj}.

In summary, $\Pr[\mathsf{Exp}^{\mathsf{unforge}}(\mathcal{A}, \lambda) = 1] = P_1 + P_2 + P_3 + P_4 \leq negl(\lambda)$.

6 Applications and Extensions

Our PAS can be used to construct many other types of signatures by invoking the Combine algorithm as a blackbox to compress the final signature. Letting dynamic threshold be the specific description and predicate function only requires the correctness of the threshold, our efficient scheme for single message also improves their state-of-the-art works in terms of trust model (relies on trusted party or non-standard assumptions) and efficiency as shown in Table 2. We explain them as follows.

(1) Our PAS implies threshold signatures with transparent setup[5] Each signer generates their public key and secret key by themselves. Some of them sign on the same message and send to the combiner. Taking the valid partial

[5] Our dynamic threshold aggregate signature with transparent setup also offers a solution for multiverse threshold signature (MTS) [8]. For any subset of users interested in forming a universe with a specific threshold, the aggregation and verification keys can be computed from their public keys. Then run the Combine algorithm to get a PAS signature with the number of signers.

signatures as input, the combiner runs the Combine algorithm to generate the final PAS signature with a threshold t. The verifier can be convinced that there are t different signers sign on this message.

(2) We get a multi-signature by letting everyone sign on the same message, aggregation is done via the Combine algorithm and the predicate only requires that the threshold number is correct.

(3) We get an aggregate signature which hides the signer identities from PAS, where aggregation is done via Combine algorithm and the predicate function is specified according to the concrete rule.

(4) We get a graded signature by letting everyone sign on the same message, aggregation is done via the Combine algorithm and the predicate only requires that the number of signers is correct. It ensures each of them can sign only once without leaking their identities.

(5) We get a threshold ring signature with prefixed threshold t by setting there is a single message and the predicate function always outputs 1 and modifying the verification algorithm a bit. Via the Combine algorithm, a PAS signature is produced. Now besides verifying whether it is valid, the verifier also checks whether the number of signers in PAS is larger than t. If yes, it is a valid threshold ring signature, otherwise not. When t is 1, it is a ring signature.

Anonymous Reputation System. An anonymous reputation system enables users to rate products they have purchased. The primary security guarantee offered by such systems is privacy, allowing users to write reviews anonymously for any purchased products. However, to prevent abuse or misuse, a *rate-once policy* is implemented. This means that if a user attempts to write multiple reviews for the same product, their reviews will become publicly traceable or linked. It requires the final signature is linear to the number of signer and the verification time is quadratic. Recent works on the anonymous reputation systems [11,12,24] achieve full anonymity at the cost of linear communication cost and quadratic verification complexity.

We consider a relaxed but reasonable setting where a combiner is allowed to know the signers' identities. It can be the shopping website who knows the user accounts when they login. But it cannot manipulate the final result even colludes with some of users. It cannot violate the rate-once policy and cannot generate review on behalf of other honest users. Malicious users and combiner cannot rate more than once or forge any other honest user's signature. The combiner produces a PAS in which the thresholds disclose the reputation states, and both the size and the verification time are logarithmic in the number of all users.

Onchain Voting System. In more extensive scenarios, there might exist more intricate voting policies that can be defined as conditions based on the identities of the voters. For instance, in blockchain governance, such as Decentralized Autonomous Organizations (DAOs), determinations might be reached by the entire community, provided their accounts possess a significant number of tokens. Certain policies necessitate that voters possess a particular property [3], and it can be denoted by their identity index. For instance, within an organization, senior members are associated with indices smaller than a threshold.

The combiner's task is to demonstrate that among the signers, there is at least one whose index is lower than a specified threshold. In our design, relying on the binary vector, the combiner only needs to establish the existence of a single position in the vector where the value is 1 and the position is smaller than a specified threshold.

6.1 Extensions

Dynamic Join. New users can seamlessly join the system without causing any disruptions to existing users. The process of joining is transparent and does not have any adverse effects on other users. A new user broadcasts his public key with PoP for registration. On verifying its validness, the combiner updates its aggregation key by adding this public key. Other honest verifier can also update the verification key by including the new public key in the commitment of all public keys. These updates are publicly verifiable and incur only a constant cost.

Weight Aggregation. In the PAS scheme, each user can associate themselves with an additional weight. This weight represents their significance or influence within the system. The weight vector $\boldsymbol{w}$ is public where each weight value w_i binds with a public key pk_i. In the Combine algorithm, the combiner additionally computes the sum of weights $W = \langle \boldsymbol{b}, \boldsymbol{w} \rangle$ as the description Δ. As a result, when the PAS generates a signature, it discloses the total weight of the signers involved. So our PAS also supports the weight aggregation like [20,22,33].

Accountability. Our PAS focuses on the privacy of signers, and it can be extended to support the accountability by adding an extra identities encryption layer. This approach bears similarity to the method employed in TAPS [15]. In this extended system, the description pertains to the minimum threshold required for the number of signers. The combiner also encrypts both the count of signers and their identities. The predicate function ensures that they are correctly encrypted under the specified public key, and that the size of the signer set surpasses the minimum threshold.

6.2 Open Problems

More Efficient Scheme. Although our construction achieves logarithmic verification time, the verifier needs to do the pairing operation in each round which is expensive. Is it possible to design a more efficient PAS scheme in which the verifier only needs to preform constant number of pairing operations and logarithmic group operations? One possible direction is studying the technology in Dory [30]. We leave it to the future work.

Multiple Layers Combination. In the current setting, our primary objectives include ensuring signer anonymity, improving efficiency, and accommodating diverse predicate requirements for the signers of different messages, which are orthogonal to aggregate multiple (already aggregated) signatures and proofs on different messages. Considering the "more layers combination" feature together with our goals presents challenges, and at this stage, it is unclear how to achieve it, which would be a very interesting open question for future study.

Acknowledgments. We would like to thank anonymous reviewers of ASIACRYPT 2023 for their insightful feedbacks. We thank Dr. Hanwen Feng for valuable suggestions. This work was supported in part by research awards from Stellar Development Foundation, Ethereum Foundation, Protocol Labs, SOAR Prize and Digital Science Initiative Pilot Project from USYD.

References

1. Quadratic moloch (2019). https://github.com/DemocracyEarth/dao
2. Quadratic voting in colorado: 2020, January 2021. https://www.radicalxchange.org/media/blog/quadratic-voting-in-colorado-2020/
3. Erc721 voting-power based on some property, February 2022. https://forum.openzeppelin.com/t/erc721-voting-power-based-on-some-property/24550
4. Daos (2023). https://ethereum.org/en/dao/
5. How to delegate votes in the unlock dao, May 2023. https://unlock-protocol.com/guides/delegation/
6. Abe, M., Fuchsbauer, G., Groth, J., Haralambiev, K., Ohkubo, M.: Structure-preserving signatures and commitments to group elements. J. Cryptol. **29**, 363–421 (2016)
7. Attema, T., Cramer, R., Rambaud, M.: Compressed σ-protocols for bilinear group arithmetic circuits and application to logarithmic transparent threshold signatures. In: Advances in Cryptology-ASIACRYPT 2021: 27th International Conference on the Theory and Application of Cryptology and Information Security, Singapore, December 6–10, 2021, Proceedings, Part IV, pp. 526–556. Springer (2021)
8. Baird, L., et al.: Threshold signatures in the multiverse. In: 2023 IEEE Symposium on Security and Privacy (SP), pp. 2057–2073. IEEE Computer Society (2023)
9. Bellare, M., Neven, G.: Multi-signatures in the plain public-key model and a general forking lemma. In: Proceedings of the 13th ACM Conference on Computer and Communications Security, pp. 390–399 (2006)
10. Bethencourt, J., Shi, E., Song, D.: Signatures of reputation. In: Sion, R. (ed.) FC 2010. LNCS, vol. 6052, pp. 400–407. Springer, Heidelberg (2010). https://doi.org/10.1007/978-3-642-14577-3_35
11. Blömer, J., Bobolz, J., Porzenheim, L.: A generic construction of an anonymous reputation system and instantiations from lattices. Cryptology ePrint Archive (2023)
12. Blömer, J., Juhnke, J., Kolb, C.: Anonymous and publicly linkable reputation systems. In: Böhme, R., Okamoto, T. (eds.) FC 2015. LNCS, vol. 8975, pp. 478–488. Springer, Heidelberg (2015). https://doi.org/10.1007/978-3-662-47854-7_29
13. Boneh, D., Drijvers, M., Neven, G.: Compact multi-signatures for smaller blockchains. In: Peyrin, T., Galbraith, S. (eds.) ASIACRYPT 2018. LNCS, vol. 11273, pp. 435–464. Springer, Cham (2018). https://doi.org/10.1007/978-3-030-03329-3_15

14. Boneh, D., Gentry, C., Lynn, B., Shacham, H.: Aggregate and verifiably encrypted signatures from bilinear maps. In: Biham, E. (ed.) EUROCRYPT 2003. LNCS, vol. 2656, pp. 416–432. Springer, Heidelberg (2003). https://doi.org/10.1007/3-540-39200-9_26
15. Boneh, D., Komlo, C.: Threshold signatures with private accountability. In: Advances in Cryptology-CRYPTO 2022: 42nd Annual International Cryptology Conference, CRYPTO 2022, Santa Barbara, CA, USA, August 15–18, 2022, Proceedings, Part IV, pp. 551–581. Springer, Cham (2022). https://doi.org/10.1007/978-3-031-15985-5_19
16. Bootle, J., Cerulli, A., Chaidos, P., Groth, J., Petit, C.: Efficient zero-knowledge arguments for arithmetic circuits in the discrete log setting. In: Fischlin, M., Coron, J.-S. (eds.) EUROCRYPT 2016. LNCS, vol. 9666, pp. 327–357. Springer, Heidelberg (2016). https://doi.org/10.1007/978-3-662-49896-5_12
17. Bootle, J., Elkhiyaoui, K., Hesse, J., Manevich, Y.: Dualdory: logarithmic-verifier linkable ring signatures through preprocessing. In: Atluri, V., Di Pietro, R., Jensen, C.D., Meng, W. (eds.) ESORICS 2022, Part II. LNCS, vol. 13555, pp. 427–446. Springer, Cham (2022). https://doi.org/10.1007/978-3-031-17146-8_21
18. Bresson, E., Stern, J., Szydlo, M.: Threshold ring signatures and applications to ad-hoc groups. In: Yung, M. (ed.) CRYPTO 2002. LNCS, vol. 2442, pp. 465–480. Springer, Heidelberg (2002). https://doi.org/10.1007/3-540-45708-9_30
19. Bünz, B., Bootle, J., Boneh, D., Poelstra, A., Wuille, P., Maxwell, G.: Bulletproofs: short proofs for confidential transactions and more. In: 2018 IEEE Symposium on Security and Privacy (SP), pp. 315–334. IEEE, San Francisco, CA, May 2018. https://doi.org/10.1109/SP.2018.00020. https://ieeexplore.ieee.org/document/8418611/
20. Chaidos, P., Kiayias, A.: Mithril: Stake-based threshold multisignatures. Cryptology ePrint Archive (2021)
21. Chow, S.S., Ma, J.P., Yuen, T.H.: Scored anonymous credentials. In: International Conference on Applied Cryptography and Network Security. pp. 484–515. Springer (2023)
22. Das, S., Camacho, P., Xiang, Z., Nieto, J., Bunz, B., Ren, L.: Threshold signatures from inner product argument: Succinct, weighted, and multi-threshold. Cryptology ePrint Archive (2023)
23. Daza, V., Ràfols, C., Zacharakis, A.: Updateable inner product argument with logarithmic verifier and applications. In: Kiayias, A., Kohlweiss, M., Wallden, P., Zikas, V. (eds.) PKC 2020. LNCS, vol. 12110, pp. 527–557. Springer, Cham (2020). https://doi.org/10.1007/978-3-030-45374-9_18
24. El Kaafarani, A., Katsumata, S., Solomon, R.: Anonymous reputation systems achieving full dynamicity from lattices. In: Meiklejohn, S., Sako, K. (eds.) FC 2018. LNCS, vol. 10957, pp. 388–406. Springer, Heidelberg (2018). https://doi.org/10.1007/978-3-662-58387-6_21
25. Fiat, A., Shamir, A.: How to prove yourself: practical solutions to identification and signature problems. In: Odlyzko, A.M. (ed.) CRYPTO 1986. LNCS, vol. 263, pp. 186–194. Springer, Heidelberg (1987). https://doi.org/10.1007/3-540-47721-7_12
26. Fuchsbauer, G., Kiltz, E., Loss, J.: The algebraic group model and its applications. In: Shacham, H., Boldyreva, A. (eds.) CRYPTO 2018. LNCS, vol. 10992, pp. 33–62. Springer, Cham (2018). https://doi.org/10.1007/978-3-319-96881-0_2
27. Garg, S., Jain, A., Mukherjee, P., Sinha, R., Wang, M., Zhang, Y.: hints: Threshold signatures with silent setup. Cryptology ePrint Archive (2023)

28. Kiayias, A., Osmanoglu, M., Tang, Q.: Graded signatures. In: Lopez, J., Mitchell, C.J. (eds.) ISC 2015. LNCS, vol. 9290, pp. 61–80. Springer, Cham (2015). https://doi.org/10.1007/978-3-319-23318-5_4
29. Lai, R.W.F., Tai, R.K.H., Wong, H.W.H., Chow, S.S.M.: Multi-key homomorphic signatures unforgeable under insider corruption. In: Peyrin, T., Galbraith, S. (eds.) ASIACRYPT 2018. LNCS, vol. 11273, pp. 465–492. Springer, Cham (2018). https://doi.org/10.1007/978-3-030-03329-3_16
30. Lee, J.: Dory: efficient, transparent arguments for generalised inner products and polynomial commitments. In: Nissim, K., Waters, B. (eds.) TCC 2021. LNCS, vol. 13043, pp. 1–34. Springer, Cham (2021). https://doi.org/10.1007/978-3-030-90453-1_1
31. Liu, J.K., Wei, V.K., Wong, D.S.: Linkable spontaneous anonymous group signature for ad hoc groups. In: Wang, H., Pieprzyk, J., Varadharajan, V. (eds.) ACISP 2004. LNCS, vol. 3108, pp. 325–335. Springer, Heidelberg (2004). https://doi.org/10.1007/978-3-540-27800-9_28
32. Maji, H.K., Prabhakaran, M., Rosulek, M.: Attribute-based signatures. In: Kiayias, A. (ed.) CT-RSA 2011. LNCS, vol. 6558, pp. 376–392. Springer, Heidelberg (2011). https://doi.org/10.1007/978-3-642-19074-2_24
33. Micali, S., Reyzin, L., Vlachos, G., Wahby, R.S., Zeldovich, N.: Compact certificates of collective knowledge. In: 2021 IEEE Symposium on Security and Privacy (SP), pp. 626–641. IEEE (2021)
34. Ristenpart, T., Yilek, S.: The Power of Proofs-of-Possession: Securing Multiparty Signatures against Rogue-Key Attacks. In: Naor, M. (ed.) EUROCRYPT 2007. LNCS, vol. 4515, pp. 228–245. Springer, Heidelberg (2007). https://doi.org/10.1007/978-3-540-72540-4_13
35. Rivest, R.L., Shamir, A., Tauman, Y.: How to leak a secret: theory and applications of ring signatures. Essays Memory Shimon Even **3895**, 164–186 (2006)
36. Schnorr, C.P.: Efficient identification and signatures for smart cards. In: Brassard, G. (ed.) CRYPTO 1989. LNCS, vol. 435, pp. 239–252. Springer, New York (1990). https://doi.org/10.1007/0-387-34805-0_22
37. Shoup, V.: Practical threshold signatures. In: Preneel, B. (ed.) EUROCRYPT 2000. LNCS, vol. 1807, pp. 207–220. Springer, Heidelberg (2000). https://doi.org/10.1007/3-540-45539-6_15
38. Zhandry, M.: To label, or not to label (in generic groups). In: Advances in Cryptology-CRYPTO 2022: 42nd Annual International Cryptology Conference, CRYPTO 2022, Santa Barbara, CA, USA, August 15–18, 2022, Proceedings, Part III, pp. 66–96. Springer, Cham (2022). https://doi.org/10.1007/978-3-031-15982-4_3

Bicameral and Auditably Private Signatures

Khoa Nguyen[1], Partha Sarathi Roy[1], Willy Susilo[1], and Yanhong Xu[2(✉)]

[1] Institute of Cybersecurity and Cryptology, School of Computing and Information Technology, University of Wollongong, Northfields Avenue, Wollongong, NSW 2522, Australia
{khoa,partha,wsusilo}@uow.edu.au

[2] School of Electronic Information and Electrical Engineering, Shanghai Jiao Tong University, 800 Dongchuan Road, Shanghai 200240, China
yanhong.xu@sjtu.edu.cn

Abstract. This paper introduces Bicameral and Auditably Private Signatures (BAPS) – a new privacy-preserving signature system with several novel features. In a BAPS system, given a certified attribute $\mathbf{x}$ and a certified policy P, a signer can issue a publicly verifiable signature Σ on a message m as long as $(m, \mathbf{x})$ satisfies P. A noteworthy characteristic of BAPS is that both attribute $\mathbf{x}$ and policy P are kept hidden from the verifier, yet the latter is convinced that these objects were certified by an attribute-issuing authority and a policy-issuing authority, respectively. By considering bicameral certification authorities and requiring privacy for both attributes and policies, BAPS generalizes the spirit of existing advanced signature primitives with fine-grained controls on signing capabilities (e.g., attribute-based signatures, predicate signatures, policy-based signatures). Furthermore, BAPS provides an appealing feature named auditable privacy, allowing the signer of Σ to verifiably disclose various pieces of partial information about P and $\mathbf{x}$ when asked by auditor(s)/court(s) at later times. Auditable privacy is intrinsically different from and can be complementary to the notion of accountable privacy traditionally incorporated in traceable anonymous systems such as group signatures. Equipped with these distinguished features, BAPS can potentially address interesting application scenarios for which existing primitives do not offer a direct solution.

We provide rigorous security definitions for BAPS, following a "sim-ext" approach. We then demonstrate a generic construction based on commonly used cryptographic building blocks, which employs a sign-then-commit-then-prove design. Finally, we present a concrete instantiation of BAPS, that is proven secure in the random oracle model under lattice assumptions. The scheme can handle arbitrary policies represented by polynomial-size Boolean circuits and can address quadratic disclosing functions. In the construction process, we develop a new technical building block that could be of independent interest: a zero-knowledge argument system allowing to prove the satisfiability of a certified-and-hidden Boolean circuit on certified-and-committed inputs.

J. Guo and R. Steinfeld (Eds.): ASIACRYPT 2023, LNCS 14439, pp. 313–347, 2023.
https://doi.org/10.1007/978-981-99-8724-5_10

Keywords: new primitive · signatures · bicamerality · auditable privacy · fine-grained information disclosure · zero-knowledge for hidden circuits

1 Introduction

A prominent line of privacy-preserving cryptography research is dedicated to the development of advanced multi-user signature systems with fine-grained controls over the signability of messages. Those controls are often based on authorities' policies, and/or users' attributes. Examples of these advanced systems include attribute-based signatures (ABS) [37], policy-based signatures (PBS) [2], functional signatures (FS) [8], predicate signatures (PS) [1] and multimodal private signatures (MPS) [39]. In ABS, a user with a certified-and-private attribute $\mathbf{x}$ can sign *any* message with respect to a *public* policy P if $P(\mathbf{x}) = 1$. PS offers a setting dual to ABS, where policies are certified-and-private while attributes are public. In PBS and FS: (i) policies/functions are also certified-and-private; (ii) one can sign messages satisfying some policy or in the range of some function; yet (iii) the notion of attributes is not considered. MPS utilizes both policies and attributes, but policies have to be public. All these systems share a common feature: each of them employs a single certification authority: either an attribute-issuing authority as in ABS/MPS, or a policy-issuing authority as in PBS/FS/PS. Furthermore, the question of simultaneously protecting the privacy of both policies and attributes was not considered.

Another active body of work in privacy-preserving signatures focuses on developing methods for realizing signers' accountability. Let us name that desirable feature accountable privacy. Among the earliest and most well-known accountably private systems are group signatures [11], in which a designated authority can trace the signer of any valid signature. Subsequent works have refined the tracing function in various directions: "who can trace" [26,43], "whether to trace" [27,45], "when to trace" [9,19], and more recently, "what can be traced" [32,39]. Nevertheless, all these systems share a common characteristic: the signer has no control over which private information can be learned by others (either the public or the tracing authorities) *after* outputting signatures.

MOTIVATIONS. This work aims to address the limitations of the advanced signature primitives mentioned above. Let us start with several motivating examples.

Consider a conference that implements a double-blind reviewing process and that allows authors to declare Conflicts of Interest (CoI) with reviewers according to some certified policies. For instance, the IACR has different policies to determine CoI[1], that can be used for IACR conferences. While such a CoI declaration system seems to work well over the years, there has not been implemented any privacy-preserving mechanism:

(i) For preventing false declarations by dishonest authors (who could attempt to avoid having their papers reviewed by some non-conflicting reviewers);

[1] https://www.iacr.org/docs/conflicts.pdf.

(ii) For the author to provide more information on a declared CoI, should the need arise at a later point while retaining the author's privacy.

Let us attempt to address the issue (i) by employing ABS/MPS for CoI declarations. Then, while authors' attributes (e.g., lists of advisors, advisees, recent affiliations, recent co-authors, and family members) are protected, the underlying policies are not. It could seriously violate authors' privacy, e.g., the disclosure of an advisor-advisee relationship could likely reveal side-channel information about the author. On the other hand, if one employs PBS/FS/PS, then the policies can be kept private, but the attributes are not protected.

Let us also try to address the issue (ii) by employing a group-signature-like system. In this case, the traditional method is to force the author to encrypt the relevant attributes, so that an authority can recover via decryption. The problem here is the encrypted attributes can already be learned by the authority at the submission time, regardless of whether there will be a need to justify the declared CoIs during the reviewing process.

We can observe that existing systems cannot offer satisfactory solutions because they do not simultaneously protect policies and attributes, and the notion of accountable privacy typically requires some escrow of private information. This inspires us to investigate a new privacy-preserving signature primitive that overcomes these limitations. How about the following arrangements?

Assume that the policies are publicly certified by some authority (e.g., the IACR). Assume further that authors have their attributes certified by some other authority. Then, when authors submit a paper, they can check whether the paper has a CoI with a given reviewer and generate a publicly verifiable signature if that is the case. Here, if the signature does not reveal any information about the underlying policy and attribute, then we have a solution for issue (i).

Next, suppose that the PC Chair wants to know some information about the circumstances of a given CoI. Depending on the context, the required information could be about which policy was activated, the list of advisees, or a recent affiliation of the author. Here, a mechanism allowing the disclosure of the exact piece of information requested by the Chair would help resolve the issue (ii).

Let us consider a further example. Suppose an author would like to apply for a visa so that they can travel to the conference. In the application process, the author submits their certified attributes (which could include financial data, criminal records, health examinations, travel records, etc.) and the associated certificates to the visa department. Suppose that the latter has several confidential policies for visa acceptance/rejection, which are certified by some higher authority. Now, assume that there is some concern about the transparency of the decision-making process. In this situation, the privacy-preserving system we have just discussed can allow the visa department to verifiably disclose to a judge certain partial information about the underlying policy and attribute, e.g., whether the policy considers the applicant's race, or the criminal records of the applicant while retaining the privacy of non-disclosed information.

More generally, many decisions regarding crucial issues, such as welfare and financial aid, employment offers, scholarship/citizenship grants, and tax audits, are taken based on organizational policies that should not be known by outsiders.

In these scenarios, the policies could be certified by some authority A, while the users' attributes could be certified by some other authority B. To show that a correct decision has been made [28], the decision-makers would need a mechanism allowing them to sign some message m and demonstrate that a private attribute $\mathbf{x}$ certified by B does satisfy a private policy P certified by A. Furthermore, for auditability purposes, it would be highly desirable if the system also allows the decision-makers to verifiably disclose the precise pieces of information about $\mathbf{x}$ and P requested by the auditors.

OUR CONTRIBUTIONS. We introduce "Bicameral and Auditably Private Signatures" (BAPS) as a new privacy-preserving signature primitive aiming to address (i) the problem of simultaneously protecting policies and attributes and (ii) the problem of secure disclosures of private information after signing. Let us first highlight several key features of BAPS.

Bicamerality. The system is "bicameral" in the sense that it involves two certification authorities, namely, attribute-issuing and policy-issuing ones, that are responsible for certifying users' attributes and organizations' policies, respectively. As discussed above, having two separate certification authorities is a commonly seen situation in practice.

More concretely, in a BAPS system, the attribute-issuing authority, given its master secret key $\mathsf{msk}_{\mathsf{X}}$, can issue a signing key $\mathsf{sk}_{\mathbf{x}}$ for attribute $\mathbf{x}$. Similarly, the policy-issuing authority can use its master secret key $\mathsf{msk}_{\mathsf{P}}$ to generate a certificate Cert_P for policy P. Note that, although the certification procedures of $\mathbf{x}$ and P are analogous, the treatments of "signing key" $\mathsf{sk}_{\mathbf{x}}$ and "certificate" Cert_P could be largely different in practice. The former typically should be kept private, unless its owner would like to have some other party to sign on their behalf. The latter normally can be made publicly available, e.g., in a list $\{(P_i, \mathsf{Cert}_{P_i})\}_i$ on an organization's website, except when the policies of the organization must be kept confidential. In our example about CoI declarations, we consider private $(\mathbf{x}, \mathsf{sk}_{\mathbf{x}})$ and public $\{(P_i, \mathsf{Cert}_{P_i})\}_i$. Meanwhile, the example with visa applications assumes that the applicant submits their credentials $(\mathbf{x}, \mathsf{sk}_{\mathbf{x}})$ to the visa department – which keeps their policies private. In any application scenario, the signer needs to know both pairs $(\mathbf{x}, \mathsf{sk}_{\mathbf{x}})$ and (P, Cert_P).

Signability and Privacy. To sign a message m, in addition to the pairs $(\mathbf{x}, \mathsf{sk}_{\mathbf{x}})$ and (P, Cert_P), the signer needs to possess a witness w such that $P(m, \mathbf{x}, w) = 1$. Here, similar to [2,32,39], witness w can be viewed as a piece of context-dependent information which intuitively serves as evidence why m is signable with respect to $\mathbf{x}$ and P. Note that our notion of "signability" is more general and does capture that of attribute-based signatures [37] (where P takes only attribute $\mathbf{x}$ as its sole input) and policy-based signatures [2,12] (where users' attributes are not considered in the syntax and P depends on (m, w) only).

If signing is successful, the signer obtains a signature Σ that is publicly verifiable. In addition, the signer stores a private clue c associated with (m, Σ), which later can be utilized for auditing purposes – should the need arise.

We demand a strong privacy property for BAPS: a valid message-signature pair (m, Σ) must not leak any information about the underlying policy P and attribute $\mathbf{x}$ (apart from the fact that $P(m, \mathbf{x}, w) = 1$ for some w). This should hold even if both authorities are fully corrupted.

Disclosures and Auditable Privacy. When asked to disclose certain partial information of P and/or $\mathbf{x}$ according to a disclosing function F (which is chosen by a court or an auditor among a public list of admitted functions), the signer of a pair (m, Σ) uses the associated clue c to generate a publicly verifiable testimony-attestation pair (t, a). Here, the attestation intuitively demonstrates that the value of the testimony is exactly determined as $t = F(P, x)$, where $(P, \mathbf{x})$ is precisely the policy-attribute pair underlying the message-signature pair (m, Σ). Such a disclosure process can be done multiple times with respect to different disclosing functions.

Here, we demand a noteworthy property for BAPS: auditable privacy. It says that no additional information about P or $\mathbf{x}$ can be learned from the pair (t, a) beyond the fact that $F(P, \mathbf{x}) = t$. In other words, it guarantees the "residual" privacy of P and $\mathbf{x}$ after (potentially many) disclosures of their partial information. It should hold against corrupted authorities and can even be defined in the strong, statistical sense.

As a summary, by considering bicameral authorities and requiring privacy for both attributes and policies, BAPS generalizes the spirit of existing advanced signature primitives with fine-grained controls on signing capabilities. Moreover, the property of auditable privacy is sharply different from and can be complementary to the notion of accountable privacy in group signatures [11] and variants [26,27,32,39,43,45], which demands that each signature contains a fixed piece of signer's information that can be recovered by a designated party. Equipped with these distinguished features, BAPS can potentially address application scenarios for which existing primitives do not offer a direct solution.

Formalizing Security Requirements for BAPS. Let us next discuss our formalizations of security for BAPS, which is a non-trivial process on its own.

We first tried to define privacy and auditable privacy for BAPS using an indistinguishability-based approach. However, with that approach, we could not manage to quantify the amount of information leaked by the disclosure processes. In fact, we need to ensure that no extra information about P and $\mathbf{x}$ is leaked, apart from the pieces of information carried by the testimonies outputted by the signer. We then observe that this requirement is quite similar to those in the contexts of zero-knowledge proofs [20], and functional encryption [5], where a simulation-based approach has been employed and proven successful. We thus adopt such an approach, which allows us to formalize privacy and auditable privacy via a unified notion of simulatability. It essentially says that the setup, signing, and disclosing processes of BAPS can be efficiently simulated in a way (statistically) indistinguishable from the real algorithms.

We next aim at formalizing other expected security properties of BAPS. On the one hand, we would like to ensure that, even if both authorities are corrupted, any valid signature Σ on any message m should be associated with some policy P, some attribute $\mathbf{x}$ and some witness w such that $P(m, \mathbf{x}, w) = 1$. Also, if $\mathsf{Judge}(m, \Sigma, F, t, a) = 1$, then it should hold that $t = F(P, \mathbf{x})$.

On the other hand, we also need to protect the security of each of the authorities, which can be divided into two orthogonal properties. Specifically, it should be infeasible to generate any valid signature, if

- One does not possess a legitimate signing key $\mathsf{sk}_{\mathbf{x}}$ for some attribute $\mathbf{x}$, even if one corrupted the policy-issuing authority;
- One does not possess a legitimate certificate Cert_P for some policy P, even if one corrupted the attribute-issuing authority.

The major technical challenge in formalizing these expected security properties is that BAPS does not readily provide a rigorous mechanism to determine whether a valid message-signature pair (m, Σ) is actually associated with some P, $\mathbf{x}$ and w such that $P(m, \mathbf{x}, w) = 1$. Therefore, for definitional purposes, we would need to introduce an extractable mode that allows us to extract additional information from (m, Σ) so that we can meaningfully explain whether and how a violation of security has occurred. As a result, we come up with a notion called intractability, which nicely captures and unifies the said properties. This is partially inspired by the "sim-ext" spirit [10], which was also employed in the context of PBS [2].

We would like to remark that our formalizations of BAPS yield a proper generalization of the PBS primitive [2]. Indeed, to obtain a PBS, one can simply remove from a BAPS the treatments of attributes and attribute-issuing authority, as well as the disclosure process. Simulatability and extractability of the resulting PBS, as defined by Bellare and Fuchsbauer [2], directly follow from those of the original BAPS. Recall that PBS is already an exceedingly powerful primitive on its own: it was shown to imply group signatures [3], attribute-based signatures [37], simulation-sound extractable NIZKs [21], and others.

Generic Constructions. Our next step is to demonstrate the feasibility of constructing secure BAPS systems from standard assumptions. Specifically, we present a generic construction that employs several commonly used cryptographic building blocks: two signature schemes, a commitment scheme, and two non-interactive zero-knowledge (NIZK) argument systems for some NP-relations. The correctness and security properties of the construction directly follow from those of the employed building blocks.

On the one hand, the two signature systems and the two NIZK systems are used in a relatively standard manner. The former systems are governed by the two authorities and are used for issuing attribute keys and policy certificates. The latter systems are utilized when generating and verifying BAPS signatures and attestations. On the other hand, our implementation of the commitment scheme is worth highlighting. We commit to policy P and attribute $\mathbf{x}$ as com_P and $\mathsf{com}_{\mathbf{x}}$, respectively, and treat them as *a bridge connecting the signing and disclosing phases.* The binding of the commitment scheme ensures that the pair $(P, \mathbf{x})$ involved in the disclosure(s) of a BAPS signature Σ is the same as the pair used for generating Σ. Furthermore, its hiding property guarantees that no additional information about $(P, \mathbf{x})$ can be learned from com_P and $\mathsf{com}_{\mathbf{x}}$. Note that in existing group-signature-like systems, a public-key encryption scheme is typically used to disclose some private information of the signer to a designated opening authority. Due to the existence of a decryption key (which is owned by the opening authority, and recoverable by an unbounded adversary), the accountable privacy property in these systems is only achieved in the computational sense. Here, in contrast, auditable privacy in the statistical sense is achievable if the commitment is statistically hiding.

In more detail, in the construction, a signature Σ on message m contains the commitments com_P and $\mathsf{com}_{\mathbf{x}}$ as well as a NIZK argument Π demonstrating that the committed values $P, \mathbf{x}$ were properly certified by the authorities, and that $P(m, \mathbf{x}, w) = 1$ for some witness w known by the signer. Verification of Σ is simply the verification of Π. The clue – which will be used for later disclosures – consists of $\mathbf{x}$, P, and the two randomnesses.

When asked to disclose certain partial information of $\mathbf{x}$ and/or P according to a disclosing function F, the signer of a message-signature pair (m, Σ), who possesses the corresponding clue, first computes $t = F(P, \mathbf{x})$ and then proves that t is well-formed w.r.t. the values P and $\mathbf{x}$ committed in the signature.

We remark that our design approach, which we term *sign-then-commit-then-prove*, effectively differs from the sign-then-encrypt-then-prove paradigm traditionally used for achieving accountable privacy in group-signature-like systems. The advantage of our approach is that the signer can preserve full privacy of the committed values (especially if the underlying commitment scheme is statistically hiding) while maintaining the capability of proving additional relations about the committed values at later times.

Our construction can serve as a proof of concept for designing secure BAPS systems based on standard assumptions in a modular manner. In particular, it can be realized in the standard model from pairings and from lattices, using the techniques for obtaining NIZKs for NP by Groth-Ostrovsky-Sahai [22] and by Peikert-Shiehian [41] (in conjunction with a lattice-based compiler by Libert et al. [31]), respectively.

A Lattice-Based Instantiation for Arbitrary Policies. Although via techniques of [31,41] it is feasible to instantiate BAPS in the standard model under lattice-based (and hence, quantum-safe) assumptions, such construction would expectedly be extremely inefficient. Our goal here is to build a concrete lattice-based BAPS that has better efficiency than the generic approach, and that can handle expressive classes of policies, e.g., polynomial-size Boolean circuits. We stress that the lattice-based BAPS scheme we provide in this paper merely serves as an illustration of how to concretely instantiate the aforementioned generic construction. It is not practical, and moreover, we do not view it as the main contribution of the paper.

At a high level, our lattice-based BAPS scheme follows the sign-then-commit-then-prove design approach of the generic construction discussed above. However, when it comes to middle-level techniques, we do introduce several novel aspects regarding the evaluation of policies in zero-knowledge and the instantiation of disclosing functions via multivariate quadratic functions.

More specifically, for both authorities, we implement the Ducas-Micciancio signature [13], which has a short public key and has a companion zero-knowledge argument of a valid message-signature pair [35]. As for commitment schemes, we employ several adaptations of the ideal-lattice-based scheme by Kawachi, Tanaka and Xagawa [25], which are used not only to commit to P and $\mathbf{x}$, but also various different objects appearing in the scheme execution. Last but not least, we need expressive zero-knowledge argument systems that can handle relatively sophisticated statements, in particular, those that capture the satisfiability of a Boolean circuit whose description is hidden, yet certified via the Ducas-Micciancio signature. To this end, we adopt a framework proposed in [30] for interactive Stern-like argument systems [44] and employ several dedicated techniques for handling the required relations. We remark that our choice of Stern-like protocols as the ZK tools has its own advantages and disadvantages. On the upside, these tools work smoothly with the statements to be proven. First, they can be directly applied to interrelated equations involving two moduli $q_1 = 2$ (representing the evaluation processes of Boolean circuits as well as disclosing functions) and $q_2 = 3^k$ for some positive integer k (representing relations capturing the Ducas-Micciancio signature verification process). Second, Stern-like protocols normally provide statistical ZK, which is crucial in attaining the desirable feature of statistical privacy for the resulting lattice-based BAPS scheme. Therefore, these zero-knowledge protocols are quite suitable for our illustration purpose. On the downside, because of the need to repeat Stern-like protocols many times to make their soundness errors negligibly small, these tools are much less efficient than the state-of-the-art Schnorr-like ZK proof/argument systems, such as [6,7,14–16,23,36,46]. While we have not been able to provide an efficient lattice-based BAPS (see more elaborations in the discussions on open questions at the end of this section), we nevertheless expect that, in the near future, practically usable lattice-based BAPS systems, if any, would likely be developed based on these state-of-the-art tools.

The major technical challenge of the construction is to prove in zero-knowledge the satisfiability of a certified-and-hidden Boolean circuit P on some input $(m, \mathbf{x}, w)$, where $\mathbf{x}$ is also certified and hidden.

Evaluating Circuits in ZK with "Imaginary Buckets". To the best of our knowledge, there has not been much work related to proving circuit satisfiability where both the circuit and input are certified and private. Ling et al. [33] proposed a code-based protocol for the restricted class of symmetric Boolean functions. Libert et al. [29] suggested a lattice-based protocol for functions in $\mathsf{NC1}$, represented by branching programs. In Libert et al.'s protocol, the prover commits to the inputs, builds a Merkle hash tree on top of the commitments, and fetches the inputs to the branching program by following the tree paths corresponding to the program's binary representation. We observe that the ideas from [29] might potentially be extended to handle Boolean circuits. However, the expected complexity of each tree-based retrieval step would be $\mathcal{O}(\log(K+N) \cdot \lambda \cdot \log \lambda)$, where λ is the security parameter, K is the bit-size of the inputs and N is the circuit size.

We, therefore, take a conceptually different approach with expected complexity $\mathcal{O}(\sqrt{K+N} + \lambda \cdot \log \lambda)$. This would yield some valuable improvement when $K+N$ is a small polynomial in λ, e.g., $K+N = o(\lambda^3)$.

Consider a circuit P whose topology is determined by two functions $g, h : [0, N-1] \to [0, K+N-2]$. Namely, if the inputs to P are $s_0, s_1, \ldots, s_{K-1}$ and the N gate outputs are ordered as $s_K, \ldots, s_{K+N-1}$, then we have

$$s_{K+i} = s_{g(i)} \text{ NAND } s_{h(i)}, \ \forall i = 0, \ldots, N-1.$$

At each step in the circuit evaluation process, we need to fetch the values of $s_{g(i)}$ and $s_{h(i)}$. The problem is that not only these values but also both the indices $g(i)$ and $h(i)$ are committed. Hence, we would need a mechanism to retrieve these values properly. Our approach employs a "bucket-based" retrieval process, the high-level ideas of which are as follows.

We divide the bits of $s_0, \ldots, s_{K+N-2}$ into ρ buckets $\mathbf{s}_0, \ldots, \mathbf{s}_{\rho-1}$, each of which is ρ-bit long. (Here, for simplicity, we assume $K+N-1 = \rho^2$.) Next, we commit to each bucket, obtaining ρ commitments: $\mathsf{com}_0, \ldots, \mathsf{com}_{\rho-1}$. To fetch the correct inputs to the gates, we will examine the binary representations of g, h, and follow them to search for the buckets where the correct inputs are committed, then identify the exact locations of the inputs within the found buckets. Such a process only requires $\mathcal{O}(\rho)$ steps, and thus, yields complexity $\mathcal{O}(\sqrt{K+N})$. We provide more detailed explanations in Sect. 4.

Handling quadratic disclosing functions. For disclosures, we consider multivariate quadratic functions. In this setting, the testimony $t = F(P, \mathbf{x})$ is a multidimensional vector, each coordinate of which has the form

$$\sum_{i,j \in [1,\bar{k}]} \alpha_{i,j} \cdot (b_i \cdot b_j) + \sum_{\ell \in [1,\bar{k}]} \beta_\ell \cdot b_\ell \bmod 2,$$

where $\alpha_{i,j}$'s, β_ℓ's are public bits and b_i's the bits determining policy P and attribute $\mathbf{x}$. This definition is thus quite general and captures arbitrary linear and quadratic relations with respect to the bits of $(P, \mathbf{x})$. By setting the coefficients appropriately, one indeed can enforce the disclosures of any bits of $(P, \mathbf{x})$, or any bit-products, or any linear and/or quadratic combinations of the bits.

To prove the well-formedness of $t = F(P, \mathbf{x})$, we will need to demonstrate in zero-knowledge the correct evaluations of many equations of the above form. This sub-task also requires several non-trivial steps, since the bits b_i's are involved not only in these linear and quadratic relations but also simultaneously satisfy various other relations, e.g., they were hashed, signed, and committed.

Open Questions. As the first work that introduces BAPS, we do not (and cannot) attempt to address all the issues around this new primitive. We pay more attention to laying the foundations for BAPS, and we view the problem of constructing a scheme with practical efficiency and/or with additional features as fascinating open questions for future investigations. In the following, we will briefly discuss several questions that we are particularly interested in.

- **Developing practically usable lattice-based BAPS schemes.** While the state-of-the-art ZK proof/argument systems from lattice assumptions and for lattice relations, such as [6,14–16,23,36], have already come close to practicality, the problem of applying these protocols in an efficiency-preserving manner to mixed relations like "correct evaluation of a certified-and-hidden Boolean circuit on a certified-and-hidden input" (which are helpful for developing BAPS) is still less well-studied. Additionally, these protocols typically only satisfy computational ZK, which could be an obstacle if one insists on achieving statistically private BAPS. Nevertheless, we do hope that some reasonably practical lattice-based BAPS schemes can be developed based on these tools in the near future, especially if one only targets computational privacy and would like to consider only some restricted classes of policies, e.g., those defined by inner-product-like relations.
- **Designing efficient BAPS without NIZK.** As we have discussed, a major barrier to constructing efficient BAPS systems is the need for NIZK systems that can handle relatively sophisticated statements. While the use of NIZKs seems unavoidable, as a BAPS satisfying our stringent security definitions does imply a PBS [2] – which in turn implies NIZK, it might be possible to circumvent this barrier by considering some relaxed security requirements for BAPS. A similar line of research was conducted with respect to group signatures [24].
- **BAPS with additional functionalities.** One interesting question along this line of research is to enable efficient user revocations, preventing revoked users from generating valid signatures while ensuring small computation/communication overheads for non-revoked users. Another appealing question is to conceptualize and realize systems that simultaneously offer both accountable privacy and auditable privacy.

ORGANIZATION. The rest of the paper is organized as follows. In Sect. 2, we present our definitions of BAPS, describe its syntax, and formalize its security requirements. Section 3 then provides a generic construction of BAPS satisfying our model, based on commonly used cryptographic building blocks. In Sect. 4, we describe our lattice-based construction of BAPS. Due to space restriction, the detailed descriptions of the zero-knowledge protocols used in our lattice-based BAPS scheme and some security analyses are deferred to the full version [40].

2 Bicameral and Auditably Private Signatures

Any Bicameral and Auditably Private Signature (BAPS) system is associated with a message space $\mathcal{M}$, an attribute space $\mathcal{X}$, a witness space $\mathcal{W}$, a disclosing space $\mathcal{DS}$, a family $\mathcal{P} := \{P : \mathcal{M} \times \mathcal{X} \times \mathcal{W} \longrightarrow \{0,1\}\}$ of policies, and a family $\mathcal{F} := \{F : \mathcal{P} \times \mathcal{X} \rightarrow \mathcal{DS}\}$ of disclosing functions.

A BAPS system is set up by a trusted party, whose jobs include generating public parameters and creating secret keys for the bicameral authorities, namely, the attribute-issuing authority and the policy-issuing authority. Policies (of organizations) and attributes (of users) are authorized and added to the system by the corresponding authorities. A signer, given a certified attribute $\mathbf{x} \in \mathcal{X}$ and a certified policy $P \in \mathcal{P}$, can issue a publicly verifiable signature Σ on a message $m \in \mathcal{M}$ if the signer possesses a witness w such that $P(m, \mathbf{x}, w) = 1$. Here, similar to [2,32,39], witness w can be viewed as a context-dependent string which serves as evidence why m is signable with respect to $\mathbf{x}$ and P. In addition, the signer stores a private clue c associated with (m, Σ), which later can be utilized for auditing purposes – should the need arise.

When asked (e.g., by a court or an auditor) to disclose certain partial information of P and/or $\mathbf{x}$ according to a disclosing function $F \in \mathcal{F}$, the signer of a pair (m, Σ) uses the associated clue c to generate a publicly verifiable testimony-attestation pair (t, a). Here, the attestation intuitively demonstrates that the value of the testimony is exactly determined as $t = F(P, \mathbf{x}) \in \mathcal{DS}$, where $(P, \mathbf{x})$ is precisely the policy-attribute pair underlying the message-signature pair (m, Σ). Such a disclosure process can be done multiple times with respect to different disclosing functions in $\mathcal{F}$.

2.1 Syntax of BAPS

A BAPS system associated with $(\mathcal{M}, \mathcal{X}, \mathcal{W}, \mathcal{DS}, \mathcal{P}, \mathcal{F})$ is a tuple of polynomial-time algorithms $(\mathsf{Setup}, \mathsf{Attribute\text{-}Iss}, \mathsf{Policy\text{-}Iss}, \mathsf{Sign}, \mathsf{Verify}, \mathsf{Disclose}, \mathsf{Judge})$, defined as follows.

$\mathsf{Setup}(1^\lambda)$: On input a security parameter λ, it outputs $(\mathsf{PP}, \mathsf{msk_X}, \mathsf{msk_P})$, where:
- PP denotes the public parameters which include, among others, the descriptions of $\mathcal{M}, \mathcal{X}, \mathcal{W}, \mathcal{DS}, \mathcal{P}, \mathcal{F}$;
- $\mathsf{msk_X}$ is the master attribute key and $\mathsf{msk_P}$ is the master policy key.

All the subsequent algorithms take PP as an implicit input.

$\mathsf{Attribute\text{-}Iss}(\mathsf{msk_X}, \mathbf{x})$: The attribute-issuing algorithm takes as inputs the key $\mathsf{msk_X}$ and an attribute $\mathbf{x} \in \mathcal{X}$. It outputs a signing key $\mathsf{sk}_\mathbf{x}$ for $\mathbf{x}$.

$\mathsf{Policy\text{-}Iss}(\mathsf{msk_P}, P)$: The policy-issuing algorithm takes as inputs the key $\mathsf{msk_P}$ and a policy $P \in \mathcal{P}$. It outputs a certificate Cert_P for P.

$\mathsf{Sign}(\mathbf{x}, \mathsf{sk}_\mathbf{x}, P, \mathsf{Cert}_P, m, w)$: The signing algorithm takes as inputs a signing key $\mathsf{sk}_\mathbf{x}$ for an attribute $\mathbf{x}$, a certificate Cert_P for a policy P, a message $m \in \mathcal{M}$ and a witness w. It outputs either a signature Σ together with a clue c, or the symbol $\bot$ indicating failure.

$\mathsf{Verify}(m, \Sigma)$: On input a message-signature pair (m, Σ), the verification algorithm outputs 1 or 0, indicating the (in)validity of the signature Σ on m.

$\mathsf{Disclose}((m, \Sigma), c, F)$: On input a message-signature pair (m, Σ), a clue c and a disclosing function $F \in \mathcal{F}$, the disclosing algorithm outputs a testimony t together with an attestation a.

$\mathsf{Judge}((m, \Sigma), F, (t, a))$: On input a message-signature pair (m, Σ), a disclosing function F and a testimony-attestation pair (t, a), this judging algorithm outputs 1 or 0, indicating the (in)validity of the disclosure.

2.2 Correctness and Security of BAPS

CORRECTNESS. Intuitively, the correctness of BAPS guarantees that honestly generated message-signature pairs are accepted by Verify, that faithfully generated testimony-attestation pairs are accepted by Judge, and that the testimony associated with $F, P, \mathbf{x}$ must precisely be $t = F(P, x)$. Formally, a BAPS scheme is correct if for any $P \in \mathcal{P}$, $\mathbf{x} \in \mathcal{X}$, $m \in \mathcal{M}$ and $w \in \mathcal{W}$ such that $P(m, \mathbf{x}, w) = 1$, and for any $F \in \mathcal{F}$, it holds that

$$\Pr\left[\begin{array}{l|l} & (\mathsf{PP}, \mathsf{msk}_{\mathsf{X}}, \mathsf{msk}_{\mathsf{P}}) \leftarrow \mathsf{Setup}(1^\lambda), \\ \mathsf{Verify}(m, \Sigma) = 1, & \mathsf{sk}_{\mathbf{x}} \leftarrow \mathsf{Attribute\text{-}Iss}(\mathsf{msk}_{\mathsf{X}}, \mathbf{x}), \\ t = F(P, x), & \mathsf{Cert}_P \leftarrow \mathsf{Policy\text{-}Iss}(\mathsf{msk}_{\mathsf{P}}, P), \\ \mathsf{Judge}(m, \Sigma, F, t, a) = 1 & (\Sigma, c) \leftarrow \mathsf{Sign}(\mathbf{x}, \mathsf{sk}_{\mathbf{x}}, P, \mathsf{Cert}_P, m, w), \\ & (t, a) \leftarrow \mathsf{Disclose}((m, \Sigma), c, F) \end{array}\right] = 1 - \mathsf{negl}(\lambda).$$

SECURITY. We will first discuss the security features that any BAPS is expected to satisfy, and then present the formal definitions that capture these features.

We expect that a secure BAPS should provide the following guarantees.

- Justifiability of signatures: Any valid signature Σ on any message m should be associated with some policy P, some attribute $\mathbf{x}$ and some witness w such that $P(m, \mathbf{x}, w) = 1$. This must hold even if both authorities are corrupted.
- Necessity of possessing attribute keys: Without possessing a legitimate signing key $\mathsf{sk}_{\mathbf{x}}$ for some attribute $\mathbf{x}$, it should be infeasible to generate any valid signature. This property captures the security of the attribute-issuing authority, and it must hold even when the policy-issuing authority is corrupted.
- Necessity of possessing policy certificates: Without possessing a legitimate certificate Cert_P for some policy P, it would be infeasible to generate any valid signature. This property is orthogonal to the preceding one: it captures the security of the policy-issuing authority in the presence of a potentially corrupted attribute-issuing authority.
- Auditability: If $\mathsf{Judge}(m, \Sigma, F, t, a) = 1$, then it should hold that $t = F(P, \mathbf{x})$, where P and $\mathbf{x}$ are the policy and attribute underlying the message-signature pair (m, Σ). This property ensures the infeasibility of misleading disclosure results, and it must hold even if both authorities are corrupted.
- Privacy: This property guarantees that a valid message-signature pair (m, Σ) does not leak any information about the underlying policy P and attribute $\mathbf{x}$ (apart from the fact that $P(m, \mathbf{x}, w) = 1$ for some w). Privacy should hold when both authorities are corrupted. Moreover, it can even be defined in the statistical sense (similar to ring signatures [4] and attribute-based signatures [37]).
- Auditable Privacy: This property says that no additional information about P or $\mathbf{x}$ can be learned from the disclosure result (t, a) beyond the fact that $F(P, \mathbf{x}) = t$. In other words, it guarantees the "residual" privacy of P and $\mathbf{x}$ after (potentially many) disclosures of their partial information. It should hold against corrupted authorities and can even be defined in the strong, statistical sense.

While other security features are somewhat reminiscent of similar properties in existing privacy-preserving signature primitives [8,11,26,27,32,39,42,43,45], auditable privacy is a distinguished property of BAPS. It allows the signer to flexibly and securely disclose selected pieces of private information when asked by different auditors. This property is sharply different from the notion of accountable privacy in group signatures [11] and variants [26,27,32,39,43,45], which demands that each signature contains a fixed piece of information about the signer that can be recovered by a designated party.

How to formalize Privacy and Auditable Privacy? In our first attempt to define privacy and auditable privacy for BAPS, we follow an indistinguishability-based approach. Specifically, the adversary provides a message m, two policies P_0, P_1, two attributes $\mathbf{x}_0, \mathbf{x}_1$, and two corresponding witnesses w_0, w_1 such that m is signable under both pairs $(P_0, \mathbf{x}_0, w_0)$ and $(P_1, \mathbf{x}_1, w_1)$, i.e., $P_0(m, \mathbf{x}_0, w_0) = 1$ and $P_1(m, \mathbf{x}_1, w_1) = 1$. The challenger then chooses a random bit b and generates a challenge signature Σ^* on m using $(P_b, \mathbf{x}_b, w_b, \mathsf{Cert}_{P_b}, \mathsf{sk}_{\mathbf{x}_b})$. Ideally, we would like to consider a strong adversary who can fully corrupt both authorities and can adaptively query the disclosing oracle with respect to the challenge message-signature pair (m, Σ^*) and any disclosing function F of its choice. However, if the adversary queries the disclosing algorithm for some F such that $F(P_0, \mathbf{x}_0) \neq F(P_1, \mathbf{x}_1)$, then it can easily guess the bit b. Hence, for the definition to be satisfiable, we must restrict the adversary's choice of $(P_0, \mathbf{x}_0, w_0)$ and $(P_1, \mathbf{x}_1, w_1)$ and require that $F(P_0, \mathbf{x}_0) = F(P_1, \mathbf{x}_1)$ for all F for which the adversary queries the disclosing algorithm.

Unfortunately, even with the above restriction, the indistinguishability-based approach might still be inadequate in capturing the expected notion of privacy. Suppose that the system only allows a single disclosing function, which is the identity function $F(P, \mathbf{x}) = (P, \mathbf{x})$. Then, to prevent the adversary from trivially winning, we must either demand that $(P_0, \mathbf{x}_0) = (P_1, \mathbf{x}_1)$ or totally prohibit disclosing queries with respect to the challenge message-signature pair.

We then take a step back and note that our major goal here is to ensure that, apart from the testimonies of the form $t = F(P, \mathbf{x})$, no additional knowledge about P and $\mathbf{x}$ is leaked. This requirement is quite similar to those in the contexts of zero-knowledge proofs [20], and functional encryption [5], where a simulation-based approach has been employed and widely accepted. We, therefore, adopt this approach, which allows us to formalize privacy and auditable privacy via a unified notion: simulatability.

Simulatability. We formalize this simulation-based notion by requiring the existence of three auxiliary algorithms SimSetup, SimSign, and SimDisclose.

$\mathsf{SimSetup}(1^\lambda)$: On input λ, this algorithm outputs public parameters PP, keys $\mathsf{msk}_\mathsf{X}, \mathsf{msk}_\mathsf{P}$ for two authorities, together with a trapdoor tr.

$\mathsf{SimSign}(\mathsf{tr}, m, P, \mathbf{x}, w)$: This algorithm takes as inputs the trapdoor tr, and a message m, a policy P, an attribute $\mathbf{x}$, and a witness w. If $P(m, \mathbf{x}, w) = 0$, it returns 0. Otherwise, it returns a simulated signature. Note that a signing key $\mathsf{sk}_\mathbf{x}$ or a certificate Cert_P is not needed here.

SimDisclose$(m, \Sigma, \mathsf{tr}, P, \mathbf{x}, F)$: This algorithm takes as inputs a valid message-signature pair (m, Σ), the trapdoor tr, a policy-attribute pair $(P, \mathbf{x})$, and a disclosing function F. It returns (t, a) as an output.

Intuitively, the simulatability of BAPS guarantees that the outputs of the above algorithms are indistinguishable from those of the real algorithms. This notion is modeled via experiment $\mathbf{Exp}^{\mathsf{sim}}_{\mathcal{A}}(\lambda)$ in Fig. 1 and is formally defined below.

$b \xleftarrow{\$} \{0,1\}$, $i \leftarrow 0$, $j \leftarrow 0$, $k \leftarrow 0$;
$(\mathsf{PP}^0, \mathsf{msk}^0_{\mathsf{X}}, \mathsf{msk}^0_{\mathsf{P}}, \mathsf{tr}) \leftarrow \mathsf{SimSetup}(1^\lambda)$; $(\mathsf{PP}^1, \mathsf{msk}^1_{\mathsf{X}}, \mathsf{msk}^1_{\mathsf{P}}) \leftarrow \mathsf{Setup}(1^\lambda)$;
$\mathsf{st} = (\mathsf{PP}^b, \mathsf{msk}^b_{\mathsf{X}}, \mathsf{msk}^b_{\mathsf{P}})$.
$b' \leftarrow \mathcal{A}^{\mathcal{O}^{\mathsf{sor}}_{\mathsf{PolicyKey}}, \mathcal{O}^{\mathsf{sor}}_{\mathsf{AttributeKey}}, \mathcal{O}^{\mathsf{sor}}_{\mathsf{Sign}}, \mathcal{O}^{\mathsf{sor}}_{\mathsf{Disclose}}}(\mathsf{st})$;
If $b = b'$, return 1; otherwise return 0.

$\mathcal{O}^{\mathsf{sor}}_{\mathsf{Sign}}(i^*, j^*, m, w)$
If $i^* \notin [1, i]$ or $j^* \notin [1, j]$, return $\perp$;
Let $P = L_{\mathcal{P}}[i^*][0]$ and $\mathbf{x} = L_{\mathcal{X}}[j^*][0]$;
If $P(m, \mathbf{x}, w) = 0$, return $\perp$;
$k \leftarrow k + 1$;
$\Sigma^{*0} \leftarrow \mathsf{SimSign}(\mathsf{tr}, m, P, \mathbf{x}, w)$;
Let $\mathsf{Cert}_P = L_{\mathcal{P}}[i^*][1]$ and $\mathsf{sk}_{\mathbf{x}} = L_{\mathcal{X}}[j^*][1]$;
$(\Sigma^{*1}, c^1) \leftarrow \mathsf{Sign}(\mathbf{x}, \mathsf{sk}_{\mathbf{x}}, P, \mathsf{Cert}_P, m, w)$;
$L_{\mathcal{S}}[k][0] = (P, \mathbf{x})$; $L_{\mathcal{S}}[k][1] = c^1$;
$L_{\mathcal{S}}[k][2] = (m, \Sigma^{*b})$;
Return Σ^{*b}.

$\mathcal{O}^{\mathsf{sor}}_{\mathsf{Disclose}}(m, \Sigma, F)$
Check if $\exists\, k^*$ such that $L_{\mathcal{S}}[k^*][2] = (m, \Sigma)$;
If k^* does not exist, return $\perp$;
Let $(P, \mathbf{x}) = L_{\mathcal{S}}[k^*][0]$; $c^1 = L_{\mathcal{S}}[k^*][1]$;
$(t^0, a^0) \leftarrow \mathsf{SimDisclose}(m, \Sigma, \mathsf{tr}, (P, \mathbf{x}), F)$;
$(t^1, a^1) \leftarrow \mathsf{Disclose}(m, \Sigma, c^1, F)$;
Return (t^b, a^b).

$\mathcal{O}^{\mathsf{sor}}_{\mathsf{PolicyKey}}(P)$
$i \leftarrow i + 1$;
$\mathsf{Cert}^0_P \leftarrow \mathsf{Policy\text{-}Iss}(\mathsf{msk}^0_{\mathsf{P}}, P)$;
$\mathsf{Cert}^1_P \leftarrow \mathsf{Policy\text{-}Iss}(\mathsf{msk}^1_{\mathsf{P}}, P)$;
$L_{\mathcal{P}}[i][0] = P$, $L_{\mathcal{P}}[i][1] = \mathsf{Cert}^1_P$;
Return Cert^b_P.

$\mathcal{O}^{\mathsf{sor}}_{\mathsf{AttributeKey}}(\mathbf{x})$
$j \leftarrow j + 1$;
$\mathsf{sk}^0_{\mathbf{x}} \leftarrow \mathsf{Attribute\text{-}Iss}(\mathsf{msk}^0_{\mathsf{X}}, \mathbf{x})$;
$\mathsf{sk}^1_{\mathbf{x}} \leftarrow \mathsf{Attribute\text{-}Iss}(\mathsf{msk}^1_{\mathsf{X}}, \mathbf{x})$;
$L_{\mathcal{X}}[j][0] = \mathbf{x}$, $L_{\mathcal{X}}[j][1] = \mathsf{sk}^1_{\mathbf{x}}$;
Return $\mathsf{sk}^b_{\mathbf{x}}$.

Fig. 1. Experiment $\mathbf{Exp}^{\mathsf{sim}}_{\mathcal{A}}(\lambda)$

Definition 1 (Simulatability). *A BAPS scheme is said to satisfy simulatability if the advantage of $\mathcal{A}$ involved in experiment $\mathbf{Exp}^{\mathsf{sim}}_{\mathcal{A}}(\lambda)$, defined as $\mathbf{Adv}^{\mathsf{sim}}_{\mathcal{A}}(\lambda) = |\Pr[\mathbf{Exp}^{\mathsf{sim}}_{\mathcal{A}}(\lambda) = 1] - 1/2|$, is $\mathsf{negl}(\lambda)$. We say that the BAPS scheme is computationally simulatable if the advantage of any PPT algorithm $\mathcal{A}$ is negligible in λ. It is statistically simulatable if the advantage of any algorithm $\mathcal{A}$ is negligible and perfectly simulatable if the advantage of any algorithm $\mathcal{A}$ is zero.*

We next aim at formalizing other expected security properties of BAPS, i.e., justifiability of signatures, auditability, necessity of possessing attribute keys, and policy certificates. This turns out to be a non-trivial task. The major reason is that the syntax of BAPS does not provide a rigorous mechanism to determine whether a valid message-signature pair (m, Σ) is actually associated with some P, $\mathbf{x}$ and w such that $P(m, \mathbf{x}, w) = 1$. Therefore, for definitional purposes, we would need to introduce some auxiliary procedure that allows us to extract additional information from (m, Σ), e.g., some P, some $\mathbf{x}$, and some w, so that we can meaningfully explain whether and how a violation of security has occurred. In addition, such extraction should be possible even in the simulated setting. Thus, we further assume the existence of algorithm Extract defined below.

$\mathsf{Extract}(\mathsf{tr}, m, \Sigma)$: Given the trapdoor tr and a valid message-signature pair (m, Σ), it returns a tuple $(P, \mathbf{x}, w) \in \mathcal{P} \times \mathcal{X} \times \mathcal{W}$.

Equipped with such an extractable mode, we are now ready to formalize the expected properties. For the sake of simpler terminology, we will consider the following three notions:

- Soundness ensures that the extracted tuple $(P, \mathbf{x}, w)$ satisfies $P(m, \mathbf{x}, w) = 1$ and $t = F(P, \mathbf{x})$, for any testimony t outputted by a disclosing process involving function F. Note that soundness captures both "justifiability of signatures" and "auditability".
- Unforgeability-I addresses the "necessity of possessing attribute keys" and aims to protect the attribute-issuing authority.
- Unforgeability-II addresses the "necessity of possessing policy certificates" and aims to protect the policy-issuing authority.

We then define extractability as the notion unifying soundness, unforgeability-I, and unforgeability-II. This is a reminiscence of the "sim-ext" spirit [10], which was also employed in the context of policy-based signatures [2].

Extractability. We model the three requirements of extractability in Fig. 2 using three experiments $\mathbf{Exp}_{\mathcal{A}}^{\mathsf{sound}}(\lambda)$, $\mathbf{Exp}_{\mathcal{A}}^{\mathsf{Uf\text{-}I}}(\lambda)$, $\mathbf{Exp}_{\mathcal{A}}^{\mathsf{Uf\text{-}II}}(\lambda)$. All experiments are run between a challenger $\mathcal{C}$ and an adversary $\mathcal{A}$.

Definition 2 (Extractability). *A BAPS scheme is said to satisfy the extractability property if there exists an additional algorithm* Extract *(as defined above) in the simulated setup, and for any PPT adversary $\mathcal{A}$ involved in the experiments* $\mathbf{Exp}_{\mathcal{A}}^{\mathsf{sound}}(\lambda)$, $\mathbf{Exp}_{\mathcal{A}}^{\mathsf{Uf\text{-}I}}(\lambda)$, $\mathbf{Exp}_{\mathcal{A}}^{\mathsf{Uf\text{-}II}}(\lambda)$, *one has*

$$\mathbf{Adv}_{\mathcal{A}}^{\mathsf{sound}}(\lambda) = \Pr[\mathbf{Exp}_{\mathcal{A}}^{\mathsf{sound}}(\lambda) = 1] \in \mathsf{negl}(\lambda);$$
$$\mathbf{Adv}_{\mathcal{A}}^{\mathsf{Uf\text{-}I}}(\lambda) = \Pr[\mathbf{Exp}_{\mathcal{A}}^{\mathsf{Uf\text{-}I}}(\lambda) = 1] \in \mathsf{negl}(\lambda);$$
$$\mathbf{Adv}_{\mathcal{A}}^{\mathsf{Uf\text{-}II}}(\lambda) = \Pr[\mathbf{Exp}_{\mathcal{A}}^{\mathsf{Uf\text{-}II}}(\lambda) = 1] \in \mathsf{negl}(\lambda).$$

The experiment $\mathbf{Exp}_{\mathcal{A}}^{\mathsf{sound}}(\lambda)$ operates in two stages which first defines an extractable mode of the scheme allowing to extract a policy P^*, an attribute $\mathbf{x}^*$, and a witness w^* from any valid message-signature pair (m, Σ). Such an extraction then enables evaluating the value $P^*(m, \mathbf{x}^*, w^*)$ a posteriori. The adversary wins the experiment if the evaluated value is 0, indicating that m is not signable with respect to P^* and $\mathbf{x}^*$. It proceeds to the second stage

$(\mathsf{PP}, \mathsf{msk_X}, \mathsf{msk_P}, \mathsf{tr}) \leftarrow \mathsf{SimSetup}(1^\lambda)$; $k \leftarrow 0$;

$\mathsf{st} = (\mathsf{PP}, \mathsf{msk_X}, \mathsf{msk_P})$; $(m, \Sigma) \leftarrow \mathcal{A}(\mathsf{st})$;

$\mathsf{st} = (\mathsf{PP}, \mathsf{msk_P})$; $(m, \Sigma) \leftarrow \mathcal{A}^{\mathcal{O}_{\mathsf{AttriKey}}, \mathcal{O}_{\mathsf{Sign}}, \mathcal{O}_{\mathsf{Dis}}}(\mathsf{st})$;

$\mathsf{st} = (\mathsf{PP}, \mathsf{msk_X})$; $(m, \Sigma) \leftarrow \mathcal{A}^{\mathcal{O}_{\mathsf{PolicyKey}}, \mathcal{O}_{\mathsf{Sign}}, \mathcal{O}_{\mathsf{Dis}}}(\mathsf{st})$;

If $(m, \Sigma) = L_S[k^\star][1]$ for $k^\star \in [1, k]$ or $\mathsf{Verify}(\mathsf{PP}, m, \Sigma) = 0$, return 0.

$(P^*, \mathbf{x}^*, w^*) \leftarrow \mathsf{Extract}(\mathsf{tr}, m, \Sigma)$;

If $P^*(m, \mathbf{x}^*, w^*) = 0$, return 1.

If $\mathbf{x}^* \notin Q_X$, return 1. If $P^* \notin Q_P$, return 1.

$(F, t, a) \leftarrow \mathcal{A}(\mathsf{st})$;
If $(m, \Sigma, F, t, a) \in Q_D$ or $\mathsf{Judge}(\mathsf{PP}, m, \Sigma, F, t, a) = 0$, return 0.
If $t \neq F(P^*, \mathbf{x}^*)$, return 1.

Return 0.

$\mathcal{O}_{\mathsf{AttriKey}}(\mathbf{x})$

$\mathsf{sk}_{\mathbf{x}} \leftarrow \mathsf{Attribute\text{-}Iss}(\mathsf{msk_X}, \mathbf{x})$;
$Q_X \leftarrow Q_X \cup \{\mathbf{x}\}$
Return $\mathsf{sk}_{\mathbf{x}}$.

$\mathcal{O}_{\mathsf{Sign}}(m, P, \mathbf{x}, w)$

If $P(m, \mathbf{x}, w) = 0$, return $\perp$;
$k \leftarrow k + 1$;
$\Sigma \leftarrow \mathsf{SimSign}(\mathsf{tr}, m, P, \mathbf{x}, w)$;
$L_S[k][0] = (P, \mathbf{x}), L_S[k][1] = (m, \Sigma)$;
Return Σ.

$\mathcal{O}_{\mathsf{PolicyKey}}(P)$

$\mathsf{Cert}_P \leftarrow \mathsf{Policy\text{-}Iss}(\mathsf{msk_P}, P)$;
$Q_P \leftarrow Q_P \cup \{P\}$;
Return Cert_P.

$\mathcal{O}_{\mathsf{Dis}}(m, \Sigma, F)$

Check if $\exists\, k^\star \in [1, k]$ such that $L_S[k^\star][1] = (m, \Sigma)$;
If $k^\star$ does not exist, return $\perp$;
Let $(P, \mathbf{x}) = L_S[k^\star][0]$;
$(t, a) \leftarrow \mathsf{SimDisclose}(m, \Sigma, \mathsf{tr}, P, \mathbf{x}, F)$;
$Q_D \leftarrow Q_D \cup \{(m, \Sigma, F, t, a)\}$;
Return (t, a).

Fig. 2. Experiments $\mathbf{Exp}_{\mathcal{A}}^{\mathsf{sound}}(\lambda)$ (excluding dotted and double solid boxes), $\mathbf{Exp}_{\mathcal{A}}^{\mathsf{Uf\text{-}I}}(\lambda)$ (excluding solid and double solid boxes), and $\mathbf{Exp}_{\mathcal{A}}^{\mathsf{Uf\text{-}II}}(\lambda)$ (excluding the solid and dotted boxes).

only if $P^*(m, \mathbf{x}^*, w^*) = 1$, i.e., the adversary did not win in the first stage. The aim of the adversary in the second stage is to output a disclosing function F and a Judge-accepted testimony-attestation pair (t, a) corresponding to (m, Σ) outputted in the first stage such that $t \neq F(P^*, \mathbf{x}^*)$. To define soundness in the strongest sense, both authorities' keys are exposed to the adversary. A BAPS system satisfies soundness if the winning probability of the adversary in $\mathbf{Exp}_{\mathcal{A}}^{\mathsf{sound}}(\lambda)$ is negligible in λ. Said otherwise, even with the help of both fully corrupted authorities, no signer can fool the system by producing valid signatures on non-signable messages or creating a testimony accompanied by an accepted attestation that does not respect the underlying disclosing value $F(P^*, \mathbf{x}^*)$.

Both experiments $\mathbf{Exp}_{\mathcal{A}}^{\mathsf{Uf\text{-}I}}(\lambda)$, $\mathbf{Exp}_{\mathcal{A}}^{\mathsf{Uf\text{-}II}}(\lambda)$ function in the extractable setting.

- Unforgeability-I is similar to the unforgeability/type-1 unforgeability notion of ABS [37]/MPS [39]. It protects the security of the attribute-issuing authority. In the experiment, the adversary fully corrupts the policy-issuing authority and can learn their signing keys on attributes of its choices via $\mathcal{O}_{\mathsf{AttriKey}}$. The adversary also makes signing queries by submitting $(m, P, \mathbf{x}, w)$ to $\mathcal{O}_{\mathsf{Sign}}$. We stress that the signing key of $\mathbf{x}$ may not be revealed to the adversary. Its goal is to output a valid pair (m, Σ) such that the extraction points to an attribute of which it has not previously learned the signing key.
- Unforgeability-II captures the spirit of the unforgeability/extractability notion in FS [8]/PS [1]/PBS [2]. This notion is orthogonal to unforgeability-I and protects the security of the policy-issuing authority. In the experiment, the adversary has access to various oracles and intends to output a valid pair (m, Σ) that is extracted to a policy $P^* \notin Q_P$.

3 A Generic Construction for BAPS

We now present a generic construction of BAPS for arbitrary policies and arbitrary disclosing functions. The construction satisfies the correctness and the security requirements defined Sect. 2.2. It employs several commonly used cryptographic building blocks: two signature schemes, a commitment scheme, and two non-interactive zero-knowledge (NIZK) argument systems for some NP-relations. As a remark, we require that the employed NIZK systems satisfy the simulation-sound extractability property [21]. We note that it could be possible to replace these building blocks with a combination of ordinary NIZK systems, (lossy) public-key encryption, and one-time signatures (similar to a construction in [2]). The resulting construction, however, would be syntactically much more complicated while relying on essentially the same high-level ideas.

We will give a technical overview of the construction in Sect. 3.1, describe it in detail in Sect. 3.2, and provide its analyses in Sect. 3.3.

3.1 Technical Overview

The construction employs the following cryptographic building blocks.

- Two secure signature schemes

$$\mathcal{S}_{\mathsf{X}} = (\mathsf{S_X.Kg}, \mathsf{S_X.Sign}, \mathsf{S_X.Ver}), \qquad \mathcal{S}_{\mathsf{P}} = (\mathsf{S_P.Kg}, \mathsf{S_P.Sign}, \mathsf{S_P.Ver});$$

- A secure commitment scheme $\mathcal{COM} = (\mathsf{C.Setup}, \mathsf{C.Com}, \mathsf{C.Open})$;
- Two simulation-sound extractable NIZK systems

$$\mathcal{NIZK}_{\mathsf{S}} = (\mathsf{ZK_S.Setup}, \mathsf{ZK_S.SimSetup}, \mathsf{ZK_S.Prove}, \mathsf{ZK_S.Ver}, \mathsf{ZK_S.Sim}, \mathsf{ZK_S.Extr}),$$
$$\mathcal{NIZK}_{\mathsf{D}} = (\mathsf{ZK_D.Setup}, \mathsf{ZK_D.SimSetup}, \mathsf{ZK_D.Prove}, \mathsf{ZK_D.Ver}, \mathsf{ZK_D.Sim}, \mathsf{ZK_D.Extr}),$$

  for the NP-relations $\mathcal{R}_{\mathsf{S}}$ and $\mathcal{R}_{\mathsf{D}}$, respectively, defined below.

The attribute-issuing authority is associated with a signing-verification key-pair $(\mathsf{msk_X}, \mathsf{vk_X})$ for $\mathcal{S}_\mathsf{X}$. A signing key $\mathsf{sk}_\mathbf{x}$ for attribute $\mathbf{x}$ is defined as a signature of the authority on "message" $\mathbf{x}$. Similarly, the policy-issuing authority is associated with a signing-verification key-pair $(\mathsf{msk_P}, \mathsf{vk_P})$ for $\mathcal{S}_\mathsf{P}$. A certificate Cert_P for policy P is then a signature of the authority on "message" P.

To sign a message m with respect to policy P, attribute $\mathbf{x}$ and witness w, the signer first checks whether $P(m, \mathbf{x}, w) = 1$, and aborts if this is not the case. Next, the signer commits to P and $\mathbf{x}$ as com_P and $\mathsf{com}_\mathbf{x}$, respectively. Then, it proves that (i) m is signable, i.e., $P(m, \mathbf{x}, w) = 1$; (ii) each of P and $\mathbf{x}$ is properly certified by the respective authority; and (iii) com_P and $\mathsf{com}_\mathbf{x}$ are valid commitments to P and $\mathbf{x}$, respectively. Specifically, the signer generates a NIZK argument Π for the following relation

$$\begin{aligned}\mathcal{R}_\mathsf{S} := \Big\{ \Big((m, \mathsf{vk_X}, \mathsf{vk_P}, \mathsf{pp_C}, \mathsf{com}_\mathbf{x}, \mathsf{com}_P),\ \ (\mathbf{x}, \mathsf{sk}_\mathbf{x}, P, \mathsf{Cert}_P, w, \mathbf{r}_{\mathsf{com},\mathbf{x}}, \mathbf{r}_{\mathsf{com},P}) \Big) :\\ \Big(P(m, \mathbf{x}, w) = 1\Big) \wedge \Big(\mathsf{S_X.Ver}(\mathsf{vk_X}, \mathbf{x}, \mathsf{sk}_\mathbf{x}) = 1\Big) \wedge \Big(\mathsf{S_P.Ver}(\mathsf{vk_P}, P, \mathsf{Cert}_P) = 1\Big)\\ \wedge \Big(\mathsf{C.Open}(\mathsf{pp_C}, \mathsf{com}_\mathbf{x}, \mathbf{x}, \mathbf{r}_{\mathsf{com},\mathbf{x}}) = 1\Big) \wedge \Big(\mathsf{C.Open}(\mathsf{pp_C}, \mathsf{com}_P, P, \mathbf{r}_{\mathsf{com},P}) = 1\Big)\Big\}.\end{aligned}$$

The signature Σ then contains the commitments com_P and $\mathsf{com}_\mathbf{x}$ as well as the argument Π. Verification of Σ is simply the verification of Π. The clue – which will be used for later disclosures – consists of $\mathbf{x}, P$ and the randomnesses $\mathbf{r}_{\mathsf{com},\mathbf{x}}$ and $\mathbf{r}_{\mathsf{com},P}$.

We remark that the design approach being used here, which we term *sign-then-commit-then-prove*, is effectively different from the sign-then-encrypt-then-prove paradigm traditionally used for achieving accountable privacy in group-signature-like systems. The advantage of our approach is that the signer can preserve full privacy of the committed values (especially if the underlying commitment scheme is statistically hiding) while maintaining the capability of proving additional relations about the committed values at later times.

When asked to disclose certain partial information of $\mathbf{x}$ and/or P according to a disclosing function $F \in \mathcal{F}$, the signer of a message-signature pair (m, Σ), who possesses the corresponding clue $c = (\mathbf{x}, P, \mathbf{r}_{\mathsf{com},P}, \mathbf{r}_{\mathsf{com},\mathbf{x}})$, first computes $t = F(P, \mathbf{x})$ and then proves that t is well-formed with respect to the values P and $\mathbf{x}$ committed in the signature. Specifically, it generates a NIZK argument a for the following relation:

$$\begin{aligned}\mathcal{R}_\mathsf{D} := \Big\{ \Big(F, t, \mathsf{com}_\mathbf{x}, \mathsf{com}_P, \mathsf{pp_C}), (\mathbf{x}, P, \mathbf{r}_{\mathsf{com},\mathbf{x}}, \mathbf{r}_{\mathsf{com},P}) \Big) : \Big(t = F(P, \mathbf{x})\Big)\\ \wedge \Big(\mathsf{C.Open}(\mathsf{pp_C}, \mathsf{com}_\mathbf{x}, \mathbf{x}, \mathbf{r}_{\mathsf{com},\mathbf{x}}) = 1\Big) \wedge \Big(\mathsf{C.Open}(\mathsf{pp_C}, \mathsf{com}_P, P, \mathbf{r}_{\mathsf{com},P}) = 1\Big)\Big\}.\end{aligned}$$

To determine the validity of a testimony-attestation pair (t, a) outputted by the disclosing algorithm, one simply verifies the NIZK argument a.

The correctness and security properties of the construction tightly follow from those of the employed building blocks. In particular, the scheme is (statistically) simulatable as long as $\mathcal{NIZK}_\mathsf{S}$ and $\mathcal{NIZK}_\mathsf{D}$ are (statistically) zero-knowledge and $\mathcal{COM}$ is (statistically) hiding. Its extractability, on the other hand, relies on the unforgeability of $\mathcal{S}_\mathsf{X}$ and $\mathcal{S}_\mathsf{P}$, the simulation-sound extractability of the NIZK systems and the binding property of $\mathcal{COM}$.

3.2 Description

In the description of the generic construction, we do not specify the choice of system parameters $(\mathcal{M}, \mathcal{X}, \mathcal{W}, \mathcal{DS}, \mathcal{P}, \mathcal{F})$. We do not make any restriction on the policies in $\mathcal{P}$ nor the disclosing functions in $\mathcal{F}$. We, however, note that these system parameters should be compatible with those of the building blocks $\mathcal{S}_\mathsf{X}$ and $\mathcal{S}_\mathsf{P}$, $\mathcal{NIZK}_\mathsf{S}$ and $\mathcal{NIZK}_\mathsf{D}$, and $\mathcal{COM}$.

$\mathsf{Setup}(1^\lambda)$: This algorithm performs the following steps:

1. Run $(\mathsf{msk}_\mathsf{P}, \mathsf{vk}_\mathsf{P}) \leftarrow \mathsf{S}_\mathsf{P}.\mathsf{Kg}(1^\lambda)$ and $(\mathsf{msk}_\mathsf{X}, \mathsf{vk}_\mathsf{X}) \leftarrow \mathsf{S}_\mathsf{X}.\mathsf{Kg}(1^\lambda)$ to obtain signing-verification key pairs for the policy-issuing authority and the attribute-issuing authority, respectively.
2. Run $\mathsf{ZK}_\mathsf{S}.\mathsf{Setup}(1^\lambda)$ and $\mathsf{ZK}_\mathsf{D}.\mathsf{Setup}(1^\lambda)$ to obtain crs_S and crs_D for the argument systems $\mathcal{NIZK}_\mathsf{S}$ and $\mathcal{NIZK}_\mathsf{D}$, respectively.
3. Generate public parameters $\mathsf{pp}_\mathsf{C} \leftarrow \mathsf{C}.\mathsf{Setup}(1^\lambda)$ for $\mathcal{COM}$.

Let $\mathsf{PP} := (\mathsf{crs}_\mathsf{S}, \mathsf{crs}_\mathsf{D}, \mathsf{pp}_\mathsf{C}, \mathsf{vk}_\mathsf{P}, \mathsf{vk}_\mathsf{X})$ and output $(\mathsf{PP}, \mathsf{msk}_\mathsf{P}, \mathsf{msk}_\mathsf{X})$.

$\mathsf{Attribute\text{-}Iss}(\mathsf{msk}_\mathsf{X}, \mathbf{x})$: Generate a signing key $\mathsf{sk}_\mathbf{x}$ for attribute $\mathbf{x}$ as

$$\mathsf{sk}_\mathbf{x} \leftarrow \mathsf{S}_\mathsf{X}.\mathsf{Sign}(\mathsf{msk}_\mathsf{X}, \mathbf{x}).$$

$\mathsf{Policy\text{-}Iss}(\mathsf{msk}_\mathsf{P}, P)$: Generate a certificate Cert_P for policy P as

$$\mathsf{Cert}_P \leftarrow \mathsf{S}_\mathsf{P}.\mathsf{Sign}(\mathsf{msk}_\mathsf{P}, P).$$

$\mathsf{Sign}(\mathbf{x}, \mathsf{sk}_\mathbf{x}, P, \mathsf{Cert}_P, m, w)$: If $P(m, \mathbf{x}, w) = 0$, the signing algorithm returns $\perp$. Otherwise, it proceeds as follows.

1. Commit to $\mathbf{x}$ as $\mathsf{com}_\mathbf{x} = \mathsf{C}.\mathsf{Com}(\mathsf{pp}_\mathsf{C}, \mathbf{x}, \mathbf{r}_{\mathsf{com},\mathbf{x}})$, and commit to P as $\mathsf{com}_P = \mathsf{Com}(\mathsf{pp}_\mathsf{C}, P, \mathbf{r}_{\mathsf{com},P})$. Here, $\mathbf{r}_{\mathsf{com},\mathbf{x}}$ and $\mathbf{r}_{\mathsf{com},P}$ are the commitment randomness.
2. Generate a NIZK argument Π to prove the knowledge of a tuple $\eta = (\mathbf{x}, \mathsf{sk}_\mathbf{x}, P, \mathsf{Cert}_P, w, \mathbf{r}_{\mathsf{com},\mathbf{x}}, \mathbf{r}_{\mathsf{com},P})$ such that the following conditions hold.
   (a) The message m is signable with respect to policy P, attribute $\mathbf{x}$ and witness w, i.e., $P(m, \mathbf{x}, w) = 1$.
   (b) $\mathsf{com}_\mathbf{x}$ and com_P are valid commitments to $\mathbf{x}$ and P, respectively, i.e.,
   $$\mathsf{C}.\mathsf{Open}(\mathsf{pp}_\mathsf{C}, \mathsf{com}_\mathbf{x}, \mathbf{x}, \mathbf{r}_{\mathsf{com},\mathbf{x}}) = 1; \quad \mathsf{C}.\mathsf{Open}(\mathsf{pp}_\mathsf{C}, \mathsf{com}_P, P, \mathbf{r}_{\mathsf{com},P}) = 1.$$
   (c) $(\mathbf{x}, \mathsf{sk}_\mathbf{x})$ is a valid (attribute, signing key) pair, i.e.,
   $$\mathsf{S}_\mathsf{X}.\mathsf{Ver}(\mathsf{vk}_\mathsf{X}, \mathbf{x}, \mathsf{sk}_\mathbf{x}) = 1.$$
   (d) (P, Cert_P) is a valid (attribute, certificate) pair, i.e.,
   $$\mathsf{S}_\mathsf{P}.\mathsf{Ver}(\mathsf{vk}_\mathsf{P}, P, \mathsf{Cert}_P) = 1.$$

This is done by running

$$\Pi \leftarrow \mathsf{ZK_S.Prove}(\ \mathsf{crs_S}, (m, \mathsf{vk_X}, \mathsf{vk_P}, \mathsf{pp_C}, \mathsf{com}_\mathbf{x}, \mathsf{com}_P), \eta\ )$$

to prove that $(\ (m, \mathsf{vk_X}, \mathsf{vk_P}, \mathsf{pp_C}, \mathsf{com}_\mathbf{x}, \mathsf{com}_P), \eta\ ) \in \mathcal{R}_\mathsf{S}$.

3. Let $\Sigma = (\mathsf{com}_\mathbf{x}, \mathsf{com}_P, \Pi)$; $\mathsf{clue} = (\mathbf{x}, P, \mathbf{r}_{\mathsf{com},\mathbf{x}}, \mathbf{r}_{\mathsf{com},P})$, return (Σ, clue).

$\mathsf{Verify}(m, \Sigma)$: Parse $\Sigma = (\mathsf{com}_\mathbf{x}, \mathsf{com}_P, \Pi)$. Then return the bit

$$b' \leftarrow \mathsf{ZK_S.Ver}(\ \mathsf{crs_S}, (m, \mathsf{vk_X}, \mathsf{vk_P}, \mathsf{pp_C}, \mathsf{com}_\mathbf{x}, \mathsf{com}_P), \Pi\ ).$$

$\mathsf{Disclose}(m, \Sigma, \mathsf{clue}, F)$: On input a valid message-signature pair (m, Σ), where $\Sigma = (\mathsf{com}_\mathbf{x}, \mathsf{com}_P, \Pi)$, a clue $\mathsf{clue} = (\mathbf{x}, P, \mathbf{r}_{\mathsf{com},\mathbf{x}}, \mathbf{r}_{\mathsf{com},P})$, and a disclosing function $F \in \mathcal{F}$, this algorithm proceeds as follows.

1. Compute $t = F(P, \mathbf{x})$.
2. Generate a NIZK argument a to show the possession of the tuple $\mathsf{clue} = (\mathbf{x}, P, \mathbf{r}_{\mathsf{com},\mathbf{x}}, \mathbf{r}_{\mathsf{com},P})$ such that the following conditions hold.
   (i) The value t is honestly computed, i.e., $t = F(P, \mathbf{x})$.
   (ii) $\mathsf{com}_\mathbf{x}$ and com_P are valid commitments to $\mathbf{x}$ and P, respectively, i.e.,

$$\mathsf{C.Open}(\mathsf{pp_C}, \mathsf{com}_\mathbf{x}, \mathbf{x}, \mathbf{r}_{\mathsf{com},\mathbf{x}}) = 1; \quad \mathsf{C.Open}(\mathsf{pp_C}, \mathsf{com}_P, P, \mathbf{r}_{\mathsf{com},P}) = 1.$$

This is done by running

$$a \leftarrow \mathsf{ZK_D.Prove}(\mathsf{crs_D}, (F, t, \mathsf{com}_\mathbf{x}, \mathsf{com}_P, \mathsf{pp_C}), \mathsf{clue})$$

to prove that $((F, t, \mathsf{com}_\mathbf{x}, \mathsf{com}_P, \mathsf{pp_C}), \mathsf{clue}) \in \mathcal{R}_\mathsf{D}$.

3. Return (t, a) as a testimony-attestation pair.

$\mathsf{Judge}(m, \Sigma, F, t, a)$: If $\mathsf{Verify}(m, \Sigma) = 0$, return 0. Otherwise, parse Σ as $\Sigma = (\mathsf{com}_\mathbf{x}, \mathsf{com}_P, \Pi)$ and return $b'' \leftarrow \mathsf{ZK_D.Ver}(\mathsf{crs_D}, (F, t, \mathsf{com}_\mathbf{x}, \mathsf{com}_P, \mathsf{pp_C}), a)$.

3.3 Analyses

Correctness. The correctness of the presented BAPS scheme follows directly from the correctness/completeness of the employed ingredients.

The correctness of the commitment scheme $\mathcal{COM}$ ensures that

$$\mathsf{C.Open}(\mathsf{pp_C}, \mathsf{com}_\mathbf{x}, \mathbf{x}, \mathbf{r}_{\mathsf{com},\mathbf{x}}) = 1, \quad \mathsf{C.Open}(\mathsf{pp_C}, \mathsf{com}_P, P, \mathbf{r}_{\mathsf{com},P}) = 1.$$

Also, it follows from the correctness of signature schemes $\mathcal{S}_\mathsf{X}$ and $\mathcal{S}_\mathsf{P}$ that

$$\mathsf{S_X.Ver}(\mathsf{vk_X}, \mathbf{x}, \mathsf{sk}_\mathbf{x}) = 1, \quad \mathsf{S_P.Ver}(\mathsf{vk_P}, P, \mathsf{Cert}_P) = 1.$$

An honest signer thus can obtain a witness $\eta = (\mathbf{x}, \mathsf{sk}_\mathbf{x}, P, \mathsf{Cert}_P, w, \mathbf{r}_{\mathsf{com},\mathbf{x}}, \mathbf{r}_{\mathsf{com},P})$ such that $(\ (m, \mathsf{vk_X}, \mathsf{vk_P}, \mathsf{pp_C}, \mathsf{com}_\mathbf{x}, \mathsf{com}_P), \eta\ ) \in \mathcal{R}_\mathsf{S}$. Then, thanks to the completeness of $\mathcal{NIZK}_\mathsf{S}$, an honestly generated proof Π will be accepted by $\mathsf{ZK_S.Ver}$. In other words, algorithm Verify returns 1 with overwhelming probability.

Next, if algorithm $\mathsf{Disclose}$ is run honestly, then one has that $t = F(P, \mathbf{x})$ and that $\mathsf{clue} = (\mathbf{x}, P, \mathbf{r}_{\mathsf{com},\mathbf{x}}, \mathbf{r}_{\mathsf{com},P})$ satisfies $((F, t, \mathsf{com}_\mathbf{x}, \mathsf{com}_P, \mathsf{pp_C}), \mathsf{clue}) \in \mathcal{R}_\mathsf{D}$. As a result, algorithm $\mathsf{ZK_D.Ver}$ returns 1 with overwhelming probability, thanks to the completeness of $\mathcal{NIZK}_\mathsf{D}$, and so does algorithm Judge.

Security. We will prove that the proposed generic construction satisfies simulatability and extractability as defined in Sect. 2.2. First, we would need to construct the following auxiliary algorithms.

$\mathsf{SimSetup}(1^\lambda)$: The changes compared to the real Setup algorithm are as follows.
- At Step 2, the common reference strings and associated trapdoors are generated via simulated algorithms $(\mathsf{crs_S}, \mathsf{tr_S}) \leftarrow \mathsf{ZK_S.SimSetup}(1^\lambda)$ for $\mathcal{NIZK}_\mathsf{S}$ and $(\mathsf{crs_D}, \mathsf{tr_D}) \leftarrow \mathsf{ZK_D.SimSetup}(1^\lambda)$ for $\mathcal{NIZK}_\mathsf{D}$.
- The algorithm outputs $\mathsf{tr} := (\mathsf{tr_S}, \mathsf{tr_D})$ in addition to $(\mathsf{PP}, \mathsf{msk_X}, \mathsf{msk_P})$.

$\mathsf{SimSign}(\mathsf{tr}, m, P, \mathbf{x}, \mathbf{w})$: If $P(m, \mathbf{x}, w) = 0$, the algorithm returns 0. Otherwise, it uses trapdoor $\mathsf{tr} = (\mathsf{tr_S}, \mathsf{tr_D})$ to simulate a signature on m as follows.
1. Compute $\mathsf{com}_\mathbf{x}$ and com_P as commitments to all-zero strings. Namely, $\mathsf{com}_\mathbf{x} = \mathsf{C.Com}(\mathsf{pp_C}, \mathbf{0}, \mathbf{r}_{\mathsf{com},\mathbf{x}})$ and $\mathsf{com}_P = \mathsf{C.Com}(\mathsf{pp_C}, \mathbf{0}, \mathbf{r}_{\mathsf{com},P})$.
2. Simulate the NIZK argument Π using $\mathsf{tr_S}$ via

$$\Pi \leftarrow \mathsf{ZK_S.Sim}(\mathsf{crs_S}, \mathsf{tr_S}, (m, \mathsf{vk_X}, \mathsf{vk_P}, \mathsf{pp_C}, \mathsf{com}_\mathbf{x}, \mathsf{com}_P)).$$

3. Output the simulated signature $\Sigma = (\mathsf{com}_\mathbf{x}, \mathsf{com}_P, \Pi)$.

$\mathsf{SimDisclose}(m, \Sigma, \mathsf{tr}, P, \mathbf{x}, F)$: If $\mathsf{Verify}(m, \Sigma) = 0$, then the algorithm returns $\perp$. Otherwise, let $\mathsf{tr} = (\mathsf{tr_S}, \mathsf{tr_D})$ and parse $\Sigma = (\mathsf{com}_\mathbf{x}, \mathsf{com}_P, \Pi)$. The disclosure process is then simulated via the following steps.
1. Compute $t = F(P, \mathbf{x})$.
2. Simulate the NIZK argument a using $\mathsf{tr_D}$ via

$$a \leftarrow \mathsf{ZK_D.Sim}(\mathsf{crs_D}, \mathsf{tr_D}, (F, t, \mathsf{com}_\mathbf{x}, \mathsf{com}_P, \mathsf{pp_C})).$$

3. Output the simulated testimony-attestation pair (t, a).

$\mathsf{Extract}(\mathsf{tr}, m, \Sigma)$: Let $\mathsf{tr} = (\mathsf{tr_S}$ and parse $\Sigma = (\mathsf{com}_\mathbf{x}, \mathsf{com}_P, \Pi)$. The algorithm uses $\mathsf{tr_S}$ to extract

$$\eta' \leftarrow \mathsf{ZK_S.Extr}(\mathsf{crs_S}, \mathsf{tr_S}, (m, \mathsf{vk_X}, \mathsf{vk_P}, \mathsf{pp_C}, \mathsf{com}_\mathbf{x}, \mathsf{com}_P), \Pi),$$

where $\eta' = (\mathbf{x}', \mathsf{sk}', P', \mathsf{Cert}', w', \mathbf{r}'_{\mathsf{com},\mathbf{x}}, \mathbf{r}'_{\mathsf{com},P})$. It then returns $(P', \mathbf{x}', w')$.

With the above auxiliary algorithms, we are ready to show that our generic construction satisfies simulatability and extractability.

Theorem 1. *Assume that the two NIZK systems for $\mathcal{R}_\mathsf{S}$ and $\mathcal{R}_\mathsf{D}$ are statistical zero-knowledge and the commitment scheme $\mathcal{COM}$ is statistically hiding. Then the proposed BAPS scheme is statistically simulatable.*

Proof. We prove the theorem via a sequence of games that are statistically indistinguishable, where the first is the experiment $\mathbf{Exp}^{\mathsf{sim}}_\mathcal{A}(\lambda)$ with b set to 1 while the last is $\mathbf{Exp}^{\mathsf{sim}}_\mathcal{A}(\lambda)$ with b set to 0. In the process, we rely on the statistical zero-knowledge property of the NIZK systems $\mathcal{NIZK}_{\mathsf{S}}$ and $\mathcal{NIZK}_{\mathsf{D}}$, and the statistical hiding property of $\mathcal{COM}$.

Game 0: We start with $\mathbf{Exp}_{\mathcal{A}}^{\mathsf{sim}|b=1}(\lambda)$. In the experiment, the challenger runs the setup algorithm $(\mathsf{PP}^1, \mathsf{msk}_{\mathsf{X}}^1, \mathsf{msk}_{\mathsf{P}}^1) \leftarrow \mathsf{Setup}(1^\lambda)$, and returns $(\mathsf{PP}^1, \mathsf{msk}_{\mathsf{X}}^1, \mathsf{msk}_{\mathsf{P}}^1)$ to $\mathcal{A}$. Regarding all the queries made by $\mathcal{A}$, the challenger replies them honestly. In particular, signature queries and disclosing queries are replied by running $\mathsf{Sign}(\mathbf{x}, \mathsf{sk}_{\mathbf{x}}, P, \mathsf{Cert}_P, m, w)$ and $\mathsf{Disclose}(m, \Sigma, c^1, F)$, respectively. The adversary can make a polynomial number of queries and outputs a bit b' eventually.

Game 1: This game introduces the following changes to Game 0. At Step 2 of the Setup algorithm, the challenger runs $(\mathsf{crs}_{\mathsf{S}}, \mathsf{tr}_{\mathsf{S}}) \leftarrow \mathsf{ZK}_{\mathsf{S}}.\mathsf{SimSetup}(1^\lambda)$ for $\mathcal{NIZK}_{\mathsf{S}}$ and $(\mathsf{crs}_{\mathsf{D}}, \mathsf{tr}_{\mathsf{D}}) \leftarrow \mathsf{ZK}_{\mathsf{D}}.\mathsf{SimSetup}(1^\lambda)$ for $\mathcal{NIZK}_{\mathsf{D}}$. It then outputs $\mathsf{tr} = (\mathsf{tr}_{\mathsf{S}}, \mathsf{tr}_{\mathsf{D}})$ in addition to $\mathsf{st} = (\mathsf{PP}^1, \mathsf{msk}_{\mathsf{X}}^1, \mathsf{msk}_{\mathsf{P}}^1)$. Similar to Game 0, only st is given to the adversary. All the queries are replied exactly the same as in Game 0. These changes are indistinguishable to the adversary due to the statistical zero-knowledge property of $\mathcal{NIZK}_{\mathsf{S}}$ and $\mathcal{NIZK}_{\mathsf{D}}$.

Game 2: This game is similar to Game 1 except that, in calls to the $\mathcal{O}_{\mathsf{sign}}^{\mathsf{sor}}$ oracle, the challenger commits to $\mathbf{x}$ and P honestly, but then simulates the proof Π instead of generating it faithfully. Simulating the proof is possible since the challenger has the trapdoor tr_{S}. Due to the statistical zero-knowledge property of $\mathcal{NIZK}_{\mathsf{S}}$, this game is statistically indistinguishable from Game 1.

Game 3: This game modifies Game 2 as follows. When $\mathcal{A}$ queries the $\mathcal{O}_{\mathsf{Disclose}}^{\mathsf{sor}}$ oracle, the challenger computes $t = F(P, \mathbf{x})$ faithfully. Then the challenger simulates the proof a without employing the witness $\mathsf{clue} = (\mathbf{x}, P, \mathbf{r}_{\mathsf{com},\mathbf{x}}, \mathbf{r}_{\mathsf{com},P})$, i.e., $a \leftarrow \mathsf{ZK}_{\mathsf{D}}.\mathsf{Sim}(\mathsf{crs}_{\mathsf{D}}, \mathsf{tr}_{\mathsf{D}}, (F, t, \mathsf{com}_{\mathbf{x}}, \mathsf{com}_P, \mathsf{pp}_{\mathsf{C}}))$. Due to the statistical ZK property of $\mathcal{NIZK}_{\mathsf{D}}$, this game is statistically indistinguishable from Game 2.

Game 4: In this game, we make a modification regarding the queries $\mathcal{O}_{\mathsf{sign}}^{\mathsf{sor}}$ again. Instead of committing to real $\mathbf{x}$ and P, we commit to the all-zero string. Specifically, $\mathsf{com}_{\mathbf{x}}$ and com_P are all commitment to the all-zero string and the proof Π is generated as $\mathsf{ZK}_{\mathsf{S}}.\mathsf{Sim}(\mathsf{crs}_{\mathsf{S}}, \mathsf{tr}_{\mathsf{S}}, (m, \mathsf{vk}_{\mathsf{X}}, \mathsf{vk}_{\mathsf{P}}, \mathsf{pp}_{\mathsf{C}}, \mathsf{com}_{\mathbf{x}}, \mathsf{com}_P))$. Due to the statistical hiding property of $\mathcal{COM}$, the views of the adversary in Game 3 and Game 4 are statistically close.

Finally, observe that Game 4 is identical to the experiment $\mathbf{Exp}_{\mathcal{A}}^{\mathsf{sim}}(\lambda)$ with b set to 0. As a result, we can deduce that the two experiments $\mathbf{Exp}_{\mathcal{A}}^{\mathsf{sim}|b=1}(\lambda)$ and $\mathbf{Exp}_{\mathcal{A}}^{\mathsf{sim}|b=0}(\lambda)$ are statistically indistinguishable. This further implies that the advantage of $\mathcal{A}$ in guessing the bit b in experiment $\mathbf{Exp}_{\mathcal{A}}^{\mathsf{sim}}(\lambda)$ is at most negligible in λ. This completes the proof. □

Theorem 2. *The proposed BAPS scheme is extractable if the two underlying NIZK systems satisfy simulation-sound extractability, $\mathcal{COM}$ is computationally binding, and the two signature schemes are* EUF-CMA *secure.*

Proof. To show our generic construction is extractable, we have to prove that the advantages of any PPT adversary $\mathcal{A}$ in experiments $\mathbf{Exp}_{\mathcal{A}}^{\mathsf{sound}}(\lambda)$, $\mathbf{Exp}_{\mathcal{A}}^{\mathsf{Uf\text{-}I}}(\lambda)$, and $\mathbf{Exp}_{\mathcal{A}}^{\mathsf{Uf\text{-}II}}(\lambda)$ are negligible in λ. Let us first consider experiment $\mathbf{Exp}_{\mathcal{A}}^{\mathsf{sound}}(\lambda)$.

Soundness. Suppose $\mathcal{A}$ wins experiment $\mathbf{Exp}_{\mathcal{A}}^{\mathsf{sound}}(\lambda)$, in which the challenger $\mathcal{C}$ possess a trapdoor $\mathsf{tr} = (\mathsf{tr}_{\mathsf{S}}, \mathsf{tr}_{\mathsf{D}})$. Then the experiment returns 1 either at Line 7 or Line 9 in Fig. 2. Let (m, Σ) be the output of $\mathcal{A}$. Hence, $\mathsf{Verify}(m, \Sigma) = 1$. At this point, the challenger runs $\mathsf{Extract}(\mathsf{tr}, m, \Sigma)$. In particular, $\mathcal{C}$ runs

$$\eta' \leftarrow \mathsf{ZK_S.Extr}(\mathsf{crs_S}, \mathsf{tr_S}, (m, \mathsf{vk_X}, \mathsf{vk_P}, \mathsf{pp_C}, \mathsf{com_{\mathbf{x}}}, \mathsf{com}_P), \Pi),$$

where $\Sigma = (\mathsf{com}_{\mathbf{x}}, \mathsf{com}_P, \Pi)$ and $\eta' = (\mathbf{x}', \mathsf{sk}', w', P', \mathsf{Cert}', \mathbf{r}'_{\mathsf{com},\mathbf{x}}, \mathbf{r}'_{\mathsf{com},P})$. If the experiment returns 1 at Line 7, implying $P'(m, \mathbf{x}', w') = 0$. This, however, will break the simulation-soundness of $\mathcal{NIZK}_{\mathsf{S}}$. Thus, the probability of outputting 1 at Line 7 is at most negligible in λ. Hence, $\mathcal{A}$ can only win the experiment by exploiting the condition of Line 9 in Fig. 2.

Let (F, t, a) be the output of $\mathcal{A}$ in this second stage. Then $(m, \Sigma, F, t, a) \notin Q_D$ and $\mathsf{Judge}(\mathsf{PP}, m, \Sigma, F, t, a) = 1$. Now, using $\mathsf{tr_D}$, the challenger runs

$$\tilde{\eta} \leftarrow \mathsf{ZK_D.Extr}(\mathsf{crs_D}, \mathsf{tr_D}, (F, t, \mathsf{com}_{\mathbf{x}}, \mathsf{com}_P, \mathsf{pp_C}), a),$$

where $\tilde{\eta} = (\tilde{\mathbf{x}}, \tilde{P}, \tilde{\mathbf{r}}_{\mathsf{com},\mathbf{x}}, \tilde{\mathbf{r}}_{\mathsf{com},P})$. On the one hand, the assumption that $\mathcal{A}$ wins the experiment in the second stage implies that $t \neq F(P', \mathbf{x}')$. On the other hand, $t = F(\tilde{P}, \tilde{\mathbf{x}})$ by the simulation soundness of $\mathcal{NIZK}_{\mathsf{D}}$. This implies that $(P', \mathbf{x}') \neq (\tilde{P}, \tilde{\mathbf{x}})$, which in turn violates the binding property of $\mathcal{COM}$. The reason is that $\mathsf{com}_{\mathbf{x}}$ and com_P are valid commitments to $(\mathbf{x}', P')$ and $(\tilde{\mathbf{x}}, \tilde{P})$ due to the simulation soundness of $\mathcal{NIZK}_{\mathsf{S}}$ and $\mathcal{NIZK}_{\mathsf{D}}$, respectively. Therefore, the probability of outputting 1 at Line 9 is also negligible in λ. Thus the probability of $\mathcal{A}$ winning $\mathbf{Exp}_{\mathcal{A}}^{\mathsf{sound}}(\lambda)$ is negligible in λ, assuming the simulation-sound extractability of two NIZK systems and the binding property of $\mathcal{COM}$.

Unforgeability-I. Let us now consider the experiment $\mathbf{Exp}_{\mathcal{A}}^{\mathsf{Uf\text{-}I}}(\lambda)$ and let ϵ_1 be the advantage of $\mathcal{A}$. Our goal is to construct a PPT adversary $\mathcal{B}$ breaking the EUF-CMA security of the signature scheme $\mathcal{S}_{\mathsf{X}}$. Given a verification key vk from the challenger in experiment $\mathbf{Exp}_{\mathcal{S}_{\mathsf{X}},\mathcal{B}}^{\mathsf{uf}}(\lambda)$, $\mathcal{B}$ first performs the following steps.

- Run $(\mathsf{msk_P}, \mathsf{vk_P}) \leftarrow \mathsf{S_P.Kg}(1^\lambda)$. Set $\mathsf{vk_X} = \mathsf{vk}$.
- Run $(\mathsf{crs_S}, \mathsf{tr_S}) \leftarrow \mathsf{ZK_S.SimSetup}(1^\lambda)$ and $(\mathsf{crs_D}, \mathsf{tr_D}) \leftarrow \mathsf{ZK_S.SimSetup}(1^\lambda)$.
- Run $\mathsf{pp_C} \leftarrow \mathsf{C.Setup}(1)^\lambda$.

Set $\mathsf{PP} := (\mathsf{crs_S}, \mathsf{crs_D}, \mathsf{pp_C}, \mathsf{vk_P}, \mathsf{vk_X})$ and $\mathsf{tr} = (\mathsf{tr_S}, \mathsf{tr_D})$. Then $\mathcal{B}$ triggers $\mathcal{A}$ by sending $(\mathsf{PP}, \mathsf{msk_P})$ to $\mathcal{A}$ as described in $\mathbf{Exp}_{\mathsf{BAPS},\mathcal{A}}^{\mathsf{Uf\text{-}I}}(\lambda)$ in Fig. 2. When $\mathcal{A}$ queries oracle $\mathcal{O}_{\mathsf{AttriKey}}$ with an attribute $\mathbf{x}$, $\mathcal{B}$ queries its own challenger in experiment $\mathbf{Exp}_{\mathcal{S}_{\mathsf{X}},\mathcal{B}}^{\mathsf{uf}}(\lambda)$, obtaining $\mathsf{sk}_{\mathbf{x}}$, which is then passed to $\mathcal{A}$. Observe that $\mathcal{B}$ can also easily answer all the queries to the oracles $\mathcal{O}_{\mathsf{Sign}}$ and $\mathcal{O}_{\mathsf{Dis}}$ since $\mathcal{B}$ holds trapdoors $\mathsf{tr_S}$ and $\mathsf{tr_D}$. Thus, $\mathcal{B}$ can simulate $\mathcal{A}$'s views in experiment $\mathbf{Exp}_{\mathsf{BAPS},\mathcal{A}}^{\mathsf{Uf\text{-}I}}(\lambda)$.

Eventually, $\mathcal{A}$ outputs a forgery (m, Σ). Suppose $\mathcal{A}$ wins the experiment $\mathbf{Exp}_{\mathsf{BAPS},\mathcal{A}}^{\mathsf{Uf\text{-}I}}(\lambda)$. We will show how $\mathcal{B}$ employs such a forgery for BAPS to find a forgery for $\mathcal{S}_{\mathsf{X}}$. Since $\mathcal{A}$ wins, then (m, Σ) is a valid message-signature pair and is never obtained from the oracle $\mathcal{O}_{\mathsf{Sign}}$ query. Now $\mathcal{B}$ can run $\mathsf{Extract}(\mathsf{tr}, m, \Sigma)$, obtaining a tuple $\eta' = (\mathbf{x}', \mathsf{sk}', w', P', \mathsf{Cert}', \mathbf{r}'_{\mathsf{com},\mathbf{x}}, \mathbf{r}'_{\mathsf{com},P})$. With overwhelming probability, $P'(m, \mathbf{x}', w') = 1$ and $\mathsf{S_X.Ver}(\mathsf{vk_X}, \mathbf{x}', \mathsf{sk}') = 1$, thanks to the simulation-soundness of the $\mathcal{NIZK}_\mathsf{S}$ system. The fact that $\mathcal{A}$ wins the experiment implies that $\mathbf{x}' \notin Q_X$. In other words, $\mathcal{B}$ never queries its challenger on $\mathbf{x}'$. Thus $(\mathbf{x}', \mathsf{sk}')$ is a valid forgery of $\mathcal{S}_\mathsf{X}$. Therefore, if ϵ_1 is non-negligible in λ, $\mathcal{B}$ is able to find a valid forgery of the $\mathcal{S}_\mathsf{X}$ scheme with non-negligible probability as well. Due to the security of the $\mathcal{S}_\mathsf{X}$ scheme, ϵ_1 is negligible.

The proof of **Unforgeability-II** is similar to that of **Unforgeability-I** and is deferred to the full version of the paper [40]. □

4 A Lattice-Based BAPS Scheme

We now present a concrete construction of BAPS, that is proven secure under lattice-based assumptions in the random oracle model. The scheme can address arbitrary policies, represented as polynomial-size Boolean circuits. Furthermore, it can handle those disclosing functions which can be expressed as quadratic functions of the bits of P and $\mathbf{x}$.

Policies as Boolean Circuits. Let integers $n, q, k_1, k_2, k_3, K, N$ be system parameters. Set $K = k_1 + k_2 + k_3$, $\delta_\mathsf{P} = \lfloor \log(K + N - 2) \rfloor + 1$, and $\bar{k} = 2N\delta_\mathsf{P} + k_1$. Our construction is associated with message space $\mathcal{M} = \{0,1\}^{k_1}$, attribute space $\mathcal{X} = \{0,1\}^{k_2}$, witness space $\mathcal{W} = \{0,1\}^{k_3}$, disclosing space $\mathcal{DS} = \{0,1\}^{\bar{k}}$, and arbitrary polynomial-size policies $\mathcal{P} = \{P : \{0,1\}^K \to \{0,1\}\}$. In particular, $P \in \mathcal{P}$ has K-bit inputs and N NAND gates, and whose topology is determined by two functions $g, h : [0, N-1] \to [0, K+N-2]$. Namely, if the inputs to P are $s_0, s_1, \ldots, s_{K-1}$ and the N gate outputs are ordered as $s_K, \ldots, s_{K+N-1}$, then

$$s_{K+i} = s_{g(i)} \ \mathsf{NAND}\ s_{h(i)}, \ \forall i = 0, \ldots, N-1.$$

Since the construction requires signing, committing, and proving relations about policies, we first need an effective method for policy representation. To this end, by running the decomposition function [34] on $g(i), h(i)$ for all $i \in [0, N-1]$, we obtain $\mathsf{idec}_\mathsf{P}(g(i)) = (g_{i,0}, \ldots, g_{i,\delta_\mathsf{P}-1})^\top$ and $\mathsf{idec}_\mathsf{P}(h(i)) = (h_{i,0}, \ldots, h_{i,\delta_\mathsf{P}-1})^\top$ for $i \in [0, N-1]$. Then we consider the following representation of the circuit P:

$$\mathbf{z}_P = (g_{0,0}, g_{0,1}, \ldots, g_{0,\delta_\mathsf{P}-1}, \ldots, g_{N-1,0}, g_{N-1,1}, \ldots, g_{N-1,\delta_\mathsf{P}-1},$$
$$h_{0,0}, h_{0,1}, \ldots, h_{0,\delta_\mathsf{P}-1}, \ldots, h_{N-1,0}, h_{N-1,1}, \ldots, h_{N-1,\delta_\mathsf{P}-1})^\top \in \{0,1\}^{2N\delta_\mathsf{P}}. \quad (1)$$

Quadratic Disclosing functions. We consider a collection $\mathcal{F} = \{F : \mathcal{P} \times \mathcal{X} \to \{0,1\}^{\bar{k}}\}$ containing polynomially many disclosing functions F, each of which is determined by two matrices $\mathbf{G}_1 \in \{0,1\}^{\bar{k} \times \bar{k}^2}$, $\mathbf{G}_2 \in \{0,1\}^{\bar{k} \times \bar{k}}$, and defined as

$$F(P, \mathbf{x}) = \mathbf{G}_1 \cdot (\mathbf{b} \otimes_{\text{Kron}} \mathbf{b}) + \mathbf{G}_2 \cdot \mathbf{b} \bmod 2, \ \text{ with } \ \mathbf{b} = (\mathbf{z}_P^\top \mid \mathbf{x}^\top)^\top \in \{0,1\}^{\bar{k}}.$$

Here, $\mathbf{b} \otimes_{\text{Kron}} \mathbf{b} \in \{0,1\}^{\bar{k}^2}$ denotes the Kronecker product, i.e., a flattening of the tensor product $\mathbf{b} \otimes \mathbf{b} \in \{0,1\}^{\bar{k} \times \bar{k}}$. According to this definition of F, each coordinate of the vector $t = F(P, \mathbf{x}) \in \{0,1\}^{\bar{k}}$ has the form

$$\sum_{i,j \in [1,\bar{k}]} \alpha_{i,j} \cdot (b_i \cdot b_j) + \sum_{\ell \in [1,\bar{k}]} \beta_\ell \cdot b_\ell \bmod 2,$$

where $\alpha_{i,j}$'s, β_ℓ's are entries of $\mathbf{G}_1, \mathbf{G}_2$ and b_i's are coordinates of $\mathbf{b}$ – which are essentially the bits determining policy P and attribute $\mathbf{x}$. This definition is thus quite general and captures arbitrary linear and quadratic relations with respect to the bits of $(P, \mathbf{x})$. By setting matrices $\mathbf{G}_1$ and $\mathbf{G}_2$ appropriately, one can enforce the disclosures of any bits of $(P, \mathbf{x})$, or any bit-products, or any linear and/or quadratic combinations of the bits.

4.1 Technical Overview

At a high level, our lattice-based BAPS scheme follows the sign-then-commit-then-prove design approach of the generic construction in Sect. 3. However, when it comes to middle-level techniques, we do introduce several adjustments.

- Policies, which often have long representations, are hashed before being signed by the policy-issuing authority.
- We handle the problem of evaluating $P(m, \mathbf{x}, w)$ in ZK via several involved sub-protocols, interconnected via the use of some extra commitments.

More concretely, we make use of the following ideal-lattice-based ingredients. Detailed descriptions can be found in the full version [40].

- A variant of the Ducas-Micciancio (DM) signature scheme [13], which is adaptively secure in the standard model. It is used to instantiate the signature systems for both authorities, i.e., $\mathcal{S}_\mathsf{X}$ and $\mathcal{S}_\mathsf{P}$. The scheme is carefully chosen among existing tools because it has asymptotically shortest keys among schemes known to admit a concrete ZK argument of a valid message-signature pair [35].
- A secure hash function family $\mathcal{H}_{m_\mathsf{P}}$, which is adapted from [38] and which will be used to hash the binary representations of policies.
- Two commitment families $\mathsf{CMT}_{\rho',m}$ and $\mathsf{CMT}_{\ell,m}$, that are adapted from [25] and that will be used to commit to various objects.
- We also need two simulation-sound extractable NIZK systems that can handle linear and quadratic relations w.r.t. two moduli q and 2, and should be compatible with the DM signature scheme. To this end, we employ a framework proposed in [30] for interactive Stern-like argument systems [44], and then apply the Fiat-Shamir transform [18] to obtain the desired properties [17]. These two systems internally employ a string commitment scheme CMT [25] and a hash function $\mathcal{H}_\mathsf{FS}$.

Proving in ZK that $P(m, \mathbf{x}, w) = 1$. The major technical challenge that we have to overcome is to prove in ZK that a hidden-and-certified policy P evaluates to 1 on a public message m, a hidden-and-certified attribute $\mathbf{x}$, and a hidden witness w. To demonstrate our techniques, we define some notations.

Let $s_0, s_1, \ldots, s_{K-1}$ be the input bits of a policy P represented by a Boolean circuit consisting of N NAND gates, whose topology is determined by functions g and h. The task is to prove that the NAND gates are computed faithfully, i.e.,

$$\begin{cases} s_K \oplus s_{g(0)} \cdot s_{h(0)} = 1 \mod 2; \\ s_{K+1} \oplus s_{g(1)} \cdot s_{h(1)} = 1 \mod 2; \\ \cdots\cdots \\ s_{K+N-2} \oplus s_{g(N-2)} \cdot s_{h(N-2)} = 1 \mod 2; \\ s_{g(N-1)} \cdot s_{h(N-1)} = 0 \mod 2, \end{cases} \tag{2}$$

where s_{K+i} is the output while $s_{g(i)}, s_{h(i)}$ are the two inputs of the i-th NAND gates for $i \in [0, N-1]$. To compute s_{K+i} as in (2), we have to retrieve the values $s_{g(i)}, s_{h(i)}$, which are either the inputs to P or some intermediate values. Most importantly, we must show that the retrieval process is honestly performed.

To this end, a first idea, inspired by [29], is to perform a dichotomic search on $\mathbf{s} = (s_0, s_1, \ldots, s_{K-1}, s_K, \ldots, s_{K+N-2}) \in \{0,1\}^{K+N-1}$. The expected complexity for a single search is $\mathcal{O}(\log(K+N) \cdot \lambda \cdot \log \lambda)$ with λ being the security parameter. We however take a different approach and perform a "bucket" search. The expected complexity for a single search is $\mathcal{O}(\sqrt{K+N} + \lambda \cdot \log \lambda)$. The new complexity is smaller if $K+N$ is a small polynomial (say $o(\lambda^3)$) in λ.

The high-level idea of our "bucket" search is as follows. We divide $\mathbf{s}$ into ρ chunks $\mathbf{s}_0, \ldots, \mathbf{s}_{\rho-1}$, each of which is ρ-bit long[2]. Next, we commit to each chunk, obtaining ρ commitments: $\mathsf{com}_0, \ldots, \mathsf{com}_{\rho-1}$. Note that $\mathsf{idec}_\mathsf{P}(g(i)) = (g_{i,0}, \ldots, g_{i,\delta_\mathsf{P}-1})^\top$ is the binary representation of $g(i)$. Let $a_{g,i}$ and $b_{g,i}$ be the integers whose binary representation are the first $\delta_\mathsf{P}/2$ bits and second $\delta_\mathsf{P}/2$ bits of $\mathsf{idec}_\mathsf{P}(g(i))$, respectively. Then the bit $s_{g(i)}$ is committed in the $a_{g,i}$-th "bucket", i.e., $\mathsf{com}_{a_{g,i}}$, and it is the $b_{g,i}$-th bit (the index starts from 0) within this bucket. To search $s_{g(i)}$, we then prove the knowledge of a bit y_i satisfying the statement "y_i is the $b_{g,i}$-th bit within the $a_{g,i}$-th bucket". Due to the correctness of the proof system, $y_i = s_{g(i)}$. Said otherwise, we can provably perform a "bucket" search for $y_i = s_{g(i)}$.

We stress that the above retrieval process would not have protected P completely if m were not committed. This is because if one sees a bit of m used in computing (2), then some partial information about P could be leaked. Thus, we commit to m even though it is public. To show the publicity of m, we output the commitment randomnesses in the final signature Σ.

Proving in ZK that $t = F(P, \mathbf{x})$. Another challenge we have to tackle is to show the correctness of disclosing value $t = F(P, \mathbf{x})$, where F is a multivariate quadratic function – as mentioned above. Although this task is not as sophisticated as the one for hidden circuits, it also requires several non-trivial steps, among which is a sub-protocol for demonstrating the well-formedness of a Knonecker product $\mathbf{b} \otimes_{\mathrm{Kron}} \mathbf{b}$, where the bits of $\mathbf{b}$ simultaneously satisfy various other relations, e.g., they were hashed, signed and committed.

4.2 Scheme Description

We now describe our lattice-based BAPS scheme in detail.

[2] For simplicity, assume that $K+N-1 = 2^{\delta_\mathsf{P}}$ for an even integer δ_P. Then $\rho = 2^{\delta_\mathsf{P}/2}$.

$\mathsf{Setup}(1^\lambda)$: Given the security parameter 1^λ, it generates parameters as follows.

- Let $n = \mathcal{O}(\lambda)$ be a power of 2, let $q = 3^k$, and $f(X) = X^n + 1$ be a irreducible polynomial. Define rings $R = \mathbb{Z}[X]/(f(X))$ and $R_q = R/(qR)$.
- Let $k_1 = k_1(\lambda)$, $k_2' = k_2'(\lambda)$, $k_3 = k_3(\lambda)$ be positive integers. The message space is $\mathcal{M} = \{0,1\}^{k_1}$, the attribute space is $\mathcal{X} = \{0,1\}^{k_2}$ with $k_2 = n \cdot k_2'$, and the witness space is $\mathcal{W} = \{0,1\}^{k_3}$. Define $K = k_1 + k_2 + k_3$.
- Lets $\mathcal{P} = \{P : \{0,1\}^K \to \{0,1\}\}$, where each P is a Boolean circuit containing N NAND gates, and is uniquely determined by two functions $g, h : [0, N-1] \to [0, K+N-2]$. Let $\delta_\mathsf{P} = \lfloor \log(K+N-2) \rfloor + 1$.
- Let $m_\mathsf{P} = \lceil (2N\delta_\mathsf{P}/n) \rceil$. Generate a random matrix $\mathbf{A}_\mathsf{hp} \xleftarrow{\$} (R_q)^{1 \times m_\mathsf{P}}$, which determines a hash function in the family $\mathcal{H}_{m_\mathsf{P}}$ and which will be used to hash the description of policies.
- Let $\kappa = \omega(\log \lambda)$ and $\mathcal{H}_\mathsf{FS} : \{0,1\}^* \to \{0,1\}^\kappa$ be a collision-resistant hash function, which will be modelled as a random oracle.
- Let CMT be a computationally binding and statistically hiding string commitment scheme (adapted from [25]) that will be used in our zero-knowledge argument system.
- Initialize $S_\mathsf{X} := 0, S_\mathsf{P} := 0$. Set $c, \alpha_0, d, c_1, \ldots, c_d, m, \overline{m}, \ell$ and generate a verification-signing key-pair $(\mathsf{vk}_\mathsf{P}, \mathsf{msk}_\mathsf{P})$ for the DM signature scheme. Denote vk_P as

$$\mathbf{A}_\mathsf{P}, \mathbf{F}_{\mathsf{P},0} \in (R_q)^{1 \times \overline{m}}, \{\mathbf{A}_{\mathsf{P},[i]}\}_{i=0}^d \in (R_q^{1 \times k})^{d+1}, \mathbf{F}_\mathsf{P}, \mathbf{F}_{\mathsf{P},1} \in (R_q)^{1 \times \ell}, u_\mathsf{P} \in R_q,$$

  and signing key msk_P as $\mathbf{R}_\mathsf{P} \in (R_q)^{m \times k}$. Looking ahead, this key pair is used to sign hashes of the description of policies.
- We also generate another verification key and signing key pair to sign the attributes. Let vk_X be

$$\mathbf{A}_\mathsf{X}, \mathbf{F}_{\mathsf{X},0} \in (R_q)^{1 \times \overline{m}}, \{\mathbf{A}_{\mathsf{X},[i]}\}_{i=0}^d \in (R_q^{1 \times k})^{d+1}, \mathbf{F}_\mathsf{X}, \mathbf{F}_{\mathsf{X},1} \in (R_q)^{1 \times \ell}, u_\mathsf{X} \in R_q,$$

  and its corresponding signing key msk_X as $\mathbf{R}_\mathsf{X} \in (R_q)^{m \times k}$.
- For simplicity, let us assume that $K + N - 1$ is a perfect square and let $\rho = \sqrt{K+N-1}$ be its square root. We also assume that ρ is a multiple of n such that $\{0,1\}^\rho \subset (R_q)^{\rho'}$ with $\rho' = \frac{\rho}{n}$. Sample $\mathbf{A}_0 \xleftarrow{\$} (R_q)^{1 \times \rho'}$ and $\mathbf{A}_1 \xleftarrow{\$} (R_q)^{1 \times m}$ from the commitment scheme $\mathsf{CMT}_{\rho', m}$. Here $\mathbf{A}_0, \mathbf{A}_1$ are used to commit ρ-bit strings.
- Sample $\mathbf{A}_c \xleftarrow{\$} (R_q)^{1 \times \ell}$. This matrix $\mathbf{A}_c$ together with $\mathbf{A}_1$ will be used to commit to $n\ell$-bit strings.

Set the master policy key as $\mathsf{msk}_\mathsf{P} = \mathbf{R}_\mathsf{P} \in (R_q)^{m \times k}$ and master attribute key as $\mathsf{msk}_\mathsf{X} = \mathbf{R}_\mathsf{X} \in (R_q)^{m \times k}$.

$\mathsf{Attribute\text{-}Iss}(\mathsf{msk}_\mathsf{X}, \mathbf{x})$: Given msk_X and $\mathbf{x} \in \{0,1\}^{nk_2'} \subset (R_q)^{k_2'}$, this algorithm computes the tag $t_\mathbf{x} = (t_0, \ldots, t_{c_d-1})^\top \in \mathcal{T}_d$ such that $S_\mathsf{X} = \sum_{j=0}^{c_d-1} 2^{c_d-1-j} t_j$ and then updates S_X to $S_\mathsf{X} + 1$. It then runs the DM signing algorithm, obtaining a signature $\mathsf{sk}_\mathbf{x} = (t_\mathbf{x}, \mathbf{r}_\mathbf{x}, \mathbf{v}_\mathbf{x}) \in \{0,1\}^{c_d} \times R^{\overline{m}} \times R^{\overline{m}+k}$ such that:

$$\begin{cases} [\ \mathbf{A_X} \mid \mathbf{A}_{\mathsf{X},[0]} + \sum_{j=1}^{d} \mathbf{A}_{\mathsf{X},[i]} \cdot t_{\mathbf{x},[i]}] \cdot \mathbf{v_x} = y_{\mathbf{x}}; \\ y_{\mathbf{x}} = u_{\mathsf{X}} + \mathbf{F_X} \cdot \mathsf{rdec}(\ \mathbf{F}_{\mathsf{X},0} \cdot \mathbf{r_x} + \mathbf{F}_{\mathsf{X},1} \cdot \mathbf{x}\ ); \\ \|\mathbf{r_x}\|_\infty \leq \beta; \quad \|\mathbf{v_x}\|_\infty \leq \beta. \end{cases} \tag{3}$$

Here, rdec is a function that decomposes a ring vector to a vector of appropriate length over $\{-1, 0, 1\}$. (See the full version [40] for formal description.)

Policy-Iss($\mathsf{msk_P}, P$): Given $\mathsf{msk_P} = \mathbf{R_P}$ and a policy P, this algorithm generates certificate Cert_P in the following manner.

- Let the binary representation of the policy P be $\mathbf{z}_P \in \{0,1\}^{2N\delta_{\mathsf{P}}} \subset (R_q)^{m_{\mathsf{P}}}$, as defined in (1).
- Compute a hash of policy P as $h_P = \mathbf{A}_{\mathsf{hp}} \cdot \mathbf{z}_P \in R_q$.
- Use the key $\mathbf{R_P}$ to generate a signature $\mathsf{Cert}_P = (t_P, \mathbf{r}_P, \mathbf{v}_P) \in \{0,1\}^{c_d} \times R^{\overline{m}} \times R^{\overline{m}+k}$ on h_P such that:

$$\begin{cases} [\ \mathbf{A_P} \mid \mathbf{A}_{\mathsf{P},[0]} + \sum_{j=1}^{d} \mathbf{A}_{\mathsf{P},[i]} \cdot t_{P,[i]}\ ] \cdot \mathbf{v}_P = y_P; \\ y_P = u_{\mathsf{P}} + \mathbf{F_P} \cdot \mathsf{rdec}(\ \mathbf{F}_{\mathsf{P},0} \cdot \mathbf{r}_P + \mathbf{F}_{\mathsf{P},1} \cdot \mathbf{h}_P\ ); \\ \mathbf{h}_P = \mathsf{rdec}(\ \mathbf{A}_{\mathsf{hp}} \cdot \mathbf{z}_P\ ) \in \{-1,0,1\}^{n\ell}; \\ \|\mathbf{r}_P\|_\infty \leq \beta; \ \|\mathbf{v}_P\|_\infty \leq \beta. \end{cases} \tag{4}$$

Sign($\mathbf{x}, \mathsf{sk_x}, m, w, P, \mathsf{Cert}_P$): If $P(m, \mathbf{x}, w) = 0$, the signing algorithm returns $\perp$. Otherwise, proceed as follows. Let $m \in \{0,1\}^{k_1}$, $\mathbf{x} \in \{0,1\}^{nk_2'} \subset (R_q)^{k_2'}$, $w \in \{0,1\}^{k_3}$. Parse $\mathsf{sk_x} = (t_\mathbf{x}, \mathbf{r_x}, \mathbf{v_x})$ and $\mathsf{Cert}_P = (t_P, \mathbf{r}_P, \mathbf{v}_P)$.

- First, we rename some inputs to facilitate the presentation. Denote $m = (s_0, \ldots, s_{k_1-1})^\top \in \{0,1\}^{k_1}$, $\mathbf{x} = (s_{k_1}, \ldots, s_{k_1+k_2-1})^\top \in \{0,1\}^{k_2}$, and $w = (s_{k_1+k_2}, \ldots, s_{K-1})^\top \in \{0,1\}^{k_3}$. Let the intermediate wires in the circuit P be $s_K, \ldots, s_{K+N-2}$ and the output wire be s_{K+N-1}. Recall that we assume $K + N - 1 = \rho^2$.
- Next, we will divide the secret bits of $\mathbf{s} = (s_0, \ldots, s_{K+N-2}) \in \{0,1\}^{\rho^2}$ into ρ-bit chunks and commit to each of the ρ chunks. To do so, for $i \in [0, \rho-1]$, let $\mathbf{s}_i = (s_{i\cdot\rho}, s_{i\cdot\rho+1}, \ldots, s_{i\cdot\rho+\rho-1})^\top$, sample randomness $\mathbf{r}_{\mathsf{com},i} \xleftarrow{\$} \{0,1\}^{nm}$ and compute $\mathsf{com}_i = \mathbf{A}_0 \cdot \mathbf{s}_i + \mathbf{A}_1 \cdot \mathbf{r}_{\mathsf{com},i} \in R_q$. Without loss of generality, assume $k_1 = \mu_1\rho$, $k_2 = \mu_2\rho$ for some integers μ_1, μ_2. Thus, $\mathsf{com}_0, \ldots, \mathsf{com}_{\mu_1-1}$ are commitments to m and $\mathsf{com}_{\mu_1}, \ldots, \mathsf{com}_{\mu_1+\mu_2-1}$ are commitments to $\mathbf{x}$. It is worth noting that we still commit to m even though m is public. This is essential in proving $P(m, \mathbf{x}, w) = 1$ without revealing P. To demonstrate that m is public, we will reveal the underlying commitment randomness in the resulting signature.
- Third, we will commit to the hash of the policy description. Let $\mathbf{z}_P \subseteq (R_q)^{m_{\mathsf{P}}}$ be the representation of P. Compute $h_P = \mathbf{A}_{\mathsf{hp}} \cdot \mathbf{z}_P \in R_q$ and $\mathbf{h}_P = \mathsf{rdec}(h_P) \in \{-1,0,1\}^{n\ell}$. We then sample randomness $\mathbf{r}_{\mathsf{com},P} \xleftarrow{\$} \{0,1\}^{nm}$ and let $\mathsf{com}_P = \mathbf{A}_c \cdot \mathbf{h}_P + \mathbf{A}_1 \cdot \mathbf{r}_{\mathsf{com},P}$ be a commitment of P.

For notational purposes, define

$$\begin{aligned}
\mathbf{s}_{else} &= (s_{k_1+k_2}, s_{k_1+k_2+1}, \ldots, s_{K+N-2})^\top \in \{0,1\}^{K+N-1-k_1-k_2},\\
\mathsf{com}_m &= (\mathsf{com}_0^\top \mid \cdots \mid \mathsf{com}_{\mu_1-1}^\top)^\top \in R_q^{\mu_1},\\
\mathsf{com}_{\mathbf{x}} &= (\mathsf{com}_{\mu_1}^\top \mid \cdots \mid \mathsf{com}_{\mu_1+\mu_2-1}^\top)^\top \in R_q^{\mu_2},\\
\mathsf{com}_{else} &= (\mathsf{com}_{\mu_1+\mu_2}^\top \mid \cdots \mid \mathsf{com}_{\rho-1}^\top)^\top \in R_q^{\rho-\mu_1-\mu_2},\\
\mathbf{r}_{\mathsf{com},m} &= (\mathbf{r}_{\mathsf{com},0}^\top \mid \cdots \mid \mathbf{r}_{\mathsf{com},\mu_1-1}^\top)^\top \in \{0,1\}^{nm\mu_1},\\
\mathbf{r}_{\mathsf{com},\mathbf{x}} &= (\mathbf{r}_{\mathsf{com},\mu_1}^\top \mid \cdots \mid \mathbf{r}_{\mathsf{com},\mu_1+\mu_2-1}^\top)^\top \in \{0,1\}^{nm\mu_2},\\
\mathbf{r}_{\mathsf{com},else} &= (\mathbf{r}_{\mathsf{com},\mu_1+\mu_2}^\top \mid \cdots \mid \mathbf{r}_{\mathsf{com},\rho-1}^\top)^\top \in \{0,1\}^{nm(\rho-\mu_1-\mu_2)}.
\end{aligned}$$

Once the commitment process is done, this algorithm then generates a NIZK argument demonstrating the knowledge of

$$\eta = (\mathbf{x}, \mathsf{sk}_{\mathbf{x}}, \mathbf{z}_P, \mathbf{h}_P, \mathsf{Cert}_P, w, s_K, \ldots, s_{K+N-2}, \mathbf{r}_{\mathsf{com},\mathbf{x}}, \mathbf{r}_{\mathsf{com},else}, \mathbf{r}_{\mathsf{com},P})$$

such that the following conditions hold.

(a) The message is signable with respect to policy P, attribute $\mathbf{x}$, and witness w, i.e., $P(m, \mathbf{x}, w) = 1$, or equivalently, equations (2) hold.

(b) $\mathsf{com}_{\mathbf{x}}$ and com_{else} are valid commitments to $\mathbf{x}$ and $\mathbf{s}_{else}$ with randomnesses $\mathbf{r}_{\mathsf{com},\mathbf{x}}$ and $\mathbf{r}_{\mathsf{com},else}$, respectively. In addition, com_P is a valid commitment to $\mathbf{h}_P$ with randomness $\mathbf{r}_{\mathsf{com},P}$. In other words, the following equations are satisfied.

$$\begin{cases} \mathsf{com}_i = \mathbf{A}_0 \cdot \mathbf{s}_i + \mathbf{A}_1 \cdot \mathbf{r}_{\mathsf{com},i}, & \forall i \in [\mu_1, \rho-1] \\ \mathsf{com}_P = \mathbf{A}_c \cdot \mathbf{h}_P + \mathbf{A}_1 \cdot \mathbf{r}_{\mathsf{com},P}. \end{cases} \tag{5}$$

(c) $\mathsf{sk}_{\mathbf{x}}$ is a valid signing key for attribute $\mathbf{x}$, i.e., $(\mathbf{x}, \mathsf{sk}_{\mathbf{x}})$ satisfies (3).

(d) Cert_P is a valid certificate for policy P, i.e., $(\mathbf{z}_P, \mathbf{h}_P, \mathsf{Cert}_P)$ satisfies (4).

This is done via a dedicated Stern-like argument (details are in the full version [40]). The protocol is repeated $\kappa = \omega(\log \lambda)$ times to achieve negligible soundness error and made non-interactive [18]. Let the resultant proof be

$$\Pi = \big(\{\mathsf{COM}_i\}_{i=0}^{\kappa-1}, \{\mathsf{CH}_i\}_{i=0}^{\kappa-1}, \{\mathsf{RSP}_i\}_{i=0}^{\kappa-1} \big), \tag{6}$$

where $(\mathsf{CH}_0, \ldots, \mathsf{CH}_{\kappa-1})^\top = \mathcal{H}_{\mathsf{FS}}(\{\mathsf{COM}_i\}_{i=0}^{\kappa-1}, \xi)$ and ξ is of the form

$$(\, m, \mathsf{vk_X}, \mathsf{vk_P}, \mathbf{A}_{\mathsf{hp}}, \mathbf{A}_c, \mathbf{A}_0, \mathbf{A}_1, \mathsf{com}_m, \mathsf{com}_{\mathbf{x}}, \mathsf{com}_{else}, \mathsf{com}_P, \mathbf{r}_{\mathsf{com},m} \,). \tag{7}$$

Return the signature as $\Sigma = (\mathsf{com}_m, \mathsf{com}_{\mathbf{x}}, \mathsf{com}_{else}, \mathsf{com}_P, \mathbf{r}_{\mathsf{com},m}, \Pi)$ and the clue as $\mathsf{clue} = (\mathbf{x}, P, \mathbf{r}_{\mathsf{com},\mathbf{x}}, \mathbf{r}_{\mathsf{com},P})$. Note that all the commitments are needed for the verification of Π. Also, as m is public, the randomnesses $\mathbf{r}_{\mathsf{com},m}$ are included in Σ.

$\mathsf{Verify}(m, \Sigma)$: This algorithm verifies the validity of the signature Σ as follows.

- Let $m = (s_0, \ldots, s_{k_1-1})^\top \in \{0,1\}^{k_1}$ and $\mathbf{s}_i = (s_{i\cdot\rho}, s_{i\cdot\rho+1}, \ldots, s_{i\cdot\rho+\rho-1})^\top$ for $i \in [0, \mu_1 - 1]$.

– Parse $\Sigma = (\mathsf{com}_m, \mathsf{com}_{\mathbf{x}}, \mathsf{com}_{else}, \mathsf{com}_P, \mathbf{r}_{\mathsf{com},m}, \Pi)$, where Π is as in (6), $\mathsf{com}_m = (\mathsf{com}_0^\top \mid \cdots \mid \mathsf{com}_{\mu_1-1}^\top)^\top$, and $\mathbf{r}_{\mathsf{com},m} = (\mathbf{r}_{\mathsf{com},0}^\top \mid \cdots \mid \mathbf{r}_{\mathsf{com},\mu_1-1}^\top)^\top$.
– Return 1 if and only if the following conditions are satisfied.
  (i) $(\mathsf{CH}_0, \ldots, \mathsf{CH}_{\kappa-1})^\top = \mathcal{H}_{\mathsf{FS}}(\{\mathsf{COM}_i\}_{i=0}^{\kappa-1}, \xi)$ with ξ as in (7).
  (ii) For all $i \in [0, \mu_1 - 1]$, $\mathsf{com}_i = \mathbf{A}_0 \cdot \mathbf{s}_i + \mathbf{A}_1 \cdot \mathbf{r}_{\mathsf{com},i}$.
  (iii) For all $j \in [0, \kappa - 1]$, response RSP_j is valid with respect to commitment COM_j and the challenge CH_j.

$\mathsf{Disclose}(m, \Sigma, \mathsf{clue}, F)$: This algorithm computes a testimony-attestation pair as follows.
– Let $\mathbf{x} = (s_{k_1}, \ldots, s_{k_1+k_2-1})^\top \in \{0,1\}^{k_2}$, and for $i \in [\mu_1, \mu_1 + \mu_2 - 1]$, let $\mathbf{s}_i = (s_{i\cdot\rho}, s_{i\cdot\rho+1}, \ldots, s_{i\cdot\rho+\rho-1})^\top$.
– Parse $\Sigma = (\mathsf{com}_m, \mathsf{com}_{\mathbf{x}}, \mathsf{com}_{else}, \mathsf{com}_P, \mathbf{r}_{\mathsf{com},m}, \Pi)$, where Π is as in (6), $\mathsf{com}_{\mathbf{x}} = (\mathsf{com}_{\mu_1}^\top | \cdots | \mathsf{com}_{\mu_1+\mu_2-1}^\top)^\top$, $\mathbf{r}_{\mathsf{com},\mathbf{x}} = (\mathbf{r}_{\mathsf{com},\mu_1}^\top | \cdots | \mathbf{r}_{\mathsf{com},\mu_1+\mu_2-1}^\top)^\top$. Return 0 if $\mathsf{Verify}(m, \Sigma) = 0$.
– Parse $\mathsf{clue} = (\mathbf{x}, P, \mathbf{r}_{\mathsf{com},\mathbf{x}}, \mathbf{r}_{\mathsf{com},P})$.
– Let the binary representation of P be $\mathbf{z}_P \in \{0,1\}^{2N\delta_P}$, and F be determined by two matrices $\mathbf{G}_1 \in \{0,1\}^{\bar{k}\times\bar{k}^2}$ and $\mathbf{G}_2 \in \{0,1\}^{\bar{k}\times\bar{k}}$. Next, denote $\mathbf{b} = (\mathbf{z}_P^\top \mid \mathbf{x}^\top)^\top$ and then compute the testimony as

$$t = \mathbf{G}_1 \cdot (\mathbf{b} \otimes_{\mathrm{Kron}} \mathbf{b}) + \mathbf{G}_2 \cdot \mathbf{b} \bmod 2.$$

– Generate a NIZK argument of knowledge of clue such that the following conditions hold.
  (i) The testimony t is honestly computed, i.e., for $\mathbf{b} = (\mathbf{z}_P^\top \mid \mathbf{x}^\top)^\top$,

$$t = F(P, \mathbf{x}) = \mathbf{G}_1 \cdot (\mathbf{b} \otimes_{\mathrm{Kron}} \mathbf{b}) + \mathbf{G}_2 \cdot \mathbf{b} \bmod 2.$$

  (ii) $\mathsf{com}_{\mathbf{x}}$ and com_P are valid commitments of $\mathbf{x}$ and P, i.e.,

$$\mathsf{com}_P = \mathbf{A}_c \cdot \mathbf{h}_P + \mathbf{A}_1 \cdot \mathbf{r}_{\mathsf{com},P}, \quad \text{with } \mathbf{h}_P = \mathsf{rdec}(\mathbf{A}_{\mathsf{hp}} \cdot \mathbf{z}_P);$$
$$\mathsf{com}_i = \mathbf{A}_0 \cdot \mathbf{s}_i + \mathbf{A}_1 \cdot \mathbf{r}_{\mathsf{com},i}, \quad \forall\, i \in [\mu_1, \mu_1 + \mu_2 - 1].$$

  This can be done by running a Stern-like argument on public input $\xi_{\mathsf{D}} = (\mathbf{G}_1, \mathbf{G}_2, t, \mathsf{com}_{\mathbf{x}}, \mathsf{com}_P, \mathbf{A}_{\mathsf{hp}}, \mathbf{A}_c, \mathbf{A}_0, \mathbf{A}_1)$ and secret input clue. The protocol is conducted $\kappa = \omega(\log\lambda)$ times in parallel to obtain negligible soundness error and then made non-interactive via the Fiat-Shamir heuristic [18]. The resultant proof a is a triple of a form

$$a = (\{\mathsf{COM}_{\mathsf{D},i}\}_{i=0}^{\kappa-1}, \{\mathsf{CH}_{\mathsf{D},i}\}_{i=0}^{\kappa-1}, \{\mathsf{RSP}_{\mathsf{D},i}\}_{i=0}^{\kappa-1}), \tag{8}$$

  where $(\mathsf{CH}_{\mathsf{D},0}, \ldots, \mathsf{CH}_{\mathsf{D},\kappa-1})^\top = \mathcal{H}_{\mathsf{FS}}(\{\mathsf{COM}_{\mathsf{D},i}\}_{i=0}^{\kappa-1}, \xi_{\mathsf{D}})$.
– Return t and a.

$\mathsf{Judge}(m, \Sigma, F, t, a)$: If $\mathsf{Verify}(m, \Sigma) = 0$, return 0. Otherwise, it proceeds to verify the validity of a, which is quite similar to the verification of Π. Return 1 if a is valid and 0 otherwise.

4.3 Analyses

Correctness. The correctness of our construction relies on two facts: (i) The employed Ducas-Micciancio signature scheme is correct with overwhelming probability; (ii) The two underlying zero-knowledge argument systems are perfectly correct. Therefore, for any policy P, any attribute $\mathbf{x}$, any message m such that $P(m, \mathbf{x}, w) = 1$ for some witness w, if a signer owns honestly-generated signing key for $\mathbf{x}$ and certificate for P, and signs the message faithfully as in the Sign algorithm, then the Verify algorithm outputs 1 with overwhelming probability. In addition, clue contains P, $\mathbf{x}$, and randomnesses for committing them. Therefore, the testimony can be correctly computed as $t = F(P, \mathbf{x})$ and the attestation a, honestly generated with the knowledge of clue, will pass the Judge algorithm.

Asymptotic Efficiency. We analyze the efficiency of our construction w.r.t. the security parameter λ, the number K of inputs in P, and the number N of NAND gates in P.

- The public parameters are dominated by $\mathsf{vk}_{\mathsf{X}}, \mathsf{vk}_{\mathsf{P}}, \mathbf{A}_{\mathsf{hp}}, \mathbf{A}_c, \mathbf{A}_0, \mathbf{A}_1$, which are of $\mathcal{O}(\ N \cdot \log(K+N) \cdot \log\lambda + \lambda \cdot (\log\lambda)^2\ )$ bits.
- The $\mathsf{msk}_{\mathsf{X}}$ and $\mathsf{msk}_{\mathsf{P}}$ have bit size $\mathcal{O}(\lambda \cdot (\log\lambda)^3)$.
- The signature size is dominated by the size of Π, which has bit size $\kappa \cdot \mathcal{O}(\ L_1 \cdot \log q + L_{\mathsf{P}}) = \kappa \cdot \mathcal{O}(\ \lambda \cdot (\log\lambda)^5 + N\sqrt{K+N}\log\lambda + N \cdot \lambda \cdot (\log\lambda)^2 + (K+N)\log\lambda + \lambda\sqrt{K+N}(\log\lambda)^2\ )$.
- The size of attestation is $\kappa \cdot \mathcal{O}(\ L_2 \cdot \log q + L_{\mathsf{D}}\ ) = \kappa \cdot \mathcal{O}(\ k_2 \cdot \log\lambda + \mu_2\lambda \cdot (\log\lambda)^2 + N^2 \cdot \log^2(K+N) + k_2^2\ )$.

Security. In the random oracle model, our construction satisfies simulatability and extractability. In particular, the construction is simulatable based on the facts that (i) the two underlying argument systems are statistical ZK and (ii) the commitment schemes $\mathsf{CMT}_{\rho',m}, \mathsf{CMT}_{\ell,m}$ are statistically hiding. Extractability relies on (i) the computational soundness of the two underlying ZKAoK systems, (ii) the computational binding property of $\mathsf{CMT}_{\rho',m}$ and $\mathsf{CMT}_{\ell,m}$, (iii) EUF-CMA security of the Ducas-Micciancio signature scheme, and (iv) the collision resistance of the hash function family $\mathcal{H}_{m_{\mathsf{P}}}$. We summarize the security in the following theorems and provide detailed proofs in the full version [40].

Theorem 3. *Assume that the two underlying zero-knowledge argument systems are statistical zero-knowledge and the commitment schemes* $\mathsf{CMT}_{\rho',m}, \mathsf{CMT}_{\ell,m}$ *are statistically hiding. Then the proposed BAPS scheme is simulatable.*

Theorem 4. *The proposed BAPS scheme is extractable if the two underlying argument systems are computationally knowledge sound, the two commitment schemes* $\mathsf{CMT}_{\rho',m}$, $\mathsf{CMT}_{\ell,m}$ *are computationally binding, the DM signature scheme is* EUF-CMA *secure, and the hash function family* $\mathcal{H}_{m_{\mathsf{P}}}$ *is collision-resistant.*

Acknowledgements. We thank the anonymous reviewers of ASIACRYPT 2023 for their helpful comments and suggestions. The work of Yanhong Xu was supported in part by the National Key Research and Development Program under Grant 2022YFA1004900. Willy Susilo was partially supported by the Australian Research Council (ARC) Discovery project (DP200100144) and the Australian Laureate Fellowship (FL230100033).

References

1. Attrapadung, N., Hanaoka, G., Yamada, S.: Conversions among several classes of predicate encryption and applications to ABE with various compactness tradeoffs. In: Iwata, T., Cheon, J.H. (eds.) ASIACRYPT 2015. LNCS, vol. 9452, pp. 575–601. Springer, Heidelberg (2015). https://doi.org/10.1007/978-3-662-48797-6_24
2. Bellare, M., Fuchsbauer, G.: Policy-based signatures. In: Krawczyk, H. (ed.) PKC 2014. LNCS, vol. 8383, pp. 520–537. Springer, Heidelberg (2014). https://doi.org/10.1007/978-3-642-54631-0_30
3. Bellare, M., Micciancio, D., Warinschi, B.: Foundations of group signatures: formal definitions, simplified requirements, and a construction based on general assumptions. In: Biham, E. (ed.) EUROCRYPT 2003. LNCS, vol. 2656, pp. 614–629. Springer, Heidelberg (2003). https://doi.org/10.1007/3-540-39200-9_38
4. Bender, A., Katz, J., Morselli, R.: Ring signatures: stronger definitions, and constructions without random oracles. J. Cryptol. **22**(1), 114–138 (2009)
5. Boneh, D., Sahai, A., Waters, B.: Functional encryption: definitions and challenges. In: Ishai, Y. (ed.) TCC 2011. LNCS, vol. 6597, pp. 253–273. Springer, Heidelberg (2011). https://doi.org/10.1007/978-3-642-19571-6_16
6. Bootle, J., Lyubashevsky, V., Nguyen, N.K., Sorniotti, A.: A framework for practical anonymous credentials from lattices. In: CRYPTO 2023, LNCS, vol. 14082, pp. 384–417. Springer (2023). https://doi.org/10.1007/978-3-031-38545-2_13
7. Bootle, J., Lyubashevsky, V., Seiler, G.: Algebraic techniques for short(er) exact lattice-based zero-knowledge proofs. In: Boldyreva, A., Micciancio, D. (eds.) CRYPTO 2019. LNCS, vol. 11692, pp. 176–202. Springer, Cham (2019). https://doi.org/10.1007/978-3-030-26948-7_7
8. Boyle, E., Goldwasser, S., Ivan, I.: Functional signatures and pseudorandom functions. In: Krawczyk, H. (ed.) PKC 2014. LNCS, vol. 8383, pp. 501–519. Springer, Heidelberg (2014). https://doi.org/10.1007/978-3-642-54631-0_29
9. Camenisch, J., Hohenberger, S., Lysyanskaya, A.: Balancing accountability and privacy using e-cash (Extended Abstract). In: De Prisco, R., Yung, M. (eds.) SCN 2006. LNCS, vol. 4116, pp. 141–155. Springer, Heidelberg (2006). https://doi.org/10.1007/11832072_10
10. Chase, M., Lysyanskaya, A.: On signatures of knowledge. In: Dwork, C. (ed.) CRYPTO 2006. LNCS, vol. 4117, pp. 78–96. Springer, Heidelberg (2006). https://doi.org/10.1007/11818175_5
11. Chaum, D., van Heyst, E.: Group Signatures. In: Davies, D.W. (ed.) Advances in Cryptology — EUROCRYPT '91, pp. 257–265. Springer Berlin Heidelberg, Berlin, Heidelberg (1991). https://doi.org/10.1007/3-540-46416-6_22
12. Cheng, S., Nguyen, K., Wang, H.: Policy-based signature scheme from lattices. Des. Codes Cryptogr. **81**(1), 43–74 (2016)
13. Ducas, L., Micciancio, D.: Improved short lattice signatures in the standard model. In: Garay, J.A., Gennaro, R. (eds.) CRYPTO 2014. LNCS, vol. 8616, pp. 335–352. Springer, Heidelberg (2014). https://doi.org/10.1007/978-3-662-44371-2_19

14. Esgin, M.F., Nguyen, N.K., Seiler, G.: Practical exact proofs from lattices: new techniques to exploit fully-splitting rings. In: Moriai, S., Wang, H. (eds.) ASIACRYPT 2020. LNCS, vol. 12492, pp. 259–288. Springer, Cham (2020). https://doi.org/10.1007/978-3-030-64834-3_9
15. Esgin, M.F., Steinfeld, R., Liu, D., Ruj, S.: Efficient hybrid exact/relaxed lattice proofs and applications to rounding and VRFs. In: CRYPTO 2023, LNCS, vol. 14085, pp. 484–517. Springer (2023). https://doi.org/10.1007/978-3-031-38554-4_16
16. Esgin, M.F., Steinfeld, R., Liu, J.K., Liu, D.: Lattice-based zero-knowledge proofs: new techniques for shorter and faster constructions and applications. In: Boldyreva, A., Micciancio, D. (eds.) CRYPTO 2019. LNCS, vol. 11692, pp. 115–146. Springer, Cham (2019). https://doi.org/10.1007/978-3-030-26948-7_5
17. Faust, S., Kohlweiss, M., Marson, G.A., Venturi, D.: On the non-malleability of the fiat-shamir transform. In: Galbraith, S., Nandi, M. (eds.) INDOCRYPT 2012. LNCS, vol. 7668, pp. 60–79. Springer, Heidelberg (2012). https://doi.org/10.1007/978-3-642-34931-7_5
18. Fiat, A., Shamir, A.: How to prove yourself: practical solutions to identification and signature problems. In: Odlyzko, A.M. (ed.) CRYPTO 1986. LNCS, vol. 263, pp. 186–194. Springer, Heidelberg (1987). https://doi.org/10.1007/3-540-47721-7_12
19. Fujisaki, E., Suzuki, K.: Traceable ring signature. In: Okamoto, T., Wang, X. (eds.) PKC 2007. LNCS, vol. 4450, pp. 181–200. Springer, Heidelberg (2007). https://doi.org/10.1007/978-3-540-71677-8_13
20. Goldwasser, S., Micali, S., Rackoff, C.: The knowledge complexity of interactive proof systems. SIAM J. Comput. **18**(1), 186–208 (1989)
21. Groth, J.: Simulation-sound NIZK proofs for a practical language and constant size group signatures. In: Lai, X., Chen, K. (eds.) ASIACRYPT 2006. LNCS, vol. 4284, pp. 444–459. Springer, Heidelberg (2006). https://doi.org/10.1007/11935230_29
22. Groth, J., Ostrovsky, R., Sahai, A.: Perfect non-interactive zero knowledge for NP. In: Vaudenay, S. (ed.) EUROCRYPT 2006. LNCS, vol. 4004, pp. 339–358. Springer, Heidelberg (2006). https://doi.org/10.1007/11761679_21
23. Jeudy, C., Roux-Langlois, A., Sanders, O.: Lattice signature with efficient protocols, application to anonymous credentials. In: CRYPTO 2023, LNCS, vol. 14082, pp. 351–383. Springer (2023). https://doi.org/10.1007/978-3-031-38545-2_12
24. Katsumata, S., Yamada, S.: Group signatures without NIZK: from lattices in the standard model. In: Ishai, Y., Rijmen, V. (eds.) EUROCRYPT 2019. LNCS, vol. 11478, pp. 312–344. Springer, Cham (2019). https://doi.org/10.1007/978-3-030-17659-4_11
25. Kawachi, A., Tanaka, K., Xagawa, K.: Concurrently secure identification schemes based on the worst-case hardness of lattice problems. In: Pieprzyk, J. (ed.) ASIACRYPT 2008. LNCS, vol. 5350, pp. 372–389. Springer, Heidelberg (2008). https://doi.org/10.1007/978-3-540-89255-7_23
26. Kiayias, A., Tsiounis, Y., Yung, M.: Traceable signatures. In: Cachin, C., Camenisch, J.L. (eds.) EUROCRYPT 2004. LNCS, vol. 3027, pp. 571–589. Springer, Heidelberg (2004). https://doi.org/10.1007/978-3-540-24676-3_34
27. Kohlweiss, M., Miers, I.: Accountable metadata-hiding escrow: a group signature case study. Proc. Priv. Enhancing Technol. **2015**(2), 206–221 (2015)
28. Kroll, J., Huey, J., Barocas, S., Felten, E., Reidenberg, J., Robinson, D., Yu, H.: Accountable algorithms. U. PA Law Rev. **165**(3), 633–705 (2017)

29. Libert, B., Ling, S., Mouhartem, F., Nguyen, K., Wang, H.: Adaptive oblivious transfer with access control from lattice assumptions. In: Takagi, T., Peyrin, T. (eds.) ASIACRYPT 2017. LNCS, vol. 10624, pp. 533–563. Springer, Cham (2017). https://doi.org/10.1007/978-3-319-70694-8_19
30. Libert, B., Ling, S., Nguyen, K., Wang, H.: Zero-knowledge arguments for lattice-based PRFs and applications to e-cash. In: Takagi, T., Peyrin, T. (eds.) ASIACRYPT 2017. LNCS, vol. 10626, pp. 304–335. Springer, Cham (2017). https://doi.org/10.1007/978-3-319-70700-6_11
31. Libert, B., Nguyen, K., Passelègue, A., Titiu, R.: Simulation-sound arguments for LWE and applications to KDM-CCA2 security. In: Moriai, S., Wang, H. (eds.) ASIACRYPT 2020. LNCS, vol. 12491, pp. 128–158. Springer, Cham (2020). https://doi.org/10.1007/978-3-030-64837-4_5
32. Libert, B., Nguyen, K., Peters, T., Yung, M.: Bifurcated signatures: folding the accountability vs. anonymity dilemma into a single private signing scheme. In: Canteaut, A., Standaert, F.-X. (eds.) EUROCRYPT 2021. LNCS, vol. 12698, pp. 521–552. Springer, Cham (2021). https://doi.org/10.1007/978-3-030-77883-5_18
33. Ling, S., Nguyen, K., Phan, D.H., Tang, H., Wang, H.: Zero-knowledge proofs for committed symmetric Boolean functions. In: Cheon, J.H., Tillich, J.-P. (eds.) PQCrypto 2021 2021. LNCS, vol. 12841, pp. 339–359. Springer, Cham (2021). https://doi.org/10.1007/978-3-030-81293-5_18
34. Ling, S., Nguyen, K., Stehlé, D., Wang, H.: Improved zero-knowledge proofs of knowledge for the ISIS problem, and applications. In: Kurosawa, K., Hanaoka, G. (eds.) PKC 2013. LNCS, vol. 7778, pp. 107–124. Springer, Heidelberg (2013). https://doi.org/10.1007/978-3-642-36362-7_8
35. Ling, S., Nguyen, K., Wang, H., Xu, Y.: Constant-size group signatures from lattices. In: Abdalla, M., Dahab, R. (eds.) PKC 2018. LNCS, vol. 10770, pp. 58–88. Springer, Cham (2018). https://doi.org/10.1007/978-3-319-76581-5_3
36. Lyubashevsky, V., Nguyen, N.K., Plançon, M.: Lattice-based zero-knowledge proofs and applications: shorter, simpler, and more general. In: CRYPTO 2022, LNCS, vol. 13508, pp. 71–101. Springer (2022). https://doi.org/10.1007/978-3-031-15979-4_3
37. Maji, H.K., Prabhakaran, M., Rosulek, M.: Attribute-based signatures. In: Kiayias, A. (ed.) CT-RSA 2011. LNCS, vol. 6558, pp. 376–392. Springer, Heidelberg (2011). https://doi.org/10.1007/978-3-642-19074-2_24
38. Micciancio, D.: Generalized compact knapsacks, cyclic lattices, and efficient one-way functions. Comput. Complex. **16**(4), 365–411 (2007)
39. Nguyen, K., Guo, F., Susilo, W., Yang, G.: Multimodal private signatures. In: CRYPTO 2022. LNCS, vol. 13508, pp. 792–822. Springer (2022). https://doi.org/10.1007/978-3-031-15979-4_27
40. Nguyen, K., Roy, P.S., Susilo, W., Xu, Y.: Bicameral and auditably private signatures. Cryptology ePrint Archive, Paper 2023/1351 (2023). https://eprint.iacr.org/2023/1351
41. Peikert, C., Shiehian, S.: Noninteractive zero knowledge for np from (plain) learning with errors. In: Boldyreva, A., Micciancio, D. (eds.) CRYPTO 2019. LNCS, vol. 11692, pp. 89–114. Springer, Cham (2019). https://doi.org/10.1007/978-3-030-26948-7_4
42. Rivest, R.L., Shamir, A., Tauman, Y.: How to leak a secret. In: Boyd, C. (ed.) ASIACRYPT 2001. LNCS, vol. 2248, pp. 552–565. Springer, Heidelberg (2001). https://doi.org/10.1007/3-540-45682-1_32

43. Sakai, Y., Emura, K., Hanaoka, G., Kawai, Y., Matsuda, T., Omote, K.: Group signatures with message-dependent opening. In: Abdalla, M., Lange, T. (eds.) Pairing 2012. LNCS, vol. 7708, pp. 270–294. Springer, Heidelberg (2013). https://doi.org/10.1007/978-3-642-36334-4_18
44. Stern, J.: A new paradigm for public key identification. IEEE Trans. Inf. Theory **42**(6), 1757–1768 (1996)
45. Xu, S., Yung, M.: Accountable ring signatures: a smart card approach. In: Quisquater, J.-J., Paradinas, P., Deswarte, Y., El Kalam, A.A. (eds.) CARDIS 2004. IIFIP, vol. 153, pp. 271–286. Springer, Boston, MA (2004). https://doi.org/10.1007/1-4020-8147-2_18
46. Yang, R., Au, M.H., Zhang, Z., Xu, Q., Yu, Z., Whyte, W.: Efficient lattice-based zero-knowledge arguments with standard soundness: construction and applications. In: Boldyreva, A., Micciancio, D. (eds.) CRYPTO 2019. LNCS, vol. 11692, pp. 147–175. Springer, Cham (2019). https://doi.org/10.1007/978-3-030-26948-7_6

Threshold Structure-Preserving Signatures

Elizabeth Crites[1], Markulf Kohlweiss[1,2], Bart Preneel[3], Mahdi Sedaghat[3(✉)], and Daniel Slamanig[4]

[1] University of Edinburgh, Edinburgh, UK
ecrites@ed.ac.uk, mkohlwei@inf.ed.ac.uk
[2] Input Output, Edinburgh, UK
[3] COSIC, KU Leuven, Leuven, Belgium
bart.preneel@esat.kuleuven.be, ssedagha@esat.kuleuven.be
[4] AIT Austrian Institute of Technology, Vienna, Austria
daniel.slamanig@ait.ac.at

Abstract. Structure-preserving signatures (SPS) are an important building block for privacy-preserving cryptographic primitives, such as electronic cash, anonymous credentials, and delegatable anonymous credentials. In this work, we introduce the first *threshold* structure-preserving signature scheme (TSPS). This enables multiple parties to jointly sign a message, resulting in a standard, single-party SPS signature, and can thus be used as a replacement for applications based on SPS.

We begin by defining and constructing SPS for indexed messages, which are messages defined relative to a unique index. We prove its security in the random oracle model under a variant of the generalized Pointcheval-Sanders assumption (PS). Moreover, we generalize this scheme to an indexed multi-message SPS for signing vectors of indexed messages, which we prove secure under the same assumption. We then formally define the notion of a TSPS and propose a construction based on our indexed multi-message SPS. Our TSPS construction is *fully non-interactive*, meaning that signers simply output partial signatures without communicating with the other signers. Additionally, signatures are short: they consist of 2 group elements and require 2 pairing product equations to verify. We prove the security of our TSPS under the security of our indexed multi-message SPS scheme. Finally, we show that our TSPS may be used as a drop-in replacement for UC-secure Threshold-Issuance Anonymous Credential (TIAC) schemes, such as Coconut, without the overhead of the Fischlin transform.

Keywords: Threshold Signatures · Structure-Preserving Signatures · Indexed Message Structure-Preserving Signatures

1 Introduction

Threshold cryptography [37–39] was designed to reduce the trust in single entities and improve the availability of keying material. It allows a secret key to

J. Guo and R. Steinfeld (Eds.): ASIACRYPT 2023, LNCS 14439, pp. 348–382, 2023.
https://doi.org/10.1007/978-981-99-8724-5_11

be shared among a set of parties [16,79] such that the task involving the key can only be performed if some threshold of them collaborates. Threshold signatures [35,80], threshold encryption [26,81], and threshold verifiable unpredictable functions [61] enable distributed protocols, such as e-voting systems [30,31] and multi-party computation [29,36].

Threshold signatures in particular have attracted significant interest recently, in part because of advances in distributed ledger technologies, cryptocurrencies, and decentralized identity management [25,33,40,68,69]. They are also the subject of current standardization efforts by NIST [20,21]. Signatures used by certification authorities to issue credentials or to secure digital wallets make attractive targets for misuse or forgery. To mitigate these risks, an (n, t)-threshold signature scheme distributes the signing key among n parties such that any quorum of at least t signers can jointly generate a signature, but the scheme remains secure as long as fewer than t key shares are known to the adversary.

A threshold signature that is *fully non-interactive* consists of a single round of communication. On input the message, each signer computes its partial signature independently of other signers, and aggregation of at least t partial signatures results in a single signature representing the group. Interactive signing protocols involving two or more rounds add complexity and are error prone [41,84]. Thus, fully non-interactive schemes are preferable, the canonical example being threshold BLS [18,19].

Structure-Preserving Signatures. Structure-preserving signatures (SPS) [4] are pairing-based signatures where the message, signature, and verification key consist of source group elements only (in one or both source groups), and signature verification consists of group membership checks and pairing product equations only. SPS have been studied extensively, with a main focus on short signatures [5,7,52,54], lower bounds [1,5,6], and (tight) security under well-known assumptions [2,8,51,62,63,65,72].

SPS are compatible with Groth-Sahai non-interactive zero-knowledge proofs (NIZKs) [60] and, more generally, help to avoid the expensive extraction of exponents in security proofs. This makes them attractive for the modular design of protocols relying on signatures and NIZKs. Indeed, SPS have seen widespread adoption in privacy-preserving applications, such as group signatures [4,72], traceable signatures [3], blind signatures [4,47], attribute-based signatures [42], malleable signatures [9], anonymous credentials [23,46,48], delegatable anonymous credentials [13,34], and anonymous e-cash [17].

For such signature-based applications, compromise of the signing key represents a single point of attack and failure. Replacing the use of SPS with TSPS together with distributed key generation (DKG) would help to reduce the trust in a single authority and increase the availability of the respective signing service. While many of the aforementioned applications of SPS would benefit from thresholdization, until now there was no known threshold construction of SPS that could serve as their basis. We provide the first candidate TSPS scheme as the main contribution of this work.

Towards Constructing a Threshold SPS. Our goal is to construct threshold SPS that are fully non-interactive, i.e., there is no coordination among signers. This puts some requirements on the used SPS and in particular prevents the use of nonlinear operations of the signing randomness and secret keys (cf. Sect. 2), which existing SPS fail to satisfy. Thus, as a starting point for our TSPS, we consider the pairing-based Pointcheval-Sanders signature scheme (PS) [76] (cf. Sect. 3.2), as its randomness is simply a random base group element and it avoids hashing during verification. We recall that the PS scheme is defined over an asymmetric bilinear group $(\mathbb{G}_1, \mathbb{G}_2, \mathbb{G}_T, p, e, g, \hat{g})$ with signing key $\mathsf{sk} = (x, y) \in (\mathbb{Z}_p^*)^2$ and corresponding verification key $\mathsf{vk} = (\hat{g}^x, \hat{g}^y) \in \mathbb{G}_2^2$. The signing algorithm takes as input a scalar message $m \in \mathbb{Z}_p$ and outputs a signature

$$\sigma = (h, s) = (g^r, h^{x+my}) \in \mathbb{G}_1^2 .$$

Importantly, the nonce r (or equivalently the base h) is sampled fresh for each signature. This scheme fails to be an SPS because the message is not a group element (or elements). Ghadafi [52] made the observation that a PS-like SPS scheme can be constructed for a group element message $(M_1, M_2) \in \mathbb{G}_1 \times \mathbb{G}_2$ for which there exists a scalar message $m \in \mathbb{Z}_p$ such that $M_1 = g^m$ and $M_2 = \hat{g}^m$. This is referred to as a Diffie-Hellman (DH) message. (cf. Sect. 1 for more on this message space.) A Ghadafi SPS signature (cf. Sect. 3.2) has the form:

$$\sigma = (h, s, t) = (g^r, M_1^r, h^x s^y) \in \mathbb{G}_1^3 .$$

Let us see how one might construct a threshold version of this scheme. Suppose each signer possesses a share $\mathsf{sk}_i = (x_i, y_i)$ of the secret key $\mathsf{sk} = (x, y)$. A first (non-interactive) attempt might have each signer output a partial signature of the form:

$$\sigma_i = (h_i, s_i, t_i) = (g^{r_i}, M_1^{r_i}, h_i^{x_i} s_i^{y_i}) ,$$

with aggregation of the third term having the form:

$$t = \prod_{i \in \mathcal{T}} t_i^{\lambda_i} = \prod_{i \in \mathcal{T}} g^{r_i x_i \lambda_i} M_1^{r_i y_i \lambda_i} ,$$

where λ_i is the Lagrange coefficient for party i in the signing set $\mathcal{T}$ of size at least t (the threshold). As with other existing SPS, this however does not allow reconstruction via Lagrange interpolation because each term in the exponent is multiplied by a distinct random integer r_i. To overcome this, due to the specific form of the signatures, the signers would have to agree on a common random element $h = g^r$. Indeed, this will be our approach to solve this issue.

A second (interactive) attempt might have each signer output randomness shares $h_i = g^{r_i}$ and corresponding $s_i = M_1^{r_i}$ in a first round of signing, followed by a second round in which each signer computes aggregate values $h = g^r = \prod_{i \in \mathcal{T}} h_i = g^{\sum_{i \in \mathcal{T}} r_i}$ and $s = \prod_{i \in \mathcal{T}} s_i$ and outputs a partial signature of the form:

$$\sigma_i = (h, s, t_i = h^{x_i} s^{y_i}) , \tag{1}$$

with aggregation of the third term having the form:

$$t = \prod_{i \in \mathcal{T}} t_i^{\lambda_i} = \prod_{i \in \mathcal{T}} g^{rx_i\lambda_i} M_1^{ry_i\lambda_i} .$$

This allows reconstruction via Lagrange interpolation. In terms of security, the unforgeability of this threshold scheme may be reduced to the unforgeability of single-party Ghadafi SPS signatures. However, the reduction needs to obtain the corrupt h_j, s_j values before revealing honest values h_i, s_i. The addition of a third signing round could achieve this, whereby all values h_i, s_i are committed to in the first round as $\mathsf{H}(h_i), \mathsf{H}'(s_i)$, for H and H' modeled as random oracles, and then revealed in the second round. However, the reduction needs to obtain the *nonces* r_j of the corrupt parties, which may be extracted from zero-knowledge proofs appending the outputs h_i, s_i in round two. These additional rounds and zero-knowledge proofs add significant overhead.

Our approach is clean and straightforward: we instead have signers obtain shared randomness $h = g^r$ via a random oracle, yielding a fully non-interactive scheme. But observe that if partial signatures have the form of Eq. (1), then $s = M_1^r$ cannot be computed without knowledge of the discrete logarithm $\mathsf{dlog}_h(M_1)$. Thus, we borrow techniques from Sonnino et al. [82] and Camenisch et al. [22], which implicitly sign *indexed* Diffie-Hellman messages (id, M_1, M_2), a concept we define and formalize rigorously in this work. Indexing can be understood as requiring the existence of an injective function f that maps each scalar message $m \in \mathbb{Z}_p$ to an index $id = f(m)$. We then have $h = \mathsf{H}(id)$, where H is modeled as a random oracle, and $M_1 = \mathsf{H}(id)^m$. Then each partial signature has the form:

$$\sigma_i = (h, s_i) = (\mathsf{H}(id), h^{x_i} M_1^{y_i}),$$

and the aggregated signature has the form:

$$\sigma = (h, s) = (\mathsf{H}(id), h^x M_1^y). \tag{2}$$

This is exactly our TSPS construction, with the underlying SPS signature defined by Eq. (2). We extend these techniques to vectors of indexed Diffie-Hellman messages $(id, \vec{M}_1, \vec{M}_2)$, which allows additional elements to be signed, e.g., attributes when used within anonymous credential systems [76,82]. It is important to note that the index is not needed for verification (and therefore $\mathsf{H}(id)$ is not computed), so our schemes are indeed structure preserving.

We define an appropriate notion of unforgeability for indexed messages: existential unforgeability under chosen indexed message attack (EUF-CiMA) and prove the security of our constructions under this notion. We discuss various ways of defining the index function, depending on the application. For example, if privacy is not required and the message and public key are known, the index function may simply be the identity function: $id = f(m) = m$, capturing the intuitive notion that each nonce r is associated with a single scalar message m.

Why Diffie-Hellman Messages? Diffie-Hellman messages can be traced back to the introduction of automorphic signatures [45] and SPS [4], and have since appeared in various other SPS constructions [52–55]. Their use is largely motivated by an impossibility result by Abe et al. [5], which proves that any SPS in the Type-III setting must have at least 3 group elements and 2 pairing product equations in the verification. Furthermore, the result rules out unilateral signatures (those containing elements from only one source group) meeting this lower bound. However, if messages are in *both* source groups, it is possible to construct a unilateral SPS meeting this lower bound. This is what Diffie-Hellman messages and the Ghadafi construction [52] achieve. We follow the same approach to construct efficient TSPS.

Constructing a TSPS over standard, unilateral message spaces remains an interesting open problem. However, such a scheme would necessarily contain more group elements in the signature and more pairing product equations to verify, due to this impossibility result. This is an important consideration when combining with Groth-Sahai NIZK proofs in applications, as the number of pairings required for verification scales linearly with the number of source pairings.

1.1 Our Contributions

Our contributions can be summarized as follows:

- We formalize the concept of indexed message spaces and formally define the notion of structure-preserving signatures (SPS) over indexed message spaces and corresponding notion of security: existential unforgeability under chosen indexed message attack (EUF-CiMA).
- We propose a concrete SPS construction over indexed Diffie-Hellman messages, called IM-SPS, and prove its EUF-CiMA security under a new variant of the generalized Pointcheval-Sanders assumption. We reduce this assumption to the hardness of the $(2, 1)$-discrete logarithm problem in the algebraic group model (AGM).
- We provide an indexed multi-message SPS construction, called IMM-SPS, which allows vectors of indexed Diffie-Hellman messages to be signed, and prove its EUF-CiMA security under the same assumption.
- We introduce the notion of a threshold structure-preserving signature (TSPS) scheme and propose a fully non-interactive TSPS based on our EUF-CiMA secure SPS scheme. Signatures contain only 2 group elements and verification consists of 2 pairing product equations. We prove the security of our TSPS under the EUF-CiMA security of IMM-SPS.
- We discuss applications of our TSPS construction and, in particular, blind signing of messages. This represents a core functionality in Threshold-Issuance Anonymous Credential (TIAC) systems. We outline how our TSPS can be used in TIAC systems as a drop-in replacement that avoids rewinding extractors for the required non-interactive zero-knowledge (NIZK) proofs.

2 Related Work

We provide an overview of pairing-based non-interactive threshold signature schemes in Table 1 and structure-preserving signature schemes (SPS) in Table 2 and discuss how these schemes fail to meet our requirements.

Table 1. Table of pairing-based non-interactive threshold signature schemes. iDH refers to indexed Diffie-Hellman messages (Definition 7). ✓: Satisfied. ✗: Not satisfied.

Scheme	Message Space	Signature Size	Structure Preserving
BLS [10,18]	$\{0,1\}^*$	$1\mathbb{G}_1$	✗
LJY ‡1 [70]	$\{0,1\}^*$	$2\mathbb{G}_1$	✗
LJY ‡2 [70]	$\{0,1\}^*$	$4\mathbb{G}_1 + 2\mathbb{G}_2$	✗
GJMMST [61]	$\{0,1\}^*$	$4\mathbb{G}_1 + 2\mathbb{G}_2$	✗
PS [82,83]	$\mathbb{Z}_p$	$2\mathbb{G}_1$	✗
Our TSPS	iDH	$2\mathbb{G}_1$	✓

Threshold Signatures. BLS [19] and its threshold version [10,18] are not structure preserving, as they map bitstring messages $\{0,1\}^*$ to the group using a random oracle. Libert et al. [70] propose a secure non-interactive threshold signature scheme based on linearly-homomorphic SPS (LHSPS) [71]. While this construction meets many of our requirements, the resulting threshold signature is not structure preserving. It either relies on random oracles to hash bitstring messages to group elements (‡1 [70]) or, when avoiding random oracles, a bit-wise encoding of the message is required (‡2 [70]). Gurkan et al. [61] propose a pairing-based threshold Verifiable Unpredictable Function (VUF), which is essentially a unique threshold signature [73]. However, their construction is not structure preserving: it hashes bitstring messages to the group using a random oracle. Sonnino et al. [82] and Tomescu et al. [83] present non-interactive threshold versions of Pointcheval-Sanders (PS) signatures; however, verification takes place over scalar vectors, and is thus not structure preserving. We note that signatures for scalar vectors are intuitively closer to SPS than ones for bitstring messages, as evidenced, for example, by Ghadafi's scheme [52]. We do not know of a general conversion technique, however.

Structure-Preserving Signatures. Most structure-preserving signatures in the literature fail to be good candidates for thresholdization due to nonlinear operations of signer-specific randomness and secret key elements, which are not amenable to Lagrange interpolation (e.g., [4,5,7,11,54,58]). However, there are two promising approaches: linearly-homomorphic SPS (LHSPS) [71] and the SPS by Ghadafi [52]. The former is a one-time signature, meaning that a key pair can only sign a single message[1]. The SPS by Ghadafi [52] lends itself to thresholdization, but it requires multiple communication rounds and incurs significant overhead. (See Sect. 1 for a discussion of this approach.)

Table 2. Table of structure-preserving signature schemes (SPS). DH refers to Diffie-Hellman messages (Definition 2), and iDH refers to indexed Diffie-Hellman messages (Definition 7). Avoids Nonlinearity refers to operations of the signing randomness and secret keys. ✓: Satisfied. ✗: Not satisfied.

Scheme	Message Space	Signature Size	Avoids Nonlinearity
AFGHO [4]	$\mathbb{G}_1$	$5\mathbb{G}_1 + 2\mathbb{G}_2$	✗
AGHO [5]	$\mathbb{G}_1 \times \mathbb{G}_2$ / $\mathbb{G}_2$	$2\mathbb{G}_1 + 1\mathbb{G}_2$	✗
AGOT [7]	$\mathbb{G}_1$	$2\mathbb{G}_1 + 1\mathbb{G}_2$	✗
BFFSST [11]	$\mathbb{G}_2$	$1\mathbb{G}_1 + 2\mathbb{G}_2$	✗
Ghadafi [54]	DH	$2\mathbb{G}_1$	✗
Ghadafi [52]	DH	$3\mathbb{G}_1$	✗
Groth [58]	$\mathbb{G}_2$	$1\mathbb{G}_1 + 2\mathbb{G}_2$	✗
LPJY [71]*	$\mathbb{G}_1$	$2\mathbb{G}_1$	✓
Our SPS	iDH	$2\mathbb{G}_1$	✓

* One-time: a key pair can only sign a single message.

3 Preliminaries and Definitions

3.1 General

Let $\kappa \in \mathbb{N}$ denote the security parameter and 1^κ its unary representation. Let p be a κ-bit prime. For all positive polynomials $f(\kappa)$, a function $\nu : \mathbb{N} \to \mathbb{R}^+$ is called *negligible* if $\exists\ \kappa_0 \in \mathbb{N}$ such that $\forall\ \kappa > \kappa_0$ it holds that $\nu(\kappa) < 1/f(\kappa)$. We denote by $\mathbb{G}^*$ the set $\mathbb{G} \setminus 1_{\mathbb{G}}$, where $1_{\mathbb{G}}$ is the identity element of the group $\mathbb{G}$. We denote the group of integers mod p by $\mathbb{Z}_p = \mathbb{Z}/p\mathbb{Z}$, its multiplicative group of units by $\mathbb{Z}_p^*$, and the polynomial ring over $\mathbb{Z}_p$ by $\mathbb{Z}_p[X]$. For a group $\mathbb{G}$ of order p with generator g, we denote the discrete logarithm $m \in \mathbb{Z}_p$ of $M \in \mathbb{G}$ base g by $\mathsf{dlog}_g(M)$ (i.e., $M = g^m$). We denote the set of integers $\{1, \ldots, n\}$ by $[1, n]$ and the vector A by $\vec{A}$. Let $Y \leftarrow\!\!\$\ F(X)$ denote running probabilistic algorithm F on input X and assigning its output to Y. Let $x \leftarrow\!\!\$\ \mathbb{Z}_p$ denote sampling an element of $\mathbb{Z}_p$ uniformly at random. All algorithms are randomized unless expressly stated otherwise. PPT refers to probabilistic polynomial time. We denote the output of a security game $\mathbf{G}^{\text{GAME}}$ between a challenger and a PPT adversary $\mathcal{A}$ by $\mathbf{G}_{\mathcal{A}}^{\text{GAME}}$, where $\mathcal{A}$ wins the game if $\mathbf{G}_{\mathcal{A}}^{\text{GAME}} = 1$.

[1] Note that the LHSPS in [71] is designed over symmetric bilinear groups with signatures consisting of 3 group elements. The authors in [70] extend this LHSPS over asymmetric bilinear groups with signatures of size 2.

Definition 1 (Bilinear Group). *A bilinear group generator $\mathcal{BG}(1^\kappa)$ returns a tuple $(\mathbb{G}_1, \mathbb{G}_2, \mathbb{G}_T, p, e, g, \hat{g})$ such that $\mathbb{G}_1$, $\mathbb{G}_2$ and $\mathbb{G}_T$ are finite groups of the same prime order p, $g \in \mathbb{G}_1$ and $\hat{g} \in \mathbb{G}_2$ are generators, and $e : \mathbb{G}_1 \times \mathbb{G}_2 \rightarrow \mathbb{G}_T$ is an efficiently computable bilinear pairing, which satisfies the following properties:*

1. *$e(g, \hat{g}) \neq 1_{\mathbb{G}_T}$ (non-degeneracy).*
2. *$\forall\ a, b \in \mathbb{Z}_p$, $e(g^a, \hat{g}^b) = e(g, \hat{g})^{ab} = e(g^b, \hat{g}^a)$ (bilinearity).*

We rely on bilinear groups $\mathbb{G}_1$ and $\mathbb{G}_2$ with no efficiently computable isomorphism between them [50], also called Type-III or asymmetric bilinear groups. To date, they are the most efficient choice for relevant security levels.

Definition 2 (Diffie-Hellman Message Space [4,45]**).** *Over an asymmetric bilinear group $(\mathbb{G}_1, \mathbb{G}_2, \mathbb{G}_T, p, e, g, \hat{g})$, a pair $(M_1, M_2) \in \mathbb{G}_1 \times \mathbb{G}_2$ belongs to the Diffie-Hellman (DH) message space $\mathcal{M}_{\mathsf{DH}}$ if there exists $m \in \mathbb{Z}_p$ such that $M_1 = g^m$ and $M_2 = \hat{g}^m$.*

One can efficiently verify whether $(M_1, M_2) \in \mathcal{M}_{\mathsf{DH}}$ by checking $e(M_1, \hat{g}) = e(g, M_2)$.

Definition 3 (Algebraic Group Model [49]**).** *An adversary is algebraic if for every group element $h \in \mathbb{G} = \langle g \rangle$ that it outputs, it is required to output a representation $\vec{h} = (\eta_0, \eta_1, \eta_2, \dots)$ such that $h = g^{\eta_0} \prod {g_i}^{\eta_i}$, where $g, g_1, g_2, \dots \in \mathbb{G}$ are group elements that the adversary has seen thus far.*

The original definition of the algebraic group model (AGM) [49] only captured regular cyclic groups $\mathbb{G} = \langle g \rangle$. Mizuide et al. [74] extended this definition to include symmetric pairing groups ($\mathbb{G}_1 = \mathbb{G}_2$), such that the adversary is also allowed to output target group elements (in $\mathbb{G}_T$) and their representations. Recently, Couteau and Hartmann [28] defined the Algebraic Asymmetric Bilinear Group Model, which extends the AGM definition for asymmetric pairings by allowing the adversary to output multiple elements from all three groups. The definition can be found in the full version [32].

3.2 Schemes

Pointcheval-Sanders Signatures [76]. The PS signature scheme is defined over the message space $\mathcal{M}$ of scalar messages $m \in \mathbb{Z}_p$ and consists of the following PPT algorithms:

- $\mathsf{pp} \leftarrow \mathsf{Setup}(1^\kappa)$: Output $\mathsf{pp} = (\mathbb{G}_1, \mathbb{G}_2, \mathbb{G}_T, p, e, g, \hat{g}) \leftarrow \mathcal{BG}(1^\kappa)$.
- $(\mathsf{sk}, \mathsf{vk}) \leftarrow \mathsf{KGen}(\mathsf{pp})$: Sample $x, y \leftarrow_\$ \mathbb{Z}_p^*$ and set $\mathsf{sk} = (\mathsf{sk}_1, \mathsf{sk}_2) = (x, y)$ and $\mathsf{vk} = (\mathsf{vk}_1, \mathsf{vk}_2) = (\hat{g}^x, \hat{g}^y)$. Output $(\mathsf{sk}, \mathsf{vk})$.
- $\sigma \leftarrow \mathsf{Sign}(\mathsf{pp}, \mathsf{sk}, m)$: Sample $r \leftarrow_\$ \mathbb{Z}_p^*$ and compute $\sigma = (h, s) = (g^r, h^{x+my})$. Output σ.
- $0/1 \leftarrow \mathsf{Verify}(\mathsf{pp}, \mathsf{vk}, m, \sigma)$: If $h \in \mathbb{G}_1, h \neq 1_{\mathbb{G}_1}$, and the pairing product equation $e(h, \mathsf{vk}_1 \mathsf{vk}_2^m) = e(s, \hat{g})$ holds, output 1 (accept); else, output 0 (reject).

Pointcheval-Sanders signatures are EUF-CMA secure under the PS assumption (Definition 5) [76].

Ghadafi SPS [52]. The Ghadafi structure-preserving signature scheme is defined over the message space $\mathcal{M}_{\mathsf{DH}}$ of Diffie-Hellman pairs $(M_1, M_2) \in \mathbb{G}_1 \times \mathbb{G}_2$ such that $e(M_1, \hat{g}) = e(g, M_2)$ and consists of the following PPT algorithms:

- $\mathsf{pp} \leftarrow \mathsf{Setup}(1^\kappa)$: Output $\mathsf{pp} = (\mathbb{G}_1, \mathbb{G}_2, \mathbb{G}_T, p, e, g, \hat{g}) \leftarrow \mathcal{BG}(1^\kappa)$.
- $(\mathsf{sk}, \mathsf{vk}) \leftarrow \mathsf{KGen}(\mathsf{pp})$: Sample $x, y \leftarrow\$ \mathbb{Z}_p^*$ and set $\mathsf{sk} = (\mathsf{sk}_1, \mathsf{sk}_2) = (x, y)$ and $\mathsf{vk} = (\mathsf{vk}_1, \mathsf{vk}_2) = (\hat{g}^x, \hat{g}^y)$. Output $(\mathsf{sk}, \mathsf{vk})$.
- $\sigma \leftarrow \mathsf{Sign}(\mathsf{pp}, \mathsf{sk}, M_1, M_2)$: Sample $r \leftarrow\$ \mathbb{Z}_p^*$ and compute $\sigma = (h, s, t) = (g^r, M_1^r, h^x s^y)$. Output σ.
- $0/1 \leftarrow \mathsf{Verify}(\mathsf{pp}, \mathsf{vk}, \sigma, M_1, M_2)$: If $h, s, t \in \mathbb{G}_1, h \neq 1_{\mathbb{G}_1}$, and both pairing product equations $e(h, M_2) = e(s, \hat{g})$ and $e(t, \hat{g}) = e(h, \mathsf{vk}_1)e(s, \mathsf{vk}_2)$ hold, output 1 (accept); else, output 0 (reject).

The Ghadafi SPS is weakly EUF-CMA secure in the generic group model (GGM) [52].

Shamir Secret Sharing [79]. An (n, t)-Shamir secret sharing divides a secret s among n shareholders such that each subset of at least t shareholders can reconstruct s, but fewer than t cannot (and s remains information-theoretically hidden). A dealer who knows the secret s forms a polynomial $f(x)$ of degree t with randomly chosen coefficients from $\mathbb{Z}_p$ such that $f(0) = s$. The dealer then securely provides each shareholder with $s_i = f(i), i \in [1, n]$. Let $\vec{s} \leftarrow\$ \mathsf{Share}(s, p, n, t)$ denote the process of computing shares $\vec{s} = (s_1, \ldots, s_n)$ of a secret s. Each subset $\mathcal{T} \subset [1, n]$ of size at least t can pool their shares to reconstruct the secret s using Lagrange interpolation, as $s = f(0) = \sum_{i \in \mathcal{T}} s_i \lambda_i$, where $\lambda_i = \prod_{j \in \mathcal{T}, j \neq i} \frac{j}{j-i}$.

3.3 Assumptions

Definition 4 ((2,1)-Discrete Logarithm Assumption [12]). *Let* $\mathsf{pp} = (\mathbb{G}_1, \mathbb{G}_2, \mathbb{G}_T, p, e, g, \hat{g}) \leftarrow \mathcal{BG}(1^\kappa)$ *be an asymmetric bilinear group. The* $(2,1)$*-discrete logarithm assumption holds with respect to* $\mathcal{BG}$ *if for all PPT adversaries* $\mathcal{A}$, *there exists a negligible function* ν *such that*

$$\Pr\left[z \leftarrow\$ \mathbb{Z}_p^*;\ (Z, Z', \hat{Z}) \leftarrow (g^z, g^{z^2}, \hat{g}^z);\ z' \leftarrow\$ \mathcal{A}(\mathsf{pp}, Z, Z', \hat{Z}) :\ z' = z\right] < \nu(\kappa)\ .$$

Definition 5 (PS Assumption [76]). *Let the advantage of an adversary* $\mathcal{A}$ *against the PS game* $\mathbf{G}^{PS}$, *as defined in Fig. 1, be as follows:*

$$Adv_{\mathcal{A}}^{PS}(\kappa) = \Pr\left[\mathbf{G}_{\mathcal{A}}^{PS} = 1\right]\ .$$

The PS assumption holds if for all PPT adversaries $\mathcal{A}$, *there exists a negligible function* ν *such that* $Adv_{\mathcal{A}}^{PS}(\kappa) < \nu(\kappa)$.

$\mathbf{G}^{\mathrm{PS}}(1^\kappa)$	$\mathcal{O}^{\mathrm{PS}}(m)$ // $m \in \mathbb{Z}_p$
$\mathsf{pp} = (\mathbb{G}_1, \mathbb{G}_2, \mathbb{G}_T, p, e, g, \hat{g}) \leftarrow \mathcal{BG}(1^\kappa)$	$h \leftarrow\!\$\, \mathbb{G}_1$
$x, y \leftarrow\!\$\, \mathbb{Z}_p^*$	$\mathcal{Q} \leftarrow \mathcal{Q} \cup \{m\}$
$(m^*, h^*, s^*) \leftarrow \mathcal{A}^{\mathcal{O}^{\mathrm{PS}}}(\mathsf{pp}, \hat{g}^x, \hat{g}^y)$	**return** (h, h^{x+my})
return $((1)\ h^* \neq 1_{\mathbb{G}_1} \wedge m^* \neq 0 \wedge$	
$(2)\ s^* = h^{*^{x+m^*y}} \wedge$	
$(3)\ m^* \notin \mathcal{Q})$	

Fig. 1. Game defining the PS assumption.

The validity of the tuple (m^*, h^*, s^*) is decidable by checking $e(s^*, \hat{g}) = e(h^*, \hat{g}^x(\hat{g}^y)^{m^*})$. The PS assumption is an interactive assumption defined by Pointcheval and Sanders [76] to construct an efficient randomizable signature and has been shown to hold in the GGM.

Kim et al. [66] introduced a generalized version of the PS assumption (GPS) that splits the PS oracle $\mathcal{O}^{\mathrm{PS}}(\cdot)$ into two oracles $\mathcal{O}_0^{\mathrm{GPS}}(), \mathcal{O}_1^{\mathrm{GPS}}(\cdot)$: the first samples $h \leftarrow\!\$\, \mathbb{G}_1$, and the second takes h and m as input and generates the PS value h^{x+my}. Recently, Kim et al. [67] extended the GPS assumption (GPS_2), replacing field element inputs, such as m, with group element inputs. The GPS_2 assumption holds under the $(2,1)$-DL assumption (Definition 4) in the AGM. Both the GPS and GPS_2 assumptions can be found in the full version [32].

Owing to the fact that our SPS and TSPS constructions rely on a different message space, we introduce an analogous generalized PS assumption (GPS_3), defined as follows.

Definition 6 (GPS_3 **Assumption**). *Let the advantage of an adversary $\mathcal{A}$ against the GPS_3 game $\mathbf{G}^{GPS_3}$, as defined in Fig. 2, be as follows:*

$$Adv_{\mathcal{A}}^{GPS_3}(\kappa) = \Pr\left[\mathbf{G}_{\mathcal{A}}^{GPS_3} = 1\right] .$$

The GPS_3 assumption holds if for all PPT adversaries $\mathcal{A}$, there exists a negligible function ν such that $Adv_{\mathcal{A}}^{GPS_3}(\kappa) < \nu(\kappa)$.

We prove that this assumption holds in the AGM if the $(2,1)$-DL problem is hard (Theorem 1).

$\mathbf{G}^{\mathsf{GPS}_3}(1^\kappa)$

$\mathsf{pp} = (\mathbb{G}_1, \mathbb{G}_2, \mathbb{G}_T, p, e, g, \hat{g}) \leftarrow \mathcal{BG}(1^\kappa)$

$x, y \leftarrow\$\ \mathbb{Z}_p^*$

$(M_1^*, M_2^*, h^*, s^*) \leftarrow \mathcal{A}^{\mathcal{O}_0^{\mathsf{GPS}_3}, \mathcal{O}_1^{\mathsf{GPS}_3}}(\mathsf{pp}, \hat{g}^x, \hat{g}^y, \boxed{g^y})$

return $((1)\ M_1^* \neq 1_{\mathbb{G}_1} \wedge h^* \neq 1_{\mathbb{G}_1} \wedge$

$(2)\ s^* = h^{*^x} M_1^{*^y} \wedge$

$(3)\ \mathsf{dlog}_{h^*}(M_1^*) = \mathsf{dlog}_{\hat{g}}(M_2^*) \wedge$

$(4)\ (\star, M_2^*) \notin \mathcal{Q}_1)$

$\mathcal{O}_0^{\mathsf{GPS}_3}()$

$h \leftarrow\$\ \mathbb{G}_1$

$\mathcal{Q}_0 \leftarrow \mathcal{Q}_0 \cup \{h\}$

return h

$\mathcal{O}_1^{\mathsf{GPS}_3}(h, M_1, M_2)$

if $(h \notin \mathcal{Q}_0 \vee \mathsf{dlog}_h(M_1) \neq \mathsf{dlog}_{\hat{g}}(M_2))$:

  return $\perp$

if $(h, \star) \in \mathcal{Q}_1$:

  return $\perp$

$\mathcal{Q}_1 \leftarrow \mathcal{Q}_1 \cup \{(h, M_2)\}$

return $h^x M_1^y$

Fig. 2. Game defining our GPS_3 assumption. The additional element in the solid box is required for blind signing only (cf. Sect. 6.1).

4 Indexed Message Structure-Preserving Signatures

In this section, we introduce the notion of structure-preserving signatures (SPS) on indexed messages as well as a corresponding notion of security: unforgeability against chosen indexed message attack (EUF-CiMA). We provide an indexed message SPS construction, called IM-SPS, and prove its EUF-CiMA security under the GPS_3 assumption (Definition 6) in the random oracle model (ROM) (Theorem 2). We also propose an indexed *multi*-message SPS construction, called IMM-SPS, which allows vectors of indexed messages to be signed, and prove its EUF-CiMA security under the same assumptions (Theorem 3). IMM-SPS are useful for applications where additional elements, such as attributes, are signed.

Indexing can be understood as requiring the existence of an injective function f that maps each message to an index. We model this by requiring that for all index/message pairs in an indexed message space $\mathcal{M}$, the following uniqueness property holds: $(id, \tilde{M}) \in \mathcal{M}$, $(id', \tilde{M}') \in \mathcal{M}$, $id = id' \Rightarrow \tilde{M} = \tilde{M}'$. That is, no two messages use the same index. We refer to index/message pairs as $M = (id, \tilde{M})$.

Indexing is useful, as signatures can depend on the index; for example, in our schemes, signing involves evaluating a hash-to-curve function H on the index to obtain a base element $h \leftarrow \mathsf{H}(id)$. Verifying a message/signature pair does not require availability of the index, making it structure preserving. Consequently, the verification message space $\tilde{\mathcal{M}}$ is obtained from $\mathcal{M}$ by omitting the index.

For our schemes, we need to consider that in verification one can provide a base element h^r obtained by randomizing the original base element h. This is due to the partial randomizability of the signatures. Thus, different messages $\tilde{M}, \tilde{M}'$ may be valid representations for the same scalar message m. Consequently, similar to SPS on equivalence classes (SPS-EQ) [48], the verification message space $\tilde{\mathcal{M}}$ is expanded to consider equivalent (randomized) messages: $\tilde{\mathcal{M}} = \{\tilde{M} \mid \exists\, (\cdot, \tilde{M}') \in \mathcal{M}\ ,\ \tilde{M} \in \mathsf{EQ}(\tilde{M}')\}$. The function EQ depends on the concrete message space and determines the respective set of equivalent messages.

Next, we define the indexed Diffie-Hellman message space used by our IM-SPS scheme (cf. Fig. 3 for its encoding function).

Definition 7 (Indexed Diffie-Hellman Message Space). *Given an asymmetric bilinear group* $(\mathbb{G}_1, \mathbb{G}_2, \mathbb{G}_T, p, e, g, \hat{g}) \leftarrow \mathcal{BG}(1^\kappa)$*, an index set* $\mathcal{I}$*, and a random oracle* $\mathsf{H} : \mathcal{I} \to \mathbb{G}_1$*,* $\mathcal{M}^{\mathsf{H}}_{\mathsf{iDH}}$ *is an indexed Diffie-Hellman (DH) message space if* $\mathcal{M}^{\mathsf{H}}_{\mathsf{iDH}} \subset \{(id, \tilde{M}) \mid id \in \mathcal{I}, m \in \mathbb{Z}_p, \tilde{M} = (\mathsf{H}(id)^m, \hat{g}^m) \in \mathbb{G}_1 \times \mathbb{G}_2\}$ *and the following index uniqueness property holds: for all* $(id, \tilde{M}) \in \mathcal{M}^{\mathsf{H}}_{\mathsf{iDH}}$*,* $(id', \tilde{M}') \in \mathcal{M}^{\mathsf{H}}_{\mathsf{iDH}}$*,* $id = id' \Rightarrow \tilde{M} = \tilde{M}'$*.*

We define the equivalence class for each message $\tilde{M} = (M_1, M_2) \in \tilde{\mathcal{M}}^{\mathsf{H}}_{\mathsf{iDH}}$ *as* $\mathsf{EQ}_{\mathsf{iDH}}(M_1, M_2) = \{(M_1^r, M_2) \mid \exists\, r \in \mathbb{Z}_p\}$*.*

$\mathsf{iDH}^{\mathsf{H}}(id, m)$	$\mathsf{H}(id)$
$h \leftarrow \mathsf{H}(id)$	**if** $\mathcal{Q}_{\mathsf{H}}[id] = \perp$:
$\tilde{M} \leftarrow (h^m, \hat{g}^m)$	$\quad \mathcal{Q}_{\mathsf{H}}[id] \leftarrow\$\ \mathbb{G}_1$
return $(id, \tilde{M})$	**return** $\mathcal{Q}_{\mathsf{H}}[id]$

Fig. 3. Encoding function of indexed Diffie-Hellman message space in the ROM.

The subset membership is efficiently decidable by checking $e(M_1, \hat{g}) = e(h, M_2)$ for $h \leftarrow \mathsf{H}(id)$. Note that, in addition, one needs to guarantee that no two messages use the same index. This is the responsibility of the signer.[2] As mentioned above, messages $\tilde{M}$ lie in a different verification message space $\tilde{\mathcal{M}}^{\mathsf{H}}_{\mathsf{iDH}}$ that is uniquely determined by $\mathcal{M}^{\mathsf{H}}_{\mathsf{iDH}}$ and $\mathsf{EQ}_{\mathsf{iDH}}$. Note that most $\tilde{M} \in \tilde{\mathcal{M}}^{\mathsf{H}}_{\mathsf{iDH}}$ are not indexed Diffie-Hellman messages. In particular, when expanding the definition of $\mathsf{EQ}_{\mathsf{iDH}}$, the verification message space is $\tilde{\mathcal{M}}^{\mathsf{H}}_{\mathsf{iDH}} = \{(M_1^r, M_2) \mid \exists\, r \in \mathbb{Z}_p\ ,\ \exists\, (\cdot, M_1, M_2) \in \mathcal{M}^{\mathsf{H}}_{\mathsf{iDH}}\}$.

[2] To highlight this responsibility, we enforce uniqueness both in the message space and later on in Line 1 of the of $\mathcal{O}_{\mathsf{Sign}}(\cdot)$ oracle of Fig. 5.

$$\underbrace{(\hat{M}_1, M_2) \xrightarrow{\mathsf{dlog}_{\hat{g}}(M_2)} m \in \mathbb{Z}_p \xrightarrow{f} id}_{\textbf{Message Indexing}} \overbrace{\xrightarrow{\mathsf{iDH}^{\mathsf{H}}(id,m)} (id, M_1, M_2) \in \mathcal{M}^{\mathsf{H}}_{\mathsf{iDH}}}^{\textbf{Indexed DH Message Space in ROM}} \underbrace{\longrightarrow (\hat{M}_1, M_2)}_{\textbf{Randomization of } M_1}$$

Fig. 4. From $\tilde{M}$ to M and back again: The first message component is randomizable; the second fixes the index.

Does $\tilde{M}$ depend on id or does id depend on $\tilde{M}$? One might observe the above apparent circularity with respect to the indexing technique. On the one hand, we require existence of an injective function f that maps (M_1, M_2) to id. On the other hand, M_1 is computed as $M_1 = \mathsf{H}(id)^{\mathsf{dlog}_{\hat{g}}(M_2)}$. This circularity is avoided by computing id from the partial message M_2, or more commonly its discrete logarithm m.

As illustrated in Fig. 4, the indexing function f assigns an index id to each scalar message $m \in \mathbb{Z}_p$. Then, a hash-to-curve function $\mathsf{H} : \{0,1\}^* \rightarrow \mathbb{G}_1$ (modeled as a random oracle) is used to generate a unique base element h. A source group message (M_1, M_2) can then be obtained using h. In an indexed message SPS, the signing algorithm takes as input the source group message together with an index and generates the underlying signature with access to H. Note that the index does not destroy the structure since the verifier does not need to know id to verify a signature on message $\tilde{M} = (M_1, M_2)$.

Indexing Function Instantiations. Depending on the application, the indexing function f can be instantiated in different ways. For example, if messages and signatures are allowed to be public, the indexing function can be instantiated by using the scalar message m itself as the index: $f(m) \mapsto m = id$.

If message and signatures must be hidden, as in the case of applications to anonymous credentials, one can take the approach of committing to the scalar message and providing a proof of well-formedness of the commitment, as done by Sonnino et al. [82]. As it is infeasible to open a well-formed commitment to two different messages, this guarantees uniqueness of the index. Camenisch et al. [22] take yet another approach for indexing messages: they assume the existence of a pre-defined and publicly available indexing function. That is, there is a unique index value for each message that is known to all signers. The corresponding base element can be obtained by evaluating the hash-to-curve function at the given index. As the authors note, if the size of the message space is polynomial and known in advance, then this approach is secure, since it is equivalent to including the base element in the public parameters. However, this is impractical for large message spaces.

4.1 Definition of Unforgeability for Indexed Message SPS

We adapt the notion of EUF-CMA security for digital signatures (Definition 16) to existential unforgeability against chosen *indexed* message attack (EUF-CiMA).

There are two adjustments: (1) the adversary makes queries to the signing oracle by providing *index*/message pairs, and (2) we expand the set of signed messages $\mathcal{Q}_{\mathsf{S}} = \{(id_i, \tilde{M}_i)\}_i$ to the set of trivially forgeable messages $\mathcal{Q}_{\mathsf{EQ}} = \{\mathsf{EQ}(\tilde{M}_i)\}_i$, i.e., all equivalent messages in the verification message space, and use it in the winning condition of the adversary.

Definition 8 (Existential Unforgeability under Chosen Indexed Message Attack (EUF-CiMA)). *A digital signature scheme over indexed message space $\mathcal{M}$ is EUF-CiMA secure if for all PPT adversaries $\mathcal{A}$ playing game $\mathbf{G}^{EUF\text{-}CiMA}$ (Fig. 5), there exists a negligible function ν such that*

$$Adv_{\mathcal{A}}^{EUF\text{-}CiMA}(\kappa) = \Pr\left[\mathbf{G}_{\mathcal{A}}^{EUF\text{-}CiMA}(1^\kappa) = 1\right] \leq \nu(\kappa).$$

$\mathbf{G}_{\mathcal{A}}^{\mathsf{EUF\text{-}CiMA}}(1^\kappa)$	$\mathcal{O}_{\mathsf{Sign}}(id, \tilde{M})$
$\mathsf{pp} \leftarrow \mathsf{Setup}(1^\kappa)$	**if** $(id, \star) \in \mathcal{Q}_{\mathsf{S}}$:
$(\mathsf{sk}, \mathsf{vk}) \leftarrow\$ \mathsf{KGen}(\mathsf{pp})$	**return** $\perp$
$(\tilde{M}^*, \sigma^*) \leftarrow\$ \mathcal{A}^{\mathcal{O}_{\mathsf{Sign}}}(\mathsf{pp}, \mathsf{vk})$	**else** : $\sigma \leftarrow \mathsf{Sign}(\mathsf{pp}, \mathsf{sk}, (id, \tilde{M}))$
return $(\tilde{M}^* \notin \mathcal{Q}_{\mathsf{EQ}} \wedge$	$\mathcal{Q}_{\mathsf{S}} \leftarrow \mathcal{Q}_{\mathsf{S}} \cup \{(id, \tilde{M})\}$
$\mathsf{Verify}(\mathsf{pp}, \mathsf{vk}, \tilde{M}^*, \sigma^*))$	$\mathcal{Q}_{\mathsf{EQ}} \leftarrow \mathcal{Q}_{\mathsf{EQ}} \cup \{\mathsf{EQ}(\tilde{M})\}$
	return σ

Fig. 5. Game $\mathbf{G}_{\mathcal{A}}^{\mathsf{EUF\text{-}CiMA}}(1^\kappa)$.

4.2 Our Indexed Message SPS

In Fig. 6, we present our indexed message SPS construction IM-SPS over the indexed Diffie-Hellman message space $\mathcal{M}_{\mathsf{iDH}}^{\mathsf{H}}$.

4.3 Security of IM-SPS

We prove that our proposed IM-SPS construction (Fig. 6) is EUF-CiMA secure under the GPS_3 assumption (Definition 6) in the random oracle model.

The GPS_3 assumption underpins both the security of IM-SPS as well as our indexed *multi*-message SPS construction IMM-SPS (Sect. 4.4). Our security reductions from IM-SPS and IMM-SPS to GPS_3 are tight. Furthermore, we show the tight security of our TSPS (Sect. 5) under the security of IMM-SPS. Figure 7 defines a roadmap for our IM-SPS, IMM-SPS, and TSPS constructions and their underlying assumptions. Thus, as a starting point, we reduce the GPS_3 assumption to the hardness of the (2, 1)-DL problem (Definition 4) in the algebraic group model.

$\mathsf{Setup}(1^\kappa)$

$(\mathbb{G}_1, \mathbb{G}_2, \mathbb{G}_T, p, e, g, \hat{g}) \leftarrow \mathcal{BG}(1^\kappa)$
$\mathsf{H} : \{0,1\}^* \rightarrow \mathbb{G}_1$
// select hash function
$\mathsf{pp} \leftarrow ((\mathbb{G}_1, \mathbb{G}_2, \mathbb{G}_T, p, e, g, \hat{g}), \mathsf{H})$
return pp

$\mathsf{KGen}(\mathsf{pp})$

$x, y \leftarrow\$ \mathbb{Z}_p^*$
$\mathsf{sk} \leftarrow (\mathsf{sk}_1, \mathsf{sk}_2) = (x, y)$
$\mathsf{vk} \leftarrow (\mathsf{vk}_1, \mathsf{vk}_2, \boxed{\mathsf{vk}_2^*})$
$\quad = (\hat{g}^x, \hat{g}^y, \boxed{g^y})$
return (sk, vk)

$\mathsf{Sign}(\mathsf{pp}, \mathsf{sk}, (id, M_1, M_2))$

$h \leftarrow \mathsf{H}(id)$
if $e(h, M_2) = e(M_1, \hat{g})$:
$\quad (h, s) \leftarrow (h, h^{\mathsf{sk}_1} M_1^{\mathsf{sk}_2})$
$\quad$ **return** $\sigma \leftarrow (h, s)$
else : **return** $\perp$

$\mathsf{Verify}(\mathsf{pp}, \mathsf{vk}, (M_1, M_2), \sigma)$

// does not invoke H
parse $\sigma = (h, s)$
return $(h \neq 1_{\mathbb{G}_1} \wedge M_1 \neq 1_{\mathbb{G}_1} \wedge$
$\quad e(h, M_2) = e(M_1, \hat{g}) \wedge$
$\quad e(h, \mathsf{vk}_1) e(M_1, \mathsf{vk}_2) = e(s, \hat{g}))$

Fig. 6. Our Indexed Message SPS Construction IM-SPS. The additional elements in solid boxes are required for blind signing only (cf. Sect. 6.1).

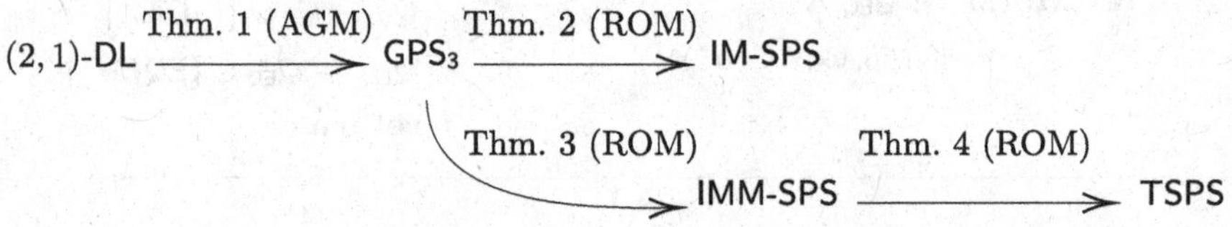

Fig. 7. The proposed constructions and underlying assumptions.

Theorem 1. *The* GPS_3 *assumption (Definition 6) holds in the asymmetric algebraic bilinear group model under the hardness of the* (2, 1)*-DL problem (Definition 4).*

The proof is provided in the full version [32].

Theorem 2. *The indexed message SPS scheme* IM-SPS *(Fig. 6) is correct and* EUF-CiMA *secure (Definition 8) under the* GPS_3 *assumption (Definition 6) in the random oracle model.*

We first present an attack to motivate the need for uniqueness in the indexed message space. Assume there were no uniqueness requirement, and suppose the redundant check in Line 1 of the of $\mathcal{O}_{\mathsf{Sign}}(\cdot)$ oracle of Fig. 5 were not present. Then, a forger could obtain two signatures $s = h^x M_1^y$, $s' = h^x M_1'^y$ and compute a forgery $s^* = s^2/s' = h^x (M_1^2/M_1')^y$.

Proof Outline. Let $\mathcal{A}$ be a PPT adversary against the EUF-CiMA security of IM-SPS. We construct a PPT reduction $\mathcal{B}$ against the GPS_3 assumption as follows. When $\mathcal{A}$ queries the random oracle H on a fresh id, $\mathcal{B}$ queries its oracle $\mathcal{O}_0^{\mathrm{GPS}_3}()$ to obtain a random base element h, which it stores and returns to $\mathcal{A}$. When $\mathcal{A}$ queries its signing oracle $\mathcal{O}_{\mathsf{Sign}}(\cdot)$ on (id, M_1, M_2), $\mathcal{B}$ looks up $h = \mathsf{H}(id)$ and queries its oracle $\mathcal{O}_1^{\mathrm{GPS}_3}(\cdot)$ on (h, M_1, M_2) to receive $h^x M_1^y$. Finally, $\mathcal{B}$ returns the signature $\sigma = (h, h^x M_1^y)$ to $\mathcal{A}$. $\mathcal{B}$ correctly simulates the $\mathsf{EUF\text{-}CiMA}$ game, and the success probability of $\mathcal{A}$ and $\mathcal{B}$ is the same.

The attack above would violate the condition $(h, \star) \notin \mathcal{Q}_1$ in Line 3 of the $\mathcal{O}_1^{\mathrm{GPS}_3}(\cdot)$ oracle in Fig. 2. The full proof is provided in the full version [32].

4.4 Our Indexed Multi-message SPS

We extend our $\mathsf{IM\text{-}SPS}$ construction to an indexed *multi*-message SPS construction $\mathsf{IMM\text{-}SPS}$, which allows vectors of indexed messages to be signed, and prove its $\mathsf{EUF\text{-}CiMA}$ security. Extending the message space to allow vectors of any length is desirable for applications in which several attributes may be signed. The number of pairings required for verification scales linearly with the length of the message vectors, but signatures remain constant sized (2 group elements).

$\mathsf{MiDH}^{\mathsf{H}}(id, \vec{m})$	$\mathsf{H}(id)$
$h \leftarrow \mathsf{H}(id)$	**if** $\mathcal{Q}_{\mathsf{H}}[id] = \perp$:
for $j \in [1, \ell]$:	$\quad \mathcal{Q}_{\mathsf{H}}[id] \leftarrow\$ \mathbb{G}_1$
$\quad M_{1j} \leftarrow h^{m_j};\ M_{2j} \leftarrow \hat{g}^{m_j}$	**return** $\mathcal{Q}_{\mathsf{H}}[id]$
return $\big(id, (\vec{M}_1, \vec{M}_2)\big)$	

Fig. 8. Encoding function of iDH multi-message space in the ROM.

We first generalize the notion of an indexed message space to the multi-message setting. In Fig. 8, we present the encoding function $\mathsf{MiDH}^{\mathsf{H}}(id, \vec{m})$ of a multi-message variant of the indexed Diffie-Hellman message space that maps, for any $\ell > 1$, ℓ-scalar message vectors $\vec{m} = (m_1, \ldots, m_\ell) \in \mathbb{Z}_p^\ell$ to 2ℓ-source group message vectors $(\vec{M}_1, \vec{M}_2) = ((M_{11}, \ldots, M_{1\ell}), (M_{21}, \ldots, M_{2\ell})) \in \mathbb{G}_1^\ell \times \mathbb{G}_2^\ell$ based on a given index id.

Definition 9 (Indexed Diffie-Hellman Multi-Message Space). *Given an asymmetric bilinear group* $(\mathbb{G}_1, \mathbb{G}_2, \mathbb{G}_T, p, e, g, \hat{g}) \leftarrow \mathcal{BG}(1^\kappa)$*, an index set* $\mathcal{I}$*, and a random oracle* $\mathsf{H} : \mathcal{I} \rightarrow \mathbb{G}_1$*,* $\mathcal{M}^{\mathsf{H}}_{\mathsf{MiDH}}$ *is an indexed Diffie-Hellman (DH) message space if* $\mathcal{M}^{\mathsf{H}}_{\mathsf{MiDH}} \subset \{(id, \tilde{M}) \mid id \in \mathcal{I}, \vec{m} \in \mathbb{Z}_p^\ell, \tilde{M} = \mathsf{MiDH}^{\mathsf{H}}(id, \vec{m})\}$ *and the following index uniqueness property holds: for all* $(id, \tilde{M}) \in \mathcal{M}^{\mathsf{H}}_{\mathsf{MiDH}}$*,* $(id', \tilde{M}') \in \mathcal{M}^{\mathsf{H}}_{\mathsf{MiDH}}$*,* $id = id' \Rightarrow \tilde{M} = \tilde{M}'$*.*

We define the equivalence class for each multi-message $\tilde{M} = (\vec{M}_1, \vec{M}_2) \in \tilde{\mathcal{M}}^{\mathsf{H}}_{\mathsf{MiDH}}$ *as* $\mathsf{EQ}_{\mathsf{MiDH}}(\vec{M}_1, \vec{M}_2) = \{(\vec{M}_1^r, \vec{M}_2) \mid \exists\, r \in \mathbb{Z}_p\}$*.*

$\mathsf{Setup}(1^\kappa)$

$(\mathbb{G}_1, \mathbb{G}_2, \mathbb{G}_T, p, e, g, \hat{g}) \leftarrow \mathcal{BG}(1^\kappa)$

$\mathsf{H} : \{0,1\}^* \rightarrow \mathbb{G}_1$

// select hash function

$\mathsf{pp} \leftarrow ((\mathbb{G}_1, \mathbb{G}_2, \mathbb{G}_T, p, e, g, \hat{g}), \mathsf{H})$

return pp

$\mathsf{KGen}(\mathsf{pp}, \ell)$

$x, y_1, \ldots, y_\ell \leftarrow\$ \mathbb{Z}_p^*$

$\vec{\mathsf{sk}} \leftarrow (\mathsf{sk}_0, \ldots, \mathsf{sk}_\ell) = (x, y_1, \ldots, y_\ell)$

$\vec{\mathsf{vk}} \leftarrow (\mathsf{vk}_0, \mathsf{vk}_1, \boxed{\mathsf{vk}_1^\star}, \ldots, \mathsf{vk}_\ell, \boxed{\mathsf{vk}_\ell^\star})$

$= (\hat{g}^x, \hat{g}^{y_1}, \boxed{g^{y_1}}, \ldots, \hat{g}^{y_\ell}, \boxed{g^{y_\ell}})$

return $(\vec{\mathsf{sk}}, \vec{\mathsf{vk}})$

$\mathsf{Sign}(\mathsf{pp}, \vec{\mathsf{sk}}, (id, \vec{M}_1, \vec{M}_2))$

$h \leftarrow \mathsf{H}(id)$

if $\exists\, j \in [1, \ell] \mid e(h, M_{2j}) \neq e(M_{1j}, \hat{g})$:

  return $\perp$

else : **return** $\sigma \leftarrow (h, s) = (h, h^{\mathsf{sk}_0} \prod_{j=1}^{\ell} M_{1j}^{\mathsf{sk}_j})$

$\mathsf{Verify}(\mathsf{pp}, \vec{\mathsf{vk}}, (\vec{M}_1, \vec{M}_2), \sigma)$

// does not invoke H

parse $\sigma = (h, s)$

return $\left(h \neq 1_{\mathbb{G}_1} \wedge \{M_{1j}\}_{j \in [1,\ell]} \neq 1_{\mathbb{G}_1} \wedge \{e(h, M_{2j}) = e(M_{1j}, \hat{g})\}_{j \in [1,\ell]} \wedge\right.$

$\left. e(h, \mathsf{vk}_0) \prod_{j=1}^{\ell} e(M_{1j}, \mathsf{vk}_j) = e(s, \hat{g})\right)$

Fig. 9. Our Indexed Multi-Message SPS Construction IMM-SPS. The additional elements in $\boxed{\text{solid boxes}}$ are required for blind signing only (cf. Section 6.1).

This generalization of the indexed Diffie-Hellman message space leads us to an indexed multi-message SPS, described in Fig. 9.

Theorem 3. *The indexed multi-message SPS scheme* IMM-SPS *(Fig. 9) is correct and EUF-CiMA secure (Definition 8) under the* GPS_3 *assumption (Definition 6) in the random oracle model.*

The proof is provided in the full version [32].

5 Threshold Structure-Preserving Signatures

We now define the syntax and security notions for non-interactive (n, t)-Threshold Structure-Preserving Signatures (TSPS) for indexed message spaces. We then propose an efficient instantiation for an indexed Diffie-Hellman multi-message space. In an (n, t)-TSPS, the signing key is distributed among n parties, and the generation of any signature requires the cooperation of a subset of at least t parties. We assume a centralized key generation algorithm for distributing the signing key, but a decentralized key generation protocol (DKG), such as Pedersen's DKG [75], may be used instead.

Definition 10 (Threshold Structure-Preserving Signature). *For a given security parameter κ and bilinear group $\mathcal{BG}$, an (n,t)-TSPS over indexed message space $\mathcal{M}$ consists of a tuple* $(\mathsf{Setup}, \mathsf{KGen}, \mathsf{ParSign}, \mathsf{ParVerify}, \mathsf{Reconst}, \mathsf{Verify})$ *of PPT algorithms defined as follows:*

- $\mathsf{pp} \leftarrow \mathsf{Setup}(1^\kappa)$*: The setup algorithm takes the security parameter 1^κ as input and returns the public parameters* pp.
- $(\vec{\mathsf{sk}}, \vec{\mathsf{vk}}, \mathsf{vk}) \leftarrow \mathsf{KGen}(\mathsf{pp}, \ell, n, t)$*: The key generation algorithm takes the public parameters* pp *and length ℓ along with two integers $t, n \in \mathsf{poly}(1^\kappa)$ such that $1 \le t \le n$ as inputs. It returns two vectors of size n of signing/verification keys $\vec{\mathsf{sk}} = (\mathsf{sk}_1, \ldots, \mathsf{sk}_n)$ and $\vec{\mathsf{vk}} = (\mathsf{vk}_1, \ldots, \mathsf{vk}_n)$ such that each party P_i for $i \in [n]$ receives a pair $(\mathsf{sk}_i, \mathsf{vk}_i)$ along with the global verification key* vk.
- $\sigma_i \leftarrow \mathsf{ParSign}(\mathsf{pp}, \mathsf{sk}_i, M)$*: The partial signing algorithm takes the public parameters* pp*, a secret signing key* sk_i*, and a message $M \in \mathcal{M}$ as inputs and returns a partial signature σ_i.*
- $0/1 \leftarrow \mathsf{ParVerify}(\mathsf{pp}, \mathsf{vk}_i, \tilde{M}, \sigma_i)$*: The partial verification algorithm is a deterministic algorithm that takes the public parameters* pp*, a verification key* vk_i*, message $\tilde{M} \in \tilde{\mathcal{M}}$, and a purported partial signature σ_i as inputs. If σ_i is a valid partial signature, it returns* 1 *(accept); else, it returns* 0 *(reject).*
- $(\sigma, \perp) \leftarrow \mathsf{Reconst}(\mathsf{pp}, \{i, \sigma_i\}_{i \in \mathcal{T}})$*: The reconstruction algorithm is a deterministic algorithm that takes public parameters* pp *and a set $\mathcal{T}$ of t partial signatures $\{i, \sigma_i\}$ with corresponding indices as inputs and returns an aggregated signature σ or $\perp$.*
- $0/1 \leftarrow \mathsf{Verify}(\mathsf{pp}, \mathsf{vk}, \tilde{M}, \sigma)$*: The verification algorithm is a deterministic algorithm that takes the public parameters* pp*, the global verification key* vk*, a message $\tilde{M} \in \tilde{\mathcal{M}}$, and a purported signature σ as inputs. If σ is a valid signature, it returns* 1 *(accept); else, it returns* 0 *(reject).*

Three main security properties for TSPS defined over indexed message spaces are *partial verification correctness*, *evaluation correctness*, and *threshold existential unforgeability against chosen indexed message attack* (Threshold EUF-CiMA). Intuitively, partial verification correctness means that any correctly generated partial signature via the ParSign algorithm passes the ParVerify verification checks, and evaluation correctness means that the Reconst algorithm for a set of well-formed partial signatures $\{i, \sigma_i\}_{i \in \mathcal{T}}$ (meaning all with the same index, on a message M) results in a valid aggregated signature σ.

Definition 11 (Partial Verification Correctness). *An (n,t)-TSPS scheme satisfies partial verification correctness if for all correctly indexed messages $M \in \mathcal{M}$,* $\mathsf{pp} \leftarrow \mathsf{Setup}(1^\kappa)$, $(\vec{\mathsf{sk}}, \vec{\mathsf{vk}}, \mathsf{vk}) \leftarrow \mathsf{KGen}(\mathsf{pp}, \ell, n, t)$ *and $i \in [1, n]$ that*

$$\Pr\left[\mathsf{ParVerify}(\mathsf{pp}, \mathsf{vk}_i, \tilde{M}, \mathsf{ParSign}(\mathsf{pp}, \mathsf{sk}_i, M)) = 1\right] = 1 .$$

Definition 12 (Evaluation Correctness). *An (n, t)-TSPS scheme satisfies evaluation correctness if for all correctly indexed messages $M \in \mathcal{M}$,* $\mathsf{pp} \leftarrow \mathsf{Setup}(1^\kappa)$, $(\vec{\mathsf{sk}}, \vec{\mathsf{vk}}, \mathsf{vk}) \leftarrow \mathsf{KGen}(\mathsf{pp}, \ell, n, t)$ *and* $\mathcal{T} \subseteq [1, n], |\mathcal{T}| = t$ *that*

$$\Pr\left[\sigma \leftarrow \mathsf{Reconst}(\mathsf{pp}, \{i, \mathsf{ParSign}(\mathsf{pp}, \mathsf{sk}_i, M)\}_{i \in \mathcal{T}}) : \mathsf{Verify}(\mathsf{pp}, \mathsf{vk}, \tilde{M}, \sigma) = 1\right] = 1.$$

Threshold Unforgeability. We next define the notion of threshold unforgeability for non-interactive (n, t)-TSPS schemes. The Threshold EUF-CiMA game is defined formally in Fig. 10. Given a set of party indices $\mathcal{P} = \{1, \ldots, n\}$, we assume that the adversary can corrupt up to $t - 1$ parties and that there is at least one honest party. We denote the set of corrupt parties by $\mathcal{C}$ and the set of honest parties by $\mathcal{H} = \mathcal{P} \setminus \mathcal{C}$.

$\mathbf{G}_{\mathcal{A}}^{\text{T-EUF-CiMA}}(1^\kappa)$

- $\mathsf{pp} \leftarrow \mathsf{Setup}(1^\kappa)$
- $\mathcal{C} \leftarrow\$ \mathcal{A}(\mathsf{pp})$ // set of corrupt signers
- **if** $\mathcal{C} \notin [1, n] \vee |\mathcal{C}| > t - 1$:
  - **return** $\perp$
- **else** : $\mathcal{H} \leftarrow [1, n] \setminus \mathcal{C}$ // set of honest signers
  - $(\vec{\mathsf{sk}}, \vec{\mathsf{vk}}, \mathsf{vk}) \leftarrow \mathsf{KGen}(\mathsf{pp}, \ell, n, t)$
  - $(\tilde{M}^*, \sigma^*) \leftarrow\$ \mathcal{A}^{\mathcal{O}_{\mathsf{PSign}}}\left(\{\mathsf{sk}_i\}_{i \in \mathcal{C}}, \vec{\mathsf{vk}}, \mathsf{vk}\right)$
  - **return** $(\tilde{M}^* \notin \mathcal{Q}_{\mathsf{EQ}} \wedge \mathsf{Verify}(\mathsf{pp}, \mathsf{vk}, \tilde{M}^*, \sigma^*))$

$\mathcal{O}_{\mathsf{PSign}}(k, id, \tilde{M})$ // $M = (id, \tilde{M})$

- **if** $(k \notin \mathcal{H} \vee (k, id, \star) \in \mathcal{Q}_{\mathsf{S}} \vee (\star, id, \tilde{M}') \in \mathcal{Q}_{\mathsf{S}}, \tilde{M}' \neq \tilde{M})$:
  - **return** $\perp$
- **else** : $\sigma_k \leftarrow \mathsf{ParSign}(\mathsf{pp}, \mathsf{sk}_k, (id, \tilde{M}))$
  - $\mathcal{Q}_{\mathsf{S}} \leftarrow \mathcal{Q}_{\mathsf{S}} \cup \{(k, id, \tilde{M})\}$
  - $\mathcal{Q}_{\mathsf{EQ}} \leftarrow \mathcal{Q}_{\mathsf{EQ}} \cup \{\mathsf{EQ}(\tilde{M})\}$
  - **return** σ_k

Fig. 10. Game $\mathbf{G}_{\mathcal{A}}^{\text{T-EUF-CiMA}}(1^\kappa)$.

In the unforgeability game, the challenger generates public parameters pp and returns them to the adversary. The adversary chooses the set of corrupted participants $\mathcal{C}$. The challenger then runs KGen to derive the global verification key vk, the individual verification keys $\{\mathsf{vk}_i\}_{i=1}^n$, and the secret signing shares $\{\mathsf{sk}_i\}_{i=1}^n$. It returns vk, $\{\mathsf{vk}_i\}_{i=1}^n$, and the set of corrupt signing shares $\{\mathsf{sk}_j\}_{j \in \mathcal{C}}$ to the adversary. We assume the adversary maintains state before and after KGen.

After key generation, the adversary can request partial signatures on messages of its choosing from honest signers by querying oracle $\mathcal{O}_{\mathsf{PSign}}(\cdot)$.

$\mathsf{Setup}(1^\kappa)$

$(\mathbb{G}_1, \mathbb{G}_2, \mathbb{G}_T, p, e, g, \hat{g}) \leftarrow \mathcal{BG}(1^\kappa);\ \mathsf{H} : \{0,1\}^* \rightarrow \mathbb{G}_1$ // select hash function
return $\mathsf{pp} \leftarrow ((\mathbb{G}_1, \mathbb{G}_2, \mathbb{G}_T, p, e, g, \hat{g}), \mathsf{H})$

$\mathsf{KGen}(\mathsf{pp}, \ell, n, t)$

$x, y_1, \ldots, y_\ell \leftarrow\!\$\ \mathbb{Z}_p^*$
$\vec{x} \leftarrow\!\$\ \mathsf{Share}(x, p, n, t), \{\vec{y}_j \leftarrow\!\$\ \mathsf{Share}(y_j, p, n, t)\}_{j \in [1,\ell]}$
for $i \in [1, n]$:
  $\mathsf{sk}_i \leftarrow (\mathsf{sk}_{i0}, \mathsf{sk}_{i1}, \ldots, \mathsf{sk}_{i\ell}) = (x_i, y_{i1}, \ldots, y_{i\ell})$
  $\mathsf{vk}_i \leftarrow (\mathsf{vk}_{i0}, \mathsf{vk}_{i1}, \boxed{\mathsf{vk}^\star_{i1}}, \ldots, \mathsf{vk}_{i\ell}, \boxed{\mathsf{vk}^\star_{i\ell}}) = (\hat{g}^{x_i}, \hat{g}^{y_{i1}}, \boxed{g^{y_{i1}}}, \ldots, \hat{g}^{y_{i\ell}}, \boxed{g^{y_{i\ell}}})$
$\vec{\mathsf{sk}} \leftarrow (\mathsf{sk}_1, \ldots, \mathsf{sk}_n)$
$\vec{\mathsf{vk}} \leftarrow (\mathsf{vk}_1, \ldots, \mathsf{vk}_n)$
$\mathsf{vk} \leftarrow (\mathsf{vk}_{00}, \mathsf{vk}_{01}, \boxed{\mathsf{vk}^\star_{01}}, \ldots, \mathsf{vk}_{0\ell}, \boxed{\mathsf{vk}^\star_{0\ell}}) = (\hat{g}^{x}, \hat{g}^{y_1}, \boxed{g^{y_1}}, \ldots, \hat{g}^{y_\ell}, \boxed{g^{y_\ell}})$
return $(\vec{\mathsf{sk}}, \vec{\mathsf{vk}}, \mathsf{vk})$

$\mathsf{ParSign}\left(\mathsf{pp}, \mathsf{sk}_i, (id, \vec{M}_1, \vec{M}_2)\right)$

$h \leftarrow \mathsf{H}(id)$
if $\exists\, j \in [1, \ell]$ |
$e(h, M_{2j}) \neq e(M_{1j}, \hat{g})$:
  return $\perp$
else : $s_i \leftarrow h^{\mathsf{sk}_{i0}} \prod_{j=1}^{\ell} {M_{1j}}^{\mathsf{sk}_{ij}}$
  return $\sigma_i \leftarrow (h, s_i)$

$\mathsf{ParVerify}\left(\mathsf{pp}, \mathsf{vk}_i, (\vec{M}_1, \vec{M}_2), \sigma_i\right)$

// does not invoke H
parse $\sigma_i = (h_i, s_i)$
return $(h_i \neq 1_{\mathbb{G}_1}\ \wedge$
  $\{M_{1j}\}_{j \in [1,\ell]} \neq 1_{\mathbb{G}_1}\ \wedge$
  $\{e(h_i, M_{2j}) = e(M_{1j}, \hat{g})\}_{j \in [1,\ell]}\ \wedge$
  $e(h_i, \mathsf{vk}_{i0}) \prod_{j=1}^{\ell} e(M_{1j}, \mathsf{vk}_{ij}) = e(s_i, \hat{g})$

$\mathsf{Reconst}\left(\mathsf{pp}, \vec{\mathsf{vk}}, (\vec{M}_1, \vec{M}_2), \{i, \sigma_i\}_{i \in \mathcal{T}}\right)$

parse $\sigma_i = (h_i, s_i)$
if $\exists\, i, j \in \mathcal{T}, i \neq j \mid h_i \neq h_j$
$\vee\ \exists\, i \in \mathcal{T}$ |
$\mathsf{ParVerify}(\mathsf{pp}, \mathsf{vk}_i, (\vec{M}_1, \vec{M}_2), \sigma_i) = 0$
  return $\perp$
else : $h \leftarrow h_i$
  return $\sigma \leftarrow (h, s) = (h, \prod_{i \in \mathcal{T}} s_i^{\lambda_i})$

$\mathsf{Verify}\left(\mathsf{pp}, \mathsf{vk}, (\vec{M}_1, \vec{M}_2), \sigma\right)$

// does not invoke H
parse $\sigma = (h, s)$
return $(h \neq 1_{\mathbb{G}_1} \wedge$
  $\{M_{1j}\}_{j \in [1,\ell]} \neq 1_{\mathbb{G}_1}\ \wedge$
  $\{e(h, M_{2j}) = e(M_{1j}, \hat{g})\}_{j \in [1,\ell]}\ \wedge$
  $e(h, \mathsf{vk}_{00}) \prod_{j=1}^{\ell} e(M_{1j}, \mathsf{vk}_{0j}) = e(s, \hat{g})$

Fig. 11. Our Threshold SPS Construction TSPS. The additional elements in solid boxes are required for blind signing only (cf. Sect. 6.1).

The adversary wins if it can produce a valid forgery $(\tilde{M}^*, \sigma^*)$ with respect to the global verification key vk representing the set of n signers, on a message $\tilde{M}^*$ for which no equivalent $\tilde{M}^{*'}$ has been previously queried to $\mathcal{O}_{\mathsf{PSign}}(\cdot)$.

Definition 13 (Threshold EUF-CiMA). *A non-interactive (n, t)-TSPS scheme over indexed message space $\mathcal{M}$ is Threshold EUF-CiMA secure if for all PPT adversaries $\mathcal{A}$ playing game $\mathbf{G}^{T\text{-}EUF\text{-}CiMA}$ (Fig. 10), there exists a negligible function ν such that*

$$Adv_{\mathcal{A}}^{T\text{-}EUF\text{-}CiMA}(\kappa) = \Pr\left[\mathbf{G}_{\mathcal{A}}^{T\text{-}EUF\text{-}CiMA}(1^\kappa) = 1\right] \leq \nu(\kappa) .$$

5.1 Our Indexed Multi-message TSPS

In Fig. 11, we present our (n, t)-TSPS scheme TSPS over an indexed Diffie-Hellman multi-message space $\mathcal{M}^{\mathsf{H}}_{\mathsf{MiDH}}$, as defined in Fig. 8.

5.2 Security of TSPS

Theorem 4. *The indexed multi-message (n, t)-Threshold SPS scheme* TSPS *is correct and Threshold EUF-CiMA secure (Definition 13) in the random oracle model under the EUF-CiMA security of* IMM-SPS *(Theorem 3).*

Proof. **Correctness.** We first show that the proposed TSPS satisfies partial verification correctness (Definition 11), i.e., any correctly generated partial signature via the ParSign algorithm passes the ParVerify verification checks. Indeed, for all $i \in [1, n]$ and correctly indexed messages $M = (id, \vec{M}_1, \vec{M}_2) \in \mathcal{M}^{\mathsf{H}}_{\mathsf{MiDH}}$, we have:

$$e(h, \mathsf{vk}_{i0}) \prod_{j=1}^{\ell} e(M_{1j}, \mathsf{vk}_{ij}) = e(h, \hat{g}^{x_i}) \prod_{j=1}^{\ell} e(M_{1j}, \hat{g}^{y_{ij}}) e(h^{x_i} \prod_{j=1}^{\ell} M_{1j}^{y_{ij}}, \hat{g}) = e(s_i, \hat{g}) .$$

Next, we show that TSPS satisfies evaluation correctness (Definition 12); that is, the Reconst algorithm for a set of partial signatures $\{i, \sigma_i\}_{i \in \mathcal{T}}, \mathcal{T} \subseteq [1, n], |\mathcal{T}| = t$, on a message $M = (id, \vec{M}_1, \vec{M}_2)$ with the same $h \leftarrow \mathsf{H}(id)$ results in a valid aggregated signature $\sigma = (h, s)$. Indeed,

$$s = \prod_{i \in \mathcal{T}} s_i^{\lambda_i} = \prod_{i \in \mathcal{T}} (h^{\mathsf{sk}_{i0}} \prod_{j=1}^{\ell} M_{1j}^{\mathsf{sk}_{ij}})^{\lambda_i} = h^{\sum_{i \in \mathcal{T}} \mathsf{sk}_{i0} \lambda_i} \prod_{j=1}^{\ell} M_{1j}^{\sum_{i \in \mathcal{T}} \mathsf{sk}_{ij} \lambda_i} = h^{\mathsf{sk}_0} \prod_{j=1}^{\ell} M_{1j}^{\mathsf{sk}_j}$$

where λ_i is the Lagrange coefficient for party P_i with respect to the signing set $\mathcal{T}$. Next, we show that verification holds for the above aggregated signature σ on message $\tilde{M} = (\vec{M}_1, \vec{M}_2)$. Indeed, $\forall\ j \in [1, \ell]$ we have that $e(h, M_{2j}) = e(h, \hat{g}^{m_j}) = e(h^{m_j}, \hat{g}) = e(M_{1j}, \hat{g})$ and

$$e(h, \mathsf{vk}_0) \prod_{j=1}^{\ell} e(M_{1j}, \mathsf{vk}_j) = e(h, \hat{g}^{x}) \prod_{j=1}^{\ell} e(M_{1j}, \hat{g}^{y_j}) = e(h^{x} \prod_{j=1}^{\ell} M_{1j}^{y_j}, \hat{g}) = e(s, \hat{g}) .$$

Note that successful partial signature verification using ParVerify and consistency of h guarantee successful reconstruction.

Need for Uniqueness. The hypothetical attack described after Theorem 2 also works with a partial signing oracle $\mathcal{O}_{\mathsf{PSign}}(\cdot)$. Assume an (n, t)-TSPS with $n > 2t$, and suppose there were no uniqueness requirement for the message space and that the redundant check in Line 2 of the $\mathcal{O}_{\mathsf{PSign}}(\cdot)$ oracle of Fig. 10 were not present. Then, a forger could obtain $2t$ partial signatures to reconstruct signatures $s = h^x M_1^y$, $s' = h^x M_1'^y$ and compute a forgery $s^* = s^2/s' = h^x(M_1^2/M_1')^y$ that is a valid signature on fresh message M_1^2/M_1'.

Threshold EUF-CiMA. Our proof of security for TSPS resembles that of threshold BLS in [18]. We wish to show that if there exists a PPT adversary $\mathcal{A}$ that breaks the Threshold EUF-CiMA security (Fig. 10) of TSPS with non-negligible probability, then we can construct a PPT adversary $\mathcal{B}$ that breaks the EUF-CiMA security (Fig. 5) of the underlying IMM-SPS scheme (Fig. 6) with non-negligible probability.

Suppose there exists such a PPT adversary $\mathcal{A}$. Then, running $\mathcal{A}$ as a subroutine, we construct a reduction $\mathcal{B}$ breaking the EUF-CiMA security of IMM-SPS as follows.

The reduction $\mathcal{B}$ is responsible for simulating oracle responses for queries to $\mathcal{O}_{\mathsf{PSign}}(\cdot)$ and H. Let $\mathcal{Q}_{\mathsf{H}}$ be the set of H queries id and their responses. $\mathcal{B}$ may program the random oracle H. Let $\mathcal{Q}_{\mathsf{S}}$ be the set of $\mathcal{O}_{\mathsf{PSign}}(\cdot)$ queries $(k, id, \tilde{M})$ and $\mathcal{Q}_{\mathsf{EQ}}$ the set of equivalence classes of messages $\tilde{M}$. $\mathcal{B}$ initializes $\mathcal{Q}_{\mathsf{H}}, \mathcal{Q}_{\mathsf{S}}, \mathcal{Q}_{\mathsf{EQ}}$ to the empty set.

Initialization. $\mathcal{B}$ takes as input public parameters $\mathsf{pp} \leftarrow (\mathbb{G}_1, \mathbb{G}_2, \mathbb{G}_T, p, e, g, \hat{g})$ and an IMM-SPS verification key vk'. In the EUF-CiMA game, $\mathcal{B}$ has access to oracles $\mathcal{O}'_{\mathsf{Sign}}(\cdot)$ and H'. $\mathcal{B}$ uses $\mathsf{vk}' = (\mathsf{vk}'_{00}, \mathsf{vk}'_{01}, \mathsf{vk}'^{\star}_{01}, \ldots, \mathsf{vk}'_{0\ell}, \mathsf{vk}'^{\star}_{0\ell})$ as the TSPS verification key $\mathsf{vk} = (\mathsf{vk}_{00}, \mathsf{vk}_{01}, \mathsf{vk}^{\star}_{01}, \ldots, \mathsf{vk}_{0\ell}, \mathsf{vk}^{\star}_{0\ell})$.

Simulating Key Generation. $\mathcal{B}$ simulates the key generation algorithm as follows.

- $\mathcal{B}$ defines the pair of secret/verification keys of the corrupted parties $P_i, i \in \mathcal{C}$, as follows. Assume without loss of generality that $|\mathcal{C}| = t - 1$. For all $i \in \mathcal{C}$, $\mathcal{B}$ samples random values $x_{i0}, y_{i1}, \ldots, y_{i\ell} \leftarrow\!\!\$\, (\mathbb{Z}_p^*)^{\ell+1}$ and defines party P_i's secret key as $\mathsf{sk}_i \leftarrow (\mathsf{sk}_{i0}, \mathsf{sk}_{i1}, \ldots, \mathsf{sk}_{i\ell}) = (x_{i0}, y_{i1}, \ldots, y_{i\ell})$ and the corresponding verification key as $\mathsf{vk}_i \leftarrow (\mathsf{vk}_{i0}, \mathsf{vk}_{i1}, \mathsf{vk}^{\star}_{i1}, \ldots, \mathsf{vk}_{i\ell}, \mathsf{vk}^{\star}_{i\ell}) = (\hat{g}^{x_{i0}}, \hat{g}^{y_{i1}}, g^{y_{i1}}, \ldots, \hat{g}^{y_{i\ell}}, g^{y_{i\ell}})$.
- To generate the verification key of the honest parties $P_k, k \in \mathcal{H}, \mathcal{H} = [1, n] \setminus \mathcal{C}$, $\mathcal{B}$ proceeds as follows:
  1. For all $i \in \tilde{\mathcal{T}} := \mathcal{C} \cup \{0\}$, it computes the Lagrange polynomials evaluated at point k:
  $$\tilde{\lambda}_{ki} = L_i^{\tilde{\mathcal{T}}}(k) = \prod_{j \in \tilde{\mathcal{T}} j \neq i} \frac{(j-k)}{(j-i)} \ . \tag{3}$$
  2. It takes the verification keys of corrupted parties $\{\mathsf{vk}_i\}_{i \in \mathcal{C}}$ and the global verification key vk and then computes

$$\begin{aligned}\mathsf{vk}_k &= (\mathsf{vk}_{k0}, \mathsf{vk}_{k1}, \mathsf{vk}^{\star}_{k1}, \ldots, \mathsf{vk}_{k\ell}, \mathsf{vk}^{\star}_{k\ell}) \\ &= \Big(\mathsf{vk}_{00}^{\tilde{\lambda}_{k0}} \prod_{i\in\mathcal{C}} \mathsf{vk}_{i0}^{\tilde{\lambda}_{ki}}, \mathsf{vk}_{01}^{\tilde{\lambda}_{k0}} \prod_{i\in\mathcal{C}} \mathsf{vk}_{i1}^{\tilde{\lambda}_{ki}}, {\mathsf{vk}^{\star}_{01}}^{\tilde{\lambda}_{k0}} \prod_{i\in\mathcal{C}} {\mathsf{vk}^{\star}_{i1}}^{\tilde{\lambda}_{ki}}, \ldots, \\ &\quad \mathsf{vk}_{0\ell}^{\tilde{\lambda}_{k0}} \prod_{i\in\mathcal{C}} \mathsf{vk}_{i\ell}^{\tilde{\lambda}_{ki}}, {\mathsf{vk}^{\star}_{0\ell}}^{\tilde{\lambda}_{k0}} \prod_{i\in\mathcal{C}} {\mathsf{vk}^{\star}_{i\ell}}^{\tilde{\lambda}_{ki}}\Big).\end{aligned}$$

$\mathcal{B}$ returns the global verification key vk, $\vec{\mathsf{vk}} = (\mathsf{vk}_1, \ldots, \mathsf{vk}_n)$, and secret keys $\{\mathsf{sk}_j\}_{j\in\mathcal{C}}$ to $\mathcal{A}$.

Simulating Random Oracle $\mathsf{H}(id)$*:* When $\mathcal{A}$ queries H on index id, if $\mathcal{Q}_{\mathsf{H}}[id] = \perp$, then $\mathcal{B}$ queries $\mathsf{H}'(id)$, receives a base element h, and sets $\mathcal{Q}_{\mathsf{H}}[id] \leftarrow h$. $\mathcal{B}$ returns $\mathcal{Q}_{\mathsf{H}}[id]$ to $\mathcal{A}$.

Simulating Signing Oracle $\mathcal{O}_{\mathsf{PSign}}(k, id, \tilde{M})$*:* When $\mathcal{A}$ queries $\mathcal{O}_{\mathsf{PSign}}(\cdot)$ on $(k, id, \tilde{M})$ for honest party identifier $k \in \mathcal{H}$ and message $M = (id, \tilde{M}) = (id, \vec{M}_1, \vec{M}_2)$, if $k \notin \mathcal{H}$ or $(k, id, \star) \in \mathcal{Q}_{\mathsf{S}}$ or $(\star, id, \tilde{M}') \in \mathcal{Q}_{\mathsf{S}}, \tilde{M}' \neq \tilde{M}$, $\mathcal{B}$ returns $\perp$. Otherwise, $\mathcal{B}$ does the following:

1. $\mathcal{B}$ looks up $h = \mathcal{Q}_{\mathsf{H}}[id]$, queries $\mathcal{O}'_{\mathsf{Sign}}(id, \vec{M}_1, \vec{M}_2)$, and receives the signature $\sigma_0 = (h, s_0)$.
2. For all $i \in \mathcal{C}$, $\mathcal{B}$ computes the partial signatures $\sigma_i = (h, s_i) = (h, h^{\mathsf{sk}_{i0}} \prod_{j=1}^{\ell} M_{1j}^{\mathsf{sk}_{ij}})$, as it knows the secret keys of corrupted parties.
3. For all $i \in \tilde{\mathcal{T}} = \mathcal{C} \cup \{0\}$, $\mathcal{B}$ computes Lagrange coefficients $\tilde{\lambda}_{ki}$ as in Equation (3).
4. $\mathcal{B}$ updates $\mathcal{Q}_{\mathsf{S}} \leftarrow \mathcal{Q}_{\mathsf{S}} \cup \{(k, id, \tilde{M})\}$ and $\mathcal{Q}_{\mathsf{EQ}} \leftarrow \mathcal{Q}_{\mathsf{EQ}} \cup \{\mathsf{EQ}(\tilde{M})\}$.
5. $\mathcal{B}$ computes $(h, s_k) = (h, s_0^{\tilde{\lambda}_{k0}} \prod_{i\in\mathcal{C}} s_i^{\tilde{\lambda}_{ki}})$ and returns $\sigma_k = (h, s_k)$ to $\mathcal{A}$.

Output. At the end of the game, $\mathcal{A}$ produces a valid forgery $\sigma^* = (h^*, s^*)$ on message $\tilde{M}^* = (\vec{M}_1^*, \vec{M}_2^*)$, and $\mathcal{B}$ returns $(\tilde{M}^*, \sigma^*)$ as its forgery.

$\mathcal{B}$ correctly simulates key generation and $\mathcal{A}$'s hash and signing queries. Since $\mathcal{A}$'s forgery satisfies $\tilde{M}^* \notin \mathcal{Q}_{\mathsf{EQ}}$ and $\mathsf{Verify}(\mathsf{pp}, \mathsf{vk}, \tilde{M}^*, \sigma^*) = 1$, $\mathcal{B}$'s winning conditions are also satisfied and $Adv^{\mathsf{T\text{-}EUF\text{-}CiMA}}_{\mathsf{TSPS},\mathcal{A}}(\kappa) \leq Adv^{\mathsf{EUF\text{-}CiMA}}_{\mathsf{IMM\text{-}SPS},\mathcal{B}}(\kappa)$. □

6 Applications to Threshold-Issuance Anonymous Credentials

Threshold-Issuance Anonymous Credential (TIAC) systems are a prime use-case of threshold SPS. TIAC systems, defined by Sonnino et al. [82], are used in various applications [64,83]. A TIAC is an anonymous credential scheme that enables a group of signers (or issuers) to jointly sign a blind message, i.e., issue a credential, without learning the original message. The core ingredient is a blind signing protocol for the used threshold signature scheme. Besides the threshold signature, this protocol relies on two main cryptographic primitives: NIZKs and commitment schemes, defined in Appendix A.3 and Appendix A.2, respectively.

The TIAC protocol of [82], known as Coconut, lacks a rigorous security proof. Recently, Rial and Piotrowska [77] conducted a security analysis that required some modifications to the original Coconut scheme, resulting in Coconut^{++}. Coconut and Coconut^{++} are based on a threshold Pointcheval-Sanders signature scheme that supports an efficient blind signing protocol.

6.1 Blind Signing for TSPS

In Fig. 12, we show that our TSPS construction also supports threshold blind signing. In addition to the TSPS parameters, the public parameters pp now contain the common reference string (CRS) of a NIZK and the public parameters of a commitment scheme.

For intuition, we note that in $\mathsf{PrepareBlindSign}$, the index is computed as a commitment to $\vec{m}$, using the generalized Pedersen commitment scheme. The single messages are also committed in a Pedersen commitment, where one commitment parameter is computed on the fly via a random oracle as $h = \mathsf{H}(id)$. The hiding property of commitments and the zero-knowledge property of NIZK ensure the blindness.

We note that the construction in Fig. 12 follows the blind signing protocol for Coconut^{++} closely, with only minor syntactical changes due to the indexed DH message space (highlighted in the figure). Consequently, the validity of the blinding operations readily follows from that of Coconut^{++}. The key generation phase is the same as in Fig. 11.

6.2 Removing Rewinding Extractors in TIAC

The TIAC constructions Coconut and Coconut^{++} combine threshold signatures (with blind signing) with generalized Schnorr proofs [78] turned into extractable (knowledge-sound) NIZK proofs via the Fiat-Shamir (FS) heuristic [43] in the random oracle model. This, however, is problematic if used within the universal composability (UC) framework [24], as extractability for such NIZK proofs requires rewinding. For instance, Coconut^{++} is modeled in the UC framework but requires rewinding to prove that it realizes $\mathcal{F}_{\mathrm{AC}}$ [77, Theorem 3]. This, in turn, makes the formal security guarantees in the UC framework questionable.

Fischlin's framework [44], also in the random oracle model, is a well-known technique to avoid rewinding. However, this adds significant overhead that negatively affects its practical applicability. Groth-Sahai (GS) NIZK proofs [60] are an efficient alternative NIZK proof system. GS proofs are secure in the standard model and support straight-line extraction of the witnesses, i.e., avoid the rewinding required by the Fischlin transform. This makes them particularly attractive if one is interested in achieving composable security, e.g., UC security. We note that there are known transformations like [27,57,59] to make GS proofs UC secure despite their malleability. However, GS proofs can only extract group elements.

$\mathsf{PrepareBlindSign}(\mathsf{pp}, \vec{m})$ // $\mathsf{pp} = (\mathsf{pp}_c, \mathsf{CRS}, \mathsf{H})$

$\quad$ **parse** $\vec{m} = (m_1, \ldots, m_\ell)$

$\quad \omega \leftarrow\!\$\, \mathbb{Z}_p^*,\ id \leftarrow \mathsf{Com}(\mathsf{pp}_c, \vec{m}, \omega) = G_0^\omega \prod_{i=1}^{\ell} G_i^{m_i}$

$\quad \left(id, (\vec{M}_1, \vec{M}_2)\right) \leftarrow \mathsf{MiDH}^{\mathsf{H}}(id, \vec{m})$

$\quad$ **for** $j \in [1, \ell]$:

$\qquad \omega_{1j}, \omega_{2j} \leftarrow\!\$\, \mathbb{Z}_p^*$

$\qquad (\mathsf{cm}_{1j}, \mathsf{cm}_{2j}) \leftarrow \left(g^{\omega_{1j}} M_{1j}\ ,\ \hat{g}^{\omega_{2j}} M_{2j} \right)$

$\quad \vec{\mathsf{cm}} = \{(\mathsf{cm}_{1j}, \mathsf{cm}_{2j})\}_{j=1}^{\ell}$

$\quad \Omega \leftarrow (\omega, \omega_{11}, \omega_{21}, \ldots, \omega_{1\ell}, \omega_{2\ell})$

$\quad \pi_s \leftarrow \mathsf{NIZK.Prove}\Big\{ \Omega, \vec{m} \mid id = G_0^\omega \prod_{i=1}^{\ell} G_i^{m_i} \wedge$

$\qquad \{\mathsf{cm}_{1j} = g^{\omega_{1j}} \mathsf{H}(id)^{m_j}\}_{j=1}^{\ell} \wedge \{\mathsf{cm}_{2j} = g^{\omega_{2j}} \hat{g}^{m_j}\}_{j=1}^{\ell} \Big\}$

$\quad$ **return** $(\Omega, id, \vec{\mathsf{cm}}, \pi_s)$

$\mathsf{BlindSign}(\mathsf{pp}, \mathsf{sk}_i, id, \vec{\mathsf{cm}}, \pi_s)$

$\quad$ **parse** $\mathsf{sk}_i = (\mathsf{sk}_1, \ldots, \mathsf{sk}_n)$

$\quad h \leftarrow \mathsf{H}(id)$

$\quad$ **if** $\mathsf{NIZK.Verify}(\mathsf{CRS}, (id, \vec{\mathsf{cm}}, h), \pi_s) = 0$:

$\qquad$ **return** $\perp$

$\quad$ **else** : $\bar{s}_i \leftarrow h^{\mathsf{sk}_{i0}} \prod_{j=1}^{\ell} {\mathsf{cm}_{1j}}^{\mathsf{sk}_{ij}}$

$\qquad$ **return** $\bar{\sigma}_i \leftarrow (h, \bar{s}_i)$

$\mathsf{AggCred}(\mathsf{pp}, \{i, \bar{\sigma}_i\}_{i \in \mathcal{T}})$

$\quad$ **parse** $\bar{\sigma}_i = (h_i, \bar{s}_i)$

$\quad$ **if** $\exists\, i, j \in \mathcal{T}, i \neq j \mid h_i \neq h_j$: **return** $\perp$

$\quad$ **else** : $h \leftarrow h_i$

$\qquad$ **return** $\bar{\sigma} \leftarrow (h, \bar{s}) = (h, \prod_{i \in \mathcal{T}} s_i^{\lambda_i})$

$\mathsf{UnBlind}(\mathsf{pp}, \mathsf{vk}, \bar{\sigma}, \Omega)$

$\quad$ **parse** $\bar{\sigma} = (h, \bar{s})$

$\quad$ **return** $\sigma := (h, s) \leftarrow (h, \bar{s} \prod_{j=1}^{\ell} (g^{y_j})^{-\omega_j})$

Fig. 12. A Threshold Blind Signature with straight-line extraction. Grey (Color figure online) boxes mark the changes from Coconut^{++}. Algorithms and notation are defined in Appendices A.2 to A.4.

Towards achieving efficient straight-line extraction without the need of rewinding, we propose to replace the blind issuance threshold Pointcheval-Sanders signature of Coconut^{++} with our blind issuance TSPS. We make the reasonable assumption that the scalar messages (attributes in the TIAC) come from some polynomially bounded message space, e.g., in practice, attributes can be encoded in small scalar values. This modification enables us to provide a GS proof of a valid signature for the showing of a credential with non-revealed messages. Noticing that GS NIZKs are commit-and-proof NIZKs, we can use an additional Schnorr NIZK obtained via Fiat-Shamir to prove a predicate over the scalar messages in the GS commitments. The interesting point is that the latter NIZK only needs to be sound, but does not need to be extractable, as GS commitments can be perfectly binding. Thus, we can avoid rewinding and, due to the polynomially bounded message space, we can extract the scalar messages (attributes in TIAC) efficiently from the straight-line extracted messages from the commitments of the GS proof.

7 Conclusion and Open Problems

In this work, we introduce the notion of a threshold structure-preserving signature (TSPS) and present an efficient fully non-interactive TSPS construction. We prove that the proposed TSPS is secure under a new variant of the generalized Pointcheval-Sanders (PS) assumption in the random oracle model. We have shown that our TSPS can be used as a drop-in replacement in TIAC systems to remove the need for rewinding extractors.

While we use a message indexing method in order to construct a non-interactive scheme, a non-interactive TSPS without indexing is an interesting open problem. Moreover, it is interesting to construct schemes that rely on weaker assumptions and avoid the use of the random oracle model. When it comes to the security model, the following two challenging problems remain open: obtaining security under adaptive corruptions more tightly than via a guessing argument from static corruptions, and achieving the strongest notion possible for fully non-interactive schemes (TS-UF-1) [14]. In general, we believe this work can open a new line of research for structure-preserving multi-party protocols, such as threshold structure-preserving encryption. Moreover, we expect that TSPS will have further applications beyond TIAC systems.

Acknowledgments. We would like to thank the anonymous reviewers for their valuable comments, and Behzad Abdolmaleki, Daniele Cozzo and Hyoseung Kim for their suggestions. Elizabeth Crites was supported by Input Output through their funding of the Blockchain Technology Lab at the University of Edinburgh. The work of Markulf Kohlweiss was done in part while visiting COSIC, KU Leuven. Mahdi Sedaghat and Bart Preneel were supported in part by the Research Council KU Leuven C1 on Security and Privacy for Cyber-Physical Systems and the Internet of Things with contract number C16/15/058 and by CyberSecurity Research Flanders with reference number VR20192203. Daniel Slamanig was supported by the European Union's Horizon 2020 research and innovation programme under grant agreement No. 871473 (Kraken) and

No. 861696 (LABYRINTH) and by the Austrian Science Fund (FWF) and netidee SCIENCE under grant agreement P31621-N38 (PROFET).

A Additional Definitions and Assumptions

A.1 Digital Signatures

Definition 14 (Digital Signature). *A digital signature scheme over message space $\mathcal{M}$ is a tuple of the following polynomial-time algorithms:*

- $\mathsf{pp} \leftarrow \mathsf{Setup}(1^\kappa)$*: Setup is a probabilistic algorithm which takes as input the security parameter* 1^κ *and outputs the set of public parameters* pp.
- $(\mathsf{sk}, \mathsf{vk}) \leftarrow \mathsf{KGen}(\mathsf{pp})$*: Key generation is a probabilistic algorithm which takes as input* pp *and outputs a pair of signing/verification keys* $(\mathsf{sk}, \mathsf{vk})$.
- $\sigma \leftarrow \mathsf{Sign}(\mathsf{pp}, \mathsf{sk}, m)$*: The signing algorithm takes as input* pp*, a secret signing key* sk*, and a message* $m \in \mathcal{M}$*, and outputs a signature* σ.
- $0/1 \leftarrow \mathsf{Verify}(\mathsf{pp}, \mathsf{vk}, m, \sigma)$*: Verification is a deterministic algorithm which takes as input* pp*, a public verification key* vk*, a message* $m \in \mathcal{M}$*, and a purported signature* σ*, and outputs either 0 (reject) or 1 (accept).*

The primary security requirements for a digital signature scheme are *correctness* and *existential unforgeability against chosen message attack* (EUF-CMA).

Definition 15 (Correctness). *A digital signature is correct if we have:*

$$\Pr\left[\begin{array}{l}\forall\ \mathsf{pp} \leftarrow \mathsf{Setup}(1^\kappa), (\mathsf{sk}, \mathsf{vk}) \leftarrow \mathsf{KGen}(\mathsf{pp}), m \in \mathcal{M} : \\ \mathsf{Verify}\,(\mathsf{pp}, \mathsf{vk}, m, \mathsf{Sign}(\mathsf{pp}, \mathsf{sk}, m)) = 1\end{array}\right] \geq 1 - \nu(\kappa) \ .$$

Definition 16 (Existential Unforgeability under Chosen Message Attack (EUF-CMA)). *A digital signature scheme over message space $\mathcal{M}$ is EUF-CMA secure if for all PPT adversaries $\mathcal{A}$ playing game* $\mathbf{G}^{\mathsf{EUF\text{-}CMA}}$ *(Fig. 13), there exists a negligible function ν such that*

$$Adv_{\mathcal{A}}^{\mathsf{EUF\text{-}CMA}}(\kappa) = \Pr\left[\mathbf{G}_{\mathcal{A}}^{\mathsf{EUF\text{-}CMA}}(1^\kappa) = 1\right] \leq \nu(\kappa) \ .$$

$\mathbf{G}_{\mathcal{A}}^{\mathsf{EUF\text{-}CMA}}(1^\kappa)$	$\mathcal{O}_{\mathsf{Sign}}(m)$
$\mathsf{pp} \leftarrow \mathsf{Setup}(1^\kappa)$	$\sigma \leftarrow \mathsf{Sign}\,(\mathsf{pp}, \mathsf{sk}, m)$
$(\mathsf{sk}, \mathsf{vk}) \leftarrow \mathsf{KGen}(\mathsf{pp})$	$\mathcal{Q} \leftarrow \mathcal{Q} \cup \{m\}$
$(m^*, \sigma^*) \leftarrow\$\ \mathcal{A}^{\mathcal{O}_{\mathsf{Sign}}}(\mathsf{pp}, \mathsf{vk})$	$\mathbf{return}\ \sigma$
$\mathbf{return}\ (m^* \notin \mathcal{Q} \wedge \mathsf{Verify}(\mathsf{pp}, \mathsf{vk}, m^*, \sigma^*))$	

Fig. 13. The EUF-CMA security game.

A.2 Commitment Schemes

Definition 17 (Commitment Scheme). *A commitment scheme over message space $\mathcal{M}$, opening space $\mathcal{T}$, and commitment space $\mathcal{C}$, consists of the following polynomial-time algorithms:*

- $\mathsf{pp}_c \leftarrow \mathsf{CSetup}(1^\kappa)$*: Setup is a probabilistic algorithm which takes as input the security parameter* 1^κ *and outputs the set of public parameters* pp_c.
- $\mathsf{cm} \leftarrow \mathsf{Com}(\mathsf{pp}_c, m, \tau)$*: The commitment algorithm takes as input* pp_c *and a message* $m \in \mathcal{M}$ *along with a trapdoor* $\tau \in \mathcal{T}$*, and outputs a commitment* $\mathsf{cm} \in \mathcal{C}$.
- $0/1 \leftarrow \mathsf{CVerify}(\mathsf{pp}_c, \mathsf{cm}, m', \tau')$*: Verification is a deterministic algorithm which takes as input* pp_c*, a commitment* $\mathsf{cm} \in \mathcal{C}$*, a message* $m' \in \mathcal{M}$*, and an opening value* $\tau' \in \mathcal{T}$*, and outputs either* 0 *(reject) or* 1 *(accept).*

Informally, the primary security requirements for a commitment scheme are *correctness*, *hiding*, and *binding*. Correctness ensures that correctly generated commitments pass the verification phase. The hiding property guarantees that the commitment does not reveal any information about the hidden value, while binding ensures that a committer cannot open a commitment to two distinct messages.

Pedersen Commitment Scheme [75]**.** Over a cyclic group $\mathbb{G}$ of prime order p with generator g, the Pedersen commitment scheme allows to commit to a scalar message $m \in \mathbb{Z}_p$ and is perfectly hiding and computationally binding. It consists of the following polynomial-time algorithms:

- $\mathsf{pp}_c \leftarrow \mathsf{CSetup}(1^\kappa)$: Sample $r \leftarrow_\$ \mathbb{Z}_p$ and set $G_1 \leftarrow g^r$. Output $\mathsf{pp}_c \leftarrow (G_0 = g, G_1, \mathcal{M})$, where $\mathcal{M} = \mathbb{Z}_p$.
- $\mathsf{cm} \leftarrow \mathsf{Com}(\mathsf{pp}_c, m, \tau)$: Compute $\mathsf{cm} \leftarrow G_0^\tau G_1^m$. Output cm.
- $0/1 \leftarrow \mathsf{CVerify}(\mathsf{pp}_c, \mathsf{cm}, m', \tau')$: Compute $\mathsf{cm}' \leftarrow G_0^{\tau'} G_1^{m'}$. Return 1 if $\mathsf{cm} = \mathsf{cm}'$ and 0 otherwise.

The Pedersen commitment scheme can be extended to allow commitment to more than one message. More precisely, the message space can be $\mathcal{M} = \mathbb{Z}_p^\ell$, where ℓ is an upper bound for the number of committed scalar messages. The extended Pedersen commitment scheme is as follows:

- $\mathsf{pp}_c \leftarrow \mathsf{CSetup}(1^\kappa)$: Sample $\alpha_1, \ldots, \alpha_\ell \leftarrow_\$ \mathbb{Z}_p$ and set $G_j \leftarrow g^{\alpha_j}$ for all $j \in [1, \ell]$. Output $(G_0 = g, G_1, \ldots, G_\ell, \mathcal{M})$, where $\mathcal{M} = \mathbb{Z}_p^\ell$.
- $\mathsf{cm} \leftarrow \mathsf{Com}(\mathsf{pp}_c, \vec{m}, \tau)$: For $\vec{m} = (m_1, \ldots, m_\ell)$, compute $\mathsf{cm} \leftarrow G_0^\tau \prod_{j=1}^\ell G_i^{m_i}$. Output cm.
- $0/1 \leftarrow \mathsf{CVerify}(\mathsf{pp}_c, \mathsf{cm}, \vec{m}', \tau')$: Compute $\mathsf{cm}' \leftarrow G_0^{\tau'} \prod_{j=1}^\ell G_i^{m'_i}$. Return 1 if $\mathsf{cm} = \mathsf{cm}'$ and 0 otherwise.

A.3 Non-interactive Zero-Knowledge Proofs

Zero-knowledge proofs enable a prover to convince a skeptical verifier of the validity of a statement without revealing any other information. *Non-interactive* zero-knowledge proofs (NIZKs) [15,56] only require one round of communication.

Definition 18 (Non-interactive Zero-Knowledge Proof [56]**).** *Consider an NP-relation $\mathcal{R}$ defined over a language $L = \{x \mid \exists\ w \text{ s.t. } (x, w) \in \mathcal{R}\}$, where x and w denote statement and witness, respectively. A NIZK over the relation $\mathcal{R}_L$ consists of the following PPT algorithms:*

- $\mathsf{CRS} \leftarrow \mathsf{Setup}(1^\kappa)$: *The setup algorithm takes as input the security parameter 1^κ and outputs a common reference string* CRS.
- $\pi \leftarrow \mathsf{Prove}(\mathsf{CRS}, x, w)$: *The prove algorithm takes as input a* CRS, *a statement x, and a witness w, and outputs a proof π.*
- $0/1 \leftarrow \mathsf{Verify}(\mathsf{CRS}, x, \pi)$: *The verification algorithm is a deterministic algorithm that takes as input a* CRS, *a statement x, and a proof π, and outputs either* 0 *(reject) or* 1 *(accept).*

A NIZK proof system is said to be *complete* if all pairs of statements and witnesses, $(x, w) \in \mathcal{R}_L$, pass verification. The *zero-knowledge* property guarantees that the proof does not reveal any information about the witness w. The *knowledge soundness* property guarantees that a malicious prover cannot convince the verifier of a false statement unless he knows the witness.

A.4 Threshold Blind Signatures

Here we recall the definition of threshold blind signatures as stated in [82]. Let pp be a given set of public parameters.

- $(\vec{\mathsf{vk}}, \vec{\mathsf{sk}}, \mathsf{vk}) \leftarrow \mathsf{TTPKeyGen}(\mathsf{pp}, \ell, n, t)$: The probabilistic key generation algorithm takes the public parameters pp and length ℓ along with two integers $t, n \in \mathsf{poly}(1^\kappa)$ such that $1 \leq t \leq n$ as inputs. It returns two vectors of size n of signing/verification keys $\vec{\mathsf{sk}} = (\mathsf{sk}_1, \ldots, \mathsf{sk}_n)$ and $\vec{\mathsf{vk}} = (\mathsf{vk}_1, \ldots, \mathsf{vk}_n)$ such that each party P_i for $i \in [n]$ receives a pair $(\mathsf{sk}_i, \mathsf{vk}_i)$ along with the global verification key vk.
- $(\Omega, id, \vec{cm}, \pi_s) \leftarrow \mathsf{PrepareBlindSign}(\mathsf{pp}, \vec{m})$: This algorithm is run by the user to blind the message $\vec{m}$ under some random blinding factors Ω.
- $(\perp, \bar{\sigma}_i) \leftarrow \mathsf{BlindSign}(\mathsf{pp}, \mathsf{sk}_i, id, \vec{cm}, \pi_s)$: The blind signing algorithm is run by each signer with secret signing key sk_i to blindly sign the messages. It either returns a blind partial signature $\bar{\sigma}_i$ as output or responds with $\perp$.
- $(\perp, \bar{\sigma}) \leftarrow \mathsf{AggCred}(\mathsf{pp}, \{i, \bar{\sigma}_i\}_{i \in \mathcal{T}})$: The reconstruction algorithm is run by the user to aggregate the received partial signatures. If a sufficient number of well-formed partial signatures are available, it returns an aggregated blind signature; otherwise it returns $\perp$.
- $\sigma \leftarrow \mathsf{Unblind}(\mathsf{pp}, \bar{\sigma}, \Omega)$: The user who knows the blinding factors Ω runs this algorithm to unblind the aggregated signature $\bar{\sigma}$. It returns σ as output.

Informally, a threshold blind signature scheme satisfies two main security properties: one-more unforgeability and blindness. One-more unforgeability requires an adversary to produce $k + 1$ valid signatures (representing a group of signers) having only queried its signing oracle k times, guaranteeing that at least one signature is a forgery. The blindness property guarantees that an adversarial signer cannot learn meaningful information about the message $\vec{m}$.

References

1. Abe, M., Ambrona, M., Ohkubo, M., Tibouchi, M.: Lower bounds on structure-preserving signatures for bilateral messages. In: Catalano, D., De Prisco, R. (eds.) SCN 2018. LNCS, vol. 11035, pp. 3–22. Springer, Cham (2018). https://doi.org/10.1007/978-3-319-98113-0_1
2. Abe, M., Chase, M., David, B., Kohlweiss, M., Nishimaki, R., Ohkubo, M.: Constant-size structure-preserving signatures: generic constructions and simple assumptions. In: Wang, X., Sako, K. (eds.) ASIACRYPT 2012. LNCS, vol. 7658, pp. 4–24. Springer, Heidelberg (2012). https://doi.org/10.1007/978-3-642-34961-4_3
3. Abe, M., Chow, S.S.M., Haralambiev, K., Ohkubo, M.: Double-trapdoor anonymous tags for traceable signatures. In: Lopez, J., Tsudik, G. (eds.) ACNS 2011. LNCS, vol. 6715, pp. 183–200. Springer, Heidelberg (2011). https://doi.org/10.1007/978-3-642-21554-4_11
4. Abe, M., Fuchsbauer, G., Groth, J., Haralambiev, K., Ohkubo, M.: Structure-preserving signatures and commitments to group elements. In: Rabin, T. (ed.) CRYPTO 2010. LNCS, vol. 6223, pp. 209–236. Springer, Heidelberg (2010). https://doi.org/10.1007/978-3-642-14623-7_12
5. Abe, M., Groth, J., Haralambiev, K., Ohkubo, M.: Optimal structure-preserving signatures in asymmetric bilinear groups. In: Rogaway, P. (ed.) CRYPTO 2011. LNCS, vol. 6841, pp. 649–666. Springer, Heidelberg (2011). https://doi.org/10.1007/978-3-642-22792-9_37
6. Abe, M., Groth, J., Ohkubo, M.: Separating short structure-preserving signatures from non-interactive assumptions. In: Lee, D.H., Wang, X. (eds.) ASIACRYPT 2011. LNCS, vol. 7073, pp. 628–646. Springer, Heidelberg (2011). https://doi.org/10.1007/978-3-642-25385-0_34
7. Abe, M., Groth, J., Ohkubo, M., Tibouchi, M.: Unified, minimal and selectively randomizable structure-preserving signatures. In: Lindell, Y. (ed.) TCC 2014. LNCS, vol. 8349, pp. 688–712. Springer, Heidelberg (2014). https://doi.org/10.1007/978-3-642-54242-8_29
8. Abe, M., Jutla, C.S., Ohkubo, M., Pan, J., Roy, A., Wang, Y.: Shorter QA-NIZK and SPS with tighter security. In: Galbraith, S.D., Moriai, S. (eds.) ASIACRYPT 2019. LNCS, vol. 11923, pp. 669–699. Springer, Cham (2019). https://doi.org/10.1007/978-3-030-34618-8_23
9. Attrapadung, N., Libert, B., Peters, T.: Computing on authenticated data: new privacy definitions and constructions. In: Wang, X., Sako, K. (eds.) ASIACRYPT 2012. LNCS, vol. 7658, pp. 367–385. Springer, Heidelberg (2012). https://doi.org/10.1007/978-3-642-34961-4_23
10. Bacho, R., Loss, J.: On the adaptive security of the threshold bls signature scheme. In: Proceedings of the 2022 ACM SIGSAC Conference on Computer and Communications Security, CCS 2022, pp. 193–207. Association for Computing Machinery, New York (2022). https://doi.org/10.1145/3548606.3560656

11. Barthe, G., Fagerholm, E., Fiore, D., Scedrov, A., Schmidt, B., Tibouchi, M.: Strongly-optimal structure preserving signatures from type II pairings: synthesis and lower bounds. In: Katz, J. (ed.) PKC 2015. LNCS, vol. 9020, pp. 355–376. Springer, Heidelberg (2015). https://doi.org/10.1007/978-3-662-46447-2_16
12. Bauer, B., Fuchsbauer, G., Loss, J.: A classification of computational assumptions in the algebraic group model. In: Micciancio, D., Ristenpart, T. (eds.) CRYPTO 2020. LNCS, vol. 12171, pp. 121–151. Springer, Cham (2020). https://doi.org/10.1007/978-3-030-56880-1_5
13. Belenkiy, M., Camenisch, J., Chase, M., Kohlweiss, M., Lysyanskaya, A., Shacham, H.: Randomizable proofs and delegatable anonymous credentials. In: Halevi, S. (ed.) CRYPTO 2009. LNCS, vol. 5677, pp. 108–125. Springer, Heidelberg (2009). https://doi.org/10.1007/978-3-642-03356-8_7
14. Bellare, M., Crites, E.C., Komlo, C., Maller, M., Tessaro, S., Zhu, C.: Better than advertised security for non-interactive threshold signatures. In: Advances in Cryptology - CRYPTO 2022. LNCS, vol. 13510, pp. 517–550. Springer (2022). https://doi.org/10.1007/978-3-031-15985-5_18
15. Ben-Or, M., Goldreich, O., Goldwasser, S., Håstad, J., Kilian, J., Micali, S., Rogaway, P.: Everything provable is provable in zero-knowledge. In: Goldwasser, S. (ed.) CRYPTO 1988. LNCS, vol. 403, pp. 37–56. Springer, New York (1990). https://doi.org/10.1007/0-387-34799-2_4
16. Blakley, G.R.: Safeguarding cryptographic keys. In: Proceedings of AFIPS 1979 National Computer Conference 48, pp. 313–317 (1979)
17. Blazy, O., Canard, S., Fuchsbauer, G., Gouget, A., Sibert, H., Traoré, J.: Achieving optimal anonymity in transferable e-cash with a judge. In: Nitaj, A., Pointcheval, D. (eds.) AFRICACRYPT 11. LNCS, vol. 6737, pp. 206–223. Springer, Heidelberg (2011)
18. Boldyreva, A.: Threshold signatures, multisignatures and blind signatures based on the gap-Diffie-Hellman-group signature scheme. In: Desmedt, Y.G. (ed.) PKC 2003. LNCS, vol. 2567, pp. 31–46. Springer, Heidelberg (2003). https://doi.org/10.1007/3-540-36288-6_3
19. Boneh, D., Lynn, B., Shacham, H.: Short signatures from the Weil pairing. J. Cryptol. **17**(4), 297–319 (2004). https://doi.org/10.1007/s00145-004-0314-9
20. Brandão, L.T., Davidson, M., Vassilev, A., et al.: Nist roadmap toward criteria for threshold schemes for cryptographic primitives. In: National Institute of Standards and Technology Internal or Interagency Report 8214A (2020). https://doi.org/10.6028/NIST.IR.8214A
21. Brandão, L., Peralta, R.: NIST first call for multi-party threshold schemes. https://nvlpubs.nist.gov/nistpubs/ir/2023/NIST.IR.8214C.ipd.pdf (2023)
22. Camenisch, J., Drijvers, M., Lehmann, A., Neven, G., Towa, P.: Short threshold dynamic group signatures. In: Galdi, C., Kolesnikov, V. (eds.) SCN 2020. LNCS, vol. 12238, pp. 401–423. Springer, Cham (2020). https://doi.org/10.1007/978-3-030-57990-6_20
23. Camenisch, J., Dubovitskaya, M., Haralambiev, K., Kohlweiss, M.: Composable and modular anonymous credentials: definitions and practical constructions. In: Iwata, T., Cheon, J.H. (eds.) ASIACRYPT 2015, Part II. LNCS, vol. 9453, pp. 262–288. Springer, Heidelberg (2015). https://doi.org/10.1007/978-3-662-48800-3_11
24. Canetti, R.: Universally composable security: a new paradigm for cryptographic protocols. In: 42nd FOCS, pp. 136–145. IEEE Computer Society Press, October 2001. https://doi.org/10.1109/SFCS.2001.959888

25. Canetti, R., Gennaro, R., Goldfeder, S., Makriyannis, N., Peled, U.: UC non-interactive, proactive, threshold ECDSA with identifiable aborts. In: Ligatti, J., Ou, X., Katz, J., Vigna, G. (eds.) ACM CCS 2020, pp. 1769–1787. ACM Press, November 2020. https://doi.org/10.1145/3372297.3423367
26. Canetti, R., Gennaro, R., Jarecki, S., Krawczyk, H., Rabin, T.: Adaptive security for threshold cryptosystems. In: Wiener, M. (ed.) CRYPTO 1999. LNCS, vol. 1666, pp. 98–116. Springer, Heidelberg (1999). https://doi.org/10.1007/3-540-48405-1_7
27. Chase, M., Kohlweiss, M., Lysyanskaya, A., Meiklejohn, S.: Malleable proof systems and applications. In: Pointcheval, D., Johansson, T. (eds.) EUROCRYPT 2012. LNCS, vol. 7237, pp. 281–300. Springer, Heidelberg (2012). https://doi.org/10.1007/978-3-642-29011-4_18
28. Couteau, G., Hartmann, D.: Shorter non-interactive zero-knowledge arguments and ZAPs for algebraic languages. In: Micciancio, D., Ristenpart, T. (eds.) CRYPTO 2020. LNCS, vol. 12172, pp. 768–798. Springer, Cham (2020). https://doi.org/10.1007/978-3-030-56877-1_27
29. Cramer, R., Damgård, I., Nielsen, J.B.: Multiparty computation from threshold homomorphic encryption. In: Pfitzmann, B. (ed.) EUROCRYPT 2001. LNCS, vol. 2045, pp. 280–300. Springer, Heidelberg (2001). https://doi.org/10.1007/3-540-44987-6_18
30. Cramer, R., Franklin, M., Schoenmakers, B., Yung, M.: Multi-authority secret-ballot elections with linear work. In: Maurer, U. (ed.) EUROCRYPT 1996. LNCS, vol. 1070, pp. 72–83. Springer, Heidelberg (1996). https://doi.org/10.1007/3-540-68339-9_7
31. Cramer, R., Gennaro, R., Schoenmakers, B.: A secure and optimally efficient multi-authority election scheme. In: Fumy, W. (ed.) EUROCRYPT 1997. LNCS, vol. 1233, pp. 103–118. Springer, Heidelberg (1997). https://doi.org/10.1007/3-540-69053-0_9
32. Crites, E., Kohlweiss, M., Preneel, B., Sedaghat, M., Slamanig, D.: Threshold Structure-Preserving Signatures. Cryptology ePrint Archive, Report 2022/839 (2022). https://eprint.iacr.org/2022/839
33. Crites, E.C., Komlo, C., Maller, M.: Fully adaptive schnorr threshold signatures. In: Handschuh, H., Lysyanskaya, A. (eds.) CRYPTO 2023, Santa Barbara, CA, USA, August 20–24, 2023, Proceedings, Part I. LNCS, vol. 14081, pp. 678–709. Springer (2023). https://doi.org/10.1007/978-3-031-38557-5_22
34. Crites, E.C., Lysyanskaya, A.: Delegatable anonymous credentials from mercurial signatures. In: Matsui, M. (ed.) CT-RSA 2019. LNCS, vol. 11405, pp. 535–555. Springer, Cham (2019). https://doi.org/10.1007/978-3-030-12612-4_27
35. Damgård, I., Koprowski, M.: Practical threshold RSA signatures without a trusted dealer. In: Pfitzmann, B. (ed.) EUROCRYPT 2001. LNCS, vol. 2045, pp. 152–165. Springer, Heidelberg (2001). https://doi.org/10.1007/3-540-44987-6_10
36. Damgård, I., Nielsen, J.B.: Universally composable efficient multiparty computation from threshold homomorphic encryption. In: Boneh, D. (ed.) CRYPTO 2003. LNCS, vol. 2729, pp. 247–264. Springer, Heidelberg (2003). https://doi.org/10.1007/978-3-540-45146-4_15
37. De Santis, A., Desmedt, Y., Frankel, Y., Yung, M.: How to share a function securely. In: 26th ACM STOC, pp. 522–533. ACM Press, May 1994. https://doi.org/10.1145/195058.195405
38. Desmedt, Y.G.: Making conditionally secure cryptosystems unconditionally abuse-free in a general context. In: Brassard, G. (ed.) CRYPTO 1989. LNCS, vol. 435, pp. 6–16. Springer, New York (1990). https://doi.org/10.1007/0-387-34805-0_2

39. Desmedt, Y., Frankel, Y.: Threshold cryptosystems. In: Brassard, G. (ed.) CRYPTO 1989. LNCS, vol. 435, pp. 307–315. Springer, New York (1990). https://doi.org/10.1007/0-387-34805-0_28
40. Doerner, J., Kondi, Y., Lee, E., shelat, A.: Threshold ECDSA from ECDSA assumptions: the multiparty case. In: 2019 IEEE Symposium on Security and Privacy, pp. 1051–1066. IEEE Computer Society Press, May 2019. https://doi.org/10.1109/SP.2019.00024
41. Drijvers, M., et al.: On the security of two-round multi-signatures. In: 2019 IEEE Symposium on Security and Privacy, pp. 1084–1101. IEEE Computer Society Press, May 2019. https://doi.org/10.1109/SP.2019.00050
42. El Kaafarani, A., Ghadafi, E., Khader, D.: Decentralized traceable attribute-based signatures. In: Benaloh, J. (ed.) CT-RSA 2014. LNCS, vol. 8366, pp. 327–348. Springer, Cham (2014). https://doi.org/10.1007/978-3-319-04852-9_17
43. Fiat, A., Shamir, A.: How to prove yourself: practical solutions to identification and signature problems. In: Odlyzko, A.M. (ed.) CRYPTO 1986. LNCS, vol. 263, pp. 186–194. Springer, Heidelberg (1987). https://doi.org/10.1007/3-540-47721-7_12
44. Fischlin, M.: Round-optimal composable blind signatures in the common reference string model. In: Dwork, C. (ed.) CRYPTO 2006. LNCS, vol. 4117, pp. 60–77. Springer, Heidelberg (2006). https://doi.org/10.1007/11818175_4
45. Fuchsbauer, G.: Automorphic signatures in bilinear groups and an application to round-optimal blind signatures. Cryptology ePrint Archive, Report 2009/320 (2009). https://eprint.iacr.org/2009/320
46. Fuchsbauer, G.: Commuting signatures and verifiable encryption. In: Paterson, K.G. (ed.) EUROCRYPT 2011. LNCS, vol. 6632, pp. 224–245. Springer, Heidelberg (2011). https://doi.org/10.1007/978-3-642-20465-4_14
47. Fuchsbauer, G., Hanser, C., Slamanig, D.: Practical round-optimal blind signatures in the standard model. In: Gennaro, R., Robshaw, M. (eds.) CRYPTO 2015. LNCS, vol. 9216, pp. 233–253. Springer, Heidelberg (2015). https://doi.org/10.1007/978-3-662-48000-7_12
48. Fuchsbauer, G., Hanser, C., Slamanig, D.: Structure-preserving signatures on equivalence classes and constant-size anonymous credentials. J. Cryptol. **32**(2), 498–546 (2019). https://doi.org/10.1007/s00145-018-9281-4
49. Fuchsbauer, G., Kiltz, E., Loss, J.: The algebraic group model and its applications. In: Shacham, H., Boldyreva, A. (eds.) CRYPTO 2018. LNCS, vol. 10992, pp. 33–62. Springer, Cham (2018). https://doi.org/10.1007/978-3-319-96881-0_2
50. Galbraith, S.D., Paterson, K.G., Smart, N.P.: Pairings for cryptographers. Discret. Appl. Math. **156**(16), 3113–3121 (2008). https://doi.org/10.1016/j.dam.2007.12.010
51. Gay, R., Hofheinz, D., Kohl, L., Pan, J.: More efficient (almost) tightly secure structure-preserving signatures. In: Nielsen, J.B., Rijmen, V. (eds.) EUROCRYPT 2018. LNCS, vol. 10821, pp. 230–258. Springer, Cham (2018). https://doi.org/10.1007/978-3-319-78375-8_8
52. Ghadafi, E.: Short structure-preserving signatures. In: Sako, K. (ed.) CT-RSA 2016. LNCS, vol. 9610, pp. 305–321. Springer, Cham (2016). https://doi.org/10.1007/978-3-319-29485-8_18
53. Ghadafi, E.: How low can you go? Short structure-preserving signatures for Diffie-Hellman vectors. In: O'Neill, M. (ed.) 16th IMA International Conference on Cryptography and Coding. LNCS, vol. 10655, pp. 185–204. Springer, Heidelberg (2017)
54. Ghadafi, E.: More efficient structure-preserving signatures - or: bypassing the type-III lower bounds. In: Foley, S.N., Gollmann, D., Snekkenes, E. (eds.) ESORICS

2017. LNCS, vol. 10493, pp. 43–61. Springer, Cham (2017). https://doi.org/10.1007/978-3-319-66399-9_3
55. Ghadafi, E.: Further lower bounds for structure-preserving signatures in asymmetric bilinear groups. In: Buchmann, J., Nitaj, A., Rachidi, T. (eds.) AFRICACRYPT 2019. LNCS, vol. 11627, pp. 409–428. Springer, Cham (2019). https://doi.org/10.1007/978-3-030-23696-0_21
56. Goldreich, O., Micali, S., Wigderson, A.: How to play any mental game or A completeness theorem for protocols with honest majority. In: Aho, A. (ed.) 19th ACM STOC, pp. 218–229. ACM Press, May 1987. https://doi.org/10.1145/28395.28420
57. Groth, J.: Simulation-sound NIZK proofs for a practical language and constant size group signatures. In: Lai, X., Chen, K. (eds.) ASIACRYPT 2006. LNCS, vol. 4284, pp. 444–459. Springer, Heidelberg (2006). https://doi.org/10.1007/11935230_29
58. Groth, J.: Efficient fully structure-preserving signatures for large messages. In: Iwata, T., Cheon, J.H. (eds.) ASIACRYPT 2015. LNCS, vol. 9452, pp. 239–259. Springer, Heidelberg (2015). https://doi.org/10.1007/978-3-662-48797-6_11
59. Groth, J., Ostrovsky, R., Sahai, A.: Perfect non-interactive zero knowledge for NP. In: Vaudenay, S. (ed.) EUROCRYPT 2006. LNCS, vol. 4004, pp. 339–358. Springer, Heidelberg (2006). https://doi.org/10.1007/11761679_21
60. Groth, J., Sahai, A.: Efficient non-interactive proof systems for bilinear groups. In: Smart, N. (ed.) EUROCRYPT 2008. LNCS, vol. 4965, pp. 415–432. Springer, Heidelberg (2008). https://doi.org/10.1007/978-3-540-78967-3_24
61. Gurkan, K., Jovanovic, P., Maller, M., Meiklejohn, S., Stern, G., Tomescu, A.: Aggregatable distributed key generation. In: Canteaut, A., Standaert, F.-X. (eds.) EUROCRYPT 2021. LNCS, vol. 12696, pp. 147–176. Springer, Cham (2021). https://doi.org/10.1007/978-3-030-77870-5_6
62. Hofheinz, D., Jager, T.: Tightly secure signatures and public-key encryption. In: Safavi-Naini, R., Canetti, R. (eds.) CRYPTO 2012. LNCS, vol. 7417, pp. 590–607. Springer, Heidelberg (2012). https://doi.org/10.1007/978-3-642-32009-5_35
63. Jutla, C.S., Roy, A.: Improved structure preserving signatures under standard bilinear assumptions. In: Fehr, S. (ed.) PKC 2017. LNCS, vol. 10175, pp. 183–209. Springer, Heidelberg (2017). https://doi.org/10.1007/978-3-662-54388-7_7
64. Kiayias, A., Kohlweiss, M., Sarencheh, A.: Peredi: privacy-enhanced, regulated and distributed central bank digital currencies. In: Proceedings of the 2022 ACM SIGSAC Conference on Computer and Communications Security, CCS 2022, pp. 1739–1752. Association for Computing Machinery, New York (2022). https://doi.org/10.1145/3548606.3560707
65. Kiltz, E., Pan, J., Wee, H.: Structure-preserving signatures from standard assumptions, revisited. In: Gennaro, R., Robshaw, M. (eds.) CRYPTO 2015, Part II. LNCS, vol. 9216, pp. 275–295. Springer, Heidelberg (2015). https://doi.org/10.1007/978-3-662-48000-7_14
66. Kim, H., Lee, Y., Abdalla, M., Park, J.H.: Practical dynamic group signature with efficient concurrent joins and batch verifications. Cryptology ePrint Archive, Report 2020/921 (2020). https://eprint.iacr.org/2020/921
67. Kim, H., Sanders, O., Abdalla, M., Park, J.H.: Practical Dynamic Group Signatures Without Knowledge Extractors. Designs, Codes and Cryptography, October 2022. https://doi.org/10.1007/s10623-022-01129-w
68. Komlo, C., Goldberg, I.: FROST: flexible round-optimized schnorr threshold signatures. In: Dunkelman, O., Jacobson, Jr., M.J., O'Flynn, C. (eds.) SAC 2020. LNCS, vol. 12804, pp. 34–65. Springer, Cham (2021). https://doi.org/10.1007/978-3-030-81652-0_2

69. Kondi, Y., Magri, B., Orlandi, C., Shlomovits, O.: Refresh when you wake up: proactive threshold wallets with offline devices. In: 2021 IEEE Symposium on Security and Privacy (SP), pp. 608–625 (2021). https://doi.org/10.1109/SP40001.2021.00067
70. Libert, B., Joye, M., Yung, M.: Born and raised distributively: fully distributed non-interactive adaptively-secure threshold signatures with short shares. Theor. Comput. Sci. **645**, 1–24 (2016). https://doi.org/10.1016/j.tcs.2016.02.031
71. Libert, B., Peters, T., Joye, M., Yung, M.: Linearly homomorphic structure-preserving signatures and their applications. In: Canetti, R., Garay, J.A. (eds.) CRYPTO 2013. LNCS, vol. 8043, pp. 289–307. Springer, Heidelberg (2013). https://doi.org/10.1007/978-3-642-40084-1_17
72. Libert, B., Peters, T., Yung, M.: Short group signatures via structure-preserving signatures: standard model security from simple assumptions. In: Gennaro, R., Robshaw, M. (eds.) CRYPTO 2015, Part II. LNCS, vol. 9216, pp. 296–316. Springer, Heidelberg (2015). https://doi.org/10.1007/978-3-662-48000-7_15
73. Micali, S., Rabin, M.O., Vadhan, S.P.: Verifiable random functions. In: 40th FOCS, pp. 120–130. IEEE Computer Society Press, October 1999. https://doi.org/10.1109/SFFCS.1999.814584
74. Mizuide, T., Takayasu, A., Takagi, T.: Tight reductions for Diffie-Hellman variants in the algebraic group model. In: Matsui, M. (ed.) CT-RSA 2019. LNCS, vol. 11405, pp. 169–188. Springer, Cham (2019). https://doi.org/10.1007/978-3-030-12612-4_9
75. Pedersen, T.P.: Non-interactive and information-theoretic secure verifiable secret sharing. In: Feigenbaum, J. (ed.) CRYPTO 1991. LNCS, vol. 576, pp. 129–140. Springer, Heidelberg (1992). https://doi.org/10.1007/3-540-46766-1_9
76. Pointcheval, D., Sanders, O.: Short randomizable signatures. In: Sako, K. (ed.) CT-RSA 2016. LNCS, vol. 9610, pp. 111–126. Springer, Cham (2016). https://doi.org/10.1007/978-3-319-29485-8_7
77. Rial, A., Piotrowska, A.M.: Security analysis of coconut, an attribute-based credential scheme with threshold issuance. Cryptology ePrint Archive, Report 2022/011 (2022). https://eprint.iacr.org/2022/011
78. Schnorr, C.P.: Efficient identification and signatures for smart cards. In: Brassard, G. (ed.) CRYPTO 1989. LNCS, vol. 435, pp. 239–252. Springer, New York (1990). https://doi.org/10.1007/0-387-34805-0_22
79. Shamir, A.: How to share a secret. Commun. Assoc. Comput. Mach. **22**(11), 612–613 (1979)
80. Shoup, V.: Practical threshold signatures. In: Preneel, B. (ed.) EUROCRYPT 2000. LNCS, vol. 1807, pp. 207–220. Springer, Heidelberg (2000). https://doi.org/10.1007/3-540-45539-6_15
81. Shoup, V., Gennaro, R.: Securing threshold cryptosystems against chosen ciphertext attack. In: Nyberg, K. (ed.) EUROCRYPT 1998. LNCS, vol. 1403, pp. 1–16. Springer, Heidelberg (1998). https://doi.org/10.1007/BFb0054113
82. Sonnino, A., Al-Bassam, M., Bano, S., Meiklejohn, S., Danezis, G.: Coconut: Threshold issuance selective disclosure credentials with applications to distributed ledgers. In: NDSS 2019. The Internet Society, February 2019
83. Tomescu, A., Bhat, A., Applebaum, B., Abraham, I., Gueta, G., Pinkas, B., Yanai, A.: UTT: Decentralized Ecash with Accountable Privacy. IACR Cryptol. ePrint Arch. p. 452 (2022), https://eprint.iacr.org/2022/452
84. Tymokhanov, D., Shlomovits, O.: Alpha-Rays: Key Extraction Attacks on Threshold ECDSA Implementations. Cryptology ePrint Archive, Report 2021/1621 (2021). https://ia.cr/2021/1621

Practical Round-Optimal Blind Signatures in the ROM from Standard Assumptions

Shuichi Katsumata[1,3], Michael Reichle[2(✉)], and Yusuke Sakai[3]

[1] PQShield Ltd., Oxford, UK
[2] ETH Zürich, Zürich, Switzerland
michael.reichle@ens.fr
[3] AIST, Tokyo, Japan

Abstract. Blind signatures serve as a foundational tool for privacy-preserving applications and have recently seen renewed interest due to new applications in blockchains and privacy-authentication tokens. With this, constructing practical *round-optimal* (i.e., signing consists of the minimum two rounds) blind signatures in the random oracle model (ROM) has been an active area of research, where several impossibility results indicate that either the ROM or a trusted setup is inherent.

In this work, we present two round-optimal blind signatures under standard assumptions in the ROM with different approaches: one achieves the smallest sum of the signature and communication sizes, while the other achieves the smallest signature size. Both of our instantiations are based on standard assumptions over asymmetric pairing groups, i.e., CDH, DDH, and/or SXDH. Our first construction is a highly optimized variant of the generic blind signature construction by Fischlin (CRYPTO'06) and has signature and communication sizes 447 B and 303 B, respectively. We progressively weaken the building blocks required by Fischlin and we result in the first blind signature where the sum of the signature and communication sizes fit below 1 KB based on standard assumptions. Our second construction is a semi-generic construction from a specific class of randomizable signature schemes that admits an *all-but-one* reduction. The signature size is only 96 B while the communication size is 2.2 KB. This matches the previously known smallest signature size while improving the communication size by several orders of magnitude. Finally, both of our constructions rely on a (non-black box) fine-grained analysis of the forking lemma that may be of independent interest.

1 Introduction

1.1 Background

Blind signature is an interactive signing protocol between a signer and a user with advanced privacy guarantees. At the end of the protocol, the user obtains a signature for his choice of message while the signer remains blind to the message

M. Reichle—Work done while employed at Inria, Paris.

J. Guo and R. Steinfeld (Eds.): ASIACRYPT 2023, LNCS 14439, pp. 383–417, 2023.
https://doi.org/10.1007/978-981-99-8724-5_12

she signed. To capture the standard notion of unforgeability, it is further required that a user interacting with the signer at most ℓ-times is not be able to produce valid signatures on more than ℓ distinct messages. The former and latter are coined as the *blindness* and *one-more unforgeability* properties, respectively.

Chaum introduced the notion of blind signatures [22] and showed its application to e-cash [22,24,48]. Since then, it has been an important building block for other applications such as anonymous credentials [16,20], e-voting [23,32], direct anonymous attestation [17], and in more recent years, it has seen a renewed interest due to new applications in blockchains [19,57] and privacy-preserving authentication tokens [37,55].

Round-Optimality. One of the main performance measures for blind signatures is *round-optimality*, where the user and signer are required to only send one message each to complete the signing protocol. While this is an ideal feature for practical applications, unfortunately, there are a few impossibility results [29,45,49] on constructing round-optimal blind signatures in the plain model (i.e., without any trusted setup) from standard assumptions (*e.g.*, non-interactive assumptions and polynomial hardness). To circumvent this, cryptographers design round-optimal blind signatures by making a minimal relaxation of relying on the random oracle model (ROM) or the trusted setup model. Considering that trusted setups are a large obstacle for real-world deployment, in this work we focus on round-optimal blind signatures in the ROM under standard assumption[1]. We refer the readers to the full version for an overview on round optimal blind signatures under non-standard assumptions (*e.g.*, interactive or super polynomial hardness) or relying on stronger idealized models such as the generic group model.

Practical Round-Optimal Blind Signatures. Constructing a *practical* round-optimal blind signature has been an active area of research. In a seminal work, Fischlin [28] proposed the first generic round-optimal blind signature from standard building blocks. While the construction is simple, an efficient instantiation remained elusive since it required a non-interactive zero-knowledge (NIZK) proof for a relatively complex language.

Recently, in the lattice-setting, del Pino and Katsumata [25] showed a new lattice-tailored technique to overcome the inefficiency of Fischlin's generic construction and proposed a round-optimal blind signature with signature and communication sizes 100 KB and 850 KB.

A different approach that has recently accumulated attention is based on the work by Pointcheval [50] that bootstraps a specific class of blind signature schemes into a fully secure one (i.e., one-more unforgeable even if polynomially many concurrent signing sessions are started). This approach has been improved by Katz et al. [41] and Chairattana-Apirom et al. [21], and the very recent work by Hanzlik et al. [36] optimized this approach leading to a round-optimal blind signature based on the CDH assumption in the asymmetric pairing setting.

[1] We note that all of our results favor well even when compared with schemes in the trusted setup model.

One of their parameter settings provides a short signature size of 5 KB with a communication size 72 KB.

Finally, there are two constructions in the pairing setting with a trusted setup which can be instantiated in the ROM under standard assumptions [2, 10][2]. Blazy et al. [10] exploited the randomizability of Waters signature [56] and constructed a blinded version of Waters signature consisting of mere 2 group elements, i.e. 96 B. While it achieves the shortest signature size in the literature, since the user has to prove some relation to his message in a bit-by-bit manner, the communication scales linearly in the message length. For example for 256 bit messages, it requires more than 220 KB in communication. Abe et al. [2] use structure-preserving signatures (SPS) and Groth-Ostrovsky-Sahai (GOS) proofs [35] to instantiate the Fischlin blind signature with signatures of size 5.8 KB with around 1 KB of communication.

While round-optimal blind signatures in the ROM are coming close to the practical parameter regime, the signature and communication sizes are still orders of magnitude larger compared to those relying on non-standard assumptions or strong idealized models such as blind RSA [7,22] or blind BLS [11]. Thus, we continue the above line of research to answer the following question:

How efficient can round-optimal blind signatures in the ROM be under standard assumptions?

1.2 Contributions

We present two round-optimal blind signatures based on standard group-based assumptions in the asymmetric pairing setting. The efficiency is summarized in Table 1, along with the assumptions we rely on. The first construction has signature and communication sizes 447 B and 303 B, respectively. It has the smallest communication size among all prior schemes and is the first construction where the sum of the signature and communication sizes fit below 1 KB. The second construction has signature and communication sizes 96 B and 2.2 KB, respectively. While it has a larger communication size compared to our first construction, the signature only consists of 2 group elements, matching the previously shortest by Blazy et al. [10] while simultaneously improving their communication size by around two orders of magnitude. Both constructions have efficient partially blind variants.

For our first construction, we revisit the generic blind signature construction by Fischlin [27]. We progressively weaken the building blocks required by Fischlin and show that the blind signature can be instantiated much more efficiently in the ROM than previously thought by a careful choice of the building blocks. At a high level, we show that the generic construction remains secure even if we

[2] Both [2,10] require a trusted setup for a common reference string crs consisting of random group elements. We can remove the trusted setup by using a random oracle to sample crs.

Table 1. Comparison of Round-Optimal Blind Signatures in the ROM

Reference	Signature size	Communication size	Assumption
del Pino et al. [25]	100 KB	850 KB	DSMR, MLWE, MSIS
Blazy et al. [10]	96 B	220 KB †	SXDH, CDH
Abe et al. [2]	5.5 KB	1 KB	SXDH
Hanzlik et al. [36]‡	5 KB	72 KB	CDH
	9 KB	36 KB	
Ours: Section 3	447 B	303 B	SXDH
Ours: Section 4	96 B	2.2 KB	DDH, CDH

All group-based assumptions are in the asymmetric paring setting, and MLWE and MSIS denote the module version of the standard LWE and SIS, respectively. DSMR denotes the decisional small matrix ratio problem, which can be viewed as the module variant of the standard NTRU. (†): Communication of [10] scales linearly with the message size, and is given here for 256 bit messages. (‡): [36] offers tradeoffs between signature and communication sizes.

replace the public-key encryption scheme (PKE) and online-extractable NIZK[3] with respectively a commitment scheme and a rewinding-extractable NIZK such as those offered by the standard Fiat-Shamir transform [8,26,51]. While these modifications may seem insignificant on the surface, it accumulates in a large saving in the concrete signature and communication sizes. Moreover, our security proof requires overcoming new technical hurdles incurred by the rewinding-extraction and relies on a fined-grained analysis of a variant of the forking lemma.

For our second construction, we revisit the idea by Blazy et al. [10] relying on randomizable signatures. However, our technique is not a simple application of their idea as their construction relies on the specific structure of the Waters signature in a non-black-box manner. Our new insight is that a specific class of signature schemes with an *all-but-one* (ABO) reduction can be used in an almost black-box manner to construct round-optimal blind signatures, where ABO reductions are standard proof techniques to prove selective security of public-key primitives (see references in [47] for examples). Interestingly, we can cast the recent blind signature by del Pino and Katsumata [25] that stated to use lattice-tailored techniques as one instantiation of our methodology.

In the instantiation of our second construction, we use the Boneh-Boyen signature [12] that comes with an ABO reduction along with an online-extractable NIZK obtained via the Fiat-Shamir transform applied to Bulletproofs [18] and a Σ-protocol for some ElGamal related statements. To the best of our knowledge, this is the first time an NIZK that internally uses Bulletproofs was proven to be

[3] This is a type of NIZK where the extractor can extract a witness from the proofs output by the adversary in an *on-the-fly* manner.

online-extractable in the ROM. Prior works either showed the non-interactive version of Bulletproofs to achieve the weaker rewinding extractability [4,5] or the stronger online simulation extractability by further assuming the algebraic group model [33]. We believe the analysis of our online extractability to be novel and may be of independent interest.

1.3 Technical Overview

We give an overview of our contributions.

Fischlin's Round-Optimal Blind Signature. We review the generic construction by Fischlin [27] as it serves as a starting point for both of our constructions. The construction relies on a PKE, a signature scheme, and an NIZK. The blind signature's verification and signing keys (bvk, bsk) are identical to those of the underlying signature scheme (vk, sk). For simplicity, we assume a perfect correct PKE with uniform random encryption keys ek and that ek is provided to all the players as an output of the random oracle. The user first sends an encryption $c \leftarrow \mathsf{PKE}(\mathsf{ek}, m; r)$ of the message m. The signer then returns a signature $\sigma \leftarrow \mathsf{Sign}(\mathsf{sk}, c)$ on the ciphertext c. The user then encrypts $\widehat{c} \leftarrow \mathsf{PKE}(\mathsf{ek}, c\|r\|\sigma; \widehat{r})$ and generates an NIZK proof π of the following fact where $(c, \sigma, r, \widehat{r})$ is the witness: $\widehat{c}$ encrypts (c, r, σ) under $\widehat{r}$; c encrypts the message m under r; and σ is a valid signature on c. The user outputs the blind signature $\sigma_{\mathsf{BS}} = (\widehat{c}, \pi)$.

It is not hard to see that the scheme is blind under the IND-CPA security of the PKE and the zero-knowledge property of the NIZK. The one-more unforgeability proof is also straight-forward: The reduction will use the adversary $\mathcal{A}$ against the one-more unforgeability game to break the euf-cma of the signature scheme. The reduction first programs the random oracle so that it knows the corresponding decryption key dk of the PKE. When $\mathcal{A}$ submits c to the blind signing oracle, the reduction relays this to its signing oracle and returns $\mathcal{A}$ the signature σ it obtains. Moreover, it makes a list L of decrypted messages $m \leftarrow \mathsf{Dec}(\mathsf{dk}, c)$. When $\mathcal{A}$ outputs the forgeries $(\sigma_{\mathsf{BS},\mathsf{i}} = (\widehat{c}_i, \pi_i), m_i)_{i \in [\ell+1]}$, it searches a m_i such that $m_i \notin L$, which is guaranteed to exist since there are at most ℓ signing queries. The reduction then decrypts $(c_i, r_i, \sigma_i) \leftarrow \mathsf{Dec}(\mathsf{dk}, \widehat{c}_i)$. Since the PKE is perfectly correct and due to the soundness of the NIZK, c_i could not have been queried by $\mathcal{A}$ as otherwise $m_i \in L$, and hence, (c_i, σ_i) breaks euf-cma security.

Source of Inefficiency. There are two sources of inefficiency when trying to instantiate this generic construction. One is the use of a *layered* encryption: the NIZK needs to prove that c is a valid encryption of m on top of proving $\widehat{c}$ is a valid encryption of (c, r, σ). This contrived structure was required to bootstrap a sound NIZK to be *online-extractable*. Specifically, the one-more unforgeability proof relied on the reduction being able to extract the (partial) witness (c_i, r_i, σ_i) in an on-the-fly manner from the outer encryption $\widehat{c}_i$ explicitly included in the blind signature. The other inefficiency stems from the heavy reliance on PKEs. As far as the correctness is concerned, the PKE seems replaceable by a computationally binding commitment scheme. This would be ideal since commitment schemes tend to be more size efficient than PKEs since decryptability is not required. [4] However, without a PKE, it is not clear how the above proof would work.

First Construction. We explain our first construction, an optimized variant of Fischlin's generic construction.

Using Rewinding-Extractable NIZKs. The first step is to relax the online-extractable NIZK with a (single-proof) rewinding-extractable NIZK. Such an NIZK allows extracting a witness from a proof output by an adversary $\mathcal{A}$ by *rewinding* $\mathcal{A}$ on a fixed random tape. NIZKs obtained by compiling a Σ-protocol using the Fiat-Shamir transform is a representative example of an efficient rewinding-extractable NIZK. The net effect of this modification is that we can remove the layer of large encryption by $\widehat{c}$, thus making the statement simpler and allowing us to remove $\widehat{c}$ from σ_{BS}.

Let us check if this rewinding-extractable NIZK suffices in the above proof of one-more unforgeability. At first glance, the proof does not seem to work due to a subtle issue added by the rewinding extractor. Observe that the reduction now needs to simulate $\mathcal{A}$ in the *rewound execution* as well. In particular, after rewinding $\mathcal{A}$, $\mathcal{A}$ may submit a new c' to the blind signing oracle, which was not queried in the initial execution. The reduction relays this c' to its signing oracle as in the first execution to simulate the signature σ'. As before, we can argue that there exists a message m_i in the forgeries output by $\mathcal{A}$ in the *first* execution such that $m_i \notin L$, but we need to further argue that $m_i \notin L'$, where L' is the list of decrypted messages $\mathcal{A}$ submitted in the *rewound* execution. Namely, we need to argue that $m_i \notin L \cup L'$ for the reduction to break euf-cma security. However, a naive counting argument as done before no longer works because $|L \cup L'|$ can be large as 2ℓ, exceeding the number of forgeries output by $\mathcal{A}$, i.e., $\ell + 1$.

We can overcome this issue by taking a closer look at the internal of a particular class of rewinding-extractable NIZK. Specifically, throughout this paper, we focus on NIZKs constructed by applying the Fiat-Shamir transform on a Σ-protocol (or in more general a public-coin interactive protocol). A standard way to argue rewinding-extractability of a Fiat-Shamir NIZK is by relying on the forking lemma [8,51], which states (informally) that if an event E happened in the first run, then it will happen in the rewound round with non-negligible probability. In the above context, we define E to be the event that the i-th message in $\mathcal{A}$'s forgeries satisfy $m_i \notin L$, where i is sampled uniformly random by the reduction at the outset of the game. Here, note that E is well-defined since the reduction can prepare the list L by decrypting $\mathcal{A}$'s signing queries. The forking lemma then guarantees that we also have $m_i \notin L'$ in the rewound execution.[5] This slightly more fine-grained analysis allows us to replace the online-extractable NIZK with a rewinding-extractable NIZK.

[4] Constructing an online extractable NIZK by adding a PKE on top of a sound NIZK is a standard method.

[5] For the keen readers, we note that we are guaranteed to have the same i-th message in both executions since these values are fixed at the forking point due to how the Fiat-Shamir transform works.

Issue with Using Commitments. The next step is to relax the PKE by a (computationally binding) commitment scheme. While the correctness and blindness hold without any issue, the one-more unforgeability proof seems to require a major reworking. The main reason is that without the reduction being able to decrypt $\mathcal{A}$'s signing queries c, we won't be able to define the list L. In particular, we can no longer define the event E, and hence, cannot invoke the forking lemma. Thus, we are back to the situation where we cannot argue that the extracted witness (c_i, r_i, σ_i) from $\mathcal{A}$'s forgeries, is a valid forgery against the euf-cma security game. Even worse, $\mathcal{A}$ could potentially be breaking the computationally binding property of the commitment scheme by finding two message-randomness pairs (m_i, r_i) and (m'_i, r'_i) such that they both commit to c_i but $m_i \neq m'_i$. In such a case, extracting from a single proof does not seem sufficient since a reduction would need at least two extracted witnesses to break the binding of the commitment scheme.

To cope with the latter issue first, we extend the one-more unforgeability proof to rely on a *multi-proof* rewinding-extractable NIZK. In general, multi-proof rewinding-extractors run in exponential time in the number of proofs that it needs to extract from [9,53]. However, in our situation, with a careful argument, we can prove that our extractor runs in strict polynomial time since $\mathcal{A}$ provides all the proofs to the extractor only at the end of the game. This is in contrast to the settings considered in [9,53] where $\mathcal{A}$ can adaptively submit multiple proofs to the extractor throughout the game.

We note that the assumption we require has not changed: a Σ-protocol for the same relation as in the single-proof setting compiled into an NIZK via the Fiat-Shamir transform. To prove multi-proof rewinding-extractability of this Fiat-Shamir NIZK, we can no longer rely on the now standard general forking lemma by Bellare and Neven [8] that divorces the probabilistic essence of the forking lemma from any particular application context. A naive extension of the general forking lemma to the multi-forking setting will incur an exponential loss in the success probability. To provide a meaningful bound, we must take into account the extra structure offered by the Fiat-Shamir transform, and thus our analysis is akin to the more traditional forking lemma analysis by Pointcheval and Stern [51] or by Micali and Reyzin [46]. To the best of our knowledge, we provide the first formal analysis of the multi-proof rewinding-extractability of an NIZK obtained by applying the Fiat-Shamir transform to a Σ-protocol. We believe this analysis to be of independent interest.

Final Idea to Finish the Proof. Getting back to the proof of one-more unforgeability, the reduction now executes the multi-proof rewinding-extractor to extract all the witnesses $(c_i, r_i, \sigma_i)_{i \in [\ell+1]}$ from the forgeries. Relying on the binding of the commitment scheme, we are guaranteed that all the commitment c_i's are distinct. Moreover, since $\mathcal{A}$ only makes ℓ blind signature queries *in the first execution*, we further have that there exists at least one c_i in the forgeries which $\mathcal{A}$ did not submit in the first execution.

However, we are still stuck since it's unclear how to argue that this particular c_i was never queried by $\mathcal{A}$ in any of the rewound executions. Our next idea is to slightly strengthen the NIZK so that the proof π is statistically binding to a portion of the witness that contains the commitments.[6] We note that this is still strictly weaker and more efficiently instantiable compared to an online-extractable NIZK required by Fischlin's construction since we do not require the full list of witnesses to be efficiently extractable from the proofs in an online manner. We use this property to implicitly fix the commitments $(c_i)_{i\in[\ell+1]}$ included in the forgeries after the end of the first execution of $\mathcal{A}$. This will be the key property to completing the proof.

The last idea is for the reduction to randomize what it queries to its signing oracle. For this, we further assume the commitment scheme is randomizable, where we emphasize that this is done for ease of explanation and we do not strictly require such an assumption (see remark 1). When $\mathcal{A}$ submits a commitment c to the blind signing oracle, the reduction randomizes c to c' using some randomness rand and instead sends c' to its signing oracle. It returns the signature σ *and* rand to $\mathcal{A}$. $\mathcal{A}$ checks if c becomes randomized to c' using rand and if σ is a valid signature on c'. It then uses c' instead of c to generate the blind signature as before. The key observation is that the reduction is invoking its signing oracle with randomness outside of $\mathcal{A}$'s control. Since the commitments $(c_i)_{i\in[\ell+1]}$ were implicitly fixed at the end of the first execution, any randomized c' sampled in the subsequent rewound execution is independent of these commitments. Hence, the probability that the reduction queries c_i to the signing oracle in any of the rewound execution is negligible, thus constituting a valid forgery against the euf-cma security game as desired.

Instantiation. We instantiate the framework in the asymmetric pairing setting, i.e. we have groups $\mathbb{G}_1, \mathbb{G}_2, \mathbb{G}_T$ of prime order p, some fixed generators $g_1 \in \mathbb{G}_1, g_2 \in \mathbb{G}_2$, and a pairing $e : \mathbb{G}_1 \times \mathbb{G}_2 \mapsto \mathbb{G}_T$. For the commitment scheme, we choose Pedersen commitments ($\mathsf{C}_{\mathsf{Ped}}$) of the form $c = g_1^m \mathsf{pp}^r$, as $\mathsf{C}_{\mathsf{Ped}}$ is randomizable and consists of a single group element. Note that the public parameter $\mathsf{pp} \in \mathbb{G}_1$ is generated via a random oracle. We then need to choose an appropriate signature scheme that allows signing $\mathsf{C}_{\mathsf{Ped}}$ commitments. We choose SPS as all components of the scheme are group elements, in particular, the message space is $\mathbb{G}_1^\ell$, where ℓ is the message length. The most efficient choice in the standard model is [39] with signatures of size 335 Byte. Instead, we optimize KPW signatures [43] to a signature size of 223 Byte (from originally 382 Byte). Our optimized variant $\mathsf{S}_{\mathsf{KPW}}$ is no longer structure-preserving, as it consists of one element τ in $\mathbb{Z}_p$, but suffices for our applications. We refer to the full version for more details. Note that $\mathsf{S}_{\mathsf{KPW}}$ would be an inefficient choice in the original Fischlin blind signature [28], as it requires encrypting the signature τ over $\mathbb{Z}_p$ to instantiate the online-extractable NIZK. In the pairing setting, this incurs an

[6] At the Σ-protocol abstraction, we call this new property f-unique extraction. It is a strictly weaker property than the *unique response* property considered in the literature [27,54].

overhead in proof size linear in the security parameter λ^7. The benefit of using our framework with the weaker rewinding-extractable NIZK is that we now only need to prove knowledge of τ, and thus can get away without encrypting it. Such an NIZK is possible with a single element in $\mathbb{Z}_p$ based on a Schnorr-type Σ-protocol (compiled with Fiat-Shamir). In the Σ-protocol, we further commit to group elements $(w_i)_i \in \mathbb{G}_1^n$ in the witness via ElGamal commitments (C_{EG}) of the form $E_i = (w_i \cdot \mathsf{pp}^{r_i}, g_1^{r_i})$, which the prover sends to the verifier in the first flow. In particular, this ensures f-unique extraction, as E_i fixes the commitment $c \in \{w_i\}_i$ statistically. Naively, this approach requires $2n$ group elements, where n is the number of group elements in the witness. Instead, we share the randomness among all commitments under different public parameters pp_i generated via a random oracle. The commitments remain secure but require only $n+1$ group elements. In particular, we set $E_i = (w_i \cdot \mathsf{pp}_i^s)$ and fix s via $S = g_1^s$. Then, we can open *all* commitments E_i in zero-knowledge with a *single* element in $\mathbb{Z}_p$, as knowledge of s is sufficient to recover the witness w_i from all E_i. Then, we compile our Σ-protocol with Fiat-Shamir to obtain a rewinding-based NIZK. We apply a well-known optimization to avoid sending some of the first flow α, and include the hash value $\beta \leftarrow \mathsf{H}(x, \alpha)$ in the proof explicitly. In total, compared to sending the witness to the verifier in the *clear*, our NIZK only has an overhead of 1 group element in $\mathbb{G}_1$ and 3 elements in $\mathbb{Z}_p$. The additional group element is S. The three additional $\mathbb{Z}_p$ elements are the hash value β, and values in the third flow required for (i) showing knowledge of s and (ii) linearizing a quadratic equation in the signature verification.

The instantiation of our framework achieves communication size of 303 Byte and signature size of 447 Byte.

Second Construction. We explain our second construction relying on randomizable signatures with an ABO reduction.

Getting Rid of NIZKs in the Signature. While the previous construction provides a small sum of signature and communication sizes, one drawback is that the blind signature has inherently a larger signature than those of the underlying signature scheme. The source of this large blind signature stems from using an NIZK to hide the underlying signature provided by the signer.

A natural approach used in the literature is to rely on techniques used to construct *randomizable* signature schemes [10,30,31,42]. Informally, a randomizable signature scheme allows to publicly randomize the signature σ on a message m to a fresh signature σ'. Many standard group-based signature schemes (in the standard model and ROM) are known to satisfy this property, *e.g.*, [12,56]. A failed attempt would be for the user to randomize the signature σ provided by the signer and output the randomized σ' as the blind signature. Clearly, this is not secure since the user is not hiding the message m, that is, σ and σ' are linkable through m thus breaking blindness. An idea to fix this would be to let

[7] For instance, with ElGamal, the message is encrypted in the exponent and decryption would require a discrete logarithm computation. Thus, the message is typically encrypted bit-wise which incurs an overhead of $\log_2(p)$.

the user send a commitment $c = \mathsf{Com}(m; r)$ to the signer and the signature signs the "message" c. However, unless the commitment c can be randomized consistently with σ, we would still need to rely on an NIZK to hide c. This calls for a signature scheme that is somehow compatible with commitments.

Signatures with All-But-One Reductions. Our main insight is that a specific class of signature schemes with an *all-but-one* (ABO) reduction is naturally compatible with blind signatures. An ABO reduction is a standard proof technique to prove selective security of public key primitives, *e.g.*, [3,13,34,52], where a formal treatment can be found in [47]. In the context of signature schemes, this is a proof technique that allows the reduction to embed the challenge message m^* (i.e., the signature for which the adversary forges) into the verification key. The reduction can simulate any signatures on $m \neq m^*$, and when the adversary outputs a forgery on m^*, then the reduction can break some hard problems.

Let us now specify the class of signature scheme. We assume an additive homomorphic commitment scheme, that is, $\mathsf{Com}(m; r) + \mathsf{Com}(m'; r') = \mathsf{Com}(m + m'; r + r')$. We then assume a signature scheme where the signing algorithm $\mathsf{Sig}(\mathsf{sk}, m)$ can be rewritten as $\widehat{\mathsf{Sig}}(\mathsf{sk}, \mathsf{Com}(m; 0) + u)$, where u is some fixed but random commitment included in the verification key. Namely, Sig first commits to the message m using no randomness, adds u to it, and proceeds with signing. Note that if $u = \mathsf{Com}(-m'; r')$ for some (m', r'), then $\mathsf{Com}(m; 0) + u = \mathsf{Com}(m - m'; r')$. While contrived at first glance, this property is naturally satisfied by many of the signature schemes that admit an ABO reduction; the ABO reduction inherently requires embedding the challenge message m^* into the verification key in an unnoticeable manner and further implicitly requires message m submitted to the signing query to interact with the "committed" m^*. Specifically, the former hints at a need for an (implicit) commitment scheme and the later hints at the need for some operation between the commitments. Finally, to be used in the security proof, we assume there is a simulated signing algorithm $\widehat{\mathsf{SimSig}}$ along with a trapdoor td such that $\widehat{\mathsf{SimSig}}(\mathsf{td}, \mathsf{Com}(m - m'; r'), m - m', r') = \widehat{\mathsf{Sig}}(\mathsf{sk}, \mathsf{Com}(m; 0) + u)$ if and only if $m \neq m'$, where recall $u = \mathsf{Com}(-m'; r')$. Specifically, $\widehat{\mathsf{SimSig}}$ can produce a valid signature if it knows the *non-zero* commitment message and randomness.

Let us explain the ABO reduction in slightly more detail. In the security proof, the reduction guesses (or the adversary $\mathcal{A}$ submits) a challenge message m^* that $\mathcal{A}$ will forge on. It then sets up the verification key while replacing the random commitment u to $u = \mathsf{Com}(-m^*; r^*)$ while also embedding a hard problem that it needs to solve. Due to the hiding property of the commitment scheme, this is unnoticeable from $\mathcal{A}$. Then, instead of using the real signing algorithm $\widehat{\mathsf{Sig}}$, the reduction uses the simulated signing algorithm $\widehat{\mathsf{SimSig}}$. As long as $m \neq m^*$, $\widehat{\mathsf{SimSig}}(\mathsf{td}, \mathsf{Com}(m - m^*; r^*), m - m^*, r^*)$ outputs a valid signature, and hence, can be used to simulate the signing oracle. Finally, given a forgery on m^*, the reduction is set up so that it can break a hard problem.

Turning it into a Blind Signature. To turn this into a blind signature, the key observation is that $\widehat{\mathsf{Sig}}$ is agnostic to the committed message and randomness of $\mathsf{Com}(m;0)+u$ — these are only used during the security proof when running $\widehat{\mathsf{SimSig}}$. Concretely, a user of a blind signature can generate a valid commitment $\mathsf{Com}(m;r)$, send it to the signer, and the signer can simply return $\sigma_r \leftarrow \widehat{\mathsf{Sig}}(\mathsf{sk}, \mathsf{Com}(m;r)+u)$. If the signature admits a way to map σ_r back to a normal signature σ for m, then we can further rely on the randomizability of the signature scheme to obtain a fresh signature σ' on the message m.

The proof of one-more unforgeability of this abstract blind signature construction is almost identical to the original ABO reduction with one exception. For the reduction to invoke the simulated $\widehat{\mathsf{SimSig}}$, recall it needs to know the message and randomness of the commitment $\mathsf{Com}(m;r)+u$. Hence, we modify the user to add an *online-extractable* NIZK to prove the correctness of the commitment $\mathsf{Com}(m;r)$ so that the reduction can extract (m,r). Here, we require online-extractability rather than rewinding-extractability since otherwise, the reduction will run exponentially in the number of singing queries [9,53]. Also, this is why the communication size becomes larger compared with our first construction. Finally, when the adversary outputs a forgery including m^*, the reduction can break a hard problem as before. Here, we note that we can simply hash the messages m with a random oracle to obtain an adaptively secure scheme using the ABO reduction.

Interestingly, while the recent lattice-based blind signature by del Pino and Katsumata [25] stated to use lattice-tailored techniques to optimize Fischlin's generic construction, the construction and the proof of one-more unforgeability follows our above template, where they use the Agrawal-Boneh-Boyen signature [3] admitting an ABO reduction. The only difference is that since lattices do not have nice randomizable signatures, they still had to rely on an NIZK for the final signature. While we focused on ABO reductions where only one challenge message m^* can be embedded in the verification key, the same idea naturally extends to all-but-*many* reductions. The blind signature by Blazy et al. [10] relying on the Waters signature can be viewed as one such instantiation. Finally, while we believe we can make the above approach formal using the ABO reduction terminology defined in [47], we focus on one class of instantiation in the main body for better readability. Nonetheless, we believe the above abstract construction will be useful when constructing round-optimal blind signatures from other assumptions.

Instantiation. We instantiate the above framework with the Boneh-Boyen signature scheme S_{BB} [12,14]. Recall that signatures of S_{BB} on a message $m \in \mathbb{Z}_p$ are of the form $\sigma = (\mathsf{sk} \cdot (u_1^m \cdot h_1)^r, g_1^r)$, where $u_1, h_1 \in \mathbb{G}_1$ are part of the verification key, sk is the secret key and $r \leftarrow \mathbb{Z}_p$ is sampled at random. We observe that S_{BB} is compatible with the Pedersen commitment scheme $\mathsf{C}_{\mathsf{Ped}}$ with generators u_1 and g_1. Roughly, the user commits to the message m via $c = u_1^m \cdot g_1^s$[8], where $s \leftarrow \mathbb{Z}_p$ blinds the message, proves that she committed to m honestly with a proof π generated via an appropriate online-extractable NIZK Π, and sends (c,π)

[8] In the actual construction, we further hash m by a random oracle; this effectively makes S_{BB} *adaptively* secure.

to the signer. The signer checks π and signs c via $(\mu_0, \mu_1) \leftarrow (\mathsf{sk} \cdot (c \cdot h_1)^r, g_1^r)$. Note that as c shares the structure u_1^m with $\mathsf{S_{BB}}$ signatures on message m, the user can recompute a valid signature on m via $\sigma \leftarrow (\mu_0 \cdot \mu_1^{-s}, \mu_1)$. Before presenting σ to a verifier, the user rerandomizes σ to ensure blindness. We refer to Sect. 4 for more details.

The main challenge is constructing an efficient *online-extractable* NIZK Π for the relation $\mathsf{R_{bb}} = \{(x, w) : c = u_1^m \cdot g_1^s\}$, where $x = (c, u_1, g_1)$ and $w = (m, s)$. As we require online-extraction, a simple Σ-protocol showing $c = u_1^m \cdot g_1^s$ compiled via Fiat-Shamir is no longer sufficient as in our prior instantiation, as the extractor needs to rewind the adversary in order to extract (m, s). For example, we could instantiate Π with the (online-extractable) GOS proofs but such a proof has a size of around 400 KB. Another well-known approach is to additionally encrypt the witness (m, s) via a PKE and include the ciphertext into the relation; recall this method was used when explaining the Fischlin blind signature. The extractor can then use the secret key to decrypt the witnesses *online*. While a common choice for the PKE would be ElGamal encryption, this is insufficient since the extractor can only decrypt group elements g_1^m and g_1^s and not the witness in $\mathbb{Z}_p$ as required. To circumvent this, a common technique is to instead encrypt the binary decompositions $(m_i, s_i)_{i \in [\ell_2]}$ of m, s, respectively, with ElGamal, where $\ell_2 = \log_2(p)$. It then proves with a (non-online extractable) NIZK that $m = \sum_{i=1}^{\ell_2} m_i 2^{i-1}$ and $s = \sum_{i=1}^{\ell_2} s_i 2^{i-1}$ are valid openings of c, while also proving that m_i, s_i encrypted in the ElGamal ciphertexts are elements in $\{0, 1\}$, where the latter can be done via the equivalent identity $x \cdot (1 - x) = 0$. The extractor can now decrypt the ElGamal encryptions of m_i to $g_1^{m_i} \in \{g_1, 1_{\mathbb{G}_1}\}$ and efficiently decide whether m_i is 0 or 1. Similarly, it can recover the decomposition s_i. Unfortunately, this approach requires at least $2\ell_2$ ElGamal ciphertexts which amount to 32 KB alone. In fact, the bit-by-bit encryption of the witness is also the efficiency bottleneck of GOS proofs for $\mathbb{Z}_p$ witnesses.

We refine the above approach in multiple ways to obtain concretely efficient online-extractable NIZKs. Instead of using the binary decomposition, we observe that the extractor can still recover x from g_1^x if $x \in [0, B-1]$ is short, i.e., $B = \mathsf{poly}(\lambda)$. Thus, we let the prover encrypt the B-ary decompositions $(m_i, s_i)_{i \in [\ell]}$ of m and s, where $\ell = \log_B(p)$. For example, setting $B = 2^{32}$ allows the extractor to recover m_i via a brute-force calculation of the discrete logarithm, and the number of encryptions is reduced by a factor of 32. Concretely, we modify the prover to prove that an ElGamal ciphertext encrypts $(m_i, s_i)_{i \in [\ell]}$ such that (i) each m_i and s_i are in $[0, B-1]$, and (ii) $m = \sum_{i=1}^{\ell} m_i B^{i-1}$, $s = \sum_{i=1}^{\ell} s_i B^{i-1}$, and $c = u_1^m \cdot g_1^s$.

To instantiate our approach, we glue two different (non-online extractable) NIZKs Π_{rp} and Π_{ped} together, each being suitable to show relations (i) and (ii), respectively. For the range relation (i), we appeal to the batched variant of Bulletproofs [4] and turn it non-interactive with Fiat-Shamir. For the linear relation (ii), we use a standard NIZK with an appropriate Σ-protocol compiled with Fiat-Shamir. We further apply three optimizations to make this composition of NIZKs more efficient:

1. While Bulletproofs require committing to the decompositions $(m_i, s_i)_{i\in[\ell]}$ in Pedersen commitments, we use the shared structure of ElGamal ciphertexts and Pedersen commitments to avoid sending additional Pedersen commitments. This also makes the relation simpler since we do not have to prove consistency between the committed components in the ElGamal ciphertext and Pedersen commitment.
2. We use a more efficient discrete logarithm algorithm during extraction with runtime $\mathcal{O}(\sqrt{B})$, which allows us to choose more efficient parameters for the same level of security. This further reduces the number of encryptions by a factor 2.
3. We perform most of the proof in a more efficient elliptic curve $\widehat{\mathbb{G}}$ of same order p without pairing structure. As both the NIZKs Π_{rp} and Π_{ped} are not reliant on pairings, this reduces the size and efficiency of the NIZK considerably.

Proof of Instantiation. Finally, we analyze the security of the optimized online-extractable NIZK Π obtained by gluing Π_{rp} and Π_{ped} together. Correctness and zero-knowledge are straightforward. Also, online-extraction seems immediate on first sight. The extractor decrypts the decomposition, reconstructs the witness (m, s), and checks whether $c = u_1^m g_1^s$. To show why it works, we rely on the soundness of the range proof Π_{rp} to guarantee that the committed values are short. This allows the extractor to decrypt efficiently. Moreover, we rely on the soundness of Π_{ped} to guarantee that the decrypted values form a proper B-ary decompositions of an opening (m, s) of c. However, this high-level idea misses many subtle issues.

First, Bulletproofs are not well-established in the non-interactive setting in the ROM. While Attema et al. [5] show that special sound multi-round proof systems are knowledge sound (or rewinding-extractable) when compiled via Fiat-Shamir, Bulletproofs are only *computationally* special sound under the DLOG assumption. An easy fix for this is to relax the relation of the extracted witness. That is we use two different relations: one to be used by the prover and the other to be used by the extractor. We define an extracted witness w to be in the relaxed relation if either w is in the original relation *or* w is a DLOG solution with respect to (part of) the statement. With this relaxation, the interactive Bulletproofs becomes special sound for the relaxed relation since we can count the extracted DLOG solution as a valid witness. Observing that the result of [5] naturally translates to relaxed relations, we can conclude the non-interactive Bulletproofs to be rewinding-extractable in the ROM.

The second subtlety is more technical. For the formal proof, when the adversary submits a proof such that the online-extraction of Π fails, we must show that the adversary is breaking either the soundness of the underlying NIZKs Π_{rp} or Π_{ped}. Recall that Π_{rp} and Π_{ped} are glued together via the ElGamal ciphertext (cf. item 1). Specifically, each witness $w \in (m_i, s_i)_{i\in[\ell]}$ are encrypted as $c = (c_0, c_1) = (g^w \mathsf{pp}^r, g^r)$ with randomness $r \leftarrow \mathbb{Z}_p$, and Π_{rp} uses the partial "Pedersen part" c_0, while Π_{ped} uses the entire "ElGamal part" c. Thus one possibility for the online-extraction of Π failing is when the adversary breaks the tie between the two NIZKs by breaking the binding property of the Pedersen commitment. That is, if the adversary finds the DLOG between (g, pp), it can break the consistency between the two NIZKs in such a way that online-extraction of Π fails.

Put differently, to show that no adversary can trigger a proof for which the online-extraction of Π fails, we must show (at the minimum) that we can use such an adversary to extract a DLOG solution between (g, pp). This in particular implies that we have to *simultaneously* extract the witness w_0 of Π_{rp} containing one opening of c_0 and the witness w_1 of Π_{ped} containing the other opening of c_0 in order to break DLOG with respect to (g, pp), or equivalently to break the binding property of the Pedersen commitment. The issue with this is that we cannot conclude that both extractions succeed at the same time even if Π_{rp} and Π_{ped} *individually* satisfy the standard notion of rewinding-extractability. For instance, using the standard notion of rewinding-extractability, we cannot exclude the case where the adversary sets up the proofs π_0, π_1 of $\Pi_{\mathsf{rp}}, \Pi_{\mathsf{ped}}$, respectively, in such a way that if the extractor of Π_{rp} succeeds, then the extractor of Π_{ped} fails. We thus show in a careful non-black box analysis that the extraction of both proofs succeeds at the same time with non-negligible probability. To the best of our knowledge, this is the first time an NIZK that internally uses Bulletproofs is proven to be online-extractable in the ROM. We believe that our new analysis is of independent interest.

2 Preliminaries

Let $\lambda \in \mathbb{N}$ be the security parameter. We use standard notations for probability, algortihms and distributions. Also, we use prime order groups $\mathbb{G}$ and pairing groups $(\mathbb{G}_1, \mathbb{G}_2, \mathbb{G}_T, e, g_1, g_2)$ of shared order p, with standard notation. We refer to the full version for more details. We denote with $[n]$ the set $\{1, \ldots, n\}$ for $n \in \mathbb{N}$. For any $\vec{h} = (h_1, \ldots, h_q)$ and $i \in [q]$, we denote $\vec{h}_{<i}$ as $(h_1, \ldots, h_{i-1})$ and $\vec{h}_{\geq i}$ as $(h_i, \ldots, h_q)$, where $\vec{h}_{<1}$ denotes an empty vector. Moreover, for any two vectors $\vec{h}, \vec{h'}$ of arbitrary length, we use $\vec{h}\|\vec{h'}$ to denote the concatenation of the two vectors. In particular, for any $i \in [q]$ and $\vec{h} \in \mathcal{H}^q$, we have $\vec{h} = \vec{h}_{<i}\|\vec{h}_{\geq i}$.

Instantiation. For our instantiations, we assume that the modulus p is of size 256 bit, and an element of $\mathbb{G}_1, \mathbb{G}_2, \mathbb{G}_T$ is of size 382, 763, 4572 bit, respectively. These are common sizes of standard BLS curves [6] with security parameter $\lambda = 128$, in particular BLS12-381 [15]. For groups that require no pairing operation, we use a curve of order p and assume that elements are of size 256 bit. We generally write $\widehat{\mathbb{G}}$ for such groups.

Assumptions. In this paper, we use the following hardness assumptions. Let $\mathbb{G}$ be an arbitrary group with generator g and $(\mathbb{G}_1, \mathbb{G}_2, \mathbb{G}_T, e, g_1, g_2) \leftarrow \mathsf{PGen}(1^\lambda)$ be a pairing description.

The discrete logarithm (DLOG) assumption in $\mathbb{G}$ states that it is hard to compute the discrete logarithm x of some random $h = g^x \in \mathbb{G}$. The decisional

Diffie-Hellman (DDH) assumption states that it is hard to distinguish tuples (g^a, g^b, g^{ab}) from tuples (g^a, g^b, g^c) with random $a, b, c \leftarrow \mathbb{Z}_p$. The symmetric external Diffie-Hellman (SXDH) assumption holds if the DDH assumption holds in $\mathbb{G}_1$ and in $\mathbb{G}_2$. Finally, the (asymmetric) computational Diffie-Hellman assumption states that given $(g_1^a, g_2^a, g_1^b, g_2^b)$, it is hard to computes g_1^{ab}..

Explaining Group Elements as Random Strings. Our frameworks generally require that public parameters pp (of commitment schemes) and common random strings crs (of NIZKs) are random bit strings. For readability, we allow that pp and crs contain random group elements $g \leftarrow \mathbb{G}$ for some group $\mathbb{G}$. This is without loss of generality, as using explainable sampling, we can explain these elements as random strings. We refer to the full version for more details.

2.1 Cryptographic Primitives

We briefly recall the primitives we use throughout the article, and refer to the full version for formal definitions.

Commitment Schemes. A *commitment scheme* C is a PPT algorithm $\mathsf{C} = \mathsf{C.Commit}$ such that

- $\mathsf{C.Commit}(\mathsf{pp}, m; r)$: given the public parameters $\mathsf{pp} \in \{0,1\}^{\ell_\mathsf{C}}$, message m and randomness r, computes a commitment c, and outputs the pair (c, r),

where $\mathsf{pp} \in \{0,1\}^{\ell_\mathsf{C}}$ are *uniform* public parameters, r is the randomness and c is the commitment. We do not explicitly define the opening algorithm since we can use the commitment randomness r as the decommitment (or opening) information and check if $c = \mathsf{Commit}(\mathsf{pp}, m; r)$ holds to verify that c is a valid commitment to message m.

We require the standard notions of correctness, hiding and binding. A commitment scheme is *correct* if honest commitments $c \leftarrow \mathsf{Commit}(\mathsf{pp}, m; r)$ always verify, i.e., $c = \mathsf{Commit}(\mathsf{pp}, m; r)$. It is hiding if it is hard to decide whether an unopened commitment c commits to message m_0 or m_1, and it is binding if it is hard to open commitments c to distinct messages.

We further say that $c = \mathsf{Commit}(\mathsf{pp}, m; r)$ is rerandomizable, if it can be rerandomized via $c' \leftarrow \mathsf{RerandCom}(\mathsf{pp}, c, \Delta r)$. We require that the new commitment c' has high min-entropy if Δr is a fresh random value, i.e., given c it is *statistically* difficult to predict c'. Also, we assume that we can recover an opening of c' via $r' \leftarrow \mathsf{RerandRand}(\mathsf{pp}, c, m, r, \Delta r)$ if an initial opening (m, r) of c and the rerandomization randomness Δr is known. That is, if compute $c' = \mathsf{RerandCom}(\mathsf{pp}, c, \Delta r)$ and $r' \leftarrow \mathsf{RerandRand}(\mathsf{pp}, c, m, r, \Delta r)$, then it holds that $c' = c''$, where $(c'', r') = \mathsf{Com}(\mathsf{pp}, m; r')$.

We note that any natural additive homomorphic commitment scheme satisfies rerandomizability if we define $\mathsf{RerandCom}(\mathsf{pp}, c, \Delta r) = c + \mathsf{Commit}(\mathsf{pp}, 0; \Delta r) = c'$. Observe that if $c = \mathsf{Commit}(\mathsf{pp}, m; r)$, the rerandomziaed randomness is $r' =$

$r + \Delta r$ since $c' = \mathsf{Commit}(\mathsf{pp}, m; r')$ by the homomorphic property. Moreover, c' has high min-entropy since $\mathsf{Commit}(\mathsf{pp}, 0)$ has high min-entropy for most natural commitment schemes. Finally, we note that while a computational variant of the high min-entropy property suffices for our generic construction, we use the statistical variant for simplicity and because our instantiation satisfies it.

Signature Schemes. We consider *deterministic* signature schemes; a scheme where the randomness of the signing algorithm is derived from the secret key and message. We can derandomize any signature scheme by using a pseudorandom function for generating the randomness used in the signing algorithm (see for example [40]). A signature scheme is a tuple of PPT algorithms $\mathsf{S} = (\mathsf{KeyGen}, \mathsf{Sign}, \mathsf{Verify})$ such that

- $\mathsf{KeyGen}(1^\lambda)$: generates a verification key vk and a signing key sk,
- $\mathsf{Sign}(\mathsf{sk}, m)$: given a signing key sk and a message $m \in \mathcal{S}_{\mathsf{msg}}$, *deterministically* outputs a signature σ,
- $\mathsf{Verify}(\mathsf{vk}, m, \sigma)$: given a verification key vk and a signature σ on message m, *deterministically* outputs a bit $b \in \{0, 1\}$.

Here, $\mathcal{S}_{\mathsf{msg}}$ is the message space. We require the standard notion of correctness and $\mathtt{euf\text{-}cma}$ security. A signature scheme is *correct* if honestly generated signatures $\sigma \leftarrow \mathsf{Sign}(\mathsf{sk}, m)$ verify correctly, i.e., $\mathsf{Verify}(\mathsf{vk}, m, \sigma) = 1$. It is *euf-cma* secure if given some vk and access to a signature oracle $\mathsf{Sign}(\mathsf{sk}, \cdot)$, it is hard to output a valid signature σ for some message m that was never queried to $\mathsf{Sign}(\mathsf{sk}, \cdot)$.

Blind Signature Scheme. We recall the definition of round-optimal blind signatures, and refer to the full version for more formal definitions of (partially) blind signatures. A blind signature scheme is a tuple of PPT algorithms $\mathsf{PBS} = (\mathsf{KeyGen}, \mathsf{User}, \mathsf{Signer}, \mathsf{Derive}, \mathsf{Verify})$ such that

- $\mathsf{KeyGen}(1^\lambda)$: generates the verification key bvk and signing key bsk,
- $\mathsf{User}(\mathsf{bvk}, m)$: given verification key bvk, and message $m \in \mathcal{BS}_{msg}$, outputs a first message ρ_1 and a state st,
- $\mathsf{Signer}(\mathsf{bsk}, \rho_1)$: given signing key bsk, and first message ρ_1, outputs a second message ρ_2,
- $\mathsf{Derive}(\mathsf{st}, \rho_2)$: given state st, and second message ρ_2, outputs a signature σ,
- $\mathsf{Verify}(\mathsf{bvk}, m, \sigma)$: given verification key bvk, and signature σ on message $m \in \mathcal{BS}_{msg}$, outputs a bit $b \in \{0, 1\}$.

In the following, we assume the state is kept implicit in the following for better readability. We consider the standard security notions for blind signatures [38].

A blind signature is *correct*, if for all messages $m \in \mathcal{BS}_{msg}$, $(\mathsf{bvk}, \mathsf{bsk}) \leftarrow \mathsf{KeyGen}(1^\lambda), (\rho_1, \mathsf{st}) \leftarrow \mathsf{User}(\mathsf{bvk}, m), \rho_2 \leftarrow \mathsf{Signer}(\mathsf{bsk}, \rho_1), \sigma \leftarrow \mathsf{Derive}(\mathsf{st}, \rho_2)$, it holds that $\mathsf{Verify}(\mathsf{bvk}, m, \sigma) = 1$.

It is *blind under malicious keys* if a malicious signer cannot distinguish whether it first signed m_0 or m_1, after engaging with a honest user in two signing sessions and being presented the obtained signatures on messages m_0, m_1 in a fixed order. Here, the honest user permutes the order of the signing sessions at random, and the verification key bvk is adversarially chosen.

It is *one-more unforgeable* if a malicious user that engages in at most Q_S signing sessions with the signer, can output at most Q_S valid distinct signature-message pairs.

Σ-Protocols. Let R be an NP relation with statements x and witnesses w. We denote by $\mathscr{L}_\mathsf{R} = \{x \mid \exists w \text{ s.t. } (x, w) \in \mathsf{R}\}$ the language induced by R. A Σ-protocol for an NP relation R for language $\mathscr{L}_\mathsf{R}$ is a tuple of PPT algorithms $\Sigma = (\mathsf{Init}, \mathsf{Chall}, \mathsf{Resp}, \mathsf{Verify})$ such that

- $\mathsf{Init}(x, w)$: given a statement $x \in \mathscr{L}_\mathsf{R}$, and a witness w such that $(x, w) \in \mathsf{R}$, outputs a first flow message (i.e., commitment) α and a state st, where we assume st includes x, w,
- $\mathsf{Chall}()$: samples a challenge $\beta \leftarrow \mathcal{CH}$ (without taking any input),
- $\mathsf{Resp}(\mathsf{st}, \beta)$: given a state st and a challenge $\beta \in \mathcal{CH}$, outputs a third flow message (i.e., response) γ,
- $\mathsf{Verify}(x, \alpha, \beta, \gamma)$: given a statement $x \in \mathscr{L}_\mathsf{R}$, a commitment α, a challenge $\beta \in \mathcal{CH}$, and a response γ, outputs a bit $b \in \{0, 1\}$.

Here, $\mathcal{CH}$ denotes the challenge space. We call the tuple (α, β, γ) the *transcript* and say that they are *valid for* x if $\mathsf{Verify}(x, \alpha, \beta, \gamma)$ outputs 1. When the context is clear, we simply say it is valid and omit x.

We recall the standard notions of correctness, high-min entropy, honest-verifier zero-knowledge, and 2-special soundness. A Σ-protocol is *correct*, if for all $(x, w) \in \mathsf{R}$, if for any honestly generated transcripts (α, β, γ), the verifier accepts, i.e., $\mathsf{Verify}(x, \alpha, \beta, \gamma) = 1$. It has *high min-entropy* if for all $(x, w) \in \mathsf{R}$, it is statistically hard to predict a honestly generated first flow α. It is *honest-verifier zero-knowledge* (HVZK), if there exists a PPT zero-knowledge simulator Sim such that the distributions of $\mathsf{Sim}(x, \beta)$ and the honestly generated transcript with Init initialized with (x, w) are computationally indistinguishable for any $x \in \mathscr{L}_\mathsf{R}$, and $\beta \in \mathcal{CH}$, where the honest execution is conditioned on β being used as the challenge. Finally, it is 2-*special sound*, if there exists a *deterministic* PPT extractor Ext such that given two valid transcripts $\{(\alpha, \beta_b, \gamma_b)\}_{b \in [2]}$ for statement x with $\beta_1 \neq \beta_2$, along with x, outputs a witness w such that $(x, w) \in \mathsf{R}$.

Note that in the above, two valid transcripts for x, with the same first flow message and different challenges, imply that statement x is in $\mathscr{L}_\mathsf{R}$. That is, we do not guarantee x to lie in $\mathscr{L}_\mathsf{R}$ when invoking Ext. While subtle, this allows us to invoke Ext properly within the security proof even if the reduction cannot decide if the statement x output by the adversary indeed lies in $\mathscr{L}_\mathsf{R}$.

In the following, we propose a new notion of *f-unique extraction*. The notion is similar to the *unique response* property [27,54] which requires that given an incomplete transcript (α, β), there is at most one response γ such that the transcript $\tau = (\alpha, \beta, \gamma)$ is valid. We relax this in two ways. First, we require that given a transcript τ and another challenge β', it is impossible to find two different responses γ_0, γ_1, such $w_0 \neq w_1$, where w_b is the witness extracted from τ and $\tau_b = (\alpha, \beta', \gamma_b)$. We further relax this by only requiring this property for a portion of the witness, defined by a function f, i.e., we require $f(w_0) \neq f(w_1)$ instead of $w_0 \neq w_1$.

While it may seem like an unnatural property, this is satisfied by many natural Σ-protocols. In particular, if the first flow α contains a perfectly binding commitment $c = \mathsf{Commit}(f(w); r)$ to $f(w)$, and the extractor extracts the appropriate r, then the Σ-protocol has f-unique extraction. We remark also that a statistical variant of f-unique extraction is sufficient for our purpose. We choose the definition below for simplicity and because our instantiation satisfies it. See Sect. 3 for more details and concrete example of f-unique extraction.

Definition 1 (f-Unique Extraction). *For a (possibly non-efficient) function f, a Σ-protocol Σ has f-*unique extraction *if for any statement x, any transcript $\tau = (\alpha, \beta, \gamma)$ and challenge $\beta' \neq \beta$, there is no γ_0, γ_1, such that for $\tau_b = (\alpha, \beta', \gamma_b)$, we have*

$$f(\mathsf{Ext}(x, \tau, \tau_0)) \neq f(\mathsf{Ext}(x, \tau, \tau_1)).$$

Non-Interactive Zero Knowledge. Given a witness w for statement x, a non-interactive zero-knowledge (NIZK) proof system allows a prover to generate a proof π that attests that she *knows* some w' such that $(w', x) \in \mathsf{R}$. Proofs π can be verified for statement x *without* revealing anything but that the statement is true. Here, we quantify "knowledge of the witness" either via *adaptive knowledge soundness* or *online-extractability*. The former informally states that if an algorithm $\mathcal{A}$ can generate a valid proof-statement pair (x, π), then there exists some extractor that when given black-box access to $\mathcal{A}$, can extract some witness w s.t. $(x, w) \in \mathsf{R}$. The latter requires that the witness w can be extracted from (x, π) "on-the-fly" without disrupting $\mathcal{A}$. In this context, we require some random oracle H on which proving and verification rely. Further, we assume that the prover and verifier are supplied with a common random string crs. As we later aim to avoid such a crs in our blind signature framework, the crs will be the output of a random oracle.

More formally, an NIZK for a relation R is a tuple of oracle-calling PPT algorithms $(\mathsf{Prove}^{\mathsf{H}}, \mathsf{Verify}^{\mathsf{H}})$ such that:

- $\mathsf{Prove}^{\mathsf{H}}(\mathsf{crs}, x, w)$: receives a common random string $\mathsf{crs} \in \{0,1\}^{\ell}$, a statement x and a witness w, and outputs a proof π,
- $\mathsf{Verify}^{\mathsf{H}}(\mathsf{crs}, x, \pi)$: receives a statement x and a proof π, and outputs a bit $b \in \{0,1\}$.

Here, ℓ is the length of common random strings. An NIZK is *correct* if for any $\mathsf{crs} \in \{0,1\}^{\ell}$, $(x, w) \in \mathsf{R}$, and $\pi \leftarrow \mathsf{Prove}^{\mathsf{H}}(\mathsf{crs}, x, w)$, it holds that $\mathsf{Verify}^{\mathsf{H}}(\mathsf{crs}, x, \pi) = 1$.

It is *zero-knowledge* if there exists a PPT simulator $\mathsf{Sim} = (\mathsf{Sim}_{\mathsf{H}}, \mathsf{Sim}_{\pi})$ that outputs simulated proofs $\pi' \leftarrow \mathsf{Sim}_{\pi}(\mathsf{crs}, x)$ that are indistinguishable from real proofs $\pi \leftarrow \mathsf{Prove}^{\mathsf{H}}(\mathsf{crs}, x, w)$ that are generated with witness w such that $(x, w) \in \mathsf{R}$. Here, $\mathsf{Sim}_{\mathsf{H}}$ simulates the random oracle H for simulated proofs.

We define adaptive knowledge soundness. We remark that the soundness relation $\mathsf{R}_{\mathsf{lax}}$ can be different from the (correctness) relation R. We are typically interested in $\mathsf{R} \subseteq \mathsf{R}_{\mathsf{lax}}$ and call $\mathsf{R}_{\mathsf{lax}}$ the *relaxed* relation.

An NIZK is *adaptively knowledge sound* for relation $\mathsf{R}_{\mathsf{lax}}$ if there exists a PPT algorithm Ext such that for any $\mathsf{crs} \in \{0,1\}^{\ell}$, given oracle access to any PPT adversary $\mathcal{A}$ (with explicit random tape ρ) that makes $Q_H = \mathsf{poly}(\lambda)$ random oracle queries, then for $(x, \pi) \leftarrow \mathcal{A}^{\mathsf{H}}(\mathsf{crs}; \rho)$, the extractor finds some $w \leftarrow \mathsf{Ext}(\mathsf{crs}, x, \pi, \rho, \vec{h})$ with $(x, w) \in \mathsf{R}_{\mathsf{lax}}$ with probability at least $\frac{\mu(\lambda) - \mathrm{negl}(\lambda)}{\mathsf{poly}(\lambda)}$. Here, $\mu(\lambda)$ is the probability that $\mathcal{A}$ outputs valid pairs (x, π) and $\vec{h}$ are the random oracle outputs in the run of $\mathcal{A}$.

An NIZK is *online-extractable* if for all PPT adversaries $\mathcal{A}$, there exists a PPT simulator SimCRS that outputs a trapdoor td and simulated $\overline{\mathsf{crs}}$ that is indistinguishable from some random $\mathsf{crs} \leftarrow \{0,1\}^{\ell}$, and a PPT extractor Ext, such that for any $Q_H = \mathsf{poly}(\lambda)$ and PPT adversary $\mathcal{A}$ that on input $\overline{\mathsf{crs}}$ makes at most Q_H random oracle queries and outputs statement-proof pairs $\{(x_i, \pi_i)\}_{i \in [Q_S]} \leftarrow \mathcal{A}^{\mathsf{H}}(\overline{\mathsf{crs}})$, Ext outputs $w_i \leftarrow \mathsf{Ext}(\overline{\mathsf{crs}}, \mathsf{td}, x_i, \pi_i)$ such that for all i it holds that $(x_i, w_i) \in \mathsf{R}$, and all proofs verify, with probability at least $\frac{\mu(\lambda) - \mathrm{negl}(\lambda)}{\mathsf{poly}(\lambda)}$. Here, $\mu(\lambda)$ denotes the probability that the proofs output by $\mathcal{A}$ verify correctly.

3 Optimizing the Fischlin Blind Signature

In this section, we provide an optimized generic construction of blind signatures compared with the Fischlin blind signature [28]. In particular, we relax the extractable (and perfect binding) commitment and multi-online extractable NIZK used as the central building block for the Fischlin blind signature by a computationally binding commitment and a standard rewinding-based NIZK built from a Σ-protocol satisfying f-unique extraction. As we show in Sect. 3.3, this relaxation allows us to minimize the sum of the communication and signature size. We construct a natural partially blind variant in the full version.

3.1 Construction

Our generic construction is based on the building blocks $(\mathsf{C}, \mathsf{S}, \Sigma)$ that satisfy some specific requirements. If $(\mathsf{C}, \mathsf{S}, \Sigma)$ satisfies these requirements, then we call it $\mathsf{BS}_{\mathsf{Rnd}}$-*suitable.*

Definition 2. ($\mathsf{BS}_{\mathsf{Rnd}}$**-Suitable** $(\mathsf{C}, \mathsf{S}, \Sigma)$). *The tuple of schemes* $(\mathsf{C}, \mathsf{S}, \Sigma)$ *are called* $\mathsf{BS}_{\mathsf{Rnd}}$-suitable, *if it holds that*

- C *is a correct and hiding* rerandomizable *commitment scheme with public parameter, message, randomness, and commitment spaces* $\{0,1\}^{\ell_{\mathsf{C}}}, \mathcal{C}_{\mathsf{msg}}, \mathcal{C}_{\mathsf{rnd}}$, *and* $\mathcal{C}_{\mathsf{com}}$, *respectively, such that* $\mathcal{C}_{\mathsf{msg}}$ *is efficiently sampleable and* $1/|\mathcal{C}_{\mathsf{msg}}| = \mathrm{negl}(\lambda)$,

- S *is a correct and* **euf-cma** *secure* deterministic *signature scheme with message space* $\mathcal{S}_{\mathsf{msg}}$ *that contains* $\mathcal{C}_{\mathsf{com}}$*, i.e.,* $\mathcal{C}_{\mathsf{com}} \subseteq \mathcal{S}_{\mathsf{msg}}$*. and we assume elements in* $\mathcal{S}_{\mathsf{msg}}$ *are efficiently checkable,*
- Σ *is a correct, HVZK,* 2*-special sound* Σ*-protocol with high min-entropy, and challenge space* $\mathcal{CH}$ *with* $1/|\mathcal{CH}| = \mathrm{negl}(\lambda)$ *for the relation*

$$\mathsf{R}_{\mathsf{rnd}} := \{x = (\mathsf{pp}, \mathsf{vk}, \overline{m}), w = (\mu, c, r) \mid \mathsf{C.Commit}(\mathsf{pp}, \overline{m}; r) = (c, r) \wedge \mathsf{S.Verify}(\mathsf{vk}, \mu, c) = 1\}.$$

We also require Σ *to be* f*-unique extraction where* $f(w) = c$*, i.e.,* f *outputs* c *and ignores* (μ, r)*.*

Let $(\mathsf{C}, \mathsf{S}, \Sigma)$ be $\mathsf{BS}_{\mathsf{Rnd}}$-suitable. Let $\mathsf{H}_{\mathsf{par}}, \mathsf{H}_{\mathsf{M}}, \mathsf{H}_{\beta}$ be a random oracles from $\{0,1\}^*$ into $\{0,1\}^{\ell_c}, \mathcal{C}_{\mathsf{msg}}, \mathcal{CH}$, respectively.

Construction. We present our blind signature $\mathsf{BS}_{\mathsf{Rnd}}$. Below, we assume that the verification key *implicitly* specifies the public parameter pp for C via $\mathsf{pp} = \mathsf{H}_{\mathsf{par}}(0)$. We assume pp is provided to all of the algorithms for readability.

- $\mathsf{BS}_{\mathsf{Rnd}}.\mathsf{KeyGen}(1^\lambda)$: samples $(\mathsf{vk}, \mathsf{sk}) \leftarrow \mathsf{S.KeyGen}(1^\lambda)$ and outputs verification key $\mathsf{bvk} = \mathsf{vk}$ and signing key $\mathsf{bsk} = \mathsf{sk}$.
- $\mathsf{BS}_{\mathsf{Rnd}}.\mathsf{User}(\mathsf{bvk}, m)$: sets $\overline{m} \leftarrow \mathsf{H}_{\mathsf{M}}(m)$ and outputs the commitment $c \in \mathcal{C}_{\mathsf{com}}$ generated via $(c, r) \leftarrow \mathsf{C.Commit}(\mathsf{pp}, \overline{m})$ as the first message and stores the randomness $\mathsf{st} = r \in \mathcal{C}_{\mathsf{rnd}}$.
- $\mathsf{BS}_{\mathsf{Rnd}}.\mathsf{Signer}(\mathsf{bsk}, c)$: checks if $c \in \mathcal{C}_{\mathsf{com}}$, samples a rerandomization randomness $\Delta r \leftarrow \mathcal{C}_{\mathsf{rnd}}$, rerandomizes the commitment c via $c' = \mathsf{C.RerandCom}(\mathsf{pp}, c, \Delta r)$, signs $\mu \leftarrow \mathsf{S.Sign}(\mathsf{sk}, c')$, and finally outputs the second message $\rho = (\mu, \Delta r)$.
- $\mathsf{BS}_{\mathsf{Rnd}}.\mathsf{Derive}(\mathsf{st}, \rho)$: parse $\mathsf{st} = r$, $\rho = (\mu, \Delta r)$ and checks $\Delta r \in \mathcal{C}_{\mathsf{rnd}}$. It then computes the randomized commitment $c'' = \mathsf{C.RerandCom}(\mathsf{pp}, c, \Delta r)$ and randomized randomness $r' \leftarrow \mathsf{C.RerandRand}(\mathsf{pp}, c, \overline{m}, r, \Delta r)$, and checks $\mathsf{S.Verify}(\mathsf{vk}, c'', \mu) = 1$ and $c'' = \mathsf{C.Commit}(\mathsf{pp}, \overline{m}; r')$. Finally, it outputs a signature $\sigma = \pi$, where $(\alpha, \mathsf{st}') \leftarrow \Sigma.\mathsf{Init}(x, w)$, $\beta \leftarrow \mathsf{H}_{\beta}(x, \alpha), \gamma \leftarrow \Sigma.\mathsf{Resp}(x, \mathsf{st}', \beta)$, $\pi = (\alpha, \beta, \gamma)$ with $x = (\mathsf{pp}, \mathsf{vk}, \overline{m})$, $w = (\mu, c'', r')$.
- $\mathsf{BS}_{\mathsf{Rnd}}.\mathsf{Verify}(\mathsf{bvk}, m, \sigma)$: parses $\sigma = \pi$ and $\pi = (\alpha, \beta, \gamma)$, sets $\overline{m} = \mathsf{H}_{\mathsf{M}}(m)$ and $x = (\mathsf{pp}, \mathsf{vk}, \overline{m})$, and outputs 1 if $\beta = \mathsf{H}_{\beta}(x, \alpha)$, $\Sigma.\mathsf{Verify}(x, \alpha, \beta, \gamma) = 1$, and otherwise outputs 0.

3.2 Correctness and Security

The correctness of $\mathsf{BS}_{\mathsf{Rnd}}$ follows directly from the correctness of the underlying schemes $(\mathsf{C}, \mathsf{S}, \Sigma)$. Blindness follows mainly from the HVZK property of Σ and the hiding property of C. The only thing to be aware of is that the user needs to check the validity of the rerandomized commitment c'' by computing a rerandomized randomness using the randomness r used to compute the original commitment c. In order to invoke the hiding property of C on c, we rely on the correctness of the randomization property so that the reduction no longer needs to check the validity of c''.

The main technical challenge is the proof of one-more unforgeability. The proof is given below, for an overview see Sect. 1. We refer to the full version for proofs of correctness and blindness.

Theorem 1. *The blind signature* $\mathsf{BS}_{\mathsf{Rnd}}$ *is correct, blind under malicious keys and one-more unforgeable if the schemes* $(\mathsf{C}, \mathsf{S}, \Sigma)$ *are* $\mathsf{BS}_{\mathsf{Rnd}}$*-suitable.*

Proof. Let $\mathcal{A}$ be a PPT adversary against one-more unforgeability. Denote by Q_S the number of signing queries, by Q_M the number of H_{M} queries, and by Q_H the number of H_β queries. Recall that we model $\mathsf{H}_{\mathsf{par}}$, H_{M}, and H_β as random oracles, where we assume without loss of generality that $\mathcal{A}$ never repeats queries. In the end of the interaction with $\mathcal{A}$, that is after Q_S signing queries, $\mathcal{A}$ outputs Q_S+1 forgeries $\{(m_i, \sigma_i)\}_{i\in[Q_S+1]}$. We write $\sigma_i = \pi_i$ and denote by c_i the Q_S first message queries to $\mathsf{BS}_{\mathsf{Rnd}}.\mathsf{Signer}(\mathsf{bsk}, \cdot)$ issued by $\mathcal{A}$. Note that if $\mathcal{A}$ is successful, then we have $\Sigma.\mathsf{Verify}(x_i, \alpha_i, \beta_i, \gamma_i) = 1$ and $\beta_i = \mathsf{H}_\beta(x_i, \alpha_i)$ for $\overline{m}_i = \mathsf{H}_{\mathsf{M}}(m_i)$, $x_i = (\mathsf{pp}, \mathsf{vk}, \overline{m}_i)$, and $\pi_i = (\alpha_i, \beta_i, \gamma_i)$. We first slightly alter the real game and remove subtle conditions to make the later proofs easier. We denote by $\mathsf{Adv}_{\mathcal{A}}^{\mathsf{H}_i}(\lambda)$ the advantage of $\mathcal{A}$ in Hybrid i for $i \in \{0, 1\}$.

- Hybrid 0 is identical to the real game.
- Hybrid 1 is the same as Hybrid 0, except it aborts if there is a collision in H_{M} or H_β, or there is some (x_i, α_i) for $i \in [Q_S + 1]$ that was never queried to H_β.

It suffices to upper bound the abort probability. A collision in H_{M} (resp. H_β) happens with probability at most $Q_M^2/|\mathcal{C}_{\mathsf{msg}}|$ (resp. $Q_H^2/|\mathcal{CH}|$) (which follows for example from a union bound). Moreover, the probability that some fixed β_i of $\mathcal{A}$'s output equals to $\mathsf{H}_\beta(x_i, \alpha_i)$ is exactly $1/|\mathcal{CH}|$, if (x_i, α_i) was never queried to H_β. Thus, it follows that $\mathsf{Adv}_{\mathcal{A}}^{\mathsf{H}_0}(\lambda) \le \mathsf{Adv}_{\mathcal{A}}^{\mathsf{H}_1}(\lambda) + \frac{Q_M^2}{|\mathcal{C}_{\mathsf{msg}}|} + \frac{Q_H^2+1}{|\mathcal{CH}|} = \mathsf{Adv}_{\mathcal{A}}^{\mathsf{H}_1}(\lambda) + \mathrm{negl}(\lambda)$.

Description of Wrapper Algorithm $\mathcal{B}$. We now present a wrapper algorithm $\mathcal{B}$ that simulates the interaction between the challenger $\mathcal{G}$ and $\mathcal{A}$ in Hybrid 1. Looking ahead we apply a generalization of the standard forking lemma on $\mathcal{B}$ to extract the witnesses from all the proof (i.e. forgery) output by $\mathcal{A}$.

Notice that $\mathcal{G}$ is deterministic once the keys $(\mathsf{vk}, \mathsf{sk})$ of the (deterministic) signature scheme S, the Q_S rerandomization randomness in $\mathcal{C}_{\mathsf{rnd}}$, and the outputs of the random oracles $\mathsf{H}_{\mathsf{par}}, \mathsf{H}_{\mathsf{M}}, \mathsf{H}_\beta$ are determined. Since $\mathsf{H}_{\mathsf{par}}$ is only used to generate the public parameter pp of the commitment scheme, we assume without loss of generality that only pp is given to $\mathcal{A}$ rather than access to $\mathsf{H}_{\mathsf{par}}$. We use coin to denote all the Q_M outputs of H_{M} and the random coins used by $\mathcal{A}$. We use $\vec{h} = (\widehat{\beta}_i, \Delta r_i)_{i\in[Q_H+Q_S]} \in (\mathcal{CH} \times \mathcal{C}_{\mathsf{rnd}})^{Q_H+Q_S}$ to explicitly denote the list that will be used to simulate the outputs of H_β and rerandomziation randomness sampled by $\mathcal{G}$. Here, we note that $\vec{h}$ is deliberately defined redundantly since $\mathcal{G}$ only needs Q_H hash outputs and Q_S rerandomziation randomness, rather than $Q_H + Q_S$ of them each. We also use $\widehat{\beta} \in \mathcal{CH}$ to denote the output of H_β to distinguish between the hash value β included in $\mathcal{A}$'s forgeries. We then define $\mathcal{B}$ as an algorithm that has oracle access to $\mathsf{S}.\mathsf{Sign}(\mathsf{sk}, \cdot)$ as follows:

$\mathcal{B}^{\mathsf{S.Sign}(\mathsf{sk},\cdot)}(\mathsf{pp}, \mathsf{vk}, \vec{h}; \mathsf{coin})$: On input pp, vk, and $\vec{h} \in (\mathcal{CH} \times \mathcal{C}_{\mathsf{rnd}})^{Q_H+Q_S}$, $\mathcal{B}$ simulates the interaction between the challenger $\mathcal{G}$ and $\mathcal{A}$ in Hybrid 1. $\mathcal{B}$ invokes $\mathcal{A}$ on the randomness included in coin and simulates $\mathcal{G}$, where it runs the same code as $\mathcal{G}$ except for the following differences:

- It uses the provided pp and vk rather than generating it on its own;
- All Q_M random oracle queries to $\mathsf{H_M}$ are answered using the hash values include in coin;
- On the i-th ($i \in [Q_H]$) random oracle query to H_β, it retrieves an unused $(\widehat{\beta}_k, \Delta r_k)$ with the smallest index $k \in [Q_H + Q_S]$ and outputs $\widehat{\beta}_k$ and discards Δr_k;
- On the i-th ($i \in [Q_S]$) first message $c_i \in \mathcal{C}_{\mathsf{com}}$ from $\mathcal{A}$, it retrieves an unused $(\widehat{\beta}_k, \Delta r_k)$ with the smallest index $k \in [Q_H + Q_S]$ and discards $\widehat{\beta}_k$. It then computes $c'_i = \mathsf{C.RerandCom}(\mathsf{pp}, c_i, \Delta r_k)$, queries the signing oracle on c'_i, obtains $\mu_i \leftarrow \mathsf{S.Sign}(\mathsf{sk}, c'_i)$, and returns the second message $\rho_i = (\mu_i, \Delta r_k)$.

At the end of the game when $\mathcal{A}$ outputs the forgeries, $\mathcal{B}$ checks if the forgeries are valid and the added condition in Hybrid 1. If the check does not pass, then $\mathcal{B}$ outputs $((0)_{i\in[Q_S+1]}, \perp)$, i.e., Q_S+1 zeros followed by a $\perp$. Otherwise, $\mathcal{B}$ finds the indices $I_i \in [Q_H + Q_S]$ such that $\mathsf{H}_\beta(x_i, \alpha_i) = \beta_i = \widehat{\beta}_{I_i}$ for $i \in [Q_S + 1]$, which are guaranteed to exist uniquely due to the modification we made in Hybrid 1. It then sets $\Lambda = (x_i, \alpha_i, \beta_i, \gamma_i)_{i\in[Q_S+1]}$ and outputs $((I_i)_{i\in[Q_S+1]}, \Lambda)$. It can be checked that $\mathcal{B}$ perfectly simulates the view of the challenger $\mathcal{G}$ in Hybrid 1. Therefore, $\mathcal{B}$ outputs $\Lambda \neq \perp$ with probability $\mathsf{Adv}^{\mathsf{H}_1}_{\mathcal{A}}(\lambda)$.

Description of Forking Algorithm $\mathsf{F}_\mathcal{B}$. We now define a generalization of the standard forking algorithm F so that F keeps on rewinding $\mathcal{B}$ until some condition is satisfied. Concretely, F takes as input (pp, vk), has oracle access to $\mathsf{S.Sign}(\mathsf{sk}, \cdot)$, and invokes $\mathcal{B}$ internally as depicted in algorithm 1, where the number of repetition T is defined below.

We show that if $\mathcal{A}$ succeeds in breaking one-more unforgeability in Hybrid 1 with non-negligible probability, then we can set a specific number of repetition T so that the forking algorithm $\mathsf{F}_\mathcal{B}$ terminates in polynomial time and succeeds in outputting a non-$\perp$ with non-negligible probability. Formally, we have the following lemma.

Lemma 1. *Let* $\epsilon = \mathsf{Adv}^{H_1}_{\mathcal{A}}(\lambda)$. *Then, if we set* $T = \left(\frac{\epsilon}{(Q_H+Q_S)(Q_S+2)^2}\right)^{-1} \cdot \log(2Q_S + 2)$, $\mathsf{F}_\mathcal{B}$ *outputs a non-*$\perp$ *with probability at least* $\frac{\epsilon}{2(Q_S+2)^2}$.

In particular, if ϵ *is non-negligible, then* $T = \mathsf{poly}(\lambda)$. *Moreover, the running time of* $\mathsf{F}_\mathcal{B}$ *is at most (roughly) a factor* $T\cdot(Q_S+1)+1$ *more of* $\mathcal{B}$ *(or equivalently* $\mathcal{A}$*), so* $\mathsf{F}_\mathcal{B}$ *runs in polynomial time.*

Algorithm 1. Description of the forking algorithm $\mathsf{F}_{\mathcal{B}}^{\mathsf{S.Sign}(\mathsf{sk},\cdot)}(\mathsf{pp}, \mathsf{vk})$

Pick coin for $\mathcal{B}$ at random.
$\vec{h} \leftarrow (\mathcal{CH} \times \mathcal{C}_{\mathsf{rnd}})^{Q_H+Q_S}$
$((I_i)_{i\in[Q_S+1]}, \Lambda) \leftarrow \mathcal{B}^{\mathsf{S.Sign}(\mathsf{sk},\cdot)}(\mathsf{pp}, \mathsf{vk}, \vec{h}; \mathsf{coin})$
if $\Lambda = \perp$ **then**
  return $\perp$ ▷ Return fail.
$D := ()$ ▷ Prepare empty list.
for $j \in [Q_S + 1]$ **do**
  $(c, \mathsf{flag}) := (1, \perp)$
  while $c \in [T] \wedge \neg\mathsf{flag}$ **do**
    $\vec{h}^{(c)}_{j,\geq I_j} \leftarrow (\mathcal{CH} \times \mathcal{C}_{\mathsf{rnd}})^{Q_H+Q_S-I_j+1}$
    $\vec{h}^{(c)}_j := \vec{h}_{<I_j} \| \vec{h}^{(c)}_{j,\geq I_j}$
    $((I^{(c)}_{j,i})_{i\in[Q_S+1]}, \Lambda^{(c)}_j) \leftarrow \mathcal{B}^{\mathsf{S.Sign}(\mathsf{sk},\cdot)}(\mathsf{pp}, \mathsf{vk}, \vec{h}^{(c)}_j; \mathsf{coin})$
    if $I^{(c)}_{j,j} = I_j$ **then**
      $D = D \cup (j, I_j, \Lambda^{(c)}_j)$
      $\mathsf{flag} = \top$ ▷ Break from while loop.
    $c = c + 1$
if $|D| < Q_S + 1$ **then** ▷ Check if $\mathcal{B}$ succeeds in all $Q_S + 1$ run.
  return $\perp$ ▷ Return fail.
return (Λ, D)

Proof. Assume $\mathcal{B}$ outputs a valid $\Lambda = (x_i, \alpha_i, \beta_i, \gamma_i)_{i\in[Q_S+1]}$ in the first execution and denote this event as E. For $i \in [Q_S + 1]$, we denote the tuple $(x_i, \alpha_i, \beta_i, \gamma_i)$ as the i-th *forgery*. For any $(i, k) \in [Q_S + 1] \times [Q_H + Q_S]$, we denote $\mathsf{E}_{i,k}$ as the event that forgery is associated to the k-th hash query, i.e., the k-th entry of $\vec{h} \in (\mathcal{CH} \times \mathcal{C}_{\mathsf{rnd}})^{Q_H+Q_S}$ includes β_i. Here, note that $\forall i \in [Q_S + 1]$, we have $\sum_{k\in[Q_H+Q_S]} \Pr[\mathsf{E}_{i,k}] = 1$. We define the set P_i as

$$P_i = \left\{ k \;\middle|\; \Pr[\mathsf{E}_{i,k} \mid \mathsf{E}] \geq \frac{1}{(Q_H + Q_S)(Q_S + 2)} \right\},$$

where for any $k \in P_i$, we have $\Pr[\mathsf{E}_{i,k}] \geq \frac{\epsilon}{(Q_H+Q_S)(Q_S+2)}$. Let us define $\mathsf{E}^{\mathsf{good}}_i = \bigvee_{k\in P_i} \mathsf{E}_{i,k}$. Then, we have $\Pr\left[\mathsf{E}^{\mathsf{good}}_i \;\middle|\; \mathsf{E}\right] \geq \frac{Q_S+1}{Q_S+2}$, since there are at most $(Q_H + Q_S)$ possible values of k's not in P_i and they can only account to a probability at most $(Q_H + Q_S) \times \frac{1}{(Q_H+Q_S)(Q_S+2)} = \frac{1}{Q_S+2}$.

Next, for any $(i, k) \in [Q_S + 1] \times P_i$, let us define $X_{i,k} = R_{\mathsf{coin}} \times (\mathcal{CH} \times \mathcal{C}_{\mathsf{rnd}})^{k-1}$ and $Y_{i,k} = (\mathcal{CH} \times \mathcal{C}_{\mathsf{rnd}})^{Q_H+Q_S-k+1}$, where R_{coin} denotes the randomness space of coin. Here, note that $(\mathsf{x}_i, \vec{h}_{\geq k}) \in X_{i,k} \times Y_{i,k}$ can be parsed appropriately to be $(\mathsf{coin}, \vec{h})$, and defines all the inputs of $\mathcal{B}$, where we assume a fixed $(\mathsf{pp}, \mathsf{vk})$. We further define $A_{i,k} \subseteq X_{i,k} \times Y_{i,k}$ to be the set of inputs that triggers event $\mathsf{E}_{i,k}$. Then using the splitting lemma with $\alpha = \frac{Q_S+1}{Q_S+2} \cdot \frac{\epsilon}{(Q_H+Q_S)(Q_S+2)}$, there exists a set $B_{i,k} \subset X_{i,k} \times Y_{i,k}$ such that

$$B_{i,k} = \left\{ (\mathsf{x}_i, \vec{h}_{\geq k}) \in X_{i,k} \times Y_{i,k} \;\middle|\; \Pr_{\vec{h'}_{\geq k} \leftarrow Y_{i,k}} \left[(\mathsf{x}_i, \vec{h'}_{\geq k}) \in A_{i,k} \right] \geq \frac{\epsilon}{(Q_H + Q_S)(Q_S + 2)^2} \right\}, \tag{1}$$

and

$$\Pr_{(\mathsf{x}_i, \vec{h'}_{\geq k}) \leftarrow X_{i,k} \times Y_{i,k}} \left[(\mathsf{x}_i, \vec{h}_{\geq k}) \in B_{i,k} \;\middle|\; (\mathsf{x}, \vec{h}_{\geq k}) \in A_{i,k} \right] \geq \frac{Q_S + 1}{Q_S + 2}. \tag{2}$$

We are now ready to evaluate the success probability of the forking algorithm $\mathsf{F}_{\mathcal{B}}$. With probability ϵ, $\mathcal{B}$ outputs $((I_i)_{i \in [Q_S+1]}, \Lambda)$ in the first execution on input $(\mathsf{coin}, \vec{h}) \in R_{\mathsf{coin}} \times (\mathcal{CH} \times \mathcal{C}_{\mathsf{rnd}})^{Q_H + Q_S}$. Then the probability that event $\mathsf{E}_i^{\mathsf{good}}$ occurrs for all $i \in [Q_S + 1]$ is at least

$$\Pr\left[\forall i \in [Q_S + 1],\ \mathsf{E}_i^{\mathsf{good}} \middle| \mathsf{E} \right] \geq 1 - \sum_{i \in [Q_S+1]} \Pr\left[\neg \mathsf{E}_i^{\mathsf{good}} \middle| \mathsf{E} \right] \geq \frac{1}{Q_S + 2},$$

where the first inequality follows from the union bound and the second inequality follows from $\Pr\left[\mathsf{E}_i^{\mathsf{good}} \middle| \mathsf{E} \right] \geq \frac{Q_S+1}{Q_S+2}$.

Then, from eq. (2) and following the same union bound argument, $\mathsf{F}_{\mathcal{B}}$ samples a good input such that $(\mathsf{coin}, \vec{h}) \in B_{i,I_i}$ for all $i \in [Q_S + 1]$ conditioned on $\mathsf{E}_i^{\mathsf{good}}$ for all $i \in [Q_S + 1]$ with probability at least $\frac{1}{(Q_S+2)}$. Therefore, by eq. 1, if $\mathsf{F}_{\mathcal{B}}$ resamples $\vec{h}_{i, \geq I_i} \in Y_{i,I_i} = (\mathcal{CH} \times \mathcal{C}_{\mathsf{rnd}})^{Q_H + Q_S - I_i + 1}$ conditioned on the set B_{i,I_i}, $\mathcal{B}$ succeeds on input $(\mathsf{coin}, \vec{h}_{i,<I_i} \| \vec{h}_{i,\geq I_i})$ with probability at least $\frac{\epsilon}{(Q_H+Q_S)(Q_S+2)^2}$. Conditioning on sampling an input $(\mathsf{coin}, \vec{h}) \in B_{i,I_i}$ for all $i \in [Q_S + 1]$ and noting the independence of each rewinding, the probability that $\mathcal{B}$ succeeds in all j-th rewinding for $j \in [Q_S + 1]$ is at least

$$\begin{aligned} \left(1 - \left(1 - \frac{\epsilon}{(Q_H + Q_S)(Q_S + 2)^2} \right)^T \right)^{Q_S+1} &\geq \left(1 - \frac{1}{e^{\log(2Q_S+2)}} \right)^{Q_S+1} \\ &= \left(1 - \frac{1}{2(Q_S + 1)} \right)^{Q_S+1} \geq \frac{1}{2}. \end{aligned}$$

Collecting all the bounds, we conclude that $\mathsf{F}_{\mathcal{B}}$ succeeds with probability at least $\frac{\epsilon}{2(Q_S+2)^2}$ as desired. Moreover, the running time of $\mathsf{F}_{\mathcal{B}}$ is roughly the same as running $\mathcal{B}$ for at most $T \cdot (Q_S + 1) + 1$ times, where the runtime of $\mathcal{B}$ is roughly the same as the runtime of $\mathcal{A}$.

Using $\mathsf{F}_{\mathcal{B}}$ to Break Binding of C or `euf-cma` of S. We are now ready to finish the proof. Assume $\epsilon = \mathsf{Adv}_{\mathcal{A}}^{\mathsf{H}_1}(\lambda)$ is non-negligible. We use $\mathsf{F}_{\mathcal{B}}$ to extract the witnesses from the proofs output by $\mathcal{A}$ with non-negligible probability and show that such witnesses can be used to break either the binding of C or the `euf-cma` security of S. Thus establishing that $\epsilon = \mathsf{negl}(\lambda)$ by contradiction.

We define adversary $\mathcal{A}_{\mathsf{C},\mathsf{S}}$ on both the binding property of C and the $\mathtt{euf\text{-}cma}$ property of S as follows. Initially, $\mathcal{A}_{\mathsf{C},\mathsf{S}}$ obtains pp from the binding challenger. Further, she receives vk and oracle access to a signing oracle $\mathsf{S.Sign}(\mathsf{sk},\cdot)$ from the $\mathtt{euf\text{-}cma}$ challenger. Then, she runs the forking algorithm $R \leftarrow \mathsf{F}_{\mathcal{B}}^{\mathsf{S.Sign}(\mathsf{sk},\cdot)}(\mathsf{pp},\mathsf{vk})$. She checks $R \neq \bot$, and parses $R = (\Lambda, D)$, where $\Lambda = (x_i, \alpha_i, \beta_i, \gamma_i)_{i\in[Q_S+1]}$ and $D = (j, I_j, \Lambda_j)_{j\in[Q_S+1]}$. Due to Lemma 1, $\mathsf{F}_{\mathcal{B}}$ runs in polynomial time and has non-negligible success probability. Below, we describe the second part of $\mathcal{A}_{\mathsf{C},\mathsf{S}}$ and analyze its success probability conditioned on $\mathsf{F}_{\mathcal{B}}$ succeeding. (If $R = \bot$, then $\mathcal{A}_{\mathsf{C},\mathsf{S}}$ outputs $\bot$ and aborts.)

For $j \in [Q_S + 1]$, we denote by $(x'_j, \alpha'_j, \beta'_j, \gamma'_j)$ the j-th element of the tuple Λ_j. Moreover, note that the same coin and values $(\widehat{\beta}_1, \Delta r_1), \dots (\widehat{\beta}_{I_j-1}, \Delta r_{I_j-1})$ are used for the initial run of $\mathcal{B}$ and the run of $\mathcal{B}$ where $\mathcal{B}$ outputs Λ_j. Thus, we have for all $j \in [Q_S + 1]$ that $(x_i, \alpha_i) = (x'_i, \alpha'_i)$. Moreover, we have $\widehat{\beta}_{I_j} \neq \widehat{\beta}_{j,I_j}$, or equivalently $\beta_j \neq \beta'_j$ for all $j \in [Q_S + 1]$ with probability at least $1 - \frac{Q_S+1}{|\mathcal{CH}|} = 1 - \mathrm{negl}(\lambda)$ since each hash outputs are sampled uniformly and independently at random. This allows $\mathcal{A}_{\mathsf{C},\mathsf{S}}$ to invoke 2-special soundness of Σ with overwhelming probability. For all $i \in [Q_S + 1]$, she runs Ext on $(x_i, (\alpha_i, \beta_i, \gamma_i), (\alpha_i, \beta'_i, \gamma'_i))$ to extract a witness $w_i = (\mu_i, c_i, r_i)$ such that $\mathsf{C.Commit}(\mathsf{pp}, \overline{m}_i; r_i) = c_i \wedge \mathsf{S.Verify}(\mathsf{vk}, \mu_i, c_i) = 1$, where $x_i = (\mathsf{pp}, \mathsf{vk}, \overline{m}_i)$.

If there exists distinct $i, j \in [Q_S + 1]$ with $c_i = c_j$, $\mathcal{A}_{\mathsf{C},\mathsf{S}}$ sends $(\overline{m}_i, \overline{m}_j, r_i, r_j)$ to the binding security game of C. Note that due to the check in Hybrid 1, the $(\overline{m}_i)_{i\in[Q_S+1]}$ are pairwise distinct, in particular $\overline{m}_i \neq \overline{m}_j$ but $\mathsf{C.Commit}(\mathsf{pp}, \overline{m}_i; r_i) = \mathsf{C.Commit}(\mathsf{pp}, \overline{m}_j; r_j)$. However, due to the binding property of C, this can happen with only negligible probability. Thus, the extracted commitments $(c_i)_{i\in[Q_S+1]}$ must be distinct with overwhelming probability.

In such a case, there must be at least one $i^* \in [Q_S + 1]$ such that c_i^* was never queried to the signing oracle $\mathsf{S.Sign}(\mathsf{sk},\cdot)$ *in the first execution* of $\mathcal{B}$ or equivalently of $\mathcal{A}$. This is because due to the one-more unforgeability game, $\mathcal{A}$ only queries the signing oracle Q_S times. Thus, $\mathcal{A}_{\mathsf{C},\mathsf{S}}$ finds such i^* with the smallest index and outputs (μ_{i^*}, c_i^*) as a forgery against the $\mathtt{euf\text{-}cma}$ security of S.

It remains to show that what $\mathcal{A}_{\mathsf{C},\mathsf{S}}$ output is a valid forgery, i.e., $\mathcal{B}$ never queried c_i^* to the signing oracle in any of the *rewound executions*. To argue this, we first show that all the extracted commitments $(c_i)_{i\in[Q_S+1]}$ are fixed *after the first execution ends* due to f-unique extraction. For any $(x_i, \tau_i := (\alpha_i, \beta_i, \gamma_i)) \in \Lambda$ defined in the first execution of $\mathcal{B}$, conditioning on $\mathsf{F}_{\mathcal{B}}$ succeeding, another valid transcript $(x_i, \tau'_i := (\alpha_i, \beta'_i, \gamma'_i)) \in \Lambda_i$ with $\beta_i \neq \beta'_i$ is guaranteed to exist with overwhelming probability. Due to f-unique extraction, for any such valid transcript the value $f(\mathsf{Ext}(x_i, \tau_i, \tau'_i)) = c_i$ is identical, where recall f simply outputs the commitment included in the witness. Put differently, conditioning on $\mathsf{F}_{\mathcal{B}}$ succeeding, (x_i, τ_i) uniquely defines c_i with overwhelming probability. We emphasize that c_i does not need to be efficiently computable given only (x_i, τ_i); we only care if c_i is determined by (x_i, τ_i) in a statistical sense.

Now, assume $\mathcal{B}$ queried c_i^* to the signing oracle in one of the rewound executions. This means $\mathcal{A}$ outputs some c^* to $\mathcal{B}$ (or equivalently the simulated challenger $\mathcal{G}$ in Hybrid 1) and $\mathcal{B}$ computed $c_i^* = \mathsf{C.RerandCom}(\mathsf{pp}, c^*, \Delta r^*)$, where Δr^* is a fresh randomness sampled by $\mathsf{F}_{\mathcal{B}}$ to be used in the rewound execution. However, this cannot happen with all but negligible probability due to the rerandomizability of C since we have established above that Δr^* is sampled independently from c_i^*. Since there are at most $T \cdot (Q_S + 1)$ rewound executions, the probability that $\mathcal{B}$ queries c_i^* to the signing oracle during in one of the rewound execution is bounded by $T \cdot (Q_S + 1) \cdot \mathrm{negl}(\lambda) = \mathrm{negl}(\lambda)$, where we use $T = \mathsf{poly}(\lambda)$ due to Lemma 1.

Thus, with overwhelming probability, what $\mathcal{A}_{\mathsf{C},\mathsf{S}}$ output is a valid forgery against the euf-cma security of S. However, due to the hardness of euf-cma security of S, this cannot happen with all but negligible probability. Combining all the arguments, we conclude that $\epsilon = \mathsf{Adv}_{\mathcal{A}}^{\mathrm{H}_1}(\lambda)$ is negligible. This completes the proof.

Remark 1 (Removing the Rerandomizability Property). As briefly noted in our technical overview, an alternative approach to using rerandomizable commitment is to let the signer (i.e., $\mathsf{BS_{Rnd}.Signer}$) sample a random string rand and run $\mu \leftarrow \mathsf{S.Sign}(\mathsf{sk}, c \| \mathsf{rand})$ instead of $\mu \leftarrow \mathsf{S.Sign}(\mathsf{sk}, c')$, where $c' = \mathsf{C.RerandCom}(\mathsf{pp}, c, \Delta r)$ is the rerandomized commitment. The signer then sends $\rho = (\mu, \mathsf{rand})$ as the second message instead of $\rho = (\mu, \Delta r)$. By observing that rand has an identical effect as Δr in the security proof, it can be checked that the same proof can be used to show blindness and one-more unforgeability of this modified protocol. While this approach works for any commitment scheme, we chose not to since it requires a slightly larger NIZK proof due to the enlarged signing space of the underlying signature scheme S.

3.3 Instantiation

We describe briefly how we instantiate the schemes $(\mathsf{C}, \mathsf{S}, \Sigma)$ in the asymmetric pairing setting. More details can be found in Sect. 1.3 and in the full version. For C, we choose Pedersen commitments in $\mathbb{G}_1$ of the form $c = g_1^{\overline{m}} \mathsf{pp}^r$, which are naturally rerandomizable and consist of a single element in $\mathbb{G}_1$.

For the signature scheme S, we use a variant of the Kiltz-Pan-Wee (KPW) structure-preserving signature (SPS) scheme [43] in the asymmetric pairing setting. The message space of KPW is $\mathbb{G}_1^{\ell}$, where $\ell \in \mathbb{N}$ is the message length.

Any SPS must contain at least three group elements, and at least one in each $\mathbb{G}_2$ and in $\mathbb{G}_1$ [1]. But as the bit size of elements in $\mathbb{G}_2$ is larger than the bit size of elements in $\mathbb{G}_1$ and $\mathbb{Z}_p$, removing elements in $\mathbb{G}_2$ in the signature is desirable. For $\mathsf{BS_{Rnd}}$, we do not require the full structure-preserving property of KPW, as we can design efficient Σ-protocols for signature verification, even if the signature contains elements in $\mathbb{Z}_p$.

Indeed, KPW signatures contain an element σ_4 in $\mathbb{G}_2$. We observe that we can safely replace σ_4 with its discrete logarithm τ. Further, we can omit two more elements in $\mathbb{G}_1$ for free, as they can be recomputed via τ and the remaining signature elements.

Our optimized variant is given below.

- $\mathsf{S_{KPW}}.\mathsf{KeyGen}(1^\lambda)$: samples $a, b \leftarrow \mathbb{Z}_p$ and sets $\boldsymbol{A} \leftarrow (1,a)^\top$ and $\boldsymbol{B} \leftarrow (1,b)^\top$. It samples $\boldsymbol{K} \leftarrow \mathbb{Z}_p^{(\ell+1)\times 2}$, $\boldsymbol{K}_0$, $\boldsymbol{K}_1 \leftarrow \mathbb{Z}_p^{2\times 2}$ and sets $\boldsymbol{C} \leftarrow \boldsymbol{K}\boldsymbol{A}$. It sets $(\boldsymbol{C}_0, \boldsymbol{C}_1) \leftarrow (\boldsymbol{K}_0\boldsymbol{A}, \boldsymbol{K}_1\boldsymbol{A})$, $(\boldsymbol{P}_0, \boldsymbol{P}_1) \leftarrow (\boldsymbol{B}^\top \boldsymbol{K}_0, \boldsymbol{B}^\top \boldsymbol{K}_1)$, $\mathsf{vk} \leftarrow ([\boldsymbol{C}_0]_2, [\boldsymbol{C}_1]_2, [\boldsymbol{C}]_2, [\boldsymbol{A}]_2)$; and $\mathsf{sk} \leftarrow (\boldsymbol{K}, [\boldsymbol{P}_0]_1, [\boldsymbol{P}_1]_1, [\boldsymbol{B}]_1)$. It outputs $(\mathsf{vk}, \mathsf{sk})$.
- $\mathsf{S_{KPW}}.\mathsf{Sign}(\mathsf{sk}, [\boldsymbol{m}]_1)$: samples $r, \tau \leftarrow \mathbb{Z}_p$ and sets $\sigma_1 \leftarrow [(1, \boldsymbol{m}^\top)\boldsymbol{K} + r(\boldsymbol{P}_0 + \tau \boldsymbol{P}_1)]_1 \in \mathbb{G}_1^2$, $\sigma_2 \leftarrow [r\boldsymbol{B}^\top]_1 \in \mathbb{G}_1^2$, and $\sigma_3 \leftarrow \tau \in \mathbb{Z}_p$. It outputs $(\sigma_1, \sigma_2, \sigma_3)$.
- $\mathsf{S_{KPW}}.\mathsf{Verify}(\mathsf{vk}, [\boldsymbol{m}]_1, (\sigma_1, \sigma_2, \sigma_3))$: checks $e(\sigma_1, [\boldsymbol{A}]_2) = e([(1, \boldsymbol{m}^\top)]_1, [\boldsymbol{C}]_2) \cdot e(\sigma_2, [\boldsymbol{C}_0]_2 \cdot \tau [\boldsymbol{C}_1]_2)$.

We show that $\mathsf{S_{KPW}}$ is `euf-cma` under the SXDH assumption in the full version. The proof relies on the computational core lemma of [44]. $\mathsf{S_{KPW}}$ can be made deterministic via a pseudorandom function.

For an efficient instantiation of the Σ-protocol Σ, we refer to the full version. In the resulting blind signature $\mathsf{BS_{Rnd}}$, the user sends 1 element in $\mathbb{G}_1$ and 1 element in $\mathbb{Z}_p$, the signer sends 4 elements in $\mathbb{G}_1$ and 1 element in $\mathbb{Z}_p$ and the final signature contains 6 elements in $\mathbb{G}_1$ and 5 elements in $\mathbb{Z}_p$. The total communication is 303 Byte and signatures are of size 447 Byte for $\lambda = 128$.

4 Blind Signatures Based on Boneh-Boyen Signature

In this section, we provide a blind signature based on randomizable signatures. Compared to the optimized generic construction of the Fischlin blind signature in Sect. 3, the resulting signature size is much smaller since it only consists of one signature of the underlying randomizable signature scheme. The construction also relies on an online-extractable NIZK which can be instantiated efficiently by carefully combining Bulletproofs and another NIZK for an ElGamal commitment (see the full version). In the full version we show how to adapt the scheme for a partially blind variant, where we modify the Boneh-Boyen signature [12,14] in order to embed the common message into the verification key.

4.1 Construction

We focus on the asymmetric pairing setting. We note that there is also a natural variant of this scheme in the symmetric setting and we omit details. First, we recall the Boneh-Boyen signatures [12,14] in the asymmetric setting. While this is implicit in our proof, we note the following is known to be selectively secure in the standard model under the CDH assumption:

- $\mathsf{S_{BB}}.\mathsf{KeyGen}(1^\lambda)$: samples $\alpha, \beta, \gamma \leftarrow \mathbb{Z}_p$, and sets $u_1 = g_1^\alpha, u_2 = g_2^\alpha, h_1 = g_1^\gamma, h_2 = g_2^\gamma, v = e(g_1, g_2)^{\alpha\beta}$, and outputs $\mathsf{vk} = (u_1, u_2, h_1, h_2, v)$ and $\mathsf{sk} = g_1^{\alpha\beta}$,
- $\mathsf{S_{BB}}.\mathsf{Sign}(\mathsf{sk}, m)$: samples $r \in \mathbb{Z}_p$ and outputs $(\sigma_1, \sigma_2) = (\mathsf{sk} \cdot (u_1^m h_1)^r, g_1^r) \in \mathbb{G}_1^2$,
- $\mathsf{S_{BB}}.\mathsf{Verify}(\mathsf{vk}, m, (\sigma_1, \sigma_2))$: outputs 1 if $e(\sigma_1, g_2) = v \cdot e(\sigma_2, u_2^m h_2)$, and otherwise outputs 0.

Let Π be an online-extractable NIZK proof system, with random oracle $\mathsf{H}_{\mathsf{zk}} : \{0,1\}^* \mapsto \{0,1\}^{\ell_{\mathsf{zk}}}$ and common reference string crs of length ℓ_{crs} for the relation

$$\mathsf{R}_{\mathsf{bb}} := \{x = (c, u_1, g_1), w = (\overline{m}, s) \mid c = u_1^{\overline{m}} \cdot g_1^s\}.$$

Let $\mathsf{H}_\mathsf{M}, \mathsf{H}_{\mathsf{crs}}$ be a random oracles mapping into $\mathbb{Z}_p, \{0,1\}^{\ell_{\mathsf{crs}}}$ respectively.

Construction. We present our blind signatures based on S_{BB}, where we assume that $\mathsf{crs} = \mathsf{H}_{\mathsf{crs}}(0)$ is provided to all of the algorithms for readability.

- $\mathsf{BS}_{\mathsf{BB}}.\mathsf{KeyGen}(1^\lambda)$: outputs $(\mathsf{bvk}, \mathsf{bsk}) \leftarrow \mathsf{S}_{\mathsf{BB}}.\mathsf{KeyGen}(1^\lambda)$, where $\mathsf{bvk} = (u_1, u_2, h_1, h_2, v)$ with $u_1 = g_1^\alpha, u_2 = g_2^\alpha, h_1 = g_1^\gamma, h_2 = g_2^\gamma, v = e(g_1, g_2)^{\alpha\beta}$ and $\mathsf{bsk} = g_1^{\alpha\beta}$.
- $\mathsf{BS}_{\mathsf{BB}}.\mathsf{User}(\mathsf{bvk}, m)$: checks validity of the verification key bvk via $e(u_1, g_2) = e(g_1, u_2)$ and $e(h_1, g_2) = e(g_1, h_2)$, sets $\overline{m} \leftarrow \mathsf{H}_\mathsf{M}(m)$ and computes a Pedersen commitment $c = u_1^{\overline{m}} g_1^s \in \mathbb{G}_1$ to $\overline{m}$ and a proof $\pi \leftarrow \Pi.\mathsf{Prove}^{\mathsf{H}_{\mathsf{zk}}}(\mathsf{crs}, x, w)$, where $s \leftarrow \mathbb{Z}_p$, $x = (c, u_1, g_1)$, and $w = (\overline{m}, s)$. It outputs the first message $\rho_1 = (c, \pi)$ and stores the randomness $\mathsf{st} = s$.
- $\mathsf{BS}_{\mathsf{BB}}.\mathsf{Signer}(\mathsf{bsk}, \rho_1)$: parses $\rho_1 = (c, \pi)$, checks $\Pi.\mathsf{Verify}^{\mathsf{H}_{\mathsf{zk}}}(\mathsf{crs}, x, \pi) = 1$ and outputs the second message $\rho_2 = (\rho_{2,0}, \rho_{2,1}) \leftarrow (\mathsf{sk} \cdot (c \cdot h_1)^r, g_1^r) \in \mathbb{G}_1^2$, where $r \leftarrow \mathbb{Z}_p$.
- $\mathsf{BS}_{\mathsf{BB}}.\mathsf{Derive}(\mathsf{st}, \rho_2)$: parses $\mathsf{st} = s$ and $\rho_2 = (\rho_{2,0}, \rho_{2,1})$, checks $e(\rho_{2,0}, g_2) = v \cdot e(\rho_{2,1}, u_2^{\overline{m}} g_2^s \cdot h_2)$, and outputs the signature $\sigma = (\rho_{2,0}/\rho_{2,1}^s \cdot (u_1^{\overline{m}} h_1)^{r'}, \rho_{2,1} \cdot g_1^{r'}) \in \mathbb{G}_1^2$ for $r' \leftarrow \mathbb{Z}_p$.
- $\mathsf{BS}_{\mathsf{BB}}.\mathsf{Verify}(\mathsf{bvk}, m, \sigma)$: sets $\overline{m} \leftarrow \mathsf{H}_\mathsf{M}(m)$ and outputs $b \leftarrow \mathsf{S}_{\mathsf{BB}}.\mathsf{Verify}(\mathsf{bvk}, \overline{m}, \sigma)$.

4.2 Correctness and Security

We prove correctness, blindness and one-more unforgeability. Correctness follows from a simple calculation. Blindness follows from the zero-knowledge property of Π, and as c statistically hides the message and σ is re-randomized. The proof follows a similar all-but-one reduction as the underlying Boneh-Boyen signature. The only difference is that we modify the Boneh-Boeyn signature which is selectively secure in the standard model, to be adaptively secure in the ROM, and to use the (multi)-online extractor to extract randomness of c submitted by the adversary. Concretely, the reduction first guesses a query $\overline{m}^* = \mathsf{H}_\mathsf{M}(m^*)$ and embeds a CDH challenge into vk such that it can sign all values in $\mathbb{Z}_p \setminus \{\overline{m}^*\}$. For each signing query, the reduction extracts the randomness of c from the proof π, simulates the signing of m as in the original euf-cma proof of S_{BB}, and finally reapplies the randomness of c to the intermediate signature. If the extracted message is $\overline{m}^*$, the reduction aborts. Here, we crucially require that Π is online-extractable. In the end, the reduction hopes to receive a valid signature on $\overline{m}^*$ with which it can solve CDH. More details can be found in Sect. 1.3. A formal security analysis is given in the full version.

Theorem 2. *The blind signature* S_{BB} *is correct, blind under malicious keys under the zero-knowledge property of* Π, *and one-more unforgeable under the* CDH *assumption and the online-extractability of* Π.

4.3 Instantiation

We give a brief overview of our online-extractable NIZK Π. More details can also be found in the full version. As our online-extraction techniques are not reliant on pairings, we use an additional group $\widehat{\mathbb{G}}$ with generators $\widehat{g}_1$ and $\widehat{\mathsf{pp}}$.

Tools. In the full version, we construct a secure Σ-protocol Σ_{ped} for relation $\mathsf{R}_{\mathsf{ped}}$. In this overview, we compile it into a NIZK Π_{ped} via Fiat-Shamir. This is kept implicit in the instantiation as we cannot rely on the security of Π_{ped} in a black-box manner. The relation $\mathsf{R}_{\mathsf{ped}}$ is defined as

$$\mathsf{R}_{\mathsf{ped}} = \{(x, w) : c = u_1^m g_1^s, E_i = \widehat{g}^{e_i} \widehat{\mathsf{pp}}^{r_i}, R_i = \widehat{g}^{r_i},$$
$$\prod_{i \in [\ell]} E_i^{B^{i-1}} = \widehat{g}^m \cdot \widehat{\mathsf{pp}}^{t_m}, \prod_{i \in [\ell]} E_{i+\ell}^{B^{i-1}} = \widehat{g}^s \cdot \widehat{\mathsf{pp}}^{t_s}\},$$

where $x = (c, u_1, g_1, \widehat{g}, \widehat{\mathsf{pp}}, (E_i, R_i)_{i \in [2\ell]}, B)$ and $w = (m, s, (e_i, r_i)_{i \in [2\ell]}, t_m, t_s)$. Note that the relation shows that $m = \sum_{i=1}^{\ell} e_i B^{i-1}$ and $s = \sum_{i=1}^{\ell} e_{i+\ell} B^{i-1}$ under the DLOG assumption. Also, we use a NIZK Π_{rp} with random oracle H_{rp} for the relation

$$\mathsf{R}_{\mathsf{rp}} = \{(x, w) : \ E_i = \widehat{g}^{e_i} \cdot \widehat{\mathsf{pp}}^{r_i}, e_i \in [0, B-1] \text{ for } i \in [2\ell]\},$$

We obtain Π_{rp} by applying the Fiat-Shamir transformation as described in [5] to the multi-round interactive proof system $\Sigma_{\mathsf{rp}}^{2\ell}$ with $\mathsf{crs} = (\widehat{g}, \widehat{\mathsf{pp}}, (\widehat{g}_i)_{i \in [\ell_{\mathsf{rp}}]})$ from [4] (Appendix F.2), for appropriate $\ell_{\mathsf{rp}} \in \mathbb{N}$. Denote with $\mathsf{R}_{\mathsf{dlog}} = \{(\mathsf{crs}, w^*)\}$ the relation that contains all non-trivial DLOG relations w^* for crs, i.e. computing w^* for random crs allows to solve the DLOG assumption. Using Theorem 4 of [5], we show in the full version that Π_{rp} is adaptively knowledge sound for the relaxed relation $\mathsf{R}_{\mathsf{lax}} := \{(x, w) : \ (x, w) \in \mathsf{R}_{\mathsf{rp}} \text{ or } (\mathsf{crs}, w) \in \mathsf{R}_{\mathsf{dlog}}\}$.

Construction of Π. Equipped with the above tools, we instantiate the online-extractable NIZK Π for relation R_{bb} with $\mathsf{crs} = (\widehat{g}, \widehat{\mathsf{pp}}, (\widehat{g}_i)_{i \in [\ell_{\mathsf{rp}}]})$ and hash function $\mathsf{H}_{\mathsf{bb}} = (\mathsf{H}_{\mathsf{rp}}, \mathsf{H}_{\beta})$, where H_{rp} (resp. H_{eg}) is the hash function for Π_{rp} (resp. Π_{ped}). Let $B = \mathsf{poly}(\lambda)$.

To generate a poof π for statement $x = (c, u_1, g_1)$, the prover decomposes the witness (m, s) into $m = \sum_{i=1}^{\ell} m_i B^{i-1}, s = \sum_{i=1}^{\ell} s_i B^{i-1}$, commits to the decompositions $\boldsymbol{e} = (m_1, \ldots, m_\ell, s_1, \ldots, s_\ell)$ via ElGamal in $R_i = \widehat{g}^{r_i}, E_i = \widehat{g}^{e_i} \widehat{\mathsf{pp}}_i^{r_i}$ for $i \in [2\ell]$, where $r_i \leftarrow \mathbb{Z}_p$, and sets $t_m \leftarrow \sum_{i=1}^{\ell} r_i B^{i-1}$ and $t_s \leftarrow \sum_{i=1}^{\ell} r_{i+\ell} B^{i-1}$, and finally outputs proofs $\pi = (\pi_0, \pi_1, (E_i, R_i)_{i \in [2\ell]})$, where π_0, π_1 are proofs generated appropriately via $\Pi_{\mathsf{rp}}, \Pi_{\mathsf{ped}}$, respectively.

To check validity of a proof π, the verifier checks both proofs π_0 and π_1 with appropriate statements x_0 and x_1, respectively, and outputs 1 iff both are valid.

Security. In the full version, we formally show that Π is correct, zero-knowledge under the DDH assumption and online-extractable under the DLOG assumption. Correctness follows immediately from the correctness of Π_{rp} and Π_{ped}. Also, zero-knowledge is easy to show via the hiding property of ElGamal commitments, the zero-knowledge property of Π_{rp} and Π_{ped}.

The proof for multi-proof extractability is more intricate. Roughly, the extractor embeds a trapdoor td for the commitment scheme in the crs. Then, given a statement-proof pair (x, π) with $x = (c, u_1, g_1)$ and $\pi = (\pi_0, \pi_1, (E_i, R_i)_{i \in [2\ell]})$, it decrypts the witnesses $(e_i)_i$ from the ElGamal commitment $(E_i, R_i)_i$ and tries to check if the extracted witness reconstructs to a witness in the relation R_{bb}. We expect that this is possible, as the range proof guarantees that the committed values are short and Σ_{ped} proves the linear relations in the exponents.

For the sake of exposition, below we only consider extracting from a single pair $(x, \pi) \leftarrow \mathcal{A}(\mathsf{crs})$ generated by some adversary $\mathcal{A}$. The argument generalizes to Q_S pairs in a straightforward manner. Note that (x, π) defines statement-proof pairs (x_0, π_1) for Π_{rp} and (x_1, π_1) as in verification.

Denote with Fail the event that online-extraction of (x, π) fails, and assume for the sake of contradiction that Fail occurs. We first try to extract a witness $w_0 = (e'_i, r'_i)_i$ from π_0 via the knowledge extractor of Π_{rp}, and a witness $w_1 = (m, s, (e_i, r_i)_i)$ from π_1 from two related transcripts obtained via rewinding $\mathcal{A}$. Here, it is important that $\mathcal{A}$ is run with the same random tape $\mathsf{coin}_{\mathcal{A}}$ for both extractions to guarantee that the statements x_0 and x_1 share the commitments $(E_i)_i$. For now, let us assume that both extractions succeed, i.e. $(x_0, w_0) \in \mathsf{R}_{\mathsf{rp}}$ and $(x_1, w_1) \in \mathsf{R}_{\mathsf{ped}}$. Assuming the soundness of Π_{rp}, we have $e'_i \in [0, B-1]$. Moreover, assuming the soundness of Π_{ped}, the extracted $(e_i)_i$ form the B-ary decomposition of a valid opening of c. Then, under the assumption that extraction fails, we must have $e'_i \neq e_i$ for some i. However, this breaks the binding property of the Pedersen commitment implicitly defined by the ElGamal commitments. In particular, we found a DLOG relation for the tuple $(\widehat{g}, \widehat{\mathsf{pp}}_i)$. Note that while the extracted DLOG relation is a trapdoor information td the extractor uses to extract the witnesses, this will not be an issue since we do not need td to analyze the success probability of the adversary.

It remains to show that extraction of w_0 and w_1 succeeds. Recall that we assumed that the extraction of w_0 and w_1 succeeds simultaneously, even if we initially run $\mathcal{A}$ on a shared random coin. We first extract w_0 with the extractor of Π_{rp}. We can argue with adaptive knowledge soundness of Π_{rp} that with a probability of $\varepsilon = \frac{\Pr[\mathsf{Fail}] - \mathsf{negl}(\lambda)}{\mathsf{poly}(\lambda)}$, we have have that $(x_0, w_0) \in \mathsf{R}_{\mathsf{rp}}$ and Fail occurs. At this point, the randomness $\mathsf{coin}_{\mathcal{A}}$ of the adversary $\mathcal{A}$ is conditioned on successful extraction of w_0. In particular, we cannot apply adaptive knowledge soundness of Π_{ped}, as the extractor of Π_{ped} has only sufficient success probability if $\mathsf{coin}_{\mathcal{A}}$ is chosen at random.

Instead, we define a specialized forking algorithm that first runs $\mathcal{A}$ on the same randomness (and same initial random oracle choices), and then rewinds $\mathcal{A}$ to obtain related transcripts. A careful non-black box analysis of the forking algorithm, similar to [51], allows us to conclude that the algorithm succeeds in finding two related transcripts in polynomial time with probability $\varepsilon/8$.

If Fail is non-negligible, then with a probability of $\varepsilon/8$, the above adversary breaks the DLOG assumption. So indeed the event Fail occurs with at most negligible probability, i.e. the extractor of Π succeeds on valid proof-statement pairs with high probability.

Efficiency of $\mathsf{BS_{BB}}$. When $\mathsf{BS_{BB}}$ is instantiated with Π for $B = \mathsf{poly}(\lambda)$, the user sends 1 element in $\mathbb{G}_1$, $2\lceil\log_2(2n\ell + \ell + 4)\rceil + 4\ell + 1$ in $\widehat{\mathbb{G}}$, and $10 + 2\ell$ elements in $\mathbb{Z}_p$ to the signer. The signer sends 2 elements in $\mathbb{G}_1$, and the final signature contains 2 elements in $\mathbb{G}_1$.

We set $B = 2^{64}$ in order to have an extractor that performs roughly $\ell \cdot 2^{32}$ group operations, where $\ell = \lceil\log_B p\rceil = 4$. The total communication is 2.2 KB and signatures are of size 96 Byte for $\lambda = 128$.

Acknowledgments. This work was partially supported by JST CREST Grant Number JPMJCR22M1, Japan, JST AIP Acceleration Research JPMJCR22U5, Japan, JSPS KAKENHI Grant Numbers JP18K18055 and JP19H01109. Also, we would like to thank Michael Klooß for helpful discussions on the soundness of Bulletproofs and Geoffroy Couteau for helpful discussions in early stages of this work.

References

1. Abe, M., Groth, J., Haralambiev, K., Ohkubo, M.: Optimal structure-preserving signatures in asymmetric bilinear groups. In: Rogaway, P. (ed.) CRYPTO 2011. LNCS, vol. 6841, pp. 649–666. Springer, Heidelberg (2011). https://doi.org/10.1007/978-3-642-22792-9_37
2. Abe, M., Jutla, C.S., Ohkubo, M., Roy, A.: Improved (Almost) tightly-secure simulation-sound QA-NIZK with applications. In: Peyrin, T., Galbraith, S. (eds.) ASIACRYPT 2018. LNCS, vol. 11272, pp. 627–656. Springer, Cham (2018). https://doi.org/10.1007/978-3-030-03326-2_21
3. Agrawal, S., Boneh, D., Boyen, X.: Efficient lattice (H)IBE in the standard model. In: Gilbert, H. (ed.) EUROCRYPT 2010. LNCS, vol. 6110, pp. 553–572. Springer, Heidelberg (2010). https://doi.org/10.1007/978-3-642-13190-5_28
4. Attema, T., Cramer, R.: Compressed Σ-protocol theory and practical application to plug and play secure algorithmics. In: Micciancio, Daniele, Ristenpart, Thomas (eds.) CRYPTO 2020. LNCS, vol. 12172, pp. 513–543. Springer, Cham (2020). https://doi.org/10.1007/978-3-030-56877-1_18
5. Attema, T., Fehr, S., Klooß, M.: Fiat-shamir transformation of multi-round interactive proofs. In: Kiltz, E., Vaikuntanathan, V. (eds.) Theory of Cryptography - 20th International Conference, TCC 2022, Chicago, IL, USA, November 7–10, 2022, Proceedings, Part I. Lecture Notes in Computer Science, vol. 13747, pp. 113–142. Springer, Cham (2022). https://doi.org/10.1007/978-3-031-22318-1_5
6. Barreto, P.S.L.M., Lynn, B., Scott, M.: Constructing elliptic curves with prescribed embedding degrees. In: Cimato, S., Persiano, G., Galdi, C. (eds.) SCN 2002. LNCS, vol. 2576, pp. 257–267. Springer, Heidelberg (2003). https://doi.org/10.1007/3-540-36413-7_19
7. Bellare, M., Namprempre, C., Pointcheval, D., Semanko, M.: The one-more-RSA-inversion problems and the security of Chaum's blind signature scheme. J. Cryptol. **16**(3), 185–215 (2003)
8. Bellare, M., Neven, G.: Multi-signatures in the plain public-key model and a general forking lemma. In: Juels, A., Wright, R.N., De Capitani di Vimercati, S. (eds.) ACM CCS 2006, pp. 390–399. ACM Press (2006). https://doi.org/10.1145/1180405.1180453

9. Bernhard, D., Fischlin, M., Warinschi, B.: Adaptive proofs of knowledge in the random oracle model. In: Katz, J. (ed.) PKC 2015. LNCS, vol. 9020, pp. 629–649. Springer, Heidelberg (2015). https://doi.org/10.1007/978-3-662-46447-2_28
10. Blazy, O., Fuchsbauer, G., Pointcheval, D., Vergnaud, D.: Short blind signatures. J. Comput. Secur. **21**(5), 627–661 (2013)
11. Boldyreva, A.: Threshold signatures, multisignatures and blind signatures based on the gap-diffie-Hellman-group signature scheme. In: Desmedt, Y.G. (ed.) PKC 2003. LNCS, vol. 2567, pp. 31–46. Springer, Heidelberg (2003). https://doi.org/10.1007/3-540-36288-6_3
12. Boneh, D., Boyen, X.: Efficient selective-ID secure identity-based encryption without random oracles. In: Cachin, C., Camenisch, J.L. (eds.) EUROCRYPT 2004. LNCS, vol. 3027, pp. 223–238. Springer, Heidelberg (2004). https://doi.org/10.1007/978-3-540-24676-3_14
13. Boneh, D., Boyen, X.: Short signatures without random oracles. In: Cachin, C., Camenisch, J.L. (eds.) EUROCRYPT 2004. LNCS, vol. 3027, pp. 56–73. Springer, Heidelberg (2004). https://doi.org/10.1007/978-3-540-24676-3_4
14. Boneh, D., Boyen, X.: Short signatures without random oracles and the SDH assumption in bilinear groups. J. Cryptol. **21**(2), 149–177 (2008). https://doi.org/10.1007/s00145-007-9005-7
15. Bowe, S.: Bls12-381: new ZK-snark elliptic curve construction. https://electriccoin.co/blog/new-snark-curve/ (2017). Accessed 02 Feb 2023
16. Brands, S.: Untraceable off-line cash in wallet with observers. In: Stinson, D.R. (ed.) CRYPTO 1993. LNCS, vol. 773, pp. 302–318. Springer, Heidelberg (1994). https://doi.org/10.1007/3-540-48329-2_26
17. Brickell, E.F., Camenisch, J., Chen, L.: Direct anonymous attestation. In: Atluri, V., Pfitzmann, B., McDaniel, P. (eds.) ACM CCS 2004, pp. 132–145. ACM Press (2004). https://doi.org/10.1145/1030083.1030103
18. Bünz, B., Bootle, J., Boneh, D., Poelstra, A., Wuille, P., Maxwell, G.: Bulletproofs: short proofs for confidential transactions and more. In: 2018 IEEE Symposium on Security and Privacy, pp. 315–334. IEEE Computer Society Press (2018). https://doi.org/10.1109/SP.2018.00020
19. Buser, M., et al.: A survey on exotic signatures for post-quantum blockchain: challenges & research directions. ACM Comput. Surv. (2022)
20. Camenisch, J., Lysyanskaya, A.: An efficient system for non-transferable anonymous credentials with optional anonymity revocation. In: Pfitzmann, B. (ed.) EUROCRYPT 2001. LNCS, vol. 2045, pp. 93–118. Springer, Heidelberg (2001). https://doi.org/10.1007/3-540-44987-6_7
21. Chairattana-Apirom, R., Hanzlik, L., Loss, J., Lysyanskaya, A., Wagner, B.: PI-cut-choo and friends: compact blind signatures via parallel instance cut-and-choose and more. In: Dodis, Y., Shrimpton, T. (eds.) CRYPTO 2022, Part III. LNCS, vol. 13509, pp. 3–31. Springer, Heidelberg (2022). https://doi.org/10.1007/978-3-031-15982-4_1
22. Chaum, D.: Blind signatures for untraceable payments. In: Chaum, D., Rivest, R.L., Sherman, A.T. (eds.) CRYPTO'82, pp. 199–203. Plenum Press, New York, USA (1982)
23. Chaum, D.: Elections with unconditionally-secret ballots and disruption equivalent to breaking RSA. In: Barstow, D., Brauer, W., Brinch Hansen, P., Gries, D., Luckham, D., Moler, C., Pnueli, A., Seegmüller, G., Stoer, J., Wirth, N., Günther, C.G. (eds.) EUROCRYPT 1988. LNCS, vol. 330, pp. 177–182. Springer, Heidelberg (1988). https://doi.org/10.1007/3-540-45961-8_15

24. Chaum, D., Fiat, A., Naor, M.: Untraceable electronic cash. In: Goldwasser, S. (ed.) CRYPTO 1988. LNCS, vol. 403, pp. 319–327. Springer, New York (1990). https://doi.org/10.1007/0-387-34799-2_25
25. del Pino, R., Katsumata, S.: A new framework for more efficient round-optimal lattice-based (partially) blind signature via trapdoor sampling. In: Dodis, Y., Shrimpton, T. (eds.) CRYPTO 2022, Part II. LNCS, vol. 13508, pp. 306–336. Springer, Heidelberg (2022). https://doi.org/10.1007/978-3-031-15979-4_11
26. Fiat, A., Shamir, A.: How to prove yourself: practical solutions to identification and signature problems. In: Odlyzko, A.M. (ed.) CRYPTO 1986. LNCS, vol. 263, pp. 186–194. Springer, Heidelberg (1987). https://doi.org/10.1007/3-540-47721-7_12
27. Fischlin, M.: Communication-efficient non-interactive proofs of knowledge with online extractors. In: Shoup, V. (ed.) CRYPTO 2005. LNCS, vol. 3621, pp. 152–168. Springer, Heidelberg (2005). https://doi.org/10.1007/11535218_10
28. Fischlin, M.: Round-optimal composable blind signatures in the common reference string model. In: Dwork, C. (ed.) CRYPTO 2006. LNCS, vol. 4117, pp. 60–77. Springer, Heidelberg (2006). https://doi.org/10.1007/11818175_4
29. Fischlin, M., Schröder, D.: On the impossibility of three-move blind signature schemes. In: Gilbert, H. (ed.) EUROCRYPT 2010. LNCS, vol. 6110, pp. 197–215. Springer, Heidelberg (2010). https://doi.org/10.1007/978-3-642-13190-5_10
30. Fuchsbauer, G., Hanser, C., Kamath, C., Slamanig, D.: Practical round-optimal blind signatures in the standard model from weaker assumptions. In: Zikas, V., De Prisco, R. (eds.) SCN 2016. LNCS, vol. 9841, pp. 391–408. Springer, Cham (2016). https://doi.org/10.1007/978-3-319-44618-9_21
31. Fuchsbauer, G., Hanser, C., Slamanig, D.: Practical round-optimal blind signatures in the standard model. In: Gennaro, R., Robshaw, M. (eds.) CRYPTO 2015. LNCS, vol. 9216, pp. 233–253. Springer, Heidelberg (2015). https://doi.org/10.1007/978-3-662-48000-7_12
32. Fujioka, A., Okamoto, T., Ohta, K.: A practical secret voting scheme for large scale elections. In: Seberry, J., Zheng, Y. (eds.) AUSCRYPT 1992. LNCS, vol. 718, pp. 244–251. Springer, Heidelberg (1993). https://doi.org/10.1007/3-540-57220-1_66
33. Ganesh, C., Orlandi, C., Pancholi, M., Takahashi, A., Tschudi, D.: Fiat-shamir bulletproofs are non-malleable (in the algebraic group model). In: Dunkelman, O., Dziembowski, S. (eds.) EUROCRYPT 2022, Part II. LNCS, vol. 13276, pp. 397–426. Springer, Heidelberg (2022). https://doi.org/10.1007/978-3-031-07085-3_14
34. Goyal, V., Pandey, O., Sahai, A., Waters, B.: Attribute-based encryption for fine-grained access control of encrypted data. In: Juels, A., Wright, R.N., De Capitani di Vimercati, S. (eds.) ACM CCS 2006, pp. 89–98. ACM Press (2006). https://doi.org/10.1145/1180405.1180418, available as Cryptology ePrint Archive Report 2006/309
35. Groth, J., Ostrovsky, R., Sahai, A.: New techniques for non-interactive zero-knowledge. J. ACM (JACM) **59**(3), 1–35 (2012)
36. Hanzlik, L., Loss, J., Wagner, B.: Rai-choo! evolving blind signatures to the next level. To Appear at EUROCRYPT (2023)
37. Hendrickson, S., Iyengar, J., Pauly, T., Valdez, S., Wood, C.A.: Private access tokens. internet-draft draft-private-access-tokens-01 (2022), https://datatracker.ietf.org/doc/draft-private-access-tokens/, work in Progress
38. Juels, A., Luby, M., Ostrovsky, R.: Security of blind digital signatures (extended abstract). In: Kaliski Jr., B.S. (ed.) CRYPTO'97. LNCS, vol. 1294, pp. 150–164. Springer, Heidelberg (1997). https://doi.org/10.1007/BFb0052233

39. Jutla, C.S., Roy, A.: Improved structure preserving signatures under standard bilinear assumptions. In: Fehr, S. (ed.) PKC 2017. LNCS, vol. 10175, pp. 183–209. Springer, Heidelberg (2017). https://doi.org/10.1007/978-3-662-54388-7_7
40. Katz, J.: Digital signatures: background and definitions. In: Digital Signatures. Springer (2010). https://doi.org/10.1007/978-0-387-27712-7_1
41. Katz, J., Loss, J., Rosenberg, M.: Boosting the security of blind signature schemes. In: Tibouchi, M., Wang, H. (eds.) ASIACRYPT 2021. LNCS, vol. 13093, pp. 468–492. Springer, Cham (2021). https://doi.org/10.1007/978-3-030-92068-5_16
42. Khalili, M., Slamanig, D., Dakhilalian, M.: Structure-preserving signatures on equivalence classes from standard assumptions. In: Galbraith, S.D., Moriai, S. (eds.) ASIACRYPT 2019. LNCS, vol. 11923, pp. 63–93. Springer, Cham (2019). https://doi.org/10.1007/978-3-030-34618-8_3
43. Kiltz, E., Pan, J., Wee, H.: Structure-preserving signatures from standard assumptions, revisited. In: Gennaro, R., Robshaw, M. (eds.) CRYPTO 2015. LNCS, vol. 9216, pp. 275–295. Springer, Heidelberg (2015). https://doi.org/10.1007/978-3-662-48000-7_14
44. Kiltz, E., Wee, H.: Quasi-adaptive NIZK for linear subspaces revisited. In: Oswald, E., Fischlin, M. (eds.) EUROCRYPT 2015. LNCS, vol. 9057, pp. 101–128. Springer, Heidelberg (2015). https://doi.org/10.1007/978-3-662-46803-6_4
45. Lindell, Y.: Lower bounds and impossibility results for concurrent self composition. J. Cryptol. **21**(2), 200–249 (2008). https://doi.org/10.1007/s00145-007-9015-5
46. Micali, S., Reyzin, L.: Improving the exact security of digital signature schemes. J. Cryptol. **15**(1), 1–18 (2002). https://doi.org/10.1007/s00145-001-0005-8
47. Nishimaki, R.: Equipping public-key cryptographic primitives with watermarking (or: A Hole Is to Watermark). In: Pass, R., Pietrzak, K. (eds.) TCC 2020. LNCS, vol. 12550, pp. 179–209. Springer, Cham (2020). https://doi.org/10.1007/978-3-030-64375-1_7
48. Okamoto, T., Ohta, K.: Universal electronic cash. In: Feigenbaum, J. (ed.) CRYPTO 1991. LNCS, vol. 576, pp. 324–337. Springer, Heidelberg (1992). https://doi.org/10.1007/3-540-46766-1_27
49. Pass, R.: Limits of provable security from standard assumptions. In: Fortnow, L., Vadhan, S.P. (eds.) 43rd ACM STOC, pp. 109–118. ACM Press (2011). https://doi.org/10.1145/1993636.1993652
50. Pointcheval, D.: Strengthened security for blind signatures. In: Nyberg, K. (ed.) EUROCRYPT 1998. LNCS, vol. 1403, pp. 391–405. Springer, Heidelberg (1998). https://doi.org/10.1007/BFb0054141
51. Pointcheval, D., Stern, J.: Security arguments for digital signatures and blind signatures. J. Cryptol. **13**(3), 361–396 (2000). https://doi.org/10.1007/s001450010003
52. Sahai, A., Waters, B.: Fuzzy identity-based encryption. In: Cramer, R. (ed.) EUROCRYPT 2005. LNCS, vol. 3494, pp. 457–473. Springer, Heidelberg (2005). https://doi.org/10.1007/11426639_27
53. Shoup, V., Gennaro, R.: Securing threshold cryptosystems against chosen ciphertext attack. In: Nyberg, K. (ed.) EUROCRYPT 1998. LNCS, vol. 1403, pp. 1–16. Springer, Heidelberg (1998). https://doi.org/10.1007/BFb0054113
54. Unruh, D.: Quantum proofs of knowledge. In: Pointcheval, D., Johansson, T. (eds.) EUROCRYPT 2012. LNCS, vol. 7237, pp. 135–152. Springer, Heidelberg (2012). https://doi.org/10.1007/978-3-642-29011-4_10
55. VPN by Google one, explained. https://one.google.com/about/vpn/howitworks (2022). Accessed 02 Feb 2023

56. Waters, B.: Efficient identity-based encryption without random oracles. In: Cramer, R. (ed.) EUROCRYPT 2005. LNCS, vol. 3494, pp. 114–127. Springer, Heidelberg (2005). https://doi.org/10.1007/11426639_7
57. Yi, X., Lam, K.Y.: A new blind ECDSA scheme for bitcoin transaction anonymity. In: Galbraith, S.D., Russello, G., Susilo, W., Gollmann, D., Kirda, E., Liang, Z. (eds.) ASIACCS 19, pp. 613–620. ACM Press (2019). https://doi.org/10.1145/3321705.3329816

A Generic Construction of an Anonymous Reputation System and Instantiations from Lattices

Johannes Blömer[1], Jan Bobolz[2], and Laurens Porzenheim[1](✉)

[1] Paderborn University, Paderborn, Germany
{bloemer,laurens.porzenheim}@upb.de
[2] University of Edinburgh, Edinburgh, UK
jan.bobolz@ed.ac.uk

Abstract. With an anonymous reputation system one can realize the process of rating sellers anonymously in an online shop. While raters can stay anonymous, sellers still have the guarantee that they can only be reviewed by raters who bought their product.

We present the first generic construction of a reputation system from basic building blocks, namely digital signatures, encryption schemes, non-interactive zero-knowledge proofs, and linking indistinguishable tags. We then show the security of the reputation system in a strong security model. Among others, we instantiate the generic construction with building blocks based on lattice problems, leading to the first module lattice-based reputation system in the random oracle model.

1 Introduction

Reputation systems are crucial for markets to function properly. They are usually a user's only indicator regarding the trustworthiness of a seller, or the quality of a product. Right now, in real-world reputation systems, ratings are centrally controlled (see, for example, Amazon or Yelp ratings) by the reputation system provider (Amazon/Yelp). This means that the reputation system provider has the ability to admit or deny users from the system, censor ratings, inject fake ratings, and trace all raters' identities. Of course, this allows a malicious provider to unilaterally undermine the reputation system, e.g. by censoring inconvenient ratings or by using knowledge of user identities to retaliate against bad ratings.

Cryptographic Reputation Systems. A *cryptographic* reputation system is a decentralized system in which the roles and abilities of the reputation system

---

J. Bobolz—Work done while at Paderborn University.
This work was partially supported by the German Research Foundation (DFG) within the Collaborative Research Centre "On-The-Fly Computing" under the project number 160364472 – SFB 901/3. Additionally, this work was partially funded by the Ministry of Culture and Science of the State of North Rhine-Westphalia.

J. Guo and R. Steinfeld (Eds.): ASIACRYPT 2023, LNCS 14439, pp. 418–452, 2023.
https://doi.org/10.1007/978-981-99-8724-5_13

provider are either fully replaced by cryptographic mechanisms or at least distributed among multiple parties, with strong anonymity guarantees for users. First, a user registers (once) with the *group manager*, who is tasked with admitting users to the system (essentially to prevent Sybil attacks). Then, when the user buys a product, he receives a *rating token* from an *issuer* (e.g., the seller), certifying that the user is indeed allowed to rate the issuer (to prevent users from rating issuers they have never interacted with). Given the membership certificate from the group manager and the rating token from the issuer, the user can create a *rating signature*. We imagine that the user posts this signature to a public *reputation board*, enabling other users to view and verify the rating. The rating signature is *anonymous*, meaning that it does not reveal who, of all users who are allowed to rate that issuer, issued this particular rating (preventing retaliation against negative ratings). However, the *opener* possesses a special key to inspect signatures and reveal the user's identity in case of misuse. Finally, even though rating signatures are otherwise anonymous to the public, anyone can efficiently check whether any two rating signatures have been created by the same user (to prevent the same user from submitting multiple ratings for the same issuer). In this setting, the role of the reputation system provider has been distributed among group manager, issuers and reputation boards. User anonymity is cryptographically guaranteed, but can be revoked by the opener. What we describe here can be seen as (a special case of) the ticket-based approach identified by [25].

Desirable Construction Types. There exists a wealth of constructions of such system in the literature (as surveyed in [25]), but they all work in the discrete logarithm setting. With the looming threat of quantum computers, there is a need for constructions that do not rely on the hardness of discrete logarithms and instead rely on some hardness assumption not likely broken by quantum computers, such as lattice-based assumptions. We are aware of only a single lattice-based reputation system in the literature, designed by El Kaafarani, Katsumata, and Solomon [20]. We can generally distinguish generic constructions from non-generic constructions. A generic construction is a prescription how to plug together (almost) arbitrary instantiations of several basic schemes (e.g., signature schemes, encryption schemes, and non-interactive zero-knowledge proofs (NIZKs)) into a secure reputation system. So far, reputation system constructions have been non-generic, i.e. there is no formally proven way to construct reputation systems from arbitrarily instantiated basic building blocks. Even beyond the lack of an *explicit* generic construction, existing constructions are also quite specific to their (discrete logarithm/lattice) setting. For example, a natural choice for rating tokens would be for the issuer to sign the buying user's public key (thereby giving that user the right to rate). However, in the discrete logarithm setting (e.g., [8,9]), rating tokens are typically (blind) signatures on the user's *secret key*, instead, because traditionally, it is easier to sign secret keys (which live in $\mathbb{Z}_p$) than public keys (which live in the group $\mathbb{G}$). In the lattice setting, the only known construction [20] accumulates all buyers' public keys in a Merkle hash tree, which is (relatively) efficient in the lattice setting, but would be absurdly inefficient and borderline impossible to implement in the discrete logarithm setting (considering the need to prove statements in zero-knowledge about the hashes).

1.1 Our Contribution

In this paper, we give the first provably secure *generic* construction of a reputation system from digital signatures, public-key encryption, linking indistinguishable tags (LITs), and NIZKs. We formally define security properties and prove that the generic construction (and hence any concrete constructions built from it) fulfills them. Furthermore, we show that this generic construction can be reasonably instantiated in both the lattice setting and the discrete logarithm setting, unifying and drawing parallels between the two settings. In particular, this results in the first reputation system based on *module* lattices, i.e. on the hardness of module lattice problems. Our construction compares favorably in its privacy properties to the only other lattice-based construction [20], as discussed later.

Generic Construction. The generic construction roughly follows a paradigm similar to the sign-encrypt-prove paradigm [15] for group signatures, similar to [8,9] (but modified to apply to both the lattice and the discrete logarithm setting). The user generates some secret key usk; his public key is $\mathsf{upk} = f(\mathsf{usk})$ for some one-way function f. To join the system, the user obtains a signature ρ on his public key under the public key gmpk of the group manager. To enable rating an issuer, who we identify by his public key ipk, the user also obtains a signature τ on his public key from the issuer. Given those two signatures, the user composes a rating text rtng and encrypts his public key upk for the opener (who holds the decryption key to reveal upk in case of misuse). For technical reasons, the user also encrypts usk under a key that nobody knows the secret key for (a trick comparable to the Naor-Yung paradigm). Furthermore, the user computes a *linking indistinguishable tag* (LIT) using his secret key usk. The LIT is the gadget that will allow anyone to check whether the user has rated the same issuer twice. Then, the user uses the NIZK essentially as a signature of knowledge [16] to create a non-interactive proof authenticating the rating text rtng by proving, in zero-knowledge, that the ciphertexts and LIT have been computed correctly, and that his public key upk has been signed by the group manager and the issuer.

Instantiation in the Discrete Logarithm Setting. In the discrete logarithm setting, we can use LIT tags in the random oracle model of the form $\mathcal{RO}(\mathsf{ipk})^{\mathsf{usk}}$ (note that this is a deterministic tag and hence enables detection of a user rating ipk twice). Because the generic construction signs *public* keys, we use a structure-preserving signature as the signature scheme. Unsurprisingly, encryption can be accomplished with ElGamal and the NIZKs can be instantiated with Schnorr-style protocols together with the Fiat-Shamir heuristic. More details can be found in Sect. 5.1.

Instantiation with Lattices. The instantiation with lattices is more difficult given that the ecosystem for privacy constructions is less mature than in the discrete logarithm setting. We need to instantiate the encryption scheme, the signature scheme, the NIZK, and the linking indistinguishable tag. For more efficiency and flexibility when setting parameters, we generally consider the *module* lattice setting. For the encryption scheme, the typical choice is between primal and dual Regev encryption (i.e. between putting the LWE error into the public key or into ciphertexts). Primal Regev is more suitable for proving statements about encryptions in zero-knowledge, since there is no added error in the ciphertext, which is why we choose it for the instantiation. In particular, we use the verifiable encryption scheme described by [38]. For the NIZK, we choose [38], which has the advantage of supporting efficient vector shortness proofs without slack, but is in the random oracle model. We use this feature to efficiently prove knowledge of, for example, a valid [19] signature. This NIZK also interfaces well with the other schemes chosen to instantiate the generic construction. Finally, we require a linking indistinguishable tag. We use a tag similar to those of [3,20], which can be seen as the lattice equivalent of DLOG-based tags mentioned above. To build a LIT tag $\mathbf{t}$ in the lattice setting, [20] use an LWE secret as the secret key, hash the message μ with the random oracle, and choose an error $\mathbf{e}$ to build an LWE sample from it, i.e. $\mathbf{t}^t = \mathbf{s}^t \cdot \mathcal{RO}(\mathsf{ipk}) + \mathbf{e}^t$. Linking works because if one tags the same message with the same secret key, the difference of the two tags is the difference of the two errors. Thus, the difference of two tags is short, iff they should link. [20] show the security of their tag under the first-are-errorless LWE assumption, a variant of LWE where the first few samples of an LWE oracle do not contain any error. When instantiating the LIT, this costs them some efficiency, so we modify their construction to show our tag secure under the Module LWE assumption. We also introduce some new security notions for LITs in order to interface better with our generic construction.

There are several signature schemes based on lattice assumptions. However, we require one that plays nicely with zero-knowledge proofs, for example the signature should not rely on random oracles. Thus, a first idea would be to use the signatures of [33] or [29], as they are designed to be compatible with current lattice-based proof systems. However, [33] present a construction based on unstructured lattices, which is too inefficient compared to a construction from structured lattices. Furthermore, their construction inherently uses a chameleon hash to achieve adaptive security, which increases the complexity of a proof of possession of a signature. On the other hand, [29] construct both a stateful ℓ-time signature and a stateless ℓ-time signature that are both directly adaptively secure. However, the former does not fit our generic construction, which requires a stateless signature scheme without a limit on the signature queries. For the latter we can argue that we can use it in our generic construction despite the ℓ-time restriction, but it suffers from a large reduction loss. Another candidate is the stateless signature scheme of [19]. Like the other two signatures, it is a tag-based signature scheme and a variant of signatures by [14], but is based on ideal lattices. [19] show their signature to be non-adaptively secure and transform it to adaptive security by employing chameleon hashes. We instead show in the full version [7] that the signature of [19] is already adaptively secure by using a proof technique as in [32]. However, the signature scheme of [19] also suffers from a high reduction loss similar to the stateless variant of [29], since they use the same proof technique. Another possible signature scheme, especially when optimizing for signature size, is the one by [11]. They design a credential system, which can be based on one of several new lattice assumptions, such as Int-NTRU-ISIS$_f$. This credential system implies a signature scheme that we can use in our generic construction. For the signature schemes of [11,29] we later give rough estimates of the size of a signature of a rating. For details, see Sect. 5.

Stateful Reputation System. We also discuss a stateful variant of our generic construction of a reputation system in Sect. 5, which is limited to ℓ users. The stateful variant works the same way as the stateless construction except for using stateful signatures as building blocks instead and having a fixed maximum number of users. The security proofs of the stateless generic construction can easily be adapted to apply to the stateful variant. Then, we can instantiate the stateful generic construction with the same schemes as discussed before, except for using the stateful signature scheme of [29]. Since their stateful scheme is more efficient than their stateless variant, this also improves the efficiency of the reputation system instantiation.

1.2 Related Work

Reputation System Constructions. Building reputation systems in the discrete logarithm setting is well-understood, with a wealth of papers with a variety of construction strategies and features. A good discussion can be found in the survey of Gurtler and Goldberg [25]. Closest to our generic construction are [8,9], they are not quite instantiations of our generic construction, but they follow a similar paradigm (changes are mostly due to the fixed discrete logarithm setting in those papers, such as the usage of blind signatures to avoid signing public keys). Other papers, such as [6,36], offer some form of privacy for issuers. In our construction, the issuer is known to all parties. We leave extensions, which offer some privacy to issuers, to future work and note that the techniques used here carry over to more complex scenarios. Another line of research considers reputation systems in a blockchain context, as surveyed by Hasan, Brunie, and Bertino [26]. Those systems usually aim for trustlessness, i.e. ideally *no* party has to be trusted, but trust is distributed and backed by incentives throughout the blockchain network. Our system makes some trust assumptions, e.g., if group manager and issuer collude, we cannot prevent Sybil attacks. We do not model any reputation board party mentioned by [26], which stores the rating signatures, but note that it can be realized by a public ledger, ensuring that ratings are not censored or deleted.

Lattice-Based Group Signatures and Credential Systems. One way to construct a reputation system is to take some group signature as base and to modify it such that linking is possible [8,9,20]. This works because the notion of group signatures is closely related to anonymous reputation systems; one can view reputation systems as a group of group signatures. Both want to protect the anonymity of users inside a group or system, where the users authenticate messages, while a privileged opener is able to de-anonymize users. Therefore, we can explore existing lattice-based group signatures as potential bases for a lattice-based reputation system. One example is the group signature of [34], which [20] used to construct their reputation system, as explained later in more detail.

Another potential group signature to build a reputation system from is the one of [13], which uses the sign-encrypt-proof paradigm. They employ the Aurora SNARK [4] for their proofs, which has the advantage of no slack and very small proofs. However, the computation time for the proofs required by the group signature seems to be too high, as [13] explain.

In their paper on very efficient NIZKs with no slack, [40] also present a group signature scheme, which is based on the constructions of [40,43]. While this scheme promises very short signatures, their group signature is static, i.e. the group does not change. This does not match our dynamic model of a reputation system. Furthermore, [40] model their user identities as single ring elements of a special set, which they sign to let the user join the group. However, in our construction we need to be able to sign the public keys of the LIT scheme, which generally do not fall into this special set.

Another group signature on which one could base a reputation system is the one by [35]. They also follow the sign-encrypt-proof paradigm, and concretely use the signatures of [19], an encryption scheme by [41] transformed to CCA security similar to the Naor-Yung paradigm and some Stern-like proof system. This group signature uses the same signature scheme and a similar encryption scheme as building blocks as we do in our first instantiation of the reputation system (note that we use different NIZKs).

Instead of basing the construction of a reputation system on some group signature, one can also look at credential system, as they are another privacy-focused primitive related to reputation systems. Two possible constructions are the systems from [11,29]. The idea of both credential systems is that they construct a blind signature, which they use to (blindly) sign some attributes, i.e. create a credential over the attributes. To sign a message, they prove possession of a credential in zero-knowledge. Thus, the idea of their constructions is different to our generic construction, which does not need a blind signature.

Lattice-Based Reputation Systems. To the best of our knowledge, the only other construction of a reputation system that is based on lattices is the construction of [20]. The idea for their construction is to start with the group signature from [34] and view the reputation system as a group of group signatures. For each item that can be rated, the group manager sets up a separate group signature via a hash-based accumulator that is a Merkle-tree of all public keys of users who may rate the item. To create a rating a user encrypts his identity, creates a tag with a LIT and proves in zero-knowledge that he encrypted and tagged correctly as well as that his public key, for which he knows the secret key, is contained in the Merkle-tree.

A drawback of their model is that there are no issuers, instead there is a single group manager who manages everything. This gives the single group manager more power in a setting where there are different people to be rated, where these people need to trust the single group manager to work honestly. By separating the group manager from issuers, we can also split up their power, allowing for a more fine-grained approach of modelling trust. This is reflected in our security model. Additionally our security model offers a slightly stronger corruption model, except for requiring the opener to be honest (cf. Sect. 4.1).

Another drawback of the construction of [20] is that due to it relying on public Merkle-trees, there exists a public record of all users who can rate an item. While this does not contradict any formal security notion, in practice it is undesirable that the whole purchase history of all users is publicly available and a construction not exhibiting this issue is preferable. Our construction prevents this drawback by using signatures instead of a Merkle-tree to add users to the group. Obviously, even in our setting malicious issuers can always share the purchase history of users who bought from them with other people, but this is unpreventable. However, [20] *requires* their group manager to publish this information in order for the system to work. Furthermore, due to their usage of first-are-errorless LWE for the LIT as mentioned before and their usage of Stern-like proofs, the construction of [20] is less efficient than ours.

The advantage that the construction of [20] has over our construction is that they can assume the opener to be corrupt in every security notion but anonymity, while our construction needs the opener to be honest-but-curious. [20] achieve this requirement by introducing a Judge algorithm with which one can publicly verify that the opener worked correctly. We note that it is straight-forward to add Judge to our generic construction and our instantiations, but we omit it for better readability.

2 Preliminaries

We denote drawing some x uniformly from a set S by $x \leftarrow S$. We overload notation and denote by $x \leftarrow D$ sampling x from a distribution D. If $A(y)$ is a (probabilistic polynomial time (ppt)) algorithm, $x \leftarrow A(y)$ denotes sampling x from the output distribution of A on input y. $[A(y)]$ denotes the set of possible outcomes of a ppt A on input y. We denote the random oracle as $\mathcal{RO}$.

We denote scalars as lowercase letters a, column vectors as bold lowercase letters $\mathbf{a}$ and matrices as bold uppercase letters $\mathbf{A}$. By $\mathbf{I}_c$ we denote the identity matrix of dimension $c \times c$. If the dimensions are clear from the context, we may only write $\mathbf{I}$. The same holds for $\mathbf{0}$, by which we denote the vector or matrix consisting of only zeroes. For the norm $\|\mathbf{a}\|$ of a vector we use the euclidian norm unless specified otherwise. We denote the infinity norm of a vector by $\|\mathbf{a}\|_\infty$.

Unless otherwise specified, let $\mathcal{R} = \mathbb{Z}[X]/(X^n+1)$ with $n \geq 16$ being a power of two and let $q > 16$ and $q = 3,5 \mod 8$. Let $\mathcal{R}_q = \mathcal{R}/q\mathcal{R}$. With such a q, $\mathcal{R}_q$

splits into $\mathcal{R}_q \cong \mathbb{F}_{q^{n/2}} \times \mathbb{F}_{q^{n/2}}$, where $\mathbb{F}_{q^{n/2}}$ denotes the field with $q^{n/2}$ elements, which we use for some results, e.g. Lemma 1. We represent elements of $\mathcal{R}_q$ as vectors over $\mathbb{Z}_q^n$. In general, we use the coefficient embedding $\theta : \mathcal{R}_q \rightarrow \mathbb{Z}_q^n$, since for the $\mathcal{R}$ we use the canonical embedding is the same as the coefficent embedding up to a factor of $\sqrt{n}$ [29]. Define $\mathcal{R}_2 = \theta^{-1}(\{0,1\}^n)$ and $\mathcal{R}_{\pm 1} = \theta^{-1}(\{-1,0,1\}^n)$. By $\tilde{x}$ we refer to the constant term of some polynomial $x \in \mathcal{R}$.

For CPA security of an encryption scheme and EUF-CMA security of a signature scheme we use the standard definitions.

2.1 Problems on Lattices

Definition 1 (MLWE). *Let $q > 2$ and $k > 0$. Let $\mathcal{R}$ be a ring and $\mathcal{R}_q = \mathcal{R}/q\mathcal{R}$. Let χ be a distribution over $\mathcal{R}_q$. For a secret $\mathbf{s} \in \mathcal{R}_q^k$, the Module Learning With Errors (MLWE) $A_\mathbf{s}$ distribution is defined as choosing $\mathbf{a} \leftarrow \mathcal{R}_q^k$ and $e \leftarrow \chi$, computing $b = \mathbf{s}^t\mathbf{a} + e \mod q$, and outputting $(\mathbf{a}, b)$.*

The MLWE problem $\mathsf{MLWE}_{q,\mathcal{R},k,\chi}$ is then defined as distinguishing between $A_\mathbf{s}$ for a secret $\mathbf{s} \leftarrow \mathcal{R}_q^k$ and the uniform distribution over $\mathcal{R}_q^{k+1}$.

It can be useful to group the $\mathbf{a}_i$ from m samples together as the column vectors of a matrix $\mathbf{A} \in \mathcal{R}_q^{k\times m}$ and the b_i as the entries of a vector $\mathbf{b} \in \mathcal{R}_q^m$, such that we have $\mathbf{s}^t\mathbf{A} + \mathbf{e}^t = \mathbf{b}^t$ for some error vector $\mathbf{e} \in \mathcal{R}_q^m$.

There exists an alternative version of the MLWE problem, where the secret is not sampled uniformly from $\mathcal{R}_q$, but instead sampled as $\mathbf{s} \leftarrow \chi^k$. This is called the *normal form* of MLWE. The described MLWE problems are decisional problems. There exist computational variants, where the goal is to compute the secret $\mathbf{s}$, given samples from the respective MLWE distribution. This is called the (normal form) *search* MLWE problem $\mathsf{sMLWE}_{q,\mathcal{R},k,\chi}$.

In some cases, we need to set the parameters of the normal form MLWE problem in such a way that the secret used to create a set of m samples is unique, meaning that with overwhelming probability there is no other secret and error vector that could produce the samples.

Lemma 1 (Short MLWE secrets are unique). *Let $q \neq 2$ be a prime with $q = 3,5 \mod 8$ (or $q = 1 \mod 2n$), $k > 0$, $n > 16$ be a power of 2, $\mathcal{R}_q = \mathbb{Z}_q[X]/(X^n + 1)$. Let $B_\beta = \{e \in \mathcal{R}_q : \|e\|_\infty \leq \beta\}$. Let $\Delta \geq 0$ such that $2\beta + \Delta < q^{1/4}$. Then, there exists an m and a negligible function negl such that*

$$\Pr\left[\begin{matrix}\exists(\mathbf{s},\mathbf{s}',\mathbf{e},\mathbf{e}') \in (B_\beta^k)^2 \times (B_\beta^m)^2 \\ \textit{with } \mathbf{s} \neq \mathbf{s}' \wedge \|\mathbf{b}\|_\infty \leq \Delta\end{matrix} : \begin{matrix}\mathbf{A} \leftarrow \mathcal{R}_q^{k\times m} \\ \mathbf{b}^t = (\mathbf{s}-\mathbf{s}')^t\mathbf{A} + (\mathbf{e}-\mathbf{e}')^t\end{matrix}\right] \leq \mathsf{negl}(n).$$

The proof can be found in the full version [7].

2.2 NIZKs

We model non-interactive zero-knowledge proof systems in the random oracle model. This is because when instantiating our generic construction of a reputation system, the NIZKs we use are in the random oracle model. The generic construction itself and the security proofs, however, do not make use of the random oracle model. There, it would suffice to model NIZKs without a random oracle by simply removing it from the syntax and security models.

Definition 2 (NIZK). *A non-interactive proof system (NIZK) for a relation* $\mathfrak{R}$ *in the random oracle model is defined as a triple* $\Pi_{\mathrm{NIZK}} = (\mathsf{Setup}, \mathcal{P}, \mathcal{V})$ *of ppt algorithms:*

- $\mathsf{Setup}(1^n)$ *outputs a common reference string* crs.
- $\mathcal{P}^{\mathcal{RO}(\cdot)}(\mathsf{crs}, x, w, m)$ *given instance* x*, witness* w*, and a message* m*, outputs a proof* π.
- $\mathcal{V}^{\mathcal{RO}(\cdot)}(\mathsf{crs}, x, m, \pi)$ *outputs a bit* b.

To simplify notation, we sometimes omit the random oracle $\mathcal{RO}(\cdot)$*, but assume implicitly that the prover and verifier have access to it. We say that the NIZK is* correct, *if for all* $(x, w) \in \mathfrak{R}$ *and* $m \in \{0,1\}^*$*, we have that*

$$\Pr[\mathcal{V}(\mathsf{crs}, x, m, \mathcal{P}(\mathsf{crs}, x, w, m)) : \mathsf{crs} \leftarrow \mathsf{Setup}(1^n)] = 1.$$

For a relation $\mathfrak{R}$, $L_{\mathfrak{R}} = \{x \mid \exists w : \ (x, w) \in \mathfrak{R}\}$ is the *language* associated with $\mathfrak{R}$. The message m is additional data bound to the proof (e.g., including m in a Fiat-Shamir hash). Its role can be observed in Definition 6.

In order to display the relation $\mathfrak{R}$ that is proven, we will use the following notation for proofs.

Definition 3. *We denote the generation of a proof* $\pi \leftarrow \mathcal{P}(\mathsf{crs}, x, w, m)$ *by*

$$\pi \leftarrow \mathrm{NIZK}\{x; w; \mathfrak{R}(x, w)\}(m),$$

where $\mathcal{P}$ *is from a non-interactive proof system* Π_{NIZK} *for the relation* $\mathfrak{R}$*. We say "Verify* π*" to mean checking that* $\mathcal{V}(\mathsf{crs}, x, m, \pi) = 1$ *and we say "*π *verifies" or "*π *is valid" if* $\mathcal{V}(\mathsf{crs}, x, m, \pi) = 1$ *holds.*

With respect to security, we require the NIZK to be zero-knowledge (i.e. proofs can be simulated without a witness), sound (i.e. one cannot prove false statements), simulation-sound (i.e. one cannot prove false statements, even in the presence of simulated proofs), and straight-line extractable (i.e. there exists an extractor that can efficiently compute a witness from a valid proof without rewinding). These definitions are standard, we list them below, starting with zero-knowledge.

Definition 4 (Zero-Knowledge). *A NIZK* Π *is* zero-knowledge *if there exists a simulator* $\mathcal{S}$ *consisting of three ppt algorithms* $\mathcal{S} = (\mathcal{S}.\mathsf{Setup}, \mathcal{S}.\mathcal{RO}, \mathcal{S}.\mathsf{Sim})$ *such that for all ppt* $\mathcal{A}$ *there exists a negligible function* negl *such that,*

$$\mathsf{Adv}^{ZK}_{\Pi,\mathcal{A}}(n) = \left| \begin{array}{l} \Pr[\mathcal{A}^{\mathcal{P}(\mathsf{crs},\cdot,\cdot,\cdot),\mathcal{RO}(\cdot)}(1^n, \mathsf{crs}) = 1 : \mathsf{crs} \leftarrow \mathsf{Setup}(1^n)] \\ - \Pr[\mathcal{A}^{\mathsf{Sim}(\cdot,\cdot,\cdot),\mathcal{S}.\mathcal{RO}(\cdot)}(1^n, \mathsf{crs}) = 1 : \mathsf{crs} \leftarrow \mathcal{S}.\mathsf{Setup}(1^n)] \end{array} \right| \leq \mathsf{negl}(n)$$

where $\mathcal{RO}$ *denotes a random oracle. The oracle* $\mathsf{Sim}(x, w, m)$ *checks if* $(x, w) \in \mathfrak{R}$ *and if so, runs* $\mathcal{S}.\mathsf{Sim}(x, m)$*. We assume that* $\mathcal{S}$ *is stateful, i.e. it implicitly keeps state between invocations of* $\mathcal{S}.\mathsf{Setup}$*,* $\mathcal{S}.\mathcal{RO}$*, and* $\mathcal{S}.\mathsf{Sim}$*.*

We give the simulator two advantages beyond a regular prover that should allow it to efficiently simulate proofs without a witness: (1) $\mathcal{S}$.Setup generates crs and that process can yield a trapdoor that $\mathcal{S}$ stores in its state. (2) $\mathcal{S}$ answers the random oracle queries of $\mathcal{A}$ with $\mathcal{S}.\mathcal{RO}(\cdot)$, so $\mathcal{S}$ can program random oracle answers.

The second requirement we have is soundness, which states it is hard for an adversary to prove a false statement.

Definition 5 (Soundness). *We say that a NIZK Π is sound if for all ppt $\mathcal{A}$, there is a negligible function* negl *such that*

$$\mathsf{Adv}^{Snd}_{\Pi,\mathcal{A}}(n) = \Pr\left[\begin{matrix}\mathcal{V}^{\mathcal{RO}(\cdot)}(\mathsf{crs}, x, m, \pi) = 1 \wedge x \notin L_{\mathfrak{R}} : \\ \mathsf{crs} \leftarrow \mathsf{Setup}(1^n), (x, m, \pi) \leftarrow \mathcal{A}^{\mathcal{RO}(\cdot)}(1^n, \mathsf{crs})\end{matrix}\right] \leq \mathsf{negl}(n)$$

Next, we require simulation soundness, i.e. even given access to an oracle creating simulated proofs (potentially for false statements), it is hard to compute an accepting proof for a wrong (not-queried) statement x.

Definition 6 (Simulation soundness). *Let $\Pi = (\mathsf{Setup}, \mathcal{P}, \mathcal{V})$ be a zero-knowledge NIZK, with simulator $\mathcal{S}$ as in Definition 4. We say that a NIZK Π is* simulation-sound *if for all ppt $\mathcal{A}$, there exists a negligible function* negl *with*

$$\mathsf{Adv}^{SS}_{\Pi,\mathcal{A}}(n) = \Pr\left[\begin{matrix}\mathcal{V}^{\mathcal{S}.\mathcal{RO}(\cdot)}(\mathsf{crs}, x, m, \pi) = 1 \\ \wedge\, x \notin L_{\mathfrak{R}} \\ \wedge\, \mathcal{A} \text{ has not queried } \mathcal{S}.\mathsf{Sim}(x, m)\end{matrix} : \begin{matrix}\mathsf{crs} \leftarrow \mathcal{S}.\mathsf{Setup}(1^n), \\ (x, m, \pi) \leftarrow \mathcal{A}^{\mathcal{S}.\mathsf{Sim}(\cdot,\cdot), \mathcal{S}.\mathcal{RO}(\cdot)}(1^n, \mathsf{crs})\end{matrix}\right] \leq \mathsf{negl}(n)$$

Note that, as usual, $\mathcal{A}$ may even query $\mathcal{S}.\mathsf{Sim}(x, m)$ for $x \notin L$. The simulation soundness property is sometimes understood to imply non-malleability of the proof π, i.e. defined with the condition "π has not been output by $\mathcal{S}.\mathsf{Sim}(x, m)$" instead of "$\mathcal{A}$ has not queried $\mathcal{S}.\mathsf{Sim}(x, m)$". We use the weaker condition here, which corresponds to the fact that we do not consider immaterial changes to rating signatures (e.g., re-randomization with no change to the rating text or the rated party) an attack (see, for example, Definition 18).

Finally, we require straight-line extractability.

Definition 7 (Straight-line extractability). *Let $\Pi = (\mathsf{Setup}, \mathcal{P}, \mathcal{V})$ be a NIZK. We say that Π is a* straight-line extractable proof of knowledge *if there are ppt algorithms $\mathcal{E}_0, \mathcal{E}_1$ such that for all ppt $\mathcal{A}_0, \mathcal{A}_1$, there exist negligible functions $\mathsf{negl}_0, \mathsf{negl}_1$ such that*

$$\mathsf{Adv}^{\mathrm{PoK}_0}_{\Pi,\mathcal{A}_0}(n) = \left|\begin{matrix}\Pr[\mathcal{A}_0(1^n, \mathsf{crs}) = 1 : \mathsf{crs} \leftarrow \mathsf{Setup}(1^n)] \\ - \Pr[\mathcal{A}_0(1^n, \mathsf{crs}) = 1 : (\mathsf{crs}, td) \leftarrow \mathcal{E}_0(1^n)]\end{matrix}\right| \leq \mathsf{negl}_0(n)$$

and

$$\mathsf{Adv}^{\mathrm{PoK}_1}_{\Pi,\mathcal{A}_1}(n) = \Pr\left[\begin{matrix}\mathcal{V}^{\mathcal{RO}}(\mathsf{crs}, x, m, \pi) = 1 \\ \wedge\, (x, w) \notin \mathfrak{R}\end{matrix} : \begin{matrix}(\mathsf{crs}, td) \leftarrow \mathcal{E}_0(1^n), \\ (x, m, \pi) \leftarrow \mathcal{A}_1(1^n, \mathsf{crs}), \\ w \leftarrow \mathcal{E}_1(td, x, m, \pi)\end{matrix}\right] \leq \mathsf{negl}_1(n)$$

In the random oracle model, $\mathcal{E}_1$ gets the list of random oracle queries that $\mathcal{A}$ made as additional input.

We give the extractor the advantage of setting up crs (allowing it to embed a trapdoor td) and, in the random oracle model, of observing the random oracle queries of $\mathcal{A}$ (as in [22]). The extractor does not have any ability to rewind $\mathcal{A}$, so extraction through rewinding is not an option. Note that in this security definition, we do not give $\mathcal{A}$ access to simulated proofs.

Later on, to instantiate the reputation system based on lattices, we want to use NIZKs over the following relation.

Definition 8. *Let $q > 0$, $\mathcal{R}$ a ring, $\mathcal{R}_q = \mathcal{R}/q\mathcal{R}$. Let $\phi, \phi_{eval}, d, e, v_d, v_e, m_1, \ell$ and k_{bin} be non-negative. Let $\psi : \mathcal{R} \to \mathcal{R}, x \mapsto x(X^{-1})$ be an automorphism. Let*

- $f_i : \mathcal{R}_q^{2(m_1+\ell)} \to \mathcal{R}_q$ *be a quadratic function for* $i \in [\phi]$,
- $F_i : \mathcal{R}_q^{2(m_1+\ell)} \to \mathcal{R}_q$ *be an evaluation function for* $i \in [\phi_{eval}]$,
- $\mathbf{D}_i \in \mathcal{R}_q^{k_i \times 2(m_1+\ell)}, \mathbf{u}_i \in \mathcal{R}_q^{k_i}$ *for* $i \in [v_d]$,
- $\mathbf{E}_i \in \mathcal{R}_q^{p_i \times 2(m_1+\ell)}, \mathbf{v}_i \in \mathcal{R}_q^{p_i}$ *for* $i \in [v_e]$,
- $(\beta_i^{(d)})_{i \in [v_d]}, (\beta_i^{(e)})_{i \in [v_e]}$ *be some bounds,*
- $\mathbf{E}_{bin} \in \mathcal{R}_q^{k_{bin} \times 2(m_1+\ell)}$ *and* $\mathbf{v}_{bin} \in \mathcal{R}_q^{k_{bin}}$.

Call the combination of these parameters pp. *Define the relation $\mathfrak{R}^R$ to consist of pairs* (pp, $\mathbf{s}$) *with* $\mathbf{s} = (\mathbf{s}_1, \psi(\mathbf{s}_1), \mathbf{m}, \psi(\mathbf{m})) \in \mathcal{R}_q^{2m_1} \times \mathcal{R}_q^{2\ell}$*, such that the following conditions hold:*

$$\forall 1 \le i \le \phi, f_i(\mathbf{s}) = 0$$
$$\forall 1 \le i \le \phi_{eval}, \tilde{F}_i(\mathbf{s}) = 0$$
$$\forall 1 \le i \le v_d, \|\mathbf{D}_i\mathbf{s} - \mathbf{u}_i\|_\infty \le \beta_i^{(d)}$$
$$\forall 1 \le i \le v_e, \|\mathbf{E}_i\mathbf{s} - \mathbf{v}_i\| \le \beta_i^{(e)}$$
$$\mathbf{E}_{bin}\mathbf{s} - \mathbf{v}_{bin} \in \{0,1\}^{dk_{bin}}$$

Recall that the notation $\tilde{F}_i(\mathbf{s})$ denotes the constant term of polynomial $F_i(\mathbf{s})$.

Lemma 2 ([38]). *There exists a NIZK for relation $\mathfrak{R}^R$ that is zero-knowledge and simulation-sound in the random oracle model.*

While [38] only claim soundness instead of simulation-soundness, their analysis ([39, Appendix B], based on [1]) applies verbatim to simulation-soundness. This is because to argue soundness for a proof π for statement x and message m, one considers only random oracle queries of the form $\mathcal{H}(\mathsf{pp}, x, m, \cdots)$. Simulated proofs for $(x', m') \neq (x, m)$, in contrast, are only concerned with random oracle queries of the form $\mathcal{H}(\mathsf{pp}, x', m', \cdots)$. Hence programming the random oracle for $\mathsf{pp}, x', m', \cdots$ does not interfere with the soundness analysis at all. We can effectively imagine that the simulator and the soundness proof use two independent random oracles.

We also want the NIZK to be straight-line extractable. For this, we use Katsumata's transform [30] as shown in [11]. Their notion of multi-proof extractability implies our straight-line extractability.

Corollary 1 ([11,30,38]). *There exists a NIZK for relation $\mathfrak{R}^R$ that is zero-knowledge and simulation-sound and straight-line extractable in the random oracle model.*

3 Linking Indistinguishable Tags

A building block we need are *linking indistinguishable tags* (LIT). The idea of such a scheme is that one can compute a tag for a given message with a secret key. An adversary should not able to tell which secret key was used to create the tag. However, if one tags the same message twice, i.e. with the same secret key, anyone can discover this by linking the tags. There also exists a function f from which we can compute a public key $\mathsf{pk} = f(\mathsf{sk})$. We typically require f to be a one-way function implicitly. This public key is not used in the scheme itself, but can be used in conjunction with other primitives. The formal model looks as follows.

Definition 9. *A linking indistinguishable tags scheme consists of a function f and the following ppt algorithms:*

- $\mathsf{KeyGen}(1^n)$: *On input a security parameter n, it outputs a secret* sk.
- $\mathsf{Tag}(\mathsf{sk}, \mu)$: *On input a secret key* sk *and a message μ, it outputs a tag t.*
- $\mathsf{Vrfy}(\mathsf{sk}, \mu, t)$: *On input a secret key* sk, *a message μ and a tag t, it outputs a bit b.*
- $\mathsf{Link}(\mu, t_0, t_1)$: *On input a message μ and two tags t_0, t_1, it outputs a bit b.*

We require that a LIT is correct. This is the case if for all security parameters n, all sk *output by* $\mathsf{KeyGen}(1^n)$, *all messages μ, all tags t_0, t_1 output by* $\mathsf{Tag}(\mathsf{sk}, \mu)$, *we have that* $\mathsf{Vrfy}(\mathsf{sk}, \mu, t_0) = 1$ *and* $\mathsf{Link}(\mu, t_0, t_1) = 1$.

The first security requirement is tag-indistinguishability. In this indistinguishability game an adversary has to decide which of two secrets was used to create the challenge, while having access to tag oracle for these secrets. We define the oracle $\mathsf{Tg}(c, \mu)$ to return t if there exists some $(c, \mu, t) \in Q$. Else, we return $t \leftarrow \mathsf{Tag}(\mathsf{sk}_c, \mu)$ and add (c, μ, t) to Q.

$$\mathsf{Anon}^{LIT}_{\Pi,\mathcal{A},b}(n)$$

$\mathsf{sk}_0, \mathsf{sk}_1 \leftarrow \mathsf{KeyGen}(1^n)$
$\mathsf{pk}_i = f(\mathsf{sk}_i), i \in \{0,1\}$
$\mu^* \leftarrow \mathcal{A}^{\mathsf{Tg}(\cdot,\cdot)}(\mathsf{pk}_0, \mathsf{pk}_1)$
$t^* \leftarrow \mathsf{Tag}(\mathsf{sk}_b, \mu^*)$
$b' \leftarrow \mathcal{A}^{\mathsf{Tg}(\cdot,\cdot)}(t^*)$
If μ^* was queried, output 0, else output b'.

Definition 10. *A LIT Π has tag-indistinguishability, if there exists a negligible function* negl *such that for all ppt adversaries $\mathcal{A}$ it holds that*

$$\mathsf{Adv}_{\Pi,\mathcal{A}}^{LIT Anon}(n) := \left|\Pr[\mathsf{Anon}_{\Pi,\mathcal{A},0}^{LIT}(n) = 1] - \Pr[\mathsf{Anon}_{\pi,\mathcal{A},1}^{LIT}(n) = 1]\right| \leq \mathsf{negl}(n).$$

The second security requirement is linkability. This asks that no adversary can produce two secret key tag pairs and a message, such that the secret key tag pairs are valid for the message, while the tags do not link. In comparison to the security model of [20], we generalize our security model for linkability and allow the adversary to output two different secret keys, but they must map to the same public key.

$\mathsf{Linkable}_{\Pi,\mathcal{A}}^{LIT}(n)$
1 : $(\mathsf{sk}_0, \mathsf{sk}_1, \mu, t_0, t_1) \leftarrow \mathcal{A}(1^n)$
2 : If $f(\mathsf{sk}_0) \neq f(\mathsf{sk}_1)$ or $\exists i \in \{0,1\}$: $\mathsf{Vrfy}(\mathsf{sk}_i, \mu, t_i) = 0$, return 0.
3 : If $\mathsf{Link}(\mu, t_0, t_1) = 0$, output 1.

Definition 11. *A LIT Π has linkability if there exists a negligible function* negl *such that for all ppt adversaries $\mathcal{A}$ it holds that*

$$\Pr[\mathsf{Linkable}_{\Pi,\mathcal{A}}^{LIT}(n) = 1] \leq \mathsf{negl}(n).$$

Another security requirement, unforgeability, is similar to the requirement for a one-way function. It requires that no adversary is able to produce a secret key, message and valid tag, such that the tag links to another valid tag. For that, we need a tag oracle QTg, that on input (sk, μ) returns t if there exists $(\mu, t) \in Q$. Else it computes $t \leftarrow \mathsf{Tag}(\mathsf{sk}, \mu)$, adds (μ, t) to $\mathcal{Q}$ and returns t.

$\mathsf{Forge}_{\Pi,\mathcal{A}}^{LIT}(n)$
1 : $\mathcal{Q} = \emptyset$
2 : $\mathsf{sk} \leftarrow \mathsf{KeyGen}(1^n), \mathsf{pk} = f(\mathsf{sk})$
3 : $(\mathsf{sk}^*, \mu, t^*) \leftarrow \mathcal{A}^{\mathsf{QTg}(\mathsf{sk},\cdot)}(\mathsf{pk})$
4 : If $\mathsf{Vrfy}(\mathsf{sk}^*, \mu, t^*) = 0$, output 0.
5 : If $\exists$ $(\mu, t) \in \mathcal{Q}$ such that $\mathsf{Link}(\mu, t, t^*) = 1$, output 1.

Definition 12. *A LIT Π is unforgeable, if there exists a negligible function* negl *such that for all ppt adversaries $\mathcal{A}$ it holds that*

$$\Pr[\mathsf{Forge}_{\Pi,\mathcal{A}}^{LIT}(n) = 1] \leq \mathsf{negl}(n).$$

The last requirement for LIT schemes is non-invertability. This asks that an adversary is not able to find a secret key to given public key, while having access to a tag oracle.

$\mathsf{Invert}_{\Pi,\mathcal{A}}(n)$
1 : $\mathsf{sk} \leftarrow \mathsf{KeyGen}(1^n)$
2 : $\mathsf{pk} = f(\mathsf{sk})$
3 : $\mathsf{sk}' \leftarrow \mathcal{A}^{\mathsf{QTg}(\mathsf{sk},\cdot)}(\mathsf{pk})$
4 : If $\mathsf{pk} = f(\mathsf{sk}')$, output 1.

Here QTg is defined as before.

Definition 13. *A LIT Π has non-invertability, if there exists a negligible function* negl *such that for all ppt adversaries $\mathcal{A}$ it holds that*

$$\Pr[\mathsf{Invert}_{\Pi,\mathcal{A}}(n) = 1] \leq \mathsf{negl}(n).$$

Construction Based on Module Lattices. Given the formal model of a LIT, we now want to construct a LIT based on module lattices of rank k. When we later use the LIT in our reputation system, we only need $k = 1$, in which case the security assumption for the LIT reduces to ideal lattices. The LIT may be of independent interest, so we construct it with general k.

The idea for the construction is that a public key is simply a batch of MLWE samples for some secret $\mathbf{s}$. A tag on a message μ is the second component of another batch of MLWE samples, i.e. $\mathbf{t}^t = \mathbf{s}^t\mathbf{A}_\mu + \mathbf{e}'^t$, for the same secret $\mathbf{s}$ and some different error $\mathbf{e}'$, where we define $\mathbf{A}_\mu = \mathcal{RO}(\mu)$. This way, if we tag the same message twice, $\mathbf{A}_\mu$ is the same for both tags, and the difference of the two tags is equal to the difference of the two errors. Since this is short, we can detect that the tags were created for the same message.

Construction 14. *Let $m, k > 0$. Let $\beta < 2^{-\frac{n}{mk}+\frac{n}{2k}\log(q)-3}$. Let χ be a distribution over $\mathcal{R}_q$. Construct the LIT Π_{LIT} consisting of the following algorithms:*

- $\mathsf{KeyGen}(1^n)$: *Choose $\mathbf{s} \leftarrow \chi^k, \mathbf{e} \leftarrow \chi^m$. Set $\mathsf{sk} = (\mathbf{s}, \mathbf{e})$.*
- $\mathsf{Tag}(\mathsf{sk}, \mu)$: *Compute $\mathbf{A}_\mu = \mathcal{RO}(\mu) \in \mathcal{R}_q^{k\times m}$ and $\mathbf{e}' \leftarrow \chi^m$. Output $\mathbf{t}^t = \mathbf{s}^t\mathbf{A}_\mu + \mathbf{e}'^t$.*
- $\mathsf{Vrfy}(\mathsf{sk}, \mu, \mathbf{t})$: *Compute $\mathbf{A}_\mu = \mathcal{RO}(\mu) \in \mathcal{R}_q^{k\times m}$. If $\|\mathbf{t} - (\mathbf{s}^t\mathbf{A}_\mu)^t\|_\infty < \beta$ and $\|\mathbf{s}\|_\infty \leq \beta$, output 1.*
- $\mathsf{Link}(\mu, \mathbf{t}_0, \mathbf{t}_1)$: *If $\|\mathbf{t}_0 - \mathbf{t}_1\|_\infty < 2\beta$, output 1.*
- *$f = f_\mathbf{A}$ for $\mathbf{A} \leftarrow \mathcal{R}_q^{k\times m}$, $f_\mathbf{A}(\mathsf{sk}) = (\mathbf{s}^t\mathbf{A} + \mathbf{e}^t)^t$*

The construction is correct, if we have that $\Pr[\|x\|_\infty \leq \beta : x \leftarrow \chi]$ with overwhelming probability.

Lemma 3. *The LIT Π_{LIT} has tag-indistinguishability (Definition 10) in the random oracle model, if normal form $\mathsf{MLWE}_{q,\mathcal{R},k,\chi}$ is hard.*

This can be proven by proving that $\mathsf{Anon}^{LIT}_{\Pi_{\mathsf{LIT}},\mathcal{A},0}(n)$ is indistinguishable from a game where the challenge tag t^* is generated uniformly at random, which is possible using the indistinguishability of the MLWE distribution from the uniform distribution. Then, one does the same for $\mathsf{Anon}^{LIT}_{\Pi_{\mathsf{LIT}},\mathcal{A},1}(n)$, from which we can see that the two games are indistinguishable if normal form MLWE is hard.

Lemma 4. *The LIT Π_{LIT} has non-invertability (Definition 13) in the random oracle model if normal form $\mathsf{sMLWE}_{q,\mathcal{R},k,\chi}$ is hard.*

Proof. Let $\mathcal{A}$ be an adversary against the invertability of the LIT. We construct an adversary $\mathcal{B}$ against normal form search-MLWE from it. $\mathcal{B}$ simulates $\mathcal{A}$ by using batching m samples from his MLWE oracle into a public key pk. By the definition of the MLWE oracle, there is some secret $\mathbf{s}$ that was used to generated these samples. When $\mathcal{A}$ asks for a tag on a previously unqueried message μ, $\mathcal{B}$ uses its MLWE oracle to get a batch of m samples $(\mathbf{A}, \mathbf{b})$, defines $\mathcal{RO}(\mu) := \mathbf{A}$ and answers with $\mathbf{b}$. If $\mathcal{A}$ asks for a tag on a previously queried μ, $\mathcal{B}$ answers with the $\mathbf{b}$ it generated before. When $\mathcal{A}$ outputs some $\mathsf{sk}' = (\mathbf{s}', \mathbf{e}')$, $\mathcal{B}$ returns $\mathbf{s}'$ to its challenger. Due to Lemma 1 we know that the secret $\mathbf{s}$ behind the tags is unique, therefore we know $\mathbf{s} = \mathbf{s}'$ if $\mathcal{A}$ wins and thus $\mathbf{s}'$ is a valid solution for normal form search-MLWE. □

Lemma 5. *The LIT Π_{LIT} is linkable (Definition 11) in the random oracle model.*

Proof. The adversary can only win, if $f(\mathsf{sk}_0) = f(\mathsf{sk}_1)$. This means, that $\mathbf{s}_0^t\mathbf{A} + \mathbf{e}_0^t = \mathbf{s}_1^t\mathbf{A} + \mathbf{e}_1^t$, where $\mathsf{sk}_i = (\mathbf{s}_i, \mathbf{e}_i)$. Due to Lemma 1 we know that the short MLWE secrets are unique, meaning $\mathbf{s}_0 = \mathbf{s}_1$. Therefore we know that $\mathbf{t}_0 - \mathbf{t}_1 = \mathbf{s}_0^t\mathbf{A}_\mu + \mathbf{e}_0'^t - \mathbf{s}_1^t\mathbf{A}_\mu - \mathbf{e}_1'^t = \mathbf{e}_0'^t - \mathbf{e}_1'^t$ for some $\mathbf{e}_i', i \in \{0, 1\}$ with $\|\mathbf{e}_i'\|_\infty \leq \beta$. Thus we have $\|\mathbf{t}_0 - \mathbf{t}_1\|_\infty \leq 2\beta$ which is why the Link algorithm always outputs 1, meaning an adversary cannot win the linking game. □

Lemma 6. *The LIT Π_{LIT} is unforgeable (Definition 12) in the random oracle model if normal form $\mathsf{sMLWE}_{q,\mathcal{R},k,\chi}$ is hard.*

Proof. Let $\mathcal{A}$ be an adversary against the unforgeability of the LIT and let Q be the number of oracle queries of $\mathcal{A}$. Construct an adversary $\mathcal{B}$ against normal form search-MLWE. $\mathcal{B}$ uses the first m samples of its oracle as the pk and gives that to $\mathcal{A}$. Then, on tag-query μ, $\mathcal{B}$ asks its oracle for m samples batched as $(\mathbf{A}, \mathbf{b})$, programs the random oracle as $\mathcal{RO}(\mu) := \mathbf{A}$ and returns $\mathbf{b}$. This way, there is a consistent $\mathbf{s}$ behind the pk and tags $\mathcal{A}$ sees, although $\mathcal{B}$ does not know it. Then, $\mathcal{A}$ outputs some sk^*, μ and t^*. If the tag is valid and links to some tag t, $\mathcal{B}$ outputs $\mathbf{s}^*$, where $\mathsf{sk}^* = (\mathbf{s}^*, \cdot)$. Now, due to Lemma 1 and the choice of β we know that the probability that $\mathbf{s} \neq \mathbf{s}^*$ is negligible. Therefore, if $\mathcal{A}$ finds a forgery, $\mathcal{B}$ outputs a solution for normal form search-MWLE with overwhelming probability. □

Other Constructions. It is also possible to base similar constructions on the security of Learning With Errors, Learning With Rounding or Module Learning With Rounding [2]. For the latter two, this simplifies all algorithms, as we no longer have to consider the error or how to sample it and can, for example, simply check for equality of tags when linking them.

4 Reputation System

The first step to our reputation system is a syntax model. We base our model on [9], but add some changes. In our model, we define four different (types of) parties: the group manager, the opener, an issuer and a user. In contrast to [9], we identify a user by some user public key upk, which he can generate himself and for which he possesses some user secret key usk. Then, he can join the reputation system by interacting with the group manager, who knows some group manager key pair $(\mathsf{gmsk}, \mathsf{gmpk})$, with which he generates a registration token ρ to give to the user. Note that the joining of new users is dynamic and the number of users is not limited. Then, the user interacts with the issuer. The latter is identified by some issuer public key ipk, for which he knows some issuer secret isk. The issuer gives the user some rating token τ enabling the user to rate the issuer. Note that in contrast to [9], the party to be rated is the issuer and not a product of an issuer. The user rates the issuer by using his usk, ρ and τ, where the latter was issued by the issuer to be rated, to create a signature for the rating. Anybody can verify the signature to check that the rating is valid, while not being able to see which user created the signature. Should the user rate the same issuer twice, anybody can use the linking algorithm to detect that two ratings were created by the same user. The last party is the opener, which in contrast to [9] is a separate party from the group manager. The opener knows some opener secret key osk for some opener public key opk. In the case that a user misbehaves, the opener open a signature to break anonymity of the user, i.e. identify the user who created the signature. Note that the group manager and opener generate their secret keys separately, which is why our model offers a stronger security model than [9]. We now give the formal definition of a reputation system.

Definition 15. *A reputation system consists of the following algorithms:*

- $\mathsf{Setup}(1^n)$*: The ppt algorithm outputs some public parameters* pp*. We implicitly assume that all algorithms have* pp *as additional input.*
- $\mathsf{KeyGen}_M(1^n)$*: The ppt algorithm outputs a pair of group manager secret and public key* $(\mathsf{gmsk}, \mathsf{gmpk})$.
- $\mathsf{KeyGen}_O(1^n)$*: The ppt algorithm outputs a pair of opening secret and public key* $(\mathsf{osk}, \mathsf{opk})$.
- $\mathsf{KeyGen}_I(1^n)$*: The ppt algorithm outputs a pair of issuer secret and public key* $(\mathsf{isk}, \mathsf{ipk})$.
- $\mathsf{KeyGen}_U(1^n)$*: The ppt algorithm outputs a pair of user secret and public key* $(\mathsf{usk}, \mathsf{upk})$.

- $\mathsf{Join}(\mathsf{gmpk}, \mathsf{usk}), \mathsf{Register}(\mathsf{gmsk}, \mathsf{upk})$: *At the end of their interaction of these interactive ppt algorithms,* Join *outputs a registration token* ρ.
- $\mathsf{Request}(\mathsf{gmpk}, \mathsf{ipk}, \mathsf{usk}, \rho), \mathsf{Issue}(\mathsf{gmpk}, \mathsf{isk}, \mathsf{upk})$: *At the end of the interaction of these interactive ppt algorithms,* Request *outputs a rating token* τ.
- $\mathsf{Sign}(\mathsf{gmpk}, \mathsf{opk}, \mathsf{ipk}, \mathsf{usk}, \rho, \tau, \mathsf{rtng})$: *The ppt algorithm outputs a signature* σ.
- $\mathsf{Vrfy}(\mathsf{gmpk}, \mathsf{opk}, \mathsf{ipk}, \mathsf{rtng}, \sigma)$. *The ppt algorithm outputs a bit* b.
- $\mathsf{Open}(\mathsf{gmpk}, \mathsf{osk}, \mathsf{ipk}, \mathsf{rtng}, \sigma)$: *The ppt algorithm outputs some* upk.
- $\mathsf{Link}(\mathsf{gmpk}, \mathsf{opk}, \mathsf{ipk}, (\mathsf{rtng}', \sigma'), (\mathsf{rtng}'', \sigma''))$: *The ppt algorithm outputs a bit* b.

Definition 16. *A reputation system is correct if for all security parameters* n, *all* $\mathsf{pp} \in [\mathsf{Setup}(1^n)]$, *all* $(\mathsf{gmsk}, \mathsf{gmpk}) \in [\mathsf{KeyGen}_M(1^n)]$, *all* $(\mathsf{osk}, \mathsf{opk}) \in [\mathsf{KeyGen}_O(1^n)]$, *all* $(\mathsf{isk}, \mathsf{ipk}) \in [\mathsf{KeyGen}_I(1^n)]$, *all* $(\mathsf{usk}, \mathsf{upk}_i) \in [\mathsf{KeyGen}_U(1^n)]$, *all* $\rho \in [\mathsf{Join}(\mathsf{gmpk}, \mathsf{usk}_i) \leftrightarrow \mathsf{Register}(\mathsf{gmsk}, \mathsf{upk})]$, *all* $\tau \in [\mathsf{Request}(\mathsf{gmpk}, \mathsf{ipk}, \mathsf{usk}_i, \rho_i) \leftrightarrow \mathsf{Issue}(\mathsf{gmpk}, \mathsf{isk}, \mathsf{upk})]$, *all ratings* rtng, *all* $\sigma \in [\mathsf{Sign}(\mathsf{gmpk}, \mathsf{opk}, \mathsf{ipk}, \mathsf{usk}_i, \rho, \tau, \mathsf{rtng})]$, *all ratings* rtng′, *all* $\sigma' \in [\mathsf{Sign}(\mathsf{gmpk}, \mathsf{opk}, \mathsf{ipk}, \mathsf{usk}, \rho, \tau, \mathsf{rtng}')]$ *it holds that*

- $\mathsf{Vrfy}(\mathsf{gmpk}, \mathsf{opk}, \mathsf{ipk}, \mathsf{rtng}, \sigma_i) = 1$
- $\mathsf{Open}(\mathsf{gmpk}, \mathsf{opk}, \mathsf{ipk}, \mathsf{rtng}, \sigma_i) = \mathsf{upk}_i$
- $\mathsf{Link}(\mathsf{gmpk}, \mathsf{opk}, \mathsf{ipk}, (\mathsf{rtng}, \sigma), (\mathsf{rtng}', \sigma')) = 1$.

4.1 Security Model

Next we define the security model of a reputation system. We consider five different notions called anonymity, non-frameability, traceability, public-linkability and joining security. These notions are inspired by the model of [9], except for non-frameability, which replaces strong-exculpability, and joining security, which is new since we split the group manager and opener into two parties.

In our security games, we model corruption differently than [9,20]. Instead of giving the adversary oracles to corrupt parties, we assume that every participant is corrupted, except for the minimal set that is needed so that the security experiment is not trivially solvable. We note that this model of corruption does not change the security level, it simply makes it easier to argue in proofs. Then, since we differentiate between the group manager and issuers, we can corrupt only one of them if needed. More importantly, this allows us model full corruption, meaning the adversary can choose the public keys *freely* for corrupted parties, where in [20] the adversary also has to output a valid secret key for the public key he outputs. We also assume that the adversary carries a state in between its calls. Note that we do not consider concurrency.

Before we define the security experiments, we define some oracles that an adversary $\mathcal{A}$ may have access to.

$\mathsf{Rg}(\mathsf{gmsk}, \mathsf{upk})$: Run $\mathcal{A} \leftrightarrow \mathsf{Register}(\mathsf{gmsk}, \mathsf{upk})$. Add upk to $\mathcal{U}$.
$\mathsf{Req}(\mathsf{gmpk}, \mathsf{ipk}, u)$: If the input was queried before, output $\perp$. Else, run $\tau_{u,\mathsf{ipk}} \leftarrow \mathsf{Request}(\mathsf{gmpk}, \mathsf{ipk}, \mathsf{usk}_u, \rho_u) \leftrightarrow \mathcal{A}$ and store the rating token $\tau_{u,\mathsf{ipk}}$.
$\mathsf{SigO}(\mathsf{gmpk}, \mathsf{opk}, \mathsf{ipk}, u, \mathsf{rtng})$: If $\tau_{u,\mathsf{ipk}}$ is undefined or the input was queried before, output $\perp$. Else, output $\sigma_{u,\mathsf{ipk}} \leftarrow \mathsf{Sign}(\mathsf{gmpk}, \mathsf{opk}, \mathsf{ipk}, \mathsf{usk}_u, \tau_{u,\mathsf{ipk}}, \mathsf{rtng})$. Add $(\mathsf{ipk}, \mathsf{rtng}, \sigma_{u,\mathsf{ipk}})$ to $\mathcal{Q}$.

$\mathsf{Iss}(\mathsf{gmpk}, \mathsf{isk}, \mathsf{upk})$: Add upk to $\mathcal{I}$. Run $\mathcal{A} \leftrightarrow \mathsf{Issue}(\mathsf{gmpk}, \mathsf{isk}, \mathsf{upk})$.

Note that in the security games, some of these parameters are fixed and cannot be chosen by the adversary. For the Rg oracle, for example, we fix gmsk, but leave upk open and thus write $\mathsf{Rg}(\mathsf{gmsk}, \cdot)$ in the JoinSecurity game.

The first security requirement for users is that they stay anonymous. In the anonymity experiment, we have two honest users that we try to protect. Except for these two users and the opener, we assume that every other party is corrupted, i.e. controlled by the adversary. In contrast to the notion of full-anonymity of group signature we only have selfless anonymity, meaning it is possible for a user to identify his own signatures. Thus, the usks of the honest users should stay hidden to the adversary.

$\mathsf{Anon}_{\Pi,\mathcal{A},b}(n)$

$\mathsf{pp} \leftarrow \mathsf{Setup}(1^n)$
$(\mathsf{osk}, \mathsf{opk}) \leftarrow \mathsf{KeyGen}_O(1^n)$
$\mathsf{gmpk} \leftarrow \mathcal{A}(\mathsf{opk})$
For $u \in \{0,1\}$
  $(\mathsf{usk}_u, \mathsf{upk}_u) \leftarrow \mathsf{KeyGen}_U(1^n)$
  $\rho_u \leftarrow \mathsf{Join}(\mathsf{gmpk}, \mathsf{usk}_u) \leftrightarrow \mathcal{A}(\mathsf{upk}_u)$
  If $\rho_u = \perp$, return 0.
$\mathsf{ipk}^* \leftarrow \mathcal{A}^{\mathsf{Req}(\mathsf{gmpk},\cdot,\cdot),\mathsf{SigO}(\mathsf{gmpk},\mathsf{opk},\cdot,\cdot,\cdot),\mathsf{Open}(\mathsf{gmpk},\mathsf{osk},\cdot,\cdot,\cdot)}$
$\tau_u \leftarrow \mathsf{Request}(\mathsf{gmpk}, \mathsf{ipk}^*, \mathsf{usk}_u, \rho_u) \leftrightarrow \mathcal{A}$ for $u \in \{0,1\}$
If $\tau_u = \perp$ for any $u \in \{0,1\}$, return 0.
$\mathsf{rtng} \leftarrow \mathcal{A}^{\mathsf{Req}(\mathsf{gmpk},\cdot,\cdot),\mathsf{SigO}(\mathsf{gmpk},\mathsf{opk},\cdot,\cdot,\cdot),\mathsf{Open}(\mathsf{gmpk},\mathsf{osk},\cdot,\cdot,\cdot)}$
$\sigma \leftarrow \mathsf{Sign}(\mathsf{gmpk}, \mathsf{opk}, \mathsf{ipk}^*, \mathsf{usk}_b, \rho_b, \tau_b, \mathsf{rtng})$
$b' \leftarrow \mathcal{A}^{\mathsf{Req}(\mathsf{gmpk},\cdot,\cdot),\mathsf{SigO}(\mathsf{gmpk},\mathsf{opk},\cdot,\cdot,\cdot),\mathsf{Open}(\mathsf{gmpk},\mathsf{isk},\cdot,\cdot,\cdot)}(\sigma)$
If there was a query to Open with $(\mathsf{gmpk}, \mathsf{osk}, \cdot, \cdot, \sigma)$ as argument, return 0.
If there was a query to SigO with $(\mathsf{gmpk}, \mathsf{opk}, \mathsf{ipk}^*, \cdot, \cdot)$ as argument, return 0.
Return b'.

Definition 17. *A reputation system Π is anonymous, if there exists a negligible function, such that for all ppt adversaries $\mathcal{A}$ it holds that*

$$\mathsf{Adv}^{anon}_{\Pi,\mathcal{A}}(n) := |\Pr[\mathsf{Anon}_{\Pi,\mathcal{A},0}(n) = 1] - \Pr[\mathsf{Anon}_{\Pi,\mathcal{A},1}(n) = 1]| \leq \mathsf{negl}(n).$$

Another security requirement for users is non-frameability. This expresses that any adversary can neither create a signature that opens to an honest user nor create a signature that links to one of an honest user, where the latter security requirement was added by [20]. In the security experiment, we have one user to be protected. In contrast to [20], here and in all further security games, we require that the keys of the opener are generated honestly. This is due to the fact that we do not include a Judge algorithm as [20] do.

$\mathsf{NFrame}_{\Pi,\mathcal{A}}(n)$

$\mathsf{pp} \leftarrow \mathsf{Setup}(1^n)$
$\mathcal{Q} = \emptyset$
$(\mathsf{osk}, \mathsf{opk}) \leftarrow \mathsf{KeyGen}_{\mathcal{O}}(1^n)$
$\mathsf{gmpk} \leftarrow \mathcal{A}(\mathsf{osk})$
$(\mathsf{usk}_0, \mathsf{upk}_0) \leftarrow \mathsf{KeyGen}_{\mathcal{U}}(1^n)$
$\rho_0 \leftarrow \mathsf{Join}(\mathsf{gmpk}, \mathsf{usk}_0) \leftrightarrow \mathcal{A}(\mathsf{upk}_0)$
$(\mathsf{ipk}, \mathsf{rtng}, \sigma) \leftarrow \mathcal{A}^{\mathsf{Req}(\mathsf{gmpk},\cdot,0),\mathsf{SigO}(\mathsf{gmpk},\mathsf{opk},\cdot,0,\cdot)}()$
$\mathsf{upk} \leftarrow \mathsf{Open}(\mathsf{gmpk}, \mathsf{osk}, \mathsf{ipk}, \mathsf{rtng}, \sigma)$
If $\mathsf{Vrfy}(\mathsf{gmpk}, \mathsf{opk}, \mathsf{ipk}, \mathsf{rtng}, \sigma) = 0$, return 0
If $(\mathsf{ipk}, \mathsf{rtng}, \cdot) \in \mathcal{Q}$, return 0
If $\mathsf{upk} = \mathsf{upk}_0$, return 1
If $\exists(\mathsf{ipk}, \mathsf{rtng}', \sigma') \in \mathcal{Q} : \mathsf{Link}(\mathsf{gmpk}, \mathsf{opk}, \mathsf{ipk}, (\mathsf{rtng}, \sigma), (\mathsf{rtng}', \sigma')) = 1$, return 1

Definition 18. *A reputation system Π has non-frameability, if there exists a negligible function* negl, *such that for all ppt adversaries $\mathcal{A}$ it holds that*

$$\Pr[\mathsf{NFrame}_{\Pi,\mathcal{A}}(n) = 1] \leq \mathsf{negl}(n).$$

An issuers requires traceability from the reputation system, which means that it is not possible to create a signature that does not open to some user or that opens to a user that was not given a rating token by an honest issuer. Here, we create one honest issuer that we want to protect.

$\mathsf{Trace}_{\Pi,\mathcal{A}}(n)$

$\mathsf{pp} \leftarrow \mathsf{Setup}(1^n)$
$\mathcal{I} = \emptyset$
$(\mathsf{osk}, \mathsf{opk}) \leftarrow \mathsf{KeyGen}_{\mathcal{O}}(1^n)$
$(\mathsf{isk}, \mathsf{ipk}) \leftarrow \mathsf{KeyGen}_{\mathcal{I}}(1^n)$
$\mathsf{gmpk} \leftarrow \mathcal{A}(\mathsf{osk}, \mathsf{ipk})$
$(\sigma, \mathsf{rtng}) \leftarrow \mathcal{A}^{\mathsf{Iss}(\mathsf{gmpk},\mathsf{isk},\cdot)}()$
If $\mathsf{Vrfy}(\mathsf{gmpk}, \mathsf{opk}, \mathsf{ipk}, \mathsf{rtng}, \sigma) = 0$, return 0
$\mathsf{upk} \leftarrow \mathsf{Open}(\mathsf{gmpk}, \mathsf{osk}, \mathsf{ipk}, \mathsf{rtng}, \sigma)$
If $\mathsf{upk} = \perp \vee \mathsf{upk} \notin \mathcal{I}$, return 1

Definition 19. *A reputation system Π has traceability, if there exists a negligible function* negl, *such that for all ppt adversaries $\mathcal{A}$ it holds that*

$$\Pr[\mathsf{Trace}_{\Pi,\mathcal{A}}(n) = 1] \leq \mathsf{negl}(n).$$

A security guarantee for the whole system is public-linkability. This requires that the outputs of Open and Link are consistent to each other, meaning it is not possible for an adversary to create two ratings for the same issuer that open to the same user, but do not link.

$\mathsf{PLinkable}_{\Pi,\mathcal{A}}(n)$

$\mathsf{pp} \leftarrow \mathsf{Setup}(1^n)$
$(\mathsf{osk}, \mathsf{opk}) \leftarrow \mathsf{KeyGen}_O(1^n)$
$(\mathsf{gmpk}, \mathsf{ipk}, (\sigma_j, \mathsf{rtng}_j)_{j\in\{0,1\}}) \leftarrow \mathcal{A}(\mathsf{osk})$
If $\exists j \in \{0,1\} : \mathsf{Vrfy}(\mathsf{gmpk}, \mathsf{opk}, \mathsf{ipk}, \mathsf{rtng}_j, \sigma_j) = 0$, return 0.
If $\mathsf{Open}(\mathsf{gmpk}, \mathsf{osk}, \mathsf{ipk}, \mathsf{rtng}_0, \sigma_0) \neq \mathsf{Open}(\mathsf{gmpk}, \mathsf{osk}, \mathsf{ipk}, \mathsf{rtng}_1, \sigma_1)$, return 0.
If $\mathsf{Link}(\mathsf{gmpk}, \mathsf{opk}, \mathsf{ipk}, (\mathsf{rtng}_0, \sigma_0), (\mathsf{rtng}_1, \sigma_1)) = 0$, return 1.

Definition 20. *A reputation system Π has public-linkability, if there exists a negligible function* negl*, such that for all ppt adversaries $\mathcal{A}$ it holds that*

$$\Pr[\mathsf{PLinkable}_{\Pi,\mathcal{A}}(n) = 1] \leq \mathsf{negl}(n).$$

The group manager also has a security requirement. He wants that every user who wants to join the system must register with him and does not circumvent him. Else, issuers can invent non-existent users to rate themselves or their products.

$\mathsf{JoinSecurity}_{\Pi,\mathcal{A}}(n)$

$\mathsf{pp} \leftarrow \mathsf{Setup}(1^n)$
$\mathcal{U} = \emptyset$
$(\mathsf{gmsk}, \mathsf{gmpk}) \leftarrow \mathsf{KeyGen}_M(1^n)$
$(\mathsf{osk}, \mathsf{opk}) \leftarrow \mathsf{KeyGen}_O(1^n)$
$(\mathsf{ipk}, \mathsf{rtng}, \sigma) \leftarrow \mathcal{A}^{\mathsf{Rg}(\mathsf{gmsk},\cdot)}(\mathsf{gmpk}, \mathsf{osk})$
If $\mathsf{Vrfy}(\mathsf{gmpk}, \mathsf{opk}, \mathsf{ipk}, \mathsf{rtng}, \sigma) = 0$, return 0.
$\mathsf{upk} \leftarrow \mathsf{Open}(\mathsf{gmpk}, \mathsf{osk}, \mathsf{ipk}, \mathsf{rtng}, \sigma)$
If $\mathsf{upk} \notin \mathcal{U}$, output 1.

Definition 21. *A reputation system Π has join-security, if there exists a negligible function* negl*, such that for all ppt adversaries $\mathcal{A}$ it holds that*

$$\Pr[\mathsf{JoinSecurity}\Pi, \mathcal{A}(n) = 1] \leq \mathsf{negl}(n).$$

4.2 Generic Construction

We construct a reputation system from a signature scheme, an encryption scheme, a LIT, and a NIZK.

Construction 22. *Let* $\Sigma = (\mathsf{KeyGen}_\Sigma, \mathsf{Sign}_\Sigma, \mathsf{Vrfy}_\Sigma)$ *be a signature scheme. Let* $\Pi_{\mathsf{Enc}} = (\mathsf{KeyGen}_{\mathsf{Enc}}, \mathsf{Enc}, \mathsf{Dec})$ *be an encryption scheme. Let* $\Pi_{\mathsf{LIT}} = (\mathsf{KeyGen}_{\mathsf{LIT}}, \mathsf{Tag}, \mathsf{Vrfy}_{\mathsf{LIT}}, \mathsf{Link}_{\mathsf{LIT}}, f)$ *be a LIT scheme. Let* Π_{NIZK} *be a non-interactive proof system for the relation listed in the "NIZK" expression below.*

- $\mathsf{Setup}(1^n)$: *Run* $\mathsf{pp} \leftarrow \Pi_{\mathrm{NIZK}}.\mathsf{Setup}(1^n)$.
- $\mathsf{KeyGen}_M(1^n)$: *Run* $(\mathsf{gmsk}, \mathsf{gmpk}) \leftarrow \mathsf{KeyGen}_\Sigma(1^n)$.
- $\mathsf{KeyGen}_O(1^n)$: *Run* $(\mathsf{sk}_{\mathsf{Enc}}, \mathsf{pk}_{\mathsf{Enc}}) \leftarrow \mathsf{KeyGen}_{\mathsf{Enc}}(1^n)$ *and* $(\mathsf{sk}'_{\mathsf{Enc}}, \mathsf{pk}'_{\mathsf{Enc}}) \leftarrow \mathsf{KeyGen}_{\mathsf{Enc}}(1^n)$. *Set* $(\mathsf{osk}, \mathsf{opk}) = (\mathsf{sk}_{\mathsf{Enc}}, (\mathsf{pk}_{\mathsf{Enc}}, \mathsf{pk}'_{\mathsf{Enc}}))$ *and forget* $\mathsf{sk}'_{\mathsf{Enc}}$.
- $\mathsf{KeyGen}_I(1^n)$: *Run* $(\mathsf{isk}, \mathsf{ipk}) \leftarrow \mathsf{KeyGen}_\Sigma(1^n)$.
- $\mathsf{KeyGen}_U(1^n)$: *Choose* $\mathsf{usk} \leftarrow \mathsf{KeyGen}_{\mathsf{LIT}}(1^n)$ *and compute* $\mathsf{upk} = f(\mathsf{usk})$.
- $\mathsf{Join}(\mathsf{gmpk}, \mathsf{usk}), \mathsf{Register}(\mathsf{gmsk}, \mathsf{upk})$: *The group manager signs* $\rho \leftarrow \mathsf{Sign}_\Sigma(\mathsf{gmsk}, \mathsf{upk})$ *and sends* ρ *to the user. If* $\mathsf{Vrfy}_\Sigma(\mathsf{gmpk}, \mathsf{upk}, \rho)$, *the user outputs it.*
- $\mathsf{Request}(\mathsf{gmpk}, \mathsf{ipk}, \mathsf{usk}, \rho), \mathsf{Issue}(\mathsf{gmpk}, \mathsf{isk}, \mathsf{upk})$: *The issuer signs* $\tau \leftarrow \mathsf{Sign}_\Sigma(\mathsf{isk}, \mathsf{upk})$ *and sends* τ *to the user. If* $\mathsf{Vrfy}_\Sigma(\mathsf{ipk}, \mathsf{upk}, \tau)$, *the user outputs it.*
- $\mathsf{Sign}(\mathsf{gmpk}, \mathsf{opk}, \mathsf{ipk}, \mathsf{usk}, \rho, \tau, \mathsf{rtng})$: *Compute* $c = \mathsf{Enc}(\mathsf{pk}_{\mathsf{Enc}}, \mathsf{upk}; r)$. *Compute* $c' = \mathsf{Enc}(\mathsf{pk}'_{\mathsf{Enc}}, \mathsf{usk}; r')$. *Compute* $l = \mathsf{Tag}(\mathsf{usk}, \mathsf{ipk}; r_t)$. *Output* $\sigma = (c, c', l, \pi)$, *where*

$$\begin{aligned}\pi = \mathrm{NIZK}\{&\mathsf{gmpk}, \mathsf{opk}, \mathsf{ipk}, \mathsf{pk}_{\mathsf{Enc}}, \mathsf{pk}'_{\mathsf{Enc}}, c, c', l;\\ &\mathsf{upk}, \mathsf{usk}, \rho, \tau, r, r' ;\mathsf{upk} = f(\mathsf{usk})\wedge\\ &\mathsf{Vrfy}_\Sigma(\mathsf{gmpk}, \mathsf{upk}, \rho) = 1\wedge\\ &\mathsf{Vrfy}_\Sigma(\mathsf{ipk}, \mathsf{upk}, \tau) = 1\wedge\\ &c = \mathsf{Enc}(\mathsf{pk}_{\mathsf{Enc}}, \mathsf{upk}; r)\wedge\\ &c' = \mathsf{Enc}(\mathsf{pk}'_{\mathsf{Enc}}, \mathsf{usk}; r')\wedge\\ &\mathsf{Vrfy}_{\mathsf{LIT}}(\mathsf{usk}, \mathsf{ipk}, l) = 1\}(\mathsf{rtng})\end{aligned}$$

- $\mathsf{Vrfy}(\mathsf{gmpk}, \mathsf{opk}, \mathsf{ipk}, \mathsf{rtng}, \sigma)$: *Verify* π *for the corresponding statement.*
- $\mathsf{Open}(\mathsf{gmpk}, \mathsf{osk}, \mathsf{ipk}, \mathsf{rtng}, \sigma)$: *Verify* π *for the corresponding statement. If* π *is valid, output* $\mathsf{upk} = \mathsf{Dec}(\mathsf{osk}, c)$.
- $\mathsf{Link}(\mathsf{gmpk}, \mathsf{opk}, \mathsf{ipk}, (\mathsf{rtng}', \sigma'), (\mathsf{rtng}'', \sigma''))$: *Verify* π', π'' *for the corresponding statements. If* π', π'' *are valid, output* $\mathsf{Link}_{\mathsf{LIT}}(\mathsf{ipk}, l', l'')$.

The correctness of the construction follows directly from the correctness of its building blocks.

4.3 Security of the Generic Construction

The encryption of usk with $\mathsf{pk}'_{\mathsf{Enc}}$ in a rating is not necessary for functionality, but a crucial component for the security proof. This is similar to the Naor-Yung paradigm to get CCA security of an encryption scheme from CPA security. Without the encryption of usk we would have to assume online simulation-extractability (we use the terminology found in [18])– that it is hard for an adversary to create a valid proof from which an extractor cannot extract, even if the adversary sees simulated proofs for possibly wrong statements not in the language, and the extractor needs to be able to extract during protocol execution, not just at the end – instead of simulation soundness from the NIZK. This is a significantly stronger assumption on the proof system, so we choose to encrypt the usk and to require simulation-soundness.

Theorem 1. *If Π_{Enc} is CPA secure , the LIT has indistinguishable tags (Definition 10) and Π_{NIZK} has zero-knowledgeness and simulation-soundness (Definitions 4 and 6), the reputation system is anonymous (Definition 17).*

Note that by our modelling of NIZKs, this theorem and the other security theorems of the generic construction hold in the random oracle model. However, as stated in Sect. 2.2, they can be adapted to hold in the standard model.

Proof. We prove this by a series of games. An overview can be found in Table 1.

Table 1. An overview of the sequence of games for the anonymity proof. The column π states whether proofs are done honestly ($\mathcal{P}$) or simulated ($\mathcal{S}$). The columns *Challenge* and *Query* state what messages are encrypted in the ciphertexts c, c' during the generation of the challenge or the signature query answer. *Tag* states which secret is used to generate a tag. *Opening* states how opening is done.

	π	Challenge	Query	Tag	Opening
Game_0	$\mathcal{P}$	$c \equiv \mathsf{upk}_0$ $c' \equiv \mathsf{usk}_0$	$c \equiv \mathsf{upk}_u$ $c' \equiv \mathsf{usk}_u$	usk_0	$\mathsf{Dec}(\mathsf{sk}_{\mathsf{Enc}}, c)$
Game_1	$\mathcal{S}$	$c \equiv \mathsf{upk}_0$ $c' \equiv \mathsf{usk}_0$	$c \equiv \mathsf{upk}_u$ $c' \equiv \mathsf{usk}_u$	usk_0	$\mathsf{Dec}(\mathsf{sk}_{\mathsf{Enc}}, c)$
Game_2	$\mathcal{S}$	$c \equiv \mathsf{upk}_0$ $c' \equiv 1^{\lvert\mathsf{usk}_0\rvert}$	$c \equiv \mathsf{upk}_u$ $c' \equiv 1^{\lvert\mathsf{usk}_u\rvert}$	usk_0	$\mathsf{Dec}(\mathsf{sk}_{\mathsf{Enc}}, c)$
Game_3	$\mathcal{S}$	$c \equiv \mathsf{upk}_0$ $c' \equiv 1^{\lvert\mathsf{usk}_0\rvert}$	$c \equiv \mathsf{upk}_u$ $c' \equiv 1^{\lvert\mathsf{usk}_u\rvert}$	usk_1	$\mathsf{Dec}(\mathsf{sk}_{\mathsf{Enc}}, c)$
Game_4	$\mathcal{S}$	$c \equiv \mathsf{upk}_0$ $c' \equiv \mathsf{usk}_1$	$c \equiv \mathsf{upk}_u$ $c' \equiv \mathsf{usk}_u$	usk_1	$\mathsf{Dec}(\mathsf{sk}_{\mathsf{Enc}}, c)$
Game_5	$\mathcal{S}$	$c \equiv \mathsf{upk}_0$ $c' \equiv \mathsf{usk}_1$	$c \equiv \mathsf{upk}_u$ $c' \equiv \mathsf{usk}_u$	usk_1	$f(\mathsf{Dec}(\mathsf{sk}'_{\mathsf{Enc}}, c'))$
Game_6	$\mathcal{S}$	$c \equiv \mathsf{upk}_1$ $c' \equiv \mathsf{usk}_1$	$c \equiv \mathsf{upk}_u$ $c' \equiv \mathsf{usk}_u$	usk_1	$f(\mathsf{Dec}(\mathsf{sk}'_{\mathsf{Enc}}, c'))$
Game_7	$\mathcal{S}$	$c \equiv \mathsf{upk}_1$ $c' \equiv \mathsf{usk}_1$	$c \equiv \mathsf{upk}_u$ $c' \equiv \mathsf{usk}_u$	usk_1	$\mathsf{Dec}(\mathsf{sk}_{\mathsf{Enc}}, c)$
Game_8	$\mathcal{P}$	$c \equiv \mathsf{upk}_1$ $c' \equiv \mathsf{usk}_1$	$c \equiv \mathsf{upk}_u$ $c' \equiv \mathsf{usk}_u$	usk_1	$\mathsf{Dec}(\mathsf{sk}_{\mathsf{Enc}}, c)$

Define $\epsilon_{\mathcal{D},a,b}(n)$ to be the advantage of some ppt $\mathcal{D}$ distinguishing $\mathsf{Game}_a(n)$ from $\mathsf{Game}_b(n)$. Let Game_0 be the Anon_0 game. Define Game_1 to be the same game as Game_0, except that the challenger uses the simulator $\mathcal{S}$ of Π_{NIZK} (Definition 4) to generate all proofs, including the challenge. We immediately see that an adversary cannot distinguish between these games, as the difference of the distribution of the proofs is negligible due to the zero-knowledge property of the proof system. Thus, we have that for all ppt distinguishers $\mathcal{D}$, there exists a ppt $\mathcal{A}_0$ such that

$$\mathsf{Adv}^{ZK}_{\Pi_{\text{NIZK}},\mathcal{A}_0}(n) = \epsilon_{\mathcal{D},0,1}(n).$$

Define Game_2 to be the same game as Game_1 except that c' in the signature queries is generated as $c' \leftarrow \mathsf{Enc}(\mathsf{pk}'_{\mathsf{Enc}}, 1^{|\mathsf{usk}_u|})$, i.e. we encrypt a string of ones instead of usk_u. Furthermore, c' in the challenge is generated as $c' \leftarrow \mathsf{Enc}(\mathsf{pk}'_{\mathsf{Enc}}, 1^{|\mathsf{usk}_0|})$, i.e. we encrypt a string of ones instead of usk_0. This is indistinguishable by the CPA security of the encryption scheme. By a standard hybrid argument we can construct a ppt $\mathcal{A}$ against the CPA security of Π_{Enc} from a distinguisher $\mathcal{D}$ such that

$$\mathsf{Adv}^{CPA}_{\Pi_{\mathsf{Enc}},\mathcal{A}_1}(n) = \frac{1}{Q+1}\epsilon_{\mathcal{D},1,2}(n).$$

Define Game_3 to be the same game as Game_2 except that tags l in the signature queries and the challenge are computed as $l \leftarrow \mathsf{Tag}(\mathsf{usk}_1, \mathsf{ipk}; r_t)$, i.e. we use usk_1 instead of usk_0. This is indistinguishable by the tag-indistinguishability of Π_{LIT} (Definition 10). Let $\mathcal{D}$ be distinguisher distinguishing Game_2 and Game_3. Construct an adversary $\mathcal{A}_2$ against the tag-indistinguishability of the LIT.

- On input $(\mathsf{pk}_0, \mathsf{pk}_1)$ set up the reputation system as in Game_2, except for setting $\mathsf{upk}_0 := \mathsf{pk}_0, \mathsf{upk}_1 := \mathsf{pk}_1$.
- Simulate $\mathcal{D}$.
- Whenever $\mathcal{D}$ asks for a signature, query the oracle for a tag l and use that to create the signature. Do the same for the challenge.
- If $\mathcal{D}$ returns a bit b, return b.

We can easily see that if $\mathcal{A}_2$'s challenger is in experiment $b = 0$, the view of $\mathcal{D}$ is the same as in Game_2, else the view is the same as in Game_3. Thus, we have the following.

$$\mathsf{Adv}^{LITAnon}_{\Pi_{\mathsf{LIT}},\mathcal{A}_2}(n) = \epsilon_{\mathcal{D},2,3}(n)$$

Define Game_4 to be the same game as Game_3 except that c' in the signature queries is generated as $c' \leftarrow \mathsf{Enc}(\mathsf{pk}'_{\mathsf{Enc}}, \mathsf{usk}_u; r')$, i.e. we again encrypt usk_u instead of $1^{|\mathsf{usk}_u|}$, and c' in the challenge is generated as $c' \leftarrow \mathsf{Enc}(\mathsf{pk}'_{\mathsf{Enc}}, \mathsf{upk}_1; r')$, i.e. we encrypt usk_1 instead of $1^{|\mathsf{usk}_0|}$. By the CPA security of the encryption scheme we immediately have the following for an adversary $\mathcal{A}_3$ that simulates a distinguisher $\mathcal{D}$ as in Game_3, by a similar argument as above:

$$\mathsf{Adv}^{CPA}_{\Pi_{\mathsf{Enc}},\mathcal{A}_3}(n) = \frac{1}{Q+1}\epsilon_{\mathcal{D},3,4}(n)$$

Define Game_5 to be the same game as Game_4 except that opening is done by remembering $\mathsf{sk}'_{\mathsf{Enc}}$ during key generation, decrypting c' to some usk and outputting $f(\mathsf{usk})$ instead of outputting the decryption of c. An adversary can only distinguish between these games if he can submit an opening query $(\mathsf{ipk}, \mathsf{rtng}, \sigma)$ with $\sigma = (c, c', l, \pi)$ such that π is valid but $\mathsf{Dec}(\mathsf{sk}_{\mathsf{Enc}}, c) \neq f(\mathsf{Dec}(\mathsf{sk}'_{\mathsf{Enc}}, c'))$ and such that σ is not an answer he received from the signature oracle. Call the event that an adversary outputs such a query Fake. However, if an adversary could submit such a query, this would break the simulation-soundness of Π_{NIZK} (Definition 6). To show this, from a distinguisher $\mathcal{D}$ between Game_4 and Game_5 we construct an adversary $\mathcal{A}_4$ against the simulation-soundness of Π_{NIZK}.

- On input some $\mathsf{pp}_{\text{NIZK}}$, set up Game_4 while remembering $\mathsf{sk}_{\mathsf{Enc}}, \mathsf{sk}'_{\mathsf{Enc}}$ and setting $\mathsf{pp} = \mathsf{pp}_{\text{NIZK}}$.
- Simulate $\mathcal{D}$. To simulate proofs, $\mathcal{A}$ uses its simulator oracle.
- Whenever $\mathcal{D}$ makes an opening query on $(\mathsf{ipk}, \mathsf{rtng}, \sigma)$, answer as in Game_4. Additionally, if $\sigma = (c, c', l, \pi)$ is not an answer from a previous signing query and $\mathsf{upk} \neq \mathsf{upk}'$, where $\mathsf{upk} \leftarrow \mathsf{Dec}(\mathsf{sk}_{\mathsf{Enc}}, c)$ and $\mathsf{upk}' \leftarrow f(\mathsf{Dec}(\mathsf{sk}'_{\mathsf{Enc}}, c'))$, stop and output the statement from σ together with π.
- If $\mathcal{D}$ stops, output a failure symbol $\perp$.

If $\mathcal{A}_4$ finds a query such that $\mathsf{upk} \neq \mathsf{upk}'$ and the σ is not from a signature query, we know that, while π is valid and is not a response from the simulator oracle, the statement is not in the language. Therefore, this σ together with the corresponding statement is a proof that breaks the simulation-soundness. Thus, we have that

$$\mathsf{Adv}^{SS}_{\Pi_{\text{NIZK}}, \mathcal{A}_4}(n) = \Pr[\mathsf{Fake}] \geq \epsilon_{\mathcal{D},4,5}(n).$$

Define Game_6 to be the same game as Game_5 except that c in the challenge σ is generated as $c \leftarrow \mathsf{Enc}(\mathsf{pk}_{\mathsf{Enc}}, \mathsf{upk}_1; r)$, i.e. we encrypt upk_1 instead of upk_0. This is again indistinguishable by the CPA security of the encryption scheme, thus for a distinguisher $\mathcal{D}$ and an adversary $\mathcal{A}_5$ constructed similarly to above we have

$$\mathsf{Adv}^{CPA}_{\Pi_{\mathsf{Enc}}, \mathcal{A}_5}(n) = \epsilon_{\mathcal{D},5,6}(n)$$

Define Game_7 to be the same game as Game_6 except that opening is done honestly again, i.e. by decrypting c. Again, from a distinguisher $\mathcal{D}$ we can construct an adversary $\mathcal{A}_6$ against the simulation-soundness of Π_{NIZK} similar to above and we get

$$\mathsf{Adv}^{SS}_{\Pi_{\text{NIZK}}, \mathcal{A}_6}(n) \geq \epsilon_{\mathcal{D},6,7}(n)$$

Define Game_8 to be the same game as Game_7 except that the proofs are generated honestly again, thus we have that Game_6 is the same as Anon_1. This is again indistinguishable due to the zero-knowledge property of Π_{NIZK}. Thus, we have that for all distinguishers $\mathcal{D}$, there exists an $\mathcal{A}_7$ such that

$$\mathsf{Adv}^{ZK}_{\Pi_{\text{NIZK}}, \mathcal{A}_7}(n) = \epsilon_{\mathcal{D},7,8}(n).$$

Therefore, in total for any ppt distinguishers $\mathcal{D}_i$ for $i \in \{0, \ldots, 7\}$ we have that

$$\begin{aligned} \mathsf{Adv}^{anon}_{\Pi,\mathcal{A}}(n) &\leq \sum_{i=0}^{7} \epsilon_{\mathcal{D}_i,i,i+1}(n) \\ &\leq 2\mathsf{Adv}^{ZK}_{\Pi_{\mathrm{NIZK}},\mathcal{A}_0}(n) + \mathsf{Adv}^{LITAnon}_{\Pi_{\mathsf{LIT}},\mathcal{A}_2}(n) \\ &\quad + (2Q+3)\mathsf{Adv}^{CPA}_{\Pi_{\mathsf{Enc}},\mathcal{A}_1}(n) \\ &\quad + 2\mathsf{Adv}^{SS}_{\Pi_{\mathrm{NIZK}},\mathcal{A}_4,\mathcal{S}}(n) = 1] \end{aligned}$$

□

Theorem 2. *If Π_{LIT} is non-invertible and unforgeable (Definitions 12 and 13) and Π_{NIZK} has zero-knowledgeness and simulation-soundness (Definition 4 and 6), the reputation system has non-frameability (Definition 18).*

Proof. When an adversary against non-frameability wins, we have that the forgery either opens to the honest user or it links to a rating of the honest user. From these cases, we construct an adversary that targets either the non-invertability or the unforgeability of Π_{LIT}. We also need to analyze the probability of some failure event, for which we use the simulation-soundness of Π_{NIZK}.

Let $\mathcal{A}$ be an adversary against the non-frameability (Definition 18) of the reputation scheme that does at most q queries to the signing oracle. Let Fail be the event that in the non-frameability game the statement of the proof contained in the forgery of $\mathcal{A}$ is wrong, i.e. it is not in the language of the relation. Construct an adversary $\mathcal{B}$ against the non-invertability (Definition 13) of Π_{LIT} as follows:

- On input pk, simulate $\mathsf{NFrame}_{\Pi,\mathcal{A}}(n)$, except for setting $\mathsf{upk}_0 = \mathsf{pk}$ and remembering $\mathsf{sk}'_{\mathsf{Enc}}$.
- When $\mathcal{A}$ queries the request oracle, use the simulator of Π_{NIZK} (cf. Definition 4) to answer the query. If it queries the signature oracle, use the tag oracle to generate a tag, generate c, c' honestly, then use the simulator of Π_{NIZK} to generate the proof.
- Eventually, $\mathcal{A}$ outputs some forgery $(\mathsf{ipk}, \mathsf{rtng}, \sigma)$ with $\sigma = (c, c', l, \pi)$. If $\mathsf{Vrfy}(\mathsf{gmpk}, \mathsf{opk}, \mathsf{ipk}, \mathsf{rtng}, \sigma) = 1$ and $u := \mathsf{Open}(\mathsf{gmpk}, \mathsf{osk}, \mathsf{ipk}, \mathsf{rtng}, \sigma) = \mathsf{upk}_0$, then $\mathsf{usk} \leftarrow \mathsf{Dec}(\mathsf{sk}'_{\mathsf{Enc}}, c')$.
- Output usk.

We can easily see that the view of $\mathcal{A}$ is perfectly simulated, except for negligible error from simulating the proofs. If $\mathcal{A}$ could distinguish the views, we could immediately construct $\mathcal{C}$ that breaks the zero-knowledgeness of Π_{NIZK}. Then, we know that if $\mathcal{A}$ manages to output a valid signature that opens to upk_0, and Fail does not happen, it holds that $\mathsf{pk} = f(\mathsf{usk})$. Thus, we have the following.

$$\Pr[\mathsf{Invert}_{\Pi_{\mathsf{LIT}},\mathcal{B}} = 1] \geq \Pr[\mathsf{NFrame}_{\Pi,\mathcal{A}} = 1 \land u = \mathsf{upk}_0 \land \neg\mathsf{Fail}] + \mathsf{Adv}^{ZK}_{\Pi_{\mathrm{NIZK}},\mathcal{C}}(n)$$

We also construct a $\mathcal{C}$ against the unforgeability of Π_{LIT} (Definition 12).

- On input pk, simulate $\mathsf{NFrame}_{\Pi,\mathcal{A}}(n)$ except for setting $\mathsf{upk}_0 = \mathsf{pk}$. Also save $\mathsf{sk}'_{\mathsf{Enc}}$.
- When $\mathcal{A}$ queries the request oracle, use Π_{NIZK} simulator to answer the query. If $\mathcal{A}$ queries the signature oracle, use the tag oracle to generate a tag, then use the simulator of Π_{NIZK} to answer the query with the corresponding statement.
- $\mathcal{A}$ outputs $(\mathsf{ipk}, \mathsf{rtng}, \sigma)$ with $\sigma = (c, c', \pi, l)$. If $\mathsf{Vrfy}(\mathsf{gmpk}, \mathsf{opk}, \mathsf{ipk}, \mathsf{rtng}, \sigma) = 1$ and $u := \mathsf{Open}(\mathsf{gmpk}, \mathsf{osk}, \mathsf{ipk}, \mathsf{rtng}, \sigma) \neq \mathsf{upk}_0$ and $\exists(\mathsf{ipk}, \hat{\mathsf{rtng}}, \hat{\sigma}) \in Q$ with $\hat{\sigma} = (\hat{c}, \hat{c}', \hat{\pi}, \hat{l})$ such that $\mathsf{Link}(\mathsf{gmpk}, \mathsf{opk}, \mathsf{ipk}, (\mathsf{rtng}, \sigma), (\hat{\mathsf{rtng}}, \hat{\sigma})) = 1$ and $\mathsf{rtng} \neq \hat{\mathsf{rtng}}$, then decrypt $\mathsf{usk} \leftarrow \mathsf{Dec}(\mathsf{sk}'_{\mathsf{Enc}}, c')$ and output $(\mathsf{usk}, \mathsf{ipk}, l)$.

Again, we can easily see that the view of $\mathcal{A}$ is perfectly simulated. If $\mathcal{A}$ outputs a forgery $(\mathsf{ipk}, \mathsf{rtng}, \sigma)$ such that

$$\begin{aligned} &\mathsf{Vrfy}(\mathsf{gmpk}, \mathsf{opk}, \mathsf{ipk}, \mathsf{rtng}, \sigma) = 1 \\ \text{and } & u := \mathsf{Open}(\mathsf{gmpk}, \mathsf{osk}, \mathsf{ipk}, \mathsf{rtng}, \sigma) \neq \mathsf{upk}_0 \\ \text{and } & \exists(\mathsf{ipk}, \hat{\mathsf{rtng}}) \in Q : \mathsf{Link}(\mathsf{gmpk}, \mathsf{opk}, \mathsf{ipk}, (\mathsf{rtng}, \sigma), (\hat{\mathsf{rtng}}, \hat{\sigma})) = 1 \\ \text{and } & \mathsf{Fail} \text{ does not happen,} \end{aligned}$$

we know that by definition we have $\mathsf{Vrfy}_{\mathsf{LIT}}(\mathsf{usk}, \mathsf{ipk}, l) = 1$ and $\mathsf{Link}_{\mathsf{LIT}}(\mathsf{ipk}, l, \hat{l}) = 1$. Therefore we have the following.

$$\Pr[\mathsf{NFrame}_{\Pi,\mathcal{A}} = 1 | \neg\mathsf{Fail} \wedge u \neq \mathsf{upk}_0] = \Pr[\mathsf{Forge}^{LIT}_{\Pi_{\mathsf{LIT}},\mathcal{C}} = 1]$$

Lastly, we want to analyze the probability $\Pr[\mathsf{Fail}]$. For this, we construct an adversary $\mathcal{D}$ against the simulation-soundness of Π_{NIZK} (Definition 6):

- On input crs, simulate $\mathsf{NFrame}_{\Pi,\mathcal{A}}(n)$ except for using the provided crs.
- Simulate $\mathcal{A}$. Whenever $\mathcal{A}$ makes an oracle query such that the answer would contain a NIZK, use the simulator oracle to generate the proof.
- $\mathcal{A}$ outputs some forgery $(\mathsf{ipk}, \mathsf{rtng}, \sigma)$. If $\mathsf{Vrfy}(\mathsf{gmpk}, \mathsf{opk}, \mathsf{ipk}, \mathsf{rtng}, \sigma) = 1$, return σ and the corresponding statement.

We can easily see that $\mathcal{A}$ is perfectly simulated and that if Fail happens, $\mathcal{D}$ wins. Therefore we can bound the non-frameability advantage of $\mathcal{A}$.

$$\begin{aligned} \Pr[\mathsf{NFrame}_{\Pi,\mathcal{A}}] \leq & \Pr[\mathsf{NFrame}_{\Pi,\mathcal{A}} \wedge \neg\mathsf{Fail}] + \Pr[\mathsf{Fail}] \\ = & \Pr[\mathsf{NFrame}_{\Pi,\mathcal{A}} = 1 \wedge \neg\mathsf{Fail} \wedge u = \mathsf{upk}_0] \\ & + \Pr[\mathsf{NFrame}_{\Pi,\mathcal{A}} = 1 \wedge \neg\mathsf{Fail} \wedge u \neq \mathsf{upk}_0] + \Pr[\mathsf{Fail}] \\ \leq & \Pr[\mathsf{NFrame}_{\Pi,\mathcal{A}} = 1 | \neg\mathsf{Fail} \wedge u = \mathsf{upk}_0] \\ & + \Pr[\mathsf{NFrame}_{\Pi,\mathcal{A}} = 1 | \neg\mathsf{Fail} \wedge u \neq \mathsf{upk}_0] + \Pr[\mathsf{Fail}] \\ = & \Pr[\mathsf{Invert}_{\Pi_{\mathsf{LIT}},\mathcal{B}} = 1] + \Pr[\mathsf{Forge}^{LIT}_{\Pi_{\mathsf{LIT}},\mathcal{C}} = 1] \\ & + \Pr[\mathsf{SimSound}_{\Pi_{\mathrm{NIZK}},\mathcal{D},\mathcal{S}} = 1] \end{aligned}$$

□

Theorem 3. *If Σ is EUF-CMA and Π_{NIZK} is straight-line extractable (Definition 7), the reputation system is traceable (Definition 19).*

Proof. Let $\mathcal{E}_0, \mathcal{E}_1$ be the extractor for Π_{NIZK} (cf. Definition 7). Let $\mathcal{A}$ be a ppt adversary against traceability. First, we define $\mathsf{Trace}'_{\Pi_{\text{NIZK}},\mathcal{A}}(n)$ to work like $\mathsf{Trace}_{\Pi_{\text{NIZK}},\mathcal{A}}(n)$, except that the public parameters pp are generated by the extractor, i.e. $(\mathsf{pp}, td) \leftarrow \mathcal{E}_0(1^n)$. From the guarantees of the extractor (Definition 7) and a straight-forward reduction, we get that $|\Pr[\mathsf{Trace}'_{\Pi_{\text{NIZK}},\mathcal{A}}(n) = 1] - \Pr[\mathsf{Trace}_{\Pi_{\text{NIZK}},\mathcal{A}}(n) = 1]| \leq \mathsf{negl}_0(n)$ for some negligible function negl_0.

We construct an adversary $\mathcal{B}$ against the unforgeability of Σ. $\mathcal{B}^{\mathsf{Sign}(\mathsf{sk},\cdot)}(\mathsf{pk})$ runs $\mathsf{Trace}'_{\Pi_{\text{NIZK}},\mathcal{A}}(n)$, except that it sets $\mathsf{ipk} = \mathsf{pk}$ and whenever $\mathcal{A}$ makes a $\mathsf{Iss}(\mathsf{gmpk}, \mathsf{isk}, \mathsf{upk})$ query, $\mathcal{B}$ answers by querying its own oracle $\mathsf{Sign}(\mathsf{sk}, \mathsf{upk})$ for the signature. Eventually, $\mathcal{A}$ outputs (σ, rtng), where $\sigma = (c, c', l, \pi)$. $\mathcal{B}$ runs $\mathcal{E}_1(td, x, \mathsf{rtng}, \pi)$ (where x is set appropriately to the proven statement) to receive a witness $w = (\mathsf{upk}, \mathsf{usk}, \rho, \tau, r, r')$. $\mathcal{B}$ outputs (upk, τ) as a candidate forgery.

Let $\mathsf{fail}_{\mathcal{E}}$ be the event that $\mathsf{Trace}'_{\Pi_{\text{NIZK}},\mathcal{A}}(n) = 1$, but $\mathcal{E}_1$ outputs an invalid witness (i.e. $(x, w) \notin \mathfrak{R}$). With a straight-forward reduction to straight-line extractability, we can show that $\Pr[\mathsf{fail}_{\mathcal{E}}] \leq \mathsf{negl}_1(n)$ for some negligible function negl_1. If $\mathsf{Trace}'_{\Pi_{\text{NIZK}},\mathcal{A}}(n) = 1$ and $\neg\mathsf{fail}_{\mathcal{E}}$, $\mathcal{B}$ outputs a valid forgery. This is because the Trace' winning condition "$\mathsf{upk} \notin \mathcal{I}$" (together with $(x, w) \in \mathfrak{R}$ and correctness of the encryption scheme guarantees that $\mathcal{B}$ has not queried its signing oracle for upk with overwhelming probability. Hence there exists a negligible function negl_2 such that

$$\begin{aligned}
&\mathsf{Adv}^{\text{EUFCMA}}_{\Sigma,\mathcal{A}}(n) \\
\geq &\Pr[\mathsf{Trace}'_{\Pi_{\text{NIZK}},\mathcal{A}}(n) = 1 \wedge \neg\mathsf{fail}_{\mathcal{E}}] - \mathsf{negl}_2(n) \\
= &\Pr[\mathsf{Trace}'_{\Pi_{\text{NIZK}},\mathcal{A}}(n) = 1] - \Pr[\mathsf{Trace}'_{\Pi_{\text{NIZK}},\mathcal{A}}(n) = 1 \wedge \mathsf{fail}_{\mathcal{E}}] - \mathsf{negl}_2(n) \\
\geq &\Pr[\mathsf{Trace}'_{\Pi_{\text{NIZK}},\mathcal{A}}(n) = 1] - \mathsf{negl}_1(n) - \mathsf{negl}_2(n)
\end{aligned}$$

□

Theorem 4. *If Σ is EUF-CMA and Π_{NIZK} is straight-line extractable (Definition 7), the reputation system has joining security (Definition 21).*

The proof is analogous to the proof of Theorem 3.

Theorem 5. *If Π_{LIT} is linkable (Definition 11) and Π_{NIZK} has soundness, the reputation system is publicly linkable (Definition 20).*

Proof. Let $\mathcal{A}$ be an adversary against the public linkability of the reputation system. We construct an adversary $\mathcal{B}$ against the linkability of Π_{LIT} from it:

- Simulate $\mathsf{PLinkable}_{\Pi,\mathcal{A}}(n)$.
- $\mathcal{A}$ outputs some gmpk and ipk and forgery-rating pairs $(\sigma_j, \mathsf{rtng}_j)_{j\in\{0,1\}}$, where $\sigma_j = (c_j, c'_j, l_j, \pi_j)$.
- If both σ_j are valid signatures in the simulated public-linkability game and do not link, decrypt c'_0, c'_1 to get $\mathsf{usk}_0, \mathsf{usk}_1$ and output $(\mathsf{usk}_0, \mathsf{usk}_1, \mathsf{ipk}, l_0, l_1)$.

If $\mathcal{A}$ outputs $\mathsf{gmpk}, \mathsf{ipk}$ with two forgeries σ_0, σ_1 that are valid for these keys and the opk, due to soundness of Π_{NIZK} we have that $\mathsf{Vrfy}_{\mathsf{LIT}}(\mathsf{usk}_j, \mathsf{ipk}, l_j) = 1$ for $j \in \{0,1\}$. Then, again due to the soundness of Π_{NIZK}, we have that $f(\mathsf{usk}_0) = f(\mathsf{usk}_1)$. Call Sound the event that $\mathcal{A}$ outputs such tags or such ciphertexts that the above conditions do not hold. Then, we can construct an adversary $\mathcal{C}$ against the soundness of Π_{NIZK}, by simply outputting the proof that $\mathcal{A}$ outputs. Thus, we know that $\Pr[\mathsf{Sound}] \leq \mathsf{Adv}^{Snd}_{\Pi,\mathcal{A}}(n)$. If the σ_j do not link, it follows that $(\mathsf{usk}_0, \mathsf{usk}_1, \mathsf{ipk}, l_0, l_1)$ is a tuple of two valid tags for the same message created with $\mathsf{usk}_0, \mathsf{usk}_1$ respectively, which do not link. Therefore, we have that

$$\Pr[\mathsf{Linkable}^{LIT}_{\Pi_{\mathsf{LIT}},\mathcal{C}}(n) = 1] = \Pr[\mathsf{PLinkable}_{\Pi,\mathcal{A}}(n) = 1] + \mathsf{Adv}^{Snd}_{\Pi,\mathcal{A}}(n).$$

□

The Role of Straight-Line Extraction. For the proof of traceability (Theorem 3) and joining security (Theorem 4), we require Π_{NIZK} to be straight-line extractable, i.e. the proof system must not rely on rewinding for extraction (which, for example, Fiat-Shamir-based proofs usually do). In our security proofs for Theorems 3 and 4, the reduction algorithm has access to a signature oracle. Similarly to what was noted in [21], this represents an issue for an extractor: when rewinding the reduction algorithm $\mathcal{B}$, the extractor needs to answer $\mathcal{B}$'s signing oracle queries. However, in standard definitions, the extractor does not have access to the signing oracle. Even if we grant access, the extractor querying the signing oracle may actually cause an extracted forgery to become invalid. This happens in case a signature on the forgery message is being requested by $\mathcal{B}$ during rewinding. There are potential ways to circumvent this issue for specific proof systems, but standard definitions of (rewinding-based) soundness are incompatible with signing oracle access in security proofs. Straight-line extraction does not suffer from this issue, as the extractor can be used without rewinding.

One can always implement straight-line extractable proofs by encrypting the witness for some honestly generated publicly known public key and proving, with a *sound* zero-knowledge proof, that the encrypted witness is valid. Note that in our security proofs for Theorems 3 and 4, the only value we need to extract from the proof is the membership certificate τ or ρ (upk is also used, but can be computed by decrypting c). For this reason, when implementing straight-line extractability, it suffices to additionally encrypt τ and ρ, there is no need to encrypt the *full* witness of the rating NIZK.

Alternatively, one can use a NIZK that is inherently straight-line extractable (e.g., using Fischlin's transform [22] or Katsumata's transform [30]). In these cases, it also suffices to extract only a part of the witness, namely ρ, τ. In practice, one can arguably even use a standard Fiat-Shamir-based construction, for which one cannot prove straight-line extractability (cf. [5]). However, to the best of our knowledge, there is no attack against Fiat-Shamir in practice that targets schemes using it in place of a straight-line extractable proof.

5 A Reputation System from Module Lattices

We now want to instantiate the generic construction with building blocks based on module lattices. Since we only used generally common concepts, we are relatively free in choosing which actual building blocks we want to use. However, we need to make sure they fit together, especially with the NIZK, meaning that we can prove the statements defined by our other building blocks. The NIZK of our choice is, as mentioned previously in Corollary 1, the proof system of [38] transformed into a straight-line extractable NIZK by Katsumata's transform [30]. With it, we can create proofs for the relation $\mathfrak{R}^R$ (cf. Definition 8), so we have to argue that we can express our statements to prove via this relation.

For the LIT, we choose the scheme presented in Construction 14. To instantiate Construction 22 with it, we need to prove possession of a secret usk and secret upk, such that $f(\mathsf{usk}) = \mathsf{upk}$. Since this boils down to showing possession of an MLWE secret for a secret $\mathbf{b}$, this can be realized as shown in Table 2. Due to our choice of the encryption scheme, we use the bit-decomposition of the upk. Thus, we also need to prove that one knows $\mathsf{upk}, \mathsf{BitD}(\mathsf{upk})$ such that $\mathsf{upk} = \mathbf{G} \cdot \mathsf{BitD}(\mathsf{upk})$ and $\mathsf{BitD}(\mathsf{upk})$ is a bit vector, which is also possible. Since this works similar to showing possession of an MLWE secret for *public* $\mathbf{b}$ as shown in [38], we roughly estimate the proof for the former to be of size 30 KB.

Table 2. Proving possession of a usk for secret upk. Define $\mathbf{A}' = [\mathbf{A}_T^t \mid \mathbf{I} \mid -\mathbf{G}]$.

variable	description	instantiation
ϕ	# of equations to prove	1
ϕ_{eval}	# of evaluations with const. coeff. zero	0
v_e	# of exact norm proofs	2
v_d	# of non-exact norm proofs	0
k_{bin}	length of the binary vector to prove	$m_U \log q$
$\mathbf{s}_1$	committed message in the Ajtai part	$(\mathbf{t}^t, \mathbf{e}^t, \mathsf{BitD}(\mathsf{upk})^t)^t$
$\mathbf{m}$	committed message in the BDLOP part	$\varnothing$ (no message)
f_1	equation to prove	$\mathbf{A}'\mathbf{s}_1 = 0$
$\mathbf{D}_1$	public matrix for proving $\Vert\mathbf{E}_1\mathbf{s} - \mathbf{u}_1\Vert_\infty \leq \beta_1^{(e)}$	$\begin{bmatrix}\mathbf{I} & \mathbf{0} & \mathbf{0}\end{bmatrix}$
$\mathbf{u}_1$	public vector for proving $\Vert\mathbf{E}_1\mathbf{s} - \mathbf{u}_1\Vert_\infty \leq \beta_1^{(e)}$	$\mathbf{0}$
$\beta_1^{(d)}$	upper bound on $\Vert\mathbf{E}_1\mathbf{s} - \mathbf{u}_1\Vert_\infty \leq \beta_1^{(e)}$	β
$\mathbf{D}_2$	public matrix for proving $\Vert\mathbf{E}_2\mathbf{s} - \mathbf{u}_2\Vert_\infty \leq \beta_2^{(e)}$	$\begin{bmatrix}\mathbf{0} & \mathbf{I} & \mathbf{0}\end{bmatrix}$
$\mathbf{u}_2$	public vector for proving $\Vert\mathbf{E}_2\mathbf{s} - \mathbf{u}_2\Vert_\infty \leq \beta_2^{(e)}$	$\mathbf{0}$
$\beta_2^{(d)}$	upper bound on $\Vert\mathbf{E}_2\mathbf{s} - \mathbf{u}_2\Vert_\infty \leq \beta_2^{(e)}$	β
$\mathbf{E}_{bin}$	matrix for proving binary	$\begin{bmatrix}\mathbf{0} & \mathbf{0} & \mathbf{I}\end{bmatrix}$
$\mathbf{v}_{bin}$	vector for proving binary	0

For the encryption scheme, we use the MLWE variant of the primal Regev encryption scheme that is presented in [38] as their verifiable encryption scheme. There they also show that one can create a proof showing the validness of a ciphertext, which we need in our generic construction. However, their scheme has a message space of $\{0,1\}^n$, while we want to encrypt a $\mathsf{upk} \in \mathcal{R}_q^m$. Thus, we instead encrypt the bit-decomposition $\mathsf{BitD}(\mathsf{upk})$ of the upk in multiple ciphertexts. Based on the parameters in [38], we estimate the proof size showing the ciphertext to be valid to be 4762KB. We expect other lattice-based encryption schemes such as Kyber [12], Saber [17] and NTRU [27] to also work for our generic construction, as [38] claim they work in their proof system.

To instantiate the signature scheme, we need it to be compatible with our NIZK. Signature schemes that use the random oracle, such as Fiat-Shamir-with-aborts signature scheme [37] or hash-then-sign signatures [23,42], are not suitable. Instead, we use signature schemes in the standard model, such as [19], and we focus on signatures that are either specifically designed for use in combination with proofs of knowledge, such as [29], or are very efficient [11]. An overview comparing the schemes can be found in Table 3.

Table 3. Overview over different candidate signature schemes to instantiate the reputation system with. For the definition of the Int-NTRU-ISIS$_f$ problem, see [11]. Proof size refers to size of a NIZK in kilobytes in the framework of [38] proving possession of a secret message-signature pair for 128-bit security. These are conservative estimates for message space $\{0,1\}^{nm \cdot \log q}$.

Scheme	State	Assumption	Proof Size
[19] and our adaption	stateless	RSIS	–
[29][28, Appendix H]	stateless	MSIS	–
[29] and our adaptions	stateful	MSIS	163584 KB
[11]	stateless	Int-NTRU-ISIS$_f$	59392 KB

The signature scheme of [19] is shown to be secure for non-adaptive queries, to be converted to adaptive security via chameleon hash. However, one can show that using a technique similar to [32] using the Rényi divergence, that the scheme has adaptive security without the chameleon hash. For details, see the full version [7], which also describes how to prove possession of a secret message-signature pair in the framework of [38]. However, the signature scheme has reduction loss dependent on the success probability of the adversary, which leads to large parameters. The stateless signature scheme of [28,29] is designed in such a way that the verification equation works well with relations that can be proven by lattice-based proofs of knowledge. In particular, [29] already show that one can show possession of a message-signature pair of their scheme in the framework of [38]. This signature scheme suffers from the same reduction loss drawback as [19] though, since they use the same proof technique of prefix-guessing of a tag.

In [11] they introduce a credential system based on novel security assumptions that are related to ISIS. Their credential system can also be seen as a (blind) signature, of which one proves possession, thus we can instantiate our signature scheme and the proof with it. The most efficient credential system they design is based on the so-called Int-NTRU-ISIS$_f$ problem and achieves a proof size of 29KB (under some heuristics) for a message space of $\{0,1\}^{16}$. If we use the construction of [11] and the other aforementioned building blocks, we arrive at a total proof size for the instantiation of the generic construction of 30KB + 4762KB + 59392KB = 64184KB. Note that this is a very rough estimate and we expect careful analysis to yield a much better proof size.

Stateful Reputation System. Parallel to the stateless variant, [29] also construct a stateful ℓ-time signature scheme based on MSIS. They show the size of a proof showing possession of a secret message-signature pair to be 693 KB for a message in $\{0,1\}^{128}$, also using the proof system of [38]. It is possible to use stateful signatures in our generic construction, by changing the model of the reputation system such that the group manager and issuers are stateful, i.e. the Join and Issue algorithms get some state as input. We also allow only a fixed number ℓ of users to join the system. The correctness and security model have to be changed accordingly, which is straight-forward. Both are not unreasonable assumptions to make in practice, as group managers have to keep track how many members there are in the system anyways and issuers have to store information about their sales, making both inherently stateful. Furthermore, for large enough ℓ, e.g. 2^{40}, this amount of users will likely not be reached in practice. The security proofs for the stateful reputation system basically work as for the stateless reputation system, except for using stateful and ℓ-time signatures instead of stateless ones.

Instead of the stateful signatures of [29], one can use an adaption presented in the full version [7], which is a slightly simplified version of the former getting rid of the commitment in the signing process. There is a second adaption, which can be more efficient than the signature of [29] depending on the degree of the ring, since its security relies on RLWE, NTRU and RSIS instead of MSIS. Details can be found in the full version [7].

5.1 Instantiation with Pairing-Based Cryptography

To instantiate the generic construction based on pairing-based cryptography, we use the following constructions for the building blocks:

- The linking indistinguishable tags are $t = \mathcal{RO}(\mathsf{ipk})^{\mathsf{usk}}$ with $f(\mathsf{usk}) = g^{\mathsf{usk}}$. Two tags t_0, t_1 link if $t_0 = t_1$.
- The signature scheme to sign the user's public key g^{usk} is a simplified version of the structure-preserving signature [24], namely $\sigma = (\tilde{R}, S, T) = (\tilde{g}^r, (y \cdot g^w)^{1/r}, (y^w \cdot M)^{1/r})$ (as in [10]), where signatures are valid iff they are of that form (can be checked using the pairing).
- The encryption scheme for the user's public key is ElGamal, the encryption scheme for $\mathsf{usk} \in \mathbb{Z}_p$ is bitwise raised ElGamal.

– The NIZK is a simple Schnorr-like protocol made straight-line extractable with Fischlin's transform [22, 31].

We leave the details of the instantiation to the reader.

Acknowledgement. We would like to thank the anonymous reviewers for their helpful comments and constructive feedback.

References

1. Attema, T., Fehr, S., Klooß, M.: Fiat-Shamir transformation of multi-round interactive proofs. In: Kiltz, E., Vaikuntanathan, V. (eds.) TCC 2022, Part I. LNCS, vol. 13747, pp. 113–142. Springer, Cham (2022). https://doi.org/10.1007/978-3-031-22318-1_5
2. Banerjee, A., Peikert, C., Rosen, A.: Pseudorandom functions and lattices. In: Pointcheval, D., Johansson, T. (eds.) EUROCRYPT 2012. LNCS, vol. 7237, pp. 719–737. Springer, Heidelberg (2012). https://doi.org/10.1007/978-3-642-29011-4_42
3. Bansarkhani, R.E., El Kaafarani, A.: Direct anonymous attestation from lattices. IACR Cryptology ePrint Archive, p. 1022 (2017). http://eprint.iacr.org/2017/1022
4. Ben-Sasson, E., Chiesa, A., Riabzev, M., Spooner, N., Virza, M., Ward, N.P.: Aurora: transparent succinct arguments for R1CS. In: Ishai, Y., Rijmen, V. (eds.) EUROCRYPT 2019. LNCS, vol. 11476, pp. 103–128. Springer, Cham (2019). https://doi.org/10.1007/978-3-030-17653-2_4
5. Bernhard, D., Nguyen, N.K., Warinschi, B.: Adaptive proofs have straightline extractors (in the random oracle model). In: Gollmann, D., Miyaji, A., Kikuchi, H. (eds.) ACNS 2017. LNCS, vol. 10355, pp. 336–353. Springer, Cham (2017). https://doi.org/10.1007/978-3-319-61204-1_17
6. Bethencourt, J., Shi, E., Song, D.: Signatures of reputation. In: Sion, R. (ed.) FC 2010. LNCS, vol. 6052, pp. 400–407. Springer, Heidelberg (2010). https://doi.org/10.1007/978-3-642-14577-3_35
7. Blömer, J., Bobolz, J., Porzenheim, L.: A generic construction of an anonymous reputation system and instantiations from lattices. Cryptology ePrint Archive, Paper 2023/464 (2023). https://eprint.iacr.org/2023/464
8. Blömer, J., Eidens, F., Juhnke, J.: Practical, anonymous, and publicly linkable universally-composable reputation systems. In: Smart, N.P. (ed.) CT-RSA 2018. LNCS, vol. 10808, pp. 470–490. Springer, Cham (2018). https://doi.org/10.1007/978-3-319-76953-0_25
9. Blömer, J., Juhnke, J., Kolb, C.: Anonymous and publicly linkable reputation systems. In: Böhme, R., Okamoto, T. (eds.) FC 2015. LNCS, vol. 8975, pp. 478–488. Springer, Heidelberg (2015). https://doi.org/10.1007/978-3-662-47854-7_29
10. Bobolz, J., Eidens, F., Krenn, S., Ramacher, S., Samelin, K.: Issuer-hiding attribute-based credentials. In: Conti, M., Stevens, M., Krenn, S. (eds.) CANS 2021. LNCS, vol. 13099, pp. 158–178. Springer, Cham (2021). https://doi.org/10.1007/978-3-030-92548-2_9
11. Bootle, J., Lyubashevsky, V., Nguyen, N.K., Sorniotti, A.: A framework for practical anonymous credentials from lattices. In: Handschuh, H., Lysyanskaya, A. (eds.) CRYPTO 2023, Part II. LNCS, vol. 14082, pp. 384–417. Springer, Cham (2023). https://doi.org/10.1007/978-3-031-38545-2_13

12. Bos, J.W., et al.: CRYSTALS - kyber: a CCA-secure module-lattice-based KEM. In: 2018 IEEE European Symposium on Security and Privacy, EuroS&P 2018, London, UK, 24–26 April 2018, pp. 353–367. IEEE (2018). https://doi.org/10.1109/EuroSP.2018.00032
13. Boschini, C., Camenisch, J., Ovsiankin, M., Spooner, N.: Efficient post-quantum SNARKs for RSIS and RLWE and their applications to privacy. In: Ding, J., Tillich, J.-P. (eds.) PQCrypto 2020. LNCS, vol. 12100, pp. 247–267. Springer, Cham (2020). https://doi.org/10.1007/978-3-030-44223-1_14
14. Boyen, X.: Lattice mixing and vanishing trapdoors: a framework for fully secure short signatures and more. In: Nguyen, P.Q., Pointcheval, D. (eds.) PKC 2010. LNCS, vol. 6056, pp. 499–517. Springer, Heidelberg (2010). https://doi.org/10.1007/978-3-642-13013-7_29
15. Camenisch, J., Stadler, M.: Efficient group signature schemes for large groups. In: Kaliski, B.S. (ed.) CRYPTO 1997. LNCS, vol. 1294, pp. 410–424. Springer, Heidelberg (1997). https://doi.org/10.1007/BFb0052252
16. Chase, M., Lysyanskaya, A.: On signatures of knowledge. In: Dwork, C. (ed.) CRYPTO 2006. LNCS, vol. 4117, pp. 78–96. Springer, Heidelberg (2006). https://doi.org/10.1007/11818175_5
17. D'Anvers, J.-P., Karmakar, A., Sinha Roy, S., Vercauteren, F.: Saber: module-LWR based key exchange, CPA-secure encryption and CCA-secure KEM. In: Joux, A., Nitaj, A., Rachidi, T. (eds.) AFRICACRYPT 2018. LNCS, vol. 10831, pp. 282–305. Springer, Cham (2018). https://doi.org/10.1007/978-3-319-89339-6_16
18. Don, J., Fehr, S., Majenz, C., Schaffner, C.: Online-extractability in the quantum random-oracle model. In: Dunkelman, O., Dziembowski, S. (eds.) EUROCRYPT 2022, Part III. LNCS, vol. 13277, pp. 677–706. Springer, Cham (2022). https://doi.org/10.1007/978-3-031-07082-2_24
19. Ducas, L., Micciancio, D.: Improved short lattice signatures in the standard model. In: Garay, J.A., Gennaro, R. (eds.) CRYPTO 2014, Part I. LNCS, vol. 8616, pp. 335–352. Springer, Heidelberg (2014). https://doi.org/10.1007/978-3-662-44371-2_19
20. El Kaafarani, A., Katsumata, S., Solomon, R.: Anonymous reputation systems achieving full dynamicity from lattices. In: Meiklejohn, S., Sako, K. (eds.) FC 2018. LNCS, vol. 10957, pp. 388–406. Springer, Heidelberg (2018). https://doi.org/10.1007/978-3-662-58387-6_21
21. Fiore, D., Nitulescu, A.: On the (in)security of SNARKs in the presence of oracles. In: Hirt, M., Smith, A. (eds.) TCC 2016, Part I. LNCS, vol. 9985, pp. 108–138. Springer, Heidelberg (2016). https://doi.org/10.1007/978-3-662-53641-4_5
22. Fischlin, M.: Communication-efficient non-interactive proofs of knowledge with online extractors. In: Shoup, V. (ed.) CRYPTO 2005. LNCS, vol. 3621, pp. 152–168. Springer, Heidelberg (2005). https://doi.org/10.1007/11535218_10
23. Gentry, C., Peikert, C., Vaikuntanathan, V.: Trapdoors for hard lattices and new cryptographic constructions. In: Dwork, C. (ed.) Proceedings of the 40th Annual ACM Symposium on Theory of Computing, Victoria, British Columbia, Canada, 17–20 May 2008, pp. 197–206. ACM (2008). https://doi.org/10.1145/1374376.1374407
24. Groth, J.: Efficient fully structure-preserving signatures for large messages. In: Iwata, T., Cheon, J.H. (eds.) ASIACRYPT 2015. LNCS, vol. 9452, pp. 239–259. Springer, Heidelberg (2015). https://doi.org/10.1007/978-3-662-48797-6_11
25. Gurtler, S., Goldberg, I.: SoK: privacy-preserving reputation systems. Proc. Priv. Enhanc. Technol. **2021**(1), 107–127 (2021). https://doi.org/10.2478/popets-2021-0007

26. Hasan, O., Brunie, L., Bertino, E.: Privacy-preserving reputation systems based on blockchain and other cryptographic building blocks: a survey. ACM Comput. Surv. **55**(2), 32:1–32:37 (2023). https://doi.org/10.1145/3490236
27. Hoffstein, J., Pipher, J., Silverman, J.H.: NTRU: a ring-based public key cryptosystem. In: Buhler, J.P. (ed.) ANTS 1998. LNCS, vol. 1423, pp. 267–288. Springer, Heidelberg (1998). https://doi.org/10.1007/BFb0054868
28. Jeudy, C., Roux-Langlois, A., Sanders, O.: Lattice signature with efficient protocols, application to anonymous credentials. Cryptology ePrint Archive, Paper 2022/509 (2022). https://eprint.iacr.org/2022/509
29. Jeudy, C., Roux-Langlois, A., Sanders, O.: Lattice signature with efficient protocols, application to anonymous credentials. In: Handschuh, H., Lysyanskaya, A. (eds.) CRYPTO 2023, Part II. LNCS, vol. 14082, pp. 351–383. Springer, Cham (2023). https://doi.org/10.1007/978-3-031-38545-2_12
30. Katsumata, S.: A new simple technique to bootstrap various lattice zero-knowledge proofs to QROM secure NIZKs. In: Malkin, T., Peikert, C. (eds.) CRYPTO 2021, Part II. LNCS, vol. 12826, pp. 580–610. Springer, Cham (2021). https://doi.org/10.1007/978-3-030-84245-1_20
31. Kondi, Y., Shelat, A.: Improved straight-line extraction in the random oracle model with applications to signature aggregation. In: Agrawal, S., Lin, D. (eds.) ASIACRYPT 2022, Part II. LNCS, vol. 13792, pp. 279–309. Springer, Cham (2022). https://doi.org/10.1007/978-3-031-22966-4_10
32. Langlois, A., Stehlé, D., Steinfeld, R.: GGHLite: more efficient multilinear maps from ideal lattices. In: Nguyen, P.Q., Oswald, E. (eds.) EUROCRYPT 2014. LNCS, vol. 8441, pp. 239–256. Springer, Heidelberg (2014). https://doi.org/10.1007/978-3-642-55220-5_14
33. Libert, B., Ling, S., Mouhartem, F., Nguyen, K., Wang, H.: Signature schemes with efficient protocols and dynamic group signatures from lattice assumptions. In: Cheon, J.H., Takagi, T. (eds.) ASIACRYPT 2016. LNCS, vol. 10032, pp. 373–403. Springer, Heidelberg (2016). https://doi.org/10.1007/978-3-662-53890-6_13
34. Ling, S., Nguyen, K., Wang, H., Xu, Y.: Lattice-based group signatures: achieving full dynamicity with ease. In: Gollmann, D., Miyaji, A., Kikuchi, H. (eds.) ACNS 2017. LNCS, vol. 10355, pp. 293–312. Springer, Cham (2017). https://doi.org/10.1007/978-3-319-61204-1_15
35. Ling, S., Nguyen, K., Wang, H., Xu, Y.: Constant-size group signatures from lattices. In: Abdalla, M., Dahab, R. (eds.) PKC 2018. LNCS, vol. 10770, pp. 58–88. Springer, Cham (2018). https://doi.org/10.1007/978-3-319-76581-5_3
36. Liu, J., Manulis, M.: pRate: anonymous star rating with rating secrecy. In: Deng, R.H., Gauthier-Umaña, V., Ochoa, M., Yung, M. (eds.) ACNS 2019. LNCS, vol. 11464, pp. 550–570. Springer, Cham (2019). https://doi.org/10.1007/978-3-030-21568-2_27
37. Lyubashevsky, V.: Fiat-Shamir with aborts: applications to lattice and factoring-based signatures. In: Matsui, M. (ed.) ASIACRYPT 2009. LNCS, vol. 5912, pp. 598–616. Springer, Heidelberg (2009). https://doi.org/10.1007/978-3-642-10366-7_35
38. Lyubashevsky, V., Nguyen, N.K., Plançon, M.: Lattice-based zero-knowledge proofs and applications: Shorter, simpler, and more general. In: Dodis, Y., Shrimpton, T. (eds.) CRYPTO 2022, Part II. LNCS, vol. 13508, pp. 71–101. Springer, Cham (2022). https://doi.org/10.1007/978-3-031-15979-4_3
39. Lyubashevsky, V., Nguyen, N.K., Plançon, M.: Lattice-based zero-knowledge proofs and applications: Shorter, simpler, and more general. IACR Cryptology ePrint Archive, p. 284 (2022). https://eprint.iacr.org/2022/284

40. Lyubashevsky, V., Nguyen, N.K., Plancon, M., Seiler, G.: Shorter lattice-based group signatures via "almost free" encryption and other optimizations. In: Tibouchi, M., Wang, H. (eds.) ASIACRYPT 2021, Part IV. LNCS, vol. 13093, pp. 218–248. Springer, Cham (2021). https://doi.org/10.1007/978-3-030-92068-5_8
41. Lyubashevsky, V., Peikert, C., Regev, O.: A toolkit for ring-LWE cryptography. In: Johansson, T., Nguyen, P.Q. (eds.) EUROCRYPT 2013. LNCS, vol. 7881, pp. 35–54. Springer, Heidelberg (2013). https://doi.org/10.1007/978-3-642-38348-9_3
42. Micciancio, D., Peikert, C.: Trapdoors for lattices: simpler, tighter, faster, smaller. In: Pointcheval, D., Johansson, T. (eds.) EUROCRYPT 2012. LNCS, vol. 7237, pp. 700–718. Springer, Heidelberg (2012). https://doi.org/10.1007/978-3-642-29011-4_41
43. del Pino, R., Lyubashevsky, V., Seiler, G.: Lattice-based group signatures and zero-knowledge proofs of automorphism stability. In: Lie, D., Mannan, M., Backes, M., Wang, X. (eds.) Proceedings of the 2018 ACM SIGSAC Conference on Computer and Communications Security. CCS 2018, Toronto, ON, Canada, 15–19 October 2018, pp. 574–591. ACM (2018). https://doi.org/10.1145/3243734.3243852

Universally Composable Auditable Surveillance

Valerie Fetzer[1,4], Michael Klooß[2], Jörn Müller-Quade[1,4], Markus Raiber[1,4], and Andy Rupp[3,4(✉)]

[1] Karlsruhe Institute of Technology, Karlsruhe, Germany
{valerie.fetzer,joern.mueller-quade,markus.raiber}@kit.edu
[2] Aalto University, Espoo, Finland
michael.klooss@aalto.fi
[3] University of Luxembourg, Esch-sur-Alzette, Luxembourg
andy.rupp@uni.lu
[4] KASTEL Security Research Labs, Karlsruhe, Germany

Abstract. User privacy is becoming increasingly important in our digital society. Yet, many applications face legal requirements or regulations that prohibit unconditional anonymity guarantees, e.g., in electronic payments where surveillance is mandated to investigate suspected crimes.

As a result, many systems have no effective privacy protections at all, or have backdoors, e.g., stored at the operator side of the system, that can be used by authorities to disclose a user's private information (e.g., lawful interception). The problem with such backdoors is that they also enable *silent mass surveillance* within the system. To prevent such misuse, various approaches have been suggested which limit possible abuse or ensure it can be detected. Many works consider auditability of surveillance actions but do not enforce that traces are left when backdoors are retrieved. A notable exception which offers retrospective and silent surveillance is the recent work on misuse-resistant surveillance by Green et al. (EUROCRYPT'21). However, their approach relies on extractable witness encryption, which is a very strong primitive with no known efficient and secure implementations.

In this work, we develop a building block for *auditable surveillance*. In our protocol, backdoors or escrow secrets of users are protected in multiple ways: (1) Backdoors are *short-term* and *user-specific*; (2) they are *shared* between trustworthy parties to avoid a single point of failure; and (3) backdoor access is given *conditionally*. Moreover (4) there are *audit trails* and public statistics for every (granted) backdoor request; and (5) surveillance remains *silent*, i.e., users do not know they are surveilled.

Concretely, we present an abstract UC-functionality which can be used to augment applications with auditable surveillance capabilities. Our realization makes use of threshold encryption to protect user secrets, and is concretely built in a blockchain context with committee-based YOSO MPC. As a consequence, the committee can verify that the conditions for backdoor access are given, e.g., that law enforcement is in possession of a valid surveillance warrant (via a zero-knowledge proof).

M. Klooß—Research was conducted at Karlsruhe Institute of Technology.

J. Guo and R. Steinfeld (Eds.): ASIACRYPT 2023, LNCS 14439, pp. 453–487, 2023.
https://doi.org/10.1007/978-981-99-8724-5_14

Moreover, access leaves an audit trail on the ledger, which allows an auditor to retrospectively examine surveillance decisions.

As a toy example, we present an Auditably Sender-Traceable Encryption scheme, a PKE scheme where the sender can be deanonymized by law enforcement. We observe and solve problems posed by retrospective surveillance via a special non-interactive non-committing encryption scheme which allows zero-knowledge proofs over message, sender identity and (escrow) secrets.

Keywords: Anonymity · Auditability · Provable Security · Universal Composability · UC · YOSO · Protocols

1 Introduction

In user-centric application scenarios such as communication services, electronic payments, internet search engines, etc. there is a strong tension between the need for user privacy and legal requirements or business interests that entail the monitoring of a user's (meta-)data. This tension is also reflected by the recent European Council Resolution on "Security through encryption and security despite encryption" [18]. On the one hand, there is a strong demand for anonymity and confidentiality supported by the European General Data Protection Regulation. On the other hand, scenario-specific laws and regulations such as the European Council Resolution on the Lawful Interception of Telecommunications [43] or the EU Directive on Anti-Money Laundering and Countering the Financing of Terrorism (AML/CFT) [44], to name just a few, make it necessary to revoke a user's anonymity or disclose its encrypted transaction data or messages under certain well-defined circumstances, e.g., when a warrant has been issued for a suspect.

The security research community has recognized and addressed the necessity to balance confidentiality/anonymity with accountability. Most proposed solutions follow a variant of the key escrow paradigm [2,3,9,19,35,41,45,49,53]. In key escrow systems one or more, typically fixed, trusted authorities (TAs) aka escrow agents, are equipped with (shares of) a trapdoor key which can be used to recover encrypted messages, revoke transaction anonymity, etc. However, this holds the risk that, by corrupting the publicly known TAs, trapdoors can be *silently* misused, e.g., for mass surveillance or spying on lawful individuals of public interest (e.g., politicians, business leaders, celebrities). Due to these issues, policymakers, security researchers, and practitioners are concerned about deploying key escrow without further measures to prevent or detect misuse, e.g., [1,32]. Moreover, the lack of transparency concerning the lawful usage of trapdoors leaves citizens with the subconscious feeling of being under permanent surveillance.

To make surveillance actions more transparent and accountable, recent work [22,29,46] has discovered the usefulness of distributed ledgers. Here, judges, law enforcement, and companies publish commitments to information about surveillance measures on the ledger and can provide zero-knowledge proofs that they behave according to the laws. However, these proposals *do not enforce* that, in order to access user trapdoors, evidence must be put onto the ledger first. That means, a secure and accountable escrow and disclosure of end-to-end encryption keys is not considered. Hence, trapdoors kept by a company are still at risk of being covertly misused without leaving any trace.

Very recently, Green et al. propose a misuse-resistant surveillance scheme [31] which compels law enforcement to leaving a warrant on the ledger in order to disclose the encrypted communication of a suspect. To this end, the authors build on extractable witness encryption (EWE) [27], instead of a key escrow scheme, where the publication of a warrant serves as the key (aka witness) to decrypt the communication. Unfortunately, it seems implausible that extractable witness encryption (for general NP languages) does actually exist [23].[1] Moreover, they prove that any protocol secure in their model would already imply extractable witness encryption (for a highly non-trivial language). The goal of our system is to combine ledger-based auditability of surveillance actions with corruption-resilient key escrow mechanisms. Similar to [31], leaving a warrant on the ledger to access trapdoors is enforced, but without relying on extractable witness encryption.

Goyal et al. [30] model storing secrets on a blockchain (via secret-sharing them among members of an evolving committee) and retrieving them under some condition. If we apply that idea to our scenario, we could secret-share user-specific trapdoors at committees who only release their shares if they find a warrant on the ledger requesting their specific shares. Benhamouda et al. [8] also model storing of a secret on a blockchain, but additionally make committee members anonymous until they finished their work to prevent targeted corruption. Both methods [8,30] can result in a lot of overhead for the committee who potentially has to manage millions of secrets. To reduce the committee's workload during the handover phase, we take this idea and combine it with a key-escrow approach. Instead of secret-sharing millions of trapdoors on the blockchain, we only secret-share one item: A secret key for a threshold encryption scheme. The trapdoors are not secret-shared on the blockchain, but encrypted under a public key and stored off-chain to reduce blockchain workload. The secret key for that ciphertext is secret-shared on the blockchain and instead of directly retrieving a secret from the blockchain, law enforcement can request the decryption of the ciphertext. To increase security, only a part of the trapdoor is decryptable by the blockchain committee; the other part is stored offline at the system operator. Thus, the system remains secure even if the blockchain committee's majority is corrupted. See the full version [21] for a discussion of important design decisions.

While some other systems [24,38] only enable *prospective* surveillance, where law enforcement must prepare surveillance of each user individually *before* this user conducts any transactions, we achieve *retrospective* surveillance, where law enforcement can also access transactions that were conducted in the past. We additionally model this functionality as a building block in the UC framework and prevent users from learning whether their trapdoor was retrieved or not

[1] Even (non-extractable) witness encryption currently has no efficient constructions.

(in contrast to [8,30]). Unlike [31], we achieve retrospective surveillance without implying EWE. Moreover, the efficiency estimate of our application shows that our system is realizable and scales favorably: The judge is only involved in granting warrants, law enforcement is only involved when surveilling users and the work on the blockchain only depends on the number of surveilled users, not the number of registered users (cf. Sect. 4.3). We thus present the first UC-secure proof of concept. Unfortunately, it is not practically efficient due to large ciphertexts (cf. Sect. 5.3).

Additionally, we add the possibility to *audit* the surveillance decisions of law enforcement. A special party, the *auditor*, has the power to retrospectively examine law enforcement's surveillance decisions and inform the public about possible abuse. Since this party is very powerful, care must be taken as to who takes on this role; for example, a neutral investigative committee might be suitable.

1.1 Contribution

We formalize an auditable surveillance system as a building block which can be used to enhance many different (existing) applications with the capability to revoke a user's anonymity or to reveal a user's transaction data under the condition that a law enforcement agency has a court-signed warrant that legally empowers them to do so. Our auditable surveillance system is the first to combine key escrow with accountability without requiring unlikely assumptions (e.g., EWE) while scaling well. We accomplish this through the following three contributions.

First and foremost, we provide an abstract ideal functionality for auditable surveillance, $\mathcal{F}_{\mathrm{AS}}$. The functionality $\mathcal{F}_{\mathrm{AS}}$ serves as a building block which allows to enhance protocols with auditable surveillance with relative ease. In particular, this provides a basic target functionality to realize and serves as a separation between the low-level implementation of the auditability mechanism, and the high-level decision of adding auditability to protocols, e.g., choosing what data to make available to law enforcement in anonymous electronic payment systems with auditable surveillance. We formalize our auditable surveillance system in the Universal Composability (UC) framework [14,15], which ensures that the system's security and privacy guarantees still hold if the system is run in combination with many different other protocols.

Our second contribution is the protocol Π_{AS} which UC-realizes $\mathcal{F}_{\mathrm{AS}}$. It uses several cryptographic building blocks like commitments, signatures and zero-knowledge proofs and is based on an ideal functionality for auditable decryption, $\mathcal{F}_{\mathrm{AD}}$, for managing the secret-shared secret key for the threshold encryption scheme and answering decryption queries. Our modeling of this building block achieves auditability of requests for secrets and privacy regarding which secrets are released. The auditable decryption functionality $\mathcal{F}_{\mathrm{AD}}$ is also modeled in the UC framework to enable a flexible use of this building block and we provide a protocol $\mathcal{F}_{\mathrm{AD}}$ that UC-realizes it. We cast our protocol $\mathcal{F}_{\mathrm{AD}}$ in the YOSO (You-Only-Speak-Once) model [25] (see Sect. 4.3 for a brief introduction). In this model, protocols are executed by roles, where each role is only allowed to send messages once. Which party is executing a specific role is hidden until it sends its messages. This prevents targeted corruption of parties that comprise the current committee, and thus allows for leveraging global honest-majority (for the set of all nodes operating the blockchain) assumptions for smaller committee sizes, and achieving security against mobile adaptive adversaries[2].

Our third contribution is a (toy) ideal functionality, $\mathcal{F}_{\text{ASTE}}$, for Auditably Sender-Traceable Encryption (ASTE). This functionality demonstrates the usefulness of $\mathcal{F}_{\text{AS}}$ as a building block. Effectively, $\mathcal{F}_{\text{ASTE}}$ allows a registered user to *anonymously* encrypt a confidential message to another registered user, while ensuring that law enforcement is able to deanonymize the resulting ciphertext. In our toy example, law enforcement does not learn the message of a ciphertext, fully separating "content" from "eidentity". But it is easy to modify the example, so that law enforcement learns any function of message and identity. At first glance, this may be a trivial application of encryption and zero-knowledge. However, to attain *retrospective* surveillance which is somewhat *practical*, we need to combine *non-interactive non-committing encryption* (NINCE) with zero-knowledge proofs, which is highly non-trivial (cf. Sect. 1.2).

To summarize our contribution:

1. We identify and define an ideal UC-functionality, called $\mathcal{F}_{\text{AS}}$, which acts as a building block for auditable surveillance systems or more generally auditable access systems.
2. We realize this functionality in a setting where the deployment of such systems is of interest (namely, the "blockchain space"). Therein we also specify a UC-functionality $\mathcal{F}_{\text{AD}}$ for auditable decryption, which may be of independent interest. We stress however, that the realization of $\mathcal{F}_{\text{AS}}$ is not in any way restricted to this setting.
3. We demonstrate the applicability of $\mathcal{F}_{\text{AS}}$ by building $\mathcal{F}_{\text{ASTE}}$ on top of it, and provide techniques to overcome the challenges posed by retrospective surveillance namely, techniques for ZK-compatible NINCE in the PROM.

1.2 Overview of Technical Challenges in Building Applications

To be used in an application, the auditable surveillance functionality $\mathcal{F}_{\text{AS}}$ must provide a suitable interface. In most applications, users need to be able to *prove* that they escrowed a secret, e.g., a secret for the current period in our messenger application ASTE. A first idea to realize that, is for $\mathcal{F}_{\text{AS}}$ to provide a digital signature on user identity, escrowed secret and current period to the user. However, formulating a usable (let alone zero-knowledge-compatible) UC signature scheme turns out to be a daunting task, since signatures in UC are riddled with subtleties [4,11,16,39], and indeed many modeling artifacts occur.

To circumvent such problems, $\mathcal{F}_{\text{AS}}$ directly provides the possibility for users to prove statements about their identity *uid*, their escrowed secret *secret*, some

[2] Mobile adversaries can adaptively corrupt and uncorrupt parties as long as they do not exceed a certain threshold of simultaneously corrupted parties.

validity period *vper* and other information. Such a proof can show a statement of interest w.r.t. *vper*, for a witness which includes (*uid*, *secret*), *and* the proof ensures that the secret *secret* for *uid* is stored for period *vper*. Overall, this approach is more general and easier to use.

Our Auditably Sender-Traceable Encryption (ASTE) functionality encapsulates the main challenges encountered with auditable systems:

Privacy: Different information must be hidden from different parties: For $\mathcal{F}_{\text{ASTE}}$, message recipients must learn the message, but not the sender's identity. Law enforcement must not learn the message, but must learn the sender's identity.

Soundness (of Surveillance): Despite anonymity of ciphertexts in $\mathcal{F}_{\text{ASTE}}$, it must be infeasible to produce ciphertexts in the name of another user.

Retrospective Surveillance: The surveillance requests of law enforcement essentially behave like *adaptive partial corruptions.*

The second point (soundness) can make good use of the non-interactive proving capabilities of $\mathcal{F}_{\text{AS}}$, which also greatly helps in achieving the first (privacy). However, the last point (retrospective surveillance) is surprisingly difficult to achieve, even with $\mathcal{F}_{\text{AS}}$. Indeed, it is a case of the well-known "simulator commitment problem" [34]: In the ideal execution, the simulator must generate a ciphertext for an unknown message (due to confidentiality) and an unknown user (due to anonymity). However, when law enforcement (lawfully) deanonymizes the user's identity *uid* in that ciphertext, it must be correct. In other words, the identity *uid* is unknown to the simulator when it generates a ciphertext c (which "commits" to *uid*). Yet, when law enforcement obtains the escrow secret, all (affected) ciphertexts must correctly decrypt to the user's identity *uid*. If non-interactive decryption for law enforcement is assumed, then the simulator must *retroactively* choose the identity *uid* of c. This asks for a (form of) *non-interactive non-committing encryption* (NINCE), which is known to be impossible in the standard model [42]. Thus, we rely on a NINCE-like construction in the programmable random oracle model (PROM). However, this entails a well-known problem, namely, that it is not possible to *prove statements about (random) oracles* with zero-knowledge proofs *for NP*—NP statements cannot have oracles. To overcome this, we use a non-trivial construction of NINCE which incorporates cut-and-choose techniques to obtain black-box proofs for statements over the NINCE-encrypted values (and even the encryption secret keys). In light of an apparent necessity for zero-knowledge-compatible NINCE, we consider this construction as part of our toolkit for basing applications on $\mathcal{F}_{\text{AS}}$.

1.3 Related Work

Key Escrow. Since the 1990s, many papers, e.g., [35,45,53], have been dealing with different variants of key escrow mechanisms in various domains, where key material is deposited with one or more trusted parties who can then decrypt targeted communications or access devices. In particular, key escrow has also been applied in the scope of e-cash [9] to balance anonymity and accountability.

Also, more recent work follows this paradigm. For instance, in [2] the authors propose protocols for secure-channel establishment of mobile communications that offer a session-specific opening mechanism. A session key is escrowed with n authorities which all need to agree for recovering the session key. The system comes with some addition of security guarantees, e.g., non-frameability. The work [49] considers lawful device access while protecting from mass surveillance. The authors propose the use of self-escrow passcodes which are written to the device itself and can only be retrieved by means of physical access, e.g., via dedicated pins.

Table 1. Comparison of our system with the most relevant related work on accountable surveillance systems

Paper	Lawful-only	Retro-spective	Silent	No EWE needed	Public Statistics	UC-secure	Flexible Framework
[38], [24]	no	no	yes	yes	no	no	no
[19]	no	yes	yes	yes	no	no	yes
[10]	no	yes	no	yes	yes	yes	no
[41]	no	yes	yes	yes	yes	no	partially
[33]	yes	yes	no	yes	no	no	partially
[31]	yes	yes	yes	no	yes	yes	no
Our System	yes	yes	yes	yes	yes	yes	yes

1 Whether a warrant is needed for surveillance actions.
2 Whether surveillance is retrospective or only prospective.
3 Whether surveillance is silent, e.g., users are not aware that they are surveilled.
4 Whether the system does not assume the existence of EWE (extractable witness encryption).
5 Whether the system supports public statistics.
6 Whether the system is UC-secure.
7 Whether the work contains a framework that can be used for many different applications.
8 The system support a limited set of applications.

Accountable Access. Some works have tried to extend key escrow with basic accountability features. We compare ourselves with the most relevant of them in Table 1. A more detailed comparison with [31] can be found in Sect. 5.4, after our application ASTE is presented.

In [3] an anonymous yet accountable access control system is proposed. Regarding accountability, the user needs to escrow its identity with a TTP which is revealed by the TTP if some previously agreed condition bound to the ID using verifiable encryption with labels (where the condition is encoded as label) is satisfied. Liu et al. [41] propose an accountable escrow system focusing on encrypted email communication. In their system users escrow their decryption capability (instead of their private key), essentially by means of a 3-party Diffie-Hellman key exchange, to trusted custodians. Custodians perform decryptions upon request by means of their own private keys and are trusted to log each decryption request to hold the government accountable. Still, the private keys of custodians can be stolen or they can be corrupted in particular as they are well-known to government organizations. The works [24,38] deal with auditable tracing techniques in the context of e-cash and cryptocurrencies, respectively. The underlying idea is to provide a user either with a randomized version of the authority's public key, where the corresponding secret key is the revocation trapdoor, or a completely random key, which is useless for tracing. The user cannot tell which key it received until later when the authority is enforced to reveal this. The big disadvantage of their approach is that the authority has to decide in advance (e.g., at the beginning of each month) which users should be traced. This could result in practical issues, e.g., when money laundering is suspected, but the transactions of suspects cannot be traced since tracing was not turned on for them. In [19] a "mutual accountability layer" is added to systems to make operators accountable for opening key-escrowed user transactions. However, this accountability feature only results in the current key escrow committee learning that *some* transaction was opened. The lawfulness of opening a transaction is not verified and information about opening requests are not persistently and publicly stored.

Some proposals try to avoid key-escrow and its misuse potential from the outset. Very recently, a misuse-resistant surveillance scheme with retrospective exceptional access to end-to-end encrypted user communication has been proposed in [31]. Instead of building on key escrow, users are forced to (additionally) encrypt their messages with extractable witness encryption [28]. Loosely speaking, witness encryption allows to define a policy under which a ciphertext can be decrypted. In their scheme, this is the case when a warrant for the corresponding user signed by a judge has been published on a public ledger. The major disadvantage of their approach is that it is implausible that extractable witness encryption schemes actually exist [23].

In [33], the authors also abstain from using key escrow. Instead, given a warrant, a user has to (verifiable) reveal the transactions of interest itself to the judge. Unfortunately, this prevents silent investigations and leaves a suspect with the option to deny cooperation.

Several works deal with the collection of auditable logs of surveillance actions. In [6] the authors propose a distributed auditing system for CALEA-compliant wiretaps. The idea is to add Encryptor devices to the wiretaps which send encrypted audit records to a log. With the help of the log, audit statistics can be computed from ciphertexts using homomorphic encryption. Kroll et al. in two not formally published manuscripts [36,37] propose different systems for accountable access control to user data. Here, law enforcement needs to interact with a set of decryption authorities to decrypt user records, for which a single encryption key is used. Accesses are logged by an auditor party with whom the other parties need to interact continuously in order to confirm the different protocol steps. No end-to-end encryption of user data or the revocation of anonymous records is considered. Also, formal security model and proofs are missing. The work [22] extending [29] uses ledgers to collect accountable information about surveillance action and a hierarchical form of MPC to compute aggregate statistics. However, a secure and accountable escrow and disclosure of user trapdoors is not considered. In particular, if such trapdoors are kept by a company, they can still be misused by the company, stolen by an intelligence agency, etc. without leaving any trace on the ledger. The work [46] addresses some of the issues of [22] like, e.g., that government agencies and companies are trusted to regularly post (correct) information on the ledger. This is done by introducing an independent party called Enforcer who serves as the conduit for interactions between them and ensure compliance. However, for this it is assumed that government agencies and companies do never directly communicate with each other. Moreover, they do not make use of ledgers to control access to user trapdoors to disclose end-to-end encrypted communication or revoke anonymous transactions.

Finally, there are number of rather unconventional proposals to impede mass surveillance. In [7], the authors introduce the concept of translucent cryptography which, based on oblivious transfer and without relying on key escrow, allows law enforcement to access encrypted messages with a certain probability p. In [52], a system is proposed where law enforcement needs to provide a hash-based proof of work in order to recover an encrypted message, intentionally resulting in a high monetary cost (e.g., \$1K-\$1M per message). The work [51] considers exceptional access schemes for unlocking devices such as smartphones. To unlock a device, law enforcement needs to get approval by a set of custodians and subsequently locate and get physical access to a randomly selected set of delegate devices to obtain an unlock token. This requires both human and monetary resources of the law enforcement agency. In [50] Scafuro introduces the concept of break-glass encryption for cloud storage where the confidentiality of encrypted cloud data can be revoked exactly once for emergency reasons. This "break" is detectable by the data owner. The author's construction relies on trusted hardware and is a feasibility result rather than a practical solution. Persiano, Phan and Yung [47] recently introduce the concept of *anamorphic encryption*. The idea behind this is that even an attacker who can dictate the messages sent and demand the surrender of a decryption key (e.g., a government), cannot prevent a second, hidden, message from being sent along that only the dedicated recipient can decipher. While this means that one cannot prevent the exchange of hidden messages despite of surveillance, law enforcement agencies still consider surveillance as a useful measure as not all criminals have the knowledge or skill set to exploit this fact or find it convenient.

Storing Secrets on a Blockchain. There are prior works which model the capabilities of storing secrets and retrieving them under certain conditions thereby replacing the need for extractable witness encryption by relying on a blockchain.

In the recently published "eWEB" system [30] a dynamic proactive secret sharing (PSS) scheme with an efficient handover phase is constructed and used in a black-box way to store and retrieve secrets on a blockchain. Their system is secure against an adversary that statically corrupts less than half of the blockchain nodes. However, the members of the current committee are publicly known and the identifier of a retrieved secret is revealed to the general public. Hence, in our case, a user would learn that law enforcement is exposing its transactions, which should be prevented.

The system by Benhamouda et al. [8] uses a similar approach. They introduce an evolving-committee PSS scheme instead, where the selection of the next committee is a part of the secret-sharing scheme itself and the members of the current committee remain anonymous (to anyone, including the members of the previous committee) until they finished their work and hand over the role to the next committee. This enables the system to handle a mobile adversary corrupting ≈29% of blockchain nodes. However, they do not clearly state how their PSS scheme can be used to retrieve secrets from the blockchain, in particular it is unclear who learns which secrets are retrieved, whether the current committee learns this witness and whether the secret is revealed to the public or not.

Our usage of a blockchain has similarities to [8,30], in particular we also use the anonymous committees from [8], but we additionally model the system as a building block in the UC framework, which [8,30] do not. Also, we prevent users from learning whether their secret was decrypted or not (in most cases).

Erwig, Faust and Riahi [20] propose a standalone protocol for threshold decryption in the YOSO model. Our building block for auditable decryption is similar to their protocol, but augmented to satisfy our auditing needs and formalized in the UC-model instead of using game-based security notions.

Brorsson et al. [10] recently published PAPR, an anonymous credential scheme with a retrospective auditable surveillance feature. PAPR and our work both model retrospective auditable surveillance with a detailed UC framework, utilizing techniques such as bulletin boards/blockchains, YOSO, secret-sharing, ZK, and TPKE. Regarding the committee structure, our system differs from PAPR as the sets of users and committee member candidates are distinct, while PAPR's sets are identical. However, it is worth mentioning that PAPR proposes this separation as future work. Notably, our system supports silent anonymity revocation, whereas anonymity revocation in PAPR is inherently non-silent. Additionally, we implement different validity periods, allowing law enforcement to revoke a user's anonymity only for specific periods, offering a more nuanced approach compared to PAPR, where revocation affects all credential showings.

2 System Overview

In this section, we provide an overview of our system. We start by introducing the parties, followed by a high-level description of their interactions. Lastly, we give a brief discussion of its (intuitively) captured security properties.

2.1 Parties

Our system consists of the following parties:

System Operator: The system operator SO operates the system (e.g., anonymous payment system, confidential instant messenger service) that is enhanced with auditable surveillance.

Law Enforcement: Law enforcement LE can access a user's escrowed secrets if it is in possession of a valid warrant.
Judge: The judge J grants or rejects warrants.
Auditor: The auditor AU can access information about all used warrants.
Users: The set $\{U_i\}$ of users who want to make use of the application provided.
Nodes: The set $\{N_i\}$ of nodes that is available to execute assigned roles on the blockchain (the shareholder committee).

There is one each of system operator, law enforcement, judge and auditor, but there may be arbitrary many users and blockchain nodes. We consider static corruption of SO, LE and the users U_i. For the nodes N_i we achieve mobile adaptive corruption since each role a node can play is cast in the YOSO model [25] and only sends messages once. J and AU[3] are assumed to always be honest. Apart from the explicitly modeled parties, some portions of our system are available for *everyone*, for example reading information from the blockchain.

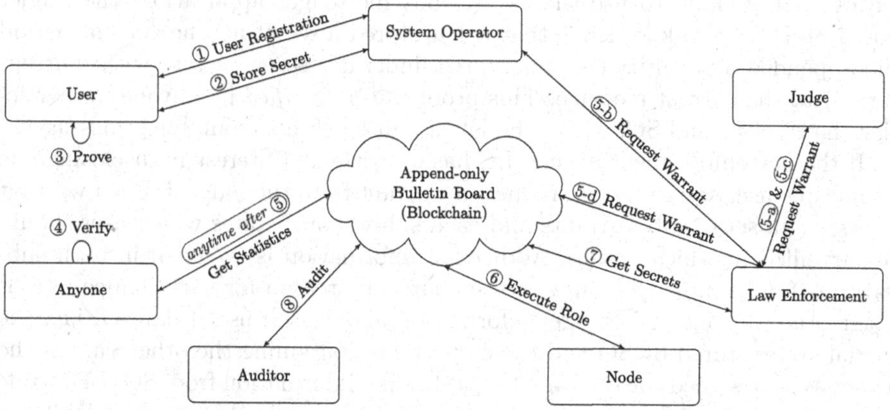

Fig. 1. High Level System Overview. The numbers represent the intended order of task execution.

2.2 High-Level System Overview

An overview of the tasks the different parties can execute can be found in Fig. 1. We now describe the intended usage of our system. In the following we focus on a specific application and instantiation to make the description clearer. We apply our functionality $\mathcal{F}_{AS}$ to an anonymous message transfer service and instantiate

[3] While a corrupt AU would learn all warrants, it is not possible for a corrupt AU to convince a third party of false claims about those warrants.

it with the protocols Π_{AS} and $\mathcal{F}_{\mathrm{AD}}$ that utilize a blockchain[4]. Note that of course different applications and instantiations are possible as well.

To initialize the system, each party generates their respective cryptographic keys. The public keys of SO, J and AU are posted on the blockchain and available to everyone. The blockchain selects its first committees and creates a threshold encryption keypair, whose public key is available to everyone and whose secret key is secret-shared among the committee members.

Users need to register themselves with SO and create an account to use the system. Each period (e.g., monthly) the user and SO create together a fresh escrow secret that could be used to expose the user's identity in messages sent during that period. The secret is then secret-shared into two *partial secrets*: One part is directly stored at SO[5] and the other part (only known to the user) is encrypted under the committee's threshold public key. The ciphertext itself reveals nothing about the user's identity, but it is linked to the user's identity and the period the secret is valid for with a zero-knowledge (ZK) proof. After depositing a secret for the current period, the user can use the messenger service during that period. To use the anonymous messenger application, the sender would *prove* in zero-knowledge that it has stored a secret for the current period and appended its identity (but encrypted under its escrow secret for the current period) to the current message. This proof can be *verified* by anyone, in particular the receiver and SO, where the latter can block non-complying messages.

If the law enforcement agency LE has a legitimate interest in disclosing one or multiple user secrets, it can request a warrant from the judge J. Each warrant consists of a set of sub-warrants and each sub-warrant states which user should be surveilled in which period. Additional information is included in each sub-warrant, for example the name of the court, the reason for surveillance, etc. If J signs the warrant, LE can get information about each user from SO, i.e., the partial secret stored by SO and the ciphertexts containing the other part of the secret. With a signed warrant and the additional information from SO, LE is able to retrieve the partial secrets for the users and periods in that warrant from the blockchain. In particular, LE convinces the current committee in zero-knowledge that it indeed has a warrant signed by J for that set of ciphertexts. Upon verifying the proof, the committee then decrypts the ciphertexts and reveals the other partial secrets to LE, who can then reconstruct the users' full secrets. Given the (anonymous) message data of the messenger system operator, LE can now match the previously anonymous messages to users in the warrant (but only for messages sent during the period specified in the warrant).

To prevent misuse of the system or even mass surveillance, several countermeasures are supported by the system. Firstly, a system-wide policy function prevents any warrants violating that policy. For example, it may disallow

[4] The features of a blockchain include publicly viewable and non-editable information as well as easy committee formation. Alternatively, an append-only bulletin board can be used. In this case, a committee has to be formed by some other means.

[5] Since we use a Blum coin toss to jointly generate the secret, SO knows a share of the secret anyway.

surveillance of an individual user for more than 12 months (by a single warrant). Secondly, LE needs to be in possession of a valid warrant signed by J to request a secret and the blockchain committee first verifies the validity of this warrant before decrypting a secret. There exists the risk that the signing key of the judge may get stolen and an attacker could use the stolen key to sign a warrant itself and thus retrieve some secrets. We cannot prevent this entirely (other than suggest that judges secure their secret keys properly), but have mitigation measures. To retrieve a decrypted secret from the blockchain, the request needs to publish some information about the respective warrant on the blockchain, thus leaving visible proof that such a request took place. What information about each warrant should be publicly available is declared by a system-wide transparency function. Choosing a suitable transparency function for the system can be a challenging task since one needs to balance the public's desire for information, the privacy of surveilled users, and LE's need for silent surveillance. The transparency function should, for example, never publish the names of the surveilled individuals. But it may, for example, publish the number of different users in the warrant, the periods in which the retrieved secrets are valid and the name of the court that signed the warrant. Assuming the latter information is published, each court can monitor the blockchain and upon seeing more warrants signed by its key than they actually signed, they can detect key theft and henceforth take appropriate measures[6]. Thirdly, assuming an appropriate transparency function, anyone can get useful information about all enforced warrants through publicly available statistics. For example, if the transparency functions reveals the number of different users in the warrant, the number of currently surveilled users becomes public. If this number suddenly skyrockets, it is an indication of misuse of power. Fourthly, the auditor AU has the capability (as it can access the "full" warrant information on the blockchain) to conduct a detailed investigation of enforced warrants. It may check for any peculiarities and prove statements about the stored warrants to an arbitrary entity without revealing any further information. For instance, such a statement might be that none of the warrants issued within a certain period of time involve a certain user.

2.3 Security Properties and Trust Assumptions

We now summarize the desired security and privacy properties of our building block for auditable surveillance in an informal and intuitive manner:

- (Non-colluding[7]) users are not aware whether LE issued a request to recover one of their secrets.

[6] Our system actually only supports a single non-revocable judge key to keep the model from being overly complex, but the extension to several different and revocable judge keys is straightforward.

[7] This security property holds for a user colluding with other users and blockchain nodes but not one colluding with SO or LE.

- To use the Prove task (cf. Fig. 1) for an application on top, e.g., to prove some statement involving the user's identity, the user needs to have escrowed a secret for the respective period.
- The privacy guarantees of the application on top are only breached if a warrant was granted. And even in that case, only the users covered by the warrant have (some of) their data exposed.
- LE can only request secrets for warrants that comply with the system policy.
- After LE requested a decryption by the blockchain, the publicly available information about the warrant (for statistical purposes) and the information about the warrant that is only available to AU are permanently stored on the blockchain and can not be modified or removed afterwards.
- Anyone is able to retrieve publicly available statistics on all enforced warrants.
- AU has the capability to provide the general public with *provably correct* statistics about the enforced warrants.[8]
- Even if SO and LE collude, they can not expose any escrowed user secrets.
- Likewise, even if a majority of the blockchain nodes collude, they can not reconstruct a user's secret.

We assume the judge J and auditor AU to be honest. Since AU has the power to read all warrants in the clear, it is a very powerful entity that could potentially misuse that power. In reality, one could decentralize that trust by having multiple auditor parties that utilize threshold cryptography or multi-party computation. Since we trust the jurisdiction, we also model J as an honest party and assume that it honestly follows the protocol. Warrants that were granted but legally not justified can be detected upon request to AU. The existence of judge-signed warrants also ensures that LE can also only request user information from SO for which it has a signed warrant.

Although SO is corruptible in our system, we implicitly have to trust it in some aspects: We assume that SO cooperates with other parties and responds to messages. A SO that ignores messages from other parties could bring the system to a halt or deny individual users' participation in the system. Since SO has a monetary motivation to keep the system running for a long time, we believe these assumptions to be reasonable. Note that while a corrupt SO cannot send false data (e.g., pretend that a ciphertext belongs to another honest user), it can omit some data (e.g., data from colluding corrupt users) when sending it to LE. This is a general problem that can be discouraged through laws.

As an exemplary application that is enhanced by auditable surveillance, we consider Auditably Sender-Traceable Encryption (ASTE). This application achieves (among others) the following core security guarantees:

- Any ciphertext which decrypts successfully (to $m \neq \bot$) for an honest user can be deanonymized by LE.
- Finding ciphertexts which falsely deanonymize to an honest user is infeasible.

[8] Since AU has access to the full warrants, its statistics can be more detailed than those the general public can compute. AU could even prove to third parties (e.g., a parliament) facts about specific warrants without revealing the full warrant.

- Plaintext and identities remain secret to parties which are not allowed access to them. That is: Without a warrant, LE learns nothing from a ciphertext. With a valid warrant, LE can deanonymize the user, but the plaintext remains hidden.

We give LE only the ability to *deanonymize* instead of reading the message (and deanonymizing), since corrupted users may use secure encryption to encrypt their messages anyway. However, by straightforward modifications, LE may learn any function of the message and the user's identity.

3 A Formal Model for Auditable Surveillance Systems

In this section we introduce the functionality $\mathcal{F}_{\mathrm{AS}}$, our formal model for our auditable surveillance system, which is independent of the application. We model our system in the Universal Composability (UC) framework [14,15]. For a very brief introduction to UC and for some writing conventions see the full version [21].

Table 2. Variables used in $\mathcal{F}_{\mathrm{AS}}$

pid	The party identifier for the UC framework (e.g., a physical identifier)
uid	The (self-chosen) identity of a user
secret	The escrowed secret
vper	The validity period for a single secret (e.g., the current month)
W	A warrant from LE to retrieve (multiple) user secrets with $W = (W_1, \ldots, W_v)$ and $W_i = (\mathit{uid}_i, \mathit{vper}_i, \mathit{meta}_i)$
v	number of subwarrants W_i inside a warrant W
meta	Meta information about a warrant. Some of it is public information and some is only meant for the auditor
W^{pub}	The information about the warrant that should be known to the public

We first introduce some variables that are essential for the functionality in Table 2. We describe how our auditable surveillance system is modeled in the

UC framework by presenting the ideal functionality $\mathcal{F}_{\mathrm{AS}}$ in Figs. 2 and 3. Note that the functionality implicitly checks the *pid* of calling parties: If the functionality description states "Input P: (...)" for P $\in$ {SO, AU, J, LE}, then the functionality first checks if the calling party has the correct role and ignores the message if the role does not match. We now also sketch the individual tasks.

System Init and Party Init. These tasks are just for initializing the system and other parties.

User Registration. To participate in the auditable surveillance system (and to use the application on top) the user needs to create an account with SO. It is ensured that each user can only create one account. The user can choose an unique identity (*uid*) under which it will be known henceforth.

Store Secret. Each period (e.g., monthly) the user needs to deposit a new secret. Since $\mathcal{F}_{\mathrm{AS}}$ is a trustworthy incorruptible entity, we do not need to encrypt it and directly store the secret inside $\mathcal{F}_{\mathrm{AS}}$. $\mathcal{F}_{\mathrm{AS}}$ first checks that the user is registered in the system and has not yet stored a secret for the current period. Then, $\mathcal{F}_{\mathrm{AS}}$ draws a fresh secret (so the user can not influence what his secret will be) and stores it in its internal storage. After this task is finished, the user can now use the application, which is not modeled directly in $\mathcal{F}_{\mathrm{AS}}$. For an example on how to use $\mathcal{F}_{\mathrm{AS}}$ for Auditably Sender-Traceable Encryption, see Sect. 5.

Request Warrant. In this task LE can request a warrant from J. The functionality itself first checks if the proposed warrant W complies with the system's policy function f_p. Then it gives J the opportunity to approve ($b = 1$) or deny ($b = 0$) that warrant. $\mathcal{F}_{\mathrm{AS}}$ also ensures that each warrant is only processed once (this ensures that the statistics calculated later will be correct).

Get Secrets. With a granted warrant LE can now retrieve the secrets for all $(uid, vper)$ pairs inside the warrant. $\mathcal{F}_{\mathrm{AS}}$ first verifies that the warrant was approved by J and then outputs all secrets corresponding to that warrant to LE.

Get Statistics. Every party of the system can query this task to enable the general public to access statistics about the warrants. For every warrant granted by J the transparency function f_t is computed to get the publicly available information W^{pub} about that warrant. The publicly available information about each warrant are then returned to the party asking for statistics.

Audit. When AU gets tasked with calculating detailed statistics or with investigating the case of a specific user, it can call this task. AU is then provided with all warrants that were approved by J. Since we assume AU to be a trustworthy entity (or a group of entities that perform this task in a multi-party computation) we can provide AU with the warrants in the clear. The actual execution of AU's task takes place outside our system, we only provide AU with the necessary information.

Prove and Verify. The zero-knowledge proof interface is used to build applications on top of $\mathcal{F}_{\mathrm{AS}}$. The Prove task allows a prover to generate a proof π for

Functionality $\mathcal{F}_{AS}$

System Parameters:
- f_t — Transparency function. Outputs public information of a warrant. Interface is $W^{pub} \leftarrow f_t(W)$.
- f_p — Policy Function. Checks whether a given warrant is allowed by system policy. Interface is $\{0,1\} \leftarrow f_p(W)$.
- $\mathcal{S}$ — Space of secrets
- $\mathcal{R}$ — an NP relation for statements about stored secrets: Contains $(stmt_R, wit_R) \in \mathcal{R}$ pairs where $stmt_R$ is a statement and wit_R is a witness for that statement
- System pids: pid_{SO}, pid_J, pid_{AU}

Functionality State:
- L_I: List of initialized parties (initially empty). Contains (pid) entries.
- L_U: List of registered users (initially empty). Contains (pid, uid) pairs.
- L_S: List of stored secrets (initially empty). Contains $(uid_i, vper_i, secret_i)$ entries.
- L_W: List of warrants that were requested by LE from J (initially empty). Entries are of the form (W, b), where b is a bit that states whether the warrant was granted or denied by the judge.
- L_π: List of proofs (initially empty). Entries are of the form $(stmt_R, wit_R, \pi, b)$, where the bit b states whether the relation is fulfilled or not.

System Init:
- Input SO & J & AU: (INIT, SO/J/AU)
  - If this is the first time, this task is invoked, do whatever is stated in "Behavior". If this is not the first time this task is invoked, ignore the messages.
  - Ignore all other messages until this task has been invoked.
- Behavior:
  1. Create empty lists L_I, L_U, L_S, L_W, and L_π
  2. Send (INIT) to the adversary
  3. Add pid_{SO} and pid_J to L_I
- Output SO & J & AU: (INITFINISHED)

Party Init:
- Input some Party P: (PINIT)
- Behavior:
  1. If $pid \notin L_I$, store pid in L_I
  2. Send (PINIT) to the adversary
- Output to P: (PINITFINISHED)

User Registration:
- Input U: (REGISTER, uid)
- Input SO: (REGISTER, uid')
- Behavior:
  1. As soon as U gave input, send (REGISTER, pid, uid) to the adversary. Wait for (OK) from the adversary and input from SO before continuing.
  2. If $uid \neq uid'$, abort. (wrong inputs)
  3. If $(pid, \cdot) \in L_U$, abort. (User already registered.)
  4. If $(\cdot, uid) \in L_U$, abort. (Identity already taken.)
  5. Store (pid, uid) of the user in list of registered Users L_U
  6. Store pid in L_I
- Output U & SO: (REGISTERED)

Store Secret:
- Input U: (STORESECRET, uid, $vper$)
- Input SO: (STORESECRET, $vper'$)
- Behavior:
  1. If SO is corrupted (and U is honest): As soon as U gave input, send (STORESECRET, $vper$) to the adversary and then wait for input from SO
  2. If $vper \neq vper'$, abort
  3. Check if user is registered: If $(pid, uid) \notin L_U$, abort.
  4. Check if user already registered a secret for the current validity period: If there exists an entry $(uid, vper, \cdot)$ in the list of stored secrets L_S, abort
  5. Generate secret: $secret \xleftarrow{r} \mathcal{S}$
  6. Store $(uid, vper, secret)$ in the list of stored secrets L_S
- Output U: (SECRETSTORED, $secret$)
- Output SO: (SECRETSTORED, uid)

Request Warrant:
- Input LE: (REQUESTWARRANT, W)
- Behavior:
  1. Check if policy function allows that warrant: If $0 \leftarrow f_p(W)$, abort (Warrant not allowed by policy function).
- Output J: (REQUESTWARRANT, W)
- Input J: (b)
- Behavior:
  1. If there already exists an entry $(W, \cdot) \in L_W$, abort (Warrant already processed).
  2. If SO is honest: If $b = 1$, send (REQUESTWARRANT, $f_t(W)$, $|\widetilde{W}|$, v) to the adversary and wait for message (OK) from the adversary
  3. If SO is corrupted: Send (REQUESTWARRANT, W, b) to the adversary and wait for message (OK) from the adversary
  4. Append (W, b) to L_W
- Output LE: (REQUESTWARRANT, b)

Fig. 2. The ideal functionality $\mathcal{F}_{AS}$

Functionality $\mathcal{F}_{\mathrm{AS}}$ (continued)

Get Secrets:
- Input LE: (GetSecrets, W)
- Behavior:
  1. Check if warrant was granted by Judge: If no entry $(W, 1)$ exists in L_W, abort. (Warrant either not requested or not granted)
  2. Parse warrant: $(W_1, \ldots, W_v) \leftarrow W$ and $(uid_i, vper_i, meta_i) \leftarrow W_i$
  3. For each i from 1 to v:
     (a) Check if secret is stored: Get $secret_i$ for which an entry $(uid_i, vper_i, secret_i)$ exists in the list of stored secrets L_S. If none exists, set $secret_i = \perp$.
  4. If LE is honest: Send (GetSecrets) to the adversary
- Output LE: (GotSecrets, $(secret_1, \ldots, secret_v)$)

Get Statistics:
- Input some Party P: (GetStatistics)
- Behavior:
  1. Send (GetStatistics) to the adversary
  2. Initialize empty list $\mathsf{L}_\mathsf{Stats}$
  3. For every $(W, b) \in \mathsf{L}_W$ with $b = 1$:
     (a) Apply transparency function to warrant: $W^{\mathrm{pub}} \leftarrow f_t(W)$
     (b) Append W^{pub} to $\mathsf{L}_\mathsf{Stats}$
- Output to P: (GotStatistics, $\mathsf{L}_\mathsf{Stats}$)

Audit:
- Input AU: (AuditRequest)
- Behavior:
  1. Send (AuditRequest) to the adversary
  2. Initialize empty list L_AU
  3. For every $(W, b) \in \mathsf{L}_W$ with $b = 1$, append W to L_AU
- Output to AU: (AuditAnswer, L_AU)

Prove:
- Input U: (Prove, $stmt_R$, wit_R)
- Behavior:
  1. Parse $(uid, secret, wit') := wit_R$
  2. Parse $(vper, stmt') := stmt_R$
  3. Let pid_U be the pid of the party calling this task
  4. If $\mathcal{R}(stmt_R, wit_R) \neq 1$ or $(pid_\mathsf{U}, uid) \notin \mathsf{L}_\mathsf{U}$ or $(uid, vper, secret) \notin \mathsf{L}_\mathsf{Secrets}$, then abort.
  5. Send urgent request (Prove, $stmt_R$) to the adversary.
  6. Wait for immediate response (Proof, π) from the adversary
  7. Store $(stmt_R, wit_R, \pi, 1)$ in L_π
- Output U (immediate): (Proof, $stmt_R$, wit_R, π)

Verify:
- Input some party P: (Verify, $stmt_R$, π)
- Behavior:
  1. If $pid \notin \mathsf{L}_\mathsf{I}$, abort (Verifier did not initialize)
  2. For $(stmt_R, \pi)$, check if there exists $(stmt_R, wit_R, \pi, b) \in \mathsf{L}_\pi$
  3. If entry exists
     (a) (Immediately) output (Verification, $stmt_R$, π, b) to P
  4. If entry does not exist
     (a) Send urgent request (Verify, $stmt_R$, π) to the adversary
     (b) Wait for immediate response (witness, wit_R) from the adversary
     (c) Set $b \leftarrow \mathcal{R}(stmt_R, wit_R)$
     (d) Only if SO is honest:
        i. Parse $(uid, secret, wit') := wit_R$
        ii. Parse $(vper, stmt') := stmt_R$
        iii. If $(uid, vper, secret) \notin \mathsf{L}_\mathsf{Secrets}$, set $b = 0$ (User has not stored a secret)
     (e) Store $(stmt_R, wit_R, \pi, b)$ in L_π
     (f) Prepare the output message (Verification, $stmt_R$, π, b)
- Output to P (immediate): (Verification, $stmt_R$, π, b)

Fig. 3. The ideal functionality $\mathcal{F}_{\mathrm{AS}}$ (continued)

a statement $stmt_R$ in some NP-relation $\mathcal{R}$, where the witness wit_R includes the user's identity and escrow secret for the chosen period. The Verify task allows to check the validity of a proof. As an example, a user may prove that it correctly encrypted its identity under its escrow secret key. Since we do not limit our system to a single application, this generic proof/verify interface enables the flexible use of different applications.

Remark 1. In the description of $\mathcal{F}_{\mathrm{AS}}$ (c.f. Figs. 2 and 3) there are several messages of the form "Send (*value*) to the adversary". This is due to modeling the system in the UC framework: In UC, privacy guarantees are modeled by explicitly sending all information that an adversary could learn in the real world to the adversary. Additionally, in UC there exists only a *single* adversarial party that can corrupt several other parties. In the real world, this corresponds to the scenario that *all* dishonest parties collude and share all the information they gathered with each other. Consequently, a UC-adversary learns a lot of information. However, one should note that in reality dishonest parties learn significantly less information if they do not cooperate.

4 Realizing the Model

After giving an idealized formalization of the system we want to achieve, we now elaborate on how to actually build such a system.

4.1 A Protocol Π_{AS} for Realizing $\mathcal{F}_{\mathrm{AS}}$

The functionality $\mathcal{F}_{\mathrm{AS}}$ represents an *ideal* version of the system we want to achieve. Since in practice we do not want to rely on trusted third parties to perform our calculations for us, we build a protocol Π_{AS} *in the real world* that achieves the same security guarantees as $\mathcal{F}_{\mathrm{AS}}$. We later prove that our constructed protocol Π_{AS} UC-realizes $\mathcal{F}_{\mathrm{AS}}$ in the $\{\mathcal{F}_{\mathrm{AD}}, \mathcal{F}_{\mathrm{CRS}}, \mathcal{F}_{\mathrm{BB}}, \mathcal{G}_{CLOCK}\}$-hybrid model. As a setup assumption, we use the well-known functionality $\mathcal{F}_{\mathrm{CRS}}$ which enables access for all parties to a *common reference string* (CRS), set up by a trusted party with a given distribution. We also use an external bulletin board functionality $\mathcal{F}_{\mathrm{BB}}$, where any party can register a single (uid, v) pair associated with its identity, where the *uid*s need to be unique. Any party can retrieve registered values v, which in our case are public encryption keys.

We modularize our realization by outsourcing the auditable decryption of ciphertexts to another hybrid functionality $\mathcal{F}_{\mathrm{AD}}$, which we describe in Sect. 4.2. This hybrid functionality idealizes the primitive of a blockchain with an evolving set of committees where the committee members are anonymous until they finished their work. The functionality is parameterized by a (threshold) PKE scheme and provides everyone with access to a public key under which secrets can be encrypted. Then, given suitable auditing and authorization information, decryption of a ciphertext can be requested. In our case this information will be a judge-signed warrant for that ciphertext. We outsource the auditable decryption for several reasons: 1. A primitive for auditable threshold decryption is an interesting building block in itself and to the best of our knowledge no UC formalization of that primitive exists yet. 2. It simplifies the security analysis of our system, since we can first assume that the decryption is handled by a trustworthy party. In a second step we then replace the auditable decryption functionality $\mathcal{F}_{\mathrm{AD}}$ with a protocol that realizes it.

Since blockchains with evolving committees generally require some concept of *time* (e.g., to ensure that the committee changes daily), the functionality $\mathcal{F}_{\mathrm{AD}}$ utilizes a global clock functionality $\mathcal{G}_{CLOCK}$ (from [5]) to model time.

We now elaborate on some of the core techniques we use in Π_{AS} and refer for the complete description of Π_{AS} and for the used hybrid functionalities (except

$\mathcal{F}_{\text{AD}}$) to the full version [21]. The hybrid functionality $\mathcal{F}_{\text{AD}}$ is briefly discussed in Sect. 4.2 and in full detail in the full version [21].

System Init. SO and J each create a signing keypair. Then SO, J, and AU initialize the auditable decryption functionality $\mathcal{F}_{\text{AD}}$ together. The functionality $\mathcal{F}_{\text{AD}}$ is then used to provide all parties with access to the needed public keys.

User Registration. Users create a signing keypair $(\mathsf{vk}_{\text{U}}, \mathsf{sk}_{\text{U}})$ during registration. To ensure at most one account per user, we use an idealized bulletin board $\mathcal{F}_{\text{BB}}$, where any party can register a single $(uid, \mathsf{vk}_{\text{U}})$ pair associated with its identity, where the *uid*s need to be unique. Any party can retrieve registered values.

Store Secret. To store a fresh secret with validity period *vper*, user and SO jointly create a fresh secret *secret* with a Blum coin toss, where each party draws a partial secret: SO draws sec_1 and the user draws sec_2. The full secret is then $secret := sec_1 \oplus sec_2$, but only learned by the user. The operator directly stores the partial secret sec_1 (along with the user's identity *uid* and the current period *vper*). The user encrypts the partial secret sec_2 under the public threshold encryption key pk of $\mathcal{F}_{\text{AD}}$, sends the resulting ciphertext *ct* to SO and proves in zero-knowledge that it calculated all values honestly. SO also stores the ciphertext *ct* and provides the user with a (blinded) signature on $(uid, vper, secret)$ (without learning *secret*). The user can then utilize this signature in the application on top to prove to another party that it indeed stored a secret for that validity period.

Request Warrant. First, J signs the warrant W proposed by LE to convince third parties that it indeed has approved the warrant. Since the auditable decryption functionality $\mathcal{F}_{\text{AD}}$ needs to know which ciphertexts should be decrypted, we need J to also sign all ciphertexts *ct* containing the partial secrets sec_2 associated with the warrant W. Therefore, we additionally include SO in this protocol: LE sends the signed warrant to SO and asks for the corresponding ciphertexts *ct* along with the stored partial secrets sec_1.[9] Afterwards, LE provides J with the ciphertexts *ct* to get a signature on $\widetilde{W}$, which is the warrant W *including* the ciphertexts.[10] LE can now utilize the hybrid functionality $\mathcal{F}_{\text{AD}}$ to request the decryption of all ciphertexts corresponding to the warrant $\widetilde{W}$.

Get Secrets. After $\mathcal{F}_{\text{AD}}$ processed the decryption request, LE can retrieve the partial secrets sec_2 for a warrant from $\mathcal{F}_{\text{AD}}$. Of course, $\mathcal{F}_{\text{AD}}$ verified the validity of all requests and partial secrets for invalid requests can not be retrieved. Then,

---

9 This of course enables SO to guess which users are or will be tracked by LE. But in practice this could be amended either by SO just sending *all* its information to LE or by LE using private information retrieval (PIR) to get just the ciphertexts for the current warrant without SO learning which ciphertexts were retrieved.

10 Before sending the request to J, LE checks the users' signatures. Before answering the request, J checks the (same) signatures as well. Since we assume that J is always honest, it would be sufficient for only J to check the signatures. But we intentionally let LE check the signatures first to filter out invalid requests before forwarding them to J, to reduce J's workload.

LE uses the already stored partial secrets sec_1 (obtained from SO) to reconstruct the full user secrets $secret := sec_1 \oplus sec_2$ for all users in the warrant.

Get Statistics and Audit. Since $\mathcal{F}_{\text{AD}}$ knows all requested[11] warrants, $\mathcal{F}_{\text{AD}}$ can directly give the desired information for those tasks.

Prove and Verify. The Prove task is a local task in which the user uses a NIZKPoK to create the proof π itself. Similarly, the Verify task is also a local task in which the validity of the statement is verified using the NIZKPoK.

Security. In the full version [21] we show that our protocol Π_{AS} UC-realizes $\mathcal{F}_{\text{AS}}$. In particular, we show the following theorem.

Theorem 1. *Π_{AS} UC-realizes $\mathcal{F}_{\text{AS}}$ in the $\{\mathcal{F}_{\text{AD}}, \mathcal{F}_{\text{CRS}}, \mathcal{F}_{\text{BB}}, \mathcal{G}_{CLOCK}\}$-hybrid model under the assumptions that* COM *is a (computationally) hiding, (statistically) binding and (dual-mode) extractable and equivocable commitment scheme, Σ is a EUF-CMA secure signature scheme,* NIZK *is a straight-line simulation-extractable non-interactive zero-knowledge proof system, and* TPKE *is IND-CPA secure against all PPT-adversaries $\mathcal{A}$ who statically corrupts either (1) a subset of the users, (2) LE and a subset of the users, (3) SO and a subset of the users, or (4) SO, LE and a subset of the users.*

4.2 Decrypting Secrets with $\mathcal{F}_{\text{AD}}$

We now want to briefly describe our ideal auditable decryption functionality $\mathcal{F}_{\text{AD}}$. The formal description can be found in the full version [21]. To enable protocols based on the YOSO approach, our functionality makes use of the global clock functionality $\mathcal{G}_{CLOCK}$ and proceeds in rounds, where a round lasts a predefined amount of time units and decryptions only become available in following rounds. The functionality is also parameterized by a (threshold) PKE scheme.

Init, Get Tasks and Interaction with $\mathcal{G}_{CLOCK}$. $\mathcal{F}_{\text{AD}}$ starts by creating an encryption keypair and registering with the global clock $\mathcal{G}_{CLOCK}$. In Π_{AS} SO and J each create a signing keypair and pass their public verification keys to $\mathcal{F}_{\text{AD}}$, where they are stored. There are also tasks to provide the parties in Π_{AS} with the public keys of SO, J and the public encryption key of the functionality. This ensures that both systems use the same keys.

Request Decryption and Retrieve Secret. LE can send a signed warrant to $\mathcal{F}_{\text{AD}}$ to request decryption of all ciphertexts *ct* listed in that warrant. $\mathcal{F}_{\text{AD}}$ checks if that warrant is valid and then adds the listed ciphertexts *ct* to a list of pending decryption requests. To allow our implementation $\mathcal{F}_{\text{AD}}$ to be YOSO, requests for decryption are only processed during committee handovers. To emulate that behavior in the ideal world, $\mathcal{F}_{\text{AD}}$ separates the *request* of a secret and the actual

[11] Note that these tasks provide the parties with information about all *requested* warrants, independently of whether the secrets were actually retrieved or not.

retrieval of a secret into two different inquiries by LE, with the requirement that the committee switches between the two calls.

Role Execute. To emulate the passing of time in the real world and the fact that YOSO parties can only send a message once, $\mathcal{F}_{\text{AD}}$ interacts with the clock $\mathcal{G}_{CLOCK}$: After all honest nodes have activated $\mathcal{F}_{\text{AD}}$, it advances the current time. After the required amount of "time" passes, $\mathcal{F}_{\text{AD}}$ emulates a committee handover as follows: $\mathcal{F}_{\text{AD}}$ handles all *pending* decryption requests and adds the decrypted (partial) secrets to a list of *processed* decryption requests. After this "committee handover", the list of processed decryption requests contains all (partial) secrets that are ready for retrieval by LE.

Get Statistics and Audit. $\mathcal{F}_{\text{AD}}$ keeps track of all warrants for which LE requested secrets. If AU initiates an investigation, $\mathcal{F}_{\text{AD}}$ provides it with all valid warrants. Likewise, $\mathcal{F}_{\text{AD}}$ can also provide a party asking for statistics with the outputs of the transparency function for all warrants. Therefore, $\mathcal{F}_{\text{AD}}$ provides the same statistics and audit information as $\mathcal{F}_{\text{AS}}$.

4.3 A Protocol $\mathcal{F}_{\text{AD}}$ for Realizing $\mathcal{F}_{\text{AD}}$

We cast our protocol $\mathcal{F}_{\text{AD}}$ in the YOSO model, which we now introduce briefly.

The YOSO Model. In the YOSO (You-Only-Speak-Once) model introduced by [25], protocols are run between roles, where each role is only allowed to send one message and has no lasting state. These roles can then be assigned to actual machines executing them through some form of role assignment mechanism. With a way to anonymously receive messages (e.g., by reading ciphertexts stored on a public blockchain) and a role assignment mechanism that privately assigns roles, this prevents targeted attack against roles: The identity of a machine executing a role can only be learned when it sends its message, but at that point it finished execution and is no longer in possession of any secret state.

This allows both resilience against denial-of-service attacks as well as against strong adversaries trying to corrupt roles that are part of a protocol execution of interest. Assuming a large enough pool of machines willing to execute roles, an attacker able to corrupt any machine of its choosing, but limited in the number of machines it can corrupt at once, cannot break the security of a protocol even when run between only a number of roles smaller than the corruption limit.

To achieve this in our protocol, we make use of a blockchain with role assignment functionality $\mathcal{F}_{\text{BCRA}}$, which provides a public append-only ledger together with a mechanism that anonymously selects parties for the next committee by posting public encryption and verification keys for the individual roles on the ledger and privately sending the corresponding decryption and signing keys to the assigned party. For more details, see Fig. 4. Note that since it is unclear how to realize the role assignment functionality provided in [25], our functionality differs from theirs in the following ways:

1. We integrated the global clock $\mathcal{G}_{CLOCK}$.

2. $\mathcal{F}_{\text{BCRA}}$ only allows assigning roles of the next committee, not roles at an arbitrary time in the future.
3. The adversary can control a portion of the public keys (and $\mathcal{F}_{\text{BCRA}}$ does not get to know the corresponding secret keys).

We deem it plausible that the committee selection protocol from [8] with suitable corruption thresholds in combination with a suitable blockchain can be used to implement this[12], although more efficient approaches such as described in [13] are also possible. We want to stress here that we are in the "near future" setting of [13], compared to the "far future" setting that would imply witness encryption. Given that the mechanisms for assigning roles and the criteria by which parties should be chosen are subject to ongoing research, we believe using $\mathcal{F}_{\text{BCRA}}$ to abstract from the details is a suitable approach that allows incorporation of future research.

Now we give a brief description of $\mathcal{F}_{\text{AD}}$ and refer to the full version [21] for further details. Our instantiation $\mathcal{F}_{\text{AD}}$ UC-realizes $\mathcal{F}_{\text{AD}}$ in the $\{\mathcal{F}_{\text{BCRA}}, \mathcal{F}_{\text{CRS}}, \mathcal{G}_{CLOCK}\}$-hybrid model.

Init, Get Tasks and Interaction with $\mathcal{G}_{CLOCK}$. During initialization, AU creates an encryption keypair and SO, J and AU post their public keys to the ledger $\mathcal{F}_{\text{BCRA}}$. The common reference string is obtained by querying $\mathcal{F}_{\text{CRS}}$, the other Get Tasks are handled by reading from the ledger $\mathcal{F}_{\text{BCRA}}$. All honest nodes N register with the clock $\mathcal{G}_{CLOCK}$ upon first activation. Additionally, the distributed key generation protocol from [20] is run by the first roles assigned through $\mathcal{F}_{\text{BCRA}}$, resulting in a public encryption key pk and a threshold-sharing of the corresponding decryption key among the first committee.

Request Decryption and Retrieve Secret. To request decryption of ciphertexts and subsequently receive user secrets, LE needs to be in possession of a judge-signed warrant listing the relevant ciphertexts ct. To ensure privacy of the warrant $\widetilde{W}$, instead of simply posting the warrant to $\mathcal{F}_{\text{BCRA}}$, LE instead posts an encryption W^{enc} of the warrant $\widetilde{W}$ under AU's public key, the output W^{pub} of the transparency function and a NIZK-proof that it knows a valid signature under J's public key on $\widetilde{W}$ and both W^{enc} and W^{pub} were computed correctly. Additionally, instead of posting the ciphertexts ct directly, LE re-randomizes them and also proves in zero-knowledge that the ciphertexts $\widehat{ct}$ are indeed re-randomizations of the ciphertexts ct listed in the warrant. This ensures that the users under surveillance can not be identified from the ciphertexts. The request additionally contains a public encryption key of LE under which the responses from the committee members will be encrypted.

After the responses have been posted, LE again reads the content of $\mathcal{F}_{\text{BCRA}}$, decrypts all responses using its decryption key, and combines the partial decryptions ct^* to obtain the secret for each ciphertext ct.

Role Execute. Nodes N read the content of $\mathcal{F}_{\text{BCRA}}$ at least once per round (this is ensured by them only sending an update-message to $\mathcal{G}_{CLOCK}$ after having done

[12] Alternatively, a suitable variant of the committee selection protocol from [8] or the "encryption to the current winner" scheme from [13] are good candidates as well.

Functionality $\mathcal{F}_{\text{BCRA}}$

The functionality is parameterized by an encryption scheme PKE, a signature scheme Σ, a threshold ϵ, a maximum delay δ_{Post} and a set MACHINE which is the set of parties allowed to use it. It has also access to a global clock $\mathcal{G}_{\text{CLOCK}}$. Upon receiving any input, $\mathcal{F}_{\text{BCRA}}$ first queries $\mathcal{G}_{\text{CLOCK}}$ and sets t_{Now} to the value returned.

Init: Let POSTED be the empty set, let ORDERED be the empty sequence.

Post: On input (POST, m) from $pid \in$ MACHINE, add (pid, t_{Now}, m) to the set POSTED and output (POST, pid, m) to the adversary.

Order: On input (ORDER, pid, m) from the adversary where some $(pid, t, m) \in$ POSTED and no $(pid, t', m) \in$ ORDERED, append (pid, t_{Now}, m) to ORDERED.

Read: On input (READ) from $pid \in$ MACHINE, leak (READ) to the adversary. For each entry $(pid, t, m) \in$ POSTED for which no $(pid, t', m) \in$ ORDERED and $t = t_{\text{Now}} - \delta_{\text{Post}}$, append (pid, t_{Now}, m) to ORDERED. Then output (ORDERED) to pid.

NextCommittee: On input (NEXTCOMMITTEE, R, n, S) from the adversary, with $|S| < \epsilon n$ containing entries of the form $(M_i \in$ MACHINE, $(\mathsf{ek}_i, \mathsf{vk}_i))$, do the following:

- For $i \in (1, \ldots, |S|)$:
  1. Mark M_i as corrupted
  2. Set $m =$ (NEXTCOMMITTEE, $R, \mathsf{ek}_i, \mathsf{vk}_i$), add $(\texttt{roleassign}, t_{\text{Now}}, m)$[a] to POSTED and leak m to the adversary
- For $i \in (|S| + 1, \ldots, n)$:
  1. Sample $\left(\mathsf{ek}_{R_i}, \mathsf{dk}_{R_i}\right) \leftarrow \mathsf{PKE.Gen}(1^\lambda)$
  2. Sample $\left(\mathsf{vk}_{R_i}, \mathsf{sk}_{R_i}\right) \leftarrow \Sigma.\mathsf{Gen}(1^\lambda)$
  3. Sample a uniformly random $M_{R_i} \in$ MACHINE
  4. Set $m = \left(\text{NEXTCOMMITTEE}, R, \mathsf{ek}_{R_i}, \mathsf{vk}_{R_i}\right)$, add $(\texttt{roleassign}, t_{\text{Now}}, m)$ to POSTED and leak m to the adversary

When $(\texttt{roleassign}, t', m)$ is later added to ORDERED output $\left(\text{GENERATE}, R, \mathsf{ek}_{R_i}, \mathsf{dk}_{R_i}, \mathsf{vk}_{R_i}, \mathsf{sk}_{R_i}\right)$ to M_{R_i} for $i \in (|S| + 1, \ldots, n)$

Forward Security: When M_R becomes corrupted, output (GENERATE, $R, \mathsf{ek}_R, \mathsf{dk}_R, \mathsf{vk}_R, \mathsf{sk}_R$) to the adversary if (NEXTCOMMITTEE, $R, \mathsf{ek}_R, \mathsf{vk}_R$) $\notin$ ORDERED.

[a] roleassign is a special pid used to represent role-assignment messages

Fig. 4. Blockchain with role assignment functionality loosely based on [25]

so). Afterwards, they check if they were assigned a role in the current round. If this is the case, they proceed as follows by parsing the content of the ledger:

- They gather all required encryption/verification keys for relevant previous and the next committee
- They gather all messages with key shares of the threshold decryption key
- They gather all requests for decryption

After gathering all relevant messages, they fulfill their role as committee member of the current round. For all messages gathered from the ledger, they validate the signature and accompanying proofs and ignore the message if they are invalid.

They gather all resharings of the threshold decryption key that were made by the previous committee and addressed to the current role and combine them to obtain their share sk_i of the threshold decryption key sk. To enable the committee in the next round to fulfill their duties as well, they reshare sk_i again and encrypt each reshare to a committee member from the next round. This is again done in the same way as in [20].

For each valid decryption request, a (partial) threshold-decryption of the ciphertext $\widehat{ct}$ is performed using sk_i. The answer (including the partial decryption

ct^* and a proof of correct decryption) is encrypted under the public key of LE contained in the request.

All messages to be sent[13] are signed using the role's signing key. Before sending any message, all state except for the prepared messages is deleted. Finally, all messages are posted to $\mathcal{F}_{\mathrm{BCRA}}$.

Get Statistics and Audit. Obtaining statistics is achieved by reading the content of $\mathcal{F}_{\mathrm{BCRA}}$ and gathering all W^{pub} accompanied by valid NIZK-proofs. Similarly, the audit is performed by AU reading the content of $\mathcal{F}_{\mathrm{BCRA}}$ and decrypting all W^{enc} accompanied by valid NIZK-proofs.

Security. In the full version [21] we show that our protocol $\mathcal{F}_{\mathrm{AD}}$ UC-realizes $\mathcal{F}_{\mathrm{AD}}$. In particular, we show the following theorem.

Theorem 2. *If* NIZK *is a straight-line simulation-extractable non-interactive zero-knowledge proof system, Σ is an EUF-CMA secure signature scheme, the* PKE *scheme used by LE and AU is an IND-CPA secure public key encryption scheme, the* PKE *scheme that is a parameter of $\mathcal{F}_{\mathrm{BCRA}}$ is a RIND-SO secure public key encryption scheme, and* TPKE *is an IND-CPA secure, randomizable and binding (t, n)-threshold PKE, then Π_{AD} UC-realizes $\mathcal{F}_{\mathrm{AD}}$ in the $\{\mathcal{F}_{\mathrm{BCRA}}, \mathcal{F}_{\mathrm{CRS}}, \mathcal{G}_{CLOCK}\}$-hybrid model with respect to adversaries $\mathcal{A}$ that may statically corrupt SO and/or LE as well as mobile adaptively corrupt at most a fraction $\frac{t}{n} - \epsilon$ of nodes N.*

Efficiency. Given the need for a suitable incentive for nodes to participate, it is important to limit the amount of work roles have to do. In our protocol, the work of roles only depends on the number of decryption requests (which correspond to the number of users under surveillance in the combined system), but not on the number of ciphertexts created (which corresponds to the number of registered users in the combined system). A current bottleneck is the role assignment process and the communication required to transmit the shared secret key to the next committee. This is an active area of research and improvements along the lines of [12,17,26] are promising.

5 Application

In this section, we present our (toy) application $\mathcal{F}_{\mathrm{ASTE}}$ for Auditably Sender-Traceable Encryption. It is intentionally kept very simplistic, and chosen to exemplify the problems one encounters with creating a system with auditable surveillance based on top of $\mathcal{F}_{\mathrm{AS}}$. The construction and techniques developed for $\mathcal{F}_{\mathrm{ASTE}}$, in particular those used for cut-and-choose-based combination of NINCE with zero-knowledge, are applicable for many functionalities of interest.

[13] These include messages to the next committee and decryption answers to LE.

5.1 The Functionality $\mathcal{F}_{\text{ASTE}}$

We briefly describe the capabilities, i.e., the tasks, offered by $\mathcal{F}_{\text{ASTE}}$. The full description is in the full version [21]. Basically, $\mathcal{F}_{\text{ASTE}}$ offers a public key encryption scheme to its users, with the tweak that only registered users can generate ciphertexts c (which honest users accept), and that such ciphertexts can be deanonymized by an authority (namely LE), holding users accountable. To simplify the definition, given a ciphertext c, the intended receiver learns only the message, while law enforcement LE learns only the identity of the encryptor (and nothing about the message). This can be easily modified, cf. Remark 2. To prevent perpetual user surveillance, "time" is partitioned into *validity periods.* Ciphertexts are bound to a period, and honest users only accepts those bound to the current period. These periods are also the granularity of surveillance of LE. That is, a warrant specifies which users are under surveillance during which (past) validity periods.

Setup and Auditability. The tasks System Init, Request Warrant, Get Statistics, and Audit, are inherited from and identical to $\mathcal{F}_{\text{AS}}$ with minimal changes to System Init to formally handle update periods (i.e., $\mathcal{G}_{CLOCK}$).

Register, Update, and Next Period. Similar to $\mathcal{F}_{\text{AS}}$, a user must first register to participate in the system, except that the user cannot choose its *uid* anymore (as it will become the public encryption key in the protocol). The Next Period task allows the system operator to advance the current validity period, in particular, validity periods are not bound to (physical) time. Honest users will only accept ciphertexts of the current validity period. Hence, when the period changes, users must execute the Update task (which, intuitively, deposits a new escrow secret for the current period).

Encrypt Message and Decrypt Ciphertext. These tasks do exactly what one expects: They encrypt a message to a (registered) user, and decrypt received ciphertexts. Decryption ensures that the ciphertext is encrypted w.r.t. the current validity period. Ciphertexts under past periods are not accepted, otherwise, a warrant specifying surveillance of a certain user in a certain period would incorrectly omit (or include) ciphertexts which do not belong to said period.

Prepare Access. Law enforcement prepares the information necessary for access to ciphertexts c covered by warrant W. This usually means that LE acquires the respective escrow secrets associated with W, i.e., it is almost identical to the Get Secrets task of $\mathcal{F}_{\text{AS}}$.

Execute Access. In this task, LE can check whether a ciphertext c was generated by the user with identity *uid* during period *vper*, where LE is supposed to have previously prepared access for a warrant which affects $(\mathit{uid}, \mathit{vper})$.

5.2 The Protocol Π_{ASTE}

To realize $\mathcal{F}_{\text{ASTE}}$, we build a protocol Π_{ASTE} (whose full description is in the full version [21]). Firstly, we work in the $\{\mathcal{F}_{\text{CRS}}, \mathcal{F}_{\text{BB}}, \mathcal{F}_{\text{AS}}, \mathcal{G}_{CLOCK}\}$-hybrid model.

Thus, we can rely on $\mathcal{F}_{AS}$ to take care of the basic requirements for adding auditability, namely, key escrow with auditable access via warrants. Our second key building block is a significantly tweaked public key encryption scheme, $\mathsf{PKE}_{\mathsf{AS}}$. In the protocol, the user identity *uid* will be set to a $\mathsf{PKE}_{\mathsf{AS}}$ public key.

The scheme $\mathsf{PKE}_{\mathsf{AS}}$ provides the promised deanonymization capabilities. This is achieved by including a proof of consistency in the ciphertext (which requires the sender's *uid* and escrow secret *usk*) which demonstrates:

- One ciphertext component encrypts a message m to the receiver (with receiver public key $\mathsf{pk}_R = uid_R$).
- Another ciphertext component encrypts the sender *uid* (i.e., sender's public key) under the sender's escrow secret key *usk* (to enable deanonymization).

This is proven via the non-interactive proof capabilities provided by $\mathcal{F}_{AS}$, which additionally ensure that the tuple $(uid, usk, vper)$ is in $\mathsf{L}_{\mathsf{Secrets}}$, i.e., it is a stored user secret. At a first glance, these two properties, combined with any secure public key encryption scheme for the receiver, seem to be enough for our purposes. However, as mentioned in the technical overview (Sect. 1.2), the simulator-commitment-problem obstructs a security proof for this direct approach.

The Scheme $\mathsf{PKE}_{\mathsf{AS}}$. To circumvent the impossibility of non-interactive non-committing encryption (NINCE) [42], we rely on the (programmable) random oracle model (PROM). It is trivial to construct public-key and secret-key NINCE schemes in the PROM, and we let $\mathsf{PKE}_{\mathsf{NCE}}$ and $\mathsf{SKE}_{\mathsf{NCE}}$ be such schemes. Intuitively, we use $\mathsf{PKE}_{\mathsf{NCE}}$ to encrypt the message for the receiver, and $\mathsf{SKE}_{\mathsf{NCE}}$ to encrypt the user's identity *uid* under its escrow key *usk* for LE. We tie the ciphertexts together with a zero-knowledge proof. Unfortunately, the random oracle RO has no "code", so it is impossible to prove (correct) encryption of a message for $\mathsf{PKE}_{\mathsf{NCE}}$ and $\mathsf{SKE}_{\mathsf{NCE}}$ with the usual (circuit-based) zero-knowledge proofs. Thus, we use a somewhat elaborate cut-and-choose technique, in order to connect traditional zero-knowledge proofs for NP with $\mathsf{PKE}_{\mathsf{NCE}}$ and $\mathsf{SKE}_{\mathsf{NCE}}$.[14]

Remark 2. For simplicity and concreteness, we only prove knowledge of the tuple $t = (m, uid, usk, vper)$ in $\mathsf{PKE}_{\mathsf{AS}}$, and prove that ciphertext components encrypt m under the receiver's key pk_R and *uid* under the escrow key *usk* (for law enforcement access). However, it is straightforward to prove any efficient relation over t. For example, choosing a receiver message function f and law enforcement message function g, one can encrypt $f(t)$ under pk_R (by modifying the shares $m_{i,0/1}$ of m to encrypt shares of $f(t)$ and adapting the proof statements), and similarly encrypt $g(t)$ under *usk* (by analogous modifications). In this sense, the code in Fig. 5 has $f(t) = m$ and $g(t) = uid$ hard-coded for concreteness.

[14] We note that avoiding a cut-and-choose approach is challenging for provably secure constructions. There are impossibilities for black-box zero-knowledge proofs, e.g., [40, 48], which we have to avoid. We do so by using a cut-and-choose approach and additionally constructing the NINCE *together* with its zero-knowledge proof. (The positive results in [40] also use this idea.).

$\mathsf{PKE}_{\mathsf{AS}}.\mathsf{Enc}(ck, \mathsf{pk}_R, m, (\mathsf{sk}_S, usk, uid, vper))$

```
// Prepare cut-and-choose encryption for LE
for i = 1, ..., ℓ(λ)
  m_{i,0} + m_{i,1} = m   // Additive secret shares
  usk_{i,0} + usk_{i,1} = usk
  uid_{i,0} + uid_{i,1} = uid
  for b ∈ {0,1}
    ct^{RE}_{i,b} = PKE_NCE.Enc(pk_R, m_{i,b}; r^{RE}_{i,b})
    ct^{LE}_{i,b} = SKE_NCE.Enc(usk_{i,b}, uid_{i,b}; r^{LE}_{i,b})
    w_{i,b} = (m_{i,b}, usk_{i,b}, uid_{i,b}, r^{RE}_{i,b}, r^{LE}_{i,b})
    com_{i,b} = COM.Com(ck, w_{i,b}; r^{com}_{i,b})
    d_{i,b} = (w_{i,b}, r^{com}_{i,b})
// Consistency proof for commitments and ctxts.
stmt = (vper, pk_R, (com_{i,b}, ct^{RE}_{i,b}, ct^{LE}_{i,b})_{i,b})
wit = (σ_vper, usk, uid, (d_{i,b})_{i,b})
π_con = NIZK_AS.Prove((usk, uid, vper),
    stmt, wit, R_PKEAS) for relation
  R_PKEAS = {(stmt, wit) |
  (uid, sk_S) = PKE_NCE.Gen(1^λ; sk_S)
  com_{i,b} = COM.Com(ck, (m_{i,b}, usk_{i,b},
    uid_{i,b}, r^{RE}_{i,b}, r^{LE}_{i,b}); r^{com}_{i,b})  for all i, b
  ∀i: m = m_{i,0} + m_{i,1}
  ∀i: usk = usk_{i,0} + usk_{i,1}
  ∀i: uid = uid_{i,0} + uid_{i,1}
  }
// Cut-and-choose: Query challenge γ
γ = RO(stmt, π_con) ∈ {0,1}^ℓ
π_cut = (d_{i,γ_i})_i
π = (π_cut, π_con)
return (pk_R, (com_{i,b}, ct^{RE}_{i,b}, ct^{LE}_{i,b})_{i,b}, π).
```

$\mathsf{PKE}_{\mathsf{AS}}.\mathsf{Gen}(1^\lambda)$

```
1 : // For simplicity, sk equals the random coins.
2 : (pk, sk) ← PKE_NCE.Gen(1^λ; sk)
```

$\mathsf{PKE}_{\mathsf{AS}}.\mathsf{Vfy}(ck, c, vper)$

```
parse c = (pk,
    ((com_{i,b}, ct^{RE}_{i,b}, ct^{LE}_{i,b})_{i,b}),
    ((d_{i,γ_i})_i, π_con))
stmt = (vper, pk_R,
    (com_{i,b}, ct^{RE}_{i,b}, ct^{LE}_{i,b})_{i,b})
γ = RO(stmt, π_con) ∈ {0,1}^ℓ
if NIZK_AS.Verify(stmt, π_con, R_PKEAS) = 0
  then return 0
// Check cut-and-choose proof
for i = 1, ..., ℓ(λ)
  b = γ_i
  parse d_{i,b} = (w_{i,b}, r^{com}_{i,b})
  parse w_{i,b} = (m_{i,b}, usk_{i,b}, uid_{i,b},
      r^{RE}_{i,b}, r^{LE}_{i,b})
  if com_{i,b} = COM.Com(ck, w_{i,b}; r^{com}_{i,b})
  or ct^{RE}_{i,b} = PKE_NCE.Enc(pk, m_{i,b}; r^{RE}_{i,b})
  or ct^{LE}_{i,b} = SKE_NCE.Enc(usk_{i,b}, uid_{i,b}; r^{LE}_{i,b})
  then return 0
return 1
```

Fig. 5. Encryption and ciphertext verification subroutines of $\mathsf{PKE}_{\mathsf{AS}}$.

Setup, encryption and ciphertext verification algorithms of $\mathsf{PKE_{AS}}$ are given in Fig. 5; the two latter algorithms depend on a public commitment key ck. Now, we explain the idea behind the proofs $(\pi_{\mathsf{cut}}, \pi_{\mathsf{con}})$ in $\mathsf{PKE_{AS}.Enc}$ and $\mathsf{PKE_{AS}.Vfy}$ (see Fig. 5). The values m, uid, usk are first secret-shared, then used in encryptions $ct^{RE}_{i,b}$, $ct^{LE}_{i,b}$. Moreover, the shares of $m_{i,b}$, $uid_{i,b}$, $usk_{i,b}$ along with the encryption randomness are also committed to in $,_{i,b}$. The $,_{i,b}$ will be important for consistency proofs which we explain now. The extractability of π_{con} (realized by $\mathcal{F}_{\mathrm{AS}}$) allows to recover the committed values in the security proof. Moreover, π_{con} ensures that the shares committed in $,_{i,b}$ are consistent with unique shared values m', uid', usk', e.g., $m' = m'_{i,0} + m'_{i,1}$ holds for all i. The proof π_{cut} is the cut-and-choose part which ensures that enough $\mathsf{PKE_{NCE}}$ resp. $\mathsf{SKE_{NCE}}$ ciphertexts encrypt m' under pk_R resp. uid' under usk'. For this, π_{cut} forces the encryptor to open a randomly chosen share $\gamma_i \in \{0,1\}$ of $ct^{RE}_{i,b}$, $ct^{RE}_{i,b}$ and $,_{i,b}$ for each $i = 1, \dots, \ell(\lambda)$, where the challenge $\gamma = \mathsf{RO}(stmt, \pi_{\mathsf{con}})$ is derived following the Fiat–Shamir paradigm. Note that if both for $\gamma_i = 0$ and $\gamma_i = 1$ can be opened, then π_{con} ensures that the value reconstructed from the shares is m' (resp. uid', usk'), unless the binding property of COM is broken. Assuming unconditionally binding COM, the latter cannot happen. Then, by a standard argument, if less than the majority of ciphertext shares reconstruct m' (resp. uid', usk'), the probability to succeed in π_{cut} is about $2^{-\ell(\lambda)/2} = 2^{-\lambda}$. Consequently, if π_{con} and π_{cut} are accepting, then with overwhelming probability, the extracted values $m'_{i,b}$, which satisfy $m' = m'_{i,0} + m'_{i,1}$, agree with the decrypted values $m_{i,b}$ which yield $m_i = m_{i,0} + m_{i,1}$ in the majority of indices i. Thus, decrypting each $ct^{RE}_{i.b}$, computing m_i, and then picking the majority value m of m_i (or $\perp$ if none exists) agrees with overwhelming probability with the extracted value m' of π_{con}. Unsurprisingly, $\mathsf{PKE_{AS}.Dec_{RE}}$ will do just that.

Observe that $\mathsf{PKE_{AS}.Vfy}$ enables public verifiability of well-formedness of ciphertexts. This verification allows the system operator to check ciphertext validity and remove any invalid ciphertexts, and it is also the first step of decryption procedures $\mathsf{PKE_{AS}.Dec_{RE}}$ and $\mathsf{PKE_{AS}.Dec_{LE}}$, which work as follows:

- $\mathsf{PKE_{AS}.Dec_{RE}}$ decrypts all $ct^{RE}_{i,b}$ using sk_R, reconstructs messages $m_i = m_{i,0} + m_{i,1}$, and outputs m if this is the absolute majority of m_i, and $\perp$ otherwise.
- $\mathsf{PKE_{AS}.Dec_{LE}}$ uses the escrow secret key usk and exploits the relation $usk_{i,1-\gamma_i} = usk - usk_{i,\gamma_i}$ to derive the second secret share $usk_{i,1-\gamma_i}$. With this, it trial-decrypts the symmetric ciphertext(s) $ct^{LE}_{i,b}$ to recover $uid_i = uid_{i,0} + uid_{i,1}$, and outputs uid if this is the absolute majority of uid_i and $\perp$ otherwise.

The majority decisions in decryption ensure that the extracted values m' and uid' from π_{con} coincide with the actual results of decryption. In particular, if $\mathsf{PKE_{AS}.Vfy}$ accepts c, then c will decrypt for the receiver and LE.

Law-Enforcement Access. To provide access to LE, the Prepare Access task uses the Get Secrets task of the underlying $\mathcal{F}_{\mathrm{AS}}$-hybrid functionality. Thus, LE obtains escrow secrets usk for all tuples $(uid, vper)$ covered by the warrant W.

In the Execute Access task, the obtained escrow secrets *usk* for (*uid*, *vper*) is used with $\mathsf{PKE}_{\mathsf{AS}}.\mathsf{Dec}_{\mathsf{LE}}$ to trial-decrypt a ciphertext c.

5.3 On Efficiency and the Necessity of (NI)NCE

We briefly sketch the apparent necessity of non-interactive (NI) non-committing encryption (NCE) to efficiently realize $\mathcal{F}_{\text{ASTE}}$. The core problem appears in the security proof, where the simulator must generate ciphertexts for users whose identities are unknown to it. Once a warrant W pertains a user with *uid*, all simulated ciphertexts $c_1, \ldots, c_n$ affected by W must correspond to that user. Thus, the simulator can (and must) not be committed to an identity *uid* for a ciphertext, unless these are affected by warrants. If the Execute Access task is non-interactive, this is very analogous to NINCE, which is impossible without (strong) setup assumptions [42].[15] As suitable setups are "black-box", e.g., random oracles, they are incompatible with circuit-based zero-knowledge. Although expensive, cut-and-choose techniques are (to our best knowledge) the only known approach. Unfortunately, the cut-and-choose proof leads to relatively large ciphertexts. For $\lambda = 128$ bits of security, an optimistic estimate yields at least 1.5 MiB for the ciphertexts, without accounting for π_{cut} and π_{con}, see the full version [21] for details. These proofs allow trade-offs between size and computational efficiency (e.g., by using SNARKs).

5.4 Comparison with [31]

Green, Kaptchuk, and Laer [31] construct (non-anonymous) messaging with auditable surveillance. They face similar challenges for their protocols, and implicitly rely on NINCE in the PROM as well. However, their setting is considerably simpler: The recipient learns all information contained in the ciphertext, so that it can simply *recompute* the encryption to ensure a ciphertext is well-formed. This approach avoids zero-knowledge proofs, but is quite limited. It can, for example, not be used as an anonymous messenger, since the receiver needs the sender's identity to recompute the ciphertext and verify the correctness of the message. Thus it cannot be used to realize ASTE. As an additional feature, [31] suggests to have the system operator remove invalid ciphertexts. This is possible for Π_{ASTE}, since ciphertext validity is publicly verifiable.[16] However, it is not possible for [31], unless the system operator can read every message, defeating the purpose of the protocol.

While both [31] and we model system security in the UC framework, our ideal functionalities differ in the following aspects: In our system it can be decided

[15] Using interactive decryption circumvents the impossibility without strong setups, but is undesirable in practice.

[16] We stress that, although $\mathsf{PKE}_{\mathsf{AS}}$ as defined in Fig. 5 encrypts only the user identity and not the message to law enforcement, this can easily be changed to also give the message to law enforcement. As noted in Remark 2, our approach allows a quite flexible choice of leakage, not just user identity and/or message.

separately for the sender identity and the content of the message whether the recipient, law enforcement (with a warrant), or both should learn it (cf. Remark 2). In [31] both parties learn both information[17]. Also, [31] is limited to the messaging application scenario, while we also specify an auditable surveillance functionality $\mathcal{F}_{\text{AS}}$ that can be used for many applications, e.g., for $\mathcal{F}_{\text{ASTE}}$.

Compared to us, [31] offers greater flexibility w.r.t. warrants. While our warrants are fixed on user (identity, validity period) pairs, in [31] a warrant may specify a predicate on metadata of a ciphertext and law enforcement can enforce access when the predicate is true. We explicitly avoid this flexibility, as it negatively affects efficiency and requires strong(er) cryptographic primitives—our approach is practically feasible, but [31] is far from it. Recall that [31] uses extractable witness encryption (EWE) [27] whose existence is implausible [23] for general NP-relations. While the relation in [31] is specific, it is quite complex, so even if such EWE existed, its practical efficiency is implausible.

5.5 Other Applications

Offering a zero-knowledge proof interface allows broad use of $\mathcal{F}_{\text{AS}}$ in applications, and our techniques to combine PROM-based encryption and zero-knowledge allow to overcome the problem of NINCE which naturally appears in most applications. For example, one may augment an anonymous e-cash or electronic payment system with auditable surveillance by adding a ciphertext for law-enforcement, which encrypts the identities of the parties of the transfer and proves that the encrypted contents (which law enforcement can learn with the escrow secret) are indeed correct and related to the transaction which was carried out.

6 Limitations and Future Work

In its current form, our building block and its realization are subject to certain limitations. Realizations of the $\mathcal{F}_{\text{BCRA}}$ hybrid functionality are still novel and experimental [8,12,17], so the actual guarantees of such a realization may differ from our assumptions. For $\mathsf{PKE}_{\mathsf{AS}}$, ciphertext size is unacceptable in practice.

A realistic protocol must also cover the existence of many judges, law enforcement agencies, and auditors. Once the judge (and auditor) are not modeled as trusted parties anymore, key-revocation mechanisms become absolutely necessary, as otherwise a single key compromise allows a (state-level) adversary permanent unauthorized surveillance. Although our system ensures that such unauthorized surveillance will be noticed, it does not prevent it. See also the full version [21] for a more fine-grained discussion of system limitations.

[17] While the ideal functionality in [31] technically only supplies some *metadata* to law enforcement (during the message sending process) and not the sender's identity, it becomes apparent later in the paper that the authors assume the sender's identity to be included in the metadata.

Moreover, to harden security, one should distribute trust over multiple parties, especially for the auditor, for example by using threshold cryptography or secure multi-party computation. Lastly, it is an interesting question how to achieve more flexibility w.r.t. warrants, e.g., surveillance based on metadata similar to [31], but without resorting to implausible primitives such as EWE.

Acknowledgements. This work was supported by funding from the topic Engineering Secure Systems of the Helmholtz Association (HGF) and by KASTEL Security Research Labs. This work has been supported by Helsinki Institute for Information Technology HIIT.

References

1. Abelson, H., Anderson, R.J., Bellovin, S.M., et al.: Keys under doormats: mandating insecurity by requiring government access to all data and communications. J. Cybersecur. **1**(1), 69–79 (2015). https://doi.org/10.1093/cybsec/tyv009
2. Arfaoui, G., et al.: How to (legally) keep secrets from mobile operators. In: Bertino, E., Shulman, H., Waidner, M. (eds.) ESORICS 2021. LNCS, vol. 12972, pp. 23–43. Springer, Cham (2021). https://doi.org/10.1007/978-3-030-88418-5_2
3. Backes, M., Camenisch, J., Sommer, D.: Anonymous yet accountable access control. In: Atluri, V., di Vimercati, S.D.C., Dingledine, R. (eds.) Proceedings of the 2005 ACM Workshop on Privacy in the Electronic Society, WPES 2005, Alexandria, VA, USA, 7 November 2005, pp. 40–46. ACM (2005). https://doi.org/10.1145/1102199.1102208
4. Backes, M., Hofheinz, D.: How to break and repair a universally composable signature functionality. In: Zhang, K., Zheng, Y. (eds.) ISC 2004. LNCS, vol. 3225, pp. 61–72. Springer, Heidelberg (2004). https://doi.org/10.1007/978-3-540-30144-8_6
5. Badertscher, C., Maurer, U., Tschudi, D., Zikas, V.: Bitcoin as a transaction ledger: a composable treatment. Cryptology ePrint Archive, Report 2017/149. https://ia.cr/2017/149.2017
6. Bates, A.M., Butler, K.R.B., Sherr, M., et al.: Accountable wiretapping -or- I know they can hear you now. In: NDSS 2012. The Internet Society, February 2012
7. Bellare, M., Rivest, R.L.: Translucent cryptography—an alternative to key escrow, and its implementation via fractional oblivious transfer. J. Cryptol. **12**(2), 117–139 (1999). https://doi.org/10.1007/PL00003819
8. Benhamouda, F., Gentry, C., Gorbunov, S., Halevi, S., Krawczyk, H., Lin, C., Rabin, T., Reyzin, L.: Can a public blockchain keep a secret? In: Pass, R., Pietrzak, K. (eds.) TCC 2020. LNCS, vol. 12550, pp. 260–290. Springer, Cham (2020). https://doi.org/10.1007/978-3-030-64375-1_10
9. Brickell, E.F., Gemmell, P., Kravitz, D.W.: Trustee-based tracing extensions to anonymous cash and the making of anonymous change. In: Clarkson, K.L. (ed.) 6th SODA. ACM-SIAM, Janurary 1995, pp. 457–466 (1995)
10. Brorsson, J., David, B., Gentile, L., Pagnin, E., Wagner, P.S.: PAPR: publicly auditable privacy revocation for anonymous credentials. In: Rosulek, M. (ed.) CT-RSA 2023. LNCS, vol. 13871, pp. 163–190. Springer, Cham (2023). https://doi.org/10.1007/978-3-031-30872-7_7

11. Camenisch, J., Enderlein, R.R., Krenn, S., Küsters, R., Rausch, D.: Universal composition with responsive environments. In: Cheon, J.H., Takagi, T. (eds.) ASIACRYPT 2016, Part II. LNCS, vol. 10032, pp. 807–840. Springer, Heidelberg (2016). https://doi.org/10.1007/978-3-662-53890-6_27
12. Campanelli, M., David, B., Khoshakhlagh, H., Konring, A., Nielsen, J.B.: Encryption to the future: a paradigm for sending secret messages to future (anonymous) committees. Cryptology ePrint Archive, Report 2021/1423 (2021). https://eprint.iacr.org/2021/1423
13. Campanelli, M., David, B., Khoshakhlagh, H., Konring, A., Nielsen, J.B.: Encryption to the future. In: Agrawal, S., Lin, D. (eds.) ASIACRYPT 2022. LNCS, vol. 13793, pp. 151–180. Springer, Cham (2022). https://doi.org/10.1007/978-3-031-22969-5_6
14. Canetti, R.: Universally composable security. J. ACM **67**(5) 28:1–28:94 (2020). https://doi.org/10.1145/3402457
15. Canetti, R.: Universally composable security: a new paradigm for cryptographic protocols. Cryptology ePrint Archive, Report 2000/067. https://ia.cr/2000/067. 2000
16. Canetti, R.: Universally composable signature, certification, and authentication. In: CSFW, p. 219. IEEE Computer Society (2004)
17. Cascudo, I., David, B., Garms, L., Konring, A.: YOLO YOSO: fast and simple encryption and secret sharing in the YOSO model. Cryptology ePrint Archive, Report 2022/242 (2022). https://ia.cr/2022/242
18. Council of the European Union: Council Resolution on Encryption - Security through encryption and security despite encryption. https://data.consilium.europa.eu/doc/document/ST-13084-2020-REV-1/en/pdf.2020
19. Daza, V., Haque, A., Scafuro, A., Zacharakis, A., Zapico, A.: Mutual accountability layer: accountable anonymity within accountable trust. In: Dolev, S., Katz, J., Meisels, A. (eds.) CSCML 2022. LNCS, vol. 13301, pp. 318–336. Springer, Cham (2022). https://doi.org/10.1007/978-3-031-07689-3_24
20. Erwig, A., Faust, S., Riahi, S.: Large-scale non- interactive threshold cryptosystems through anonymity. Cryptology ePrint Archive, Report 2021/1290. https://eprint.iacr.org/2021/1290.2021
21. Fetzer, V., Klooß, M., Müller-Quade, J., Raiber, M., Rupp, A.: Universally composable auditable surveillance. Cryptology ePrint Archive, Paper 2023/1343 (2023). https://eprint.iacr.org/2023/1343
22. Frankle, J., Park, S., Shaar, D., Goldwasser, S., Weitzner, D.J.: Practical accountability of secret processes. In: Enck, W., Felt, A.P. (eds.) USENIX Security 2018, pp. 657–674. USENIX Association, August 2018
23. Garg, S., Gentry, C., Halevi, S., Wichs, D.: On the implausibility of differing-inputs obfuscation and extractable witness encryption with auxiliary input. In: Garay, J.A., Gennaro, R. (eds.) CRYPTO 2014, Part I. LNCS, vol. 8616, pp. 518–535. Springer, Heidelberg (2014). https://doi.org/10.1007/978-3-662-44371-2_29
24. Garman, C., Green, M., Miers, I.: Accountable privacy for decentralized anonymous payments. In: Grossklags, J., Preneel, B. (eds.) FC 2016. LNCS, vol. 9603, pp. 81–98. Springer, Heidelberg (2017). https://doi.org/10.1007/978-3-662-54970-4_5
25. Gentry, C., et al.: YOSO: you only speak once. In: Malkin, T., Peikert, C. (eds.) CRYPTO 2021, Part II. LNCS, vol. 12826, pp. 64–93. Springer, Cham (2021). https://doi.org/10.1007/978-3-030-84245-1_3
26. Gentry, C., Halevi, S., Lyubashevsky, V.: Practical noninteractive publicly verifiable secret sharing with thousands of parties. In: Dunkelman, O., Dziembowski, S.

(eds.) EUROCRYPT 2022. LNCS, vol. 13275, pp. 458–487. Springer, Cham (2022). https://doi.org/10.1007/978-3-031-06944-4_16
27. Gentry, C., Lewko, A., Waters, B.: Witness encryption from instance independent assumptions. In: Garay, J.A., Gennaro, R. (eds.) CRYPTO 2014, Part I. LNCS, vol. 8616, pp. 426–443. Springer, Heidelberg (2014). https://doi.org/10.1007/978-3-662-44371-2_24
28. Goldwasser, S., Kalai, Y.T., Popa, R.A., Vaikuntanathan, V., Zeldovich, N.: How to run Turing machines on encrypted data. In: Canetti, R., Garay, J.A. (eds.) CRYPTO 2013, Part II. LNCS, vol. 8043, pp. 536–553. Springer, Heidelberg (2013). https://doi.org/10.1007/978-3-642-40084-1_30
29. Goldwasser, S., Park, S.: Public accountability vs. secret laws: can they coexist?: A cryptographic proposal. In: Thuraisingham, B.M., Lee, A.J. (eds.) Proceedings of the 2017 on Workshop on Privacy in the Electronic Society, Dallas, TX, USA, 30 October–3 November 2017, pp. 99–110. ACM (2017). https://doi.org/10.1145/3139550.3139565
30. Goyal, V., Kothapalli, A., Masserova, E., Parno, B., Song, Y.: Storing and retrieving secrets on a blockchain. In: Hanaoka, G., Shikata, J., Watanabe, Y. (eds.) PKC 2022. LNCS, vol. 13177, pp. 252–282. Springer, Cham (2022). https://doi.org/10.1007/978-3-030-97121-2_10
31. Green, M., Kaptchuk, G., Van Laer, G.: Abuse resistant law enforcement access systems. In: Canteaut, A., Standaert, F.-X. (eds.) EUROCRYPT 2021, Part III. LNCS, vol. 12698, pp. 553–583. Springer, Cham (2021). https://doi.org/10.1007/978-3-030-77883-5_19
32. Encryption Working Group: Moving the Encryption Policy Conversation Forward. Technical report, Carnegie Endowment for International Peace (2019)
33. Jarecki, S., Shmatikov, V.: Handcuffing big brother: an abuse-resilient transaction escrow scheme. In: Cachin, C., Camenisch, J.L. (eds.) EUROCRYPT 2004. LNCS, vol. 3027, pp. 590–608. Springer, Heidelberg (2004). https://doi.org/10.1007/978-3-540-24676-3_35
34. Jost, D., Maurer, U.: Overcoming impossibility results in composable security using interval-wise guarantees. In: Micciancio, D., Ristenpart, T. (eds.) CRYPTO 2020. LNCS, vol. 12170, pp. 33–62. Springer, Cham (2020). https://doi.org/10.1007/978-3-030-56784-2_2
35. Kilian, J., Leighton, T.: Fair cryptosystems, revisited. In: Coppersmith, D. (ed.) CRYPTO 1995. LNCS, vol. 963, pp. 208–221. Springer, Heidelberg (1995). https://doi.org/10.1007/3-540-44750-4_17
36. Kroll, J.A., Felten, E.W., Boneh, D.: Secure protocols for accountable warrant execution (2014). https://www.jkroll.com/papers/warrant_paper.pdf
37. Kroll, J.A., Zimmerman, J., Wu, D.J., et al.: Accountable Cryptographic Access Control (2018). https://www.cs.yale.edu/homes/jf/kroll-paper.pdf
38. Kügler, D., Vogt, H.: Offline payments with auditable tracing. In: Blaze, M. (ed.) FC 2002. LNCS, vol. 2357, pp. 269–281. Springer, Heidelberg (2003). https://doi.org/10.1007/3-540-36504-4_19
39. Kurosawa, K., Furukawa, J.: Universally composable undeniable signature. In: Aceto, L., Damgård, I., Goldberg, L.A., Halldórsson, M.M., Ingólfsdóttir, A., Walukiewicz, I. (eds.) ICALP 2008. LNCS, vol. 5126, pp. 524–535. Springer, Heidelberg (2008). https://doi.org/10.1007/978-3-540-70583-3_43
40. Liang, X., Pandey, O.: Towards a unified approach to black-box constructions of zero-knowledge proofs. In: Malkin, T., Peikert, C. (eds.) CRYPTO 2021, Part IV. LNCS, vol. 12828, pp. 34–64. Springer, Cham (2021). https://doi.org/10.1007/978-3-030-84259-8_2

41. Liu, J., Ryan, M.D., Chen, L.: Balancing societal security and individual privacy: accountable escrow system. In: Datta, A., Fournet, C. (eds.) CSF 2014 Computer Security Foundations Symposium, pp. 427–440. IEEE Computer Society Press (2014). https://doi.org/10.1109/CSF.2014.37
42. Nielsen, J.B.: Separating random oracle proofs from complexity theoretic proofs: the non-committing encryption case. In: Yung, M. (ed.) CRYPTO 2002. LNCS, vol. 2442, pp. 111–126. Springer, Heidelberg (2002). https://doi.org/10.1007/3-540-45708-9_8
43. Official Journal of the European Communities. Council Resolution on on the lawful interception of telecommunications (1995). https://eur-lex.europa.eu/legal-content/EN/TXT/PDF/?uri=CELEX:31996G1104&from=EN
44. Official Journal of the European Communities. Directive (EU) 2018/843 of the European Parliament and of the Council amending Directive (EU) 2015/849 on the prevention of the use of the financial system for the purposes of money laundering or terrorist & financing, and amending Directives 2009/138/EC and 2013/36/EU (2018). https://eur-lex.europa.eu/legal-content/EN/TXT/PDF/?uri=CELEX:31996G1104&from=EN
45. Paillier, P., Yung, M.: Self-escrowed public-key infrastructures. In: Song, J.S. (ed.) ICISC 1999. LNCS, vol. 1787, pp. 257–268. Springer, Heidelberg (2000). https://doi.org/10.1007/10719994_20
46. Panwar, G., Vishwanathan, R., Misra, S., Bos, A.: SAMPL: scalable auditability of monitoring processes using public ledgers. In: Cavallaro, L., Kinder, J., Wang, X.F., Katz, J. (eds.) ACM CCS 2019, pp. 2249–2266. ACM Press, November 2019. https://doi.org/10.1145/3319535.3354219
47. Persiano, G., Phan, D.H., Yung, M.: Anamorphic encryption: private communication against a dictator. In: Dunkelman, O., Dziembowski, S. (eds.) EUROCRYPT 2022, Part II. LNCS, vol. 13276, pp. 34–63. Springer, Cham (2022). https://doi.org/10.1007/978-3-031-07085-3_2
48. Rosulek, M.: Must you know the code of f to securely compute f? In: Safavi-Naini, R., Canetti, R. (eds.) CRYPTO 2012. LNCS, vol. 7417, pp. 87–104. Springer, Heidelberg (2012). https://doi.org/10.1007/978-3-642-32009-5_7
49. Savage, S.: Lawful device access without mass surveillance risk: a technical design discussion. In: Lie, D., Mannan, M., Backes, M., Wang, X.F. (eds.) ACM CCS 2018, pp. 1761–1774. ACM Press, October 2018. https://doi.org/10.1145/3243734.3243758
50. Scafuro, A.: Break-glass encryption. In: Lin, D., Sako, K. (eds.) PKC 2019. LNCS, vol. 11443, pp. 34–62. Springer, Cham (2019). https://doi.org/10.1007/978-3-030-17259-6_2
51. Servan-Schreiber, S., Wheeler, A.: Judge, jury & encryptioner: exceptional access with a fixed social cost. CoRR abs/1912.05620 (2019). http://arxiv.org/abs/1912.05620
52. Wright, C.V., Varia, M.: Crypto crumple zones: enabling limited access without mass surveillance. In: 2018 IEEE European Symposium on Security and Privacy, EuroS&P 2018, London, United Kingdom, 24–26 April 2018, pp. 288–306. IEEE (2018). https://doi.org/10.1109/EuroSP.2018.00028
53. Young, A., Yung, M.: Auto-recoverable auto-certifiable cryptosystems. In: Nyberg, K. (ed.) EUROCRYPT 1998. LNCS, vol. 1403, pp. 17–31. Springer, Heidelberg (1998). https://doi.org/10.1007/BFb0054114

Author Index

J. Guo and R. Steinfeld (Eds.): ASIACRYPT 2023, LNCS 14439, p. 489, 2023.
https://doi.org/10.1007/978-981-99-8724-5

Printed in the United States
by Baker & Taylor Publisher Services